Clinical Coding Workout:

Practice Exercises
for Skill Development

With Answers

2010 Edition

Melanie Endicott, MBA/HCM, RHIA, CCS, CCS-P,
Kathy Giannangelo, MA, RHIA, CCS, CPHIMS, FAHIMA,
Karen Kostick, RHIT, CCS, CCS-P,
Lynn Kuehn, MS, RHIA, CCS-P, FAHIMA, and
Tanai Nelson, RHIT, CCS, CCS-P,
Editors

AHIMA
PRESS

ISBN: 978-1-58426-241-1
AHIMA Product No. AC201510

AHIMA Staff:
Claire E. Blondeau, MBA, Senior Editor
Katherine Greenock, Editorial and Production Coordinator
Ashley Sullivan, Assistant Editor
Ken Zielske, Director of Publications

American Health Information Management Association
233 North Michigan Avenue, 21st Floor
Chicago, Illinois 60601-5800

http://www.ahima.org

Contents

Preface

The *Clinical Coding Workout* is designed to challenge coding professionals and students alike to develop expert skills in the assignment of clinical codes required for administrative use.

The coding process requires a range of skills that combines knowledge and practice. Someone new to this discipline must conquer the basic principles of using the required code sets. A student at the intermediate level learns to apply code set conventions, guidelines, and principles in various combinations, settings, and scenarios. A person with advanced coding skills analyzes complex health data and determines what needs to be reported to accurately reflect each patient's condition and treatment. Like a violinist or a gymnast, the coding professional develops virtuosity step-by-step through systematic exercise. At each level of skill development, practice enhances performance.

The AHIMA Practice Resources team has gathered coding scenarios and case studies together to create a resource for skill development and review of guidelines and conventions applied in code selection. Practice exercises take the user from beginning concepts and selection of codes, through intermediate applications using short code assignment scenarios, to advanced case studies that are based on excerpts from health records and that require complex clinical analysis skills and multiple code assignments. The user is encouraged to reference the American Hospital Association's *Coding Clinic*, National Center for Health Statistics' *ICD-9-CM Official Guidelines for Coding and Reporting*, and American Medical Association's *CPT Assistant* cited within select case scenarios to further enhance learning. Not all cases include a reference and not all references are cited for a particular case or topic. Coding challenges in the final chapter include exercises for ICD-10-CM and ICD-10-PCS, CPT modifiers, HCPCS Level II modifiers, home health, LTAC coding, and rehabilitation and SNF cases. Appendix A contains tables that link each exercise to the AHIMA certifications and competencies to which it pertains. Lastly, the annotated answer key serves as a unique instructional guide not only providing the correct answer to each question, but also explaining why the answer is correct and why the incorrect answers are not appropriate.

Ways in which this valuable resource can be used include the following:

- Health information management (HIM) educators and coding program trainers can use the exercises to supplement basic- and intermediate-level course materials for students seeking extra credit or advanced preparation.

- HIM students can use the exercises for self-directed learning.

- Coding professionals can use the exercises to gain additional coding experience in a variety of specialties and settings that may not be available to them in their current workplace.

- Employers can use this resource to challenge new coding professionals who are ready to sharpen their skills to the intermediate and advanced levels of coding performance.

- Coding managers can use this material as a tool to assess the competency of coding staff for complex coding practice.

- Employers seeking high-level competency in the more difficult coding practice areas can use the case studies as a means of screening for advanced coding skills.

Clinical Coding Workout is also an excellent tool for:

- Preparing to sit for the mastery-level coding exams offered by AHIMA (CCS and CCS-P) to gain additional insight into a variety of specialty coding topics.

- Evaluating or instructing coding professionals as part of ongoing compliance initiatives.

Acknowledgments

1st edition through 2009 edition contributors

June Bronnert, RHIA, CCS, CCS-P
Kathy DeVault, RHIA, CCS
Susan M. Hull, MPH, RHIA, CCS, CCS-P
Anita Majerowicz, MS, RHIA
Rita Scichilone, MHSA, RHIA, CCS, CCS-P
Mary H. Stanfill, MBI, RHIA, CCS, CCS-P
Ann Zeisset, RHIT, CCS, CCS-P

How to Use This Book

Unlike coding instructional books that are based on one coding classification system, *Clinical Coding Workout* uses the full range of administrative code sets applicable in today's healthcare environment for reporting diagnoses, procedures, and services in various settings and specialty practice areas.

The actual codes used in the exercises and answer key for this book are those that were confirmed or already in effect at the time of publication, as follows:

- *International Classification of Diseases, 9th Revision, Clinical Modification (ICD-9-CM)*, 2010 edition, codes effective October 1, 2009

- *Current Procedural Terminology (CPT)*, 2009 edition, codes effective January 1, 2009

- *Healthcare Common Procedural Coding System Level II (HCPCS)*, 2009 edition, codes effective January 1, 2009

Use of different versions of coding books with this resource will require attention to the code changes after the effective date. Revised answer keys will be created that are consistent with coding changes for the upcoming year soon after the effective date of the new codes. All answer keys are available to instructors in online format from the individual book page in the AHIMA Bookstore (http://imis.ahima.org/orders), and also are posted on the AHIMA Assembly on Education Community of Practice (AOE CoP) Web site. Instructors who are AHIMA members can sign up for this private community by clicking on the help icon within the CoP home page and requesting additional information on becoming an AOE CoP member. An instructor who is not an AHIMA member or a member who is not an instructor may contact the publisher at publications@ahima.org.

As in actual practice, ICD-9-CM codes are used for diagnoses and inpatient procedures for hospital reporting in this book; whereas for ambulatory facility and physician service reporting, ICD-9-CM codes are used for diagnoses, and HCPCS/CPT codes are used for procedures and services.

Federal Register notices and other regulatory updates are available from the Centers for Medicare and Medicaid Services at www.cms.hhs.gov. HCPCS Level II codes are updated each quarter and are available by download from www.cms.hhs.gov/HCPCSReleaseCodeSets/. CPT code sets are generally released in mid-September for implementation by January 1 of the following year.

Refer to the instructions in each chapter for additional information. Please report any potential inconsistencies or inaccuracies in this book to publications@ahima.org.

Part I
Beginning Coding Exercises

Chapter 1

Basic Principles of ICD-9-CM Coding

Note: The exercises in this chapter are based on the 2010 edition of the ICD-9-CM Classification System but are suitable for other editions in most instances. Annual updates are made to the ICD-9-CM coding system with changes effective October 1 of each year.

The Centers for Medicare and Medicaid Services (CMS) and the National Center for Health Statistics (NCHS) provide the *ICD-9-CM Official Guidelines for Coding and Reporting*, which should be used as a companion document to the official version. The guidelines have been approved by the four organizations that make up the Cooperating Parties for the ICD-9-CM: the American Hospital Association (AHA), the American Health Information Management Association (AHIMA), CMS, and NCHS.

The guidelines are a set of rules that have been developed to accompany and complement the official conventions and instructions provided within ICD-9-CM. The guidelines are based upon the coding and sequencing instructions found in ICD-9-CM, and they provide additional instruction. Adherence to the guidelines is required under the Health Insurance Portability and Accountability Act (HIPAA). The guidelines are organized into sections. Section I includes the structure and conventions of the classification, general guidelines that apply to the entire classification, and chapter-specific guidelines that correspond to the chapters as they are arranged in the classification. This section is applicable to all healthcare settings unless otherwise indicated. Section II includes guidelines for selecting principal diagnoses for non-outpatient settings. Section III includes guidelines for reporting additional diagnoses in non-outpatient settings. Section IV is for outpatient coding (including physician) and reporting.

These guidelines are regularly updated and are available at: www.cdc.gov/nchs/datawh/ftpserv/ftpicd9/ftpicd9.htm#guide.

Instructions: Circle the correct answer, fill in the blank, or assign the correct code(s) for each of the following exercise items.

Characteristics and Conventions of the ICD-9-CM Classification System

1.1.   Nonessential modifiers are enclosed in:

   a. Brackets
   b. Parentheses
   c. Slanted brackets
   d. Boxes

1.2.   A diagnostic descriptor that is listed in italics is a(n):

   a. Manifestation code
   b. Inappropriate principal diagnosis
   c. CC exclusion
   d. Code that must be reported first

1.3.   The abbreviation UHDDS refers to the _____.

1.4.   Diagnoses described as "possible," "probable," "likely," and "rule out" are reported if present for _____ records.

1.5.   For patients seen in the outpatient setting for chemotherapy, radiation therapy, or rehabilitation, the first reported diagnosis is:

   a. The diagnosis toward which the treatment is directed
   b. The appropriate V code
   c. Either a or b
   d. The diagnosis that the physician lists first on the order

1.6.   When multiple burns are present, the first sequenced diagnosis is the:

   a. Burn that is treated surgically
   b. Burn that is closest to the head
   c. Highest-degree burn
   d. Any of the above

1.7.   A coding professional may assume a cause-and-effect relationship between hypertension and which of the following complications?

   a. Hypertension and heart disease
   b. Hypertension and chronic kidney disease
   c. Hypertension and heart and chronic kidney disease
   d. None of the above

1.8.   ICD-9-CM codes that describe the behavior of cells in neoplasms are called _____.

1.9.   New ICD-9-CM codes go into effect on _____ of each year.

1.10. Supplementary classifications include:

    a. V codes
    b. V codes and E codes
    c. V codes, E codes, and M codes
    d. None of the above

1.11. The neoplasm table includes:

    a. The nature and status (primary, secondary, in situ) for malignancies
    b. A listing of the morphology codes
    c. The stage of benign neoplasms
    d. E codes for reactions to chemotherapy

1.12. V codes can be used as:

    a. Principal diagnosis only
    b. Secondary diagnosis only
    c. Either principal diagnosis or secondary diagnosis, depending on the code and the circumstances of the admission
    d. Secondary diagnosis only on inpatient stays and principal diagnosis only on outpatient visits

1.13. Terms listed in the Alphabetic Index in boldface type are known as _____.

1.14. Manifestation codes:

    a. Can never be reported first
    b. Are printed in italics in the Tabular List
    c. Describe a condition that results from another, underlying condition
    d. All of the above

1.15. Codes that contain the descriptive abbreviation NOS are to be used:

    a. When the record itself is not available for review
    b. When the coder lacks sufficient information to assign a more specific code
    c. When only outpatient diagnostic records are being coded
    d. All the time

Infectious and Parasitic Diseases

1.16. Meningitis due to ECHO virus

    Code(s): _____

1.17. Chickenpox

    Code(s): _____

1.18.   Cutaneous anthrax

Code(s): _____

1.19.   *Aerobacter aerogenes* is an example of a gram-_____
bacterial organism.

1.20.   Genital herpes

Code(s): _____

1.21.   Patients with any known prior diagnosis of an HIV-related illness should be
reported with this ICD-9-CM code: _____.

1.22.   Acute salpingitis due to gonococcal infection

Code(s): _____

1.23.   A patient with known AIDS is admitted to the hospital for treatment of
Pneumocystis carinii pneumonia. Assign the principal diagnosis.

a. 042
b. 486
c. 136.3
d. Any of the above

1.24.   A patient with known chronic hepatitis C is seen in the outpatient department
for interferon treatment. Assign the primary diagnosis.

a. 070.51
b. 070.44
c. 070.54
d. 070.32

1.25.   Paratyphoid fever A

Code(s): _____

1.26.   Food poisoning due to *Staphylococcus* organism

Code(s): _____

1.27.   Infectious diarrhea

Code(s): _____

1.28.   Pulmonary tuberculosis, bacilli identified with microscopy

Code(s): _____

1.29.   Scarlatina

Code(s): _____

1.30. Streptococcal septicemia

Code(s): _____

1.31. Dermatophytosis of scalp

Code(s): _____

1.32. Pneumonia as a complication of measles

Code(s): _____

1.33. Mumps

Code(s): _____

1.34. Plantar wart

Code(s): _____

1.35. Infectious mononucleosis

Code(s): _____

Neoplasms

1.36. Hodgkin's disease of thoracic lymph nodes

Code(s): _____

1.37. Benign neoplasm of bronchus

Code(s): _____

1.38. When a patient is admitted to the hospital for radiation therapy for a primary malignancy that is still present, what code is reported as the principal diagnosis? _____

1.39. A patient is admitted as an inpatient to receive radiation and chemotherapy for distal esophageal carcinoma. What is the appropriate principal diagnosis?

    a. V58.0
    b. V58.11
    c. 150.5
    d. Either a or b

1.40. Carcinoma of the broad ligament (confined to this location)

Code(s): _____

1.41. Adenoma of the islet cells of the pancreas

Code(s): _____

1.42. Neoplasms at the cellular level that are incapable of spreading to distant sites are called _____ neoplasms.

1.43. Malignant melanoma of the skin of the chest wall

Code(s): _____

1.44. Adenocarcinoma of the lesser curvature of the stomach

Code(s): _____

1.45. Secondary carcinoma of the submandibular salivary gland

Code(s): _____

1.46. Benign neoplasm of the appendix

Code(s): _____

1.47. Carcinoma in situ of breast

Code(s): _____

1.48. Rhabdomyosarcoma is an example of which of the following kinds of neoplasms?

a. Benign
b. Malignant
c. Uncertain behavior
d. Unspecified

1.49. Myxofibrosarcoma is a malignant neoplasm that affects what type of tissue?

_____

1.50. The site at which a malignant neoplasm originated is known as the _____ site.

1.51. Bronchogenic carcinoma

Code(s): _____

1.52. Carcinoma in situ of the uterine cervix

Code(s): _____

1.53. In coding for neoplasms of the lymphatic and hematopoietic systems (200–202), a fifth digit of 4 refers to which organs?

a. Lymph nodes of inguinal region and lower limb
b. Lymph nodes of head, face, and neck
c. Lymph nodes of axilla and upper limb
d. Intrapelvic lymph nodes

1.54. Multiple myeloma in remission

Code(s): _____

1.55. Acute myelogenous leukemia in relapse

Code(s): _____

Endocrine, Nutritional and Metabolic Diseases, and Immunity Disorders

1.56. Congenital dysgammaglobulinemia

Code(s): _____

1.57. Hyponatremia

Code(s): _____

1.58. Primary hypercholesterolemia

Code(s): _____

1.59. Bartter's syndrome is a form of which of the following?

    a. Diabetic neuropathy
    b. Hyperaldosteronism
    c. Hypertriglyceridemia
    d. Polycystic ovarian disease

1.60. Type I diabetes mellitus with diabetic renal nephrosis, out of control

Code(s): _____

1.61. Diabetes mellitus

Code(s): _____

1.62. Type I diabetes mellitus with proliferative retinopathy

Code(s): _____

1.63. Type I diabetes mellitus with ketoacidosis

Code(s): _____

1.64. Type I diabetes mellitus with ophthalmic manifestations

Code(s): _____

1.65. Hypoinsulinemia following total pancreatectomy

Code(s): _____

1.66. Code 255.2 (adrenogenital disorders) includes which of the following?

a. Achard-Thiers syndrome
b. Macrogenitosomia praecox in the male
c. Congenital adrenal hyperplasia
d. All of the above

1.67. Hypophyseal dwarfism

Code(s): _____

1.68. Hypopotassemia

Code(s): _____

1.69. Cystic fibrosis with pulmonary manifestations

Code(s): _____

1.70. Hurler's syndrome, gargoyle syndrome, and Sanfilippo's syndrome are all forms of _____.

1.71. Morbid obesity with a BMI of 40

Code(s): _____

1.72. Polycystic ovaries

Code(s): _____

1.73. Renal glycosuria

Code(s): _____

1.74. Nodular goiter with hyperthyroidism

Code(s): _____

1.75. Congenital hypothyroidism

Code(s): _____

Disorders of the Blood and Blood-Forming Organs

1.76. Iron-deficiency anemia secondary to chronic blood loss

Code(s): _____

1.77. Sickle cell anemia and thalassemia are both types of:

a. Iron deficiency anemias
b. Hereditary hemolytic anemias
c. Aplastic anemia
d. Coagulation defects

1.78.   Sickle cell trait

Code(s): _____

1.79.   Anemia due to acute blood loss

Code(s): _____

1.80.   Anemia in end-stage renal disease

Code(s): _____

1.81.   Which of the following is (are) not an example(s) of constitutional red blood cell aplasia (284.01)?

a. Fanconi's anemia
b. Familial hypoplastic anemia
c. Blackfan-Diamond syndrome
d. All of the above

1.82.   von Willebrand's disease

Code(s): _____

1.83.   Agranulocytosis is a disease of the _____ blood cells.

1.84.   Aplastic anemia

Code(s): _____

1.85.   Folate deficiency anemia due to drugs

Code(s): _____

1.86.   Refractory megaloblastic anemia

Code(s): _____

1.87.   Osteosclerotic anemia

Code(s): _____

1.88.   Purpura fulminans

Code(s): _____

1.89.   Thrombocytopenic purpura

Code(s): _____

1.90.   Thrombocytopenia following massive blood transfusions

Code(s): _____

1.91. Anemia

Code(s): _____

1.92. Congenital aplastic anemia

Code(s): _____

1.93. Eosinophilic leukocytosis

Code(s): _____

1.94. Anemia secondary to vitamin B_{12} deficiency

Code(s): _____

1.95. Hemophilia

Code(s): _____

Mental Disorders

Because the code assignment for mental disorders can have significant impact on the patient, coding professionals must take special care to ensure that codes are based on diagnostic statements clearly provided in physician documentation.

1.96. To report Jakob-Creutzfeldt disease with dementia, you would need:

    a. One code
    b. Two codes
    c. Either one or two codes
    d. More than two codes

1.97. Chronic alcoholic brain syndrome

Code(s): _____

1.98. Chronic paranoid schizophrenia with acute exacerbation

Code(s): _____

1.99. Hypomanic personality disorder

Code(s): _____

1.100. Panic attack

Code(s): _____

1.101. Which of the following is a synonym for multiple personality disorder?

    a. Dissociative identity disorder
    b. Factitious illness
    c. Adjustment reaction
    d. Multiple psychoses

1.102. Munchausen syndrome

Code(s): _____

1.103. Which of the following is a sexual deviation or disorder per ICD-9-CM?

    a. Bestiality
    b. Pedophilia
    c. Voyeurism
    d. All of the above

1.104. Alcoholism with acute intoxication

Code(s): _____

1.105. Morphine addiction, in remission

Code(s): _____

1.106. Heroin and diazepam addiction

Code(s): _____

1.107. Psychogenic torticollis

Code(s): _____

1.108. Gilles de la Tourette's syndrome

Code(s): _____

1.109. Nervous depression

Code(s): _____

1.110. Separation anxiety disorder

Code(s): _____

1.111. Mental retardation, measured IQ of 42

Code(s): _____

1.112. Attention deficit/hyperactivity disorder

Code(s): _____

1.113. Alcoholic paranoia

Code(s): _____

1.114. DTs due to alcohol withdrawal

Code(s): _____

1.115. Multi-infarct dementia with depression

Code(s): _____

Nervous System and Sense Organs

1.116. Acute endophthalmitis

Code(s): _____

1.117. Duchenne muscular dystrophy

Code(s): _____

1.118. Which of the following are the correct codes for proliferative diabetic retinopathy?

a. 250.53, 362.01
b. 362.02, 250.50
c. 250.50, 362.02
d. 362.02, 250.00

1.119. Central retinal artery occlusion

Code(s): _____

1.120. Nuclear cataract

Code(s): _____

1.121. Retinal detachment, traction type

Code(s): _____

1.122. Senile cataract, posterior subcapsular

Code(s): _____

1.123. Angle closure glaucoma, acute

Code(s): _____

1.124. According to the notes in the Tabular List of ICD-9-CM, tritan defect color blindness causes difficulty distinguishing between:

    a. Green and red
    b. All colors
    c. Blue and yellow
    d. Red and blue

1.125. Bullous keratopathy

    Code(s): _____

1.126. Temporal sclerosis

    Code(s): _____

1.127. All but one of the following conditions are examples of strabismus (category 378). Identify the condition that is not a form of strabismus.

    a. Esotropia
    b. Exotropia
    c. Presbyopia
    d. Heterotropia

1.128. Chronic serous otitis media

    Code(s): _____

1.129. Acute suppurative otitis media with eardrum rupture due to pressure

    Code(s): _____

1.130. Cholesteatoma involving middle ear and mastoid

    Code(s): _____

1.131. Hyperactive labyrinth, right side

    Code(s): _____

1.132. Anisocoria

    Code(s): _____

1.133. Malignant otitis externa

    Code(s): _____

1.134. Otitis media

    Code(s): _____

1.135. Reflex sympathetic dystrophy, both arms

    Code(s): _____

Circulatory System

1.136. Left ventricular aneurysm

Code(s): _____

1.137. Malignant hypertension with hypertensive heart disease and congestive heart failure is coded:

    a. 402.01
    b. 402.01, 428.9
    c. 428.0, 402.11
    d. 402.01, 428.0

1.138. Mitral valve stenosis and aortic valve insufficiency

Code(s): _____

1.139. Hospital discharge diagnosis: Acute inferolateral myocardial infarction

Code(s): _____

1.140. A myocardial infarction is considered to be acute when it is less than _____ _____ weeks old.

1.141. Hypertension

Code(s): _____

1.142. Identify the main term in the diagnostic statement "idiopathic hypertrophic subaortic stenosis (IHSS)": _____

1.143. Atrial flutter

Code(s): _____

1.144. Ventricular fibrillation

Code(s): _____

1.145. Chronic diastolic heart failure

Code(s): _____

1.146. Preinfarction angina

Code(s): _____

1.147. Pulmonary infarction

Code(s): _____

1.148. ASHD of transplanted heart

Code(s): _____

1.149. Atherosclerosis of left internal mammary artery bypass graft

Code(s): _____

1.150. Dysarthria secondary to old stroke (cerebrovascular disease)

Code(s): _____

1.151. Cerebral infarct due to stenosis of the vertebral artery

Code(s): _____

1.152. Chronic pulmonary embolism

Code(s): _____

1.153. Orthostatic hypotension

Code(s): _____

1.154. Varicose veins of the legs with ulceration

Code(s): _____

1.155. Abdominal aortic aneurysm, ruptured

Code(s): _____

Respiratory System

1.156. Acute bronchitis

Code(s): _____

1.157. Acute laryngitis with airway obstruction

Code(s): _____

1.158. Hypertrophy of tonsils and adenoids

Code(s): _____

1.159. Maxillary sinus polyp(s)

Code(s): _____

1.160. The correct code assignment(s) for pneumonia due to the RSV organism is (are):

   a. 486 and 079.6
   b. 480.1
   c. 466.11
   d. 079.6

1.161. Pneumonia due to gram-negative anaerobic organisms

   Code(s): _____

1.162. Acute exacerbation of chronic obstructive pulmonary disease

   Code(s): _____

1.163. Emphysema

   Code(s): _____

1.164. Bilateral granulomatous hemorrhagic septic pneumonia

   Code(s): _____

1.165. Aspiration pneumonia

   Code(s): _____

1.166. Chronic obstructive asthma with status asthmaticus

   Code(s): _____

1.167. Postoperative pneumothorax

   Code(s): _____

1.168. Chronic respiratory failure

   Code(s): _____

1.169. Tracheostomy stenosis

   Code(s): _____

1.170. Postinfective bronchiectasis

   Code(s): _____

1.171. What is the correct code assignment for extrinsic asthma with acute exacerbation and status asthmaticus?

   a. 493.02
   b. 493.00
   c. 493.01
   d. 493.02, 493.01

1.172. Spontaneous pneumothorax

Code(s): _____

1.173. Childhood asthma

Code(s): _____

1.174. Radiation pneumonitis

Code(s): _____

1.175. Common cold

Code(s): _____

Digestive System

1.176. Dental caries

Code(s): _____

1.177. Acute duodenal ulcer with bleeding

Code(s): _____

1.178. Gastric ulcer

Code(s): _____

1.179. Leukoplakia of tongue

Code(s): _____

1.180. Identify the appropriate code for reflux esophagitis

    a. 530.81
    b. 530.11
    c. 530.10
    d. 530.89

1.181. Select the correct code for acute peptic ulcer of stomach with perforation

    a. 533.10
    b. 531.50
    c. 533.60
    d. 531.10

1.182. Angiodysplasia of the stomach

Code(s): _____

1.183. Alcoholic gastritis with hemorrhage

Code(s): _____

1.184. Acute obstructive appendicitis

Code(s): _____

1.185. Incisional hernia

Code(s): _____

1.186. Bilateral inguinal hernia, recurrent

Code(s): _____

1.187. Incarcerated right femoral hernia

Code(s): _____

1.188. Crohn's disease of the small bowel

Code(s): _____

1.189. Ulcerative colitis

Code(s): _____

1.190. Ileus due to gallstones impacting the intestine

Code(s): _____

1.191. Select the correct code for diverticulosis of the colon

a. 562.11
b. 562.00
c. 562.10
d. 562.12

1.192. Postoperative peritoneal adhesions

Code(s): _____

1.193. Cholelithiasis with acute and chronic cholecystitis

Code(s): _____

1.194. Acute pancreatitis

Code(s): _____

1.195. Pouchitis

Code(s): _____

Genitourinary System

1.196. Acute renal failure

Code(s): _____

1.197. Ureterolithiasis

Code(s): _____

1.198. Acute pyelonephritis

Code(s): _____

1.199. Urethrolithiasis

Code(s): _____

1.200. Hydronephrosis

Code(s): _____

1.201. UTI

Code(s): _____

1.202. Overactive bladder

Code(s): _____

1.203. Hematuria

Code(s): _____

1.204. Select the appropriate code for urethral stricture.

    a. 598
    b. 598.9
    c. 598.00
    d. 598.8

1.205. In the diagnostic statement "urinary tract infection due to *Escherichia coli,*" which condition is coded as the principal diagnosis?

    a. The *E coli*
    b. The urinary tract infection
    c. Either may be coded as the principal diagnosis.
    d. The circumstances of the admission determine which condition is coded as the principal diagnosis.

1.206. Select the appropriate code for benign prostatic hypertrophy

    a. 222.2
    b. 600.20
    c. 600.00
    d. 600.90

1.207. PIN II

Code(s): _____

1.208. In the diagnostic statement "tuberculous prostatitis," which condition is coded as the principal diagnosis?

    a. The tuberculosis
    b. The prostatitis
    c. Either may be coded as the principal diagnosis.
    d. The circumstances of the admission determine which condition is coded as the principal diagnosis.

1.209. Micromastia

Code(s): _____

1.210. Acute PID

Code(s): _____

1.211. Endometriosis of the broad ligament

Code(s): _____

1.212. Corpus luteum cyst of ovary

Code(s): _____

1.213. Dysmenorrhea

Code(s): _____

1.214. Postmenopausal atrophic vaginitis

Code(s): _____

1.215. CIN II

Code(s): _____

Pregnancy, Childbirth, and the Puerperium

1.216. Contracted pelvis, infant delivered vaginally

Code(s): _____

1.217. Gestational diabetes, admitted for control, not delivered

Code(s): _____

1.218. Maternal hypotension syndrome, onset 10 minutes after delivery

Code(s): _____

1.219. The postpartum period begins immediately following delivery and lasts for _____ weeks following delivery.

1.220. By ICD-9-CM definition, an "elderly primigravida" is a woman who is _____ years or older at the time of her first delivery.

1.221. Large-for-dates baby, delivered this admission (maternal record)

Code(s): _____

1.222. Primary uterine inertia, delivered this admission

Code(s): _____

1.223. Vaginal delivery with fourth-degree perineal laceration

Code(s): _____

1.224. Postpartum puerperal sepsis, patient readmitted 2 weeks after delivery

Code(s): _____

1.225. Hyperemesis gravidarum at 16 weeks, with dehydration, not delivered

Code(s): _____

1.226. False labor, 39 weeks, not delivered

Code(s): _____

1.227. Pregnancy in bicornuate uterus, 20 weeks, undelivered this admission

Code(s): _____

1.228. Dehiscence of cesarean section wound requiring readmission 1 week after delivery

Code(s): _____

1.229. Postpartum amniotic fluid embolism occurring while patient is still in the hospital

Code(s): _____

1.230. The fifth digit to describe a delivery that was accompanied by a postpartum complication while the patient was still in the hospital is _____.

1.231. If a patient is admitted for treatment of an antepartum condition and does not deliver during the stay, the appropriate fifth digit is

_____.

1.232. Oligohydramnios, reported with code 658.0X, is:

    a. Infection of the amniotic fluid
    b. Excessive amount of amniotic fluid
    c. Deficient amount of amniotic fluid
    d. Embolism of amniotic fluid

1.233. Missed abortion

Code(s): _____

1.234. When an abortion is complicated by septic shock, the appropriate fourth digit is _____.

1.235. Ectopic pregnancies include which of the following types?

    a. Tubal
    b. Abdominal
    c. Septic
    d. a and b

Skin and Subcutaneous Tissue

1.236. Carbuncle of the hand

Code(s): _____

1.237. Paronychia of finger

Code(s): _____

1.238. Sunburn

Code(s): _____

1.239. Cellulitis of chin

Code(s): _____

1.240. Pilonidal cyst

Code(s): _____

1.241. Poison ivy

Code(s): _____

1.242. Dermatitis due to cat dander

Code(s): _____

1.243. Lupus erythematosus

Code(s): _____

1.244. Keloid scar

Code(s): _____

1.245. Actinic keratosis

Code(s): _____

1.246. Alopecia areata

Code(s): _____

1.247. Hidradenitis suppurativa

Code(s): _____

1.248. Select the correct code for pressure ulcer of heel

    a. 707.15
    b. 707.14
    c. 707.07
    d. 707.10

1.249. In the diagnostic statement "diabetic foot ulcer," what condition should be assigned as the principal diagnosis?

    a. The ulcer
    b. The diabetes mellitus
    c. Either condition
    d. The circumstances of the admission will determine which condition is classified as the principal diagnosis.

1.250. Lichen planus, generalized

Code(s): _____

1.251. Contact dermatitis due to new detergent

Code(s): _____

1.252. Abscess of axilla

Code(s): _____

1.253. Ammonia dermatitis from soiled diapers

Code(s): _____

1.254. Erythema multiforme

Code(s): _____

1.255. Second-degree sunburn

Code(s): _____

Musculoskeletal System and Connective Tissue

1.256. Pyogenic arthritis of the hip

Code(s): _____

1.257. Rheumatoid arthritis involving the hands

Code(s): _____

1.258. Aseptic necrosis of femoral head

Code(s): _____

1.259. Osteoarthritis of the knees

Code(s): _____

1.260. DJD, generalized

Code(s): _____

1.261. Chronic bucket handle tear of the lateral meniscus of the knee

Code(s): _____

1.262. Chondromalacia patellae

Code(s): _____

1.263. Hemarthrosis of the elbow, chronic

Code(s): _____

1.264. Ankylosing spondylitis

Code(s): _____

1.265. Osteoarthritis of the cervical spine with cord compression documented at surgery

Code(s): _____

1.266. HNP, L4–5, with left lower extremity sciatica

Code(s): _____

1.267. Degenerative disk disease of lumbar spine

Code(s): _____

1.268. Low back pain

Code(s): _____

1.269. Synovial cyst of wrist

Code(s): _____

1.270. SLE

Code(s): _____

1.271. Osteomyelitis, acute, of first and second metatarsi

Code(s): _____

1.272. Postmenopausal osteoporosis

Code(s): _____

1.273. Pathologic fracture of neck of femur

Code(s): _____

1.274. Hallux valgus

Code(s): _____

1.275. Kyphosis

Code(s): _____

Newborn/Congenital Disorders

1.276. Spina bifida of lumbar region

Code(s): _____

1.277. Branchial cleft cyst

Code(s): _____

1.278. VSD

Code(s): _____

1.279. Coarctation of the aorta

Code(s): _____

1.280. Bilateral complete cleft palate

Code(s): _____

1.281. Hypospadias

Code(s): _____

1.282. Polycystic kidney disease

Code(s): _____

1.283. Congenital dislocation of left hip, with subluxation of right hip

Code(s): _____

1.284. Syndactyly of fingers involving soft tissues only

Code(s): _____

1.285. Spondylolisthesis, L5–S1

Code(s): _____

1.286. Gastroschisis

Code(s): _____

1.287. Klinefelter's syndrome

Code(s): _____

1.288. Osteogenesis imperfecta

Code(s): _____

1.289. Congenital CMV infection

Code(s): _____

1.290. Meconium aspiration syndrome

Code(s): _____

1.291. Hemolytic disease of newborn due to Rh maternal/fetal incompatibility

Code(s): _____

1.292. Omphalocele

Code(s): _____

1.293. Drug withdrawal syndrome in newborn

Code(s): _____

1.294. In the diagnostic statement "newborn male with meconium aspiration syndrome, subarachnoid hemorrhage, and neonatal jaundice due to prematurity," what is the principal diagnosis?

    a. 772.2
    b. V30.00
    c. 770.1
    d. 774.2

1.295. Necrotizing enterocolitis of the newborn

Code(s): _____

Symptoms, Signs, and Ill-Defined Conditions

1.296. Anorexia

Code(s): _____

1.297. Failure to thrive, 35-year-old patient

Code(s): _____

1.298. Fussy infant

Code(s): _____

1.299. Fever

Code(s): _____

1.300. Syncope

Code(s): _____

1.301. Chronic fatigue syndrome

Code(s): _____

1.302. Chest pain

Code(s): _____

1.303. Nervousness

Code(s): _____

1.304. Polydipsia

Code(s): _____

1.305.   Abnormal GTT

Code(s): _____

1.306.   Nausea and vomiting

Code(s): _____

1.307.   Colic

Code(s): _____

1.308.   Urinary frequency

Code(s): _____

1.309.   RUQ abdominal pain

Code(s): _____

1.310.   Abnormal EEG

Code(s): _____

1.311.   Nonvisualization of gallbladder on x-ray examination

Code(s): _____

1.312.   Abnormal mammogram

Code(s): _____

1.313.   SIDS

Code(s): _____

1.314.   Cachexia

Code(s): _____

1.315.   Hyperventilation

Code(s): _____

Trauma/Poisoning

1.316.   Open skull fracture with subarachnoid and subdural hemorrhage, expired without regaining consciousness

Code(s): _____

1.317.   Fracture of C3 with complete transection of spinal cord at that level

Code(s): _____

1.318. Fracture ribs 2 to 4 right and 2 to 5 left

Code(s): _____

1.319. Multiple fractures of pelvis with loss of continuity of pelvic circle

Code(s): _____

1.320. Comminuted, impacted fracture of surgical neck of right humerus

Code(s): _____

1.321. Torus fracture of radius and ulna

Code(s): _____

1.322. Nursemaid's elbow

Code(s): _____

1.323. Missile fracture of patella due to bullet

Code(s): _____

1.324. Dislocation of jaw

Code(s): _____

1.325. Sprained wrist

Code(s): _____

1.326. Pneumothorax with knife wound of chest wall

Code(s): _____

1.327. Mosquito bite, buttocks, with secondary infection

Code(s): _____

1.328. Third-degree burns of palm of hand

Code(s): _____

1.329. Poisoning by salicylate ingestion

Code(s): _____

1.330. Anaphylactic shock due to ingestion of pecans

Code(s): _____

1.331. Frostbite of face

Code(s): _____

1.332. Leakage of prosthetic heart valve

Code(s): _____

1.333. Rejection of transplanted liver

Code(s): _____

1.334. Accidental laceration of aorta during laminectomy procedure

Code(s): _____

1.335. Battered spouse

Code(s): _____

E Codes

There is a separate Alphabetic Index to External Causes of Injury and Poisoning. Depending on the publisher, this index may be found in different locations within the book. E codes are not indexed in the main Alphabetic Index to Diseases.

1.336. Assign the appropriate E code for injury due to tackle in a football game.

Code(s): _____

1.337. Assign the appropriate E code for fall from ladder.

Code(s): _____

1.338. Assign the appropriate E code for burns due to ignition of clothing from fireplace in restaurant.

Code(s): _____

1.339. Assign the appropriate E code for injury from rattlesnake bite.

Code(s): _____

1.340. Assign the appropriate E code for injury in an avalanche.

Code(s): _____

1.341. Assign the appropriate E code for injury to the toe due to bumping into the table.

Code(s): _____

1.342. Assign the appropriate E code for drowning in the bathtub.

Code(s): _____

1.343. Assign the appropriate E code for injury from fireworks.

Code(s): _____

1.344. Assign the appropriate E code for injury involving rappelling.

Code(s): _____

1.345. Laceration of hand from assault with knife. Assign both the diagnosis code and the E code.

Code(s): _____

1.346. Cervical strain due to motor vehicle accident, secondary to loss of control and collision with tree. Patient was the restrained driver. Assign both the diagnosis code and the E code.

Code(s): _____.

1.347. Fracture of ulna due to fall from motorcycle. Patient was passenger on the back of the motorcycle. Assign both the diagnosis code and the E code.

Code(s): _____

1.348. Assign the appropriate E code for injury due to riding a rollercoaster.

Code(s): _____

1.349. Assign the appropriate E code for injury from dog bite.

Code(s): _____

1.350. What is the appropriate place of occurrence code for an accident occurring on a street or highway?

Code(s): _____

1.351. Assign the appropriate E code for foreign body left inside a patient during a surgical procedure.

Code(s): _____

1.352. Assign the appropriate E code for injury during earthquake.

Code(s): _____

1.353. Assign the appropriate E code for injury from a lathe.

Code(s): _____

1.354. Assign the appropriate E code for burn from boiling water.

Code(s): _____

1.355. Laceration of pinna of the ear from accidental human bite, with secondary infection. Assign both the diagnosis code and the E code.

Code(s): _____

V Codes

1.356. Encounter for artificial insemination

Code(s): _____

1.357. Hepatitis B carrier

Code(s): _____

1.358. History of carcinoma of the breast

Code(s): _____

1.359. History of colonic polyps

Code(s): _____

1.360. Family history of ovarian cancer

Code(s): _____

1.361. Well-baby visit

Code(s): _____

1.362. Incidental pregnancy

Code(s): _____

1.363. Liveborn male twin, delivered by cesarean section

Code(s): _____

1.364. Encounter for amniocentesis for screening for chromosomal anomalies

Code(s): _____

1.365. Exposure to mold

Code(s): _____

1.366. Renal dialysis status

Code(s): _____

1.367. Cardiac pacemaker status, without complications

Code(s): _____

1.368. Encounter for reprogramming of AICD

Code(s): _____

1.369. Aftercare for pathological fracture of L4 vertebra

Code(s): _____

1.370. Admission for change of tracheostomy tube and stoma revision

Code(s): _____

1.371. Admission for planned colostomy closure

Code(s): _____

1.372. Admission for chemotherapy

Code(s): _____

1.373. Admission to donate kidney

Code(s): _____

1.374. Observation of child post MVA with no apparent injury and no complaints

Code(s): _____

1.375. Encounter for screening mammogram

Code(s): _____

ICD-9-CM Procedure Coding

1.376. Vasectomy

Code(s): _____

1.377. Stapling of left atrial appendage (LAA)

Code(s): _____

1.378. Right thyroid lobectomy

Code(s): _____

1.379. Lamellar keratoplasty with donor corneal tissue

Code(s): _____

1.380. Myringotomy with placement of pressure equalization tube

Code(s): _____

1.381. Cleft palate repair

Code(s): _____

1.382. Lung volume reduction surgery

Code(s): _____

1.383. Open-heart surgery for repair of atrial septal defect with mesh

Code(s): _____

1.384. Right coronary artery PTCA

Code(s): _____

1.385. Coronary artery bypass grafting using left and right internal mammary arteries

Code(s): _____

1.386. Bilateral radical neck dissection

Code(s): _____

1.387. Total intra-abdominal colectomy performed by laparoscope

Code(s): _____

1.388. Whipple procedure

Code(s): _____

1.389. Right direct inguinal herniorrhaphy with mesh

Code(s): _____

1.390. Transplant nephrectomy

Code(s): _____

1.391. Paraurethral suspension utilizing Pereyra suture

Code(s): _____

1.392. Pelvic exenteration for ovarian cancer

Code(s): _____

1.393. Repair of fourth-degree laceration of rectum during delivery

Code(s): _____

1.394. Right total hip replacement

Code(s): _____

1.395. Reattachment of arm amputated through humerus

Code(s): _____

1.396. Mid-forceps extraction with episiotomy

Code(s): _____

1.397. Retropubic prostatectomy

Code(s): _____

1.398. Subtotal jejunectomy with end-to-end anastomosis

Code(s): _____

1.399. Percutaneous transmyocardial revascularization

Code(s): _____

1.400. Insertion of drug-eluting coronary artery stent

Code(s): _____

Review Questions

1.401. A patient with known acquired immunodeficiency syndrome (AIDS) is admitted to the hospital as an inpatient with acute appendicitis and undergoes an open appendectomy. The patient's AIDS is under treatment, and he is presently asymptomatic. The appropriate principal diagnosis in this case would be:

  a. 042
  b. 540.9
  c. V08
  d. Any of the above

1.402. When the diagnosis is stated as "septic shock," _____ is coded as the principal diagnosis.

1.403. The four types of neoplasms are benign, malignant, uncertain behavior, and

_____.

1.404. When a patient is admitted to the hospital for treatment of a secondary malignancy, and the primary is still present, the principal diagnosis is the _____ malignancy.

1.405. A patient is admitted for treatment of dehydration secondary to chemotherapy for primary liver cancer. Which condition should be sequenced as the principal diagnosis?

   a. Liver carcinoma
   b. Complication of chemotherapy
   c. Dehydration
   d. Any of the above

1.406. What code(s) are assigned for a patient with acute bronchitis and chronic obstructive bronchitis?

   a. 466.0
   b. 491.22
   c. 491.21
   d. 466.0, 491.21

1.407. Coding professionals may assume a cause-and-effect relationship between hypertension and which of the following conditions?

   a. Chronic kidney disease
   b. Heart failure
   c. Both heart and chronic kidney disease
   d. Neither condition

1.408. When a patient is admitted in respiratory failure due to/associated with a chronic nonrespiratory condition, the respiratory failure is the _____ diagnosis.

1.409. When a patient is admitted with respiratory failure due to/associated with an acute nonrespiratory condition (e.g., myocardial infarction), the principal diagnosis will be:

   a. Respiratory failure
   b. Nonrespiratory condition
   c. Dependent on the circumstances of the admission
   d. None of the above

1.410. Code 484.5 and its descriptor "Pneumonia in anthrax" are printed in italics. This convention identifies this code as a _____ code that must not be coded first.

1.411. Per *ICD-9-CM Official Guidelines for Coding and Reporting,* chapter 11 codes have sequencing priority over:

   a. Codes from all other chapters
   b. V codes only
   c. No other codes
   d. All codes except V codes

1.412. Chapter 11 codes are reported on:

    a. The mother's and the baby's record
    b. The mother's record
    c. The baby's record
    d. Either mother's record only or mother's and baby's records, depending on departmental coding policies

1.413. Which of the following criteria must be met to assign a diagnosis code of 650?

    a. Full-term normal delivery
    b. Single, healthy infant
    c. No maternal complications during the delivery, antepartum, or postpartum episode
    d. All of the above

1.414. According to official coding guidelines, which of the following statements is true about the assignment of code 650?

    a. It can never be assigned with any other code from chapter 11.
    b. V27.0 is the only appropriate outcome of delivery code with 650.
    c. It can be assigned if a patient had a complication at some time during her pregnancy, but it is no longer present at the time of delivery.
    d. All of the above

1.415. In the diagnostic statement "arthritis of bilateral knee joints secondary to primary hyperparathyroidism," which condition is sequenced as the principal diagnosis?

    a. The arthritis
    b. The primary hyperparathyroidism
    c. Either condition
    d. The circumstances of the admission will determine the appropriate sequencing.

1.416. Codes from categories 764 and 765 are assigned based on review of:

    a. Documented weights and dates per office and hospital records
    b. Nursing assessment of fetal maturity
    c. Attending physician's documented clinical assessment of the maturity of the infant
    d. Any of the above

1.417. The diagnostic statement "cholelithiasis with acute cholecystitis without obstruction" is reported with one code, 574.00. This is referred to as a _____ code.

1.418. In order for a condition to be considered a late effect, how much time must elapse between the acute event and the late effect?

    a. No more than 24 hours
    b. Six weeks
    c. There is no set time.
    d. One year

1.419. Per coding guidelines, a "significant procedure" must meet which of the following conditions:

    a. It is surgical in nature.
    b. It carries an anesthetic and/or surgical risk.
    c. It requires specialized training.
    d. All of the above

1.420. When two procedures meet the criteria for principal procedure, the one coded first is:

    a. The one performed first
    b. The one most closely related to the principal diagnosis
    c. The one that was performed by the attending physician
    d. The one with the highest reimbursement

1.421. A patient was admitted for a total hip replacement for arthritis of the hip. Just prior to the surgery, he developed a fever; pneumonia was seen on the chest x-ray. The patient was discharged and the surgery was rescheduled. What is the principal diagnosis for this admission?

    a. 486, Pneumonia
    b. 715.95, Osteoarthritis of the hip
    c. 780.60, Fever
    d. V64.1, Surgical or other procedure not carried out because of contraindication

1.422. A patient was admitted for evaluation of abdominal pain. In the evening after eating dinner, she fell out of bed and sustained a fracture of the femur. The next day she underwent hip replacement surgery and was eventually discharged to a skilled nursing facility for follow-up care. What is the principal diagnosis of this admission?

    a. Fracture of hip
    b. Abdominal pain
    c. Either abdominal pain or fracture of hip per the attending physician's final diagnosis statement
    d. Either abdominal pain or fracture of hip, whichever has the higher reimbursement

1.423. A patient was admitted with nausea and vomiting, and the final diagnosis stated acute gastroenteritis versus food poisoning. What are the diagnoses reported?

    a. Nausea with vomiting is reported as the principal diagnosis, and acute gastroenteritis and food poisoning are reported as secondary diagnoses.

    b. Acute gastroenteritis or food poisoning is reported as the principal diagnosis, and nausea with vomiting is reported as a secondary diagnosis.

    c. Only the nausea and vomiting are reported.

    d. Only the acute gastroenteritis and food poisoning are reported.

1.424. Diabetic foot ulcers may result from:

    a. Diabetic peripheral vascular complications

    b. Diabetic neurological complications

    c. Diabetic ketoacidosis

    d. Either a or b

1.425. Which of the following statements is true of gestational diabetes?

    a. It involves abnormal glucose tolerance test findings/results in pregnant women without previous history of diabetes.

    b. It is a form of true diabetes mellitus.

    c. It usually does not resolve after the patient delivers.

    d. It only occurs in patients with juvenile-onset type diabetes.

1.426. What is meant by a provider?

    a. Physician

    b. Physician, nurse-practitioner, or physician assistant

    c. Physician or any qualified healthcare practitioner who is legally accountable for establishing the patient's diagnosis

    d. Anyone documenting in the patient record.

Chapter 2

Basic Principles of CPT Coding

The following exercises are designed to review CPT coding guidelines and to provide practice in assigning CPT codes. Because CPT indexes procedures in many different ways, the rationale for the selection of a particular code may be different from the approach that you use. The information included in the rationale is not meant to describe the only way to obtain an appropriate code but to represent one possible way. Unless the coder is specifically instructed to assign modifiers, no modifiers will appear in the rationale.

Note: These exercises were developed to be used with the 2009 edition of CPT but are suitable for other editions in most cases.

Instructions: Circle the correct answer, fill in the blank, or assign the correct code(s) for each of the following exercise items.

CPT Organization, Structure, and Guidelines

2.1.   Category II codes cover all but one of the following topics. Which is not addressed by Category II codes?

    a. Patient management
    b. New technology
    c. Therapeutic, preventive, or other interventions
    d. Patient safety

2.2.   In CPT, the symbols ▶◀ are used to indicate:

    a. Changes in verbiage within code descriptions
    b. A new code
    c. Changes in verbiage other than that in code descriptions; for example, changes in coding guidelines or parenthetical notes
    d. A code for which there is a corresponding HCPCS Level II code

2.3.   During the performance of a femoral angioplasty, a patient develops additional areas of occlusion. A diagnostic angiogram of the affected artery is performed. Is it appropriate to code this diagnostic study in addition to the therapeutic procedure?

    a. No. All diagnostic procedures are included in therapeutic interventional procedures.

    b. Yes. Per revised coding guidelines, if there is a clinical change during an interventional procedure that requires further diagnostic study, the diagnostic angiogram may be reported in addition to the therapeutic procedure.

2.4.   Per CPT coding guidelines, a "complete" diagnostic ultrasound of the retroperitoneum includes at least the following organs:

    a. Kidneys, abdominal aorta, common iliac artery origins, inferior vena cava

    b. Kidneys, abdominal aorta, common iliac artery origins, inferior vena cava, and urinary bladder

    c. Liver, gallbladder, common bile duct, pancreas, spleen, kidneys, upper aorta, inferior vena cava

    d. Kidneys, abdominal aorta, common iliac artery origins

2.5.   A list of codes describing procedures that include conscious sedation, if administered by the same surgeon as performs the procedure, can be found in:

    a. Appendix E

    b. Appendix F

    c. Appendix G

    d. Appendix H

2.6.   True or false? Category II codes may be used as the first-listed CPT code when the patient is seen only for counseling.

    a. True

    b. False

2.7.   Which of the newly added appendices would a neurologist's practice consult to determine the nerve conduction code to assign for a study of the suprascapular motor nerve to the infraspinatus?

    a. Appendix I

    b. Appendix J

    c. Appendix K

    d. Appendix L

2.8.   In order to be included in the CPT manual, a procedure must meet which of the following criteria?

    a. It must be commonly performed by many physicians across the country.

    b. It must be consistent with contemporary medical practice.

    c. It must be covered by Medicare.

    d. Both a and b

2.9. Which of the following statements about CPT Category III codes is false?

    a. They are updated only once every 2 years.
    b. They were developed to reflect emerging technologies and procedures.
    c. They are archived after 5 years if the code has not been accepted for inclusion in the main body of CPT.
    d. Reimbursement for these services is dependent on individual payer policy.

2.10. Per CPT guidelines, a separate procedure:

    a. Is coded when it is performed as a part of another, larger procedure
    b. Is considered to be an integral part of another, larger service
    c. Is never coded under any circumstances
    d. Both a and b above

2.11. Which of the following statements is (are) true of CPT codes?

    a. They are numeric.
    b. They describe nonphysician services.
    c. They are updated annually by CMS.
    d. All of the above

2.12. What does the symbol ▲ before a code in the CPT manual signify?

    a. The code is new for this year.
    b. The code is exempt from bundling requirements.
    c. The code can only be used as an add-on code, never reported alone or first.
    d. The code has been revised in some way this year.

2.13. What does the symbol ● before a code in the CPT manual signify?

    a. The code is new for this year.
    b. The code is exempt from bundling requirements.
    c. The code can only be used as an add-on code, never reported alone or first.
    d. The code has been revised in some way this year.

2.14. CPT was developed and is maintained by:

    a. CMS
    b. AMA
    c. The Cooperating Parties
    d. WHO

2.15. CPT is updated:

    a. Annually for the main body of codes and every 6 months for Category III codes
    b. Annually
    c. Every 6 months
    d. As often as required by new technology

2.16.   The Alphabetic Index to CPT includes listings for:

a. Procedures/services
b. Examinations/tests
c. Anatomic sites
d. All of the above

2.17.   The use of the term "for" followed by a diagnosis in CPT means that:

a. The procedure must be reported for that diagnosis.
b. The procedure can only be reported for that diagnosis.
c. The diagnosis is an example of the types of diagnoses for which this procedure could be done.
d. None of the above

2.18.   If a surgeon performs a procedure for which there is no CPT code and no HCPCS Level II code, what code should be reported on the CMS 1500 form?

a. CPT code 99999
b. An unlisted procedure code from the appropriate chapter of CPT
c. An ICD-9-CM procedure code
d. A procedure that does not have a valid CPT code should not be reported.

2.19.   There are six sections to CPT: E/M, anesthesia, surgery, radiology, medicine, and _____.

2.20.   The symbol + before a code in CPT means that:

a. This code can never be reported alone.
b. This code can never be reported first.
c. This is an add-on code.
d. All of the above

2.21.   A listing of all current modifiers is found in which appendix of CPT?

a. Appendix A
b. Appendix B
c. Appendix C
d. Appendix D

2.22.   The codes in the musculoskeletal section of CPT may be used by:

a. Orthopedic surgeons only
b. Orthopedic surgeons and emergency department physicians
c. Any physician
d. Orthopedic surgeons and neurosurgeons

Evaluation and Management (E/M) Services

2.23.   A nursing facility patient develops an acute illness and is seen by her attending physician. He performs a detailed interval history, detailed physical examination, and performs medical decision making of moderate complexity. What code should the physician use to report these services?

   a. 99304
   b. 99305
   c. 99309
   d. 99310
   e. 99318

2.24.   For reporting of physician services, E/M codes are usually based on:

   a. Documentation of history, physical examination, and medical decision making
   b. The final diagnosis for the visit
   c. The amount of time spent with the patient
   d. Documentation of medical decision making

2.25.   Select the appropriate E/M code for a new patient office visit in which a comprehensive history and comprehensive physical examination were performed and medical decision making was of high complexity.

_____

2.26.   Select the appropriate E/M code for a new patient office visit in which a comprehensive history and comprehensive physical examination were performed and medical decision making was of straightforward complexity. _____

2.27.   Select the appropriate E/M code for an established patient visit in which a comprehensive history and expanded problem-focused physical examination was performed and medical decision making was of low complexity.

_____

2.28.   When counseling consumes more than half the total visit time, _____ may be used as the criterion for assigning the E/M code.

2.29.   Observation E/M codes (99218–99220) are used when:

   a. A patient is admitted and discharged on the same date.
   b. A patient is admitted for routine nursing care following surgery.
   c. A patient does not meet admission criteria.
   d. A patient is placed in designated observation status.

2.30.   A physician sees a patient in his office in the morning, then again in the early afternoon, at which time he sends the patient to the hospital in observation status. Later that day he visits the patient in the hospital and admits him as a full inpatient. What E/M codes should be assigned for this day of care?

   a. Two E/M codes for the office visits: one for the observation care, and one for the inpatient admission
   b. One code combining the two office visits: one for the observation care, and one for the inpatient admission
   c. One code for the observation care and one for the inpatient admission
   d. One code for the inpatient admission only

2.31.   History, physical examination, and medical decision making are the _____ components considered in assigning an E/M code.

2.32.   Which of the following are considered components of the social history?

   a. Occupational history
   b. Marital history
   c. Allergic history
   d. a and b above

2.33.   Documentation in history of use of drugs, alcohol, and/or tobacco is considered part of the_____.

   a. Past medical history
   b. Social history
   c. Systems review
   d. History of present illness

2.34.   Per CPT guidelines, a presenting problem of moderate severity is one that:

   a. May not require the presence of a physician, but for which care is provided under the supervision of a physician
   b. Runs a definite and prescribed course, is transient in nature and is not likely to permanently alter health status, or has a good prognosis with management and compliance
   c. Has a low risk of morbidity without treatment, little or no risk of mortality without treatment, with full recovery expected without functional impairment
   d. Has a moderate risk of morbidity without treatment, a moderate risk of mortality without treatment, uncertain prognosis, or increased probability of functional impairment

2.35.   Pediatric inpatient critical care, patient 6 months of age, first day

   Code(s): _____

2.36. Dr. Smith sees a patient in consultation in the hospital at the request of Dr. Jones. He renders an opinion. He then takes over the management of a portion of the patient's care. What codes should Dr. Smith use to bill for his subsequent hospital visits?

    a. Inpatient consultation codes
    b. Initial inpatient hospital care codes
    c. Subsequent hospital care codes
    d. No codes; the initial consultation includes all subsequent visits

2.37. Assign the appropriate E/M code for an outpatient office consultation in which the physician performed a detailed history, a comprehensive physical examination, and medical decision making of moderate complexity.

_____

2.38. Per CPT guidelines, a concise statement describing the symptom, problem, condition, diagnosis, or other factor that is the reason for the encounter, usually stated in the patient's words, is the definition of the:

    a. History of present illness
    b. Chief complaint
    c. Admission diagnosis
    d. Past history

2.39. Which of the following are parts of medical decision making?

    a. Number of possible diagnoses or management options that must be considered
    b. Amount or complexity of medical record, diagnostic tests, or other information that must be obtained, reviewed, and analyzed
    c. Risk of significant complications, morbidity, and/or mortality associated with the patient's presenting problem, the diagnostic procedures, and/or the management options
    d. All of the above

2.40. Which E/M codes are used to report services to patients in a facility that provides room, board, and other personal assistance services, generally on a long-term basis?

    a. Outpatient services
    b. Nursing facility care
    c. Domiciliary, rest home, or custodial care services
    d. Care plan oversight services

2.41. Preventive medicine services are based on which of the following criteria?

    a. Documentation of history, physical examination, and medical decision making
    b. Age of the patient
    c. Amount of time spent with the patient
    d. The final diagnosis for the visit

2.42. AHIMA Hospital has a "fast-track" department attached to the emergency department. This area is staffed by emergency department physicians on a rotating basis, treats minor problems, and is open from 5:00 a.m. until 8:00 p.m. What codes should be used to report services rendered in this department?

    a. Emergency department services codes

    b. Office or other outpatient services codes

    c. These are not codable services because the department is not open 24 hours per day.

    d. Either office or emergency department codes may be used.

2.43. In order to report a critical care code, a physician must spend at least _____ minutes with a critically ill patient.

Anesthesia Services

2.44. Per CPT guidelines, anesthesia time begins when the anesthesiologist begins to prepare the patient for induction, and ends:

    a. When the patient leaves the operating room

    b. When the anesthesiologist is no longer in personal attendance on the patient

    c. When the patient has fulfilled postanesthesia care unit criteria for recovery

    d. When the patient leaves the postanesthesia care unit

2.45. A physical status anesthesia modifier of P3 means that a patient:

    a. Has a mild systemic disease

    b. Has a severe systemic disease

    c. Has a severe systemic disease that is a constant threat to life

    d. Is moribund

2.46. Qualifying circumstances anesthesia codes are used:

    a. In addition to the anesthesia codes

    b. To describe provision of anesthesia under particularly difficult circumstances

    c. To describe circumstances that impact the character of the anesthesia

    d. All of the above

2.47. The qualifying circumstance code to assign when anesthesia services are provided under emergency circumstances is _____.

2.48. Anesthesia for total repair of cleft palate, patient 4 years of age

    Code(s): _____

2.49. Anesthesia for tracheal reconstruction, patient 6 months of age

    Code(s): _____

2.50. Anesthesia for permanent transvenous pacemaker insertion

    Code(s): _____

2.51. Anesthesia for lumbar laminectomy with fusion and insertion of rods and hooks

Code(s): _____

2.52. Anesthesia for ventral hernia repair, patient a 76-year-old female

Code(s): _____

2.53. Anesthesia for donor nephrectomy

Code(s): _____

2.54. Anesthesia for left knee arthroscopy with medial meniscectomy

Code(s): _____

2.55. Anesthesia for total hip replacement

Code(s): _____

2.56. Anesthesia for vasectomy

Code(s): _____

2.57. Anesthesia for cesarean section following failed attempt at vaginal delivery under spinal anesthesia

Code(s): _____

2.58. Anesthesia for emergency completion of near-total amputation through the midthigh with laceration of femoral artery with imminent exsanguination

Code(s): _____

2.59. Anesthesia for ORIF of fracture of the distal tibia and fibula

Code(s): _____

2.60. Anesthesia for left ventricular reduction surgery with heart–lung bypass and systemic hypothermia

Code(s): _____

2.61. Anesthesia for Whipple procedure

Code(s): _____

2.62. Anesthesia for direct coronary artery bypass grafting with pump oxygenator

Code(s): _____

2.63. Anesthesia for laparoscopically-assisted vaginal hysterectomy

Code(s): _____

Integumentary System

2.64. A patient undergoes placement of brachytherapy after loading catheters into her right breast under conscious sedation. The physician who performs the procedure administers the Versed® himself, and a nurse is present throughout the procedure to monitor the patient. Is it appropriate for the surgeon to report the conscious sedation for this procedure?

    a. Yes
    b. No

2.65. Tissue transplanted from one individual to another of the same species but different genotype is called a(n):

    a. Autograft
    b. Xenograft
    c. Allograft or allogeneic graft
    d. Heterograft

2.66. True or false? Per coding guidelines, skin grafting codes cannot be used unless there is surgical fixation of the graft to the recipient tissue.

    a. True
    b. False

2.67. When a malignant lesion is excised and the resultant skin defect is closed with a Z-plasty, what code(s) should be reported?

    a. A code for the Z-plasty only (14000–14061)
    b. A code for the malignant lesion excision (11600–11646) and a code for the Z-plasty (14000–14061)
    c. A code for the malignant lesion excision only (11600–11646)
    d. A code for the complex repair only (13100–13160)

2.68. When lesions are excised from multiple sites, which of the following is the correct coding protocol?

    a. Add all the dimensions and assign one code based on the total area.
    b. Code each lesion separately.
    c. Code only the largest lesion.
    d. Add all the dimensions for each body part, such as arms, legs, and so on, and assign as many codes as there are body parts treated.

2.69. A patient presents with a palpable lump in the left breast. The surgeon dissects down to the mass and removes it entirely. The procedure is described as "Biopsy of mass of left breast." Assign the appropriate CPT code (omitting modifiers).

    a. 19120
    b. 19101
    c. 19125
    d. 19301

2.70. When calculating dimensions for assigning a lesion excision code, which of the following is the appropriate method?

    a. Measurement of the lesion documented by the surgeon preexcision

    b. Measurement of the lesion plus circumferential margins documented by the surgeon preexcision

    c. Measurement of the lesion documented by the pathologist postexcision

    d. Measurement of the lesion plus circumferential margins documented by the pathologist postexcision

2.71. "The sharp removal by transverse incision or horizontal slicing to remove epidermal and dermal lesions without a full-thickness dermal excision" is the CPT definition of_____.

2.72. Débridement of skin, subcutaneous tissue, and muscle

Code(s): _____

2.73. Excision of 0.5 cm solar keratosis of the cheek with no significant margins

Code(s): _____

2.74. Excision of basal cell carcinoma, abdominal wall, 1.2 cm in diameter, with 1-cm skin margin all around

Code(s): _____

2.75. Excision of skin and subcutaneous tissue from the right groin for hidradenitis, with layered closure

Code(s): _____

2.76. Insertion and injection of tissue expander, scalp

Code(s): _____

2.77. Repair of 5.2-cm laceration of the left hand, dorsum, with layered closure

Code(s): _____

2.78. Repair of 3.4-cm laceration of the left forearm, single-layer closure with 4-0 Dexon; repair of 2.0-cm laceration of the left upper arm, single-layer closure

Code(s): _____

2.79. Repair of 3.0-cm laceration of the scalp, 2.5-cm laceration of the left foot, and 6.0-cm laceration of the left lower leg

Code(s): _____

2.80. Repair of 5.0-cm laceration of the left cheek, 3.2-cm laceration of the forehead, and 16.0-cm complex laceration of the left chest wall, utilizing multilayered closure

Code(s): _____

2.81. Simple repair of 2-inch laceration of the right neck area

Code(s): _____

2.82. A wound repair that involves layered closure of one or more of the deeper layers of subcutaneous tissue and superficial (nonmuscle) fascia or extensive cleaning of heavily contaminated wounds is a (an) _____ repair.

2.83. Open excisional biopsy of breast lesion identified by preoperative placement of radiological marker

Code(s): _____

2.84. Mohs micrographic surgery involves the surgeon acting as:

a. Both plastic surgeon and general surgeon
b. Both surgeon and pathologist
c. Both plastic surgeon and dermatologist
d. Both dermatologist and pathologist

2.85. Excision of nonpalpable suspicious area of possible microcalcification identified on mammogram (needle identifying the site placed at an outside radiologist's suite)

Code(s): _____

2.86. Excision of 2-cm squamous cell carcinoma from left chest with repair of resultant 8-cm^2 defect using V-Y plasty

Code(s): _____

Musculoskeletal System

2.87. Per coding guidelines, the type of fracture does not have a coding correlation to the type of treatment provided.

a. True
b. False

2.88. True or false? If a bone biopsy is performed in conjunction with a kyphoplasty procedure, it is separately coded.

a. True
b. False

2.89. Per the description of code 22523, fracture reduction and bone biopsy, if performed, are included in the procedure and are not separately coded. 3D reconstruction is not to be reported with which of the following base modalities?

a. CT angiography
b. MR angiography
c. PET scans
d. All of the above

2.90. Which of the following terms does not describe an open fracture?

    a. Missile
    b. Comminuted
    c. Infected
    d. Compound

2.91. Open fracture treatment includes which of the following scenarios?

    a. The fractured bone is exposed to the environment.
    b. The bone ends are visualized and internal fixation inserted.
    c. The fractured bone is opened remote from the fracture site and an intramedullary nail is inserted across the fracture site.
    d. All of the above

2.92. If an orthopedic surgeon attempted to reduce a fracture but was unsuccessful in obtaining acceptable alignment, what type of code should be assigned for the procedure?

    a. A "with manipulation" code
    b. A "without manipulation" code
    c. An unlisted procedure code
    d. An E/M code only

2.93. Keller bunionectomy

    Code(s): _____

2.94. Diagnostic arthroscopy, left knee, with medial meniscectomy

    Code(s): _____

2.95. Open reduction of knee dislocation with repair of the anterior cruciate ligament by anchor suture

    Code(s): _____

2.96. Percutaneous vertebroplasty, L5 (Do not assign radiological supervision and interpretation code.)

    Code(s): _____

2.97. Incision and drainage of infected shoulder bursa

    Code(s): _____

2.98. Putti-Platt procedure, left shoulder

    Code(s): _____

2.99. Open reduction, internal fixation humerus shaft fracture with cast application

    Code(s): _____

2.100. Wrist fusion with bone graft from iliac crest

Code(s): _____

2.101. Closed reduction of distal radial wrist fracture

Code(s): _____

2.102. Total hip arthroplasty

Code(s): _____

2.103. Casting is separately reported:

    a. When applied to stabilize or for comfort, by a separate physician
    b. For initial application by a physician who does not perform the fracture care
    c. When recasting is done during fracture follow-up
    d. All of the above

2.104. Anterior removal of artificial cervical disc

Code(s): _____

2.105. Bone biopsy obtained from iliac crest

Code(s): _____

2.106. Application of short leg walking cast for severe sprain of ankle

Code(s): _____

2.107. Arthroscopy of shoulder with complete rotator cuff repair

Code(s): _____

2.108. Midthigh amputation of leg

Code(s): _____

2.109. Closed reduction, temporomandibular joint dislocation

Code(s): _____

Respiratory System

2.110. A pulmonologist performed a diagnostic bronchoscopy with biopsy. The endoscope was introduced into the bronchus, and attachments were used to perforate the bronchial wall. Tissue was obtained and submitted to the pathologist, who identified it as "lung parenchyma." What type of biopsy was performed?

    a. Transbronchial lung biopsy
    b. Bronchial biopsy
    c. Bronchoalveolar lavage
    d. Protected specimen brush biopsy

2.111. Submucous resection of nasal turbinates

Code(s): _____

2.112. Control of epistaxis, anterior, by packing and silver nitrate cautery

Code(s): _____

2.113. Nasal sinus endoscopy with total ethmoidectomy

Code(s): _____

2.114. Total laryngectomy with left radical neck dissection

Code(s): _____

2.115. Direct laryngoscopy with vocal cord stripping using the operating microscope

Code(s): _____

2.116. Bronchoscopy with transbronchial lung biopsy

Code(s): _____

2.117. Thoracentesis with placement of tube

Code(s): _____

2.118. Thoracoscopy of the mediastinal space with biopsy

Code(s): _____

2.119. Open Caldwell-Luc procedure of maxillary sinuses

Code(s): _____

2.120. Emergency endotracheal intubation

Code(s): _____

2.121. Flexible bronchoscopy with placement of catheters for afterloading of radiotherapeutic agents

Code(s): _____

2.122. Right lung middle lobectomy

Code(s): _____

2.123. Double-lung transplant with cardiopulmonary bypass

Code(s): _____

2.124. Functional endoscopic sinus surgery (FESS) with frontal sinus polyp removal

Code(s): _____

2.125. Endoscopic control of nasal hemorrhage

Code(s): _____

2.126. When a bronchoscopy is performed under fluoroscopic guidance, how are the codes assigned per CPT coding guidelines?

    a. The fluoroscopy guidance code is assigned as a secondary procedure code with the bronchoscopy code.
    b. The fluoroscopy guidance code is assigned as the first procedure code.
    c. The fluoroscopy is included in the bronchoscopy and no code is assigned for it.
    d. Individual hospital coding guidelines determine whether the fluoroscopy is separately coded.

2.127. Talc pleurodesis for pneumothorax

Code(s): _____

2.128. Laryngoplasty for reconstruction following third-degree chemical burns of the larynx

Code(s): _____

2.129. Anterovertical hemilaryngectomy

Code(s): _____

Cardiovascular System

2.130. Codes describing endovascular repair of the descending thoracic aorta include all of the following procedures except one. Which procedure is not included in the repair code?

    a. Intravascular ultrasound
    b. Angiography of the thoracic aorta
    c. Fluoroscopic guidance in delivery of the endovascular components
    d. Preprocedure diagnostic imaging

2.131. True or false? Separate codes exist for ligation and stripping of the long saphenous vein and ligation and stripping of the short saphenous vein.

    a. True
    b. False

2.132. In coding arterial catheterizations, when the tip of the catheter is manipulated from the insertion into the aorta and then out into another artery, this is called:

    a. Selective catheterization
    b. Nonselective catheterization
    c. Manipulative catheterization
    d. Radical catheterization

2.133. Subtotal pericardiectomy

Code(s): _____

2.134. Insertion of permanent pacemaker with atrial and ventricular transvenous leads

Code(s): _____

2.135. When coding a selective catheterization, how are codes assigned?

    a. One code for each vessel entered
    b. One code for the point of entry vessel
    c. One code for the final vessel entered
    d. One code for the vessel of entry and one for the final vessel, with intervening vessels not coded

2.136. Replacement of the mitral valve with cardiopulmonary bypass

Code(s): _____

2.137. CABG using saphenous vein to the LAD

Code(s): _____

2.138. LIMA graft to the circumflex coronary artery and sequentially to the right coronary artery

Code(s): _____

2.139. Insertion of intra-aortic balloon pump, percutaneous

Code(s): _____

2.140. Introduction of catheter into the aorta

Code(s): _____

2.141. Venipuncture by cutdown, patient 32 years of age

Code(s): _____

2.142. A 35-year-old patient required implantation of a tunneled central venous catheter with insertion of a Life-Port® vascular access device (VAD).

Code(s): _____

2.143. Creation of Brescia-Cimino fistula for chronic hemodialysis

Code(s): _____

2.144. Ligation and stripping of long and short saphenous veins

Code(s): _____

2.145. Laparoscopic splenectomy

Code(s): _____

2.146. Injection for identification of sentinel node

Code(s): _____

2.147. Temporal artery biopsy

Code(s): _____

2.148. A tunneled centrally-inserted central venous catheter is placed in a 57-year-old patient.

Code(s): _____

2.149. Blood transfusion

Code(s): _____

2.150. Aortobifemoral bypass graft

Code(s): _____

2.151. Percutaneous transluminal popliteal angioplasty

Code(s): _____

Digestive System

2.152. Primary repair of bilateral cleft lip, one-stage procedure

Code(s): _____

2.153. Biopsy of floor of mouth

Code(s): _____

2.154. Uvulopalatopharyngoplasty for sleep apnea

Code(s): _____

2.155. T&A, 6-year-old patient

Code(s): _____

2.156. Upper gastrointestinal endoscopy with biopsy of lesion of esophagus

Code(s): _____

2.157. Per CPT coding guidelines, if a lesion is biopsied and then the remainder of the lesion is removed, what code(s) is (are) assigned?

    a. A code for the biopsy and one for the lesion excision
    b. A code for the lesion excision only
    c. A code for the biopsy only
    d. Hospital-specific coding procedures determine what is coded

2.158. Rigid esophagoscopy with removal of impacted food

Code(s): _____

2.159. EGD with esophageal dilation over guidewire

Code(s): _____

2.160. When the physician does not specify the method used to remove a lesion during an endoscopy, what is the appropriate procedure?

    a. Assign the removal by snare technique code.
    b. Assign the removal by hot biopsy forceps code.
    c. Assign the ablation code.
    d. Query the physician as to the method used.

2.161. ERCP with sphincterotomy

Code(s): _____

2.162. Laparoscopic Nissen fundoplication

Code(s): _____

2.163. Esophageal dilation with bougies

Code(s): _____

2.164. Endoscopic percutaneous gastrostomy tube placement

Code(s): _____

2.165. Left partial colectomy with end-to-end anastomosis

Code(s): _____

2.166. Laparoscopic partial colectomy with end colostomy (Hartmann procedure)

Code(s): _____

2.167. Revision of colostomy with repair of paracolostomy herniation

Code(s): _____

2.168. Small bowel endoscopy with control of hemorrhagic site in ileum using bipolar cautery

Code(s): _____

2.169. Colonoscopy with removal of five colonic polyps using hot biopsy forceps

Code(s): _____

2.170. Flexible sigmoidoscopy with decompression of volvulus

Code(s): _____

2.171. Laparoscopic cholecystectomy with cholangiography duct

Code(s): _____

Urinary System

2.172. Percutaneous needle biopsy of kidney

Code(s): _____

2.173. Donor nephrectomy, live donor

Code(s): _____

2.174. Surgical laparoscopy with ablation of renal cysts

Code(s): _____

2.175. Extracorporeal sound wave lithotripsy of large kidney stone

Code(s): _____

2.176. Change of ureterostomy tube

Code(s): _____

2.177. Total cystectomy with continent diversion using large intestine

Code(s): _____

2.178. Placement of indwelling bladder catheter

Code(s): _____

2.179. Cystourethroscopy with fulguration of three bladder tumors ranging in size from 0.4 to 1.6 cm

Code(s): _____

2.180. Cystourethroscopy with insertion of urethral stent

Code(s): _____

2.181. Cystourethroscopy with insertion of double-J ureteral stent

Code(s): _____

2.182. Cystourethroscopy with balloon dilation of UPJ stenosis

Code(s): _____

2.183. Transurethral resection of prostate with control of postoperative bleeding

Code(s): _____

2.184. Insertion of inflatable urethra–bladder neck sphincter

Code(s): _____

2.185. Repeat dilation of urethral stricture with filiforms and followers, male patient

Code(s): _____

2.186. Laparoscopic ureterolithotomy

Code(s): _____

2.187. Urethral pressure profile

Code(s): _____

2.188. Anterior vesicourethropexy by Marshall-Marchetti-Krantz procedure

Code(s): _____

2.189. Cystourethroscopy with biopsy of bladder wall

Code(s): _____

2.190. Cystourethroscopy with diagnostic ureteroscopy and removal of ureteral stones

Code(s): _____

2.191. Repeat transurethral resection of prostate tissue 4 years after original procedure

Code(s): _____

Male/Female Genital System and Laparoscopy

2.192. Laser destruction of condylomata of penis

Code(s): _____

2.193. Insertion of inflatable penile prosthesis

Code(s): _____

2.194. Removal and replacement of semirigid penile prosthesis from infected site, with irrigation and débridement of infected and necrotic tissue

Code(s): _____

2.195. Laparoscopic orchiopexy for undescended (intra-abdominal) testicle

Code(s): _____

2.196. Vasectomy

Code(s): _____

2.197. Needle biopsy of prostate

Code(s): _____

2.198. Radical retropubic prostatectomy

Code(s): _____

2.199. Incision and drainage of Bartholin's abscess

Code(s): _____

2.200. Colposcopy of cervix with cervical curettage

Code(s): _____

2.201. Total abdominal hysterectomy with concurrent Marshall-Marchetti-Krantz urethropexy

Code(s): _____

2.202. Vaginal hysterectomy (weight of uterus, 283 g) with bilateral salpingo-oophorectomy

Code(s): _____

2.203. Vaginal hysterectomy (weight of uterus, 230 g) with enterocele repair

Code(s): _____

2.204. Laparoscopic myomectomy with removal of eight intramural myomas

Code(s): _____

2.205. Ligation of fallopian tubes for elective sterilization

Code(s): _____

2.206. Laparoscopic sterilization procedure with Falope-rings®, bilateral

Code(s): _____

2.207. Bilateral salpingo-oophorectomy for ovarian malignancy with pelvic lymph node and peritoneal biopsies

Code(s): _____

2.208. Catheterization with dye injection for hysterosalpingogram

Code(s): _____

2.209. Penile plethysmography

Code(s): _____

2.210. Third-stage hypospadias repair

Code(s): _____

2.211. Laparoscopic fulguration of endometrial implants on the peritoneum and broad ligament

Code(s): _____

Endocrine System

2.212. Incision and drainage of infected thyroglossal duct cyst

Code(s): _____

2.213. Percutaneous needle biopsy of thyroid gland

Code(s): _____

2.214. Excision of adenoma of thyroid

Code(s): _____

2.215. Partial right-sided thyroidectomy

Code(s): _____

2.216. Partial right-sided thyroid lobectomy with isthmusectomy and subtotal resection of left thyroid

Code(s): _____

2.217. Left total thyroid lobectomy

Code(s): _____

2.218. Total right-sided thyroid lobectomy with isthmusectomy and subtotal resection of left thyroid

Code(s): _____

2.219. Total thyroidectomy

Code(s): _____

2.220. Total thyroidectomy for thyroid carcinoma with partial neck dissection

Code(s): _____

2.221. Thyroidectomy for thyroid carcinoma with radical neck dissection

Code(s): _____

2.222. Parathyroidectomy

Code(s): _____

2.223. Thyroidectomy (with sternal portion of thyroid) via cervical approach

Code(s): _____

2.224. Excision of recurrent thyroglossal duct cyst

Code(s): _____

2.225. Parathyroidectomy with mediastinal exploration

Code(s): _____

2.226. Transthoracic thymectomy

Code(s): _____

2.227. Exploration and biopsy of adrenal glands, transabdominal

Code(s): _____

2.228. Laparoscopic adrenalectomy

Code(s): _____

2.229. Excision of carotid body tumor and carotid artery

Code(s): _____

2.230. Thymectomy with radical mediastinal dissection

Code(s): _____

2.231. Aspiration of thyroid gland cyst

Code(s): _____

Nervous System

2.232. Cranial burr holes for drainage of subdural hematoma

Code(s): _____

2.233. Decompression craniectomy for treatment of intracranial hypertension

Code(s): _____

2.234. Excision of posterior fossa meningioma tumor via craniectomy

Code(s): _____

2.235. Percutaneous transcatheter embolization, brachiocephalic artery

Code(s): _____

2.236. Sterotactic radiosurgery for eradication of a 2.0 cm pituitary tumor

Code(s): _____

2.237. Ventriculoperitoneal shunt procedure

Code(s): _____

2.238. Diagnostic lumbar spinal tap

Code(s): _____

2.239. Implantation of cranial neurostimulator pulse generator

Code(s): _____

2.240. Injection of bupivacaine and Depo-Medrol®, L4 facet

Code(s): _____

2.241. Transforaminal epidural injection of Depo-Medrol®, C4–5 interspace

Code(s): _____

2.242. Excision neuroma, digital nerve, right fourth finger. Assign the CPT code and appropriate modifier.

Code(s): _____

2.243. Subtemporal decompression procedure for pseudotumor cerebri

Code(s): _____

2.244. Repair of 20-mm aneurysm, vertebrobasilar circulation

Code(s): _____

2.245. Stereotactic biopsy of intracranial lesion with magnetic resonance (MR) guidance. (Do not assign the radiological supervision and interpretation code.)

Code(s): _____

2.246. Intracranial neuroendoscopy with excision of pituitary tumor

Code(s): _____

2.247. Reprogramming of programmable cerebrospinal fluid shunt

Code(s): _____

2.248. Anterior diskectomy, T2–3 interspace

Code(s): _____

2.249. Injection of lidocaine, brachial plexus

Code(s): _____

2.250. Suture of digital nerves to the left third and fourth fingers. Assign the appropriate modifier(s) in addition to the CPT code.

Code(s): _____

2.251. Phenol injection for destruction of the infraorbital branch of the trigeminal nerve

Code(s): _____

Eye/Ocular Adnexa

2.252. Removal of corneal foreign body using slit lamp

Code(s): _____

2.253. Penetrating keratoplasty, aphakic eye

Code(s): _____

2.254. Radial keratotomy

Code(s): _____

2.255. Extracapsular cataract extraction by phacoemulsification with placement of posterior chamber IOL

Code(s): _____

2.256. Scleral buckle for retinal detachment

Code(s): _____

2.257. YAG laser photocoagulation of diabetic retinopathy

Code(s): _____

2.258. Strabismus surgery with recession of lateral and medial rectus muscles

Code(s): _____

2.259. Strabismus surgery with recession of superior oblique muscle

Code(s): _____

2.260. Strabismus surgery with 6-mm recession of superior rectus muscle and 3-mm recession of inferior rectus muscle, with placement of adjustable suture at inferior rectus

Code(s): _____

2.261. Repair of blepharoptosis by frontalis muscle fascial sling

Code(s): _____

2.262. Repair of entropion by thermocauterization

Code(s): _____

2.263. Dacryocystorhinostomy

Code(s): _____

2.264. Probing of nasolacrimal duct with stent placement

Code(s): _____

2.265. Excision of chalazions (three) from left upper and left lower eyelids

Code(s): _____

2.266. Laser photocoagulation of retina for prophylaxis of retinal detachment

Code(s): _____

2.267. Trabeculectomy ab externo

Code(s): _____

2.268. Enucleation of eyeball with implant, muscle controlled

Code(s): _____

2.269. Removal of foreign body from posterior chamber using magnet

Code(s): _____

2.270. Excision of pterygium with normal conjunctival tissue graft

Code(s): _____

2.271. Subtotal vitrectomy with endolaser panretinal photocoagulation

Code(s): _____

Auditory System

2.272. Removal of exostosis, external ear canal

Code(s): _____

2.273. Myringotomy with aspiration under general anesthesia

Code(s): _____

2.274. Myringotomy with PE tube insertion

Code(s): _____

2.275. Tympanoplasty with mastoidectomy with ossicular chain reconstruction

Code(s): _____

2.276. Decompression of internal auditory canal

Code(s): _____

2.277. Drainage of abscess of external ear canal

Code(s): _____

2.278. Removal of bead from a toddler's external ear canal using conscious sedation

Code(s): _____

2.279. Pin-back procedure for protruding ear

Code(s): _____

2.280. Removal of impacted cerumen, bilateral

Code(s): _____

2.281. Tympanoplasty without mastoidectomy, with placement of PORP

Code(s): _____

2.282. Tympanostomy with ventilation tube insertion under general anesthesia

Code(s): _____

2.283. Transmastoid excision of glomus tumor of ear

Code(s): _____

2.284. Repair of tympanic membrane perforation using synthetic patch

Code(s): _____

2.285. Stapedotomy with footplate drillout

Code(s): _____

2.286. Implantation of cochlear device

Code(s): _____

2.287. Oval window fistula repair

Code(s): _____

2.288. Transcanal labyrinthectomy with mastoidectomy

Code(s): _____

2.289. Removal and replacement of electromagnetic hearing aid in temporal bone

Code(s): _____

2.290. Débridement of mastoid cavity under general anesthesia

Code(s): _____

2.291. Removal of ventilation tubes under general anesthesia

Code(s): _____

Radiology Services

2.292. True or false? Code 76856 Ultrasound, pelvic (nonobstetrical), real time with image documentation, complete, can be used to describe examinations of either the male or female pelvis.

   a. True
   b. False

2.293. X-ray of mandible, five views

Code(s): _____

2.294. X-ray, including fluoroscopy, of pharynx for foreign body

Code(s): _____

2.295. CT scan of the brain, with and without contrast

Code(s): _____

2.296. Chest x-ray, AP and lateral

Code(s): _____

2.297. MRI of brain with contrast

Code(s): _____

2.298. X-ray, neck, six views, including oblique and flexion

Code(s): _____

2.299. Cervical myelogram, radiological supervision and interpretation

Code(s): _____

2.300. Shoulder arthrogram, radiological supervision and interpretation

Code(s): _____

2.301. X-ray of fractured hip in the operating room to confirm reduction

Code(s): _____

2.302. Barium enema with KUB

Code(s): _____

2.303. Percutaneous transhepatic cholangiography, radiological supervision and interpretation

Code(s): _____

2.304. Intravenous pyelogram with KUB and tomograms

Code(s): _____

2.305. Left external carotid angiography, selective, radiological supervision and interpretation

Code(s): _____

2.306. Ultrasound, pregnant uterus, first trimester

Code(s): _____

2.307. Nonselective pulmonary angiography, radiological supervision and interpretation

Code(s): _____

2.308. SPECT bone scan

Code(s): _____

2.309. Percutaneous transcatheter introduction of vascular stent, external iliac artery, radiological supervision and interpretation

Code(s): _____

2.310. Mammographic guidance for preoperative needle placement in breast, radiological supervision and interpretation

Code(s): _____

2.311. Retroperitoneal ultrasound

Code(s): _____

2.312. Acute gastrointestinal blood loss imaging scan

Code(s): _____

Pathology/Laboratory Services

2.313. The symbol ✗ added to the Laboratory and Pathology section, means:

   a. This is an add-on laboratory code.
   b. The code is sex specific.
   c. This code should only be reported for Medicare patients.
   d. FDA approval of the vaccine is pending.

2.314. Mr. Smith is seen in his primary care physician's office for his annual physical examination. He has a digital rectal examination and is given three small cards to take home and return with fecal samples to screen for colorectal cancer. Assign the appropriate CPT code to report this occult blood sampling.

   a. 82270
   b. 82271
   c. 82272
   d. 82274

2.315. True or false? Code 80048, basic metabolic panel, can be assigned with a modifier of 52, reduced services, if only seven of the eight tests are performed.

   a. True
   b. False

2.316. Code 87900, infectious agent drug susceptibility phenotype prediction using regularly updated genotypic bioinformatics, is used in the management of patients with what disease?

   a. Cancer patients on toxic chemotherapy agents
   b. HIV patients on antiretroviral therapy
   c. Tuberculosis patients on rifampin therapy
   d. Organ transplant patients on immunosuppressive therapy

2.317. Creatine phosphokinase isoenzymes

Code(s): _____

2.318. Iron-binding capacity

Code(s): _____

2.319. Screen for mercury

Code(s): _____

2.320. Spinal fluid pH

Code(s): _____

2.321. Protein, by refractometry

Code(s): _____

2.322. Urine sodium

Code(s): _____

2.323. Automated CBC with automated differential

Code(s): _____

2.324. Duke bleeding time

Code(s): _____

2.325. Protime

Code(s): _____

2.326. Antinuclear antibody titer

Code(s): _____

2.327. VDRL

Code(s): _____

2.328. HBsAb

Code(s): _____

2.329. Chlamydia antibody, IgM

Code(s): _____

2.330. Erythrocyte sedimentation rate, automated

Code(s): _____

2.331. Surgical pathology, examination (gross and microscopic) of arterial biopsy

Code(s): _____

2.332. Surgical pathology, examination (gross and microscopic) of breast and regional lymph nodes

Code(s): _____

2.333. Lyme disease antibody

Code(s): _____

2.334. Protoporphyrin screen

Code(s): _____

2.335. Infrared spectroscopy of renal calculus

Code(s): _____

2.336. Blood culture

Code(s): _____

Medicine

2.337. An infusion that lasts less than 15 minutes would be reported with a(n) _____ code.

    a. Intravenous infusion
    b. Intravenous piggyback
    c. Intravenous or intra-arterial push
    d. Intravenous hydration

2.338. Codes 90760 and 90761 are used to report infusion of:

    a. Chemotherapeutic agents
    b. Sequential drugs of the same drug family
    c. Hormonal antineoplastics
    d. Prepackaged fluids and/or electrolytes

2.339. The code for moderate conscious sedation is determined by:

    a. Who administers the sedation
    b. The age of the patient
    c. The duration of the sedation
    d. All of the above

2.340. A prostate cancer patient is seen in the office for infusion of luteinizing hormone-releasing hormone agonist therapy, given subcutaneously. Assign the appropriate CPT code.

    a. 96401
    b. 96402
    c. 96413
    d. 96405

2.341. True or false? The "initial service" code under Hydration, Infusions and Chemotherapy is chosen based on the first substance infused.

    a. True
    b. False

2.342. Select the appropriate code(s) to report an injection of rabies immune globulin performed under direct physician supervision.

    a. 90772
    b. 90471
    c. 90375, 90772
    d. 90375, 90473

2.343. Psychotherapy that involves the use of physical aids and nonverbal communication to overcome barriers to therapeutic intervention is called _____ psychotherapy.

2.344. Individual psychotherapy, inpatient hospital, 50 minutes

Code(s): _____

2.345. Esophageal motility study with acid perfusion testing

Code(s): _____

2.346. Fluorescein angiography

Code(s): _____

2.347. Reprogramming of cochlear implant device, patient 3 years of age

Code(s): _____

2.348. Transcatheter placement of coronary artery stent, right coronary artery

Code(s): _____

2.349. EKG, physician interpretation and report, using hospital equipment

Code(s): _____

2.350. Combined right heart catheterization and retrograde left heart catheterization via femoral artery approach

Code(s): _____

2.351. Electronic analysis of pacing cardioverter-defibrillator, dual chamber, with reprogramming

Code(s): _____

2.352. Duplex scan of bilateral lower extremity arteries

Code(s): _____

2.353. Pulmonary stress testing with measurements of CO_2 production, O_2 uptake, and electrocardiographic recordings

Code(s): _____

2.354. EEG, awake and asleep

Code(s): _____

2.355. Therapeutic exercises, 23 minutes

Code(s): _____

2.356. Chiropractic manipulation of the spine, cervical, thoracic, lumbar, and sacral regions

Code(s): _____

2.357. EMG testing of both upper extremities and related paraspinal musculature

Code(s): _____

2.358. Bronchospasm provocation evaluation

Code(s): _____

2.359. Lymphatic drainage (15 minutes of manual traction)

Code(s): _____

2.360. Chemotherapy administration via IV push

Code(s): _____

2.361. Comprehensive electrophysiologic testing with induction of arrhythmia

Code(s): _____

Modifiers

2.362. In physician professional fee coding, when multiple procedures other than E/M services are provided on the same date by the same provider, modifier _____ should be appended to the second and all subsequent procedures.

2.363. The modifier used to report therapeutic interventional procedures on the right coronary artery is_____.

2.364. Which of the following circumstances can be described by the use of a HCPCS modifier?

a. A service has been increased or reduced.
b. Only part of a service was performed.
c. A service was provided more than once.
d. All of the above

2.365. A radiologist interprets x-rays for a community hospital. The equipment belongs to the hospital. What modifier should the radiologist append to his CPT codes? _____

2.366. A patient underwent repair of an ectropion of the left upper eyelid by tarsal wedge technique. Assign the appropriate CPT code and modifier(s).
_____

2.367. A pediatric thoracic and cardiovascular surgeon performs a curative procedure on an infant but does not see the child again. Instead, a pediatric cardiologist does all follow-up. What modifier should the surgeon append to his CPT procedure code? _____

2.368. A surgeon performs a palmar fasciotomy for Dupuytren's contracture of the right hand by open technique. Assign the appropriate CPT code(s) and modifier(s). _____

2.369. A patient is scheduled for a colonoscopy, but due to sudden drop in blood pressure, the procedure is canceled just as the scope is introduced into the rectum. Because of moderately severe mental retardation, the patient is given a general anesthetic prior to the procedure. How should this procedure be coded by the hospital?

    a. Assign the code for a colonoscopy with modifier -74.
    b. Assign the code for a colonoscopy with modifier -52.
    c. Assign no code because no procedure was performed.
    d. Assign an anesthesia code only.

2.370. When clinical laboratory tests are repeated on the same day, what modifier should be assigned? _____

2.371. When a surgeon performs a procedure and a separately identifiable E/M service on the same date, how should codes and modifiers be assigned?

    a. Assign a code for the procedure only.
    b. Assign a code for the procedure and one for the E/M service without any modifiers.
    c. Assign a code for the procedure and one for the E/M service, with modifier -25 appended to the E/M code.
    d. Assign a code for the procedure and one for the E/M service, with modifier -25 appended to both the E/M code and the procedure code.

2.372. When absolutely identical procedures are performed on both members of a set of paired organs, such as kidneys, what modifier is assigned?
_____

2.373. Planned rigid proctosigmoidoscopy with removal of foreign body under conscious sedation, procedure not completed due to hypotension. How would the physician report this?

    Code(s): _____

2.374. When a separately identifiable evaluation and management service is performed by the same physician on the same day of a procedure of their service, what modifier should be reported with the E/M code?

_____

2.375. When a physician performs a consultation as a required second opinion for an HMO, what modifier should be appended to the consultation code?

_____

2.376. When a patient is seen in two hospital outpatient departments in 1 day, what modifier should be appended to the second E/M code to ensure appropriate reimbursement? _____

2.377. When a hospital provides ambulance services by arrangement with a transport company, what modifier should be appended to the codes for ambulance services? _____

2.378. Because of language barriers and patient agitation, the performance of a consultation takes approximately twice as long as the "usual" time for a level 5 service. What modifier should be attached to the consultation code to reflect this situation? _____

2.379. In addition to the claim submitted by the surgeon, the assistant surgeon also bills for his or her services. What modifier does the assistant surgeon attach to the procedure code? _____

2.380. When two surgeons work together as primary surgeons performing distinct parts of a procedure, each surgeon should report which modifier to the procedure code(s)? _____

2.381. Some reconstructive plastic surgical procedures are performed in multiple stages. What modifier should the surgeon report when the patient is returned to surgery for a planned-staged procedure? _____

Category III Codes

2.382. Which of the following statements about Category III CPT codes is true?

a. They are temporary.
b. They are updated more frequently than the rest of CPT.
c. They are intended to allow for the coding of new technologies, services, and procedures.
d. All of the above

2.383. Both a regular CPT unlisted procedure code and a Category III code may exist to report the same procedure. Which code(s) should be reported?

a. Report the CPT unlisted procedure code.
b. Report the Category III code.
c. Report both the CPT unlisted procedure code and the Category III code.
d. Report the Category III code with modifier -59.

2.384. After 5 years, all Category III codes:

    a. Will be archived unless there is evidence that a temporary code is still needed
    b. Will be automatically renewed for another 5 years
    c. Will be automatically retired
    d. Will be replaced with a regular CPT code

2.385. Insertion of posterior spinous process distraction device into L2 and L3

Code(s): _____

2.386. Holotranscobalamin, quantitative

Code(s): _____

2.387. Excision of rectal tumor via TEMS approach

Code(s): _____

2.388. Lumbar discectomy and arthrodesis utilizing pre-sacral interbody fusion technique

Code(s): _____

2.389. How frequently are Category III codes updated?

    a. Annually
    b. Semiannually
    c. Every two years
    d. Every four months

2.390. Antiprothrombin antibody

Code(s): _____

2.391. Remote real-time interactive video-conferenced critical care, evaluation and management of a critically ill patient for 60 minutes

Code(s): _____

2.392. Repair of anorectal fistula with plug

Code(s): _____

2.393. Suprachoroidal delivery of pharmacologic agent

Code(s): _____

2.394. Anterior diskectomy and total arthroplasty, utilizing artificial disk, of C3 and C4.

Code(s): _____

2.395. Category III codes can be used by what groups of providers?

    a. Hospital outpatient providers only
    b. Physicians only
    c. Hospitals, physicians, insurers, health services researchers
    d. Medicare-approved providers only

2.396. 64-lead electrocardiogram with tracing and graphics, without interpretation and report

Code(s): _____

2.397. Photocoagulation of macular drusen

Code(s): _____

2.398. Laparotomy with removal of gastric stimulation electrodes of the lesser curvature

Code(s): _____

2.399. Diagnostic virtual colonoscopy

Code(s): _____

2.400. Exhaled breath condensate pH

Code(s): _____

2.401. Cerebral perfusion study using CT with contrast

Code(s): _____

Review Questions

2.402. Surgical knee arthroscopy with medial meniscectomy and lateral retinacular release

Code(s): _____

2.403. Functional endoscopic sinus surgery with bilateral anterior ethmoidectomy and bilateral maxillary antrostomy with curettage of maxillary polyps

Code(s): _____

2.404. Excision of 2.3-cm (including margins) squamous cell skin cancer from the right arm with closure of the resultant defect with rotational flap advancement

Code(s): _____

2.405. Repair of multiple lacerations of the right upper extremity, including 7.6-cm laceration of the upper arm, closed with single layer of 3-0 Dexon; 5.4-cm laceration of the upper arm requiring layered closure; 3.5-cm laceration of the dorsum of the right hand, closed in layers; and 16-cm laceration of the forearm, closed in a single layer of 3-0 Dexon

Code(s): _____

2.406. Spinal fusion, L2–3 and L3–4, with laminectomy and placement of bone graft harvested from sacral spinous processes

Code(s): _____

2.407. Decompression fasciotomy of the forearm, flexor and extensor compartments, with débridement of necrotic muscle and nerve tissue

Code(s): _____

2.408. Banding of the pulmonary artery in a 4-week-old infant weighing 3,650 g. Assign modifier(s) as appropriate.

Code(s): _____

2.409. Coronary artery bypass graft (CABG) using vein grafts to the left anterior descending coronary artery and internal mammary artery graft to the lateral circumflex coronary artery. Due to severe lower extremity vascular disease, vein was harvested from the right basilic vein.

Code(s): _____

2.410. Transcatheter placement of stent, abdominal aorta, using intravascular ultrasound monitoring. Assign both surgical and radiological supervision and interpretation codes.

Code(s): _____

2.411. Diagnostic upper gastrointestinal (GI) endoscopy to the jejunum, with injection of esophageal varices, and biopsy of gastrojejunal junction and body of stomach

Code(s): _____

2.412. Proctosigmoidoscopy with removal of one polyp by hot biopsy forceps and biopsy of hemorrhagic area

Code(s): _____

2.413. Bronchoscopy with tracheal biopsy, and dilation and placement of tracheal stent

Code(s): _____

2.414. Needle biopsy of inguinal lymph nodes

Code(s): _____

2.415. Endoscopic retrograde cholangiopancreatography (ERCP) with manipulation and removal of stone from the common bile duct

Code(s): _____

2.416. Cystourethroscopy with resection of bladder tumor, 2.3 cm in diameter, and ureteral catheterization with manipulation of ureteric stone

Code(s): _____

2.417. Radical perineal prostatectomy with complete bilateral pelvic lymph node dissection

Code(s): _____

2.418. Colposcopy of cervix with endocervical curettage

Code(s): _____

2.419. VBAC, including routine prenatal and postpartum care

Code(s): _____

2.420. Transnasal hypophysectomy

Code(s): _____

2.421. Repair of laceration of cornea, penetrating, with excision of devitalized uveal tissue

Code(s): _____

2.422. Right shoulder arthrogram. Assign surgical and radiological supervision and interpretation codes, as well as any appropriate modifiers for hospital reporting.

Code(s): _____

2.423. Liver and spleen imaging with vascular flow

Code(s): _____

2.424. High-sensitivity C-reactive protein

Code(s): _____

2.425. TEE for congenital cardiac anomalies, placement of probe only

Code(s): _____

2.426. Intramuscular (IM) injection of HepB-Hib vaccine

Code(s): _____

Chapter 3

HCPCS Level II Coding

> **Note:** These exercises are intended for use with the 2009 version of the Healthcare Common Procedure Coding System (HCPCS) Level II codes. HCPCS codes are revised annually by the Centers for Medicare and Medicaid Services (CMS) and become effective January 1 each calendar year. Books are available from a variety of publishers. An electronic file is available for downloading from the Internet at http://www.cms.hhs.gov/MedHCPCSGenInfo/01_Overview.asp. Click on HCPCS Annual Update.
>
> **Instructions:** Circle the correct answer, fill in the blank, or assign the correct code(s) for each of the following exercise items.

Drugs

3.1.   HCPCS Level II contains codes for drugs that are administered:

   a. Subcutaneously
   b. Intramuscularly
   c. Intravenously
   d. All of the above

3.2.   Injection Unasyn®, 1.5 g

   Code(s): _____

3.3.   Injection baclofen, 50 mcg intrathecal

   Code(s): _____

3.4.   Injection Botox®, three units

   Code(s): _____

3.5.   Injection Anzemet®, 10 mg

   Code(s): _____

3.6.   Injection RhoGam®, 300 mcg

Code(s): _____

3.7.   Injection Cytosar-U®, 100 mg

Code(s): _____

3.8.   Injection mitomycin, 40 mg

Code(s): _____

3.9.   Injection digoxin, 0.5 mg

Code(s): _____

3.10.   Intra-articular injection of Synvisc®, 16 mg, left knee

Code(s): _____

Supplies

3.11.   CPAP device

Code(s): _____

3.12.   Blood tubing, venous, for hemodialysis

Code(s): _____

3.13.   Urinary ostomy pouch with barrier attached

Code(s): _____

3.14.   Alginate dressing, 36-in^2 pad

Code(s): _____

3.15.   Radiopharmaceutical technetium medronate (Tc-99m)

Code(s): _____

3.16.   Therapeutic radiopharmaceutical agent Strontium 89 chloride, 1 mCi

Code(s): _____

3.17.   Tracheal suction, closed system, for 72 or more hours of use

Code(s): _____

3.18.   Blood glucose reagent strips for home glucose monitor, bottle of 50 strips

Code(s): _____

3.19. Distilled water used with nebulizer, 1,000 mL

Code(s): _____

3.20. Surgical trays used in physician office surgery

Code(s): _____

Ambulance

3.21. BLS defibrillation supplies

Code(s): _____

3.22. The two-digit modifier to indicate that a patient was taken from the acute hospital to a skilled nursing facility by ambulance is:

Code(s): _____

3.23. Basic life support ambulance services

Code(s): _____

3.24. Ground ambulance transport services are reported:

a. Per trip
b. Per mile
c. Per minute of travel time
d. Per hour of travel time

3.25. Helicopter transport, per mile

Code(s): _____

3.26. Because of the patient's condition, an additional EMT is required for the transport. What is the code for the presence of the extra attendant?

_____

3.27. Ambulance waiting time is measured in:

a. Minutes
b. Hours
c. Half hours
d. 10-minute increments

3.28. Routine disposable supplies used during a basic life support transport

Code(s): _____

3.29. Neonatal transport

Code(s): _____

3.30.   Oxygen administered during advanced life support transport

Code(s): _____

Durable Medical Equipment

3.31.   Rental of portable liquid oxygen system

Code(s): _____

3.32.   Totally electric hospital bed, without mattress, and alternating pressure mattress for hospital bed

Code(s): _____

3.33.   Cycler dialysis machine for peritoneal dialysis

Code(s): _____

3.34.   Portable whirlpool

Code(s): _____

3.35.   Wheelchair, amputee, with detachable arms and detachable, swing-away footrests

Code(s): _____

3.36.   Adult transport chair

Code(s): _____

3.37.   Wheelchair accessories tray

Code(s): _____

3.38.   Eggcrate dry pressure pad

Code(s): _____

3.39.   Four-lead TENS unit

Code(s): _____

3.40.   Recording apnea monitor

Code(s): _____

Procedures/Services

3.41.   Glaucoma screening for high-risk patients

Code(s): _____

3.42. Colorectal cancer screening by barium enema

Code(s): _____

3.43. Diagnostic mammography, unilateral

Code(s): _____

3.44. PET scanning, whole body, for diagnosis of esophageal carcinoma, for restaging

Code(s): _____

3.45. Direct hospital observation admission for patient with diagnosis of congestive heart failure (CHF), chest pain, or asthma

Code(s): _____

3.46. Transcatheter placement of drug-eluting stent, coronary artery, percutaneous

Code(s): _____

3.47. Services of clinical social worker in home health setting per 15 minutes

Code(s): _____

3.48. Diabetes self-management training, group session, per 30 minutes

Code(s): _____

3.49. Trimming of dystrophic nails

Code(s): _____

3.50. Influenza virus vaccine

Code(s): _____

Part II
Intermediate Coding Exercises

Chapter 4

Case Studies from Inpatient Health Records

Note: Even though the specific cases are divided by setting, most of the information pertaining to the diagnosis is applicable to most settings. If you practice or apply codes in a particular type of setting, you may find additional information in other sections of this publication that may be pertinent to you.

Every effort has been made to follow current recognized coding guidelines and principles, as well as nationally recognized reporting guidelines. The material presented may differ from some health plan requirements for reporting. The ICD-9-CM codes used are effective October 1, 2009, through September 30, 2010, and the HCPCS (CPT and HCPCS Level II) codes are in effect January 1, 2009, through December 31, 2009. The current standard transactions and code sets named in HIPAA have been utilized, which require ICD-9-CM Volume III procedure codes for inpatients.

Instructions: Cases are presented as either multiple choice or fill in the blank.

- For multiple-choice cases:
  —Select the letter of the appropriate code set
- For the fill-in-the-blank cases:
  —Assign the MS-DRG, where indicated.
  —Assign present on admission (POA) indicator for each diagnosis code.
  - Y-Yes (POA)
  - N-No (Not POA)
  - U-Unknown (Documentation is insufficient to determine if condition is POA.)
  - W-Clinically undetermined (Provider is unable to clinically determine whether or not the condition was POA.)
  - Leave blank for the exercises in this book all codes that are exempt from POA reporting. See the Exempt List as published in the *ICD-9-CM Official Guidelines for Coding and Reporting*. These codes are exempt because they represent circumstances regarding healthcare encounters or factors influencing health status that do not represent a current disease or injury, or are always present on admission. Reporting exempt codes for Medicare claims requires a number 1 to be entered, rather than a blank, per CMS Transmittal 1240 dated 5/11/07.
  —Sequence the ICD-9-CM principal diagnosis in the first diagnosis position.

—Assign all reportable secondary diagnosis codes including V codes and E codes (both cause of injury and place of occurrence).

—Sequence the ICD-9-CM principal procedure code in the first procedure position.

—Assign all reportable secondary ICD-9-CM procedure codes.

The scenarios are based on selected excerpts from health records. In practice, the coding professional should have access to and refer to the entire health record. Health records are analyzed and codes assigned based on physician documentation. Documentation for coding purposes must be assigned based on medical record documentation. A physician may be queried when documentation is ambiguous, incomplete, or conflicting. The queried documentation must be a permanent part of the medical record.

The objective of the cases and scenarios reproduced in this publication is to provide practice in assigning correct codes, not necessarily to emulate complete coding, which can be achieved only with the complete medical record. For example, the reader may be asked to assign codes based on only an operative report when in real practice, a coder has access the entire medical record.

The *ICD-9-CM Official Guidelines for Coding and Reporting*, published by the National Center for Health Statistics (NCHS), includes Present on Admission (POA) Reporting Guidelines in Appendix I. These guidelines supplement the official conventions and instructions provided within ICD-9-CM. Adherence to these guidelines when assigning ICD-9-CM diagnosis codes is required under the Health Insurance Portability and Accountability Act (HIPAA) of 1996. Additional official coding guidance can be found in the American Hospital Association (AHA)'s *Coding Clinic* publication.

Disorders of the Blood and Blood-Forming Organs

4.1. This 45-year-old man underwent colon resection for carcinoma of the transverse colon. The physician progress note on postoperative day 2 states anemia. Hemoglobin and hematocrit levels dropped significantly after surgery and a blood transfusion was ordered. How is the anemia coded?

   a. 285.1
   b. 998.11
   c. 998.11, 285.1
   d. Unable to code, the physician must be queried

4.2. The discharge diagnoses included for this 82-year-old woman admitted for acute exacerbation of chronic obstructive pulmonary disease are: neutropenia, anemia, pancytopenia, and thrombocytopenia. A blood transfusion was given. What codes are assigned for this case?

   a. 491.21, 284.1, 99.03
   b. 491.21, 284.1, 285.9, 288.00, 287.5, 99.03
   c. 496, 284.1, 99.03
   d. 491.21, 285.9, 288.00, 287.5, 99.02

4.3. This 35-year-old female patient has carcinoma of the upper-outer left breast. She had a lumpectomy performed and a sentinel lymph node biopsy of the axillary lymph node. The pathology report for the lymph node states no pathological change. What codes are assigned in this case?

Code(s) with POA indicator: _____

4.4. An 8-year-old male hemophiliac is admitted with acute blood loss anemia due to uncontrolled bleeding. He is given clotting factor and six units of whole blood. Which of the following answers would be correct?

    a. 286.0, 99.06, 99.03
    b. 285.1, 286.0, 99.06, 99.03
    c. 286.0, 285.1, 99.06, 99.03
    d. 285.1, 99.06, 99.03

4.5. What code(s) is/are assigned for a patient admitted for chemotherapy for a chemotherapy drug induced aplastic anemia?

Code(s) with POA indicator and MS-DRG: _____

Disorders of the Cardiovascular System

4.6. When a diagnostic statement lists hypertension and chronic kidney disease, which of the following coding guidelines applies?

    a. The conditions are reported with two separate codes unless the physician specifically states that there is a cause-and-effect relationship.
    b. Code 403.9X is assigned, with an additional code to identify the stage of chronic kidney disease.
    c. A cause-and-effect relationship is never assumed.
    d. Code 403.9X is assigned, with an additional code to specify the type of hypertension.

4.7. This 52-year-old male was admitted to City Hospital with chest pain that was determined to be due to an acute inferior wall myocardial infarction. He was subsequently transferred to Anytown Medical Center for cardiac catheterization. A right and left heart catheterization with Judkins coronary angiography and right and left angiocardiography were performed. New onset atrial fibrillation was diagnosed, and the patient was discharged on the fourth day in stable condition. What codes are reported at Anytown Medical Center?

Code(s) with POA indicator: _____

4.8.   A patient is readmitted to the acute care hospital from a long-term care facility for treatment of heart failure. She had an acute anterior wall myocardial infarction (MI) 4 weeks ago. She was placed in the intensive care unit and monitored on telemetry. She was also found to have urinary tract infection (UTI) due to *Escherichia coli.* After intense drug therapy, she continued to improve and was transferred back to the long-term care facility. The acute systolic and diastolic heart failure was improved, but she will be monitored. What codes are assigned in this case?

a. 428.21, 428.31, 410.12, 599.0, 041.4, 89.54
b. 428.41, 410.12, 599.0, 041.4, 89.54
c. 428.0, 412, 599.0, 041.4, 89.54
d. 428.41, 410.11, 599.0, 041.4, 89.54

4.9.   A patient with severe arteriosclerotic heart disease (ASHD) of native arteries and severe chronic obstructive pulmonary disease (COPD) was admitted for coronary artery bypass graft (CABG) × 4 with cardiopulmonary bypass. Postoperatively, the patient developed pulmonary emboli that required treatment and extended the inpatient stay.

Code(s) with POA indicator and MS-DRG: _____

4.10.   The following was documented in the history and physical:

This patient was admitted with a diagnosis of acute myocardial infarction. He was hospitalized for pneumonia last year and 2 years ago had surgery for a bleeding gastric ulcer. Additional history is that he was diagnosed 5 years ago with Parkinson's disease, which is getting progressively worse. He is being treated with levodopa. History also notes emphysema being treated with bronchodilators and corticosteroids.

Discharge Summary: The discharge summary repeats the information in the history and physical examination (H&P), plus adds the following information. During the hospital stay, the patient developed congestive heart failure confirmed by x-ray and started Lasix p.o.

Discharge Diagnoses: Acute myocardial infarction, Parkinson's disease, congestive heart failure, emphysema, history of pneumonia, and history of bleeding gastric ulcer. What conditions are coded in this example?

a. Acute myocardial infarction, congestive heart failure, Parkinson's disease, emphysema
b. Acute myocardial infarction, congestive heart failure
c. Acute myocardial infarction, congestive heart failure, Parkinson's disease, emphysema, pneumonia, bleeding ulcer
d. Acute myocardial infarction, pneumonia, congestive heart failure, emphysema

4.11. The following documentation is from the health record of a cardiac service patient.

Discharge Summary

Admit Date:	1/9/XX
Discharge Date:	1/12/XX
Final Diagnoses:	1. Coronary artery disease (CAD)
	2. Sick sinus syndrome
Procedures:	1. Permanent dual chamber pacemaker insertion
	2. Percutaneous transluminal coronary angioplasty (PTCA) with stent insertion

History of Present Illness: The patient is a 60-year-old female who was admitted to another hospital on 1/8/XX, after experiencing tachycardia. There she underwent a cardiac catheterization, showing the presence of severe single-vessel coronary artery disease. The patient has a history of sick sinus syndrome. She was transferred to our hospital to undergo a percutaneous transluminal angioplasty.

Physical Examination: No physical abnormalities were found on the cardiovascular examination. Pulse 50, blood pressure 100/66. HEENT: PERRLA, faint carotid bruits. Lungs: Clear to percussion and auscultation. Heart: Normal sinus rhythm with a 2.6 systolic ejection murmur. Extremities and abdomen were negative.

Laboratory Data: Unremarkable

Hospital Course: To manage the patient's sick sinus syndrome, a permanent dual chamber pacemaker with atrial and ventricular leads was implanted on 1/9. On 1/10, the patient underwent a PTCA with insertion of a drug-eluting stent in the right coronary artery without complications, and good results were obtained. Postoperatively, the patient was stable and was subsequently discharged. Patient was discharged on the following medications: Cardizem®, 30 mg p.o. q 6 hours; ASA, 5 grains q. a.m.; Metamucil® and Colace® p.r.n.; Nitro paste 1/2 inch q. 6 hours.

Code(s) with POA indicator and MS-DRG: _____

4.12. This 62-year-old male patient was admitted to the hospital with progressive episodes of chest pain determined to be crescendo angina. He had myocardial infarction 5 years ago and progressively has been having more frequent episodes of chest pain. During the hospital stay, he was given IV nitroglycerin and was subsequently placed on Cardizem for further treatment of his angina. He is scheduled for cardiac catheterization next week because he refused to have it performed during this admission. No other complications arose during the hospitalization. What is the code assignment?

a. 411.0, 412
b. 413.9, 412
c. 411.1, 412
d. 413.0, 412

4.13.   This 55-year-old female patient is admitted with occlusion of the cerebral arteries resulting in an infarction. The patient suffered a stroke 2 years ago with residual hemiplegia affecting her dominant side. What would be the correct code assignment for this case?

Code(s) with POA indicator and MS-DRG: _____

4.14.   What code is assigned to show the long-term use of aspirin in a patient with osteoarthritis and heart disease?

    a. V58.64
    b. V58.61
    c. V58.69
    d V58.66

4.15.   What code(s) is/are assigned for PTCA of two arteries using three nondrug-eluting stents and infusion of thrombolytic?

    a. 00.66
    b. 00.66, 00.47, 00.41, 99.10
    c. 00.66, 36.06, 00.47, 00.41, 99.10
    d. 36.02, 36.06

Disorders of the Digestive System

4.16.   This 44-year-old male patient is known to have diverticulitis of the colon. He has noticed melena occasionally for the past week. The initial impression was that this is bleeding from diverticulitis. Patient was scheduled for colonoscopy. Colonoscopy identified the cause of the bleeding to be angiodysplasia of the ascending colon. What are the codes assigned for this case?

Code(s) with POA indicator: _____

4.17.   The patient was admitted because of severe abdominal pain. There has been a history of abdominal pain and some bleeding, but never this severe. Because of the symptoms, the patient underwent emergency surgery to repair the perforation in the antrum of the stomach by suturing. The physician states: acute peptic ulcer with perforation and bleeding. What codes are assigned for this case?

Code(s) with POA indicator: _____

4.18.   This patient with chronic systolic congestive heart failure was admitted because of melena. Patient had EGD with biopsy. No other findings were found to determine the source of the melena. What codes are assigned in this case?

Code(s) with POA indicator and MS-DRG: _____

4.19. The patient is a 44-year-old male who started having abdominal pain the day before yesterday. Subsequently he had diarrhea. He had 4 episodes of diarrhea last night and then 4 episodes in the morning. The stools have turned to fairly frank blood. Also the abdominal pain got worse, and he said he felt dizzy when he stood up. Patient admitted with acute gastroenteritis with resulting mild dehydration. Patient has frank blood coming out from his bowels. Stool culture and sensitivity revealed Salmonella. Patient put on Levaquin IV and also rehydrated. Patient responded well and was discharged. What codes are assigned?

Code(s) with POA indicator: _____

4.20. A patient with hypertension, chronic obstructive pulmonary disease (COPD), and end-stage renal disease is admitted for bilateral inguinal hernia repair. The H&P states that the left side is recurrent. The operative report states that the surgeon repaired left direct and right indirect inguinal hernias with mesh. What is the correct code assignment?

Code(s) with POA indicator and MS-DRG: _____

4.21. An 80-year-old patient with hypertension was admitted to the hospital for cholecystectomy. The patient underwent an open cholecystectomy with exploration of the common duct and choledocholithotomy. Final diagnostic statement: 1. Acute and chronic cholecystitis with choledocholithiasis and cholelithiasis. 2. Hypertension. Correct code assignment would be:

Code(s) with POA indicator: _____

4.22. This 58-year-old patient recently had biopsy done showing adenocarcinoma of the sigmoid colon. He is admitted now for resection of the sigmoid colon. An end-to-end anastomosis was performed. CT scan shows metastasis to the liver. Final diagnosis: Adenocarcinoma of sigmoid colon with metastases to the liver. What codes are assigned in this case?

Code(s) with POA indicator and MS-DRG: _____

4.23 **Discharge Summary**

Date of Discharge: 02/12/XX

This is a 29-year-old male who comes in to the cardiology specialists. He had presented with an acute inferior wall myocardial infarction and was given tissue plasminogen activator (tPA). Apparently, this was unsuccessful, and he was transferred to Memorial Hospital for an acute angiogram and an attempt to revascularize percutaneously.

The patient had a creatine phosphokinase level (CPK) of 1,488 initially, going up to 3,021, and then down to 2,622. On his emergency angiogram there was 40 to 50 percent stenosis in a proximal diagonal. The circumflex was said to be normal. The right coronary artery had 20% stenosis at the crux and an occlusion of the posterolateral left ventricular branch. There was an attempt made to salvage the posterolateral left ventricular branch with no success. His left ventricle showed an inferobasilar hypokinesis. The patient was monitored throughout his hospitalization and did have episodes of nonsustained ventricular tachycardia. His cholesterol was noted to be 192 with a low-density lipoprotein of 113 and a high-density lipoprotein of 49. He had problems with the smallest and next smallest toes on his right leg which he says began giving him problems before he even had his transfer here to this hospital and clearly before he had his angiogram. These toes were noted to have cyanosis on the plantar aspect and were painful unless held dependently. Examination was remarkable for the absence of any pulse deficits. He was sent for a duplex to see if there was a problem with his arteries. The preliminary report was that there was none. He had no more cardiovascular symptoms following his angiogram, but his toes were giving him problems. This is going to be treated conservatively as an outpatient. He will need to return to see the doctor in a couple of weeks.

He did have his treadmill exercise test before leaving the hospital, and this was thought to be negative for any acute ischemia. He went 10.5 minutes to a heart rate of 108 with no chest pain, arrhythmia, or blood pressure change.

Discharge Medications:
1. Lopressor 50 mg 1 b.i.d.
2. Aspirin 325 mg 1 every day
3. Nitroglycerin 0.4 sublingual p.r.n.
4. Motrin as tolerated.

History and Physical Examination

Reason for Admission: Acute inferior myocardial infarction.

Present Illness: This is a 29-year-old man with the acute onset of nausea and vomiting early this morning with referral to subsequent change to chest discomfort radiating into the neck. He presented to County Hospital to receive morphine, nitroglycerin, and aspirin and tPA. There were no thrombolytic contraindications. His pain had improved but it diminished and he still had persistent ST elevation despite improvement in his symptoms. Given his young age, he was referred for attempted salvage revascularization.

Past Medical History: Unremarkable.

Review of Systems: Negative for stroke, bleeding, fevers or chills, or nausea, vomiting, or recent flu-like illness.

Social History: He smokes, works a cement truck, heavy drinker, heavy alcohol use on occasions.

Family History: Positive for coronary artery disease in both parents.

Physical Examination: This is a pleasant young gentleman in no acute distress. His blood pressure is 110/70, heart rate 80, respirations 16. HEENT: Unremarkable. Neck: Neck veins are nondistended. Chest: Clear. Heart: Normal 81, 82 without murmurs, gallops or rubs. Abdomen: 80 ft and nontender. Extremities: 2+ pulses and no edema. Neurologic: He is intact.

EKG showed an acute inferior injury pattern with inferior Q wave present. His admission laboratories are pending. His Chem-7 is normal. His CBC and cardiac enzymes are pending.

Impression: Acute inferior myocardial infarction

Plan: Attempt at salvage PTCA after failed reperfusion with thrombolytic therapy, risk factor modification, tobacco cessation, and checking his lipids. We will treat him with beta blockers, aspirin, and heparin in the interim.

Cardiology

Procedure: Left heart catheterization, coronary angiography, left ventriculography, and attempted PTCA of the right posterior lateral branch.

Indications: This is a 29-year-old male who presented to County Hospital earlier this morning with evolving acute inferior myocardial infarction. The symptoms improved with morphine and nitrates, aspirin, and thrombolytic therapy but had no evidence of reperfusion by total EKG or reperfusion arrhythmias. He is still having low-grade arm discomfort when he was transferred for attempted salvage revascularization.

Procedure: Informed consent was obtained.

He was brought to the cardiac catheterization suite, prepped, draped in the usual sterile manner. 1 percent Xylocaine was used for local anesthesia. A 6 French sheath was placed in the right femoral artery by the modified Seldinger technique. Coronary angiography was performed using the Judkins 5 French four curved left angiographic catheters. We then checked the baseline ACT, gave 5,000 units of intra-arterial heparin and subsequent ACT in 2 hours and 50 seconds. A 6 French JR-4 guiding catheter was chosen and a 300-cm, 14 reflux guidewire was used to cross the stenosis in the distal right posterolateral branch with some difficulty.

We performed a total of four inflations with a 2.0 × 20 mm rocket balloon without evidence of restoration of flow. He received 400 mcg. of intracoronary Nitroglycerin in three divided doses. The symptoms had not changed. He was thought to be clinically stable. This is a small vessel in the distal distribution. It is thought not prudent to warrant further attempted angioplasty. The dilating catheters, the guidewire, and the guiding catheter were removed. A 5 French straight pigtail catheter was advanced to the left ventricle for pressure recordings. Single plain left ventriculogram was performed in the right anterior oblique using power-inducted contrast. Pull-back across the aortic valve revealed no gradient. The sheath was secured. The patient was taken to the holding area in hemodynamically stable condition with intact distal pulses.

Results: Pressures: Aortic pressure 120/70. Left ventricular pressure 120/8.

Left ventriculography: Single plain left ventriculography reveals inferobasal hypokinesis with an ejection fraction estimated to be 50 percent without mitral regurgitation.

Coronary angiography: Left main: Left main coronary divided into the left anterior descending artery (LAD) and circumflex vessel and is normal.

Left anterior descending artery gives rise to two diagonal branches in the central perforator branch and traverses to an apical recurrent branch. There is a 40% tapering at the proximal aspect of the first diagonal branch, otherwise there are no flow-limiting lesions in the LAD, diagonal system.

Left circumflex: Left circumflex coronary artery consists of one very high obtuse marginal branch as well as subsequent second and third obtuse marginal branches and atrioventricular groove continuation and is normal.

Right coronary: Right coronary artery is a dominant vessel for the posterior circulation giving rise to a posterior descending artery, posterior lateral left ventricular branch, and right ventricular marginal branches as well as atrial branches. There is a 20% taper in the proximal right coronary artery and a flush occlusion in the mid to distal segment of the right posterolateral branch with some staining of contrast present there.

Post PTCA of the right posterior lateral branch: there is no significant change with persistent TIMI grade 0 flow in the small distal vessel, which is judged to be approximately 2.0 to 2.2 mm. There is no disruption in the main body of the right coronary artery as a result of procedure.

Impression:

1. Evolution of acute inferior myocardial infarction secondary to occluded distal right posterior lateral branch with unsuccessful attempted salvage (PTCA after failing thrombolytic therapy.

2. Preserved left ventricular systolic function.

3. Family history of heart disease and tobacco use.

Plan: The patient will be treated medically at this point with aspirin, beta blockers, and risk factor modification.

Which of the following code sets will be reported for the above admission?

a. 410.42, 414.01, 729.5, 782.5, 305.1, V17.3, 00.66, 00.40, 37.22, 88.56, 88.53
b. 410.41, 414.01, 729.5, 782.5, 305.1, V17.3, 00.66, 00.40, 37.22, 88.56, 88.53
c. 410.41, 414.01, 305.1, V17.3, 37.22, 88.56, 88.53
d. 410.42, 414.01, 305.1, V17.3, 37.22, 88.56, 88.53

Endocrine, Nutritional and Metabolic Diseases, and Immunity Disorders

4.24.   This 75-year-old female admitted because of chronic diarrhea and dehydration. History of herpes zoster, right upper extremity leading to monoparesis right upper extremity with postherpetic neuralgia on the right side of the chest. She has been treated with heavy doses of Neurontin with no significant relief. On admission her chest x-ray showed resolving lingular and left lower lobe pneumonia and pneumonia in the right perihilar region. The patient is being treated with Levaquin. She had colonoscopy in the hospital for her iron deficiency anemia. Colonoscopy with biopsies taken of the small bowel as well as the rectosigmoid area showed no specific etiology. What codes are assigned?

Code(s) with POA indicator and MS-DRG: _____

4.25. This patient, who has type II diabetes, is admitted because of diabetic coma. He has nephrotic syndrome due to the diabetes and gangrene of several toes. What codes would be assigned?

    a. 250.30, 250.40, 581.81, 250.70, 785.4

    b. 250.30, 581.81, 785.4

    c. 250.30, 250.41, 581.81, 785.4

    d. 250.31, 250.41, 250.71

4.26. The following information is contained in the health record.

Chief Complaint: History of nausea with severe vomiting for the past 2 to 3 days. Diabetes mellitus diagnosed at the age of 12 years.

Hospital Course: This 31-year-old male patient has a history of type I diabetes mellitus and is on 15 units of NPH and 10 of Regular in the morning, and 10 units of NPH and 5 of Regular in the evening. The patient started having symptoms of nausea. The patient at the same time had increased frequency of urination and polydipsia with evidence of uncontrolled diabetes. The patient was severely dehydrated on admission. There was no evidence of thrombophlebitis, varicosities, or edema on examination of the extremities. The patient was hydrated and, as a result, his blood sugar decreased from more than 600 to normal levels. The patient was discharged with the diagnosis of diabetic ketoacidosis, type 1.

What code(s) are assigned for this admission?

Code(s) with POA indicator: _____

4.27. From the health record of a patient requiring thyroid surgery:

History: Patient is a 50-year-old female who noted a swelling in the neck. Workup was done, which included thyroid scan and thyroid sonogram, revealing moderate enlargement of the left lobe of the thyroid gland measuring 1.1 × 2.2 cm, a solid nodule at the anterior aspect of the mid of the left lobe of thyroid measuring approximately 1 × 1.9 cm, a small cyst in the middle of the left lobe of the thyroid measuring 2.4 cm; normal right lobe of the thyroid; a small cyst in the mid of the right lobe measuring 2.3 mm. Thyroid scan showed hot nodule, which is usually negative for malignancy. The fine-needle aspiration was strongly suspicious for papillary carcinoma.

Impression: Papillary carcinoma of the thyroid

Report of Operation:

Preoperative Diagnosis: Steroid nodule left lobe, rule out papillary carcinoma

Postoperative Diagnosis: Papillary carcinoma of thyroid

Procedure: Left thyroid lobectomy with isthmectomy and frozen section. Subsequently, patient underwent total thyroid right lobectomy

Anesthesia: General endotracheal

Estimated Blood Loss: 50 cc. Replacement: IV fluids, sponge count, needle count times two correct

Technique: After patient was well anesthetized with general endotracheal anesthesia, a sand bag was placed underneath the shoulder blades. The neck was extended and stabilized and placed on a foam head pillow. Entire neck and anterior chest was prepped and draped in the usual manner. The skin incision site was marked with 2-0 VICRYL® suture with pressure. Preempt analgesia was obtained with infiltration of .25 percent Marcaine®. Transverse skin incision was made in the anterior part of the neck, which was deepened through the subcutaneous tissue and the platysma. Upper and lower flaps were raised, upper flap up to the thyroid cartilage, lower flap up to the sternal notch. Hemostasis obtained with cautery as well as 3-0 VICRYL sutures. Midline fascia was incised. Strap muscles on the left side were separated from the underlying thyroid gland. Strap muscles were retracted laterally with a Green retractor. Middle thyroid veins were identified, divided between the clamps, ligated with 3-0 VICRYL suture. Patient was noted to have palpable thyroid nodule on the left lower part of the thyroid gland. Superior thyroid vessels were identified. External of the superior laryngeal nerve was identified and protected. Superior thyroid vessels were divided close to the thyroid clamp between the Mixter clamp and ligated with 2-0 VICRYL suture. Recurrent laryngeal nerve was identified and protected throughout the procedure. Superior and inferior parathyroids were identified, protected with their vasculature. Inferior thyroid vessels were divided close to the thyroid capsule after its branching to preserve the blood supply to the parathyroid gland. Isthmus was divided between the clamps, and the entire thyroid lobe was removed and sent for frozen section, which was reported to be a papillary carcinoma. After the pathology report, the decision was made to proceed with the total thyroidectomy, which was carried out in the following manner:

Strap muscles on the right side were separated from the right thyroid gland. Middle thyroid vessels were divided between the clamps, ligated with 3-0 VICRYL suture. Superior and inferior thyroid poles were identified. Superior thyroid vessels were divided close to the upper pole. During the procedure, the external branch of the superior laryngeal nerve was identified and protected. The divided vessels were ligated with 2-0 VICRYL suture. Recurrent laryngeal nerve was identified and protected. Inferior and superior parathyroid glands were identified and protected with vasculature. Inferior thyroid vessel branches were divided between the clamps; thereby the blood supply to the parathyroid glands was preserved. Care was taken to protect the recurrent laryngeal nerve throughout the procedure. The right lobe of the thyroid was completely removed after satisfactory hemostasis. No drains were placed. The strap muscles were approximated with interrupted 3-0 VICRYL suture. Platysma and subcutaneous tissue was approximated with interrupted 4-0 VICRYL suture. Skin approximated with subcuticular 4-0 Dexon. Sterile dressings were applied. At the end of the procedure the vocal cords were inspected. They were moving equally well. The patient tolerated the entire procedure well and was discharged in stable condition to the recovery room.

Discharge Information: Patient discharged after 2 days, with no complications.

Diagnosis: Papillary carcinoma of the thyroid, left and right lobes, with follicular pattern. Papillary carcinoma positive in one cervical lymph node. Will follow up with me in the office.

What are the correct codes in this case?

Code(s) with POA indicator and MS-DRG: _____

4.28. This 51 year-old male is a Type I insulin-dependent diabetic admitted for treatment of a grade III foot ulcer on the left foot with abscess and gangrenous changes resulting from diabetic neuropathy, atherosclerosis, and chronic peripheral vascular insufficiency. Debridement of the wound is accomplished by use of a water jet appliance and application of sterile dressings.

Which of the following answers would be correct?

a. 250.71, 440.23, 250.61, 357.2, 86.28
b. 250.71, 440.24, 250.61, 357.2, 707.15, 86.28
c. 250.01, 440.20, 785.4, 357.2, 707.15, 86.22
d. 250.71, 440.24, 250.61, 357.2, 707.15, 86.22

Disorders of the Genitourinary System

4.29. From the health record of a patient with urinary retention admitted through the emergency department:

Discharge Summary

Pertinent History: The patient is a 34-year-old female admitted through the ER with severe, stabbing, low back pain and inability to urinate. The patient has a long history of pelvic inflammatory disease, with three surgical episodes to remove implants. CT scan revealed a mass in the area of the kidneys.

Hospital Course: The patient was admitted, prepped, and taken to surgery. Exploratory laparotomy revealed an area of pelvic inflammatory disease involving both kidneys in dense adhesions. Cultures indicate chlamydia. Both ureters were almost totally blocked. Dense adhesions were painstakingly taken down. This was done very carefully and required several hours of surgery. Care was taken not to sever the kidneys or ureters. INTERCEED® adhesion barrier was applied.

Postoperatively, the patient was pain free.

Discharge Instructions: The patient was discharged home to return to see me in the office in 1 week.

Diagnosis: Severe pelvic adhesions, chlamydia infection.

Which of the following code sets would be reported for this admission?

a. 614.9, 079.98, 59.02
b. 614.6, 079.98, 59.02, 99.77
c. 614.6, 079.88, 54.59, 99.77
d. 614.3, 079.98, 59.02, 99.77

4.30.   From the health record of a patient requiring radical surgery:

Discharge Summary

Pertinent History: The patient is a 68-year-old female admitted through the ER. The patient's abdomen is enlarged to about 18-week size; however, the patient states she has actually lost 22 pounds over the past few weeks. Patient says her appetite has disappeared. Patient is admitted for workup and definitive treatment.

Hospital Course: The patient's CT scan and MRI revealed a suspicious mass in the pelvis. Patient was taken to surgery, where exploration revealed and pathology report later confirmed ovarian cancer. A radical abdominal hysterectomy was performed with regional lymph node dissection and bilateral salpingo-oophorectomy. The patient tolerated the procedure well.

Discharge Instructions: The patient was discharged home to see me in the office in 1 week for removal of staples and scheduling for oncologist consultation.

Which of the following code sets should be reported for this admission?

a. 183.0, 68.41, 65.61, 40.3
b. 183.0, 68.69, 65.61, 40.3
c. 198.6, 68.61, 65.61, 40.3
d. 183.0, 68.69, 65.61, 40.59

4.31.   This 80-year-old female patient was admitted with fever, malaise, and left flank pain. A urinalysis was performed and showed bacteria more than 100,000/ mL. This was followed by a culture, showing *Escherichia coli* growth documented as *E. coli* urinary tract infection (UTI). On day 2 the patient had an exacerbation of chronic obstructive pulmonary disease (COPD) and was treated with inhaler. This resolved the same day. Patient is also on current medication therapy for hypertension and arteriosclerotic heart disease (ASHD). What codes are assigned for this encounter?

Code(s) with POA indicator and MS-DRG: _____

4.32.   This 65-year-old male was admitted to the hospital in acute urinary retention. A transurethral resection of the prostate was performed and the diagnosis of benign nodular hyperplasia of the prostate was made. When the pathology report was reviewed, there was documentation of BPH and microscopic foci of adenocarcinoma of the prostate, which was confirmed by the physician. What codes are reported?

Code(s) with POA indicator: _____

4.33.   This 38-year-old mother of four children has been treated for nearly 20 years for severe cystic breast disease. The patient has elected to have her breasts removed to relieve the pain. She is also very worried about developing breast cancer because her mother died from breast cancer at age 42 years. She has had numerous breast biopsies, and each time they are benign. She may consider plastic reconstruction later, but is not interested in it now. She is in good health. She was taken to surgery, and bilateral simple mastectomies were performed. The pathology report shows severe cystic breast disease. What codes are assigned?

Code(s) with POA indicator: _____

4.34. This elderly patient has been treated for hypertension for many years. Otherwise he is in relatively good condition considering his age. He was brought to the ER and admitted in acute renal failure due to severe dehydration with hyponatremia. What code(s) are assigned for this case?

Code(s) with POA indicator and MS-DRG: _____

4.35. The 56-year-old patient who has type I diabetes mellitus is admitted with acute renal failure. Past medical history includes: hypertension, diabetic nephropathy, and chronic kidney disease stage IV. What codes are assigned?

Code(s) with POA indicator and MS-DRG: _____

4.36. What code is assigned to show that a 35-year-old patient is having prophylactic removal of her breasts because of a strong family history of breast cancer and positive laboratory results demonstrating genetic susceptibility to breast cancer?

    a. V50.41, V84.01, V16.3
    b. V16.3, V84.01
    c. 174.9, V16.3
    d. V50.41, V84.01, V10.3

Infectious Diseases

4.37. This is a 35-year-old HIV-positive male with progressive lymphadenopathy and unexplained fevers, night sweats, and chills. CT scan of the chest, abdomen, pelvis, and neck showed extensive lymphadenopathy involving mediastinum and left hilum, paratracheal nodal chains, retroperitoneum, right iliac nodal chains, and right inguinal nodes. There were several areas of atelectasis evident in the right lung. Lymph node biopsy suspicious for tuberculosis and in fact was AFB-positive. The patient was placed on respiratory isolation and serial sputums were obtained. The patient's sputum contained positive AFB on concentrated specimen. Also during the course of hospitalization the patient complained of swelling in the bilateral lower extremities. Dopplers were negative for DVT. The patient will be referred to the clinic for management of his HIV disease and associated tuberculosis. What codes are assigned?

Code(s) with POA indicator and MS-DRG: _____

4.38. The discharge diagnosis for a patient admitted with urosepsis due to streptococcus and white blood cell count of 15,000. Urine culture and blood cultures were positive for streptococcus. After query to the physician regarding the meaning of the term *urosepsis*, an addendum was added to the record: Sepsis with streptococcal septicemia and urinary tract infection (UTI) due to streptococcus B. What codes are assigned?

Code(s) with POA indicator and MS-DRG: _____

4.39. This 25-year-old patient was admitted with difficulty breathing. She has AIDS and is in the 21st week of pregnancy. Workup shows *Pneumocystis carinii* pneumonia. What codes are assigned in this case?

Code(s) with POA indicator and MS-DRG: _____

4.40. This 53-year-old male with emphysema, previous lung transplant 2 years ago, was admitted with history of elevated temperature of 101 degrees with associated malaise, fatigue and headache. The patient continued to have temperature elevations after admission. He was started on intravenous ganciclovir and intravenous Imipenem. Blood and urine cultures were basically nondiagnostic. He underwent a bronchoscopy for bronchoalveolar lavage from his left transplanted lung, which did not show any evidence of viral or bacterial pathogens. Blood CMV antigen test was positive and hence he was diagnosed with CMV infection. He has had a persistent cough, and microscopy confirmed the presence of pulmonary tuberculosis. The physician documentation shows the infiltrating pulmonary tuberculosis and CMV are HIV-related. Patient was treated with ethambutol. What codes are assigned?

Code(s) with POA indicator and MS-DRG: _____

4.41. This 23-year-old female is admitted with pneumonia. She also has multiple bilateral lesions of the vulva and vagina with fluid-filled blisters. The history includes fever, and pain for 2 days. Sputum cultures show group A streptococcus. History also includes pain, particularly with urination, and itching of the genitals. Physician documents group A streptococcus pneumonia, vulvovaginitis due to herpes. What codes are assigned?

Code(s) with POA indicator: _____

Disorders of the Skin and Subcutaneous Tissue

4.42. An elderly nursing home patient was admitted for pneumonia. He has frequent aspiration because of difficulty swallowing due to a previous stroke. This pneumonia was documented as aspiration pneumonia. He was also found on admission to have stage one decubitus ulcer on the hip. The patient received skin care by the nursing staff for this ulcer. What codes are assigned in this case?

Code(s) with POA indicator and MS-DRG: _____

4.43. This patient had surgery 2 weeks ago for appendicitis. She is admitted now because of fever, pain, and redness at the operative site. There is evidence of cellulitis of the operative wound, and cultures confirm *Staphylococcus aureus* as the cause. She received IV antibiotics. She also has type II diabetes mellitus on oral antidiabetic medication. What codes are assigned?

Code(s) with POA indicator: _____

4.44. This nursing home patient was admitted to the hospital with severe cellulitis in the lower extremity. The cultures grew streptococcus B, and this was documented by the physician as the cause of the cellulitis. Patient was given IV antibiotics. He also has right-sided hemiplegia from an old cerebrovascular accident (CVA) and was found to have decubitus ulcers in the gluteal region. What code(s) are assigned?

Code(s) with POA indicator and MS-DRG: _____

4.45. This 85-year-old patient, who is a resident at the skilled nursing facility, was admitted with a severe decubitus ulcer on the right buttock, stage II, and a small chronic ulcer on the heel. Patient also has Alzheimer's disease. The treatment was an excisional debridement of the heel and an excisional debridement into the muscle of the buttock. What is the code assignment?

Code(s) with POA indicator and MS-DRG: _____

4.46. This 29-year-old female patient is admitted for wide excision of melanoma on the back. She also has a history of asthma. After surgery, she had an acute exacerbation of her asthma treated with two nebulizer treatments. The wide excision was performed and a full-thickness skin graft was applied. What codes are assigned?

Code(s) with POA indicator: _____

Behavioral Health Conditions

4.47. **Case Scenario:** A patient in a state of acute intoxication presented for care. The patient's 12-year alcohol dependence is consistent with a high level of daily alcohol consumption. The patient was admitted for alcohol detoxification and rehabilitation. On the second day of admission, he began experiencing withdrawal symptoms of sweating and nausea. On the third day, the sweating became more profuse, and he developed irregular tremors and tachycardia. The delirium tremors were managed medically. The patient did not experience any seizures. Hallucinations abated by day 4. By day 5, the patient was resting more comfortably, and plans for rehabilitation were initiated. The patient expressed a desire to reduce his alcohol abuse to a "controlled" level. A treatment plan was developed and implemented, with the short-term goal of assisting the patient in reaching a stable level of use; that is, controlled drinking and a long-range goal of motivating the patient to accept a goal of total abstinence. Initially, the patient actively participated in the program, but his motivation waned, and he left the program after signing out AMA without meeting any of the rehabilitation goals.

Which of the following code sets most accurately reflects this case scenario?

a. 291.81, 303.01, 94.63
b. 291.81, 303.90, 94.62
c. 291.0, 303.01, 94.63
d. 291.0, 303.90, 94.62

4.48. This 30-year-old male was admitted after being transferred from the outpatient therapy services because of severe major depressive disorder with psychotic features. After a complete psychological evaluation, the risks and benefits of ECT were reviewed and explained to the patient and his family. ECT was administered three times per week. The patient tolerated the therapy well and responded quickly with overall improvement in the acute phase of his depressive disorder. After establishing adequate therapeutic levels of lithium, the patient was discharged to be managed as an outpatient. What codes are assigned?

Code(s) with POA indicator and MS-DRG: _____

4.49. This patient has been living at home, but his dementia has been getting progressively worse. He was diagnosed with Alzheimer's disease over 2 years ago. The family called the police because he was missing from home. A search was conducted and an observant passerby called in a report of an elderly man who seemed to be disoriented at a nearby park. He was found after several hours and brought to the hospital. He had fallen and had a laceration on his knee that required sutures. What codes are reported in this case?

Code(s) with POA indicator and MS-DRG: _____

4.50. The patient was brought to the ER and then admitted because of acute alcohol inebriation. The discharge diagnosis is acute and chronic alcoholism, continuous. What codes are assigned?

Code(s) with POA indicator: _____

4.51. This 65-year-old chronic smoker was admitted to the hospital with acute exacerbation of her chronic obstructive pulmonary disease. She has a history of anxiety syndrome due to hypothyroidism, maintained on medications for both the anxiety and the hypothyroidism. No symptomatology at the time of admission. On hospital day 2, she developed extreme anxiety over being in the hospital environment and a psychiatric consultation was ordered. What codes are assigned in this case?

Code(s) with POA indicator and MS-DRG: _____

Disorders of the Musculoskeletal System and Connective Tissue

4.52. This patient was admitted for treatment of a left metatarsal fracture. The fracture site was opened and reduced, followed by placement of three internal Kirschner wires. Two pins were then placed and an external fixator frame was connected to the pins to provide pressure and hold them in reduction. What codes are assigned in this case?

Code(s) with POA indicator: _____

4.53. A patient is admitted with an infected partial hip prosthesis. The prosthesis was removed and the patient underwent a total hip arthroplasty. What are the correct code assignments?

Code(s) with POA indicator and MS-DRG: _____

4.54. A patient was admitted for recurrent dislocation of the shoulder. The operation included débridement of the acromion, subacromial bursectomy, division of the coracoacromial ligament, and an abrasion acromioplasty with Mitek suture placement. Which of the following is the correct code assignment?

    a. 718.31, 81.82
    b. 718.31, 81.82, 83.5
    c. 831.00, 81.82, 83.5
    d. 831.00, 81.82, 83.5, 80.41

4.55. This is a 65-year-old lady with complaints of low back pain with radiation down her right leg to her foot. This pain has been progressively worse over the last several months. MRI scan showed degenerative disc disease at L2–3, L3–4, and L4–5, L3–L4 with mild central canal stenosis, and facet arthropathy at L3–L4 and L4–L5. Past medical history includes coronary artery disease, hypertension, and arthritis. Her current medications include Lipitor, Avapro, Ecotrin, Imdur, Lasix, K-Dur, calcium, and Vioxx. She had a CABG two years ago and PTCA with cardiac stents placed three years ago. Patient admitted for lumbar epidural steroid injections for her lumbar radiculopathy as noted on MRI results. Which of the following answers would be correct?

    a. 722.52, 721.3, 414.00, 401.9, 03.92, 99.23, 88.93
    b. 722.52, 721.3, 724.02, 724.4, 414.00, 401.9, 03.92, 99.23, 88.93
    c. 724.4, 414.00, 401.9, 03.92, 99.23, 88.93
    d. 722.52, 721.3, 414.00, 401.9, 03.91, 88.93

4.56. This 70-year-old female has been treated for progressive increasing pain in her back. She is to the point that she is unable to move. She was brought to the ER and admitted after x-ray shows severe compression fractures of the lumbar vertebrae due to her senile osteoporosis. An injection of anesthetic was done into the spinal canal. What codes are assigned?

Code(s) with POA indicator: _____

4.57. This 45-year-old male patient in whom conservative treatment for degenerative disk disease of the lumbar spine has failed came to the hospital. The discectomy was performed at L5 and total spinal disk prosthesis inserted to restore disk function and anatomy. What procedure code(s) are assigned?

    a. 80.51
    b. 80.51, 84.65
    c. 84.65, 80.51
    d. 84.65

4.58. What procedure code(s) are assigned for a patient with limb deformity due to trauma? An implantation of an internal limb-lengthening device with kinetic distraction was performed on the tibia.

    a. 84.53, 78.37
    b. 84.53
    c. 78.37
    d. 84.54, 78.37

4.59.   **Discharge Summary**

DATE OF ADMISSION: 06/28/XX **DATE OF DISCHARGE:** 07/07/XX

Diagnoses: 1. Status post fractured right femoral neck.
2. Chronic obstructive pulmonary disease.
3. Rheumatoid arthritis, steroid dependent.
4. Osteoporosis.

Pertinent History: The patient was admitted on the 28th of June after a fall. She did not pass out but just fell and fractured her hip. She fell off of a stool. She underwent surgery for this. She had a hemiarthroplasty. She tolerated the procedure well and was transferred to A Pavilion for continued physical therapy and rehabilitation.

Pertinent Laboratory: CBC initially showed a white count of 15,400, subsequently the white count is 10,900 with 78 neutrophils. H&H was stable at 12.2 and 36.9. Theophylline level was 10.3, therapeutic.

Hospital Course: The patient tolerated physical therapy well. She was able to give her own Lovenox shots. She was anxious to go home on Saturday. Orthopedics had planned for 14 more days of Lovenox, and that will be given by the patient and prescribed by Dr. Thomas's group. She will be back in about 3 weeks. She will continue with her current medications which are proventil 2 puffs q.i.d., Fosamax 10 mg q.a.m., Soma 350 mg q.i.d., Lovenox 30 mg q. 12 hours, folic acid 1 mg q. day, Lasix 40 mg b.i.d., Atrovent 2 puffs q. 6 hours, synthroid 0.075 q. day, potassium 20 mEq b.i.d., prednisone 20 mg a day, Theo-Dur 100 mg in the morning and 200 mg in the evening. She takes Sonata and she will continue with 5 mg q.h.S. She will continue with her laxative of choice. She will restart her Nasonex, Celebrex, Vicodin, and Vanceril when she gets home. She will stay on a regular diet. Activities per her primary care physician. She will see me back in 3 weeks.

History and Physical Examination

Admission Date: 6/28

Chief Complaint: Hip fracture.

Present Illness: The patient is a 79-year-old, white female who slipped off of a stool while talking to her daughter. She was apparently trying to do too many things at one time, trying to clean some books or something like that and then just slipped and fell off and fractured her hip. She lives alone, had to call for help. She denies any type of passing out, no head injury, and no history of falling a lot before.

Past Medical History: The patient denies any kind of past history of chest pains, exertional chest pain. She stopped smoking some time ago but continues to be mildly short of breath and that has been stable.

She has no gastrointestinal (GI) symptoms, only occasionally some mild stress incontinence.

Medications: 1. Nasonex nasal spray.
2. Soma 350 mg 1 g.i.d.
3. Potassium 10 mEq. 2 b.i.d.
4. Celebrex 200 mg q.d.

5. Synthroid 0.075 q.d.
6. Vicodin p.r.n.
7. Fosamax 10 mg q. a.m.
8. Theo Dur 200 mg ~ in the morning and 1 in the evening
9. Folic acid 1 q.d.
10. Lasix 40 mg b.i.d.
11. Prednisone 10 mg.2 g.d.
12. Vanceril inhaler
13. Atrovent inhaler
14. Albuterol inhaler

Allergies: Halcion, which causes her to hallucinate.

Medical History: Her medical history includes rheumatoid arthritis, chronic obstructive pulmonary disease (COPD), osteoporosis, and congestive heart failure (CHF).

Social History: She is a widow, stopped smoking 12 years ago. Does not use any alcohol.

Family History: Noncontributory.

Physical Examination: Finds her alert and oriented in no acute distress. Her blood pressure is 140/68, pulse 74, respirations 18. She was afebrile. HEENT: Examination was negative. Neck: Supple without any adenopathy, no bruit was heard. Chest: Clear to auscultation. Heart: Sounds regular without any murmur or gallop. Abdomen; Soft, positive bowel sounds, nontender, no bruits heard. Extremities: Showed normal vascular status.

Laboratory and X-Ray Data: Mild renal insufficiency is present. She has a complete blood count (CBC) and urinalysis essentially normal. EKG shows no acute changes. Chest x-ray is pending at this time. If that is normal, she will be able to go on to surgery; that is decided on by Dr. Rowan.

Impression(s):   1.   Fracture right femoral neck.
2. Chronic obstructive pulmonary disease and rheumatoid arthritis. She is steroid dependent so we are going to increase the amount of steroids that she is taking right now. Continue her on her inhalers and restart her oral medications as directed later.

Operative Report

Date: 06/28

Preoperative Diagnosis: Displaced right femoral neck hip fracture.

Postoperative Diagnosis: Displaced right femoral neck hip fracture.

Operation: Right hip hemiarthroplasty (Zimmer LDFX cemented monopolar).

Anesthesia: Spinal.

Indications: This is a 79-year-old, previously ambulatory female with a history of rheumatoid arthritis, osteoporosis, steroid-dependent emphysema, and renal insufficiency with the above diagnosis. Risks, benefits, and alternatives of the above procedure were explained to the patient in detail and she consented to proceed.

Operative Procedure: The patient was taken to the operating room and placed in the lateral position on the transfer bed where spinal anesthesia was administered. She was transferred to the left lateral decubitus position on a beanbag on the operative table. Padded all bony prominences. Peritoneum was sealed off with Steri-Drape. The right hip was prepped and draped in the usual sterile fashion. Longitudinal incision over the greater trochanter and proximal femur was performed curving posteriorly proximally along the gluteus maximus. Sharp dissection to the skin, Bovie dissection to the subcutaneous tissues down to tensor fascia lata, identifying the greater trochanter. Besides the tensor fascia lata and along with the incision splitting the fibrous gluteus maximus, controlling bleeders with Bovie cautery. Piriformis was identified and short external rotators were tagged with a #5 Tycron suture. These are moved from their insertion. T capsulotomy was performed. Displaced hip fracture was identified, femoral head was removed and measured, copious irrigation was performed, acetabular was visibly and palpable normal appearing. Sagittal saw was used to make cut in the femoral neck. Box osteotome was used to gain lateral entrance to the canal. The canal finder was used, easily locating the femoral canal. Sequential broaching was performed up to a 14, which fit well. Stating the appropriate anteversion. Trawled with an endofemoral head. Had full range of motion without instability and grossly equal leg lengths. I could bring the hip and knee up to 90 degrees of flexion, neutral adduction, start to internally rotate to 30 degrees before it would become unstable. Hip was redislocated, trial components were removed. Measured the canal for a centralizer. I placed a distal cement restrictor 2 cm distal to the component. Copious lavage of the canal was performed and brushed. Acetabulum was irrigated clean; palpable and visibly free of loose fragments. It was packed off with lap sponge. Dried the femoral canal. Placed cement in the femoral canal with retrograde manor using proximal pressurizer. Place the 14-mm Zimmer LDFX with a distal centralizer in the appropriate anteversion, held in place with a cement set. Copious irrigation was performed. After the cement set, placed the final endo head, tapped into position with Morris taper, reduced the head. Could take the hip through the same range of motion without any instability. The short external rotator is in the drill holes in the greater trochanter. The tensor fascia lata closed with interrupted 0-0 VICRYL suture. We copiously irrigated each layer. Subcutaneous tissue closed with interrupted 2-0 VICRYL sutures, skin was closed with staples. Sterile dressing was applied.

Code(s) with POA indicator and MS-DRG: _____

Neoplasms

4.60.   The following documentation is from the health record of a terminally ill oncology patient.

Discharge Summary

History of Present Illness: The patient is an 80-year-old white female with a known history of advanced metastatic carcinoma of the breast, widely metastatic. The patient was admitted because of increasing shortness of breath and severe pain. The pain, which was worse in her left chest, was associated with increasing shortness of breath. At the time of admission, the patient was in so much pain that she was unable to remember her history. The patient initially presented for congestive heart failure over 1 year ago. This was subsequently found to be secondary to metastatic breast cancer, post left mastectomy, 3 years ago. The patient had previously been on chemotherapy.

Laboratory Data and Hospital Course: The patient was treated initially with IV pain medication to control her pain. Subsequently, she became able to be stable on oral medication. By the time of discharge, the patient was stable on oral Vicodin®, and she was able to eat. Blood sugars were improved, and her Tolinase® was withheld. Laboratory results at time of discharge included BUN 17, creatinine 1, sodium 141, potassium 4.5, chloride 105, CO_2 25, alkaline phosphatase elevated at 170 with GGT 267, SGOT 68. Admission BUN was up to 38 with creatinine 1.3 secondary to dehydration. By the time of discharge, these had improved. Admission glucose 225, down to 110 at discharge. Patient treated with Lanoxin® and Lasix® for CHF.

Medications at Discharge Include: Aldactone®, 25 mg twice a day; Lanoxin, 0.125 mg daily; Metamucil, 5 cc in four ounces of juice twice a day; Tolinase, 250 mg half tablet b.i.d. (but hold if preceding Accu-Chek® is less than 125); Reglan®, 10 mg p.o. a.c.; Pepcid, 20 mg b.i.d.; Lasix, 40 mg daily (only if pedal edema is present); Vicodin tablets, 1 every 3 hours p.r.n. for pain.

Discharge Diagnoses:
1. Uncontrolled pain, secondary to widely metastatic breast carcinoma
2. Dehydration
3. Type II diabetes mellitus, uncontrolled
4. Congestive heart failure

Which of the following is the correct ICD-9-CM code assignment?

a. 338.3, 199.0, V10.3, 276.51, 250.02, 428.0
b. 174.9, 276.51, 250.02, 428.0
c. 199.0, V10.3, 276.51, 250.02, 428.0
d. 786.59, 199.0, 276.51, 250.02, 428.0

4.61. This 60-year-old male was admitted with a diagnosis of bone metastasis originating from the right upper lobe (RUL) of the lung. The pathology was consistent with oat cell carcinoma. This admission is for chemotherapy that was administered. What codes are assigned for this admission?

Code(s) with POA indicator: _____

4.62. This patient with terminal carcinoma of the breast, metastatic to the liver and brain, was admitted with dehydration. Patient rehydrated with IVs and discharged, with no treatment given to the cancer. What are the codes assigned?

Code(s) with POA indicator and MS-DRG: _____

4.63. This 45-year-old female patient was diagnosed with right breast carcinoma 3 years ago, at which time she had a mastectomy performed with chemotherapy administration. She has been well since that time with no further treatment but yearly checkups. She had metastasis in three axillary lymph nodes. She is admitted now with visual disturbances, dizziness, headaches, and blurred vision. Workup was done that revealed metastasis to the brain. What is the correct code assignment for this admission?

Code(s) with POA indicator: _____

4.64. This patient was admitted for chemotherapy following recent diagnosis of cancer of the small intestines. The tumor was in the area where the duodenum and jejunum join. It was resected 1 month ago and she has been receiving chemotherapy. After the chemotherapy administration, the patient developed severe nausea and vomiting, which led to dehydration and an extra day's stay. Medications were given for the nausea and vomiting. IV fluids were given to rehydrate the patient. What codes are assigned?

Code(s) with POA indicator and MS-DRG: _____

4.65. This patient was admitted with a large pelvic mass and underwent an exploratory laparotomy. Pathology confirmed carcinoma of the left ovary with extensive metastasis to the omentum. A total omentectomy, excision of left ovarian mass, and radical abdominal hysterectomy with bilateral salpingo-oophorectomy were performed. What codes are assigned?

Code(s) with POA indicator and MS-DRG: _____

4.66. This 55-year-old male patient was diagnosed with prostate cancer 3 years ago. He has been treated and followed with bone metastasis, and last year the CT scan showed extensive liver mets. He has been having increasing amounts of pain. He is admitted now to have a PORT-A-CATH® VAD inserted because of intractable pain from his liver cancer. What codes are assigned in this case?

Code(s) with POA indicator: _____

Disorders of the Nervous System and Sense Organs

4.67. This is one of multiple hospital admissions for this 37-year-old white male with a history of meningoencephalitis 20 years ago. He developed obstructive hydrocephalus and underwent ventriculoperitoneal shunting of the right lateral ventricle using a high-pressure valve. The patient is now complaining of numbness in his right leg, headaches, and diplopia. The patient had CT head scan which showed a slight increase in the hydrocephalus involving the fourth ventricle. Cisternogram was done, and the dye went into the fourth ventricle but never into the lateral ventricles. Impression was shunt malfunction. He is admitted this time for VP shunt revision. Ventricular shunt was replaced and was functioning well at the time of discharge. Which of the following is the correct ICD-9-CM code assignment?

a. 996.2, 331.4, 326, 02.42, 87.02, 87.03
b. 331.4, 326, 02.42, 87.02, 87.03
c. 996.63, 331.4, 02.42
d. 996.2, 02.42, 87.03

4.68. This 32-year-old female patient was admitted with intractable partial epilepsy after an MRI showed medial temporal sclerosis on the right side with hippocampal atrophy. The neurosurgeon carried out a selective amygdalohippocampectomy with intraoperative electrocorticography. The rest of her hospital stay was uneventful. What codes are assigned?

Code(s) with POA indicator: _____

4.69. This 19-year-old college student was brought to the ER and admitted with high fever, stiff neck, chest pain, cough, and nausea. A lumbar puncture was performed, and results were positive for meningitis. Chest x-ray revealed pneumonia. Sputum cultures grew *Pneumococcus*. Patient was treated with IV antibiotics and was discharged with the diagnosis of pneumococcal meningitis and pneumococcal pneumonia. What codes are assigned?

Code(s) with POA indicator and MS-DRG: _____

4.70. This patient was admitted when MRI revealed cerebral aneurysm. After admission, a cerebral angiogram was performed and showed nonruptured arteriosclerotic aneurysm of the anterior cerebral artery. An aneurysmectomy by anastomosis was performed using Marlex® graft replacement. What codes are assigned?

Code(s) with POA indicator: _____

4.71. This is a 71-year-old female admitted with a complaint of right-sided weakness. She denies any fever, shortness of breath, cough, headaches, or chest pain. Patient has NIDDM, controlled by diet. Patient currently smokes one pack of cigarettes a day. Mild right-sided paralysis was found on physical examination. Patient is right-handed. Brain MRI demonstrated subacute infarct in the left basal ganglia. Discharge diagnosis was CVA—subacute infarct. Physical therapy and speech therapy for her hemiparalysis and dysphasia started and will continue at the rehabilitation facility where she was transferred.

Which of the following answers would be correct?

a. 434.91, 438.21, 438.12, 250.00, 305.1, 88.91, 93.39, 93.72
b. 434.91, 342.91, 784.5, 250.00, 305.1, 88.91, 93.39, 93.74
c. 436, 250.00, 305.1, 88.91, 93.39, 93.74
d. 434.91, 342.91, 784.5, 250.00, 305.1, 88.91, 93.39, 93.72

Newborn/Congenital Disorders

4.72. A 6-month-old baby with a left-sided, incomplete cleft lip and palate is admitted and undergoes surgical repair of both deformities.

Which of the following codes would be correct?

a. 749.02, 749.12, 27.62, 27.54
b. 749.22, 27.54, 27.63
c. 749.02, 749.12, 27.69
d. 749.22, 27.62, 27.54

4.73. The patient is an 18-day-old baby girl admitted after it was noticed she was developing drainage from the umbilical cord. Upon admission she was placed on intravenous Cefotaxime and Ampicillin, later changed to Cefotaxime and Clindamycin. A culture taken from the umbilical stump grew Staphylococcus aureus and Group H Streptococcus. After the first day, there was great improvement, and the baby continued to improve. She remained afebrile, has continued to eat very well, and she shows no sign of abdominal tenderness or peritonitis. The mother was instructed to watch the child closely and to notify the office if there is any redevelopment of the redness, swelling, or discharge. Recheck in two weeks for one month check-up. Discharge diagnosis: omphalitis of the newborn. What codes are assigned?

Code(s) with POA indicator: _____

4.74. An infant is born by cesarean section at 27 weeks' gestation. The baby weighs 945 g. The baby's lungs are immature, and the baby develops respiratory distress syndrome, requiring a 25-day hospital stay in the NICU. Discharge diagnosis: Extreme immaturity, with 27-week gestation, with respiratory distress syndrome, delivered by cesarean section.

Which of the following diagnosis codes would be correct?

a. V30.01, 765.03, 765.24
b. 765.03, 769
c. V30.01, 765.03, 765.24, 769
d. V30.01, 769

4.75. The patient is a 6-month-old infant born with the US2 type of Usher syndrome. He was admitted for bilateral cochlear hearing implants to treat his bilateral mixed hearing loss. The day after admission the patient was taken to surgery and the implants were inserted without incident. The patient tolerated the procedure and anesthesia without incident. The patient was discharged home on the second postoperative day to be followed in the office.

Which of the following answers is correct to code this admission?

a. 389.9, 20.96
b. 389.22, 759.89, 20.96, 20.96
c. 389.20, 759.89, 20.95
d. 389.22, 20.96, 20.96

4.76. This full-term female infant was born in this hospital by vaginal delivery. Her mother has been an alcoholic for many years and would not stop drinking during her pregnancy. The baby was born with fetal alcohol syndrome and was placed in the NICU. What codes are assigned?

Code(s) with POA indicator: _____

Pediatric Conditions

4.77. A child has second- and third-degree burns of the lower leg and second- and third-degree burns of the back with a total of 16% total body surface area (TBSA), 9% third-degree. What is the correct code assignment?

Code(s) with POA indicator and MS-DRG: _____

4.78. Patient admitted with cervical lymphadenopathy. Lymph node biopsy confirmed Hodgkin's sarcoma disease. Megavoltage radiotherapy begun.

Which of the following is the correct code set?

a. 201.21, 40.40, 92.29
b. 201.91, 40.40, 92.29
c. 201.21, 40.11, 92.24
d. 201.91, 40.11, 92.24

4.79. This 7-year-old child was brought to the emergency room with difficulty breathing. He did not respond to aminophylline and was placed in the ICU with acute asthma attack with bronchospasm. Discharge diagnosis was refractory asthma with persistent bronchospasm. What codes are assigned?

Code(s) with POA indicator: _____

4.80. The 2-year-old female was admitted to the hospital after being seen in the ER because of vomiting and diarrhea. She received Phenergan suppositories but the vomiting and diarrhea persisted. She was given an intravenous bolus of normal saline followed by intravenous D5 one-quarter, with potassium added, to correct the 5% dehydration. At the time of admission, mucous membranes were tacky. The abdominal examination revealed markedly increased bowel sounds; abdomen was mildly distended, but nontender. There were no masses and no organomegaly. Laboratory evaluation at the time of admission included a Chem-7 profile, which was remarkable for a BUN of 22 and a CO_2 of 19.5. On repeat the following day, the Chem-7 revealed values that were essentially within normal limits. The CBC on admission revealed a white blood cell count of 13,500 with hemoglobin increased at 54.1%, and there was a left shift. On repeat evaluation, the white cell count was down to 5,100, and the indices were within normal limits. Throat culture revealed normal flora, Rotavirus antigen was positive and found to be the cause of the gastroenteritis.

Which of the following answers would be correct?

a. 008.61, 276.51
b. 276.51, 558.9
c. 276.51, 008.61
d. 008.8

4.81. This 3-month-old infant was brought to the ER by the babysitter after she did not wake up from a nap. The babysitter admits to shaking the baby because she would not stop crying earlier in the day. She was admitted to ICU and was unconscious for 8 hours. Diagnosis at discharge: Shaken infant syndrome, subdural hematoma, loss of consciousness for 8 hours, and total retinal detachment, right eye. What codes are assigned?

Code(s) with POA indicator and MS-DRG: _____

Conditions of Pregnancy, Childbirth, and the Puerperium

4.82. The patient presented through the ED with severe abdominal pain, amenorrhea. Serum human chorionic gonadotropin (hCG) was lower than normal. There were also endometrial and uterine changes. Patient diagnosed with tubal pregnancy. A unilateral salpingectomy with removal of tubal pregnancy was performed. Which of the following is the correct code assignment?

a. 633.80, 66.62
b. 633.10, 66.62
c. 633.10, 66.4
d. 633.10, 66.02

4.83. From the health record of a patient experiencing a spontaneous abortion:

Diagnosis: Incomplete spontaneous abortion

Postoperative Diagnosis: Same

Operation: Dilatation and curettage

History: This 22-year-old female, gravida IV, para II, AB I, comes in today because of crampy abdominal pain and passing fetal tissue at home. Apparently her last menstrual period was 9 weeks ago, and she had been doing well, and this problem just started today.

Procedure: The patient was placed on the operating table in the lithotomy position, prepped, and draped in the usual manner. Under satisfactory intravenous sedation, the cervix was visualized by means of weighted speculum, grasped in the anterior lip with a sponge forceps. Cord was prolapsed through the cervix and vagina, and a considerable amount of placental tissue was in the vagina and cervix. This was removed. A sharp curet was used to explore the endometrial cavity, and a minimal amount of curettings was obtained. The patient tolerated the procedure well. What codes are assigned?

a. 635.91, 69.09
b. 634.91, 69.09
c. 634.91, 69.02
d. 635.91, 69.02

4.84. This 25-year-old female was admitted in labor. She has had a normal pregnancy and this is a term delivery. The single liveborn infant was delivered with spontaneous delivery. A first-degree perineal laceration was repaired. What codes are assigned?

Code(s) with POA indicator: _____

4.85. This is a 26-year-old patient who had previous cesarean section for delivery for fetal distress. She had normal antepartum care and has had no complications. We are going to attempt a VBAC for this delivery. She is admitted in her 39th week in labor. The fetus is in cephalic position and no rotation is necessary. The labor continues to progress and 5 hours later she is taken to delivery. During the delivery she was fatigued, so outlet forceps were required over a midline episiotomy. A single liveborn infant was delivered. What codes are reported?

Code(s) with POA indicator and MS-DRG: _____

4.86. This patient was admitted in labor at 39 weeks' gestation. She has had gestational diabetes during her pregnancy. The labor was very difficult, and finally a low cervical cesarean section was performed because of obstructed labor due to an unusually large baby causing disproportion. A single liveborn infant was delivered. What codes are assigned in this case?

Code(s) with POA indicator and MS-DRG: _____

Disorders of the Respiratory System

4.87. The patient was admitted with increasing shortness of breath, weakness, and nonproductive cough. Treatment included oxygen therapy. Final diagnoses listed as acute respiratory insufficiency and acute exacerbation of chronic obstructive pulmonary disease (COPD). Which of the following is the correct ICD-9-CM diagnostic code assignment?

a. 491.21
b. 491.21, 518.82
c. 518.81, 491.21
d. 518.82, 491.21

4.88. A ventilator-dependent patient (due to chronic obstructive pulmonary disease emphysema) is admitted to the hospital at 10 a.m. on January 1. He is admitted for dehydration and is placed on the hospital's ventilator upon admission. The patient is discharged January 5 at 1 p.m. What is the appropriate code assignment?

a. 492.8, 276.51, 96.72
b. 276.51, 492.8, V46.11, 96.72
c. 276.51, 496, V46.11, 96.71
d. 492.8, 276.51, V46.11, 96.72

4.89. The patient is a 59-year-old female who is quadriplegic after C5–6 fracture from motor vehicle one year ago. Admitted because of a two day history of shortness of breath, fevers, and productive cough of green yellow sputum. She has not had much of an appetite and has not been eating or drinking much for the past two days. The patient is allergic to Penicillin. An x-ray revealed left sided pneumonia. She was admitted to the hospital and given intravenous antibiotics for her pneumonia, IV fluids for dehydration, and oxygen. Her pO$_2$ in the Emergency Room was 50 on room air. She was started on hand-held nebulizer treatment, and her hypoxemia rapidly improved. Serum electrolytes were normal except for potassium of 3.3. This was corrected with additional potassium. At the time of discharge, she was breathing easy on room air and was discharged home. What codes are assigned?

Code(s) with POA indicator and MS-DRG: _____

4.90. This nursing home patient presents with aspiration pneumonia with superimposed staphylococcal pneumonia. The patient aspirated food particles in the nursing home because of his dysphagia after a CVA last year. Treatment included clindamycin 600 mg IV q. 6 hours. Condition resolved with treatment and patient discharged home. The correct code assignment is:

Code(s) with POA indicator and MS-DRG: _____

4.91. A 75-year-old male was admitted to the hospital in acute respiratory failure. He has emphysema due to his continuous smoking for over 50 years. Sputum cultures showed streptococcus A pneumonia. He was intubated in the ER and started on mechanical ventilation. Thirty-six hours later he was extubated and was able to breathe on his own. Diagnosis: Acute respiratory failure, pneumonia due to streptococcus A, and emphysema. What codes are assigned?

Code(s) with POA indicator and MS-DRG: _____

Trauma and Poisoning

4.92. From the health record of a high school athlete:

Discharge Summary: The patient is a 16-year-old male who received a hard tackle while playing football. He was unconscious at the playing field and was brought by ambulance to the emergency department. MRI showed a right subdural hematoma. Repeat MRI 1 hour later showed the hematoma to be growing. The patient remained unconscious. Vital signs were continuously monitored and remained within normal limits. The patient was taken to the OR, where the hematoma was evacuated. Postoperative course has been uneventful. The patient awakened and stated he was hungry. He has no memory of the event or the period of the football game. The patient is now discharged on the seventh postoperative day.

Which of the following code sets would be correct for this scenario?

a. 852.23, E886.0, 01.31, 88.91, 88.91
b. 852.26, E886.0, 01.31, 88.91, 88.91
c. 852.33, E886.0, 01.39, 88.91, 88.91
d. 852.26, E886.0, 01.39, 88.91, 88.91

4.93. From the health record of a patient requiring continuing care after surgery:

Discharge Summary: The patient is a 32-year-old male who was admitted for revision of the amputation site above the knee on the right leg. He sustained the amputation in a motorcycle accident 8 years ago and now presents with a neuroma of the stump. The patient was taken to surgery, where the bony stump was revised and nerve and scar tissue were removed without event. The patient has undergone this type of revision several times since the accident. The patient was discharged on the second day postop.

Which of the following would be coded?

a. 997.61, E929.0; 84.3
b. 905.9, E929.0; 84.3
c. 997.61, 905.9, E929.0; 84.3
d. 997.61, V49.76; 84.10

4.94. This 35-year-old female patient was a driver involved in an automobile accident when she was rear-ended by another driver. She was seen in the emergency room complaining of pain in the arm and neck. She was brought into the hospital by the EMTs on a backboard and after proper splinting to the right arm. It was evident that there was a compound fracture present. After a CT scan of the head and neck, the patient was removed from the backboard.

She was admitted to the hospital for an open reduction, internal fixation of the radius and ulna. The surgery was completed without problems. Postoperative x-rays show the radial and ulnar shafts in good alignment. Patient was advised to wear a collar for her cervical strain.

Final Diagnoses, in Order of Significance:
Compound radius and ulna shaft fractures
Cervical spine strain

What are the correct codes to report for this service?

Code(s) with POA indicator: _____

4.95. This 32-year-old patient was brought to the emergency department after a gas leak caused an explosion at his home. He was admitted with third-degree burns of the back involving 20 percent of the body surface. What codes are assigned?

Code(s) with POA indicator and MS-DRG: _____

4.96. This nursing home patient is admitted with extensive cellulitis of the abdominal wall. The examination performed reveals that his existing gastrostomy site is infected. He had a feeding tube inserted 4 months ago because of carcinoma of the middle esophagus. The physician confirms that the responsible organism is *Staphylococcus aureus*.

Code(s) with POA indicator and MS-DRG: _____

4.97. This patient was walking along the railroad tracks when a train hit him. He was taken to the Medical Center by ambulance. Surprisingly, there were no internal injuries, and the only injury sustained was significant trauma to both legs. Discharge diagnosis was bilateral traumatic amputation. He had a long hospital stay because of delayed healing, which was appropriately treated. A revision of the traumatic amputation with reconstruction was performed on both legs.

What are the correct ICD-9-CM codes?

Code(s) with POA indicator and MS-DRG: _____

4.98. From the health record of a patient who is status post joint replacement:

Discharge Summary: The patient is an active 61-year-old male, who underwent right total hip arthroplasty approximately 3 years ago. The patient is very active and walks several miles every day and enjoys playing golf. He has recently experienced several instances of failure of the right hip prosthesis. This is well documented in several ED visits for dislocation of the prosthetic hip. The patient was now admitted for scheduled replacement of the right hip arthroplasty. The patient was taken to surgery, where the old prosthesis was found to be eroded and bent, causing the repeated dislocations. The prosthesis was removed and replaced with a titanium prosthesis without incident. The patient was begun on physical therapy for gait training while in the hospital to help regain mobility. The patient was discharged on the fifth day postop to continue the physical therapy as an outpatient.

Which of the following codes would be used to report the above scenario?

Code(s) with POA indicator: _____

4.99. From the health record of a patient sustaining a fracture:

Discharge Summary: The patient is a 50-year-old female who fell down the icy front steps of her house and sustained a closed trimalleolar fracture of the medial and lateral malleolus, confirmed by x-ray done in the ED. She also hit her head on the concrete step and suffered a slight concussion but no loss of consciousness. The patient was admitted and taken to surgery, where open reduction and pinning was accomplished with good alignment of fracture fragments. Postop course was uneventful, and the patient was discharged home with daily physical therapy.

What codes are assigned in this case?

Code(s) with POA indicator and MS-DRG: _____

Chapter 5

Case Studies from Ambulatory Health Records

Note: Even though the specific cases are divided by setting, most of the information pertaining to the diagnosis is applicable to most settings. Even the CPT codes in the ambulatory and physician sections may be reported in the same manner. The differences in coding in these two settings may involve modifier reporting, evaluation and management CPT code reporting, and other health plan reporting guidelines unique to settings. If you practice or apply codes in a particular type of setting, you may find additional information in other sections of this publication that may be pertinent to you.

Every effort has been made to follow current recognized coding guidelines and principles, as well as nationally recognized reporting guidelines. The material presented may differ from some health plan requirements for reporting. The ICD-9-CM codes used are effective October 1, 2009, through September 30, 2010, and the HCPCS (CPT and HCPCS Level II) codes are in effect January 1, 2009, through December 31, 2009. The current standard transactions and code sets named in HIPAA have been utilized.

Instructions: Assign all applicable ICD-9-CM diagnosis including V codes and E codes. Assign all CPT Level I procedure codes and HCPCS Level II codes. Assign Level I (CPT) and Level II (HCPCS) modifiers as appropriate. Outpatient healthcare settings represented in the case examples include emergency room (ER), urgent care, outpatient surgery, observation, ancillary outpatient, wound care, interventional radiology, radiation therapy, or other outpatient department. Final codes for billing occur after codes are passed through payer edits. Medicare utilizes the National Correct Coding Initiative (NCCI) edits. CMS developed the NCCI edit list to promote national correct coding methodologies and to control improper coding leading to improper payments for Medicare Part B. The purpose of the NCCI edits is to ensure the most comprehensive code is assigned and billed rather than the component codes. In addition, NCCI edits check for mutually exclusive pairs.

Cases are presented as either multiple choice or fill in the blank.

- For multiple-choice cases:
  —Select the letter of the appropriate code set.

- For the fill-in-the-blank cases:
  —Assign up to three reasons for visit ICD-9-CM codes to describe the reason for unscheduled visits such as emergency room. Reason for visit coding is required on the UB-04 for all "unscheduled" outpatient visits.
  —Sequence the primary diagnosis first followed by the secondary diagnoses including any appropriate V codes and E codes (both cause of injury and place of occurrence).
  —Sequence the CPT procedure code first followed by additional procedure codes including modifiers as appropriate (both CPT Level I and HCPCS Level II modifiers).
  —Assign HCPCS level II codes **only if instructed** (case specific).
  —Assign evaluation and management (E/M) codes **only if instructed** (case specific).
    - Type A provider-based emergency department visits are reported with CPT level I codes 99281–99285 and critical care codes 99291 and 99292.
    - Type B provider-based urgent care visits are reported with level II HCPCS codes G0380–G0384.

The scenarios are based on selected excerpts from health records. In practice, the coding professional should have access to and refer to the entire health record. Health records are analyzed and codes assigned based on physician documentation. Documentation for coding purposes must be assigned based on medical record documentation. A physician may be queried when documentation is ambiguous, incomplete, or conflicting. The queried documentation must be a permanent part of the medical record.

The objective of the cases and scenarios reproduced in this publication is to provide practice in assigning correct codes, not necessarily to emulate complete coding that can be achieved only with the complete medical record. For example, the reader may be asked to assign codes based on only an operative report; in real practice, a coder has access to documentation in the entire medical record.

The *ICD-9-CM Official Guidelines for Coding and Reporting* of Outpatient Services, published by the National Center for Health Statistics (NCHS), supplements the official conventions and instructions provided within ICD-9-CM. Adherence to these guidelines when assigning ICD-9-CM diagnosis codes is required under the Health Insurance Portability and Accountability Act (HIPAA) of 1996. Additional official coding guidance can be found in the American Hospital Association (AHA)'s *Coding Clinic* publication.

Disorders of the Blood and Blood-Forming Organs

5.1. This 35-year-old patient was brought to the ER for GI bleeding. He was given three units of packed red cells. He was taken to the same-day surgery suite, and colonoscopy showed angiodysplasia of the transverse colon, which was controlled with laser. What codes are assigned for this case?

   a. 569.85, 45382, 36430
   b. 578.9, 569.84, 45382, 36430, 36430, 36430
   c. 578.9, 45382, 36430
   d. 569.84, 578.9, 45382

5.2. This 20-year-old female came to the outpatient procedure area with a diagnosis of anemia. A bone marrow aspiration was performed in the following manner.

Manubrial area was prepped with Betadine®. Skin and periosteum anesthetized with 2 percent Xylocaine®. Skin incision was made with #11 Bard Parker blade, and marrow aspirations performed with U of IL sternal needle. Patient tolerated the procedure with no complaints or complications. Advised to resume normal activity.

Diagnosis: Iron deficiency anemia

Pathology Report

Specimen Received: Bone marrow aspiration and biopsy

Pathologic Diagnosis: Slightly hypercellular marrow with diminished iron consistent with iron deficiency anemia

Microscopic Description: The bone marrow specimen is adequate. The marrow appears to be slightly hypercellular with a cell to fat ratio of 60/40. Megakaryocytes are easily found. Most of them are of normal morphology. There is nothing to suggest a primary or metastatic neoplastic proliferation. Granuloma is not found. The maturation of myeloid cells is complete. A Prussian blue stain obtained on both specimens shows diminished stainable iron. The specimen appears to be marrow aspiration. Bone trabecula are not seen in any of it. A reticulin stain was obtained. There is no evidence of significant increase in reticulin in the marrow stroma.

The marrow smears show adequate number of spicules. The complete maturation of myeloid cells is confirmed. Hemoglobinization of erythroid cells is slightly deficient. There is no evidence of excessive number of blasts. The myeloid/erythroid ratio is within normal limits. Plasma cells amount to less than 1 percent of the cells counted.

A review of the peripheral blood smear received shows no abnormal morphological changes in any of the cell lines.

What would be the correct codes assigned in this case?

a. 285.9, 38220
b. 280.9, 38220
c. 285.9, 38220, 38221-59
d. 280.8, 38230

5.3. This 18-year-old patient with abnormal blood test underwent bone marrow aspiration from the sternum. The area was cleaned with antiseptic solution and a local anesthetic was injected. The needle was inserted beneath the skin and rotated into the cortex and the sample taken. The needle was repositioned slightly, and a new syringe attached, and a second sample was obtained. These were sent to the laboratory for analysis. The results show acute lymphocytic leukemia. How is this coded?

Code(s): _____

5.4.   A 40-year-old female had recent surgery for melanoma of the left arm, documented as Clark level IV. She has no obvious signs of metastasis or adenopathy, but staging needs to be done. Under general anesthesia, a sentinel node biopsy of the deep axillary nodes is performed with a gamma counter probe. An injection of isosulfan blue dye was performed, and the nodes followed carefully to the single bright blue node. This node was excised and sent for frozen section, which proved to be positive for melanoma. Before the procedure, lymphoscintigraphy was performed. What are the appropriate codes to report in this case?

Code(s): _____

5.5.   This 12-year-old male African-American patient is admitted to the ER with chest pain and pulmonary infiltrates. He has sickle cell anemia. Treatment was aimed at reducing the chest pain to improve breathing. He was transferred to a larger children's hospital for admission for his sickle cell crisis and acute chest syndrome. What code(s) would be assigned for the diagnosis in this case?

Reason for visit code(s): _____

Code(s): _____

Disorders of the Cardiovascular System

5.6.   A 42-year-old patient with severe varicose veins presents to the ambulatory surgery center for stripping of the long saphenous veins in the right leg, and the long and short saphenous veins in the left leg. She has had increasing pain and edema in her legs and has not responded to conservative therapy. What codes will be submitted on the claim form for this service?

a. 454.9, 37718-50
b. 454.8, 37722-50
c. 454.8, 37722-50, 37718-LT
d. 454.2, 37722-50, 37718-50

5.7.   A pediatric patient requires a transesophageal echocardiogram to evaluate an atrioventricular canal defect present since birth. Which codes are reported for this outpatient service?

a. 745.4, 93315
b. 745.69, 93315
c. 745.69, 93312
d. 429.71, 93312

5.8.   This 45-year-old patient is scheduled for the ambulatory surgical center to have an INFUSAID pump installed. He has primary liver cancer and the pump is being inserted for continuous administration of 5-FU.

The right subclavian vein was cannulated without difficulty and the guidewire passed centrally. The subcutaneous tunnel and pocket was then created and the catheter passed through the tunnel. The central venous catheter was placed and connected to the secured pump. The pump was filled with the chemotherapy agent provided by the hospital, and the patient is observed for adverse reaction and then is discharged home.

What codes are assigned for this episode?

Code(s): _____

5.9. This 55-year-old patient has a history of unstable angina, hypertension, and chronic systolic heart failure. He is seen in the ER after prolonged chest pain that was not relieved by medication. Cardiac enzymes are elevated, and EKG shows anterior infarct. A decision was made to admit patient to observation and perform a cardiac catheterization and coronary angiography. Left heart catheterization was performed in order to perform a left ventriculogram. He tolerated the procedure well and will be discharged. Diagnosis: Acute anterior myocardial infarction, chronic systolic heart failure, hypertension. What are the correct codes?

Reason for visit code(s): _____

Code(s): _____

5.10. This 82-year-old male patient was shoveling snow and collapsed in his driveway. He arrived in the emergency department unresponsive and in asystole. A "code blue" was called and CPR was administered without a return to consciousness. The final diagnosis on the ER record was "Cardiopulmonary arrest, probably secondary to an acute myocardial infarction induced by exertion." Which diagnosis codes are reported?

Reason for visit code(s): _____

Code(s): _____

5.11. Under local anesthesia and ultrasound guidance, a patient underwent radiofrequency ablation of an incompetent greater saphenous vein in the right lower extremity. Assign the appropriate CPT code(s).

    a. 36475-RT
    b. 36475-RT, 36000
    c. 36478-RT
    d. 36475-RT, 76942

Disorders of the Digestive System

5.12. The following documentation is from the health record of a female patient.

Outpatient Operative Report

This patient with hiatal hernia is admitted to same-day surgery for repair.

Description of Procedure: The patient was placed under satisfactory general endotracheal anesthesia. She was then placed in the lithotomy position. Foley was placed. Orogastric tube was inserted. The abdomen was prepped and draped in normal sterile fashion. A supraumbilical incision was made to the midline, and the fascia was incised to enter the abdomen. Under direct visualization, a 0 VICRYL®

stitch was placed on each side of the fascia, and a blunt Hasson trocar was inserted. The abdomen was insufflated with CO_2. Under direct visualization, two 11-mm ports were placed in the left subcostal region, and 11-mm and 12-mm ports were placed in the right subcostal region.

The liver bed was then lifted up off the gastrohepatic ligament. The gastrohepatic ligament was taken down with harmonic scalpel. The right crus of the diaphragm was identified and dissected out with harmonic scalpel and blunt dissection. I dissected out the phrenicoesophageal ligament anteriorly and came around identifying the left crus. I then took down the short gastrics from the midportion of the greater curvature of the stomach up to the GE junction, using harmonic scalpel and taking care to not damage the spleen. Once we had adequately taken down the short gastrics, the posterior ligament was then mobilized behind the esophagus, and the stomach easily pulled through with no tension and no twist on the esophagus and easily laid in place.

The hiatal hernia was then repaired with a posterior cruropexy stitch of 0 ETHIBOND®. The wrap was then brought around and was placed approximately 2 cm into the esophagus with a horizontal mattress pledgeted 0 ETHIBOND stitch. A second interrupted stitch was placed just through-and-through on the stomach below this. At the end of the procedure, there was no tension or twist on the esophagus and no bleeding apparent. All ports were removed under direct visualization and there appeared to be hemostasis. The fascia at the supraumbilical incision was closed with 0 VICRYL®. The skin was anesthetized with local anesthetic and then closed with 4-0 subcuticular MONOCRYL®.

Which codes are reported for this case?

a. 553.3, 39502
b. 553.3, 43280
c. 551.3, 43280
d. 553.3, 43324

5.13. This 59-year-old female patient came into the emergency room because of passing melanic stools. The emergency room physician initially saw her. The gastroenterologist was called into consultation. Because of the massive amounts of bleeding, it was decided to proceed with endoscopy. The endoscope was passed into the esophagus, stomach, and duodenum. Blood and clots were noted. This patient could possibly have a duodenal ulcer, but because of the amount of blood, it was difficult to delineate an ulcer crater. Diagnosis: Gastrointestinal hemorrhage, melanic stools, and possibly duodenal ulcer. What codes are assigned in this case?

Reason for visit code(s): _____

Code(s): _____

5.14. This 77-year-old patient admitted to the special procedures room is having an endoscopic-directed percutaneous endoscopic gastrostomy tube placed because of moderate malnutrition. The patient has had a stroke, with residual right dominant-sided hemiparesis. Assign the codes that the hospital would use to bill this service, including the radiologic supervision and interpretation.

Code(s): _____

5.15. A 39-year-old male has been treated for symptomatic cholelithiasis without improvement. Patient comes to outpatient surgery for a laparoscopic cholecystectomy. Due to previous abdominal surgery, adhesions were encountered. During the course of the laparoscopic cholecystectomy procedure, the adhesions were lysed, but this did not prolong the procedure.

What codes are assigned?

Code(s): _____

5.16. The following documentation is from the health record of an outpatient surgical patient.

Preoperative Diagnosis:	Rectal mass
	Change in bowel habits
Postoperative Diagnosis:	Rectal prolapse
	Colonic polyps. Biopsies × 2
	Significant sigmoid diverticulosis with nonspecific colitis
Procedure:	Colonoscopy performed to the level of the cecum, 110 cm

Procedure: The 62-year-old male patient was prepped in the usual fashion, followed by placement in the left lateral decubitus position. I administered 3 mg of Versed. Monitoring of sedation was assisted by a trained registered nurse. Next, the Pentax® Video Endoscope was passed through the rectal verge after a negative digital examination and advanced to the level of the cecum. The scope was then slowly retracted with a circular tip motion. There was mild nonspecific colitis noted. She did have significant sigmoid diverticulosis and several small polyps just inside the rectum, as well as a large prolapsing mass of mucosa approximately 5 cm inside the rectum. This appears to have prolapsed previously. Two of the small polyps were biopsied using the cold biopsy forceps and sent to pathology for examination. The remainder of the examination was unremarkable. The patient tolerated the procedure well.

Pathology Report

Clinical Information: Change in bowel habits. Colonoscopy performed.

Gross Examination: The specimen is labeled polyps × 2 at 3 cm. Submitted are two fragments of tan tissue measuring tip to 0.3 cm in greatest dimension.

Microscopic Examination: Sections examined at multiple levels show two fragments of rectal mucosa in which the surfaces and subjacent crypts show no evidence of adenomatous or neoplastic changes.

Diagnosis: Rectum, biopsies at 3 cm: rectal polyps

What codes are assigned in this case?

Code(s): _____

5.17. The following documentation is from the health record of an outpatient surgical patient.

Preoperative Diagnosis:	Right inguinal hernia
Postoperative Diagnosis:	Right inguinal hernia, direct and indirect
Procedures:	Repair of right inguinal hernia with mesh

Procedure: This 45-year-old male was prepped in the usual manner for an initial hernia repair. After satisfactory spinal anesthesia, the inguinal area was draped in the usual sterile manner. A transverse incision was made above the inguinal ligament and carried down to the fascia of the external oblique, which was then opened and the cord was mobilized. The ilioinguinal nerve was identified and protected. A relatively large indirect hernia was found. However, there was an extension of the hernia, such that one could definitely tell there had been a long-standing hernia here that probably had enlarged fairly recently. The posterior wall, however, was quite dilated and without a great deal of tone and bulging, and probably fit the criteria for a hernia by itself. Nonetheless, the hernia sac was separated from the cord structures, and a high ligation was done with a purse-string suture of 2-0 silk and a suture ligature of the same material prior to amputating the sac. The posterior wall was repaired with Marlex mesh, which was sewn in place in the usual manner, anchoring two sutures at the pubic tubercle tissue, taking one lateral up the rectus sheath and one lateral along the shelving border of Poupart's ligament past the internal ring. The mesh had been incised laterally to accommodate the internal ring. Several sutures were used to tack the mesh down superiorly and laterally to the transversalis fascia. Then the two limbs of the mesh were brought together lateral to the internal ring and secured to the shelving border of Poupart's ligament. The mesh was irrigated with gentamicin solution. The subcutaneous tissue was closed with fine VICRYL®, as was the internal oblique. Marcaine was infiltrated in the subcutaneous tissue and skin. The wound was closed with fine nylon. The patient tolerated the procedure well.

Pathology Report

Gross Description

Specimen: Right inguinal hernia sac

The specimen consists of a pink to blue-gray membranous piece of tissue measuring 5.5 cm in maximum dimension. Blocks are made.

Clinical: Right inguinal hernia

What codes would be assigned?

Code(s): _____

5.18. The following documentation is from the health record of an outpatient surgical patient.

Preoperative Diagnosis:	Chronic cholelithiasis
Postoperative Diagnosis:	Chronic cholelithiasis
	Subacute cholecystitis
Operation:	Laparoscopic cholecystectomy
	Intraoperative cholangiogram

Procedure: The patient is a 44-year-old female brought to the operating room, placed in supine position, and underwent general endotracheal anesthesia. After adequate induction of anesthesia, the abdomen was prepped and draped in the usual fashion. The patient had several previous lower midline incisions and right flank incision; therefore, the pneumoperitoneum was created via epigastric incision to the left of the midline with a Verres needle. After adequate pneumoperitoneum was created, the 11-mm trocar was placed through the extended incision in the left epigastrium just to the left of the midline. The trocar was placed, and the laparoscope and camera were in place. Inspection of the peritoneal cavity revealed it to be free of adhesions, and an 11-mm trocar was then placed under direct vision through a small infraumbilical incision. The scope and camera were then moved to this position, and the gallbladder was easily visualized. The gallbladder was elevated, and Hartmann's pouch was grasped. Using a combination of sharp and blunt dissection, the cystic artery was identified. The gallbladder was somewhat tense and subacutely inflamed. Therefore, a needle was passed through the abdominal wall into the gallbladder, and the gallbladder was aspirated free until it collapsed. One of the graspers was held over this region to prevent any further leakage of bile. Again, direction was turned to the area of the triangle of Calot. The cystic duct was dissected free with sharp and blunt dissection. A small opening was made in the duct, and the cholangiogram catheter was passed. The cholangiogram revealed no stones or filling defects in the bile duct system. The biliary tree was normal. There was good flow into the duodenum, and the catheter was definitely in the cystic duct. The catheter was removed, and the cystic duct was ligated between clips, as was the cystic artery. The gallbladder was then dissected free from the hepatic bed using electrocautery dissection, and it was removed from the abdomen through the umbilical port. Inspection of the hepatic bed noted that hemostasis was meticulous. The region of dissection was irrigated and aspirated dry. The trocars were removed, and the pneumoperitoneum was released. The incisions were closed with Steri-Strips™, and the umbilical fascial incision was closed with 2-0 Maxon. The patient tolerated the procedure well; there were no complications. She was returned to the recovery room awake and alert.

What codes would be assigned?

Code(s): _____

5.19. A 61-year-old male patient is being assessed for possible colon cancer and treated in the special procedure unit of the hospital. He undergoes a colonoscopy into the ascending colon with biopsy of a suspicious area in the transverse colon using the cold biopsy forceps. In addition, a colonic ultrasound of the area is performed, with transmural biopsy of an area of the mesentery adjacent to the transverse colon. Assign the appropriate CPT codes.

   a. 45384, 45342
   b. 45380, 45391
   c. 45384, 45392
   d. 45380, 45392

5.20.   Colonoscopy

Surgery Date: 03/30/XX

Preoperative Diagnosis:	Please see indications.
Postoperative Diagnosis:	Please see impressions.
Operative Procedure:	Flexible colonoscopy beyond the splenic flexure with biopsy.
Anesthesia:	Fentanyl 200 mcg IV; midazolam 5 mg IV total; oxygen 3 L nasal cannula.
Indications for Procedure:	Question of eosinophilic gastroenteritis.
Instrument:	Olympus PCF 160-AL video colonoscope.
Preparation:	Fleet Phospho-Soda.

Description of Procedure: The patient was last seen in outpatient evaluation on March 5, 200X. No contraindications of colonoscopy were noted then nor have any developed in the interval. On the day of the procedure she was awake, alert, understood the reasons for the procedure as well as its attendant risks and benefits. History and physical examination done just prior to the procedure revealed no contraindications to colonoscopy.

After explaining the procedure and obtaining informed consent, she was placed in the left lateral decubitus position, and intravenous sedation was administered through an indwelling intravenous line. Calculation of the dose of sedative analgesic medication, its administration, intraoperative monitoring, and postoperative recovery were directly under the supervision of the endoscopist. Following normal digital rectal examination, the colonoscope was manually inserted into the rectum and advanced under direct vision to the cecum without difficulty. Cecal position was confirmed by intubation of the ileocecal valve.

Findings: The ileum and mucosa of the distal terminal ileum was normal. The ileocecal valve was normal.

The colonic mucosal preparation was fair. A modest amount of retained liquid and semisolid fecal debris obscured examination of the colon at all colonic levels, but especially the right colon. The colonic mucosa visualized *en face* was normal. No acute or chronic inflammatory mucosal changes were seen. The left colon was somewhat tortuous with an acutely angulated splenic flexure. Extensive sigmoid diverticulosis with sigmoid diverticula deformity, sigmoid haustral hypertrophy, and luminal narrowing limited both colonic visualization and reintubation of the cecum. No active diverticulitis was seen. In the midsigmoid colon, a 3- to 4-mm sessile area of polypoid mucosa was removed in three fragments with a biopsy forceps. No other polyps or masses were seen. There were a few punctate ulcerations in the distal rectum that did not readily bleed when biopsied. The dentate line was fully seen on retroflexion and was otherwise normal.

Segmental biopsies were obtained from the terminal ileum, right colon, transverse colon, descending colon, sigmoid colon, and rectum and submitted separately for histopathological analysis. An attempt was made to intubate the colon twice; however, acutely angulated sigmoid descending junction and abdominal pain precluded a second cecal intubation.

She tolerated the procedure well and was sent to the recovery room in satisfactory condition.

Impression:	1. Abdominal bloating and gas symptoms, upper GI endoscopic biopsies suggestive of eosinophilic esophagitis, rule out eosinophilic colitis.
	2. Rule out proctitis.
	3. Colon polyp, rule out neoplasia.
	4. Diverticulosis coli.
Recommendations:	1. Pending pathology.
	2. Return to office in 4 to 6 weeks.
	3. Continue to follow with primary care physician.

Pathology Addendum: Eosinophilic colitis, possibly a component of eosinophilic gastroenteritis. Hyperplastic polyps sigmoid colon and rectum.

Which codes are assigned for the ambulatory surgery center?

a. 558.9, 211.3, 569.0, 562.10, 45384, 45380-59
b. 558.9, 211.3, 569.0, 562.10, 45380
c. 787.3, 211.3, 569.0, 562.10, 45384, 45380-59
d. 558.9, 211.3, 562.10, 45384, 45380

Endocrine, Nutritional and Metabolic Diseases, and Immunity Disorders

5.21. This 17-year-old patient presents to the emergency room with a chief complaint of severe right lower quadrant abdominal pain. The patient describes the pain as tightness and an intense cramping feeling. She has had increased bowel movements that provide some relief from the cramping. The pain seems much more intense after milk or ice cream. The patient is also currently menstruating but describes these cramps as different and worse. She is on no medication, no birth control, and is not sexually active.

Discharge diagnoses: Lactose intolerance, menstrual cramps

Reason for visit Code(s): _____

Code(s): _____

5.22.   This 57-year-old female patient with known type I diabetes mellitus presents for laboratory work as an ancillary outpatient at the hospital for evaluation of blood sugar levels. What is the correct coding and/or sequencing for this encounter?

Code(s): _____

5.23.   A 45-year-old female presents to the outpatient surgery unit of the hospital with a complaint of neck swelling. The physician noted diffuse swelling of the neck with enlargement of the thyroid gland. The patient exhibits no clinical signs of hyperthyroidism. The physician suspects lymphoma and a biopsy is performed. A large, hollow core needle is passed through the skin into the thyroid. Tissue is sent for histopathology. A diagnosis of nodular lymphoma is confirmed and chemotherapy is planned.

What is the correct code assignment?

Code(s): _____

Disorders of the Genitourinary System

5.24.   A 55-year-old female patient presents to the same-day surgical unit with stress incontinence and requires repair for midline cystocele and incomplete vaginal prolapse. The physician elects to perform a paravaginal defect repair on both sides. An abdominal incision is made and entry into the space of Retzius is gained. Six sutures are placed through the anterior lateral edge of the vaginal wall and then through the fascia condensation over the obturator internus muscle from the inferior aspect of the pubic bone along the arcus tendinous to the ischial spine. Additional anchors were placed at the level of the urethrovesical junction on both sides to correct the cystocele.

Which of the following code sets is reported for this service?

a. 625.6, 618.01, 618.2, 57284, 51840
b. 625.6, 57284-50
c. 618.02, 57240
d. 618.01, 625.6, 57284

5.25.   This 77-year-old male patient is a nursing home patient who is admitted to the special procedure unit at the hospital. Patient is stress incontinent and continually leaks urine. To treat this, the urologist introduces a mechanical obstruction in the urethra that prevents leakage. Using an endoscope, the physician injects a solution of polytetrafluoroethylene into the region of the distal sphincter of the urethra; then inserts an inflatable bladder neck sphincter with pump, reservoir, and cuff. Which of the following code sets is reported for this surgery?

a. 788.37, 53445, 51715
b. 788.39, 51715
c. 788.37, 53440
d. 788.37, 53445

5.26. This 35-year-old male is treated in the outpatient surgery suite with the diagnosis of renal calculus diagnosed per x-ray. Endoscopes are used to pass through the patient's urethra into the bladder and then the ureter identifying the renal calculus. An electrohydraulic lithotriptor probe is used to pulverize the stone. An indwelling double-J stent is placed to facilitate passing of any residual stones.

   a. 592.1, 52353, 52332
   b. 592.0, 52353-RT
   c. 592.0, 52353, 52332
   d. 592.0, 52352, 52332-51

5.27. This patient, a 47-year-old male with adenoma of the prostate, is being treated in the outpatient surgery suite. The urologist inserts an endoscope in the penile urethra and dilates the structure to allow instrument passage. After endoscope placement, a radiofrequency stylet is inserted, and the diseased prostate is excised with radiant energy. Bleeding is controlled with electrocoagulation. Following instrument removal, a catheter is inserted and left in place. Which of the following code sets will be reported for this service?

   a. 600.20, 53852
   b. 600.20, 52601
   c. 600.00, 53852
   d. 222.2, 53850

5.28. The patient is a 22-year-old male with left testicular pain and scrotal swelling over the past 3 hours. No dysuria, no penile discharge, no fever and is able to void well. No trauma to groin. Pain 5/10. The physician orders an ultrasound which demonstrates a testicle that is free floating in the scrotum with the spermatic cord looped once around the middle of the testicle. The patient was against surgical intervention and opted to try manual detorsion. The patient was warmed with hot packs to loosen the scrotal skin, and the physician manipulated the testicle until the spermatic cord felt loosened. Reultrasound confirmed proper position and the patient's pain was substantially relieved. The patient was sent home with a list of precautions, and instructions to return with any increase in pain.

What codes are reported by the facility? Do not include an E/M code for this case.

Reason for visit Code(s): _____

Code(s): _____

5.29. A 90-year-old female nursing home patient with a long history of chronic urinary tract infections is brought to the emergency room, after developing a fever of 102°F with generalized abdominal pain. The patient has senile dementia with delirium and is unable to communicate. The history was obtained from nursing home transfer records. Nonautomated urinalysis with microscopy was performed but was not remarkable. The physician's assessment stated "fever of unknown origin." The patient was treated with

Tylenol® and started on a broad-spectrum antibiotic and referred to her primary care physician for follow-up first thing in the morning.

What codes are reported by the ER facility coding? Do not include E/M codes in this example, but do include laboratory codes, even though they would be reported by the chargemaster.

Reason for visit Code(s): _____

Code(s): _____

5.30.   Patient is a 59-year-old admitted to the same day surgery suite. Patient is a type I diabetic with diabetic nephropathy and end-stage renal disease now requiring dialysis. A Cimino-type direct arteriovenous anastomosis is performed by incising the skin of the left antecubital fossa. Vessel clamps are placed on the vein and adjacent artery. The vein is dissected free and the downstream portion of the vein is sutured to an opening in the artery using an end-to-side technique. The skin incision is closed in layers.

What codes are reported for this service?

Code(s): _____

5.31.   A 28-year-old patient admitted for same-day surgery with a history of abdominal surgery and is experiencing sharp pain in the pelvic area. Diagnostic workup has presented no etiology. An exploratory laparoscopy was performed and revealed adhesions around the fallopian tubes and ovaries. The adhesions were taken down during the procedure. What codes will be reported?

Code(s): _____

5.32.   A 59-year-old male is admitted to the special procedure unit of the hospital. He has been having increasing difficulty in urinating. A transurethral resection of the bladder neck is performed to treat urinary obstruction and retention due to vesicourethral obstruction with benign prostatic hypertrophy. What codes are reported?

Code(s): _____

5.33.   A patient with advanced renal cell carcinoma is admitted to the interventional radiology department to undergo percutaneous radiofrequency ablation of four tumors of the right kidney. Assign the appropriate CPT code for this procedure.

Code(s): _____

Infectious Diseases

5.34.   A 22-year-old male patient presents to the emergency room with symptoms of right upper quadrant pain, fever, profound malaise, and bloody diarrhea. An infectious consultation was obtained and diagnosis was made of acute *Entamoeba histolytica* dysentery. What code(s) are assigned?

Reason for visit Code(s): _____

Code(s): _____

5.35. A 29-year-old male patient presents to the hospital emergency room with a vesicular eruption and severe itching on the penis, scrotum, buttocks, and groin. Itching is severe at night. Assessment: Infestation with *Sarcoptes scabiei*. Plan: PMS-Lindane is applied to the affected area and a prescription provided for treatment of the entire household. What diagnosis code is reported for this encounter?

Reason for visit Code(s): _____

Code(s): _____

5.36. This 3-year-old patient presents to the emergency department with history of sudden bloody diarrhea. The stool culture demonstrated *Escherichia coli*. The patient went swimming with his child care center the previous day at a nearby water park. The physician documented: acute enteritis, due to enterotoxigenic *E. coli*. What is the correct ICD-9-CM diagnostic code for this encounter?

Reason for visit Code(s): _____

Code(s): _____

5.37. The patient is seen for latent TB infection. He had a positive TB skin test last week and presents today for counseling on the start of INH 300 mg day, orally. The patient also has moderate Bipolar I disorder and is currently depressed. Because of this, the physician spends considerable time discussing the need to take the INH daily, along with all other prescribed medication.

What diagnosis code(s) describe this case?

Reason for visit Code(s): _____

Code(s): _____

Disorders of the Skin and Subcutaneous Tissue

5.38. A 55-year-old female patient who has had a lesion removal 2 weeks ago returns now for a wide excision of a malignant melanoma on the back. The area excised consists of a 3-cm diameter area. A layer closure is required to close the defect. The pathology report shows clear margins.

What are the correct codes to report? The procedure is performed in the outpatient surgery suite at the hospital.

   a. 172.5, 11603
   b. 709.9, 11603
   c. 172.5, 11603, 12032
   d. V76.43, 11603, 13121

5.39. An ambulatory surgery operative report for a 75-year-old male patient states that the patient received a full-thickness graft of the cheek following lesion removal of a basal carcinoma. The lesion plus margins are documented to be 3.2 cm in diameter. A 10 sq cm graft is applied with donor skin from his thigh, closed by suture.

Which of the following code sets is correct for this surgery?

a. 173.3, 15240, 11646
b. 173.3, 15240, 15004
c. 173.3, 15350, 15004, 11644
d. 173.3, 15240, 11644

5.40. From the health record of a patient undergoing foot surgery in the outpatient surgical unit:

Indication for Procedure: The patient is a 60-year-old female who has a persistently ingrowing great toenail on the right foot that has had two past infections. The infection is now clear and the patient presents for wedge resection of the toenail. She also has pernicious anemia, Friedrich's ataxia, and heart disease. Because of these conditions, a digital block will be used for the procedure.

Procedure: Wedge resection of toenail

Procedure Description: The patient is placed in the supine position, with the knees flexed and the right foot is flat on the table. The toe is prepped and cleansed. A standard digit block is performed with 1% lidocaine using a 10-ml syringe and a 30 gauge needle. Approximately 3 ml is instilled on each side of the toe.

After waiting 10 minutes, a sterilized rubber band is placed around the base of the toe. The toe is resterilized and draped with the toe protruding. A nail elevator is slid under the cuticle to separate the nail plate from the overlying proximal nail fold. The lateral one fourth of the nail plate is identified as the site for the partial lateral nail removal. A bandage scissors is used to cut from the distal end of the nail straight back beneath the proximal nail fold. A straight, smooth, new lateral edge to the nail plate is created. The lateral piece of nail is grasped with a hemostat and removed in one piece, pulling straight out.

Electrocautery ablation is used to destroy the nail matrix where the nail was removed. The matrix is treated twice. Antibiotic ointment is applied and a bulky gauze dressing is placed. The foot is placed in a surgical boot. Post-op instructions are given for daily cleansing with warm water and strenuous exercise is to be avoided completely for at least one week. The patient tolerated the procedure well and understands the discharge instructions.

What codes would be assigned for reporting the facility services? Report all ICD-9-CM, CPT and/or HCPCS codes.

Reason for visit Code(s): _____

Code(s): _____

5.41. A 17-year-old male patient presents to the hospital outpatient surgery center for surgery. Destruction was performed on eight viral warts on the left arm. Destruction was done using cryosurgery and curettage. What codes are reported?

Code(s): _____

5.42. This 4-year-old boy is seen in the emergency room today. He was helping his father, who was installing a new bedroom window, and the window fell. The glass broke, cutting the boy on his hand, arm, and leg. He received a 2-cm laceration on his left hand, a 3-cm laceration on his left arm, and a 2.5-cm laceration on his lower right leg. The lacerations on the hand and arm were repaired with a simple repair. The laceration on the leg was deeper and required a layered repair. What are the diagnosis and CPT procedure codes for this ER visit?

Reason for visit Code(s): _____

Code(s): _____

5.43.

Preoperative Diagnosis:	Burn scar contracture with hypertrophic and keloid scarring anterior neck.
Postoperative Diagnosis:	Burn scar contracture with hypertrophic and keloid scarring anterior neck.
Procedure Performed:	Excision of keloid and release of anterior neck (20 × 8 cm).
Anesthesia:	General.
Estimated Blood Loss:	Minimal.

Indications For Procedure: This 18-year-old male had very severe hypertrophic burn scar to his anterior neck region. He is a keloid former by his previous history. He has been successfully treated with an acellular dermal replacement in the past. Our plan today after release of his neck and excision of the keloid is application of Integra to the defect on the anterior neck.

Description Of Procedure: The patient was brought to the operating room and placed in the supine position on the OR table where general anesthesia and endotracheal intubation were accomplished without difficulty. After this was done, the patient was placed in a slightly hyper-extended position on the neck with a roll behind his shoulders and with sterile towels in the usual manner. A line was then drawn across the site of maximal contracture on the anterior neck and this was incised, carried down to scar into the platysma muscle. A large amount of hypertrophic and keloid scar was excised from the upper part of the flap. After this was released, the face was not distorted anymore and the contracture had been alleviated. The size of the defect with this was 20 × 8 cm. After bleeding was controlled with electrocautery, Integra was prepared and one sheet was meshed 1:1 and applied on to the wound and secured with staples. Following this, stretched burn netting was applied over the Integra for support by Reston foam wet, irrigation catheters, and wet burn dressings. Spandex was used to complete the dressing.

The patient was then awakened, extubated, and transferred to the recovery room in good condition.

Code(s): _____

5.44. A 38-year-old female patient underwent a left lumpectomy and placement of an afterloading balloon catheter into the left breast in the special procedure room. Assign the appropriate CPT code(s).

    a. 19297-LT
    b. 19301-LT, 19297-LT
    c. 19301-RT
    d. 19120-LT

5.45. A 75-year-old female patient is treated in the wound care clinic. She presents with a large sacral decubitus and a small decubitus on her buttock. Procedure performed by the surgeon: Full-thickness excisional débridement to the sacral decubitus. Scalpel was used to remove devitalized tissue down to bleeding. Patient tolerated the procedure well. Code the diagnosis and CPT procedure code(s).

    a. 707.0, 97602
    b. 707.03, 707.05, 11040
    c. 707.03, 97597
    d. 707.03, 707.05, 11041

Behavioral Health Conditions

5.46. A 35-year-old female patient presents to the Community Mental Health Center for group therapy with the diagnosis of obsessive compulsive disorder. A psychiatrist provides group therapy for obsessive-compulsive disorder. Which of the following code sets would be reported for the facility code?

    a. 301.4, 90853
    b. 300.3, 90857
    c. 300.3, 90853
    d. 300.3, 90847

5.47. A 66-year-old patient is seen as an outpatient in the community mental health center and receives individual insight-oriented psychotherapy for 25 minutes. Diagnosis: Posttraumatic stress disorder, acute. List the diagnosis and CPT procedure codes for facility reporting.

Code(s): _____

5.48. A 15-year-old depressed male is seen in the emergency department after a failed suicide attempt. Right wrist with a 3-cm laceration with no injury to the tendon. Left wrist with a 2.0-cm laceration with no injury to the tendon. Both wrists required simple suture repair. Patient used a razor to cut himself in a suicide attempt while at home in the bathroom today. He stated he has become increasingly depressed and has not experienced these types of symptoms before. He denies psychotic symptoms. Assessment: Laceration to both wrists, repaired. Major depression, severe. Plan: A 24-hour hold was instituted and the patient was transferred for psychiatric care. Stitches removed in 10 days. List the diagnosis and CPT procedure codes for facility reporting.

Reason for visit Code(s): _____

Code(s): _____

5.49. This 25-year-old female was brought to the ER because of an overdose of prescription drugs. Her roommate found her and called 911. She has been treated recently for depression, and her bottle of amitriptyline was empty. The roommate also reports that her bottle of diazepam was empty. Roommate estimates that there may have been about 20 pills in each bottle. According to the evidence, it appears as if she used alcohol to take the pills, and this was confirmed during drug screening. She left a suicide note stating that she could not go on living. Aggressive measures included stomach pumping to remove pill fragments and cardiopulmonary resuscitation. She could not be revived and was pronounced dead at 2305. List the diagnosis and CPT procedure codes for facility reporting.

Reason for visit Code(s): _____

Code(s): _____

Disorders of the Musculoskeletal System and Connective Tissue

5.50. A patient fell from a ladder at his home, which resulted in a nondisplaced compression fracture of L1 and L2 vertebral bodies. The patient was placed in a back brace and will be followed for potential complications. Do not code the supply in this example.

Which codes are appropriate for reporting?

a. 805.5, E881.0, 22325
b. 805.4, E881.0, E849.0, 22310
c. 806.4, E881.0, E849.0, 22315
d. 805.01, 805.02, E881.0, E849.0, 22326

5.51. From the health record of a 16-year-old male patient requiring fracture care in outpatient surgical unit:

Operative Report

Preoperative Diagnosis: Displaced comminuted fracture of the lateral condyle, right elbow

Postoperative Diagnosis: Same

Procedure: Open reduction, internal fixation

Description: The patient was anesthetized and prepped with Betadine. Sterile drapes were applied, and the pneumatic tourniquet was inflated around the arm. An incision was made in the area of the lateral epicondyle through a Steri-Drape™, and this was carried through subcutaneous tissue, and the fracture site was easily exposed. Inspection revealed the fragment to be rotated in two planes about 90 degrees. It was possible to manually reduce this quite easily, and the judicious manipulation resulted in an almost anatomic reduction. This was fixed with two pins driven across the humerus. These pins were cut off below skin level. The wound was closed with some plain catgut suture subcutaneously and 5-0 nylon in the skin. Dressings were applied to the patient and tourniquet released. A long arm cast was applied.

Which of the following is the correct code assignment? Do not assign supplies codes.

a. 812.52, 24577, 29065
b. 812.42, 24579, 29065
c. 812.42, 24579-RT
d. 812.52, 24579-RT

5.52. The patient was hit in the face by a soccer ball on the neighborhood soccer field, sustaining a 2.3 cm superficial laceration to the medial cheek. X-rays revealed a nasal fracture that required stabilization. The emergency room physician stabilizes the fracture with a splint and tape and repairs the laceration.

Reason for visit Code(s): _____

Code(s): _____

5.53. This 52-year-old male was brought to the same-day surgery area for treatment of an open fracture of the distal phalanx of his index finger on the right hand. Patient is right-handed and this injury occurred when the food-processing machine at work tipped over and his hand got caught. He works in the local food factory here in town. The patient had open treatment performed to remove the fracture fragments without any internal or external fixation hardware used. What diagnosis and CPT code(s) are reported?

Code(s): _____

5.54. This 32-year-old male had an ORIF of a fractured metacarpal bone done 3 months ago. The fracture has completely healed, and he is scheduled for removal of deep internal fixation hardware involving the metacarpals of this left wrist. The plate and pins were removed without incident. Which codes would be reported for this service in a hospital-based outpatient surgery center where anesthesia is available?

Code(s): _____

5.55. The procedure that involves transplantation of a piece of articular cartilage and attached subchondral bone from a cadaver donor to a damaged region of the articular surface of the knee joint is called a(n):

a. Osteochondral autograft
b. Osteochondral allograft
c. Autologous chondrocyte implantation
d. Anterior cruciate ligament repair

5.56. From the health record of a 47-year-old patient admitted for outpatient surgery on his knee:

Operative Report

Preoperative Diagnosis: Severe chondromalacia patellar right knee.

Postoperative Diagnosis: Severe chondromalacia patella and medial femoral condylar right knee.

Procedure Performed: 1. Arthroscopy.
         2. Chondroplasty/débridement of patella and medial femoral condyle.
         3. Lateral retinacular release right knee.

Anesthesia: General.

Indications: This 47-year-old man has a history of severe patellofemoral and anteromedial joint line pain. This has been treated with anti-inflammatory medications and physical therapy with persistent symptoms. He has tightness of his lateral retinaculum associated with lateral patellar compression syndrome and patellofemoral pain. He presents now for surgical treatment after failed conservative management.

Details of Operation: Patient was brought to the operating room and placed on the operating table in a supine position. After instillation of successful general anesthesia, the right knee was examined. Range of motion was full; no laxity to stress testing was noted. Marked patellofemoral crepitus was noted. The leg was then placed in the arthroscopic leg holder and the knee sterilely prepped and draped. The knee was injected with a total of 30 cc of 0.25 percent Marcaine with epinephrine. Standard arthroscopic portals were established. There were grade III changes over the superior aspect and medial aspect of the patella. The trochlear groove of the femur was softened and minimally fissured. The medial compartment was entered and showed grade III chondromalacia over the majority of the weight-bearing surface of the medial femoral condyle. The tibial plateau was mildly softened, as was the medial meniscus. Intercondylar notch revealed a normal anterior cruciate ligament. The lateral compartment also revealed mild degeneration of the posterior horn of the lateral meniscus, and minimal chondromalacia of the tibial plateau. At that point, a full radius resector was placed, and a chondroplasty débridement was carried out of the patella and medial femoral condyle. An internal lateral retinacular release was then carried out using arthroscopic electrocautery to help decompress the patellofemoral area. The patient returned to the recovery room without complications.

What are the correct code assignments for this outpatient surgical case?

a. 719.46. 717.7, 29873-RT, 29877-RT-59
b. 719.46, 717.7, 27425-RT
c. 717.7, 29877-RT
d. 719.46, 717.7, 29999-RT, 29877-RT

Neoplasms

5.57.   A patient has squamous cell carcinoma of the posterior pharyngeal wall and metastasis to the cervical lymph nodes. Following consultation with the oncology team, the patient refused surgical intervention and elected to begin radiation therapy daily on a 6-MV linear accelerator. The radiation was delivered by hyperfractionation technique. Each field was treated twice each day, through a pair of large opposing lateral head and neck fields covering the primary cancer, the suspected areas of extension, and the lymph nodes in the neck. (Three separate treatment areas are involved, and customized shielding blocks are employed to shield normal tissue and shape the field to follow the anatomic boundaries.) Prior to the encounter under consideration, the clinical treatment parameters and dosimetry calculations have been completed, and the simulation-aided field settings have been accomplished.

Which of the following codes will be reported by the hospital for the encounters for radiation therapy, keeping in mind the number of treatments that will be reported in the unit's field on the UB-04?

a. V58.0, 77413
b. 149.0, 77408
c. V58.0, 149.0, 196.0, 77413
d. 149.0, 196.0, 77412

5.58.   A patient with a lung mass discovered on prior x-ray presents to the outpatient surgery area for a diagnostic bronchoscopy. Following anesthetic to the airway, a fiberoptic bronchoscope is introduced into the bronchial tree. A needle is advanced through a channel in the scope, and tissue is aspirated from the lung mass for pathologic evaluation under fluoroscopic guidance. Pathology report confirmed parenchymal tissue of the lung was obtained and reported a diagnosis of oat cell carcinoma.

Which of the following is the correct code assignment?

a. 162.9, 31629
b. 162.9, 31629, 77002
c. 162.9, 31625
d. 235.7, 31629, 77002

5.59.   A Medicare patient is scheduled for breast biopsy of a palpable lump in the right breast. A much smaller lesion in the left breast is identified by a radiological marker shown on mammography. An excisional biopsy is performed on both sides. The specimen on the right is diagnostic for breast malignancy with clear margins, whereas the small lesion in the left breast is found to be only fibrocystic disease, without evidence of malignancy. Which of the following is reported?

a. 174.9, 610.1, 19120-RT, 19125-LT, 19290-LT
b. 611.72, 610.1, 19120-50
c. 174.9, 610.1, 19120-50, 19125-50, 19290-50
d. 174.9, 610.2, 19120, 19125-59, 19290

5.60.   A 50-year-old male patient with a personal history of colonic polyps presents to the outpatient surgery department for a colonoscopy to rule out colon cancer. The patient has been experiencing rectal bleeding for approximately 6 weeks and has lost a significant amount of weight. A colonoscopy to the terminal ileum is performed. Just beyond the rectal vault, two polyps are found and excised by hot biopsy forceps. Further up into the sigmoid colon, a lesion was biopsied. The pathology report confirms a diagnosis of colon cancer in the lesion found, and the polyps were found to be villous adenoma.

What codes are assigned in this case?

Code(s): _____

5.61. A patient presents to the hospital outpatient department for chemotherapy treatment. She is a 15-year-old female with acute lymphocytic leukemia. The chemotherapy agent is listed as an injection of lyophilized cyclophosphamide, 200 mg IV push. What codes, including the medication, would be reported?

Code(s): _____

Disorders of the Nervous System and Sense Organs

5.62. A 36-year-old female patient presents to the ED with a severe headache, listlessness, light sensitivity, nausea, and vomiting. The headache has been growing in intensity over the last 3 days. The patient does not have a fever. The patient has a programmable cerebrospinal fluid shunt in place and after MRI of both the head and the abdomen, it is determined that there is fluid accumulation in the intracranial portion of the shunt, indicating malfunction. The neurosurgeon takes the patient to the outpatient surgical suite and performs a magnetic adjustment of the valve pressure. The diagnoses are documented as headache and idiopathic normopressure hydrocephalus.

Excluding the E/M code and the MRI codes assigned by the chargemaster, what codes would be assigned for the facility in this case?

Code(s): _____

5.63. A patient with Lou Gehrig's disease presents to the hospital-based outpatient neurology department for EMG testing. A needle electromyography of the legs and both of the eyes was conducted. Which of the following code sets would be reported?

a. 335.20, 92265-50, 95861
b. 335.24, 95868-59, 95861
c. 335.20, 95861, 92265
d. 335.29, 95861

5.64. From the health record of a patient requiring outpatient eye surgery:

Operative Report

Preoperative Diagnosis: Type I diabetes patient with severe retinal microaneurysmal diabetic retinopathy, OU

Postoperative Diagnosis: Same

Operation: Vitrectomy followed by laser photocoagulation, OU

Description of Procedure: An Ocutome® is used to go behind the iris and cut and suction the vitreous mechanically. After vitreous removal, a laser is used to treat the remaining retinal disorders in all four retinal quadrants and prevent further retinal hemorrhage. Procedure repeated.

Which of the following code sets is reported for this service?

a. 250.51, 362.01, 67040-50
b. 362.01, 362.81, 67040-50
c. 250.50, 362.02, 67039-LT-RT
d. 250.51, 362.02, 67105, 67145

5.65. From the health record of a patient with cataracts treated in outpatient surgery at the Eye Center:

Operative Report

Procedure: Extracapsular cataract extraction with intraocular lens implantation, left eye

Diagnosis: Bilateral cataracts

Technique: The patient was given a retrobulbar injection of 2.5 to 3.0 cc of a mixture of equal parts of 2 percent lidocaine with epinephrine and 0.75 percent Marcaine with Wydase®. The area about the left eye was infiltrated with an additional 6 to 7 cc of this mixture in a modified Van Lint technique. A self-maintaining pressure device was applied to the eye, and a short time later, the patient was taken to the OR.

The patient was properly positioned on the operating table, and the area around the left eye was prepped and draped in the usual fashion. A self-retaining eyelid speculum was positioned and 4-0 silk suture passed through the tendon of the superior rectus muscle, thereby deviating the eye inferiorly. A 160° fornix-based conjunctival flap was created, followed by a 150° corneoscleral groove with a #64 Beaver blade. Hemostasis was maintained throughout with gentle cautery. A 6-0 silk suture was introduced to cross this groove at the 12 o'clock position and looped out of the operative field. The anterior chamber was then entered superiorly temporally, and after injecting Occucoat, an anterior capsulotomy was performed without difficulty. The nucleus was easily brought forward into the anterior chamber. The corneoscleral section was opened with scissors to the left and the nucleus delivered with irrigation and gentle lens loop manipulation. Interrupted 10-0 nylon sutures were placed at both the nasal and lateral extent of the incision. A manual irrigating aspirating setup then was used to remove remaining cortical material from both the anterior and posterior chambers.

At this point, a modified C-loop posterior chamber lens was removed from its package and irrigated and inspected. It then was positioned into the inferior capsular bag without difficulty, and the superior haptic was placed behind the iris at the 12 o'clock location. The lens was rotated to a horizontal orientation in an attempt to better enhance capsular fixation. Miochol® was used to constrict the pupil, and a peripheral iridectomy was performed in the superior nasal quadrant. In addition, three or four interrupted 10-0 nylon sutures were used to close the corneal scleral section. The silk sutures were removed, and the conjunctiva advanced back into its normal location and was secured with cautery burns at the 3 o'clock and 9 o'clock positions. Approximately 20 to 30 mg of both gentamicin and Kenalog® were injected into the inferior cul-de-sac in a subconjunctival and sub-Tenon fashion. After instillation of 2 percent pilocarpine and Maxitrol® ophthalmic solution, the eyelid speculum was removed and the eye dressed in a sterile fashion. The patient was discharged to the recovery room in good condition.

What codes are assigned in this case?

Code(s): _____

5.66. This 45-year-old female was admitted through the emergency room after a grand mal seizure. She did not respond to treatment and was transferred with the diagnosis of intractable epilepsy to a higher level of care at the neurology institute. What diagnosis code is reported?

Reason for visit Code(s): _____

Code(s): _____

5.67. The patient has known chronic glaucoma, more severe in the left eye. She is brought to the outpatient procedure suite and anesthetized with a periocular anesthetic. The left eye is prepared and sterilely draped, followed by insertion of a lid speculum. A clear corneal incision is made temporally with the diamond blade approximately 3.4 mm in width. Viscoelastic material is injected into the anterior chamber over the pupil and lens to increase and maintain anterior chamber depth. Viscoelastic is then injected under the iris for 180° to visualize the ciliary body processes with the endoscope. The endoscope is inserted through the temporal incision viewing the nasal ciliary processes. The ciliary processes are coagulated through the endoscope with the endpoint of shrinkage and whitening.

Assign the appropriate CPT code for the described procedure.

- a. 66710-LT
- b. 66711-LT
- c. 66720-LT
- d. 66700-LT

5.68. From the health record of a patient scheduled for eye surgery:

Surgery Date:	04/10/XX
Preoperative Diagnosis:	Endophthalmitis, left eye.
Postoperative Diagnosis:	Endophthalmitis, left eye.
Operative Procedure:	1. Pars plana vitrectomy, left eye.
	2. Intravitreal vancomycin (1 mg left eye).
	3. Intravitreal ceftazidime (2 mg left eye).
	4. Intravitreal triamcinolone (4 mg left eye.)

Anesthesia: Retrobulbar anesthesia with 5 cc of a 50/50 mixture of 2 percent lidocaine and 0.75 percent Marcaine.

Indications: This patient is status post tap and injection on April 1, 20XX. She presents with vitreous debris, poor vision, and a history of endophthalmitis.

Description of Procedure: After informed written consent was obtained, the patient was brought to the operating room and was prepped and draped in the usual sterile fashion. Retrobulbar anesthesia was performed with 5 cc of a 50/50 mixture of 2 percent lidocaine and 0.75 percent Marcaine in the retrobulbar space of the left eye without any complications. She was then prepped and draped in the usual sterile fashion. A speculum was placed in the left eye.

A standard 20-gauge pars plana vitrectomy was carried out with the pars placed 3 mm posterior to the limbus. A full vitrectomy was performed. Posterior vitreous detachment was induced and then further vitrectomy was carried out. The sclerotomy was closed with 7-0 VICRYL®, as was the conjunctiva. Then, 0.1 mL of vancomycin (1 mg),

0.1 mL of ceftazidime (2 mg), and 0.1 mL of triamcinolone (4 mg) were injected into the vitreous cavity at the end of the case.

The patient was patched after atropine and Maxitrol were applied to the eye. The patient will follow-up tomorrow at 8 a.m.

No qualified resident was available for the case.

What are the correct codes for this ambulatory surgery?

a. 360.00, 67036-LT, 66030-LT
b. 360.03, 67036-LT, 66030-LT
c. 360.00, 67036-RT
d. 998.59, 360.00, 67036-LT, 66030-LT

Newborn/Congenital Disorders

5.69. A baby was born in the hospital to a woman who lacked prenatal care and contracted rubella during pregnancy, passing it on to her fetus. The baby was born with multiple deformities, including a congenital cortical and zonular cataract of the left eye. The baby is now 7 months old and ready for extracapsular phacoemulsification with intraocular lens replacement.

Which of the following code sets would be reported for the surgery?

a. 743.30, 760.2, 66984-50
b. 366.03, 66984-LT
c. V30.00, 771.0, 743.32
d. 743.32, 66984-LT

5.70. A newborn female is born with polydactyly of the right foot with a total of five normal toes and two extra digits that do not contain bony structures. Which of the following code sets would be reported by the ASC facility tying off and removing these digits at the age of 2 weeks?

a. 755.02, 11200
b. 755.02, 11200-RT, 11200-59
c. 755.00, 28899
d. 755.02, 26587

5.71. A baby boy is born with hypospadias. At 7 months of age, the first stage of surgical correction is undertaken, which requires transplantation of the prepuce, but no skin flaps. What are the correct codes for this ambulatory surgery, as reported by the hospital?

Code(s): _____

5.72. This child was born with a bilateral hydrocele. He also has reducible inguinal hernias on both sides. The condition has become troublesome, and the parents and pediatrician have decided that surgical correction is warranted for this 3 year old. Surgeon performed a bilateral hernia repair with hydrocelectomy.

Postoperative Diagnosis: Bilateral hernia repair with hydrocelectomy.

Report diagnosis and CPT procedure codes.

Code(s): _____

Pediatric Conditions

5.73. A 3-year-old child was brought to the ER with fever, cough, and chest pain. Chest x-ray reveals diffuse bronchopneumonia. Gram stain of sputum shows numerous, small gram-negative coccobacilli. Patient treated with ampicillin 250 mg orally t.i.d. Diagnosis: *Haemophilus influenzae* pneumonia. Which of the following is the correct ICD-9-CM diagnostic code assignment?

    a. 487.0, 482.2
    b. 487.0
    c. 482.2, 487.0
    d. 485, 482.2

5.74. Emergency Room Service

Chief Complaint: Coughing, history of asthma, on Albuterol MDI, no allergies.

S: Patient is a 11 year old male, who is seen today with cough that started 3 days ago, growing progressively worse. He states that he coughs when walking short distances. Peak flows have been around 200 at home but hard to measure due to coughing. Personal best is 300. Has been using Albuterol MDI with little success today. He had some loose stools yesterday, and Mom says that his activity level is severely reduced. Appetite moderate to minimal, totally unlike him. Some nasal allergy symptoms due to tree season. No chest pain. No nausea or vomiting.

O: Young white male in moderate respiratory distress. W: 81 lbs P: 64 RR: 24 T: 100.4 HEENT: PERRLA. TMs bilaterally are clear. Nose: Congested with rhinorrhea. Oropharynx: mild erythema. Neck: supple. Full ROM. Thyroid normal. Lungs have bilateral wheeze in the left lower lobe. Heart RRR w/o gallop or murmur. Abdomen positive bowel sounds, soft, nontender. No organomegaly is noted.

Data: Peak flows here are 200, 210, 200 with coughing. Pulse Ox is 97. Albuterol 0.5 cc aerosol via nebulizer is given with resulting peak flows of 230, 240, and 220 and repeat nebulizer at .05 cc in 15 minutes with improvement to 250.

A: Cough, acute asthma exacerbation due to seasonal allergies.

P: Albuterol 2 puffs QID. Prednisone 40 mg qd x 3 days, rest at least today, until appetite and energy improve. Follow up with PMD in 3 days for adjustment in asthma care plan or sooner if symptoms don't improve.

Excluding the E/M code, what codes are submitted for the facility?

Reason for visit code(s): _____

Code(s): _____

5.75. From the health record of a patient requiring hernia repair:

Outpatient Surgery

Preoperative Diagnosis: Right inguinal hernia

Postoperative Diagnosis: Same

Operation: Right inguinal herniorrhaphy

Indications: The patient is a 13-year-old male with reducible right inguinal hernia who now presents for definitive care.

Procedure: The patient was brought to the operating room and placed in the supine position. After the adequate general endotracheal anesthesia, a 4-cm incision was made in the right inguinal region. The subcutaneous tissues were divided and hemostasis achieved with electrocautery. The external oblique fascia was identified and cleaned using Metzenbaum scissors. An incision was made in the external oblique and carried down to the external ring using Metzenbaum scissors. The external oblique was freed from the underlying cord using two pair of forceps. The cremasteric fibers were divided and the hernia sac grasped. Pulling the hernia sac up on some tension, we were then able to tease off the cremasteric fibers, as well as the vas and vessels. At this point, we were able to control the hernia sac between the two hemostats. We then teased it off of the vas and vessels as we dissected proximally toward the internal ring. At this point, the sac was twisted, sutured, ligated times two, amputated, and then the sac was allowed to fall back into the peritoneal cavity. We continued the dissection distally. The anterior wall was opened using electrocautery. At this point, we placed the cord back into the inguinal canal. The external oblique fascia was closed using interrupted 4-0 silk sutures. The external oblique fascia and the structures below it were infiltrated using .05 percent Marcaine. The Scarpa's fascia was closed using 5-0 VICRYL. The skin was closed using interrupted 5-0 subcuticular stitches. Steri-Strips were applied. The patient was taken to the recovery room in satisfactory condition.

Which of the following code sets is correct for reporting this surgery?

a. 550.91, 49520-RT
b. 550.90, 49525-RT
c. 550.92, 49505-50
d. 550.90, 49505-RT

5.76. This four-year-old child was brought to the ER because of cough and fever. The mother was worried about pneumonia, and the physician's office was closed for the weekend. X-ray was negative. Diagnosis: upper respiratory infection with bilateral acute conjunctivitis. What diagnosis code(s) are assigned?

Reason for visit code(s): _____

Code(s): _____

Conditions of Pregnancy, Childbirth, and the Puerperium

5.77. A patient in the 26th week of pregnancy had a 1-hour glucose screening test. Results of this test showed a blood sugar level of 160 mg/dL. Subsequently, the patient presents to the outpatient laboratory department with a physician order for a 3-hour glucose tolerance test. The reason for the test as documented on the order is: abnormal glucose on screening, rule out gestational diabetes. What is the correct code set for this outpatient ancillary services encounter?

    a. 790.22, V22.2, 82951
    b. 648.83, 82951
    c. 648.83, 82950
    d. 648.80, 82951, 82952, 82952

5.78. This 26-year-old gravida 1, para 0 female has been having spotting and has been on bedrest. She awoke this morning with severe cramping and bleeding. Her husband brought her to the hospital. After examination it was determined that she has had an incomplete early spontaneous abortion. She is in the 10th week of her pregnancy. She was taken to outpatient surgery, and a dilatation and curettage was performed. There were no complications from the procedure. She is discharged home with instructions to follow up with the physician in the office.

Which of the following is the correct code set?

    a. 637.91, 58120
    b. 634.91, 59812
    c. 634.91, 58120
    d. 634.92, 59812

5.79. This 23-year-old female is expecting her first child. She comes into the radiology department for an outpatient antenatal ultrasound to confirm the gestational age of the fetus and rule out fetal growth retardation. A real-time image was taken of the fetus estimated to be at 16 weeks. What diagnosis codes and associated CPT codes (even though they may be chargemaster-assigned codes) are assigned?

Code(s): _____

5.80. This patient has a history of infertility and has been seeing her OB/GYN physician for more than 2 years. It was elected to perform a hysterosalpingogram at the outpatient surgery center to assess the patency of the fallopian tubes.

Procedure Report

The patient was prepped and draped in the usual manner. The cervical os was cannulated and Sinografin® injected in retrograde fashion under fluoroscopic control. The body of the uterus appears normal. No filling defects are seen. There is no evidence of synechiae. The right fallopian tube is occluded approximately 1 cm from the body of the uterus. The left fallopian tube is patent and demonstrates free spill of contrast into the peritoneal cavity.

What codes are appropriate for this case?

Code(s): _____

Disorders of the Respiratory System

5.81.   A patient with chronic obstructive asthma and an acute exacerbation of chronic bronchitis presents to the ED in respiratory distress.

Which answer represents the correct diagnosis coding for this case?

a. 493.22
b. 493.21, 491.21
c. 493.20
d. 491.21

5.82.   This 65-year-old smoker with hemoptysis and chronic cough is scheduled for an outpatient bronchoscopy with an endobronchial biopsy of the lesion in the bronchus. The pathology report states "well-differentiated oat cell carcinoma of the upper bronchus." What codes would be reported?

Code(s): _____

5.83.   This 59-year-old male patient presents to the emergency room with severe epistaxis, causing him to nearly choke on blood in the back of the throat. Extensive bilateral anterior cautery and packing is required to control the hemorrhage. What codes are reported?

Reason for visit Code(s): _____

Code(s): _____

Trauma and Poisoning

5.84.   A 10-year-old choking on a small latex balloon is rushed from the amusement park to the emergency department. The balloon is lodged in the trachea just past the larynx and threatening to obstruct her breathing. The piece of latex balloon is carefully removed from the trachea by use of biopsy forceps through flexible fiberoptic laryngoscope following administration of topical anesthesia.

Which codes are reported for this service in addition to the ED visit code?

a. 934.0, E912, E849.4, 31577
b. 934.0, E912, E849.4, 31511
c. 784.99, E912, E849.4, 31530
d. 933.1, 31577

5.85. This 23-year-old female is brought to the emergency department after being found by her college roommate. Sometime within the last hour and a half after the roommate left, the patient ingested her entire bottle of verapamil (estimated at over 20 pills) as a suicide attempt, evidenced by a note. The physician ordered a high-dose glucagon HCl administration as an antidote, consisting of 10 mg/100 ml of D5W in an IV over 2 minutes, followed by a 5 mg/100 ml of D5W per hour for 2 more hours. A gastric lavage and aspiration were also performed. The patient's vital signs stabilized and lab work returned to normal over the next several hours. The patient was transferred to an inpatient psychiatric facility for follow-up treatment on her suicide attempt.

Excluding the E/M code, what are the correct codes for the facility services?

Code(s): _____

5.86. This 32-year-old female was burned by hot grease in her kitchen 1 week ago. She is seen in the hospital-based wound clinic for large dressing changes on both upper extremities following second-degree burns to both arms. This is accomplished without requiring anesthesia.

What codes are assigned for this service?

Code(s): _____

5.87. A physician performed an aspiration via thoracentesis on a patient in observation status in the hospital. The patient has advanced lung cancer with malignant pleural effusion. Later the same day, due to continued accumulation of fluid, the patient was returned to the procedure room and the same physician performed a repeat thoracentesis.

Report diagnosis and CPT procedure codes. Do not report observation codes.

Code(s): _____

5.88. A 12-year-old boy presents with his father to the ER due to open wounds to his arm, hand, and upper leg. The injury occurred when the boy fell on a barbed-wire fence at the farm. Diagnosis: Multiple open wounds to the right forearm, right hand, and left thigh. Procedure: Suture repair of the following: single-layer closure, 4.0 cm, forearm; layered closure 3.0 cm, hand; 6.0 simple repair, thigh.

Report the diagnosis and CPT procedure codes for this visit.

Reason for visit Code(s): _____

Code(s): _____

5.89. From the health record of a patient seen in the emergency room/observation area for an allergic reaction:

Discharge Summary

Date of Discharge: 01/08/XX

Chief Complaint: Allergic reaction to Bactrim, resulting in angioedema and mild respiratory distress.

Hospital Course: Fifty-six-year-old male admitted for angioedema after taking Bactrim for an ear infection. The patient had mild respiratory distress and marked swelling of his hands, face, and his oropharynx. The patient was given IV steroids in the Emergency Room and was admitted overnight for observation. The patient's swelling rapidly improved and by the morning after his admission he was back to baseline. He had no complaints of shortness of breath and desired to go home.

Condition on Discharge: Good. Activity: As tolerated. Diet: As tolerated.

Medications: Home medications only including:

1. Celebrex 200 mg one b.i.d.

2. Isosorbide 30 mg once a day.

3. Atenolol 25 mg per day.

4. Lipitor 10 mg per day.

Follow-Up: Will be as needed with primary care physician if ear problem returns and/or if he has any evidence of recurrent swelling and/or respiratory distress.

Emergency Assessment

Chief Complaint: Swelling, itching, and change in voice.

Present Illness: This is a 56-year-old, white male with a history of allergic reaction to an antibiotic in the past, who presents today after taking his second dose of Bactrim this morning at home. He then had acute onset of swelling, redness, itching, and change in voice, also states that he was slightly short of breath but no wheezing. He denies any nausea, vomiting, fevers, chills.

Past Medical History: Coronary artery disease, MI 2 years ago, is currently taking Celebrex, Isosorbide, Atenolol, Lipitor, and Bactrim that he just started on this morning.

Physical Examination: Appears very red, swollen diffusely with erythematous rash, macular type rash. Blood pressure is 146/77, heart rate of 120, respiration rate 18 and 02; saturation is 96%. On room air. HEENT: He does have swollen eyelids, both upper and lower eyelids with also some facial swelling and some uvular swelling as well as some lateral pharyngeal and uvular swelling, which appears to be allergic in nature. His tongue appears also slightly swollen, does not have any neck swelling, also has an erythematous rash. Lungs: Clear to auscultation with no wheezing noted. Abdomen: Soft, nontender.

Ed Course: Received Benadryl 25 mg IV, Pepcid 20 mg IV, Solu-Medrol 125 mg IV. At this point, his voice was still changing and decision was made to admit the patient to the hospital for observation and then to observe and given a second dose of Solu-Medrol and Benadryl. Consultation between patient's private physician.

Select the correct codes for this observation patient.

a. 961.0, 786.09, 995.1, 693.0, E857, E849.0
b. 995.20, E931.0, E849.0
c. 995.1, 786.09, E931.0, E849.0
d. 995.1, 786.09, 693.0, E930.9, E849.0

5.90. From the health record of a patient treated in the emergency room for finger injury.

Operative Report

Preoperative Diagnosis: Circular saw injury with complex laceration of left index finger with laceration of extensor tendon and joint capsule; laceration collateral ligament, radial side; compound fracture at base of the middle phalanx, articular involvement.

Postoperative Diagnosis: Circular saw injury with complex laceration of left index finger with laceration of extensor tendon and joint capsule; laceration collateral ligament, radial side; compound fracture base of the middle phalanx, articular involvement.

Operation Performed

Débridement and repair extensor tendon and joint capsule. Repair radial collateral ligament and wound closure.

Anesthesia: Digital block

This is a 42-year-old white male who accidentally injured his left index finger on a circular saw while working at home in his garage. The patient sustained a jagged laceration over the dorsal radial aspect of the index finger at the proximal interphalangeal joint. The wound was deep, involving the joint capsule, extensor tendon, and collateral ligament. The bone also involved, especially at the base of the middle phalanx into the apical surface. The sensation to the tip of the finger was intact, especially all of the radial side. The wound measured about 3 cm in length.

Procedure: 0.5 percent Marcaine was used as local anesthetic digital block. After anesthesia had been obtained, the hand was prepped and draped in the usual manner. Tourniquet then was placed at the base of the fingers. The wound was then débrided. The minute loose bone and articular surface had to be removed. Some skin débrided also was removed. After satisfactory débridement, the joint capsule and extensor tendon then were repaired with 5-0 PDS suture material. The radial collateral ligament also was repaired with the same suture material. The skin then was carefully approximated with 5-0 nylon. After completion, a dressing was applied. The tourniquet was released and there was good perfusion throughout the fingers. An aluminum splint was placed.

The patient received 1 g of Ancef in the emergency room. He will continue to take Keftab 500 mg twice daily for 4 days and Vicodin one tablet q.4h. p.r.n. for pain. The postoperative instructions were given. Also the patient was informed about his injury and complications, especially wound infection and some stiffness of the finger. The patient will be followed up in my office.

List the diagnosis and procedure codes:

Reason for visit Code(s): _____

Diagnosis Code(s): _____

Procedure Code(s): _____

Chapter 6

Case Studies from Physician-based Health Records

Note: Although the specific cases are divided by setting, much of the information pertaining to the diagnosis is applicable in most settings. Even the CPT codes in the ambulatory and physician sections may be reported in the same manner. The differences in coding in these two settings may involve modifier reporting, evaluation and management CPT code reporting, and other health plan reporting guidelines unique to settings. If you practice or apply codes in a particular type of setting, you may find additional information in other sections of this publication that may be pertinent to you.

Every effort has been made to follow current recognized coding guidelines and principles, as well as nationally recognized reporting guidelines. The material presented may differ from some health plan requirements for reporting. The ICD-9-CM codes used are effective October 1, 2009, through September 30, 2010, and the HCPCS (CPT and HCPCS Level II) codes are in effect January 1, 2009, through December 31, 2009. The current standard transactions and code sets named in HIPAA have been utilized.

Instructions:

Assign all applicable ICD-9-CM diagnosis including V codes and E codes. Assign all CPT level I procedure codes and HCPCS level II codes. Assign level I (CPT) and level II (HCPCS) modifiers as appropriate. Final codes for billing occur after codes are passed through payer edits. Medicare utilizes the National Correct Coding Initiative (NCCI) edits. CMS developed the NCCI edit list to promote national correct coding methodologies and to control improper coding leading to improper payments for Medicare Part B. The purpose of the NCCI edits is to ensure the most comprehensive code is assigned and billed rather than the component codes. In addition, NCCI edits check for mutually exclusive pairs.

Cases in this workbook are presented as either multiple choice or fill in the blank.

- For multiple-choice cases:
  —Select the letter of the appropriate code set.
- For fill-in-the-blank cases:
  —Sequence the primary diagnosis first followed by the secondary diagnoses including appropriate V codes and E codes (both cause of injury and place of occurrence).

—Sequence the primary CPT procedure code first followed by additional procedure codes including modifiers as appropriate (both CPT level I and HCPCS level II modifiers).

—Assign HCPCS level II codes **only if instructed** (case specific).

—Assign evaluation and management (E/M) codes **only if instructed** (case specific).

The scenarios are based on selected excerpts from health records. In practice, the coding professional should have access to and refer to the entire health record. Health records are analyzed and codes assigned based on physician documentation. In physician practice, valuable information for coding purposes is available on the superbill; however, documentation for coding purposes must be assigned based on medical record documentation. A physician may be queried when documentation is ambiguous, incomplete, or conflicting. The queried documentation must be a permanent part of the medical record.

The objective of the cases and scenarios reproduced in this publication is to provide practice in assigning correct codes, not necessarily to emulate complete coding which can only be achieved with the complete medical record. For example, the reader may be asked to assign codes based on only an operative report; in real practice, a coder has access to documentation in the entire medical record.

The *ICD-9-CM Official Guidelines for Coding and Reporting* of Outpatient Services, published by the National Center for Health Statistics (NCHS), supplements the official conventions and instructions provided within ICD-9-CM. Adherence to these guidelines when assigning ICD-9-CM diagnosis codes is required under the Health Insurance Portability and Accountability Act (HIPAA) of 1996. Additional official coding guidance can be found in the American Hospital Association (AHA)'s *Coding Clinic* publication.

Anesthesia Services

Note: The reporting of the anesthesia section code versus the CPT code is a payer-specific policy. For these exercises, the anesthesia section code is to be reported for practice in assigning these codes. The exercises in this section are not based on payer-specific requirements.

6.1.   Correctly apply the anesthesia code for 19367, a breast reconstruction with TRAM flap. Use your CPT book and/or Anesthesia Crosswalk, if available. Do not assign modifiers in this example.

  a. 00404
  b. 00406
  c. 00402
  d. 00400

6.2. An epidural was given during labor. Subsequently, it was determined that the patient would require a C-section for cephalopelvic disproportion because of obstructed labor. Assign the correct anesthesia code and ICD-9-CM codes. Modifiers are not used in this example.

    a. 660.11, 653.41, 64475
    b. 660.11, 653.01, 01961
    c. 660.11, 653.41, 01967, 01968
    d. 660.11, 653.91, 01996

6.3. A 3-year-old child came to the outpatient surgery center to have dental caries filled and caps placed on his teeth due to nursing bottle decay syndrome. Anesthesia was provided by an anesthesiologist. Assign the correct CPT and ICD-9-CM codes for the anesthesia services. Modifiers are included in this example.

    a. 521.00, 00170-AA-23
    b. 521.00, 00170-AA, 99100-23
    c. 520.7, 00170-P1-23-AA
    d. 521.30, 00170, 99100–23–AA

6.4. A 5-year-old patient was brought into the emergency room with a deep 2-cm laceration of his scalp. The child was combative and would not allow staff to cleanse the wound. The mother held the child in her lap while the ED physician administered 10 mg of Versed intranasally. When the child was sufficiently sedated, one of the ED nurses monitored the patient's vital signs, and the physician performed a layered repair of the laceration. The intra-service time for the procedure did not exceed 30 minutes.

Assign the correct CPT code for the CPT procedure and sedation for this case:

    a. 12031, 99143
    b. 12031, 99144
    c. 12031-47
    d. 12031-QS

6.5. A 2-month-old infant is brought to the operating room for repair of coarctation of the aorta with pump oxygenator. Anesthesia is provided by an anesthesiologist. The infant is in critical condition and may not survive. Assign the correct ICD-9-CM and CPT codes, including physical status, Level I and II modifiers, and qualifying conditions for this procedure.

Code(s):_____

Disorders of the Blood and Blood-Forming Organs

6.6.   This patient with an abnormal blood test underwent bone marrow aspiration from the sternum. Results show acute lymphocytic leukemia. How is this coded?

   a. 204.90, 38221
   b. 208.00, 20220
   c. 204.90, 38220
   d. 204.00, 38220

6.7.   A patient is admitted with cervical lymphadenopathy. A needle biopsy of a cervical lymph node is performed, and Hodgkin's sarcoma disease is confirmed. Which of the following is the correct code assignment?

   a. 201.21, 38505
   b. 201.91, 38505
   c. 201.21, 38500
   d. 785.6, 38510

6.8.   From the physician services documentation of a 39-year-old male:

History of Present Illness: The patient is a 39-year-old, African-American male who has a known history of sickle cell anemia. He was admitted to the hospital with diffuse extremity pains with minor complaints of pain along the right inguinal area. They started on Friday, became a little bit better on Saturday, then improved, and started again in the past 24 hours. He denies any problems with cough or sputum or production. He denies any problems with fever.

Past Medical History: See recent medical records in charts. He does have a new onset of diabetes, probably related to his hemochromatosis. He does have evidence of iron overload with high ferritins.

Review of Systems: Otherwise unremarkable except for those related to his pain. He denies any problems with fever or night sweats. No cough or sputum production. Denies any changes in gastrointestinal or genitourinary habits. No blood from the rectum or urine.

Physical Examination: This is a 39-year-old, African-American male who is conscious and cooperative. He is oriented x 3 and appears in no acute distress. Vital signs are stable. HEENT is remarkable for icterus present in oral mucosa and conjunctivae, which is a chronic event for him. The neck is supple. No evidence of any gross lymphadenopathy of the cervical, supraclavicular, or axillary areas. The heart is abnormally irregular in rate without any murmurs heard. Lungs are clear to auscultation and percussion. The abdomen is soft and benign without any gross organomegaly. Extremities reveal no edema. No palpable cords. He does have some tenderness along the inner aspects of his right lower extremity near the inguinal area; however, no masses were palpable and no point tenderness is noted.

The patient was treated for his painful sickle cell crisis with IV fluids and pain medications. He had a problem with his right inguinal area. He had evidence of pain.

There was some pain on abduction of his right lower extremity. The examination really was unremarkable. There was no evidence of any Holman, no palpable cords, no masses were palpable.

Because of his sickle cell anemia, rule out the possibility of osteonecrosis of the femur. Complete x-rays of his femur and hip were carried out. However, these were both negative. Patient is being discharged after improvement. To follow up with me in 1 week.

Diagnoses:
1. Painful sickle cell crisis
2. Type II diabetes mellitus
3. Chronic atrial fibrillation

Condition on Discharge: Stable

What diagnosis codes would the physician report on this case?

a. 282.61, 789.09, 427.31, 250.00
b. 282.62, 733.42, 427.31, 250.00
c. 282.62
d. 282.62, 427.31, 250.00

6.9. This established patient comes to the physician's office and after evaluation requires a glucose tolerance test. The physician drew the three specimens and performed the test at the office. List the correct procedure codes.

Code(s):_____

6.10. The physician prepares the patient's stem cell sample by thawing it and depleting the T cells. The cells are then transplanted back into the patient.

What is the correct CPT code assignment for the services provided by the physician?

a. 38206, 38210, 38241
b. 38208, 38210, 38241
c. 38209, 38211, 38240
d. 38209, 38241

Disorders of the Cardiovascular System

6.11. **Chief complaint:** Left knee pain

Reason for Admission: Hypotension, bradycardia, and possible GI bleed

This 83-year-old patient presented to my office this morning complaining of knee pain and wanting to see an orthopedic surgeon for a knee replacement. My first impression of the patient was that he appeared lethargic and extremely tired looking. Upon questioning, he stated that he was far more tired than normal and "just didn't feel good," attributing this to the chronic pain in the knee. I reviewed his meds and completed a 10 point review of systems which revealed increasing bouts of periodic diarrhea with dark stool. He has overall poor health with multiple previous surgeries and hypertension that has been difficult to control. Other systems are negative for new complaints today. At the completion of our office visit, I arranged for a direct admission to the hospital. I saw him again at the hospital and continued the diagnostic workup.

No known allergies. Takes Lisinopril 40 mg daily, Coreg, half of a 25 mg pill twice per day and Protonix daily. He is married and lives with his second wife. The first wife died in 1996. His mother lived to 93 and father lived to 96. He reports that they died of "old age".

Vital signs: Blood pressure is 96/62. RR 18, P 54, T 97.3, Wt 197, down 6 pounds from last month with BMI of 28.67. General: Elderly male in no acute distress. Skin: Laminectomy scar on his lower back. No clubbing or cyanosis of his fingers and no suspicious lesions. Neurologic: He is alert and oriented but his timeline is unclear, especially relating to the diarrhea. Is far more concerned about his knee than anything else. Cranial nerves grossly intact and motor strength is 5/5. HEENT: Atraumatic, normocephalic. Anicteric sclera. No sinus tenderness. Posterior oropharynx is very irritated. Lips without cyanosis. NECK: Supple without adenopathy. No thyromegaly, nodules or carotid bruits. CHEST: Normal symmetry. CARDIOVASCULAR: Rate is somewhat bradycardiac and very difficult tones to auscultate. Regular rhythm. LUNGS: Clear. ABDOMEN: Soft, nontender, nondistended, decreased bowel sounds, no hepatosplenomegaly, rebound or rigidity. No inguinal adenopathy, 2+ inguinal pulses bilaterally. MUSCULOSKELETAL: Left leg shows some atrophy in the muscles and left knee looks larger than the right knee. No real swelling appreciated. Not warm. GU: Normal scrotal exam. No hernia. RECTAL: Perianal area is somewhat irritated. There is a large external hemorrhoid. Prostate is slightly enlarged. Stool is dark brown but heme negative.

Labs are pending. EKG shows a significant sinus bradycardia around 50-55 beats per minute. This does not appear to be atrial fibrillation. He has a somewhat widened QRS complex or intraventricular conduction delay. He does not peak T waves or any other significant issues regarding arrhythmia.

Assessment:

1. Hypotension, potentially due to antihypertensive medication or based on decreased volume due to diarrhea and potential GI bleed.
2. Sinus bradycardia. Cause unclear but could also be due to volume depletion.
3. Diarrhea. Has had problems with anemia in the past but not currently. Potentially upper GI source since stool is dark.
4. Localized osteoarthrosis of left knee.

Plan: IV fluids, 2L over 8 hours and then will switch to 100 ml/hour of D5 normal saline. Blood was drawn in the office. Recheck comprehensive metabolic panel after IV hydration. Hold Lisinopril and Coreg until blood pressure stabilizes. Cardiology consult requested. GI consult requested. Will hold on evaluating any orthopedic issues until seen in follow-up in the office.

Code(s):_____

6.12. The following documentation is from the health record of a 63-year-old female patient.

Admission Date: 11/19/XX

Discharge Date: 11/24/XX

Final Diagnoses:
1. Coronary artery disease
2. Sick sinus syndrome

Procedures:
1. Permanent AV sequential pacemaker insertion
2. Percutaneous transluminal coronary angioplasty

History of Present Illness: The patient is a 63-year-old female who was admitted to another hospital on 11/19, after experiencing tachycardia. At that hospital, she underwent a cardiac catheterization, showing the presence of severe single-vessel coronary artery disease. The patient has a history of sick sinus syndrome. She was transferred to our hospital to undergo a percutaneous transluminal angioplasty.

Physical Examination: No physical abnormalities were found on the cardiovascular examination. Pulse 50, blood pressure 100/66. HEENT: PERRLA, faint carotid bruits. Lungs: Clear to percussion and auscultation. Heart: Normal sinus rhythm with a 2.6 systolic ejection murmur. Extremities and abdomen were negative. Laboratory data: Unremarkable.

Hospital Course: To manage the patient's sick sinus syndrome, a permanent AV sequential pacemaker was implanted by transvenous technique on 11/19. On 11/20, the patient underwent a PTCA without complications and good results were obtained. Postoperatively, the patient was stable and was subsequently discharged. Patient was discharged on the following medications: Cardizem, 30 mg p.o. q. 6 hours; ASA, 5 grains q. a.m.; Metamucil and Colace p.r.n; Nitro paste 1/2 inch q. 6 hours.

Which of the following is the correct code assignment for the procedures performed?

a. 427.0, 414.01, 92982, 33206
b. 414.01, 427.81, 92995, 33208
c. 414.01, 427.81, 92982, 33208
d. 427.81, 414.01, 92982, 33200

6.13. A patient is seen in the hospital with a diagnosis of congestive heart failure due to hypertensive heart disease. The patient responds positively to Lasix therapy. The patient also has chronic kidney disease stage V and is a type I diabetic. Assign the correct diagnostic codes.

Code(s):_____

6.14. This 55-year-old male was brought to the ER with chest pain. The final diagnostic statement on the patient's record stated "preinfarction syndrome." What is the correct diagnostic code?

Code(s):_____

6.15. A patient had an implantable vascular access device placed 7 weeks ago for chemotherapy administered each week in the ambulatory surgery department of the hospital. The full cycle is now complete and it is no longer needed. The physician surgically removed the centrally tunneled central venous catheter. No services for the carcinoma of the sigmoid colon are provided. The cancer has not been resected yet, because the chemotherapy was utilized in an attempt to shrink the tumor before surgery was initiated. The correct codes for reporting by the physician will be:

Code(s):_____

Disorders of the Digestive System

6.16. This 30-year-old male patient has exhausted all types of conservative treatment for his morbid obesity. He has been treated by me in this clinic for 3 years. He has also been treated for hypertension and hypercholesterolemia. With these risk factors and with careful review of his condition and symptoms and with multiple consultations with him regarding the risks and benefits of the surgery, it is decided to perform a vertical-banded gastroplasty.

What diagnosis and procedure codes are used in this surgical case?

a. 278.00, 43842, 43846–51
b. 278.01, 401.9, 272.0, 43842
c. 278.01, 401.1, 272.0, 43842, 43843–59
d. 278.01, 43848

6.17. This 25-year-old woman has been treated for Crohn's disease of the small intestine since 18 years of age. She has had several exacerbations but has been maintained on drug therapy. She is being seen now for extreme pain, which on x-ray shows small bowel obstruction. Patient is taken to surgery immediately. During the surgery, a partial excision of the terminal ileum is performed to release the obstruction. There is also a section of the jejunum that is very inflamed. This section is also resected. An end-to-end anastomosis is completed on all segments. The patient tolerates the procedure well. Which of the following is the correct code assignment?

a. 560.89, 555.0, 44120, 44121-51
b. 555.0, 560.89, 44120, 44121-51
c. 555.0, 560.89, 44120, 44121
d. 555.2, 560.89, 44020

6.18. During a colonoscopy, the surgeon biopsies an inflamed area in the ascending colon and removes a polyp in the descending colon with use of hot biopsy forceps. What is the correct CPT coding assignment?

Code(s):_____

6.19. The patient has a history of abdominal pain and blood in the stool. A colonoscopy was done earlier today and did not identify a bleed. As a further evaluation, the patient is undergoing a capsule endoscopy of the entire GI tract. The physician documentation states:

The patient was able to swallow the capsule orally without difficulty. Images were downloaded. The capsule was seen traversing the small bowel all of the way down to the cecum. Gastric images demonstrated no ulceration. Gastric passage time was 1 hour and 37 minutes. Careful review of small bowel images, which were of good quality, did not demonstrate any significant mucosal lesion. There was one single site suggestive of possible erosion seen in the ileum. The capsule was seen entering the ileocecal valve into the cecum.

Code(s):_____

6.20. This 50-year-old male patient had a cholecystectomy done with exploration of the common duct for stones. During the procedure an incidental appendectomy was performed. How are the procedure codes reported if the third-party payer requires that both procedures be reported?

Code(s):_____

6.21. The patient has thrombosed external hemorrhoids. The surgeon incises two hemorrhoids. What codes would be assigned?

Code(s):_____

6.22. A laparoscopic cholecystectomy with cholangiography was performed on a 35-year-old female patient due to symptomatic cholelithiasis. The pathology report showed acute and chronic cholecystitis with lithiasis and was documented by the physician. What codes would be assigned?

Code(s):_____

6.23. The patient's gastric band has been adjusted so many times that it is losing its elasticity and starting to slip on her stomach and migrate up around her esophagus. She enters to undergo removal of her current gastric band and placement of a new adjustable band. Her weight loss has been steady and appropriate. Assign the CPT code(s) for the procedure of laparoscopic removal and replacement of an adjustable gastric band.

    a. 43773
    b. 43771, 43770
    c. 43774, 43770
    d. 43888

Evaluation and Management (E/M) Services

6.24. A 45-year-old patient was found unconscious in a park and was brought to the emergency department by ambulance. A comprehensive physical examination was performed, and the medical decision-making was of high complexity. The

ED physician documents that he was unable to obtain a history due to the condition of the patient.

What is the correct E/M code assignment for the physician's services for this encounter?

a. 99284
b. 99285
c. 99285-52
d. 99291

6.25. Dr. Jones saw Mr. Stone at the VA domiciliary after the patient had an episode of severe choking at the noon meal. He did not aspirate any food. The patient stubbornly refused to go to the clinic but agreed to be seen if the doctor came over. Mr. Stone has had several episodes of choking in the past few days, which he attributed completely to his sinus medication causing a very dry mouth. Dr. Jones documented a problem-focused interval history and an expanded problem-focused examination on this established patient. Medical decision-making was of low complexity. Another medication was substituted. He was advised to drink liquids with his meals and take smaller bites. Give the correct ICD-9-CM and CPT codes for this visit.

a. 784.99, 783.3, 99335
b. 933.1, 99334
c. 933.1, 99335
d. 783.3, 99334

6.26. A 59-year-old male established patient is scheduled for his routine physical examination; however, the physician finds a mass in the abdomen, schedules an abdominal CT scan, and orders laboratory for blood work and a UA. The physician performs a detailed history and an expanded problem-focused examination with medical decision making of moderate complexity. The patient has been a patient of this physician for several years. What E/M code(s) are assigned?

Code(s):_____

6.27. An elderly patient is brought to the emergency department by an ambulance due to a cardiac arrest suffered at home. The ED physician provides and documents critical care services to the patient for a total duration of 2 hours before the attending physician admits the patient to the cardiac care unit.

What codes are assigned for the ED physician? (Include E/M code(s).)

Code(s):_____

6.28. Summary of the clinic record of a family practice physician:

The patient is a 3-year-old male with Down's Syndrome who was seen in the office yesterday for bilateral otitis media. He was given a prescription for Septra liquid suspension. On repeat visit today, the mother reports that the patient complained of a "tummy ache" after the first dose and has vomited six times since being seen yesterday. PO intake is decreased but still sufficiently hydrated. Has not been able to keep down any antibiotic. A detailed history is documented.

Documentation states that the ears have increased redness with the right TM bulging more than yesterday. Considerable wheezing is noted on lung exam. No other significant findings are documented on the detailed exam.

The patient is treated with 500 mg of Ceftriaxone sodium, IM, and given a prescription for an albuterol metered dose inhaler with spacer. The patient and mother are taught the proper use of the inhaler.

The physician documents the diagnoses as: 1. Acute otitis media with effusion, 2. First time wheezer, 3. Vomiting, 4. Down's Syndrome.

What ICD-9 and CPT codes would be reported for this visit (include E/M code)?

Code(s):_____

6.29. Dr. Smith sees his patient, Bob Jones, in the nursing home where he has resided for 11 months. Bob is pretty stable and happy, and Dr. Smith performs an annual physical examination and completes the minimum data set instrument. He performs and documents a detailed interval history, comprehensive examination, and performs medical decision making of low complexity. Assign the appropriate CPT code.

 a. 99304
 b. 99308
 c. 99318
 d. 99306

Endocrine, Nutritional and Metabolic Diseases, and Immunity Disorders

6.30. A repeat thyroidectomy is performed after a previous right partial thyroidectomy was completed several years ago. All thyroid tissue is removed from the right side, and a total left thyroidectomy is performed. The parathyroid glands are separated from the thyroid tissue and replanted. What is the correct CPT code assignment for the services of the surgeon?

 a. 60220-50
 b. 60240
 c. 60260-50, 60512
 d. 60260-RT, 60220-LT, 60512

6.31. A 6-year-old child, an established patient, is seen in the pediatrician's office for routine immunization. The physician speaks with the child's father about national immunization recommendations, risks and benefits of vaccine provided, and gives follow-up instructions for possible side-effect treatment. The patient receives a DtaP immunization IM. Assign the appropriate CPT procedure code(s).

 a. 90467, 90700
 b. 99213, 90465, 90700
 c. 90465, 90700
 d. 90465

6.32. A 35-year-old man was referred to the endocrinology clinic for symptoms that involved headaches, deepening voice, and enlargement and coarsening of facial features, hands, and feet. This has been gradual over the past 3 years. The patient was referred by his dentist, who noticed increased spacing between his teeth over the same time period. Growth hormone levels tested by the endocrinology clinic were elevated for an adult male. Follow-up IGF-1 tests confirmed the diagnosis. The patient was scheduled for a CT scan of the brain to rule out pituitary tumor. Diagnosis after the second clinic visit was acromegaly and ruled out pituitary adenoma. Give the correct ICD-9-CM code for the second clinic visit.

   a. 253.0, 225.0
   b. 253.0
   c. 227.3
   d. 253.0, 227.3

6.33. A 62-year-old postmenopausal female is seen in the clinic for a refill of her estrogen patch. On review of systems, she relays that she has no complaints. Physical exam is unremarkable and prescription for the estrogen patch is refilled.

   Assessment: Menopause

   Assuming documentation meets the requirements for a level II established visit, which of the following is the correct code set for this clinic visit?

   a. V07.4, V49.81, 99212
   b. 627.2, 99212
   c. 256.31, 99212
   d. V58.69, V49.81, 99212

6.34. This 45-year-old female diabetic patient comes in for her quarterly evaluation of her condition. She has type I diabetes, which has been in good control now. She has diabetic nephropathy and retinopathy. What diagnosis codes are assigned?

   Code(s):_____

6.35. From the hospital record of a patient requiring diabetic management:

   Hospital Course: This 49-year-old female patient has a history of type I diabetes mellitus and is on 15 units of NPH and 10 of Regular in the morning, and 10 units of NPH and 5 of Regular in the evening. The patient started having symptoms of nausea and vomiting. The patient at the same time had increased frequency of urination and polydipsia. The patient was severely dehydrated on admission. There was no evidence of thrombophlebitis, varicosities, or edema on examination of the extremities. The patient was hydrated and, as a result, her blood sugar decreased from more than 600 to normal levels. The patient was discharged with the diagnosis of diabetic ketoacidosis, dehydration, polydipsia, and increased frequency of urination.

What diagnosis codes would be assigned for this admission for the physician's services?

Code(s):_____

6.36. Assign the code(s) for a patient with type II diabetic gastroparesis who is presently on insulin.

    a. 250.60, 536.3, V58.67
    b. 250.60, 586.3, 337.1, V58.67
    c. 250.61, 536.3
    d. 250.62, 536.3, V58.67

6.37. A 65-year-old female patient has a long history of type II diabetes mellitus with diabetic retinopathy. She is being seen today for her retinal ischemia and diabetic macular edema. What codes are assigned for this proliferative retinopathy?

    a. 250.50, 362.07
    b. 250.50, 362.06, 362.07
    c. 250.50, 362.02, 362.07
    d. 362.02, 363.07

Disorders of the Genitourinary System

6.38. A patient in end-stage renal failure requires outpatient hemodialysis three times a week while he is awaiting kidney transplant. He has an A-V fistula in his left arm for vascular access. Which of the following code sets is appropriate for reporting physician services for this 55-year-old male for the month of August?

    a. 585.6, 90925
    b. V56.0, 90921
    c. 585.6, V56.8, 90999
    d. 585.6, 90921

6.39. From the health record of a patient receiving endoscopy services:

The patient presents to the hospital outpatient department for follow-up cystoscopy for a history of high-grade bladder cancer. This was resected 7 years ago and was found to be grade III with superficial muscle invasion. A cycle of chemotherapy was provided, but no radiation. No recurrence has been noted since then. CT scan of the pelvis 6 months ago was negative for masses. Sometimes the patient experiences painful ejaculation, but no hematospermia has been found. Cytology to date has been negative, so a biopsy will not be performed, because there has been 7 years without recurrence.

Cystoscopy examination today shows a normal anterior urethra and prostatic urethra. There is some lateral lobe prostatic hypertrophy, just barely touching in the midline. The bladder is nontrabeculated. There are no tumors, stones, or carcinoma in situ evident on examination. There is clear efflux from each orifice. The area of resection was around the right ureteral orifice, which appears a little atrophic, but patent.

Impression: Stable transitional cell of the bladder without recurrence with mild benign prostatic hypertrophy.

Which of the following code sets is appropriate for this case?

a. V67.6, V10.51, 600.00, 52000
b. 188.9, 600.0, 52000
c. 600.00, V10.51, 52010
d. V67.00, 188.9, 52000

6.40. This 40-year-old with ureterolithiasis will have a planned cystourethroscopy with stone removal performed. One stone is removed, and after several attempts, the second stone cannot be removed through the scope. Ultrasonic fragmentation is then used on the second stone. What codes would be assigned in this case?

Code(s):_____

6.41. This 35-year-old female has had four cesarean births in the past 6 years and has decided to proceed with sterilization.

Operative Report

Procedure: Laparoscopic tubal ligation with application of Falope-Rings

Diagnosis: Multiparity; desired sterilization

Anesthesia: General

Under general anesthesia and in the supine lithotomy position, the patient was prepped and draped in the usual sterile fashion. A two-puncture laparoscopy was performed in the usual manner with insufflation through a Verres needle inserted infraumbilically. Through the first puncture, a trocar was inserted infraumbilically, followed by the laparoscope. A second trocar was inserted suprapubically in the midline, followed initially by a probe and then a Falope-Ring applicator. Both tubes were ligated in their midsegment. On the left side, two rings were applied because of the round position of the Falope-Ring director. The right tube was singly ligated. The operation was completed, and the trocar sites were closed with subcuticular sutures of 2-0 VICRYL. The patient was transferred to the recovery room in good condition.

What are the correct codes to assign for this service?

Code(s):_____

6.42. This 35-year-old man has had an eruption of molluscum contagiosum on the penis for several months. He finally sought medical attention. He was advised to have these lesions removed. He is here now for the procedure. The patient had destruction of a penile molluscum contagiosum performed by cryosurgery and laser surgery. What are the correct code(s)?

Code(s):_____

Infectious Diseases

6.43. The patient is a 10-year-old girl who presents with a sore throat, fever of 101.4, swollen glands in the neck, red blotchy rash over the neck, face, chest, and back. She has significant nausea and has vomited three times since this morning and is complaining of severe pain when swallowing. A detailed history and examination are documented, with medical decision making of moderate complexity. The physician ordered a rapid strep test which was performed in the office and was positive. Because of the significant nausea and questionable antibiotic compliance in the past, the physician administers 2.4 million units of long-acting Penicillin G/Penicillin G Procaine via a deep intramuscular injection. The patient will be seen again in 5 days. Diagnoses were documented as strep throat with scarlatina.

List the diagnosis and procedure codes, including E/M codes and laboratory codes, for this case.

Code(s):_____

6.44. The employees of this clinic who work in the patient care areas are receiving the vaccination for hepatitis B in the employee health clinic. What codes would be reported for this service given as an IM injection?

Code(s):_____

6.45. This 5-year-old child is here in the office for her routine annual child exam. She has been healthy, and there were no problems encountered. Active immunization with live measles, mumps, and rubella virus vaccine was given during her annual preventive medicine visit for this established patient. What are the correct codes?

Code(s):_____

Disorders of the Skin and Subcutaneous Tissue

6.46. An elderly patient has an abscess formation around a pacemaker pocket on his chest wall that requires that the device be removed and the pocket reformed in another location. Which of the following code sets is appropriate for this outpatient surgical service? Do not assign E codes in this case.

a. 996.61, 682.2, 33222
b. 682.2, 33222
c. 996.61, 33233
d. 996.72, 682.2, 33999

6.47. This 18-year-old male patient has pustular acne that requires periodic opening and/or removal of milia and comedones from his face in the dermatology clinic on a recurring basis. These visits do not include medical history or examination by the physician—only the procedure. List diagnosis and CPT procedure code(s).

Code(s):_____

6.48. This 54-year-old female has noticed areas of raised skin on her face, mostly on her forehead. She states that they have grown quickly with the size almost doubling in 3 weeks. She has concerns that this may be skin cancer and wants an evaluation. She is scheduled for surgery, and the physician abraded six areas on the patient's face. They were determined to be keratoses. What codes would be assigned for the surgery episode of care?

Code(s):_____

6.49. A patient with significant second- and third-degree burns over his back and buttocks underwent débridement of approximately 175 sq cm of necrotic eschar tissue and application of 325 sq cm of Mediskin® as a temporary wound closure. Assign the appropriate CPT code(s).

Code(s):_____

6.50. This patient received 45 sq cm of TranCyte® to an ulcer of the lateral left foot. Assign the appropriate CPT procedure code(s).

Code(s):_____

Behavioral Health Conditions

6.51. A patient in a clinic received individual insight-oriented psychotherapy for more than 25 minutes. The physician also provided E/M services that included a problem-focused history, problem-focused examination, and straightforward level of medical decision making. What CPT codes(s) would this physician report?

a. 90805
b. 90804, 99212
c. 90811
d. 90810, 99212

6.52. A young adult who is self referred presents as a new patient in the clinic with complaints of an increasing inability to concentrate and complete tasks. He states that he has always been easily distracted and often leaves tasks uncompleted, but in recent years his restlessness has increased. He is perceived as unreliable at work and is concerned about future job advancements. The physician takes a comprehensive history and exam and performs medical decision making of moderate complexity. The physician's diagnosis is attention deficit disorder, DSM-IV 314.9, and the plan of treatment is to begin Ritalin and to follow up to assess dosage and efficacy. The physician documents that he spent 45 minutes in counseling with the patient.

What are the correct ICD-9-CM and CPT codes to report this encounter?

a. 314.00, 99214
b. 314.00, 99204
c. 314.01, 99204
d. 314.9, 99214

6.53. This 25-year-old man is admitted to the hospital for acute alcohol inebriation. He was brought in by the police because he was causing a disturbance. He is well known to me due to his continuous alcoholism. He has refused treatment or admission to alcohol rehabilitation. What diagnosis code(s) are assigned in this case?

Code(s):_____

6.54. Physician progress note states: This patient is a 75-year-old female who has severe Alzheimer's disease. The patient shows no acute change in mental status from her last visit. She requires continuous care because of her dementia, but the family is insistent on keeping her at home. She has made repeated attempts to leave and has wandered off in the past, hence the need for continuous care. She at times recognizes her daughter, the primary caregiver, but most of the time she is unaware of her identity. What diagnosis codes are reported for this visit?

Code(s):_____

Disorders of the Musculoskeletal System and Connective Tissue

6.55. A patient had an osteopathic physician as a primary care provider. The patient suffered from sternoclavicular somatic dysfunction. An evaluation was done using a detailed history and an expanded problem-focused examination with low medical decision making. The physician performed osteopathic manipulation to the affected body region. What codes should be assigned to this office visit?

a. 739.7, 99213-25, 98925
b. 739.2, 98925
c. 786.59, 99212-25, 98925
d. 739.8, 99213

6.56. From the health record of a young athlete:

Preoperative Diagnosis: Fracture of fibula, left

Postoperative Diagnosis: Left distal fracture of fibula

Procedure: Reduction of fibular fracture

Indications and Description: This 14-year-old girl who is a gymnast felt pain in her leg after vaulting at practice. She is unable to bear any weight on her left leg.

Physical examination revealed foot and ankle to be normal. The neurovascular status of the foot is normal. The ankle is nontender and not swollen. Findings are confined to the distal fibula, 2 inches proximal to the lateral malleolus. There is point tenderness in this area. An x-ray of the tibia and fibula shows a displaced fracture of the distal fibula.

The fracture was reduced, and the patient was put in a short leg splint molded for her from fiberglass, with extensive padding placed over the fracture site. Crutches were provided, and she is instructed not to place any weight on the foot. She was given a supply of Tylenol 3 for pain and will follow up at the clinic in 10 days.

Which of the following is the correct code assignment?

a. 824.8, E917.0, 27788, Q4046
b. 824.2, E917.0, 27788, 29515–51
c. 823.81, E917.0, 27786, L4350
d. 824.4. E917.0, 27810, 29515–51, L4396

6.57. This 16-year-old was tackled during a football game 3 weeks ago and received fracture care with a cast for a fracture of the fibula. He is coming in today for a walking cast, which was applied after a two-view x-ray in the clinic. This converted an existing cast to one that did not require crutches. What are the codes that will appear on the CMS-1500 form that is sent to the insurance company?

Code(s):_____

6.58. The physician treats a patient who has osteomyelitis of the scapula following an injury. A piece of dead bone is removed from the body of the scapula.

What CPT code is assigned by the surgeon?

a. 23140
b. 23172
c. 23182
d. 23190

6.59. From the health record of a patient having hand surgery:

Operative Report

Preoperative Diagnosis: Foreign body on the left little finger at the metacarpophalangeal joint is a broken piece of glass.

Postoperative Diagnosis: Same.

Operation: Exploration of the MP joint of the left little finger with excision and removal of foreign body.

Indication of Surgery: The patient was a passenger in a vehicle that was struck by a large rock. The rock from a hillside hit the windshield, breaking the glass. She tried to brace herself with her left hand and sustained a laceration on the dorsum of the metacarpal phalangeal joint of the left little finger. The injury didn't seem significant at the time and she did not even see a physician. The wound subsequently healed, but she stated noticing some pain in that region. Over three months later, she accidentally hit the metacarpal phalangeal joint of the left little finger against something and since then she has been complaining of severe pain and numbness. She had an x-ray of her left hand which revealed a foreign body in the metacarpal phalangeal joint of the left little finger. The patient was referred to me. I explained to the patient I need to open up the wound, explore the area, and remove the foreign body. The possible risks, benefits, and possible complication of the procedure were explained.

Technique: The patient was placed on the OR bed assuming the supine position. Blood pressure monitoring and pulse oximetry monitoring were in progress. The left hand and forearm were then prepped and draped. Initially, I tried to palpate the metacarpophalangeal joint until I found the area that had the most tenderness. This area is located at the dorsum of the MP joint of the left little finger proximal to the previously healed scar. This area was then marked out and infiltrated with 1% Carbocaine solution. An oblique incision was then made over the area parallel to the old scar. Incision was deepened and bleeders were fulgurated with high temperature. By careful sharp and blunt dissection, the foreign body was searched for. For a while, I could not find the foreign body. Therefore, the incision was extended distally towards the previous area of the laceration. After searching for some time, it was found that the dorsal digital nerve in this area was intact. It was retracted out of harms way and the area near the extensor tendon towards the foot of the extensor tendon. The foreign body was wedged in the soft tissue of the joint capsule. It was a piece of broken glass and measures about $2 \times 3 \times 1$ mm. It was completely extracted and removed. The wound was irrigated with a large amount of saline solution. Wound closure was accomplished with 5-0 nylon interrupted mattress sutures. Compression dressing was applied. The patient withstood the procedure well. She was advised to keep the hand elevated and keep it dry and clean. She was advised ice compress and change dressing in 48 hours. The patient was placed on Vicodin 1 tablet q.4h p.r.n. for pain. She was cautioned not to take pain medicine if she was driving. She was instructed to return to my office in six days.

Code(s):_____

6.60. When back pain is due to a psychological condition, how is this coded?

a. 724.5
b. 724.5, 307.89
c. 307.89
d. 307.89, 724.5

Neoplasms

6.61. A non-Medicare patient with carcinoma of the oral cavity and lip is receiving daily intramuscular injections of interferon alfa-2a (3 million units) in the outpatient cancer center. Which of the following will be reported for this service? The payer does accept HCPCS Level II codes for drugs.

a. V58.11, 149.8, 96401, J9213
b. 149.8, 96372, J9213
c. 145.9, 140.9, 96372
d. V58.11, 96549

6.62. This 32-year-old female with asthma and known cervical dysplasia is admitted for an endoscopic cervical biopsy with endocervical curettage. The procedure was performed without incident. The pathology report shows carcinoma in situ of the cervix. What diagnosis and CPT procedure codes are assigned?

Code(s):_____

6.63. This patient had a history of carcinoma of the colon 5 years ago without reoccurrence or metastasis. After several tests he is admitted now for probable renal cell carcinoma, thought to be a new primary. Laparoscopic partial nephrectomy of the kidney was performed without incident. Frozen-section pathology report reveals a lipoma. What diagnosis and CPT procedure codes are assigned for the procedure performed in the hospital?

Code(s):_____

6.64. This 56-year-old female recently had an abdominal sonogram performed for elevated liver enzymes and abdominal pain. This showed a mass in the liver and a needle biopsy was done. The patient is now admitted with hepatocellular carcinoma. Wedge resection is performed without incident. What are the appropriate diagnosis and CPT procedure codes for this hospital admission?

Code(s):_____

6.65. This 42-year-old female patient has known ovarian carcinoma, and she is being admitted for right oophorectomy. Patient has type I diabetes mellitus, and during her stay we had a hard time controlling her blood sugar level. Right oophorosalpingectomy with lymph node samplings and peritoneal biopsies was completed to stage the cancer. Diagnosis: Ovarian carcinoma, without metastasis, and diabetes out of control. What are the correct diagnosis and CPT procedure codes for this admission?

Code(s):_____

Disorders of the Nervous System and Sense Organs

6.66. A patient has right trigeminal neuralgia, and it is decided that gamma knife stereotactic radiosurgery will be performed. A Leksell® stereotactic head frame was placed prior to the procedure, which consisted of a single shot to a total dose of 7,500 cGy delivered to the 50 percent isodose line.

What are the CPT level I procedure codes reported for this service?

a. 61793, 20660
b. 61793
c. 64600, 61795
d. 61795

6.67. The following documentation is from the health record of a surgical patient.

A Medicare beneficiary has a procedure to promote nerve regeneration at a pain management center. The patient is placed in a prone position, and a midline incision overlying the affected vertebrae is made. The fascia is divided and the paravertebral muscles are retracted. The physician places the inductive electrode pads in the epidural space proximal to the damaged spinal segment. The pulse generator is sutured over the muscles, just below the skin, and closed with a layer closure.

What CPT procedure code is reported by the physician?

a. 63655
b. 63685
c. 63650
d. 63688

6.68. From the health record of a patient having eye surgery:

Operative Report

Preoperative Diagnosis: Open-angle glaucoma, right eye; diabetes mellitus, type I

Postoperative Diagnosis: Same

Operation: Initial trabeculectomy, right eye

Anesthesia: Local

Procedure: Full-thickness lid speculums were placed. A fornix-based, conjunctival flap was performed in the superior temporal quadrant. An angulated blade breaker was used to make grooves at the site of the future scleral flap at approximately the 10 o'clock position. Next, a three-sided, partial-thickness, scleral flap was created using a #64 Beaver blade. A trabeculectomy was performed using a sharp blade. A peripheral iridectomy was performed. The scleral flap was irrigated and found to be free flowing. The conjunctiva was closed using two 8-0 collagen sutures at the 12 o'clock position and one 8-0 collagen at the nine o'clock position. Decadron® 10 mg was injected subconjunctivally in the inferior fornix. Maxitrol ointment, patch, and shield were applied.

What are the correct codes for this procedure performed in the hospital surgery center?

a. 365.9, 250.00, 66172–RT
b. 365.11, 250.01, 65850
c. 250.51, 365.44, 66170–52
d. 365.10, 250.01, 66170–RT

6.69. From the health record of a patient having office-based surgery:

Operative Report

Preoperative Diagnosis: Bilateral entropion

Postoperative Diagnosis: Bilateral entropion

Operation: Repair of entropion of right eye

Anesthesia: Local

Procedure: The patient was sterilely prepped and draped for ocular solution of 2 percent lidocaine, mixed in equal proportions with 0.75 percent Marcaine with the addition of Wydase, and a modified Van Lint technique was performed on the right eye. Incision was made in the inferior lid margin extended inferiorly. This consisted of a diamond shape, with 6-mm lengthwise incisions interconducted. Hemostasis was obtained using wet-field cautery. The incision was then sutured using a tapered needle. The first suture was placed through the approximate lash line, in addition to one suture through the area of the meibomian gland. Using the tapered needle, the tarsal plate was approximated and reapproximated. The incision was then reapproximated with subcuticular sutures. This was followed by implantation of approximately four interrupted skin sutures using 6-0 nylon.

What are the correct codes for this procedure performed in the hospital surgery center?

a. 374.00, 67921–RT
b. 374.00, 67921–50
c. 374.10, 67921–RT
d. 374.00, 67923

6.70. This 71-year-old male had a stroke 6 months ago. He is being followed during his therapy for the residuals of his stroke with evaluation of progress. He has right-sided hemiplegia and aphasia. He also has hypertension and diabetes mellitus, type II. What diagnosis codes are assigned?

Code(s):_____

Newborn/Congenital Disorders

6.71. A neonatologist is treating a spontaneously delivered newborn with respiratory failure and erythroblastosis fetalis due to Rh antibodies. An exchange transfusion is required to stabilize this critically ill baby receiving services in the neonatal intensive care unit. The baby remains on CPAP to assist breathing and prevent further respiratory failure.

Which of the following code sets is reported by the neonatologist for this second day of care following birth?

a. 773.0, 770.84, 99469
b. V30.00, 99468, 36450, 94657
c. V30.00, 773.0, 770.84, 99469, 36450
d. 773.0, 770.84, 99469

6.72. A 22-year-old patient presents for a closure of a patent ductus arteriosus. The patient's thorax is opened posteriorly and the vagus nerve is isolated away. The PDA is divided and sutured individually in the aorta and pulmonary artery. How is this procedure coded?

a. 33813
b. 33820
c. 33822
d. 33824

6.73. A congenital bilateral hydrocele has become troublesome, along with reducible inguinal hernias on both sides, and the parents and pediatrician have decided that surgical correction is warranted for their 2-year-old son.

When the surgeon reports the surgical service, including bilateral hernia repair with hydrocelectomy, which of the following CPT codes are used?

    a. 49495–50, 55041–51
    b. 49500–50
    c. 49500–RT, 49500–LT
    d. 55041, 49500

6.74. A hospital-based pediatric clinic is treating a newborn with talipes equinovarus by manipulation and short leg casting. Which of the following code sets is reported for a visit where the condition is evaluated with a problem-focused history and examination and parents' questions are answered, followed by foot and ankle manipulation and replacement of the plaster cast?

    a. 754.69, 29450
    b. 736.71, 29405
    c. 754.51. 29405
    d. 754.51, 99212–25, 29450

6.75. From the health record of a newborn delivered in a birthing room setting:

This infant was born in the New Beginnings Birthing Center adjacent to Children's Hospital at 10:58 a.m. on September 1. He weighed 8 lb, 5 oz and was 21 inches long with Apgar scores of 9 and 9. Dr. Smith performed a history and examination immediately following the vaginal delivery with no abnormal findings. Parents declined circumcision or administration of hepatitis B. Ricky was discharged at 6:30 p.m. with his mother.

Which of the following code sets is appropriate for Dr. Smith's services on September 1?

    a. V30.2, 99431, 99238
    b. V30.00, 99435
    c. V30.2, 99431
    d. V30.2, 99435

Pediatric Conditions

6.76. A 6-month-old infant, born prematurely, presents for his monthly injection for RSV. The nurse documents Synagis® 40 mg, IM.

Which of the following code sets is correct for reporting this office visit?

    a. 99212, 90378, 96372
    b. 90378, 90471
    c. 99212, J1565
    d. 90378, 96372

6.77. This 5-year-old female patient presents to the office for bilateral ear drainage, fever, and ear pain. There is a large perforation in the left eardrum visible. She was given Augmentin twice a day for 7 days and will be seen in follow-up.

Diagnosis: Acute suppurative otitis media. An expanded problem-focused history and examination was performed, with medical decision making of moderate complexity.

What are the correct diagnosis and CPT procedure codes (including E/M) for this case?

Code(s):_____

6.78. The same patient in item 6.76 is scheduled for tubes now after the acute otitis media has resolved.

Surgery Center Report

Preoperative Diagnosis: Chronic recurrent suppurative otitis media

Postoperative Diagnosis: Same

Operation: Bilateral myringotomy, placement of permanent ventilating tube

Anesthesia: General

Procedure: A standard myringotomy incision was made and a copious amount of serous fluid suctioned from the middle ear cleft. A Goode T-tube was placed without problems. The procedure was then repeated on the left side in the same manner.

What are the diagnosis and CPT procedure codes (including E/M) reported by the surgeon for this procedure. The procedure was performed in the hospital same-day day surgery center?

Code(s):_____

6.79. This 7-year-old child with an acute attack of his childhood asthma is taken to ER. Spirometry, both pre- and post-bronchodilator reveal continued bronchospasm with intractable wheezing. An expanded problem-focused history and examination were performed with moderate medical decision making. He is subsequently admitted to the hospital. What diagnosis and CPT procedure codes (including E/M) are assigned by the ER physician?

Code(s):_____

Conditions of Pregnancy, Childbirth, and the Puerperium

6.80. This 29-year-old female has had two spontaneous abortions because of incompetent cervix. Because of this, she had a cervical cerclage placed in the third month of this pregnancy. She is coming in now to have the cerclage removed under general anesthesia. She was taken to surgery, and the cerclage was removed without complication. She was discharged that evening. There are no signs of labor, and the membranes are intact. She was instructed on the signs of labor and will see me in the office in 2 days. Estimated due date is in 2 weeks, but labor could begin at any time.

What are the correct code assignments for this case?

a. 654.53, 59871
b. 654.53 (The cerclage removal is part of the global package.)
c. 622.5, with appropriate E/M procedure
d. 622.5, 59871

6.81.   This 29-year-old patient is being admitted for evacuation of uterus for blighted ovum. She is in her second month of pregnancy and has had two antepartum visits. What are the correct codes to report?

a. 632, 59820
b. 632, 59851, 59425
c. 631, 59820
d. 631, 59820, plus appropriate E/M code

6.82.   This 26-year-old gravida 1 para 1 female has been spotting and has been on bed rest. She awoke this morning with severe cramping and bleeding. Her husband brought her to the hospital. After examination, it was determined that she has had an incomplete early spontaneous abortion. She is in the 12th week of her pregnancy. She was taken to surgery, and a dilation and curettage was performed. There were no complications from the procedure. She is to follow up with me in the office. She has had four antepartum visits during her pregnancy.

What are the correct codes to assign?

a. 637.91, 59812
b. 634.91, 59812, 59425
c. 634.91, 58120
d. 634.92, 58120, 59425

6.83.   This 30-year-old female comes to the clinic because of excessive vomiting. She has been vomiting for 3 days. She has had no problems with vomiting in her early pregnancy. She is now estimated to be in her 24th week. What is the correct ICD-9-CM diagnostic code assignment for this case?

Code(s):_____

6.84.   This 29-year-old female is admitted to the hospital with pneumonia due to *Pneumocystis carinii*. She is in her 30th week of pregnancy and has AIDS. What ICD-9-CM codes are assigned?

Code(s):_____

Disorders of the Respiratory System

6.85. A patient is respirator dependent and has a tracheostomy in need of revision due to redundant scar tissue formation surrounding the site. Under general anesthesia and establishing the airway to maintain ventilation, the scar tissue is resected and then repair is accomplished using skin flap rotation from the adjacent tissue of the neck. What codes will be used to report this procedure performed in the hospital short-stay surgery area?

    a. 519.00, V46.11, 31614
    b. V55.0, V46.11, 31614
    c. V55.0, 31610
    d. 519.00, 31613

6.86. This 60-year-old patient was admitted with emphysematous nodules. A thoracoscopic wedge resection was performed in the left lung to remove the lung nodules. A resection was done in the upper and lower lobes. Which of the following answers is correct?

    a. 518.89, 32657
    b. 492.8, 32657, 32657-51
    c. 518.89, 32500
    d. 492.8, 32657

6.87. From the health record of a patient newly diagnosed with a malignancy:

Preoperative Diagnosis: Suspicious lesions, main bronchus

Postoperative Diagnosis: Carcinoma, in situ, main bronchus

Indications: Previous bronchoscopy showed two suspicious lesions in the main bronchus. Laser photoresection is planned for destruction of these lesions, because bronchial washings obtained previously showed carcinoma in situ.

Procedure: Following general anesthesia in the hospital same-day surgery area, with a high-frequency jet ventilator, a rigid bronchoscope is inserted and advanced through the larynx to the main bronchus. The areas were treated with laser photoresection.

Which codes are reported for this service?

    a. 231.2, 31641
    b. 162.2, 31641, 31623-59
    c. 231.2, 31641, 31623–59
    d. 162.2, 31641

6.88. This 80-year-old male presented to the ER with acute pulmonary edema after experiencing a 3-day history of increasing shortness of breath and cough. He was admitted to the critical care unit with a diagnosis of congestive heart failure and treated with Procardia®, Nitro Paste, and Lasix with resolution of his respiratory distress.

The patient responded to treatment with increasing nitroglycerin and Lasix. The patient was also given intravenous fluids and low-dose dopamine to maintain an adequate wedge pressure and cardiac output.

Final Diagnosis: Acute pulmonary edema with congestive heart failure.

What diagnosis code(s) are reported?

Code(s):_____

6.89.   This 82-year-old nursing home patient presents with aspiration pneumonia. The patient aspirated food particles. Treatment included clindamycin 600 mg IV q 6 hours. He also has superimposed staphylococcal pneumonia. The condition resolved with treatment, and patient transferred back to the nursing home. What is the correct diagnosis code assignment?

Code(s):_____

6.90.   Under conscious sedation, administered by the endoscopist, a patient underwent a bronchoscopy with biopsy of the walls of the left upper lobe bronchus and left mainstem bronchus, dilation of the left mainstem bronchus, and placement of a bronchial stent in the left mainstem bronchus. Assign the appropriate CPT codes.

a. 31622, 31625, 31636, 99144
b. 31628, 31632, 31636
c. 31625, 31636
d. 31625, 31636, 99144

Trauma and Poisoning

6.91.   Assign the correct ICD-9-CM diagnosis codes for a 29-year-old patient with deep third-degree burns of the chest and right leg. He was the victim of a house fire. He has third-degree burns over 25 percent of his body.

Code(s):_____

6.92.   The patient in question 6.91 was treated with skin grafting over a period of time until his burns healed. Six months later, he is being seen with severe scarring due to third-degree burns of his right leg and chest received in a house fire. What ICD-9-CM codes are assigned for this case?

Code(s):_____

6.93. This 79-year-old patient had a gastrostomy performed because of dysphagia due to a stroke. He has been doing fairly well but is now admitted with extensive cellulitis of the abdominal wall. Examination reveals that the existing gastrostomy site is infected. The physician confirms that the responsible organism is *Staphylococcus aureus*. What diagnosis codes are assigned?

Code(s):_____

6.94. What CPT code(s) would be assigned for a simple repair of a 1.5-cm laceration of the left upper arm and an intermediate repair of a 1-cm laceration of the left hand?

Code(s):_____

6.95. What diagnosis codes are reported for an encounter where the patient is seen for a crushing injury of the left toes, foot, and ankle? He was crushed in a metal rolling mill machine at work.

Code(s):_____

Part III
Advanced Coding Exercises

Chapter 7

Case Studies from Inpatient Health Records

Note: Even though the specific cases are divided by setting, most of the information pertaining to the diagnosis is applicable to most settings. If you practice or apply codes in a particular type of setting, you may find additional information in other sections of this publication that may be pertinent to you.

Every effort has been made to follow current recognized coding guidelines and principles, as well as nationally recognized reporting guidelines. The material presented may differ from some health plan requirements for reporting. The ICD-9-CM codes used are effective October 1, 2009 through September 30, 2010, and the HCPCS (CPT and HCPCS Level II) codes are in effect January 1, 2009 through December 31, 2009. The current standard transactions and code sets named in HIPAA have been utilized, which require ICD-9-CM Volume III procedure codes for inpatients.

Instructions: Cases are presented as either multiple choice or fill in the blank.

- For multiple-choice cases:
  —Select the letter of the appropriate code set
- For the fill-in-the-blank cases:
  —Assign present on admission (POA) indicator for each diagnosis code.
    - Y-Yes (POA)
    - N-No (Not POA)
    - U-Unknown (Documentation is insufficient to determine if condition is POA.)
    - W-Clinically undetermined (Provider is unable to clinically determine whether or not the condition was POA.)
    - Leave blank for the exercises in this book all codes that are exempt from POA reporting. See the Exempt List as published in the *ICD-9-CM Official Guidelines for Coding and Reporting*. These codes are exempt because they represent circumstances regarding healthcare encounters or factors influencing health status that do not represent a current disease or injury, or are always present on admission. Reporting exempt codes for Medicare claims requires a number 1 to be entered, rather than a blank, per CMS Transmittal 1240 dated 5/11/07.
  —Assign all reportable secondary diagnosis codes including V codes and E codes (both cause of injury and place of occurrence).
  —Sequence the ICD-9-CM principal procedure code in the first procedure position.
  —Assign all reportable secondary ICD-9-CM procedure codes.

The scenarios are based on selected excerpts from health records. In practice, the coding professional should have access to and refer to the entire health record. Health records are analyzed and codes assigned based on physician documentation. Documentation for coding purposes must be assigned based on medical record documentation. A physician may be queried when documentation is ambiguous, incomplete, or conflicting. The queried documentation must be a permanent part of the medical record.

The objective of the cases and scenarios reproduced in this publication is to provide practice in assigning correct codes, not necessarily to emulate complete coding that can be achieved only with the complete medical record. For example, the reader may be asked to assign codes based on only an operative report; in real practice, a coder has access to documentation in the entire medical record.

The *ICD-9-CM Official Guidelines for Coding and Reporting*, published by the National Center for Health Statistics (NCHS), includes Present on Admission (POA) Reporting Guidelines in Appendix I. These guidelines supplement the official conventions and instructions provided within ICD-9-CM. Adherence to these guidelines when assigning ICD-9-CM diagnosis codes is required under the Health Insurance Portability and Accountability Act (HIPAA) of 1996. Additional official coding guidance can be found in the American Hospital Association (AHA)'s *Coding Clinic* publication.

Disorders of the Blood and Blood-Forming Organs

7.1.   The following documentation is from the health record of an 87-year-old female patient.

Discharge Summary

History of Present Illness: The patient is an 87-year-old female who was admitted from a nursing home with dehydration and pleural effusion, as well as urinary tract infection and thrombocytopenia with petechial hemorrhage. On admission, she was found to have a platelet count of 77,000 and a hematology consultation was done. The patient denied any bleeding diathesis in the past. She stated that she had recent bruising of the hands related to needle sticks but otherwise has not had any past history of any bleeding disorder. She stated she was taking aspirin on a regular basis. No specific history of hematuria, hematemesis, gross rectal bleeding, or black stools.

Past Medical History: Significant for congestive heart failure, diabetes

Medications: Coreg®, isosorbide, aspirin, Actos®, digoxin, glyburide, hydralazine, furosemide, Ditropan®, and potassium

Family History: No family history of any bleeding disorder

Physical Examination: She is an elderly-appearing white female, somewhat short of breath, using supplemental oxygen. Examination of the head and neck revealed no scleral icterus. Throat was clear. Tongue was papillated. There was no thyromegaly or JVD. There was no cervical supraclavicular, axillary, or inguinal adenopathy. Chest examination revealed rales, bilaterally. There were decreased breath sounds at the right base. There were coarse rales heard in the right midlung field. Heart examination showed rhythm was irregularly irregular. Abdomen examination was difficult to perform. I was unable to palpate the liver or spleen. Bowel sounds were active. Extremities revealed no clubbing, cyanosis, or edema. There were diffuse ecchymoses, especially in the dorsum of the right hand.

Laboratory Studies: Hematocrit was 43, white blood cell count 9,000 with 82 percent neutrophils, and the platelet count 77,000. The MCCV was 102. Creatinine was 1.7. Bilirubin was 1.7. The alkaline phosphatase was 122. AST 498, ALT 493, and albumin 3.6. The prothrombin time was 18 seconds, the PTT was 25 seconds. The chest x-ray showed a right pleural effusion.

Course in Hospital: The patient was admitted and started on IV fluids. Her diuretics were increased, and she showed a good response with a resolution of her pleural effusion and better control of her congestive heart failure. Hematology consult recommended holding platelet transfusion unless there was evidence of active bleeding. No platelets were given during this admission.

The patient was discharged back to the nursing home on day 6 in improved condition to continue with the same medication regimen as previous to hospitalization.

Final Diagnoses: 1. Pleural effusion from congestive heart failure
2. Dehydration
3. Primary thrombocytopenia with petechial hemorrhage and hematoma of the eyelids and arms and hands
4. Urinary tract infection
5. Type II diabetes mellitus

Which of the following code sets would be correct for this hospitalization?

a. 428.0, 276.51, 287.30, 599.0, 250.00
b. 428.0, 276.51, 287.5, 599.0, 250.00
c. 428.0, 511.9, 276.51, 287.30, 599.0, 250.00
d. 276.51, 511.9, 428.0, 287.30, 782.7, 599.0, 250.00

Optional MS-DRG Exercise (for users with access to MS-DRG software or tables)

What is the correct MS-DRG for this case? _____

Which of the following is an incorrect statement regarding the MS-DRG assignment on this case?

a. MS-DRG assignment in this case is based on the principal diagnosis; the secondary codes do not impact the DRG.
b. A principal diagnosis of CHF results in a higher-paying DRG than a principal diagnosis of dehydration.
c. This patient's LOS exceeded the average length of stay for the assigned DRG.
d. All of the above are true.

7.2.   The following documentation is from the health record of a 34-year-old male patient.

Admission Diagnosis: Sickle cell pain crisis.

Discharge Diagnosis: Sickle cell pain crisis/Staph (Staphylococcus) aureus bacteremia.

Secondary Diagnosis: Sickle cell disease, priapism, chronic lower back pain secondary to sickle cell diagnosis, asthma, gastroesophageal reflux disease (GERD) and hemorrhoids.

Consults: None.

Procedures: PICC line placement, bone scan and transesophageal echocardiogram.

Hospital Course: The patient is a 34-year-old, African-American male with history of sickle cell disease who presented with back pain and whole body pain, a remote history of some diarrhea and nausea, and some fevers and chills. Blood cultures taken on admission and during his first night as an inpatient grew four out of four bottles of Staph. aureus. The patient received 1 gm of ceftriaxone in the Emergency Department and received approximately six days of vancomycin IV as an inpatient. Thereafter he was switched to Ancef 1 gm IV g.8 hours.

In order to find a source for the patient's Staph. bacteremia, a transesophageal echocardiogram was done which did not show evidence of any cardiac vegetations. A bone scan was also done which did not show any deep-seated abscesses or any evidence of osteomyelitis. In light of the fact that the patient had Staph. bacteremia of unknown source, Infectious Disease was consulted. As per their recommendation, the patient is to be on five weeks of IV Ancef.

At the time of admission, the patient was placed on a PCA pump. He was rapidly weaned off of this and he was also placed on some oxygen and was bolused with fluids and kept on maintenance fluids. The patient's clinical status improved rapidly. He was soon weaned off the oxygen, fluids and pain medications.

At the time of discharge, the patient is afebrile and stable. A PICC line was placed in order to ensure access for the next five weeks during which he will receive his IV antibiotics. Home care and home IV teaching was arranged for the patient and his family.

Follow-Up: Hematology was contacted and follow-up will be arranged within the next two weeks. Follow-up will also be arranged with Infectious Disease in five weeks. Home medications include folate 1 mg p.o. q.d.; Flexeril 10 mg p.o. b.i.d.; Ancef 2 gm q.12 IV times five weeks; Phenergan 12.5 mg p.o. q.4 p.r.n. nausea and Zantac 150 mg p.o. b.i.d. The patient was told to return for fevers, chills, sweats, nausea, vomiting, bone or muscle pain.

Disposition is to home with home care.

Code Assignment including POA indicator:

Principal diagnosis: _____

Additional diagnoses: _____

Procedure: _____

Issues to clarify: _____

7.3. The following documentation is from the inpatient record of a patient with anemia.

Discharge Summary

Date of Admission:	11/19/XX
Date of Discharge:	11/21/XX

Discharge Diagnoses:
1. Anemia of chronic disease.
2. Chronic renal insufficiency.
3. Diabetes mellitus, insulin-dependent.
4. Hypertension.
5. Coronary artery disease.
6. Congestive heart failure.
7. Hypokalemia.

Attending Physician for Service:	Family Practice Service.
Consultations:	None.
Procedures:	None.

Hospital Course: The patient is a 66-year-old gentleman with multiple medical problems including: Coronary artery disease, insulin dependent diabetes mellitus, chronic renal insufficiency, who presented to the Emergency Department at Anytown Hospital on 11/19/07 complaining of shortness of breath. He had been seen in the office earlier that week and seemed to be doing reasonably well at that point in time.

On admission he said that over the last 2-3 days his shortness of breath has been increasing, he had orthopnea and a nonproductive cough. He denies chest pain at that point in time. He denied other symptomatology.

In the Emergency Department he was noted to have significant anemia with hemoglobin of 7.0 and a hematocrit of 21.2 with an MCV of 78.3. He was given two units of packed red blood cells and admitted to the Transitional Care Unit to rule out myocardial infarction and to receive blood.

Problems

1. Anemia. Initial H&H of 7.0 and 21.2. He received two units of packed red blood cells and at discharge his H&H was 9.1 and 27.0, respectively. His reticulocyte count was pending at discharge. Iron level was 51, total iron binding capacity was 371, ferritin level of 14. He had been on iron as an outpatient. This was stopped secondary to diarrhea, which he felt was probably from the iron. We will restart this at this time consisting of Niferex one p.o. q day. Follow his H&H as an outpatient. I would consider him for erythropoietin therapy at some point in time.

2. Cardiac. History of coronary artery disease and congestive heart failure. He had one elevated troponin on day 1 of hospitalization. He had had two normal troponins previous to this and two post this. I am uncertain of the significance of this one elevation of his troponin to 1.6. He had no chest pain throughout. Electrocardiogram

showed no changes. He was briefly started on heparin. This was subsequently discontinued the following day. We will send him home on his regular cardiac regimen consisting of Digoxin, an ACE inhibitor, diuretics consisting of Lasix and Carbatolol. He will also be given p.r.n. nitrates. From a congestive heart failure perspective on admission he was felt to have mild congestive heart failure. He diuresed well, and once he was transfused, his shortness of breath, orthopnea improved significantly.

3. Hypokalemia. The day after admission revealed this and his potassium was replaced. Being we were restarting his Lasix therapy, we will send him home on potassium supplementation as well.

4. Diabetes mellitus. Well-controlled. Continue Glucotrol at 5 mg p.o. b.i.d

5. Hypertension. Controlled. Continue Lotensin, Coreg, and will add Lasix as above.

6. Gastrointestinal. He had weakly heme-positive stools on admission. He has had this recently, has actually undergone upper and lower endoscopy twice this year already. He has had no complaints of melena or bright red blood. I am wondering if this was not secondary to trauma during the rectal examination. We will continue to follow for now.

Code Assignment with POA indicators:

Principal diagnosis: _____

Additional diagnoses: _____

Principal procedure: _____

Additional procedures: _____

Disorders of the Cardiovascular System

7.4. The following documentation is from the health record of a 66-year-old male patient.

Discharge Summary

Admission Date: 6/19/XX

Discharge Date: 6/28/XX

History of Present Illness: This patient is a 66-year-old man admitted on 6/19 because of unstable postinfarct angina. He underwent cardiac bypass surgery here 15 years ago. He did well until 1989, when he developed angina and underwent angioplasty here. On 6/9, he was awakened with severe chest pain and was taken to a nearby community hospital where he was found to have a small anterior wall myocardial infarction, with the CPK only slightly elevated.

Because of this small infarction, he was referred here for consideration for further coronary arteriography. He was discharged from the hospital on 6/16. On 6/19, as the patient was walking from the car to the office, he developed quite significant chest pain and was therefore admitted to rule out further infarction.

Hospital Course: He was taken to the cardiac catheterization laboratory the day after admission. At that time, complete left heart catheterization, left ventricular cineangiography, coronary arteriography, and bypass visualization were performed. We found that his left ventricle showed severe anterior hypokinesis, although it did still move. The left main coronary artery was narrowed by about 70 percent.

The bypass to the circumflex looked good, but the bypass to the left anterior descending had a very severe stenosis in the body of the graft. There was a very large, marginal circumflex artery that had an orificial 80 percent stenosis. I felt that he was not a candidate for angioplasty but should have bypass surgery. He was seen in consultation by Dr. Reed, who agreed with this, so he was taken to the operating room on 6/21 for that procedure.

Using extracorporeal circulation, the left internal mammary artery was anastomosed to the left anterior descending coronary artery and a venous graft was placed from the aorta to the marginal circumflex. It was found that the old venous graft to the main circumflex was in excellent condition with very soft, pliable walls so that vessel was left intact. There were no complications of this surgery.

His postoperative course was singularly uncomplicated. He never had any arrhythmia problems; his wounds healed nicely. He had a tiny left pleural effusion that never needed to be tapped. He was walking about the ward participating in the cardiac rehab program at the time of discharge.

Discharge Instructions: Discharge medications will simply be aspirin grains 5 q. d., Tylenol with Codeine 1 or 2 p.r.n. for pain, Lopressor 50 mg a day, and Colace, as necessary. He was instructed to contact his private physician upon return home for resumption of his medical care. He is to call me here at the medical center if there are any questions or problems that he wishes to discuss.

Discharge Diagnoses:
1. Unstable angina (intermediate coronary syndrome)
2. Recent incomplete anterior wall myocardial infarction
3. Coronary atherosclerosis, three vessel
4. Successful double-bypass surgery

What are the correct codes for this admission?

a. 414.01, 414.05, 410.12, 411.1, V45.82, 36.11, 36.15, 39.61, 37.22, 88.53, 88.57
b. 414.01, 414.05, 410.12, 411.1, V45.81, 36.12, 39.61, 37.22, 88.53, 88.57
c. 414.00, 414.05, 410.11, 411.1, 36.11, 36.15, 39.61, 37.22, 88.53, 88.57
d. 414.01, 414.05, 410.12, 411.1, 412, V45.81, 36.11, 36.15, 39.61, 37.22, 88.53, 88.57

Optional MS-DRG Exercise (for users with access to MS-DRG software or tables)

Indicate the principal diagnosis: _____

Which of the codes affects the MS-DRG assignment on this case?

_____

True or False: For this MS-DRG the presence of a complication/comorbid condition affects the MS-DRG assignment?

7.5.   An inpatient undergoes insertion of an AICD and lead testing subsequent to the implant. What is the appropriate code to assign for the lead testing?

   a. 37.26 Catheter-based invasive electrophysiologic testing
   b. There is no ICD-9-CM code to report a lead check; it is included in the lead insertion.
   c. 89.49 Automatic implantable cardioverter-defibrillator (AICD) check
   d. Either code 89.49 or 37.26 may be assigned to report the lead check; they are essentially synonymous.

7.6.   A patient is admitted with severe atherosclerosis of the left carotid artery. He undergoes a percutaneous atherectomy of the artery, along with infusion of streptokinase to assist with clot resolution. A carotid artery stent was also inserted to ensure that the artery would remain open. Assign the appropriate ICD-9-CM procedure code(s) to report this procedure.

   a. 00.61, 99.10, 00.63
   b. 00.61, 99.10, 00.64
   c. 00.61, 00.63
   d. 00.61

7.7.   Joe Jones was admitted to the hospital with severe angina. At cardiac catheterization he was found to have major atheromatous involvement of the left anterior descending coronary artery, with near-total occlusion, but well-preserved flow in the remainder of the coronary arteries. Because only one vessel was involved, the attending physician decided on a percutaneous treatment and stent placement. Mr. Jones underwent percutaneous atherectomy of the LAD with placement of two sirolimus-eluting stents. Urokinase was injected following the procedure to assist with clot dissolution. Assign the appropriate ICD-9-CM procedure code(s) for the hospital to report this inpatient procedure. Do not assign codes for the cardiac catheterization for this exercise.

   a. 00.66, 00.40, 36.07, 36.07, 99.10
   b. 00.66, 36.07
   c. 00.66, 00.40, 00.46, 36.07, 99.10
   d. 36.09, 00.40, 00.46, 36.06, 99.10

7.8.   A patient with severe arterial disease involving the lower abdominal aorta and the iliac bifurcation is admitted to the hospital as an inpatient for endovascular repair. Incisions are made over each femoral artery, and a catheter with modular attachments is inserted via the right femoral artery. The catheter carries a self-deploying endovascular prosthesis, which consists of an aortic component with a modular bifurcated prosthesis to extend into each of the iliac arteries. Via the femoral incisions, the components are aligned and are noted to be secure. The small incisions are closed, and the patient is taken to the recovery area for further observation. Assign the appropriate ICD-9-CM procedure code(s) to describe this procedure.

   a. 38.44
   b. 39.79
   c. 39.71
   d. 39.7

7.9. **History and Physical:** The patient is a 67-year-old male who was transferred from Down-the-Street Hospital where he was admitted with chest pain, shortness of breath, and EKG changes. His cardiac enzymes were elevated and, subsequently, underwent a cardiac catheterization, which revealed significant four-vessel disease. He was transferred here for a coronary artery bypass procedure once his angina is stabilized.

Past History: Diabetes, hypercholesterolemia and status post appendectomy

Medications: See transfer list

Allergies: None known

Physical Exam:

General: Normal appearing male in no acute distress

Cardio: Rate and rhythm regular

Lungs: Normal

Tests: Chest x-ray normal; EKG nonspecific T-wave changes

Impression and Plan: Unstable angina, coronary artery disease, diabetes mellitus; patient will undergo CABG tomorrow.

Operative Report

Preoperative Diagnosis: CAD

Postoperative Diagnosis: same

Procedure: Bypass graft of obtuse marginal and posterior descending arteries and left anterior descending artery. Cardiopulmonary bypass.

Description of Procedure: After obtaining adequate anesthesia, the patient was prepped and draped in the usual fashion. A primary median sternotomy incision was made, and the pericardium was opened. The left internal mammary artery was dissected as a pedicle using electrocautery and small hemoclips at the same time that the greater saphenous vein was harvested from the left lower extremity. Cardiopulmonary bypass was instituted, and the patient was taken to a mild degree of hypothermia.

The aorta was cross-clamped, and electrical arrest effect was administered via cold blood cardioplegia. The saphenous vein graft was placed end-to-side with the posterior descending artery, and then a separate graft was placed to the obtuse marginal artery. Each anastomosis was done with running 7-0 Prolene® suture and verified no bleeders were present. The left internal mammary artery was subsequently brought through a subthalamic tunnel and placed end-to-side with the left anterior descending coronary artery.

Following completion of the grafts, warm blood cardioplegia was administered. During this time, two atrial and ventricular pacing wires were attached to the heart's surface; in addition, mediastinal tubes also were placed. The cross clamps were released following this, and sinus rhythm returned spontaneously. The patient was weaned from cardiobypass without incident.

After all grafts were checked for diastolic flow by Doppler interrogation, which revealed no problems, the incisions were closed. The patient was taken to the recovery room in good condition and will be monitored in the intensive care unit for complications.

Progress Notes

Day 1: Patient progressing well; all vital signs are stable. Will transfer to step-down unit today.

Day 2: Heart rate stable and incision healing nicely. If patient continues to progress will be ready for discharge in a few days.

Day 3: Stable; patient ambulating in hallway without difficulty

Day 4: Continues to progress in ambulation; ready for discharge tomorrow

Day 5: Discharge patient today to follow up with myself next week.

What is the correct code assignment for this admission?

a. 411.1, 414.01, 250.00, 272.0, 36.12, 36.15, 39.61
b. 414.01, 411.1, 250.00, 272.0, 36.12, 36.15, 39.61
c. 414.00, 413.9, 995.89, 250.00, 36.12, 36.15, 39.61
d. 414.01, 411.1, 272.0, 250.00, 36.13, 39.61

7.10. The following documentation is from the health record of a patient admitted with angina.

Coronary Artery Bypass Graft

Surgery Date: 03/14/XX

Preoperative Diagnosis: Unstable postinfarct angina, mitral insufficiency, and severe left ventricular dysfunction.

Postoperative Diagnosis: Unstable postinfarct angina, mitral insufficiency, and severe left ventricular dysfunction.

Operative Procedure: On-pump coronary artery bypass surgery × 3: Saphenous vein to the right, saphenous vein to the marginal, internal mammary to the left anterior descending, and mitral valve reconstruction with a #26 Future ring and posteromedial papillary muscle repositioning.

Anesthesia: General endotracheal, Dr. Anesthesiologist.

Operative Findings: The patient had marked RV and LV dysfunction, ejection fraction of left ventricle about 20 percent. There was moderately severe mitral insufficiency related to tethering of the posteromedial papillary muscle. Vein and mammary were adequate.

Description of Procedure: Patient brought to the OR and placed on the OR table in supine position. Arterial line and Swan-Ganz catheter were placed, general endotracheal anesthesia induced, and the patient prepped and draped in usual fashion. Midline sternotomy performed. Left saphenous vein endoscopically harvested, left mammary harvested. Cooled the patient to 32 degrees, gave 1,200 cc of antegrade cardioplegia, and performed a distal anastomosis to the right with 7-0 Prolene. 500 cc of cardioplegia given. Distal anastomosis to the OM completed with 7-0 Prolene. Another 1,000 cc of cardioplegia given antegrade and retrograde as well as down the graft. The extended transseptal approach to the mitral valve was utilized, the mitral valve exposed, and the papillary muscle repositioned using pledgeted two Gore-Tex sutures sutured to the annulus. Complete partially flexible, partially rigid ring #26 Future was then implanted with 2-0 Ethibond sutures, the left atrial appendage oversewn in two layers, and left and right atria closed with running 4-0 Prolene, the mammary anastomosis with 8-0 Prolene, and the proximal anastomosis with 6-0 Prolene. Cardioplegia given every 15 to 20 minutes at 500- to 1,000-cc boluses. Warm blood potassium cardioplegia given prior to removal of crossclamp. Left atrium, left ventricle, and ascending aorta were deaired. Pericardial wall flooded with CO_2 to minimize air emboli. The aortic crossclamp was removed and the patient discontinued from cardiopulmonary bypass on epinephrine, Levophed, Neo-Synephrine, vasopressin, and milrinone, as well as inhaled Flolan. Cannulae were removed, heparin reversed with protamine, and the wound closed in layers with antibiotic irrigation of soft tissue. Sterile dressing applied.

Which of the following is the correct code set for this inpatient?

a. 411.1, 424.0, 429.81, 36.12, 36.15, 39.61, 35.12, 35.31
b. 411.1, 424.0, 36.12, 36.15, 39.61, 35.12, 35.31
c. 411.1, 424.0, 429.81, 36.13, 39.61, 35.12, 35.31
d. 411.0, 424.0, 429.81, 36.12, 36.15, 39.61, 35.12, 35.31

Disorders of the Digestive System

7.11. The following documentation is from the health record of an 81-year-old female patient.

Operative Report

Diagnoses: Acute gallstone pancreatitis with acute cholecystitis, evidence of bile duct obstruction.

History: The patient is an 81-year-old female admitted 48 hours ago with evidence of acute gallstone pancreatitis. The patient had some thickening of her gallbladder wall and pericholecystic fluid. The patient had marked elevation of amylase and was given 48 hours of medical therapy with chemical clearance of her pancreatitis. The patient was thought to be a candidate for open exploration of her biliary tract, with concomitant cholecystectomy and possible common duct exploration.

Description of Procedure: After discussion with the patient and her family and obtaining informed consent, she was taken to the operating room where, after induction of general anesthesia, the abdomen was prepped and draped in a standard fashion. Following this, a right upper quadrant incision was used to gain access to the abdominal cavity. Manual exploration revealed no abnormalities of the uterus, ovaries, colon, or stomach. The pancreas was enlarged and edematous in the area of the head. Attention was then turned to the right upper quadrant, where the gallbladder was noted to be somewhat distended. This decompressed with a 2-0 VICRYL® pursestring stitch using the trocar.

Following this, dissection of the hepatoduodenal ligament revealed arterial anomaly of the right hepatic artery, coursing from behind the common duct over the top of the cystic duct prior to giving off the cystic artery. The cystic artery was dissected free and double clipped proximally, singly distally, and divided. The duct was then dissected free and subsequently clipped proximally.

Cholangiogram was then obtained by opening the cystic duct and placing a cholangiogram catheter. Real-time cholangiography revealed marked dilation of the bile duct, which was noted prior to placing the catheter. The common bile duct measured roughly 1.5 cm in size. The duct tapered out in the area of the intraduodenal portion of the common duct to near-occlusion. There was a very scant amount of contrast, which went beyond the ampulla into the duodenum. With this structure itself, the patient may well have a distal impacted stone. The gallbladder was removed by transecting the cystic duct and removing it in a retrograde fashion. The gallbladder contained no stone.

Following removal of the gallbladder, attention was turned to the common bile duct, which was opened. No stones were retrieved initially from the bile duct. A biliary Fogarty was passed distally and, with some difficulty, was negotiated into the duodenum. On return, no calculus material was obtained. Palpation of the distal duct revealed thickening because of the pancreatic inflammation, which was noted to improve somewhat over the inside portion of the C-loop to the duodenum. The patient was thought to have possible impacted stone or perhaps some primary common duct process other than inflammation that was causing her distal duct picture. Choledochoscopy was performed, but distal visualization of the bile duct was not adequate. As such, it was thought that evaluation of the duct from both inside the duodenum and within the duct was profitable. Inspection of the ampulla directly revealed no abnormalities from within the duodenal lumen. Palpation of the ampulla and passage of the biliary Fogarty revealed what appeared to be just diffuse soft-tissue thickening and no strong evidence for calculus disease.

Following this, cholangiography revealed some mild emptying of the distal common duct into the duodenum, with filling of the pancreatic duct as well. With the overall picture, it was thought that the patient might benefit from a feeding jejunostomy, because she might well sustain postoperative or perioperative complications of respiratory insufficiency or perhaps other imponderables. As such, jejunum was identified roughly one foot beyond the ligament of Treitz, and 2-0 VICRYL® purse-string stitches × 2 were placed. The jejunotomy was performed, and a 16 French T-tube was then placed and brought out through a stab wound in the left upper quadrant. The tube was anchored anteriorly with interrupted 2-0 silk stitches and externally with 2-0 stitches. Jackson-Pratt drain was placed through a lateral stab wound in the right upper quadrant and used to drain the duodenotomy and choledochotomy. This was anchored with several 3-0 silk stitches.

Following this, the wound was irrigated with Kantrex® irrigation, 1 g/L, and the wound was closed by closing the posterior rectus sheath with running 1 VICRYL® suture. The sub-q was irrigated and the skin was closed with staples. The wound was then dressed, and the patient was taken to the recovery room postop in stable condition. Estimated blood loss was 400 cc. Sponge and needle counts were correct × 2.

Code Assignment:

Principal diagnosis: _____

Additional diagnoses: _____

Principal procedure: _____

Additional procedures: _____

7.12. The following documentation is from the health record of a 67-year-old female patient.

Clinical Resumé

Reasons for Admission: 1. The patient has abdominal pain.
2. The patient has nausea and vomiting.
3. The patient has elevated amylase level, also lipase level.

History of Present Illness: The patient is a 67-year-old white female who has a history of diabetes mellitus, type II, and also hypertension. The patient remained in stable condition until approximately 3 p.m. yesterday afternoon when she was shopping and was not feeling well. Subsequently, the patient went home, and developed nausea and vomiting associated with excruciating abdominal pain; however, the patient did not call for medical attention until almost midnight. The patient was noted to have recurrent abdominal pain. Because of this, the patient was subsequently seen in the emergency room. While she was in the ER, the patient was noted to have amylase level of 2,319. Lipase was 6,312. Because of this, the patient was admitted to the hospital for further evaluation and therapy.

Past Medical History: The patient has diabetes mellitus, type II. Surgical history includes partial hysterectomy 20 years ago. The patient also had surgery done on her left knee. She has also had a cyst removed from her ankle.

Allergies: The patient is not allergic to any medications.

Social History: The patient does not smoke or drink.

Review of Systems: The patient has complained of abdominal pain associated with nausea and vomiting. This has been present for the past 24 hours, but there is no chest pain and no shortness of breath.

Physical Examination: The patient's blood pressure is 134/70. Pulse is 78. HEENT reveals pupils that seem to be reactive. The fundi show sharp disks. There is some exudate, but there is no hemorrhage. Ears: The tympanic membranes are clear. The neck is supple. Thyroid is palpable, but not enlarged. Negative for hepatojugular reflux and negative for jugular venous distention. Chest revealed decreased breath sounds. Cardiac is regular. Abdominal examination is soft. There is only very minimal tenderness on palpation in the right upper quadrant area. Bowel sounds are present. Extremities: There is no cyanosis, there is no clubbing. The deep tendon reflexes seem to be symmetrical and bilateral. Neurological examination: The patient is oriented × 3. The cranial nerves II–XII are grossly intact. Sensory and motor strength are within normal limits. There is no clonus. There is no Babinski. Cerebellar sign is normal.

EKG reveals normal sinus rhythm.

Laboratory Data: The lipase level is 6,312. Amylase level is 2,319. The patient's white blood cell count is 14.4 with RBC of 4.51, hemoglobin of 13.8 with hematocrit of 40.0, MCV of 88, MCH of 30.7. Platelet count is 279,000. The patient's glucose level is 200, BUN of 19, and creatinine of 0.7, sodium of 136, potassium of 4.0, chloride of 93. Total bilirubin is 1.8. Calcium is 9.6. AST is 435. Total protein is 6.3.

Impressions: 1. Suspected gallstones; rule out possible common bile duct obstruction with stones.
2. The patient has abdominal pain due to pancreatitis.
3. The patient has diabetes mellitus, type II.
4. The patient has hypertension.
5. The patient is obese.

Plan: The patient will be admitted to the hospital. I will get abdominal ultrasound, and GI consultation will be obtained. The patient needs to have ERCP or surgical consultation. Pending above, further diagnostic therapy to follow.

Operative Report

Preoperative Diagnosis: Abnormal liver function tests. Biliary pancreatitis. Chronic cholecystitis with lithiasis.

Postoperative Diagnoses: 1. Dilated common bile duct
2. Small filling deficit in the distal common bile duct, status post sphincterotomy, and balloon extraction of common bile duct stones

Surgery Performed: Endoscopic retrograde cholangiopancreatography with sphincterotomy and balloon extraction of stone.

Anesthesia: Demerol® 100 mg IV, Versed 6 mg IV, glucagon 2 mg IV in intermittent doses.

Procedure: After obtaining informed consent, the patient was brought to the fluoroscopy unit. IV Demerol and IV Versed were given in intermittent doses to a total of Demerol 100 mg and 6 mg of Versed, as well as 2 mg of glucagon during the whole procedure.

The Olympus® System V-System(tm) ERCP scope was inserted from the mouth up to the second portion of the duodenum. Duodenal papilla was identified. Using the glow-tipped cannula, the common bile duct and pancreatic duct were cannulated. The pancreatic duct was then slightly dilated. The common bile duct was also dilated, and there were three small filling defects noted in the distal common bile duct causing obstruction. Then the common bile duct was selectively cannulated, and a guidewire was passed. Using a papillotome and current, the sphincterotomy was done. Then the 11.5 balloon was used to sweep the common bile duct. The balloon sweep was done three times. After the balloon sweep, cholangiogram was obtained again, which showed no evidence of any obstruction.

Recommendations: Recommend cholecystectomy for the chronic cholecystitis with lithiasis as soon as possible after acute illness is past. She was discharged after 3 days in the hospital. We will schedule the cholecystectomy for next week as an outpatient.

Final Diagnoses: 1. Calculus of common bile duct and gallbladder with cholecystitis
2. Biliary pancreatitis
3. Diabetes mellitus, type II
4. Obesity
5. Hypertension

Which of the following is the correct ICD-9-CM code assignment?

a. 574.70, 577.0, 250.00, 401.9, 278.00, 52.93, 51.85, 51.10
b. 574.71, 577.0, 250.00, 401.9, 278.00, 52.93, 51.85, 51.88, 87.53
c. 574.81, 577.0, 52.93, 51.85, 87.53
d. 574.80, 577.2, 250.00, 401.9, 278.00, 52.93, 51.85, 51.88

Optional MS-DRG Exercise (for users with access to MS-DRG software or tables)

What are the results when you group this case with and without the intraoperative cholangiogram procedure code?

MS-DRG assignment with the intraoperative cholangiogram code:

_____

MS-DRG assignment without the intraoperative cholangiogram code:

_____

Which MS-DRG is appropriate for this case?

Excluding the principal diagnosis, what other code affects the MS-DRG assignment for this admission? _____

7.13. Discharge Summary

Principal Diagnosis: Morbid obesity

Principal Procedure: Open Roux-en-Y gastric bypass, removal of gastroplasty ring, gastric (G) tube prior placement.

History of Present Illness: The patient is a 55-year-old white female with a history of gastroplasty ring placement in 1979 who comes to Dr. Smart for revision by doing a Roux-en-Y gastric bypass because of recurrence of her morbid obesity. Her morbid obesity is complicated by gastroesophageal reflux disease (GERD), and obstructive sleep apnea (OSA).

Past Medical History: (1) Morbid obesity. (2) OSA. (3) GERD.

Past Surgical History: (1) Gastroplasty in 1979. (2) Laminectomy.

Allergies: Keflex® **Medications:** Pepcid q. d.

Physical Examination: VITAL SIGNS Afebrile, vital signs stable. General: No acute distress. CV RRR. PULMONARY CTAB. Abdomen: Soft, nontender, nondistended.

Impression: A 55-year-old white female with a history of gastroplasty, needing a revision into a Roux-en-Y gastric bypass after morbid obesity not secured.

Hospital Admission: The patient was admitted through same-day surgery and taken to the operating room for open Roux-en-Y gastric bypass with removal of a gastroplasty ring, liver biopsy, and G tube placement. Afterward, she was taken to the ICU because of her obstructive sleep apnea. She was monitored closely, did very well, and afterward, she was transferred to the floor. She was full advanced to activities of daily living through our gastric bypass protocol. She advanced to gastric bypass soft diet by postoperative day 4. She did well with this. On postoperative day 5, she was deemed ready to go home. She understands her discharge instructions and will be given pain medications as well as continue prescription for Zantac® for her GERD and for marginal ulcer prophylaxis.

Condition on Discharge: Stable on postoperative day 5 from open Roux-en-Y gastric bypass.

Disposition: The patient was discharged home with family.

Medications: Resume previous home medications. The patient can resume her Pepcid, or she can continue taking Zantac 150 b.i.d.

Follow-up: The patient will follow up with Dr. Smart.

Diet on Discharge: Gastric bypass soft diet. She has been instructed by a dietician two times already.

Operative Report

Preoperative Diagnosis: Morbid obesity with gastroplasty dysfunction

Postoperative Diagnosis: The same

Operation: Revision gastroplasty to Roux-en-Y gastric bypass and liver biopsy.

Indications: This 55-year-old lady had undergone a Silastic® ring gastroplasty by another surgeon in 1979 at a weight of more than 250 lb. She had done well for a long time and then had started regaining her weight and also developed significant gastroesophageal reflux disease. A gastric endoscopy done preoperatively showed that the Silastic ring of her gastroplasty had eroded into the gastric lumen with a wide outlet from the pouch and also with a separate dehiscence of the staple line. In the interim, she had developed sleep apnea but did not have hypertension or diabetes. Following the endoscopy and because of being on disability related to a laminectomy and to spinal problems, the excess weight seemed to aggravate her disability and seemed a justifiable reason for a surgical intervention.

Description of Procedure: With the patient supine on the operating table and under satisfactory general anesthesia, we attempted a right and then left subclavian line but had difficulties with the wire guide. Subsequently, a neck central line was placed and the abdomen was prepped and draped in a sterile manner. An upper midline incision was made and carried through the fat by tearing and through the fascia with the cautery. There were adhesions immediately of omentum to the anterior abdominal wall and also to the lower abdominal wall where a paramedian incision had been. These were all lysed, which was not difficult. A Tru-Cut needle was used to obtain a biopsy from the left lobe, which was moderately fatty by examination. The gallbladder was emptied sufficiently to know that there were no stones. The uterus and ovaries were surgically absent. We began by lysing adhesions on the undersurface of the left lobe of the liver to the stomach until we were able to uncover the old gastric pouch and appreciate the location of the staple line. I could also appreciate where the Silastic ring was, separate from the nasogastric tube, which was brought inside. We dissected around the distal esophagus and brought a long Penrose drain around it for retraction purposes. I held up the portion of the stomach near the lesser curve where the Silastic ring was palpable, and we used the cautery to enter into the lumen to find the ring. Its suture was cut and the ring was removed and sent to pathology. The opening made for the gastrotomy was closed with interrupted 2-0 silk sutures. We then dissected a little more proximal to this location along the lesser curve to go around the serosa of the stomach to its backside. A 12 French Robinson catheter was put along this tract and turned around to come to hold the lesser omentum on traction. We also divided some of the gastrocolic omentum to gain access from the lateral side to the posterior lesser sac. We then used a 45-mm blue load endoscopic autosuture stapler to staple and transect the stomach at the lesser curve transversely to create the posterior part of our pouch. When this was done, there was still a small hole into the distal stomach and perhaps into the proximal pouch where the staples had found the tissue too thick to seal completely. On the gastric pouch side, this was managed by an over-and-over suture of 2-0 Prolene from one edge to the other. On the gastric side, this was managed with interrupted 2-0 silk sutures. We then dissected behind the stomach up to the angle of His and eventually were able to pass the 12 French Robinson catheter through the angle of His and around the stomach to represent the pathway for the stapler to go at a later time. We lifted the omentum upward and identified the ligament of Treitz. The jejunum was divided a measured 7.5 inches beyond that ligament, and the mesentery at that level was divided using the endoscopic stapler. The small bowel was then measured from that point to the cecum, which proved to be 204 inches, and we selected a 72-inch Roux limb length. The side-to-side jejunojejunostomy was created with the biliopancreatic limb and the Roux limb using an outer running 3-0 Prolene seromuscular layer and an inside GIA stapled anastomosis. The Prolene was continued over the holes made for the stapler and also used to invert the stapled edge of the biliopancreatic limb. The aperture between the 2 mesenteric leaves was closed with a couple of 3-0 silk sutures. We then made a channel through the omentum up to the transverse colon and then across the gastrocolic omentum to allow the Roux limb to lie easily antecolic up near the pouch. When this placement was assured, the Roux limb was fixed to the end of our pouch with 3 interrupted 3-0 silk seromuscular sutures. The cautery was used to make an opening in the jejunum in the gastric wall and the posterior part of the anastomosis was done with interrupted 3-0 VICRYL suture. An opening was made in the Roux limb through which a 10-mm Hegar dilator was passed through the jejunal and gastric sides of the anastomosis. That anastomosis was then sutured with the VICRYL over the dilator and then further reinforced with interrupted 3-0 silk seromuscular sutures. When this was done, we removed the dilator and passed the nasogastric tube through the anastomosis to lie in the Roux limb. The end of the Roux limb was then oversewn with a running 3-0 Prolene suture. After this, we used the 60-mm blue load endoscopic stapler to begin to transect the gastric pouch from the remainder of the stomach, going vertically towards the angle of His. It ultimately took three 45-mm cartridges after the first 60-mm cartridge in order to complete this, but it was done satisfactorily. We used 2-0 Prolene to oversew that vertical staple line throughout its length. We also used the 2-0 Prolene to oversew the gastric staple line throughout its length. The anastomosis in the pouch looked fine, and we made sure that the nasogastric tube was movable within the pouch. We then created a gastrostomy to the distal stomach with a 2-0 silk purse-string suture near the greater curve. A 22 French Foley catheter was brought through a left upper quadrant stab wound and on into the stomach and the balloon was filled. A pursestring suture was tied, and a couple of 2-0 silk sutures between stomach and abdominal wall were placed. After this, we irrigated the abdomen with an antibiotic solution containing Kantrex and bacitracin. All of the bowel and omentum was laid back in its normal position, and there was no tension on the Roux limb. The fascia was then closed with a running #1 loop PDS suture. The subcutaneous fat was cleaned with antibiotic solution and the skin was closed with 3-0 VICRYL dermal sutures and 3-0 VICRYL subcuticular sutures. The patient tolerated the procedure well and was taken to the SICU. Estimated blood loss was 350 mL, and the sponge count was correct.

Code Assignment:

Principal diagnosis: _____

Additional diagnoses: _____

Principal procedure: _____

Additional procedures: _____

Optional MS-DRG Exercise (for users with access to MS-DRG software or tables)

What is the MS-DRG assignment for this admission?

Which of the following would change the MS-DRG assignment of this admission?

a. Secondary diagnosis of a complication/comorbid condition or a major complication/comorbid condition.
b. Additional procedure codes
c. If one of the current diagnoses was not present on admission
d. All of the above

Endocrine, Nutritional and Metabolic Diseases, and Immunity Disorders

7.14.   This 56-year-old female was admitted for resection of an adrenal mass. The patient has had hypertension and palpitations of several years' duration treated with Toprol under good control. Ultrasound was done in consideration of the possibility of a mass, and catecholamine studies have been normal. A 4- to 5-cm right adrenal mass was identified. Dr. White had obtained a 24-hour urinary free cortisol, ACTH, and short suppression tests, all of which confirmed the presence of Cushing's syndrome. The patient was not diabetic. She did report weight gain, some shift in body configuration, and easy bruising of several years' duration. The easy bruising was identified on examination in the hospital.

Surgery: A 5-cm, well-circumscribed round cortical tumor was resected from the adrenal gland 2 days ago.

Allergies: No known drug allergies

Medications on Discharge: Hydrocortisone, rapidly tapering dose, currently on 40 mg daily; Toprol® 50 mg q. a.m.; Prevacid® 30 mg q. d.; Lipitor® 10 mg q. a.m.; Prempro® 0.625/2.5

Physical Exam: Vital signs stable. HEENT: Sclerae and conjunctivae clear. Neck: Supple. No palpable thyroid. Lungs: Somewhat decreased breath sounds currently. There is mild splinting with deep breathing. Abdomen: Tenderness in the incision area. She has active bowel sounds at this time. Extremities: No definite bruises currently. No edema noted.

Discharge Diagnosis: Right adrenal tumor with Cushing's syndrome secondary to tumor.

Plan: The patient appears to have tolerated the surgery well. She will require steroid replacement. Excess cortisol output is presumed entirely due to her tumor, and her ACTH was suppressed previously. As with exogenous steroid therapy, there will be contralateral adrenal suppression. The patient will be tapered rapidly to replacement hydrocortisone levels. We will try the remaining hydrocortisone withdrawal over the next 6 months or so, depending on her ACTH and cortisol responses. She is discharged to home with follow-up in my office in 1 week.

Which of the following is the correct code set for this hospitalization?

a. 239.7, 255.0, 401.9, 785.1, 07.21
b. 194.0, 401.9, 785.1, 07.22
c. 227.0, 255.0, 401.9, 785.1, 07.21
d. 227.0, 255.0, 07.29

Optional MS-DRG Exercise (for users with access to MS-DRG software or tables)

Which of the following MS-DRGs is correct for this admission?

a. 644, Endocrine Disorders with CC
b. 615, Adrenal and Pituitary Procedures without CC/MCC
c. 614, Adrenal and Pituitary Procedures with CC/MCC
d. 628, Other Endocrine, Nutritional and Metabolic OR Procedures with MCC

7.15. The following documentation is from the health record of a 57-year-old male patient.

Discharge Diagnoses:
1. Lung cancer currently undergoing chemotherapy with Taxol® and carboplatin with dexamethasone
2. Type II diabetes, with neuropathy and nephropathy, not controlled
3. Hyperlipidemia
4. Hepatomegaly

History: This patient is a 57-year-old man who presented for outpatient chemotherapy. He had surgery for lung cancer in September and is now undergoing chemotherapy with Taxol and carboplatin, including dexamethasone as part of his chemo and prophylaxis for nausea. He has done very well with the chemotherapy. When he presented for outpatient treatment on the day of admission, he was found to be hypoglycemic. He is a known type II diabetic. His diabetes is complicated by neuropathy and nephropathy. Due to his blood glucose levels, it was decided to postpone this chemo session, and he was admitted for control of his diabetes. Dr. Johnson consulted with the patient to manage his diabetes regimen. He has been on 70/30 insulin, 25 units in the morning and 15 units in the evening. He had problems in the hospital with hypoglycemia several times the first day, with blood sugar levels ranging from 30 to greater than 450. An IV insulin drip was started, and he also had q. 1 hour Accu-Cheks. His hepatomegaly has enlarged from the last time that I saw him. Question whether this is fatty infiltration due to poor diabetes control, or whether there is now some involvement with metastatic carcinoma.

Laboratory Data: Sodium 128, potassium 5.5, chloride 89, CO_2 34, BUN 13, creatinine 0.8, glucose range 30–460, with final glucose of 210. Calcium 9.4, WBC 9.8, hemoglobin 11.6, hematocrit 34.3, platelets 277,000.

Plan: One difficulty here is the cyclic nature of his chemo treatment regimen, likely to produce major shifts in his glucose, which is already difficult to control. The patient will need to monitor his glucose levels closely. He is discharged on 70/30 insulin, 35 units in the morning and 20 units in the evening. Dr. Johnson will be managing his diabetes, and the patient has instructions to call into his nurse on a daily basis for the next week. He is to follow up with me for further chemotherapy in the oncology clinic next week.

Code Assignment including POA indicator:

Principal diagnosis: _____

Additional diagnoses: _____

Procedures: _____

Issues to clarify: _____

7.16.   The following documentation is from the health record of a 52-year-old patient.

Discharge Summary

Admission Date: 11/14/XX

Discharge Date: 11/17/XX

Discharge Diagnosis: (1)   Diabetic ketoacidosis
(2)   Dehydration
(3)   Congestive heart failure
(4)   Aortic valve disorder
(5)   Urinary tract infection
(6)   Hyperkalemia
(7)   Peripheral vascular disease

(8) Hypertension
(9) *Escherichia coli* infection
(10) Hyperlipidemia
(11) Renal ureteral disease
(12) Old myocardial infarction
(13) Tobacco use
(14) Coronary atherosclerosis with native coronaries

Admitting Diagnosis: (1) Diabetic ketoacidosis
(2) Diabetes mellitus Type I
(3) Dehydration
(4) Congestive heart failure
(5) Hyperkalemia
(6) Hyperlipidemia
(7) Hypertension
(8) Tobacco abuse
(9) Severe peripheral vascular disease
(10) Atherosclerotic coronary artery disease
(11) Urinary tract infection
(12) Renal insufficiency

Present Illness: A 52-year-old, white female with known diabetes mellitus Type I, CVA's, cellulitis, hypertension, chronic hypertension, hyperlipidemia, poorly compliant diabetic. Most recently in hospital from September 3rd to September 8th with cellulitis, congestive heart failure, poorly controlled diabetes. Most recently in the hospital with diabetic ketoacidosis. Discharged home. She was supposed to be following up with her primary care physician doing b.i.d. Accu-Cheks. She was nauseated for the previous 2 weeks. As soon as she got nauseated, she quit checking her blood sugar level. She cancelled her doctor's appointment because she was "too sick to go". She had decreased appetite, and feeling poorly overall. She came to the emergency room with a blood sugar of 737. She had ketones 200 to 250. Her blood urea nitrogen was 75, creatinine 1.8. her potassium is 6.1, chloride 5, bicarb at 13. Patient is a poor historian, although she is awake and alert at the time of evaluation, on an insulin drip. Overnight her nausea had resolved. The nausea probably occurred because she was in the beginning stages of diabetic ketoacidosis.

Hosptial Course: The patient was put on insulin drip. Blood sugars got down. She was put on q.i.d. Accu-Cheks. Once her blood sugar level came down to the 100s, potassium was lowered. I had a very lengthy discussion with patient about the need for keeping doctor's visits and checking blood sugars. The patient was placed on Cipro. Her electrocardiogram showed a prolonged Q T. The patient went to ultrasound and had sludge and possible small stones in her gallbladder, and it was felt that she was able to be discharged home improved.

Discharged Medications/Instructions: Insulin 70/30, 20 units in the a.m., 20 in the p.m, Rezulin 400 mg q. a.m., Tenormin 50 q.d., Plavix 75 q.d., Monoket 10 mg b.i.d., Lasix 20 mg b.i.d., aspirin 325 q. a.m., Zocor 20 once a day, Oxycontin 20 b.i.d., Prozac 20 q. a.m., Vasotec 5 mg q. a.m., Propulsid 10 mg at Ac and HS, Bactrim DS 1 tablet every 12 hours. She is to see her primary care physician in one week. She is to call if she has any difficulties.

Dispositon: Discharged home.

History and Physical

Past Medical History: The patient has history of renal insufficiency with a blood urea nitrogen of 30 to 40 with a creatinine a 1.2 to 1.4. She has had a CVA, severe peripheral arterial disease. Echocardiogram done shows aortic sclerosis, mitral leaflet thickening, normal left ventricular size, normal diabetes, smoked 3 to 4 packs of cigarettes a day. She has hypertension. She has hyperlipidemia. She is dehydrated. She has a history of atherosclerotic coronary artery disease.

Medications: At the time of admission included Rezulin 40 mg q.d., Prozac 20 q.d., Propulsid 10 a.c. and h.s., Vasotec 2.5 2 every morning, Atenolol 50 q. a.m, Plavix 75 q. a.m, Lasix 20 milligrams b.i.d., Novolin 70 /30 20 units every a.m., aspirin 325 q. a day, vitamin E, iron, Oxycotan 20 a.m. and h.s., Zocor 20 mg at dinner. The patient has no known drug allergies.

Social History: She is married but her husband lives out of state and works there. She has one daughter. She does not drink and has smoked about 3 to 4 packs a day since a teenager.

Physical Exam: At the present time, the patient is afebrile, vital signs are stable. She is awake and alert, oriented × 3.

Heent: Pupils equal, round, reactive to light and accommodation, extraocular muscles intact, oropharynx benign.

Neck: Supple without adenopathy or jugular venous distention.

Lungs: Clear to auscultation.

Heart: Reveals a regular rate and rhythm without murmurs, gallops or rubs.

Abdomen: Soft, nontender, positive bowel sounds, no masses noted.

GU: Deferred.

Extremities: No edema. She has a baseline edema currently. Pulses are absent, pedal pulses.

Laboratory: At the time of admission, her glucose was 737, blood urea nitrogen 75, creatinine 1.8, acetone greater than 200, less than 250, sodium 136, potassium 6.1, chloride 95, bicarb of 13. Her hemoglobin was 13.9 and hematocrit of 44.1 and white blood cell count of 9.2 with a left shift showing 80.2 percent neutrophils, 16.2 percent lymphocytes. Platelets were 241,000. Urinalysis shows positive nitrites, greater than 1,000 glucose, 30 protein, 15 ketones, trace hemoglobin. She had 13 white blood count per high power field. Rare red per high power field, 2+ bacteria. Gram stain on her u/a showed no organisms seen.

Impression(s):
1. Diabetic ketoacidosis
2. Diabetes mellitus type I
3. Dehydration
4. Congestive heart failure
5. Hyperkalemia
6. Hyperlipidemia
7. Hypertension

8. Tobacco abuse
9. Severe peripheral vascular disease, arterial in nature
10. Atherosclerotic coronary artery disease
11. Urinary tract infection
12. Renal insufficiency

Plan: Admit, hydrate. She has been on insulin drip, we will d/c this now and change to q. 4 Accu-cheks and continue sliding scale. Hopefully on 16th be able to reinstitute her routine meds. Her potassium has now come down to the mid 4's secondary to her hydration and her sugar being driven intracellular with the insulin drip. I have impressed upon the patient the need for checking blood sugars and keeping M.D. appointment versus death in the future. The patient is on Cipro for her urinary tract infection. Further work up as indicated during hospital stay.

Exam: 9005 EK EKG REG
Compared with 9/25/07 no change.

Impression: Normal EKG

Assign the correct codes including POA indicators for this case:

Principal diagnosis: _____

Additional diagnoses: _____

_____

Issues to clarify: _____

Disorders of the Genitourinary System

7.17. The following documentation is from the health record of a 48-year-old female patient.

Discharge Summary

Discharge Diagnoses:

1. Dysfunctional uterine bleeding.
2. Anemia.

Therapies:

1. Transfusion of 4 units of packed red blood cells.
2. Fractional D&C.
3. ThermaChoice balloon endometrial ablation.

Discharge Medications: Tylenol III and iron supplementation.

Hospital Course: The patient presented to the emergency department with complaints of heavy vaginal bleeding which had progressively gotten worse over the previous three months. Prior to the patient's admission, she was using 7 Maxi pads in an hour. Assessment at that time showed that she was hemodynamically stable. However, she did have a hemoglobin of 8.5 and was continuing to bleed. She was admitted for IV premarin therapy and transfusion.

The patient has a mechanical heart valve and for this reason, she was on Coumadin. A PT with INR was obtained to make sure that the patient was not supra therapeutic. However, she was in the normal range. Despite the Premarin, the patient did continue to bleed. After the first two units of blood were transfused, her hemoglobin was only 8.8. She was given two additional units and scheduled for a D&C and a balloon ablation of her endometrium. This was performed. The procedure was uncomplicated. She was discharged home to follow-up in the office.

History & Physical Exam

Admission: For surgery

Present Illness: This is a 48-year-old gravida 10, para 7 who had been seen in the office with complaints of some bleeding after being menopausal for approximately one year. On examination, her uterus was found to be slightly enlarged, six to eight weeks' sized, the adnexa were non palpable. An ultrasound was performed which showed the endometrial thickness was 25 rom and had a complex echogenicity to it. Uterus measured $10.5 \times 8.2 \times 6.1$ cm, right ovary $3.7 \times 3.8 \times 3.5$ cm, left ovary $3.1 \times 2.1 \times 3.2$ cm. There is no evidence of fluid in the cul-de-sac. An endometrial biopsy was performed which showed a small amount of proliferative-type endometrium with breakdown consistent with dysfunctional uterine bleeding. She was scheduled to have a D&C later this month. However, the patient presented to the Emergency Department with complaints of very heavy vaginal bleeding requiring the use of seven maxi pads in an hour. The patient was found to be hemodynamically stable, blood pressure and pulse were in the normal range. However, hemoglobin was found to be 8.5. She was bleeding rather heavily; there was a large amount of clot in her vagina. She was admitted for a blood transfusion. She received two units of packed red cells and was also started on IV Premarin 25 mg every six hours. The patient has a history of having a mechanical heart valve for which she takes Coumadin, the fear was that, perhaps, she was overly anticoagulated. However, a PT with INR was found to be in the therapeutic range. Due to the patient's heavy bleeding, I felt that a D&C with some kind of therapeutic intervention was warranted. In this particular circumstance, an endometrial ablation would serve the patient very well. Plan is to perform a D&C with a balloon thermo-ablation.

Past Medical History: Significant for mechanical valve placement.

Surgery: Valve replacement

Current Medications: Lasix, Lanoxin, Coumadin. Allergies: No drug allergies.

Obstetrical History: Gravida 10, para 7.

Social History: No tobacco, alcohol, or drugs.

Family History: Significant for diabetes in her mother.

Physical Exam: Blood pressure 120/80, weight 224.

HEENT: Moist mucous membranes without thyromegaly or lymphadenopathy.

Breasts: Symmetrical without additional mass, nipple discharge.

Lungs: Clear to auscultation.

Heart: Regular rate and rhythm.

Abdomen: Soft, no mass. No lesions are seen on the vulva, vagina or the cervix. Uterus is approximately six to eight weeks' sized. The adnexa were not palpable.

Assessment and Plan: 48-year-old gravida 10, para 7 with dysfunctional uterine bleeding. Plan is to perform a D&C (dilation and curettage) with a ThermaChoice balloon ablation. The patient is currently in-house and this is scheduled for Thursday morning at 8 a.m.

Operative Report

Pre-Operative Diagnoses:

1. Dysfunctional uterine bleeding.
2. Anemia.

Post-Operative Diagnoses: Same.

Operations: Fractional D&C. & Therma-Choice balloon endometrial ablation.

Anesthesia: General with endotracheal tube intubation.

Complications: None.

Estimated Blood Loss: Less than 50 cc. Drains: None.

Specimen(s) to Lab:

1. Endocervical curettings.
2. Endometrial curettings.

Operative Procedure: The patient was taken to the Operating Room and under adequate general anesthesia. She was prepped and draped in the dorsolithotomy position for a vaginal procedure. The uterus was sounded to approximately 9-10 cm. Using Pratt cervical dilators, the cervix was dilated to the point that a Sims sharp curette could be inserted. A Kevorkian curette was first used to obtain endocervical curettings and the Sims sharp curette was passed to obtain endometrial curettings. After the curettings were obtained, the Therma-Choice system was assembled and primed. The catheter with the balloon was placed inside the endometrial cavity and slowly filled with fluid until it stabilized at a pressure of approximately 175 to 180 mmHg. The system was then preheated and after preheating to 87 degrees C. eight minutes of therapeutic heat was applied to the lining of the endometrium. The fluid was allowed to drain from the balloon and the system was removed. The procedure was then discontinued.

All sponge, instrument, and needle counts were correct. The patient tolerated the procedure well and was taken to the Recovery Room. She will be discharged home when stable.

Pathology Report

Endocervical mucosa with squamous metaplasia, negative for dysplasia.

Inactive endometrium with features of non-cycling endometrium.

No evidence of hyperplasia or malignancy

Code Assignment including POA indicator:

Principal diagnosis: _____

Additional diagnoses: _____

Procedures: _____

Issues to clarify: _____

Optional MS-DRG Exercise (for users with access to MS-DRG software or tables)

What are the results when you group this case with the code for acute blood loss anemia versus anemia due to blood loss?

MS-DRG assignment with the acute blood loss anemia code:

_____

MS-DRG assignment with anemia due to blood loss code:

_____

Which MS-DRG is appropriate for this case?

7.18.   The following documentation is from the health record of a 92-year-old female patient.

Admission Diagnoses:

1. Fever
2. Delirium

Discharge Diagnoses:

1. Left lower extremity cellulitis

2. Probable urosepsis with streptococcal bacteremia

3. Status post acute renal failure likely secondary to acute tubular necrosis

4. Insulin-requiring diabetes mellitus

5. Probable chronic obstructive pulmonary disease

6. Hypothyroidism

7. Hypertension

Consultations: Infectious Disease.

Procedures Performed:

1. Doppler ultrasound of the left lower extremity which showed no evidence of DVT

2. Transthoracic echocardiogram which showed normal left ventricular function

Hospital Course: The patient is a 92-year-old white female with past medical history significant for hypertension, hypothyroidism, and non-insulin-dependent diabetes mellitus who was brought to the Emergency Room for evaluation of fever and dyspnea. The patient at that time was a poor historian; however, family corroborated abrupt onset of symptoms with no clear source. Generally the patient has been healthy although she is minimally active and most of her activities of daily living consist of ambulating around her bedroom with the assistance of family.

In the Emergency Room the patient was febrile to 40:C. Urinalysis was significant for pyuria with evident bacteria. No focal infiltrate was seen on chest x-ray. The patient had marked leukocytosis with a white count of 25,000, 80 polys and 15 band forms. She was admitted for intravenous antibiotics. She was treated with Ceftriaxone and by the following morning was noticeably brighter and more alert. She remained afebrile for the duration of her hospital course. Also on the morning of first hospital day blood cultures were reported as positive for gram positive cocci in chains. This was subsequently confirmed as group C streptococcus which was Penicillin sensitive. Urinalysis grew out mixed flora. It was somewhat unclear as to the specific source of the patient's bacteremia. It is somewhat unusual for a UTI to yield this organism. The patient had some mild erythema on her left lower extremity and had marked discomfort to touch over both of her ankles, which she attributed to her "diabetes". She remained on Rocephin and was actually tolerating near normal diet.

On the evening of the second hospital day, the patient complained of increased pain and was noted to be increasingly incoherent. She had been placed on nasal cannula overnight for have markedly increased erythema in her left lower extremity concerning for desaturation. On evaluation by cross covering physician, she was noted to have markedly increased erythema in her left lower extremity concerning for possible DVT. Doppler ultrasound showed no evidence of clot. She was started on Vancomycin for improved gram positive coverage. Respiratory status remained stable. However the patient was minimally arousable later that morning. She had been administered a 1 mg dose of morphine for leg pain. Chest x-ray showed increased interstitial edema possibly consistent with heart failure. The patient received Narcan with some improvement in her mental status. Arterial blood gas showed evidence of significant CO_2 retention with pH of 7.19, pCO_2 70, pO_2 50, serum bicarbonate of 26. She was diuresed and administered nebulizer treatments. She was moved to the Medical Intensive Care Unit for possible ventilation with BiPAP. Echocardiogram showed no wall motion abnormalities and no left ventricular dysfunction. Chemstix remained greater than 100 mg/dl. The patient had prompt improvement in her respiratory status with diuresis and prevision of Narcan. No further invasive ventilation was necessary.

Of note during these events the patient's family was in close attendance including her three daughters and grandson. There was extensive consultation with them regarding any advanced directives that the patient might have specified previously. It was the consensus of the family that reasonable attempts at aggressive intervention were indicated as long as there was a possibility of a reversible etiology for her problems. Fortunately the patient's condition stabilized.

For the remainder of her hospital course intervention focused on improving her pulmonary status as well as renal function. Her creatinine had increased from prior baseline of 1.2 up to 1.7 with noticeable drop-off in her urine output. The patient had received intravenous antibiotics during her hospital course but had not had any noticeable hypotensive episodes. She was receiving diuretics, which complicated calculation of her urine sodium; however, overall picture appeared consistent with acute tubular necrosis. Renal ultrasound was obtained and showed no evidence of hydronephrosis or obstruction. She was restarted on her oral Indapamide and continued to have steady improvement in her pulmonary status. She did not require any supplemental oxygen following resolution of her pulmonary edema.

Infectious Disease was consulted with regards to her cellulitis and was concerned that it was not resolving as would be expected with a streptococcal organism. Therefore she was continued on Vancomycin for an additional five days and by the time of this dictation erythema had completely resolved and the patient was consistently alert, sitting up in bed and actually ambulating around her room. Leukocytosis resolved and as noted above renal function normalized. The plan was to continue her on oral Dicloxacillin for an additional ten days of oral antibiotic therapy. Only additional intervention was provision of a combined albuterol Atrovent inhaler given the patient's signs of chronic interstitial lung disease. This appeared to improve her ventilatory status as she had no further episodes of nocturnal desaturation. The patient at this time is stable for discharge.

I briefly discussed her hospital course with her primary physician, who will continue to follow her. Family is requesting the assistance of home health nurse for overall assessment over the next two weeks while the patient continues to recuperate at home. Other peripheral issues addressed during this hospitalization included the patient's probable iron deficiency anemia. Recent colonoscopy and endoscopy showed evidence of diverticular disease but no other pathology. The patient has had upper GI bleeding. She was guaiaced during this admission, had stable hematocrit. B-12 and folate were checked and were within normal limits. Other issue was the patient's diet and she was evaluated by a speech therapist who noted that she did fine without any aspiration as long as she was provided with somewhat *thickened* feeds and had her usual foods provided. It was particularly requested that she be given pills, tablets and capsules with a spoonful of pudding, applesauce or yogurt instead of fluid. It was also recommended that she continue to have thickener available. The family was aware of these recommendations and is extraordinarily attentive to the patient's needs.

Medications on Discharge: Insulin NPH 10 units qam; Synthroid .05 mg po qd; Aspirin 325 mg po qd; Lorazepam .5 mg po qhs; Iron 324 mg po tid; Colace 100 mg po qd; Dulcolax 10 mg prn constipation; Combivent MDI 2 puffs bid; Indapamide 2.5 mg po qd; Dicloxacillin 125 mg po qid × 10 days.

Follow-up: The patient's family has been instructed to call for appointment.

Diet: Soft mechanical 1800 calorie ADA.

Activities: The patient may ambulate to a chair with assistance.

Special Instructions: The patient should seek prompt medical attention for any recurrent fever, increased erythema in her lower extremity or mental status changes as reported by the family.

Code Assignment including POA indicator:

Principal diagnosis: _____

Additional diagnoses: _____

Procedures: _____

Issues to clarify: _____

7.19. The following documentation is from the health record of a 14-year-old male patient.

Discharge Summary

The patient is a 14-year-old male with history of renal failure and failed kidney transplant. The patient was admitted for his second kidney transplant.

Prior to surgery, the patient underwent hemodialysis, through the existing AV fistula. The transplant was accomplished within 48 hours of the harvesting of the donor organ. Tissue samples confirmed adequate donor match. The previously transplanted, now failing, kidney was first removed; then the new kidney was placed.

One postoperative dialysis session was required before the transplanted kidney was functioning adequately. Postoperatively, the patient was watched carefully for signs of rejection. Patient's postoperative course was relatively uneventful.

The patient was discharged, to be followed weekly in the office.

Which of the following code sets will be reported for the above admission?

a. 996.81, 586, 55.53, 55.69, 39.95 × 2
b. 586, 996.81, 55.69, 39.95 × 2
c. 586, V42.0, 55.53, 55.69, 39.95
d. 584.9, V42.0, 55.69, 39.95

7.20. The following is from the health record of a 77-year-old female.

Discharge Summary

Admission Date:	04/12/XX
Discharge Date:	04/15/XX
Discharge Diagnosis:	1. Acute renal failure
	2. Congestive heart failure
	3. Chronic obstructive pulmonary disease (COPD)
	4. Leg cellulitis
	5. Seizure disorder
	6 Venous insufficiency
	7. Osteoarthritis
	8. Morbid obesity
	9. Acute ankle arthritis, likely pseudogout
Discharge Medications:	Resume home medications.
Procedures:	None.
Consults:	None.

Present Illness: This is a 77-year-old female transferred to the acute care ward from a subacute unit for treatment of renal insufficiency. She was originally admitted with a BUN of 32, creatinine 1.4. While on the subacute unit she was diuresed for congestive heart failure and developed acute renal failure. Her BUN rose to 78, creatinine to 2.3. She was transferred to the trauma care unit (TCU) for IV fluids and monitoring for her redevelopment of congestive heart failure. She was developing some rales with IV fluids on the subacute unit. She was monitored closely over the next 3 days. As her BUN and creatinine fell she seemed to tolerate it fairly well symptomatically, having some rales. She had a BUN of 60 and a creatinine of 1.3 on the day of discharge. She was released by the cardiologist that day when he felt she was in no significant congestive heart failure and her BUN and creatinine were improving. She should follow up with the cardiologist in the near future for follow-up electrolytes and reevaluation of her congestive heart failure.

While the patient was on the TCU, she also developed some ankle pain. It was somewhat swollen and was given a dose of steroids. She had quick resolution to the pain and swelling and likely this was an episode of pseudogout.

History and Physical Exam

Admission Date: 04/12/XX

Chief Complaint: Acute chronic renal failure.

Present Illness: This is a 77-year-old white female who was transferred down from the subacute unit to the acute care unit for increasing renal insufficiency. The patient was originally admitted on 03/28 with a BUN, creatinine of 32 and 1.4. The patient has been treated with I.V. Ancef and I.V. Lasix for cellulitis and pulmonary edema. Yesterday, her BUN and creatinine were found to be 78 and 2.3. She was transferred to the acute care unit for I.V. fluids and to monitor her renal function. This a.m., she complains of right ankle pain. She denies any trauma to the right ankle, but she does give a history of osteoarthritis. She reports that there is excruciating pain with weight bearing and with any movement. In addition, she reports that the right ankle is very tender to touch.

Past Medical History:	1. Obesity
	2. Renal failure
	3. Bilateral lower extremity cellulitis
	4. Hypertension
	5. Anemia
	6. COPD
	7. Seizure disorder
	8. Intertrigo

Current Medications:	1. Lotrisone, b.i.d. topical to breast and groin
	2. prinivil, 40 mg po q.day
	3. Dilantin — mg po b.i.d.
	4. Benadryl, 25 mg q. 4 hours prn
	5. Catapres, 0.1 mg prn
	6. Hydrocortisone cream, 1% topical b.i.d. prn
	7. Tylox, 1-2 tabs po q.i.d. prn
	8. Norvasc, 5 mg po q.day

Allergies: No known drug allergies.

Review of Systems: The patient reports that she does have arthritis in her back and multiple joints. She denies a history of gout. She denies sporadic fevers, chills, cough, abdominal pain, GI or GU complaints.

Social History: The patient is a smoker, she has smoked two packs per day for the previous 20 years.

Physical Exam: BP 140/70, pulse 100, respirations 24, temperature 97.5. In general, this is an obese white female in no acute distress. HEENT: Atraumatic, normocephalic. Pupils equal, round and reactive. Oropharynx is clear. Neck: Supple; no lymphadenopathy; trachea midline. Lungs: Lungs reveal few crackles, right base. Heart: Regular rate and rhythm; SI, S2, no murmur, click, gallop, or rub. Abdomen: Protuberant, positive bowel sounds, and nontender. Extremities: Chronic venous changes bilaterally with trace edema. Right lateral malleolus is very tender to palpation, range of motion is limited by pain. There is no calf or thigh tenderness.

Laboratory Data/Clinical Tests: Glucose 98; BUN 76; creatinine 2.1; calcium 8.2; sodium 134; potassium 4.4; chloride 94; total CO_2 30.

Assessment/Plan:

1. Renal failure. This is most likely prerenal secondary to overdiuresis. We will hold her diuretics and continue with general I.V. fluids. Her BUN, creatinine is slightly improved today since yesterday with this therapy. Urine electrolytes and eosinophils are currently pending.

2. Right ankle pain. Etiology not completely certain. There is no history of trauma. I question if this could possibly be an inflammatory arthritis monoarticular such as gout or pseudogout. We will check a sed rate and a rheumatoid factor. We will hold off on giving the patient any nonsteroidal anti-inflammatories, in light of her renal failure. We'll continue with the Tylox and give her a trial of SoluMedrol. We'll also check a foot x-ray.

3. Cellulitis. This is stable, off of her antibiotics.

4. Hypertension. We will continue her current treatment.

Which of the following is the correct ICD-9-CM code assignment?

a. 584.9, 428.0, 496, 345.90, 459.81, 721.90, 715.89, 278.01, 275.49, 712.37, 401.9
b. 403.90, 584.9, 428.0, 496, 345.90, 459.81, 721.90, 715.89, 278.01, 275.49, 712.37
c. 586, 428.0, 496, 345.90, 459.81, 721.90, 715.89, 278.01, 275.49, 712.37
d. 404.90, 584.9, 428.0, 496, 345.90, 459.81, 721.90, 715.89, 278.01, 275.49, 712.37

Optional MS-DRG Exercise (for users with access to MS-DRG software or tables)

True or False: The assigned MS-DRG for this admission contains a CC or MCC.

Infectious Diseases

7.21. The following documentation is from the health record of a 71-year-old male patient.

Discharge Summary

History and Physical Findings: This 71-year-old male is a nursing home resident as a result of a cerebrovascular accident 2 years ago. He has had numerous hospital admissions for pneumonia and other infectious complications. On the day of admission (4/21), the patient was noted to be clammy, with tachypnea, to have decreased level of responsiveness, and to show increased fever. He was seen in the ER, where evaluation revealed the presence of probable urosepsis. The patient was also found to have renal insufficiency with BUN and creatinine elevated. His WBC count was 23,000 with decreased hemoglobin and hematocrit. He was admitted for treatment of *Escherichia coli* septicemia. Physical examination revealed an elderly male who was aphasic and with a right hemiplegia from a previous CVA. The heart had a regular rhythm. The lungs were clear. The abdomen was soft.

Significant Lab, X-Ray, and Consult Findings: Follow-up chemistry showed progressive decline in the BUN and creatinine to near-normal levels. Initial white blood cell count was 23,700. Final blood count was 9,000. The urinalysis showed white cells too numerous to count. The urine culture had greater than 100,000 colonies of *E. coli* and group D strep, which revealed the cause of the UTI. Repeated blood cultures grew *E. coli* with the same sensitivities as that of the urine. There were no acute abnormalities noted. EKG showed sinus tachycardia and low lead voltage, otherwise was normal and unchanged.

Course in Hospital: The patient was initially started empirically on Primaxin®. He underwent fluid rehydration and his electrolytes were followed closely. Electrolytes improved through his hospital stay. He was continued on IV Primaxin until the date of discharge, when he was changed to Cipro® by tube. All of the bacteria grown in the urine and in the blood were sensitive to the Cipro. The chest x-ray showed no change from previous admissions, and he was followed closely with additional oxygen as needed. The patient does have a history of chronic obstructive lung disease and has required intermittent oxygen therapy at the nursing home. At this time, the patient had reached maximal hospital benefit. He was switched to oral antibiotics. He was to continue on tube feedings, which he was tolerating quite well. The patient was discharged back to the nursing home on 5/4.

Discharge Diagnoses: *E. coli* septicemia
UTI
Renal insufficiency
Chronic obstructive lung disease
CVA with right hemiplegia

Code Assignment including POA indicator:

Principal diagnosis: _____

Additional diagnoses: _____

Issues to clarify: _____

Optional MS-DRG Exercise (for users with access to MS-DRG software or tables)

What is the correct MS-DRG for this case?

_____

7.22. The following documentation is from the health record of a 34-year-old male.

Discharge Summary

History of Present Illness: The patient is a 34-year-old male who was transferred to the hospital with the diagnosis of rule out AIDS. The patient dates the onset of his current illness to two months prior to admission when he had a tooth extraction. The patient doesn't know whether he was treated with antibiotics at that time; however, he does note that the socket was packed. The patient states that after the above tooth extraction, he developed a fever with shaking chills, night sweats, and anorexia. He lost about 12 pounds. He also notes the onset of mild right flank pain associated with foam in urine and urinary frequency. There was no hematuria, dysuria, incontinence, urinary retention, hesitancy, or slow stream. The patient also complains of occasional diarrhea but no melena or bright red blood per rectum. Medications on transfer are Codeine, Lasix, Amphojel, Mylanta, Penicillin, Ranitidine, Halcion. Social history is remarkable for continuous IV drug abuse, both heroin and cocaine. There's no history of homosexual activity. He doesn't drink alcohol, but smokes a half-pack of cigarettes a day.

Pertinent Lab, X-Ray, and Consult Findings: This patient is a 34-year-old, well-developed, well-nourished male in no acute distress. Mucous membranes are moist. There is a questionable white area at the outer aspect of the right lower gingiva near second tricuspid. There are small mobile submandibular and posterior cervical nodes. The patient also has bilateral inguinal adenopathy and two left epitrochlear nodes. Chest X ray showed minimal blunting of both costophrenic angles, no definite effusions are noted. There are confluent patches of infiltration in the left midlung field spanning from the hilum to the periphery as well as in the right lower lung. These findings are nonspecific, but could very well fit in with the diagnosis of Pneumocystis carinii pneumonia. Urinalysis negative. CBC: hemoglobin 9.0, hematocrit 27.2, MCV 87, WBC 5.1, 11 lymphs, S monos, platelets 206,000. Sodium 130, potassium 3.98, chloride 112, C02 10, BUN 50, creatinine 4.7, glucose 82, calcium 7.0, albumin 0.80. Sputum culture showed normal respiratory flora with normal Enterobacter aerogens. Urine culture showed no growth.

Hospital Course by Problem List:

Problem #1. Acquired immunodeficiency syndrome: The patient's history was significant for weight loss. Social history significant for IV drug abuse. Physical examination revealed diffuse lymphadenopathy. Laboratory data revealed neutropenia with lymphopenia. Serological test was positive for HIV.

Problem #2. Pneumocystic carinii pneumonia: The patient underwent bronchoscopy and washings revealed changes consistent with pneumocystic carinii and reactive bronchial cells and pneumocytes. The patient was treated with two weeks of intravenous Septra therapy. However, there was no improvement in his clinical status.

After two weeks of therapy, the patient was still afebrile. His chest x-ray did not improve and WBC count progressively declined to a low of 2.5. The infectious disease service recommended Pentamidine therapy at that point. The patient became afebrile.

Problem #3. Chronic renal failure: The patient's renal failure deteriorated during his hospitalization prior to transfer. Workup was negative and the etiology remains unclear. The patient's renal function remained stable throughout this hospitalization. At the time of transfer, his BUN and creatinine were 50 and 5.0, respectively. He was started on Bicitra therapy to correct the metabolic acidosis felt secondary to his renal failure.

Problem #4. Nephrotic syndrome secondary to renal failure: The patient was found to have edema, hypoalbuminemia, proteinuria, and high triglyceride levels, all consistent with the diagnosis of nephrotic syndrome. The patient did have a renal biopsy done prior to transfer to this hospital and the results per phone report are as follows: interstitial nephritis, no deposits over capillary loops, no immunofluorescence of CMV. The patient was treated with bed rest, a low-sodium, high-protein fluid restriction diet. In spite of this therapy, the patient's albumin level had not improved at the time of transfer.

Problem #5. Chronic normocytic normochromic anemia secondary to external hemorrhoid bleeding. The patient required transfusion of 2 units of packed red blood cells. Otherwise, his hematocrit remained relatively stable throughout the admission. Physical examination revealed swollen hemorrhoids with stool heme negative.

The patient was transferred in stable condition to the local hospital. Medications at the time of transfer were Bicitra, Pentamidine, Restoril, Lorazepam.

Which of the following is the correct ICD-9-CM code assignment for this admission?

a. 042, 136.3, 276.2, 581.89, 585.9, 280.0, 305.61, 305.51, 455.5, 305.1, 33.24, 99.04
b. 042, 136.3, 276.2, 581.89, 585.9, 280.0, 455.5, 33.24, 99.04
c. 042, 136.3, 581.89, 585.9, 280.0, 305.61, 305.51, 305.1, 33.24, 99.04
d. 136.3, 042, 581.89, 585.9, 280.0, 305.61, 305.51, 305.1, 33.24, 99.04

7.23. The following documentation is from the health record of a 2-year-old boy.

Discharge Summary

Admission Date:	7/18/20XX
Discharge Date:	7/20/20XX
Admitting Diagnosis:	Fever of unknown origin
Discharge Diagnosis:	1. Primary herpetic gingivostomatitis 2. Kawasaki's disease 3. Strep pharyngitis

History: The patient is a 2-year-old male who presented to the ER this evening from his primary medical doctor's office with 4 days of fever, rash, cracked lips, and drooling. Mom states that he has had a decreased activity level, decreased p.o. intake, and increased irritability. He has received Tylenol and Motrin® at home. Mom denies vomiting or diarrhea. He has had a sick contact at day care. He also has dysphagia and rhinorrhea.

Past Medical History: Significant for a VSD that has not been repaired. He is followed by a cardiologist and the abnormality is currently stable.

Physical Exam: This young male is quite irritable. He has bulbar conjunctival injection without discharge. His tympanic membranes are dull bilaterally. His tonsils are enlarged. He also has an exudate in his oropharynx. Heart shows regular rate and rhythm with a IV–VI systolic murmur at the left lower sternal border. He has a diffuse maculopapular rash on his lower extremities, trunk, back, and diaper area. He also has perineal desquamation.

Hospital Course: Patient presented to the ER with a 4- to 5-day history of fever, rash, cracked lips, drooling, and sore throat. Due to lymphadenopathy, perineal desquamation, bilateral bulbar conjunctivitis, and rash found on physical exam, he was treated for Kawasaki's disease with IVIG 2 g/kg and aspirin 80 mg per day. He was also tested for herpes due to the perioral, paranasal, and oral lesions. His test came back positive for herpes I virus and he was treated with Kefzol®. Cardiologist performed an echocardiogram to evaluate his VSD. His lesions slowly improved and are largely healed at this time. He remained afebrile for the past 4 nights. His medications were changed to oral form. He is no longer taking antibiotics, and he will be continued on oral acyclovir. Follow-up with cardiologist is in 4 weeks.

Which of the following is the correct code set for this hospitalization?

a. 523.10, 054.9, 745.4, 446.1, 034.0
b. 054.2, 745.4, 034.0, 446.1, 785.6, 372.30, 782.1
c. 054.2, 745.4, 446.1, 034.0
d. 054.2, 446.1, 034.0

7.24. History

The patient is a 78-year-old female who was initially admitted to the intensive care unit for sepsis and urinary tract infection and decreased level of consciousness. After admission to the intensive care unit, the patient was found to have a massive right-sided cerebrovascular accident, which was felt to be secondary to an embolic phenomenon. The patient also had severe mitral regurgitation, moderate tricuspid regurgitation, and aortic insufficiency. CT of the head revealed an acute left middle cerebral arterial infarction involving the temporal and parietal lobes with localized mass effect and mild midline shift. No hemorrhage was seen.

The patient's sepsis was treated with IV antibiotics as was her urinary tract infection. Discussion was undertaken with the patient's next of kin as to the patient's resuscitation status. The patient was made a Do Not Resuscitate. Decision was made to keep the patient comfortable, and she was transferred to a medical bed. The patient's antibiotics were adjusted by an infectious disease group. Her renal failure was followed by nephrology. Neurology was consulted for the patient's cerebrovascular accident. They did an EEG, which showed marked slowing, however, there was no total absence of brain activity. Cardiology consultation was obtained because of new onset atrial fibrillation. Cardiology felt that no aggressive intervention was needed; however, she would be given medicine to control her ventricular rate. The patient remained unresponsive. She was started on tube feeding and her antibiotics were continued. The patient was noted to have some thrombocytopenia as well as her continued renal failure and anemia. Diuresis was attempted with IV diuretics by nephrology in an attempt to help the patient's congestive heart failure. The patient was retaining copious amounts of fluid despite the diuretics. Her prothrombin time eventually normalized. Her blood sugar was elevated, and she was placed on insulin once per day at bedtime to cover her tube feedings. The patient was found without audible or visible respirations and no heart tones. She was pronounced dead at 12:40, and her body was released to the funeral home.

Which of the following code sets would be assigned by the hospital for this admission?

a. 038.9, 995.91, 599.0, 434.11, 394.1, 397.0, 398.91, 427.31, 287.5, 285.9
b. 995.91, 599.0, 586, 434.11, 424.0, 397.0, 428.0, 427.31, 287.5, 285.9
c. 038.9, 995.92, 599.0, 586, 434.11, 396.3, 397.0, 398.91, 427.31, 287.5, 285.9
d. 434.11, 038.9, 995.92, 586, 428.0, 424.0, 397.0, 427.31, 287.5, 285.9

Optional MS-DRG Exercise (for users with access to MS-DRG software or tables)

What is the correct MS-DRG for this case?

a. 064, Intracranial Hemorrhage or Cerebral Infarction with MCC
b. 871, Septicemia without mechanical ventilation 96+ hours with MCC
c. 872, Septicemia without mechanical ventilation 96+ hours without MCC
d. 868, Other Infectious and Parasitic Disease Diagnoses with CC

7.25.   Discharge Diagnosis

1. *Escherichia coli* and *Staphylococcus aureus* urinary tract infection with sepsis
2. Sepsis syndrome
3. Advanced dementia
4. Hypothroidism
5. Hypertension
6. Protein calorie malnutrition
7. Dysphagia

Discharge Medications: Levoxyl® 88mcg p.o. q. a.m., Paxil® 20mg p.o. q. a.m., Namenda® 10mg p.o. q. a.m., and Ativan® .5 q. 8 hours agitation, Augmentin 500 mg p.o. b.i.d. for 15 days, and Megace® 400 mg p.o. b.i.d.

Discharge Disposition: Improved and home with home healthcare.

History of Present Illness: The patient is an 85-year-old female who was apparently brought into the emergency room by her family this evening for multiple problems. According to the family, she has not been eating recently and has been getting extremely weak. She has not been unable to stand without assistance for quite some time now. The patient, although awake and alert, will not answer any questions. All history is obtained from the computer records, as well as the ER staff and ER physician. Initial workup reveals significant urinary tract infection. She is also most likely septic secondary to her presentation given her hypotension and acute encephalopathy.

Laboratory/Radiology: Admission labs significant for a white blood cell count of 9.8, hemoglobin 14.9, platelets of 328,000 with a BUN of 29 and creatinine of 1.4. Urinalysis was small bilirubin, 15 mg ketones, large blood, 100 mg protein, positive nitrates, large leukocytes, and too many WBCs to count, with many bacteria and many red cells. CT of the head was normal. Portable chest x-ray showed hyperexpanded lung fields but no mass.

Hospital Course: The patient was admitted to the general medical floor with the diagnosis of sepsis. After discussion with family, she was made DNR III and was hydrated and started on IV ciprofloxacin. She has a significant advanced dementia and does not speak but was somewhat more encephalopathic secondary to her sepsis, and this improved to her baseline. Her BUN and creatinine normalized, and she was continued on her usual medications for dementia. Her hydrochlorothiazide was held, but she was continued on her Toprol. Levoxyl was held and a TSH was within normal limits. She was continued on her Paxil. Subsequently, her urine culture grew out *E. coli,* pan sensitive and *S. aureus,* pan sensitive, and she was changed from ciprofloxacin to Augmentin 500 mg p.o. b.i.d., which she tolerated well. Speech therapy was consulted, and an MBS was performed. Diet with thin liquids was recommended. She does have protein calorie malnutrition.

Disposition: The daughter has been contacted because the patient is stable for discharge. She is discharged to her daughter's care with physical and occupational therapy.

Code Assignment including POA indicator:

Principal Diagnosis: _____

Secondary Diagnosis: _____

Behavioral Health Conditions

7.26. In the following case scenario, a 26-year-old white male was admitted after being transferred from the outpatient evaluation service with severe homicidal and suicidal ideation. Admitting diagnosis was severe major depressive disorder with psychotic features. Pharmacologic treatment was initiated and suicide precautions were instituted. After a thorough psychologic evaluation, the risks and benefits of ECT were reviewed. Due to the severity of the psychotic episode and the patient's delusional state, it was determined that ECT was warranted. Extensive efforts were made to secure informed consent from the patient, and a course of ECT was begun.

ECT was administered three times per week, and the course of therapy was completed in a 3-week period. On the fourth treatment of ECT, postictal observation was notable for cardiac arrhythmia, which subsided without sequelae. Otherwise, the patient tolerated the therapy well and responded quickly with resolution of the psychotic features and overall improvement in the acute phase of his depressive disorder. Suicide precautions could be lifted after the fifth treatment with ECT. After establishing adequate therapeutic levels of lithium, the patient was discharged to be managed as an outpatient.

Discharge Diagnosis: Severe major depressive disorder with suicidal ideation, stabilized after a course of ECT.

Which is the correct code set for reporting this case scenario?

a. 296.24, V62.84, 94.27, 94.22, 94.08
b. 296.23, V62.84, 94.27, 94.22, 94.08
c. 296.24, V62.84, 427.9, 94.26, 94.22, 94.08
d. 296.23, V62.84, 997.1, 427.9, 94.27, 94.22, 94.08

7.27.   The following documentation is from the health record of a 56-year-old male patient.

Final Diagnosis

Axis I: Chronic schizophrenia, paranoid type with acute exacerbation, improved
Axis II: None
Axis III: Cardiomyopathy secondary to hypertension
            COPD
            Type II diabetes mellitus
Axis IV: Psychosocial and environmental stressors are severe
Axis V: Admission GAF 25 to 30
            Discharge GAF 55

Physical Examination: For pertinent findings on medical examination, see the medical doctor's dictation.

Pertinent Laboratory Results: Electrolyte panel within normal limits. Digoxin level was 0.6, hemoglobin A1C 6.5, triglycerides 138, CBC unremarkable. TSH 1.3, urinalysis negative. EKG showed normal sinus rhythm.

Hospital Course: This is a 56-year-old male who was admitted due to decompensating at his apartment where he thought people were trying to get into his apartment, and he continued to decompensate with his paranoia and persecutory-type delusions, so that it was felt he needed longer hospitalization. During this time he also switched his medications from Zyprexa® to Seroquel® to Risperdal®, and then he was admitted on Prolixin®. We reviewed his records, and it appears he did quite well on Risperdal so he went back to taking that, and he was titrated up to 30 mg q. h.s. of Risperdal and 100 mg of trazodone. These two medications helped significantly to eliminate his delusions and paranoid ideation. He slept better. Patient started going on therapeutic passes that went well. His sister reports that he is doing the best that she has seen him in quite some time. During his stay here his mother passed away from a long medical illness, and he was able to go to the funeral and dealt with that loss in an appropriate way. He continued to show improvement and was placed on Level E. He continued to go to psychosocial programming. A discharge meeting was held, and it was agreed that he could get most of his services through the outpatient program. It was felt by everyone that the patient was stable enough to be discharged, and discharge was scheduled.

Pertinent Findings on Mental Status at Discharge: 45 minutes spent in the final examination with the patient. Appearance: Pleasant, white male who looks his stated age. Behavior is cooperative, fair eye contact. Speech is of normal rate and volume. Not rapid or pressured. Mood euthymic, affect appropriate. Thought process is goal directed, decreased paranoid ideation. Negative for racing thoughts and flight of ideas. Thought content: He denies signs of active psychosis, denies current suicidal or homicidal intent. Insight and judgment improved. Impulse control is fair.

Prognosis: Fair. The main problem is that the patient is on so many medications for his medical problems. He did do well with the pill organizer and self-medications, but his mental illness may be exacerbated if his medical conditions are not well controlled.

Discharge Medications: Digoxin .25 mg q. d, Glucotrol® 2.5 mg a.m. and 7.5 mg q. 5:00 pm, potassium 10 mEq q. a.m., Spironolactone 25 mg q. a.m., an aspirin 325 mg q. a.m., Lasix 10 mg q. d., lisopril 2.5 mg q. d., Atrovent inhaler two puffs q. i.d., isosorbide dinitrate 10 mg t.i.d., beclomethasone inhaler 4 puffs b.i.d., Risperdal 3 mg q. h.s., Colace 100 mg b.i.d., and trazodone 100 mg q. h.s.

Aftercare Recommendations: The patient will be discharged to his apartment. Social services will follow the patient. He will follow up with a psychiatrist and medical care through the outpatient program. Also, a home health nurse will come to see the patient.

Which of the following code sets is correct for reporting this inpatient hospitalization?

a. 295.34, 425.4, 401.9, 496, 250.01, 94.25
b. 295.32, 402.90, 496, 250.01, 94.25
c. 295.34, 402.90, 496, 250.00, 94.25
d. 295.84, 402.90, 496, 250.00, 94.25

7.28. The following documentation is from the health record of a 17-year-old male patient.

History of Present Illness: The patient is a 17-year-old white male who was brought to the ED after being found passed out in the town park. The patient was in restraints and accompanied by two police officers. The patient was combative and aggressive, threatening physical harm to himself as well as the physician and hospital staff. The patient has a long history of alcohol and drug abuse, was in the local treatment center, and walked off campus 2 days ago.

Allergies:	NKDA
PMH:	Attention deficit hyperactivity disorder (ADHD), drug and alcohol dependence, aggressive behavior
Family History:	Noncontributory
ROS:	As above

Physical Examination: Vital signs: Temp. 100.1 degrees; BP 144/88 mm Hg; General: Alternating between lethargy and combativeness; HEENT: Pupils pinpoint, 1 mm bilaterally; Skin: Cool, clammy to touch, feet and hands cold, slightly diaphoretic; Heart: Rate tachy, no murmurs; Lungs: Clear, respiratory rate 28 and shallow; Abdomen: Benign; Neurological: Mental status as above; follows commands inconsistently, responds to voice; cranial nerves: pupils as noted, gag intact; Motor: Moving all four extremities with equal power; Sensory: Responds to touch in all four extremities; deep tendon reflexes +3 throughout, but plantar reflexes down going bilaterally.

Laboratory: U/A shows 2+ blood, done after Foley catheter was placed; drug screen positive for amphetamines; ETOH 0.30; ABG within normal limits; EKG sinus tachycardia.

Hospital Course: Family was contacted, IV fluids were initiated, and the patient was admitted to ICU with suicide protocol, Ativan 1 to 2 mg IV q. 2 hours p.r.n. He was maintained on soft restraints with checks every 15 minutes and monitored with telemetry and neuro checks through the night. By the morning he was no longer tachycardic. By hospital day 3 he was medically stable, but still saying he wants to "kill himself." Psychiatric consult requested; see dictated report.

Disposition: Discharge to psych. Psychiatric liaison service agreed to accept him in transfer to the inpatient adolescent psychiatric unit at children's hospital.

Discharge Diagnoses: Drug overdose with amphetamines and alcohol
Apparent suicide attempt
Continued verbalization of suicidal ideation

Which of the following code sets would be correct for this case?

a. 969.7, 785.0, 304.40, E950.3, 980.0, 303.00, E950.9, 314.01, 312.00
b. 785.0, E939.7, 305.90, 314.01, 312.00
c. 969.7, 785.0, 304.00, E980.3, 303.00, 314.01, 312.00
d. 785.0, 303.00, 304.40, 969.7, E950.3, 980.0, E950.9, 314.01, 312.00

Disorders of the Musculoskeletal System and Connective Tissue

7.29.   The following documentation is from the health record of a 42-year-old male patient.

Discharge Summary

Hospital Course: This is a 42-year-old male admitted through the ED with a right thumb crush injury, the result of a farm accident. See ED report and admitting H&P for details of the accident. The patient was admitted and taken to surgery for repair. Postoperative course was uncomplicated.

Prognosis: Long-term prognosis is mixed because of the severity of injury. The patient had severe crush injury and is at high risk for partial- or full-thickness skin loss, entire loss of thumb, stiffness, osteoarthritis, sepsis, osteomyelitis, septic arthritis, and generalized dysfunction of thumb. The patient may require further reconstructive surgery at a later date. Discharge medications include Lortab® 5 p.r.n., Anaprox® DS prn for pain, and Duricef® 500 mg for infection. The patient will be followed in my office in three to five days.

Discharge Diagnoses: Right thumb crush injury
Open fracture of proximal phalanx
Pollicis longus tendon transection

Operative Report

Pre- and Postoperative Diagnosis: Right thumb crush injury

1. Open articular fracture of head of proximal phalanx
2. Extensor pollicis longus tendon transection

Procedure Details: The patient was taken to the operating room. Given preoperatively 1g of Ancef® and 80 mg of tobramycin IV in the emergency room. Axillary block was previously administered, as well as a standard metacarpal block, by myself. Standard prep and drape was done. The extremity was exsanguinated and tourniquet was inflated to 250 mm Hg. The entire procedure was performed with 3.5 loupe magnification.

The complex, radially based laceration was opened, vigorously irrigated with normal saline and bacitracin. Neurovascular bundle identified, visualized, and noted to be intact, though contused. Laceration was extended dorsally to facilitate exposure. Because of the complexity of the fracture, the entire fracture was opened. Fracture site was irrigated and debrided. Fracture site was curetted. Multiple loose bone fragments were removed. The linear complex radial intra-articular fracture was stabilized to the proximal ulnar fracture with 0.35 crossed K-wires, resulting in excellent bony fixation. The split T-condylar fracture was then anatomically reduced and transfixed with transverse 0.35 K-wires. Anatomic reduction of the articular surface was achieved. This was confirmed clinically and then with intraoperative AP and lateral C-arm. Fracture was clinically stable and anatomically reduced.

The area was irrigated with normal saline with bacitracin again. All potential bleeders were electrocauterized. The distal interphalangeal joint was stabilized in 0 degrees of extension with a 0.45 K-wire that was originally driven retrograde followed by antegrade with excellent purchase. Extensor pollicis longus was formally repaired with interrupted 4-0 MERSILENE® followed by 6-0 nylon epitenon repair. Strong anatomic repair was achieved. The area was again irrigated. Skin was closed with interrupted 4-0 and 5-0 nylon with no skin loss.

At this point, the hand was cleansed with hydrogen peroxide. Proximal metacarpal and median nerve block was performed with 0.5 percent Marcaine. The hand was then further dressed with Neosporin®, Adaptic®, 4×4, 1-inch TubeGauz®. A complex static volar splint was then applied, which was forearm based and covering the thumb. Tourniquet was released. Patient tolerated the procedure well and was transferred to the recovery room in stable condition. Estimated blood loss was none.

Which of the following is the correct ICD-9-CM code assignment?

a. 816.01, 813.18, 79.24, 79.22
b. 816.01, 813.08, 79.34, 79.32, 82.45
c. 927.3, 816.11, 813.18, 79.24, 79.22, 82.45
d. 927.3, 816.11, 813.18, 79.34, 79.32, 82.45

Optional MS-DRG Exercise (for users with access to MS-DRG software or tables)

What is the correct MS-DRG for this case?

Which MDC does this MS-DRG belong to? _____

7.30.   The following documentation is from the health record of a 29-year-old male patient.

Discharge Summary

Hospital Course: This is a 29-year-old white male who was involved in a motor vehicle accident on 11/21 and initially taken to Care Community Hospital and thought to have a T6–7 paraplegia at that time. CT of the head was ordered at that time, but apparently not done. The patient was transferred here for further treatment and evaluation. On evaluation here, a fracture at C7 was indeed noted. Evaluation revealed a C7 quadriplegic, Frankel B, with a neurogenic bladder. The patient apparently was already in traction and that was maintained on admission here. There is no mention in the chart of plane x-ray abnormalities at that time, and he was subsequently scheduled for an MRI and CT scan. The patient was also placed on steroid protocol and sub-q heparin, as well as sequential compression hose.

Urology consultation was also obtained, as well as neurosurgical consultation. MRI was done on 11/22, which showed a decreased amount of cord C7, which suggested a central cord contusion and also a ventral defect at C6–7. CT contrast also showed a diffuse ventral lesion at C5–6; however, there was no displacement of the cord, and no cord encasement was identified, so decompression of the cord was not recommended by neurosurgery. The patient was continued on pain medications as needed, and traction via the halo placed at Care Community Hospital was maintained.

An odontoid fracture was also identified on plane films on flexion and extension of the neck. A halo vest was applied, and traction was discontinued on 11/28. X-rays were taken, and good fracture alignment was obtained at that time. Follow-up films were again taken, and, on 12/11, displacement of the odontoid fracture was noted. The halo itself was repositioned the following day on 12/12. Good position was initially confirmed by x-ray; however, after 2 days' time, the fracture had redisplaced. Once again, the halo was readjusted on 12/14. On review of films on 12/16, for the second time, again, the odontoid had displaced from its initially reduced position. Surgery was recommended for stabilization of the odontoid fracture; however, the patient initially refused to have this done. After several days of encouragement, the patient finally consented to surgery, which was performed on 12/21. He had posterior cervical wiring and fusion with a left iliac crest bone graft C1 to C2. He had no intraoperative complications and was followed postoperatively. He experienced no neurologic changes and had a well-healed surgical incision. Follow-up x-rays postoperatively showed good alignment and stable fixation of the fracture. The patient's course was undergoing full-team evaluation and treatment. At this time, nutrition was concerned and good p.o. intake was stressed. Other services were also working with him, including a speech pathologist, who was working with him for difficulty swallowing. He was maintained in the halo postoperatively after his fusion, and this was checked periodically.

The hospital course was complicated by several episodes of urinary tract infection that were addressed by practitioners from urology. He was placed on antibiotics for these problems. The patient also had one episode of vomiting coffee ground emesis on 1/24. This was treated with antacids and n.p.o. for a temporary period of time. His hemoglobin and hematocrit levels were checked and were stable.

On 1/25, the patient was noted to have some left scrotal swelling. Ultrasound of the testicles was done, and diagnosis of epididymitis was obtained. This was followed by practitioners from infectious disease and urology, who placed him on appropriate antibiotics, which were later switched to p.o. Cipro. Organism was Pseudomonas. After a few days, this resolved, and he had no further sequelae from his epididymitis.

Follow-up x-rays continued to show good reduction and healing of the fracture. His halo vest was discontinued on 2/14, and he was then maintained on a hard collar for approximately 2 weeks. It was then later removed on 2/25. The patient continued in a full rehabilitation program during this time. The patient's hospitalization at this point was getting fairly lengthy, and he was becoming impatient with his rehab and did not cooperate with his therapist, as his discharge date was pushed back some; however, he began to be more cooperative and did show a better attitude in meeting his goals. He continued with his rehab and did relatively well, meeting the majority of his goals, however not doing this willingly sometimes. He was subsequently discharged to home on 4/12 to the care of his mother. He will be followed as an outpatient in the clinic at 8 weeks postdischarge.

Final Diagnoses: Cervical fracture at C-6/7 with central cord contusion and a ventral defect
C7 Quadriplegic, Frankel B, with neurogenic bladder
Odontoid fracture, C1
UTI
Epididymitis

Procedures: Posterior cervical wiring and fusion with a left iliac crest bone graft C1 to C2
Traction maintenance with halo previously placed

Which of the following is the correct ICD-9-CM code assignment?

a. 806.00, E819.9, 344.61, 599.0, 787.20, 604.90, 041.7, 81.01, 93.41, 02.94
b. 806.09, 805.01, E819.9, 344.61, 599.0, 604.90, 81.01, 93.41, 02.94
c. 806.08, 805.01, E819.9, 344.61, 599.0, 787.20, 604.90, 041.7, 81.00, 93.42
d. 806.08, 806.07, 805.01, E819.9, 344.61, 599.0, 787.20, 604.90, 041.7, 81.01, 93.41

7.31. The following documentation is from the health record of an ORIF patient.

Operative Report

Preoperative Diagnosis: Displaced comminuted fracture of the lateral condyle, right elbow

Postoperative Diagnosis: Same

Procedure: Open reduction, internal fixation

Description: The patient, with malignant hypertension and type I diabetes mellitus, was anesthetized and prepped with Betadine, sterile drapes were applied, and the pneumatic tourniquet was inflated around the arm. An incision was made in the area of the lateral epicondyle through a Steri-Drape, and this was carried through subcutaneous tissue, and the fracture site was easily exposed. Inspection revealed the fragment to be rotated in two planes about 90 degrees. It was possible to manually reduce this quite easily, and the judicious manipulation resulted in an almost anatomic reduction. This was fixed with two pins driven across the humerus. These pins were cut off below skin level. The wound was closed with some plain catgut subcutaneously and 5-0 nylon in the skin. Dressings were applied to the patient and tourniquet released. A long arm cast was applied.

Which of the following is the correct ICD-9-CM code assignment?

a. 812.52, 401.9, 250.01, 79.32
b. 812.42, 401.0, 250.01, 79.31
c. 812.42, 401.0, 250.01, 78.52
d. 812.52, 401.9, 250.00, 79.32

7.32. Discharge Summary

Admission Date: November 15, 20XX

Discharge Date: November 20, 20XX

Description: The patient is a 49-year-old male who was admitted on November 15. He underwent revision laminectomy and stabilization of his lumbar spine with a Dynesys® system. The patient tolerated the procedure well and had an uneventful hospital course, except experienced acute pain after the surgery requiring additional physical therapy and pain control.

By postoperative day 5, he was tolerating a regular diet, had obtained pain control, and cleared physical therapy. He was subsequently discharged home with written instructions. He is to follow up in 3 weeks after discharge. He was given Percocet® and Flexeril® for pain and spasms, as needed.

History and Physical

Admit Diagnosis: Recurrent herniated disc

Procedure: Lumbar laminectomy, disc stabilization with Dynesys

History of Present Illness: Forty-nine-year-old male with left leg and back pain. Diagnosed with recurrent disc herniation

Past Medical History: Status post laminectomy and diskectomy 2 years ago

Physical Examination

Neck: Supple

Heart: Regular rate and rhythm

Lungs: Clear to auscultation

Neuro: Left leg weakness, numbness and pain

Skin: No lesions, masses or rashes

Assessment and Plan: Recurrent HNP L5 to S1

Operative Report

Preoperative Diagnosis: Radiculopathy and degenerative disc disease at L5–S1 with recurrent disc herniation at L5–S1

Postoperative Diagnosis: Same

Procedure Performed: Revision L5 laminectomy, revision S1 laminectomy and diskectomy, stabilization of L5 to S1 with flexible rod Dynesys system.

Anesthesia: General

Blood Loss: Minimal

Complications: Intraoperative dural tear, which was repaired with watertight seal with interrupted 4-0 Nurolon® sutures.

Description of the Procedure: Under sterile conditions, the patient was brought to the operating room and was placed under general endotracheal anesthesia and placed in a prone position. Lumbar spine was then prepped and draped in the usual sterile manner with a Betadine prep. A lateral x-ray was obtained with an 18-gauge spinal needle placed for level localization. Based upon the x-ray, a direct posterior approach to the lumbar spine was performed. This was carried down to the transverse process of L5 and the sacral ala bilaterally. After adequate exposure, complete laminectomy was performed in a subperiosteal fashion with a combination Leksell and Kerrison rongeurs at the L5 and S1 levels. Mobilization of the left S1 and L5 nerve roots was performed, although there was a significant amount of scar tissue. There was a large free L5-S1 recurrent disc fragment, which was removed with a pituitary rongeur. There was a small dural tear within the axilla of the L5 nerve root repaired with watertight seal with interrupted 4-0 Nurolon® sutures. After adequate decompression, attention was brought to stabilization. Using the usual internal and external landmarks, pedicle screws were placed in the L5 and S1 pedicles bilaterally. These were drilled, probed, dilated, and then a combination of 7.2 × 40 mm screws and 7.2 mm by 45 mm screws were placed in the L5 and S1 pedicles bilaterally. AP and lateral x-rays were obtained, noting appropriate placement of the screws. Measuring of the cord device was performed bilaterally. The cord was placed in the usual fashion, tensioned and then finally tightened. The wound was copiously irrigated with bacitracin solution. No drain was utilized. The fascia was closed with interrupted 0 VICRYL® suture. The subcutaneous tissue and skin were closed in three sequential layers. The patient was awakened in the operating room, extubated, and brought to the recovery room in satisfactory condition.

Code Assignment including POA indicator:

Principal diagnosis: _____

Additional diagnoses: _____

Procedures: _____

Neoplasms

7.33. In the following scenario, the discharge summary states: The patient is a 67-year-old male with cancer of the prostate 3 years ago, which was treated with prostatectomy and radiation therapy. He has also been diagnosed with metastases to the testes and the lymph nodes in the groin. He has been having increasingly severe lower back pain, and a recent radioisotope bone scan showed a "hot" spot in the lower lumbar vertebrae. The patient was admitted five days ago through the ED, complaining of severe lower back pain upon getting out of bed that day. Lumbar x-ray revealed fracture of the L4 vertebrae. The patient was admitted and placed in Buck's traction for 24 hours in an attempt to relieve his pain, which was unsuccessful. MRI the next day also revealed metastasis to the spinal cord and vertebrae at the L4 fracture site. The patient was begun on MS Contin® to relieve pain, and arrangements were made for transfer to a skilled nursing facility for palliative care. Hospice services were offered to the patient and family.

Which of the following code sets would be correct for reporting the diagnoses in this scenario?

a. 198.5, 733.13, 198.3, 198.82, 196.5, 185
b. 198.3, 805.4, 198.5, 198.82, 196.5, V10.46
c. 805.4, 198.5, 198.3, 198.82, 196.5, 185
d. 733.13, 198.5, 198.3, 198.82, 196.5, V10.46

Optional MS-DRG Exercise (for users with access to MS-DRG software or tables)

1. Recall the UHDDS definition of the principal diagnosis. What is the principal diagnosis on this case? _____

2. What is the correct MS-DRG assignment? _____

3. If this patient had any additional complications/comorbidities, would it change the MS-DRG assignment and why or why not? _____

_____

7.34. The following documentation is from the health record of a 72-year-old male patient.

Discharge Summary

History of Present Illness: This 72-year-old male was admitted with shortness of breath. The patient had a prior history of right pleuritic chest pain in January, with a chest x-ray that showed right pleural reaction and mass versus infiltrate on the right. The episode of pain resolved. A follow-up chest x-ray in March showed a decrease in the lung infiltrates, as well as a small bleb not seen on prior films. Over the 3 to 4 days prior to admission, the patient complained of increasing shortness of breath, dyspnea on exertion, sweats, and myalgias at the legs and arms, with decreased p.o. intake and abdominal soreness. The patient also had chills once in a while. He denied cough, sputum, and chest pain. There was no nausea, vomiting, diarrhea, or constipation, and there was no dysuria. He was a former 50-pack/year smoker.

Physical Examination: Heart rate 96 to 104, respiratory rate 30 to 36, temperature 96 po, blood pressure 115/80. Neck showed no nodes or jugular venous distention. Lungs showed resonant breath sounds equally with left basilar rales. Back was nontender. Heart tones are S1 and S2 with a I/VI systolic murmur. Abdomen was soft and he had positive bowel sounds. The patient had positive right upper quadrant and epigastric tenderness with no rebound or guarding. There was a liver edge palpable at 1 to 2 cm below the right costal margin. Extremities showed no edema, and there was a darkish/bluish tinge to the lips. Neuro: Patient was alert, oriented, and grossly intact. The patient was admitted to the hospital with respiratory distress, left-sided rales, and pallor. Primary consideration at that time was given to infection (pulmonary) versus exacerbation of chronic obstructive pulmonary disease.

Lab Data: Admission blood values were obtained and showed a white blood cell count of 14,600 with 83 bands and 10 lymphs. Hemoglobin was 12, hematocrit 36. Platelet count was 430,000. Initial Profile I was within normal limits except for a CO PO_2 of 21, BUN of 36, and glucose of 145. Initial Profile II was remarkable only for an albumin of 3.3. Chest x-ray was obtained, which showed cardiomegaly with no infiltrate or masses seen. Blood gases obtained showed a pH of 7.46, PCO_2 of 22, and PO_2 of 63 on room air. A CT scan of the chest was obtained, which showed mediastinal adenopathy and a right-sided mass; massive acute pericardial effusion was also visualized.

Hospital Course: The patient had an emergency consultation with Cardiology. An echocardiogram was obtained that showed acute pericardial effusion. The patient was seen by thoracic surgery, and a percutaneous drainage of the malignant pericardial effusion was performed. With drainage, the patient received almost immediate symptomatic improvement in his dyspnea and chest discomfort. Over the next few days, his dyspnea remained stable, he had no more epigastric pain, and there was improvement in his abdominal exam. Pericardial fluid cytology showed an undifferentiated carcinoma. Once the patient was stabilized, he had a pericardial window placed, as well as a bronchoscopy with transbronchial biopsy, which was interpreted as adenocarcinoma of the lung. He subsequently received a course of chemotherapy with mitomycin, Velban®, and platinum. This was tolerated without major difficulty. The patient was discharged hemodynamically stable; to be seen in the office.

Final Diagnoses: 1. Adenocarcinoma of the lung
2. Acute pericardial effusion
3. Chronic obstructive pulmonary disease

Code Assignment including POA indicator:

Principal diagnosis: _____

Additional diagnoses: _____

Procedures: _____

Issues to clarify: _____

Optional MS-DRG Exercise (for users with access to MS-DRG software or tables)

Which of the following is the correct MS-DRG assignment for this case?

a. 164, Major chest procedures with CC
b. 167, Other respiratory system OR procedures with CC
c. 163, Major chest procedures with MCC
d. 181, Respiratory neoplasms with CC

7.35.   The following documentation is from the health record of a 71-year-old female patient.

Discharge Summary

History of Present Illness: This patient is a 71-year-old female with carcinoma of the left breast. She was admitted for reexcision of the left breast mass and left axillary dissection with mirror image biopsy of the right breast. The patient has a history of hypertension, COPD, heavy smoker, and chronic alcohol dependence. She was in her usual state of health until December, when she noted a lump in her left breast that was painless, without discharge, without retraction. Mammography was reportedly within normal limits. The patient was followed closely.

During recheck in July, a repeat mammography revealed a mass in the left breast with calcifications. The patient underwent an excisional biopsy of the left breast mass, which was positive for in situ intraductal and lobular carcinoma. The initial biopsy specimen showed a positive margin. The patient is, therefore, admitted at this time for extended excision of the left breast. Mirror image biopsy of the right breast and a left axillary lymph node resection are also to be done.

The patient had menarche at age 12 and has given birth to a single child. The patient has no family history of breast carcinoma. Past medical history: Positive for hypertension and chronic obstructive bronchitis. Medications include: Aldomet®, 250 mg p.o. b.i.d.; Dyazide®, one p.o. b.i.d.; Theo-Dur; Premarin; and Provera®. Otherwise unremarkable.

Physical Examination: Exam revealed a well-developed, well-nourished female in no apparent distress. The vital signs are stable, afebrile. The HEENT examination is within normal limits. The neck is supple, the trachea is midline. There are no masses or adenopathy present. The lungs are clear to auscultation and percussion. The cardiovascular examination is within normal limits. The left breast shows a contusion with overlying skin incision and surrounding erythema. The right breast is within normal limits. The right axilla is normal without adenopathy. The left axilla reveals small (less than 1 cm), nonfixed, not matted lymph nodes. The abdominal examination is within normal limits. The rectal examination is normal, with guaiac negative stool present in the vault.

Hospital Course: After adequate preoperative preparation, the patient was taken to the operating room. A left breast excision was performed with left axillary lymph node excision. A right breast local excision was performed for the indication of lobular carcinoma in situ of the left breast. The patient's postoperative course was unremarkable.

The patient is discharged with a large Jackson-Pratt in place, continuing to drain from the left axilla. She is on a regular diet. The patient will be followed up in general surgery clinic. Pathology: Small residual of in situ intraductal lobular carcinoma, left breast. Negative nodes in right breast.

Final Diagnoses: 1. Carcinoma left breast
2. Chronic bronchitis
3. Hypertension

Procedures: 1. Local excision, right breast
2. Simple excision of left breast with left axillary lymph node dissection

Which of the following is the most accurate ICD-9-CM code assignment?

a. 233.0, 491.9, 401.9, 85.41, 40.23, 85.12
b. 174.9, 491.20, 401.9, 305.1, 303.90, 85.43, 85.21
c. 233.0, 491.20, 401.9, 305.1, 303.90, 85.43, 85.21
d. 174.9, 491.9, 401.9, 85.41, 40.23, 85.21

7.36. The following documentation is from the health record of a 72-year-old male patient.

Discharge Summary

History of Present Illness: The patient is a 72-year-old male with a history of abdominal perineal resection for colon cancer in 1985 and left hemicolectomy in 1995 for splenic flexure recurrence of cancer. Subsequent right nephrectomy, right adrenalectomy, right posterior hepatic wedge resection in February for metastatic colon carcinoma. The patient is admitted with complaints of lower back pain and bilateral thigh pain for 2 months, increasing in intensity.

Physical Examination: Examination on admission: temperature 99°F, pulse 72, respirations 24, blood pressure 150/90. The examination was remarkable for left lower quadrant colostomy from previous operation, mildly tender lumbar spine, and the patient was barely able to stand. It was also noted that the patient had decreased sharp/dull discrimination on the neural examination of the lateral thighs.

Laboratory Data: On admission the laboratory values were: Urinalysis: Specific gravity 1.021, pH 5; chem. tests were negative; nitrite negative; blood negative, 12 white cells, moderate bacteria. The clinical chemistry results were: Serum sodium 141, BUN 42, potassium 4.9, chloride 104, CO_2 28, glucose 99, creatinine 1.8, SGOT 12, SGPT 16, alkaline phosphatase 68, total protein 6.6, albumin 3.8, total bilirubin 0.7, direct bilirubin 0.0, GGT 87, calcium 10.3, magnesium 2.0, phosphorus 3.2, uric acid 5.7, PT 12.9, PTT 28.4, white blood cell count 8.0, hemoglobin 15.0, hematocrit 43.8, platelets 223,000. The CEA level was noted to be 508 nanograms per mL on admission. Metastatic workup for the colon carcinoma revealed no evidence of metastatic disease to the head or the thoracic and cervical spine.

Radiologic Studies: CT and MRI revealed left celiac ganglion node plexus enlarged, diagnosed as metastasis. Multiple small lung nodules, bilaterally, suspicious for metastasis. Pathological fractures of L2 and L4, with compression of L2, effacement of the spinal canal space and apparent cord compression at the L2 level. Subsequent urine culture grew out greater than 10 to the 5th *Pseudomonas aeruginosa,* which was sensitive to ciprofloxacin. The patient was treated for this UTI with ciprofloxacin 500 mg p.o. q. 8 hours and subsequent urine culture showed no growth.

Hospital Course: The patient went to the operating room for L2 laminectomy with decompression and anterior allograft bone fusion. The patient fell 3 days after surgery while ambulating without significant injuries. Further physical therapy was marked by continued improvement in ambulation with walker and no further setbacks. Clinically, the patient is afebrile without signs and symptoms of infection, no CVA tenderness, and no dysuria. The patient will be discharged home today. Condition on discharge fairly good.

Treatment: The patient will go home on Vicodin p.o. q 4 to 6 hours for pain, and Capoten®. He will resume Capoten b.i.d. dosing per his internist's recommendations for his hypertension, 25 p.o. b.i.d. Prognosis: The long-term prognosis is poor as the patient has extensive metastatic colon CA; short-term prognosis is fairly good with improvement in ambulation. Ambulation is with walker assistance. Follow-up: The patient will return to see me next Wednesday.

Final Diagnoses: Metastatic colon cancer to lung and bone
Pathologic fracture of L2 secondary to metastasis, with cord compression

Code Assignment including POA indicator:

Principal diagnosis: _____

Additional diagnoses: _____

Procedures: _____

7.37.   The following documentation is from the health record of a 59-year-old cancer patient.

History and Physical Examination

Present Illness: The patient is a 59-year-old female admitted with a diagnosis of seizure disorder and acute seizure. This patient's illness began last year when she was diagnosed with a metastatic lesion in her brain, which was a metastatic hypernephroma from her kidney. She had the isolated metastasis removed surgically, had been on Tegretol since then, but she has only been taking her nighttime dosages. The dosages she felt kind of wiped her out a little bit. She then was scheduled for renal surgery but developed chest pain, and a coronary angiogram revealed severe three-vessel disease, inoperable and not a candidate for any kind of surgical procedure. Since then her treatment has been expectant with treatment of chemotherapy per usual protocols. She did not have any radiation to the brain previously. Her CT scan in the ER last night was showing some questionable areas.

Past Medical History: She has had the metastatic lesion to the head, renal carcinoma, and severe coronary artery disease. She had no prior surgeries or illnesses.

Review of Systems: Was doing well until yesterday, but she was taking the treatment and taking her Tegretol mainly at night. Her level was 5.9 where 8 or 9 is therapeutic.

Family History: She is adopted but has a brother. She is divorced with two children. She is living with her daughter. She is on disability from work. She was employed actively.

Physical Examination: She is a well-developed, well-nourished, white female.

Heent: Negative

Neck: No bruits

Chest: Clear

Heart: Regular sinus rhythm

Abdomen: Soft; no masses

Pelvic/Rectal: Deferred at this time

Extremities: Negative

Neurologic: Negative. At this time, the daughter states that her right leg and arm stiffened out during her seizure.

Impression(s): Seizure disorder secondary to metastatic renal to brain. She is to get an MRI done today, and we are going to increase dosage to the Tegretol. I think she can go home and if she does have metastatic lesion, she will probably need to have radiation done and will be set up through a radiation oncologist whom I think has been consulted previously on her condition.

Discharge Summary

Admission Date:	06/01/XX
Discharge Date:	06/03/XX
Consultants:	1. Oncologist
	2. Neurosurgeon

Discharge Diagnosis:

1. Convulsion, secondary to malignant neoplasm of the brain secondary to a hypernephroma.

Hospital Course: The patient was seen by the neurosurgeon, who felt conservative management was needed. She is going to begin radiation treatment to her head. This will be done as an outpatient in order to control the metastatic disease to the brain.

Discharge Medications/Instructions: She was discharged home on:

1. Lopressor 50 mg each morning.
2. Decadron 4 mg twice a day.
3. Tegretol 200 t.i.d. Her Tegretol level was a little low at the time of admission.

So, she will be followed then to begin radiation treatment on Monday for follow-up there.

Consultation

Physical Examination: She is a well-developed, well-nourished white female with partial baldness to the right side of her head. Her neck exam reveals turbulence transmitted from the thorax bilaterally to both carotids. On lung exam there were no crackles or wheezes and her respiratory effort is normal. Cardiac exam reveals S1 and S2 to be physiologic with no S3 or S4 gallop. There is a murmur at the left ventricular apex most compatible with a flow murmur. The apex is not well palpated. She has no gallop or rub appreciated. Abdominal exam is supple without organomegaly. The back exam is normal. Her extremity exam reveals no clubbing, cyanosis, or edema. HEENT exam reveals partial baldness of the right side of the scalp. There is a well healed craniotomy scar. She has no xanthelasma nor is there any gum bleeding. Her musculature and gait are relatively normal without any obvious lateralizing signs.

Final Assessment: This is a lady who has incredibly severe coronary disease and a poor prognosis with regard to her heart. She tolerated a craniotomy 6 months ago before knowledge of her coronary artery disease. She could probably tolerate another craniotomy but would be at increased risk for a perioperative infarction during general anesthesia. This would be obviously magnified if she had hemodynamic instability. The anticipated surgery would not involve a vascular challenge as would the nephrectomy. Nonetheless, the general anesthetic would pose a cardiovascular risk that seems to be unpreventable. The plan is to proceed with radiation and, reserve surgery for nonavoidable indication. I have discussed this with the radiation oncologist, and the patient is most agreeable with this sort of approach as well. I hope this information can be of some help to you. Thanks again.

History of Present Illness: This 59-year-old woman is well known to me, undergoing craniotomy for resection of a metastatic renal cell carcinoma in January of 200X. At that time she presented with weakness of her left upper and lower extremity. She was continued on a daily Tegretol dose as she did not tolerate Dilantin. She was doing well until she presented with a generalized tonic clonic seizure yesterday and postictal Todd's paralysis which is now resolving. She was brought to the hospital, underwent a CT scan and subsequent MRI scan that does show a solitary lesion in the postoperative bed consistent with recurrence of her metastatic disease. She has never received whole brain radiation postoperatively. Currently she tells me her kidney was never resected as she has significant cardiovascular disease and was thought by the cardiologist not to be able to tolerate a nephrectomy. Currently treatment options include:

1. Whole brain radiation.
2. Surgical removal of the lesion followed by whole brain radiation if she can obtain surgical clearance.
3. Possibility of doing stereotactic radiosurgery on the lesion again followed by whole brain radiation.

Recommendations: Currently, I have placed the patient on Decadron 400 mg twice daily and will ask the neurosurgeon and his associates to evaluate the possibility of a craniotomy on the patient.

Which of the following is the correct code assignment?

a. 198.3, 189.0, 780.39, 414.01
b. 780.39, 198.3, 189.0, 414.01
c. 189.0, 198.3, 780.39, 414.01
d. 198.3, 189.0, 414.01

Optional MS-DRG Exercise (for users with access to MS-DRG software or tables)

What is the correct MS-DRG for this case?

Which MDC does this MS-DRG belong to?

Disorders of the Nervous System and Sense Organs

7.38. The following documentation is from the health record of a 62-year-old male patient.

Discharge Summary

Admission Diagnosis: Transient ischemic attack, possible stroke.

Final Diagnoses

1. Transient vertigo versus posterior circulation transient ischemic attack.
2. Noninsulin dependent diabetes.
3. Coronary artery disease status post coronary bypass grafting.
4. Hyperlipidemia.

Consultants: Neurology

History

This is a 62-year-old white male who was admitted through the Emergency Department with a variety of symptoms, somewhat vague, describing components of dizziness, double vision, slightly slurred speech, vague numbness and tingling of the upper extremities for two or possibly three days. He has had intermittent different episodes off and on over the last two to three months. The patient has several risk factors including coronary disease, hyperlipidemia, and he is a smoker. He was admitted with possible TIAs or CVA.

Hospital Course: After being admitted to the Intermediate Care Unit and Stepdown Unit for monitoring and being started on Heparin, his symptoms resolved very rapidly.

Diagnostics: A CT of the brain indicated a possible ischemic event in the right frontoparietal region and an old lacunar infarct to the basal ganglia on the right. The chest x-ray showed mild congestive heart failure, although this was not clinically apparent. Carotid studies showed minimal abnormalities with approximately 30% disease on the left internal carotid. The right side was normal.

An echocardiogram of the heart indicated minor valvular abnormalities of no significance and an ejection fraction of 35-40% and no embolic clots were noted. A routine cardiogram showed some old findings of left anterior hemiblock.

As mentioned, the patient's symptoms rapidly resolved. He was seen in consultation by Dr. G the following morning who felt that he did not need IV heparin for the current event and that aspirin should be sufficient. Some consideration was given that if he had future episodes, of starting either Plavix or possible long-term Coumadin. Arrangements were made for discharge, as the patient's basic clinical status has returned to baseline.

Discharge Medications

1. Glucophage 500 mg b.i.d.
2. Glyburide 5 mg b.i.d.
3. Lipitor 20 mg daily.
4. Ecotrin 325 mg daily.

Discharge Instructions

Diet—ADA diet, low fat. He was advised at length about smoking cessation. Activity—As tolerated, but no heavy exertion. It was suggested that at some point the patient have an MRI and an MRA as an outpatient and consideration be given to stronger anticoagulation if he has further episodes. Follow-up in the office in approximately one to two weeks.

Emergency Department

History of Present Illness: This is a 62-year-old male who complains of five days of dizziness and three days of weakness, decreasing ambulation, and unsteadiness. He complains of no pain or numbness of the lower extremities, chest pain, fever, or headache. He does complain of having mild vision blurring with turning when he turns his head. The patient has also had slurring of his speech. He was seen yesterday by his private physician who noticed his ataxia and has him scheduled for a magnetic resonance imaging today.

Past Medical History:

1. Diabetes mellitus.
2. Myocardial infarction times three in the past.
3. Coronary artery bypass graft done in the last five years.
4. Hypertension.
5. Mild neuropathy secondary to his diabetes mellitus.

Social History: The patient lives in a private home by himself. He smokes two packs of cigarettes a day. He denies any drinking.

Medications:

1. Glucophage.
2. Talacen.

Allergies: No known allergies.

Review of Systems: Negative except for the pertinent positives and negatives noted in the history of present illness.

Physical Examination

Vital Signs: Temperature is 97. Pulse of 84. Respirations 20. Blood pressure 132/73. GENERAL: The patient is mildly sleepy but very alert and cooperative with the examination. HEENT: He is normocephalic. Atraumatic. He has some mild preauricular swelling on the right as compared to the left. His tympanic membranes were normal bilaterally. Extraocular muscles intact. Pupils equal, round, reactive to light and accommodation. Oral pharynx is normal. He did have some staining consistent with tobacco.

Neck: Supple. No adenopathy.

Heart: Regular rate and rhythm without any murmurs, thrills, or rubs. He has 2+ pulses radial and brachial bilaterally.

Lungs: Breath sounds are clear bilaterally with no tachypnea or retraction.

Abdomen: Mildly tender at the left upper quadrant over the rib area. Otherwise the abdomen was soft and nondistended.

Extremities: He had upper and lower extremity strength of +5.

Neurology: There is 212 and grossly intact. He had no pitting edema or other lesions noted. The patient was ataxic.

Laboratory and Diagnostics: Labs were obtained. Basic metabolic profile showed a sodium of 138, potassium 4.0, chloride of 107, bicarbonate of 22, glucose of 106, blood urea nitrogen of 21, and creatinine of 0.8. Calcium is 9.4. PT and partial prothrombin time were 13.2 and 29.8. White blood cell count was 11.4. H&H is 15.4 and 45.7. He had 222,000 platelets, 62 segs, 29 lymphs, 4 monocytes, 3 eosinopllils, and no basophils. CT scan of the head showed a new infarction of the brain and old lacunar infarct.

Emergency Room Course: We talked to the primary care doctor who agreed with the admission of this patient.

Plan: The patient was admitted to a monitored bed. Assisting physician helped coordinate the care, management, and treatment of this patient with myself. The patient is being admitted to the primary care doctor's service.

Neurologic Consultation

History: This is a 62-year-old white male whom we were asked to evaluate regarding dizziness and a possible new stroke.

The patient's neurologic history recently appears to date back to approximately one month ago when he developed what he described as some double vision. He was seeing things side by side. He did see his primary care physician who felt this may have been due to a diabetic extraocular movement palsy, and the patient was given a patch. After three weeks, his symptoms resolved. Around that same time, about a month ago, he noticed some numbness and tingling in his fingertips which at times is still bothersome. He was doing fine until this past Saturday when he had the onset of what sounds like dysequilibrium or vertigo where he had difficulty walking. This was transient and then seemed to resolve. This is not currently a problem for him now, and he is much better. The patient tells me that his son told him he may have had some slurred speech, but he is not aware of it. He reported no other specific symptoms. Specifically, he reported no headache. He denies any new change in his vision in the last week. He reported no other areas of focal numbness or tingling. He reported no trouble with focal weakness. He felt like his balance was only off for a short period of time, but then resolved. His bowel and bladder function had been fine. He has had no nausea or vomiting. He denies any chest pain, palpitations, or shortness of breath. He did see his primary care physician who told him that some of his problems may have been related to recent medication change and felt that otherwise he would be okay. However, when seeing the physician the day of admission, he was noted to be somewhat ataxic and was admitted to rule out a new stroke.

Laboratory Data: Current blood work on admission showed normal electrolytes. Digoxin level was less than 0.3. CPK levels have been normal. White count was 11.4 with the remainder of his CBC normal. INR was normal at 1.3. He has remained neurologically stable since admission.

Diagnostics: MRI and MRA are pending. Echocardiogram was grossly suboptimal with an ejection fraction of 35% to 40%. Carotid ultrasound preliminarily showed no stenosis. Heparin is on hold at this time pending our evaluation and the results of the MRI and MRA.

Current Medications

1. Glucophage.
2. Insulin coverage.
3. Lasix.
4. DiaBeta.
5. Lipitor.

Neurologic Examination: On exam, the patient is awake and alert. He is fully oriented. He is able to name and repeat. Attention, concentration, and memory are okay. Cranial nerves II–XII are grossly intact. Neck is supple with no bruits. Motor exam appears symmetric with no significant focal weakness. He has fairly good bulk and tone. There is no tremor. Sensory exam is remarkable for stocking glove sensory loss. Reflexes are symmetric and somewhat diminished in the lower extremities. Gait is only minimally wide based and he is able to ambulate on his own without any clear ataxia noted at this time. Coordination testing is symmetric. Romberg is negative. He does have difficulty with heel to toe walk.

Impression: The patient presents now with transient vertigo along with some slurred speech. This combined with the recent history of double vision certainly warrants a workup for vertebrobasilar insufficiency.

Recommendations

Echocardiogram as done.

Carotid ultrasound as done.

MRI and MRA as done.

IF MRI and MRA are negative, along with the other studies, then treatment with antiplatelet therapy is certainly reasonable.

Physical therapy.

Blood pressure and blood sugar control while avoiding relative hypotension.

We will likely need to stop heparin or discontinue its use even while being held, as long as studies appear normal. If all of this is okay, and the patient is stable on his feet, discharge then could be shortly.

Assign the diagnosis correct codes including POA indicators for this case:

Principal diagnosis: _____

Additional diagnoses: _____

Issues to clarify: _____

7.39. The following documentation is from the health record of a 67-year-old female patient.

Discharge Summary

This is a 67-year-old lady with complaints of low back pain, with radiation down her right leg to her foot. This pain has been progressively worse over the past 6 months. She had an MRI scan that showed degenerative disc disease at L2–3, L3–4, and L4–5; L3–L4 with mild central canal stenosis; and facet arthropathy at L3–-L4 and L4–L5. She has a past medical history of coronary artery disease, hypertension, and arthritis. Her current medications include Lipitor, Avapro®, Ecotrin®, Imdur®, Lasix, K-Dur®, calcium, and Vioxx®. She had a CABG 2 years ago. She also had PTCA with cardiac stents placed 3 years ago. Patient is admitted for lumbar epidural steroid injections for her lumbar radiculopathy—as noted on MRI results.

Which of the following is the correct ICD-9-CM code assignment?

a. 722.52, 721.3, 724.02, 724.4, 414.00, 401.9, V45.81, V45.82, 03.92, 99.23, 88.91
b. 724.4, 414.00, 401.9, V45.81, V45.82, 03.92, 99.23, 88.91
c. 722.52, 721.3, 414.00, 401.9, V45.81, V45.82, 03.92, 99.23, 88.91
d. 722.52, 721.3, 414.00, 401.9, V45.81, V45.82, 03.91, 88.91

Optional MS-DRG Exercise (for users with access to MS-DRG software or tables)

Which of the following statements is true regarding the MS-DRG assignment for this case?

a. This case is assigned to a medical MS-DRG.
b. This case is assigned to a surgical MS-DRG.
c. MS-DRG assignment is changed based on the procedure code (03.92).
d. The MS-DRG assigned to this case falls into MDC 1, diseases and disorders of the nervous system.

Newborn/Congenital Disorders

7.40.   The following documentation is from the health record of an 18-day-old baby boy.

Discharge Summary

This is an 18-day-old male infant who was admitted after he was noticed to be developing omphalitis. He was immediately placed on intravenous cefotaxime and ampicillin, later changed to cefotaxime and clindamycin. A culture taken from the umbilical stump grew *Staphylococcus aureus* and group H Streptococcus.

After the first day, there was great improvement, and the patient continued to improve completely. Now there is no redness or swelling whatsoever. The child has remained afebrile and has continued to eat very well. He shows no sign of abdominal tenderness or peritonitis. I feel that we have treated this well. He has had 5 days of intravenous antibiotics. I will finish the treatment with Keflex by mouth seeing that both *Streptococcus pyogenes* and *Staphylococcus aureus* are sensitive. The mother will watch the child closely and let me know if any problems occur. I have instructed her to watch for any more redevelopment of the redness, swelling, or discharge. We will recheck this in 2 weeks at his 1-month checkup.

Which of the following answers contains the correct diagnostic code(s) for this admission?

a. 771.2, 041.09
b. 686.9, 041.11, 041.09
c. 771.4
d. 771.4, 041.11, 041.09

7.41.   The following documentation is from the health record of a 3-day-old baby boy.

Discharge Summary

The patient is a 3-day-old male infant. He was born at home after approximately 38 weeks' gestation and brought to the Emergency Room shortly thereafter with difficulty breathing. The baby's respirations were very quick and shallow. This was the mother's fourth child, all of whom have been born at home. This was the first child born with complications.

The newborn was resuscitated and placed in the NICU under continuous oxygen therapy.

Admission history and physical examination were otherwise unremarkable. Chest x-ray showed wet lungs. Repeat chest x-ray 24 hours later showed the lungs had cleared. PKU specimen was taken and sent to the state laboratory, as required.

By the second day of hospitalization, the patient was able to be weaned off the oxygen and discharged from the NICU to a bassinet.

The mother requested that the baby be circumcised. This was accomplished without incident.

The infant is discharged to be seen in the clinic at 1 month for a well-baby visit.

Which of the following answers is correct to code this admission?

a. 770.6, V30.10, V50.2, 96.04
b. V30.1, 770.6, V50.2, 64.0, 93.93, 93.96
c. V30.1, 769, V50.2, 64.0, 96.04
d. V30.10, 768.6, V50.2, 64.0, 96.05, 93.96

Optional MS-DRG Exercise (for users with access to MS-DRG software or tables)

In addition to the principal diagnosis, the MS-DRG for this admission is based upon which of the following factors listed below?

a. Complication or comorbid condition
b. Major complication or comorbid condition
c. Procedure code
d. Other significant problems

7.42. The patient is a 3-year-old child with congenital patent ductus arteriosus. The patient has had several open-heart surgeries attempting to correct the defect. The patient was born prematurely at 34 weeks' gestation. The patient continues to be below average on standard growth charts in size and weight, and the mother states the child is not very active.

Recent echocardiogram revealed an area of the aorta leaking blood into the pulmonary artery. The child is now admitted for further corrective surgery.

On the day after admission, the child was taken to the OR. Open-chest surgery was performed through the existing scar, and the ribs were spread to gain access to the operative field. Several areas of communication between the aorta and the pulmonary artery were identified and closed. The chest was then closed. Throughout the procedure, the patient's vital signs were monitored and remained at satisfactory levels. The patient tolerated the procedure well.

The day after surgery, the patient was allowed to be up and walking. The child appeared to have increased energy and was a healthy pink color. The child was eating and asking for more.

The patient was discharged on the third postop day to be followed as an outpatient in the cardiac education center.

Final Diagnosis: Patent ductus arteriosus

Which of the following answers is correct to code this admission?

a. 747.0, 765.10, 765.27, 38.85
b. 745.9, 35.39
c. 747.0, 38.85
d. 745.0, 38.85

7.43.   The following documentation is from the health record of a 5-year-old girl.

Discharge Summary

The patient is a 5-year-old female child born with myelomeningocele spina bifida. The patient has previously undergone several procedures to cover the defect at the bottom of her spine, including the insertion of a ventriculoperitoneal (VP) shunt to drain the cerebrospinal fluid (CSF) fluid accumulation from her hydrocephalus.

The patient was admitted this morning through the emergency department with a plugged shunt. The child was rushed to the OR for emergent irrigation of the shunt. Irrigation was attempted several times but was unsuccessful. Therefore, the shunt was removed and replaced with another VP shunt.

The patient tolerated the procedure, although she was very anxious about having surgery and being in the hospital. Her parents were very caring and present to calm her at all times.

The patient was discharged on the second day postop to be followed in the office.

Final Diagnoses: Congenital myelomeningocele spina bifida
Plugged VP shunt

Which of the following answers is correct to code this admission?

a. 996.75, 741.03, 02.42
b. 996.2, 741.03, 02.41, 02.42
c. 741.03, V45.2, 02.42, 02.43
d. 996.75, 742.3, 741.00, 02.42

Pediatric Conditions

7.44.   The following documentation is from the health record of a 13-year-old boy.

Preoperative Diagnosis: Right inguinal hernia, hypospadias

Postoperative Diagnosis: Same

Operation: Right inguinal herniorrhaphy, repair of hypospadias

Indications: The patient is a 13-year-old male with reducible right inguinal hernia and hypospadias who now presents for definitive care.

Procedure: The patient was brought to the operating room and placed in the supine position. After the adequate general endotracheal anesthesia, a 4-cm incision was made in the right inguinal region. The subcutaneous tissues were divided, and hemostasis achieved with electrocautery. The external oblique fascia was identified and cleaned using Metzenbaum scissors. An incision was made in the external oblique and carried down to the external ring using Metzenbaum scissors. The external oblique was freed from the underlying cord using two pairs of forceps. The cremasteric fibers were divided and the hernia sac grasped. Pulling the hernia sac up on some tension, we were then able to tease off the cremasteric fibers, as well as the vas and vessels. At this point, we were able to control the hernia sac between the two hemostats. We then teased off the vas and vessels as we dissected proximally toward the internal ring. At this point, the sac was twisted, sutured ligated, × 2, amputated, and then the sac was allowed to fall back into the peritoneal cavity. We continued the dissection distally. The anterior wall was opened using electrocautery. At this point, we placed the cord back into the inguinal canal. The external oblique fascia was closed using interrupted 4-0 silk sutures. The external oblique fascia and the structures below it were infiltrated using .05 percent Marcaine. The Scarpa's fascia was closed using 5-0 VICRYL®. The skin was closed using interrupted 5-0 subcuticular stitches. Steri-Strips were applied.

With this completed, attention was then turned to repairing the hypospadias. Procedure commenced by placing a 4-0 Prolene stay suture through the glans for traction and observing the distal shaft hypospadias without chordee and with a dorsal hooded foreskin.

The urethroplasty was begun by making parallel lines with a marking pen on either side of the urethral meatus, going out to the tip of the glans, connecting these proximally from the meatus for a distance of about 2.5 cm. With a tourniquet used intermittently, an incision was made in these lines to create two rectangular flaps connected at the urethral meatus. On the left side of the meatus there was a small nevus just lateral to the incision line, and the incision was extended around this to excise a small nevus, less than .6 cm in diameter, which will be sent for pathology. After mobilization of both skin flaps, the proximal one off of the shaft and the ventral one off of the underlying tissue of the glans, optical magnification was used to convert these two flaps into a neourethral tube using 6-0 PDS sutures. The neourethral tube came together quite well.

Next, an incision was made in the midline, out to the tip of the glans, through the incision point at the previous site of the distal flap, to accomplish mobilization of the urethra and advance this urethra out to the tip of the glans. Wedge-shaped areas of glandular tissue were excised to make a smooth passageway for the neourethra. Then the neourethra was sutured into position at the tip of the glans with 6-0 and 5-0 PDS sutures.

Next, a second layer was created by approximating the subcutaneous tissue, adventitial tissue, and elements of the corpus spongiosum over the neourethral reconstruction at the corona, and carrying this with a running 6-0 PDS suture proximally to provide a second layer of coverage.

When this was done, the glans itself was approximated with 4-0 PDS sutures, placing about three sutures into position to firmly reconnect the wings of the glans and to keep them from pulling apart. This left an aperture for the neourethra, which was then sutured into position with 4-0 and 5-0 PDS sutures. When this was done, a #11 French Silastic catheter was used, and a portion of its wall was cut out to turn it into a splint. It was positioned into the urethra and sutured into place at the meatus with a 4-0 Prolene suture to hold it into position. The next step was to close the skin defect on the ventral shaft with interrupted 3-0 chromic catgut suture.

The next part of the operation involved performing circumcision of the redundant dorsal and lateral preputial tissue. First, this was marked with a marking pen, and then an incision was made in the pen lines to allow excision of the redundant foreskin. Hemostasis was obtained with electrocautery, and 3-0 chromic catgut suture was used to complete the circumcision.

The next step was to consider the ability of this patient to void. Because of his hernial repair and this operation on the prepuce, I was afraid he would be in urinary retention. I, therefore, inserted an #8 French feeding tube through the #11 French Silastic catheter, passed it all the way into the bladder, and allowed it to drain urine freely. Then a light sterile dressing of 1-inch Adaptic roller gauze soaked in tincture of benzoin was loosely wrapped around the shaft for mild compression and hemostasis. The last few wraps of this incorporated the catheter.

The patient was taken to the recovery room in satisfactory condition.

Which of the following code sets is correct for reporting this operative episode?

a. 752.61, 550.91, 752.69, 58.49, 53.02, 64.0, 57.94
b. 752.61, 605, 550.90, 239.5, 58.47, 53.01, 64.2, 57.94
c. 752.61, 550.91, 752.69, 58.49, 53.00, 57.94
d. 752.61, 605, 550.90, 222.1, 58.45, 53.02, 64.0, 64.2, 57.94

7.45.   The following documentation is from the health record of an 11-year-old boy.

Preoperative Diagnoses: 1. Ewing sarcoma, left scapula
                              2. Down syndrome

Postoperative Diagnosis: Same

Findings: This is an 11-year-old boy with Down syndrome who presented 4 days ago with a large mass in the left scapular region. X-ray and CT scan showed laminated new bone with a large, expansile, permeative lesion in the scapular body. It did not appear to involve the glenohumeral joint. Bone scan showed marked increased uptake and questionable area of uptake in the right seventh rib and left first vertebral body. CT of the lungs was reportedly normal. At the time of biopsy, there was obvious stretching of the posterior trapezius and deltoid musculature over the mass and a very soft calcific mass noted within the central area of the substance. Frozen pathology sections showed many small cells, but definitive diagnosis could not be made off the frozen section. Final pathologic diagnosis was malignant bone tumor consistent with Ewing sarcoma. He will be started on a chemotherapy program, and definitive surgery will be planned.

Procedure: Following an adequate level of general endotracheal anesthesia, the patient was turned to the right lateral decubitus position with the left side up. The left shoulder region was prepped and draped in routine sterile fashion. Before beginning the biopsy, a venous access device, a MediPort® catheter, was inserted on the right side.

A 3-cm incision was then made over the spine of the scapula. Electrocautery was used for hemostasis and the incision deepened with electrocautery. When we were in the area of the soft-tissue mass noted on the CT scan, biopsies were taken. The initial biopsies showed primarily muscle fibers, so we deepened the incision at this point and obtained some of the obvious calcific soft-tissue mass. These cultures were more consistent with tumor, and, at this point, hemostasis was achieved with a combination of bone wax, packing, and electrocautery. Meticulous hemostasis was achieved prior to closure, and then a two-layer interrupted closure was performed, closing the skin with a running subcuticular suture of 4-0 VICRYL®. Bulky dry sterile dressing was applied, and the patient was awakened and returned to the recovery room in good condition.

Which of the following is the correct code set to report this procedure?

a. 170.4, 758.0, 77.41
b. 170.4, 170.3, 170.2, 77.81
c. 170.4, 758.0, 77.61, 86.07
d. 170.4, 758.0, 77.41, 86.07

Optional MS-DRG Exercise (for users with access to MS-DRG software or tables)

What is the correct MS-DRG assignment for this admission?

a. 517, Other musculoskeletal system and connective tissue OR procedure without CC/MCC
b. 497, Local excision and removal internal fixation devices except hip and femur without CC/MCC
c. 479, Biopsies of musculoskeletal system and connective tissue without CC/MCC
d. 477, Biopsies of musculoskeletal system and connective tissue with MCC

Conditions of Pregnancy, Childbirth, and the Puerperium

7.46.   The following documentation is from the health record of a 19-year-old female patient.

Discharge Diagnosis:
1. Term Pregnancy.
2. Previous cesarean section.
3. Failed attempt at vaginal birth after cesarean delivery.
4. Arrest of descent, secondary to occiput posterior position.

Procedures Performed: Repeat low transverse cesarean delivery.

History of Present Illness: The patient is a 19-year-old, gravida 3, para 1 with an estimated date of delivery in two weeks. She is with a thirty-seven plus week pregnancy. She has prior beta strep culture, positive. She underwent spontaneous rupture of membranes. Upon admission, the patient's membranes were ruptured.

Hospital Course: The patient was started on intravenous Clindamycin for positive group B strep. Further, she was started on Pitocin for induction of labor because of the premature rupture of membranes. The patient had a slow labor course, eventually establishing a good labor curve. She dilated completely to a zero station but failed to descend with pushing. Then the decision was made to perform a primary low transverse cesarean delivery because of arrest of descent. She underwent a cesarean delivery without complications. Estimated blood loss was 600 cc. This resulted in delivery of a live male infant weighing 7 pounds 4 ounces having Apgars of 9 at one minute and 9 at five minutes.

Postoperatively, the patient did well. She was ambulating and tolerating her diet. She was afebrile and her incision looked clear so the patient was discharged home on the third postoperative day.

Medications/aftercare plan:

1. The patient is to limit her activity around the home for a one week period.
2. She will be followed up in the office in one to two weeks.
3. Birth control method was discussed and the patient is considering Depo-Provera. She will finalize her decision on this and let us know in the office.

The patient's discharge medications consist of:

1. Motrin 800 mg one every eight hours p.r.n.
2. Tylenol #3 1-2 every four hours p.r.n.
3. The patient should continue her prenatal vitamins and irons.
4. Colace 100 mg b.i.d.
5. There are no diet restrictions.

Assign the correct codes:

Principal diagnosis: _____

Additional diagnoses: _____

Procedures: _____

Issues to clarify: _____

7.47.   The following documentation is from the health record of a 33-year-old female patient.

OB Record

Admit Note: 2/27/XX

This is a 33-year-old G2 P0, estimated delivery date of 2/28, and estimated gestational age of 40 weeks. She presents for induction secondary to gestational diabetes mellitus. She has required insulin since 28 weeks, with adequate control. PNL: O positive, rubella immune. PE: AVSS, Abdomen FH 40 cm, EFW 3,800 to 4,000 g. Cervix is closed/50 percent/-3/post/ceph. Plan is for Prostin E2® induction and insulin infusion when in active labor.

Progress Note: 2/28/XX, 0915

Patient is having uterine contractions every three to eight minutes. Cervix is 1 cm/100 percent/floating. Patient desires not to start Prostin E2 induction yet. Feels that she is in labor. FHR reactive, baseline 120s with accelerations.

Progress Note: 2/28/XX, 1925

Patient's uterine contractions have resolved. Cervix unchanged. Discussed options, would like to go home to sleep and return in a.m. for Pitocin induction. Discharged home for tonight to sleep. Admit in a.m., start IV Pitocin as per protocol, start insulin drip, clear liquid diet.

Which of the following is the correct code assignment?

a. 648.83, V58.67, 73.4
b. 648.81, V58.67, 73.01
c. 648.83, V58.67
d. 659.13, 648.83

Optional MS-DRG Exercise (for users with access to MS-DRG software or tables)

What is the MS-DRG assignment for this admission?

7.48. The following documentation is from the health record of a 32-year-old female patient.

Delivery Record

Admit Note: 7/20: Patient is a 32-year-old female with EDC 7/22 and EGA of +39 weeks. She has been having uterine contractions for 2 days, mild, more severe this a.m. with contractions every 2 to 4 minutes at admission. Cervix is 1 cm/20 percent/-1 station. EFW 3500 g.

Delivery Record Summary: 7/21: Patient progressed to 5 cm and exhausted! NO sleep for 2 nights. Also in extreme pain of labor. Vacuum-assisted vaginal delivery of a live male. Episiotomy. Fourth-degree laceration repaired with 2-0 and 3-0 VICRYL®. EBL 450 mL.

Progress Note: 7/22: Patient weak, slightly dizzy, sore perineum. VSS, afebrile, fundus firm. H/H 8.5/24.6; A – s/p VD with fourth degree laceration; postpartum anemia. Slow Fe® #30.

Progress Note: 7/23: PPD #2 – S – feeling better, ambulating without dizziness; O – VSS, afebrile, fundus firm; A – s/p VD with 4th-degree laceration; P – home today, FU 4 weeks, DC meds Vicodin #20, Colace #20, and Slow Fe #30.

Code Assignment including POA indicator:

Diagnoses: _____

Procedures: _____

7.49. **Discharge Summary**

Admission Diagnosis: A 38-week intrauterine pregnancy with leaking amniotic fluid

Discharge Diagnosis: Postpartum female—status post classical cesarean section secondary to prolonged second stage of labor; endomyometritis, postoperative ileus, persistent fever—suspected septic pelvic thrombophlebitis; wound seroma

Operative Procedure: Classical cesarean section

Admission History: This is a 26-year-old gravida 1, para 0 female who presented at 38 weeks gestation complaining of leaking fluid in the morning. She had very mild leaking noted. She had positive nitrazine. She had no gush of fluid at that time and good fetal movement. She had some mild cramping and minimal contractions. No nausea, vomiting, headache, or shortness of breath. No chest pain. Her pregnancy had been uncomplicated. She has had mildly elevated blood pressures over the past couple of weeks, but otherwise nothing significant.

Past medical and social history is negative.

Ob-Gyn History: She is gravida 1

OB Laboratory Data: Blood type is O positive. Antibody screen negative. HIV negative. GBS negative. Rubella nonimmune. RPR nonreactive. Hepatitis B negative.

Objective

Vital Signs: stable; BP: Elevated at 152/102; it did come down between the 130 to 140s/70 to 80

Lungs: Clear to auscultation

Heart: Regular rate and rhythm

Abdomen: Soft and nontender

Pelvic: Cervix is 1 cm, 70% effaced, and -2 station. The amniotic bag could still be palpated, but it was thought that the patient might be leaking fluid; therefore, artificial rupture of membranes was performed with clear fluid. Tocol showed irregular contractions.

Assessment and Plan: Term intrauterine pregnancy at 38 weeks with mild leaking of fluid. The patient is admitted, and she is given an IV Hep-lock with expectant management.

Hospital Course: The patient did require Pitocin augmentation, as after several hours, she was not contracting adequately. She progressed slowly, but adequately over the next 24 hours. She was completely dilated at approximately 7:00 in the morning. She began pushing. She pushed for 3 hours. The baby progressed from a +1 to a +2-3 station. She had no further progression. She was counseled on the risks regarding cesarean section versus forceps delivery. The patient did elect for a cesarean section. She is, therefore, taken for a C-section, see operative report for details. The patient did undergo a classical cesarean section due to the fact that the fetal head could not be reduced from the vagina, and a classical was performed in order to grab the fetal feet and deliver in a breech fashion.

Postoperatively the patient did become febrile within a few hours, and this was felt to be caused by endomyometritis due to the prolonged rupture, prolonged labor, and the significant manipulation of the uterus with cesarean section. The patient was started on Ancef during the procedure and was started on gentamicin within 12 hours of the surgery. The patient continued on IV antibiotics. Her temperature continued to spike on a fairly regular basis over the next 2 postoperative days. She was tolerating a regular diet and ambulating, in addition to passing minimal flatus. On postoperative day 1 she did have a fever as high as 103°F with a tachycardic episode in the 160s. She was somewhat lightheaded when she was out of bed to go to the restroom, but improved with rest. Her heart rate did decrease at that point. An EKG was done and this showed sinus tachycardia. She denied any shortness of breath or chest pain. No nausea or vomiting. Her laboratory studies showed her hemoglobin to be 8.9, white count 12, with a morning repeat of 8.8 and a white count of 9. Blood cultures also were done at that time.

On postoperative day 2, the patient was beginning to feel distended. Her pain was getting worse secondary to the descent. She denied any shortness of breath or chest pain. She was still passing some flatus, but minimal. No nausea or vomiting. On examination her temperature was 103.3°F, which was the maximum. Her abdomen is soft; however, she did have moderate to severe distention at that time. She had good bowel sounds in all the quadrants. Her incision was intact. The extremities showed no calf tenderness. A chest x-ray was done because of the continued elevated temperature; there was bowel distension and suspected ileus. Abdominal x-rays were then done which did confirm an ileus, but no signs of bowel obstruction. Her hemoglobin was repeated and showed 7.4 with stable platelets. Blood cultures were negative, as well as her urine. BUN and creatinine were normal. The patient was made n.p.o. and given an NG tube for the postoperative ileus. She did note some relief to her abdominal discomfort and pain. She was afebrile throughout most of the day at that time. The NG tube had 250 cc out initially.

On postoperative day 3, the NG tube was continued, and her belly was somewhat less distended. She continued to pass flatus and her pain was otherwise controlled. Her temperature was 101.6°F, and clindamycin was added to the antibiotic regimen to treat the persistent fevers. On examination, her distention was improved. She was still having some bowel sounds, although hypoactive. The incision showed no significant erythema. Blood cultures remained negative, and the NG tube was continued with intermittent suction.

On postoperative day 4, the patient was feeling better and producing stools. No nausea or vomiting or shortness of breath, chest pain, dizziness, or lightheadedness. She was having normal lochia and pain was controlled. The NG tube had collected a minimal amount overnight, and her temperature was 101.6°F. She was then started on a clear diet and, if tolerated, the NG tube was to be discontinued. Her hemoglobin level was 6.9, with a decreased potassium level of 3.2. All other lab work was essentially normal. The NG tube was discontinued, and she was given KCl to replace her potassium.

On postoperative day 5, she continued to be febrile with a temperature of 101.5°F. The abdomen was soft and nondistended. She was appropriately tender, more on the left side than the right. The incision still appeared well. Laboratory studies showed the hemoglobin to be 6.8 and stable. Her potassium continued to decrease to 3.1. At that time a CT of the abdomen and pelvis was ordered to rule out a pelvic abscess.

C. difficile was ordered due to continued diarrhea. Another physician was consulted. A suspicion of septic pelvic thrombophlebitis was then entertained as her fever continued despite adequate antibiotic therapy. The patient was started on Lovenox®, and the CT scan showed normal postoperative changes, but no evidence of an abscess.

On postoperative day 6, she was feeling better and had no further diarrhea. *C. difficile* was negative and she was tolerating a regular diet. Her incision did show some erythema, and it was probed with some serosanguineous drainage from the left side, but no purulent drainage. Her laboratory studies were stable, and she was continued on Lovenox and antibiotics. The incision was to be cleaned twice daily.

Postoperative day 7, the patient continued to improve and was feeling well. She was tolerating a regular diet and remained afebrile in which she remained for 27 hours and therefore was discharged home.

Consultation Report: The patient is 26-year-old female who is gravida 1, now para 1. The patient required a C-section because of prolonged labor and maternal exhaustion. The patient was ruptured for a little over 24 hours prior to delivery. The C-section was complicated by the inability to reduce the fetal head from the vaginal canal and was converted to a breech extraction; therefore, the patient had a primary low transverse C-section that had to be converted to a classical C-section. The patient had some tachycardia on the date of delivery. Ancef was continued and gentamicin was started. On postoperative day 1, she developed a temperature up to 103°F. Urinalysis was unremarkable, along with blood cultures. A chest x-ray revealed some atelectasis at the bases, which the radiologist ultimately felt was possibly consistent with bibasilar pneumonia. At that point the patient was switched from Ancef to ceftriaxone; clindamycin was added on postoperative day 2.

It was noted on the chest x-ray that she had a probable ileus, which was confirmed on the abdominal films. She was placed n.p.o. and an NG tube to intermittent suction was started. The fevers persisted with concomitant chills through today, postoperative day 5; however, now her temperature spikes are more in the 101°F range. The patient's ileus has resolved, and she is tolerating a normal diet. The patient clinically had endometritis after the delivery with a tender lower abdomen. However, this has gradually improved even though her fevers are persisting.

Review of systems performed in addition to physical examination.

Data Interpretation: Laboratory data reviewed; chest x-ray also reviewed by myself revealed some atelectatic changes in the lung bases with bibasilar patchy infiltrates read as possible hypostatic pneumonia. Follow-up x-ray 3 days later revealed definite improvement with less bibasilar infiltrated, now with just some minimal atelectatic changes in the left lung base. CT scan today revealed an enlarged uterus with prominent endometrial stripes, felt to be probably iatrogenic from the surgery. There was some pelvic cobwebbing, but no obvious abscess and some subcutaneous edema anterior in the abdomen with some pockets of gas, also felt to be iatrogenic. With all of these factors, infection could not be entirely excluded. No obvious evidence of thrombophlebitis was seen.

Assessment: Persistent postpartum fever with clinical evidence of endometritis initially that has improved. The patient has had good broad-spectrum antibiotic coverage and with persistent fever, the possibility of a pelvic septic thrombophlebitis must be entertained.

Diarrhea with negative *C. difficile,* possibly still related to antibiotics, also Prevacid has been shown to cause diarrhea.

Postoperative anemia—stable.

Heart murmur—likely secondary to her anemia and being immediately postpartum.

Hypokalemia, which has been difficult to normalize—-likely related to GI losses.

Plan: She has received appropriate IV antibiotic coverage for her endomyometritis and no other source of infection is identified; would recommend that anticoagulation be initiated for the possibility of pelvic septic thrombophlebitis or ovarian vein thrombosis.

Would recommend continuing the patient's current antibiotic coverage; however, because the most recent x-ray did not show significant evidence of pneumonia, the ceftriaxone could be discontinued.

Would recommend adding potassium to her IV fluids to try to correct her hypokalemia. The hypokalemia could add to her ileus.

If the patient does not improve in the next couple of days, other considerations would be to add amp or Unasyn to her regimen for possible resistant organism, such as *Enterococcus.* Also agree with continued intermittent blood cultures if she continues to spike.

Her anemia is stable, would recommend continuing to watch for now; however, if it drops or she becomes symptomatic, transfuse.

Consider echo if fever persists to rule out endocarditis.

Operative Report

Preoperative diagnosis: Gravida 1 para 0 female at 38 weeks' gestation; prolonged rupture of membranes; prolonged second stage of labor with failure to descend

Postoperative Diagnosis: Same

Operation: Primary cesarean section-classical

Anesthesia: Epidural

Complications: Classical extension of initially low transverse incision

Findings: Viable female infant; complete placenta with three-vessel cord; normal uterus, tubes, and ovaries

Indications: This is a 26-year-old female gravida 1 para 0 who presented at 38 weeks' gestation with complaints of leaking fluid. The patient was approximately 1 cm dilated and 80% effaced at that time. She was felt to be having some leaking, although membranes could still be palpated. Therefore, artificial rupture of membranes was performed. The patient progressed very slowly in labor and required Pitocin augmentation. Over the next 24 hours, she progressed to finally complete dilation and began pushing for 3 hours. She started at approximately 0 to +1 station and progressed to + 2 or 3 station. Fetal head was seen with separation of the labia;

however, after 3 hours and maternal exhaustion, she made no further progression of the fetal head over the last hour of pushing. The patient was counseled regarding the need for assistance, and forceps assistance versus cesarean section were offered. The risk and benefits of both were explained, and the patient opted for a cesarean section.

Technique: The patient was taken to the operating room and placed under epidural anesthesia. She was prepped and draped in the normal sterile fashion in dorsal supine position with leftward tilt. Pfannenstiel skin incision was made two fingerbreadths above the symphysis pubis in the midline and carried through to the underlying fascia. The fascia was incised in the midline and extended laterally with Mayo scissors. The rectus muscles were dissected off the fascia using both blunt and sharp dissection. Rectus muscles were then separated in the midline. The peritoneum was entered bluntly and extended superiorly and inferiorly. The bladder blade was inserted. The vesicouterine peritoneum was grasped with pickups and entered with Metzenbaum scissors. This was extended laterally, and the bladder flap was created digitally. The bladder blade was reinserted. The lower uterine segment was incised in a transverse fashion with a scalpel and extended laterally with blunt dissection. The infant's head was very low in the pelvis. Attempt to deliver the fetal head was difficult, and we were unable to reduce the fetal head from the vaginal canal. Nursing staff did apply pressure to the fetal head from the vaginal canal, but still was unable to be dislodged. An attempt was made to retract on the shoulders of the infant in order to dislodge the fetal head from the vaginal canal, but again this was unsuccessful. For this reason, the uterine incision was extended vertically in a classical fashion, and the feet were grasped and pulled to the uterine incision. The feet were then delivered, and the infant was delivered in a breech fashion. Nose and mouth were suctioned and cord was clamped and cut. The infant was then handed off to the waiting pediatrician.

Cord gas was obtained. The cord blood was inadvertently not obtained. The placenta was removed. The uterus was cleared of clots and debris. The uterus was exteriorized for better visualization; 0 VICRYL® sutures were used to close the vertical incision in the uterus in several layers. Two layers were done initially, then the transverse portion of the incision was closed. There was a cervical extension distally, and this was also closed with 0 VICRYL® sutures. Once the transverse portion of the incision was closed, attention was again turned back to the vertical incision. The uterus was returned to the abdomen and inspection of the incision appeared to be hemostatic. With all the layers being closed and the sponge, lap, and needle counts were correct × 2. The patient tolerated the procedure well and was taken to the recovery room in stable condition.

Progress Notes:

Postop day 1: Patient with episode of tachycardia consistent with endomyometritis

Postop day 2: Abdomen feels distended endomyometritis, suspect ileus

Postop day 3: Endomyometritis, ileus

Postop day 4: Ileus resolved, temperature improving

Postop day 5: Continued fever, endomyometritis, internal med consult

Postop day 6: Prolonged postpartum fever with initial endometritis, probable pelvic septic thrombophlebitis—on Lovenox, postop anemia, stable; hypokalemia—improved

Postop day 7: Patient improved; will discharge home

Code Assignment including POA indicator:

Principal diagnoses: _____

Additional diagnoses: _____

Procedures: _____

Disorders of the Respiratory System

7.50.   The following documentation is from the health record of a 67-year-old female patient.

Brief History: This 67-year-old female was transferred here for further evaluation of continued respiratory failure. She has a long history of asthma and chronic obstructive pulmonary disease. Current medications: Claforan® one gram q. 6 h. Cardizem SR 90 mg b.i.d., Solu-Medrol® 125 mg intravenously q. 8 h. Trental® one p.o. b.i.d., DiaBeta® 1.25 mg p.o. q. a.m. and 2.5 mg q. p.m., Klonopin® 1 mg p.o. q. 6 h., Ibuprofen 800 mg p.o. b.i.d., Lortab 5 mg q. 6 h. p.r.n. headache, Atrovent and Proventil® inhalers at bedside.

Physical Examination: She was intubated. Admission ABGs were PO_2 40, PCO_2 55, and pH 7.30. Blood pressure 156/89, heart rate 130 beats per minute, temperature 100.7°F. Neck: No jugular venous distention. Carotid normal upstroke without audible bruits. Pulmonary exam: Decreased breath sounds throughout. Expiratory wheezes were auscultated. Cardiac exam: Sinus tachycardiac rhythm. No murmurs or gallops. Extremities: No edema.

Hospital Course: Upon admission, emergent pulmonary consultation was obtained, and a fiberoptic bronchoscopy was performed without difficulty. Copious, thin white pus was noted in all of her inflamed airways. She had no cough despite airway suctioning. A #7.5 nasotracheal tube was inserted via her right naris without difficulty, and airways were aspirated clear. The patient was placed on Ventolin 2 mg p.o. q 6 h. placed on Proventil inhaler 1 mg q. 4 h. and q. 2 h. p.r.n., placed on oxygen, was given intravenous Lasix, and intravenous Solu-Medrol. A Dobbhoff NG tube was placed the day after admission without difficulty. Two days later, she developed a temperature of 103°F and developed chills. All cultures obtained on admission revealed no growth thus far, and a chest x-ray was clear.

Infectious disease consultation was obtained, and a workup was ordered to rule out sinusitis, viral upper respiratory tract infection, drug fever, collagen vascular disease, or occult abdominal source. Antibiotic coverage in the form of Unasyn and tobramycin ordered along with yeast coverage. Other problems included hypokalemia, which required potassium repletion, frequent premature atrial contractions, and marked metabolic alkalosis preventing weaning from her intubation. The only source of fever seemed to be the maxillary and ethmoidal sinusitis on the CT scan, and her head was elevated to decrease venous congestion of the sinuses.

GI consultation was obtained when she started developing abdominal distention and coffee-ground emesis; hematocrit level had dropped from 37.8 to 24.2 for which she was given two units of packed red blood cells. The consultant felt that a GI bleed could possibly be related to stress, nonsteroidal anti-inflammatory drugs, or gastritis and that the abdominal distention was probably aerophagia related to the ventilator. The recommendation was made to stop the tube feedings and decompression with nasogastric tube and checking stools for hemoccult. Gallbladder ultrasound revealed gallstones in the thick walls of the ducts.

The patient continued to have abdominal pain. Surgical consultation was ordered and confirmed acute cholecystitis, which could be worse secondary to the steroids. The day of consultation, the patient underwent exploratory laparotomy, bilateral salpingo-oophorectomy, cholecystectomy, cholangiogram, and omental biopsy. Cystadenofibroma of borderline malignancy of the right ovary was reported on pathological findings.

The patient developed anasarca and required intravenous diuretics. She underwent another fiberoptic bronchoscopy 6 days postop, which revealed diffused edema and slight inflammation with yellow plugs in the left upper lobe and right middle lobe, and scant secretions otherwise clear and foamy. She also underwent tube feedings with hyper Osmolite®. Seven days later, she started developing increasing respiratory distress and a tracheostomy was performed. Tracheal aspirate revealed gram-negative herpetic tracheobronchitis. Within 48 hours, she developed bradycardia and increasing ventilation pressures. Emergency tap of the right pleural space was done, which revealed tension pneumothorax. A trocar chest tube was inserted with good air return. Attempts to see airways via left nares with fiberoptic bronchoscopy revealed all mucosa to be obstructed at the level of the retropharynx. A retap of the left chest revealed air not under pressure, opened with scissors, but still unable to ventilate by tracheal tube. Heart rate was zero, and blood pressure was zero. The futility of cardiopulmonary resuscitation for further events, based on inability to ventilate, led to cessation of efforts and the patient was pronounced dead at 11:15 a.m.

Final Diagnoses:	Acute respiratory failure
	Long history of asthma
	Chronic obstructive pulmonary disease
	Metabolic alkalosis with ventilator dependence for the last week or more of her hospitalization
	Gram-negative herpetic tracheobronchitis
	Acute cholecystitis and cholelithiasis
	Anemia due to GI bleed from undetermined cause
	Maxillary and ethmoidal sinusitis
	Pneumothorax
	Premature atrial contractions
	Cystadenofibroma right ovary
	Hypokalemia
Procedures:	Intubation, mechanical ventilation
	Tracheostomy
	Fiberoptic bronchoscopy × 3
	Cholecystectomy with cholangiogram
	Bilateral salpingo-oophorectomy
	Omental biopsy
	Thoracentesis and chest tube

Code Assignment including POA indicator:

Principal diagnoses: _____

Additional diagnoses: _____

Procedures: _____

Optional MS-DRG Exercise (for users with access to MS-DRG software or tables)

What is the MS-DRG assignment on this case?

Which of the following had the greatest impact on MS-DRG assignment for this case?

a. The secondary diagnosis of acute cholecystitis and cholelithiasis
b. There was an extensive OR procedure unrelated to the principal diagnosis
c. The fact that the patient had a tracheostomy
d. All of the above

7.51. The following documentation is from the health record of an 80-year-old male patient.

Discharge Summary

History: The patient is an 80-year-old male with a 4- to 5-week history of pulmonary disease, apparently developing out of an acute influenzalike illness. He was admitted to his local hospital approximately 22 days ago with right middle lobe and right lower lobe alveolar filling infiltrates. Initial cultures were negative. Treatment with intravenous Ancef was not effective. The patient's hospital course was manifested by progressive pulmonary infiltrates unresponsive to erythromycin, Claforan, and Primaxin. Complications of nasogastric feeding tube placement in the right pleural space and administration of 1 L of Osmolite into the pleural space apparently occurred during hospitalization. The patient had a chest tube placed with effective removal of the Osmolite. Because of fatigue, the patient was twice placed on a ventilator but has been off the ventilator for approximately 1 week. He has become severely malnourished and was placed on TPN. Diarrhea has intervened with tube feedings. Cultures and ova and parasite findings showed *Trichomonas*. Because of failure to resolve pneumonia, malnutrition, and persistent fever, he was transferred here.

Physical Examination: The patient is a chronically ill-appearing, thin man, responsive but unable to talk secondary to a very dry mouth. Blood pressure 144/70, pulse rate 110 per minute and regular, temperature 99.4°F, respirations 28. He is on nasal oxygen. Skin is dry. Lymph nodes are negative. Head: No deformity. Eyes: Increased bilateral purulent drainage. Sclerae are not red. Pupils round and equal. Throat very dry with caked secretions on teeth and palate. Neck is supple. Jugular venous pulse flat, carotids equal. Chest nontender. He ventilates with the left chest fairly well with scattered rhonchi. The right chest, however, showed decreased breath sounds with a line of consolidation about halfway up. Scattered rhonchi were noted above the area of consolidation. No friction rub was heard. The patient had evidence of a right pleural effusion versus right pleural thickening. Heart: PMI was at the midclavicular line. A regular rhythm was noted, no significant murmur, gallop, or rub. Abdomen: Soft and scaphoid, no organomegaly or tenderness, bowel sounds active. The patient passed a green watery stool during examination. Rectal: Slightly decreased sphincter tone, no masses were felt. Prostate was +2 enlarged, no nodules. Extremities showed no edema, clubbing, or cyanosis.

Initial Laboratory and X-Ray Findings: Blood gas on 4 L of nasal oxygen showed pH 7.48, pCO$_2$ 37, pO$_2$ 65. Initial chest x-ray showed bilateral mixed infiltrate and consolidation throughout both lungs, most prominently in the right midlung and right lung base. A left subclavian venous catheter was seen. Initial hematocrit level was 40. Within 2 days after hydration, this was noted to be 27. Sed rate 96 mm per hour. White blood cell count 16,000 with 5 bands, 73 segs, 15 lymphs, 5 monos, 2 eosinophils. Platelets 464,000. PT and PTT negative. SMA profile: Cholesterol 113, triglycerides 110, electrolytes normal except chloride of 96, CO$_2$ 34. Blood sugar 120. BUN 20, creatinine 0.8. Serum osmolality was 338. Urine osmolality was 456. Creatinine clearance was 81 mL per minute. Urinalysis was negative, except for an initial elevated specific gravity of 1.032. The patient was malnourished by low albumin and transferrin levels. IV albumin was ordered. Cryptococcal antigen of spinal fluid positive at a titer of 1:32.

Hospital Course: The day after admission on 1/9, the patient was submitted to bronchoalveolar lavage. His culture showed beta hemolytic streptococcus A, *Proteus mirabilis,* and a gram-negative bacillus that was not further identified. Legionella culture was negative. Stool showed no pathogens. Spinal tap was done with the finding of cryptococcal antigen of 1:32 in spinal fluid, the patient was started on amphotericin B for his meningitis, but he could not tolerate this and was thus switched to fluconazole. On 1/12, it became evident that the large volume of sputum he was required to mobilize and his generally weakened state resulted in increasing fatigue resulting in acute respiratory failure, such that it was necessary to transfer the patient to the ICU, intubate, and place him on ventilatory assistance. Because of continued deterioration, antibiotics were modified to include vancomycin and imipenem. Because of the inability to obtain a fully established diagnosis, the patient was submitted to open-lung biopsy. The open-lung biopsy showed advanced fibrosis and scarring. Despite therapy with aggressive pulmonary toilet and ventilatory support, his condition continued to deteriorate. The patient experienced cardiac arrest on 1/16.

Final Diagnosis:	Pneumonia, apparently due to Gram-negative bacteria
Additional Diagnoses:	Acute respiratory failure
	Cardiac arrest
	Cryptococcal meningitis
	Severely malnourished
Procedures:	Open-lung biopsy
	Ventilatory assistance

Code Assignment including POA indicator:

Principal diagnoses: _____

Additional diagnoses: _____

Procedures: _____

Issues to clarify: _____

Optional MS-DRG Exercise (for users with access to MS-DRG software or tables)

Which of the following is the correct MS-DRG for this case?

a. 163, Major Chest Procedures with MCC
b. 853, Infectious and Parasitic Diseases with OR Procedure with MCC
c. 178, Respiratory Infections and Inflammations with CC
d. 003, ECMO or Tracheostomy with Mechanical Ventilation 96+ Hours or Principal Diagnosis Except Face, Mouth and Neck with Major OR

7.52. The following documentation is from the health record of a 29-year-old male.

Brief History: This patient is a 29-year-old male who presented to the emergency room with cough and shortness of breath. On examination, his skin was very warm and moist. His color was pale. He states he has been coughing and short of breath and febrile for several days. On admission, his temperature was 102.3°F, respirations 26 per minute and regular, pulse 126 per minute, blood pressure 150/90. He appeared ill.

Pertinent Physical Examination Findings: The patient had decreased breath sounds in the left lower lobe with basilar rales in that area. His heart was tachycardiac. There was no significant murmur, gallop, or rub. The abdomen was soft, no organomegaly. Extremities showed no edema, clubbing, or cyanosis.

Laboratory and X-Ray Findings: Chest x-ray showed consolidation involving the basal segments of the left lower lobe, as well as a subsegmental infiltrate involving the anterior segment of the right upper lobe. Hematocrit was 38.9, white count 5,900, 80 percent granulocytes. SMA profile was normal, including a cholesterol of 135, SGOT of 48. UA was clear. Gram stain of sputum showed few gram-positive cocci in clusters and many polymorphonuclear cells. Final sputum culture showed the usual throat flora. This culture, however, was taken after the patient had taken Augmentin orally for several days prior to admission. Blood and urine cultures showed no growth. Patient experienced episodes of tachycardia of unknown etiology. This will be followed up on an outpatient basis.

Hospital Course: It was the impression that the patient had lobar pneumonia due to *Pneumococcus*. However, because of the apparent failure of Augmentin, other etiologies were considered, and he was started on ceftizoxime. The patient responded promptly and felt well enough to be discharged with plans for follow-up in 2 weeks.

Which of the following is the correct code assignment?

a. 482.89
b. 483.8, 427.2
c. 481, 785.0
d. 482.9, 785.0

7.53.   The following documentation is from the health record of a 65-year-old male patient.

Hospital Course: This unfortunate gentleman was discharged from the hospital yesterday after being treated for several days for congestive heart failure. He presented back to the hospital within 24 hours after he developed significant respiratory discomfort and shortness of breath. He was found to be in respiratory failure and have pneumonia. The patient required ventilation in the emergency room. His x-ray showed diffuse infiltrates bilaterally, a condition also consistent with possible congestive heart failure. The patient did not have an elevated BNP. He was taken to the intensive care unit for further evaluation and treatment. It was explained to his wife and family that he was critically ill, and his survival was very guarded. The patient required blood pressure support. He was treated for pneumonia and his sputum cultures grew methicillin-resistant *Staphylococcus aureus.* He was treated with vancomycin. He had a stroke while admitted and had right-sided hemiparesis. He was found to have a left-sided internal carotid artery stenosis. He was felt not to be a surgical candidate because he was critically ill. He was placed on Bumex® infusion for his congestive heart failure. His respiratory status remained very tenuous despite maximum medical management. He was placed on TPN. His condition never improved despite all efforts. He remained poorly responsive, and he developed acute renal failure, as well. On day 15, it was clear that his survival was unlikely. His family asked that his ventilator support be discontinued. Shortly after, the ventilator was discontinued.

Discharge Diagnoses:

Acute respiratory failure secondary to pneumonia and congestive heart failure

Cerebrovascular accident with infarction

Methicillin-resistant *S. aureus* infection

Coronary artery disease

Acute renal failure

Lung mass

Chronic obstructive pulmonary disease

Diabetes mellitus

Paroxysmal ventricular tachycardia

Hemiplegia secondary to stroke

Hyperlipidemia

Anemia

Operative Procedures:

Mechanical ventilation greater than 96 hours

Packed red blood cell transfusion × 2

Placement of central venous line

Code Assignment including POA indicator:

Principal diagnoses: _____

Additional diagnoses: _____

Procedures: _____

Optional MS-DRG Exercise (for users with access to MS-DRG software or tables)

Which of the following is the correct MS-DRG for this case?

a. 189, Pulmonary Edema and Respiratory Failure
b. 291, Heart Failure and Shock with MMC
c. 207, Respiratory System Diagnosis with Ventilator Support 96+ Hours
d. 064, Intracranial Hemorrhage or Cerebral Infarction with MCC

7.54. History and Physical Exam

Present Illness: This 74-year-old male presented to the emergency room last night with complaints of increased weakness and shortness of breath. In the emergency room, he was found to be hypotensive. Blood pressure 83/42 apparently—actually that was the recording at home. In the emergency room, it was 130/80. He was afebrile, tachypneic per usual, respiratory rate of 32, and admitted with acute pneumonia. He was started on Levaquin®. He has a history of purulent sputum for several days. Since admission, he feels better; tachypnea and weakness have improved. His blood pressure readings have somewhat improved. His peripheral edema improved with a diuretic.

Past Medical History: End-stage pulmonary disease, atherosclerotic heart disease and congestive heart failure, gastroesophageal reflux disease, gout, and hypothyroidism.

Family History: Unremarkable

Social History: Has six children and is a widower

Physical Exam: On physical examination, blood pressure 102/70, pulse 90, respirations 28. He is pleasant, alert. Color is good. No JVD.

Chest: He has bilateral rales, which are chronic.

Heart: There is a systolic ejection murmur, grade 3, with an S4 gallop.

Abdomen: The abdomen is soft, nontender. No palpable organomegaly.

Extremities: Extremities reveal trace to +1 peripheral edema. He does have some stasis pigmentary changes. He does have clubbing of his fingers.

Musculoskeletal: No atrophic changes

Skin: Unremarkable except as noted

Neurological: He has no focal sensory or motor deficits and reflexes are physiologic.

Impressions: I suspect he probably just has purulent bronchitis and that is the cause of his deterioration. He is on Levaquin and seems to be improving. We will observe until tomorrow. If still doing reasonably well, we will let him go.

Discharge Summary

History of Present Illness: This 74-year-old male with end-stage pulmonary fibrosis was admitted via the emergency room with increased breathlessness. The admitting diagnosis was pneumonia. While here, he did not develop any significant fever.

Laboratory Studies: On admission PO_2 58, PCO_2 37, pH 7.45 on 3.5 L, his electrolytes were normal with the exception of BUN 28, creatinine 1.3, white blood cell count 8.6, hemoglobin 11.4, platelet count slightly low 117, urinalysis fairly unremarkable with trace protein, rare red and white blood cells.

Hospital Course: The patient was continued on Levaquin, which had been started 1 day previously. His chest x-ray showed decreased cardiac size from the previous examination, chronic infiltrates bilaterally, no acute infiltrates; pneumonia ruled out. Electrocardiogram showed sinus rhythm, right bundle branch block, left anterior hemiblock. He did receive intravenous diuretic and with this did achieve significant diuresis. My concern at the time of admission was the possible hypotension, which was recorded at home, but all blood pressure recordings here varied from the 100 to 130 systolic range.

Discharge Diagnosis: Probably acute bronchitis with possible mild congestive heart failure.

What are the correct code sets for this admission?

a. 466.0, 515, 428.0
b. 491.22, 428.0
c. 491.22, 466.0, 515, 428.0
d. 428.0, 466.0, 515e

7.55.   **Admission Diagnosis:** Pneumonia, hypoxemia

Discharge Diagnosis: Bilateral pneumonia, respiratory failure, dehydration, quadriplegia with old C5–C6 fracture, atonic bladder, tobacco use

Disposition: The patient is being discharged to home. Her daughter stays with her full time to care for her. She is to come to our office in one week to get a repeat chest x-ray and then further treatment with her pending results.

Hospital Course: The patient is a 50-year-old female who is a quadriplegic after a motor vehicle accident in which she suffered a C5–C6 fracture. She had a fever 2 days prior to admission, so we called her in a prescription for Keflex. She did not improve on this medication, and she came to the emergency room on the day of admission complaining of shortness of breath and cough. She reported a 2-day history of shortness of breath, fever, and cough productive of green and yellow sputum. There was no elevation in her temperature. A chest x-ray in the emergency room showed bilateral lower lobe infiltrates. She was admitted to the hospital for intravenous antibiotics for her pneumonia and treatment of her hypoxemia. Her pO_2 in the emergency room was 50 on room air. Her temperature was 102.6°F.

After admission to the hospital, the patient was placed on Biaxin®, and she did become afebrile and started to feel better. Her caretaker, who is her daughter, felt that she could care for her at home. The patient is being discharged to the daughter's care.

Work-up during this admission included a glucose of 81, a BUN of 6, a creatinine of .5. Electrolytes were normal. Her arterial blood gases show a pH of 7.482, a pCO_2 of 33, a pO_2 low at 50, HCO_3 324, and total CO_2 was 55. Her O_2 saturation was only 88 percent on room air. She was started on handheld nebulizer treatments, and she rapidly improved.

At the time of discharge, she was breathing easy on room air. She was benefiting from her handheld nebulizer treatments, and she wants to return home.

The work-up during admission, in addition to that above, included serum electrolytes, which were normal, except for a potassium level of 3.3. This was corrected with additional potassium. Her hemoglobin level on admission was 13.5. Hematocrit was 40.1, RBC was 4.40. Her MCV was 91. Her MCH was 33.6. RDW was 12.7. The urinalysis showed a moderate amount of hemoglobin but no red cells. Her chest x-ray did show a definite infiltrate in her left lower lobe and a questionable infiltrate in her right lower lobe. There is question that possibly her paraplegia may affect her ability to breathe, necessitating her seeing us for respiratory infections. The patient is discharged to home. She will be seeing Dr. Jones in 2 weeks after repeat chest x-ray.

Code Assignment including POA indicator:

Principal diagnoses: _____

Secondary diagnoses: _____

7.56. Discharge Summary

Admit Date: 3/19/20XX

Discharge Date: 3/25/20XX

Admitting Diagnoses: Acute exacerbation of asthma, chronic obstructive pulmonary disease, acute bronchitis, hormonal replacement therapy

Discharge Diagnoses: Acute exacerbation of asthma, chronic obstructive pulmonary disease, acute bronchitis, hormonal replacement therapy

Discharge Instructions: Patient is to follow up in the office in 1 week.

Discharge Medications: Spiriva® as directed daily, Pulmicort® inhaler two puffs p.o. every 12 hours, Serevent® Diskus® one puff p.o. every 12 hours, Augmentin 500 mg p.o. three times a day for 6 days, prednisone 35 mg to decrease by 5 mg every day until gone.

Brief History: The patient is a 57-year-old white female who presents with an approximate 1-day history of increasing dyspnea to the point where any ambulation required increasing effort as she could not catch her breath. The patient also had mild complaints of sore throat, neck pain, and headache. She denied any fever, although a low grade one was present on admission. The patient also admitted to a nonproductive cough.

The patient had an acute exacerbation of asthma and was admitted to observation. However, this did not clear with IV steroids, nebulizer treatments, or supportive therapy so she was admitted for inpatient treatment of acute exacerbation of asthma with possible bronchitis and respiratory distress. During her initial 2-day stay, Z-Pak®, Decadron, and albuterol and Atrovent treatments were continued because her respiratory distress did not significantly improve. The patient had increased anxiety secondary to her nebulized treatments and her medication was changed to Xopenex® with some improvement.

Chest x-ray was checked on the second hospital day, and a two-dimensional echocardiogram was ordered in addition to a pulmonary consult. The patient's Zithromax® was changed to Augmentin to better cover *Haemophilus influenzae* as a possibility. Inhaled steroids were added as the bronchodilators were continued. The patient's respiratory distress subsequently improved with less agitation with continued high-dose Xopenex. The two-dimensional echocardiogram was normal. The patient's respiratory condition improved with less dyspnea with her lung exam overall cleared. The patient was discharged in stable condition.

History and Physical: This is a 57-year-old female who presents with an approximate 1-day history of increasing dyspnea to the point where any ambulation required increasing effort, and she could not catch her breath. The patient stated that approximately 1 month ago some cold medication was phoned in for her, which cleared up her congestion but did not feel she totally got well. She was admitted from the emergency room to observation, but her symptoms did not resolve so she is being admitted for inpatient treatment. Patient smokes approximately one pack of cigarettes a day and denies any alcohol use.

Physical Exam:

General:	The patient is alert and oriented, appearing in mild to moderate respiratory distress
Lungs:	Showed decreased breath sounds throughout with no wheezing present
Abdomen:	Soft and nontender, with good bowel sounds present
Extremities:	No cyanosis or edema

The patient is currently on 2 L of nasal cannula with O_2 saturations at approximately 92 percent. Her chest x-ray is unremarkable.

Assessment and Plan: Acute exacerbation of asthma/chronic obstructive pulmonary disease/acute bronchitis. The patient will continue with Zithromax given at 500 mg p.o. q. 24 hours. Continued on 10 mg of Decadron q. 8 hours, given albuterol as well as Atrovent treatments on a daily basis.

Hormone replacement therapy on Premarin .625 mg/day

Consultant Report:

Reason for Consultation: Asthmatic bronchitis

Impression: Asthmatic bronchitis either representing acute exacerbation of chronic bronchitis and/or asthma. Cigarette use greater than 40-pack-years.

Recommendations: Change Zithromax to Augmentin because she has had antibiotics in the past 90 days, and there is a high incidence of resistant *H. influenzae* and streptococcal pneumonia.

Handheld steroids

Prophylactic H_2 blockers and low molecular with heparin

Check sputum for eosinophils

Cigarette cessation

Discussion: The patient has purulent bronchitis and wheezing on top of chronic daily shortness of breath and wheezing. This is compounded by at least 40-pack-years of smoking history. It is difficult to tell if this is just chronic obstructive pulmonary disease exacerbation due to infection or whether or not she has a large component of asthma. Whatever the initial diagnosis is, she would benefit with albuterol and Atrovent, inhaled steroids, and antibiotics.

On the long-term basis, she will need PFTs and a long-acting bronchodilator, Spiriva or Advair® depending on the way she responds on her pulmonary function test abnormalities. Advair is recommended if the FEV1 is less than 50 percent, Spiriva would be a better choice if this is all chronic obstructive pulmonary disease.

Emergency Room Report: Chief Complaint: Shortness of breath

History of Present Illness: The patient is a 57-year-old female complaining of shortness of breath since yesterday evening. She states that breathing difficulty became very severe to the point that she felt like she could not catch her breath. She could not walk across the room without becoming severely dyspneic. Also complaining of soreness in her neck bilaterally and of a headache.

Impression/Management Plan: Breathing difficulty with marked bronchospasm, possible fever with chills present. Rule out superimposed pneumonia. Symptoms consistent with exacerbation of asthma. Initial oxygen saturation on presentation to the emergency department 89 percent on room air.

Course in the Emergency Department: The patient received intravenous fluids, Decadron, magnesium. The patient did develop a fever in the emergency department with temperature up to 100.7°F, for which she received Tylenol. The patient received multiple nebulizer treatments in the emergency department and has persistent expiratory wheezes with somewhat labored respirations. Chest x-ray read negative for acute changes by my reading. The patient received initial dose of Zithromax in the emergency department. Decision for further treatment was made with an admission to the observation unit.

Final Diagnosis: Status asthmaticus.

What is the correct code assignment for this admission?

a. 493.91, 305.1, V07.4
b. 466.0, 493.22, 305.1, V07.4
c. 493.22, 305.1, V07.4
d. 493.21

7.57.   **Discharge Summary**

Date of Admission:	12/18/XX
Date of Discharge:	12/22/XX

Admitting Diagnoses:
1. Right lung mass.
2. Postobstructive pneumonia.
3. COPD.
4. Respiratory acidosis.

Procedure: Fiberoptic bronchoscopy on 12/20/XX.

History of Present Illness: This 80-year-old white male was admitted with a 4-day history of increasing dyspnea, fever, and productive cough. Initial evaluation suggested a right lower lobe pneumonia based on ER data. He was known to have underlying chronic obstructive pulmonary disease, and labs verified the presence of respiratory acidosis.

Physical Examination: He presented with a temperature of 97.9, respiratory rate of 28, pulse 127, blood pressure 162/80. There were coarse crackles heard in the right base with poor air flow throughout.

Hospital Course: The patient was admitted for treatment of right lower lobe pneumonia and acute exacerbating COPD. He was initially placed on Zinacef one gram q8 hours and Solumedrol 60 mg q6 hours. He was also provided supplemental oxygen as required and supervised inhalation therapy. On the 20th, the Solumedrol was changed to Prednisone 50 mg per day and the Zinacef changed to Ceftin 500 mg po b.i.d. With that, the cough, etc., began to improve.

Further investigation in the right lower lobe abnormality via a CT scan of the chest showed a 2-cm inferior hilar mass obstructing the right lower lobe bronchi associated with post productive infiltrate and/or atelectasis. This was suspicious for right inferior hilar neoplasm. Biapical scarring was also suggested. On 12/20/XX, fiberoptic bronchoscopy was performed. Fortunately, this showed no distinct endobronchial lesion. Any obstruction was peripheral to the area visible. Washings were negative for acid-fast bacilli. Brushings showed only atypical cells. Perioperatively, the patient had some worsening of his CO_2 retention, which was transiently benefited by Bi-PAP for his sleep. He had not required this prior to this admission and his sedation has not resolved. It was felt that this was a long-term need.

Laboratory Data: During this stay, an SMA7 was done on the 18th, showing glucose 126, BUN 26, and creatinine 1. Sodium 145, Potassium 3.8, Chloride 96, CO_2 32. The most recent blood gas was on the 22nd, showing a pH 7.4, pCO_2 67, pO_2 43, on 2 L nasal cannula. Theophylline level was 15.9. Hemoglobin of 14.4 and hematocrit of 42.4. White blood cell count 14,600 with 9 percent Bands.

Discharge Summary

Disposition/Recommendations: The patient is being discharged home with plans for continued antibiotics therapy and steroid taper, and arrangements for an outpatient fine needle aspirate of the lung abnormality.

Discharge Medications:
1. Atrovent 2 puffs inhalation q6 hours.
2. Albuterol 2 puffs q4 hours while awake prn.
3. Ceftin 500 mg po q12 hours for 10 more days.
4. Prednisone 30 mg per day for 6 days and then decrease by 5 mg every other day until weaned.

Activity and Diet: As tolerated.

As mentioned, request will be made for Radiology to arrange for an outpatient fine-needle aspiration of the lung abnormality. The patient understands that there is a risk of pneumothorax and if such occurs, he may return to the hospital for treatment of same.

Condition on Discharge: Improved.

History and Physical Exam

Date of Admission: 12/18/XX

History-Present Illness: This is an 80-year-old gentleman who presented to the emergency room last night. He had called me earlier in the evening with complaints of increasing breathlessness of about 4 days' duration. His evaluation in the emergency room suggested a right lower lung zone pneumonic infiltrate, and he did have a leukocytosis. He was admitted.

I have known this patient for approximately 3 years. For many years he has been treated for chronic obstructive pulmonary disease secondary to a long history of tobacco use. He has been oxygen-dependent for at least 3 years. In this interval, he has had one admission that I am aware of for exacerbation of COPD. His recent history is that of 4 days of increasing cough, purulent sputum production, and probably fever. He does describe chills and diaphoretic episodes.

Past Medical History: His past medical history is relatively unremarkable with the exception of his chronic obstructive pulmonary disease. As far as I know, he has no prior history of cardiovascular disease, stroke, or myocardial infarction.

Physical Examination: He is pleasant, alert, feels a bit more comfortable this morning. His blood pressure is 162/80, pulse 100, respirations 26. HEENT: Mouth and oropharynx are adequately hydrated. He does have a scar on his left lip at the site of corrective surgery for a harelip. Neck: Supple. There is no jugular venous distention. Chest: He does have somewhat of a pectus excavatum deformity with slight sternal retraction. He has coarse rales over his right chest laterally and posteriorly with a congested cough. Breath sounds are diminished on the left side. Heart: Regular rhythm without murmur or gallop. Abdomen: Soft, nontender. No masses. No organomegaly. Back and extremities: No clubbing, cyanosis, or peripheral edema. Distal pulses are easily palpable. Neurological: There are no focal neurological deficits.

Impression: 1. COPD. Plan: IV steroids and inhaled beta agonists. 2. Pneumonia. Plan: IV Zinacef. We will add Zithromax for community-acquired organisms.

EKG

Impression: Sinus tachycardia with premature ventricular contractions. Cannot exclude old inferior myocardial infarction, stable pattern.

Progress Notes

12/18   80 y/o admitted with 4 day hx of SOB, fever, and productive cough. #1
Pneumonia #2 COPD

12/19   CXR mass of lung neoplasm

12/19   Plan bronchoscopy

12/20   Bronchoscopy note dictated. No lesions noted. Pt. tolerated procedure well.

12/20   House Doctor: Pt. apparently very sedated after bronchoscopy –Demerol
12.5 mg and Phenergen 12.5 mg. Has now gotten 3 doses of Narcan with
noticeable alertness with each dose but then drifts off to deep sleep again.
V: BP 130/70 P 70 to 80s. SaO$_2$ now 95 to 97 on 2 L. Pt open eyes briefly
with prompting but not enough to answer ?'s or follow commands. CV:
RRR, Lungs: occ rales B Extremities: - edema. A/P: Excessive sedation is
what I suspect. Continue Narcan as needed. Will discuss with Dr. X.

12/21   S: No complaints
O: Afebrile, VSS, Lungs: poor air flow, Bronchial washings neg.
A: Lung Mass, Post obstructive pneumonia, Respiratory acidosis
P: D/C home for outpatient for FNA, Scenario discussed with family

12/22   Discharged home with family.

Operative Report

Operation Performed: Bronchoscopy.

Premedication: 12.5 mg. Demerol and 12.5 mg. Phenergan and Atropine 0.4 mg.

Description of Procedure: The patient was taken to the endoscopy room. The
nasopharynx and upper airway were anesthetized with 1 percent Xylocaine. The
Olympus fiberoptic bronchoscope was introduced into the left nostril without
difficulty. The nasopharynx and upper airway appeared normal. The vocal cords
moved anatomically to the midline. The trachea was then entered. The carina was
sharp. The right main stem bronchus was entered. There were inflammatory changes.

The bronchoscope was advanced into the right middle lobe. The mucosa was
somewhat friable, but no endobronchial lesions were identified. The bronchoscope
was then introduced further into the right lower lobe and brushings were obtained.
The area was then irrigated with saline, and washings were recovered. The
bronchoscope was then passed quickly to the left, side and no endobronchial lesions
were present.

The patient was monitored via blood pressure, pulse, and oximetry throughout,
maintaining oximetry in the 85 to 92 range, and other vital signs were normal.

Following the procedure, the patient was given an amp of Narcan.

Impression: Bronchoscopy suggestive of inflammatory process in the right lower lobe.

Code Assignment including POA indicator:

Principal diagnoses: _____

Additional diagnoses: _____

Procedure(s): _____

Optional MS-DRG Exercise (for users with access to MS-DRG software or tables)

What is the MS-DRG assignment for this admission?

Trauma and Poisoning

7.58. The following documentation is from the health record of a 4-year-old male patient.

Case Summary: The patient is a 4-year-old male child who, at the age of 2 years, swallowed some drain cleaner while playing in the bathroom. He was found at that time with acid burns of the mouth, throat, trachea, and esophagus. Plastic repair has been performed on the mouth and throat. He is now being admitted by a plastic surgeon for plastic reconstruction and removal of scar tissue to the trachea. The patient was admitted, prepped, and taken to surgery where the scar tissue of the trachea was removed, and plastic repair was accomplished. The patient's recovery was uneventful, and the patient was discharged in satisfactory condition three days postsurgery.

Which of the following code sets is correct for reporting the diagnoses of the most recent admission?

a. 709.2, 909.1, E929.2
b. 478.9, 909.1, 906.8, E929.2
c. 709.2, 909.5, 906.8, E864.2
d. 478.9, 909.5, E864.2

Optional MS-DRG Exercise (for users with access to MS-DRG software or tables)

What is the MS-DRG assignment for this admission?

7.59. The following documentation is from the health record of a 22-year-old male patient.

Case Summary: The patient is a 22-year-old male, admitted through the emergency department after the motorcycle he was driving collided with an elk on a mountain highway. The patient was not wearing a helmet and sustained a skull fracture over the left temporal and orbital roof areas with depressed zygomatic arch on the left side. The patient was unconscious at the scene and upon examination in the ED, with a GCS score of 12. Left pupil was blown (fixed and dilated), indicating intracranial injury. Hypoxemia, hypotension, and brain swelling were noted. The patient was admitted to the ICU with monitoring of intracranial pressure. The patient experienced increasing periods of apnea and was placed on a ventilator following endotracheal intubation. The patient also had numerous friction burns all over his body, but no other fractures were apparent. The patient's family (in another state) was notified and arrived 2 days later. There was no improvement in the patient's status over the next 4 days. The patient continued to be monitored and was unconscious. Attempts to wean from ventilation were unsuccessful. Brain wave monitoring showed no brain wave function. The family made the decision to discontinue life support and the life-sustaining efforts were discontinued.

Which of the following is the correct code set for this case scenario?

a. 804.45, E815.2, E849.5, 96.72
b. 803.45, 919.0, E815.2, E849.5, 96.72, 96.04
c. 801.05, 802.85, 802.45, E815.2, E849.5, 96.72, 96.04, 01.18
d. 801.45, 802.4, 919.0, E815.2, E849.5, 96.72, 96.04, 01.18

7.60. The following documentation is from the health record of a 28-year-old female patient.

Case Summary: The patient is a 28-year-old female passenger in a motor vehicle accident traveling at high speed on the freeway. Upon arrival in the ED the patient was complaining of severe abdominal pain. CT scan revealed laceration of the liver and increasing hematoma. The patient was taken immediately to the OR, where exploratory laparotomy revealed a traumatic rupture approximately 2 cm deep. It was felt that the parenchyma could not be adequately repaired, so a lobectomy was carried out with evacuation of the hematoma. The patient's postoperative course was stormy. The patient developed infection and dehiscence of the operative wound, necessitating return to the OR for opening and drainage of the wound. The patient was also given a 10-day course of IV gentamicin. The patient was finally able to be discharged on the 12th day postop in satisfactory condition.

Code Assignment including POA indicator:

Principal diagnoses: _____

Additional diagnoses: _____

Procedure(s): _____

Issues to clarify: _____

7.61. The following documentation is from the health record of a 32-year-old male patient.

History of Present Illness: A 32-year-old male was brought to the ED via ambulance. He was the unrestrained front-seat passenger in a single-vehicle crash that occurred because of a tire blow-out at high speed; the car collided with a barricade off the highway. The patient was ejected from the vehicle and had brief loss of consciousness witnessed at the scene. Paramedics reported the following vital signs en route: BP 110/palp; heart rate 90, respiratory rate 20. A large bore intravenous access was established, and fluids were begun.

Physical Examination:
Vital signs: Unchanged
HEENT: 2-cm superficial laceration over left eyebrow
Lungs: Clear to auscultation

CV: Regular rate, S1/S2; NSR on EKG monitor
Abdomen: Mild epigastric tenderness without rebound
Pelvis: Stable, no crepitans
Extremities: No deformities
Neuro: GCS 13, nonfocal exam

Radiology: Chest x-ray, lateral C-spine, and pelvis film all are reviewed by the chief resident on call and noted to be normal. CT scan of the patient's abdomen demonstrated free intra-abdominal fluid, perisplenic hematoma, and splenic laceration. Patient remained hemodynamically stable during the scan.

Because of the patient's young age and hemodynamic stability, nonoperative management of his splenic injury was begun. The patient was admitted to the ICU for hemodynamic monitoring, serial measurement of hematocrit, and serial abdominal examinations. He was transferred to the floor on hospital day 2 and made an uneventful recovery.

Diagnoses: 1. Minor concussion with 10 minutes of loss of consciousness
                2. Perisplenic hematoma and splenic laceration of capsule

Which of the following code sets for the diagnoses would be correct?

a. 865.11
b. 865.02, 850.9, E816.1, E849.5
c. 865.02, 850.11, E816.1, E849.5
d. 865.01, 865.02, 850.11, E816.1, E849.5

Chapter 8

Case Studies from Ambulatory Health Records

Note: Even though the specific cases are divided by setting, most of the information pertaining to the diagnosis is applicable to most settings. If you practice or apply codes in a particular type of setting, you may find additional information in other sections of this publication that may be pertinent to you.

Every effort has been made to follow current recognized coding guidelines and principles, as well as nationally recognized reporting guidelines. The material presented may differ from some health plan requirements for reporting. The ICD-9-CM codes used are effective October 1, 2009 through September 30, 2010, and the HCPCS (CPT and HCPCS Level II) codes are in effect January 1, 2009 through December 31, 2009. The current standard transactions and code sets named in HIPAA have been utilized.

Instructions: Assign all applicable ICD-9-CM diagnoses including V codes and E codes. Assign all CPT Level I procedure codes and HCPCS Level II codes. Assign Level I (CPT) and Level II (HCPCS) modifiers as appropriate. Outpatient health care settings represented in the case examples include emergency room (ER), urgent care, outpatient surgery, observation, ancillary outpatient, wound care, interventional radiology, radiation therapy, or other outpatient department. Final codes for billing occur after codes are passed through payer edits. Medicare utilizes the National Correct Coding Initiative (NCCI) edits. CMS developed the NCCI edit list to promote national correct coding methodologies and to control improper coding leading to improper payments for Medicare Part B. The purpose of the NCCI edits is to ensure the most comprehensive code is assigned and billed rather than the component codes. In addition, NCCI edits check for mutually exclusive pairs.

Cases are presented as either multiple choice or fill in the blank.

- For multiple-choice cases
  —Select the letter of the appropriate code set.
- For the fill-in-the-blank cases
  —Assign up to three reason for visit ICD-9-CM codes to describe the reason for unscheduled visits such as emergency room. Reason for visit coding is required on the UB-04 for all "unscheduled" outpatient visits.

—Sequence the primary diagnosis first followed by the secondary diagnoses, including any appropriate V codes and E codes (both cause of injury and place of occurrence).

—Sequence the CPT procedure code first followed by additional procedure codes including modifiers as appropriate (both CPT Level I and HCPCS Level II modifiers).

—Assign HCPCS Level II codes **only if instructed** (case specific).

—Assign evaluation and management (E/M) codes **only if instructed** (case specific).

- Type A provider-based emergency department visits are reported with CPT Level I codes 99281–99285 and critical care codes 99291 and 99292.
- Type B provider-based urgent care visits are reported with Level II HCPCS codes G0380–G0384.

The scenarios are based on selected excerpts from health records. In practice, the coding professional should have access to and refer to the entire health record. Health records are analyzed and codes assigned based on physician documentation. Documentation for coding purposes must be assigned based on medical record documentation. A physician may be queried when documentation is ambiguous, incomplete, or conflicting. The queried documentation must be a permanent part of the medical record.

The objective of the cases and scenarios reproduced in this publication is to provide practice in assigning correct codes, not necessarily to emulate complete coding that can be achieved only with the complete medical record. For example, the reader may be asked to assign codes based on only an operative report; in real practice, a coder has access to documentation in the entire medical record.

The *ICD-9-CM Official Guidelines for Coding and Reporting of Outpatient Services,* published by the National Center for Health Statistics (NCHS), supplements the official conventions and instructions provided within ICD-9-CM. Adherence to these guidelines when assigning ICD-9-CM diagnosis codes is required under the Health Insurance Portability and Accountability Act (HIPAA) of 1996. Additional official coding guidance can be found in the American Hospital Association (AHA)'s *Coding Clinic* publication.

Disorders of the Blood and Blood-Forming Organs

8.1.   The following documentation is from the health record of a 39-year-old male.

Emergency Department Services

History of Present Illness: The patient is a 39-year-old African-American male who has a known history of sickle cell anemia and who presented to the emergency department with diffuse extremity pain and pain along the right inguinal area. The pains started on Friday, became a little bit better on Saturday; then improved, and again started in the past 24 hours. He denies any problems with cough or sputum production. He denies any problems with fever.

Past Medical History: See recent medical records in charts. He does have a new onset of diabetes, probably related to his hemochromatosis. He does have evidence of iron overload with high ferritins.

Review of Systems: Otherwise unremarkable except for those related to his pain. He denies any problems with fever or night sweats. No cough or sputum production. Denies any changes in gastrointestinal or genitourinary habits. No blood per rectum or urine.

Physical Examination: This is a 39-year-old African-American male who is conscious and cooperative. He is oriented × 3 and appears in no acute distress. Vital signs are stable. HEENT is remarkable for icterus present in oral mucosa and conjunctivae, which is a chronic event for him. The neck is supple. No evidence of any gross lymphadenopathy of the cervical, supraclavicular, or axillary areas. The heart is irregular in rate without any murmurs heard. Lungs are clear to auscultation and percussion. The abdomen is soft and benign without any gross organomegaly. Extremities reveal no edema. No palpable cords. He does have some tenderness along the inner aspects of his right lower extremity near the inguinal area; however, no masses were palpable and no point tenderness is noted.

He had a problem with his right inguinal area. He had evidence of pain. There was some pain on abduction of his right lower extremity. The rest was unremarkable. There was no evidence of any Holman, no palpable cords, no masses were palpable.

Because of his sickle cell anemia, rule out the possibility of osteonecrosis of the femur. Complete x-rays of his femur and hip were carried out. However, these were both negative.

Patient is being transferred to a larger facility for treatment of his sickle cell crisis. Doppler studies should also be carried out to rule out any venous thrombosis.

Diagnoses: 1. Painful sickle cell crisis
            2. Type II diabetes mellitus
            3. Chronic atrial fibrillation

Condition on Discharge: Stable on pain meds

What codes would the facility report for this Medicare service? The patient met the fourth acuity level in the facility's criteria for evaluation and management in the ED.

a. 282.61, 789.09, 427.31, 250.00, 99285
b. 282.62, 733.42, 99284, 73550, 73510
c. 282.62, 427.31, 250.00, 73550, 73510
d. 282.62, 427.31, 250.00, 99284-25, 73550, 73510

8.2. The following documentation is from the health record of a 66-year-old male patient.

Outpatient Hospital Department Services

History: This is a 66-year-old male who had coronary artery bypass graft in February. He did well. He was discharged home. Some time after that when he was home, he had 2 days of black stools. He mentioned it to the nurse, but I'm not sure anything was done about it. He has not had any other evidence of hematemesis, melena, or hematochezia but was feeling rather weak and fatigued. He had blood work done that showed a hemoglobin of 5.7, hematocrit of 20.9, MCV of 80. Serum iron of 8, 2 percent saturation. No indigestion or heartburn. No abdominal pain of any kind. No past history of anemia or GI bleed.

Past Medical History: General health has been good.

Allergies: None known

Previous Surgeries: Coronary artery bypass graft

Medications: At the time of admission include Glucotrol, Lasix, potassium, and aspirin

Review of Systems: Endocrine: He does have diabetes controlled with medication. Cardiovascular: History of coronary artery disease with coronary artery bypass graft. No recent symptoms of chest pain or shortness of breath. Respiratory: No chronic cough or sputum production. GU: No dysuria, hematuria, history of stones, or infections. Musculoskeletal: No arthritic complaints or muscle weakness. Neuropsychiatric: No syncope, seizures, weakness, paralysis, depression.

Family History: Is positive for cardiovascular disease and diabetes in his mother. No history of cancer.

Social History: The patient is married. Never smoked. Doesn't drink any alcohol. Works in a factory.

On physical examination, a well-developed, well-nourished, alert male in no acute distress. Blood pressure: 146/82. Respirations: 18. Heart rate: 78. Skin: Good turgor and texture. Eyes: No scleral icterus. Pupils are round, regular, equal, and react to light. Neck: No jugular venous distention. No carotid bruits. Thyroid is not enlarged. Trachea in the midline. Lungs are clear. Heart: No murmur noted. Abdomen is soft. Bowel sounds present. No masses, no tenderness. Liver and spleen are not palpably enlarged. Extremities: Good pulses. Trace edema of the feet.

Laboratory values show severe anemia with a hemoglobin of 5.7. Hemoccult is also positive. His iron studies showed low iron and low ferritin, consistent with chronic blood loss anemia. His B_{12} and folate levels were normal. His SMA-12 was essentially unremarkable.

Impression: 1.   Anemia. Probably he is anemic after bypass and then had stress gastritis with a little bit of bleeding and has never recovered from that. No evidence of acute or active bleeding at this time. The patient is stable. Possibility of occult malignancy or active peptic ulcer disease does exist.
2. Arteriosclerotic heart disease of native vessel, stable

Recommendations: Admit patient as an outpatient for blood transfusion. Patient is being transfused. He should have an esophagogastroduodenoscopy and colonoscopy, possible biopsy or polypectomy, which has been explained to the patient along with potential risks and complications including bleeding, transfusion, perforation, and surgery. These tests will be scheduled as soon as possible.

Discharge Note

Final Diagnoses:
1. Severe blood loss anemia; weakness
2. Type II diabetes mellitus
3. History of coronary artery disease status post coronary artery bypass graft

The patient received three units of packed red blood cells, leukoreduced, CMV negative. He felt better, with subsidence of his shortness of breath, and his weakness improved. His last hemoglobin was 8.4, with a hematocrit of 27.7.

The patient was scheduled for EGD to rule out peptic ulcer disease and colonoscopy to rule out occult malignancy in 1 week. The patient will be discharged home, and he will have a clear liquid diet. He is to call for any problems. He will continue with his home medications, and he was placed on ferrous sulfate, one tablet twice a day.

What codes are reported for this outpatient encounter? The facility purchases its blood from the blood bank.

a. 280.0, 792.1, 414.01, 250.00, V45.81, V17.40, 36430, P9051 (3 units)
b. 285.9, 780.79, 36430, P9051 (3 units)
c. 280.0, 578.1, 414.01, 250.00, V45.81, V17.40, 36430
d. 285.9, 792.1, 414.01, 250.00, V45.81, V17.49, P9051 (3 units)

8.3. The following documentation is from the health record of an 87-year-old female patient.

Emergency Department Services

History: The patient is an 87-year-old white female brought to the ED because of pleural effusion, urinary tract infection, and dehydration. She had been taking medication. She lives at the nursing home and has been doing fairly well. Today she was found to be weak and not eating well. Then she was sent to the emergency room for evaluation and found to have pleural effusion and dehydration, urinary tract infection, also thrombocytopenia with petechial hemorrhage. She was found to have a platelet count of 77,000.

Past History: She has a history of cholecystectomy.

Social History: She is a retired woman. No smoking, no drinking, no allergies.

Family History: Noncontributory

Systemic Review: Otherwise normal

Physical Examination: Today reveals blood pressure is 163/62. Pulse of 80. Respirations of 15. Temperature of 98.6°F. General condition of the patient showed chronically ill, confused, disoriented. No jaundice, no cyanosis. No pallor, no edema. The patient has dehydration +3. Scalp and skull are normal. There was a bluish color around the eyes and petechial hemorrhage at the eyelid and conjunctiva. Ears, nose, and throat are normal. Neck showed normal cervical spine. The neck veins are flat. No bruits of the carotid arteries. The trachea is midline. Thyroid gland cannot be palpated. Lymph glands cannot be palpated. Chest shows normal contour. The breasts are normal. Movement of the chest equal on both sides. There is dullness of the chest with some rales and rhonchi. Heart shows apex beat is at the fifth intercostal space, left midclavicular line. No diffuse precordial pulsation, no thrill. Heart rate is 80, regular, with premature ventricular contraction, no murmur. Back is normal. Abdomen showed normal contour, soft, nontender, no guarding, no rigidity. Liver, spleen, and kidneys cannot be palpated, no mass is palpable. Bowel sounds are positive. No fluid thrill. No shifting dullness. No bruits of the abdominal vessels. Extremities show no clubbing of the fingers. No varicose veins. No phlebitis. Hematoma of the right hand. Peripheral pulses are normal. The deep tendon reflexes are normal. Babinski sign is negative.

Laboratory Studies: Hematocrit was 43, white count 9,000 with 82 percent neutrophils, and the platelet count 77,000. The MCV was 102. Creatinine was 1.7. Bilirubin was 1.7. The alkaline phosphatase was 122. AST 498, ALT 493, and albumin 3.6. The prothrombin time was 18 seconds, the PTT was 25 seconds. The chest x-ray showed a right pleural effusion.

Impression:
1. Urinary tract infection
2. Dehydration
3. Pleural effusion from congestive heart failure
4. Primary thrombocytopenia with petechial hemorrhage
5. Type II diabetes mellitus

Plan of Treatment: The patient will be stabilized and started on IV fluids. Also will start IV antibiotic for urinary tract infection.

Patient will be transferred at the family's request to a larger facility. A consultation with hematology will be arranged, and a transfusion of platelets may be indicated.

What are the appropriate diagnosis codes for this service?

a. 599.0, 276.51, 428.0, 287.5, 250.00
b. 599.0, 276.51, 428.0, 511.9, 287.5, 250.00
c. 599.0, 276.51, 428.0, 287.30, 250.00
d. 599.0, 276.51, 428.0, 511.9, 287.30, 782.7, 250.00

8.4. The following documentation is from the health record of a 39-year-old female patient.

Hospital Outpatient Department Services

This 39-year-old female was diagnosed with breast cancer 2 years ago. At that time she had a mastectomy performed, with no evidence of metastases to the lymph nodes. About 8 months ago, metastases were discovered in her liver. The patient was given chemotherapy. She has been losing weight and developing increased fatigue. Patient was referred to hospice care program, with a life expectancy of 4 to 6 months. Progressive weight loss due to loss of appetite led to cachexia and program of home intravenous hyperalimentation. Progressive, unrelenting abdominal pain led to chronic use of analgesics. Patient is awake, alert, and desires to spend more time with family. Progressive weakness and dropping hemoglobin led to the decision to transfuse the patient every 2 weeks with two units of packed cells. Patient is stable and more comfortable on this regimen.

She is coming into the outpatient department now for transfusion.

Diagnosis: History of breast cancer, current liver metastases, anemia due to the neoplasm and chemotherapy.

What are the correct diagnosis codes assigned in this case?

a. 285.22, 197.7, V10.3, E933.1
b. 285.9, 197.7, V10.3, E933.1
c. 197.7, 285.22, V10.3, E933.1
d. 285.9, 197.7, V10.3

Disorders of the Cardiovascular System

8.5.   The following documentation is from the health record of a 60-year-old male patient.

Outpatient Hospital Diagnostic Services

A 60-year-old man was given a stress test for recent left arm pain that occurred with exercise the day before. His only medication was Dyazide 1 daily. He was exercised by the Bruce protocol for a duration of 6 minutes, 2 seconds using the treadmill. Maximum heart rate achieved was 137, 85 percent maximum predicted was 136. His blood pressure during the stress test went up to 182/80. He denied any arm pain with the exercise. He did have 2 mm of ST depression at a point of maximum exercise in 2, 3, AVF, but these were all upsloping. Also in V5, V6, he had 1.4-mm ST depression, also upsloping.

Following exercise he was placed at rest. At about 1 minute, 45 seconds post exercise, his STT waves changed. He had STT wave depression with T-wave inversion in the interior and V5 and V6 leads. The patient remained asymptomatic throughout, with no arrhythmias. His blood pressure dropped to a low of 38 systolic over 0 at 6 minutes post exercise and remained low for several minutes. During this time period, an IV was started and D5 1/2 normal saline at 200 cc/hour was given to elevate the blood pressure. IV started at 12:30 and stopped at 13:20. The patient remained pain free during this episode and felt fine during the entire episode. At the 10-minute mark, the T-wave inversion started resolving, and the STT waves returned to normal.

Upon consultation with Dr. Jones at Magic Memorial, the patient was advised to report for a cardiac catheterization to rule out ischemic heart disease.

Which codes are reported by the hospital for this outpatient service?

Note: The cardiologist is not employed by the hospital reporting the test. _— Tracings Only_

a. 786.50, 796.3, 93015, 90760
b. 729.5, 796.3, 93015, 90760
c. 414.8, 458.29, 93017, 90765
d. 729.5, 458.9, 93017, 90760

8.6.   The following documentation is from the health record of a patient who received hospital outpatient surgical services.

Preoperative Diagnosis: Hypertensive cardiovascular with end stage renal disease and congestive heart failure

Postoperative Diagnosis: Same

Procedure: Placement of AV fistula with Gore-Tex® graft of the right forearm for dialysis access

Description: After placement on the operating table, the patient was premedicated with .05 mg of Versed. The right arm was prepped and draped in the usual sterile fashion. Following the infiltration of 1 percent lidocaine, a transverse incision was made just beyond the antecubital fossa. Dissection was carried down, the basilic vein and artery were identified and mobilized, and Silastic loops were placed. Another incision was then made, just above the wrist. After the area was infiltrated with lidocaine, a 6-mm Gore-Tex graft was tunneled through the loop. Anastomosis to the artery was accomplished after the patient received 2,000 units of IV heparin. End-to-side anastomosis was accomplished with 6-0 and 7-0 Prolene sutures. The end areas were interrupted and the edges approximated with running sutures. On removal of the clamps, excellent blood flow was evident. Anastomosis was deemed satisfactory. Venous anastomosis was then accomplished with 6-0 and 7-0 Prolene sutures. Flushing and back-bleeding was allowed prior to completion of the anastomosis. Upon completion, excellent flow was evident through the vein. After a period of observation with no bleeding, both wounds were closed with subcutaneous 3-0 VICRYL® in a running fashion, and the skin was closed with 4-0 Prolene sutures. Dressings were applied and the patient returned to the outpatient recovery area in stable condition.

Which of the following is the correct code set?

a. 404.92, 36830
b. 404.93, 585.6, 428.0, 36830
c. 585.6, 428.0, 401.9, 36821
d. 404.93, 36821

8.7.   The following documentation is from the health record of a patient who received hospital outpatient diagnostic services.

Preoperative Diagnosis: Angina

Postoperative Diagnosis: Patent coronary arteries and grafts, ASHD present

Procedure: Right and left heart cath with coronary angiography

The patient was brought to the cath lab in a fasting state. The right groin was prepped and draped in the usual sterile fashion. After local anesthesia was administered, sheaths were placed percutaneously into the right femoral artery and vein. IV heparin 3,000 units, were given.

Using a thermodilution catheter, right heart pressures were measured, and thermodilution cardiac outputs and AV oxygen differences were obtained. A pigtail catheter was inserted into the left ventricular cavity, and simultaneous left ventricular pressures were measured. A pullback was obtained across the aortic valve.

Using a 7R4 catheter, angiography was performed of the right coronary artery and both vein grafts. A 7L4 was used for angiography of the left coronary artery. Additional attempts were made to image the vein graft to the right coronary artery with a right coronary artery bypass catheter. The pigtail catheter was reinserted, and left ventricular angiography and aortic root angiography was performed. The patient tolerated the procedure well and returned to the recovery room in good condition.

Which codes are assigned for this service?

a. 414.00, 413.9, V45.81, 93526, 93543, 93540, 93544, 93555, 93556
b. 414.01, 414.02, 93526, 93543, 93540, 93544, 93555, 93556
c. 414.00, 413.9, V45.81, 93526, 93543, 93540, 93544
d. 414.01, 414.02, 413.9, V45.81, 93510, 93543, 93544

8.8. This 21-month-old male presents to the Emergency Department with nausea and vomiting since 10 pm last night, at least 8 times, which is nonbloody but bilious. Temp of 39.8 since last night. He has a history of Tetralogy of Fallot, s/p repair 2 months ago. He has known immunodeficiency, laryngomalacia and a gastrostomy tube. After examination, working differential diagnoses are acute gastroenteritis, bacteremia, or possible septicemia. Symptoms similar to episode about 1 month ago that was determined to be bacteremia with G-tube site infection. The patient is treated with Zofran 2 mg IV, followed by Ceftriaxone 600 mg IV. The patient is discharged after resolution of vomiting and fever. Diagnosis listed as acute gastroenteritis.

Assign the correct ICD-9-CM codes for the facility services provided today.

a. 279.3, 558.9, 748.3, V13.69, V15.1, V44.1
b. 558.9, 790.7, V15.1, V44.1
c. 787.01, 558.9, V44.1
d. 787.03, 780.60, 558.9, 745.2, V15.1, V44.1

8.9. A patient with rapid atrial fibrillation that is resistant to medical management is referred to the EP laboratory for AV node ablation. He undergoes placement of catheters in the right atrial septum for mapping and in the right ventricle for temporary pacing. The appropriate location for ablation is mapped and the designated area is ablated to achieve complete heart block. Assign the appropriate CPT code(s) to report this procedure.

a. 93650, 93620
b. 93650, 93620-59
c. 93650
d. 93650, 93620, 93622

8.10. This 63-year-old male patient presents to the ED by ambulance after collapsing while mowing the lawn at home. He has a diminished level of consciousness but says that he had palpitations and lightheadedness followed by apparent syncope. His wife saw him fall and immediately called 9-1-1. He has a prior history of MI 3 years ago and coronary atherosclerosis of the native vessels. His vital signs on presentation show hypotension with a heart rate of 110. His EKG shows arrhythmia. While on the heart monitor the patient's rhythm changes to ventricular fibrillation. 150-J biphasic cardioversion shock is performed, following standard advanced cardiac life support protocols. Arrhythmia continues following cardioversion, and the patient arrests. CPR is performed, and the patient is resuscitated.

The physician documents: 35 minutes of critical care provided, exclusive of the time spent performing cardioversion, for a patient with acute ventricular tachycardia, ventricular fibrillation, prior MI, coronary atherosclerosis of native vessels, and cardiac arrest, successfully resuscitated.

What are the correct diagnosis and procedure codes for this patient?

8.11.   The following documentation is from the health record of a patient who received hospital outpatient radiology department services.

Preoperative Diagnosis: Left carotid aneurysm, internal extracranial portion

Postoperative Diagnosis: Same

Procedure: Left carotid artery test occlusion

Procedure Description: With the patient properly prepared and draped in sterile fashion, a 6-French sheath was inserted in antegrade fashion into the right femoral artery. A diagnostic catheter was inserted coaxially through the sheath and used to select the left internal carotid artery. An exchange 018 wire was placed through the catheter and then the catheter was removed. A 6 mm × 2 cm balloon catheter was threaded over the wire and positioned with the balloon across the lumen of the proximal left internal carotid artery. The balloon was inflated to 0.5 atmosphere while slowly injecting contrast through the end of the balloon around the wire. Complete stasis of the carotid artery was documented. Neurologic testing was performed for 5 minutes. The patient was placed on heparin prior to this procedure, and a 5,000-unit bolus was administered in the left carotid artery just prior to balloon inflation. Another 1,000 units of heparin were slowly administered through the tip of the balloon over a 5-minute period, along with saline. Only a small amount of total fluid was administered, and contrast was found to be static in the carotid artery during the entire period. After 5 minutes, the balloon was deflated and the patient was sent to the recovery area in good condition.

What is the correct code assignment?

a. 437.3, 36100, 37204, 75894
b. 442.81, 36620
c. 442.81, 36100, 37204, 75894
d. 442.81, 61626, 36100, 75894

8.12.   The following documentation is from the health record of a cardiac catheterization patient.

Procedures Performed: Left heart catheterization.
Coronary angiography.
Right coronary artery mid in-stent restenotic lesion;
Percutaneous transluminal coronary balloon angioplasty;
Placement of intracoronary stent.

Right coronary artery-distal stent edge lesion;
Percutaneous transluminal coronary balloon angioplasty;
Placement of intracoronary stent.
Adjunct use of intravenous Aggrastat infusion.

Complications: None.

Indication: This is a 70-year-old white male with known history of hyperlipidemia, TIA and coronary artery disease status, post PTCA with stent placement of the mid right coronary artery on July 27, 20XX, who presented with recurrence of chest pain. The stress MIBI cardiac scan performed on January 29, 20XX revealed proximal inferior wall perfusion defects extending to the LV apex.

Diagnostic Angiography: After obtaining informed consent, the patient was brought to the cardiac catheterization laboratory in a fasting state. The bilateral femoral areas were prepped sterilely in the standard fashion, and ECG monitoring was established. Using the modified Seldinger technique, arterial access was obtained in the right femoral artery.

The #7 French Cordis JL-4 HF and JR-4 HF catheters were used to perform the diagnostic coronary angiography. The left main artery was large and essentially normal. The left anterior descending artery was moderate sized, long, and wrapped around the apex without significant lesion. The first diagonal branch artery was large, bifurcated, and essentially normal. The second diagonal branch artery was small sized and normal. The left circumflex artery was large and had 40 to 50 percent ostial stenosis. The first and second obtuse marginal arteries were small and normal. The right coronary artery was dominant and had 90 to 95 percent multifocal in-stent restenosis in the mid artery. There was also 60 to 70 percent distal stent edge stenosis in the early distal right coronary artery. The PDA and PLB arteries were normal.

Procedure: Mid right coronary artery (RCA) in-stent restenosis and distal stent edge lesions: Following the diagnostic coronary angiography, Aggrastat 16.1 cc IV bolus was then given to the patient with continuous infusion at rate of 14 cc/hour for 50 minutes. Heparin, 5,400-unit IV bolus, was also given to the patient to control ACT around 200 to 300 seconds. After this, a #8 French Cordis JR-4/side hole guiding catheter was used to engage into the ostium of the right coronary artery. After baseline angiography was performed, a Guidant 0.014 inch Hi-Torque floppy extra support guidewire was then advanced out of the guide into the RCA. The guidewire was then advanced across the mid RCA in-stent restenotic lesion and positioned in the distal PLB artery without difficulty. After this, an NC Ranger balloon, 2.75 mm in diameter by 22 mm in length, was advanced over the guidewire into the mid RCA in-stent restenotic lesion. The balloon was positioned across the lesion and inflated twice at 18 atmospheres and 20 atmospheres for 60 seconds, respectively. The patient had transient chest pain and ST-T wave elevation in the inferior leads.

Following this, the balloon was then advanced further to cross the distal stent edge lesion in the early distal right coronary artery and inflated at 10 atmospheres for 60 seconds. Repeat angiogram still revealed some residual narrowing at the distal stent edge lesion. After this, the balloon was then exchanged out for a BX Velocity, 2.75 mm × 8 mm, coronary stent that was advanced to deploy cover in the distal stent edge lesion at 12 atmospheres for 15 seconds; however, the stent did not overlap with the mid RCA previously stented segment. Repeat angiogram revealed a small dissection at the distal RCA in the gap between the old and the new coronary stent. The operator then elected to deploy another short stent to cover the dissection. The second BX Velocity, 2.75 mm × 8 mm, coronary stent was then advanced to position to cover the dissection, overlapping with the mid RCA and distal RCA stented segment. The stent was then successfully deployed at 12 atmospheres for 30 seconds. Follow-up angiogram revealed good luminal dilatation in the distal RCA stented segment; however, there was increased renarrowing within the mid RCA in-stent restenotic lesion with irregular border. The operator decided to deploy another stent to cover within the mid RCA in-stent restenotic lesion. The third BX Velocity, 2.75 mm × 18 mm, coronary stent was then advanced to position within the mid RCA in-stent restenotic lesion and successfully deployed at 14 atmospheres for 30 seconds. After this, the stent balloon was used to post dilate sequentially within the entire mid RCA and distal RCA stented segment at 10 atmospheres and 12 atmospheres for three minutes of total duration.

Final orthogonal angiogram revealed no residual stenosis in the overlapping stented mid and distal RCA in-stent restenotic lesion and distal stent edge lesion. There was no angiographic evidence of dissection or thrombus. Flow to the distal vessel was TIMI grade 3. Plavix, 375 mg, was given to the patient after the stent deployment. At this point, it was elected to conclude the procedure. Balloon, wires, and catheters were removed. The hemostatic sheaths were sewn in place. The patient was transferred back to the ward in stable condition.

Conclusions: 1. Significant multifocal in-stent restenotic lesion in the mid RCA with distal stent edge lesion in the distal RCA.
2. Successful percutaneous transluminal coronary balloon angioplasty and placement of three overlapping coronary stents (BX Velocity 2.75 mm × 18 mm, 2.75 mm × 8 mm, and 2.75 mm × 8 mm) in the mid RCA in-stent restenotic lesion and distal stent edge lesion in the early distal right coronary artery.

What are the correct diagnosis and procedure codes for this patient?

Code(s): _____

Disorders of the Digestive System

8.13.   The following documentation is from the health record of a 68-year-old female patient.

Emergency Department and Hospital Observation Services

The patient presented to the ER per ambulance from the nursing home for G-tube placement. According to nursing staff at Happy Acres, there has been a foul-smelling green drainage for the past several days. Today the bulb was deflated and was found lying on the stomach. Nurses attempted to place the tube without success. Patient has redness surrounding the stoma.

Procedure: Gastrostomy tube placement

Date: 11/30/2000

The patient was taken to the GI treatment room where the wound site was scrubbed with Betadine. A wire was placed into the stomach with relative ease. At this point, because the tract appeared to be closed, an 8-mm balloon was then applied across the tract with some dilatation. A 16-gauge MIC tube was attempted to be placed through the site, but could not be accomplished, even with multiple attempts. Therefore, a 12-gauge Foley was attempted, also without much result. The patient will have to proceed with endoscopic replacement of the gastrostomy tube. The patient was sent to an observation bed in good condition, and tube placement was arranged in the GI lab for tomorrow.

Procedure: Esophagogastroduodenoscopy with percutaneous endoscopic gastrostomy tube replacement

Date: 12/01/20XX

Record Review: This is a 68-year-old white female with an astrocytoma with seizure disorders who requires feeding by gastrostomy tube due to inability to swallow. Yesterday an attempt was made to replace the feeding tube by manipulation of the abdominal wound site and use of an MIC tube and a 12-gauge Foley, both of which were unable to be placed through the tract, even after dilating with a 10-mm balloon. The patient is noncommunicative but has no history of prior surgery other than the previous placement of the PEG tube. Physical exam shows blood pressure of 130/76, pulse 60. Lungs show a few rales. Heart, regular rhythm. Abdomen soft, nontender, with an obvious wound site where the previous gastrostomy tube was placed.

Procedure Description: The patient is prepared in the GI treatment room with IV sedation. The Pentax upper endoscope was passed beyond the cricopharyngeus muscle in the left lateral decubitus position. Examination of the mid and distal esophagus was relatively normal. The scope was advanced into the stomach where a prior gastrostomy site was seen. The antrum was otherwise unremarkable. The pylorus was normal. The scope was then advanced to the second, then the third portion of the duodenum. The third portion, second portion, and duodenal bulb were normal. The scope was brought back into the antrum. The abdominal wound site was cleaned in the usual fashion. After taking a culture of the drainage, I chose a site next to the prior site. However, even after using a 22-gauge spinal needle, I was unable to locate the stomach, even 1 cm away from the prior site. Therefore, because a wire could be advanced through the prior site, it was decided to place the wire of the gastrostomy tube kit into the stomach, which went in easily. A snare was used to grab the scope and pull it out in the usual fashion via the mouth. At this time, a 20-gauge Bard Mushroom gastrostomy tube was easily pulled out via the prior abdominal wound site and fixed in the usual manner. Betadine scrub was used to clean the infected wound. Betadine antibiotic ointment was used around the gastrostomy tube site. The bumper was applied in minimal fashion, and the patient returned to the observation bed in good condition.

The patient was held an additional 8 hours to receive IV Ancef to prevent cellulitis, then transferred to a skilled care bed in the nursing facility. Close observation by nursing home staff is recommended for signs of infection or other problems. The wound site was strongly positive for *Staphylococcus aureus*.

What codes will be reported for the outpatient care of this Medicare observation patient for services from 11/30 to 12/1?

a. V55.1, 191.9, 345.9, 43246, 43760-52
b. 191.9, 345.9, V55.1, 43246, 43760-74
c. 536.41, 041.11, 787.20, 191.9, 345.9, 43246, 43760-52
d. 996.69, 041.11, 787.20, 191.9, 345.9, 43246

8.14.   A patient reported to the ambulatory surgery department at the request of her general surgeon.

Operative Report: Hospital Outpatient Surgery Department

Preoperative Diagnoses: 1. Inguinal hernia
                                2. Postcolorectal resection for CA

Postoperative Diagnosis: Same

Procedure: Right inguinal herniorrhaphy

Description of Procedure: Under general anesthetic, an incision was made over the anterior wall of the inguinal canal, which was opened. The cord was isolated, taking care to protect the nerve. The hernia sac was seen, which has direct hernia on the medial aspect of the wound. This was reduced and held in place using mesh that was stapled into place with a hole being made for the cord. The anterior wall of the inguinal canal was then closed with VICRYL®, a hemostasis was achieved, and the wound closed with skin clips. Following this, the attention was turned to a screening colonoscopy, which was performed to the ileocecal valve without difficulty. Ascending, transverse, and descending colon were normal. There was no true evidence of diverticula. The sigmoid was normal, and a retroflex view of the rectosigmoid anastomosis in the rectum shows no gross abnormalities. The patient tolerated the procedure well and will be followed in the office.

Which code set is reported by the facility for this outpatient surgery?

a. 550.90, 562.10, V10.05, 49505-RT, G0105
b. 550.90, V76.51, V10.06, 49505-RT, 45378
c. 550.91, V76.51, V10.05, 49505-RT, 49568-RT
d. 550.90, V10.06, 49520-RT, 45330

8.15.   The following documentation is from the health record of a 70-year-old Medicare patient who received hospital outpatient services.

Operative Report

History and Indications: The patient is a 70-year-old female who has complained of altered bowel habits, abdominal pain, and a 2- to 3-g documented decline in hemoglobin, confirming blood loss anemia. Her stools are heme negative, but there is suspicion that she may have pathology in the colon. She presents today for a diagnostic colonoscopy.

Procedure: Incomplete colonoscopy

In the endoscopy suite, with appropriate monitoring of pulse, oxygenation, temperature, blood pressure, and respiration, a digital rectal examination was performed. IV sedation was administered. Following the digital exam, the Pentax video colonoscope was inserted through the anus and was advanced almost to the midsigmoid colon. At this point, anatomic factors precluded any further advancement. In this instance, it was felt that a conservative approach was warranted in view of the patient's cardiovascular symptoms, including elevation of blood pressure and tachycardia and generally frail state. We elected to terminate the procedure and removed the air using suction and removed the instrument. The patient stabilized and she was sent to recovery in good condition, but the examination was incomplete. No evidence of malignancy was seen in the section of the colon that could be visualized. The patient will be further evaluated using alternative methods.

Which code set will be submitted for this Medicare patient for the services described?

a. 789.00, 787.99, 280.0, 796.2, 785.0, V64.3, 45378-74
b. V71.1, V64.3, 45378-52
c. 789.00, 787.99, 280.0, 796.2, 785.0, V64.3, 45378
d. 789.00, 787.99, 280.0, 997.1, V64.3, 45330

8.16. The following documentation is from the health record of a 65-year-old male who received hospital outpatient GI laboratory services.

Endoscopy Record

Preoperative Diagnosis: Guaiac positive stools

Postoperative Diagnosis: Multiple colon polyps, diverticulosis

Procedure: Total colonoscopy with biopsy and polypectomy

Indications: This is a 65-year-old male who was found to have guaiac positive stools on a routine exam, no change in bowel habits or appreciable weight loss.

The patient was brought to the endoscopy suite and placed in the left lateral decubitus position. 50 mg of Demerol and 2 mg Versed were administered. Digital rectal exam was performed, which was normal. Olympus colonoscope was inserted and passed under direct vision. A large polyp was seen immediately at 20 cm. This appeared to be pedunculated and approximately 1.5 cm long. Scope was passed all the way to the cecum and then slowly withdrawn. Cecum, ascending colon, hepatic flexure, transverse colon all appeared normal except for fairly extensive diverticula in the cecum and scattered throughout the rest of the sets. At the splenic flexure at 80 cm, there was a lesion, which was biopsied with a hot biopsy probe. At 60 cm, there was another small polyp, which was cauterized at the base with the probe and excised. At 20 cm, the pedunculated rectal polyp was snared and removed. The exam of the base revealed complete excision. The rest of the sigmoid and the rectum were unremarkable.

The pathology report showed mucus polypoid tissue at 80 cm and adenomatous polyps at 60 cm and 20 cm.

Which of the following code sets should be reported?

a. 211.3, 211.4, 562.10, 45385, 45384-59, 45380-59
b. 211.3, 569.0, 45384
c. 211.3, 569.0, 45385, 45384-59, 45380-59
d. 792.1, 211.3, 569.0, 562.10, 45385, 45384

8.17.   The following documentation is from the health record of a 40-year-old female patient.

Emergency Department Services

HPI: This is a 40-year-old female with a 3-year history of diarrhea and a 1-year history of epigastric discomfort. She had a CT scan with a mass on the tail of the pancreas, as well as gastrin level greater than 1,000 while taking Prilosec®. She has been amenorrheic for the past 4 months.

The patient presents to the ED with severe diarrhea and dehydration after discontinuing medications to allow for a repeat gastrin level off medications to eliminate the compounding effect of Prilosec on gastrin levels. Unfortunately, she was unable to stay off medication long enough, and she developed severe diarrhea with dehydration and a creatinine greater than 3, and she was admitted to observation services. Gastrin level is 1,023 with VIP of 290.

Patient was rehydrated and orally treated with 200 mEq of potassium. The patient had significantly elevated calcium, which normalized with rehydration. Vitamin D level is pending, and PTH level also has returned elevated, concurrent with a calcium of 9.9. MRI of the abdomen has revealed multiple lesions in the liver with a density consistent with metastatic malignancy. Additionally on the MRI, a 6-cm pancreatic mass was noted at the tail of the pancreas.

This scenario is most consistent with multiple endocrine neoplasia syndrome (MEN-1) with parathyroid hyperplasia leading to hypercalcemia when dehydrated. Most likely, the recent normal calcium is due to a concurrent hypovitaminosis D, which is, in turn, secondary to chronic diarrhea. Dostinex® has been initiated today at 0.25 mg two times a week. Most likely she has MEN-1 given the current pancreatic and pituitary evidence of adenoma.

She is transferred to Memorial Hospital for CT-guided biopsy of a possible adenocarcinoma and to rule out the possibility of MEN-1.

Discharge Diagnoses:	1. Pancreatic and pituitary adenomas with multiple lesions on the liver consistent with metastasis
	2. Probable carcinoid syndrome (MEN-1)
	3. Hypercalcemia while dehydrated with normalization on rehydration
	4. Severe chronic diarrhea with hypokalemia and hypomagnesemia
	5. Amenorrhea

Discharge Medications: Prevacid 30 mg, one p.o. b.i.d.

Magnesium oxide 400 mg, one p.o. t.i.d.
Sandostatin® ampules 0.5 amp of 1 mg per amp every 8 hours
Trazodone 50 p.o. q. h.s. p.r.n. insomnia
Darvocet N® 100 mg p.o. q. 4–6 hours p.r.n.
Dostinex 0.5 mg 1/2 tab every Wednesday and Saturday

Which of the following is the correct ICD-9-CM code set for this observation service?

a. 237.4, 573.8, 275.42, 276.51, 787.91, 276.8, 275.2, 626.0
b. 211.6, 227.3, 197.7, 275.42, 276.51, 787.91, 276.8, 275.2, 626.0
c. 235.5, 237.0, 197.7, 275.42, 276.51, 787.91, 276.8, 275.2, 626.0
d. 237.4, 573.8, 259.2, 275.42, 276.51, 787.91, 276.8, 275.2, 626.0

8.18. The following documentation is from the health record of a 57-year-old male patient.

Hospital Outpatient Department Services

Diagnoses:
1. Lung cancer
2. Chemotherapy with Taxol and carboplatin with dexamethasone
3. Type II diabetes with neuropathy and nephropathy, uncontrolled
4. Hyperlipidemia
5. Hepatomegaly

This patient is a 57-year-old male who presents to the outpatient department for chemotherapy, which has been complicated by his diabetes because it has been difficult to control. He had surgery for lung cancer in September and has now undergone chemotherapy with Taxol and carboplatin, including dexamethasone as part of his chemo and prophylaxis for nausea. He has done very well with the chemotherapy. His diabetes is complicated by neuropathy and nephropathy. Dr. Johnson consulted with the patient to manage his diabetes. He has been on 70/30 insulin, 25 units in the morning and 15 units in the evening, for over 1 year. His hepatomegaly has enlarged from the last time that I saw him. I question whether this is fatty infiltration due to poor diabetes control, or whether there is now some involvement with metastatic carcinoma.

Taxol and carboplatin were infused today, followed by dexamethasone; see infusion sheet. The patient appears to have tolerated the chemotherapy well.

Laboratory Data: Sodium 128, potassium 5.5, chloride 89, CO_2 34, BUN 13, creatinine 0.8, glucose 210, calcium 9.4, WBC 9.8, hemoglobin 11.6, hematocrit 34.3, platelets 277,000.

Plan: One difficulty here is the cyclic nature of his treatment regimen, likely to produce major shifts in his glucose, which is already difficult to control. The patient will need to monitor his glucose levels closely and follow up with Dr. Johnson. The patient has instructions to call in to Dr. Johnson's nurse on a daily basis for the next week. He is to follow up with me for further chemotherapy next week.

Which of the following is the correct ICD-9-CM code set for this outpatient visit?

a. 162.9, 250.62, 357.2, 250.42, 583.81, V58.67, 272.4, 789.1
b. V58.11, 250.62, 250.42, V58.67, 272.4, 789.1
c. V58.11, 162.9, 250.62, 357.2, 250.42, 583.81, V58.67, 272.4, 789.1
d. 162.9, 250.02, V58.67, 272.4, 789.1

Disorders of the Genitourinary System

8.19.   The following documentation is from the health record of a 22-year-old male patient who received hospital outpatient surgery services.

A patient with chronic benign hypertension and stage V chronic kidney disease requiring chronic dialysis, replacement of a permanent Quinton catheter, and the formation of an arteriovenous graft in the left forearm. Following heparinization, the anastomosis was performed, which resulted in a good pulse, but no thrill. The vein was then explored where an area of stenosis was found. This was opened and a dilator passed, but no more than 2-mm diameter was possible. Therefore, the anastomosis was taken down, a tunnel formed, and a 4 × 7 Impra® graft used. The graft originated at the antecubital fossa, which was opened transversely. The vein here was about 4 mm, so there were no problems passing a dilator. The graft was then anastomosed over a distance of approximately 5 mm, resulting in good flow. Wounds were closed in layer fashion with 3-0 VICRYL® for deep tissues and continuous suture of 6-0 Prolene.

Following completion of the graft, the patient was reprepped and draped for the changing of the Quinton catheter. Following administration of local anesthesia, an incision was made high in the neck close to the point of insertion in the internal jugular. A guidewire was then tunneled centrally through the existing catheter. The old Quinton catheter was removed and an obturator placed. Then a peel-away introducer was inserted easily. The wounds were then closed and a confirmatory x-ray obtained for placement. This showed the Quinton catheter extended well into the internal jugular. Dialysis was provided the same day.

Which of the following code sets will be assigned for this?

a. 585.6, 401.1, 36830, 90935
b. 403.90, 36825, 90935
c. 403.11, 585.5, 36830, 36581-59
d. 403.11, 585.6, 36830, 36581-59, 90935

8.20.   The following documentation is from the health record of a patient who received hospital radiology department services.

A patient who has had his bladder removed due to carcinoma without recurrence is ordered to have a radiology procedure to evaluate the patency of his ileal conduit, including a ureteropyelography using contrast media. The chief complaint and reason for service line in the progress note is blank. The entire procedure is performed in the radiology suite with the radiologist's impression of "normal functioning ileal conduit."

Which of the following procedure codes should be reported for the UB-04 in this case? Do not assign ICD-9-CM Volume III procedure codes.

a. V55.6, V45.74, V10.51, 50684, 74425
b. V55.2, V10.51, 74425
c. 596.8, 188.9, 74425
d. Contact the ordering physician to obtain a diagnosis before coding this encounter.

8.21. The following documentation is from the health record of a 47-year-old female.

Hospital Outpatient Surgery Services

Preoperative Diagnosis: Menorrhagia, failure of conservative treatment

Postoperative Diagnosis: Same

Procedure: Hysteroscopy with biopsy, dilatation and curettage

Diagnosis: Menorrhagia

Anesthesia: General

Indications: The patient is a 47-year-old multigravida female with increasing irregular vaginal bleeding. The uterus is very tender, and ultrasound reveals no specific adnexal masses. A Pap smear shows some chronic inflammatory cells. Bleeding has not been controlled in the past month with conservative therapy; thus, the patient is admitted for dilatation and curettage, and a hysteroscopy and biopsy will be carried out.

Technique: Under general anesthesia, the patient was prepped and draped in the usual manner with Betadine, with her cervix retracted outward. Secondary uterine prolapse was noted with minimal cystocele, large rectocele, enterocele, and moderate cervical erosions. The vaginal vault appeared to be clear, as did both adnexa. However, the uterus was thought to be slightly enlarged. Sound was passed into the intrauterine cavity after the cervix was found to be 8 cm deep. The cervix was dilated with Hegar dilators up to #5. The 5-mm Wolff scope, with normal saline irrigation, was then inserted. An inspection of the endocervical canal showed no abnormalities.

Upon entering the uterine cavity, some irregular shedding of the endometrium was noted. Endometrial shedding was noted more to be the patient's left cornu area than the right. The contour of the cavity appeared to be normal; no bulging masses or septation were noted. The Wolff scope was removed, and the cervix was further dilated with Hegar dilators up to #12. A medium-sharp curette was inserted into the uterine cavity and the uterus was curettaged in a clockwise manner, with a moderate amount of what appeared to be irregular proliferative endometrium being obtained. Again, the contour of the cavity appeared to be normal. Endometrial biopsies also were taken. The patient was transferred to the recovery room in good condition.

Pathology report reveals secretory proliferative endometrium without additional abnormalities noted.

Which of the following code sets will be reported?

a. 626.2, 618.4, 618.6, 616.0, 58558
b. 626.2, 58558
c. 626.2, 618.4, 618.6, 616.0, 58100, 58120
d. 618.4, 618.6, 616.0, 58558

Infectious Diseases/Disorders of the Skin and Subcutaneous Tissue

8.22. The following documentation is from the health record of a 62-year-old female patient.

Hospital Outpatient Surgery Services

The patient is a 62-year-old female who has been in generally good health until last month, when she developed a crusty lesion inside the left naris. She initially treated it with Vicks® ointment. When it failed to heal, she decided to seek medical attention. Her primary care physician biopsied this lesion, and the pathologic diagnosis was squamous cell carcinoma of the left internal nasal ala. She is posthysterectomy (10 years) for endometrial carcinoma. She has smoked $1^1/_2$ packs of cigarettes each day for the past 40 years.

The patient presented to the outpatient surgery center of the hospital for wide excision of the left internal nasal alar lesion, which is less than .5 cm in diameter. This procedure included a full-thickness resection in the middle and posterior thirds of the lateral cartilage, along with vestibular skin and mucous membrane. Nasal reconstruction was required to provide an acceptable cosmetic appearance following excision. A flap graft composite reconstruction was utilized for primary closure of the defect that was left following excision, using donor tissue from the right arm and requiring primary closure of a 2-cm graft.

Which of the following code sets is appropriate for this case?

a. 173.3. V10.42, 30118, 30400
b. 160.0, V10.42, 305.1, 30150, 15760
c. 160.0, 15760, 30150
d. 173.3, V10.42, 305.1, 14060

8.23. The following documentation is from the health record of a 44-year-old female patient.

Hospital Outpatient Surgery Services

Preoperative Diagnosis:	Extensive superficial partial-thickness wounds to the abdomen, secondary to poor wound healing; status post abdominoplasty
Postoperative Diagnosis:	Same
Operation:	Split-thickness skin graft

History: This is a 44-year-old white female who underwent abdominoplasty for morbid obesity in October 20XX, and had poor wound healing after the procedure. The patient underwent several débridements and presently has an extensive superficial, partial-thickness abdominal wound that is granulating well, but it was felt the patient would benefit significantly from split-thickness skin graft to decrease wound pain and decrease convalescence time.

Details of Procedure: The patient was taken to the operating room, and prepared, and draped in the usual sterile fashion, preparing the donor site of the right thigh as well as abdominal superficial partial-thickness wound. First, two donor grafts were taken with the Brown dermatome, adjusted to a #10 blade, 10:1000 of an inch size. The grafts were placed over the abdominal superficial partial-thickness wound in the abdomen after it was prepared by a sharp débridement with Bard-Parker #10 blade. The graft was scored with a #10 blade Bard-Parker in a meshing fashion The graft was then sewn into place with multiple 5-0 VICRYL® sutures. The wounds as well as the donor site were then covered with an Owens dressing. Sutures were placed, and the Owens was reinforced with wet saline cotton balls and with a fluff dressing. The stents were then tied in place and covered with a pressure dressing of Elastoplast®, while the donor site received wet-to-dry dressing with ABD burn pad taped into place. The patient was extubated in the operating room. All needle and sponge counts were correct, and the patient was taken to the PAR in stable condition.

Pathology Report: None

Which of the following code sets is correct for this case?

a. 998.59, E878.8, 15100
b. 998.59, 15002, 15100
c. 998.83, E878.8, 15100, 15002
d. 998.83, 278.01, 15200

8.24. The following documentation is from the health record of a patient who received hospital outpatient surgery services.

Preoperative Diagnosis: 1. Biopsy-proven malignant melanoma, Clark Level I, right shoulder
  2. Neoplasm on left heel

Postoperative Diagnosis: Same

Operation: 1. Wide excision of malignant melanoma, Clark Level I, right shoulder with wide undermining, rotation, and advancement flap reconstruction

  2. Excision of left heel 2 cm × 1 cm × .5 cm pigmented neoplasm, rule out dysplasia vs. malignant melanoma, with wide undermining, rotation, and advancement flap reconstruction

Description of Procedure: The patient was placed on the operating table in the prone position with the back and left heel prepped and draped in sterile fashion. Utilizing 1 percent Xylocaine with epinephrine, a block of the two sites was performed.

The right shoulder lesion was outlined with Brilliant Green in the lines of relaxation, excised in full-thickness fashion down to the fascial level. Undermining over the fascial level was then performed with rotation flaps elevated into position and sutured deeply at the fascial level with #5-0 PDS interrupted, #6-0 PDS, superficial dermis, and #6-0 PDS running intracuticular on the skin. Total area slightly over 10.2 sq cm.

Attention was then turned to the left heel where the pigmented neoplasm was outlined with Brilliant Green, excised in full-thickness fashion, and closed at the fascial level with #4-0 PDS interrupted and 4-0 black nylon interrupted on the skin.

The patient tolerated the procedure quite well and was taken to the recovery room.

Pathology Report

Preoperative Diagnosis: Melanoma right shoulder and lesion left heel

Postoperative Diagnosis: Same

Macroscopic: Specimen 1: Received in formalin, labeled "melanoma right shoulder; biopsy proven Clark Level I" is one ellipse of tan skin, 5 × 1.3 × 1.8 cm. In the center is a healing pink ulcer, 0.6 × 0.4 cm.

The specimen is serially sectioned, and the central lesion is totally submitted in multiple cassettes.

Specimen 2: Received in formalin, labeled "lesion left heel" is one ellipse of tan skin, 1.8 × 0.9 × 0.4 cm. In the center is a brown macular lesion that covers much of the center of the specimen. The specimen is totally submitted in multiple cross sections.

Microscopic and Summary

Specimen 1: Right shoulder excision. Healing ulcer of skin overlying eschar. There is mild scarring and focal foreign body response.

Specimen 2: Left heel. Compatible with a giant pigmented dysplastic nevus.

Which of the following codes sets would be reported for this ambulatory surgery?

a. 172.6, 216.7, 14001, 15002
b. 216.7, 216.6, 14000
c. 216.6, 238.2, 14001, 11606, 11423
d. 172.6, 238.2, 14001, 11423-59, 12041

8.25.   The following documentation is from the health record of a patient who received hospital outpatient surgery services.

Preoperative Diagnosis:	Nevus of the left auricle
Postoperative Diagnosis:	Nevus of the left auricle
Operation:	Excision of nevus, left auricle, with reconstruction with full-thickness skin graft, postauricular area

Description of Procedure: The patient was brought to the operating suite and placed under satisfactory general anesthetic using an indwelling endotracheal tube. The left ear and postauricular areas were prepped with Betadine.

A total of 6 cc of 1 percent Xylocaine with 1:200,000 adrenalin were utilized during the procedure. The lesion measured about 6 mm and was superficially infiltrating at its margins with some variegated color being present as well. The lesion was at a 2 o'clock position on the auricular helix. Margins of about 5 mm were made around the lesion. The tissues were submitted for permanent section.

The resulting defect could not be closed primarily. The postauricular incision was outlined for development of postauricular skin graft centered at the level of the cephaloauricular groove. The graft measured about 8 mm × 10 mm in its form and was elliptical in its orientation. The resulting defect postauricularly was closed in layers with 4-0 VICRYL® to the subcutaneous layer and 4-0 nylon in an interrupted fashion to the skin.

The skin graft was placed and sutured in place with four sutures peripherally with 4-0 silk and then was tied over bolster sutures of 4-0 silk with a bacitracin-impregnated section of sponge rubber. The patient is to avoid contact sports and to keep a prescription for Duricef 250 mg twice a day for 10 days. A prescription for Cap elixir with codeine 1 to 2 tsp, 8 oz was also given. The patient is to be followed in approximately 1 week in the office.

Pathology Report

Tissues/Specimen: Skin of external ear, nevus of left auricle

Clinical History: Left ear nevus

Gross Description: "Nevus left auricle" consists of small 4-mm fragment of skin. Entire specimen submitted.

Microscopic: Sections show the specimen to consist of an ellipse of skin showing a benign compound nevus. There is no evidence of malignancy.

Which of the following code sets will be reported for this service?

a. 216.8, 15240, 15004, 12051
b. 216.2, 15260, 11442
c. 173.2, 15260, 11442
d. 216.2, 14060

8.26.   The following documentation is from the health record of a male patient who received emergency department services (Type A provider-based emergency room).

ED Report

A patient who is a known heroin addict is brought in significant distress to the emergency room by friends. His genitalia are covered with many lesions. Due to his IV drug habit and sexual preference, he is at risk for HIV exposure and hepatitis. He has experienced febrile jaundice for three days. He is unable to provide a medical history, but the physician is able to get some information from his girlfriend. Although severely ill, he is not comatose. Medical decision making was stated to be of high complexity. The ER acuity system used by the hospital for medical visits indicated a Level IV service.

Physical examination reveals multiple excoriations covering the penis and scrotum with fluid-filled blisters. The patient is jaundiced and in significant distress. The last "fix" was 3 hours ago per the girlfriend, and the patient has been using heroin daily for the past 2 months. A number of laboratory tests were run, and it was determined that the patient should be transferred to a tertiary care center for definitive treatment and an infectious disease consultation and substance abuse rehabilitation when stable.

The physician's dictated report that details the test results shows the following diagnostic assessment:

1. Herpes simplex virus-2 infection, culture confirmed, severe outbreak

2. Hepatitis suspected, pending laboratory results for type, abnormal liver function studies confirmed; febrile jaundice $\times$ 3 days

3. HIV seropositive; recommend Western blot to confirm

4. High-risk lifestyle; sexual habits and drug addict

Which of the following code sets will be reported in addition to chargemaster-reported codes?

a. 054.10, 782.4, 794.8, 042, 99284
b. 054.19, 573.3, 795.71, 305.51, V69.8, 99214
c. 054.13, 054.19, 070.1, 794.8, 795.71, 305.51, V69.2, 99284
d. 042, 305.51, 070.1, 99291

Behavioral Health Conditions

8.27. The following documentation is from the health record of a 26-year-old male.

Hospital Outpatient Services

On 1/15, a 26-year-old white male was admitted after being transferred from the outpatient evaluation service with severe homicidal and suicidal ideation. Admitting diagnosis was severe major depressive disorder with psychotic features. Pharmacological treatment was initiated, and suicide precautions were instituted. After a thorough diagnostic evaluation, the risks and benefits of ECT were reviewed. Due to the severity of the psychotic episode and the patient's delusional state, it was determined that ECT was warranted. Extensive efforts were made to secure informed consent from the patient, and a course of ECT was begun.

On 1/23, the psychiatrist reviewed the patient's status noting any changes in his physical condition and his response to the treatment. He performed a problem-focused interval history, a problem-focused examination, and medical decision making of low complexity. At this visit, the psychiatrist again reviewed the treatment options and confirmed the patient's continued consent for ECT. Subsequently on 1/23, the fourth treatment of ECT was administered via placement of a stimulus electrode frontotemporally. Sufficient electrical stimulus was applied to produce an adequate ictal response. A generalized seizure was monitored via EEG. EKG, blood pressure, and pulse remained acceptable throughout. Postictal observation was notable for cardiac arrhythmia, which subsided without sequelae. The patient tolerated the procedure well and was returned to his inpatient room in good condition.

He was discharged to a group home on 1/25 and returned to the hospital as an outpatient for his final planned ECT treatment. Again, sufficient electrical stimulus was applied to produce an adequate ictal response. A generalized seizure was monitored via EEG. EKG, blood pressure, and pulse remained acceptable throughout. Postictal observation was notable for cardiac arrhythmia, which subsided without sequelae. The patient tolerated the procedure well and was held in observation for 4 hours posttreatment, then discharged to the care of his group home supervisor in good condition.

Which of the following code sets is reported for the 1/25 outpatient hospital service?

a. 296.24, 90870
b. 296.24, 90870, 95812, 93040
c. 296.24, 90870, 99211-25
d. 296.24, 90870, 95812, 93040, 99234-25

8.28. The following documentation is from the health record of a 56-year-old man.

Emergency Department and Hospital Observation Services

Final Diagnosis: Chronic schizophrenia, paranoid type with acute exacerbation, improved, compensated congestive heart failure

Pertinent Laboratory Results: Electrolyte panel within normal limits. Digoxin level was 0.6, hemoglobin A1C 6.5, triglycerides 138, CBC unremarkable. TSH 1.3, urinalysis negative. EKG showed normal sinus rhythm.

Assessment: This is a 56-year-old male who presented to the Emergency Room with his sister after decompensating at a hotel where he thought people were trying to get into his apartment, and he continued to decompensate with his paranoia and persecutory-type delusions, so that she felt he needed evaluation for hospitalization. Psychiatric consultation was initiated with Dr. Brown.

Recently, his personal physician has been switching his medications from Zyprexa to Seroquel to Risperdal, and then he started Prolixin. We requested and reviewed his records, and it appears he did quite well on Risperdal, so he went back to taking that, and he was titrated up to 30 mg q. h.s. of Risperdal and 100 mg of trazodone. These two medications helped significantly to eliminate his delusions and paranoid ideation. He was admitted to observation status and slept peacefully for 6 hours. His sister reported that he is doing the best that she has seen him in quite some time, and we were conversing at the time of discharge. After consultation with this psychiatrist about the change in medication, the patient was released in the custody of his sister to follow up with his personal physician next Tuesday.

Pertinent Findings on Mental Status at Discharge: Patient spent 45 minutes in the final examination. Behavior is cooperative, fair eye contact. Speech is of normal rate and volume. Not rapid or pressured. Mood euthymic, affect appropriate. Thought process is goal directed, decreased paranoid ideation. Negative for racing thoughts and flight of ideas. Thought content: He denies signs of active psychosis, denies current suicidal or homicidal intent. Insight and judgment improved. Impulse control is fair.

Prognosis: Fair. The main problem is that the patient did not respond well to medication changes. He did do well with the changes we made, but his mental illness may be exacerbated if his medical conditions are not well controlled or if he is noncompliant with dosages.

Aftercare Recommendations: The patient will be discharged to his sister's care and will be followed by his personal psychiatrist, Dr. X. Social services will follow the patient from his hometown.

The hospital acuity system used showed this to be a Level 4 ER service.

Which of the following code sets is correct for reporting this service?

a. 295.34, 428.0, 99201
b. 295.32, 99283
c. 295.34, 428.0, 99284
d. 295.84, 99234

8.29. The following documentation is from the health record of a female patient who received psychiatrist treatment services in a hospital outpatient–based clinic.

XX/XX/XX 6:20 p.m. Dialectical behavior therapy (DBT), individual therapy— 1:1 × 45 minutes at 5 p.m.

Subjective/Objective: Patient and I reviewed diary card and target hospitalizable behaviors and increased skills to stay out of the hospital and complete the outpatient program. Target goals 1 through 3 were reviewed today. Patient did not engage or act on urges for self-harm and urges for suicide after self-injurious behavior on XX/XX/XX. We focused on reinforcing skills of emotion regulation, highlighting times she used these while at work and with family members. Suicidal ideation today was minimal with sense of increased willingness to learn to apply skills. Discussed need to address ETOH dependence because patient notes increased risk of suicidal ideation with ETOH use. She identifies "fear" of "running in panic" will be what keeps her from staying with chemical dependency (CD) program. We addressed treatment plan (see below) to increase skills associated with CD treatment follow-through as well as structuring environment to "keep me in CD treatment."

Assessment: Major depressive disorder, recurrent; posttraumatic stress disorder, ETOH dependent; borderline personality disorder. Continued suicidal risk, patient has had some success over urges but is now coping well with the outpatient treatment where she receives therapy four times a week.

Plan: Patient and I identified targeting emotion regulation and distress tolerance in individual therapy to increase control over urges for suicidal thoughts, as well as follow-through with substance abuse treatment. Extended structuring continues with increased resources for managing son's behavior at home. Patient wants family meeting to orient family to DBT to increase chance they will be supportive of her treatment after discharge as opposed to disparaging, which, according to the patient, has increased her emotional vulnerability leading to increased suicidal urges. I gave times I would be available for a family meeting.

Addendum: Patient now has few suicidal urges and wants to do target behaviors. She reviewed skills with me to "get through" the rest of her week at home and at work. She notes that level of urges right now is manageable for her, and she believes she is improving.

Which of the following code sets is correct for reporting the outpatient services provided to this patient?

a. 296.20, 309.81, 303.92, 301.83, 300.9, 90819
b. 296.30, 309.81, 303.90, 301.83, 300.9, 90845
c. 296.30, 309.81, 303.90, 301.83, 90818
d. 296.30, 309.81, 303.90, 301.83, 300.9, 90818

8.30. The following documentation is from the health record of a 45-year-old female patient.

Mental Health Clinic Visit (Facility Services)

The 45-year-old patient is seen today for 20-minute medication review in the Community Mental Health Center. Patient continues to be somewhat elevated in her mood with some evidence of grandiosity but overall is goal directed and seems to be doing reasonably well with her subchronic schizophrenia in the structured setting. Patient currently is now off Seroquel and will continue to transition from oral Prolixin to Prolixin Decanoate®. She did receive Prolixin Decanoate 12.5 mg IM on XX/XX/XX. When I try to decrease her oral Prolixin dosage, we notice some more increased grandiosity as well as more impulsive behavior and more thought disorganization, so on XX/XX/XX we increased her Prolixin back to 5 mg q. h.s. orally. On seeing her today, she seems to be improving somewhat on that. Her appetite and sleep pattern were fine over the weekend. She had no evidence of aggressive behavior. I decided at this time to maybe increase her Prolixin Decanoate® to 25 mg IM every 2 weeks, and that will start today. Will continue with the oral Prolixin for a period of time and then will be able to eliminate that. There is a meeting with her family this upcoming Wednesday and we'll discuss patient's care and how they feel she is doing and also discuss discharge and aftercare planning if that's appropriate.

Mental Status Exam: Appearance: The patient is a female who looks her stated age. Behavior: Cooperative, fair eye contact. Speech: Normal rate and volume. Mood slightly elevated. Affect less labile. Thought process: More goal directed. Negative for racing thoughts, flight of ideas. Thought content: Has delusional belief system, but it has decreased in intensity. No evidence of auditory, visual, or olfactory hallucinations. Denies current suicide or homicide intent. Insight: Judgment remains impaired. Impulse control improving.

Impression: Axis I: Schizophrenia, paranoid type, acute exacerbation
               Axis II: None known
               Axis III: Hypercholesterolemia; currently on Lipitor

Plan: At this time will continue on the Prolixin Decanoate but increase to 25 mg IM every 2 weeks. Will continue with the oral Prolixin at 5 mg q. h.s.

Which of the following is the correct code set for reporting this clinic service?

a. 295.33, 272.0, 90862
b. 295.30, 272.0, 90862
c. 295.30, 272.0, 90862, 99231
d. 295.33, 272.0, M0064, 99231

8.31. The following documentation is from the health record of a female patient who received services in a community mental health center.

Reason for Encounter: The patient has not had any self-injurious behavior or behavioral problems this past week except that she has used marijuana, which she endorses. Today we discussed her treatment and overall she is happy with the DBT program and her chemical dependency program. She and I discussed future care and the need for her to get away from her current living arrangements.

Counseling/Coordination of Care: We reviewed how her DBT is going and what skills she could use when she has high urges to use marijuana. We also discussed that I would be doing periodic drug screenings.

Response to/Complications of Current Medications: None. The patient is happy with her medications as they are.

Examination:	WNL	Abnormal
General appearance	X	
Muscle strength/tone, gait		
Speech		
Thought process	X	
Associations/psychosis		
Suicidal/homicidal ideation	X	
Judgment and insight	X	
Attention span/concentration		
Orientation	X	
Recent and remote memory	X	
Fund of knowledge	X	
Mood and affect	X	

Assessment of Current Status: The patient appears to be stabilizing; however, she does appear to have a need for ongoing chemical dependency treatment and support, perhaps on an inpatient basis if the outpatient treatment plan fails to control relapses.

Diagnosis: Borderline personality disorder; major depression, recurrent; cannabis dependence.

Plan: Continue DBT and chemical dependency treatment. The social worker and the patient should begin to work on alternative living arrangements because the patient is exposed to substance abuse in the current living arrangements and has conflicts with others living in the same apartment. We will not be changing any medications at this time.

Session Time: 25 minutes

Over 50 percent Counseling/Coordination of Care? __ Yes _x_ No

History: Problem focused

Examination: Problem focused

Decision Making: Straightforward

Which of the following code sets is correct for reporting this clinic visit with a psychiatrist?

a. 301.83, 296.30, 304.31, 99214
b. 301.83, 296.30, 304.30, 99212
c. 301.83, 296.30, 304.30, 90805
d. 301.83, 296.30, 304.31, 90805

Disorders of the Musculoskeletal System and Connective Tissue

8.32.   The following documentation is from the health record of a 39-year-old female patient.

Hospital Outpatient Surgery Services

Admission Diagnosis: Possible rotator cuff repair

Discharge Diagnosis: Partial rotator cuff tear, right shoulder

Procedure: Arthroscopy, right shoulder, with subacromial decompression and excision of the distal clavicle

Short-Stay History and Physical
Age, Sex, Diagnosis, Operation: 39-year-old female for right shoulder arthroscopy.
Patient has complained of pain in shoulder since injury 1 week ago.
Past Surgery: D&C in 1986
Anesthetic Complications: None
Allergies: NKDA
Medications: HCTZ for hypertension. Last dose taken before admission.
Respiratory Assessment: Clear, smokes cigarettes, 1/2 pack per day
Cardiovascular: Normal sinus rhythm, normal heart sounds. Blood pressure 168/90 on medication.
Bleeding: Negative history
Renal: No complaints
Hepatic: Negative history
Neuromuscular: Negative, except as above
Metabolic: Negative
Diagnostics: Chest x-ray shows mild cardiomegaly, otherwise normal
Physical Status: Cleared for arthroscopic surgery, pain in right shoulder, possible rotator cuff; monitor blood pressure

Operative Report

Preoperative Diagnosis: Probable rotator cuff

Postoperative Diagnoses: 1. Partial rotator cuff tear and anterior labral tear, right shoulder
2. Chronic bursitis

Procedure Description: The patient was taken to surgery. After adequate induction of general anesthesia, the patient was placed in the left lateral decubitus position and prepped and draped in standard orthopedic fashion. The arthroscope was introduced through a standard posterior portal. On visualizing the glenohumeral joint, the glenoid and humeral head appeared to be normal. The instruments were then transferred to the subacromial bursa. There was evidence of chronic bursitis that was resected away. There was also a large acromial spur with corresponding lesion on the superior surface of the rotator cuff, appearing to be a traumatic-type injury with a partial rotator cuff tear. This was débrided and anterior acromioplasty was performed with the shaver in the lateral and posterior portals. The coracoacromial ligament was excised down to the coracoid, the AC joint was carefully examined, and it was thought that the distal clavicle was moderately arthritic, and resection of the distal clavicle was accomplished as well. Once this had been completed, the instruments were withdrawn from the shoulder and Marcaine injected into the portals and intra-articularly. Sterile dressing was applied, and the patient was sent to recovery in stable condition.

Which of the following is the correct code assignment?

a. 840.4, 29822
b. 726.10, 401.9, 23415-RT, 23120-RT
c. 840.4, 726.10, 29820, 29805-59
d. 840.4, 726.10, 401.9, 29826-RT, 29824-RT

8.33.   The following documentation is from the health record of a 47-year-old male patient.

Hospital Outpatient Surgery Services

Operative Report

Preoperative Diagnosis: Torn medial meniscus and DJD right knee

Postoperative Diagnosis: Large flap tear, posterior horn, medial meniscus; chondral loose bodies; significant degenerative arthritis right knee

Operation: Arthroscopy of the right knee with partial medial meniscectomy; arthroscopy of the right knee, with removal of chondral loose bodies

Procedure Description: This 47-year-old male was taken to the operating room and placed in the supine position. General anesthesia was accomplished without complication. Evaluation under anesthesia of the right knee showed it was stable with a negative Lachman's test and firm end point. Negative anterior and posterior drawer, stable to varus and valgus testing. A tourniquet was placed on the midright thigh. The right leg was prepped and draped free in the usual sterile manner. Tourniquet inflated to 325 mm Hg. There were loose bodies throughout the knee, which were flushed and removed. The patient had a large flap tear of the posterior horn of the medial meniscus that was unstable. He underwent a partial medial meniscectomy with small basket forceps and small synovial resector removing the torn portion of the meniscus, leaving about a 2-mm rim posteriorly and then saucerizing this to smooth margins anteriorly. The anterior cruciate ligament and posterior cruciate ligament were normal. The lateral compartment could not be entered because of significant arthritis medially. The knee joint was thoroughly irrigated and the portals closed with interrupted 3-0 nylon mattress sutures. Sterile dressing was applied. No complications occurred. The tourniquet was deflated after 20 minutes. The patient went to the recovery room in stable condition.

Which of the following is the correct code assignment?

a. 717.2, 717.6, 715.96, 29881-RT
b. 717.43, 718.16, 29881-RT, 29874-RT
c. 844.8, 717.6, 29881-RT, 29877-RT
d. 717.2, 715.96, 29881-RT, 29874-RT

8.34. The following documentation is from the health record of a 68-year-old male patient.

Hospital Outpatient Surgery Services

This patient presented to the podiatrist for surgical evaluation at the request of the primary care physician. After surgery was completed, a copy of the evaluation and operative report was sent to the primary care office.

Preoperative Evaluation This 68-year-old male of Italian descent presents with degenerative arthritis and bunion formation. On 6/30/00, patient was sent by Dr. Brown for bunionectomy evaluation. A problem-focused history was conducted followed by an expanded problem-focused examination.

Impression: Painful left foot due to: (1) Bunion with degenerative joint disease in the toes. (2) Metatarsus primus varus. (3) Hammer toe, second digit. (4) Elongated metatarsal, second digit, left.

Plan: Surgery scheduled for 8:00 a.m. 7/12/00, at the Hospital

Procedures: Keller bunionectomy; Austin bunionectomy; arthroplasty, second digit; and excision of the metatarsal head, second digit, left foot

Operative Report: The patient was placed in the semisupine position where Dr. Graybeard administered spinal anesthesia. After prepping and draping the patient in the usual aseptic manner and under ankle hemostasis, the left foot was approached. A dorsal linear incision was performed medial to the extensor hallucis longus tendon. Incision was carried through the skin and subcutaneous tissue and extended from midshaft metatarsal to distal proximal phalanx. The superficial fascia was separated from the deep fascia using sharp and blunt dissection techniques. An inverted L-capsulotomy was performed and sharp capsular periosteal dissection was performed with a #15 blade to expose the first metatarsal and base of the proximal phalanx. The medial eminence was resected with a micro-oscillating saw.

Next, attention was directed to the base of the proximal phalanx, where the Keller procedure was performed. One third of the proximal phalanx was resected and excised in toto.

Attention was next directed to the head of the first metatarsal where an Austin osteotomy was performed in the usual manner with screw fixation. The area was flushed with copious amounts of antibiotic flush. The capsular periosteal layer was next closed with 3-0 VICRYL®. The subcutaneous tissue was reapproximated with 4-0 VICRYL®.

Attention was next directed to the second digit and MPJ area, where a dorsal curvilinear incision was performed. The incision was deepened and the PIPJ was exposed. A transverse incision was performed through the capsular periosteal tissue at the PIPJ. Medial and lateral capsulotomies were performed, exposing the head of the proximal phalanx. The head of the proximal phalanx was resected and excised in toto.

Attention was next directed to the second MPJ. The incision at this area was deepened. A dorsal linear capsulotomy was performed and the head of the second metatarsal was resected and excised in toto. The surgical sites were next flushed with copious amounts of antibiotic flush. The second digit was noted to be aligned without pressure on the neurovascular structures.

Next, a .45 K-wire was placed percutaneously into the hallux distal to proximal. Capsular periosteal closure was next performed with 3-0 VICRYL®. Subcutaneous closure was performed with 4-0 VICRYL®. The skin was closed in 4-0 nylon. Postop anesthesia consisted of 17 cc 5.0 percent Marcaine plain and 1 cc of Decadron 4 mg/mL. Next, the sterile dressing was applied, which consisted of Betadine ointment, 4 × 4 gauze, and 4-inch Kling. The tourniquet was released, and the patient was returned to recovery in stable condition.

Which of the following is the correct code assignment for this outpatient procedure?

a. 727.1, 735.4, 99242-25, 28202, 28285
b. 727.1, 715.97, 754.52, 735.4, 754.59, 28299-TA, 28285-T1
c. 735.4, 754.52, 28296
d. 727.2, 715.97, 754.52, 735.4, 754.59, 28296-TA and 28292-TA-59, 28285-T1

8.35.   The following documentation is from the health record of a patient who received hospital outpatient surgery services.

Preoperative Diagnosis: Deep laceration, left hand with extensive tendon disruption of the fourth and fifth digits, secondarily of the third digit, middle finger; and open fracture with chip fracture from the MCP joint of the fifth digit; open fracture of the middle phalanx of the index finger.

Postoperative Diagnosis: Deep laceration, left hand with extensive tendon disruption of the fourth and fifth digits, secondarily of the third digit, middle finger; open fracture with chip fracture from the MCP joint of the fifth digit; open fracture of the middle phalanx of the index finger.

Operation: Extensive tendon repair, fourth and fifth digits, third digit longitudinally, index finger second digit with extensor hood, and débridement, open fracture middle phalanx, and intra-articular laceration of fourth and fifth digit.

Anesthesia: Intravenous Bier block

The patient was brought to the operating theater and anesthetized with a Bier block. We explored the wound, and the joint capsule to fourth and fifth was excised into the joint. The superior pole of the articular surface of the distal metacarpal on the fifth digit was avulsed, and we excised this because it was impregnated with a lot of dirt.

The tendon of the extensor indices communis to the fifth digit was lacerated. The extensor indices proprius ulnarly was still intact. The extensor hood over the MCP joint of #4 was torn, as was the capsule. The extensor tendon along the central hood of the third digit was torn longitudinally and the point was spared. The index finger had a longitudinal tear of the extensor hood in the central portion of the midphalanx, with the lateral band on the radial side torn. The wound was copiously irrigated with bacitracin saline with a pulsatile lavage. The joint surface of the fourth and fifth were irrigated. The open fracture of the fifth digit was removed. The open fracture of the middle phalanx of the index was débrided and irrigated.

We then began the definitive repairs. We sutured the joint capsule of the fourth and fifth with a 4-0 VICRYL® continuous. We sutured the extensor digitorum communis tendon to #5 with 5-0 Prolene and to #4 over the central hood, over the MCP joint with a 5-0 Prolene continuous. The extensor tendon of the third or middle finger was sutured longitudinally, and a lateral band on the radial side was repaired with a 5-0 VICRYL®. The longitudinal tear, which was really a split or a double split, was sutured with over-and-over 5-0 VICRYL® as well. We then increased her incision in an S-shaped fashion over the index finger to expose the central hood, which was torn, and lateral on the radial aspect, which was torn as well. This was repaired with 5-0 VICRYL® and the main extensor hood was repaired with 5-0 Prolene simple sutures. We then irrigated again with a liter of bacitracin pulsatile figure-of-8 mattress sutures, alternating with simple sutures. A bulky dressing was then applied, with a volar slab with the hand in the position of function, extension of the wrist, extension of the MCP joint, flexion of the PIP, and DIP of 30 degrees. The patient then had the tourniquet deflated fully and was sent to the recovery room in good condition.

Which of the following is the correct code assignment? Report the codes a hospital outpatient surgery department would report for this hand surgery. Do not assign E codes.

a. 882.1. 817.1, 26418, 26735, 26746, 11012
b. 842.12, 817.0, 26746-F4, 11010-F1, 11012-F4
c. 842.12, 817.1, 26418–F1, 26418–F2, 26418–F3, 26418–F4
d. 882.2, 816.11, 26418–F1, 26418–F2, 26418–F3, 26418–F5, 11010–F1, 11012–F4

Neoplasms

8.36. The following documentation is from the health record of a patient who received hospital outpatient surgery services.

Operative Report

A patient with an elevated (35.7) prostate-specific antigen (PSA) comes to the outpatient surgery center for a transrectal ultrasonic-guided (TRUS) prostate biopsy.

Technique: The patient is placed in the Sims position with the left side down. The anus was generously lubricated with 2 percent Xylocaine jelly. The ultrasound probe was then introduced and scanning initiated. A great deal of calcification was noted in the outer margin of the central zone. The area proximal and anterior to the calcifications was hypoechoic but may have been influenced by the prostate stones. There was very thin peripheral zone tissue available. Three needle biopsies were taken from each side, starting in the periphery and working toward the midline and trying to biopsy anterior to the prostate stones on the more medial biopsies from each side.

The pathology report confirmed carcinoma in situ of the prostate.

Which codes will be reported for this service? This facility does not assign ICD-9-CM Volume III procedure codes to radiologic procedures but reports CPT procedure codes for reimbursement.

a. 185, 55700
b. 233.4, 790.93, 55705, 76872
c. 233.4, 602.0, 55700, 76872, 76942
d. 185, 790.93, 602.0, 55700, 76872, 76942

8.37. The following documentation is from the health record of an 88-year-old female patient.

Hospital-Based Oncology Department Services

This 88-year-old white female is here to rule out the possibility of myeloma. She has been followed by Dr. Black as an outpatient and has sustained a 13-lb weight loss over a 6-week period. She seemed to stabilize at a weight of 82 lb but has recently dropped an additional 2 pounds. She is experiencing recurrent pain in the chest. Three weeks ago, she was treated by Dr. Black for a sinus infection, and sinus films showed lytic lesions of the skull, as well as the left maxillary sinus.

The patient had a left radical mastectomy 38 years ago for carcinoma of the breast without recurrence. The right breast is atrophic and without masses. Laboratory tests are attached and without noteworthy comments, except for urinalysis culture revealing over 100,000 *Escherichia coli*. A bone scan shows multiple areas of increased bony uptake and two areas of increased rib uptake and present healing osteoporotic fractures. There are multiple areas of increased uptake throughout the bony skull, suggestive of progressive metastatic disease or perhaps myeloma.

This is a delightful elderly woman who has markedly abnormal bone films and severe osteoporosis. General appearance of the bone is metastatic malignancy, supported by the weight loss history. Myeloma is consistent with her symptoms, but a normal sed rate and relatively normal globulin level are somewhat contradictory of that diagnosis. Certainly light chain myeloma is a possibility. In addition, some other metastatic disease, including the previous breast cancer, could give this appearance, but that seems unusual. I have never seen recurrent breast cancer this late (38 years).

Pertinent studies have been ordered, but I believe it would also be worthwhile to do Beta II microglobulin, which may be helpful in confirming myeloma. The UTI due to *E. coli* is being treated with antibiotics. Additional x-rays of the lateral skull and long bones have also been ordered. In addition, I performed a bone marrow aspiration today from the left posterior iliac crest.

At this point, my recommendation is to wait and see what the additional tests show. If we can determine that this is a myeloma, then it would be worth treating her with an alkylator-prednisone combination. In terms of any other metastatic disease, there is little we can do short of palliative radiation therapy. If this looks like recurrent breast cancer; then it may be useful to try tamoxifen. I would probably do that at any rate, if the carcinoma is further collaborated in any fashion by the bone marrow biopsy or other studies.

I cannot make any more definitive recommendations at this point. When I return next week and we see the studies ordered, we will go from there.

Procedure Note

Bone Marrow Biopsy Results: Metastatic poorly differentiated carcinoma and hyperplastic marrow with decreased iron stores

Comment from Pathologist: The features of the tumor do not suggest a definite site or origin. The most common tumors causing extensive lytic lesions of the bone are breast carcinoma, lung carcinoma, and renal cell carcinoma. With regard to the patient's previous history of breast cancer, although late recurrence has been described after more than 20 years, 38 years is an extreme interval.

Which of the following are assigned for the services performed on this date of service?

a. 203.01, 199.1, 38221
b. 198.5, 199.1, 733.19, 733.00, V10.3, 599.0, 041.4, 38221
c. 199.0, 27299
d. 198.5, 203.01, 174.9, 38221

8.38. The following documentation is from the health record of a female patient who received hospital outpatient surgery services.

Operative Report

A 52-year-old female presented with abdominal pain and change in bowel habits. A barium enema suggested a diverticular stricture, so a sigmoidoscopy was performed in the clinic, finding a stricture at 25 cm. The patient was then scheduled for exploratory laparoscopy in the hospital outpatient surgical center to treat the stricture.

Preoperative Diagnosis: Stricture of the sigmoid colon, rule out carcinoma

Postoperative Diagnosis: Carcinoma of the sigmoid with invasion into adjacent tissue and suspected metastasis to the liver

The patient was brought to the surgical suite, and an NG tube was placed in the stomach and a Foley catheter in the bladder. She was placed in the lithotomy position and routine prep and draping performed. A small incision was made in the right upper quadrant directly into the peritoneal cavity with CO_2. Once we had a good tent, we examined the peritoneal cavity and could not really see the liver because we were too close to it, but one view suggested surface lesions. After placement of the three cannulas (12 mm in the RUQ, 10 mm LLQ, and 5 mm in LUQ) we mobilized the sigmoid off the pelvic gutter and dissected down towards the bladder. She had undergone a previous hysterectomy, but there were no adhesions. We could not get the small bowel to easily come up out of the pelvis and lesions were evident surrounding the colon, so biopsies were taken. We then used a colonoscope through the rectum and advanced to 25 cm where we saw, not a stricture, but carcinoma, and biopsies were taken for pathologic evaluation. Complete evaluation of the colon was performed with no other pathology found. The surgery was discontinued, the trocars removed, and the patient returned to recovery in stable condition. The patient will undergo evaluation and consultation with oncology before further treatment is undertaken.

Pathology report confirms invasive adenocarcinoma, moderate to poorly differentiated, of the sigmoid colon with extension to the pericolic adipose.

Which codes are assigned to this surgery?

a. 153.3, 197.4, 49329
b. 153.9, 49321-74, 45380-59
c. 197.4, 153.3, 197.7, 49321, 45380
d. 153.3, 198.89, 49321, 45380

8.39.   The following documentation is from the health record of a female patient who received hospital outpatient surgery services.

Operative Report

Preoperative Diagnosis: Vulvar lesion.

Postoperative Diagnosis: Carcinoma in situ of the vulva.

Operative Procedure: Vulvectomy.

Indicationas for Procedure: This 74-year-old patient was found to have a suspicious looking lesion on her vulva. Medically, she is diabetic, has Parkinson's disease, and is obese. On the day of surgery, her cardiac, pulmonary and mental status were adequate.

Operative Findings: On the posterior vulva was a vulvar lesion which was superficially ulcerated and extended along the posterior vaginal introitus involving the perineum. The urethra was normal. The bladder was negative for tumor. The vaginal mucosa and remainder of the vulva appeared without any lesions.

Description of Operation: The patient received general anesthesia, was intubated, and placed in the dorsal lithotomy position. A pelvic examination was performed. A vaginal prep with Betadine was done and she was draped for a vaginal procedure.

An incision was made transversely along the perineum half way between the vaginal introitus and the rectum. The skin was dissected towards the vaginal introitus bilaterally and posteriorly. The lesion was then excised with a good margin at the posterior vagina and laterally, along the vulva. Dimensions were approximately 4 cm × 3 cm × 1 cm in a triangular shape. Bleeding points were either ligated with 3-0 Vicryl or cauterized with electrocautery. The specimen was submitted for pathology evaluation with a suture marker designating the rectal margin.

The vaginal mucosa, which was undermined for at least 2 cm, was approximated to the perineal skin by interrupted 2-0 Vicryl sutures. The entire wound was closed in this way. The patient tolerated the surgical procedure well and left the operating room in satisfactory condition.

Tissue Consultation Report

Preoperative Diagnosis: Vulvar lesion

Postoperative Diagnosis: Carcinoma in situ of the vulva

Specimen: #1. Vulvar lesion with anal margin

Gross Description: #1. Received in formalin labeled "vulvar lesion and margin tag" is a roughly triangular shaped fragment of tissue covered on one surface with wrinkled pink-white focally hair-bearing skin and on the other surface with fibrous pink tissue. There is a suture at one apex. The specimen measures 3.5 × 2.5 cm. with a thickness that ranges from 0.3 to 0.4 cm. The surface is slightly hypopigmented and slightly rough and granular in some areas. The margins are inked. A portion of the margin containing the suture is additionally marked with yellow ink. A line diagram is drawn. The specimen is sectioned and entirely submitted in eight cassettes.

Microscopic Description: #1. The specimen consists of squamous mucosa. In the center of the specimen, there is epithelial hyperplasia with markedly abnormal maturation extending from the basal layer to the surface. The surface is composed of compact hyperkeratosis. The abnormal cells display nuclear enlargement, hyperchromasia, a disorganized growth pattern, and increased mitotic figures many of which are abnormal. Invasive squamous cell carcinoma is not identified.

Diagnosis:

#1. Vulvar lesion, including anal margin, excision:

    Carcinoma in situ (vulvar epithelial neoplasia VIN III), with clear margins.

Which of the following code sets is assigned?

a. 239.5, 250.00, 332.0, 278.00, 57410, 56620
b. 624.02, 250.00, 332.0, 278.00, 56630
c. 233.32, 250.00, 57410, 11626, 12042
d. 233.32, 250.00, 332.0, 278.00, 56620

Disorders of the Nervous System and Sense Organs

8.40. The following documentation is from the health record of a 22-year-old male patient who received hospital outpatient surgery services.

Operative Report

A patient injured his foot using a razor-sharp garden hoe in his yard and severed the superficial branch of the external plantar nerve and the flexor digiti minimi brevis tendon in his left foot. The patient experienced loss of sensation on the outer side of the fifth toe and across the side of the foot, so a neurology consultation was requested, and the patient was taken directly to surgery. Following exploration of the wound and identification of the nerve avulsion, a repair of the nerve was undertaken using a nerve graft from the sural nerve. A lateral incision was made on the lateral malleolus of the ankle. The nerve was identified and freed for grafting, and the proximal and distal sural nerve endings were anastomosed. The wound was dissected, and the damaged area of the nerve was removed. The innervation of the external digital nerve was restored by suturing the 1.5-cm graft to the proximal and digital ends of the damaged nerve, using the operating microscope. Tenoplasty was performed on the tendon injury, and the wound closed in layers.

Which of the following would be correct? Do not assign evaluation and management service codes for the ER visit or consultation service.

a. 956.5, E920.4, E849.0, 64831, 28200
b. 892.2, 956.5, E920.4, E849.0, 64891, 28202, 69990
c. 892.2, 956.5, E920.4, E849.0, 64890-LT, 28200-LT, 69990
d. 956.5, 64890-LT, 28200-LT

8.41. The following documentation is from the health record of a patient who received hospital outpatient surgery services.

Preoperative Diagnosis:	Reflex sympathetic dystrophy
Postoperative Diagnosis:	Same
Operation:	Right stellate ganglion block #1
Location:	Outpatient Pain Clinic Surgery Center
Anesthesia:	Local with conscious sedation

Details: The patient was placed in the supine position to start the IV in his left hand for the sedation of 4 mg of Versed. Then he was positioned using a shoulder roll with the neck extended. Betadine was used for preparation. Following local anesthesia, a #22, 1.5-cm needle was introduced paratracheally at the level of the cricoid cartilage towards the stellate ganglion. Ten cc of .05 percent Marcaine with epinephrine 1:200,000 was injected, and the patient tolerated this very well. There was no paresthesia, heme, or CSF detected. The patient swallowed copiously during the procedure, but we were able to obtain an adequate block with the patient's right hand temperature changing from 90.1 to 93 °F following the block. He was moved to the outpatient recovery area where he tolerated fluids and nutrition and was able to be discharged home to his caregiver.

Assign the correct diagnosis and procedure codes. Do not assign HCPCS level II codes for the drug(s) injected.

Code Assignment:

Diagnosis code: _____

Procedure code: _____

8.42. The following documentation is from the health record of a 48-year-old female patient.

Emergency Department Services

This is a 48-year-old female presenting to the ER in the middle of the night with a complaint of unexpected right-sided weakness. It occurred during sleep, and the patient awoke and found it difficult to use her right arm or leg. She denies fever, shortness of breath, cough, headache, or other symptoms, and related that she was asymptomatic until this occurred.

Medication: Glucophage® for type II diabetes mellitus control. Has never used oral contraceptives

Allergies: None

Habits: Tobacco, one pack per day; social use of alcohol

Family History: Positive for early stroke in maternal grandmother at 52; father deceased at 53 due to lung cancer

Physical Exam: Patient is alert and oriented times three. HEENT: Pupils are round, regular, equal, and reactive to light and accommodation. Extraocular muscles are intact. Oral mucosa moist and pink. Decreased nasolabial fold on the right side and slight drooping of the angle of the mouth on the right. Neck supple, without lymphadenopathy, carotid bruit, or thyromegaly. She has impaired speech. Chest: Negative. Cardiovascular: Negative. Abdomen: Benign. Neurologic: Mild paralysis evident. Cranial nerves II through XII intact. Marked decrease in power and tone on the right side when compared to the left. Decrease in sensation on the right compared to the left. She has no visual disturbances or vertigo.

CT scan without contrast shows a small infarction in the left basal ganglia near the internal capsule. This is a small to medium-size arterial occlusion causing the stroke.

Plan: Will transfer for further neurologic consultation to University Medical Center for lab work per Dr. Smith on the neurology service. MRI, carotid Doppler, and two-dimensional echocardiogram were ordered to be completed there also.

Acuity Level: IV

Which of the following code sets will be used for reporting this ER visit for the facility?

a. 436, 99284-25, 70450
b. 434.91, 99283, 70470
c. 434.91, 342.90, 784.5, 305.1, 250.00, 99284-25, 70450
d. 436, 342.90, 784.5, 305.1, 250.00, 99284, 70470

8.43. The following documentation is from the health record of a 35-year-old female patient.

Hospital Outpatient Surgery Services

Operative Report

Preoperative Diagnosis: Right trigeminal neuralgia

Postoperative Diagnosis: Right trigeminal neuralgia

Operation: Right radiofrequency coagulation of the trigeminal nerve

Indications: This is a 35-year-old lady with intractable trigeminal neuralgia causing her considerable pain and inability to eat or speak, and who was referred for treatment of her affliction. Indications, potential complications, and risks were explained to the patient and family.

Operative Procedure: After the patient was positioned supine, intravenous sedation with propofol was administered. Lateral skull x-ray fluoroscopy was set. The right cheek was infiltrated dermally with Xylocaine and a small nick in the skin 2.5 cm lateral to the corner of the mouth was made with an 18-gauge needle. The radiofrequency needle with 2-mm exposed tip was then introduced using the known anatomical landmarks and under lateral fluoroscopy guidance into the foramen ovale. Confirmation of the placement of the needle was done by the patient grimacing to pain and by the lateral x-ray. The first treatment, 90 seconds in length, was administered with the tip of the needle 3 mm below the clival line at a temperature of 75 °C. The needle was then advanced further to the midclival line and another treatment of similar strength and duration was also administered. Finally, the third and last treatment was administered with the tip of the needle approximately 3 cm above the line. The cerebrospinal fluid was noted. The needle was removed. The patient tolerated the procedure well and had adequate tearing and corneal sensation and had reduction, if not complete cure, of her pain by the end of the procedure.

Which of the following code sets is correct?

a. 350.1, 64600, 77003
b. 350.1, 64610, 77003
c. 350.1, 64610
d. 350.1, 64605

8.44. The following documentation is from the health record of a 33-year-old female patient.

Hospital Outpatient Surgery Services

Operative Report

Preoperative Diagnosis: Left frontal lesion

Postoperative Diagnosis: Left frontal lesion

Operation: Stereotactic biopsy of left frontal lesion

Indications for Procedure: The patient is a 33-year-old female transferred to the university neurosurgical service for outpatient treatment from Blank Memorial Hospital, where she is an inpatient. She presents with neurologic deterioration, nausea, neck pain, and headache. A CT and MRI revealed a left frontal cystic mass. It was recommended that the patient undergo stereotactic biopsy and aspiration. The risks and benefits of the procedure were explained in detail to the patient and her family, who requested the procedure be performed, and the patient returned to Blank for further therapy.

Procedure: The patient was first taken to the CT suite, where a stereotactic halo was placed on the patient's head with the four-pin system using local anesthesia. The stereotactic CT was then performed, and the patient was transported to the operating room. The patient was placed on the operating room table in the supine position. General endotracheal anesthesia was smoothly induced. The left frontal area was then clipped and shaved, and the area was then prepped and draped in the usual sterile fashion. The stereotactic arm was then brought into the field and placed on the stereotactic ring. The localizing arm and the pointer were used to mark the left frontal area for skin incision. The area was then infused with 1 percent lidocaine with epinephrine, and a 2-cm skin incision was created in the left frontal region. The self-retaining retractor was placed, and hemostasis was obtained. The pointer was again used to mark the spot on the skull to make the burr hole, and a perforator was used to create a left frontal burr hole. The dura was coagulated and incised using a #15 bladed knife. The pia was then also coagulated and nicked with a #11 blade knife. The biopsy needle was then placed into the stereotactic localizing arm. The coordinates were dialed into the arm, and the biopsy needle was advanced to the appropriate depth. Upon entering the lesion, 25 cc of yellowish fluid was withdrawn from the cyst. The fluid was sent for cytology and bacteriology. The biopsy needle was then removed, and the incision was irrigated with bacitracin irrigation. The self-retaining retractor was then removed, and the incision was closed using #00 Dexon for the galea and staples for the skin. Estimated blood loss was 15 cc. No transfusion was given. The sponge, needle, and instrument counts were reported as correct at the end of the case. The patient was removed from the stereotactic halo ring. She was allowed to wake up and was extubated and taken to the recovery area. She will be transferred by ambulance back to Blank as soon as she has recovered from the anesthesia.

Assign the correct CPT codes for this procedure.

Code(s):_____

8.45. The following documentation is from the health record of a patient seen for retinal detachment.

Ophthalmologic Procedure—Nervous/Sense

Surgery Date: 04/20/XX

Preoperative Diagnosis:
1. Retinal detachment, left eye.
2. Vitreous hemorrhage, left eye.
3. Traumatic iritis, left eye.

Postoperative Diagnosis: 1. Retinal detachment, left eye.
2. Vitreous hemorrhage, left eye.
3. Traumatic iritis, left eye.

Operative Procedure: 1. Scleral buckle, left eye.
2. Pars plana vitrectomy, left eye.
3. Air fluid exchange, left eye.
4. Endolaser, left eye.
5. Injection of 16% C3F8 gas, left eye.

Anesthesia: General.

Indications: The patient presents with count-fingers vision in the left eye 4 days after blunt trauma to the left eye caused by a punch. B-scan revealed moderate vitreous hemorrhage and retinal detachment with tear at 4:30 with macula off.

Description of Procedure: After informed written consent was obtained, patient was brought to the operating room, prepped and draped in the usual sterile fashion after he was induced under general anesthesia. Speculum was placed in the left eye. A 360-degree peritomy was performed with a 0.12 forceps and Westcott scissors. Each quadrant was dissected bluntly with the curved Stevens scissors. Muscles were looped with a muscle hook and threaded with a 2-0 silk and then isolated with 2-0 silk. Quadrants were inspected and found to be pathology free. Then a Gill knife and corneal dissector were used to perform scleral buckle procedure, 1 belt loop in each quadrant, 3 mm posterior to the muscle insertion, 3 mm long and 3 mm wide. The 41-band was threaded through each belt loop and under each muscle, tied with a Watzke sleeve superonasally. A standard 20-gauge pars plana vitrectomy was then performed with sclerotomies placed 3.5 mm posterior to the limbus with an MVR blade. The first sclerotomy placed was inferotemporal and the trocar was used to place the cannula. Infusion line screwed into place and turned on after it was visualized in the vitreous cavity. Other two cannulas were placed with trocars, and the BIOM viewing system was used to perform a complete vitrectomy. Tears were noted not only at 4:30, but also at the 5 o'clock that were out near the vitreous base, and there was a large tear running radially along the edge of the detachment and traction of vitreous from 6:30 all the way past the equator and about three disc diameters from the optic nerve head. After vitreous was removed, air fluid exchange was performed to flatten the retina and endolaser was performed 360 degrees and around the tears. Air was exchanged for 16% C3F8 gas and sclerotomies were tied with 7-0 VICRYL, as was the conjunctiva. Retrobulbar block was given, a total of 6 cc of a 50/50 mixture of 2 percent lidocaine and 0.75 percent Marcaine. Maxitrol and atropine were applied to the eye. The eye was patched with a soft pad followed by a hard pad. The patient left the room awake in a stable condition and will follow up tomorrow morning at 8 a.m.

Which of the following is the correct code assignment for this outpatient surgery?

a. 361.02, 379.23, 364.3, 67108
b. 361.9, 379.23, 364.3, 67108
c. 361.02, 364.3, 67108
d. 361.02, 379.23, 364.10, 67107, 67036

8.46. The following documentation is from the health record of a 17 year old admitted for endoscopic sinus surgery.

Preoperative diagnosis: Nasal septal deviation, hypertrophic inferior turbinates, nasal airway obstruction, chronic frontal ethmoid and maxillary sinusitis with sinus polyposis.

Postoperative diagnosis: Same

Procedure: Nasal/sinus endoscopy, surgical, with frontal sinus exploration, right.
Nasal/sinus endoscopy, surgical, with frontal sinus exploration, left.
Nasal/sinus endoscopy, surgical, with anterior and posterior ethmoidectomy, right.
Nasal/sinus endoscopy, surgical, with anterior and posterior ethmoidectomy, left.
Septoplasty.
Nasal/sinus endoscopy, surgical, with maxillary antrotomy and polypectomy, right.
Nasal/sinus endoscopy, surgical, with maxillary antrotomy and polypectomy, left.
Submucous resection of inferior turbinate, right.
Submucous resection of inferior turbinate, left.

History: The patient is a 17-year-old, Caucasian male presenting with a history of chronic nasal obstruction and chronic sinusitis. He has been refractory to conservative therapy. Preop evaluation reveals an obvious gross nasal septal deformity, with hypertrophic inferior turbinates, causing bilateral nasal airway obstruction. His preop CT scan confirms these findings, along with evidence of polypoid degeneration involving the maxillary, ethmoid, and frontal sinuses. The recommendations for septoplasty with endoscopic sinus surgery were given to the patient and his mother. All benefits, risks, alternate therapies, expected outcomes were discussed. Consent form signed. The patient presents at this time for this procedure.

Details of Procedure: The patient was taken to the operating suite and placed in the supine position. General anesthesia with endotracheal intubation was carried out by the Department of Anesthesia. Following adequate anesthesia, the table was turned.

Further preparation of the nasal cavity was carried out in the usual manner. Following this, the patient was properly draped and the procedure begun.

A #15 blade was used to make a Killian incision into the left aspect of the mucoperichondrium. A mucoperichondrial and mucoperiosteal flap was then developed. The cartilaginous septum was detached from the maxillary crest and from the bony septum, and a portion of reflected bony septum causing obstruction was taken down with a Gorney scissors and a biting Takahashi forceps. The large bony spur coming out the maxillary crest was then taken down with a curved chisel and mallet technique. Bone fragments were removed with a biting forceps. Following this, the cartilaginous septum was allowed to swing to the midline and attention was turned to the endoscopic portion of the procedure.

The zero-degree endoscope was inserted into the left nasal cavity and brought up to the head of the left middle turbinate. The left middle turbinate was medialized. An infundibulotomy incision was made, followed by uncinectomy. The maxillary antrum was then entered. The antrotomy opening was widened with the Xomed straight shot microdébrider. Polypoid tissue encountered in the left maxillary sinus was then visualized and evacuated with a series of biting forceps. Following this, the débrider was used to gain access to the anterior, then the posterior, ethmoid air cells, removing diseased mucoperiosteal tissue along the way. The nasal frontal recess was then identified. Polypoid tissue in this region was evacuated. The nasofrontal duct was then cannulated. Further disease around the duct was removed with the débrider. Following these maneuvers, submucous resection of the left inferior turbinate was then carried out. Next, attention was turned to the opposite maxillary, ethmoid, and frontal sinuses. Identical procedures and findings were noted here. Submucous resection of the right inferior turbinate was then carried out.

The middle turbinates were then sutured in the midline, utilizing 4-0 VICRYL on a PS2 cutting needle. Silastic splints, Merocel sinus and nasal packs were then placed. The oral cavity was then suctioned of all blood and debris. The patient tolerated these procedures well. He was turned back over to the Department of Anesthesia, and was taken to the recovery room in satisfactory condition.

Report of Surgical Pathology

Final Diagnosis: Nasal sinus mucosa with septal bone and cartilage
Mild chronic allergic sinusitis; nasal bone and cartilage showing no specific gross abnormality
specimen(s)
Nasal septum—with sinus products
Clinical diagnosis: recurrent sinusitis.

Gross Examination: Received are multiple portions of somewhat mucinous mucosa accompanying bits of platelike, wedge-shaped, and sail-shaped bone and cartilage. The latter present no specific gross abnormalities. The mucosa has an estimated aggregate volume of 2 cc and is submitted for histologic processing (1 block).

Microscopic Examination: Sections disclose edematous sinonasal mucosa with mild chronic inflammation, basement membrane thickening, and a somewhat mucinous epithelium. The inflammatory infiltrate is dominantly lymphoplasmacytic with foci of eosinophilic admixture. There is no evidence of squamous metaplasia or dysplasia.

Select the correct code set to report for this patient.

a. 470, 478.0, 519.8, 473.0, 473.2, 473.1, 471.8, 31276-50, 31255-50, 30140-50-59, 30520, 31256-50
b. 470, 478.0, 519.8, 473.0, 473.2, 473.1, 471.8, 31276, 31255, 30140, 30520, 31256
c. 470, 478.0, 519.8, 461.0, 461.1, 461.2, 471.8, 31276-50, 31255-50, 30520, 31256-50
d. 470, 478.0, 519.8, 461.0, 461.1, 461.2, 471.8, 31276-50, 31255-50, 30140-50-59, 30520, 31256-50

Newborn/Congenital Disorders

8.47.   The following documentation is from the health record of a 3-year-old child.

Hospital-Based Clinic Outpatient Services

Parents bring their three-year-old boy, who was born with hydrocephalus, to the pediatric neurology clinic at University Hospital to have the child evaluated by the pediatric neurologist and have his VP shunt lengthened to accommodate a growth spurt. Their pediatrician requested a consultation to evaluate the shunt and replace the peritoneal catheter if needed. Outpatient surgery had been previously scheduled tentatively pending this evaluation for the afternoon.

The catheter used in the shunt was removed and replaced in the outpatient surgery suite following a follow-up consultation, which included a detailed interim history, a detailed examination, and medical decision making of moderate complexity. Findings documented in the consultation include "Assessment: Shunt valve malfunction requiring replacement." The VP shunt valve was replaced, along with a new peritoneal catheter in a longer length.

Which of the following code sets will be reported for this service?

a. V53.01, 62230
b. 996.2, 742.3, 62230
c. 742.3, V53.01, 62225
d. 742.3, 62230

8.48.   The following documentation is from the health record of a 4-week-old baby.

Emergency Department Services

A 4-week-old baby is rushed to the hospital after the parents found her cyanotic. While in the ER, she suffered respiratory arrest followed by cardiac arrest and was given cardiopulmonary resuscitation. The baby was born at 36 weeks, with a birth weight of 2400 g. Her current weight is 2700 g. An emergency intubation was performed, and then she was placed on a ventilator and transferred to the neonatal intensive care unit at the university hospital across town for monitoring and further workup. The ER physician provided 1 hour and 20 minutes of critical care, not including the cardiopulmonary resuscitation. His final diagnosis for the ER service is "Hypoxia with respiratory failure in a preterm infant—etiology unknown."

Which of the following code sets (diagnoses and CPT codes) will be reported for the hospital emergency room encounter?

a. Diagnoses: 770.84, 765.19; 99285
b. Diagnoses: 770.84, 779.89, 427.5, 765.18; 99291, 92950, 31500
c. Diagnoses: 770.84, 779.89, 765.18; 99295, 92950
d. Diagnoses: 770.84, 779.89, 427.5, 765.18; 99291

Pediatric Conditions

8.49. The following documentation is from the health record of a male patient who received emergency department services.

Chief Complaint: Tommy was playing basketball today, and fell when he was pushed by an opposing player. He hurt his left wrist. He is right-hand dominant.

Allergies: NKA

Examination: Tenderness and swelling of the wrist, especially the volar aspect. There is a slight abrasion over the swelling. The x-ray shows a fracture of the ulnar styloid and distal radial epiphyseal plate fracture with slight posterior displacement of the distal fragment of about 4 mm. CMS is intact. Short arm cast is applied for comfort measures.

Diagnosis: Colles' fracture

Condition: Good

Disposition: He is to follow up with the orthopedist in the next day or two to determine if reduction is necessary and return if problems occur. Tylenol 3 q. 4 h p.r.n. pain.

Acuity level III.

Which is the correct code set for this emergency service, in addition to the codes for the x-ray and cast supplies captured via the chargemaster?

a. 813.41, E886.0, E849.4, 29075-LT, 99283
b. 813.44, E886.0, E849.4, 29075-LT, 99283-25
c. 813.44, E886.0, E849.4, 25600-LT, 99283-25
d. 813.41, E886.0, E849.4, 25600-LT, 99283-25

Conditions of Pregnancy, Childbirth, and the Puerperium

8.50. The following documentation is from the health record of a 33-year-old woman who received hospital observation services.

Observation Patient

Admit Note: 2/28/XX, 07:30

This is a 33-year-old G2, P0, estimated delivery date of 2/28 and estimated gestational age of 40 weeks. She presents for induction secondary to gestational DM. She has required insulin since 28 weeks with adequate control. PNL: O positive, rubella immune. PE: AVSS, abdomen FH 40 cm, EFW 3800–4000 g. Cervix is closed/50 percent/-3/post/ceph. Plan is for Prostin EZ induction and insulin infusion when in active labor.

Progress Note: 2/28/XX, 09:15

Patient is having uterine contractions every 3 to 8 minutes. Cervix is 1 cm/100 percent/floating. Patient does not want to start Pitocin yet. Feels that she is in labor. FHR reactive, baseline 120s with accelerations.

Progress Note: 2/28/XX, 19:25

Patient's uterine contractions have resolved. Cervix unchanged. Discussed options, would like to go home to sleep and return in a.m. for Pitocin induction. Discharged home for tonight to sleep. Admit in a.m., start IV Pitocin as per protocol, start insulin drip, clear liquid diet.

Which of the following is the correct code set for this outpatient encounter?

a. 648.81, 250.01, V58.67, 99235
b. 648.83, 250.81, 99235
c. 648.83, V58.67, 99235
d. 648.83, 790.29, V58.67, 99235

8.51. The following documentation is from the health record of a female patient who was seen in the Emergency Department.

Emergency Department Record

This is a 30-year-old G2 P1 female who is 13 weeks pregnant who came in following a motor vehicle crash today. The patient was a passenger in the vehicle and appeared unhurt at the scene. She accompanied her daughter, who had obvious injuries, to the ED in the ambulance. During the initial exam of the child, this patient became lightheaded and had mild abdominal cramping. She was triaged and care began for her. She has had passage of 2 clots since the initial cramping episode. Pregnancy was confirmed as intrauterine on ultrasound at 7 weeks. There has been no dizziness, no syncope and no other complaints on review of systems. She has a history of a left-sided conductive hearing loss following several childhood illnesses. The patient has a poor obstetrical history with pre-term labor during her first pregnancy.

Vital signs: 37.0. 78, 18, 132/73, 98%. Alert and oriented × 3. HEENT is generally normal with significant hearing loss demonstrated on the left. Chest is clear to auscultation bilaterally. Heart shows RRR. Back is normal. Normal bowel sounds, nontender and nondistended. + VB from cervical OS. No POC seen. Musculoskeletal does show tenderness over the right olecranon and proximal ulna on palpation. Motion is slightly painful but full. Neuro, Nodes and Skin are all normal. Fetal heart tones are appropriate for gestational age. On re-exam after two hours of bedrest, VB appears to have stopped. Fetal heart tones continue to be strong. Patient's VS are stable.

30-year-old female with threatened AB and contusion to right elbow, status post MVA, restrained passenger. Doubt ectopic given positive IUP on ultrasound. She is anxious to join her daughter at her bedside and agrees that she will be re-seen here if she has any further symptoms. Agrees that nurses on pediatric floor will monitor her closely, and they are alerted to the situation. She will be seen by her OB tomorrow AM if she is not seen here in the ED later today.

Code(s): _____

8.52. The following documentation is from the health record of a 36-year-old female patient.

Hospital Outpatient Surgery Services

Preoperative Diagnosis: Left ectopic pregnancy

Postoperative Diagnosis: Same

Anesthesia: General

Operation: Diagnostic laparoscopy
Left salpingostomy with removal of ectopic pregnancy

Rationale for Surgery: This patient is a 36-year-old gravida III, para I, AB I, who has a positive pregnancy test with left adnexal mass that is a gestational sac with FHTs, and left ectopic pregnancy diagnosis was made. She was admitted at this time for laparoscopy with removal of this left ectopic pregnancy. We did talk about possibly sacrificing the tube on that side if we did get into problems with bleeding. This patient has a history of pelvic adhesions with blocked right tube. She is aware that we may have to sacrifice the left tube and that essentially she would be unable to become pregnant in all probability if we're not able to save the tube. She is also aware of the risks and benefits of surgery, including hemorrhage, bowel and bladder injury, and infection.

Procedure: With the patient in the lithotomy position and under satisfactory general anesthesia, the abdomen and perineum were prepped and draped in the usual manner. A weighted speculum was placed in the vaginal vault. The anterior lip of the cervix was grasped with a single-toothed tenaculum. The uterus was sounded to about 9 cm, and it was retroverted. The endocervical canal was dilated with Pratt dilators, and Zumi™ uterine manipulator was placed and the bulb insufflated with approximately 8 cc of air. A red rubber catheter was placed to gravity and attached to the Zumi uterine manipulator. Attention was then turned to the abdominal area, where a small skin incision was made with a scalpel. A large trocar was placed in the direct insertion technique, and pneumoperitoneum was established without difficulty. It is noted she did have some blood in the cul-de-sac. The right tube and ovary looked grossly within normal limits except the fimbriated end on the right was somewhat blunted. The ectopic pregnancy was really at the fimbriated end and had a small clot that was extruded from the fimbriated end. She also had the ovarian cyst on that side, which was not complicating this pregnancy. It was opened and drained. She also had a peritubular cyst, which I left intact. I isolated the ectopic pregnancy and then made a small cut using the needle coagulator over the ectopic pregnancy and extruded this with the needle nose forceps. Had some oozing along the fimbriated end. I did put Avitene™ in this area and then topped it with some Surgicel®. We watched it for several minutes, and it seemed to control the small amount of oozing. We irrigated the pelvic region with copious amounts of irrigation and then aspirated it. We again checked the operative field, and it seemed to be dry. We watched it as we deflated the abdominal pressure. I then removed all the instruments, used .25 mg of Marcaine injection at the injection sites, and closed the incisions with staples. Vaginal instruments were removed. She was taken to the recovery room in good condition. Estimated blood loss approximately 50 cc. Sponge and needle count was correct ×2. Patient did tolerate the procedure well and left the operating room in good condition.

Which of the following is the correct code set for this outpatient surgery?

a. 633.20, 620.2, 59121, 49320
b. 633.10, 620.2, 620.8, 59150, 58662
c. 633.10, 620.2, 58673, 49320
d. 633.20, 654.43, 58673, 58662

Disorders of the Respiratory System

8.53. A patient is respirator dependent and has a tracheostomy in need of revision due to redundant scar tissue formation surrounding the site. Under general anesthesia and establishing the airway to maintain ventilation, the scar tissue is resected, and then repair is accomplished using skin flap rotation from the adjacent tissue of the neck. What codes will be used to report this procedure, which was performed in the hospital outpatient surgical department?

Code Assignment:

Diagnosis code(s): _____

Procedure code(s): _____

8.54. The following documentation is from the health record of a 72-year-old female patient.

Hospital-Based Clinic Services

This 72-year-old female presented to the hospital-based urgent care clinic with a chief complaint of recurrent epistaxis for 3 days prior to admission. The bleeding occurred in the right nostril. She also complained of weakness and dizziness when standing. At the last clinic visit, hematocrit was 35, and this morning it is 27. Her past medical history is positive for COPD, with a negative surgical history.

A right anterior limited nasal pack was placed in the clinic treatment room. Because of the weakness and dizziness, we decided to admit the patient to an observation bed. In the evening, the anterior pack required replacement with extensive cauterization in the right nares because of refractory bleeding. Due to falling hematocrit, two units of packed red cells were transfused for the blood loss anemia resulting. The next morning, the patient was still experiencing some bleeding around the anterior nasal pack. For this reason, she was taken back to the treatment room, and a posterior nasopharyngeal pack in the right nares was placed by another physician. No further bleeding occurred throughout the day, and the patient was discharged to home healthcare follow-up following pack removal.

Which of the following should appear on the UB-04 claim for the outpatient services rendered to this Medicare patient? **Note:** The facility purchases its blood from the blood bank.

a. 784.7, 30901-RT, 30903-RT, 30905-RT, 36430-RT
b. 784.7, 280.0, 496, 30901-RT, 30901-RT-76, 30905-RT-77, P9021
c. 784.7, 285.9, 30901-RT, 30903-RT-59, 30905-RT-77, 36430-RT, P9021 (two units)
d. 784.7, 280.0, 496, 30901-RT, 30903RT–59, 30905-RT-59, 36430-RT, P9021 (two units)

8.55. The following documentation is from the health record of a 66-year-old male patient.

Emergency Department Services

The patient is a 66-year-old male who presented to the Emergency Department with a two-day history of severe shortness of breath, nonproductive cough, and slight fever. His medical history includes non-small cell lung cancer in the right middle lobe, 2 months post completion of radiation therapy. Surgery was contraindicated because of atrial fibrillation and long-term use of Coumadin. The Oncologist documented that chemotherapy was not indicated in this case and felt that the tumor was eradicated. The patient also has been plagued with dermatitis over the radiation port area on the right lateral chest wall following the 2nd radiation treatment. The skin showed no infection on exam. A two-view chest x-ray showed consolidation in the right lower lobe of the lung.

The physician diagnosed pneumonitis as an after effect of radiation therapy and prescribed both the inhaled corticosteroid, Beclomethasone Dipropionate, and long term oral corticosteroids on a tapering dose.

Which of the following represents correct coding for this service, including the chargemaster-assigned codes?

a. 486, 692.3, V10.11, E879.2, 71010
b. 508.0, 692.82, 427.31, V58.61, V10.11, E879.2, 71020
c. 508.0, 990, E926.5, 162.4, 427.31, V58.69, 71030
d. 508.1, 692.82, 162.4, 427.31, V58.69, E926.5, 71020

8.56. The following documentation is from the health record of a patient who received hospital outpatient surgery services.

Operative Report

Preoperative Diagnosis: Chronic sinusitis

Postoperative Diagnosis: Sinusitis of the maxillary, ethmoid, and sphenoid sinuses

Procedure: Bilateral endoscopic sinusotomies, anterior and posterior ethmoidectomies, sphenoidotomy, with debris removal in all sites

EBL: <100 cc

Description of Operation: The patient was placed in the supine position after appropriate preparation, draping, and induction of endotracheal anesthesia. The nose was cocainized and injected with Xylocaine 2 percent with 1:100,000 epinephrine.

The endoscope was then used to examine the maxillary sinus structures on the left side. There were several polyps present, and these were carefully injected with Xylocaine 0.5 percent with 1:200,000 epinephrine and removed. The maxillary sinus opening was identified by blunt dissection and was then opened, and with various rongeurs, the tissue was débrided. We then started through the posterior of the middle meatus region involving the ethmoid floors. Care was taken to preserve the parietal mucosa while performing the ethmoidectomies; then we proceeded posteriorly and entered into the sphenoid posteriorly and inferiorly. Gelfilm® was folded and placed in the areas involved.

Attention was then directed to the right side in similar fashion. Again, polyps were removed from the maxillary sinus. The uncinate was prominent and was resected, and more polyps were débrided. We then identified the maxillary sinus opening on the right and opened it in a satisfactory manner. We then proceeded anterior through posterior ethmoidal cells into the sphenoid cavity posteriorly, opening and removing large amounts of polypoid mucosa, polyps, and some mild purulence. When this was completed to our satisfaction, Gelfilm was folded and placed. The posterior throat was suctioned clear, and the patient was awakened and taken to recovery in good condition.

Which codes will be reported for this ambulatory surgery service?

a. 473.9, 31256-50, 31287
b. 473.0, 473.2, 473.3, 471.8, 31256-50, 31287–50
c. 473.0, 473.2, 473.3, 471.8, 31255-50, 31267–50, 31288–50
d. 473.0, 473.2, 473.3, 471.8, 31255, 31267

Trauma and Poisoning

8.57.   The following documentation is from the health record of a 25-year-old female patient.

Emergency Department Services

A 25-year-old female fell off of her horse in the morning, sustaining an injury and fracture of the spinal cord and vertebra at the C4 level. The patient was brought to the nearest ED by ambulance in a full-body air splint. CT scan revealed the injury to be a complete injury to the spinal cord (tetraplegia). The patient was having some difficulty breathing, and after endotracheal intubation, ventilator support was initiated. Vital signs were unstable in the ED. The patient had no feeling below the level of the injury. The patient was closely monitored throughout her stay in the ED. Later that day, when it was thought that she was stable enough for transport, she was transferred to the neurosurgical intensive care unit at the teaching hospital downtown for definitive treatment at the fracture site.

Critical care services were provided according to the acuity system. The ED physician who managed this patient recorded extensive progress notes, which included the specific time he spent with the patient on and off throughout the day. Times noted included the following: 0800–0900, 1000–1030, 1100–1115, 1300–1315, 1500–1600.

Which of the following sets of codes would be appropriate for facility reporting of this ED service in addition to the CT scan, 72125, assigned via the chargemaster?

a. 805.04, 344.01, E828.2, 99291, 31500
b. 805.04, 344.01, E828.2, 99291, 31500
c. 806.01, E828.2, 99291, 31500
d. 806.01, E828.2, 99291, 31500, 22305

8.58. The following documentation is from the health record of a male patient with a hand injury.

Hospital Outpatient Surgery Services

Preoperative diagnosis: Open fracture, shaft of the middle phalanx of the left small finger, on the oblique

Postoperative diagnosis: Open fracture, shaft of the middle phalanx of the left small finger, on the oblique with disruption of collateral ligament and extensor tendon

Procedure: Irrigation and debridement, open reduction of fracture, repair of extensor tendon and lateral collateral ligament, left small finger.

Indications: This 42-year-old man sustained this injury at home while using a powered hedge trimmer which slipped and caused a 60% amputation of the left little finger through the middle phalanx on the oblique, disrupting the extensor tendon and lateral collateral ligament. The medial ligament, soft tissue, and skin are intact. Because of this wound, the patient was brought to the operating room today.

Description: Two grams of Ancef were administered prior to the start of the case. The patient was identified by site of surgery, by direct communication with the patient, and by consent form. Following induction of general anesthesia, the left upper extremity was prepped and draped in the usual manner. A tourniquet was placed. Attention was first directed to the wound, and the margins of the wound were trimmed of devascularized tissue. There was a significant amount of debris in the wound. It was debrided of bone chips using the operating microscope and lavaged with 4 liters of Kantrex saline solution. Following this, the oblique fracture of the middle phalanx was approximated over a metal pin using fluoroscopic guidance. This provided excellent alignment of the fracture and appropriate positioning of the finger. The extensor tendon was repaired with acceptable extension being achieved. The lateral collateral ligament was repaired and the PIP joint was again stable. The wound was closed using 4-0 nylon suture, apposing his soft tissues. The tourniquet was released. Tourniquet time was 40 minutes. Vascularization appeared adequate. Sterile bandage of bacitracin, Adaptic, 2 × 2s and a tube gauze bandage were applied. Estimated blood loss was minimal during the procedure.

Which of the following code sets is appropriate for this service?

a. 816.00, 26756-F4, 13131-F4
b. 816.01, E920.1, 11012, 26735-F4
c. 816.11, E920.1, E849.0, 26735-F4
d. 816.11, E920.1, E849.0, 26756-F4, 26418-F4, 26540-F4, 11012, 13131

Chapter 9

Case Studies from Physician-based Health Records

> **Note:** Although the specific cases are divided by setting, much of the information pertaining to the diagnosis is applicable in most settings. If you practice or apply codes in a particular type of setting, you may find additional information in other sections of this publication that may be pertinent to you.
>
> Every effort has been made to follow current recognized coding guidelines and principles, as well as nationally recognized reporting guidelines. The material presented may differ from some health plan requirements for reporting. The ICD-9-CM codes used are effective October 1, 2009, through September 30, 2010, and the HCPCS (CPT Level I and HCPCS Level II) codes are in effect January 1, 2009, through December 31, 2009. The current standard transactions and code sets named in HIPAA have been utilized, which require ICD-9-CM Volume III procedure codes for inpatients.
>
> **Instructions:** Assign all applicable ICD-9-CM diagnosis including V codes and E codes. Assign all CPT level I procedure codes and HCPCS level II codes. Assign level I (CPT) and level II (HCPCS) modifiers as appropriate. Final codes for billing occur after codes are passed through payer edits. Medicare utilizes the National Correct Coding Initiative (NCCI) edits. CMS developed the NCCI edit list to promote national correct coding methodologies and to control improper coding leading to improper payments for Medicare Part B. The purpose of the NCCI edits is to ensure the most comprehensive code is assigned and billed rather than the component codes. In addition, NCCI edits check for mutually exclusive pairs.
>
> Cases in this workbook are presented as either multiple choice or fill in the blank.
>
> - For multiple-choice cases:
>   - Select the letter of the appropriate code set.
> - For fill-in-the-blank cases:
>   - Sequence the primary diagnosis first followed by the secondary diagnoses including appropriate V codes and E codes (both cause of injury and place of occurrence).
>   - Sequence the primary CPT procedure code first followed by additional procedure codes including modifiers as appropriate (both CPT level I and HCPCS level II modifiers).
>   - Assign HCPCS level II codes **only if instructed** (case specific).
>   - Assign evaluation and management (E/M) codes **only if instructed** (case specific).

The scenarios are based on selected excerpts from health records. In practice, the coding professional should have access to and refer to the entire health record. Health records are analyzed and codes assigned based on physician documentation. Documentation for coding purposes must be assigned based on medical record documentation. A physician may be queried when documentation is ambiguous, incomplete, or conflicting. The queried documentation must be a permanent part of the medical record.

The objective of the cases and scenarios reproduced in this publication is to provide practice in assigning correct codes, not necessarily to emulate complete coding, which can be achieved only with the complete medical record. For example, the reader may be asked to assign codes based on only an operative report; in real practice, a coder has access to documentation in the entire medical record.

The *ICD-9-CM Official Guidelines for Coding and Reporting* of Outpatient Services, published by the National Center for Health Statistics (NCHS), supplements the official conventions and instructions provided within ICD-9-CM. Adherence to these guidelines when assigning ICD-9-CM diagnosis codes is required under the Health Insurance Portability and Accountability Act (HIPAA) of 1996. Additional official coding guidance can be found in the American Hospital Association (AHA)'s *Coding Clinic* publication.

Anesthesia Services

9.1.   A neonatal patient is brought to the operating room for repair of complete transposition of the great arteries under cardiopulmonary bypass. The infant is in critical condition and may not survive. Assign the correct ICD-9-CM diagnosis codes and CPT codes to report the administration of anesthesia, including physical status, Level I and II modifiers, and qualifying conditions for this procedure.

    a. 745.10, 00562–AA–23, 99100
    b. 745.11, 00561–AD–P5, 99140
    c. 745.10, 00561–AA–P5
    d. 745.19, 00563–AA–P5, 99100, 99140

9.2.   A patient came into the pain clinic for management of chronic neck and shoulder pain after a car accident 1 year ago. The pain extended down into her left hand, and the patient had difficulty lifting or moving anything with that hand. She also reported inability to sleep well due to pain. Her attending physician requested a consultation with Dr. Jones, a pain specialist. Dr. Jones performed a brief history and expanded problem-focused physical exam with medical decision making of low complexity. He and the patient discussed the injection of Marcaine and steroids into the cervical plexus for relief. The patient agreed to this plan, and after consents were signed, the injection was performed. The patient noted approximately 40 percent relief in pain almost immediately. Dr. Jones requested that the patient come back in 1 week and again in 2 weeks for another injection.

Diagnosis: Cervicobrachial syndrome, due to auto accident 1 year ago.

Assign the correct diagnosis and CPT codes (including E/M) for this scenario.

a. 723.3, 907.3, E929.0, 99241, 64413
b. 907.3, 723.3, E929.0, 99242, 64413
c. 723.3, 907.3, E929.0, 99212, 64415
d. 907.3, E929.0, 99245, 64470

9.3. A 55-year-old patient is brought into the operating room for elective decompression of the median nerve for carpal tunnel syndrome. She is in excellent health otherwise. The surgeon places an Esmarch bandage on the arm, and the arm is exsanguinated. A tourniquet is then placed and the surgeon administers Bier block anesthesia.

Tourniquet time was approximately 50 minutes. Assign the ICD-9-CM diagnosis code and CPT surgical and anesthesia codes with any applicable modifiers.

a. 354.0, 64719
b. 354.0, 64722–47
c. 354.0, 64721–47
d. 354.1, 64721, 01810

Disorders of the Blood and Blood-Forming Organs

9.4. A 32-year-old female has recently had surgery for melanoma of the right arm, Clark level IV. She had no other signs of metastasis or adenopathy. Under general anesthesia, a sentinel node biopsy of the deep axillary nodes was performed with a gamma counter probe. An injection of isosulfan blue dye was performed and the nodes followed carefully to the single bright-blue node. This node was excised and sent for frozen section, which proved to be negative for melanoma. Before the procedure, the radiologist performed a lymphoscintigraphy. Which of the following code sets would the surgeon report? (Do not report supplies.)

a. 173.6, 38525
b. 172.6, 38525, 38792
c. 172.6, 38525, 38792–51, 78195
d. 172.9, 38525, 38790–51

9.5. The following documentation is from the health record of a male patient.

History: This is a 66-year-old male who had a coronary artery bypass graft in February. He did well. He was discharged home. Some time after that when he was home, he had 2 days of black stools. He mentioned it to the nurse, but I'm not sure anything was done about it. He has not had any other evidence of hematemesis, melena, or hematochezia but was feeling rather weak and fatigued. He had blood work done, which showed a hemoglobin of 5.7, hematocrit of 20.9, MCV of 80. Serum iron of 8, 2 percent saturation. No indigestion or heartburn. No abdominal pain of any kind. No past history of anemia or GI bleed.

Past Medical History: General health has been good.

Allergies: None known

Previous Surgeries: Coronary artery bypass graft

Medications: At the time of admission include Glucotrol, Lasix, potassium, and aspirin

Review of Systems: Endocrine: He does have diabetes, controlled with medication. Cardiovascular: History of coronary artery disease with coronary artery bypass graft. No recent symptoms of chest pain or shortness of breath. Respiratory: No chronic cough or sputum production. GU: No dysuria, hematuria, history of stones, or infections. Musculoskeletal: No arthritic complaints or muscle weakness. Neuropsychiatric: No syncope, seizures, weakness, paralysis, or depression.

Family History: His mother had cardiovascular disease and diabetes. No history of cancer.

Social History: The patient is married. Never smoked. Doesn't drink any alcohol. Works in a factory.

On physical examination, a well-developed, well-nourished, alert male in no acute distress. Blood pressure 146/82. Respirations 18. Heart rate 78. Skin: Good turgor and texture. Eyes: No scleral icterus. Pupils are round, regular, equal, and react to light. Neck: No jugular venous distention. No carotid bruits. Thyroid is not enlarged. Trachea in the midline. Lungs are clear. No heart murmur noted. Abdomen is soft. Bowel sounds present. No masses, no tenderness. Liver and spleen are not palpably enlarged. Extremities: Good pulses. Trace edema of the feet.

Laboratory values show severe anemia with a hemoglobin of 5.7. Hemoccult is also positive. His iron studies showed low iron and low ferritin, consistent with chronic blood loss anemia. His B_{12} and folate levels were normal. His SMA-12 was essentially unremarkable.

Impression: 1. Anemia. Probably he is anemic post bypass and then had stress gastritis with a little bit of bleeding and has never recovered from that. No evidence of acute or active bleeding at this time. The patient is stable. Possibility of occult malignancy or active peptic ulcer disease does exist.
2. Arteriosclerotic heart disease of native vessel, stable.

Recommendations: Admit patient as an outpatient for blood transfusion. Patient is being transfused. He should have an esophagogastroduodenoscopy and colonoscopy, possible biopsy or polypectomy, which has been explained to the patient along with potential risks and complications, including bleeding, transfusion, perforation, and surgery. These tests will be scheduled for a later date.

Discharge Note

Final Diagnosis: Severe blood loss anemia, weakness, diabetes mellitus, history of coronary artery disease status post coronary artery bypass graft.

The patient received three units of packed red blood cells; he felt better with subsidence of his shortness of breath and his weakness improved. His last hemoglobin was 8.4, with a hematocrit of 27.7.

The patient was scheduled for EGD to rule out peptic ulcer disease and colonoscopy to rule out occult malignancy in 1 week. The patient will be discharged home, and he will have a clear liquid diet. He is to call for any problems. He will continue with his home medications, and he was placed on ferrous sulfate one tablet twice a day.

What diagnosis codes are reported for this hospital outpatient encounter reported by the physician?

a. 280.0, 792.1, 414.01, 250.00, V45.81
b. 285.9, 780.79
c. 280.0, 578.1, 414.01, 250.00, V45.81
d. 998.11, 285.1, 792.1, 414.01, 250.00, V45.81

Disorders of the Cardiovascular System

9.6. A patient who is 6 weeks post anterior MI with congestive heart failure has been taking Lanoxin and is experiencing nausea and vomiting and profound fatigue. The evaluation and treatment were focused on adjustment of medication only. Blood levels show 4 ng/mL. Which of the following diagnosis codes will be reported?

a. 972.1, E858.3, 787.01
b. 410.12, 428.0
c. 787.01, 780.79, E858.3
d. 787.01, 780.79, E942.1, 410.12, 428.0

9.7. The following documentation is from the health record of a female patient.

History: This is a 70-year-old female who had noted exertional tachyarrhythmia described as palpitations, diaphoresis, and presyncope. She had noted no frank syncopal episodes. Prior to this admission, she had been on Lopressor, Norpace®, and Lanoxin in combination but was still experiencing breakthrough atrial flutter.

Hospital Course: Upon admission, the patient underwent echocardiography. This revealed moderate left ventricular dysfunction, mild to moderate aortic regurgitation, mild mitral regurgitation, and the left atrium proved to be within the upper limits of normal. At that time, it was recommended that the patient begin on amiodarone therapy due to drug refractory atrial flutter. Pulmonary function test and thyroid function test were also performed. Thyroid function test results proved within normal limits. Pulmonary function test results revealed normal lung volumes with mild loss of alveolar capacity. Amiodarone loading continued. The patient was taken to the electrophysiology lab, and overdrive pacing was attempted. This was unsuccessful. The patient therefore underwent direct-current external atrial cardioversion and at that time converted to normal sinus rhythm. The patient was discharged with a scheduled follow-up in 1 month.

Final Diagnoses: 1. Drug refractory atrial flutter
                       2. Successful cardioversion to normal sinus rhythm

Which of the following is the correct code assignment?

a. 429.9, 424.0, 92961
b. 429.9, 394.1, 33240
c. 427.32, 394.1, 429.9, 33211
d. 427.32, 396.3, 429.9, 92960

9.8.   The following documentation is from the health record of a 66-year-old male patient.

Discharge Summary

Admission Date: 6/19/XX

Discharge Date: 6/28/XX

History of Present Illness: This patient is a 66-year-old male admitted on June 19 because of unstable postinfarct angina. He underwent cardiac bypass surgery here 15 years ago. He did well until 1989, when he developed angina and underwent angioplasty here. On 6/9, he was awakened by severe chest pain and was taken to a nearby community hospital where he was found to have a small anterior wall myocardial infarction with the CPK only slightly elevated. He had cardiac catheterization performed at that time. Because of this small infarction, he was referred here for consideration for further surgical intervention. He was discharged from the hospital on 6/16. On 6/19, as the patient was walking from the car to the office, he developed significant chest pain and was therefore admitted to rule out further infarction.

Documentation of recent cardiac catheterization showed that complete left heart catheterization, left ventricular cineangiography, coronary arteriography, and bypass visualization were performed. The left ventricle showed severe anterior hypokinesis; although it did still move. The left main coronary artery was narrowed by about 70 percent. The bypass to the circumflex looked good, but the bypass to the left anterior descending had a very severe stenosis in the body of the graft. There was a very large, marginal circumflex artery that had an orificial, 80 percent stenosis. He was thought not to be a candidate for angioplasty but bypass surgery instead.

Surgical Procedure: Using extracorporeal circulation, the left internal mammary artery was anastomosed to the left anterior descending coronary artery, and a venous graft was placed from the aorta to the marginal circumflex. It was found that the old venous graft to the main circumflex was in excellent condition with very soft, pliable walls so that the vessel was left intact. There were no complications of this surgery. His postoperative course was singularly uncomplicated. He never had any arrhythmia problems; his wounds healed nicely. He had a tiny left pleural effusion that never needed to be tapped. He was walking about the ward participating in the cardiac rehab program at the time of discharge.

Discharge Instructions: Discharge medications will simply be aspirin grains 5 q.d., Tylenol with Codeine 1 or 2 p.r.n. for pain, Lopressor 50 mg a day, and Colace, as necessary. He was instructed to contact his private physician upon return home for resumption of his medical care. He is to call me here at the medical center if there are any questions or problems that he wishes to discuss.

Discharge Diagnoses: 1. Unstable angina (intermediate coronary syndrome)
2. Recent incomplete, anterior wall myocardial infarction
3. Coronary atherosclerosis, three vessel
4. Successful double-bypass surgery

What are the correct codes for this admission?

a. 414.01, 414.05, 410.12, 411.1, V45.81, 33517, 33533, 33530
b. 414.01, 414.05, 410.12, 411.1, V45.81, 33510, 33533
c. 414.00, 414.05, 410.11, 411.1, V45.81, 33530
d. 414.01, 414.05, 410.12, 412, V45.81, 33518, 33530

9.9. The following documentation is from the health record of an 85-year-old female patient.

Admission Date: 12/10/XX

Discharge Date: 12/22/XX

Discharge Diagnoses: 1. Acute pulmonary edema with congestive heart failure
2. Myocardial infarction ruled out
3. Chronic obstructive pulmonary disease
4. Pneumonia
5. Senile dementia

History of Present Illness: This 85-year-old female was admitted via the emergency room from the nursing home with shortness of breath, confusion, and congestion. There was no history of fever or cough noted. Patient has a history of senile dementia and COPD. Prior to admission, the patient was on the following medications: Prednisone, Lasix, Haldol, and Colace.

Physical Examination: Blood pressure 140/70, heart rate of 125 beats per minute, respirations were 30, temperature of 101.4°F. The eyes showed postsurgical eyes, nonreactive to light. The lungs showed bilaterally bibasilar crackles. The heart showed S1 and S2, with no S3. The abdomen was soft and nontender. The extremities showed leg edema. The neurological exam revealed no deficits, and she was alert × 3.

Laboratory Data: ABGs were 7.4, PO_2 of 63, CO_2 of 43, bicarbonate 26, saturation of 89. Hemoglobin 11.7, hematocrit was 31.5, platelets of 207,000. Sodium 139, chloride 107, potassium 4.4, BUN 42, creatinine 1.2. The EKG was unremarkable.

Hospital Course: Basically, this patient was admitted to the coronary care unit with acute pulmonary edema, rule out myocardial infarction. Serial cardiac enzymes were done, which were within normal limits, therefore ruling out myocardial infarction. A chest x-ray performed on the day of admission confirmed congestive heart failure and pneumonia. The patient was started on Unasyn and tobramycin for the pneumonia, which improved. The congestive heart failure; however, was not improving with administration of Lasix. The patient was not taking foods and liquids well and, at the family's request, she was labeled DNR. On hospital day 12, she was found without respirations, with no heart sounds, and pupils were fixed. She was pronounced dead by the physician, and the family was notified.

Which of the following answers demonstrates the correct ICD-9-CM code assignment?

a. 428.0, 486, 496, 290.0
b. 428.0, 518.4, 486, 496, 290.0
c. 428.0, 410.91, 486, 496, 290.0
d. 518.4, 428.0, 486, 496, 290.0

9.10. Dr. Hiram performs an endovascular repair of a very long aneurysm of the descending thoracic aorta, with placement of two distal extension components due to the extensive length of the aneurysm. The left subclavian artery was not covered during this procedure. Assign the appropriate CPT code(s) to report this procedure.

a. 33880
b. 33779
c. 33881
d. 33881, 33883, 33884

9.11. Ms. Jones has a pseudoaneurysm of her left iliac artery that has developed proximal to an area of occlusion. She is admitted to Community Hospital for an endovascular repair. She undergoes a percutaneous transluminal balloon angioplasty of the area of occlusion, with placement of a drug-eluting stent, and an endovascular graft placement to repair the area of the pseudoaneurysm. An endovascular ultrasound is performed after the procedure to assure patency of the vessel. Assign the appropriate CPT code(s) that her surgeon, Dr. Vessel, would report. You do not need to assign modifiers for this exercise.

a. 35454, 34900, 37205, 37250
b. 35473, 34900, 37205, 37250
c. 35454
d. 35492, 34900, 37205

9.12. In the cardiac catheterization laboratory of Big City Hospital, Dr. Hart performed a PTCA on a patient's right coronary artery, with placement of a drug-eluting stent. He also performed a PTCA of the left circumflex coronary artery and placement of two stents. The patient had undergone a complete diagnostic cardiac catheterization at an outlying hospital the previous day, so complete cardiac catheterization was not performed. Dr. Hart performed the procedure via femoral artery cutdown without left heart catheterization. Assign the appropriate CPT codes and HCPCS Level II modifiers that Dr. Hart would use to report these procedures. You do not need to assign CPT Level I modifiers for this exercise.

a. 93508, 92980-RC, 92981-LC
b. 93508, 92982-RC, 92984-LC, 92980-RC, 92981-LC × 2
c. 93510, 92980-RC, 92981-LC
d. 93510, 92982-RC, 92984-LC, 92980-RC, 92981-LC × 2

Disorders of the Digestive System

9.13. A 48-year-old man came in to the emergency department complaining of vomiting material resembling coffee grounds several times within the past hour. He has abdominal pain and has been unable to eat for the past 24 hours. He is dizzy and lightheaded. Two stools today have been black and tarry. While in the emergency department, he vomited bright-red blood and some material resembling coffee grounds. A nasogastric tube was inserted by the ED physician and attached to suction. An abdominal exam showed a fluid wave consistent with ascites. CBC and clotting studies were drawn. A detailed history and physical exam with high-complexity medical decision making were documented. A GI consultant was called and the patient was taken to Endoscopy for further evaluation of upper GI bleeding. Diagnosis: Hematemesis, rule out esophageal varices; blood loss anemia, acute; ascites.

Which of the following is the correct diagnosis and CPT procedure code assignment for the independent ED physician?

a. 578.0, 285.1, 789.59, 99285, 43752
b. 578.0, 789.00, 780.4, 99284–25, 91105
c. 789.51, 578.0, 280.0, 99284, 43752
d. 578.0, 285.1, 789.59, 99284–25, 43752

9.14. This 35-year-old man has had a history of diverticulosis with frequent bleeding in the past. He came in to have a colonoscopy and rule out any other pathology, such as carcinoma. During the colonoscopy, severe diverticulosis was noted. This is definitely the cause of the bleeding. Also noted were a polyp at the splenic flexure and a polyp in the transverse colon. The polyp at the splenic flexure was removed by hot biopsy, and the second polypectomy was done by snare technique. The polyps were both classified as adenomatous with no signs of malignancy. What are the correct codes for this case?

a. 562.12, 211.3, 45385, 45384–51 or 45384–59
b. 211.3, 562.10, 578.1, 45384
c. 562.12, 211.3, 578.9, 45385
d. 562.12, 211.3, 45384

9.15. The patient had a laparoscopic Nissen fundoplasty performed for gastroesophageal reflux with esophagitis. He also has Barrett's esophagus. These conditions have not been responding to conservative treatment, and the patient wishes to undergo surgery at this time. The patient has also had many instances of treatment for chronic cholecystitis. It has been decided to pursue a laparoscopic cholecystectomy at the same time that the fundoplasty is done. Which of the following is the correct code assignment?

a. 530.81, 530.85, 47562, 43289-51
b. 530.11, 530.85, 574.10, 43324, 47600–52
c. 530.11, 530.89, 575.11, 43326
d. 530.11, 530.85, 575.11, 43280, 47562–51

9.16. This 52-year-old female has chronic cholecystitis with cholelithiasis. She has been having increasing abdominal pain. A laparoscopic cholecystectomy was performed, and an ERCP was also done to rule out obstruction of the common bile duct. The findings showed an obstructed common bile duct with stones. A sphincterotomy was performed, and then lithotripsy of the stones was done. The largest particles of stones were removed. Which of the following is the correct code assignment?

a. 574.11, 47564
b. 574.70, 47562, 43265–51
c. 574.71, 47562, 43265–51, 43264–51
d. 574.71, 47562, 43265–51, 43262–51, 43264–51

9.17. The following documentation is from the health record of a 33-year-old female patient.

History and Physical

The patient is scheduled for surgery today.

Chief Complaint: Anal pain with bleeding

History of Present Illness: This is a 33-year-old woman with a 2-year history of anal pain and bleeding, which has been markedly worse lately. Has been on stool softener and sitz baths; symptoms have not improved. She presents for ligation of internal hemorrhoids.

Past History: General health is good. There are no major medical illnesses. She has had a tubal ligation in the past.

Family History and Review of Systems: Otherwise noncontributory

Physical Examination: HEENT: Grossly intact. Neck: Supple. Chest: Clear. Heart: Regular rate and rhythm. Abdomen: Soft, without mass, tenderness, or organomegaly. Anal exam: There is marked posterior tenderness and pain.

Impression: Bleeding, prolapsed internal hemorrhoids, not responding to conservative therapy

Recommendations: Internal rubber band ligation. The procedure has been explained in detail to the patient, and she understands and accepts.

Operative Report

Preoperative Diagnosis: Internal prolapsing hemorrhoids

Postoperative Diagnosis: Same

Surgery Performed: Proctosigmoidoscopy, rubber band ligation of the internal hemorrhoids, done with an anoscope

Procedure: The patient was placed on the operating table in a sitting position. The patient was placed in prone jackknife position and the buttocks were retracted.

Proctosigmoidoscopy was then carried out to 20 cm and was normal except for the anal findings mentioned above. The proctoscope was withdrawn, and the anus was prepped and draped in antiseptic fashion. A field block with Marcaine 0.25 percent was then placed. The anoscope was inserted. There was a prolapsing hemorrhoid in the anterior midline. This was rubber-band ligated above the dentate line by applying two bands. In the posterior midline, there was another hemorrhoid, which was banded in the same manner. Bleeding was checked, and none was noted.

The patient was taken to the recovery room in stable condition. Blood loss was negligible. Counts correct; no drains.

Which of the following is the correct code assignment?

a. 455.2, 46221, 45300–51, 46600–51
b. 455.2, 46221, 46221–59, 45300
c. 455.0, 46945, 45300
d. 455.8, 46934, 45300–51, 46600–51

Evaluation and Management (E/M) Services

9.18.   Dr. Bill admitted a patient to observation after seeing him in the emergency department with severe nausea, vomiting, and dizziness from dehydration. IVs were started, and the plan was to hydrate the patient and discharge him to home the next morning. The patient, however, had not improved enough the next day (day 2) and was kept an additional 24 hours. On day 3, the patient was discharged home.

Assuming documentation guidelines have been met, choose the correct sequence of CPT procedure E/M codes for Dr. Bill's observation service coding.

a. 99219, 99231, 99217
b. 99219, 99499, 99217
c. 99283, 99219, 99217
d. 99283, 99231, 99217

9.19.   Dr. Smith sent a patient to observation care at the local hospital following his visit to the nursing facility. The patient was admitted for observation to rule out stroke due to a change in mental status. The next morning, Dr. Smith left town, and his partner, Dr. Johnson, admitted the patient to inpatient care because of sudden worsening symptoms. The patient expired later the same day. Assuming documentation guidelines were met, how would E/M services for these two physicians be coded?

a. Dr. Smith: 99315, 99219; Dr. Johnson: 99236
b. Dr. Smith: 99219; Dr. Johnson: 99217, 99236
c. Dr. Smith: 99219; Dr. Johnson: 99236
d. Dr. Smith: 99315, 99222; Dr. Johnson: 99238

9.20. An 85-year-old patient of Dr. Smith's was brought to the clinic from her home after her family failed to get her to respond to their phone calls. She was poorly nourished, dehydrated, and confused. Dr. Smith admitted her to the hospital to stabilize her, then discharged her to a nursing facility the next day. Assuming that all documentation guidelines for each level of service have been met, assign the correct CPT codes for Dr. Smith's services to the hospital and nursing home.

    a. 99214, 99222, 99239, 99305
    b. 99222, 99239, 99305
    c. 99214, 99235, 99305
    d. 99222, 99305

9.21. Dr. Donahue had an elderly Hispanic male come to his office for an initial visit. The patient had multiple medical problems and had not had any care for at least 10 years. The patient brought his 12-year-old granddaughter to interpret; however, she was of minimal assistance due to her unfamiliarity with medical terms and problems. Dr. Donahue's nurse called the local hospital and requested the services of their Spanish-speaking interpreter. By putting the interpreter on speakerphone, Dr. Donahue was able to finish his examination of the patient, prescribe medications, and give instructions for follow-up care. He documented a comprehensive history, and physical examination, and medical decision making that was moderate. He spent an additional 50 minutes counseling and coordinating the care of this patient, for a total of 95 minutes of care.

Assign the correct CPT code for Dr. Donahue's services.

    a. 99204, 99354
    b. 99205, 99354, 99355
    c. 99205, 99354
    d. 99204

9.22. The following documentation is from the health record of a 56-year-old female.

Preventive Medicine Visit

This patient is a 56-year-old female who comes in today for a complete physical, which is covered by her insurance company. Patient is known to me, although has not been in to see me since last year.

Past Medical History:
1. History of proctosigmoiditis, probably ischemic, treated 1/93
2. History of TAH-BSO for endometriosis
3. History of NSVD × 2
4. History of correction of bunion and hammer toe, 1996

The only concern that she has is some problems with headaches in the frontal area in the morning. The headaches seem to be worse fairly consistently in the morning. She has also had some problems with hips aching, and her eyes occasionally have been a little blurry. Other than that, she has no other concerns on ROS. She has no jaw claudication, joint pains, etc.

Family History: Her mother died of CVA and colon cancer at age 76. Her father died of heart disease at age 80.

Social History: She has been married for 25 years. She has two children and is a homemaker. She does not smoke or drink. Her husband is a farmer.

Allergies: No known allergies

Medications: ASA, Premarin, Caltrate®

ROS is otherwise entirely unremarkable.

Physical Exam: She appears to be in no acute distress.

HEENT:	Head is normocephalic. PERRLA: Fundi benign. TMs are clear. Pharynx is negative. There is no temporal artery tenderness.
Neck:	Without adenopathy or thyromegaly
Lungs:	Clear
Heart:	Showed a normal S1, S2, with regular rate and rhythm and no murmur
Breasts:	Without masses. Self breast examination was taught and encouraged on a monthly basis. Axillary is unremarkable.
Abdomen:	Soft and nontender with no hepatosplenomegaly present
Genitalia:	External genitalia normal. Cervix was absent. Vaginal Pap smear was done. Bimanual exam revealed an absent uterus and nonpalpable ovaries. Rectal exam was normal.
Neurological:	Exam intact

Assessment:
1. Headaches, exact etiology not clear. I am going to check her sed rate. If that is normal, then will proceed with CT scan of the head.
2. Routine physical

I will write to her with the test results. If she does not hear from me in 2 weeks, she will give me a call. Otherwise I will see her right after her head CT.

Assign the correct ICD-9-CM and CPT codes for this visit:

a. V72.31, V76.47, V45.77, 99396; 784.0, 99213–25
b. V70.9, 99396, 784.0, 99213
c. V76.2, V76.47, V45.77, G0101, Q0091; 784.0, 99213–25
d. 784.0, V72.31, V76.47, V45.77, 99214

9.23. The following scenario involves a female patient in the intensive care unit.

Hospital Emergency Visit

Subjective: I was called regarding endotracheal tube cuff leak and copious secretions suctioned through ETT. N/G sounds not heard in stomach per nurse, though no evidence by exam that N/G was withdrawn partially. Anesthesia called in. Patient is very afraid of losing airway.

Objective: Vital signs stabilized. Endotracheal tube replaced by anesthesia and verified with good bilateral breath sounds. There are a few mild right expiratory rhonchi. Cor 50s to 60s. O_2 saturation remained in the 90s.

Assessment:	1. Respiratory failure: Holding own; chest x-ray ordered
	2. Congestive heart failure: Retaining fluid despite increased diuretics
	3. Nutrition: Improved
	4. Heart: Remains in normal sinus rhythm
	5. Atelectasis and pneumonia: Now afebrile, still needs frequent pulmonary toilet
	6. INR 1.9
Critical care time:	2 a.m. to 3 a.m. – Emergent
Plan:	1. Transfer to ICU
	2. Increase Coumadin
	3. Continue respiratory care and IV antibiotics
	4. Increase diuresis: She is above her dry weight

Determine the correct E/M code for the ER physician for this scenario.

a. 99233
b. 99291, 99292
c. 99233, 99354
d. 99291

9.24.   The following documentation is from the health record of a female patient.

Office Consultation

Reason for Consultation: Recurrent right costal margin pain from about the midclavicular line in the midline. Recurred 4 to 5 weeks ago. Pain daily. The patient tends to vomit if she eats much, so she hasn't been eating well. Describes the pain as "just a continuous pain. Sometimes it doubles me up. It goes through to my back" (that is, to the right medial lower posterior thoracic region). She has had a thorough evaluation for right upper quadrant pain in the recent past. Her last study and treatment was the ERCP with sphincterotomy 11/7/XX. Recurrence of pain suggests that this procedure was not successful; thus, the pain is not related to sphincter of Oddi dysfunction. However, it is not entirely out of the question that sphincterotomy may have been inadequate or that she may have scarring of the sphincterotomy site.

Review of Systems: She took a week off from work because of pain, and since then she has missed additional work because of pain. She doesn't know what pain pills she is taking, but she takes three to four of them per day and notes that if pain is really bad, she is allowed to double up on her pills. She notes that when she vomits, pain is worse, and "it seems to be sharper."

For the past several weeks, at least, she has had dizziness. This is probably vertigo because it bothers her when she lies flat in bed and also when she rolls over in bed. Her head has been hurting all of the time, "but it's not like a headache." Light bothers her at times. She has been on meclizine 25 mg pills 2 times a day, without much improvement.

Allergies: Sulfa and Tylenol 3

Medications: Meclizine 25 mg pills 2 q.i.d. and two medicines, the names of which she doesn't know

Physical Exam:

Chest:	Clear
Heart:	Regular rate and rhythm
Abdomen:	Manifests a midline scar from about the midepigastrium down to the pubis. Extending across the right lower quadrant is a horizontal scar that reaches to the midline and extends across both lowermost abdominal regions. There appears to be a small hernia through the medial aspect of the horizontal RLQ scar. I can't feel liver, spleen, or masses. There is mild to moderate tenderness in the right medial epigastrium. This feels quite localized. I can't feel a clear-cut defect. There is no tenderness along the rib margin in this region. I can create tenderness, however, by pushing both downward and upward underneath the rib margin, and I think that this tenderness is coming from abdominal wall structures rather than from something within the abdomen.

Impression:
1. Recurrent right medial epigastric pain of 4 to 5 weeks' duration, etiology uncertain. This pain may well be of abdominal wall origin. She may have a trigger point in the right medial epigastric region. Another possibility is that she might have a small midline hernia, though I doubt that.
2. Small incisional hernia, RLQ
3. Vertigo of a number of weeks' duration, etiology uncertain. There is some associated headache.

Recommendations: CBC, sed rate, chemistry panel, amylase. Recommend anesthesiology for consideration of injection therapy directed at right medial epigastric region and recommend neurology for headaches and vertigo.

I spent 25 minutes interviewing and examining this patient and another 40 minutes discussing the etiology of her problem and answering multiple questions she had.

Give the correct CPT procedure code for the E/M service.

a. 99205
b. 99244
c. 99243
d. 99354

Endocrine, Nutritional and Metabolic Diseases, and Immunity Disorders

9.25.   A 13-year-old male patient is being evaluated in the children's clinic for growth problems. He is 4'1" and does not exhibit any signs of puberty or secondary sexual characteristics. His parents wonder if the necrotizing enterocolitis that he had at birth is the cause of his short stature. Other than his short stature, the patient seems in normal health. Blood tests indicated a deficiency of growth hormone. The patient returned to the clinic for follow-up of test results and parents were given the option of starting him on growth hormone treatments. Diagnosis on the second visit is HGH deficiency. Give the ICD-9-CM codes for both the first and second visits.

   a. First visit: 259.4, 259.0; second visit: 253.3
   b. First visit: 783.43, 259.0; second visit: 253.3
   c. First visit: 259.0; second visit: 253.4
   d. First visit: 259.4; second visit: 253.4

9.26.   An 18-year-old male was referred to an endocrinologist by his family doctor with symptoms of gynecomastia, hypogonadism, and failure to develop secondary sexual characteristics. The family reported no exposure to industrial chemicals and lived in a town far from any large industrial areas. The patient's mother reported that the family did live on a farm briefly when the patient was a small child, and there was a large amount of crop dusting that took place at that time. The endocrinologist reviewed the case and performed a physical exam that confirmed the findings of the family doctor. The endocrinologist initiated several diagnostic studies. Assessment: Gynecomastia, hypogonadism, and failure to develop secondary sexual characteristics, possible pesticide exposure, etiology pending further study.

   Which of the following is the correct code set for this initial visit to the endocrinologist?

   a. 611.1, 257.2
   b. 257.1, 611.1, 259.0
   c. 257.8, 909.1
   d. 257.2, 259.0

9.27.   The following documentation is from the health record of a 69-year-old female.

   HPI: The patient is a 69-year-old female with a large pituitary tumor found after lymph node biopsy that demonstrated lung cancer. The lung cancer is apparently non-small cell adenocarcinoma. This is being followed by Dr. Smith who is planning chemotherapy, I believe, for the future. The pituitary gland appears to be nonfunctioning. She underwent transphenoidal surgery 3 days ago and is doing well without complaints.

Physical Exam: Vital signs normal. General: Elderly white female in no acute distress. HEENT: Normocephalic and atraumatic. Pupils are equal, round, and reactive to light. Lids and conjunctivae are normal. Throat unremarkable. No blurred vision. Lungs: Clear, but with decreased basilar breath sounds. Cardiac: Regular rate and rhythm without any murmurs. Abdomen: Positive bowel sounds. Soft and nontender, without hepatosplenomegaly. Extremities: Negative; no edema. Neuro: Oriented $\times$ 3. Cranial nerves II—XII intact.

Lab Data: WBC 6.9, hemoglobin 12.1, hematocrit 36.2, platelets 314,000.

Glucose 116, BUN 9, creatinine 0.7, sodium 134, potassium 3.9, Chloride 85, CO_2 26, calcium 8.2

Assessment and Plan: Pituitary tumor, status post resection. Currently on steroids, 50 mg q. 8 hours. Wean to 20 mg in the morning and 10 mg in the evening starting tomorrow. Recommend follow-up in 2 weeks with Dr. Smith; he will further evaluate that. We will watch urine output and look for any evidence of diabetes insipidus.

Which of the following is the correct ICD-9-CM code set for this physician?

a. 227.3, 162.9, V77.1
b. 194.3, 162.9
c. 239.7, 162.9, 253.5
d. 239.7, 162.9

Disorders of the Genitourinary System

9.28. A patient has a transrectal ultrasound-guided placement of prostatic radiation palladium seeds with a cystoscopy for localized adenocarcinoma of the prostate.

Procedure Description: The patient was given general anesthesia, placed in the lithotomy position, and prepped and draped in sterile fashion. The bladder was drained, and 100 cc of half contrast and half saline were placed into the bladder. The scrotum was then draped up out of the way. The BUK 7.5 MHz transrectal ultrasound probe was then introduced into the rectum, and the prostate was imaged. The probe was placed into the stabilization bar mechanism. We then centered the prostate image on the template screen and established our base image. Stabilization needles were then put into position. We then passed the needles using a perineal approach at the corresponding positions to the corresponding depth, using ultrasound and fluoroscopy for guidance. After satisfactory placement of all the needles, the ultrasound probe and needles were removed. A total of 60 palladium seeds were put in place. We had good distribution of the seeds and good images on the ultrasound. Using the #22 French cystoscope, a cystoscopy was performed, and the bladder was fully inspected with the 30- and 70-degree lenses without notable findings. The bladder demonstrated no tumors, lesions, or other abnormalities, and there were no seeds present and very minimal bleeding. The bladder was drained and the patient was taken to the recovery room in stable condition.

Which of the following code sets would be reported for this service in addition to the HCPCS Level II supply codes for the implants and contrast used? The procedure was performed in the cancer center.

a. 233.4, 55859, 52000, 77763, 76965, 76000
b. 185, 55859, 77778, 76965, 76000
c. 185, 55859, 77787, 76872, 77790
d. 185, 52000, 77762

9.29. A Medicare patient is scheduled for breast biopsy of a palpable lump in the right breast. In the left breast is a much smaller lesion as shown on mammography and identified by a radiological marker. An excisional biopsy is performed on both sides. The specimen on the right is diagnostic for breast malignancy with clear margins, while the small lesion in the left breast is found to be only fibrocystic disease without evidence of malignancy.

Which of the following is reported for the physician services? The procedure is completed at the hospital surgery center.

a. 611.72, 610.1, 19120-50
b. 174.9, 610.1, 19125-50, 19290-50, 19120–50
c. 174.9, 610.1, 19120-RT, 19125–LT-51, 19290–LT-51
d. 174.9, 610.2, 19120, 19125–59, 19290–59

9.30. The following documentation is from the health record of a 48-year-old female patient.

Surgical Procedure

The patient is here for office hysteroscopy. She has a long history of dysfunctional bleeding. She is known to have multiple fibroids. Recent ultrasound did demonstrate normal appearing ovaries but several large fibroids, the largest of which is 5 cm in diameter.

After informed consent and taking the preop medication, the patient was sterilely prepped. We then injected her with a total of 12 cc of 2% Lidocaine without Epinephrine. We then performed an office hysteroscopy using a uterine sound. The uterus sounded to 8 cm. We then dilated the cervical OS with Pratt dilators. The hysteroscope was placed with good visualization of all portions of the endometrium. We were able to identify both tubal ostium. There was a very large fibroid posterior that does press in on the endometrium and occupies much of it. This is not a pedunculated endometrium and is intramural. There are other fibroids that also affect the cavity size and shape but again these are intramural fibroids and not accessible through the hysteroscope. D&C was performed without difficulty and the patient tolerated the procedure well. Instrument, needle and sponge count were correct.

I advised the patient to see how her symptoms proceed in the next few months. Her last FSH level was 30, suggesting a perimenopausal state. She does understand that the fibroids should shrink in size or at least remain the same once she is menopausal. However, if she feels her bleeding problems are persistent, we may have to consider hysterectomy. The patient will follow-up in three or four months and will document her bleeding.

Which diagnosis and CPT procedure codes does the surgeon assign?

a. 626.8, 218.1, 58558
b. 626.8, 218.9, 57800, 58558
c. 627.0, 218.9, 58558, 58120
d. 627.0, 218.1, 58558

9.31. The following documentation is from the health record of a female patient.

Operative Report

Preoperative Diagnosis: Recurrent right ureteral malignancy

Postoperative Diagnosis: Same

Description of Procedure: Under satisfactory standby anesthesia, the patient was placed in the dorsolithotomy position. Her external genitalia were prepped and draped in sterile fashion for a cystourethroscopy examination.

Two percent Xylocaine jelly was instilled into the urethra for topical anesthesia. Using a #20 Wappler panendoscope sheath, right angle, and four oblique fiberoptic telescopes, a cystourethroscopy was performed with a normal urethra noted. The bladder was also unremarkable but showed evidence of past reimplantation of one of the right ureters. Using a flexible ureteroscope, retrograde ureteroscopy was performed all the way to the renal pelvis. Two tumors were found in the right upper ureter, one at the ureteropelvic junction and one below. Each was less than .5 cm in size. Using the rigid ureteroscope, the tumors were reached and, using a Bugbee electrode, fulguration of the tumors was carried out. Tissue that remained on the Bugbee electrode was retained and sent to pathology for microscopic study. All of the instruments were removed, and the patient was moved to recovery in good condition. She will receive Bactrim® 1 b.i.d. for 10 days.

Pathology Results: Carcinoma of the ureter, recurrent

Which of the following code sets is reported for the surgeon for this hospital-based ambulatory surgical service?

a. 188.6, 52354-RT
b. 188.6, 52224-RT
c. 189.2, 52354-RT
d. 189.2, 52354-RT, 52330-RT

9.32. The following documentation is from the health record of a male patient.

Operative Report

A patient with an elevated prostate-specific antigen (PSA) of 35.7 comes to the surgery center for a transrectal, ultrasonic-guided (TRUS) prostate biopsy.

Technique: The patient is placed in the Sims position with the left side down. The anus was generously lubricated with 2 percent Xylocaine jelly. The ultrasound probe was then introduced and scanning initiated. A great deal of calcification was noted in the outer margin of the central zone. The area proximal and anterior to the calcifications was hypoechoic but may have been influenced by the stones. There was very thin peripheral zone tissue available. Three needle biopsies were taken from each side, starting in the periphery and working toward the midline and trying to biopsy anterior to the stones on the more medial biopsies from each side.

The pathology report confirmed carcinoma in situ of the prostate.

Which codes will be reported for this service? The facility bills for the technical and professional components and also reports procedure codes for radiologic procedures for reimbursement. Do not include surgical supplies in this example.

a. 185, 55700
b. 233.4, 790.93, 55705, 76872
c. 185, 790.93, 602.0, 55700, 76872, 76942
d. 233.4, 602.0, 55700, 76872, 76942

Infectious Diseases/Disorders of the Skin and Subcutaneous Tissue

9.33.   A 53-year-old male is seen in the office for a skin problem on the left shin. It started 2 days ago as mild redness and has developed into an area of severe itching, is swollen with dark red blotches and has an area of open weeping. The patient has Type II Diabetes Mellitus, diabetic peripheral vascular disease and a previous MRSA infection. A detailed history and a comprehensive examination are documented.

The physician diagnoses cellulitis of the left leg and obtains cultures from the open area. To speed the start of treatment, the physician administers one dose of 300 mg Clindamycin IV push at the office before sending the patient to the observation unit at the hospital for continued doses of antibiotic every 6 hours for the next 48 hours. The patient's primary insurance is Blue Cross.

Which of the following code sets is appropriate for physician reporting of these services? Do not code laboratory services.

a. 686.9, V12.04. 250.00, 443.81, 99214, 96372
b. 682.6, V02.54, 250.70, 443.81, 99214, 96374, S0077
c. 682.6, V12.04, 250.70, 443.81, 99215, 96374, S0077
d. 891.1, V02.54, 250.70, 443.81, 99215, 96372, J3490

9.34.   The following documentation is from the health record of a 73-year-old male patient.

Physician Office Record

This 73-year-old male slipped and fell while carrying a pane of glass. He was changing a window at home. He sustained three lacerations—one on his left ankle, one on his right ankle and one on his left hand.

Left ankle: 3.5 cm laceration, involving deep subcutaneous tissue and fascia, was repaired with layered closure using 1 percent lidocaine local anesthetic.

Right ankle: 4.2 cm laceration was repaired under local anesthetic with a single-layer closure.

Left hand: 2.5 cm laceration of the dermis was repaired with simple closure using DERMABOND® tissue adhesive.

Assessment: Wounds of both ankles and left hand requiring repair.

Plan: Follow-up in 10 days for suture removal. Call office if there are any problems or complications.

What are the correct ICD-9-CM and CPT procedure codes?

a. 891.0, 882.0, E920.8, E849.0, 12004
b. 891.1, 882.0, 12002, 12032–51
c. 894.0, 12032, 12002, supply code for the DERMABOND adhesive
d. 891.0, 882.0, E920.8, E849.0, 12032, 12002–51, G0168

9.35. An operative report provides the following information:

Excision lesion on right shoulder, 2.5 × 1.0 × .5 cm, including circumferential margins. Excision lesion, skin of left cheek, 1.0 × 1.0 × .5 cm, including margins. Pathology report states that the skin lesion on the right shoulder is a lipoma, and the lesion on the left cheek is a squamous cell carcinoma. The physician progress note states that the right shoulder was sutured with a layered closure, and the cheek was repaired with a simple repair.

What are the correct code sets?

a. 173.3, 214.1, 11641, 11403–51, 12031–51
b. 173.3, 214.9, 11403, 11441–51
c. 214.1, 195.0, 11603, 11641–51, 12031–51
d. 173.3, 11643, 12031–51

9.36. The following documentation is from the health record of a patient who received outpatient surgical services.

Operative Report

Preoperative Diagnosis:	Full-thickness burn wound to anterior left lower leg
Postoperative Diagnosis:	Same
Operation:	Split-thickness skin graft, approximately 35 cm; preparation of the wound
Anesthesia:	General

Procedure: The left lower leg was prepped and draped in the usual sterile fashion. The ulcer, which measured approximately 8 × 4 to 4.5 cm, was débrided sharply with Goulian knife until healthy bleeding was seen. The bleeding was controlled with epinephrine-soaked lap pads. Split-thickness skin graft was harvested from the left lateral buttock area approximately 4.5 to 5 cm × 8 cm at the depth of 14/1000 of an inch. The graft was meshed to 1 to 1.5 and placed over the prepared wound. This was stabilized with staples, and then Xeroform dressings and dry dressings, wrapped with gauze and finally immobilized in a posterior splint. The donor site was covered with Xeroform and dry dressings.

What are the correct procedure codes reported by the physician for this procedure performed in the hospital outpatient surgical suite?

a. 15220, 15221–51, 15002–51
b. 15100
c. 14021, 15002–51
d. 15100, 15002–51

9.37. The following documentation is from the health record of a patient who received outpatient surgical services.

Operative Report

Preoperative Diagnosis: Basal cell carcinoma of the forehead

Postoperative Diagnosis: Same

Procedure: Excision of basal cell carcinoma with split-thickness skin graft

The patient was given a local IV sedation and taken to the operating room suite. The face and left thigh were prepped with pHisoHex® soap. The cancer was outlined for excision. The cancer measured approximately 2.5 cm in diameter. The forehead was infiltrated with 1 percent Xylocaine with 1:1,000,000 epinephrine.

The cancer was excised and carried down to the frontalis muscle. The area of the excision measured 5 × 4 cm in toto. A suture was placed at the 12 o'clock position. The specimen was sent to pathology for frozen section.

Attention was then turned to the skin graft. A pattern of the defect was transferred to the left anterior thigh using a new needle. A local infiltration was performed on the thigh. Using a free-hand knife, a split-thickness skin graft was harvested. The thigh was treated with Tegaderm™ and a wraparound Kerlix® and ACE® wrap. The skin graft was applied and sutured to the forehead defect with running 5-0 plain catgut.

Xeroform with cotton soaked in glycerin was sutured with 4-0 silk. A sterile dressing was applied. The patient tolerated the procedure well with no complications or blood loss.

What are the correct codes reported by the physician for this procedure performed in the hospital outpatient surgical suite?

a. 195.0, 15120
b. 173.3, 15120
c. 173.3, 15100, 11646
d. 195.0, 15004, 15120

9.38. The physician sees an established patient in the office. She is a 2-year-old girl with a 2 day history of fever to 100.5, fuzziness, fatigue and headache. She also has been complaining for 5 days of pain in the left buttock with an area that is swollen and red as of today, with no known injury. She is a known asthmatic. A detailed history is obtained. Physical exam reveals a 4 cm × 4 cm abscess over the left upper buttock that is fluctuant and red, as the only finding on a comprehensive exam. Laboratory done in the office today reveals: Elevated WBC on the automated Complete CBC with Differential and an abnormal automated

Urinalysis with microscopy. A moderate level of medical decision making is used.

After obtaining consent, the physician and the staff observer prepare the patient for conscious sedation in the procedure room. The physician injects 5 cc's 2% Lidocaine as anesthetic and incises the abscess with a #11 blade straight scalpel. 10 cc of pus is drained and the area is packed with Iodoform gauze. Culture and sensitivity of the drainage is sent to an outside laboratory for evaluation. Total intra-service time was 30 minutes. The patient was given Ceftin 300 mg BID for 10 days to treat both the UTI and the abscess and will return to clinic in 2 days for a wound check.

What are the correct ICD-9-CM and CPT procedure codes for the services provided?

a. 599.0, 682.5, 780.60, 493.90, 99214-25, 99143, 10061, 99000
b. 599.0, 682.5, 780.61, 99215, 99143, 10061, 36415, 85025, 85009, 81001
c. 599.0, 682.2, 99214, 99144, 10060, 99000, 36415, 85025, 81003
d. 599.0, 682.5, 99214-25, 99143, 10060, 99000, 36415, 85025, 81001

Behavioral Health Conditions

9.39.   A patient was brought to the emergency department by her mother after she was found to be groggy after an intentional overdose of a "handful" of aspirin approximately 1/2 hour before. The mother thought the bottle was almost empty. The patient was beginning to experience dizziness and loud ringing of the ears. The physician inserted a gastric tube. The patient was stabilized in the ED, during which time bleeding studies and urinalysis were completed. A detailed history and physical examination were performed, and medical decision making was of moderate complexity. The diagnosis was suicide attempt with unknown quantity of aspirin, dizziness, and tinnitus. A psychiatric consult was arranged, and the patient was transferred to the psychiatric hospital by ambulance.

What are the correct ICD-9-CM and CPT codes for this visit?

a. 965.1, 780.4, 388.30, E950.0, 99284-25, 91105
b. 965.1, 780.4, E980.0, 99284
c. 780.4, 388.30, E935.3, 99284-25, 43752
d. 780.4, 388.30, 965.1, E935.3, 99284, 43752

9.40.   A 20-year-old patient was brought into the emergency department in nearly comatose condition following an evening of drinking beer and vodka with friends. Vital signs were depressed. A blood-alcohol level was measured, which was reported as 0.38. The patient had vomited several times before passing out. There was a 1-cm laceration on the patient's eyebrow. This was treated with a Steri-Strip. The patient was stabilized in the emergency department for 1-1/2 hours and admitted to intensive care by the Internal Medicine physician on call. Documentation in the ED record supports a level 5 emergency department visit. Diagnosis was alcohol poisoning, acute alcohol intoxication, and 1-cm laceration, right eyebrow.

What is the correct ICD-9-CM and CPT code assignment?

a. 303.00, 980.9, 99291, 99292
b. 980.9, 305.00, 99285–25, 12011
c. 980.0, 305.00, 873.42, E860.0, 99285
d. 980.0, 303.00, 99291, 12011

9.41. The following documentation is from the health record of a 22-year-old female patient.

Date of Admission: 02/10/XX

Date of Evaluation: 02/12/XX

Amount of Time of Evaluation: Patient participated in a direct interview for 40 minutes.

Sources of Information: The patient participated in a 40-minute direct interview. Patient's commitment documents from ABC facility were also reviewed. Patient's records from Dr. S. were also reviewed.

Chief Complaint: "I came here because someone was hurting me, and they thought that I wasn't eating enough and that I was throwing up too much."

History of Present Illness: The patient is a 22-year-old female with a past history of anorexia nervosa and attention deficit disorder. She was committed after a 6-week stay at ABC. Her parents brought her to this facility after her mother noticed that she was fasting and vomiting and was not sleeping. Her mother also noted that she was more weak than usual and was only able to work her job for 1 or 2 hours rather than a full day. It was also noticed that she was losing track of time, appearing confused, fearful, and angry. Patient notes that, prior to admission, she was actually sleeping fairly normally for her, about 5 hours of sleep per night, though she does agree that she was eating rather little and vomiting because of some abuse that was troubling her. On admission, she was noted to be withdrawn and refused to talk to staff and was very tearful. Later that day, however, she did not remember this incident of being tearful. On admission she was noted to be 84 lb at a height of 5 feet. She at that time admitted to vomiting as much as three times a day and that she had to have her teeth resurfaced due to purging. At ABC facility, staff noted she was hoarding condiments in her room and was also noted to purge in front of staff during her stay there. The patient, however, does not think that her purging was due to an eating disorder; rather, she thinks that it was due to stress and anxiety over a previous abuse. Previous records reveal potassium levels as low as 2.0. She states that the low potassium is due to a kidney disorder; however, a nephrologist thought that the low potassium was most likely due to her purging behavior. Her weight at discharge from ABC was 85.5 pounds. Patient notes that her sleep has not been disrupted prior to her hospital stay. She states that she usually gets about 5 hours of sleep per night, which is normal for her. She notes that her appetite has been decreased for the past several months because of stress regarding prior abuse. She denies any thought racing or excessive energy for the past several months. She also denies any suicidal thoughts or behaviors. She also denies any obsessive-compulsive actions. She denies feeling hopeless or depressed.

Chemical Dependency History: Patient denies any current or previous use of alcohol or drugs.

Current Prescribed Medications: Claritin® 10 mg p.o. q. d.; potassium chloride 20 mEq t.i.d. to q. i.d. p.r.n. hypokalemia; Dexedrine® SR 40 mg t.i.d.

Past Psychiatric History: Patient has a history of problems with eating disorders that goes back to the age of 14. Over the past 8 years she has been involved in a variety of treatment programs. She was first treated in an inpatient setting at the age of 14. She was subsequently hospitalized at the age of 15, age 16 × 2, and age 17. From the age of 17 to 18 she was placed in foster care. She has attempted suicide three times in her life. Each time the attempt was made by trying to overdose on her asthma medication, theophylline. She has been hospitalized five times for hypokalemia. She notes that she currently sees a psychiatrist and a psychologist as an outpatient. In the past, she has exhibited some features of self-injurious behavior. She burned a cross into her arm at age 13. She also has a past history of scratching her arm.

Family Psychiatric History: She notes that her younger sister attempted to overdose one time in the past and that her father has been treated for depression with ECT, which was successful.

Mental Status Examination: The patient is a petite, too-thin young female who appears younger than her stated age of 22. She is clean, well groomed, and dressed in jeans and a large hooded sweatshirt. Her general behavior is noted to be normal and appropriate throughout the interview. She is cooperative throughout our question-and-answer session. Her mood is somewhat subdued, and she seems slightly anxious. Her affect is rather flat throughout the interview. No abnormal movements are noted during the interview. Her speech is fairly soft and rather monotone in nature. Speech is noted to be of normal speed. Stream of mental activity is normal and appropriate. The form of thought processes appears to be normal without any tangential thinking. Thought content appears to be normal as well. She denies delusions, hallucinations, and suicidal or homicidal ideation at present. She does not seem to be impulsive in her speech or thought processes throughout the interview. She does seem to have some insight into her illness in that she is able to name her illness as anorexia. She states that her weight now is OK. Her judgment, concentration, orientation all appear to be within normal limits. Recent and remote memory appears intact. Her general fund of knowledge is above average. Her calculations, abstractions, proverbs, similarities, are all within normal limits. Estimated IQ would be 120 based on educational background and verbal skills. The patient does not appear to be dangerous or suicidal at present.

Biopsychosocial Discussion and Discussion of Differential Diagnosis: The patient is a 22-year-old female with a past history of anorexia and subsequent hypokalemia. She notes that recent exacerbation in her anorexia and vomiting seems to be due to stress over abuse in the past by a physician with whom she had previous professional contact and subsequently became friends. She has limited insight into her eating disorder in that she is able to name it as anorexia now. In the past, however, she has denied the existence of an eating disorder. In the past, she has had suicidal attempts. However, at this time she does not appear to be depressed and does not indicate any suicidal thoughts or plans. At this time, she does not indicate feeling particularly anxious but, rather, regards her main symptom as stress. She states that her only fear right now is that of being in the hospital for her first commitment. She appears to have a long history of hospitalizations for her eating disorder and subsequent hypokalemia. Her family history does appear to have a history of mental illness, with depression in her father and a suicide attempt by her younger sister. She also was noted to have burned a cross into her arm as a young child, as well as a history of scratching her arm. There is a possibility that she has a personality disorder with borderline features. Though she does not seem to be in danger of suicide right now or hurting others, it is felt that because of her history of severe hypokalemia and history of anorexia, as well as purging behavior, she will require a long-term inpatient hospitalization for her safety.

Admitting Diagnosis:

Axis I	1. Anorexia nervosa, purging type
	2. Attention deficit hyperactive disorder
Axis II	Personality disorder with predominant borderline features
Axis III	1. History of hypokalemia
	2. Asthma
	3. Hypokalemic periodic paralysis (per patient report)
Axis IV	Severe with stresses incurred due to previous abuse
Axis V	Current GAF—50 to 60

Prognosis: Guarded due to her history of multiple hospitalizations for her eating disorder

Strengths:
1. Patient is very intelligent.
2. Patient is enrolled in school and has had a high level of education.
3. Patient has a therapeutic relationship with her therapist and psychiatrist as an outpatient.
4. Patient's weight is near her target weight already.
5. The patient has some insight into her eating disorder.

Problems
1. Patient lacks a deep insight into her eating disorder.
2. Patient clings to a diagnosis of hypokalemia periodic paralysis, which she claims is a kidney disorder that she has. Nephrologist cannot corroborate this theory.
3. Patient has a high rate of recidivism in the hospital system for treatment of her eating disorder.

Short-Term Goals
1. Patient will identify and discuss high-risk situations.
2. She will listen.
3. She will demonstrate four alternative coping skills to purging.
4. She will seek out assistance from staff before acting on urges to purge.
5. Patient will identify triggers.
6. Patient will be able to discuss short- and long-term consequences of her eating disorder.
7. Patient will complete a crisis plan to control purging urges.

8. Patient will maintain personal safety by not engaging in purging.
9. Patient will maintain her current weight or increase that weight up to 90 lb.

Long-Term Goals
1. Patient will reduce the frequency of purging.
2. Patient will complete community passes without reports of purging in preparation for transition to home.
3. Patient will develop the ability to control impulses and demonstrate strategies to deal with dysphoric moods.
4. Patient will maintain her current weight or increase that weight.
5. Patient will maintain normal potassium levels and will not require supplemental potassium treatment.

Biopsychosocial Treatment Plan
1. Because of her anorexia nervosa and possible personality disorder, she would likely benefit from a referral to dialectical behavior therapy.
2. She would also benefit from a referral to the eating disorders group.
3. Because of her history of hypokalemia, we will regularly monitor her potassium level and treat accordingly with supplemental potassium.
4. We will weigh her three times a week in order to monitor her progress here. We will expect that she maintain her current weight or increase it.
5. She will be allowed initially to go to the cafeteria on her own and choose what she eats, assuming that her weight stays at her current level or increases.
6. She will be started at level B privileges.

Discharge Criteria
1. She will maintain or increase her weight during her stay here.
2. She will maintain normal potassium levels during her stay here.
3. She will participate in dialectical behavior therapy as well as eating disorders group.
4. She will reduce the frequency of her purging behaviors while here.
5. She will complete community passes without reports of purging in preparation for transition to home.

Estimated Length of Stay as Per UM Norms: 45 days

Which of the following is the correct code set for reporting this physician's service?

a. 307.1, 314.01, 301.83, 493.90, V17.0, 90801
b. 301.1, 314.01, 301.83, 276.8, 493.90, 359.3, 90801
c. 307.1, 314.01, 301.83, 493.90, V17.0, 99223
d. 301.1, 314.01, 301.83, 276.8, 493.90, 359.3, 99223

Disorders of the Musculoskeletal System and Connective Tissue

9.42.   A Monteggia fracture-dislocation with a large contaminated open wound is treated with open reduction and external fixation, extensive subcutaneous fracture site débridement, and application of a posterior splint. Which codes are assigned for the surgical services?

   a. 813.32, 24650, 11010-51, 20692–51
   b. 813.18, 24685, 11010–51, 29105–51
   c. 813.02, 24635, 20692, 29105–51
   d. 813.13, 24635, 11010–51

9.43.   The following documentation is from the health record of a patient having orthopedic surgery on the leg.

Operative Report

Preoperative Diagnosis: Left distal femur osteosarcoma

Postoperative Diagnosis: Left distal femur osteosarcoma

Operation:

1. Resection of left distal femur
2. Prosthetic reconstruction of the left knee
3. Osteotomy of the left femur
4. Femoral artery exploration

Anesthesia: General

Estimated Blood Loss: 500 ml. The patient received 4 units of packed RBCs.

Complications: None

Indications for procedure: The patient is a 23-year-old female who was diagnosed with a left distal femur osteosarcoma on biopsy and has undergone preoperative chemotherapy. Risks, benefits, complications, and alternatives of resection and reconstruction were discussed with her, and consent was obtained.

Description of procedure: The patient was seen in the preoperative area and a history and physical examination was performed. Consents were reviewed. She was taken to the operating room, given general anesthesia. She received preoperative antibiotics, and a Foley catheter was placed. Both legs were prepped and draped out. An external incision was made on the anteromedial aspect of the left thigh, extending towards the anterior aspect of the proximal tibia, including excision of the previous biopsy tract.

Dissection was carried down to the subcutaneous tissue leaving a cuff of healthy tissue on the biopsy tract and also a cuff of muscle was left. Dissection was carried subvastus, elevating the muscle but leaving the fat and other loose tissue including fascia on the tumor. Medially the vastus medialis was elevated off the medial septum. Dissection was carried further subvastus as well as laterally. The patella was preserved. Distally the subpatellar tendon fat pad was left with the knee to be resected. Following dissection, an Osteotomy site was located further laterally and proximally at 16 cm from the articular surface of the femoral condyle. This was based on the recent MRI. An osteotomy was performed and parts of the posterior cortex were curetted and marrow was removed and passed off to the pathologist for evaluation. Both of these were read on frozen sections as being normal and not containing any malignant tissue.

With these findings known, the remaining posterior attachments to the femur were dissected/transected. The femoral artery extending towards the popliteal space was carefully explored, retracted, and any branches of the tumor were either clipped or suture ligated. The tumor was dissected and the resection was carried out under tourniquet at 270 mmHg.

The tourniquet was let down and hemostasis was achieved with Bovie cautery, vascular clips, or suture ligations. The wound was slightly irrigated. The specimen was sent off to the pathologist for evaluation. The tibial surface was reamed and trial implants were placed. The femoral canal was reamed to 15 mm, which gave satisfactory chatter suggestive of a good fit. A 15 mm diameter, 150 mm long stem was placed into the femur with various length trials. A regular femoral condyle was chosen along with a regular tibial component. Following adequate leg length, which gave us satisfactory soft tissue tensioning, rotation as well as ability to close the wound and patella tracking, but also about 1 extra cm length on the left side, the appropriate components were chosen. The tibial plastic component was cemented into place. An uncemented 150-mm-long, 15-mm-diameter stem with the components in place was gently impacted into the femur and was checked under fluoroscopy. It was noted to be satisfactorily placed. After placement of the bushings, the hinge, and the bumper, the components were reduced. The soft tissue tension was adequate and the vessels seemed to be without any undue stress, and adequate pulsation of the femoral artery was present extending down to the popliteal space. With these findings, patella tracking was again checked and noted to be satisfactory. A lateral retinacular release was carried out to allow further appropriate tracking. The wound was thoroughly irrigated, 2 drains were placed, and the various layers were reapproximated with either #1 Ethibond, #1, 0 or 2-0 Vicryl sutures, and then the skin was closed with 4-0 Monocryl. Steri-strips were applied, and the dressings were applied as well as the knee immobilizer with a slight flexion of the knee.

Postoperatively, the foot showed adequate blood flow with a palpable dorsalis pedis pulse. The patient was extubated. She will be admitted for postoperative pain control as well as rehabilitation and discharged when stable.

Which of the following is the correct code assignment for the services of the surgeon?

a. 170.7, 27360, 27447, 35741, 27448, 76000
b. 170.7, 27365, 27445, 35721, 27448, 27425, 76000-26
c. 238.0, 27329, 27445, 27448, 76000-26
d. 239.2, 27360, 27447, 27448, 27425, 76000

9.44. The following documentation is from the health record of a 42-year-old male patient.

Physician Office Record Entries

Hospital Copy: History and Physical

Admitting Diagnosis: Herniation of intervertebral disc, L5–S1 right side

Present Medical History: Patient is a 42-year-old Native American male, who initially developed problems with his back in July of this year. He was treated with anti-inflammatory agents and started on an exercise program; his condition improved enough to return to work. About 1 month ago, he had recurrence of pain, which has become steadily worse in the past week. He noticed some numbness of his right foot, primarily the toes and right heel. The patient was initially evaluated by his family physician and is now admitted to the orthopedic service for microdiskectomy after MRI revealed herniation and protrusion of the disc encroaching on the nerve root.

Past Medical History: Patient denied any known allergies or drug sensitivities. He has been taking Advil® on a p.r.n. basis. Also takes Lotensin® 10 mg daily for hypertension and has a history of incomplete bundle branch block, hyperlipidemia (no meds), hiatus hernia with gastroesophageal reflux.

Previous Surgeries: Tonsillectomy as a child and also tendon repair to the right hand in 1989. Does state that he injured his kidney in a motorcycle accident at age 21 years and was hospitalized with viral pneumonia in 1983.

Family History: Father is 62 years with heart disease and hypertension problems. Mother is 64 years and in good health, without significant illness. Three siblings, all in good health.

Social History: Patient is employed full-time at the Harley-Davidson® dealership. At the present time, he is divorced and has one child who lives with her mother. He does not smoke, is sexually active, and admits to sporadic alcohol use.

Review of Systems

HEENT: Patient denies any unusual problems with headaches and dizziness, or visual or hearing difficulty. Cardiorespiratory: Denies chest pain; does have occasional asthma symptoms with some wheezing but does not use medications. Hypertension for 2 years, well controlled on medication. Gastrointestinal: Denies distention, diarrhea, and constipation. Genitourinary: Negative. Musculoskeletal: See present complaint.

Physical Examination: Reveals a well-developed, well-nourished male in no acute distress. Does have a hard time sitting due to pain on the right side. Height 6'1", Weight 210 lb, Blood Pressure 122/90, pulse 72, respiration 20. Skin is clear, normal temperature and texture. HEENT: Head normal cephalic. Pupils are round, equal, and reactive to light accommodation. Canals are clear. Tympanic membranes, nose, and throat are clear of infection. Neck: Supple, thyroid negative. No adenopathy, no distomegaly or carotid bruits. Chest: Symmetrical, lungs clear to P & A. Heart: Normal sinus rhythm, no thrills or murmurs. Abdomen: Soft, no tenderness or masses. No organomegaly. Normal male genitalia. Extremities: Normal development. Patient does have tenderness in the area of the right sciatic knot and in the lower lumbar area on the right side. Has positive leg raising and some decrease in the deep tendon reflexes on the side.

Impression: Herniation of intervertebral disc at L5–S1 right side

Plan: Microdiskectomy tomorrow morning

Operative Report

Preoperative Diagnosis: Herniated nucleus pulposus, right

Postoperative Diagnosis: Same

Operation: Right L5–S1 diskectomy with minifacetectomy foraminotomy

Complications: None

Indications: The patient is an otherwise healthy 42-year-old Native American male who has had 6 months of disabling right leg pain. He has tried extensive physical therapy, nonsteroidal anti-inflammatory drugs, and an epidural injection, without relief. He has a positive straight leg-raising test on the right side and an absent ankle jerk. MRI scan confirms the disk herniation at L5–S1 on the right side.

Description of Procedure: The patient was brought to the operating room, and general anesthesia was administered in the usual fashion. He was positioned in the prone position onto a well-padded Andrews frame. All pressure points were well padded. The back was prepped and draped in a sterile fashion. He received 1 g of Ancef prior to the beginning of the case, along with 30 mg of IV Toradol®.

Initially, an x-ray was checked that showed we were at the L4–5 interspace, so we went down one level. A 3/4 skin incision was made in the midline of the lumbar sacral spine, and this was carried down to the subcutaneous tissue. The fascia over the L5–S1 lamina was then dissected away. The paraspinal muscles were then elevated above the lamina, and a laminotomy was performed in between L5 and S1. The superior facet of S1 was undercut using a Kerrison rongeur. The S1 nerve root was well visualized and this area was protected throughout the procedure. Following this, a foraminotomy was performed over the top of the S1 nerve root. The S1 nerve root was then gently retracted medially, and a very large extrusive disk fragment was pulled out from underneath the S1 nerve root. The annulotomy that had been made from the disc herniation was then explored, and no further fragments could be found. The wound was thoroughly irrigated with a bacitracin solution. Gelfoam® and thrombin were placed over the top of the dura, and the deep fascia was closed with interrupted 0 VICRYL® sutures. The subcutaneous tissue was closed with 2–0 VICRYL® suture, and the skin was closed with 4–0 VICRYL® suture. Benzoin and Steri-Strips were applied to the wound. The patient was returned to recovery in stable condition. EBL 10 cc.

Pathologic Diagnosis: Intervertebral disc L5–S1 resection, herniated nucleus pulposus

Which of the following is the correct code assignment for physician service? Code for surgical services only.

a. 722.52, 401.9, 63047
b. 722.73, 401.9, 63030
c. 722.10, 63047
d. 722.10, 401.9, 63030

9.45. The following documentation is from the health record of a male patient.

Operative Report

Preoperative Diagnosis: 1. ACL deficient, right knee
2. Medial and lateral meniscal tear, right knee

Operation: 1. Examination under anesthesia, right knee
2. Arthroscopic-assisted anterior cruciate ligament reconstruction, right knee
3. Partial medial and partial lateral meniscectomy

Anesthesia: General

Complications: None

The patient was identified and taken to the operating room and general anesthesia administered. The patient's lower extremity was examined under anesthesia. The patient had evidence of +2 Lachman and +2 pivot shift. After examination under anesthesia, the right lower extremity was prepped and draped in the usual sterile fashion. Routine arthroscopic portals were placed. Examination of the patellofemoral joint was fairly unremarkable. Coming down the medial gutter and the medial compartment, there was a complex tear of the posterior horn of the medial meniscus. Using a combination of basket and 4.2 shaver, partial medial meniscectomy was carried out. This resected about 50 percent of the posterior horn of the medial meniscus. There was a horizontal cleavage component remaining, that was stable to probing; it was left alone. Intercondylar notch revealed a complete tear of the anterior cruciate ligament. Going to the lateral compartment, there was a flap tear of the posterior horn of the lateral meniscus, and, again utilizing the lateral meniscus, partial lateral meniscectomy was carried out. This resected about 30 percent of the posterior horn. At this point, the scope was removed from the knee. We did make a longitudinal incision based upon the tibial tubercle medially. This was carried down through the skin and down the subcutaneous tissue. We readily identified the hamstring tendon and harvested the gracilis and semitendinosus. These were taken to the back table and a #2 ETHIBOND leader was placed on the leading edge, and the graft was doubled over for quadruple graft. The scope was placed back into the knee. Notchplasty was performed. Subsequently, we made a tibial tunnel utilizing the Arthrex® tibial guide referenced off the posterior cruciate ligament. We then made a femoral tunnel again utilizing the Arthrex femoral guide referenced off the posterior cortex. Both of these were 8-mm tunnels. We subsequently placed the graft on the knee, and we fixed it on the femoral side with 8 × 23 Arthrex bioabsorbable screw. Visualization of the graft revealed no evidence of impingement, no roughing on the medial aspect of the lateral wall. We subsequently held the knee in just short of full extension with appropriate amount of tension and fixed it on the tibial side with an 8 × 28 Arthrex bioabsorbable screw. Examination after placement of the graft revealed a negative Lachman and negative pivot shift. Multiple intraoperative photos were obtained. At the end of the procedure, subcutaneous tissue was closed with 2-0 VICRYL®, the skin with running 2-0 nylon, and portals with 3-0 nylon. Sterile dressing was placed followed by ACE® wrap and total thigh and knee immobilizer. The patient tolerated the procedure well, and there were no complications.

Assign the correct codes for this case:

Primary (first listed) diagnosis: _____

Additional diagnoses: _____

Procedures: _____

9.46. The following documentation is from the health record of a patient admitted for a right total hip.

Preoperative Diagnosis:	Right hip osteonecrosis, Ficat stage IV.
Postoperative Diagnosis:	Right hip osteonecrosis, Ficat stage IV.
Procedure Performed:	Right total hip arthroplasty.
Blood Loss:	350 cc.
Complications:	None.
Implants Used:	1. DePuy Articul/eze femoral head 28 mm + 1.5 lot #1169939.
	2. DePuy large AML femoral component, 150 mm long, 45-mm offset, lot #YDZCV1000.
	3. DePuy hole eliminator lot #YH9DH1000.
	4. DePuy pinnacle acetabular liner 28 mm, lot #X69AR1000.
	5. DePuy cancellous bone screw 25 mm long, lot #X2BEN1000.
	6. DePuy acetabular cup 36 mm, lot #X60CK1000.

Indications for Operation: The patient is a 54-year-old man who is presented with long-standing right hip pain secondary to osteonecrosis. Nonsurgical treatment was unsuccessful. After risks, benefits, and alternatives of the surgery were explained to the patient, informed consent was obtained for this procedure.

Details of Procedure: Patient was taken back to the operating room and placed on the operating table in a supine position. After induction of general anesthesia, the patient was placed in the left lateral decubitus position and the left lower extremity was prepped and draped in usual sterile manner. Lateral incision was made over the greater trochanter. This incision was approximately 15 cm long. It was carried down through subcutaneous tissue to the iliotibial band, which was incised longitudinally. The gluteus medius was identified and split in line with its fibers down to the level of the greater trochanter. The gluteus medius was then split. This ran along with greater trochanter and was lifted anteriorly off the greater trochanter in line with vastus lateralis as well. These structures were dissected off of the greater trochanter. The gluteus minimus was exposed and its tendon was transected longitudinally as well. Capsule was delineated just lying underneath the gluteus adducted and placed in a sterile bag as it was dislocated. The neck was cut with an oscillating saw. Retractors were placed inferiorly, posteriorly along the acetabulum as well as superiorly. The acetabulum was then débrided off the remaining capsular and labral tissue as well as ligamentaries. The acetabulum was then reamed starting with a 49-mm reamer and reamed sequentially in 1-mm increments to 55, 56 was trailed and it was deemed to be appropriate. Version was checked at each sequential reaming. The 56-mm acetabular component was then inserted and hammered into place. Trial liner was placed. The limb was then placed in the bag and the medial aspect of the greater trochanter was cut with the use of a box cutter. The femoral canal was then reamed sequentially and increments to a 13.5. The lateral side cutter was then used to cut out the cancellous bone from the calcar. A small broach was replaced with 13.5 large broach. The head component was placed and was trailed. The hip was deemed to be too tight. Intraoperative x-ray was obtained and demonstrated the femoral neck cut to be insufficient. The hip was dislocated. The trial head and neck were removed and the femur was then reamed further distally. The calcar planar was used to take down the femoral neck cut. The broach was placed prior to calcar planning often reaming the femoral canal sufficiently, the 13.5 large broach did in fact sink further end of the canal and after the hip was reduced it was deemed to be both stable and not in too much tension. The hip was then dislocated. The broach was removed as well as the trial liner. The true liner was then placed as well as the femoral stem component was then placed. Femoral head was placed and the hip was located. Tension was deemed to be adequate. The hip was tested and position of instability was deemed to be stable. The wound was copiously irrigated to sterile saline. The minimus was repaired with interrupted #0 VICRYL sutures. The medius was reapproximated with running #0 VICRYL sutures as well as drill holes placed into greater troch and #5 Tycron sutures. The IT band was repaired with interrupted #0 VICRYL sutures and subcutaneous tissue was repaired with interrupted #2-0 VICRYL sutures. The skin was closed with staples. Sterile dressings were applied. The patient was extubated and recovered in a holding area uneventfully.

Code the orthopedic surgeon's code sets:

Diagnoses: _____

Procedure(s): _____

Neoplasms

9.47.   The patient is a 4-year-old male with acute lymphocytic leukemia who has had a fever for the last 24 hours. It has been 9 days since his last chemotherapy, which was his first. A comprehensive history is documented. On examination, the skin over his Hickman site is extremely red and starting to break down. No other abnormal findings are noted in the comprehensive exam. Labs show that the patient is not neutropenic. The physician lists the diagnoses as: ALL not in remission, infected Hickman. The patient is given 770 mg of Ceptaz over 10 minutes, through a new peripheral IV site and admitted for continued treatment. Medical decision making is moderate.

What is code set is reported for the services of the emergency physician?

a. 204.00, 996.62, 780.60, 99284–25, 96374
b. 204.00, 999.31, E878.2, 99284
c. 208.00, 996.69, 780.61, 99285
d. 208.00, 999.31, 99285–25, 96374

9.48. A patient with a chronic cough and shortness of breath is scheduled for a pleural biopsy following a chest x-ray that revealed a significant mass in the left lower lobe of the lung. Due to the position of the mass, a pleural biopsy is planned rather than a bronchoscopic biopsy.

Following the administration of local anesthetic in the interventional radiology suite of the hospital, a pleural biopsy needle is passed over the left side of the ribs. Fluoroscopic guidance is used to guide needle placement into the mass, so that tissue is obtained for pathologic evaluation.

Which of the following code sets would the physician assign for this procedure if carcinoma of the lung is diagnosed?

a. 162.9, 32400, 77002
b. 786.09, 786.2, 32405
c. 162.5, 32405, 77002–26
d. 162.5, 786.09, 786.2, 32405, 77002–26

9.49. A patient with hemoptysis, hoarseness, and chronic cough is scheduled for an outpatient flexible fiberoptic laryngoscopy including a biopsy of the cricoid. Procedure: Patient was taken to operating outpatient suite #2. I administered IV sedation at 1300 and applied topical anesthetic spray. Next, I introduced a flexible fiberoptic laryngoscope. Biopsies are taken from multiple sites of the affected areas. The pathology report states "metastatic carcinoma of the arytenoid cartilage and the posterior commissure and well-differentiated carcinoma of the cricoid and extrinsic larynx." The operative note states suspected involvement of the thyroid cartilage with primary malignancy believed to be from the esophagus. The patient experienced an increase in blood pressure after the biopsies were obtained, and the procedure was discontinued at 1316. An esophagoscopy will be scheduled after the patient's blood pressure is stabilized.

Which of the following code sets would the physician report?

a. 197.3, 199.1, 796.2, 31576, 99144
b. 161.8, 198.89, 401.9, 31510
c. 150.9, 197.3, 197.3, 197.3, 197.3, 997.1, 31576–53
d. 150.9, 161.8, 796.2, 31576, 99144, 99145

9.50. A Medicare patient with a personal history of colon cancer, considered to be at high risk for recurrent disease, presents to the office for a screening colonoscopy. The gastroenterologist also examines the anastomosis sites following a previous hemicolectomy.

Procedure: The patient was prepped in the usual fashion, followed by placement in the left lateral decubitus position. I administered 3 mg of Versed. Monitoring of sedation was assisted by a trained RN.

A colonoscopy to the terminal ileum was performed with lesions found just beyond the splenic flexure, which were biopsied. In the sigmoid colon, two polyps were found and excised by hot biopsy forceps.

The pathology report showed the descending colon lesions to be a recurrence of the malignancy and the polyps to be adenomatous.

Which of the following code sets would be reported for the procedure performed in the office?

a. 153.2, 45384
b. 153.2, 211.3, 45384, 45380–59
c. V67.09, V10.05, 153.2, G0105, 45384–59
d. 153.9, V10.05, V45.89, 45384, 45380

9.51. A Medicare beneficiary visits the oncology clinic for follow-up. Following a comprehensive history and detailed physical examination, including pelvic and breast examinations, the physician elects to perform a hysteroscopy with endometrial biopsy to evaluate postmenopausal bleeding and rule out a neoplastic source. The patient also has a suspicious lump (enlarged lymph nodes) under the arm, which is suspected to be a recurrence of breast cancer resected 8 years ago that will require a future biopsy to stage. According to the clinic form, the physician's medical decision making was considered moderate complexity. The pathology report from the biopsy indicates primary endometrial cancer.

Which of the following will be reported for this clinic service?

a. 182.0, 627.1, V10.3, 58558, 99214–59
b. 182.0, 785.6, V10.3, 58558, 99214–25
c. 182.0, 785.6, V10.3, 58558–25
d. 182.0, 785.6, V10.3, 58555, 58100, 99214–25

9.52. The following documentation is from the health record of a 78-year-old male patient.

Preoperative Diagnosis: Need for permanent venous access

Postoperative Diagnosis: Same

Description of Procedure: Placement of Infuse-A-Port®, right subclavian vein

The patient is a 78-year-old Hispanic male with disseminated metastatic colon carcinoma under chemotherapy management. His oncologist has requested placement of a permanent venous access catheter.

The patient was brought to the operating room and placed in the supine position. The initial request was for placement in the left subclavian vein. However, after cannulation of the vein and injection of contrast, there was not adequate flow to allow passage of the guidewire through the vein into the superior vena cava. Therefore, the left-sided procedure was aborted.

The right subclavian vein was cannulated without difficulty, and the guidewire was passed centrally down into the superior vena cava. The location was confirmed with fluoroscopy. A subcutaneous pocket and tunnel was then created for the port. The port was placed just above the pectoral fascia. The dilator and peel-away catheter and sheath were passed off the guidewire into the subclavian vein. The sheath was peeled away, and the catheter that had been previously trimmed to the appropriate length and flushed with heparinized saline was passed through the sheath into the subclavian vein. The sheath was peeled away, and hemostasis was achieved. The port was sutured into the pocket with 3-0 Dexon. The 2.5 cm wound was irrigated with saline and closed in layers with 3-0 Dexon subcutaneously followed with 4-0 Dexon subcuticular for the skin. Steri-Strips were applied with sterile dressing and tape. Following the procedure, a chest x-ray in the holding area revealed no pneumothorax and the catheter in excellent position.

Which of the following code sets would the surgeon report for this ambulatory surgical service performed at the hospital?

a. 199.0, 153.9, 36561, 36556–59
b. 153.9, 36563, 36410–53
c. 199.0, 153.9, 36561, 36410–59
d. V58.81, 199.0, 153.9, 36561, 12031

9.53. The following documentation is from the health record of a patient with a lesion on the left calf.

Comprehensive Visit

History

Referring Doctor:	Primary care physician
Chief Complaint:	Lesion Lt. calf
History of Present Illness:	4 to 5 yr. HX pigmented lesion posterior Lt. calf. Lesion changed (divided into 2, became rough). Pt. saw primary care physician and lesion was biopsied. Path positive for malignant melanoma in situ. Pt. referred for wide re-excision.
Medications:	Indural 40 mg 2 qd, Norvasc 5 mg 1 qd, Lasix 80 mg 2 qd, Potassium 20 meq 2 qd.
Allergies:	Septra
Medical History:	Basal Carcinoma 1995, wears glasses, High BP
Surgery:	Tonsillectomy 1945, Partial Hysterectomy 1963—Lumpectomy Rt. Breast 1965—Lumpectomy Rt. Breast 1967

Family History

Physical

HT:	5'1"
WT:	147
TEMP:	
BP:	160/72
P:	64
R:	
General:	NDWF
HEENT:	No bruits or JVD
Heart:	RSR without murmur

Extremities:	Lt. posterior calf recent biopsy site—greater than 1 cm diameter defect—dermal based.
Diagnosis:	Melanoma in-situ Lt. posterior calf
Plan:	Will need wide local excision with STSG to excision site. Donor site—thigh or hip.

Select the correct ICD-9-CM code set for this physician.

a. 172.7
b. 232.7
c. 232.7, 172.7
d. 172.7, 709.9

Disorders of the Nervous System and Sense Organs

9.54. A patient presents to the neurology clinic for assessment of apraxia at the request of her primary care physician. The patient has a history of CVA and has expressive aphasia. She is unable to carry out purposeful movements, even though she has normal muscle tone and coordination. A full assessment is performed using the Boston Diagnostic Aphasia Examination including interpretation and report (1 hour). The consulting neurologist conducts a detailed history and examination, performs medical decision making of low complexity, and dictates a complete report to the requesting physician, along with the finding of the aphasia assessment.

Which of the following code sets is reported for this service?

a. 438.11, 438.81, 99203, 96105
b. 784.3, 784.69, 99244
c. 438.81, 99243
d. 438.11, 438.81, 99243–25, 96105

9.55. This 35-year-old female patient was admitted with the diagnosis of cerebral aneurysm. The following procedure was performed: intracranial aneurysm repair by intracranial approach with microdissection, carotid circulation. The patient continued to improve with no residual defects. During the hospital stay, she did experience postoperative pneumonia due to *Pseudomonas*.

In addition to the E/M codes submitted by the office, what ICD-9-CM codes and CPT codes are assigned?

a. 437.3, 61700
b. 430, 482.1, 61700, 69990-51
c. 437.3, 997.3, 482.1, 61700, 69990
d. 747.81, 997.3, 61703, 69990

9.56. A patient presents to the neurology clinic for a consultation with a neurologist for intention tremors with periodic muscle weakness in the upper body.

Short-latency somatosensory-evoked potential studies were conducted immediately following a comprehensive history, comprehensive neurologic examination, and decision making of moderate complexity. Both arms and the head and trunk were tested. The results of the interpretation of the tests state "Rule out MS," and a report was sent to the requesting physician stating that a diagnosis of multiple sclerosis could not be ruled out at this time and further testing would be undertaken at a later date. Which of the following is correct?

a. 333.1, 728.9, 99244–25, 95925, 95927–51
b. 340, 99245–25, 95927
c. 333.1, 728.9, 99204, 95925, 95927–51
d. 728.9, 781.0, 99244–25, 95927

9.57.   A Medicare patient has a persistent pain syndrome of the low back and leg subsequent to an automobile accident 5 years ago in which he sustained back injuries. The patient is brought to the outpatient surgery center nerve block area and is premedicated so he is relaxed enough to be positioned appropriately. The sacral area is prepped with Betadine and a 25-gauge needle, followed by a 22-gauge needle, is placed under lidocaine anesthesia in the caudal space. The area was injected with 29 cc of solution containing 150 cc of Xylocaine and 16 mg of Decadron LA®. The patient remained in good condition in the block room and the recovery area.

Which of the following procedure code sets is reported?

a. 64449
b. 62319
c. 62311
d. 62311, 77003

9.58.   This 45-year-old patient has been followed for left ear conductive hearing loss. It was decided to proceed with surgery to correct the condition. The postoperative diagnosis is left ear otosclerosis. During the procedure, a markedly thickened stapes footplate was observed; however, the eustachian tube was intact, and there was normal mobility of the malleus and incus. The left ear stapedectomy with drillout of the footplate proceeded uneventfully. During recovery, the patient experienced atrial fibrillation. This was felt to be due to the surgery because the EKG was normal during the preoperative evaluation. The patient was admitted to the hospital from the outpatient surgical area, and a consultation was requested from the cardiologist. I will continue to follow the patient.

With the exception of E/M codes, what are the correct diagnosis and procedure codes for physician reporting?

a. 387.9, 997.1, 427.31, 69661–LT
b. 387.9, 69661–LT
c. 387.9, 427.31, 69661–LT
d. 387.9, 69660–LT

Newborn/Congenital Disorders

9.59. The following documentation is from the health record of a newborn infant.

Newborn Care

Delivery Note: 11/20/XX, 2300. Called to provide pediatric standby during delivery for suspected nuchal cord. Mother G2, P1. Onset of labor 0730 with normal progression. Entered stage 2 labor at 2100. Fetal monitor showed occasional decelerations. Spontaneous rupture of membranes at 2110, fluid was clear. Noted to have nuchal cord at time of delivery. Otherwise uneventful course.

O: Initial Apgar score 8/9. Weight 3,340 g. Approximate gestational age 38 weeks.

General: Pink with lusty cry. HEENT: Normal, moderate molding, minimal caput. Spine intact. Lungs: Clear bilaterally. Cardiovascular: No murmur noted, capillary refill less than 2 seconds.

Assessment: Normal full-term newborn, noted to have nuchal cord with occasional decels, otherwise uneventful delivery.

Plan: No further intervention at this time. Transferred to newborn nursery for routine newborn care and monitoring.

Progress Note: 11/21/XX, 0630

Subjective: Female newborn, gestational age 39 3/7 wks. Product of full-term pregnancy, NSVD, SROM epidural anesthesia, sl nuchal cord. Initial Apgar score 8/9.

Mother is 32-year-old G2 P1. Pregnancy was significant for maternal hypothyroidism and vanishing twin syndrome. See delivery note for labor course. EDC 24 Nov, initial prenatal care at 10 3/7 wks. Maternal labs: blood type O positive, ABS neg, Rub immune, VDRL nonreactive, HIV neg, GBS neg, 1hr GTT 82, HBsAg neg, GC/Chlm neg.

Objective: Birth wt 7 lb 6 oz, head circ 14″, length 19 3/4″, head: normocephalic, fontanelles soft nonbulging. Mild caput, moderate molding. Skin: Pink and warm. Eyes: + red reflux × 2, PERRL. ENT: Nares patent, palate intact. TMs clear bilaterally. Lungs: Bilateral breath sounds equal, no accessory muscle use noted. Cardiovascular: regular rate and rhythm, no murmur appreciated. Well-perfused, normal pulses. Capillary refill less than 2 seconds. Abdomen: Normal active bowl sounds, soft no masses, three-vessel cord. No erythema or discharge at umbilical stump. Genitalia: Normal female minimal engorement, anus patent. Neuro: Lusty cry, good suck, reflexes: + rooting, + morrow, + grip, + Babinski reflex present bilaterally. Skeletal: Clavicle is intact. Spine: No dimples or defects noted. Hips: Normal range of motion, no click noted.

Assessment: Healthy, full-term infant. No defects noted.

Plan: Continue routine newborn care and monitoring. Hearing screen ordered. Check bili, ABO, CBC, and Coombs given Rh+ mother. Continue breast feeding, no supplemental feeding at this time.

Discharge Exam: 11/22/XX, 1000

Subjective: 2 d/o female infant. Breast feeding q. 2 h.r., 10 min ea breast; mother denies diff with latching on (+ breast fed previous infant), + lusty cry when hungry, easily consoled. + Wet diapers q. 2–3 hours, + meconium diapers × 3 since birth.

Objective: wt 7 lbs 1.5 oz, afebrile throughout admission

See Newborn D/C Pe Form

Laboratory: Coombs neg, blood type B neg, bili 12, HTC 37, hearing screen pass, initial PKU pending

Assessment: Normal, healthy term infant, s/p SVD

Plan: D/C to home. Continue breast feeding. Follow up in clinic for wt check and repeat bili in three days. Hep B and 2nd PKU in 2 weeks. RT ER for temp >100.5°F, no wet diapers > 12 hours, lethargy, or resp distress. Education given to parents regarding use of car seat, + verbalized understanding.

Which of the following CPT code sets accurately represents the physician's services for this newborn hospital stay?

	11/20	11/21	11/22
a.	99460	99462	99238
b.	99460, 99464	99462	99238
c.	99460, 99360	99233	99238
d.	99464	99232	99238

9.60 The following documentation is from the health record of a two-year-old boy.

Patient Name: Johnny Jones

CC: Routine checkup

HPI: Johnny is 2 1/2-years old and has Down syndrome and a ventricular septal defect, surgically corrected. Mother reports he is pulling at his ears and has been running a temp of 99 to 100°F in the past two evenings. Tylenol liquid has been effective in fever resolution according to mother. Development is coming along as expected. Walks with an ataxic gait but does not run. One-word speech pattern. No two-word sentences yet. Appetite is good. Child appears happy, well groomed, and well nourished. Mother reports no specific behavior or social-adjustment concerns.

Past History: Normal SVB, 8 lb 5 oz, 24" long. Heart surgery at 7 months. No known allergies. No medication at this time. Takes daily multivitamins.

Social: Lives at home with mother, father, and older brother. Receives physical, speech, and occupational therapy services from area education services in the home on a periodic basis.

Review of Systems: See patient data sheet and pediatric growth profile chart, not remarkable other than notation concerning recurrent ear infections. No cyanotic episodes, difficulty breathing, or other cardiac symptoms reported. Johnny had a follow-up visit to the cardiologist last month and his findings were reviewed; no significant problems. No voiding or digestive complaints by mother. Child still in diapers. All other systems negative (see detailed history).

Physical Exam: Weight 27 lb, Height 36" HEENT: Both ears positive for redness and otitis media with effusion evident on the left, eyes PERRLA, nose slightly congested clear discharge, neck supple without adenopathy. Throat slightly red.

Temperature 99.6°F, Blood pressure 108/82, R 15, P 72. Heart regular rate and rhythm; lungs clear to auscultation and percussion, no rales or wheezing. Abdomen soft without tenderness.

Extremities negative. (Detailed)

Assessment: Acute serous otitis media and slight throat infection, likely viral. Inject Bicillin C-R, 600,000 units and follow-up appointment in 3 days. No immunizations needed at this time. Fifteen additional minutes spent in counseling the mother concerning developmental expectations and reviewing cardiologist findings and answering questions about future cardiac risks.

Which of the following code sets is assigned for reporting the pediatrician's services?

a. 381.01, 462, 758.0, V45.89, 99214, 96372, J0530
b. V20.2, 381.01, 462, 758.0, V45.89, 99392, 99214-25
c. 381.01, 462, 99214, 96372
d. 758.0, V45.89, 99213, J0530

9.61.   The following documentation is from the health record of a 10-year-old boy.

Preoperative Diagnosis: Status post palatoplasty, history of bilateral incomplete cleft palate with recurrent tonsillitis

Postoperative Diagnosis: Same

Operation: Second-stage palatoplasty with attachment of pharyngeal flap and incidental tonsillectomy

Indications: A 10-year-old patient scheduled for revision of palatoplasty with incidental tonsillectomy requested by pediatrician due to repeated infections

Description of Procedure: The patient was prepped and draped in normal sterile fashion. A midline incision was made through the soft palate, exposing the posterior pharyngeal wall. A flap was then taken by incising the mucosa, submucosa, and underlying muscle, and securely sutured to the soft palate.

Bilateral tonsillectomy was then performed by grasping with a tonsil clamp and capsule dissection. Bleeders were controlled with electrocautery and gauze packing. Sponge and instrument counts were taken and correct, and the patient was transferred to the recovery room in good condition. Follow-up in the office in 3 days.

Which of the following code sets will be reported?

a. 749.04, 42225, 42825
b. 749.04, 474.00, 42225
c. 749.04, 474.00, 42225, 42825–51
d. V50.8, 749.04, 474.00, 42200, 42826–51

9.62.   The following documentation is from the health record of a 10-month-old baby.

Hospital Outpatient Services

A 10-month-old boy is seen in the Gastroenterology Lab to insert a gastrostomy tube. The child pulled out his previous G-tube during the night. He is being followed for congenital cytomegalovirus infection and GERD with erosion of the esophagus. Conscious sedation is provided by the anesthesiologist. The gastroenterologist positions the patient and probes the site with a catheter, injects contrast medium into the tract for assessment and maneuvers a wire through the tract into the stomach under fluoroscopic guidance. The physician advances the gastrostomy tube over the wire and into position and then secures the device internally and externally. The system is put to gravity drainage and a sterile dressing is applied.

Which of the following code sets is reported by the pediatric gastroenterologist?

a. 536.49, 079.99, 530.81, 49440
b. 536.41, 771.1, 530.81, 530.89, 43760, 76000-26
c. V55.1, 530.81, 530.89, 771.1, 49450
d. V55.1, 530.81, 079.99, 49450, 76000-26

Pediatric Conditions

9.63. A 3-year-old child was brought to the emergency department after inhaling a peanut. The child had a brassy cough that was not present prior to the incident. X-rays showed congestion in the lungs but no obvious foreign body in the larynx. The child was given Versed intravenously and placed on a papoose board. The emergency department physician could see the peanut on indirect laryngoscopy but could not grasp it with multiple attempts. An ENT specialist took the patient to surgery for removal under anesthesia. An expanded, problem-focused history, problem-focused physical exam, and medical decision making of low complexity were documented.

Give the correct CPT codes for reporting the independent ED physician's service:

a. 99281–25, 31505
b. 99281–25, 31511
c. 99282, 31505
d. 99281, 31511

9.64. The patient is a 5-week-old male infant brought in by ambulance after the mother called 9-1-1. The baby was taking a bottle feeding normally and suddenly was blue in the face, appeared to stop breathing and went limp. Breathing returned spontaneously as the mother moved the baby into various different positions but was still reportedly labored. A comprehensive history was obtained. A comprehensive physical exam in the ED revealed only mild tachycardia and increased work of breathing. The patient was transferred to the local pediatric hospital for continued evaluation, with a diagnosis of apparent life threatening event, cyanosis, apnea, rule out respiratory syncytial virus infection, rule out asphyxia by aspiration.

Which of the following diagnoses will be reported?

a. 770.83, 079.6, 933.1, E911, 99284
b. 782.5, 799.82, 99285
c. 799.82, 99285
d. 782.5, 799.82, 99291

9.65. The following documentation is from the health record of a boy with a fracture.

Office Visits

3/31 Office Visit (Primary Care Physician)

S: Peter was playing basketball today, fell, and hurt his wrist.

O: Tenderness and swelling of the wrist, especially the volar aspect. There is a slight abrasion over the swelling. X-ray shows a fracture of the ulnar styloid and possibly the distal radius. There is some question of dorsal displacement of the epiphysis. Short arm cast is applied for comfort measures.

A: Fracture of the ulnar styloid

P: I am going to have the orthopedist look at the x-ray and obtain a consult to determine if reduction is necessary. Return to clinic in 2 days for ortho appt, sooner if problems.

4/1 Office Visit (Primary Care Physician)

S: Peter has pain inside his cast.

O: We thought this was pressure, so I split the cast and it really didn't relieve the pain much at all. I asked him what was hurting about it, and he said it was hurting further up his arm. Then he told me that at the time he had the injury he noticed a great big bulge there. He thought it was the bone poking through, pushed on it, and it sort of went down by itself. His x-ray clearly shows there is no bony injury at that area, but that he has the fracture down by the epiphyseal plate. This is probably a torn muscle.

A: Torn muscle left arm with fracture.

P: Keep the appointment with ortho tomorrow. In the meantime, symptomatic care, and we left the cast split because it is probably going to have to be removed for adequate exam tomorrow anyway.

4/2 Office Visit (Primary Care Physician)

S: Peter injured the left wrist playing basketball. He is right-hand dominant. He is currently in a short arm cast, which had been split previously because it was a bit too snug. With the cast he has wrist in extension at least 15 degrees despite the fact that he has the epiphyseal plate fracture with slight posterior displacement of the distal fragment of about 4 mm. He has seen the orthopod in consultation, who felt that this did not require further reduction.

O: He has intact CMS today. Cast is removed, and he is placed in a short arm cast with anterior flexion of about 10 degrees with very slight ulnar deviation. The position of the distal epiphysis of the radius appears to be about the same as it was on the original x-rays taken 1 week ago. This position alignment should be quite satisfactory.

A: Distal radial fracture, Colles' type, with ulnar styloid fracture

P: We will continue with the short arm cast for a duration of 6 weeks. He is to return to see me in 2 weeks for repeat x-ray through the cast and follow up sooner if any problems.

Which of the following is the correct code set to report these visits with the primary care physician?

a. 3/31: 813.43, 25600, A4580
   4/1: 813.43, 840.9, 99024
   4/2: 813.44, 99024, A4580
b. 3/31: 813.43, 29075, A4580
   4/1: 840.9, 813.43, 99213
   4/2: 813.44, 25600, A4580
c. 3/31: 813.43, 25605, A4580
   4/1: 840.9, 813.43, 99213
   4/2: 813.44, 29075, A4580
d. 3/31: 813.43, 29075, A4580
   4/1: 840.9, 813.43, 99213
   4/2: 813.44, 25605, A4580

9.66. The following documentation is from the health record of a 14-year-old male patient.

Admission Date:	2/2/XX
Discharge Date:	2/3/XX
Admission Diagnosis:	Peritonsillar abscess
Discharge Diagnoses:	1. Peritonsillar abscess
	2. Chronic tonsillitis
	3. Mononucleosis
	4. Type I diabetes

Reason for Hospitalization: This patient is a 14-year-old white male with a history of right peritonsillar abscess in December who presented with a 4- to 5-day history of progressively increasing sore throat. He had previously been started on amoxicillin as an outpatient, but the severity of his symptoms increased. He presented to the ER on 2/2 with findings consistent with a peritonsillar abscess.

Hospital Course: He was admitted and started on IV Unasyn. Blood glucose levels were drawn and showed only slight hypoglycemia, no doubt as a result of decreased intake due to throat pain. Insulin dosage was adjusted accordingly. An ENT consult was performed, and I&D was recommended. An endocrinology consult was obtained, and he was cleared for surgery. The patient was taken to the operating room that same day. An I&D of the right peritonsillar abscess was performed with a unilateral right tonsillectomy, given his history of recurrent peritonsillar abscesses. The patient was continued on IV antibiotics overnight. The following day, the patient reported significant improvement in his throat pain. He was noted to be afebrile. His Monospot was positive and consistent with acute infectious mononucleosis. Blood glucose levels were adequate. Later, on 2/3, he was seen by the surgeon, who thought he was doing well from a surgical standpoint. The patient was tolerating p.o. well, and the decision was made to discharge the patient home later that same day.

The patient is in satisfactory condition at the time of discharge. Discharge medications include Roxicet® p.r.n. for throat pain, Augmentin, and insulin.

He was instructed to comply with a soft diet until further follow-up. Extra time was spent reviewing his insulin regimen and making adjustments (35 minutes with patient and family). Additionally, he was educated about activity restrictions, including no vigorous exercise or contact sports for the next 3 to 4 weeks because of his mononucleosis. The patient was instructed to follow up with the surgeon in 2 weeks.

Which of the following code sets is correct for reporting the attending physician's services on the day of discharge?

a. 475, 474.00, 075, 250.01, 99239
b. 475, 474.00, 075, 250.81, 99238
c. 475, 075, 250.01, 99238
d. 475, 474.0, 075, 250.81, 99239

Conditions of Pregnancy, Childbirth, and the Puerperium

9.67. The following documentation is from the health record of a female patient.

Discharge Summary

Admission Date:	03/12/XX
Discharge Date:	03/23/XX

Discharge Diagnoses:
1. Term intrauterine pregnancy, delivered, single liveborn
2. Maternal obesity
3. Iron deficiency anemia
4. Herpes simplex virus type II with spontaneous rupture of membranes
5. Retained placenta
6. Endometritis

Procedures Performed: Right paramedian episiotomy, low outlet forceps vaginal delivery, repair of right paramedian episiotomy with repair of partial fourth-degree extension, manual removal of placenta 3/13/XX. Dilatation and suction curettage 3/22/XX.

Hospital Course: This patient presented at 39 weeks' gestation with rupture of membranes of clear fluid. She was not in active labor, her cervix was unfavorable for induction. She was initially managed expectantly, and oxytocin was used to facilitate labor. She progressed throughout the active phase of labor without complications. The fetal evaluations were reassuring throughout the labor process.

The fetal head presented on the perineum in the OA position; and because of maternal exhaustion and inability to allow further descent because there was a single nuchal cord released, low outlet forceps were placed after right paramedian episiotomy was performed, and the fetal head was delivered without difficulty. Upon delivery, there was a partial fourth-degree extension just through the anal mucosa. There was retained placenta and manual extraction was required. The episiotomy was repaired by using 000 VICRYL® suture, closing the rectal mucosa.

The postpartum course was complicated by the patient developing endometritis. The patient was placed on IV antibiotics and showed some sign of improvement with a dropping white blood cell count; however, her temperature continued to spike. An initial ultrasound revealed some intrauterine products that appeared to be retained placenta. The following day, however, she passed these retained products without difficulty, and her bleeding subsided. Her temperature, however, continued to develop intermittent fever, the antibiotics were switched to the IV, and she again showed a good clinical response with decreased uterine tenderness. Because of the fever continuing, however, a follow-up ultrasound was performed, and no placental products were appreciated. However, there were some clots and unidentifiable tissues still remaining in the intrauterine cavity. Thus, a dilatation and curettage was performed on 3/22/XX, and some amniotic membranes were removed, which appeared to be infected. There were no placental products noted in the curettage.

After removal of the amniotic membrane, her temperature defervesced, and she remained afebrile throughout the remainder of the hospitalization. On discharge, she was tolerating a regular diet, ambulatory without complaints, very scant vaginal spotting, and on oral antibiotics.

It should be noted that because of the excessive blood loss she was given two units of transfused blood to maintain hemoglobin levels from 8 to 9. She was asymptomatic with this hemoglobin, and thus was placed on iron and Colace therapy throughout the remainder of her hospitalization.

Discharge Medications: Include iron sulfate, Colace, and Augmentin

Which of the following is the correct code set presuming this physician provided the antepartum and postpartum care?

a. 667.02, 646.62, 670.02, 664.31, 663.31, V27.0; 59400, 59160–78
b. 667.04, 646.62, 670.02, 664.31, 663.31, V27.0; 59400, 59300–51, 58120–78
c. 667.02, 664.31, 663.31, V27.0; 59400, 59300, 59160
d. 667.04, 646.62, 670.02, 664.31, V27.0; 59400, 58120

9.68. The following documentation is from the health record of a female patient.

Anesthesia:　IV sedation by CRNA, combined with paracervical block

Preop DX:　Anembryonic gestation

Operation:　Suction curettage

Postop DX:　Anembryonic gestation

History: Problem list includes G4, P2, L2, and missed abortion. Patient has asthma with medications including albuterol p.r.n.

Findings: The laminaria that had been placed in the office yesterday had dilated the cervix, which easily fit a #20 Hanks dilator. The uterus sounded 12 cm. The uterus was 10-week size. There was a moderate amount of tissue obtained from the uterine cavity.

Procedure: Under satisfactory intravenous medication, the patient was prepped and draped in the dorsolithotomy position. A speculum was placed. Paracervical block was administered. The laminaria was removed. Using a #9 rigid curved Vacurette, curettage was performed. There was good clamping down effect of the uterus. The intrauterine contents were expelled. There were no complications of the procedure. There was a satisfactory amount of bleeding following the procedure. Estimated blood loss was negligible.

Path report demonstrates histological sections of the uterine contents, which show multiple chorionic villi. This is accompanied by fragments of decidualized tissue and gestational-type endometrium. These histological findings represent products of conception.

Which of the following code sets would be reported for this procedure?

a. 632, 493.90, 59820, 59200–51
b. 630, 493.90, 59870
c. 631, 59856, 59200
d. 631, 493.90, 59820

Disorders of the Respiratory System

9.69.   Patient seen in the office with increasing shortness of breath, weakness, and ineffective cough. This patient is seen frequently for this chronic condition. Orders were given for chest x-ray and lab work. Antibiotics were also prescribed. This patient already is on oxygen at home. I will try to manage this patient at home, per his wishes. A detailed history was done with an expanded problem-focused exam and medical decision making of moderate complexity. Diagnoses listed as acute respiratory insufficiency and acute exacerbation of COPD. Which of the following is the correct ICD-9-CM diagnostic code assignment?

a. 491.21, 518.82, 99214
b. 518.81, 491.21, 99213
c. 518.82, 491.21, 99203
d. 491.21, 99214

9.70.   A patient has recurrent polyposis with right pansinusitis and left anterior polyposis with blocked maxillary ostiomeatal units on both sides. The surgeon performs a bilateral intranasal sphenoethmoidectomy and maxillary antrostomy with polypectomy.

The patient was placed under general anesthesia and appropriately prepped and draped. The nose was anesthetized with cocaine flakes, 200 to 300 mg, and topical adrenaline 1:1000. A large polyposis on the right side was removed to gain access for more vasoconstriction using a Robert's snare. Injections of Xylocaine and epinephrine were also used, and the procedure was essentially the same on both sides.

On the left side, there was extensive scarring of the middle turbinate, so through-cutting punches were used to open up the ethmoidectomy bilaterally. While manipulating the left middle turbinate, there was a small CSF leak noted at the junction of the turbinate with the equivaform area. No instrumentation had been done in this area, and it was only a slitlike small leak. This was packed with topical Gelfoam and topical thrombin with Gelfoam at the end of the case and held unto the pack. The nasal antral windows were opened bilaterally and were cannulated, using the right-angle ethmoid curet until palpation showed the natural ostium of the maxillary sinus. The uncinate process was still there from the previous surgery, and this was removed with back-biting forceps and opened into the maxillary sinus widely.

Both sphenoides were widely opened. There was an adhesion from the head of the middle turbinate to the nasal septum on the left side, and this was lysed. A Cottle speculum and the through-cutting forceps were used throughout the case as well as the 1.7 power magnification operating microscope. The patient had a moderate bout of bleeding bilaterally that was controlled with towel clip pledgets of 1:10,000 of adrenaline. Silastic splints were placed on both sides of the nose to prevent adhesions and were sewn in with 4-0 Prolene sutures. Expandable foam packs were then placed and expanded with 1 g and 10 cc of Ancef. The procedure was then terminated with estimated blood loss at 300 cc for the entire case. The patient tolerated the procedure well and there were no CSF leaks found at the end of the procedure.

Which diagnosis and procedure codes are assigned for this procedure performed in the outpatient surgical department of the hospital?

a. 473.8, 471.8, 349.81, 31201–50, 31051–50, 31020–50, 69990
b. 473.8, 471.8, 998.2, E870.0, E849.7, 31201–50, 31051–50, 31020–50
c. 478.19, 473.8, 31267–50, 31288–50, 31254–50, 69990
d. 473.8, 471.8, 998.11, 998.2, E870.0, E849.7, 31090–50, 69990

9.71. A patient with bilateral partial vocal cord paralysis requires removal of the arytenoid cartilage to improve breathing. Following a temporary tracheostomy, a topical anesthetic is applied to the oral cavity, pharynx, and larynx, and the laryngoscope with operating microscope is inserted. After adequate visualization is established, the arytenoid cartilage is exposed by excision of the mucosa overlying it. The procedure is performed in the outpatient surgery center of the hospital. Which diagnosis and procedure code(s) is going to be reported for this procedure?

a. 478.33, 31561, 31600
b. 478.30, 31560
c. 478.33, 31561
d. 478.33, 31560, 69990

9.72. A 54-year-old male patient with bronchial carcinoma, right lower lobe, has an obstructed bronchus in the right lower lobe of the lung. The pulmonologist views the airway using a bronchoscope introduced through the oral airway following administration of conscious sedation. Thirty minutes of moderate sedation services were performed. The obstruction is identified with the assistance of fluoroscopic guidance. A laser probe is introduced through the bronchoscope to eradicate the obstruction and relieve the stenosis. The procedure was performed in the physician's clinic/surgery center. What codes are reported for physician services for the procedure performed at the outpatient ambulatory surgery center?

a. 162.5, 31641, 99144
b. 162.5, 31641, 76001
c. 239.1, 31640, 99144–51
d. 239.1, 31641, 99144, 76001

9.73. A 78-year-old-patient is scheduled for a transbronchial needle aspiration biopsy with fluoroscopic guidance for a lung mass. Following the administration of conscious sedation by the anesthetist, the patient experiences a run of atrial fibrillation, and the physician elects to terminate the procedure before the biopsy is obtained. The procedure is done in the hospital's same-day surgery department.

Which of the following shows correct code assignment for physician services?

a. 239.1, V64.1, 31629, 76000
b. 786.6, 427.31, 31629–52
c. 786.6, 427.31, V64.1, 31628–53
d. 786.6, 427.31, V64.1, 31629–53

9.74. This patient was admitted to have a thoracoscopic lobectomy performed. The patient has a malignant neoplasm of the left lower lobe. Because of extensive pleural effusion, I was unable to complete the endoscopic procedure. We converted to an open technique, and a successful lobectomy was performed. The patient tolerated the procedure well. What are the correct procedure codes?

a. 32480, 32663–53
b. 32663, 32480
c. 32480
d. 32484, 32663–52

9.75. The following documentation is from the health record of a 2-year-old boy seen in the pediatric clinic.

Chief Complaint: Difficulty breathing.

History of Present Illness: Patient is a 2-year-old black male with a 1-day history of difficulty breathing and a cough. No fever or chills. He otherwise has been acting normally.

Past Medical History: Unremarkable. No history of asthma.

Medications: Over-the-counter cough medicine.

Allergies: None.

Physical Examination:

General:	Alert, playful black male in no apparent distress.
Vitals:	Temperature 98.5 °F; pulse 125; respiration 28; blood pressure 95/64.
Head, Ears, Eyes, Nose and Throat:	Conjunctivae clear. Pupils are equal and reactive to light. Tympanic membranes normal. Oropharynx negative.
Neck:	Supple without adenopathy.
Heart:	Regular. No murmurs or gallops noted.
Lungs:	Breath sounds equal bilaterally with mild wheezing. Minimal retractions.
Abdomen:	Benign.

Diagnosis: Acute bronchitis with bronchospasm.

Disposition and Plan: The patient was given two breathing treatments and his wheezing cleared. He was no longer retracting. He was discharged home on albuterol syrup 3/4 teaspoon q 8 hours; Amoxil 250 mg per 5 mL one teaspoon three times a day. Follow-up in 2 to 3 days with primary care physician. Return if worse.

Which of the following is the correct ICD-9-CM code set for this physician?

a. 466.0
b. 466.0, 519.11
c. 519.11
d. 466.19

Trauma and Poisoning

9.76. An adult patient is seen in the emergency department after sustaining second- and third-degree burns of the chest and both upper and lower arm after pulling a pan of boiling soup out of the microwave onto his right side. The burn size was documented as 18 cm × 24 cm on the chest, and 26 cm × 8 cm on the right arm. The chest burn was full thickness and the arm burn was partial thickness. The total size was estimated to be about 13% of the total body surface area. Due to the associated pain, local anesthesia, including IM Demerol, was administered. The wound was débrided, and a sterile dressing was applied. The patient was transferred to a local burn unit for further treatment.

What are the correct CPT and ICD-9-CM code assignments for this procedure as reported and billed by the emergency department physician, who performed a detailed medical history, performed an expanded problem-focused physical examination to rule out other injuries, and rendered moderately complex medical decision making before undertaking the burn care?

a. 942.32, 943.29, 948.10, E924.0, E015.2, 99283–25, 16030
b. 942.32, 948.00, E924.0, 16025
c. 942.23, 942.33, E924.0, E015.2, 99284, 16025
d. 942.22, 943.20, 948.10, E924.0, 11000, 11001

9.77. A motorcyclist is brought into the Emergency Department after a motorcycle accident. The ED physician confirms an open tibia (proximal) fracture and performs extensive débridement of gravel, glass, and other matter, down to and including part of the muscle, at the site of the fracture in preparation for surgery. The orthopedic surgeon then takes the patient to surgery to perform the reduction of the fracture, and the patient is subsequently admitted to the hospital.

In addition to the evaluation and management service, what is the correct code assignment for the ED physician's services?

a. 823.10, E819.2, 27535, 11011–51
b. 823.12, E819.2, 11043
c. 823.10, E819.2, 11011
d. 823.90, E819.2, 27535, 11043–51

9.78. A 35-year-old patient was a passenger on a motorcycle involved in an accident and sustained three severely broken ribs and a fractured femur. Chest x-ray showed a 45 percent collapse of the left lung and air in the pleural space. The patient complained of increasing shortness of breath and was cyanotic. A chest tube was inserted into the third intercostal space by the ED physician. Subsequent chest x-ray showed marked improvement to only 5 percent collapse. The patient was thoroughly evaluated by the emergency department physician for possible internal injuries. The emergency department physician documented a comprehensive history, comprehensive physical examination, and complex medical decision making. Final diagnosis was tension pneumothorax; fractured femur, midshaft; and multiple rib fractures. The patient was taken to surgery by the on-call orthopedic surgeon to care for the fractured femur sustained in the accident.

Which of the following is the correct code set for reporting the ED physician's services?

a. 512.0, 821.01, 807.03, E819.3; 99284–25, 32020
b. 860.0, 821.01, 807.03, E819.3; 99285–25, 32020
c. 860.0, 821.00, 807.09, E819.3; 99285, 32002
d. 512.0, 821.00, 807.09, E819.3; 99284, 32002

9.79. In the same accident as described in question 9.78, the 23-year-old driver of the motorcycle, who was not wearing a helmet, was brought to the ED, unresponsive, with tachypnea and tachycardia. The diagnosis was a severe head injury with multiple skull fractures. Dr. Smith, following intubation with an 8 mm endotracheal tube, placed a percutaneous nontunneled centrally inserted central venous line. History was unobtainable from the patient. The patient was hand-bagged by Dr. Smith for approximately 20 minutes until the neurosurgeon arrived and assumed care of the patient.

Which of the following code sets would be reported by Dr. Smith?

a. 803.06, E819.2, 99291, 36556
b. 803.46, E819.3, 99291, 31500
c. 803.33, E819.2, 99285, 31500, 36556–51
d. 803.46, E819.2, 99285, 31500, 36556–51

9.80. A patient arrived in the ED in full cardiopulmonary arrest following a gunshot wound to the chest. He was intubated, and large-bore IVs of lactated Ringer's solution were started in each arm. A STAT type and cross-match was ordered, along with six units of PRBCs. Dr. Jones, a private trauma surgeon, was on call and was present in the ED when the patient arrived. The patient's chest was opened, and cardiac massage was begun. Despite all efforts at resuscitation, the patient expired of massive blood loss after approximately 85 minutes in the ED.

What CPT codes will be reported by Dr. Jones?

a. 99291, 99292, 32160, 31500
b. 99291, 99292, 32160
c. 99291, 99292, 31500–51
d. 99291, 32160, 31500

9.81. A surgeon performs an evacuation of an epidural hematoma. The physician incises the scalp and peels it away from the area to be drilled. After drilling a burr hole in the cranium and identifying the hematoma via CT scan, the hematoma is decompressed and bleeding is controlled. The hematoma is located outside the dura just under the periosteum. The scalp is repositioned and sutured into place. The patient tolerates the procedure well and is sent to recovery.

What is the correct code set for physician reporting of this procedure?

a. 852.40, 61154
b. 853.00, 61108
c. 852.40, 61156
d. 853.00, 61156

9.82. The following documentation is from the health record of a 19-month-old with a burn.

Preoperative Diagnosis: Full-thickness burn with deep necrosis and limb loss involving bilateral lower extremities and posterior buttocks area.

Postoperative Diagnosis: Full-thickness burn with deep necrosis and limb loss involving bilateral lower extremities and posterior buttocks area and a small portion of the left flank.

Procedure Performed: Cultured skin placement to bilateral lower extremities and right buttock with autografting to bilateral buttocks and left flank and a small portion of the left stump. Total area covered was 1,030 cm^2, of which 720 cm^2 was cultured skin.

Anesthesia: General

Estimated Blood Loss: 100 mL

IV Fluids: 250 mL of Normosol
140 mL of blood
350 mL of Pitkin

Urine Output: 42 mL

Indications For Procedure: The patient is 19-month-old male who has undergone multiple excision and grafting procedures in the past for a 72 percent total body surface area (TBSA) burn. He most recently underwent removal of allograft on his bilateral extremities and buttocks area in preparation for skin grafting today. He also has a small area on his left flank where he has not received grafting in the past for which he will also receive skin if sufficient skin is available. His grandmother is present and knows the initial attempt will be to see if the cultured skin is sufficient to cover everything without donor site. However, given the recent fact that 900 cm^2 was reduced to 700 cm^2 and 20 cm^2, this may not be sufficient and the donor site will then be taken from the scalp and lower abdomen. The grandmother is aware of risks and we are proceeding today.

Description of Procedure: After successful induction of general anesthesia, time out for patient identification and surgery planned, the patient was placed in the supine position. His dressings were removed to level of the red rubber catheter. A 0 Prolene was placed into the bilateral stumps in order to allow for easy access to the lower extremities with elevation. The dressings were removed down and revealed a nice healthy base. Hemostasis was obtained using Epinephrine-soaked laparotomy pads as well as electrocautery. Cultures were taken from the left lower extremity for the cultured skin study as well as biopsies from the past autograft of the lower abdomen and cultured skin. The cultured skin was placed in serial fashion along each of the lower extremities with coverage attained with all but a small portion of the left lower extremity stump. 3 pieces remained which will be placed on the abdomen, but since donor site will be necessary, the skin was then harvested from the upper scalp and lower abdomen after Pitkin infiltration using the Padgett dermatome at a thickness of 0.015 inches. Once complete, this was meshed 2:1 and the donor sites were covered with Kaltostat and dry gauze. The patient was then flipped into the prone position. Dressings were removed and patient was re-prepped and draped and then the final dressing lying over the base was removed revealing a nice healthy base. Hemostasis was obtained again with electrocautery and Epinephrine-soaked laparotomy pads. When complete, the meshed skin was placed over the defect and the remaining three pieces of cultured skin on the right upper buttock area. These were all secured with surgical staples and covered with a layer of fine mesh gauze, burn gauze, red rubber catheters, burn gauze and a spandex stent. A small piece skin was placed on to the left flank where Bacitracin and sterile nonadherent dressing was used as coverage due to the small size. The patient was then returned to the supine position with no shearing of the cultured skin. The distal area on the left stump was covered with meshed graft with a final dressing being attained using a layer of fine mesh gauze, burn gauze, red rubber catheter, burn gauze, and Ace wrap for the right lower extremity, then a Spandex stent for the left lower extremity in order to keep the upper thigh protected and avoid maceration.

Which codes does this surgeon assign?

a. 945.50, 942.44, 942.43, 11100–59, 15150, 15151, 15152 × 7, 15100, 15101 × 3
b. 945.50, 942.49, 11100–59, 15150, 15151, 15152 × 7, 15100, 15101 × 3
c. 945.50, 942.44, 942.43, 11100, 15150, 15151, 15152 × 7, 15100, 15101 × 3
d. 945.50, 942.44, 942.43, 11100-59, 15150, 15151, 15152, 15100, 15101 × 3

Part IV
Coding Challenge

Chapter 10

Coding Challenge: Nonacute Settings; ICD-10-CM and ICD-10-PCS Code Sets; CPT Modifiers, HCPCS Level II Modifiers

Note: Even though the specific cases are divided by setting, most of the information pertaining to the diagnosis is applicable to most settings. If you practice or apply codes in a particular type of setting, you may find additional information in other sections of this publication that may be pertinent to you.

Every effort has been made to follow current recognized coding guidelines and principles, as well as nationally recognized reporting guidelines. The material presented may differ from some health plan requirements for reporting. The ICD-10-CM/PCS code sets utilized are the 2009 draft codes published in 2009, and the HCPCS (CPT and HCPCS II) codes are in effect January 1, 2009 through December 31, 2009. The current standard transactions and code sets named in HIPAA have been utilized, which require ICD-9-CM Volume III procedure codes for inpatients.

Instructions: Assign all applicable ICD-9-CM codes appropriate for the setting for the case studies presented. Some of the cases provide multiple-choice answers, and the reader must select the appropriate code set. In other instances, the reader is expected to assign codes without any prompts.

The scenarios are based on selected excerpts from health records without reproducing the entire health record. However, in practice, the coding professional should have access to the entire health record. Health records are analyzed and codes are selected only with the physician's complete and appropriate documentation available. According to coding guidelines, codes are not assigned without physician documentation.

The objective of the cases and scenarios reproduced in this publication is to provide practice in assigning correct codes, not necessarily to emulate actual health record analysis. For example, the reader may be asked to assign codes based only on an operative report or discharge summary. Labeled excerpts are used as source documentation for coding skill practice.

Home Health

10.1. A patient is being followed for postoperative care after surgery for a bleeding gastric ulcer. What code would be assigned in M0230?

a. V code for aftercare of surgery
b. Bleeding gastric ulcer
c. Traumatic wound of abdomen
d. None of the above

10.2. This 85-year-old female lives alone. She recently was in the hospital with aspiration pneumonia. There are infiltrates still present on the chest x-ray, and home health care is focused on the treatment of the pneumonia. She also has type II diabetes mellitus. She had partial colectomy last year for acute diverticulitis. What diagnosis would be reported in M0240?

a. Aspiration pneumonia
b. Diverticulitis
c. Diabetes mellitus
d. Acute diverticulitis and diabetes mellitus

10.3. This patient had colon resection because of carcinoma of the transverse colon. He has skilled nursing services for management of the surgical wound, which has a surgical drain not scheduled to be removed for several days. He lives alone and has right hemiplegia after a stroke. What code is reported in M0230?

a. 438.20
b. 153.1
c. V58.42
d. V58.31

10.4. A 72-year-old female patient recently had rectal resection for rectal cancer. She is scheduled for radiation and chemotherapy treatments. Home health services will provide visits four times per week to teach colostomy care and assess compliance with medication. What coding is the best?

a. M0230: V58.42; M0240: 154.1, V55.3
b. M0230: V55.3; M0240: 154.1, V58.42
c. M0230: 154.1; M0240: V55.3, V58.42
d. M0230: V55.3; M0240: V10.06, V58.42

10.5. What code is assigned for a patient who had prostate cancer 2 years ago? He underwent a proctectomy and received chemotherapy. He has had no treatment in the past year. How is the cancer reported in M0240?

a. 185
b. V10.46
c. V16.42
d. The status of the cancer would not be reported.

10.6. This 80-year-old female patient recently had cholecystectomy for chronic cholecystitis and cholelithiasis. She developed postoperative infection and is being seen for monitoring of antibiotics, vital signs, and observation of the wound, with frequent surgical wound dressing changes. What code is assigned in M0230?

a. 998.59
b. V58.31
c. 879.2
d. 574.10

10.7. Patient is status post total hip replacement secondary to localized osteoarthritis and was experiencing problems with ambulation and gait following hip surgery. The patient was discharged with home health services twice weekly. Home care was ordered for wound care. The patient also received physical therapy for gait training and strengthening to increase the patient's ability to ambulate. How should this encounter be coded? **Note:** Include codes for M0230, M0240, and M0246 (if applicable). _____

10.8. The patient is a 75-year-old man with chronic stasis ulcer of the leg, but he also has two diabetic toe ulcers at this time. Patient has chronic lower extremity edema, CHF, HTN. He has daily caregivers through the Medicaid program. The nurse is seeing him four times per week to change leg dressings (using Polymem® and covering with stretch bandage), monitor/adjust medications, teach medication management, teach caregivers to provide a low-sodium diet, and keep leg elevated. The nurse hopes to teach a neighbor to change the dressing at least once per week. Physical therapy is ordered every other week for exercise, transfer training, and gait training. Patient ambulates minimally, only with close assistance and a walker. He needs assistance with all ADLs. What codes are assigned? **Note:** Include codes for M0230, M0240, and M0246 (if applicable). _____

10.9. A 69-year-old right-handed woman is discharged from the hospital 4 days after a left modified radical mastectomy for breast cancer. Her only medications are oral tamoxifen and pain medications. She is scheduled to begin chemotherapy in the next 2 weeks. Skilled nursing is prescribed for management of the surgical wound, including dressing changes. The surgical drain is not scheduled to be removed for several days. The patient lives alone and has residual dysfunction of her right arm due to monoplegia after a stroke. The nurse will also supervise the patient's performance of the exercises ordered to improve her shoulder range of motion on the affected side and to monitor for the development of lymphedema in her arm. What codes are assigned? **Note:** Include codes for M0230, M0240, and M0246 (if applicable). _____

10.10. Section I of the *Official Coding Guidelines for Coding and Reporting* must be followed for:

a. Hospital inpatients
b. Physician services
c. Home health agencies
d. All of the above

10.11. A 74-year-old patient was discharged from the hospital after surgical amputation of the right foot due to diabetic osteomyelitis. The patient has type II diabetes. She was admitted to home healthcare for wound care consisting of assessment for signs and symptoms of a wound infection, instructing the patient and her husband on wound care, and surgical wound dressing changes. She will also receive physical therapy to improve her gait. What codes are assigned? **Note:** Include codes for M0230, M0240, and M0246 (if applicable).

_____

10.12. An 89-year-old man fell in his home, sustaining a right hip fracture. An open reduction with internal fixation was performed 6 days ago. The patient was discharged home, where his daughter now cares for him. The patient does not bear weight on the right lower extremity but can perform supervised pivot transfers with contact guard assistance in and out of bed. The physician orders the agency to provide physical therapy for gait training and exercise three times per week for 5 weeks. What codes are assigned? **Note:** Include codes for M0230, M0240, and M0246 (if applicable). _____

10.13. What code(s) is/are assigned for a patient receiving home care after a kidney transplant?

    a. V58.44
    b. V58.44, V42.0
    c. 585.6
    d. V42.0

10.14. How many categories are there for neurology disorders in the HH-PPS?

    a. Three
    b. Four
    c. Five
    d. Six

ICD-10-CM and ICD-10-PCS

Introduction:

HIM professionals across the country will lead the transition from ICD-9-CM to ICD-10-CM and ICD-10-PCS. In preparation they need to take steps to become experts on how ICD-10-CM and ICD-10-PCS differ from ICD-9-CM. Coding professionals will need to become proficient in coding with the ICD-10 systems. The following exercises are designed to increase your familiarity with ICD-10-CM and ICD-10-PCS.

Selected sections of the code sets are included with the exercises where possible. Current drafts of the ICD-10-CM index and tabular volumes are available on the Web site for the National Center for Health Statistics (NCHS). You may download the volumes at www.cdc.gov/nchs/about/otheract/icd9/abticd10.htm

The current draft of the ICD-10-PCS coding system and reference manual is available on the Web site for the Centers for Medicare and Medicaid Services (CMS). You may access this information at www.cms.hhs.gov/ICD9ProviderDiagnosticCodes/08_ICD10.asp

ICD-10-CM

10.15. A myocardial infarction is considered acute for _____ weeks according to the ICD-10-CM Official Guidelines for Coding and Reporting.

    a. 2
    b. 4
    c. 6
    d. 8

10.16. Which of the following conditions is not represented by a code from the J44 category?

    a. Asthma with chronic obstructive pulmonary disease
    b. Chronic bronchitis with emphysema
    c. Chronic emphysematous bronchitis
    d. Emphysema

10.17. ICD-10-CM codes will be utilized by all healthcare settings to assign diagnosis codes.

    a. True
    b. False

10.18. What would be the appropriate ICD-10-CM code for acute gangrenous cholecystitis?

    a. K81.0
    b. K81.2
    c. K80.13
    d. K81.9

10.19. Assign the appropriate ICD-10-CM diagnosis code(s) for cataract due to hypoparathyroidism.

    a. E88.9, H28
    b. H28
    c. E20.9, H28
    d. H28, E20.9

10.20. Assign the appropriate ICD-10-CM diagnosis code(s) for aspiration pneumonia due to inhalation of food.

    a. J15.9
    b. J69.0
    c. J18.9
    d. J69.1

ICD-10-PCS

10.21. ICD-10-PCS is based on a 7-character alphanumeric code. The meaning of each individual character changes according to the needs of the clinical section.

   a. True
   b. False

10.22. Recall that the first character of an ICD-10-PCS code specifies the section within ICD-10-PCS. Using the list of ICD-10-PCS sections provided below, identify the first character that would be assigned to the following procedures.

Sections of ICD-10-PCS

0	Medical and surgical
1	Obstetrics
2	Placement
3	Administration
4	Measurement and monitoring
5	Extracorporeal assistance and performance
6	Extracorporeal therapies
7	Osteopathic
8	Other procedures
9	Chiropractic
B	Imaging
C	Nuclear medicine
D	Radiation oncology
F	Physical rehabilitation and diagnostic audiology
G	Mental health
H	Substance abuse treatment

   a. _____ Cranioplasty
   b. _____ Cholecystectomy
   c. _____ Gait training
   d. _____ Computerized Tomography, Spine
   e. _____ Application of lower extremity pressure dressing
   f. _____ Acupuncture

10.23. Using the list of ICD-10-PCS root operations provided below, identify the root operation used to describe each of the following procedures.

ICD-10-PCS Medical and Surgical Root Operations

0	Alteration		J	Inspection
1	Bypass		K	Map
2	Change		L	Occlusion
3	Control		M	Reattachment
4	Creation		N	Release
5	Destruction		P	Removal
6	Detachment		Q	Repair
7	Dilation		R	Replacement
8	Division		S	Reposition
9	Drainage		T	Resection
B	Excision		U	Supplement
C	Extirpation		V	Restriction
D	Extraction		W	Revision
F	Fragmentation		X	Transfer
G	Fusion		Y	Transplantation
H	Insertion			

a. _____ Kidney transplant

b. _____ Appendectomy

c. _____ Diagnostic bronchoscopy

d. _____ Lithotripsy, bladder stone

e. _____ Varicose vein stripping

f. _____ Fallopian tube ligation

10.24. Match the approach term with the correct definition:

ICD-10-PCS Character-Approach

0   Open

2   Open Endoscopic

3   Percutaneous

4   Percutaneous Endoscopic

7   Via Natural or Artificial Opening

8   Via Natural or Artificial Opening Endoscopic

X   External

Definition:

a. _____ Entry, by puncture or minor incision, of instrumentation through the skin or mucous membrane and any other body layers necessary to reach the site of the procedure.

b. _____ Entry of instrumentation through a natural or artificial external opening to reach the site of the procedure.

c. _____ Cutting through the skin or mucous membrane and any other body layers necessary to expose the body site of the procedure.

d. _____ Cutting through the skin or mucous membrane and any other body layers necessary to expose a body part, and introduction of instrumentation to reach and visualize the site of the procedure.

e. _____ Entry, by puncture or minor incision, of instrumentation through the skin or mucous membrane and any other body layers necessary to reach and visualize the site of the procedure.

f. _____ Entry of instrumentation through a natural or artificial external opening to reach and visualize the site of the procedure.

g. _____ Procedures performed directly on the skin or mucous membrane and procedures performed indirectly by the application of external force through the skin or mucous membrane.

10.25. Using the definitions listed in item 10.24 above, match the following:

Procedure	**Approach**
a. ____ Total abdominal hysterectomy	1. Via Natural or Artificial Opening
b. ____ Needle biopsy of the pancreas	2. Open
c. ____ Endotracheal intubation	3. Percutaneous Endoscopic
d. ____ Arthroscopy	4. Percutaneous

10.26. What is the correct ICD-10-PCS code for complete removal of the appendix performed laparoscopically? _____

ICD-10-CM/PCS Application Exercise

10.27. You are a coding professional at General Medical Center. One of your responsibilities includes responding to requests for coded data. Facility data in the registry has been coded in ICD-10-CM and ICD-10-PCS for 2 years. Prior to that, data was coded in ICD-9-CM. You receive requests for data that spans the most recent 5 years for the following cases. How will you find all applicable cases in the registry for these two requests?

a. Request for cases with an initial acute myocardial infarction of the anterior wall: _____

_____

b. Request for cases with exploration of the common bile duct during an open cholecystectomy: _____

_____

CPT Modifiers

10.28. Dr. Raddy, staff radiologist, interprets a chest x-ray that was obtained in the hospital radiology department. Dr. Raddy is contracted with the hospital to read radiographs. The equipment and staff are owned and/or employed by the hospital. What modifier, if any, should Dr. Raddy report with the chest x-ray code?

a. No modifier is necessary because Dr. Raddy interpreted the x-ray under contract with the hospital. The hospital will bill the global and pay Dr. Raddy from the reimbursement.

b. Modifier -26, Professional component

c. Modifier -TC, Technical component

d. Modifier -59

10.29. Tiny Patti Sue Smith, 15 days old, currently weighs 1,652 g. She is taken to the operating room for small bowel resection for necrotizing enterocolitis, a frequent complication of prematurity. The remaining portions of the small bowel were anastomosed end to end. CPT code 44120 reports a small bowel resection with anastomosis. Is a modifier necessary, and if so, which modifier?

    a. No modifier is needed for the surgery, although the anesthesiologist might need a modifier.

    b. Modifier -63 is reported because the baby weighs less than 4 kg and thus is a higher surgical risk than a larger neonate.

    c. No modifier is needed because code 44120 already applies to neonates who are very low weight.

    d. A modifier is optional and may or may not be assigned depending on the departmental coding guidelines.

10.30. A patient is seen in the emergency department because of hyperkalemia due to an inadvertent overdose of his potassium medication. Over the course of the next 6 hours he receives infusions and his potassium is measured three times. What is the appropriate modifier to report with the second and third potassium determinations?

    a. Modifier -59, to show that these were not duplicate charges, but indeed separate incidents.

    b. No modifier is necessary for repeat laboratory tests, only for repeat surgical procedures.

    c. Modifier -91

    d. Modifier -91 and -59 should be reported for the second and third determinations.

10.31. A patient who was high on PCP stabbed himself in the chest, causing a pneumothorax. He was seen in the emergency department, and Dr. Jones inserted a chest tube. Approximately 1 hour later, despite soft restraints, the patient managed to free himself and pull out his chest tube. Dr. Jones reinserted the chest tube via a fresh incision. What modifier should be reported on each procedure?

    a. Modifier -76, Repeat procedure by the same physician, should be reported for each chest tube insertion.

    b. Modifier -76 should be reported with the second procedure; no modifier on the first procedure.

    c. Modifier -59 should be reported with the second procedure; no modifier with the first procedure.

    d. Either modifier -59 or -76 may be reported on the first and second procedure.

10.32. A patient underwent gallbladder removal by Dr. Pitts on 4/1 and was discharged home on 4/2. On 4/16, he developed right lower quadrant abdominal pain and evaluation was strongly suggestive of acute appendicitis. Dr. Pitts performed an exploratory laparotomy and appendectomy for an acutely inflamed appendix. What modifier, if any, should be reported with the appendectomy code?

    a. No modifier is needed because the ICD-9-CM diagnosis code and the CPT procedure code clearly identify that this was a procedure not related to the cholecystectomy.

    b. Modifier -79, Unrelated procedure or service by the same physician during the postoperative period, should be reported with the appendectomy code.

    c. Modifier -78, Return to the operating room for a related procedure during the postoperative period, should be reported with the appendectomy code.

    d. Modifier -58, Staged or related procedure or service by the same physician during the postoperative period.

HCPCS Level II Modifiers

10.33. A patient is brought to the emergency department of Community Hospital following a motor vehicle accident. He appears to have an avulsion of the aortic root and is rushed to the operating room where repair is attempted. The patient expires on the operating room table just as the surgery is being completed and before he can be admitted to the hospital. The CPT code for repair of avulsion of the aortic root is designated as an "inpatient only" code under the outpatient prospective patient system (OPPS). Is there a modifier that the hospital can report to obtain reimbursement for this procedure when performed as an outpatient?

    a. No, if an "inpatient only" procedure is performed on an outpatient basis, the hospital cannot obtain reimbursement under any circumstances.

    b. Modifier -CA, Procedure payable only in the inpatient setting when performed emergently on an outpatient who expires prior to admission, may be appended to the CPT procedure code.

    c. Modifier -ST, Related to trauma or injury, may be appended and a 50 percent reimbursement will be available to the hospital.

    d. Modifier -SC, Medically necessary service or supply, may be appended and a 25 percent reimbursement will be available to the hospital.

10.34. A patient undergoes a bunionectomy on the big toe of the right foot. What modifier is appended to report the location of this procedure?

    a. No modifier. By definition, bunionectomy is performed on the big toe.

    b. Modifier -T5

    c. Modifier -RT

    d. Modifier -TA

10.35. A hospice patient, under hospice care for terminal COPD, falls out of bed and fractures his wrist. He is taken to the emergency department at the local hospital and has a cast applied to the nondisplaced fracture. What modifier is reported to show that these services are not related to the patient's hospice-qualifying condition?

  a. Modifier -GW
  b. Modifier -AT
  c. Modifier -GZ
  d. Modifier -SC

10.36. HCPCS Level II modifiers can be used with which of the following code sets?

  a. CPT codes
  b. HCPCS Level II codes
  c. ICD-9-CM Volume III codes
  d. Both a and b

10.37. Modifiers -G1 through -G5, which report the levels of Urea Reduction Ratio (URR) in the blood, are reported with codes for _____, and measure the efficacy of this modality.

  a. Laboratory tests
  b. Dialysis codes
  c. Coronary artery interventional procedures
  d. Oxygen therapy

10.38. Match the HCPCS Level II modifier in column 2 with its application in column 1.

1. The patient was pronounced dead after the ambulance was called. Ambulance company is entitled to reimbursement.	a. -KA
2. Left hand, fourth digit	b. -SG
3. The beneficiary has been informed of rent/purchase option and has decided to rent the item.	c. -GH
4. Service furnished in an ambulatory surgery center.	d. -QY
5. Left circumflex coronary artery	e. -E4
6. Monitored anesthesia care	f. -QL
7. Diagnostic mammogram converted from screening mammogram same day	g. -F3
8. Add-on option or accessory for wheelchair	h. -QS
9. Lower right eyelid	i. -BR
10. Medical supervision of one CRNA by an anesthesiologist	j. -LC

10.39   After a tragic accident where a 75-year-old patient's eye was injured, the patient received a court order for provision of an extended wear, hydrophilic contact lens. What HCPCS Level II modifier(s) should be appended to code V2523?

_____

Long-term Acute Care (LTAC) Coding

10.40.   Patient Julie Jones suffers a massive intracerebral hemorrhage due to right basilar artery bleed. She is admitted to City Acute Hospital where she remains for 8 days undergoing acute care and regulation of anticoagulation.

Following her acute hospital stay, she is transferred to City LTAC for continued management. Treatment at City LTAC will focus on continued management and intensive physical, occupational, and speech-language therapy for rehabilitation from the following sequelae of her intracranial bleed:

Left (dominant sided) hemiplegia involving her upper and lower extremities

Expressive aphasia

Severe dysphagia with impaired swallowing and risk for aspiration

Assign the admission diagnoses that CLTAC will report.

a. 433.00, 438.21, 438.11, 438.82
b. V57.89, 438.21, 438.11, 438.82
c. V58.9, 438.21, 438.11, 438.82
d. V57.2, V57.3, V57.89

10.41.   The patient developed buttock and heel decubiti, both stage II, following an extended stay in the acute hospital. He has had resolution of the underlying acute condition that occasioned his admission there and is transferred to the LTAC for treatment of the decubitus ulcers. While in LTAC, he undergoes nonexcisional debridement of the decubiti. He also has underlying diabetes without documented complications and COPD. Assign the appropriate ICD-9-CM diagnoses and procedural codes for this admission.

a. 707.05, 707.07, 707.22, 250.00, 496, 86.28
b. V57.89, 707.05, 707.07, 707.22, 250.00, 496, 86.28
c. 707.05, 707.07, 707.22, 86.28
d. 707.05, 707.07, 707.22, 86.22

10.42.   This patient is admitted for pulmonary rehabilitation in a setting of advanced COPD. She also has ASHD and type II diabetes mellitus with peripheral neuropathy. She has been ventilator-dependent at the local acute hospital but was weaned from the ventilator prior to transfer to LTAC. Which are the principal diagnosis and secondary diagnoses that the LTAC personnel will report for her stay?

a. 496, 414.00, 250.60, 337.1
b. V57.0, 496
c. V57.89, 496, 414.00, 250.60, 337.1
d. V57.89

10.43. This patient underwent an above-knee amputation of her left leg for severe vascular trauma with transaction of the posterior tibial artery just below the level of the knee and loss of viability of the distal leg, after a motor vehicle accident. She has had continued stump infections and healing has not occurred, now 4 weeks after amputation. She is transferred to the long-term acute care hospital for management of the stump infection, eventual rehabilitation, and possible prosthetic fitting. What is the principal diagnosis that the LTAC personnel should report for this admission?

    a. V57.89

    b. V52.1

    c. 904.53

    d. 997.62

Outpatient Rehabilitation Cases

10.44. Physician Order:

Diagnosis: Congenital CP, scoliosis, bilateral congenital dislocated hips

Treatment Goals: Increase in ADLs, strengthening

Therapy Provided:

PT: ROM exercises, strengthening, stretching

OT: ADLs, upper extremity strengthening/ROM

What are the correct diagnosis codes for this outpatient therapy visit? (Procedure codes are captured via the chargemaster.) _____

10.45. Physician Order:

PT to evaluate and treat neck pain

Therapy Provided:

PT: Evaluation and treatment in the weight room

What are the correct diagnosis codes for this outpatient therapy visit? (Procedure codes are captured via the chargemaster.) _____

Inpatient Rehabilitation Cases

10.46. History and Physical for Inpatient Case

Purpose of Consultation: Physical medicine and rehabilitation evaluation at the request of Dr. Brown, status post trochanteric femoral nailing of left IT fracture on May 19 with touch weight-bearing restrictions.

History of Present Illness: Joe is a 52-year-old male with a history of mental retardation. He resides at home with parents whom I believe are near their 70s. Joe apparently fell in the home setting and sustained a left intertrochanteric femur fracture and was admitted to Regional Hospital on May 16. He was evaluated by

Dr. Smith and then operated on 5/19 with trochanteric femoral nailing, Synthes® type, placed by Dr. Brown.

The patient has been followed by Dr. Smith secondary to difficulties with prior arrhythmia and A Fib flutter with him having been on Coumadin chronically until this admission. His INR today is 2.7, his platelets are 283,000, and his hemoglobin preoperative on 5/16 was 15.6 g/dL. His hemoglobin on 5/22 was 13.2 g/dl.

Chemistries of today, 5/25, are sodium 138, potassium 4.3, chloride 99, CO2 31, BUN 20, creatinine 0.8, glucose 105, magnesium low at 1.4.

He has been working with a physical therapist and has been very slow to progress until significantly improving and tolerating activities and instructions yesterday on 5/24. At that time, he was able with touch to non-weight bearing on the left lower limb with walker ambulate 15 to 20 feet to the doorway and back with contact-guard assistance. He is tall in stature at 6′2″. His admission weight was recorded at 119.3 kg, weight today is 138.5 kg, with a discrepancy likely in his admission weight recording. Pain scores have ranged from a 1 to 2 of 10 today. He has noted some cramping and tightness in his calf, although nontender. He has been working on stretching this out. His medications are as per MAR. He currently remains on telemetry.

Past Medical History: 1. As above, notable for mental retardation and living with parents. He lives in a trilevel home, which he describes as having no stairs to enter the main floor or second level. He lives in the lower level with stair access and frequently is at the upper or higher level. Please refer to the occupational therapy evaluation of tub and difficulties with transfers therein.
2. History of A Fib flutter as above
3. History of gastroesophageal reflux
4. History of chronic Coumadin

Allergies: No known drug allergies

Current Medications: Per MAR, as above

Family History: Noncontributory

Social History: As per above. His care is monitored by his parents. His father has stated that he needs to be more mobile and able to care for himself before returning home. He has been very concerned about his disposition at this time. There is a history of tobacco use approximately 10 years ago. He has a dental bridge prosthesis. He wears glasses for vision and has had a history of night terrors. He is disabled. He is single. His primary care physician is Dr. Allen Smith.

Review of Systems: As per admission H&P of Dr. Brown, as well as ER evaluation of Dr. Canter. See also Dr. Smith evaluation and ongoing care. He has recommended telemetry until discharged from Regional Hospital.

Physical Examination: Admission height: 6′2″

Admission weight: As above I believe is in error at 119.3 kg.

Most Recent Weights: These have been in the 130 to 140 kg range. Today is 138.5.

Vital Signs: BP 133/73, afebrile at 97.6, heart rate in the mid 70s.

General: He is alert and conversant. He is sitting up in a chair. He is reading a magazine. He has his lenses in place. He is able to demonstrate functional range of the shoulders and upper extremities and denies any aggravation or irritation with use of the walker for the touch or no weight-bearing on the left. He does have a saline lock. He has significant ecchymotic change about the left posterior elbow and forearm; this is nontender. He is able to demonstrate good strength, and this limits symmetric reflexes.

Lungs: Clear to auscultation

Cardiovascular: Regular rate and rhythm without A Fib at this time

Abdomen: Soft, normoactive bowel sounds

GU: He is voiding spontaneously.

Extremities: Lower limbs demonstrate +1 reflexes, left knee jerk does evoke some left hip discomfort. He is able to ankle plantar flex, somewhat pain-inhibited on the left. There is no distal swelling. He has TED hose in place, knee high. He is able to follow instructions.

Assessment
1. Status post fall with left intertrochanteric femur fracture on 5/16 in the home setting
2. Status post 5/19 ORIF with trochanteric femoral nailing
3. Touch weight-bearing limitations, left lower extremity
4. History of arrhythmia and A Fib flutter; on chronic Coumadin
5. Gastroesophageal reflux disorder
6. Mild mental retardation; living with parents
7. Pain issues
8. Slow progress but now improving and tolerating therapies per my discussion with his physical therapist

Plan/Comment: I had the pleasure of evaluating Joe today. He appears to be a good candidate for rehab intervention to maximize his functional status so that he can return home with his parents. We will anticipate his admission therein on 5/27 if he continues to progress as well.

Discharge Summary

Date of Discharge:	6/21/20XX
Date of Admission:	5/28/20XX

Discharging Diagnoses:
1. Status post fall with left intertrochanteric femur fracture 5/16/XX, in home setting
2. Status post open reduction and internal fixation with intertrochanteric femoral nailing 5/19/XX, by Dr. Brown, with touch weight-bearing restrictions left lower limb
3. History of arrhythmia and atrial fibrillation flutter, on Coumadin chronically
4. Gastroesophageal reflux disorder
5. Postoperative pain issues
6. Mild cognitive issues, chronic
7. Mobility and self-care deficits

History of Present Illness: The patient is a 52-year-old Caucasian male. He has a history of some mild mental retardation and resides with his parents who are in their 70s.

His primary physician is Dr. Smith, and he is being followed by Dr. Brown in current hospitalization since being admitted on 5/16/XX, at Regional Hospital.

The patient was evaluated by myself in consultation on 5/25/XX, for rehabilitation needs with him coming to the Rehabilitation Hospital on 5/28/XX. Please refer to my consultation of 5/25/XX for specifics.

Hospital Course: The patient was brought to Rehabilitation Hospital for comprehensive therapy programming. He and his parents were in agreement with this.

He is a large Caucasian male who is pleasant and cooperative. He has had problems with pain limitations and some swelling in the left leg. He has remained on Coumadin and was on this chronically before. He has been followed by cardiology and is scheduled to see Dr. Smith in follow-up on 6/22/XX, at 11:15 a.m. He remains on Coumadin, which is followed by his primary physician with him to have further pro time/INR on 6/23/XX, Thursday.

His physical mobility has continued to progress. He has been maintaining touch weight bearing much better with contact guard assistance for gait using front-wheeled walker for 50-feet distances × 2. He has been able to perform total hip arthroplasty exercise program and is independent in 10 repetitions of each.

He has been followed for lymphedema of the left lower limb and has been issued Juzo® garments, and his parents were instructed by the physical therapist on his day of discharge on how to don and doff these garments.

With self-care skills, his upper extremities remained with 4/5 strength and active range of motion. Sensation was intact. Somewhat slower on the right side than the left side for 9-Hole peg coordination: 38 seconds right, 24 seconds left. Sitting balance was good. Endurance was within functional limits. He has some mild problems with cognition in terms of problem solving and judgment. Visual perceptive skills were thought to be good using his lenses. FIM-level scores were improved by two levels for all tasks except for toileting, which improved from a 3 to a 4. He is independent in feeding and dressing. Dressing lower extremities FIM level 5, grooming 6, toileting 4, showering 5. Discharge equipment includes commode.

Medications at Discharge:

1. Fentanyl patch 25 mcg per hour with this having been decreased the day prior to discharge from 50 mcg to 25 mcg with him noting no substantial change in pain levels. He is provided with refill for five patches or 15 days with these to be changed every 72 hours with it to then be discontinued.
2. He has also been using oral medications for pain relief, using Percocet (oxycodone/acetaminophen) 5/325 with 10.100 provided for one to two p.o. every 4 to 6 hours p.r.n. No refills.
3. Coumadin 3 mg daily currently with 2-week supply issued on 6/21/XX.
4. Durable medical equipment includes:

   Front-wheeled walker with large fixed wheels

   Bedside commode

Rental wheelchair, 20 inches wide. This gentleman is 6'2"
or 6'3" in height and weighs 116 kg secondary to left hip
fracture and mobility defects with limited weight bearing.

5. Ferrous sulfate 650 mg p.o. b.i.d. with meals
6. He has been on Prevacid, but will resume his previous proton
pump inhibitor at home for which he has a prescription. His
home PPI is Aciphex®.
7. He is on Betapace® 160 mg p.o. b.i.d.
8. Lanoxin 0.25 mg p.o. every evening
9. Cardizem CD 120 mg p.o. daily
10. He may use over-the-counter stool softeners as needed.

Discharge Instructions:
1. He is to wear his Juzo stockings on the left leg, being placed
initially in the morning, removed at bedtime.
2. Fall precautions should be in place.
3. Patient and family chose Regional Hospital Home Health Care
for ongoing home health PT, OT, visiting nurse, and aid, with his
parents involved in all care decisions.

His prognosis is fair for continued compliance and ongoing follow-up care.

a. What are the correct diagnosis codes (admit, principal, and secondary) for
reporting on the UB-04? _____

b. What are the correct diagnosis (etiology and comorbidities) codes for the
Patient Assessment Instrument (IRF-PAI)? _____

10.47. Neurology Rehabilitation H&P for Inpatient Case

Date of Consultation: 4/10/XX

Introduction: Rehabilitation consultation is requested to evaluate this 30-year-old
man who was injured in a motorcycle accident on 4/3. At that time, he was thrown
from his bike and apparently sustained a transient loss of consciousness consistent
with concussion. He also apparently had quadriparesis at the scene. He was
transported to Regional Hospital where he was ultimately found to have, I believe, a
significant hyperflexion injury without major fracture dislocation. He did not require
emergency stabilization surgery.

He was clinically and radiographically diagnosed with a cervical spinal cord contusion.
This was most prominent at the C3–4 level. There was some initial respiratory
impairment, and he was transiently placed on a ventilator. He has since been extubated.

The patient's clinical course has been consistent with a central type of spinal cord
contusion such that he has had paralysis of his arms and paresis of the legs. The
sensory deficits follow similarly. Patient is now being considered for eventual
transfer to the Rehab Hospital.

Current Medications:
1. Insulin by sliding scale
2. Bacitracin
3. Dulcolax®, p.r.n.

4. Decadron, 4 mg q.6 h. and eventually will be tapered according to protocol

5. Lovenox, 90 mg subcutaneously q.12 h.

6. Prevacid, 30 mg p.o. b.i.d.

7. Claritin, 10 mg p.o. daily

8. Senokot®, 8.6 mg p.o. b.i.d.

9. Tylenol, p.r.n.

10. Benadryl®, 25 mg p.o. q. 6 h. p.r.n.

11. Ativan, 0.5 mg was used 1 time only

12. Percocet, 5/325, 1 to 2 hours p.o. q. 4 to 6 h. p.r.n.

13. Ambien®, p.r.n.

14. Zofran®, p.r.n.

Allergies: He has no known medication allergies but has a history of intolerance to morphine and to Motrin. These tend to cause significant itching. He is having some mild itching with his Percocet, but this is relieved with Benadryl.

Past Medical History: He has a torn anterior cruciate ligament.

Review of Systems: Prior to admission, the patient has had no fever, chills, sweats, or weight loss. No change in his vision. No ear, nose, or throat complaints. No chest pains or palpitations. No shortness of breath, coughing, or wheezing. No nausea, vomiting, diarrhea, or constipation. No bladder or kidney dysfunction. No bone or joint problems outside of the anterior cruciate tear. No skin lesions such as rash. No mental illness. No other neurologic problems. No diabetes, thyroid disease, blood or bleeding problems, swollen lymph nodes, or allergic or asthmatic problems.

Family History: Parents are in good health. No neurologic problems.

Social History: He is divorced. Lives in Watson. He is a corrections officer for County Jail. Parents live in Plainsville. He has two children; however they do not reside with him.

General Exam: Appearance: The appearance is that of a well-developed, athletic-appearing young man who is lying on his back. He has a rigid cervical collar in place. The rigid collar is not to be removed.

Vital Signs: His temperature reached a maximum of 100.3°F but is now down to 99°F. Blood pressure 121/68, pulse is at 72. Respirations 18.

General: He appears normocephalic. The left arm is swollen and wrapped with an ACE®-type wrap. No obvious head trauma.

Heart: Is beating at a regular rate and rhythm without murmur. Carotid pulsations cannot be examined at this time. Peripheral pulses cannot easily be examined at this time.

Neurological Exam: He is a bit sleepy. He has received some narcotics and Benadryl. He arouses easily to voice. He is oriented to place and person and thought the date was 4/17. His recent and remote memory is grossly intact, although he has some amnesia for the accident when he was rendered unconscious. His attention span and concentration is grossly normal. Receptive expressive language normal. Fund of knowledge appropriate. His pupils are equal, round, and reactive to light.

Funduscopic exam is benign. Visual fields are intact. Visual acuity is grossly normal. Eye movements are intact. Facial sensation, corneal responses, muscles of mastication are normal. Facial movement symmetrical and normal. Hearing intact. Tongue and palate move normally. The sternocleidomastoid is not examined at this time due to the rigid collar. Trapezius testing was not attempted because of his immobilized neck.

He has complete plegia of the upper extremities bilaterally. In the legs, he does have some leg extension, hip extension, and thigh adduction with abduction. He has some ability to extend the legs bilaterally. There is a limited ability to lift the heels off the bed. There is virtual absence of foot dorsiflexion bilaterally; however, there is a weak plantar flexion response bilaterally. Muscle tone slightly increased in the legs. Babinski responses were not attempted. The muscle stretch reflexes are absent in the upper extremities and hyperactive at the knees and ankles. Sensation grossly intact to light touch and temperature in the legs bilaterally. There is anesthesia of the arms bilaterally and reduced sensation of the lower abdomen. The chest sensation and upper shoulders have essentially normal light touch sensation.

Coordination cannot be attempted. Patient obviously not ambulatory at this time.

Lab Studies: Most recent lab studies of note: Glucose is 137, BUN is at 23, creatinine 1.1. Sodium is at 136. The other chemistry parameters are normal. White count is elevated at 12,100, hemoglobin normal at 15.

Imaging Studies: Are most pertinent for the MRI scans. The MRI is most noteworthy for the abnormal signal within the spinal cord, primarily at the C3–C4 disk space level. An additional small area of signal abnormality noted at the C5–C6 disk level. The abnormality within the spinal cord is consistent with spinal cord edema and contusion. There is an additional abnormality in the soft tissues with interspinous ligamentous edema at C3–4 and C5–C6. Patient coincidentally also has a relatively small spinal canal that appears congenital.

Assessment: Thirty-year-old man with spinal cord injury without significant fracture but is associated with severe cervical spinal cord contusion, primarily at the C3–C4 disk level. Clinically patient has a "central cord" syndrome with paralysis of his arms and paresis of the legs.

Plan: 1. Patient should be an excellent candidate for comprehensive rehabilitation.
2. We will follow along and facilitate transfer when needed.

Interim Discharge Summary for Inpatient Rehab Case

Discharge Diagnosis

1. Cervical instability with plans for cervical fusion and stabilization procedure by Dr. Johnson, neurosurgery
2. Status post motor vehicle accident with cervical trauma and cord myelopathy
3. Quadriparesis and central cord syndrome
4. Neurogenic bowel and neurogenic bladder
5. Dysesthetic pain and numbness
6. Mobility and self-care deficits

John is a 30-year-old, Caucasian male who was involved in motor vehicle trauma with subsequent spinal injury and quadriparesis. Please refer to admission H&P for details. He was admitted in transfer from Regional Hospital for comprehensive rehabilitation programming given his quadriparesis. He has been undergoing spinal recovery program with comprehensive therapies and intervention to include neuropsychology.

He has remained somewhat unrealistic and has deferred many of the spinal education efforts that have been offered to him. He is returning on 5/13/XX to Regional Hospital for cervical stabilization procedure, with Dr. Johnson planning a C3 through C6 anterior cervical diskectomy and fusion.

He has had significant motor recovery from his initial presentation, with his lower extremity strength now +3/5 at the hip extensors and knee extensors. Quadriceps +3/5 bilaterally. Knee flexors, hamstrings were 2/5. Ankle dorsiflexion +1/5. Plantar flexion 3/5. Spasticity and tone does interfere with gait patterning and does limit his ability to progress, with him needing assistance. Bed mobility is rolling with minimal assistance to his stronger right side. Sliding board transfers to bed and chair were with moderate assistance of 1. Supine to sit was with moderate to maximum assist of 1. Gait with ARJO Walker with heavy truncal support is 75 feet with moderate assistance of 1, knee brace on the right, and AFO on the right. Steps and stairs have not yet been attempted.

In terms of self-care skills, the patient remains essentially dependent although he is beginning to show almost antigravity strength being -2 to +2 in the upper limbs with some flicker of hand movement. Palmer grasp on the right 3 lb and left 1 lb. He continues to have a greater degree of sensation proximally than distally; although deep pressure is intact. Light touch is impaired. He is unable to complete a 9-Hole Peg Test and is unable to functionally use the hands bilaterally. Visual perceptive skills are intact.

Medications as per MARS

Plans are for return within 72 hours to the Rehabilitation Hospital if medically stable to resume acute rehabilitation program.

Plan: Disposition is home with support of family and possible spinal cord attendant program via state services. Equipment needs are still to be determined. The patient remains optimistic.

a. What are the correct diagnosis codes (admit, principal, and secondary) for reporting on the UB-04? _____
b. What are the correct diagnosis (etiology and comorbidities) codes for the Patient Assessment Instrument (IRF-PAI)? _____

10.48. Interim History and Physical for Inpatient Case

Subjective: This is an interim history and physical for a 73-year-old woman who sustained an acute right hemisphere ischemic stroke on 03/30/XX. The patient was actually in preadmission at Regional Hospital where she was planning to undergo an orthopedic procedure when she developed acute left hemiparesis. She was transported immediately to the emergency department. It was determined that she had an acute ischemic stroke and received TPA. Despite the TPA, however, the patient was left with severe residual deficits in the form of left hemineglect, left facial weakness, left arm plegia, left leg paresis, and inability to walk. In the course of her workup, she was found to have atrial fibrillation but no significant stenosis of the internal carotid arteries. She was determined to be a suitable candidate for chronic Coumadin therapy.

The patient was fairly stable neurologically, although she had chronic debilitation prior to her admission. This debilitation was related to multiple medical problems, but she was ambulatory, I believe, with a walker. Because of her severe deficits, the patient is now being transferred to the Rehabilitation Hospital for a complete rehabilitation program.

The patient has several comorbid medical problems, including atrial fibrillation, diabetes mellitus, morbid obesity, hyperlipidemia, and degenerative arthritis to include a particular problem with her hip, which was being considered for replacement.

At the time of transfer, she has a temperature of 97.8°F, pulse 108, respirations 20, and blood pressure 134/93. She is awake, alert, and oriented. Her speech is fluent. Her eyes tend to gaze to the right. There is left facial droop consistent with central-type facial weakness. There is left upper extremity plegia, left neglect, and left lower extremity paresis. She is unable to walk.

Assessment:
1. Right hemisphere ischemic infarction with severe residual deficits
2. There are several complicating comorbid problems, which are likely to aggravate her stroke deficit. In particular, these include degenerative arthritis, diabetes, heart disease, and chronic mobility problems.

Plan:
1. Transfer to Rehabilitation Hospital
2. Physical therapy, occupational therapy, speech therapy, and therapeutic recreation
3. Primary goals of therapy will be to improve her ability to ambulate and take care of herself with regard to independence of ADLs.
4. It is anticipated the patient will require 3 to 4 weeks of inpatient rehabilitation.
5. It is anticipated disposition would be to home with the care of family, if possible.

Rehab Hospital Discharge Summary for Inpatient Rehab

Date of Admission: 4/7/XX

Date of Discharge: 5/10/XX

Admission Diagnosis: Right hemisphere infarction with severe residual deficits.

Secondary or Comorbid Conditions:
1. Degenerative arthritis
2. Diabetes
3. Coronary artery disease
4. Chronic mobility problems

Discharge Diagnoses:
1. Right hemisphere infarction with severe residual deficits
2. Degenerative arthritis

3. Diabetes
4. Coronary artery disease
5. Chronic mobility problems

History of Present Illness: Patient is a 73-year-old female who sustained a right hemisphere infarction on 3/30/XX. Patient apparently was in the process of undergoing preadmittance for orthopedic procedure when she developed acute left hemiparesis. She was transferred to the emergency room. She received TPA. However, she was left with severe left deficits in the form of left hemineglect, left facial weakness, left arm plegia, and left leg paresis, and an inability to walk.

In the course of her workup, she was found to have atrial fibrillation. It was thought that she was a suitable candidate for chronic Coumadin. Patient was stabilized in the Regional Hospital setting, and it was thought that she would be an appropriate rehabilitation candidate. Her examination at the transfer to the Rehabilitation Hospital showed her general medical exam to be stable. Neurologically, she was awake, alert, and oriented on mental status, and her speech was fluent. The cranial nerves showed a right gaze preference with a left facial droop that was central in nature. There was left upper extremity plegia and left neglect and left lower extremity paresis, and the patient was unable to walk.

During the course of her rehab stay, the patient did undergo some laboratory workup. This consisted of a series of PT and INR values. Initial PT/INR from 4/8/XX, showed PT of 24.0 with an INR of 2.2. Prior to discharge on 5/01/XX, the PT was 26.7 with an INR of 2.5. The patient did undergo some limited metabolic profiles including one from 4/22/XX, showing elevated glucose of 143 with a sodium low at 123, chloride low at 88. Uric acid was 6.2. The osmolality was 0.273. On repeat metabolic profile from 4/23/XX, showed an elevated glucose of 126 with a sodium low at 123, and a low chloride at 88. On 4/26/XX, glucose was 131. Sodium was 127, chloride 92. On 5/5/XX, patient had sodium level checked and it was at 130. It had improved to 134. Patient had a series of Glucometer® checks done throughout the course of her rehabilitation stay. These levels appeared to have remained fairly consistently elevated with values at times near 190, but no values were noted below grossly 120.

During the course of her rehabilitation stay, she underwent some radiographic imaging including a swallowing study from 4/8/XX, which showed some delay in oral phase of swallowing, likely the result of sensory issues. She had a right hip x-ray from 4/10/XX, showing relatively severe arthritic involvement of the right hip. Right shoulder x-ray from 4/10/XX, showed a degenerative change with history of previous surgery. A CT of the right shoulder from 4/19/XX showed previous surgery with screws in the proximal right humerus. There were arthritic changes with subluxation of the humeral head superiorly, suggesting a chronic degenerative rotator cuff tear.

During the course of her rehabilitation stay, the patient was seen by the various therapy services. This included speech therapy who felt that she had trouble swallowing, the patient was to undergo dysphagia management techniques and diet texture modification and full supervision with p.o. She had speech trouble and was to undergo oromotor exercises. She had communication and language deficits and was to undergo standard speech therapy protocol assessment. She had memory trouble and was to undergo assessment, and she was to be 79 percent accurate with auditory and visual memory exercises. The occupational therapy team thought she had decreased independence with ADLs, and she was to be seen three to five times per week to be educated in ADL techniques and in AE. She had decreased use of the left lower extremity and was to be seen for education and weight-bearing techniques and self-range of motion. She had decreased independence with functional transfers and was to be educated in safety with functional transfers. She had decreased independence with leisure participation and was to be seen for education in leisure exploration. The therapeutic recreation team thought she had decreased leisure participation due to hospitalization and was to be provided an opportunity for successful leisure involvement in an activity of choice. The physical therapy team thought that the patient was dependent on transfers and was to undergo transfer training. She had decreased lower extremity strength and was to undergo strengthening exercise. She had dependence with standing and gait and was to undergo standing and gait training.

Rehab Hospital Course: Patient was admitted for an aggressive inpatient rehabilitation stay. The patient was able to participate with rehabilitation efforts and did make slow but steady progress throughout the course of her rehabilitation stay. She was followed by internal medicine during her stay, and various medical issues were addressed in that regard. Patient had no major setbacks during the course of her stay. She was seen by Dr. Benson for a chronic rotator cuff tear and physical therapy was recommended. The patient's hyponatremia gradually improved throughout the course of her rehabilitation stay.

By 5/10/XX, it was thought that the patient had optimized her rehabilitation hospital benefits. As of that date, the various therapy services noted as follows: Occupational therapy thought that the patient had met some but not all of her goals due to inconsistency and poor attention to task. Physical therapy felt that the patient had met almost all of her goals except the first goal of bed mobility and also her standing goal because she still needed moderate assistance. Therapeutic recreation felt that she had met her established goals with recommendations to continue with social and leisure interest and community involvement. Speech therapy staff thought her condition had improved.

On 5/10/XX, the patient was discharged home with outpatient physical therapy, occupational therapy, speech therapy, and nursing. She was on a diabetic, pureed food, full-supervision diet and was to be encouraged to eat a consistent diet. Her activity was as tolerated, and she was not allowed to drive. She was transfer with 2 on a sliding board, and she was to continue with her knee-high T.E.D. hose. She was to get a PT/INR on 5/11/XX. She was to check her blood sugar before breakfast and evening meals. She was to have a drop-arm shower and transport in a commode. She was to get a hospital bed with rails and a slide board.

Discharge Medications:

1. Baby aspirin daily
2. Lemon juice b.i.d. to t.i.d.
3. Over-the-counter stool softeners
4. Novolin® insulin subcu b.i.d. on a sliding-scale basis
5. Sinemet® 25/100 at bedtime for restless legs
6. Coreg 6.25 mg b.i.d.
7. Klonopin 0.5 mg at bedtime
8. Lanoxin 0.125 mg daily

9. Surfak® 240 mg b.i.d.

10. Zetia® 5 mg b.i.d.

11. Neurontin® 600 mg b.i.d. and then 900 mg at 10 p.m.

12. Prevacid 30 mg b.i.d.

13. Levothyroxine 100 mcg at bedtime

14. Cozaar® 100 mg at 8 a.m.

15. Magnesium oxide 400 mg at 8 a.m.

16. Glucophage 1000 mg b.i.d., 500 mg at noon

17. Singulair® 10 mg at 10 p.m.

18. Actos 45 mg at 8 a.m.

19. Zoloft 50 mg b.i.d.

20. Zocor® 80 mg at 6 p.m.

21. Coumadin 1 mg at 4 p.m.

a. What are the correct diagnosis codes (admit, principal, and secondary) for reporting on the UB-04? _____

b. What are the correct diagnosis (etiology and comorbidities) codes for the Patient Assessment Instrument (IRF-PAI)? _____

Skilled Nursing Facility (SNF) Cases

10.49. The patient was admitted to the acute hospital with a pathological fracture of the left femur due to underlying metastatic cancer from the breast (resected years ago). She underwent percutaneous fixation in the hospital. She had been largely nonambulatory prior to the injury, and remains so. She is admitted to the skilled nursing facility for continued healing of the fracture and for general conditioning. Assign the appropriate diagnosis codes for the skilled facility to report.

a. V54.25, 198.5, V10.3
b. 733.14, 198.5, V10.3
c. V57.89, 733.14, 198.5, V10.3
d. V54.15, 821.00

10.50. This patient had been residing at home until an episode of pneumonia resulted in his hospitalization. While there, it was determined that he really was not able to remain in his home on his own due to rapidly advancing Alzheimer's dementia and episodes where he tried to wander away from the hospital. He was transferred to the skilled nursing facility because of this condition, although no specific therapy was ordered. The pneumonia had completely resolved in the acute hospital, and no further treatment was needed in the skilled nursing facility. The patient does have underlying chronic obstructive pulmonary disease, hypertension, and ASHD that require daily medication. Assign the appropriate diagnosis for this long-term admission.

a. 486, 496, 401.9, 414.00
b. 331.0, 294.11
c. 331.0, 294.11, 496, 401.9, 414.00
d. V57.89, 331.0, 294.11, 496, 401.9, 414.00

10.51. This patient underwent a subtotal colectomy in the acute hospital for resection of a carcinoma of the transverse colon. She was left significantly weak and debilitated following her surgery and was admitted to the skilled nursing facility for conditioning. The surgery appears to have been successful in eradicating the malignancy, and she was receiving no chemotherapy or radiation therapy at the time of her transfer. Assign the appropriate codes for the skilled nursing facility to report for this admission.

a. V58.75, 780.79, V10.05
b. V58.75, 997.99, 780.79, V10.05
c. V10.05, 780.79
d. V58.75, 780.79, 153.1

References

American Hospital Association. 1985–2009. *Coding Clinic for ICD-9-CM*. Chicago: American Hospital Association.

American Medical Association. 2009. *Current Procedural Terminology (CPT)*. Chicago: American Medical Association.

American Medical Association. 1992–2009. *CPT Assistant*. Chicago: American Medical Association.

Hazelwood, Anita, and Carol Venable. 2010. *ICD-9-CM Diagnostic Coding and Reimbursement for Physician Services*. Chicago: American Health Information Management Association.

ICD-9-CM Professional for Hospitals: Volumes 1, 2, and 3. 2010. Salt Lake City, UT: Ingenix.

ICD-10-CM: The Complete Official Draft Code Set. 2009. Salt Lake City, UT: Ingenix.

ICD-10-PCS: The Complete Official Draft Code Set. 2009. Salt Lake City, UT: Ingenix.

Kuehn, Lynn. 2009. *CPT/HCPCS Coding and Reimbursement for Physician Services*. Chicago: American Health Information Management Association.

National Center for Health Statistics. 2008 (Oct. 1). *ICD-9-CM Official Guidelines for Coding and Reporting and Present on Admission Reporting Guidelines*. Hyatsville, MD: US Department of Health and Human Services.

Schraffenberger, Lou Ann. 2010. *Basic ICD-9-CM Coding*. Chicago: American Health Information Management Association.

Smith, Gail. 2009. *Basic Current Procedural Terminology (CPT) and HCPCS Coding*. Chicago: American Health Information Management Association.

Appendix A

Certification Competencies

To ensure that its members meet professional standards of excellence, AHIMA issues credentials in health information management, coding, and healthcare privacy and security. Members earn credentials through a combination of education and experience and, finally, performance on national certification exams. Following their initial certification, AHIMA members must maintain their credentials and, thereby, the highest level of competency for their employers and consumers through rigorous continuing education requirements.

This appendix contains tables that link each exercise to AHIMA certifications and competencies to which it pertains. Linkages for the following three certifications (Certified Coding Associate, Certified Coding Specialist, and Certified Coding Specialist—Physician-based) are detailed herein, and are detailed by certification and also by question number. Additional information, including certification candidate handbooks, is available online from www.ahima.org/certification/.

Certified Coding Associate (CCA)

The Certified Coding Associate (CCA) is the entry-level certification for coders without any related job experience. CCA holders distinguish themselves from noncredentialed coders and those who hold credentials from other organizations that do not require the higher level of expertise necessary to earn AHIMA certification. The CCA should be viewed as the starting point for a career as a coder. The CCS and/or CCS-P exams demonstrate the mastery level skills that the CCA would strive for to advance his or her career.

CCA Competencies

Domain I: Health Records and Data Content

1. Collect and maintain health data.
2. Analyze health records to ensure that documentation supports the patient's diagnosis and procedures, reflects progress, clinical findings, and discharge status.
3. Request patient-specific documentation from other sources (such as ancillary departments, physician offices, and the like).
4. Apply clinical vocabularies and terminologies used in the organization's health information systems.

Domain II: Health Information Requirements and Standards

1. Evaluate the accuracy and completeness of the patient record as defined by organizational policy and external regulations and standards.
2. Monitor compliance with organization-wide health record documentation guidelines.
3. Report compliance findings according to organizational policy.
4. Assist in preparing the organization for accreditation, licensing, and/or certification surveys.

Domain III: Clinical Classification Systems

1. Utilize electronic applications to support clinical classification and coding (such as encoders).
2. Assign secondary diagnosis procedure codes using ICD-9-CM official coding guidelines:
   a. Assign principal diagnosis (Inpatient) or first listed diagnosis (Outpatient).
   b. Assign secondary diagnosis(es), including complications and comorbidities (CC).
   c. Assign principal and secondary procedure(s).
3. Assign procedure codes using CPT coding guidelines.
4. Assign appropriate HCPCS codes.
5. Identify discrepancies between coded data and supporting documentation.
6. Consult reference materials to facilitate code assignment.

Domain IV: Reimbursement Methodologies

1. Validate the data collected for appropriate reimbursement:
   a. Validate Medicare Severity Diagnosis-Related Groups (MS-DRGs).
   b. Validate Ambulatory Payment Classifications (APCs).
2. Comply with the National Correct Coding Initiative.
3. Verify the National and Local Coverage Determinations (NCD/LCD) for medical necessity.

Domain V: Information and Communication Technologies

1. Use personal computer to ensure data collection, storage, analysis, and reporting of information.
2. Use common software applications (such as word processing; spreadsheets; e-mail; and the like) in the execution of work processes.
3. Use specialized software in the completion of HIM processes.

Domain VI: Privacy, Confidentiality, Legal, and Ethical Issues

1. Apply policies and procedures for access and disclosure of personal health information.
2. Release patient-specific data to authorized individuals.
3. Apply ethical standards of practice.
4. Recognize and report privacy issues/problems.
5. Protect data integrity and validity using software or hardware technology.

Certified Coding Associate (CCA) Competencies

CCA Exam Competency	CCA Exam Level	Question	CCA Exam Competency	CCA Exam Level	Question
II.1.a	Application	10.13	III.2.a	Application	1.57
III.2.a	Application	1.5	III.2.a	Application	1.58
III.2.a	Application	1.16	III.2.a	Application	1.60
III.2.a	Application	1.17	III.2.a	Application	1.61
III.2.a	Application	1.18	III.2.a	Application	1.62
III.2.a	Application	1.20	III.2.a	Application	1.63
III.2.a	Application	1.21	III.2.a	Application	1.64
III.2.a	Application	1.22	III.2.a	Application	1.65
III.2.a	Application	1.23	III.2.a	Application	1.67
III.2.a	Application	1.24	III.2.a	Application	1.68
III.2.a	Application	1.25	III.2.a	Application	1.69
III.2.a	Application	1.26	III.2.a	Application	1.71
III.2.a	Application	1.27	III.2.a	Application	1.72
III.2.a	Application	1.28	III.2.a	Application	1.73
III.2.a	Application	1.29	III.2.a	Application	1.74
III.2.a	Application	1.30	III.2.a	Application	1.75
III.2.a	Application	1.31	III.2.a	Application	1.76
III.2.a	Application	1.32	III.2.a	Application	1.78
III.2.a	Application	1.33	III.2.a	Application	1.79
III.2.a	Application	1.34	III.2.a	Application	1.80
III.2.a	Application	1.35	III.2.a	Application	1.82
III.2.a	Application	1.36	III.2.a	Application	1.84
III.2.a	Application	1.37	III.2.a	Application	1.85
III.2.a	Application	1.38	III.2.a	Application	1.86
III.2.a	Application	1.39	III.2.a	Application	1.87
III.2.a	Application	1.40	III.2.a	Application	1.88
III.2.a	Application	1.41	III.2.a	Application	1.89
III.2.a	Application	1.42	III.2.a	Application	1.90
III.2.a	Application	1.43	III.2.a	Application	1.91
III.2.a	Application	1.44	III.2.a	Application	1.92
III.2.a	Application	1.45	III.2.a	Application	1.93
III.2.a	Application	1.46	III.2.a	Application	1.94
III.2.a	Application	1.47	III.2.a	Application	1.95
III.2.a	Application	1.51	III.2.a	Application	1.97
III.2.a	Application	1.52	III.2.a	Application	1.98
III.2.a	Recall	1.53	III.2.a	Application	1.99
III.2.a	Application	1.54	III.2.a	Application	1.100
III.2.a	Application	1.55	III.2.a	Application	1.102
III.2.a	Application	1.56	III.2.a	Application	1.104

CCA Exam Competency	CCA Exam Level	Question	CCA Exam Competency	CCA Exam Level	Question
III.2.a	Application	1.105	III.2.a	Application	1.151
III.2.a	Application	1.106	III.2.a	Application	1.152
III.2.a	Application	1.107	III.2.a	Application	1.153
III.2.a	Application	1.108	III.2.a	Application	1.154
III.2.a	Application	1.109	III.2.a	Application	1.155
III.2.a	Application	1.110	III.2.a	Application	1.156
III.2.a	Application	1.111	III.2.a	Application	1.157
III.2.a	Application	1.112	III.2.a	Application	1.158
III.2.a	Application	1.113	III.2.a	Application	1.159
III.2.a	Application	1.114	III.2.a	Application	1.160
III.2.a	Application	1.115	III.2.a	Application	1.161
III.2.a	Application	1.116	III.2.a	Application	1.162
III.2.a	Application	1.117	III.2.a	Application	1.163
III.2.a	Application	1.119	III.2.a	Application	1.164
III.2.a	Application	1.120	III.2.a	Application	1.165
III.2.a	Application	1.121	III.2.a	Application	1.166
III.2.a	Application	1.122	III.2.a	Application	1.167
III.2.a	Application	1.123	III.2.a	Application	1.168
III.2.a	Application	1.125	III.2.a	Application	1.169
III.2.a	Application	1.126	III.2.a	Application	1.170
III.2.a	Application	1.128	III.2.a	Application	1.171
III.2.a	Application	1.129	III.2.a	Application	1.172
III.2.a	Application	1.130	III.2.a	Application	1.173
III.2.a	Application	1.131	III.2.a	Application	1.174
III.2.a	Application	1.132	III.2.a	Application	1.175
III.2.a	Application	1.133	III.2.a	Application	1.176
III.2.a	Application	1.134	III.2.a	Application	1.177
III.2.a	Application	1.135	III.2.a	Application	1.178
III.2.a	Application	1.136	III.2.a	Application	1.179
III.2.a	Application	1.138	III.2.a	Application	1.180
III.2.a	Application	1.139	III.2.a	Application	1.181
III.2.a	Application	1.141	III.2.a	Application	1.182
III.2.a	Application	1.143	III.2.a	Application	1.183
III.2.a	Application	1.144	III.2.a	Application	1.184
III.2.a	Application	1.145	III.2.a	Application	1.185
III.2.a	Application	1.146	III.2.a	Application	1.186
III.2.a	Application	1.147	III.2.a	Application	1.187
III.2.a	Application	1.148	III.2.a	Application	1.188
III.2.a	Application	1.149	III.2.a	Application	1.189
III.2.a	Application	1.150	III.2.a	Application	1.190

CCA Exam Competency	CCA Exam Level	Question	CCA Exam Competency	CCA Exam Level	Question
III.2.a	Application	1.191	III.2.a	Application	1.239
III.2.a	Application	1.192	III.2.a	Application	1.240
III.2.a	Application	1.193	III.2.a	Application	1.241
III.2.a	Application	1.194	III.2.a	Application	1.242
III.2.a	Application	1.195	III.2.a	Application	1.243
III.2.a	Application	1.196	III.2.a	Application	1.244
III.2.a	Application	1.197	III.2.a	Application	1.245
III.2.a	Application	1.198	III.2.a	Application	1.246
III.2.a	Application	1.199	III.2.a	Application	1.247
III.2.a	Application	1.200	III.2.a	Application	1.248
III.2.a	Application	1.201	III.2.a	Application	1.249
III.2.a	Application	1.202	III.2.a	Application	1.250
III.2.a	Application	1.203	III.2.a	Application	1.251
III.2.a	Application	1.204	III.2.a	Application	1.252
III.2.a	Application	1.206	III.2.a	Application	1.253
III.2.a	Application	1.207	III.2.a	Application	1.254
III.2.a	Application	1.208	III.2.a	Application	1.255
III.2.a	Application	1.209	III.2.a	Application	1.256
III.2.a	Application	1.210	III.2.a	Application	1.257
III.2.a	Application	1.211	III.2.a	Application	1.258
III.2.a	Application	1.212	III.2.a	Application	1.259
III.2.a	Application	1.213	III.2.a	Application	1.260
III.2.a	Application	1.214	III.2.a	Application	1.261
III.2.a	Application	1.215	III.2.a	Application	1.262
III.2.a	Application	1.216	III.2.a	Application	1.263
III.2.a	Application	1.217	III.2.a	Application	1.264
III.2.a	Application	1.218	III.2.a	Application	1.265
III.2.a	Application	1.221	III.2.a	Application	1.266
III.2.a	Application	1.222	III.2.a	Application	1.267
III.2.a	Application	1.223	III.2.a	Application	1.268
III.2.a	Application	1.224	III.2.a	Application	1.269
III.2.a	Application	1.225	III.2.a	Application	1.270
III.2.a	Application	1.226	III.2.a	Application	1.271
III.2.a	Application	1.227	III.2.a	Application	1.272
III.2.a	Application	1.228	III.2.a	Application	1.273
III.2.a	Application	1.229	III.2.a	Application	1.274
III.2.a	Application	1.233	III.2.a	Application	1.275
III.2.a	Application	1.236	III.2.a	Application	1.276
III.2.a	Application	1.237	III.2.a	Application	1.277
III.2.a	Application	1.238	III.2.a	Application	1.278

CCA Exam Competency	CCA Exam Level	Question		CCA Exam Competency	CCA Exam Level	Question
III.2.a	Application	1.279		III.2.a	Application	1.319
III.2.a	Application	1.280		III.2.a	Application	1.320
III.2.a	Application	1.281		III.2.a	Application	1.321
III.2.a	Application	1.282		III.2.a	Application	1.322
III.2.a	Application	1.283		III.2.a	Application	1.323
III.2.a	Application	1.284		III.2.a	Application	1.324
III.2.a	Application	1.285		III.2.a	Application	1.325
III.2.a	Application	1.286		III.2.a	Application	1.326
III.2.a	Application	1.287		III.2.a	Application	1.327
III.2.a	Application	1.288		III.2.a	Application	1.328
III.2.a	Application	1.289		III.2.a	Application	1.329
III.2.a	Application	1.290		III.2.a	Application	1.330
III.2.a	Application	1.291		III.2.a	Application	1.331
III.2.a	Application	1.292		III.2.a	Application	1.332
III.2.a	Application	1.293		III.2.a	Application	1.333
III.2.a	Application	1.294		III.2.a	Application	1.334
III.2.a	Application	1.295		III.2.a	Application	1.335
III.2.a	Application	1.296		III.2.a	Application	1.336
III.2.a	Application	1.297		III.2.a	Application	1.337
III.2.a	Application	1.298		III.2.a	Application	1.338
III.2.a	Application	1.299		III.2.a	Application	1.339
III.2.a	Application	1.300		III.2.a	Application	1.340
III.2.a	Application	1.301		III.2.a	Application	1.341
III.2.a	Application	1.302		III.2.a	Application	1.342
III.2.a	Application	1.303		III.2.a	Application	1.343
III.2.a	Application	1.304		III.2.a	Application	1.344
III.2.a	Application	1.305		III.2.a	Application	1.345
III.2.a	Application	1.306		III.2.a	Application	1.346
III.2.a	Application	1.307		III.2.a	Application	1.347
III.2.a	Application	1.308		III.2.a	Application	1.348
III.2.a	Application	1.309		III.2.a	Application	1.349
III.2.a	Application	1.310		III.2.a	Application	1.350
III.2.a	Application	1.311		III.2.a	Application	1.351
III.2.a	Application	1.312		III.2.a	Application	1.352
III.2.a	Application	1.313		III.2.a	Application	1.353
III.2.a	Application	1.314		III.2.a	Application	1.354
III.2.a	Application	1.315		III.2.a	Application	1.355
III.2.a	Application	1.316		III.2.a	Application	1.356
III.2.a	Application	1.317		III.2.a	Application	1.357
III.2.a	Application	1.318		III.2.a	Application	1.358

CCA Exam Competency	CCA Exam Level	Question		CCA Exam Competency	CCA Exam Level	Question
III.2.a	Application	1.359		III.2.a	Application	5.36
III.2.a	Application	1.360		III.2.a	Application	5.37
III.2.a	Application	1.361		III.2.a	Application	5.66
III.2.a	Application	1.362		III.2.a	Application	5.81
III.2.a	Application	1.363		III.2.a	Application	6.14
III.2.a	Application	1.364		III.2.a	Application	6.32
III.2.a	Application	1.365		III.2.a	Application	6.53
III.2.a	Application	1.366		III.2.a	Application	6.83
III.2.a	Application	1.367		III.2.a	Application	6.88
III.2.a	Application	1.368		III.2.a	Analysis	9.53
III.2.a	Application	1.369		III.2.a	Analysis	9.75
III.2.a	Application	1.370		III.2.a	Recall	10.1
III.2.a	Application	1.371		III.2.a	Recall	10.2
III.2.a	Application	1.372		III.2.a	Application	10.3
III.2.a	Application	1.373		III.2.a	Application	10.4
III.2.a	Application	1.374		III.2.a	Application	10.5
III.2.a	Application	1.375		III.2.a	Application	10.6
III.2.a	Application	1.401		III.2.a	Application	10.7
III.2.a	Recall	1.402		III.2.a	Application	10.8
III.2.a	Recall	1.404		III.2.a	Application	10.9
III.2.a	Recall	1.405		III.2.a	Application	10.11
III.2.a	Application	1.406		III.2.a	Application	10.12
III.2.a	Recall	1.408		III.2.a,b	Application	10.41
III.2.a	Recall	1.409		III.2.a,b	Application	1.118
III.2.a	Recall	1.410		III.2.a,b	Application	4.5
III.2.a	Recall	1.411		III.2.a,b	Application	4.6
III.2.a	Recall	1.415		III.2.a,b	Application	4.10
III.2.a	Recall	1.421		III.2.a,b	Application	4.12
III.2.a	Recall	1.422		III.2.a,b	Application	4.13
III.2.a	Application	4.1		III.2.a,b	Application	4.19
III.2.a	Application	4.14		III.2.a,b	Application	4.24
III.2.a	Application	4.36		III.2.a,b	Application	4.25
III.2.a	Application	4.50		III.2.a,b	Application	4.26
III.2.a	Application	4.79		III.2.a,b	Application	4.28
III.2.a	Application	4.87		III.2.a,b	Application	4.31
III.2.a	Application	4.89		III.2.a,b	Application	4.34
III.2.a	Application	5.10		III.2.a,b	Application	4.35
III.2.a	Application	5.22		III.2.a,b	Application	4.38
III.2.a	Application	5.34		III.2.a,b	Application	4.39
III.2.a	Application	5.35		III.2.a,b	Application	4.40

CCA Exam Competency	CCA Exam Level	Question
III.2.a,b	Application	4.41
III.2.a,b	Application	4.42
III.2.a,b	Application	4.43
III.2.a,b	Application	4.44
III.2.a,b	Application	4.51
III.2.a,b	Application	4.60
III.2.a,b	Application	4.62
III.2.a,b	Application	4.63
III.2.a,b	Application	4.74
III.2.a,b	Application	4.76
III.2.a,b	Application	4.77
III.2.a,b	Application	4.80
III.2.a,b	Application	4.81
III.2.a,b	Application	4.90
III.2.a,b	Application	4.95
III.2.a,b	Application	4.96
III.2.a,b	Application	5.5
III.2.a,b	Analysis	5.20
III.2.a,b	Application	5.21
III.2.a,b	Application	5.45
III.2.a,b	Application	5.48
III.2.a,b	Application	5.49
III.2.a,b	Application	5.73
III.2.a,b	Application	5.76
III.2.a,b	Application	6.8
III.2.a,b	Application	6.11
III.2.a,b	Application	6.13
III.3	Application	6.30
III.2.a,b	Application	6.34
III.2.a,b	Application	6.35
III.2.a,b	Application	6.36
III.2.a,b	Application	6.37
III.2.a,b	Application	6.54
III.2.a,b	Application	6.70
III.2.a,b	Application	6.84
III.2.a,b	Application	6.89
III.2.a,b	Application	6.91
III.2.a,b	Application	6.92
III.2.a,b	Application	6.93
III.2.a,b	Application	6.95

CCA Exam Competency	CCA Exam Level	Question
III.2.a,b	Analysis	7.1
III.2.a,b	Analysis	7.15
III.2.a,b	Analysis	7.21
III.2.a,b	Analysis	7.24
III.2.a,b	Analysis	7.25
III.2.a,b	Analysis	7.28
III.2.a,b	Analysis	7.33
III.2.a,b	Analysis	7.38
III.2.a,b	Analysis	7.40
III.2.a,b	Analysis	7.47
III.2.a,b	Analysis	7.52
III.2.a,b	Analysis	7.54
III.2.a,b	Analysis	7.55
III.2.a,b	Analysis	7.56
III.2.a,b	Analysis	7.58
III.2.a,b	Analysis	8.3
III.2.a,b	Application	8.4
II.2.a,b/III.3	Application	8.10
III.2.a,b	Analysis	8.17
III.2.a,b	Analysis	8.18
III.2.a,b	Analysis	9.5
III.2.a,b	Application	9.6
III.2.a,b	Application	9.9
III.2.a,b	Analysis	9.25
III.2.a,b	Analysis	9.26
III.2.a,b	Analysis	9.27
II.2.a,b/III.3	Analysis	9.47
III.4	Recall	10.38
III.4	Application	10.39
III.2.a,b	Application	10.40
III.2.a,b	Application	10.42
III.2.a	Application	10.43
III.2.a,b	Application	10.44
III.2.a,b	Application	10.45
III.2.a,b	Application	10.46
III.2.a,b	Application	10.47
III.2.a,b	Application	10.48
III.2.a,b	Application	10.49
III.2.a,b,c	Application	4.2
III.2.a,b,c	Application	4.3

CCA Exam Competency	CCA Exam Level	Question
III.2.a,b,c	Application	4.4
III.2.a,b,c	Application	4.7
III.2.a,b,c	Application	4.8
III.2.a,b,c	Application	4.9
III.2.a,b,c	Application	4.11
III.2.a,b,c	Application	4.16
III.2.a,b,c	Application	4.17
III.2.a,b,c	Application	4.18
III.2.a,b,c	Application	4.20
III.2.a,b,c	Application	4.21
III.2.a,b,c	Application	4.22
III.2.a,b,c	Analysis	4.23
III.2.a,b,c	Application	4.27
III.2.a,b,c	Application	4.29
III.2.a,b,c	Application	4.32
III.2.a,b,c	Application	4.33
III.2.a,b,c	Application	4.37
III.2.a,b,c	Application	4.45
III.2.a,b,c	Application	4.46
III.2.a,b,c	Application	4.47
III.2.a,b,c	Application	4.49
III.2.a,b,c	Application	4.53
III.2.a,b,c	Application	4.55
III.2.a,b,c	Application	4.56
III.2.a,b,c	Application	4.61
III.2.a,b,c	Application	4.64
III.2.a,b,c	Application	4.65
III.2.a,b,c	Application	4.66
III.2.a,b,c	Application	4.67
III.2.a,b,c	Application	4.69
III.2.a,b,c	Application	4.71
III.2.a,b,c	Application	4.73
III.2.a,b,c	Application	4.75
III.2.a,b,c	Application	4.84
III.2.a,b,c	Application	4.85
III.2.a,b,c	Application	4.86
III.2.a,b,c	Application	4.88
III.2.a,b,c	Application	4.91
III.2.a,b,c	Application	4.92
III.2.a,b,c	Application	4.93

CCA Exam Competency	CCA Exam Level	Question
III.2.a,b,c	Application	4.94
III.2.a,b,c	Application	4.97
III.2.a,b,c	Application	4.99
III.2.a,b,c	Analysis	7.2
III.2.a,b,c	Analysis	7.4
III.2.a,b,c	Analysis	7.9
III.2.a,b,c	Analysis	7.11
III.2.a,b,c	Analysis	7.12
III.2.a,b,c	Analysis	7.13
III.2.a,b,c	Analysis	7.14
III.2.a,b,c	Analysis	7.17
III.2.a,b,c	Analysis	7.18
III.2.a,b,c	Analysis	7.19
III.2.a,b,c	Analysis	7.22
III.2.a,b,c	Analysis	7.23
III.2.a,b,c	Analysis	7.26
III.2.a,b,c	Analysis	7.27
III.2.a,b,c	Analysis	7.29
III.2.a,b,c	Analysis	7.30
III.2.a,b,c	Analysis	7.31
III.2.a,b,c	Analysis	7.32
III.2.a,b,c	Analysis	7.34
III.2.a,b,c	Analysis	7.35
III.2.a,b,c	Analysis	7.36
III.2.a,b,c	Analysis	7.39
III.2.a,b,c	Analysis	7.41
III.2.a,b,c	Analysis	7.43
III.2.a,b,c	Analysis	7.44
III.2.a,b,c	Analysis	7.45
III.2.a,b,c	Analysis	7.46
III.2.a,b,c	Analysis	7.48
III.2.a,b,c	Analysis	7.49
III.2.a,b,c	Analysis	7.50
III.2.a,b,c	Analysis	7.51
III.2.a,b,c	Analysis	7.53
III.2.a,b,c	Analysis	7.59
III.2.a,b,c	Analysis	7.60
III.2.a,b,c	Analysis	7.61
III.2.a,b/III.3	Application	5.4
III.2.a,b/III.3	Application	5.9

CCA Exam Competency	CCA Exam Level	Question
III.2.a,b/III.3	Application	5.14
III.2.a,b/III.3	Application	5.16
III.2.a,b/III.3	Application	5.18
III.2.a,b/III.3	Application	5.24
III.2.a,b/III.3	Application	5.29
III.2.a,b/III.3	Application	5.30
III.2.a,b/III.3	Application	5.50
III.2.a,b/III.3	Application	5.53
III.2.a,b/III.3	Application	5.57
III.2.a,b/III.3	Application	5.59
III.2.a,b/III.3	Application	5.60
III.2.a,b/III.3	Application	5.64
III.2.a,b/III.3	Application	5.72
III.2.a,b/III.3	Application	5.82
III.2.a,b/III.3	Application	5.84
III.2.a,b/III.3/III.4	Application	5.85
III.2.a,b/III.3	Application	5.87
III.2.a,b/III.3	Application	5.88
III.2.a,b/III.3	Application	6.2
III.2.a,b/III.3	Application	6.5
III.2.a,b/III.3	Application	6.12
III.2.a,b/III.3	Application	6.15
III.2.a,b/III.3	Application	6.16
III.2.a,b/III.3	Application	6.17
III.2.a,b/III.3	Application	6.22
III.2.a,b/III.3/III.4	Application	6.28
III.2.a,b/III.3	Application	6.33
III.2.a,b/III.3	Application	6.39
III.2.a,b/III.3	Application	6.41
III.2.a,b/III.3	Application	6.46
III.2.a,b/III.3	Application	6.56
III.3	Application	6.58
III.2.a,b/III.3	Application	6.59
III.2.a,b/III.3	Application	6.62
III.2.a,b/III.3	Application	6.63
III.2.a,b/III.3	Application	6.65
III.2.a,b/III.3	Application	6.71
III.2.a,b/III.3	Application	6.85
III.2.a,b/III.3	Application	8.1
III.2.a,b/III.3	Application	8.5

CCA Exam Competency	CCA Exam Level	Question
III.2.a,b/III.3	Application	8.6
III.2.a,b/III.3	Analysis	8.7
III.2.a,b/III.3	Analysis	8.13
III.2.a,b/III.3	Application	8.14
III.2.a,b/III.3	Analysis	8.15
III.2.a,b/III.3	Analysis	8.16
III.2.a,b/III.3	Analysis	8.19
III.2.a,b/III.3	Analysis	8.20
III.2.a,b/III.3	Analysis	8.21
III.2.a,b/III.3	Analysis	8.22
III.2.a,b/III.3	Analysis	8.23
III.2.a,b/III.3	Analysis	8.24
III.2.a,b/III.3	Analysis	8.26
III.2.a,b/III.3	Analysis	8.28
III.2.a,b/III.3	Application	8.29
III.2.a,b/III.3	Analysis	8.30
III.2.a,b/III.3	Analysis	8.31
III.2.a,b/III.3	Analysis	8.32
III.2.a,b/III.3	Analysis	8.33
III.2.a,b/III.3	Analysis	8.34
III.2.a,b/III.3	Analysis	8.35
III.2.a,b/III.3	Analysis	8.36
III.2.a,b/III.3	Analysis	8.37
III.2.a,b/III.3	Application	8.38
III.2.a,b/III.3	Analysis	8.40
III.2.a,b/III.3	Analysis	8.42
III.2.a,b/III.3	Analysis	8.47
III.2.a,b/III.3	Analysis	8.48
III.2.a,b/III.3	Application	8.50
II.2.a,b	Analysis	8.51
III.2.a,b/III.3	Analysis	8.52
III.2.a,b/III.3	Analysis	8.53
III.2.a,b/III.3	Analysis	8.54
III.2.a,b/III.3	Analysis	8.55
III.2.a,b/III.3	Analysis	8.56
III.2.a,b/III.3	Application	8.57
III.2.a,b/III.3/IV.2	Analysis	8.58
III.2.a,b/III.3	Analysis	9.2
III.2.a,b/III.3	Application	9.7
III.2.a,b/III.3	Analysis	9.8

CCA Exam Competency	CCA Exam Level	Question
III.2.a,b/III.3	Analysis	9.13
III.2.a,b/III.3	Analysis	9.14
III.2.a,b/III.3	Analysis	9.15
III.2.a,b/III.3	Analysis	9.22
III.2.a,b/III.3	Analysis	9.29
III.2.a,b/III.3	Analysis	9.32
II.2.a,b/III.3	Analysis	9.34
III.2.a,b/III.3	Analysis	9.35
II.2.a,b/III.3	Analysis	9.38
III.2.a,b/III.3	Analysis	9.39
III.2.a,b/III.3	Analysis	9.40
III.2.a,b/III.3	Analysis	9.41
II.2.a,b/III.3	Analysis	9.43
III.2.a,b/III.3	Analysis	9.44
III.2.a,b/III.3	Analysis	9.45
III.2.a,b/III.3	Analysis	9.49
III.2.a,b/III.3	Analysis	9.50
III.2.a,b/III.3	Analysis	9.51
III.2.a,b/III.3	Analysis	9.52
III.2.a,b/III.3	Analysis	9.54
III.2.a,b/III.3	Analysis	9.55
III.2.a,b/III.3	Application	9.56
III.2.a,b/III.3	Analysis	9.58
III.2.a,b/III.3	Analysis	9.61
II.2.a,b/III.3	Analysis	9.64
III.2.a,b/III.3	Analysis	9.66
III.2.a,b/III.3	Analysis	9.67
III.2.a,b/III.3	Analysis	9.68
III.2.a,b/III.3	Analysis	9.70
III.2.a,b/III.3	Application	9.73
III.2.a,b/III.3	Analysis	9.76
III.2.a,b/III.3	Analysis	9.77
III.2.a,b/III.3	Analysis	9.78
III.2.a,b/III.3	Analysis	9.79
III.2.a,b/III.3	Application	5.40
III.2.a,b/III.3	Application	5.52
III.2.a,b/III.3/ III.4	Application	5.61
III.2.a,b/III.3	Application	5.62

CCA Exam Competency	CCA Exam Level	Question
III.2.a,b/III.3/ III.4	Analysis	8.2
II.2.a,b/III.3/III.4	Analysis	9.33
III.2.a,b/III.3/ III.4	Analysis	9.60
III.2.a,b/III.3/III.4	Analysis	9.65
III.2.a,c	Application	4.30
III.2.a,c	Application	4.48
III.2.a,c	Application	4.52
III.2.a,c	Application	4.54
III.2.a,c	Application	4.68
III.2.a,c	Application	4.70
III.2.a,c	Application	4.72
III.2.a,c	Application	4.78
III.2.a,c	Application	4.82
III.2.a,c	Application	4.83
III.2.a,c	Application	4.98
III.2.a,c	Analysis	7.42
III.2.a.3.	Analysis	5.68
III.2.a.b	Analysis	5.89
III.2.a.b.	Analysis	7.16
III.2.a.b.	Analysis	7.20
III.2.a.b.	Analysis	7.37
III.2.a.b./III.3	Analysis	9.46
III.2.a.b.3	Analysis	8.12
III.2.a.b.3	Analysis	8.45
III.2.a.b.3	Analysis	8.46
III.2.a.b.3.	Analysis	5.90
III.2.a.b.c	Analysis	4.59
III.2.a.b.c	Analysis	7.3
III.2.a.b.c	Analysis	7.10
III.2.a.b.c	Analysis	7.57
III.2.a.b//II.3	Analysis	5.56
III.2.a.b/III.3	Analysis	9.82
III.2.a/III.2.b	Application	1.137
III.2.a/III.2.b	Recall	1.423
III.2.a/III.3	Application	5.1
III.2.a/III.3	Application	5.2
III.2.a/III.3	Application	5.3
II.2.a/III.3	Application	5.6

CCA Exam Competency	CCA Exam Level	Question
III.2.a/III.3	Application	5.7
III.2.a/III.3	Application	5.8
III.2.a/III.3	Application	5.12
III.2.a/III.3	Application	5.13
III.2.a/III.3	Application	5.15
III.2.a/III.3	Application	5.17
III.2.a/III.3	Application	5.23
III.2.a/III.3	Application	5.25
III.2.a/III.3	Application	5.26
III.2.a/III.3	Application	5.27
III.2.a/III.3	Application	5.28
III.2.a/III.3	Application	5.31
III.2.a/III.3	Application	5.32
III.2.a/III.3	Application	5.38
III.2.a/III.3	Application	5.39
III.2.a/III.3	Application	5.41
III.2.a/III.3	Application	5.43
III.2.a/III.3	Application	5.46
III.2.a/III.3	Application	5.51
III.2.a/III.3	Application	5.54
III.2.a/III.3	Application	5.58
III.2.a/III.3	Application	5.63
III.2.a/III.3	Application	5.65
III.2.a/III.3	Application	5.69
III.2.a/III.3	Application	5.70
III.2.a/III.3	Application	5.71
III.2.a,b/III.3/ III.4	Application	5.74
III.2.a/III.3	Application	5.75
III.2.a/III.3	Application	5.77
III.2.a/III.3	Application	5.78
III.2.a/III.3	Application	5.79
III.2.a/III.3	Application	5.80
III.2.a/III.3	Application	5.83
III.2.a/III.3	Application	5.86
III.2.a/III.3	Application	6.3
III.2.a/III.3	Application	6.6
III.2.a/III.3	Application	6.7
III.2.a,b/III.3	Application	6.19
III.2.a/III.3	Application	6.21
III.2.a/III.3	Application	6.25

CCA Exam Competency	CCA Exam Level	Question
III.2.a/III.3	Application	6.27
III.2.a/III.3	Application	6.38
III.2.a/III.3	Application	6.40
III.2.a/III.3	Application	6.42
III.2.a,b/III.3/ III.4	Application	6.43
III.2.a/III.3	Application	6.44
III.2.a/III.3	Application	6.45
III.2.a/III.3	Application	6.47
III.2.a/III.3	Application	6.48
III.2.a/III.3	Application	6.52
III.2.a/III.3	Application	6.55
III.2.a/III.3	Application	6.57
III.2.a/III.3	Application	6.60
III.2.a/III.3	Application	6.64
III.2.a/III.3	Application	6.68
III.2.a/III.3	Application	6.69
III.3	Application	6.72
III.2.a/III.3	Application	6.74
III.2.a/III.3	Application	6.75
III.2.a/III.3	Application	6.77
III.2.a/III.3	Application	6.78
III.2.a/III.3	Application	6.79
III.2.a/III.3	Application	6.80
III.2.a/III.3	Application	6.81
III.2.a/III.3	Application	6.82
III.2.a/III.3	Application	6.86
III.2.a/III.3	Application	6.87
III.2.a/III.3	Analysis	8.11
III.2.a/III.3	Analysis	8.25
III.2.a/III.3	Analysis	8.27
II.2.a,b/III.3	Analysis	8.39
III.2.a/III.3	Application	8.41
III.2.a/III.3	Application	8.43
III.2.a/III.3	Analysis	8.49
III.2.a/III.3	Analysis	9.1
III.2.a/III.3	Analysis	9.3
III.2.a/III.3	Analysis	9.4
III.2.a/III.3	Application	9.16
III.2.a/III.3	Analysis	9.17
III.2.a/III.3	Analysis	9.28

CCA Exam Competency	CCA Exam Level	Question	CCA Exam Competency	CCA Exam Level	Question
II.2.a,b/III.3	Analysis	9.30	III.2.c	Analysis	7.5
III.2.a/III.3	Analysis	9.31	III.2.c	Analysis	7.6
III.2.a/III.3	Analysis	9.37	III.2.c	Analysis	7.7
III.2.a/III.3	Analysis	9.42	III.2.c	Analysis	7.8
III.2.a/III.3	Analysis	9.48	III.3	Application	2.23
II.2.a,b/III.3	Analysis	9.62	III.3	Application	2.25
III.2.a/III.3	Analysis	9.69	III.3	Application	2.26
III.2.a/III.3	Analysis	9.71	III.3	Application	2.27
III.2.a/III.3	Application	9.72	III.3	Application	2.35
III.2.a/III.3	Application	9.81	III.3	Application	2.37
III.2.a/III.3/III.4	Application	6.61	III.3	Application	2.47
III.2.c	Application	1.376	III.3	Application	2.48
III.2.c	Application	1.377	III.3	Application	2.49
III.2.c	Application	1.378	III.3	Application	2.50
III.2.c	Application	1.379	III.3	Application	2.51
III.2.c	Application	1.380	III.3	Application	2.52
III.2.c	Application	1.381	III.3	Application	2.53
III.2.c	Application	1.382	III.3	Application	2.54
III.2.c	Application	1.383	III.3	Application	2.55
III.2.c	Application	1.384	III.3	Application	2.56
III.2.c	Application	1.385	III.3	Application	2.57
III.2.c	Application	1.386	III.3	Application	2.58
III.2.c	Application	1.387	III.3	Application	2.59
III.2.c	Application	1.388	III.3	Application	2.60
III.2.c	Application	1.389	III.3	Application	2.61
III.2.c	Application	1.390	III.3	Application	2.62
III.2.c	Application	1.391	III.3	Application	2.63
III.2.c	Application	1.392	III.3	Application	2.69
III.2.c	Application	1.393	III.3	Application	2.72
III.2.c	Application	1.394	III.3	Application	2.73
III.2.c	Application	1.395	III.3	Application	2.74
III.2.c	Application	1.396	III.3	Application	2.75
III.2.c	Application	1.397	III.3	Application	2.76
III.2.c	Application	1.398	III.3	Application	2.77
III.2.c	Application	1.399	III.3	Application	2.78
III.2.c	Application	1.400	III.3	Application	2.79
III.2.c	Recall	1.420	III.3	Application	2.80
III.2.c	Application	4.15	III.3	Application	2.81
III.2.c	Application	4.57	III.3	Application	2.83
III.2.c	Application	4.58	III.3	Application	2.85

CCA Exam Competency	CCA Exam Level	Question	CCA Exam Competency	CCA Exam Level	Question
III.3	Application	2.86	III.3	Application	2.138
III.3	Application	2.89	III.3	Application	2.139
III.3	Application	2.93	III.3	Application	2.140
III.3	Application	2.94	III.3	Application	2.141
III.3	Application	2.95	III.3	Application	2.142
III.3	Application	2.96	III.3	Application	2.143
III.3	Application	2.97	III.3	Application	2.144
III.3	Application	2.98	III.3	Application	2.145
III.3	Application	2.99	III.3	Application	2.146
III.3	Application	2.100	III.3	Application	2.147
III.3	Application	2.101	III.3	Application	2.148
III.3	Application	2.102	III.3	Application	2.149
III.3	Application	2.104	III.3	Application	2.150
III.3	Application	2.105	III.3	Application	2.151
III.3	Application	2.106	III.3	Application	2.152
III.3	Application	2.107	III.3	Application	2.153
III.3	Application	2.108	III.3	Application	2.154
III.3	Application	2.109	III.3	Application	2.155
III.3	Application	2.111	III.3	Application	2.156
III.3	Application	2.112	III.3	Application	2.158
III.3	Application	2.113	III.3	Application	2.159
III.3	Application	2.114	III.3	Application	2.161
III.3	Application	2.115	III.3	Application	2.162
III.3	Application	2.116	III.3	Application	2.163
III.3	Application	2.117	III.3	Application	2.164
III.3	Application	2.118	III.3	Application	2.165
III.3	Application	2.119	III.3	Application	2.166
III.3	Application	2.120	III.3	Application	2.167
III.3	Application	2.121	III.3	Application	2.168
III.3	Application	2.122	III.3	Application	2.169
III.3	Application	2.123	III.3	Application	2.170
III.3	Application	2.124	III.3	Application	2.171
III.3	Application	2.125	III.3	Application	2.172
III.3	Application	2.127	III.3	Application	2.173
III.3	Application	2.128	III.3	Application	2.174
III.3	Application	2.129	III.3	Application	2.175
III.3	Application	2.133	III.3	Application	2.176
III.3	Application	2.134	III.3	Application	2.177
III.3	Application	2.136	III.3	Application	2.178
III.3	Application	2.137	III.3	Application	2.179

CCA Exam Competency	CCA Exam Level	Question
III.3	Application	2.180
III.3	Application	2.181
III.3	Application	2.182
III.3	Application	2.183
III.3	Application	2.184
III.3	Application	2.185
III.3	Application	2.186
III.3	Application	2.187
III.3	Application	2.188
III.3	Application	2.189
III.3	Application	2.190
III.3	Application	2.191
III.3	Application	2.192
III.3	Application	2.193
III.3	Application	2.194
III.3	Application	2.195
III.3	Application	2.196
III.3	Application	2.197
III.3	Application	2.198
III.3	Application	2.199
III.3	Application	2.200
III.3	Application	2.201
III.3	Application	2.202
III.3	Application	2.203
III.3	Application	2.204
III.3	Application	2.205
III.3	Application	2.206
III.3	Application	2.207
III.3	Application	2.208
III.3	Application	2.209
III.3	Application	2.210
III.3	Application	2.211
III.3	Application	2.212
III.3	Application	2.213
III.3	Application	2.214
III.3	Application	2.215
III.3	Application	2.216
III.3	Application	2.217
III.3	Application	2.218
III.3	Application	2.219

CCA Exam Competency	CCA Exam Level	Question
III.3	Application	2.220
III.3	Application	2.221
III.3	Application	2.222
III.3	Application	2.223
III.3	Application	2.224
III.3	Application	2.225
III.3	Application	2.226
III.3	Application	2.227
III.3	Application	2.228
III.3	Application	2.229
III.3	Application	2.230
III.3	Application	2.231
III.3	Application	2.232
III.3	Application	2.233
III.3	Application	2.234
III.3	Application	2.235
III.3	Application	2.236
III.3	Application	2.237
III.3	Application	2.238
III.3	Application	2.239
III.3	Application	2.240
III.3	Application	2.241
III.3	Application	2.242
III.3	Application	2.243
III.3	Application	2.244
III.3	Application	2.245
III.3	Application	2.246
III.3	Application	2.247
III.3	Application	2.248
III.3	Application	2.249
III.3	Application	2.250
III.3	Application	2.251
III.3	Application	2.252
III.3	Application	2.253
III.3	Application	2.254
III.3	Application	2.255
III.3	Application	2.256
III.3	Application	2.257
III.3	Application	2.258
III.3	Application	2.259

CCA Exam Competency	CCA Exam Level	Question	CCA Exam Competency	CCA Exam Level	Question
III.3	Application	2.260	III.3	Application	2.301
III.3	Application	2.261	III.3	Application	2.302
III.3	Application	2.262	III.3	Application	2.303
III.3	Application	2.263	III.3	Application	2.304
III.3	Application	2.264	III.3	Application	2.305
III.3	Application	2.265	III.3	Application	2.306
III.3	Application	2.266	III.3	Application	2.307
III.3	Application	2.267	III.3	Application	2.308
III.3	Application	2.268	III.3	Application	2.309
III.3	Application	2.269	III.3	Application	2.310
III.3	Application	2.270	III.3	Application	2.311
III.3	Application	2.271	III.3	Application	2.312
III.3	Application	2.272	III.3	Application	2.314
III.3	Application	2.273	III.3	Application	2.317
III.3	Application	2.274	III.3	Application	2.318
III.3	Application	2.275	III.3	Application	2.319
III.3	Application	2.276	III.3	Application	2.320
III.3	Application	2.277	III.3	Application	2.321
III.3	Application	2.278	III.3	Application	2.322
III.3	Application	2.279	III.3	Application	2.323
III.3	Application	2.280	III.3	Application	2.324
III.3	Application	2.281	III.3	Application	2.325
III.3	Application	2.282	III.3	Application	2.326
III.3	Application	2.283	III.3	Application	2.327
III.3	Application	2.284	III.3	Application	2.328
III.3	Application	2.285	III.3	Application	2.329
III.3	Application	2.286	III.3	Application	2.330
III.3	Application	2.287	III.3	Application	2.331
III.3	Application	2.288	III.3	Application	2.332
III.3	Application	2.289	III.3	Application	2.333
III.3	Application	2.290	III.3	Application	2.334
III.3	Application	2.291	III.3	Application	2.335
III.3	Application	2.293	III.3	Application	2.336
III.3	Application	2.294	III.3	Application	2.338
III.3	Application	2.295	III.3	Application	2.340
III.3	Application	2.296	III.3	Application	2.342
III.3	Application	2.297	III.3	Application	2.344
III.3	Application	2.298	III.3	Application	2.345
III.3	Application	2.299	III.3	Application	2.346
III.3	Application	2.300	III.3	Application	2.347

CCA Exam Competency	CCA Exam Level	Question	CCA Exam Competency	CCA Exam Level	Question
III.3	Application	2.348	III.3	Application	2.410
III.3	Application	2.349	III.3	Application	2.411
III.3	Application	2.350	III.3	Application	2.412
III.3	Application	2.351	III.3	Application	2.413
III.3	Application	2.352	III.3	Application	2.414
III.3	Application	2.353	III.3	Application	2.415
III.3	Application	2.354	III.3	Application	2.416
III.3	Application	2.355	III.3	Application	2.417
III.3	Application	2.356	III.3	Application	2.418
III.3	Application	2.357	III.3	Application	2.419
III.3	Application	2.358	III.3	Application	2.420
III.3	Application	2.359	III.3	Application	2.421
III.3	Application	2.360	III.3	Application	2.422
III.3	Application	2.361	III.3	Application	2.423
III.3	Application	2.366	III.3	Application	2.424
III.3	Application	2.368	III.3	Application	2.425
III.3	Application	2.373	III.3	Application	2.426
III.3	Application	2.385	III.3	Application	5.11
III.3	Application	2.386	III.3	Application	5.19
III.3	Application	2.387	III.3	Application	5.33
III.3	Application	2.388	III.3	Application	5.42
III.3	Application	2.390	III.3	Application	5.44
III.3	Application	2.391	III.3	Application	5.47
III.3	Application	2.392	III.3	Application	5.67
III.3	Application	2.393	III.3	Application	6.1
III.3	Application	2.394	III.3	Application	6.4
III.3	Application	2.396	III.3	Application	6.9
III.3	Application	2.397	III.3	Application	6.10
III.3	Application	2.398	III.3	Application	6.18
III.3	Application	2.399	III.3	Application	6.20
III.3	Application	2.400	III.3	Application	6.23
III.3	Application	2.401	III.3	Application	6.24
III.3	Application	2.402	III.3	Application	6.26
III.3	Application	2.403	III.3	Application	6.29
III.3	Application	2.404	III.3	Application	6.31
III.3	Application	2.405	III.3	Application	6.49
III.3	Application	2.406	III.3	Application	6.50
III.3	Application	2.407	III.3	Application	6.51
III.3	Application	2.408	III.3	Application	6.66
III.3	Application	2.409	III.3	Application	6.73

CCA Exam Competency	CCA Exam Level	Question	CCA Exam Competency	CCA Exam Level	Question
III.3	Application	6.76	III.4	Application	3.15
III.3	Application	6.90	III.4	Application	3.16
III.3	Application	6.94	III.4	Application	3.17
III.3	Application	8.9	III.4	Application	3.18
III.3	Analysis	8.44	III.4	Application	3.19
III.3	Application	9.10	III.4	Application	3.20
III.3	Application	9.11	III.4	Application	3.21
III.3	Application	9.12	III.4	Application	3.22
III.3	Application	9.18	III.4	Application	3.23
III.3	Application	9.19	III.4	Recall	3.24
III.3	Application	9.20	III.4	Application	3.25
III.3	Analysis	9.21	III.4	Application	3.26
III.3	Analysis	9.23	III.4	Recall	3.27
III.3	Analysis	9.24	III.4	Application	3.28
III.3	Application	9.36	III.4	Application	3.29
III.3	Application	9.57	III.4	Application	3.30
III.3	Analysis	9.59	III.4	Application	3.31
III.3	Analysis	9.63	III.4	Application	3.32
III.3	Analysis	9.74	III.4	Application	3.33
III.3	Application	9.80	III.4	Application	3.34
III.3	Application	10.27	III.4	Application	3.35
III.3	Application	10.28	III.4	Application	3.36
III.3	Application	10.29	III.4	Application	3.37
III.3	Application	10.30	III.4	Application	3.38
III.3	Application	10.31	III.4	Application	3.39
III.3/III.4	Application	6.67	III.4	Application	3.40
II.2.a,b	Application	8.8	III.4	Application	3.41
III.4	Recall	3.1	III.4	Application	3.42
III.4	Application	3.2	III.4	Application	3.43
III.4	Application	3.3	III.4	Application	3.44
III.4	Application	3.4	III.4	Application	3.45
III.4	Application	3.5	III.4	Application	3.46
III.4	Application	3.6	III.4	Application	3.47
III.4	Application	3.7	III.4	Application	3.48
III.4	Application	3.8	III.4	Application	3.49
III.4	Application	3.9	III.4	Application	3.50
III.4	Application	3.10	III.4	Application	10.32
III.4	Application	3.11	III.4	Application	10.33
III.4	Application	3.12	III.4	Application	10.34
III.4	Application	3.13	III.4	Recall	10.35
III.4	Application	3.14	III.4	Recall	10.36

CCA Exam Competency	CCA Exam Level	Question	CCA Exam Competency	CCA Exam Level	Question
III.4	Recall	10.37	III.6	Recall	1.407
III.6	Recall	1.1	III.6	Recall	1.412
III.6	Recall	1.2	III.6	Recall	1.413
III.6	Recall	1.3	III.6	Recall	1.414
III.6	Recall	1.4	III.6	Recall	1.416
III.6	Recall	1.6	III.6	Recall	1.417
III.6	Recall	1.7	III.6	Recall	1.418
III.6	Recall	1.8	III.6	Recall	1.419
III.6	Recall	1.9	III.6	Recall	1.424
III.6	Recall	1.10	III.6	Recall	1.425
III.6	Recall	1.11	III.6	Recall	1.426
III.6	Recall	1.12	III.6	Recall	2.1
III.6	Recall	1.13	III.6	Recall	2.2
III.6	Recall	1.14	III.6	Recall	2.3
III.6	Recall	1.15	III.6	Recall	2.4
III.6	Application	1.19	III.6	Recall	2.5
III.6	Recall	1.48	III.6	Recall	2.6
III.6	Application	1.49	III.6	Recall	2.7
III.6	Recall	1.50	III.6	Recall	2.8
III.6	Application	1.59	III.6	Recall	2.9
III.6	Recall	1.66	III.6	Recall	2.10
III.6	Application	1.70	III.6	Recall	2.11
III.6	Recall	1.77	III.6	Recall	2.12
III.6	Recall	1.81	III.6	Recall	2.13
III.6	Recall	1.83	III.6	Recall	2.14
III.6	Recall	1.96	III.6	Recall	2.15
III.6	Recall	1.101	III.6	Recall	2.16
III.6	Recall	1.103	III.6	Recall	2.17
III.6	Recall	1.124	III.6	Recall	2.18
III.6	Recall	1.127	III.6	Recall	2.19
III.6	Recall	1.140	III.6	Recall	2.20
III.6	Recall	1.142	III.6	Recall	2.21
III.6	Recall	1.205	III.6	Recall	2.22
III.6	Recall	1.219	III.6	Recall	2.24
III.6	Recall	1.220	III.6	Recall	2.28
III.6	Recall	1.230	III.6	Recall	2.29
III.6	Recall	1.231	III.6	Recall	2.30
III.6	Recall	1.232	III.6	Recall	2.31
III.6	Recall	1.234	III.6	Recall	2.32
III.6	Recall	1.235	III.6	Recall	2.33
III.6	Recall	1.403	III.6	Recall	2.34

CCA Exam Competency	CCA Exam Level	Question	CCA Exam Competency	CCA Exam Level	Question
III.6	Recall	2.36	III.6	Recall	2.343
III.6	Recall	2.38	III.6	Application	2.362
III.6	Recall	2.39	III.6	Application	2.363
III.6	Recall	2.40	III.6	Recall	2.364
III.6	Recall	2.41	III.6	Application	2.365
III.6	Recall	2.42	III.6	Application	2.367
III.6	Recall	2.43	III.6	Application	2.369
III.6	Recall	2.44	III.6	Application	2.370
III.6	Recall	2.45	III.6	Recall	2.371
III.6	Recall	2.46	III.6	Application	2.372
III.6	Recall	2.64	III.6	Application	2.374
III.6	Recall	2.65	III.6	Application	2.375
III.6	Recall	2.66	III.6	Application	2.376
III.6	Recall	2.67	III.6	Application	2.377
III.6	Recall	2.68	III.6	Application	2.378
III.6	Recall	2.70	III.6	Application	2.379
III.6	Recall	2.71	III.6	Application	2.380
III.6	Recall	2.82	III.6	Application	2.381
III.6	Recall	2.84	III.6	Recall	2.382
III.6	Recall	2.87	III.6	Recall	2.383
III.6	Recall	2.88	III.6	Recall	2.384
III.6	Recall	2.90	III.6	Recall	2.389
III.6	Recall	2.91	III.6	Recall	2.395
III.6	Recall	2.92	III.6	Application	5.55
III.6	Recall	2.103	III.6	Recall	10.10
III.6	Recall	2.110	I.4	Recall	10.14
III.6	Recall	2.126	N/A	ICD-10	10.15
III.6	Recall	2.130	N/A	ICD-10	10.16
III.6	Recall	2.131	N/A	ICD-10	10.17
III.6	Recall	2.132	N/A	ICD-10	10.18
III.6	Recall	2.135	N/A	ICD-10	10.19
III.6	Recall	2.157	N/A	ICD-10	10.20
III.6	Recall	2.160	N/A	ICD-10	10.21
III.6	Recall	2.292	N/A	ICD-10	10.22
III.6	Recall	2.313	N/A	ICD-10	10.23
III.6	Recall	2.315	N/A	ICD-10	10.24
III.6	Recall	2.316	N/A	ICD-10	10.25
III.6	Recall	2.337	N/A	ICD-10	10.26
III.6	Recall	2.339	III.2.a,b	Application	10.50
III.6	Recall	2.341	III.2.a,b	Application	10.51

Certified Coding Specialist (CCS)

Certified Coding Specialists are professionals skilled in classifying medical data from patient records, generally in the hospital setting. These coding practitioners review patients' records and assign numeric codes for each diagnosis and procedure. To perform this task, they must possess expertise in the ICD-9-CM coding system and the surgery section within the CPT coding system. In addition, the CCS is knowledgeable about medical terminology, disease processes, and pharmacology.

Hospitals or medical providers report coded data to insurance companies or the government, in the case of Medicare and Medicaid recipients, for reimbursement of their expenses. Researchers and public health officials also use coded medical data to monitor patterns and explore new interventions. Coding accuracy is thus highly important to healthcare organizations because of its impact on revenues and describing health outcomes. Accordingly, the CCS credential demonstrates tested data quality and integrity skills in a coding practitioner. The CCS certification exam assesses mastery or proficiency in coding rather than entry-level skills.

CCS Coding Competencies

Domain I: Health Information Documentation

1. Interpret health record documentation using knowledge of anatomy, physiology, clinical disease processes, pharmacology, and medical terminology to identify codeable diagnoses and/or procedures.
2. Determine when additional clinical documentation is needed to assign the diagnosis and/or procedure code(s).
3. Consult with physicians and other healthcare providers to obtain further clinical documentation to assist with code assignment.
4. Consult reference materials to facilitate code assignment.
5. Identify patient encounter type.
6. Identify and post charges for healthcare services based on documentation

Domain II. Diagnosis Coding

1. Select the diagnoses that require coding according to current coding and reporting requirements for acute care (inpatient) services.
2. Select the diagnoses that require coding according to current coding and reporting requirements for outpatient services.
3. Interpret conventions, formats, instructional notations, tables and definitions of the classification system to select diagnoses, conditions, problems or other reasons for the encounter that require coding.
4. Sequence diagnoses and other reasons for encounter according to notations and conventions of the classification system and standard data set definitions [such as Uniform Hospital Discharge Data Set (UHDDS)].
5. Apply the official ICD-9-CM coding guidelines.

Domain III: Procedure Coding

1. Select the procedures that require coding according to current coding and reporting requirements for acute care (inpatient) services.
2. Select the procedures that require coding according to current coding and reporting requirements for outpatient services.

3. Interpret conventions, formats, instructional notations, and definitions of the classification system and/or nomenclature to select procedures/services that require coding.
4. Sequence procedures according to notations and conventions of the classification system/ nomenclature and standard data set definitions (such as UHDDS).
5. Apply the official ICD-9-CM coding guidelines.
6. Apply the official CPT/HCPCS Level II coding guidelines.

Domain IV: Regulatory Guidelines and Reporting Requirements for Acute Care (Inpatient)

1. Select the principal diagnosis, principal procedure, complications, comorbid conditions, other diagnoses and procedures that require coding according to UHDDS definitions and Coding Clinic for ICD-9-CM.
2. Evaluate the impact of code selection on Diagnosis Related Group (DRG) assignment.
3. Verify DRG assignment based on Inpatient Prospective Payment System (IPPS) definitions.
4. Assign the appropriate discharge disposition.

Domain V: Regulatory Guidelines and Reporting Requirements for Outpatient Services

1. Select the reason for encounter, pertinent secondary conditions, primary procedure, and other procedures that require coding according to UHDDS definitions, *CPT Assistant, Coding Clinics for ICD-9-CM*, and HCPCS.
2. Apply Outpatient Prospective Payment System (OPPS) reporting requirements:
   a. Modifiers
   b. CPT/ HCPCS Level II
   c. Medical necessity
   d. Evaluation and Management code assignment (facility reporting)

Domain VI: Data Quality and Management

1. Assess the quality of coded data.
2. Educate health care providers regarding reimbursement methodologies, documentation rules and regulations related to coding.
3. Analyze health record documentation for quality and completeness of coding.
4. Review the accuracy of abstracted data elements for data base integrity and claims processing.
5. Review and resolve coding edits (such as Correct Coding Initiative (CCI), Medicare Code Editor (MCE), and Outpatient Code Editor (OCE).

Domain VII: Information and Communication Technologies

1. Use computer to ensure data collection, storage, analysis, and reporting of information.
2. Use common software applications (for example, word processing, spreadsheets, and e-mail) in the execution of work processes.
3. Use specialized software in the completion of HIM processes.

Domain VIII: Privacy, Confidentiality, Legal and Ethical Issues

1. Apply policies and procedures for access and disclosure of personal health information.
2. Apply AHIMA Code of Ethics/Standards of Ethical Coding.

3. Recognize/report privacy issues/problems.
4. Protect data integrity and validity using software or hardware technology.

Domain IX: Compliance

1. Participate in the development of institutional coding policies to ensure compliance with official coding rules and guidelines.
2. Evaluate the accuracy and completeness of the patient record as defined by organizational policy and external regulations and standards.
3. Monitor compliance with organization-wide health record documentation and coding guidelines.
4. Recognize/report compliance concerns/findings.

Certified Coding Specialist (CCS) Competencies

CCS Exam Competency	CCS Exam Level	Question
I.1	Recall	1.8
I.1	Recall	1.48
I.1	Recall	1.59
I.1	Recall	1.101
I.1	Recall	1.103
I.1	Application	1.142
I.1	Application	1.208
I.1	Recall	1.235
I.1	Recall	1.403
I.1	Recall	1.406
I.1	Recall	1.416
I.1	Recall	1.424
I.1	Recall	1.425
I.1	Recall	1.426
I.1	Recall	2.96
I.1	Recall	2.116
I.1	Application	5.55
I.1/II.1/II.3/II.4/II.5/ III.1/III.3/III.4/III.5/ IV.1	Application	7.22
I.1/I.2/II.1/II.3/II.4/ II.5/III.1/III.3/III.4/ III.5/IV.1	Analysis	7.38
I.1/I.2/II.1/II.3/II.4/ II.5/IV.1/IV.3	Application	4.89
I.1/I.2/II.1/II.3/II.4/ II.5/III.1/III.3/III.4/ III.5/IV.1	Analysis	7.2

CCS Exam Competency	CCS Exam Level	Question
I.1/I.2/II.1/II.3/II.4/ II.5/III.1/III.3/III.4/ III.5/IV.1	Analysis	7.18
I.1/I.2/II.1/II.3/II.4/ II.5/III.1/III.3/III.4/ III.5/IV.1/IV.2/IV.3	Analysis	7.17
I.1/II.1/II.3/II.4/II.5/ III.1/III.3/III.4/III.5/ IV.1	Analysis	7.46
I.1/II.1/II.3/II.4/II.5/ IV.1	Application	4.19
I.1/II.1/II.3/II.4/II.5/ IV.1	Application	4.73
I.1/II.1/II.3/II.4/II.5/ IV.1	Application	4.80
I.1/II.1/II.3/II.4/II.5/ III.1/III.3/III.4/III.5/ IV.1	Application	4.28
I.1/II.1/II.3/II.4/II.5/ III.1/III.3/III.4/III.5/ IV.1	Application	4.55
I.1/II.1/II.3/II.4/II.5/ III.1/III.3/III.4/III.5/ IV.1	Application	4.71
I.1/II.1/II.3/II.4/II.5/ III.1/III.3/III.4/III.5/ IV.1/IV.3	Application	4.37
I.1/II.1/II.3/II.4/II.5/ III.1/III.3/III.4/III.5/ IV.1/IV.3	Application	4.40
I.2/II.2/III.2	Application	5.28
I.2/I.4/II.1/II.4	Analysis	7.55

CCS Exam Competency	CCS Exam Level	Question
I.2/I.4/II.3	Application	4.1
I.2/II.1/II.4	Analysis	7.16
I.2/II.1/II.4/III.1/III.4	Analysis	7.26
I.2/II.2/II.4/III.2	Application	8.5
I.2/II.2/II.4/III.2/III.4/V.2.a/V.2.b	Analysis	8.54
I.2/II.2/II.4/III.2/III.4/V.2.b	Analysis	8.2
I.3	Recall	2.144
I.4.II.3	Application	4.25
I.4/II.1	Application	4.50
I.4/II.1	Application	4.79
I.4/II.1/II.4	Application	4.39
I.4/II.1/II.4	Application	4.31
I.4/II.1/II.4	Application	4.38
I.4/II.1/II.4	Application	4.81
I.4/II.1/II.4	Analysis	7.1
I.4/II.1/II.4	Analysis	7.15
I.4/II.1/II.4	Analysis	7.21
I.4/II.1/II.4	Analysis	7.24
I.4/II.1/II.4	Analysis	7.56
I.4/II.1/II.4/III.1	Application	4.32
I.4/II.1/II.4/III.1	Application	4.47
I.4/II.1/II.4/III.1	Analysis	4.59
I.4/II.1/II.4/III.1	Application	4.66
I.4/II.1/II.4/III.1	Application	4.74
I.4/II.1/II.4/III.1	Analysis	7.2
I.4/II.1/II.4/III.1	Analysis	7.3
I.4/II.1/II.4/III.1/III.4	Application	4.91
I.4/II.1/II.4/III.1/III.4	Analysis	7.13
I.4/II.1/II.4/III.1/III.4	Analysis	7.19
I.4/II.1/II.4/III.1/III.4	Analysis	7.39
I.4/II.1/II.4/III.2	Analysis	7.57
I.4/II.1/III.1	Application	4.16
I.4/II.1/III.1	Application	4.18
I.4/II.1/III.1/III.4	Application	4.53
I.4/II.1/III.1/III.4	Analysis	7.53
I.4/II.2	Application	5.45

CCS Exam Competency	CCS Exam Level	Question
I.4/II.2/II.4	Analysis	8.3
I.4/II.2/II.4	Analysis	8.18
I.4/II.2/II.4/III.2	Application	5.16
I.4/II.2/II.4/III.2	Application	5.24
I.4/II.2/II.4/III.2	Application	8.1
I.4/II.2/II.4/III.2/III.4	Application	5.9
I.4/II.2/II.4/III.2/III.4	Analysis	8.20
I.4/II.2/II.4/III.2/III.4/V.2.a	Analysis	8.33
I.4/II.2/II.4/III.2/III.4/V.2.a	Analysis	8.46
I.4/II.2/II.4/III.2/III.4/V.2.a/VI.5	Analysis	8.19
I.4/II.2/II.4/III.2/V.2.a	Analysis	8.15
I.4/II.2/III.1	Application	4.3
II.2/III.2	Analysis	8.39
II.1	Recall	1.4
II.1	Application	1.23
II.1	Recall	1.38
II.1	Application	1.39
II.1	Application	1.139
II.1	Application	1.221
II.1	Application	1.222
II.1	Application	1.224
II.1	Application	1.227
II.1	Application	1.228
II.1	Application	1.229
II.1	Application	1.294
II.1	Application	1.336
II.1	Application	1.337
II.1	Application	1.338
II.1	Application	1.339
II.1	Application	1.340
II.1	Application	1.341
II.1	Application	1.342
II.1	Application	1.343
II.1	Application	1.344
II.1	Application	1.345
II.1	Application	1.346

CCS Exam Competency	CCS Exam Level	Question	CCS Exam Competency	CCS Exam Level	Question
II.1	Application	1.347	II.1/II.2	Application	1.28
II.1	Application	1.348	II.1/II.2	Application	1.29
II.1	Application	1.349	II.1/II.2	Application	1.30
II.1	Application	1.350	II.1/II.2	Application	1.31
II.1	Application	1.351	II.1/II.2	Application	1.32
II.1	Application	1.352	II.1/II.2	Application	1.33
II.1	Application	1.353	II.1/II.2	Application	1.34
II.1	Application	1.354	II.1/II.2	Application	1.35
II.1	Application	1.355	II.1/II.2	Application	1.36
II.1	Application	4.9	II.1/II.2	Application	1.37
II.1	Application	4.11	II.1/II.2	Application	1.40
II.1	Application	4.12	II.1/II.2	Application	1.41
II.1	Application	4.14	II.1/II.2	Application	1.42
II.1	Application	4.20	II.1/II.2	Application	1.43
II.1	Application	4.21	II.1/II.2	Application	1.44
II.1	Application	4.22	II.1/II.2	Application	1.45
II.1	Application	4.51	II.1/II.2	Application	1.46
II.1	Application	4.87	II.1/II.2	Application	1.47
V.2.a	Application	10.38	II.1/II.2	Application	1.49
V.2.a	Application	10.39	II.1/II.2	Application	1.50
II.1	Application	10.40	II.1/II.2	Application	1.51
II.2	Application	10.43	II.1/II.2	Application	1.52
II.2	Application	10.44	II.1/II.2	Application	1.54
II.1	Application	10.45	II.1/II.2	Application	1.55
II.1	Application	10.46	II.1/II.2	Application	1.56
II.1	Application	10.47	II.1/II.2	Application	1.57
II.1	Application	10.48	II.1/II.2	Application	1.58
II.1	Application	10.49	II.1/II.2	Application	1.60
II.1/II.2	Recall	1.6	II.1/II.2	Application	1.61
II.1/II.2	Recall	1.7	II.1/II.2	Application	1.62
II.1/II.2	Application	1.16	II.1/II.2	Application	1.63
II.1/II.2	Application	1.17	II.1/II.2	Application	1.64
II.1/II.2	Application	1.18	II.1/II.2	Application	1.65
II.1/II.2	Application	1.19	II.1/II.2	Application	1.67
II.1/II.2	Application	1.20	II.1/II.2	Application	1.68
II.1/II.2	Application	1.21	II.1/II.2	Application	1.69
II.1/II.2	Application	1.22	II.1/II.2	Application	1.70
II.1/II.2	Application	1.25	II.1/II.2	Application	1.71
II.1/II.2	Application	1.26	II.1/II.2	Application	1.72
II.1/II.2	Application	1.27	II.1/II.2	Application	1.73

CCS Exam Competency	CCS Exam Level	Question	CCS Exam Competency	CCS Exam Level	Question
II.1/II.2	Application	1.74	II.1/II.2	Application	1.121
II.1/II.2	Application	1.75	II.1/II.2	Application	1.122
II.1/II.2	Application	1.76	II.1/II.2	Application	1.123
II.1/II.2	Application	1.78	II.1/II.2	Application	1.125
II.1/II.2	Application	1.79	II.1/II.2	Application	1.126
II.1/II.2	Application	1.80	II.1/II.2	Application	1.128
II.1/II.2	Application	1.82	II.1/II.2	Application	1.129
II.1/II.2	Application	1.84	II.1/II.2	Application	1.130
II.1/II.2	Application	1.85	II.1/II.2	Application	1.131
II.1/II.2	Application	1.86	II.1/II.2	Application	1.132
II.1/II.2	Application	1.87	II.1/II.2	Application	1.133
II.1/II.2	Application	1.88	II.1/II.2	Application	1.134
II.1/II.2	Application	1.89	II.1/II.2	Application	1.135
II.1/II.2	Application	1.90	II.1/II.2	Application	1.136
II.1/II.2	Application	1.91	II.1/II.2	Application	1.137
II.1/II.2	Application	1.92	II.1/II.2	Application	1.138
II.1/II.2	Application	1.93	II.1/II.2	Application	1.141
II.1/II.2	Application	1.94	II.1/II.2	Application	1.143
II.1/II.2	Application	1.95	II.1/II.2	Application	1.144
II.1/II.2	Application	1.97	II.1/II.2	Application	1.145
II.1/II.2	Application	1.98	II.1/II.2	Application	1.146
II.1/II.2	Application	1.99	II.1/II.2	Application	1.147
II.1/II.2	Application	1.100	II.1/II.2	Application	1.148
II.1/II.2	Application	1.102	II.1/II.2	Application	1.149
II.1/II.2	Application	1.104	II.1/II.2	Application	1.150
II.1/II.2	Application	1.105	II.1/II.2	Application	1.151
II.1/II.2	Application	1.106	II.1/II.2	Application	1.152
II.1/II.2	Application	1.107	II.1/II.2	Application	1.153
II.1/II.2	Application	1.108	II.1/II.2	Application	1.154
II.1/II.2	Application	1.109	II.1/II.2	Application	1.155
II.1/II.2	Application	1.110	II.1/II.2	Application	1.156
II.1/II.2	Application	1.111	II.1/II.2	Application	1.157
II.1/II.2	Application	1.112	II.1/II.2	Application	1.158
II.1/II.2	Application	1.113	II.1/II.2	Application	1.159
II.1/II.2	Application	1.114	II.1/II.2	Application	1.160
II.1/II.2	Application	1.115	II.1/II.2	Application	1.161
II.1/II.2	Application	1.116	II.1/II.2	Application	1.162
II.1/II.2	Application	1.117	II.1/II.2	Application	1.163
II.1/II.2	Application	1.119	II.1/II.2	Application	1.164
II.1/II.2	Application	1.120	II.1/II.2	Application	1.165

CCS Exam Competency	CCS Exam Level	Question	CCS Exam Competency	CCS Exam Level	Question
II.1/II.2	Application	1.166	II.1/II.2	Application	1.207
II.1/II.2	Application	1.167	II.1/II.2	Application	1.209
II.1/II.2	Application	1.168	II.1/II.2	Application	1.210
II.1/II.2	Application	1.169	II.1/II.2	Application	1.211
II.1/II.2	Application	1.170	II.1/II.2	Application	1.212
II.1/II.2	Application	1.171	II.1/II.2	Application	1.213
II.1/II.2	Application	1.172	II.1/II.2	Application	1.214
II.1/II.2	Application	1.173	II.1/II.2	Application	1.215
II.1/II.2	Application	1.174	II.1/II.2	Application	1.216
II.1/II.2	Application	1.175	II.1/II.2	Application	1.217
II.1/II.2	Application	1.176	II.1/II.2	Application	1.218
II.1/II.2	Application	1.177	II.1/II.2	Application	1.223
II.1/II.2	Application	1.178	II.1/II.2	Application	1.225
II.1/II.2	Application	1.179	II.1/II.2	Application	1.226
II.1/II.2	Application	1.180	II.1/II.2	Application	1.233
II.1/II.2	Application	1.181	II.1/II.2	Application	1.236
II.1/II.2	Application	1.182	II.1/II.2	Application	1.237
II.1/II.2	Application	1.183	II.1/II.2	Application	1.238
II.1/II.2	Application	1.184	II.1/II.2	Application	1.239
II.1/II.2	Application	1.185	II.1/II.2	Application	1.240
II.1/II.2	Application	1.186	II.1/II.2	Application	1.241
II.1/II.2	Application	1.187	II.1/II.2	Application	1.242
II.1/II.2	Application	1.188	II.1/II.2	Application	1.243
II.1/II.2	Application	1.189	II.1/II.2	Application	1.244
II.1/II.2	Application	1.190	II.1/II.2	Application	1.245
II.1/II.2	Application	1.191	II.1/II.2	Application	1.246
II.1/II.2	Application	1.192	II.1/II.2	Application	1.247
II.1/II.2	Application	1.193	II.1/II.2	Application	1.248
II.1/II.2	Application	1.194	II.1/II.2	Application	1.250
II.1/II.2	Application	1.195	II.1/II.2	Application	1.251
II.1/II.2	Application	1.196	II.1/II.2	Application	1.252
II.1/II.2	Application	1.197	II.1/II.2	Application	1.253
II.1/II.2	Application	1.198	II.1/II.2	Application	1.254
II.1/II.2	Application	1.199	II.1/II.2	Application	1.255
II.1/II.2	Application	1.200	II.1/II.2	Application	1.256
II.1/II.2	Application	1.201	II.1/II.2	Application	1.257
II.1/II.2	Application	1.202	II.1/II.2	Application	1.258
II.1/II.2	Application	1.203	II.1/II.2	Application	1.259
II.1/II.2	Application	1.204	II.1/II.2	Application	1.260
II.1/II.2	Application	1.206	II.1/II.2	Application	1.261

CCS Exam Competency	CCS Exam Level	Question	CCS Exam Competency	CCS Exam Level	Question
II.1/II.2	Application	1.262	II.1/II.2	Application	1.303
II.1/II.2	Application	1.263	II.1/II.2	Application	1.304
II.1/II.2	Application	1.264	II.1/II.2	Application	1.305
II.1/II.2	Application	1.265	II.1/II.2	Application	1.306
II.1/II.2	Application	1.266	II.1/II.2	Application	1.307
II.1/II.2	Application	1.267	II.1/II.2	Application	1.308
II.1/II.2	Application	1.268	II.1/II.2	Application	1.309
II.1/II.2	Application	1.269	II.1/II.2	Application	1.310
II.1/II.2	Application	1.270	II.1/II.2	Application	1.311
II.1/II.2	Application	1.271	II.1/II.2	Application	1.312
II.1/II.2	Application	1.272	II.1/II.2	Application	1.313
II.1/II.2	Application	1.273	II.1/II.2	Application	1.314
II.1/II.2	Application	1.274	II.1/II.2	Application	1.315
II.1/II.2	Application	1.275	II.1/II.2	Application	1.316
II.1/II.2	Application	1.276	II.1/II.2	Application	1.317
II.1/II.2	Application	1.277	II.1/II.2	Application	1.318
II.1/II.2	Application	1.278	II.1/II.2	Application	1.319
II.1/II.2	Application	1.279	II.1/II.2	Application	1.320
II.1/II.2	Application	1.280	II.1/II.2	Application	1.321
II.1/II.2	Application	1.281	II.1/II.2	Application	1.322
II.1/II.2	Application	1.282	II.1/II.2	Application	1.323
II.1/II.2	Application	1.283	II.1/II.2	Application	1.324
II.1/II.2	Application	1.284	II.1/II.2	Application	1.325
II.1/II.2	Application	1.285	II.1/II.2	Application	1.326
II.1/II.2	Application	1.286	II.1/II.2	Application	1.327
II.1/II.2	Application	1.287	II.1/II.2	Application	1.328
II.1/II.2	Application	1.288	II.1/II.2	Application	1.329
II.1/II.2	Application	1.289	II.1/II.2	Application	1.330
II.1/II.2	Application	1.290	II.1/II.2	Application	1.331
II.1/II.2	Application	1.291	II.1/II.2	Application	1.332
II.1/II.2	Application	1.292	II.1/II.2	Application	1.333
II.1/II.2	Application	1.293	II.1/II.2	Application	1.334
II.1/II.2	Application	1.295	II.1/II.2	Application	1.335
II.1/II.2	Application	1.296	II.1/II.2	Application	1.356
II.1/II.2	Application	1.297	II.1/II.2	Application	1.357
II.1/II.2	Application	1.298	II.1/II.2	Application	1.358
II.1/II.2	Application	1.299	II.1/II.2	Application	1.359
II.1/II.2	Application	1.300	II.1/II.2	Application	1.360
II.1/II.2	Application	1.301	II.1/II.2	Application	1.361
II.1/II.2	Application	1.302	II.1/II.2	Application	1.362

CCS Exam Competency	CCS Exam Level	Question
II.1/II.2	Application	1.363
II.1/II.2	Application	1.364
II.1/II.2	Application	1.365
II.1/II.2	Application	1.366
II.1/II.2	Application	1.367
II.1/II.2	Application	1.368
II.1/II.2	Application	1.369
II.1/II.2	Application	1.370
II.1/II.2	Application	1.371
II.1/II.2	Application	1.372
II.1/II.2	Application	1.373
II.1/II.2	Application	1.374
II.1/II.2	Application	1.375
II.1/II.4	Application	4.13
II.1/II.4	Application	4.26
II.1/II.4	Application	4.34
II.1/II.4	Application	4.35
II.1/II.4	Application	4.36
II.1/II.4	Application	4.41
II.1/II.4	Application	4.42
II.1/II.4	Application	4.43
II.1/II.4	Application	4.44
II.1/II.4	Application	4.60
II.1/II.4	Application	4.62
II.1/II.4	Application	4.63
II.1/II.4	Application	4.77
II.1/II.4	Application	4.84
II.1/II.4	Application	4.90
II.1/II.4	Application	4.95
II.1/II.4	Application	4.96
II.1/II.4	Analysis	7.20
II.1/II.4	Analysis	7.25
II.1/II.4	Analysis	7.28
II.1/II.4	Analysis	7.33
II.1/II.4	Analysis	7.37
II.1/II.4	Analysis	7.40
II.1/II.4	Analysis	7.47
II.1/II.4	Analysis	7.52
II.1/II.4	Analysis	7.54
II.1/II.4	Analysis	7.58

CCS Exam Competency	CCS Exam Level	Question
II.1/II.4/III.1	Analysis	4.23
II.1/II.4/III.1	Application	4.27
II.1/II.4/III.1	Application	4.29
II.1/II.4/III.1	Application	4.30
II.1/II.4/III.1	Application	4.33
II.1/II.4/III.1	Application	4.45
II.1/II.4/III.1	Application	4.46
II.1/II.4/III.1	Application	4.49
II.1/II.4/III.1	Application	4.56
II.1/II.4/III.1	Application	4.61
II.1/II.4/III.1	Application	4.64
II.1/II.4/III.1	Application	4.65
II.1/II.4/III.1	Application	4.67
II.1/II.4/III.1	Application	4.69
II.1/II.4/III.1	Application	4.70
II.1/II.4/III.1	Application	4.75
II.1/II.4/III.1	Application	4.76
II.1/II.4/III.1	Application	4.78
II.1/II.4/III.1	Application	4.85
II.1/II.4/III.1	Application	4.86
II.1/II.4/III.1	Application	4.88
II.1/II.4/III.1	Application	4.93
II.1/II.4/III.1	Application	4.94
II.1/II.4/III.1	Application	4.99
II.1/II.4/III.1	Analysis	7.14
II.1/II.4/III.1	Analysis	7.23
II.1/II.4/III.1	Analysis	7.27
II.1/II.4/III.1	Analysis	7.29
II.1/II.4/III.1	Analysis	7.31
II.1/II.4/III.1	Analysis	7.43
II.1/II.4/III.1/III.4	Application	4.7
II.1/II.4/III.1/III.4	Application	4.8
II.1/II.4/III.1/III.4	Application	4.48
II.1/II.4/III.1/III.4	Application	4.92
II.1/II.4/III.1/III.4	Application	4.97
II.1/II.4/III.1/III.4	Analysis	7.4
II.1/II.4/III.1/III.4	Analysis	7.9
II.1/II.4/III.1/III.4	Analysis	7.10
II.1/II.4/III.1/III.4	Analysis	7.11
II.1/II.4/III.1/III.4	Analysis	7.12

CCS Exam Competency	CCS Exam Level	Question	CCS Exam Competency	CCS Exam Level	Question
II.1/II.4/III.1/III.4	Analysis	7.30	II.2/II.4	Application	5.48
II.1/II.4/III.1/III.4	Analysis	7.32	II.2/II.4	Application	5.49
II.1/II.4/III.1/III.4	Analysis	7.34	II.2/II.4	Application	5.73
II.1/II.4/III.1/III.4	Analysis	7.35	II.2/II.4	Application	5.76
II.1/II.4/III.1/III.4	Analysis	7.36	II.2/II.4	Analysis	5.89
II.1/II.4/III.1/III.4	Analysis	7.41	II.2/II.4	Application	8.4
II.1/II.4/III.1/III.4	Analysis	7.44	II.2/III.2	Application	8.10
II.1/II.4/III.1/III.4	Analysis	7.45	II.2/II.4	Analysis	8.17
II.1/II.4/III.1/III.4	Analysis	7.48	II.2/II.4	Application	8.57
II.1/II.4/III.1/III.4	Analysis	7.49	II.2/II.4/III.2	Application	5.18
II.1/II.4/III.1/III.4	Analysis	7.50	II.2/II.4/III.2	Application	5.29
II.1/II.4/III.1/III.4	Analysis	7.51	II.2/II.4/III.2	Application	5.30
II.1/II.4/III.1/III.4	Analysis	7.59	II.2/II.4/III.2	Application	5.32
II.1/II.4/III.1/III.4	Analysis	7.60	II.2/II.4/III.2	Application	5.50
II.1/II.4/III.1/III.4	Analysis	7.61	II.2/II.4/III.2	Application	5.53
II.1/II.4/III.2	Analysis	8.45	II.2/II.4/III.2	Application	5.58
II.1/III.1	Application	4.4	II.2/II.4/III.2	Application	5.64
II.1/III.1	Application	4.17	II.2/II.4/III.2	Application	5.82
II.1/III.1	Application	4.52	II.2/II.4/III.2	Application	5.84
II.1/III.1	Application	4.54	II.2/II.4/III.2	Application	8.6
II.1/III.1	Application	4.82	II.2/II.4/III.2	Analysis	8.21
II.1/III.1	Application	4.83	II.2/II.4/III.2	Analysis	8.26
II.1/III.1	Analysis	7.42	II.2/II.4/III.2	Analysis	8.28
II.1/III.1/III.4	Application	4.68	II.2/II.4/III.2	Application	8.29
II.1/III.1/III.4	Application	4.98	II.2/II.4/III.2	Analysis	8.30
II.1/III.1/III.4	Application	4.72	II.2/II.4/III.2	Analysis	8.31
II.1/IV.1	Application	4.10	II.2/II.4/III.2	Analysis	8.37
II.2	Recall	1.5	II.2/II.4/III.2	Application	8.50
II.2	Application	1.24	II.2	Analysis	8.51
II.2	Application	5.22	II.2/II.4/III.2	Analysis	8.53
II.2	Application	5.34	II.2/II.4/III.2/III.4	Application	5.4
II.2	Application	5.35	II.2/II.4/III.2/III.4	Application	5.14
II.2	Application	5.36	II.2/II.4/III.2/III.4	Application	5.60
II.2	Application	5.37	II.2/II.4/III.2/V.2.b	Application	5.85
II.2	Application	5.66	II.2/II.4/III.2/III.4	Application	5.88
II.2	Application	5.81	II.2/II.4/III.2/III.4	Analysis	8.7
II.1	Application	10.41	II.2/II.4/III.2/III.4	Analysis	8.22
II.1	Application	10.42	II.2/II.4/III.2/III.4	Analysis	8.23
II.2/II.4	Application	5.5	II.2/II.4/III.2/III.4	Analysis	8.36
II.2/II.4	Application	5.21	II.2/II.4/III.2/III.4	Analysis	8.47

CCS Exam Competency	CCS Exam Level	Question
II.2/II.4/III.2/III.4	Analysis	8.48
II.2/II.4/III.2/III.4	Analysis	8.52
II.2/III.2	Analysis	8.55
II.2/II.4/III.2/III.4/ V.2.a	Application	5.59
II.2/II.4/III.2/III.4/ V.2.a	Application	5.87
II.2/II.4/III.2/III.4/ V.2.a	Analysis	5.90
II.2/II.4/III.2/III.4/ V.2.a	Analysis	8.13
II.2/II.4/III.2/III.4/ V.2.a	Analysis	8.34
II.2/II.4/III.2/III.4/ V.2.a	Analysis	8.35
II.2/II.4/III.2/III.4/ V.2.a	Analysis	8.40
II.2/II.4/III.2/III.4/ V.2.a	Analysis	8.42
II.2/III.2	Analysis	8.58
II.2/II.4/III.2/III.4/ V.2.a/ V.2.b	Application	8.14
II.2/II.4/III.2/III.4/ V.2.a/VI.5	Analysis	5.20
II.2/II.4/III.2/III.4/ V.2.a/VI.5	Analysis	5.56
II.2/II.4/III.2/III.4/ V.2.a/VI.5	Analysis	8.12
II.2/II.4/III.2/III.4/ V.2.a/VI.5	Analysis	8.32
II.2/II.4/III.2/III.4/ V.2.a/VIL.5	Analysis	8.16
II.2/II.4/III.2/III.4/ VI.5	Analysis	8.24
II.2/II.4/III.2/III.4/ VI.5	Application	8.38
II.2/II.4/III.2/V.2.a	Application	5.72
II.2/II.4/III.2/V.2.b	Application	5.61
II.2/II.4/III.2	Application	5.62
II.2/II.4/III.2	Application	5.52
II.2/III.2	Application	4.6
II.2/III.2	Application	5.2
II.2/III.2	Application	5.3
II.2/III.2	Application	5.7
II.2/III.2	Application	5.8
II.2/III.2	Application	5.10

CCS Exam Competency	CCS Exam Level	Question
II.2/III.2	Application	5.12
II.2/III.2	Application	5.13
II.2/III.2	Application	5.15
II.2/III.2	Application	5.23
II.2/III.2	Application	5.27
II.2/III.2	Application	5.31
II.2/III.2	Application	5.43
II.2/III.2	Application	5.46
II.2/III.2	Application	5.54
II.2/III.2	Application	5.69
II.2/III.2	Application	5.70
II.2/III.2	Application	5.71
II.2/III.2	Application	5.77
II.2/III.2	Application	5.78
II.2/III.2	Application	5.79
II.2/III.2	Application	5.86
II.2/III.2	Analysis	8.27
II.2/III.2	Application	8.41
II.2/III.2/III.4	Application	5.1
II.2/III.2/III.4	Application	5.25
II.2/III.2/III.4	Application	5.26
II.2/III.2/III.4	Application	5.38
II.2/III.2/III.4	Application	5.39
II.2/III.2/III.4	Application	5.41
II.2/III.2/III.4	Application	5.63
II.2/III.2/III.4	Application	5.80
II.2/III.2/III.4	Analysis	8.11
II.2/III.2/III.4	Analysis	8.25
II.2/III.2/III.4	Application	8.43
II.2/III.2/III.4/V.2.a	Analysis	5.68
II.2/III.2/III.4/V.2.a	Analysis	8.49
II.2/III.2/III.4/V.2.a	Analysis	8.56
II.2/III.2/III.4/V.2.a/ VI.5	Application	5.6
II.2/III.2/V.2.a	Application	5.17
II.2/III.2/V.2.a	Application	5.51
II.2/III.2/V.2.a	Application	5.65
II.2/III.2/V.2.a	Application	5.74
II.2/III.2/V.2.a	Application	5.75
II.2/III.2/V.2.a	Application	5.83
II.2/III.2	Application	5.40

CCS Exam Competency	CCS Exam Level	Question
II.3	Recall	1.1
II.3	Recall	1.2
II.3	Recall	1.10
II.3	Recall	1.11
II.3	Recall	1.12
II.3	Recall	1.13
II.3	Recall	1.14
II.3	Recall	1.15
II.3	Recall	1.53
II.3	Recall	1.66
II.3	Recall	1.77
II.3	Recall	1.81
II.3	Recall	1.83
II.3	Recall	1.96
II.3	Application	1.118
II.3	Recall	1.124
II.3	Recall	1.127
II.3	Recall	1.140
II.3	Recall	1.219
II.3	Recall	1.220
II.3	Recall	1.230
II.3	Recall	1.231
II.3	Recall	1.232
II.3	Recall	1.234
II.3	Recall	1.402
II.3	Recall	1.407
II.3	Recall	1.410
II.3	Recall	1.412
II.3	Recall	1.413
II.3	Recall	1.414
II.3	Recall	1.417
II.3	Recall	1.418
II.3	Application	4.2
II.3	Application	4.5
II.4	Recall	1.205
II.4	Recall	1.249
II.4	Application	1.401
I.1/II.1/II.3/II.4/II.5/III.1/III.3/III.4/III.5/IV.1/IV.3	Application	4.24
II.4/IV.1	Recall	1.3

CCS Exam Competency	CCS Exam Level	Question
II.4/IV.1	Recall	1.404
II.4/IV.1	Recall	1.405
II.4/IV.1	Recall	1.408
II.4/IV.1	Recall	1.409
II.4/IV.1	Recall	1.411
II.4/IV.1	Recall	1.415
II.4/IV.1	Application	1.421
II.4/IV.1	Application	1.422
II.5	Recall	1.423
II.9/III.2	Application	5.57
III.1	Application	4.57
III.1	Analysis	7.5
III.1	Analysis	7.8
III.1/III.2	Application	1.376
III.1/III.2	Application	1.377
III.1/III.2	Application	1.378
III.1/III.2	Application	1.379
III.1/III.2	Application	1.380
III.1/III.2	Application	1.381
III.1/III.2	Application	1.382
III.1/III.2	Application	1.383
III.1/III.2	Application	1.384
III.1/III.2	Application	1.385
III.1/III.2	Application	1.386
III.1/III.2	Application	1.387
III.1/III.2	Application	1.388
III.1/III.2	Application	1.389
III.1/III.2	Application	1.390
III.1/III.2	Application	1.391
III.1/III.2	Application	1.392
III.1/III.2	Application	1.393
III.1/III.2	Application	1.394
III.1/III.2	Application	1.395
III.1/III.2	Application	1.396
III.1/III.2	Application	1.397
III.1/III.2	Application	1.398
III.1/III.2	Application	1.399
III.1/III.2	Application	1.400
III.1/III.2	Recall	1.419
III.1/III.4	Application	4.15

CCS Exam Competency	CCS Exam Level	Question
III.1/III.4	Application	4.58
III.1/III.4	Analysis	7.6
III.1/III.4	Analysis	7.7
III.2	Application	2.40
III.2	Application	2.41
III.2	Application	2.42
III.2	Application	2.43
III.2	Application	2.44
III.2	Application	2.45
III.2	Application	2.46
III.2	Application	2.47
III.2	Application	2.48
III.2	Application	2.49
III.2	Application	2.50
III.2	Application	2.51
III.2	Application	2.52
III.2	Application	2.53
III.2	Application	2.54
III.2	Application	2.55
III.2	Application	2.58
III.2	Application	2.61
III.2	Application	2.62
III.2	Application	2.63
III.2	Application	2.64
III.2	Application	2.65
III.2	Application	2.66
III.2	Application	2.67
III.2	Application	2.68
III.2	Application	2.69
III.2	Application	2.70
III.2	Application	2.71
III.2	Application	2.72
III.2	Application	2.74
III.2	Application	2.75
III.2	Application	2.79
III.2	Application	2.80
III.2	Application	2.81
III.2	Application	2.82
III.2	Application	2.83
III.2	Application	2.84

CCS Exam Competency	CCS Exam Level	Question
III.2	Application	2.85
III.2	Application	2.86
III.2	Application	2.87
III.2	Application	2.88
III.2	Recall	2.89
III.2	Application	2.90
III.2	Application	2.91
III.2	Application	2.92
III.2	Application	2.93
III.2	Application	2.94
III.2	Application	2.95
III.2	Application	2.97
III.2	Application	2.98
III.2	Application	2.99
III.2	Application	2.100
III.2	Application	2.101
III.2	Application	2.102
III.2	Application	2.103
III.2	Application	2.104
III.2	Application	2.105
III.2	Application	2.106
III.2	Application	2.107
III.2	Application	2.108
III.2	Application	2.109
III.2	Application	2.110
III.2	Application	2.111
III.2	Application	2.113
III.2	Application	2.114
III.2	Application	2.115
III.2	Application	2.117
III.2	Application	2.118
III.2	Application	2.120
III.2	Application	2.121
III.2	Application	2.122
III.2	Application	2.123
III.2	Application	2.124
III.2	Application	2.125
III.2	Application	2.126
III.2	Application	2.127
III.2	Application	2.128

CCS Exam Competency	CCS Exam Level	Question	CCS Exam Competency	CCS Exam Level	Question
III.2	Application	2.129	III.2	Application	2.171
III.2	Application	2.130	III.2	Application	2.172
III.2	Application	2.131	III.2	Application	2.173
III.2	Application	2.132	III.2	Application	2.174
III.2	Application	2.133	III.2	Application	2.175
III.2	Application	2.134	III.2	Application	2.176
III.2	Application	2.135	III.2	Application	2.177
III.2	Application	2.136	III.2	Application	2.178
III.2	Application	2.137	III.2	Application	2.179
III.2	Application	2.138	III.2	Application	2.180
III.2	Application	2.139	III.2	Application	2.181
III.2	Application	2.140	III.2	Application	2.182
III.2	Application	2.142	III.2	Application	2.183
III.2	Application	2.143	III.2	Application	2.184
III.2	Application	2.145	III.2	Application	2.185
III.2	Application	2.146	III.2	Application	2.186
III.2	Application	2.147	III.2	Application	2.187
III.2	Application	2.148	III.2	Application	2.188
III.2	Application	2.149	III.2	Application	2.189
III.2	Application	2.150	III.2	Application	2.190
III.2	Application	2.151	III.2	Application	2.191
III.2	Application	2.152	III.2	Application	2.192
III.2	Application	2.153	III.2	Application	2.193
III.2	Application	2.154	III.2	Application	2.194
III.2	Application	2.155	III.2	Application	2.195
III.2	Application	2.156	III.2	Application	2.196
III.2	Application	2.157	III.2	Application	2.197
III.2	Application	2.158	III.2	Application	2.198
III.2	Application	2.159	III.2	Application	2.199
III.2	Application	2.160	III.2	Application	2.200
III.2	Application	2.161	III.2	Application	2.201
III.2	Application	2.162	III.2	Application	2.202
III.2	Application	2.163	III.2	Application	2.203
III.2	Application	2.164	III.2	Application	2.204
III.2	Application	2.165	III.2	Application	2.205
III.2	Application	2.166	III.2	Application	2.206
III.2	Application	2.167	III.2	Application	2.207
III.2	Application	2.168	III.2	Application	2.208
III.2	Application	2.169	III.2	Application	2.209
III.2	Application	2.170	III.2	Application	2.210

CCS Exam Competency	CCS Exam Level	Question	CCS Exam Competency	CCS Exam Level	Question
III.2	Application	2.211	III.2	Application	2.251
III.2	Application	2.212	III.2	Application	2.252
III.2	Application	2.213	III.2	Application	2.253
III.2	Application	2.214	III.2	Application	2.254
III.2	Application	2.215	III.2	Application	2.255
III.2	Application	2.216	III.2	Application	2.256
III.2	Application	2.217	III.2	Application	2.257
III.2	Application	2.218	III.2	Application	2.258
III.2	Application	2.219	III.2	Application	2.259
III.2	Application	2.220	III.2	Application	2.260
III.2	Application	2.221	III.2	Application	2.261
III.2	Application	2.222	III.2	Application	2.262
III.2	Application	2.223	III.2	Application	2.263
III.2	Application	2.224	III.2	Application	2.264
III.2	Application	2.225	III.2	Application	2.265
III.2	Application	2.226	III.2	Application	2.266
III.2	Application	2.227	III.2	Application	2.267
III.2	Application	2.228	III.2	Application	2.268
III.2	Application	2.229	III.2	Application	2.269
III.2	Application	2.230	III.2	Application	2.270
III.2	Application	2.231	III.2	Application	2.271
III.2	Application	2.232	III.2	Application	2.272
III.2	Application	2.233	III.2	Application	2.273
III.2	Application	2.234	III.2	Application	2.274
III.2	Application	2.235	III.2	Application	2.275
III.2	Application	2.236	III.2	Application	2.276
III.2	Application	2.237	III.2	Application	2.277
III.2	Application	2.238	III.2	Application	2.278
III.2	Application	2.239	III.2	Application	2.279
III.2	Application	2.240	III.2	Application	2.280
III.2	Application	2.241	III.2	Application	2.281
III.2	Application	2.242	III.2	Application	2.282
III.2	Application	2.243	III.2	Application	2.283
III.2	Application	2.244	III.2	Application	2.284
III.2	Application	2.245	III.2	Application	2.285
III.2	Application	2.246	III.2	Application	2.286
III.2	Application	2.247	III.2	Application	2.287
III.2	Application	2.248	III.2	Application	2.288
III.2	Application	2.249	III.2	Application	2.289
III.2	Application	2.250	III.2	Application	2.290

CCS Exam Competency	CCS Exam Level	Question		CCS Exam Competency	CCS Exam Level	Question
III.2	Application	2.291		III.2	Application	2.332
III.2	Application	2.292		III.2	Application	2.333
III.2	Application	2.293		III.2	Application	2.334
III.2	Application	2.294		III.2	Application	2.335
III.2	Application	2.295		III.2	Recall	2.337
III.2	Application	2.296		III.2	Recall	2.338
III.2	Application	2.297		III.2	Application	2.340
III.2	Application	2.298		III.2	Recall	2.342
III.2	Application	2.299		III.2	Application	2.343
III.2	Application	2.300		III.2	Recall	2.344
III.2	Application	2.301		III.2	Recall	2.346
III.2	Application	2.302		III.2	Recall	2.350
III.2	Application	2.303		III.2	Recall	2.351
III.2	Application	2.304		III.2	Application	2.359
III.2	Application	2.305		III.2	Application	2.360
III.2	Application	2.306		III.2	Application	2.361
III.2	Application	2.307		III.2	Application	2.382
III.2	Application	2.308		III.2	Application	2.383
III.2	Application	2.309		III.2	Application	2.384
III.2	Application	2.310		III.2	Application	2.385
III.2	Application	2.311		III.2	Application	2.386
III.2	Application	2.312		III.2	Application	2.387
III.2	Application	2.313		III.2	Application	2.388
III.2	Application	2.314		III.2	Application	2.389
III.2	Application	2.315		III.2	Application	2.390
III.2	Application	2.316		III.2	Application	2.391
III.2	Application	2.318		III.2	Application	2.392
III.2	Application	2.319		III.2	Application	2.393
III.2	Application	2.320		III.2	Application	2.394
III.2	Application	2.321		III.2	Application	2.395
III.2	Application	2.322		III.2	Application	2.396
III.2	Application	2.323		III.2	Application	2.397
III.2	Application	2.324		III.2	Application	2.398
III.2	Application	2.325		III.2	Application	2.399
III.2	Application	2.326		III.2	Application	2.400
III.2	Application	2.327		III.2	Application	2.401
III.2	Application	2.328		III.2	Application	2.402
III.2	Application	2.329		III.2	Application	2.403
III.2	Application	2.330		III.2	Application	2.404
III.2	Application	2.331		III.2	Application	2.405

CCS Exam Competency	CCS Exam Level	Question	CCS Exam Competency	CCS Exam Level	Question
III.2	Application	2.406	III.2/V2.a	Application	3.11
III.2	Application	2.407	III.2/V2.a	Application	3.12
III.2	Application	2.408	III.2/V2.a	Application	3.13
III.2	Application	2.409	III.2/V2.a	Application	3.14
III.2	Application	2.410	III.2/V2.a	Application	3.15
III.2	Application	2.411	III.2/V2.a	Application	3.16
III.2	Application	2.412	III.2/V2.a	Application	3.17
III.2	Application	2.413	III.2/V2.a	Application	3.18
III.2	Application	2.414	III.2/V2.a	Application	3.19
III.2	Application	2.415	III.2/V2.a	Application	3.20
III.2	Application	2.416	III.2/V2.a	Application	3.23
III.2	Application	2.417	III.2/V2.a	Application	3.25
III.2	Application	2.418	III.2/V2.a	Application	3.28
III.2	Application	2.419	III.2/V2.a	Application	3.29
III.2	Application	2.420	III.2/V2.a	Application	3.30
III.2	Application	2.421	III.2/V2.a	Application	3.31
III.2	Application	2.422	III.2/V2.a	Application	3.32
III.2	Application	2.423	III.2/V2.a	Application	3.33
III.2	Application	2.424	III.2/V2.a	Application	3.34
III.2	Application	2.425	III.2/V2.a	Application	3.35
III.2	Application	2.426	III.2/V2.a	Application	3.36
III.2	Application	5.33	III.2/V2.a	Application	3.37
III.2	Application	5.44	III.2/V2.a	Application	3.38
III.2	Application	5.47	III.2/V2.a	Application	3.39
III.2	Application	5.67	III.2/V2.a	Application	3.40
III.2	Application	8.9	III.2/V2.a	Application	3.41
III.2	Analysis	8.44	III.2/V2.a	Application	3.42
III.2/III.4	Application	5.19	III.2/V2.a	Application	3.43
III.2/III.4	Application	5.42	III.2/V2.a	Application	3.44
II.2/II.4	Application	8.8	III.2/V2.a	Application	3.45
III.2/V.2.a	Application	5.11	III.2/V2.a	Application	3.46
III.2/V2.a	Application	3.2	III.2/V2.a	Application	3.47
III.2/V2.a	Application	3.3	III.2/V2.a	Application	3.48
III.2/V2.a	Application	3.4	III.2/V2.a	Application	3.49
III.2/V2.a	Application	3.5	III.2/V2.a	Application	3.50
III.2/V2.a	Application	3.6	III.3	Recall	2.1
III.2/V2.a	Application	3.7	III.3	Recall	2.2
III.2/V2.a	Application	3.8	III.3	Recall	2.3
III.2/V2.a	Application	3.9	III.3	Recall	2.4
III.2/V2.a	Application	3.10	III.3	Recall	2.5

CCS Exam Competency	CCS Exam Level	Question
III.3	Recall	2.6
III.3	Recall	2.7
III.3	Recall	2.8
III.3	Recall	2.9
III.3	Recall	2.10
III.3	Recall	2.11
III.3	Recall	2.12
III.3	Recall	2.13
III.3	Recall	2.14
III.3	Recall	2.15
III.3	Recall	2.16
III.3	Recall	2.17
III.3	Recall	2.18
III.3	Recall	2.19
III.3	Recall	2.20
III.3	Recall	2.21
III.3	Recall	2.22
III.3	Recall	2.23
III.3	Recall	2.24
III.3	Recall	2.25
III.3	Recall	2.26
III.3	Recall	2.27
III.3	Recall	2.28
III.3	Recall	2.29
III.3	Recall	2.30
III.3	Recall	2.31
III.3	Recall	2.32
III.3	Recall	2.33
III.3	Recall	2.34
III.3	Recall	2.35
III.3	Recall	2.36
III.3	Recall	2.37
III.3	Recall	2.38
III.3	Recall	2.39
III.3	Recall	2.56
III.3	Recall	2.57
III.3	Recall	2.59
III.3	Recall	2.60
III.3	Recall	2.73
III.3	Recall	2.76

CCS Exam Competency	CCS Exam Level	Question
III.3	Recall	2.77
III.3	Recall	2.78
III.3	Recall	2.119
III.3	Recall	2.141
III.3	Recall	2.317
III.3	Recall	2.356
III.3	Recall	2.357
III.3	Recall	2.358
III.3/V.2.a	Recall	3.1
III.4/IV.1	Recall	1.420
III.5	Recall	2.112
IX.1	Recall	1.9
N/A	N/A	2.336
N/A	N/A	2.339
N/A	N/A	2.341
N/A	N/A	2.345
N/A	N/A	2.347
N/A	N/A	2.348
N/A	N/A	2.349
N/A	N/A	2.352
N/A	N/A	2.353
N/A	N/A	2.354
N/A	N/A	2.355
N/A	N/A	3.21
N/A	N/A	3.22
N/A	N/A	3.24
N/A	N/A	3.26
N/A	N/A	3.27
N/A	N/A	6.1
N/A	N/A	6.2
N/A	N/A	6.3
N/A	N/A	6.4
N/A	N/A	6.5
N/A	N/A	6.6
N/A	N/A	6.7
N/A	N/A	6.8
N/A	N/A	6.9
N/A	N/A	6.10
N/A	N/A	6.11
N/A	N/A	6.12

CCS Exam Competency	CCS Exam Level	Question	CCS Exam Competency	CCS Exam Level	Question
N/A	N/A	6.13	N/A	N/A	6.53
N/A	N/A	6.14	N/A	N/A	6.54
N/A	N/A	6.15	N/A	N/A	6.55
N/A	N/A	6.16	N/A	N/A	6.56
N/A	N/A	6.17	N/A	N/A	6.57
N/A	N/A	6.18	N/A	N/A	6.58
N/A	N/A	6.19	N/A	N/A	6.59
N/A	N/A	6.20	N/A	N/A	6.60
N/A	N/A	6.21	N/A	N/A	6.61
N/A	N/A	6.22	N/A	N/A	6.62
N/A	N/A	6.23	N/A	N/A	6.63
N/A	N/A	6.24	N/A	N/A	6.64
N/A	N/A	6.25	N/A	N/A	6.65
N/A	N/A	6.26	N/A	N/A	6.66
N/A	N/A	6.27	N/A	N/A	6.67
N/A	N/A	6.28	N/A	N/A	6.68
N/A	N/A	6.29	N/A	N/A	6.69
N/A	N/A	6.30	N/A	N/A	6.70
N/A	N/A	6.31	N/A	N/A	6.71
N/A	N/A	6.32	N/A	N/A	6.72
N/A	N/A	6.33	N/A	N/A	6.73
N/A	N/A	6.34	N/A	N/A	6.74
N/A	N/A	6.35	N/A	N/A	6.75
N/A	N/A	6.36	N/A	N/A	6.76
N/A	N/A	6.37	N/A	N/A	6.77
N/A	N/A	6.38	N/A	N/A	6.78
N/A	N/A	6.39	N/A	N/A	6.79
N/A	N/A	6.40	N/A	N/A	6.80
N/A	N/A	6.41	N/A	N/A	6.81
N/A	N/A	6.42	N/A	N/A	6.82
N/A	N/A	6.43	N/A	N/A	6.83
N/A	N/A	6.44	N/A	N/A	6.84
N/A	N/A	6.45	N/A	N/A	6.85
N/A	N/A	6.46	N/A	N/A	6.86
N/A	N/A	6.47	N/A	N/A	6.87
N/A	N/A	6.48	N/A	N/A	6.88
N/A	N/A	6.49	N/A	N/A	6.89
N/A	N/A	6.50	N/A	N/A	6.90
N/A	N/A	6.51	N/A	N/A	6.91
N/A	N/A	6.52	N/A	N/A	6.92

CCS Exam Competency	CCS Exam Level	Question		CCS Exam Competency	CCS Exam Level	Question
N/A	N/A	6.93		N/A	N/A	9.38
N/A	N/A	6.94		N/A	N/A	9.39
N/A	N/A	6.95		N/A	N/A	9.40
N/A	N/A	9.1		N/A	N/A	9.41
N/A	N/A	9.2		N/A	N/A	9.42
N/A	N/A	9.3		N/A	N/A	9.43
N/A	N/A	9.4		N/A	N/A	9.44
N/A	N/A	9.5		N/A	N/A	9.45
N/A	N/A	9.6		N/A	N/A	9.46
N/A	N/A	9.7		N/A	N/A	9.47
N/A	N/A	9.8		N/A	N/A	9.48
N/A	N/A	9.9		N/A	N/A	9.49
N/A	N/A	9.10		N/A	N/A	9.50
N/A	N/A	9.11		N/A	N/A	9.51
N/A	N/A	9.12		N/A	N/A	9.52
N/A	N/A	9.13		N/A	N/A	9.53
N/A	N/A	9.14		N/A	N/A	9.54
N/A	N/A	9.15		N/A	N/A	9.55
N/A	N/A	9.16		N/A	N/A	9.56
N/A	N/A	9.17		N/A	N/A	9.57
N/A	N/A	9.18		N/A	N/A	9.58
N/A	N/A	9.19		N/A	N/A	9.59
N/A	N/A	9.20		N/A	N/A	9.60
N/A	N/A	9.21		N/A	N/A	9.61
N/A	N/A	9.22		N/A	N/A	9.62
N/A	N/A	9.23		N/A	N/A	9.63
N/A	N/A	9.24		N/A	N/A	9.64
N/A	N/A	9.25		N/A	N/A	9.65
N/A	N/A	9.26		N/A	N/A	9.66
N/A	N/A	9.27		N/A	N/A	9.67
N/A	N/A	9.28		N/A	N/A	9.68
N/A	N/A	9.29		N/A	N/A	9.69
N/A	N/A	9.30		N/A	N/A	9.70
N/A	N/A	9.31		N/A	N/A	9.71
N/A	N/A	9.32		N/A	N/A	9.72
N/A	N/A	9.33		N/A	N/A	9.73
N/A	N/A	9.34		N/A	N/A	9.74
N/A	N/A	9.35		N/A	N/A	9.75
N/A	N/A	9.36		N/A	N/A	9.76
N/A	N/A	9.37		N/A	N/A	9.77

CCS Exam Competency	CCS Exam Level	Question
N/A	N/A	9.78
N/A	N/A	9.79
N/A	N/A	9.80
N/A	N/A	9.81
N/A	N/A	9.82
N/A	Home Health	10.1
N/A	Home Health	10.2
N/A	Home Health	10.3
N/A	Home Health	10.4
N/A	Home Health	10.5
N/A	Home Health	10.6
N/A	Home Health	10.7
N/A	Home Health	10.8
N/A	Home Health	10.9
N/A	Home Health	10.10
N/A	Home Health	10.11
N/A	Home Health	10.12
N/A	Home Health	10.13
I.4	Home Health	10.14
N/A	ICD-10	10.15
N/A	ICD-10	10.16
N/A	ICD-10	10.17
N/A	ICD-10	10.18
N/A	ICD-10	10.19
N/A	ICD-10	10.20
N/A	ICD-10	10.21
N/A	ICD-10	10.22
N/A	ICD-10	10.23
N/A	ICD-10	10.24
N/A	ICD-10	10.25
N/A	ICD-10	10.26
V.2.a	Application	2.362

CCS Exam Competency	CCS Exam Level	Question
V.2.a	Recall	2.363
V.2.a	Application	2.364
V.2.a	Application	2.365
V.2.a	Application	2.366
V.2.a	Application	2.367
V.2.a	Application	2.368
V.2.a	Recall	2.369
V.2.a	Application	2.370
V.2.a	Application	2.371
V.2.a	Application	2.372
V.2.a	Application	2.373
V.2.a	Application	2.374
V.2.a	Application	2.375
V.2.a	Application	2.376
V.2.a	Application	2.377
V.2.a	Application	2.378
V.2.a	Application	2.379
V.2.a	Application	2.380
V.2.a	Application	2.381
N/A	ICD-10	10.27
V.2.a	Application	10.28
V.2.a	Application	10.29
V.2.a	Application	10.30
V.2.a	Application	10.31
V.2.a	Application	10.32
V.2.a	Application	10.33
V.2.a	Application	10.34
V.2.a	Application	10.35
V.2.a	Recall	10.36
V.2.a	Recall	10.37
II.1	Application	10.50
II.1	Application	10.51

Certified Coding Specialist—Physician-based (CCS-P)

The CCS-P is a coding practitioner with expertise in physician-based settings such as physician offices, group practices, multispecialty clinics, or specialty centers. This coding practitioner reviews patients' records and assigns numeric codes for each diagnosis and procedure. To perform this task, the individual must possess in-depth knowledge of the CPT coding system and familiarity with the ICD-9-CM and HCPCS Level II coding systems. The CCS-P is also expert in health information documentation, data integrity, and quality. Because patients' coded data is submitted to insurance companies or the government for expense reimbursement, the CCS-P plays a critical role in the health provider's business operation. The CCS-P certification exam assesses mastery or proficiency in coding rather than entry-level skills.

CCS-P Coding Competencies

Domain I: Health Information Documentation

1. Locate appropriate source documents within the health record for coding or data collection.
2. Interpret health record documentation using knowledge of anatomy, physiology, clinical disease processes, pharmacology, and medical terminology to identify codeable diagnoses and/or procedures.
3. Determine when additional clinical documentation is needed to assign and/or validate the diagnosis and/or procedure code(s).
4. Consult with/query physicians and/or nonphysician practitioners when additional information is needed for coding and/or to clarify conflicting or ambiguous information.
5. Consult clinical reference materials to enable interpretation of health information documentation.
6. Determine those elements of the documentation that are extraneous or unnecessary for coding purposes.

Domain II: ICD-9-CM Diagnosis Coding

1. Apply ICD-9-CM conventions, formats, instructional notations, tables, and definitions to select diagnoses, conditions, problems, or other reasons for the encounter.
2. Assign ICD-9-CM code by applying Diagnostic Coding and Reporting Guidelines for Outpatient Services (Hospital-based and Physician Office).
3. Consult AHA *Coding Clinic* to assist in proper assignment of diagnostic codes.

Domain III: CPT and HCPCS II Coding

1. Apply CPT guidelines, format, and instructional notes to select services, procedures, and supplies that require coding.
2. Assign CPT code(s) for procedures and/or services rendered during the encounter:
   a. Evaluation and Management (E/M) services
   b. Anesthesia
   c. Surgery
   d. Radiology
   e. Pathology and Laboratory
   f. Medicine
   g. Category III

3. Apply HCPCS II guidelines and instructional notes to select services, procedures, drugs, and supplies that require coding.
4. Assign HCPCS II codes for services, procedures, drugs, and/or supplies provided.
5. Append modifiers to CPT and/or HCPCS II codes when applicable.

Domain IV: Reimbursement

1. Create and maintain encounter form or charge tickets and/or electronic equivalents.
2. Apply bundling and unbundling guidelines (for example, National Correct Coding Initiative [NCCI]).
3. Apply reimbursement methodologies for billing and/or reporting (for example, OIG, CMS, and *Federal Register*).
4. Link diagnosis code to the associated procedure code for billing or reporting.
5. Identify, post, and submit charges for healthcare services based on documentation and payer guidelines.
6. Evaluate payer remittance or payment (for example, RA, EOB, and EOMB) reports for reimbursement and/or denials.
7. Process claim denials and/or appeals.

Domain V: Data Quality and Analysis

1. Validate accuracy and completeness of coded data by comparing the documentation to the encounter form or electronic equivalent.
2. Assess the quality of coding and billing using generated reports.
3. Verify the accuracy and completeness of the data on the claim.
4. Conduct coding and billing audits for compliance and trending.
5. Educate healthcare providers and/or staff regarding reimbursement methodologies, documentation rules, and regulations related to coding.

Domain VI: Information and Communication Technologies

1. Use computer systems to ensure data collection, storage, analysis and reporting of information.
2. Use common software applications (for example, word processing, spreadsheets, e-mail, and encoders) in the execution of work processes.

Domain VII: Compliance and Regulatory Issues

1. Apply policies and procedures for access to and disclosure of personal health information.
2. Release patient-specific data to authorized individuals.
3. Apply AHIMA Code of Ethics and Standards of Ethical Coding.
4. Recognize/report privacy issues/problems.
5. Protect data integrity and validity using software or hardware technology.
6. Participate in the development of coding policies to ensure compliance with official coding rules and guidelines.
7. Evaluate the accuracy and completeness of the patient record as defined by organizational policy and external regulations and standards (for example, signature, teaching physician rules, PA co-sign requirements).
8. Recognize/report compliance concerns/findings.

Certified Coding Specialist—Physician-Based (CCS-P) Competencies

CCS-P Exam Competency	CCS-P Exam Level	Question	CCS-P Exam Competency	CCS-P Exam Level	Question
VII.7	Recall	1.426	II.2	Application	1.41
I.2	Recall	1.48	I.2	Application	1.42
I.2	Recall	1.59	II.2	Application	1.43
I.2	Recall	1.101	II.2	Application	1.44
I.1	Recall	1.103	II.2	Application	1.45
I.1	Application	1.142	II.2	Application	1.46
N/A	N/A	1.208	II.2	Application	1.47
I.2	Recall	1.235	I.2	Application	1.49
I.2	Recall	1.403	I.2	Application	1.50
I.2	Recall	1.406	II.2	Application	1.51
II.2	Recall	1.416	II.1,II.2	Application	1.52
I.2	Recall	1.424	II.2	Application	1.54
I.2	Recall	1.425	II.2	Application	1.55
III.2.c	Recall	2.96	II.2	Application	1.56
III.2.c	Recall	2.116	II.2	Application	1.57
I.3	Recall	1.6	II.2	Application	1.58
III.2.c	Recall	2.144	II.2	Application	1.60
II.2	Application	1.16	II.2	Application	1.61
II.2	Application	1.17	II.2	Application	1.62
II.2	Application	1.18	II.2	Application	1.63
II.2	Application	1.19	II.2	Application	1.64
II.2	Application	1.20	II.2	Application	1.65
II.2	Application	1.21	II.2	Application	1.67
II.2	Application	1.22	II.2	Application	1.68
II.2	Application	1.23	II.2	Application	1.69
II.2	Application	1.24	II.2	Application	1.70
II.2	Application	1.25	II.2	Application	1.71
II.2	Application	1.26	II.2	Application	1.72
II.2	Application	1.27	II.2	Application	1.73
II.2	Application	1.28	II.2	Application	1.74
II.2	Application	1.29	II.2	Application	1.75
II.2	Application	1.30	II.2	Application	1.76
II.2	Application	1.31	II.2	Application	1.78
II.2	Application	1.32	II.2	Application	1.79
II.2	Application	1.33	II.2	Application	1.80
II.2	Application	1.34	II.2	Application	1.82
II.2	Application	1.35	II.2	Application	1.84
II.2	Application	1.36	II.2	Application	1.85
II.2	Application	1.37	II.2	Application	1.86
II.2	Application	1.40	II.2	Application	1.87

CCS-P Exam Competency	CCS-P Exam Level	Question	CCS-P Exam Competency	CCS-P Exam Level	Question
II.2	Application	1.88	II.2	Application	1.135
II.2	Application	1.89	II.2	Application	1.136
II.2	Application	1.90	II.2	Application	1.137
II.2	Application	1.91	II.2	Application	1.138
II.2	Application	1.92	II.2	Application	1.139
II.2	Application	1.93	II.2	Application	1.141
II.2	Application	1.94	II.2	Application	1.143
II.2	Application	1.95	II.2	Application	1.144
II.2	Application	1.97	II.2	Application	1.145
II.2	Application	1.98	II.2	Application	1.146
II.2	Application	1.99	II.2	Application	1.147
II.2	Application	1.100	II.2	Application	1.148
II.2	Application	1.102	II.2	Application	1.149
II.2	Application	1.104	II.2	Application	1.150
II.2	Application	1.105	II.2	Application	1.151
II.2	Application	1.106	II.2	Application	1.152
II.2	Application	1.107	II.2	Application	1.153
II.2	Application	1.108	II.2	Application	1.154
II.2	Application	1.109	II.2	Application	1.155
II.2	Application	1.110	II.2	Application	1.156
II.2	Application	1.111	II.2	Application	1.157
II.2	Application	1.112	II.2	Application	1.158
II.2	Application	1.113	II.2	Application	1.159
II.2	Application	1.114	II.2	Application	1.160
II.2	Application	1.115	II.2	Application	1.161
II.2	Application	1.116	II.2	Application	1.162
II.2	Application	1.117	II.2	Application	1.163
II.2	Application	1.119	II.2	Application	1.164
II.2	Application	1.120	II.2	Application	1.165
II.2	Application	1.121	II.2	Application	1.166
II.2	Application	1.122	II.2	Application	1.167
II.2	Application	1.123	II.2	Application	1.168
II.2	Application	1.125	II.2	Application	1.169
II.2	Application	1.126	II.2	Application	1.170
II.2	Application	1.128	II.2	Application	1.171
II.2	Application	1.129	II.2	Application	1.172
II.2	Application	1.130	II.2	Application	1.173
II.2	Application	1.131	II.2	Application	1.174
II.2	Application	1.132	II.2	Application	1.175
II.2	Application	1.133	II.2	Application	1.176
II.2	Application	1.134	II.2	Application	1.177

CCS-P Exam Competency	CCS-P Exam Level	Question	CCS-P Exam Competency	CCS-P Exam Level	Question
II.2	Application	1.178	II.2	Application	1.222
II.2	Application	1.179	II.2	Application	1.223
II.2	Application	1.180	II.2	Application	1.224
II.2	Application	1.181	II.2	Application	1.225
II.2	Application	1.182	II.2	Application	1.226
II.2	Application	1.183	II.2	Application	1.227
II.2	Application	1.184	II.2	Application	1.228
II.2	Application	1.185	II.2	Application	1.229
II.2	Application	1.186	II.1	Application	1.233
II.2	Application	1.187	II.2	Application	1.236
II.2	Application	1.188	II.2	Application	1.237
II.2	Application	1.189	II.2	Application	1.238
II.2	Application	1.190	II.2	Application	1.239
II.2	Application	1.191	II.2	Application	1.240
II.2	Application	1.192	II.2	Application	1.241
II.2	Application	1.193	II.2	Application	1.242
II.2	Application	1.194	II.2	Application	1.243
II.2	Application	1.195	II.2	Application	1.244
II.2	Application	1.196	II.2	Application	1.245
II.2	Application	1.197	II.2	Application	1.246
II.2	Application	1.198	II.2	Application	1.247
II.2	Application	1.199	II.2	Application	1.248
II.2	Application	1.200	II.2	Application	1.250
II.2	Application	1.201	II.2	Application	1.251
II.2	Application	1.202	II.2	Application	1.252
II.2	Application	1.203	II.2	Application	1.253
II.2	Application	1.204	II.2	Application	1.254
N/A	N/A	1.205	II.2	Application	1.255
II.2	Application	1.206	II.2	Application	1.256
II.2	Application	1.207	II.2	Application	1.257
II.2	Application	1.209	II.2	Application	1.258
II.2	Application	1.210	II.2	Application	1.259
II.2	Application	1.211	II.2	Application	1.260
II.2	Application	1.212	II.2	Application	1.261
II.2	Application	1.213	II.2	Application	1.262
II.2	Application	1.214	II.2	Application	1.263
II.2	Application	1.215	II.2	Application	1.264
II.2	Application	1.216	II.2	Application	1.265
II.2	Application	1.217	II.2	Application	1.266
II.2	Application	1.218	II.2	Application	1.267
II.2	Application	1.221	II.2	Application	1.268

CCS-P Exam Competency	CCS-P Exam Level	Question
II.2	Application	1.269
II.2	Application	1.270
II.2	Application	1.271
II.2	Application	1.272
II.2	Application	1.273
II.2	Application	1.274
II.2	Application	1.275
II.2	Application	1.276
II.2	Application	1.277
II.2	Application	1.278
II.2	Application	1.279
II.2	Application	1.280
II.2	Application	1.281
II.2	Application	1.282
II.2	Application	1.283
II.2	Application	1.284
II.2	Application	1.285
II.2	Application	1.286
II.2	Application	1.287
II.2	Application	1.288
II.2	Application	1.289
II.2	Application	1.290
II.2	Application	1.291
II.2	Application	1.292
II.2	Application	1.293
II.2	Application	1.295
II.2	Application	1.296
II.2	Application	1.297
II.2	Application	1.298
II.2	Application	1.299
II.2	Application	1.300
II.2	Application	1.301
II.2	Application	1.302
II.2	Application	1.303
II.2	Application	1.304
II.2	Application	1.305
II.2	Application	1.306
II.2	Application	1.307
II.2	Application	1.308
II.2	Application	1.309
II.2	Application	1.310

CCS-P Exam Competency	CCS-P Exam Level	Question
II.2	Application	1.311
II.2	Application	1.312
II.2	Application	1.313
II.2	Application	1.314
II.2	Application	1.315
II.2	Application	1.316
II.2	Application	1.317
II.2	Application	1.318
II.2	Application	1.319
II.2	Application	1.320
II.2	Application	1.321
II.2	Application	1.322
II.2	Application	1.323
II.2	Application	1.324
II.2	Application	1.325
II.2	Application	1.326
II.2	Application	1.327
II.2	Application	1.328
II.2	Application	1.329
II.2	Application	1.330
II.2	Application	1.331
II.2	Application	1.332
II.2	Application	1.333
II.2	Application	1.334
II.2	Application	1.335
II.2	Application	1.336
II.2	Application	1.337
II.2	Application	1.338
II.2	Application	1.339
II.2	Application	1.340
II.2	Application	1.341
II.2	Application	1.342
II.2	Application	1.343
II.2	Application	1.344
II.2	Application	1.345
II.2	Application	1.346
II.2	Application	1.347
II.2	Application	1.348
II.2	Application	1.349
II.2	Application	1.350
II.2	Application	1.351

CCS-P Exam Competency	CCS-P Exam Level	Question
II.2	Application	1.352
II.2	Application	1.353
II.2	Application	1.354
II.2	Application	1.355
II.2	Application	1.356
II.2	Application	1.357
II.2	Application	1.358
II.2	Application	1.359
II.2	Application	1.360
II.2	Application	1.361
II.2	Application	1.362
II.2	Application	1.363
II.2	Application	1.364
II.2	Application	1.365
II.2	Application	1.366
II.2	Application	1.367
II.2	Application	1.368
II.2	Application	1.369
II.2	Application	1.370
II.2	Application	1.371
II.2	Application	1.372
II.2	Application	1.373
II.2	Application	1.374
II.2	Application	1.375
N/A	N/A	1.401
N/A	N/A	1.404
N/A	N/A	1.405
II.2	Recall	1.411
N/A	N/A	1.415
III.2.e	Application	2.336
III.1	Recall	2.337
III.1	Recall	2.338
III.1	Recall	2.339
III.1	Recall	2.341
III.2.f	Application	2.342
III.2.f	Application	2.344
III.2.f	Application	2.345
III.2.f	Application	2.346
III.2.f	Application	2.348
III.2.f	Application	2.349
III.2.f	Application	2.350

CCS-P Exam Competency	CCS-P Exam Level	Question
III.2.f	Application	2.351
III.2.f	Application	2.352
III.2.f	Application	2.353
III.2.f	Application	2.354
III.2.f	Application	2.355
N/A	N/A	3.21
N/A	N/A	3.22
II.2	Application	6.8
II.2	Application	6.11
II.2	Application	6.13
II.2	Application	6.14
II.2/III.2.a/III.3/ III.4	Application	6.28
III.2.a	Application	6.29
III.2.c/III.5	Application	6.30
III.2.f	Application	6.31
II.2	Application	6.32
II.2/III.2.c	Application	6.46
II.2/III.2.c	Application	6.62
II.2/III.2.a	Application	6.75
III.2.f	Application	6.76
II.2/III.2.c	Application	6.80
II.2/III.2.c	Application	6.81
II.2/III.2.c	Application	6.82
II.2	Application	6.83
II.2	Application	6.84
II.2/III.2.c	Application	6.86
II.2	Application	6.88
II.2	Application	6.89
II.2	Application	6.91
II.2	Application	6.92
II.2	Application	6.93
II.2	Application	6.95
II.2	Application	9.5
II.2	Application	9.6
II.2	Application	9.25
II.2	Application	9.26
II.2	Application	9.27
II.2/III.2.c/III.5	Application	9.45
II.2	Application	9.53
II.2	Application	9.75
N/A	ICD-10	10.27

CCS-P Exam Competency	CCS-P Exam Level	Question
III.5	Application	10.28
III.5	Application	10.29
III.5	Application	10.30
III.5	Application	10.31
III.5	Application	10.32
III.5	Application	10.33
III.5	Application	10.34
III.5	Recall	10.35
III.5	Recall	10.36
III.5	Recall	10.37
N/A	LTAC	10.41
N/A	LTAC	10.42
II.2/III.2.b/III.5	Application	6.3
III.2.c/III.2.f	Application	6.4
II.2/III.2.b/III.5	Application	6.5
III.2.c/III.5	Application	6.20
II.2/III.2.c/III.5	Application	6.21
II.1/II.10	Application	6.35
II.2/III.2.c	Application	6.48
II.1/II.10	Application	6.60
II.2/III.2.f/III.4	Application	6.61
II.2/III.2.c	Application	6.65
III.2.c	Application	6.66
II.2/III.2.b	Application	9.1
II.2/III.2.c	Application	9.3
II.2/II.2.c	Application	9.29
II.2/III.2.a,c/ III.4	Analysis	9.65
II.2/III.2.c	Application	6.49
III.2.c/III.5	Application	6.73
II.2/III.2.c	Application	9.35
II.2/III.2.c	Application	9.37
II.2/III.2.f	Application	9.41
II.2/III.2.a,c/ III.5	Application	9.51
II.2/III.2.c	Application	9.57
II.2/III.2.c/III.5	Application	9.67
II.2/III.2.c/III.5	Application	9.70
II.2/III.2.c	Analysis	9.71
II.2/III.2.c,f	Application	9.72
II.2/III.2.a,c	Application	9.76
II.2/III.2.b	Application	6.2

CCS-P Exam Competency	CCS-P Exam Level	Question
II.2/III.2.c	Application	6.6
II.2/III.2.c	Application	6.7
II.2/III.2.c/ III.2.f	Application	6.12
II.2/III.2.c	Application	6.15
II.2/III.2.c/III.5	Application	6.16
II.2/III.2.c/III.5	Application	6.17
III.2.c/III.5	Application	6.18
II.2/III.2.f	Application	6.19
II.2/III.2.a	Application	6.33
II.2	Application	6.34
II.2	Application	6.36
II.2	Application	6.37
II.2/III.2.c	Application	6.39
II.2/III.2.c	Application	6.41
II.2/III.2.c	Application	6.42
II.2/III.2.a,e,f/ III.4	Application	6.43
II.2/III.2.a,f	Application	6.45
III.2.c	Application	6.50
III.2.f	Application	6.51
II.2	Application	6.54
II.2/III.2.a,c	Application	6.55
II.2/III.2.f/III.4	Application	6.56
II.2/III.2.c,d	Application	6.57
II.2/III.2.c	Application	6.63
II.2/III.2.c	Application	6.64
II.2	Application	6.70
II.2/III.2.a,c	Application	6.74
II.2/III.2.a	Application	6.77
II.2/III.2.c	Application	6.78
II.2/III.2.a,f	Application	6.79
II.2/III.2.c	Application	6.87
II.2/III.2.c	Application	9.4
II.2/III.2.f	Application	9.7
II.2/III.2.c	Application	9.8
II.2/III.2.c/III.5	Application	9.17
II.2/III.2.c,d	Application	9.28
II.2/III.2.c	Application	9.34
II.2/III.2.a,f/ III.4	Application	9.39
II.2/III.2.c/III.5	Application	9.42

CCS-P Exam Competency	CCS-P Exam Level	Question	CCS-P Exam Competency	CCS-P Exam Level	Question
II.2/III.2.c	Application	9.44	II.2/III.2.c/III.5	Application	9.50
II.2/III.2.c/III.5	Application	9.46	II.2/III.2.c/III.5	Application	9.52
II.2/III.2.c,d/ III.5	Application	9.48	II.2	Application	6.53
II.2/III.2.a,f/ III.5	Application	9.54	II.2/III.2.a,f/ III.4	Application	9.33
II.2/III.2.a,f/ III.4	Application	9.60	III.2.a	Application	9.59
II.2/III.2.c	Application	9.62	II.2/III.2.c,d	Application	9.32
II.2/III.2.a	Application	9.64	II.2/III.2.c	Application	9.30
II.2/III.2.a	Application	9.66	II.2/III.2.c/III.5	Application	9.31
II.2/III.2.c/III.5	Application	9.68	II.2/III.2.a	Application	9.47
III.2.a,c	Application	9.80	II.1	Recall	1.1
II.2/III.2.c	Application	9.81	II.1	Recall	1.2
II.2/III.2.c/III.5	Application	9.14	II.1	Recall	1.4
II.2/III.2.c/III.5	Application	9.15	II.1	Application	1.5
II.2/III.2.c/III.5	Application	9.16	II.2	Recall	1.8
II.2/III.2.a	Application	9.69	II.1	Recall	1.9
III.2.c/III.5	Application	9.74	II.1	Recall	1.10
II.2/III.2.c/III.5	Application	9.82	II.1	Recall	1.11
II.2/III.2.a,c	Application	6.71	II.1	Recall	1.12
III.2.c	Application	6.72	II.1	Recall	1.13
II.2/III.2.a,c	Analysis	9.2	II.1	Recall	1.14
III.2.a,c/III.5	Analysis	9.63	II.1	Recall	1.15
II.2/III.2.c,f	Analysis	9.49	II.1	Recall	1.53
III.2.a	Application	6.24	I.2	Recall	1.66
II.2/III.2.a	Application	6.25	I.2	Recall	1.77
III.2.a/III.5	Application	6.26	I.2	Recall	1.81
II.2/III.2.a	Application	6.27	I.1	Recall	1.83
II.2/III.2.f	Application	6.38	II.2	Recall	1.96
II.2/III.2.c/III.5	Application	6.40	II.2	Application	1.118
II.2/III.2.a	Application	6.52	I.2	Recall	1.124
III.2.c	Application	6.67	I.2	Recall	1.127
II.2/III.2.c/ III.5	Application	6.69	II.2	Recall	1.140
II.2/III.2.a	Application	9.22	I.2	Recall	1.219
II.2/III.2.a,c,f	Application	9.38	I.2	Recall	1.220
II.2/III.2.a	Application	9.40	II.1	Recall	1.230
II.2/III.2.c	Application	9.55	II.1	Recall	1.231
II.2/III.2.c	Application	9.77	II.1	Recall	1.232
II.2/III.2.a,c	Application	9.13	II.2	Recall	1.234
II.2/III.2.c,d/ III.5	Application	9.43	N/A	N/A	1.249
			N/A	N/A	1.402
			II.2	Recall	1.407

CCS-P Exam Competency	CCS-P Exam Level	Question
II.1	Recall	1.410
II.1	Recall	1.412
II.2	Recall	1.413
II.2	Recall	1.414
II.1	Recall	1.417
II.1	Recall	1.418
II.2/III.2.c	Application	6.47
III.2.c	Application	6.58
II.2	Application	9.9
III.1	Recall	2.1
III.1	Recall	2.2
III.1	Recall	2.3
III.1	Recall	2.4
III.1	Recall	2.5
III.1	Recall	2.6
III.1	Recall	2.7
III.1	Recall	2.8
III.1	Recall	2.9
III.1	Recall	2.10
III.1	Recall	2.11
III.1	Recall	2.12
III.1	Recall	2.13
III.1	Recall	2.14
III.1	Recall	2.15
III.1	Recall	2.16
III.1	Recall	2.17
III.1	Recall	2.18
III.1	Recall	2.19
III.1	Recall	2.20
III.1	Recall	2.21
III.1	Recall	2.22
III.2.a	Application	2.23
III.1	Recall	2.24
III.2.a	Application	2.25
III.2.a	Application	2.26
III.2.a	Application	2.27
III.1	Recall	2.28
III.1	Recall	2.29
III.2.a	Application	2.30
III.1	Recall	2.31
III.1	Recall	2.32

CCS-P Exam Competency	CCS-P Exam Level	Question
III.1	Recall	2.33
III.1	Recall	2.34
III.2.a	Application	2.35
III.1	Recall	2.36
III.2.a	Recall	2.37
III.1	Recall	2.38
III.1	Recall	2.39
III.2.b	Application	2.56
III.2.b	Application	2.57
III.2.b	Application	2.59
III.2.b	Application	2.60
III.2.c	Application	2.73
III.2.c	Application	2.76
III.2.c	Application	2.77
III.2.c	Application	2.78
III.1	Recall	2.89
III.2.c	Application	2.119
III.2.c	Application	2.141
III.2.e	Application	2.317
III.2.f	Application	2.356
III.2.f	Application	2.357
III.2.f	Application	2.358
III.5	Recall	2.363
III.5	Recall	2.369
III.3	Recall	3.1
N/A	N/A	3.24
N/A	N/A	3.27
II.2/III.2.c	Application	6.85
II.2/III.2.c/III.5	Application	9.36
II.2/III.2.c/III.5	Application	9.73
II.2/III.2.a,c/ III.5	Application	9.79
II.2/III.2.c	Application	6.22
III.1	Application	2.40
III.1	Application	2.41
III.1	Application	2.42
III.1	Application	2.43
III.1	Application	2.44
III.1	Application	2.45
III.1	Application	2.46
III.1	Application	2.47

CCS-P Exam Competency	CCS-P Exam Level	Question	CCS-P Exam Competency	CCS-P Exam Level	Question
III.2.b	Application	2.48	III.2.c	Application	2.98
III.2.b	Application	2.49	III.2.c	Application	2.99
III.2.b	Application	2.50	III.2.c	Application	2.100
III.2.b	Application	2.51	III.2.c	Application	2.101
III.2.b	Application	2.52	III.2.c	Application	2.102
III.2.b	Application	2.53	III.1	Application	2.103
III.2.b	Application	2.54	III.2.c	Application	2.104
III.2.b	Application	2.55	III.2.c	Application	2.105
III.2.b	Application	2.58	III.2.c	Application	2.106
III.2.b	Application	2.61	III.2.c	Application	2.107
III.2.b	Application	2.62	III.2.c	Application	2.108
III.2.b	Application	2.63	III.2.c	Application	2.109
III.1	Application	2.64	III.1	Application	2.110
III.1	Application	2.65	III.2.c	Application	2.111
III.1	Application	2.66	III.2.c	Application	2.113
III.2.c	Application	2.67	III.2.c	Application	2.114
III.1	Application	2.68	III.2.c	Application	2.115
III.2.c	Application	2.69	III.2.c	Application	2.117
III.1	Application	2.70	III.2.c	Application	2.118
III.1	Application	2.71	III.2.c	Application	2.120
III.2.c	Application	2.72	III.2.c	Application	2.121
III.2.c	Application	2.74	III.2.c	Application	2.122
III.2.c	Application	2.75	III.2.c	Application	2.123
III.2.c	Application	2.79	III.2.c	Application	2.124
III.2.c	Application	2.80	III.2.c	Application	2.125
III.2.c	Application	2.81	III.1	Application	2.126
III.1	Application	2.82	III.2.c	Application	2.127
III.2.c	Application	2.83	III.2.c	Application	2.128
III.1	Application	2.84	III.2.c	Application	2.129
III.2.c	Application	2.85	III.1	Application	2.130
III.2.c	Application	2.86	III.1	Application	2.131
III.1	Application	2.87	III.1	Application	2.132
III.1	Application	2.88	III.2.c	Application	2.133
III.1	Application	2.90	III.2.c	Application	2.134
III.1	Application	2.91	III.1	Application	2.135
III.1	Application	2.92	III.2.c	Application	2.136
III.2.c	Application	2.93	III.2.c	Application	2.137
III.2.c	Application	2.94	III.2.c	Application	2.138
III.2.c	Application	2.95	III.2.c	Application	2.139
III.2.c	Application	2.97	III.2.c	Application	2.140

CCS-P Exam Competency	CCS-P Exam Level	Question
III.2.c	Application	2.142
III.2.c	Application	2.143
III.2.c	Application	2.145
III.2.c	Application	2.146
III.2.c	Application	2.147
III.2.c	Application	2.148
III.2.c	Application	2.149
III.2.c	Application	2.150
III.2.c	Application	2.151
III.2.c	Application	2.152
III.2.c	Application	2.153
III.2.c	Application	2.154
III.2.c	Application	2.155
III.2.c	Application	2.156
III.1	Application	2.157
III.2.c	Application	2.158
III.2.c	Application	2.159
III.1	Application	2.160
III.2.c	Application	2.161
III.2.c	Application	2.162
III.2.c	Application	2.163
III.2.c	Application	2.164
III.2.c	Application	2.165
III.2.c	Application	2.166
III.2.c	Application	2.167
III.2.c	Application	2.168
III.2.c	Application	2.169
III.2.c	Application	2.170
III.2.c	Application	2.171
III.2.c	Application	2.172
III.2.c	Application	2.173
III.2.c	Application	2.174
III.2.c	Application	2.175
III.2.c	Application	2.176
III.2.c	Application	2.177
III.2.c	Application	2.178
III.2.c	Application	2.179
III.2.c	Application	2.180
III.2.c	Application	2.181
III.2.c	Application	2.182

CCS-P Exam Competency	CCS-P Exam Level	Question
III.2.c	Application	2.183
III.2.c	Application	2.184
III.2.c	Application	2.185
III.2.c	Application	2.186
III.2.c	Application	2.187
III.2.c	Application	2.188
III.2.c	Application	2.189
III.2.c	Application	2.190
III.2.c	Application	2.191
III.2.c	Application	2.192
III.2.c	Application	2.193
III.2.c	Application	2.194
III.2.c	Application	2.195
III.2.c	Application	2.196
III.2.c	Application	2.197
III.2.c	Application	2.198
III.2.c	Application	2.199
III.2.c	Application	2.200
III.2.c	Application	2.201
III.2.c	Application	2.202
III.2.c	Application	2.203
III.2.c	Application	2.204
III.2.c	Application	2.205
III.2.c	Application	2.206
III.2.c	Application	2.207
III.2.c	Application	2.208
III.2.c	Application	2.209
III.2.c	Application	2.210
III.2.c	Application	2.211
III.2.c	Application	2.212
III.2.c	Application	2.213
III.2.c	Application	2.214
III.2.c	Application	2.215
III.2.c	Application	2.216
III.2.c	Application	2.217
III.2.c	Application	2.218
III.2.c	Application	2.219
III.2.c	Application	2.220
III.2.c	Application	2.221
III.2.c	Application	2.222

CCS-P Exam Competency	CCS-P Exam Level	Question		CCS-P Exam Competency	CCS-P Exam Level	Question
III.2.c	Application	2.223		III.2.c	Application	2.263
III.2.c	Application	2.224		III.2.c	Application	2.264
III.2.c	Application	2.225		III.2.c	Application	2.265
III.2.c	Application	2.226		III.2.c	Application	2.266
III.2.c	Application	2.227		III.2.c	Application	2.267
III.2.c	Application	2.228		III.2.c	Application	2.268
III.2.c	Application	2.229		III.2.c	Application	2.269
III.2.c	Application	2.230		III.2.c	Application	2.270
III.2.c	Application	2.231		III.2.c	Application	2.271
III.2.c	Application	2.232		III.2.c	Application	2.272
III.2.c	Application	2.233		III.2.c	Application	2.273
III.2.c	Application	2.234		III.2.c	Application	2.274
III.2.c	Application	2.235		III.2.c	Application	2.275
III.2.c	Application	2.236		III.2.c	Application	2.276
III.2.c	Application	2.237		III.2.c	Application	2.277
III.2.c	Application	2.238		III.2.c	Application	2.278
III.2.c	Application	2.239		III.2.c	Application	2.279
III.2.c	Application	2.240		III.2.c	Application	2.280
III.2.c	Application	2.241		III.2.c	Application	2.281
III.2.c	Application	2.242		III.2.c	Application	2.282
III.2.c	Application	2.243		III.2.c	Application	2.283
III.2.c	Application	2.244		III.2.c	Application	2.284
III.2.c	Application	2.245		III.2.c	Application	2.285
III.2.c	Application	2.246		III.2.c	Application	2.286
III.2.c	Application	2.247		III.2.c	Application	2.287
III.2.c	Application	2.248		III.2.c	Application	2.288
III.2.c	Application	2.249		III.2.c	Application	2.289
III.2.c	Application	2.250		III.2.c	Application	2.290
III.2.c	Application	2.251		III.2.c	Application	2.291
III.2.c	Application	2.252		III.1	Application	2.292
III.2.c	Application	2.253		III.2.d	Application	2.293
III.2.c	Application	2.254		III.2.d	Application	2.294
III.2.c	Application	2.255		III.2.d	Application	2.295
III.2.c	Application	2.256		III.2.d	Application	2.296
III.2.c	Application	2.257		III.2.d	Application	2.297
III.2.c	Application	2.258		III.2.d	Application	2.298
III.2.c	Application	2.259		III.2.d	Application	2.299
III.2.c	Application	2.260		III.2.d	Application	2.300
III.2.c	Application	2.261		III.2.d	Application	2.301
III.2.c	Application	2.262		III.2.d	Application	2.302

CCS-P Exam Competency	CCS-P Exam Level	Question	CCS-P Exam Competency	CCS-P Exam Level	Question
III.2.d	Application	2.303	III.2.c/III.5	Application	2.368
III.2.d	Application	2.304	III.5	Application	2.370
III.2.d	Application	2.305	III.5	Application	2.371
III.2.d	Application	2.306	III.5	Application	2.372
III.2.d	Application	2.307	III.2.c/III.5	Application	2.373
III.2.d	Application	2.308	III.5	Application	2.374
III.2.d	Application	2.309	III.5	Application	2.375
III.2.d	Application	2.310	III.5	Application	2.376
III.2.d	Application	2.311	III.5	Application	2.377
III.2.d	Application	2.312	III.5	Application	2.378
III.1	Application	2.313	III.5	Application	2.379
III.2.e	Application	2.314	III.5	Application	2.380
III.1	Application	2.315	III.5	Application	2.381
III.1	Application	2.316	III.1	Application	2.382
III.2.e	Application	2.318	III.1	Application	2.383
III.2.e	Application	2.319	III.1	Application	2.384
III.2.e	Application	2.320	III.2.g	Application	2.385
III.2.e	Application	2.321	III.2.g	Application	2.386
III.2.e	Application	2.322	III.2.g	Application	2.387
III.2.e	Application	2.323	III.2.g	Application	2.388
III.2.e	Application	2.324	III.2.g	Application	2.389
III.2.e	Application	2.325	III.2.g	Application	2.390
III.2.e	Application	2.326	III.2.g	Application	2.391
III.2.e	Application	2.327	III.2.g	Application	2.392
III.2.e	Application	2.328	III.2.g	Application	2.393
III.2.e	Application	2.329	III.2.g	Application	2.394
III.2.e	Application	2.330	III.1	Application	2.395
III.2.e	Application	2.331	III.2.g	Application	2.396
III.2.e	Application	2.332	III.2.g	Application	2.397
III.2.e	Application	2.333	III.2.g	Application	2.398
III.2.e	Application	2.334	III.2.g	Application	2.399
III.2.e	Application	2.335	III.2.g	Application	2.400
III.2.f	Application	2.359	III.2.g	Application	2.401
III.2.f	Application	2.360	III.2.c	Application	2.402
III.2.f	Application	2.361	III.2.c	Application	2.403
III.5	Application	2.362	III.2.c	Application	2.404
III.5	Application	2.364	III.2.c	Application	2.405
III.5	Application	2.365	III.2.c	Application	2.406
III.5	Application	2.366	III.2.c	Application	2.407
III.5	Application	2.367	III.2.c	Application	2.408

CCS-P Exam Competency	CCS-P Exam Level	Question
III.2.c	Application	2.409
III.2.c	Application	2.410
III.2.c	Application	2.411
III.2.c	Application	2.412
III.2.c	Application	2.413
III.2.c	Application	2.414
III.2.c	Application	2.415
III.2.c	Application	2.416
III.2.c	Application	2.417
III.2.c	Application	2.418
III.2.c	Application	2.419
III.2.c	Application	2.420
III.2.c	Application	2.421
III.2.c	Application	2.422
III.2.d	Application	2.423
III.2.e	Application	2.424
III.2.f	Application	2.425
III.2.f	Application	2.426
N/A	N/A	3.28
N/A	N/A	3.29
N/A	N/A	3.30
III.4	Application	3.31
III.4	Application	3.32
III.4	Application	3.33
III.4	Application	3.34
III.4	Application	3.35
III.4	Application	3.36
III.4	Application	3.37
III.4	Application	3.38
III.4	Application	3.39
III.4	Application	3.40
III.4	Application	3.41
III.4	Application	3.42
III.4	Application	3.43
III.4	Application	3.44
III.4	Application	3.45
III.4	Application	3.46
III.4	Application	3.47
III.4	Application	3.48
III.4	Application	3.49

CCS-P Exam Competency	CCS-P Exam Level	Question
III.4	Application	3.50
III.2.b	Application	6.1
III.2.c,f	Application	6.90
III.2.c	Application	6.94
III.2.c	Application	9.10
III.2.c	Application	9.11
III.2.f/III.5	Application	9.12
II.2/III.2.a,f/III.5	Application	9.56
III.2.f	Application	2.340
III.1	Recall	2.343
III.2.f	Application	2.347
II.2/III.2.f	Application	6.44
II.2/III.2.c	Application	6.59
II.2/III.2.c/ III.5	Application	6.68
III.2.c/III.2.e	Application	6.9
III.2.c	Application	6.10
III.2.c	Application	6.23
III.2.a	Analysis	9.18
III.2.a	Analysis	9.19
III.2.a	Analysis	9.20
III.2.a	Application	9.21
III.2.a	Application	9.23
III.2.a	Application	9.24
II.2/III.2.c/III.5	Application	9.58
II.2/III.2.c/III.5	Application	9.61
II.2/III.2.a,c/III.5	Application	9.78
III.2.c	Application	2.112
III.4	Application	3.2
III.4	Application	3.3
III.4	Application	3.4
III.4	Application	3.5
III.4	Application	3.6
III.4	Application	3.7
III.4	Application	3.8
III.4	Application	3.9
III.4	Application	3.10
III.4	Application	3.11
III.4	Application	3.12
III.4	Application	3.13
III.4	Application	3.14

CCS-P Exam Competency	CCS-P Exam Level	Question
III.4	Application	3.15
III.4	Application	3.16
III.4	Application	3.17
III.4	Application	3.18
III.4	Application	3.19
III.4	Application	3.20
N/A	N/A	3.23
N/A	N/A	3.25
N/A	N/A	3.26
II.3	Recall	1.7
N/A	N/A	1.3
N/A	N/A	1.38
N/A	N/A	1.39
N/A	N/A	1.294
N/A	N/A	1.376
N/A	N/A	1.377
N/A	N/A	1.378
N/A	N/A	1.379
N/A	N/A	1.380
N/A	N/A	1.381
N/A	N/A	1.382
N/A	N/A	1.383
N/A	N/A	1.384
N/A	N/A	1.385
N/A	N/A	1.386
N/A	N/A	1.387
N/A	N/A	1.388
N/A	N/A	1.389
N/A	N/A	1.390
N/A	N/A	1.391
N/A	N/A	1.392
N/A	N/A	1.393
N/A	N/A	1.394
N/A	N/A	1.395
N/A	N/A	1.396
N/A	N/A	1.397
N/A	N/A	1.398
N/A	N/A	1.399
N/A	N/A	1.400
N/A	N/A	1.408

CCS-P Exam Competency	CCS-P Exam Level	Question
N/A	N/A	1.409
N/A	N/A	1.419
N/A	N/A	1.420
N/A	N/A	1.421
N/A	N/A	1.422
N/A	N/A	1.423
N/A	N/A	4.1
N/A	N/A	4.2
N/A	N/A	4.3
N/A	N/A	4.4
N/A	N/A	4.5
N/A	N/A	4.6
N/A	N/A	4.7
N/A	N/A	4.8
N/A	N/A	4.9
N/A	N/A	4.10
N/A	N/A	4.11
N/A	N/A	4.12
N/A	N/A	4.13
N/A	N/A	4.14
N/A	N/A	4.15
N/A	N/A	4.16
N/A	N/A	4.17
N/A	N/A	4.18
N/A	N/A	4.19
N/A	N/A	4.20
N/A	N/A	4.21
N/A	N/A	4.22
N/A	N/A	4.23
N/A	N/A	4.24
N/A	N/A	4.25
N/A	N/A	4.26
N/A	N/A	4.27
N/A	N/A	4.28
N/A	N/A	4.29
N/A	N/A	4.30
N/A	N/A	4.31
N/A	N/A	4.32
N/A	N/A	4.33
N/A	N/A	4.34

CCS-P Exam Competency	CCS-P Exam Level	Question		CCS-P Exam Competency	CCS-P Exam Level	Question
N/A	N/A	4.35		N/A	N/A	4.74
N/A	N/A	4.36		N/A	N/A	4.75
N/A	N/A	4.37		N/A	N/A	4.76
N/A	N/A	4.38		N/A	N/A	4.77
N/A	N/A	4.39		N/A	N/A	4.78
N/A	N/A	4.40		N/A	N/A	4.79
N/A	N/A	4.41		N/A	N/A	4.80
N/A	N/A	4.42		N/A	N/A	4.81
N/A	N/A	4.43		N/A	N/A	4.82
N/A	N/A	4.44		N/A	N/A	4.83
N/A	N/A	4.45		N/A	N/A	4.84
N/A	N/A	4.46		N/A	N/A	4.85
N/A	N/A	4.47		N/A	N/A	4.86
N/A	N/A	4.48		N/A	N/A	4.87
N/A	N/A	4.49		N/A	N/A	4.88
N/A	N/A	4.50		N/A	N/A	4.89
N/A	N/A	4.51		N/A	N/A	4.90
N/A	N/A	4.52		N/A	N/A	4.91
N/A	N/A	4.53		N/A	N/A	4.92
N/A	N/A	4.54		N/A	N/A	4.93
N/A	N/A	4.55		N/A	N/A	4.94
N/A	N/A	4.56		N/A	N/A	4.95
N/A	N/A	4.57		N/A	N/A	4.96
N/A	N/A	4.58		N/A	N/A	4.97
N/A	N/A	4.59		N/A	N/A	4.98
N/A	N/A	4.60		N/A	N/A	4.99
N/A	N/A	4.61		N/A	N/A	5.1
N/A	N/A	4.62		N/A	N/A	5.2
N/A	N/A	4.63		N/A	N/A	5.3
N/A	N/A	4.64		N/A	N/A	5.4
N/A	N/A	4.65		N/A	N/A	5.5
N/A	N/A	4.66		N/A	N/A	5.6
N/A	N/A	4.67		N/A	N/A	5.7
N/A	N/A	4.68		N/A	N/A	5.8
N/A	N/A	4.69		N/A	N/A	5.9
N/A	N/A	4.70		N/A	N/A	5.10
N/A	N/A	4.71		N/A	N/A	5.11
N/A	N/A	4.72		N/A	N/A	5.12
N/A	N/A	4.73		N/A	N/A	5.13

CCS-P Exam Competency	CCS-P Exam Level	Question	CCS-P Exam Competency	CCS-P Exam Level	Question
N/A	N/A	5.14	N/A	N/A	5.53
N/A	N/A	5.15	N/A	N/A	5.54
N/A	N/A	5.16	N/A	N/A	5.55
N/A	N/A	5.17	N/A	N/A	5.56
N/A	N/A	5.18	N/A	N/A	5.57
N/A	N/A	5.19	N/A	N/A	5.58
N/A	N/A	5.20	N/A	N/A	5.59
N/A	N/A	5.21	N/A	N/A	5.60
N/A	N/A	5.22	N/A	N/A	5.61
N/A	N/A	5.23	N/A	N/A	5.62
N/A	N/A	5.24	N/A	N/A	5.63
N/A	N/A	5.25	N/A	N/A	5.64
N/A	N/A	5.26	N/A	N/A	5.65
N/A	N/A	5.27	N/A	N/A	5.66
N/A	N/A	5.28	N/A	N/A	5.67
N/A	N/A	5.29	N/A	N/A	5.68
N/A	N/A	5.30	N/A	N/A	5.69
N/A	N/A	5.31	N/A	N/A	5.70
N/A	N/A	5.32	N/A	N/A	5.71
N/A	N/A	5.33	N/A	N/A	5.72
N/A	N/A	5.34	N/A	N/A	5.73
N/A	N/A	5.35	N/A	N/A	5.74
N/A	N/A	5.36	N/A	N/A	5.75
N/A	N/A	5.37	N/A	N/A	5.76
N/A	N/A	5.38	N/A	N/A	5.77
N/A	N/A	5.39	N/A	N/A	5.78
N/A	N/A	5.40	N/A	N/A	5.79
N/A	N/A	5.41	N/A	N/A	5.80
N/A	N/A	5.42	N/A	N/A	5.81
N/A	N/A	5.43	N/A	N/A	5.82
N/A	N/A	5.44	N/A	N/A	5.83
N/A	N/A	5.45	N/A	N/A	5.84
N/A	N/A	5.46	N/A	N/A	5.85
N/A	N/A	5.47	N/A	N/A	5.86
N/A	N/A	5.48	N/A	N/A	5.87
N/A	N/A	5.49	N/A	N/A	5.88
N/A	N/A	5.50	N/A	N/A	5.89
N/A	N/A	5.51	N/A	N/A	5.90
N/A	N/A	5.52	N/A	N/A	7.1

CCS-P Exam Competency	CCS-P Exam Level	Question	CCS-P Exam Competency	CCS-P Exam Level	Question
N/A	N/A	7.2	N/A	N/A	7.40
N/A	N/A	7.3	N/A	N/A	7.41
N/A	N/A	7.4	N/A	N/A	7.42
N/A	N/A	7.5	N/A	N/A	7.43
N/A	N/A	7.6	N/A	N/A	7.44
N/A	N/A	7.7	N/A	N/A	7.45
N/A	N/A	7.8	N/A	N/A	7.46
N/A	N/A	7.9	N/A	N/A	7.47
N/A	N/A	7.10	N/A	N/A	7.48
N/A	N/A	7.11	N/A	N/A	7.49
N/A	N/A	7.12	N/A	N/A	7.50
N/A	N/A	7.13	N/A	N/A	7.51
N/A	N/A	7.14	N/A	N/A	7.52
N/A	N/A	7.15	N/A	N/A	7.53
N/A	N/A	7.16	N/A	N/A	7.54
N/A	N/A	7.17	N/A	N/A	7.55
N/A	N/A	7.18	N/A	N/A	7.56
N/A	N/A	7.19	N/A	N/A	7.57
N/A	N/A	7.20	N/A	N/A	7.58
N/A	N/A	7.21	N/A	N/A	7.59
N/A	N/A	7.22	N/A	N/A	7.60
N/A	N/A	7.23	N/A	N/A	7.61
N/A	N/A	7.24	N/A	Home Health	10.1
N/A	N/A	7.25	N/A	Home Health	10.2
N/A	N/A	7.26	N/A	Home Health	10.3
N/A	N/A	7.27	N/A	Home Health	10.4
N/A	N/A	7.28	N/A	Home Health	10.5
N/A	N/A	7.29	N/A	Home Health	10.6
N/A	N/A	7.30	N/A	Home Health	10.7
N/A	N/A	7.31	N/A	Home Health	10.8
N/A	N/A	7.32	N/A	Home Health	10.9
N/A	N/A	7.33	N/A	Home Health	10.10
N/A	N/A	7.34	N/A	Home Health	10.11
N/A	N/A	7.35	N/A	Home Health	10.12
N/A	N/A	7.36	N/A	Home Health	10.13
N/A	N/A	7.37	I.5	Home Health	10.14
N/A	N/A	7.38	N/A	ICD-10	10.15
N/A	N/A	7.39	N/A	ICD-10	10.16

CCS-P Exam Competency	CCS-P Exam Level	Question
N/A	ICD-10	10.17
N/A	ICD-10	10.18
N/A	ICD-10	10.19
N/A	ICD-10	10.20
N/A	ICD-10	10.21
N/A	ICD-10	10.22
N/A	ICD-10	10.23
N/A	ICD-10	10.24
N/A	ICD-10	10.25
N/A	ICD-10	10.26
III.5	Recall	10.38

CCS-P Exam Competency	CCS-P Exam Level	Question
III.5	Application	10.39
N/A	LTAC	10.40
N/A	LTAC	10.43
II.1	Application	10.44
II.1	Application	10.45
N/A	IRF	10.46
N/A	IRF	10.47
N/A	IRF	10.48
N/A	SNF	10.49
N/A	SNF	10.50
N/A	SNF	10.51

Question Number Index to Competencies

Chapter 1

Question	CCA Exam Competency	CCA Exam Level	CCS Exam Competency	CCS Exam Level	CCS-P Exam Competency	CCS-P Exam Level
1.1	III.6	Recall	II.3	Recall	II.1	Recall
1.2	III.6	Recall	II.3	Recall	II.1	Recall
1.3	III.6	Recall	II.4/IV.1	Recall	N/A	N/A
1.4	III.6	Recall	II.1	Recall	II.1	Recall
1.5	III.2.a	Application	II.2	Recall	II.1	Recall
1.6	III.6	Recall	II.1/II.2	Recall	I.3	Recall
1.7	III.6	Recall	II.1/II.2	Recall	II.3	Recall
1.8	III.6	Recall	I.1	Recall	II.2	Recall
1.9	III.6	Recall	IX.1	Recall	II.2	Recall
1.10	III.6	Recall	II.3	Recall	II.1	Recall
1.11	III.6	Recall	II.3	Recall	II.1	Recall
1.12	III.6	Recall	II.3	Recall	II.1	Recall
1.13	III.6	Recall	II.3	Recall	II.1	Recall
1.14	III.6	Recall	II.3	Recall	II.1	Recall
1.15	III.6	Recall	II.3	Recall	II.1	Recall
1.16	III.2.a	Application	II.1/II.2	Application	II.2	Application
1.17	III.2.a	Application	II.1/II.2	Application	II.2	Application
1.18	III.2.a	Application	II.1/II.2	Application	II.2	Application
1.19	III.6	Application	II.1/II.2	Application	II.2	Application
1.20	III.2.a	Application	II.1/II.2	Application	II.2	Application
1.21	III.2.a	Application	II.1/II.2	Application	II.2	Application
1.22	III.2.a	Application	II.1/II.2	Application	II.2	Application
1.23	III.2.a	Application	II.1	Application	II.2	Application
1.24	III.2.a	Application	II.2	Application	II.2	Application
1.25	III.2.a	Application	II.1/II.2	Application	II.2	Application
1.26	III.2.a	Application	II.1/II.2	Application	II.2	Application
1.27	III.2.a	Application	II.1/II.2	Application	II.2	Application
1.28	III.2.a	Application	II.1/II.2	Application	II.2	Application
1.29	III.2.a	Application	II.1/II.2	Application	II.2	Application
1.30	III.2.a	Application	II.1/II.2	Application	II.2	Application
1.31	III.2.a	Application	II.1/II.2	Application	II.2	Application
1.32	III.2.a	Application	II.1/II.2	Application	II.2	Application
1.33	III.2.a	Application	II.1/II.2	Application	II.2	Application
1.34	III.2.a	Application	II.1/II.2	Application	II.2	Application
1.35	III.2.a	Application	II.1/II.2	Application	II.2	Application
1.36	III.2.a	Application	II.1/II.2	Application	II.2	Application
1.37	III.2.a	Application	II.1/II.2	Application	II.2	Application
1.38	III.2.a	Application	II.1	Recall	N/A	N/A

Question	CCA Exam Competency	CCA Exam Level	CCS Exam Competency	CCS Exam Level	CCS-P Exam Competency	CCS-P Exam Level
1.39	III.2.a	Application	II.1	Application	N/A	N/A
1.40	III.2.a	Application	II.1/II.2	Application	II.2	Application
1.41	III.2.a	Application	II.1/II.2	Application	II.2	Application
1.42	III.2.a	Application	II.1/II.2	Application	I.2	Application
1.43	III.2.a	Application	II.1/II.2	Application	II.2	Application
1.44	III.2.a	Application	II.1/II.2	Application	II.2	Application
1.45	III.2.a	Application	II.1/II.2	Application	II.2	Application
1.46	III.2.a	Application	II.1/II.2	Application	II.2	Application
1.47	III.2.a	Application	II.1/II.2	Application	II.2	Application
1.48	III.6	Recall	I.1	Recall	I.2	Recall
1.49	III.6	Application	II.1/II.2	Application	I.2	Application
1.50	III.6	Recall	II.1/II.2	Application	I.2	Application
1.51	III.2.a	Application	II.1/II.2	Application	II.2	Application
1.52	III.2.a	Application	II.1/II.2	Application	II.1/II.2	Application
1.53	III.2.a	Recall	II.3	Recall	II.1	Recall
1.54	III.2.a	Application	II.1/II.2	Application	II.2	Application
1.55	III.2.a	Application	II.1/II.2	Application	II.2	Application
1.56	III.2.a	Application	II.1/II.2	Application	II.2	Application
1.57	III.2.a	Application	II.1/II.2	Application	II.2	Application
1.58	III.2.a	Application	II.1/II.2	Application	II.2	Application
1.59	III.6	Application	I.1	Recall	I.2	Recall
1.60	III.2.a	Application	II.1/II.2	Application	II.2	Application
1.61	III.2.a	Application	II.1/II.2	Application	II.2	Application
1.62	III.2.a	Application	II.1/II.2	Application	II.2	Application
1.63	III.2.a	Application	II.1/II.2	Application	II.2	Application
1.64	III.2.a	Application	II.1/II.2	Application	II.2	Application
1.65	III.2.a	Application	II.1/II.2	Application	II.2	Application
1.66	III.6	Recall	II.3	Recall	I.2	Recall
1.67	III.2.a	Application	II.1/II.2	Application	II.2	Application
1.68	III.2.a	Application	II.1/II.2	Application	II.2	Application
1.69	III.2.a	Application	II.1/II.2	Application	II.2	Application
1.70	III.6	Application	II.1/II.2	Application	II.2	Application
1.71	III.2.a	Application	II.1/II.2	Application	II.2	Application
1.72	III.2.a	Application	II.1/II.2	Application	II.2	Application
1.73	III.2.a	Application	II.1/II.2	Application	II.2	Application
1.74	III.2.a	Application	II.1/II.2	Application	II.2	Application
1.75	III.2.a	Application	II.1/II.2	Application	II.2	Application
1.76	III.2.a	Application	II.1/II.2	Application	II.2	Application
1.77	III.6	Recall	II.3	Recall	I.2	Recall
1.78	III.2.a	Application	II.1/II.2	Application	II.2	Application

Question	CCA Exam Competency	CCA Exam Level	CCS Exam Competency	CCS Exam Level	CCS-P Exam Competency	CCS-P Exam Level
1.79	III.2.a	Application	II.1/II.2	Application	II.2	Application
1.80	III.2.a	Application	II.1/II.2	Application	II.2	Application
1.81	III.6	Recall	II.3	Recall	I.2	Recall
1.82	III.2.a	Application	II.1/II.2	Application	II.2	Application
1.83	III.6	Recall	II.3	Recall	II.2	Recall
1.84	III.2.a	Application	II.1/II.2	Application	II.2	Application
1.85	III.2.a	Application	II.1/II.2	Application	II.2	Application
1.86	III.2.a	Application	II.1/II.2	Application	II.2	Application
1.87	III.2.a	Application	II.1/II.2	Application	II.2	Application
1.88	III.2.a	Application	II.1/II.2	Application	II.2	Application
1.89	III.2.a	Application	II.1/II.2	Application	II.2	Application
1.90	III.2.a	Application	II.1/II.2	Application	II.2	Application
1.91	III.2.a	Application	II.1/II.2	Application	II.2	Application
1.92	III.2.a	Application	II.1/II.2	Application	II.2	Application
1.93	III.2.a	Application	II.1/II.2	Application	II.2	Application
1.94	III.2.a	Application	II.1/II.2	Application	II.2	Application
1.95	III.2.a	Application	II.1/II.2	Application	II.2	Application
1.96	III.6	Recall	II.3	Recall	II.2	Recall
1.97	III.2.a	Application	II.1/II.2	Application	II.2	Application
1.98	III.2.a	Application	II.1/II.2	Application	II.2	Application
1.99	III.2.a	Application	II.1/II.2	Application	II.2	Application
1.100	III.2.a	Application	II.1/II.2	Application	II.2	Application
1.101	III.6	Recall	I.1	Recall	I.2	Recall
1.102	III.2.a	Application	II.1/II.2	Application	II.2	Application
1.103	III.6	Recall	I.1	Recall	II.1	Recall
1.104	III.2.a	Application	II.1/II.2	Application	II.2	Application
1.105	III.2.a	Application	II.1/II.2	Application	II.2	Application
1.106	III.2.a	Application	II.1/II.2	Application	II.2	Application
1.107	III.2.a	Application	II.1/II.2	Application	II.2	Application
1.108	III.2.a	Application	II.1/II.2	Application	II.2	Application
1.109	III.2.a	Application	II.1/II.2	Application	II.2	Application
1.110	III.2.a	Application	II.1/II.2	Application	II.2	Application
1.111	III.2.a	Application	II.1/II.2	Application	II.2	Application
1.112	III.2.a	Application	II.1/II.2	Application	II.2	Application
1.113	III.2.a	Application	II.1/II.2	Application	II.2	Application
1.114	III.2.a	Application	II.1/II.2	Application	II.2	Application
1.115	III.2.a	Application	II.1/II.2	Application	II.2	Application
1.116	III.2.a	Application	II.1/II.2	Application	II.2	Application
1.117	III.2.a	Application	II.1/II.2	Application	II.2	Application
1.118	III.2.a,b	Application	II.3	Application	II.2	Application

Question	CCA Exam Competency	CCA Exam Level	CCS Exam Competency	CCS Exam Level	CCS-P Exam Competency	CCS-P Exam Level
1.119	III.2.a	Application	II.1/II.2	Application	II.2	Application
1.120	III.2.a	Application	II.1/II.2	Application	II.2	Application
1.121	III.2.a	Application	II.1/II.2	Application	II.2	Application
1.122	III.2.a	Application	II.1/II.2	Application	II.2	Application
1.123	III.2.a	Application	II.1/II.2	Application	II.2	Application
1.124	III.6	Recall	II.3	Recall	I.2	Recall
1.125	III.2.a	Application	II.1/II.2	Application	II.2	Application
1.126	III.2.a	Application	II.1/II.2	Application	II.2	Application
1.127	III.6	Recall	II.3	Recall	I.2	Recall
1.128	III.2.a	Application	II.1/II.2	Application	II.2	Application
1.129	III.2.a	Application	II.1/II.2	Application	II.2	Application
1.130	III.2.a	Application	II.1/II.2	Application	II.2	Application
1.131	III.2.a	Application	II.1/II.2	Application	II.2	Application
1.132	III.2.a	Application	II.1/II.2	Application	II.2	Application
1.133	III.2.a	Application	II.1/II.2	Application	II.2	Application
1.134	III.2.a	Application	II.1/II.2	Application	II.2	Application
1.135	III.2.a	Application	II.1/II.2	Application	II.2	Application
1.136	III.2.a	Application	II.1/II.2	Application	II.2	Application
1.137	III.2.a/III.2.b	Application	II.1/II.2	Application	II.2	Application
1.138	III.2.a	Application	II.1/II.2	Application	II.2	Application
1.139	III.2.a	Application	II.1	Application	II.2	Application
1.140	III.6	Recall	II.3	Recall	II.2	Recall
1.141	III.2.a	Application	II.1/II.2	Application	II.2	Application
1.142	III.6	Recall	I.1	Application	II.1	Application
1.143	III.2.a	Application	II.1/II.2	Application	II.2	Application
1.144	III.2.a	Application	II.1/II.2	Application	II.2	Application
1.145	III.2.a	Application	II.1/II.2	Application	II.2	Application
1.146	III.2.a	Application	II.1/II.2	Application	II.2	Application
1.147	III.2.a	Application	II.1/II.2	Application	II.2	Application
1.148	III.2.a	Application	II.1/II.2	Application	II.2	Application
1.149	III.2.a	Application	II.1/II.2	Application	II.2	Application
1.150	III.2.a	Application	II.1/II.2	Application	II.2	Application
1.151	III.2.a	Application	II.1/II.2	Application	II.2	Application
1.152	III.2.a	Application	II.1/II.2	Application	II.2	Application
1.153	III.2.a	Application	II.1/II.2	Application	II.2	Application
1.154	III.2.a	Application	II.1/II.2	Application	II.2	Application
1.155	III.2.a	Application	II.1/II.2	Application	II.2	Application
1.156	III.2.a	Application	II.1/II.2	Application	II.2	Application
1.157	III.2.a	Application	II.1/II.2	Application	II.2	Application
1.158	III.2.a	Application	II.1/II.2	Application	II.2	Application

Question	CCA Exam Competency	CCA Exam Level	CCS Exam Competency	CCS Exam Level	CCS-P Exam Competency	CCS-P Exam Level
1.159	III.2.a	Application	II.1/II.2	Application	II.2	Application
1.160	III.2.a	Application	II.1/II.2	Application	II.2	Application
1.161	III.2.a	Application	II.1/II.2	Application	II.2	Application
1.162	III.2.a	Application	II.1/II.2	Application	II.2	Application
1.163	III.2.a	Application	II.1/II.2	Application	II.2	Application
1.164	III.2.a	Application	II.1/II.2	Application	II.2	Application
1.165	III.2.a	Application	II.1/II.2	Application	II.2	Application
1.166	III.2.a	Application	II.1/II.2	Application	II.2	Application
1.167	III.2.a	Application	II.1/II.2	Application	II.2	Application
1.168	III.2.a	Application	II.1/II.2	Application	II.2	Application
1.169	III.2.a	Application	II.1/II.2	Application	II.2	Application
1.170	III.2.a	Application	II.1/II.2	Application	II.2	Application
1.171	III.2.a	Application	II.1/II.2	Application	II.2	Application
1.172	III.2.a	Application	II.1/II.2	Application	II.2	Application
1.173	III.2.a	Application	II.1/II.2	Application	II.2	Application
1.174	III.2.a	Application	II.1/II.2	Application	II.2	Application
1.175	III.2.a	Application	II.1/II.2	Application	II.2	Application
1.176	III.2.a	Application	II.1/II.2	Application	II.2	Application
1.177	III.2.a	Application	II.1/II.2	Application	II.2	Application
1.178	III.2.a	Application	II.1/II.2	Application	II.2	Application
1.179	III.2.a	Application	II.1/II.2	Application	II.2	Application
1.180	III.2.a	Application	II.1/II.2	Application	II.2	Application
1.181	III.2.a	Application	II.1/II.2	Application	II.2	Application
1.182	III.2.a	Application	II.1/II.2	Application	II.2	Application
1.183	III.2.a	Application	II.1/II.2	Application	II.2	Application
1.184	III.2.a	Application	II.1/II.2	Application	II.2	Application
1.185	III.2.a	Application	II.1/II.2	Application	II.2	Application
1.186	III.2.a	Application	II.1/II.2	Application	II.2	Application
1.187	III.2.a	Application	II.1/II.2	Application	II.2	Application
1.188	III.2.a	Application	II.1/II.2	Application	II.2	Application
1.189	III.2.a	Application	II.1/II.2	Application	II.2	Application
1.190	III.2.a	Application	II.1/II.2	Application	II.2	Application
1.191	III.2.a	Application	II.1/II.2	Application	II.2	Application
1.192	III.2.a	Application	II.1/II.2	Application	II.2	Application
1.193	III.2.a	Application	II.1/II.2	Application	II.2	Application
1.194	III.2.a	Application	II.1/II.2	Application	II.2	Application
1.195	III.2.a	Application	II.1/II.2	Application	II.2	Application
1.196	III.2.a	Application	II.1/II.2	Application	II.2	Application
1.197	III.2.a	Application	II.1/II.2	Application	II.2	Application
1.198	III.2.a	Application	II.1/II.2	Application	II.2	Application

Question	CCA Exam Competency	CCA Exam Level	CCS Exam Competency	CCS Exam Level	CCS-P Exam Competency	CCS-P Exam Level
1.199	III.2.a	Application	II.1/II.2	Application	II.2	Application
1.200	III.2.a	Application	II.1/II.2	Application	II.2	Application
1.201	III.2.a	Application	II.1/II.2	Application	II.2	Application
1.202	III.2.a	Application	II.1/II.2	Application	II.2	Application
1.203	III.2.a	Application	II.1/II.2	Application	II.2	Application
1.204	III.2.a	Application	II.1/II.2	Application	II.2	Application
1.205	III.6	Recall	II.4	Recall	NA	N/A
1.206	III.2.a	Application	II.1/II.2	Application	II.2	Application
1.207	III.2.a	Application	II.1/II.2	Application	II.2	Application
1.208	III.2.a	Application	I.1	Application	NA	N/A
1.209	III.2.a	Application	II.1/II.2	Application	II.2	Application
1.210	III.2.a	Application	II.1/II.2	Application	II.2	Application
1.211	III.2.a	Application	II.1/II.2	Application	II.2	Application
1.212	III.2.a	Application	II.1/II.2	Application	II.2	Application
1.213	III.2.a	Application	II.1/II.2	Application	II.2	Application
1.214	III.2.a	Application	II.1/II.2	Application	II.2	Application
1.215	III.2.a	Application	II.1/II.2	Application	II.2	Application
1.216	III.2.a	Application	II.1/II.2	Application	II.2	Application
1.217	III.2.a	Application	II.1/II.2	Application	II.2	Application
1.218	III.2.a	Application	II.1/II.2	Application	II.2	Application
1.219	III.6	Recall	II.3	Recall	I.2	Recall
1.220	III.6	Recall	II.3	Recall	I.2	Recall
1.221	III.2.a	Application	II.1	Application	II.2	Application
1.222	III.2.a	Application	II.1	Application	II.2	Application
1.223	III.2.a	Application	II.1/II.2	Application	II.2	Application
1.224	III.2.a	Application	II.1	Application	II.2	Application
1.225	III.2.a	Application	II.1/II.2	Application	II.2	Application
1.226	III.2.a	Application	II.1/II.2	Application	II.2	Application
1.227	III.2.a	Application	II.1	Application	II.2	Application
1.228	III.2.a	Application	II.1	Application	II.2	Application
1.229	III.2.a	Application	II.1	Application	II.2	Application
1.230	III.6	Recall	II.3	Recall	II.1	Recall
1.231	III.6	Recall	II.3	Recall	II.1	Recall
1.232	III.6	Recall	II.3	Recall	II.2	Recall
1.233	III.2.a	Application	II.1/II.2	Application	II.1	Application
1.234	III.6	Recall	II.3	Recall	II.2	Application
1.235	III.6	Recall	I.1	Recall	I.2	Recall
1.236	III.2.a	Application	II.1/II.2	Application	II.2	Application
1.237	III.2.a	Application	II.1/II.2	Application	II.2	Application
1.238	III.2.a	Application	II.1/II.2	Application	II.2	Application

Question	CCA Exam Competency	CCA Exam Level	CCS Exam Competency	CCS Exam Level	CCS-P Exam Competency	CCS-P Exam Level
1.239	III.2.a	Application	II.1/II.2	Application	II.2	Application
1.240	III.2.a	Application	II.1/II.2	Application	II.2	Application
1.241	III.2.a	Application	II.1/II.2	Application	II.2	Application
1.242	III.2.a	Application	II.1/II.2	Application	II.2	Application
1.243	III.2.a	Application	II.1/II.2	Application	II.2	Application
1.244	III.2.a	Application	II.1/II.2	Application	II.2	Application
1.245	III.2.a	Application	II.1/II.2	Application	II.2	Application
1.246	III.2.a	Application	II.1/II.2	Application	II.2	Application
1.247	III.2.a	Application	II.1/II.2	Application	II.2	Application
1.248	III.2.a	Application	II.1/II.2	Application	II.2	Application
1.249	III.2.a	Application	II.4	Recall	N/A	N/A
1.250	III.2.a	Application	II.1/II.2	Application	II.2	Application
1.251	III.2.a	Application	II.1/II.2	Application	II.2	Application
1.252	III.2.a	Application	II.1/II.2	Application	II.2	Application
1.253	III.2.a	Application	II.1/II.2	Application	II.2	Application
1.254	III.2.a	Application	II.1/II.2	Application	II.2	Application
1.255	III.2.a	Application	II.1/II.2	Application	II.2	Application
1.256	III.2.a	Application	II.1/II.2	Application	II.2	Application
1.257	III.2.a	Application	II.1/II.2	Application	II.2	Application
1.258	III.2.a	Application	II.1/II.2	Application	II.2	Application
1.259	III.2.a	Application	II.1/II.2	Application	II.2	Application
1.260	III.2.a	Application	II.1/II.2	Application	II.2	Application
1.261	III.2.a	Application	II.1/II.2	Application	II.2	Application
1.262	III.2.a	Application	II.1/II.2	Application	II.2	Application
1.263	III.2.a	Application	II.1/II.2	Application	II.2	Application
1.264	III.2.a	Application	II.1/II.2	Application	II.2	Application
1.265	III.2.a	Application	II.1/II.2	Application	II.2	Application
1.266	III.2.a	Application	II.1/II.2	Application	II.2	Application
1.267	III.2.a	Application	II.1/II.2	Application	II.2	Application
1.268	III.2.a	Application	II.1/II.2	Application	II.2	Application
1.269	III.2.a	Application	II.1/II.2	Application	II.2	Application
1.270	III.2.a	Application	II.1/II.2	Application	II.2	Application
1.271	III.2.a	Application	II.1/II.2	Application	II.2	Application
1.272	III.2.a	Application	II.1/II.2	Application	II.2	Application
1.273	III.2.a	Application	II.1/II.2	Application	II.2	Application
1.274	III.2.a	Application	II.1/II.2	Application	II.2	Application
1.275	III.2.a	Application	II.1/II.2	Application	II.2	Application
1.276	III.2.a	Application	II.1/II.2	Application	II.2	Application
1.277	III.2.a	Application	II.1/II.2	Application	II.2	Application
1.278	III.2.a	Application	II.1/II.2	Application	II.2	Application

Question	CCA Exam Competency	CCA Exam Level	CCS Exam Competency	CCS Exam Level	CCS-P Exam Competency	CCS-P Exam Level
1.279	III.2.a	Application	II.1/II.2	Application	II.2	Application
1.280	III.2.a	Application	II.1/II.2	Application	II.2	Application
1.281	III.2.a	Application	II.1/II.2	Application	II.2	Application
1.282	III.2.a	Application	II.1/II.2	Application	II.2	Application
1.283	III.2.a	Application	II.1/II.2	Application	II.2	Application
1.284	III.2.a	Application	II.1/II.2	Application	II.2	Application
1.285	III.2.a	Application	II.1/II.2	Application	II.2	Application
1.286	III.2.a	Application	II.1/II.2	Application	II.2	Application
1.287	III.2.a	Application	II.1/II.2	Application	II.2	Application
1.288	III.2.a	Application	II.1/II.2	Application	II.2	Application
1.289	III.2.a	Application	II.1/II.2	Application	II.2	Application
1.290	III.2.a	Application	II.1/II.2	Application	II.2	Application
1.291	III.2.a	Application	II.1/II.2	Application	II.2	Application
1.292	III.2.a	Application	II.1/II.2	Application	II.2	Application
1.293	III.2.a	Application	II.1/II.2	Application	II.2	Application
1.294	III.2.a	Application	II.1	Application	NA	N/A
1.295	III.2.a	Application	II.1/II.2	Application	II.2	Application
1.296	III.2.a	Application	II.1/II.2	Application	II.2	Application
1.297	III.2.a	Application	II.1/II.2	Application	II.2	Application
1.298	III.2.a	Application	II.1/II.2	Application	II.2	Application
1.299	III.2.a	Application	II.1/II.2	Application	II.2	Application
1.300	III.2.a	Application	II.1/II.2	Application	II.2	Application
1.301	III.2.a	Application	II.1/II.2	Application	II.2	Application
1.302	III.2.a	Application	II.1/II.2	Application	II.2	Application
1.303	III.2.a	Application	II.1/II.2	Application	II.2	Application
1.304	III.2.a	Application	II.1/II.2	Application	II.2	Application
1.305	III.2.a	Application	II.1/II.2	Application	II.2	Application
1.306	III.2.a	Application	II.1/II.2	Application	II.2	Application
1.307	III.2.a	Application	II.1/II.2	Application	II.2	Application
1.308	III.2.a	Application	II.1/II.2	Application	II.2	Application
1.309	III.2.a	Application	II.1/II.2	Application	II.2	Application
1.310	III.2.a	Application	II.1/II.2	Application	II.2	Application
1.311	III.2.a	Application	II.1/II.2	Application	II.2	Application
1.312	III.2.a	Application	II.1/II.2	Application	II.2	Application
1.313	III.2.a	Application	II.1/II.2	Application	II.2	Application
1.314	III.2.a	Application	II.1/II.2	Application	II.2	Application
1.315	III.2.a	Application	II.1/II.2	Application	II.2	Application
1.316	III.2.a	Application	II.1/II.2	Application	II.2	Application
1.317	III.2.a	Application	II.1/II.2	Application	II.2	Application
1.318	III.2.a	Application	II.1/II.2	Application	II.2	Application

Question	CCA Exam Competency	CCA Exam Level	CCS Exam Competency	CCS Exam Level	CCS-P Exam Competency	CCS-P Exam Level
1.319	III.2.a	Application	II.1/II.2	Application	II.2	Application
1.320	III.2.a	Application	II.1/II.2	Application	II.2	Application
1.321	III.2.a	Application	II.1/II.2	Application	II.2	Application
1.322	III.2.a	Application	II.1/II.2	Application	II.2	Application
1.323	III.2.a	Application	II.1/II.2	Application	II.2	Application
1.324	III.2.a	Application	II.1/II.2	Application	II.2	Application
1.325	III.2.a	Application	II.1/II.2	Application	II.2	Application
1.326	III.2.a	Application	II.1/II.2	Application	II.2	Application
1.327	III.2.a	Application	II.1/II.2	Application	II.2	Application
1.328	III.2.a	Application	II.1/II.2	Application	II.2	Application
1.329	III.2.a	Application	II.1/II.2	Application	II.2	Application
1.330	III.2.a	Application	II.1/II.2	Application	II.2	Application
1.331	III.2.a	Application	II.1/II.2	Application	II.2	Application
1.332	III.2.a	Application	II.1/II.2	Application	II.2	Application
1.333	III.2.a	Application	II.1/II.2	Application	II.2	Application
1.334	III.2.a	Application	II.1/II.2	Application	II.2	Application
1.335	III.2.a	Application	II.1/II.2	Application	II.2	Application
1.336	III.2.a	Application	II.1	Application	II.2	Application
1.337	III.2.a	Application	II.1	Application	II.2	Application
1.338	III.2.a	Application	II.1	Application	II.2	Application
1.339	III.2.a	Application	II.1	Application	II.2	Application
1.340	III.2.a	Application	II.1	Application	II.2	Application
1.341	III.2.a	Application	II.1	Application	II.2	Application
1.342	III.2.a	Application	II.1	Application	II.2	Application
1.343	III.2.a	Application	II.1	Application	II.2	Application
1.344	III.2.a	Application	II.1	Application	II.2	Application
1.345	III.2.a	Application	II.1	Application	II.2	Application
1.346	III.2.a	Application	II.1	Application	II.2	Application
1.347	III.2.a	Application	II.1	Application	II.2	Application
1.348	III.2.a	Application	II.1	Application	II.2	Application
1.349	III.2.a	Application	II.1	Application	II.2	Application
1.350	III.2.a	Application	II.1	Application	II.2	Application
1.351	III.2.a	Application	II.1	Application	II.2	Application
1.352	III.2.a	Application	II.1	Application	II.2	Application
1.353	III.2.a	Application	II.1	Application	II.2	Application
1.354	III.2.a	Application	II.1	Application	II.2	Application
1.355	III.2.a	Application	II.1	Application	II.2	Application
1.356	III.2.a	Application	II.1/II.2	Application	II.2	Application
1.357	III.2.a	Application	II.1/II.2	Application	II.2	Application
1.358	III.2.a	Application	II.1/II.2	Application	II.2	Application

Question	CCA Exam Competency	CCA Exam Level	CCS Exam Competency	CCS Exam Level	CCS-P Exam Competency	CCS-P Exam Level
1.359	III.2.a	Application	II.1/II.2	Application	II.2	Application
1.360	III.2.a	Application	II.1/II.2	Application	II.2	Application
1.361	III.2.a	Application	II.1/II.2	Application	II.2	Application
1.362	III.2.a	Application	II.1/II.2	Application	II.2	Application
1.363	III.2.a	Application	II.1/II.2	Application	II.2	Application
1.364	III.2.a	Application	II.1/II.2	Application	II.2	Application
1.365	III.2.a	Application	II.1/II.2	Application	II.2	Application
1.366	III.2.a	Application	II.1/II.2	Application	II.2	Application
1.367	III.2.a	Application	II.1/II.2	Application	II.2	Application
1.368	III.2.a	Application	II.1/II.2	Application	II.2	Application
1.369	III.2.a	Application	II.1/II.2	Application	II.2	Application
1.370	III.2.a	Application	II.1/II.2	Application	II.2	Application
1.371	III.2.a	Application	II.1/II.2	Application	II.2	Application
1.372	III.2.a	Application	II.1/II.2	Application	II.2	Application
1.373	III.2.a	Application	II.1/II.2	Application	II.2	Application
1.374	III.2.a	Application	II.1/II.2	Application	II.2	Application
1.375	III.2.a	Application	II.1/II.2	Application	II.2	Application
1.376	III.2.c	Application	III.1/III.2	Application	N/A	N/A
1.377	III.2.c	Application	III.1/III.2	Application	N/A	N/A
1.378	III.2.c	Application	III.1/III.2	Application	N/A	N/A
1.379	III.2.c	Application	III.1/III.2	Application	N/A	N/A
1.380	III.2.c	Application	III.1/III.2	Application	N/A	N/A
1.381	III.2.c	Application	III.1/III.2	Application	N/A	N/A
1.382	III.2.c	Application	III.1/III.2	Application	N/A	N/A
1.383	III.2.c	Application	III.1/III.2	Application	N/A	N/A
1.384	III.2.c	Application	III.1/III.2	Application	N/A	N/A
1.385	III.2.c	Application	III.1/III.2	Application	N/A	N/A
1.386	III.2.c	Application	III.1/III.2	Application	N/A	N/A
1.387	III.2.c	Application	III.1/III.2	Application	N/A	N/A
1.388	III.2.c	Application	III.1/III.2	Application	N/A	N/A
1.389	III.2.c	Application	III.1/III.2	Application	N/A	N/A
1.390	III.2.c	Application	III.1/III.2	Application	N/A	N/A
1.391	III.2.c	Application	III.1/III.2	Application	N/A	N/A
1.392	III.2.c	Application	III.1/III.2	Application	N/A	N/A
1.393	III.2.c	Application	III.1/III.2	Application	N/A	N/A
1.394	III.2.c	Application	III.1/III.2	Application	N/A	N/A
1.395	III.2.c	Application	III.1/III.2	Application	N/A	N/A
1.396	III.2.c	Application	III.1/III.2	Application	N/A	N/A
1.397	III.2.c	Application	III.1/III.2	Application	N/A	N/A
1.398	III.2.c	Application	III.1/III.2	Application	N/A	N/A

Question	CCA Exam Competency	CCA Exam Level	CCS Exam Competency	CCS Exam Level	CCS-P Exam Competency	CCS-P Exam Level
1.399	III.2.c	Application	III.1/III.2	Application	N/A	N/A
1.400	III.2.c	Application	III.1/III.2	Application	N/A	N/A
1.401	III.2.a	Application	II.4	Application	N/A	Application (N/A)
1.402	III.2.a	Recall	II.3	Recall	N/A	Recall (N/A)
1.403	III.6	Recall	I.1	Recall	I.2	Recall
1.404	III.2.a	Recall	II.4/IV.1	Recall	N/A	N/A
1.405	III.2.a	Recall	II.4/IV.1	Recall	N/A	N/A
1.406	III.2.a	Application	I.1	Recall	I.2	Recall
1.407	III.6	Recall	II.3	Recall	II.2	Recall
1.408	III.2.a	Recall	II.4/IV.1	Recall	N/A	N/A
1.409	III.2.a	Recall	II.4/IV.1	Recall	N/A	N/A
1.410	III.2.a	Recall	II.3	Recall	II.1	Recall
1.411	III.2.a	Recall	II.4/IV.1	Recall	II.2	Recall
1.412	III.6	Recall	II.3	Recall	II.1	Recall
1.413	III.6	Recall	II.3	Recall	II.2	Recall
1.414	III.6	Recall	II.3	Recall	II.2	Recall
1.415	III.2.a	Recall	II.4/IV.1	Recall	N/A	Recall (N/A)
1.416	III.6	Recall	I.1	Recall	II.2	Recall
1.417	III.6	Recall	II.3	Recall	II.1	Recall
1.418	III.6	Recall	II.3	Recall	II.1	Recall
1.419	III.6	Recall	III.1/III.2	Recall	N/A	N/A
1.420	III.2.c	Recall	III.4/IV.1	Recall	N/A	N/A
1.421	III.2.a	Recall	II.4/IV.1	Application	N/A	N/A
1.422	III.2.a	Recall	II.4/IV.1	Application	N/A	N/A
1.423	III.2.a/III.2.b	Recall	II.5	Recall	N/A	N/A
1.424	III.6	Recall	I.1	Recall	I.2	Recall
1.425	III.6	Recall	I.1	Recall	I.2	Recall
1.426	III.6	Recall	I.1	Recall	VII.7	Recall

Chapter 2

Question	CCA Exam Competency	CCA Exam Level	CCS Exam Competency	CCS Exam Level	CCS-P Exam Competency	CCS-P Exam Level
2.1	III.6	Recall	III.3	Recall	III.1	Recall
2.2	III.6	Recall	III.3	Recall	III.1	Recall
2.3	III.6	Recall	III.3	Recall	III.1	Recall
2.4	III.6	Recall	III.3	Recall	III.1	Recall
2.5	III.6	Recall	III.3	Recall	III.1	Recall
2.6	III.6	Recall	III.3	Recall	III.1	Recall
2.7	III.6	Recall	III.3	Recall	III.1	Recall
2.8	III.6	Recall	III.3	Recall	III.1	Recall
2.9	III.6	Recall	III.3	Recall	III.1	Recall
2.10	III.6	Recall	III.3	Recall	III.1	Recall
2.11	III.6	Recall	III.3	Recall	III.1	Recall
2.12	III.6	Recall	III.3	Recall	III.1	Recall
2.13	III.6	Recall	III.3	Recall	III.1	Recall
2.14	III.6	Recall	III.3	Recall	III.1	Recall
2.15	III.6	Recall	III.3	Recall	III.1	Recall
2.16	III.6	Recall	III.3	Recall	III.1	Recall
2.17	III.6	Recall	III.3	Recall	III.1	Recall
2.18	III.6	Recall	III.3	Recall	III.1	Recall
2.19	III.6	Recall	III.3	Recall	III.1	Recall
2.20	III.6	Recall	III.3	Recall	III.1	Recall
2.21	III.6	Recall	III.3	Recall	III.1	Recall
2.22	III.6	Recall	III.3	Recall	III.1	Recall
2.23	III.3	Application	III.3	Recall	III.2.a	Application
2.24	III.6	Recall	III.3	Recall	III.1	Recall
2.25	III.3	Application	III.3	Recall	III.2.a	Application
2.26	III.3	Application	III.3	Recall	III.2.a	Application
2.27	III.3	Application	III.3	Recall	III.2.a	Application
2.28	III.6	Recall	III.3	Recall	III.1	Recall
2.29	III.6	Recall	III.3	Recall	III.1	Recall
2.30	III.6	Recall	III.3	Recall	III.2.a	Application
2.31	III.6	Recall	III.3	Recall	III.1	Recall
2.32	III.6	Recall	III.3	Recall	III.1	Recall
2.33	III.6	Recall	III.3	Recall	III.1	Recall
2.34	III.6	Recall	III.3	Recall	III.1	Recall
2.35	III.3	Application	III.3	Recall	III.2.a	Application
2.36	III.6	Recall	III.3	Recall	III.1	Recall
2.37	III.3	Application	III.3	Recall	III.2.a	Recall
2.38	III.6	Recall	III.3	Recall	III.1	Recall
2.39	III.6	Recall	III.3	Recall	III.1	Recall

Question	CCA Exam Competency	CCA Exam Level	CCS Exam Competency	CCS Exam Level	CCS-P Exam Competency	CCS-P Exam Level
2.40	III.6	Recall	III.2	Application	III.1	Application
2.41	III.6	Recall	III.2	Application	III.1	Application
2.42	III.6	Recall	III.2	Application	III.1	Application
2.43	III.6	Recall	III.2	Application	III.1	Application
2.44	III.6	Recall	III.2	Application	III.1	Application
2.45	III.6	Recall	III.2	Application	III.1	Application
2.46	III.6	Recall	III.2	Application	III.1	Application
2.47	III.3	Application	III.2	Application	III.1	Application
2.48	III.3	Application	III.2	Application	III.2.b	Application
2.49	III.3	Application	III.2	Application	III.2.b	Application
2.50	III.3	Application	III.2	Application	III.2.b	Application
2.51	III.3	Application	III.2	Application	III.2.b	Application
2.52	III.3	Application	III.2	Application	III.2.b	Application
2.53	III.3	Application	III.2	Application	III.2.b	Application
2.54	III.3	Application	III.2	Application	III.2.b	Application
2.55	III.3	Application	III.2	Application	III.2.b	Application
2.56	III.3	Application	III.3	Recall	III.2.b	Application
2.57	III.3	Application	III.3	Recall	III.2.b	Application
2.58	III.3	Application	III.2	Application	III.2.b	Application
2.59	III.3	Application	III.3	Recall	III.2.b	Application
2.60	III.3	Application	III.3	Recall	III.2.b	Application
2.61	III.3	Application	III.2	Application	III.2.b	Application
2.62	III.3	Application	III.2	Application	III.2.b	Application
2.63	III.3	Application	III.2	Application	III.2.b	Application
2.64	III.6	Recall	III.2	Application	III.1	Application
2.65	III.6	Recall	III.2	Application	III.1	Application
2.66	III.6	Recall	III.2	Application	III.1	Application
2.67	III.6	Recall	III.2	Application	III.2.c	Application
2.68	III.6	Recall	III.2	Application	III.1	Application
2.69	III.3	Application	III.2	Application	III.2.c	Application
2.70	III.6	Recall	III.2	Application	III.1	Application
2.71	III.6	Recall	III.2	Application	III.1	Application
2.72	III.3	Application	III.2	Application	III.2.c	Application
2.73	III.3	Application	III.3	Recall	III.2.c	Application
2.74	III.3	Application	III.2	Application	III.2.c	Application
2.75	III.3	Application	III.2	Application	III.2.c	Application
2.76	III.3	Application	III.3	Recall	III.2.c	Application
2.77	III.3	Application	III.3	Recall	III.2.c	Application
2.78	III.3	Application	III.3	Recall	III.2.c	Application
2.79	III.3	Application	III.2	Application	III.2.c	Application

Question	CCA Exam Competency	CCA Exam Level	CCS Exam Competency	CCS Exam Level	CCS-P Exam Competency	CCS-P Exam Level
2.80	III.3	Application	III.2	Application	III.2.c	Application
2.81	III.3	Application	III.2	Application	III.2.c	Application
2.82	III.6	Recall	III.2	Application	III.1	Application
2.83	III.3	Application	III.2	Application	III.2.c	Application
2.84	III.6	Recall	III.2	Application	III.1	Application
2.85	III.3	Application	III.2	Application	III.2.c	Application
2.86	III.3	Application	III.2	Application	III.2.c	Application
2.87	III.6	Recall	III.2	Application	III.1	Application
2.88	III.6	Recall	III.2	Application	III.1	Application
2.89	III.3	Application	III.2	Recall	III.1	Recall
2.90	III.6	Recall	III.2	Application	III.1	Application
2.91	III.6	Recall	III.2	Application	III.1	Application
2.92	III.6	Recall	III.2	Application	III.1	Application
2.93	III.3	Application	III.2	Application	III.2.c	Application
2.94	III.3	Application	III.2	Application	III.2.c	Application
2.95	III.3	Application	III.2	Application	III.2.c	Application
2.96	III.3	Application	I.1	Recall	III.2.c	Application
2.97	III.3	Application	III.2	Application	III.2.c	Application
2.98	III.3	Application	III.2	Application	III.2.c	Application
2.99	III.3	Application	III.2	Application	III.2.c	Application
2.100	III.3	Application	III.2	Application	III.2.c	Application
2.101	III.3	Application	III.2	Application	III.2.c	Application
2.102	III.3	Application	III.2	Application	III.2.c	Application
2.103	III.6	Recall	III.2	Application	III.1	Application
2.104	III.3	Application	III.2	Application	III.2.c	Application
2.105	III.3	Application	III.2	Application	III.2.c	Application
2.106	III.3	Application	III.2	Application	III.2.c	Application
2.107	III.3	Application	III.2	Application	III.2.c	Application
2.108	III.3	Application	III.2	Application	III.2.c	Application
2.109	III.3	Application	III.2	Application	III.2.c	Application
2.110	III.6	Recall	III.2	Application	III.1	Application
2.111	III.3	Application	III.2	Application	III.2.c	Application
2.112	III.3	Application	III.5	Recall	III.2.c	Application
2.113	III.3	Application	III.2	Application	III.2.c	Application
2.114	III.3	Application	III.2	Application	III.2.c	Application
2.115	III.3	Application	III.2	Application	III.2.c	Application
2.116	III.3	Application	I.1	Recall	III.2.c	Application
2.117	III.3	Application	III.2	Application	III.2.c	Application
2.118	III.3	Application	III.2	Application	III.2.c	Application
2.119	III.3	Application	III.3	Recall	III.2.c	Application

Question	CCA Exam Competency	CCA Exam Level	CCS Exam Competency	CCS Exam Level	CCS-P Exam Competency	CCS-P Exam Level
2.120	III.3	Application	III.2	Application	III.2.c	Application
2.121	III.3	Application	III.2	Application	III.2.c	Application
2.122	III.3	Application	III.2	Application	III.2.c	Application
2.123	III.3	Application	III.2	Application	III.2.c	Application
2.124	III.3	Application	III.2	Application	III.2.c	Application
2.125	III.3	Application	III.2	Application	III.2.c	Application
2.126	III.6	Recall	III.2	Application	III.1	Application
2.127	III.3	Application	III.2	Application	III.2.c	Application
2.128	III.3	Application	III.2	Application	III.2.c	Application
2.129	III.3	Application	III.2	Application	III.2.c	Application
2.130	III.6	Recall	III.2	Application	III.1	Application
2.131	III.6	Recall	III.2	Application	III.1	Application
2.132	III.6	Recall	III.2	Application	III.1	Recall
2.133	III.3	Application	III.2	Application	III.2.c	Application
2.134	III.3	Application	III.2	Application	III.2.c	Application
2.135	III.6	Recall	III.2	Application	III.1	Application
2.136	III.3	Application	III.2	Application	III.2.c	Application
2.137	III.3	Application	III.2	Application	III.2.c	Application
2.138	III.3	Application	III.2	Application	III.2.c	Application
2.139	III.3	Application	III.2	Application	III.2.c	Application
2.140	III.3	Application	III.2	Application	III.2.c	Application
2.141	III.3	Application	III.3	Recall	III.2.c	Application
2.142	III.3	Application	III.2	Application	III.2.c	Application
2.143	III.3	Application	III.2	Application	III.2.c	Application
2.144	III.3	Application	I.3	Recall	III.2.c	Application
2.145	III.3	Application	III.2	Application	III.2.c	Application
2.146	III.3	Application	III.2	Application	III.2.c	Application
2.147	III.3	Application	III.2	Application	III.2.c	Application
2.148	III.3	Application	III.2	Application	III.2.c	Application
2.149	III.3	Application	III.2	Application	III.2.c	Application
2.150	III.3	Application	III.2	Application	III.2.c	Application
2.151	III.3	Application	III.2	Application	III.2.c	Application
2.152	III.3	Application	III.2	Application	III.2.c	Application
2.153	III.3	Application	III.2	Application	III.2.c	Application
2.154	III.3	Application	III.2	Application	III.2.c	Application
2.155	III.3	Application	III.2	Application	III.2.c	Application
2.156	III.3	Application	III.2	Application	III.2.c	Application
2.157	III.6	Recall	III.2	Application	III.1	Recall
2.158	III.3	Application	III.2	Application	III.2.c	Application
2.159	III.3	Application	III.2	Application	III.2.c	Application

Question	CCA Exam Competency	CCA Exam Level	CCS Exam Competency	CCS Exam Level	CCS-P Exam Competency	CCS-P Exam Level
2.160	III.6	Recall	III.2	Application	III.1	Application
2.161	III.3	Application	III.2	Application	III.2.c	Application
2.162	III.3	Application	III.2	Application	III.2.c	Application
2.163	III.3	Application	III.2	Application	III.2.c	Application
2.164	III.3	Application	III.2	Application	III.2.c	Application
2.165	III.3	Application	III.2	Application	III.2.c	Application
2.166	III.3	Application	III.2	Application	III.2.c	Application
2.167	III.3	Application	III.2	Application	III.2.c	Application
2.168	III.3	Application	III.2	Application	III.2.c	Application
2.169	III.3	Application	III.2	Application	III.2.c	Application
2.170	III.3	Application	III.2	Application	III.2.c	Application
2.171	III.3	Application	III.2	Application	III.2.c	Application
2.172	III.3	Application	III.2	Application	III.2.c	Application
2.173	III.3	Application	III.2	Application	III.2.c	Application
2.174	III.3	Application	III.2	Application	III.2.c	Application
2.175	III.3	Application	III.2	Application	III.2.c	Application
2.176	III.3	Application	III.2	Application	III.2.c	Application
2.177	III.3	Application	III.2	Application	III.2.c	Application
2.178	III.3	Application	III.2	Application	III.2.c	Application
2.179	III.3	Application	III.2	Application	III.2.c	Application
2.180	III.3	Application	III.2	Application	III.2.c	Application
2.181	III.3	Application	III.2	Application	III.2.c	Application
2.182	III.3	Application	III.2	Application	III.2.c	Application
2.183	III.3	Application	III.2	Application	III.2.c	Application
2.184	III.3	Application	III.2	Application	III.2.c	Application
2.185	III.3	Application	III.2	Application	III.2.c	Application
2.186	III.3	Application	III.2	Application	III.2.c	Application
2.187	III.3	Application	III.2	Application	III.2.c	Application
2.188	III.3	Application	III.2	Application	III.2.c	Application
2.189	III.3	Application	III.2	Application	III.2.c	Application
2.190	III.3	Application	III.2	Application	III.2.c	Application
2.191	III.3	Application	III.2	Application	III.2.c	Application
2.192	III.3	Application	III.2	Application	III.2.c	Application
2.193	III.3	Application	III.2	Application	III.2.c	Application
2.194	III.3	Application	III.2	Application	III.2.c	Application
2.195	III.3	Application	III.2	Application	III.2.c	Application
2.196	III.3	Application	III.2	Application	III.2.c	Application
2.197	III.3	Application	III.2	Application	III.2.c	Application
2.198	III.3	Application	III.2	Application	III.2.c	Application
2.199	III.3	Application	III.2	Application	III.2.c	Application

Question	CCA Exam Competency	CCA Exam Level	CCS Exam Competency	CCS Exam Level	CCS-P Exam Competency	CCS-P Exam Level
2.200	III.3	Application	III.2	Application	III.2.c	Application
2.201	III.3	Application	III.2	Application	III.2.c	Application
2.202	III.3	Application	III.2	Application	III.2.c	Application
2.203	III.3	Application	III.2	Application	III.2.c	Application
2.204	III.3	Application	III.2	Application	III.2.c	Application
2.205	III.3	Application	III.2	Application	III.2.c	Application
2.206	III.3	Application	III.2	Application	III.2.c	Application
2.207	III.3	Application	III.2	Application	III.2.c	Application
2.208	III.3	Application	III.2	Application	III.2.c	Application
2.209	III.3	Application	III.2	Application	III.2.c	Application
2.210	III.3	Application	III.2	Application	III.2.c	Application
2.211	III.3	Application	III.2	Application	III.2.c	Application
2.212	III.3	Application	III.2	Application	III.2.c	Application
2.213	III.3	Application	III.2	Application	III.2.c	Application
2.214	III.3	Application	III.2	Application	III.2.c	Application
2.215	III.3	Application	III.2	Application	III.2.c	Application
2.216	III.3	Application	III.2	Application	III.2.c	Application
2.217	III.3	Application	III.2	Application	III.2.c	Application
2.218	III.3	Application	III.2	Application	III.2.c	Application
2.219	III.3	Application	III.2	Application	III.2.c	Application
2.220	III.3	Application	III.2	Application	III.2.c	Application
2.221	III.3	Application	III.2	Application	III.2.c	Application
2.222	III.3	Application	III.2	Application	III.2.c	Application
2.223	III.3	Application	III.2	Application	III.2.c	Application
2.224	III.3	Application	III.2	Application	III.2.c	Application
2.225	III.3	Application	III.2	Application	III.2.c	Application
2.226	III.3	Application	III.2	Application	III.2.c	Application
2.227	III.3	Application	III.2	Application	III.2.c	Application
2.228	III.3	Application	III.2	Application	III.2.c	Application
2.229	III.3	Application	III.2	Application	III.2.c	Application
2.230	III.3	Application	III.2	Application	III.2.c	Application
2.231	III.3	Application	III.2	Application	III.2.c	Application
2.232	III.3	Application	III.2	Application	III.2.c	Application
2.233	III.3	Application	III.2	Application	III.2.c	Application
2.234	III.3	Application	III.2	Application	III.2.c	Application
2.235	III.3	Application	III.2	Application	III.2.c	Application
2.236	III.3	Application	III.2	Application	III.2.c	Application
2.237	III.3	Application	III.2	Application	III.2.c	Application
2.238	III.3	Application	III.2	Application	III.2.c	Application
2.239	III.3	Application	III.2	Application	III.2.c	Application

Question	CCA Exam Competency	CCA Exam Level	CCS Exam Competency	CCS Exam Level	CCS-P Exam Competency	CCS-P Exam Level
2.240	III.3	Application	III.2	Application	III.2.c	Application
2.241	III.3	Application	III.2	Application	III.2.c	Application
2.242	III.3	Application	III.2	Application	III.2.c	Application
2.243	III.3	Application	III.2	Application	III.2.c	Application
2.244	III.3	Application	III.2	Application	III.2.c	Application
2.245	III.3	Application	III.2	Application	III.2.c	Application
2.246	III.3	Application	III.2	Application	III.2.c	Application
2.247	III.3	Application	III.2	Application	III.2.c	Application
2.248	III.3	Application	III.2	Application	III.2.c	Application
2.249	III.3	Application	III.2	Application	III.2.c	Application
2.250	III.3	Application	III.2	Application	III.2.c	Application
2.251	III.3	Application	III.2	Application	III.2.c	Application
2.252	III.3	Application	III.2	Application	III.2.c	Application
2.253	III.3	Application	III.2	Application	III.2.c	Application
2.254	III.3	Application	III.2	Application	III.2.c	Application
2.255	III.3	Application	III.2	Application	III.2.c	Application
2.256	III.3	Application	III.2	Application	III.2.c	Application
2.257	III.3	Application	III.2	Application	III.2.c	Application
2.258	III.3	Application	III.2	Application	III.2.c	Application
2.259	III.3	Application	III.2	Application	III.2.c	Application
2.260	III.3	Application	III.2	Application	III.2.c	Application
2.261	III.3	Application	III.2	Application	III.2.c	Application
2.262	III.3	Application	III.2	Application	III.2.c	Application
2.263	III.3	Application	III.2	Application	III.2.c	Application
2.264	III.3	Application	III.2	Application	III.2.c	Application
2.265	III.3	Application	III.2	Application	III.2.c	Application
2.266	III.3	Application	III.2	Application	III.2.c	Application
2.267	III.3	Application	III.2	Application	III.2.c	Application
2.268	III.3	Application	III.2	Application	III.2.c	Application
2.269	III.3	Application	III.2	Application	III.2.c	Application
2.270	III.3	Application	III.2	Application	III.2.c	Application
2.271	III.3	Application	III.2	Application	III.2.c	Application
2.272	III.3	Application	III.2	Application	III.2.c	Application
2.273	III.3	Application	III.2	Application	III.2.c	Application
2.274	III.3	Application	III.2	Application	III.2.c	Application
2.275	III.3	Application	III.2	Application	III.2.c	Application
2.276	III.3	Application	III.2	Application	III.2.c	Application
2.277	III.3	Application	III.2	Application	III.2.c	Application
2.278	III.3	Application	III.2	Application	III.2.c	Application
2.279	III.3	Application	III.2	Application	III.2.c	Application

Question	CCA Exam Competency	CCA Exam Level	CCS Exam Competency	CCS Exam Level	CCS-P Exam Competency	CCS-P Exam Level
2.280	III.3	Application	III.2	Application	III.2.c	Application
2.281	III.3	Application	III.2	Application	III.2.c	Application
2.282	III.3	Application	III.2	Application	III.2.c	Application
2.283	III.3	Application	III.2	Application	III.2.c	Application
2.284	III.3	Application	III.2	Application	III.2.c	Application
2.285	III.3	Application	III.2	Application	III.2.c	Application
2.286	III.3	Application	III.2	Application	III.2.c	Application
2.287	III.3	Application	III.2	Application	III.2.c	Application
2.288	III.3	Application	III.2	Application	III.2.c	Application
2.289	III.3	Application	III.2	Application	III.2.c	Application
2.290	III.3	Application	III.2	Application	III.2.c	Application
2.291	III.3	Application	III.2	Application	III.2.c	Application
2.292	III.6	Recall	III.2	Application	III.1	Application
2.293	III.3	Application	III.2	Application	III.2.d	Application
2.294	III.3	Application	III.2	Application	III.2.d	Application
2.295	III.3	Application	III.2	Application	III.2.d	Application
2.296	III.3	Application	III.2	Application	III.2.d	Application
2.297	III.3	Application	III.2	Application	III.2.d	Application
2.298	III.3	Application	III.2	Application	III.2.d	Application
2.299	III.3	Application	III.2	Application	III.2.d	Application
2.300	III.3	Application	III.2	Application	III.2.d	Application
2.301	III.3	Application	III.2	Application	III.2.d	Application
2.302	III.3	Application	III.2	Application	III.2.d	Application
2.303	III.3	Application	III.2	Application	III.2.d	Application
2.304	III.3	Application	III.2	Application	III.2.d	Application
2.305	III.3	Application	III.2	Application	III.2.d	Application
2.306	III.3	Application	III.2	Application	III.2.d	Application
2.307	III.3	Application	III.2	Application	III.2.d	Application
2.308	III.3	Application	III.2	Application	III.2.d	Application
2.309	III.3	Application	III.2	Application	III.2.d	Application
2.310	III.3	Application	III.2	Application	III.2.d	Application
2.311	III.3	Application	III.2	Application	III.2.d	Application
2.312	III.3	Application	III.2	Application	III.2.d	Application
2.313	III.6	Recall	III.2	Application	III.1	Application
2.314	III.3	Application	III.2	Application	III.2.e	Application
2.315	III.6	Recall	III.2	Application	III.1	Application
2.316	III.6	Recall	III.2	Application	III.1	Application
2.317	III.3	Application	III.3	Recall	III.2.e	Application
2.318	III.3	Application	III.2	Application	III.2.e	Application
2.319	III.3	Application	III.2	Application	III.2.e	Application

Question	CCA Exam Competency	CCA Exam Level	CCS Exam Competency	CCS Exam Level	CCS-P Exam Competency	CCS-P Exam Level
2.320	III.3	Application	III.2	Application	III.2.e	Application
2.321	III.3	Application	III.2	Application	III.2.e	Application
2.322	III.3	Application	III.2	Application	III.2.e	Application
2.323	III.3	Application	III.2	Application	III.2.e	Application
2.324	III.3	Application	III.2	Application	III.2.e	Application
2.325	III.3	Application	III.2	Application	III.2.e	Application
2.326	III.3	Application	III.2	Application	III.2.e	Application
2.327	III.3	Application	III.2	Application	III.2.e	Application
2.328	III.3	Application	III.2	Application	III.2.e	Application
2.329	III.3	Application	III.2	Application	III.2.e	Application
2.330	III.3	Application	III.2	Application	III.2.e	Application
2.331	III.3	Application	III.2	Application	III.2.e	Application
2.332	III.3	Application	III.2	Application	III.2.e	Application
2.333	III.3	Application	III.2	Application	III.2.e	Application
2.334	III.3	Application	III.2	Application	III.2.e	Application
2.335	III.3	Application	III.2	Application	III.2.e	Application
2.336	III.3	Application	N/A	N/A	III.2.e	Application
2.337	III.6	Recall	III.2	Recall	III.1	Recall
2.338	III.3	Application	III.2	Recall	III.1	Recall
2.339	III.6	Recall	N/A	N/A	III.1	Recall
2.340	III.3	Application	III.2	Application	III.2.f	Application
2.341	III.6	Recall	N/A	N/A	III.1	Recall
2.342	III.3	Application	III.2	Recall	III.2.f	Application
2.343	III.6	Recall	III.2	Application	III.1	Recall
2.344	III.3	Application	III.2	Recall	III.2.f	Application
2.345	III.3	Application	N/A	N/A	III.2.f	Application
2.346	III.3	Application	III.2	Recall	III.2.f	Application
2.347	III.3	Application	N/A	N/A	III.2.f	Application
2.348	III.3	Application	N/A	N/A	III.2.f	Application
2.349	III.3	Application	N/A	N/A	III.2.f	Application
2.350	III.3	Application	III.2	Recall	III.2.f	Application
2.351	III.3	Application	III.2	Recall	III.2.f	Application
2.352	III.3	Application	N/A	N/A	III.2.f	Application
2.353	III.3	Application	N/A	N/A	III.2.f	Application
2.354	III.3	Application	N/A	N/A	III.2.f	Application
2.355	III.3	Application	N/A	N/A	III.2.f	Application
2.356	III.3	Application	III.3	Recall	III.2.f	Application
2.357	III.3	Application	III.3	Recall	III.2.f	Application
2.358	III.3	Application	III.3	Recall	III.2.f	Application
2.359	III.3	Application	III.2	Application	III.2.f	Application

Question	CCA Exam Competency	CCA Exam Level	CCS Exam Competency	CCS Exam Level	CCS-P Exam Competency	CCS-P Exam Level
2.360	III.3	Application	III.2	Application	III.2.f	Application
2.361	III.3	Application	III.2	Application	III.2.f	Application
2.362	III.6	Application	V.2.a	Application	III.5	Application
2.363	III.6	Application	V.2.a	Recall	III.5	Recall
2.364	III.6	Recall	V.2.a	Application	III.5	Application
2.365	III.6	Application	V.2.a	Application	III.5	Application
2.366	III.3	Application	V.2.a	Application	III.5	Application
2.367	III.6	Application	V.2.a	Application	III.5	Application
2.368	III.3	Application	V.2.a	Application	III.2.c/III.5	Application
2.369	III.6	Application	V.2.a	Recall	III.5	Recall
2.370	III.6	Application	V.2.a	Application	III.5	Application
2.371	III.6	Recall	V.2.a	Application	III.5	Application
2.372	III.6	Application	V.2.a	Application	III.5	Application
2.373	III.3	Application	V.2.a	Application	III.2.c/III.5	Application
2.374	III.6	Application	V.2.a	Application	III.5	Application
2.375	III.6	Application	V.2.a	Application	III.5	Application
2.376	III.6	Application	V.2.a	Application	III.5	Application
2.377	III.6	Application	V.2.a	Application	III.5	Application
2.378	III.6	Application	V.2.a	Application	III.5	Application
2.379	III.6	Application	V.2.a	Application	III.5	Application
2.380	III.6	Application	V.2.a	Application	III.5	Application
2.381	III.6	Application	V.2.a	Application	III.5	Application
2.382	III.6	Recall	III.2	Application	III.1	Application
2.383	III.6	Recall	III.2	Application	III.1	Application
2.384	III.6	Recall	III.2	Application	III.1	Application
2.385	III.3	Application	III.2	Application	III.2.g	Application
2.386	III.3	Application	III.2	Application	III.2.g	Application
2.387	III.3	Application	III.2	Application	III.2.g	Application
2.388	III.3	Application	III.2	Application	III.2.g	Application
2.389	III.6	Recall	III.2	Application	III.2.g	Application
2.390	III.3	Application	III.2	Application	III.2.g	Application
2.391	III.3	Application	III.2	Application	III.2.g	Application
2.392	III.3	Application	III.2	Application	III.2.g	Application
2.393	III.3	Application	III.2	Application	III.2.g	Application
2.394	III.3	Application	III.2	Application	III.2.g	Application
2.395	III.6	Recall	III.2	Application	III.1	Application
2.396	III.3	Application	III.2	Application	III.2.g	Application
2.397	III.3	Application	III.2	Application	III.2.g	Application
2.398	III.3	Application	III.2	Application	III.2.g	Application
2.399	III.3	Application	III.2	Application	III.2.g	Application

Question	CCA Exam Competency	CCA Exam Level	CCS Exam Competency	CCS Exam Level	CCS-P Exam Competency	CCS-P Exam Level
2.400	III.3	Application	III.2	Application	III.2.g	Application
2.401	III.3	Application	III.2	Application	III.2.g	Application
2.402	III.3	Application	III.2	Application	III.2.c	Application
2.403	III.3	Application	III.2	Application	III.2.c	Application
2.404	III.3	Application	III.2	Application	III.2.c	Application
2.405	III.3	Application	III.2	Application	III.2.c	Application
2.406	III.3	Application	III.2	Application	III.2.c	Application
2.407	III.3	Application	III.2	Application	III.2.c	Application
2.408	III.3	Application	III.2	Application	III.2.c	Application
2.409	III.3	Application	III.2	Application	III.2.c	Application
2.410	III.3	Application	III.2	Application	III.2.c	Application
2.411	III.3	Application	III.2	Application	III.2.c	Application
2.412	III.3	Application	III.2	Application	III.2.c	Application
2.413	III.3	Application	III.2	Application	III.2.c	Application
2.414	III.3	Application	III.2	Application	III.2.c	Application
2.415	III.3	Application	III.2	Application	III.2.c	Application
2.416	III.3	Application	III.2	Application	III.2.c	Application
2.417	III.3	Application	III.2	Application	III.2.c	Application
2.418	III.3	Application	III.2	Application	III.2.c	Application
2.419	III.3	Application	III.2	Application	III.2.c	Application
2.420	III.3	Application	III.2	Application	III.2.c	Application
2.421	III.3	Application	III.2	Application	III.2.c	Application
2.422	III.3	Application	III.2	Application	III.2.c	Application
2.423	III.3	Application	III.2	Application	III.2.d	Application
2.424	III.3	Application	III.2	Application	III.2.e	Application
2.425	III.3	Application	III.2	Application	III.2.f	Application
2.426	III.3	Application	III.2	Application	III.2.f	Application

Chapter 3

Question	CCA Exam Competency	CCA Exam Level	CCS Exam Competency	CCS Exam Level	CCS-P Exam Competency	CCS-P Exam Level
3.1	III.4	Recall	III.3/V.2.a	Recall	III.3	Recall
3.2	III.4	Application	III.2/V2.a	Application	III.4	Application
3.3	III.4	Application	III.2/V2.a	Application	III.4	Application
3.4	III.4	Application	III.2/V2.a	Application	III.4	Application
3.5	III.4	Application	III.2/V2.a	Application	III.4	Application
3.6	III.4	Application	III.2/V2.a	Application	III.4	Application
3.7	III.4	Application	III.2/V2.a	Application	III.4	Application
3.8	III.4	Application	III.2/V2.a	Application	III.4	Application
3.9	III.4	Application	III.2/V2.a	Application	III.4	Application
3.10	III.4	Application	III.2/V2.a	Application	III.4	Application
3.11	III.4	Application	III.2/V2.a	Application	III.4	Application
3.12	III.4	Application	III.2/V2.a	Application	III.4	Application
3.13	III.4	Application	III.2/V2.a	Application	III.4	Application
3.14	III.4	Application	III.2/V2.a	Application	III.4	Application
3.15	III.4	Application	III.2/V2.a	Application	III.4	Application
3.16	III.4	Application	III.2/V2.a	Application	III.4	Application
3.17	III.4	Application	III.2/V2.a	Application	III.4	Application
3.18	III.4	Application	III.2/V2.a	Application	III.4	Application
3.19	III.4	Application	III.2/V2.a	Application	III.4	Application
3.20	III.4	Application	III.2/V2.a	Application	III.4	Application
3.21	III.4	Application	N/A	N/A	N/A	N/A
3.22	III.4	Application	N/A	N/A	N/A	N/A
3.23	III.4	Application	III.2/V2.a	Application	N/A	N/A
3.24	III.4	Recall	N/A	N/A	N/A	N/A
3.25	III.4	Application	III.2/V2.a	Application	N/A	N/A
3.26	III.4	Application	N/A	N/A	N/A	N/A
3.27	III.4	Recall	N/A	N/A	N/A	N/A
3.28	III.4	Application	III.2/V2.a	Application	N/A	N/A
3.29	III.4	Application	III.2/V2.a	Application	N/A	N/A
3.30	III.4	Application	III.2/V2.a	Application	N/A	N/A
3.31	III.4	Application	III.2/V2.a	Application	III.4	Application
3.32	III.4	Application	III.2/V2.a	Application	III.4	Application
3.33	III.4	Application	III.2/V2.a	Application	III.4	Application
3.34	III.4	Application	III.2/V2.a	Application	III.4	Application
3.35	III.4	Application	III.2/V2.a	Application	III.4	Application
3.36	III.4	Application	III.2/V2.a	Application	III.4	Application
3.37	III.4	Application	III.2/V2.a	Application	III.4	Application
3.38	III.4	Application	III.2/V2.a	Application	III.4	Application
3.39	III.4	Application	III.2/V2.a	Application	III.4	Application

Question	CCA Exam Competency	CCA Exam Level	CCS Exam Competency	CCS Exam Level	CCS-P Exam Competency	CCS-P Exam Level
3.40	III.4	Application	III.2/V2.a	Application	III.4	Application
3.41	III.4	Application	III.2/V2.a	Application	III.4	Application
3.42	III.4	Application	III.2/V2.a	Application	III.4	Application
3.43	III.4	Application	III.2/V2.a	Application	III.4	Application
3.44	III.4	Application	III.2/V2.a	Application	III.4	Application
3.45	III.4	Application	III.2/V2.a	Application	III.4	Application
3.46	III.4	Application	III.2/V2.a	Application	III.4	Application
3.47	III.4	Application	III.2/V2.a	Application	III.4	Application
3.48	III.4	Application	III.2/V2.a	Application	III.4	Application
3.49	III.4	Application	III.2/V2.a	Application	III.4	Application
3.50	III.4	Application	III.2/V2.a	Application	III.4	Application

Chapter 4

Question	CCA Exam Competency	CCA Exam Level	CCS Exam Competency	CCS Exam Level	CCS-P Exam Competency	CCS-P Exam Level
4.1	III.2.a	Application	I.2/I.4/II.3	Application	N/A	N/A
4.2	III.2.a,b,c	Application	II.3	Application	N/A	N/A
4.3	III.2.a,b,c	Application	I.4/II.2/III.1	Application	N/A	N/A
4.4	III.2.a,b,c	Application	II.1/III.1	Application	N/A	N/A
4.5	III.2.a,b	Application	II.3	Application	N/A	N/A
4.6	III.2.a,b	Application	II.2/III.2	Application	N/A	N/A
4.7	III.2.a,b,c	Application	II.1/II.4/III.1/III.4	Application	N/A	N/A
4.8	III.2.a,b,c	Application	II.1/II.4/III.1/III.4	Application	N/A	N/A
4.9	III.2.a,b,c	Application	II.1	Application	N/A	N/A
4.10	III.2.a,b	Application	II.1/IV.1	Application	N/A	N/A
4.11	III.2.a,b,c	Application	II.1	Application	N/A	N/A
4.12	III.2.a,b	Application	II.1	Application	N/A	N/A
4.13	III.2.a,b	Application	II.1/II.4	Application	N/A	N/A
4.14	III.2.a	Application	II.1	Application	N/A	N/A
4.15	III.2.c	Application	III.1/III.4	Application	N/A	N/A
4.16	III.2.a,b,c	Application	I.4/II.1/III.1	Application	N/A	N/A
4.17	III.2.a,b,c	Application	II.1/III.1	Application	N/A	N/A
4.18	III.2.a,b,c	Application	I.4/II.1/III.1	Application	N/A	N/A
4.19	III.2.a,b	Application	I.1/II.1/II.3/II.4/II.5/IV.1	Application	N/A	N/A
4.20	III.2.a,b,c	Application	II.1	Application	N/A	N/A
4.21	III.2.a,b,c	Application	II.1	Application	N/A	N/A
4.22	III.2.a,b,c	Application	II.1	Application	N/A	N/A
4.23	III.2.a,b,c	Analysis	II.1/II.4/III.1	Analysis	N/A	N/A
4.24	III.2.a,b	Application	I.1/II.1/II.3/II.4/II.5/III.1/III.3/III.4/III.5/IV.1/IV.3	Application	N/A	N/A
4.25	III.2.a,b	Application	I.4/II.3	Application	N/A	N/A
4.26	III.2.a,b	Application	II.1/II.4	Application	N/A	N/A
4.27	III.2.a,b,c	Application	II.1/II.4/III.1	Application	N/A	N/A
4.28	III.2.a,b	Application	I.1/II.1/II.3/II.4/II.5/III.1/III.3/III.4/III.5/IV.1	Application	N/A	N/A
4.29	III.2.a,b,c	Application	II.1/II.4/III.1	Application	N/A	N/A
4.30	III.2.a,c	Application	II.1/II.4/III.1	Application	N/A	N/A
4.31	III.2.a,b	Application	I.4/II.1/II.4	Application	N/A	N/A
4.32	III.2.a,b,c	Application	I.4/II.1/II.4/III.1	Application	N/A	N/A
4.33	III.2.a,b,c	Application	II.1/II.4/III.1	Application	N/A	N/A
4.34	III.2.a,b	Application	II.1/II.4	Application	N/A	N/A
4.35	III.2.a,b	Application	II.1/II.4	Application	N/A	N/A
4.36	III.2.a	Application	II.1/II.4	Application	N/A	N/A

Question	CCA Exam Competency	CCA Exam Level	CCS Exam Competency	CCS Exam Level	CCS-P Exam Competency	CCS-P Exam Level
4.37	III.2.a,b,c	Application	I.1/II.1/II.3/II.4/ II.5/III.1/III.3/ III.4/III.5/IV.1/IV.3	Application	N/A	N/A
4.38	III.2.a,b	Application	I.4/II.1/II.4	Application	N/A	N/A
4.39	III.2.a,b	Application	I.4/II.1/II.4	Application	N/A	N/A
4.40	III.2.a,b	Application	I.1/II.1/II.3/II.4/ II.5/III.1/III.3/III.4/ III.5/IV.1/IV.3	Application	N/A	N/A
4.41	III.2.a,b	Application	II.1/II.4	Application	N/A	N/A
4.42	III.2.a,b	Application	II.1/II.4	Application	N/A	N/A
4.43	III.2.a,b	Application	II.1/II.4	Application	N/A	N/A
4.44	III.2.a,b	Application	II.1/II.4	Application	N/A	N/A
4.45	III.2.a,b,c	Application	II.1/II.4/III.1	Application	N/A	N/A
4.46	III.2.a,b,c	Application	II.1/II.4/III.1	Application	N/A	N/A
4.47	III.2.a,b,c	Application	I.4/II.1/II.4/III.1	Application	N/A	N/A
4.48	III.2.a,c	Application	II.1/II.4/III.1/III.4	Application	N/A	N/A
4.49	III.2.a,b,c	Application	II.1/II.4/III.1	Application	N/A	N/A
4.50	III.2.a	Application	I.4/II.1	Application	N/A	N/A
4.51	III.2.a,b	Application	II.1	Application	N/A	N/A
4.52	III.2.a,c	Application	II.1/III.1	Application	N/A	N/A
4.53	III.2.a,b,c	Application	I.4/II.1/III.1/III.4	Application	N/A	N/A
4.54	III.2.a,c	Application	II.1/III.1	Application	N/A	N/A
4.55	III.2.a,b,c	Application	I.1/II.1/II.3/II.4/ II.5/III.1/III.3/ III.4/III.5/IV.1	Application	N/A	N/A
4.56	III.2.a,b,c	Application	II.1/II.4/III.1	Application	N/A	N/A
4.57	III.2.c	Application	III.1	Application	N/A	N/A
4.58	III.2.c	Application	III.1/III.4	Application	N/A	N/A
4.59	III.2.a.b.c	Analysis	I.4/II.1/II.4/III.1	Analysis	N/A	N/A
4.60	III.2.a,b	Application	II.1/II.4	Application	N/A	N/A
4.61	III.2.a,b,c	Application	II.1/II.4/III.1	Application	N/A	N/A
4.62	III.2.a,b	Application	II.1/II.4	Application	N/A	N/A
4.63	III.2.a,b	Application	II.1/II.4	Application	N/A	N/A
4.64	III.2.a,b,c	Application	II.1/II.4/III.1	Application	N/A	N/A
4.65	III.2.a,b,c	Application	II.1/II.4/III.1	Application	N/A	N/A
4.66	III.2.a,b,c	Application	I.4/II.1/II.4/III.1	Application	N/A	N/A
4.67	III.2.a,b,c	Application	II.1/II.4/III.1	Application	N/A	N/A
4.68	III.2.a,c	Application	II.1/III.1/III.4	Application	N/A	N/A
4.69	III.2.a,b,c	Application	II.1/II.4/III.1	Application	N/A	N/A
4.70	III.2.a,c	Application	II.1/II.4/III.1	Application	N/A	N/A
4.71	III.2.a,b,c	Application	I.1/II.1/II.3/II.4/ II.5/III.1/III.3/ III.4/III.5/IV.1	Application	N/A	N/A

Question	CCA Exam Competency	CCA Exam Level	CCS Exam Competency	CCS Exam Level	CCS-P Exam Competency	CCS-P Exam Level
4.72	III.2.a,c	Application	II.1/III.1/III.4	Application	N/A	N/A
4.73	III.2.a,b,c	Application	I.1/II.1/II.3/II.4/II.5/IV.1	Application	N/A	N/A
4.74	III.2.a,b	Application	I.4/II.1/II.4/III.1	Application	N/A	N/A
4.75	III.2.a,b,c	Application	II.1/II.4/III.1	Application	N/A	N/A
4.76	III.2.a,b	Application	II.1/II.4/III.1	Application	N/A	N/A
4.77	III.2.a,b	Application	II.1/II.4	Application	N/A	N/A
4.78	III.2.a,c	Application	II.1/II.4/III.1	Application	N/A	N/A
4.79	III.2.a	Application	I.4/II.1	Application	N/A	N/A
4.80	III.2.a,b	Application	I.1/II.1/II.3/II.4/II.5/IV.1	Application	N/A	N/A
4.81	III.2.a,b	Application	I.4/II.1/II.4	Application	N/A	N/A
4.82	III.2.a,c	Application	II.1/III.1	Application	N/A	N/A
4.83	III.2.a,c	Application	II.1/III.1	Application	N/A	N/A
4.84	III.2.a,b,c	Application	II.1/II.4	Application	N/A	N/A
4.85	III.2.a,b,c	Application	II.1/II.4/III.1	Application	N/A	N/A
4.86	III.2.a,b,c	Application	II.1/II.4/III.1	Application	N/A	N/A
4.87	III.2.a	Application	II.1	Application	N/A	N/A
4.88	III.2.a,b,c	Application	II.1/II.4/III.1	Application	N/A	N/A
4.89	III.2.a	Application	I.1/I.2/II.1/II.3/II.4/II.5/IV.1/IV.3	Application	N/A	N/A
4.90	III.2.a,b	Application	II.1/II.4	Application	N/A	N/A
4.91	III.2.a,b,c	Application	I.4/II.1/II.4/III.1/III.4	Application	N/A	N/A
4.92	III.2.a,b,c	Application	II.1/II.4/III.1/III.4	Application	N/A	N/A
4.93	III.2.a,b,c	Application	II.1/II.4/III.1	Application	N/A	N/A
4.94	III.2.a,b,c	Application	II.1/II.4/III.1	Application	N/A	N/A
4.95	III.2.a,b	Application	II.1/II.4	Application	N/A	N/A
4.96	III.2.a,b	Application	II.1/II.4	Application	N/A	N/A
4.97	III.2.a,b,c	Application	II.1/II.4/III.1/III.4	Application	N/A	N/A
4.98	III.2.a,c	Application	II.1/III.1/III.4	Application	N/A	N/A
4.99	III.2.a,b,c	Application	II.1/II.4/III.1	Application	N/A	N/A

Chapter 5

Question	CCA Exam Competency	CCA Exam Level	CCS Exam Competency	CCS Exam Level	CCS-P Exam Competency	CCS-P Exam Level
5.1	III.2.a/III.3	Application	II.2/III.2/III.4	Application	N/A	N/A
5.2	III.2.a/III.3	Application	II.2/III.2	Application	N/A	N/A
5.3	III.2.a/III.3	Application	II.2/III.2	Application	N/A	N/A
5.4	III.2.a,b/III.3	Application	II.2/II.4/III.2/III.4	Application	N/A	N/A
5.5	III.2.a,b	Application	II.2/II.4	Application	N/A	N/A
5.6	III.2.a/III.3	Application	II.2/III.2/III.4/V.2.a/VI.5	Application	N/A	N/A
5.7	III.2.a/III.3	Application	II.2/III.2	Application	N/A	N/A
5.8	III.2.a/III.3	Application	II.2/III.2	Application	N/A	N/A
5.9	III.2.a,b/III.3	Application	I.4/II.2/II.4/III.2/III.4	Application	N/A	N/A
5.10	III.2.a	Application	II.2/III.2	Application	N/A	N/A
5.11	III.3	Application	III.2/V.2.a	Application	N/A	N/A
5.12	III.2.a/III.3	Application	II.2/III.2	Application	N/A	N/A
5.13	III.2.a/III.3	Application	II.2/III.2	Application	N/A	N/A
5.14	III.2.a,b/III.3	Application	II.2/II.4/III.2/III.4	Application	N/A	N/A
5.15	III.2.a/III.3	Application	II.2/III.2	Application	N/A	N/A
5.16	III.2.a,b/III.3	Application	I.4/II.2/II.4/III.2	Application	N/A	N/A
5.17	III.2.a/III.3	Application	II.2/III.2/V.2.a	Application	N/A	N/A
5.18	III.2.a,b/III.3	Application	II.2/II.4/III.2	Application	N/A	N/A
5.19	III.3	Application	III.2/III.4	Application	N/A	N/A
5.20	III.2.a,b	Analysis	II.2/II.4/III.2/III.4/V.2.a/VI.5	Analysis	N/A	N/A
5.21	III.2.a,b	Application	II.2/II.4	Application	N/A	N/A
5.22	III.2.a	Application	II.2	Application	N/A	N/A
5.23	III.2.a/III.3	Application	II.2/III.2	Application	N/A	N/A
5.24	III.2.a,b/III.3	Application	I.4/II.2/II.4/III.2	Application	N/A	N/A
5.25	III.2.a/III.3	Application	II.2/III.2/III.4	Application	N/A	N/A
5.26	III.2.a/III.3	Application	II.2/III.2/III.4	Application	N/A	N/A
5.27	III.2.a/III.3	Application	II.2/III.2	Application	N/A	N/A
5.28	II.2.a/III.3	Application	I.2/II.2/III.2	Application	N/A	N/A
5.29	III.2.a,b/III.3	Application	II.2/II.4/III.2	Application	N/A	N/A
5.30	III.2.a,b/III.3	Application	II.2/II.4/III.2	Application	N/A	N/A
5.31	III.2.a/III.3	Application	II.2/III.2	Application	N/A	N/A
5.32	III.2.a/III.3	Application	II.2/II.4/III.2	Application	N/A	N/A
5.33	III.3	Application	III.2	Application	N/A	N/A
5.34	III.2.a	Application	II.2	Application	N/A	N/A
5.35	III.2.a	Application	II.2	Application	N/A	N/A
5.36	III.2.a	Application	II.2	Application	N/A	N/A
5.37	III.2.a	Application	II.2	Application	N/A	N/A
5.38	III.2.a/III.3	Application	II.2/III.2/III.4	Application	N/A	N/A

Question	CCA Exam Competency	CCA Exam Level	CCS Exam Competency	CCS Exam Level	CCS-P Exam Competency	CCS-P Exam Level
5.39	III.2.a/III.3	Application	II.2/III.2/III.4	Application	N/A	N/A
5.40	III.2.a,b/III.3	Application	II.2/III.2	Application	N/A	N/A
5.41	III.2.a/III.3	Application	II.2/III.2/III.4	Application	N/A	N/A
5.42	III.3	Application	III.2/III.4	Application	N/A	N/A
5.43	III.2.a/III.3	Application	II.2/III.2	Application	N/A	N/A
5.44	III.3	Application	III.2	Application	N/A	N/A
5.45	III.2.a,b	Application	I.4/II.2	Application	N/A	N/A
5.46	III.2.a/III.3	Application	II.2/III.2	Application	N/A	N/A
5.47	III.3	Application	III.2	Application	N/A	N/A
5.48	III.2.a,b	Application	II.2/II.4	Application	N/A	N/A
5.49	III.2.a,b	Application	II.2/II.4	Application	N/A	N/A
5.50	III.2.a,b/III.3	Application	II.2/II.4/III.2	Application	N/A	N/A
5.51	III.2.a/III.3	Application	II.2/III.2/V.2.a	Application	N/A	N/A
5.52	III.2.a,b/III.3	Application	II.2/II.4/III.2	Application	N/A	N/A
5.53	III.2.a,b/III.3	Application	II.2/II.4/III.2	Application	N/A	N/A
5.54	III.2.a/III.3	Application	II.2/III.2	Application	N/A	N/A
5.55	III.6	Application	I.1	Application	N/A	N/A
5.56	III.2.a.b//II.3	Analysis	II.2/II.4/III.2/ III.4/V.2.a/VI.5	Analysis	N/A	N/A
5.57	III.2.a,b/III.3	Application	II.9/III.2	Application	N/A	N/A
5.58	III.2.a/III.3	Application	II.2/II.4/III.2	Application	N/A	N/A
5.59	III.2.a,b/III.3	Application	II.2/II.4/III.2/ III.4/V.2.a	Application	N/A	N/A
5.60	III.2.a,b/III.3	Application	II.2/II.4/III.2/III.4	Application	N/A	N/A
5.61	III.2.a,b/III.3/ III.4	Application	II.2/II.4/III.2/ V.2.b	Application	N/A	N/A
5.62	III.2.a,b/III.3	Application	II.2/II.4/III.2	Application	N/A	N/A
5.63	III.2.a/III.3	Application	II.2/III.2/III.4	Application	N/A	N/A
5.64	III.2.a,b/III.3	Application	II.2/II.4/III.2	Application	N/A	N/A
5.65	III.2.a/III.3	Application	II.2/III.2/V.2.a	Application	N/A	N/A
5.66	III.2.a	Application	II.2	Application	N/A	N/A
5.67	III.3	Application	III.2	Application	N/A	N/A
5.68	III.2.a.3.	Analysis	II.2/III.2/III.4/ V.2.a	Analysis	N/A	N/A
5.69	III.2.a/III.3	Application	II.2/III.2	Application	N/A	N/A
5.70	III.2.a/III.3	Application	II.2/III.2	Application	N/A	N/A
5.71	III.2.a/III.3	Application	II.2/III.2	Application	N/A	N/A
5.72	III.2.a,b/III.3	Application	II.2/II.4/III.2/V.2.a	Application	N/A	N/A
5.73	III.2.a,b	Application	II.2/II.4	Application	N/A	N/A
5.74	III.2.a,b/III.3/ III.4	Application	II.2/III.2/V.2.b	Application	N/A	N/A
5.75	III.2.a/III.3	Application	II.2/III.2/V.2.a	Application	N/A	N/A

Question	CCA Exam Competency	CCA Exam Level	CCS Exam Competency	CCS Exam Level	CCS-P Exam Competency	CCS-P Exam Level
5.76	III.2.a,b	Application	II.2/II.4	Application	N/A	N/A
5.77	III.2.a/III.3	Application	II.2/III.2	Application	N/A	N/A
5.78	III.2.a/III.3	Application	II.2/III.2	Application	N/A	N/A
5.79	III.2.a/III.3	Application	II.2/III.2	Application	N/A	N/A
5.80	III.2.a/III.3	Application	II.2/III.2/III.4	Application	N/A	N/A
5.81	III.2.a	Application	II.2	Application	N/A	N/A
5.82	III.2.a,b/III.3	Application	II.2/II.4/III.2	Application	N/A	N/A
5.83	III.2.a/III.3	Application	II.2/III.2/V.2.a	Application	N/A	N/A
5.84	III.2.a,b/III.3	Application	II.2/II.4/III.2	Application	N/A	N/A
5.85	III.2.a,b/III.3/ III.4	N/A	II.2/II.4/III.2/V.2.b	N/A	N/A	N/A
5.86	III.2.a/III.3	Application	II.2/III.2	Application	N/A	N/A
5.87	III.2.a,b/III.3	Application	II.2/II.4/III.2/ III.4/V.2.a	Application	N/A	N/A
5.88	III.2.a,b/III.3	Application	II.2/II.4/III.2/III.4	Application	N/A	N/A
5.89	III.2.a.b	Analysis	II.2/II.4	Analysis	N/A	N/A
5.90	III.2.a.b.3.	Analysis	II.2/II.4/III.2/ III.4/V.2.a	Analysis	N/A	N/A

Chapter 6

Question	CCA Exam Competency	CCA Exam Level	CCS Exam Competency	CCS Exam Level	CCS-P Exam Competency	CCS-P Exam Level
6.1	III.3	Application	N/A	N/A	III.2.b	Application
6.2	III.2.a,b/III.3	Application	N/A	N/A	II.2/III.2.b	Application
6.3	III.2.a/III.3	Application	N/A	N/A	II.2/III.2.b/ III.5	Application
6.4	III.3	Application	N/A	N/A	III.2.c/III.2.f	Application
6.5	III.2.a,b/III.3	Application	N/A	N/A	II.2/III.2.b/ III.5	Application
6.6	III.2.a/III.3	Application	N/A	N/A	II.2/III.2.c	Application
6.7	III.2.a/III.3	Application	N/A	N/A	II.2/III.2.c	Application
6.8	III.2.a,b	Application	N/A	N/A	II.2	Application
6.9	III.3	Application	N/A	N/A	III.2.c/III.2.e	Application
6.10	III.3	Application	N/A	N/A	III.2.c	Application
6.11	III.2.a,b	Application	N/A	N/A	II.2	Application
6.12	III.2.a,b/III.3	Application	N/A	N/A	II.2/III.2.c/ III.2.f	Application
6.13	III.2.a,b	Application	N/A	N/A	II.2	Application
6.14	III.2.a	Application	N/A	N/A	II.2	Application
6.15	III.2.a,b/III.3	Application	N/A	N/A	II.2/III.2.c	Application
6.16	III.2.a,b/III.3	Application	N/A	N/A	II.2/III.2.c/ III.5	Application
6.17	III.2.a,b/III.3	Application	N/A	N/A	II.2/III.2.c/ III.5	Application
6.18	III.3	Application	N/A	N/A	III.2.c/III.5	Application
6.19	III.2.a,b/III.3	N/A	N/A	N/A	II.2/III.2.f	Application
6.20	III.3	Application	N/A	N/A	III.2.c/III.5	Application
6.21	III.2.a/III.3	Application	N/A	N/A	II.2/III.2.c/ III.5	Application
6.22	III.2.a,b/III.3	Application	N/A	N/A	II.2/III.2.c	Application
6.23	III.3	Application	N/A	N/A	III.2.c	Application
6.24	III.3	Application	N/A	N/A	III.2.a	Application
6.25	III.2.a/III.3	Application	N/A	N/A	II.2/III.2.a	Application
6.26	III.3	Application	N/A	N/A	III.2.a/III.5	Application
6.27	III.2.a/III.3	Application	N/A	N/A	II.2/III.2.a	Application
6.28	III.2.a,b/III.3/ III.4	Application	N/A	N/A	II.2/III.2.a/ III.3/III.4	Application
6.29	III.3	Application	N/A	N/A	III.2.a	Application
6.30	III.3	Application	N/A	N/A	III.2.c/III.5	Application
6.31	III.3	Application	N/A	N/A	III.2.f	Application
6.32	III.2.a	Application	N/A	N/A	II.2	Application
6.33	III.2.a,b/III.3	Application	N/A	N/A	II.2/III.2.a	Application
6.34	III.2.a,b	Application	N/A	N/A	II.2	Application
6.35	III.2.a,b	Application	N/A	N/A	II.2	Application

Question	CCA Exam Competency	CCA Exam Level	CCS Exam Competency	CCS Exam Level	CCS-P Exam Competency	CCS-P Exam Level
6.36	III.2.a,b	Application	N/A	N/A	II.2	Application
6.37	III.2.a,b	Application	N/A	N/A	II.2	Application
6.38	III.2.a/III.3	Application	N/A	N/A	II.2/III.2.f	Application
6.39	III.2.a,b/III.3	Application	N/A	N/A	II.2/III.2.c	Application
6.40	III.2.a/III.3	Application	N/A	N/A	II.2/III.2.c/ III.5	Application
6.41	III.2.a,b/III.3	Application	N/A	N/A	II.2/III.2.c	Application
6.42	III.2.a/III.3	Application	N/A	N/A	II.2/III.2.c	Application
6.43	III.2.a,b/III.3/ III.4	Application	N/A	N/A	II.2/III.2.a,e,f/ III.4	Application
6.44	III.2.a/III.3	Application	N/A	N/A	II.2/III.2.f	Application
6.45	III.2.a/III.3	Application	N/A	N/A	II.2/III.2.a,f	Application
6.46	III.2.a,b/III.3	Application	N/A	N/A	II.2/III.2.c	Application
6.47	III.2.a/III.3	Application	N/A	N/A	II.2/III.2.c	Application
6.48	III.2.a/III.3	Application	N/A	N/A	II.2/III.2.c	Application
6.49	III.3	Application	N/A	N/A	II.2/III.2.c	Application
6.50	III.3	Application	N/A	N/A	III.2.c	Application
6.51	III.3	Application	N/A	N/A	III.2.f	Application
6.52	III.2.a/III.3	Application	N/A	N/A	II.2/III.2.a	Application
6.53	III.2.a	Application	N/A	N/A	II.2	Application
6.54	III.2.a,b	Application	N/A	N/A	II.2	Application
6.55	III.2.a/III.3	Application	N/A	N/A	II.2/III.2.a,c	Application
6.56	III.2.a,b/III.3	Application	N/A	N/A	II.2/III.2.f/ III.4	Application
6.57	III.2.a/III.3	Application	N/A	N/A	II.2/III.2.c,d	Application
6.58	III.3	Application	N/A	N/A	III.2.c	Application
6.59	III.2.a/III.3	Application	N/A	N/A	II.2/III.2.c	Application
6.60	III.2.a/III.3	Application	N/A	N/A	II.2	Application
6.61	III.2.a/III.3/ III.4	Application	N/A	N/A	II.2/III.2.f/ III.4	Application
6.62	III.2.a,b/III.3	Application	N/A	N/A	II.2/III.2.c	Application
6.63	III.2.a,b/III.3	Application	N/A	N/A	II.2/III.2.c	Application
6.64	III.2.a/III.3	Application	N/A	N/A	II.2/III.2.c	Application
6.65	III.2.a,b/III.3	Application	N/A	N/A	II.2/III.2.c	Application
6.66	III.3	Application	N/A	N/A	III.2.c	Application
6.67	III.3/III.4	Application	N/A	N/A	III.2.c	Application
6.68	III.2.a/III.3	Application	N/A	N/A	II.2/III.2.c/ III.5	Application
6.69	III.2.a/III.3	Application	N/A	N/A	II.2/III.2.c/ III.5	Application
6.70	III.2.a,b	Application	N/A	N/A	II.2	Application
6.71	III.2.a,b/III.3	Application	N/A	N/A	II.2/III.2.a,c	Application

Question	CCA Exam Competency	CCA Exam Level	CCS Exam Competency	CCS Exam Level	CCS-P Exam Competency	CCS-P Exam Level
6.72	III.3	Application	N/A	N/A	III.2.c	Application
6.73	III.3	Application	N/A	N/A	III.2.c/III.5	Application
6.74	III.2.a/III.3	Application	N/A	N/A	II.2/III.2.a,c	Application
6.75	III.2.a/III.3	Application	N/A	N/A	II.2/III.2.a	Application
6.76	III.3	Application	N/A	N/A	III.2.f	Application
6.77	III.2.a/III.3	Application	N/A	N/A	II.2/III.2.a	Application
6.78	III.2.a/III.3	Application	N/A	N/A	II.2/III.2.c	Application
6.79	III.2.a/III.3	Application	N/A	N/A	II.2/III.2.a,f	Application
6.80	III.2.a/III.3	Application	N/A	N/A	II.2/III.2.c	Application
6.81	III.2.a/III.3	Application	N/A	N/A	II.2/III.2.c	Application
6.82	III.2.a/III.3	Application	N/A	N/A	II.2/III.2.c	Application
6.83	III.2.a	Application	N/A	N/A	II.2	Application
6.84	III.2.a,b	Application	N/A	N/A	II.2	Application
6.85	III.2.a,b/III.3	Application	N/A	N/A	II.2/III.2.c	Application
6.86	III.2.a/III.3	Application	N/A	N/A	II.2/III.2.c	Application
6.87	III.2.a/III.3	Application	N/A	N/A	II.2/III.2.c	Application
6.88	III.2.a	Application	N/A	N/A	II.2	Application
6.89	III.2.a,b	Application	N/A	N/A	II.2	Application
6.90	III.3	Application	N/A	N/A	III.2.c,f	Application
6.91	III.2.a,b	Application	N/A	N/A	II.2	Application
6.92	III.2.a,b	Application	N/A	N/A	II.2	Application
6.93	III.2.a,b	Application	N/A	N/A	II.2	Application
6.94	III.3	Application	N/A	N/A	III.2.c	Application
6.95	III.2.a,b	Application	N/A	N/A	II.2	Application

Chapter 7

Question	CCA Exam Competency	CCA Exam Level	CCS Exam Competency	CCS Exam Level	CCS-P Exam Competency	CCS-P Exam Level
7.1	III.2.a,b	Analysis	I.4/II.1/II.4	Analysis	N/A	N/A
7.2	III.2.a,b,c	Analysis	I.1/I.2/II.1/II.3/ II.4/II.5/III.1/III.3/ III.4/III.5/IV.1	Analysis	N/A	N/A
7.3	III.2.a,b,c	Analysis	I.4/II.1/II.4/III.1	Analysis	N/A	N/A
7.4	III.2.a,b,c	Analysis	II.1/II.4/III.1/III.4	Analysis	N/A	N/A
7.5	III.2.c	Analysis	III.1	Analysis	N/A	N/A
7.6	III.2.c	Analysis	III.1/III.4	Analysis	N/A	N/A
7.7	III.2.c	Analysis	III.1/III.4	Analysis	N/A	N/A
7.8	III.2.c	Analysis	III.1	Analysis	N/A	N/A
7.9	III.2.a,b,c	Analysis	II.1/II.4/III.1/III.4	Analysis	N/A	N/A
7.10	III.2.a,b,c	Analysis	II.1/II.4/III.1/III.4	Analysis	N/A	N/A
7.11	III.2.a,b,c	Analysis	II.1/II.4/III.1/III.4	Analysis	N/A	N/A
7.12	III.2.a,b,c	Analysis	II.1/II.4/III.1/III.4	Analysis	N/A	N/A
7.13	III.2.a,b,c	Analysis	I.4/II.1/II.4/III.1/ III.4	Analysis	N/A	N/A
7.14	III.2.a,b,c	Analysis	II.1/II.4/III.1	Analysis	N/A	N/A
7.15	III.2.a,b	Analysis	I.4/II.1/II.4	Analysis	N/A	N/A
7.16	III.2.a,b	Analysis	I.2/II.1/II.4	Analysis	N/A	N/A
7.17	III.2.a,b,c	Analysis	I.1/I.2/II.1/II.3/ II.4/II.5/III.1/ III.3/III.4/III.5/ IV.1/IV.2/IV.3	Analysis	N/A	N/A
7.18	III.2.a,b,c	Analysis	I.1/I.2/II.1/II.3/ II.4/II.5/III.1/III.3/ III.4/III.5/IV.1	Analysis	N/A	N/A
7.19	III.2.a,b,c	Analysis	I.4/II.1/II.4/III.1/ III.4	Analysis	N/A	N/A
7.20	III.2.a,b	Analysis	II.1/II.4	Analysis	N/A	N/A
7.21	III.2.a,b	Analysis	I.4/II.1/II.4	Analysis	N/A	N/A
7.22	III.2.a,b,c	Analysis	I.1/II.1/II.3/II.4/ II.5/III.1/III.3/ III.4/III.5/IV.1	Application	N/A	N/A
7.23	III.2.a,b,c	Analysis	II.1/II.4/III.1	Analysis	N/A	N/A
7.24	III.2.a,b	Analysis	I.4/II.1/II.4	Analysis	N/A	N/A
7.25	III.2.a,b	Analysis	II.1/II.4	Analysis	N/A	N/A
7.26	III.2.a,b,c	Analysis	I.2/II.1/II.4/III.1/ III.4	Analysis	N/A	N/A
7.27	III.2.a,b,c	Analysis	II.1/II.4/III.1	Analysis	N/A	N/A
7.28	III.2.a,b	Analysis	II.1/II.4	Analysis	N/A	N/A
7.29	III.2.a,b,c	Analysis	II.1/II.4/III.1	Analysis	N/A	N/A
7.30	III.2.a,b,c	Analysis	II.1/II.4/III.1/III.4	Analysis	N/A	N/A
7.31	III.2.a,b,c	Analysis	II.1/II.4/III.1	Analysis	N/A	N/A
7.32	III.2.a,b,c	Analysis	II.1/II.4/III.1/III.4	Analysis	N/A	N/A

Question	CCA Exam Competency	CCA Exam Level	CCS Exam Competency	CCS Exam Level	CCS-P Exam Competency	CCS-P Exam Level
7.33	III.2.a,b	Analysis	II.1/II.4	Analysis	N/A	N/A
7.34	III.2.a,b,c	Analysis	II.1/II.4/III.1/III.4	Analysis	N/A	N/A
7.35	III.2.a,b,c	Analysis	II.1/II.4/III.1/III.4	Analysis	N/A	N/A
7.36	III.2.a,b,c	Analysis	II.1/II.4/III.1/III.4	Analysis	N/A	N/A
7.37	III.2.a.b.	Analysis	II.1/II.4	Analysis	N/A	N/A
7.38	III.2.a,b	Analysis	I.1/I.2/II.1/II.3/ II.4/II.5/III.1/III.3/ III.4/III.5/IV.1	Analysis	N/A	N/A
7.39	III.2.a,b,c	Analysis	I.4/II.1/II.4/III.1/ III.4	Analysis	N/A	N/A
7.40	III.2.a,b	Analysis	II.1/II.4	Analysis	N/A	N/A
7.41	III.2.a,b,c	Analysis	II.1/II.4/III.1/III.4	Analysis	N/A	N/A
7.42	III.2.a,c	Analysis	II.1/III.1	Analysis	N/A	N/A
7.43	III.2.a,b,c	Analysis	II.1/II.4/III.1	Analysis	N/A	N/A
7.44	III.2.a,b,c	Analysis	II.1/II.4/III.1/III.4	Analysis	N/A	N/A
7.45	III.2.a,b,c	Analysis	II.1/II.4/III.1/III.4	Analysis	N/A	N/A
7.46	III.2.a,b,c	Analysis	I.1/II.1/II.3/II.4/ II.5/III.1/III.3/ III.4/III.5/IV.1	Analysis	N/A	N/A
7.47	III.2.a,b	Analysis	II.1/II.4	Analysis	N/A	N/A
7.48	III.2.a,b,c	Analysis	II.1/II.4/III.1/III.4	Analysis	N/A	N/A
7.49	III.2.a,b,c	Analysis	II.1/II.4/III.1/III.4	Analysis	N/A	N/A
7.50	III.2.a,b,c	Analysis	II.1/II.4/III.1/III.4	Analysis	N/A	N/A
7.51	III.2.a,b,c	Analysis	II.1/II.4/III.1/III.4	Analysis	N/A	N/A
7.52	III.2.a,b	Analysis	II.1/II.4	Analysis	N/A	N/A
7.53	III.2.a,b,c	Analysis	I.4/II.1/III.1/III.4	Analysis	N/A	N/A
7.54	III.2.a,b	Analysis	II.1/II.4	Analysis	N/A	N/A
7.55	III.2.a,b	Analysis	I.2/I.4/II.1/II.4	Analysis	N/A	N/A
7.56	III.2.a,b	Analysis	I.4/II.1/II.4	Analysis	N/A	N/A
7.57	III.2.a.b.c	Analysis	I.4/II.1/II.4/III.2	Analysis	N/A	N/A
7.58	III.2.a,b	Analysis	II.1/II.4	Analysis	N/A	N/A
7.59	III.2.a,b,c	Analysis	II.1/II.4/III.1/III.4	Analysis	N/A	N/A
7.60	III.2.a,b,c	Analysis	II.1/II.4/III.1/III.4	Analysis	N/A	N/A
7.61	III.2.a,b,c	Analysis	II.1/II.4/III.1/III.4	Analysis	N/A	N/A

Chapter 8

Question	CCA Exam Competency	CCA Exam Level	CCS Exam Competency	CCS Exam Level	CCS-P Exam Competency	CCS-P Exam Level
8.1	III.2.a,b/III.3	Application	I.4/II.2/II.4/III.2	Application	N/A	N/A
8.2	III.2.a,b/III.3/ III.4	Analysis	I.2/II.2/II.4/III.2/ III.4/V.2.b	Analysis	N/A	N/A
8.3	III.2.a,b	Analysis	I.4/II.2/II.4	Analysis	N/A	N/A
8.4	III.2.a,b	Application	II.2/II.4	Application	N/A	N/A
8.5	III.2.a,b/III.3	Application	I.2/II.2/II.4/III.2	Application	N/A	N/A
8.6	III.2.a,b/III.3	Application	II.2/II.4/III.2	Application	N/A	N/A
8.7	III.2.a,b/III.3	Analysis	II.2/II.4/III.2/III.4	Analysis	N/A	N/A
8.8	II.2.a,b	Application	II.2/II.4	Application	N/A	N/A
8.9	III.3	Application	III.2	Application	N/A	N/A
8.10	II.2.a,b/III.3	Application	II.2/III.2	Application	N/A	N/A
8.11	III.2.a/III.3	Analysis	II.2/III.2/III.4	Analysis	N/A	N/A
8.12	III.2.a.b.3	Analysis	II.2/II.4/III.2/ III.4/V.2.a/VI.5	Analysis	N/A	N/A
8.13	III.2.a,b/III.3	Analysis	II.2/II.4/III.2/ III.4/V.2.a	Analysis	N/A	N/A
8.14	III.2.a,b/III.3	Application	II.2/II.4/III.2/ III.4/V.2.a/ V.2.b	Application	N/A	N/A
8.15	III.2.a,b/III.3	Analysis	I.4/II.2/II.4/III.2/ V.2.a	Analysis	N/A	N/A
8.16	III.2.a,b/III.3	Analysis	II.2/II.4/III.2/ III.4/V.2.a/VIL.5	Analysis	N/A	N/A
8.17	III.2.a,b	Analysis	II.2/II.4	Analysis	N/A	N/A
8.18	III.2.a,b	Analysis	I.4/II.2/II.4	Analysis	N/A	N/A
8.19	III.2.a,b/III.3	Analysis	I.4/II.2/II.4/III.2/ III.4/V.2.a/VI.5	Analysis	N/A	N/A
8.20	III.2.a,b/III.3	Analysis	I.4/II.2/II.4/III.2/ III.4	Analysis	N/A	N/A
8.21	III.2.a,b/III.3	Analysis	II.2/II.4/III.2	Analysis	N/A	N/A
8.22	III.2.a,b/III.3	Analysis	II.2/II.4/III.2/III.4	Analysis	N/A	N/A
8.23	III.2.a,b/III.3	Analysis	II.2/II.4/III.2/III.4	Analysis	N/A	N/A
8.24	III.2.a,b/III.3	Analysis	II.2/II.4/III.2/ III.4/VI.5	Analysis	N/A	N/A
8.25	III.2.a/III.3	Analysis	II.2/III.2/III.4	Analysis	N/A	N/A
8.26	III.2.a,b/III.3	Analysis	II.2/II.4/III.2	Analysis	N/A	N/A
8.27	III.2.a/III.3	Analysis	II.2/III.2	Analysis	N/A	N/A
8.28	III.2.a,b/III.3	Analysis	II.2/II.4/III.2	Analysis	N/A	N/A
8.29	III.2.a,b/III.3	Application	II.2/II.4/III.2	Application	N/A	N/A
8.30	III.2.a,b/III.3	Analysis	II.2/II.4/III.2	Analysis	N/A	N/A
8.31	III.2.a,b/III.3	Analysis	II.2/II.4/III.2	Analysis	N/A	N/A
8.32	III.2.a,b/III.3	Analysis	II.2/II.4/III.2/ III.4/V.2.a/VI.5	Analysis	N/A	N/A
8.33	III.2.a,b/III.3	Analysis	I.4/II.2/II.4/III.2/ III.4/V.2.a	Analysis	N/A	N/A

Question	CCA Exam Competency	CCA Exam Level	CCS Exam Competency	CCS Exam Level	CCS-P Exam Competency	CCS-P Exam Level
8.34	III.2.a,b/III.3	Analysis	II.2/II.4/III.2/III.4/V.2.a	Analysis	N/A	N/A
8.35	III.2.a,b/III.3	Analysis	II.2/II.4/III.2/III.4/V.2.a	Analysis	N/A	N/A
8.36	III.2.a,b/III.3	Analysis	II.2/II.4/III.2/III.4	Analysis	N/A	N/A
8.37	III.2.a,b/III.3	Analysis	II.2/II.4/III.2	Analysis	N/A	N/A
8.38	III.2.a,b/III.3	Application	II.2/II.4/III.2/III.4/VI.5	Application	N/A	N/A
8.39	II.2.a,b/III.3	Application	II.2/III.2	Application	N/A	N/A
8.40	III.2.a,b/III.3	Analysis	II.2/II.4/III.2/III.4/V.2.a	Analysis	N/A	N/A
8.41	III.2.a/III.3	Application	II.2/III.2	Application	N/A	N/A
8.42	III.2.a,b/III.3	Analysis	II.2/II.4/III.2/III.4/V.2.a	Analysis	N/A	N/A
8.43	III.2.a/III.3	Application	II.2/III.2/III.4	Application	N/A	N/A
8.44	III.3	Analysis	III.2	Analysis	N/A	N/A
8.45	III.2.a.b.3	Analysis	II.1/II.4/III.2	Analysis	N/A	N/A
8.46	III.2.a.b.3	Analysis	I.4/II.2/II.4/III.2/III.4/V.2.a	Analysis	N/A	N/A
8.47	III.2.a,b/III.3	Analysis	II.2/II.4/III.2/III.4	Analysis	N/A	N/A
8.48	III.2.a,b/III.3	Analysis	II.2/II.4/III.2/III.4	Analysis	N/A	N/A
8.49	III.2.a/III.3	Analysis	II.2/III.2/III.4/V.2.a	Analysis	N/A	N/A
8.50	III.2.a,b/III.3	Application	II.2/II.4/III.2	Application	N/A	N/A
8.51	II.2.a,b	Application	II.2	Application	N/A	N/A
8.52	III.2.a,b/III.3	Analysis	II.2/II.4/III.2/III.4	Analysis	N/A	N/A
8.53	III.2.a,b/III.3	Analysis	II.2/II.4/III.2	Analysis	N/A	N/A
8.54	III.2.a,b/III.3	Analysis	I.2/II.2/II.4/III.2/III.4/V.2.a/V.2.b	Analysis	N/A	N/A
8.55	II.2.a,b/III.3	Application	II.2/III.2	Application	N/A	N/A
8.56	III.2.a,b/III.3	Analysis	II.2/III.2/III.4/V.2.a	Analysis	N/A	N/A
8.57	III.2.a,b/III.3	Application	II.2/II.4	Application	N/A	N/A
8.58	III.2.a,b/III.3/IV.2	Analysis	II.2/III.2	Analysis	N/A	N/A

Chapter 9

Question	CCA Exam Competency	CCA Exam Level	CCS Exam Competency	CCS Exam Level	CCS-P Exam Competency	CCS-P Exam Level
9.1	III.2.a/III.3	Analysis	N/A	N/A	II.2/III.2.b	Application
9.2	III.2.a,b/III.3	Analysis	N/A	N/A	II.2/III.2.a,c	Application
9.3	III.2.a/III.3	Analysis	N/A	N/A	II.2/III.2.c	Application
9.4	III.2.a/III.3	Analysis	N/A	N/A	II.2/III.2.c	Application
9.5	III.2.a,b	Analysis	N/A	N/A	II.2	Application
9.6	III.2.a,b	Application	N/A	N/A	II.2	Application
9.7	III.2.a,b/III.3	Application	N/A	N/A	II.2/III.2.f	Application
9.8	III.2.a,b/III.3	Analysis	N/A	N/A	II.2/III.2.c	Application
9.9	III.2.a,b	Application	N/A	N/A	II.2	Application
9.10	III.3	Application	N/A	N/A	III.2.c	Application
9.11	III.3	Application	N/A	N/A	III.2.c	Application
9.12	III.3	Application	N/A	N/A	III.2.f/III.5	Application
9.13	III.2.a,b/III.3	Analysis	N/A	N/A	II.2/III.2.a,c	Application
9.14	III.2.a,b/III.3	Analysis	N/A	N/A	II.2/III.2.c/ III.5	Application
9.15	III.2.a,b/III.3	Analysis	N/A	N/A	II.2/III.2.c/ III.5	Application
9.16	III.2.a/III.3	Application	N/A	N/A	II.2/III.2.c/ III.5	Application
9.17	III.2.a/III.3	Analysis	N/A	N/A	II.2/III.2.c/ III.5	Application
9.18	III.3	Application	N/A	N/A	III.2.a	Analysis
9.19	III.3	Application	N/A	N/A	III.2.a	Analysis
9.20	III.3	Application	N/A	N/A	III.2.a	Analysis
9.21	III.3	Analysis	N/A	N/A	III.2.a	Application
9.22	III.2.a,b/III.3	Analysis	N/A	N/A	II.2/III.2.a	Application
9.23	III.3	Analysis	N/A	N/A	III.2.a	Application
9.24	III.3	Analysis	N/A	N/A	III.2.a	Application
9.25	III.2.a,b	Analysis	N/A	N/A	II.2	Application
9.26	III.2.a,b	Analysis	N/A	N/A	II.2	Application
9.27	III.2.a,b	Analysis	N/A	N/A	II.2	Application
9.28	III.2.a/III.3	Analysis	N/A	N/A	II.2/III.2.c,d	Application
9.29	III.2.a,b/III.3	Analysis	N/A	N/A	II.2/II.2.c	Application
9.30	II.2.a,b/III.3	Application	N/A	N/A	II.2/III.2.c	Application
9.31	III.2.a/III.3	Analysis	N/A	N/A	II.2/III.2.c/ III.5	Application
9.32	III.2.a,b/III.3	Analysis	N/A	N/A	II.2/III.2.c,d	Application
9.33	II.2.a,b/III.3/ III.4	Application	N/A	N/A	II.2/III.2.a,f/ III.4	Application
9.34	II.2.a,b/III.3	Application	N/A	N/A	II.2/III.2.c	Application
9.35	III.2.a,b/III.3	Analysis	N/A	N/A	II.2/III.2.c	Application
9.36	III.3	Application	N/A	N/A	II.2/III.2.c/ III.5	Application
9.37	III.2.a/III.3	Analysis	N/A	N/A	II.2/III.2.c	Application
9.38	II.2.a,b/III.3	Application	N/A	N/A	II.2/III.2.a,c,f	Application

Question	CCA Exam Competency	CCA Exam Level	CCS Exam Competency	CCS Exam Level	CCS-P Exam Competency	CCS-P Exam Level
9.39	III.2.a,b/III.3	Analysis	N/A	N/A	II.2/III.2.a,f/ III.4	Application
9.40	III.2.a,b/III.3	Analysis	N/A	N/A	II.2/III.2.a	Application
9.41	III.2.a,b/III.3	Analysis	N/A	N/A	II.2/III.2.f	Application
9.42	III.2.a/III.3	Analysis	N/A	N/A	II.2/III.2.c/ III.5	Application
9.43	II.2.a,b/III.3	Application	N/A	N/A	II.2/III.2.c,d/ III.5	Application
9.44	III.2.a,b/III.3	Analysis	N/A	N/A	II.2/III.2.c	Application
9.45	III.2.a,b/III.3	Analysis	N/A	N/A	II.2/III.2.c/ III.5	Application
9.46	III.2.a.b./III.3	Analysis	N/A	N/A	II.2/III.2.c/ III.5	Application
9.47	II.2.a,b/III.3	Application	N/A	N/A	II.2/III.2.a	Application
9.48	III.2.a/III.3	Analysis	N/A	N/A	II.2/III.2.c,d/ III.5	Application
9.49	III.2.a,b/III.3	Analysis	N/A	N/A	II.2/III.2.c,f	Application
9.50	III.2.a,b/III.3	Analysis	N/A	N/A	II.2/III.2.c/ III.5	Application
9.51	III.2.a,b/III.3	Analysis	N/A	N/A	II.2/III.2.a,c/ III.5	Application
9.52	III.2.a,b/III.3	Analysis	N/A	N/A	II.2/III.2.c/ III.5	Application
9.53	III.2.a	Analysis	N/A	N/A	II.2	Application
9.54	III.2.a,b/III.3	Analysis	N/A	N/A	II.2/III.2.a,f/ III.5	Application
9.55	III.2.a,b/III.3	Analysis	N/A	N/A	II.2/III.2.c	Application
9.56	III.2.a,b/III.3	Application	N/A	N/A	II.2/III.2.a,f/ III.5	Application
9.57	III.3	Application	N/A	N/A	II.2/III.2.c	Application
9.58	III.2.a,b/III.3	Analysis	N/A	N/A	II.2/III.2.c/ III.5	Application
9.59	III.3	Analysis	N/A	N/A	III.2.a	Application
9.60	III.2.a,b/III.3/ III.4	Analysis	N/A	N/A	II.2/III.2.a,f/ III.4	Application
9.61	III.2.a,b/III.3	Analysis	N/A	N/A	II.2/III.2.c/ III.5	Application
9.62	II.2.a,b/III.3	Application	N/A	N/A	II.2/III.2.c	Application
9.63	III.3	Analysis	N/A	N/A	III.2.a,c/III.5	Application
9.64	II.2.a,b/III.3	Application	N/A	N/A	II.2/III.2.a	Application
9.65	III.2.a,b/III.3/ III.4	Analysis	N/A	N/A	II.2/III.2.a,c/ III.4	Analysis
9.66	III.2.a,b/III.3	Analysis	N/A	N/A	II.2/III.2.a	Application
9.67	III.2.a,b/III.3	Analysis	N/A	N/A	II.2/III.2.c/ III.5	Application
9.68	III.2.a,b/III.3	Analysis	N/A	N/A	II.2/III.2.c/ III.5	Application

Question	CCA Exam Competency	CCA Exam Level	CCS Exam Competency	CCS Exam Level	CCS-P Exam Competency	CCS-P Exam Level
9.69	III.2.a/III.3	Analysis	N/A	N/A	II.2/III.2.a	Application
9.70	III.2.a,b/III.3	Analysis	N/A	N/A	II.2/III.2.c/ III.5	Application
9.71	III.2.a/III.3	Analysis	N/A	N/A	II.2/III.2.c	Application
9.72	III.2.a/III.3	Application	N/A	N/A	II.2/III.2.c,f	Application
9.73	III.2.a,b/III.3	Application	N/A	N/A	II.2/III.2.c/ III.5	Application
9.74	III.3	Analysis	N/A	N/A	III.2.c/III.5	Application
9.75	III.2.a	Analysis	N/A	N/A	II.2	Application
9.76	III.2.a,b/III.3	Application	N/A	N/A	II.2/III.2.a,c	Application
9.77	III.2.a,b/III.3	Analysis	N/A	N/A	II.2/III.2.c	Application
9.78	III.2.a,b/III.3	Analysis	N/A	N/A	II.2/III.2.a,c/ III.5	Application
9.79	III.2.a,b/III.3	Analysis	N/A	N/A	II.2/III.2.a,c/ III.5	Application
9.80	III.3	Application	N/A	N/A	III.2.a,c	Application
9.81	III.2.a/III.3	Application	N/A	N/A	II.2/III.2.c	Application
9.82	III.2.a.b/III.3	Analysis	N/A	N/A	II.2/III.2.c/ III.5	Application

Chapter 10

Question	CCA Exam Competency	CCA Exam Level	CCS Exam Competency	CCS Exam Level	CCS-P Exam Competency	CCS-P Exam Level
10.1	III.2.a	Recall	N/A	Home Health	N/A	Home Health
10.2	III.2.a	Recall	N/A	Home Health	N/A	Home Health
10.3	III.2.a	Application	N/A	Home Health	N/A	Home Health
10.4	III.2.a	Application	N/A	Home Health	N/A	Home Health
10.5	III.2.a	Application	N/A	Home Health	N/A	Home Health
10.6	III.2.a	Application	N/A	Home Health	N/A	Home Health
10.7	III.2.a	Application	N/A	Home Health	N/A	Home Health
10.8	III.2.a	Application	N/A	Home Health	N/A	Home Health
10.9	III.2.a	Application	N/A	Home Health	N/A	Home Health
10.10	III.6	Recall	N/A	Home Health	N/A	Home Health
10.11	III.2.a	Application	N/A	Home Health	N/A	Home Health
10.12	III.2.a	Application	N/A	Home Health	N/A	Home Health
10.13	II.1.a	Application	N/A	Home Health	N/A	Home Health
10.14	I.4	Recall	I.4	Home Health	I.5	Home Health
10.15	N/A	ICD-10	N/A	ICD-10	N/A	ICD-10
10.16	N/A	ICD-10	N/A	ICD-10	N/A	ICD-10
10.17	N/A	ICD-10	N/A	ICD-10	N/A	ICD-10
10.18	N/A	ICD-10	N/A	ICD-10	N/A	ICD-10
10.19	N/A	ICD-10	N/A	ICD-10	N/A	ICD-10
10.20	N/A	ICD-10	N/A	ICD-10	N/A	ICD-10
10.21	N/A	ICD-10	N/A	ICD-10	N/A	ICD-10
10.22	N/A	ICD-10	N/A	ICD-10	N/A	ICD-10
10.23	N/A	ICD-10	N/A	ICD-10	N/A	ICD-10
10.24	N/A	ICD-10	N/A	ICD-10	N/A	ICD-10
10.25	N/A	ICD-10	N/A	ICD-10	N/A	ICD-10
10.26	N/A	ICD-10	N/A	ICD-10	N/A	ICD-10
10.27	N/A	ICD-10	N/A	ICD-10	N/A	ICD-10
10.28	III.3	Application	V.2.a	Application	III.5	Application
10.29	III.3	Application	V.2.a	Application	III.5	Application
10.30	III.3	Application	V.2.a	Application	III.5	Application
10.31	III.3	Application	V.2.a	Application	III.5	Application
10.32	III.3	Application	V.2.a	Application	III.5	Application
10.33	III.4	Application	V.2.a	Application	III.5	Application
10.34	III.4	Application	V.2.a	Application	III.5	Application
10.35	III.4	Application	V.2.a	Application	III.5	Application
10.36	III.4	Recall	V.2.a	Recall	III.5	Recall
10.37	III.4	Recall	V.2.a	Recall	III.5	Recall
10.38	III.4	Recall	V.2.a	Recall	III.5	Recall
10.39	III.4	Application	V.2.a	Application	III.5	Application
10.40	III.2.a,b	Application	II.1	Application	N/A	LTAC
10.41	III.2.a,b	Application	II.1	Application	N/A	LTAC

Question	CCA Exam Competency	CCA Exam Level	CCS Exam Competency	CCS Exam Level	CCS-P Exam Competency	CCS-P Exam Level
10.42	III.2.a,b	Application	II.1	Application	N/A	LTAC
10.43	III.2.a	Application	II.2	Application	N/A	LTAC
10.44	III.2.a,b	Application	II.2	Application	II.1	Application
10.45	III.2.a,b	Application	II.1	Application	II.1	Application
10.46	III.2.a,b	Application	II.1	Application	N/A	IRF
10.47	III.2.a,b	Application	II.1	Application	N/A	IRF
10.48	III.2.a,b	Application	II.1	Application	N/A	IRF
10.49	III.2.a,b	Application	II.1	Application	N/A	SNF
10.50	III.2.a,b	Application	II.1	Application	N/A	SNF
10.51	III.2.a,b	Application	II.1	Application	N/A	SNF

Exercise Answer Key

Part I

Beginning Coding Exercises

Chapter 1. Basic Principles of ICD-9-CM Coding

Characteristics and Conventions of the ICD-9-CM Classification System

1.1.   b. Parentheses

Rationale: Square brackets in ICD-9-CM are used to enclose synonyms, alternative wordings, abbreviations, and explanatory phrases. Slanted brackets are found only in the Alphabetic Index and enclose a code that must be used in conjunction with a code that immediately precedes it. Boxes are not a defined convention of ICD-9-CM.

1.2.   a. Manifestation code

Rationale: Manifestation codes are secondary to the code representing the etiology of the condition. A CC exclusion is a term related to the prospective payment system based on diagnosis-related groups (MS-DRGs), which use ICD-9-CM codes. If the code is designated as an exclusion, the reporting of that code will not affect MS-DRG assignment. In the Alphabetic Index to diseases, the first code represents the underlying condition, and the second code, enclosed in italicized brackets, is the manifestation.

1.3.   Uniform Hospital Discharge Data Set

1.4.   Inpatient

Rationale: If a condition has not been ruled out at the termination of an inpatient stay, it may be reported to avoid data loss of a condition that consumed work or resources during an inpatient stay and could not be ruled out. For all other settings, diagnoses are reported only to their highest degree of specificity, and this rule is not applied. Rather, known signs or symptoms are assigned codes.

1.5. b. The appropriate V code

Rationale: This is an official guideline in ICD-9-CM.

1.6. c. Highest-degree burn

Rationale: This is an ICD-9-CM guideline. Treatment and anatomic location are not factors in the sequencing of burn conditions.

1.7. b. Hypertension and chronic kidney disease

Rationale: ICD-9-CM presumes a cause-and-effect relationship between hypertension and chronic kidney disease unless documentation in the health record states the hypertension is secondary. This is not the case with other conditions with hypertension, including heart disease.

1.8. Morphology codes, M codes

1.9. October 1, 10/1, 10/01, the first of October

1.10. b. V codes and E codes

Rationale: The ICD-9-CM system includes only two supplementary classifications:

- Supplementary Classification of Factors Influencing Health Status and Contact with Health Services
- Supplemental Classification of External Causes of Injury and Poisoning

The morphology codes are considered an appendix (A) to ICD-9-CM.

1.11. a. The nature and status (primary, secondary, in situ) for malignancies

Rationale: The neoplasm table included in the Alphabetic Index of ICD-9-CM provides code numbers by anatomic site. It includes benign, malignant, uncertain behavior, and unspecified categories, and for malignancies only, provides a method to reflect primary, secondary, or in situ status. Morphology codes are not found in the neoplasm table. A benign neoplasm is not reported according to stage because metastasis is not a characteristic of that behavior.

1.12. c. Either principal diagnosis or secondary diagnosis, depending upon the code and the circumstances of the admission

Rationale: Review the explanation of this supplementary classification included in the ICD-9-CM book for details. The rules for reporting depend on the circumstances of the encounter.

1.13. Main terms

1.14. d. All of the above

1.15.   b. When the coder lacks sufficient information to assign a more specific code

Rationale: The Not Otherwise Specified (NOS) designation means that the documentation used to select the code does not provide additional specificity to allow a more granular code assignment. This can be contrasted with Not Elsewhere Classified (NEC), which would be assigned when specific details of a condition are available, but the classification system does not include a specific category or code that exactly reflects the concept. Codes are not assigned without appropriate source documents reflecting the physician's diagnosis, even in the outpatient setting.

Infectious and Parasitic Diseases

1.16.   047.1

Rationale: Alphabetic Index term is Meningitis, subterm ECHO virus.

1.17.   052.9

Rationale: Alphabetic Index term is Chickenpox, with an instruction to "*see also* Varicella." Unless this is an encounter for a vaccination against the disease (reported with code V05.4), the code to represent that the patient actually has the disease is 052.9.

1.18.   022.0

Rationale: The main term in the Alphabetic Index is Anthrax, and the subterm is cutaneous. Without further specification, the code is 022.9, and if a manifestation was provided in the documentation that is not classified to the other possible codes in this category (NEC), then 022.8 is reported.

1.19.   Negative

Rationale: Alphabetic term is Infection, subterm Aerobacter aerogenes, which is classified to an NEC code, 041.85. When the Tabular List is consulted to verify the code, you will note that it appears in the code for "other Gram-negative organisms."

1.20.   054.10

Rationale: Alphabetic term is Herpes, subterm genital. If a specific site is included in the documentation that does not have its own code, code 054.19 is reported. The 054.10 code would be reported only if the condition is not further described.

1.21.   042

Rationale: There are specific guidelines for reporting human immunodeficiency virus (HIV) infections. Code 042 is assigned to confirmed cases of HIV infection based on a physician's diagnostic statement. Once a patient develops an HIV-related illness, the 042 code will be assigned on every subsequent admission for disease management of this condition. Once the 042 code is reported, it is inappropriate to assign codes 795.71 or V08, because the infection is confirmed.

1.22. 098.17

Rationale: The Alphabetic Index entries, main term Salpingitis, subterms venereal, acute; Salpingitis, subterms gonococcal, acute; or main term Gonorrhea, subterms fallopian tube, acute, are used to assign code 098.17.

1.23. a. 042

Rationale: AIDS stands for acquired immunodeficiency syndrome, frequently called human immunodeficiency infection. When a patient is treated for a complication associated with HIV infection, the 042 code is assigned as the principal diagnosis, followed by the code for the complication—in this case, a specific type of pneumonia. Alphabetic Index main term is Pneumonia, subterm Pneumocystis (carinii). Whenever an HIV person is admitted with an HIV-related condition, the principal diagnosis should be 042, followed by additional ICD-9-CM codes for all reported HIV-related conditions.

1.24. c. 070.54

Rationale: The Alphabetic Index main term is Hepatitis, subterms viral, type C, chronic. An outpatient would not have hepatic coma, and this was also not mentioned in the diagnostic statement. Reporting for acute disease is different than for chronic disease.

1.25. 002.1

Rationale: Alphabetic Index main term is Fever, subterm paratyphoid A.

1.26. 005.0

Rationale: Alphabetic Index main term is Poisoning, subterms food, Staphylococcus.

1.27. 009.2

Rationale: Alphabetic Index main term is Diarrhea, subterm infectious. A different code is assigned if the organism responsible is known.

1.28. 011.93

Rationale: Alphabetic Index main term is Tuberculosis, subterm pulmonary. A fifth digit of 3 is required to show that the tubercle bacilli (in sputum) have been identified by microscopic examination.

1.29. 034.1

Rationale: Alphabetic Index main term is Scarlatina. The code 034.1 is assigned alone because there are no further qualifications documented as manifestations.

1.30. 038.0

Rationale: Official coding guidelines state that if the documentation states septicemia, only code 038.0 should be assigned; however, the provider should be queried whether the patient has sepsis, an infection with SIRS.

1.31. 110.0

Rationale: Alphabetic Index main term is Dermatophytosis, subterm scalp. Codes are specific to anatomic location.

1.32. 055.1

Rationale: Alphabetic Index main term is Pneumonia, subterms in, measles.

1.33. 072.9

Rationale: Alphabetic Index main term is the same because mumps without stated complications is assigned to code 072.9. This code is assigned only when the patient has confirmed disease, not for vaccination (V04.6).

1.34. 078.12

Rationale: Alphabetic Index main term is Wart, subterm plantar.

1.35. 075

Rationale: Alphabetic Index main term is Mononucleosis, infectious. This is an example of a three-digit category.

Neoplasms

1.36. 201.92

Rationale: Alphabetic Index main term is the eponym Hodgkin's, subterm disease, with the fifth digit 2 added to indicate the location of the lymph nodes involved.

1.37. 212.3

Rationale: The neoplasm table in the Alphabetic Index may be used for code selection. In the neoplasm table, the main term is bronchus. Because the character of the disease is stated to be benign, the fourth column of the table is used for selection. Note that all anatomic locations are assigned to the same code when the disease is benign, but to separate codes when a malignancy is diagnosed in the bronchus. The code is 212.3.

1.38. V58.0

Rationale: Encounters for chemotherapy and radiation therapy without other diagnostic workup or disease management are reported with a V code from the supplementary classification in first position. For a hospital inpatient, that is known as the principal diagnosis.

1.39. d. Either a or b

Rationale: When both treatment methods are used in the same admission, ICD-9-CM allows the reporting of either one as the principal diagnosis, according to guidelines. The disease is not reported in this position when the encounter is specifically for receipt of treatment rather than for diagnosis or disease management.

1.40. 183.3

Rationale: The Alphabetic Index of ICD-9-CM, under the main term Carcinoma, instructs the coder to "*see also* neoplasm, by site, malignant." Turning to the neoplasm table, we go to the subterm for broad ligament and choose the code in the first column under the "malignant" heading. Because the cancer has not spread (metastasized), it is considered "primary."

1.41. 211.7

Rationale: The Alphabetic Index indicates that the main term Adenoma is a benign neoplasm. Note the instructions to the coder to "*see also* neoplasm, by site, benign." Turning to the neoplasm table, we go to the subterms pancreas, islet cells, and assign code 211.7. Note that this code is different than the codes for benign growths in other parts of the pancreas.

1.42. Benign

Rationale: Knowledge of the disease process is critical for accurate code assignment and correct classification.

1.43. 172.5

Rationale: The Alphabetic Index term Melanoma shows a nonessential modifier (malignant), so it is clear how this disease will be classified. If the coder relies on the subterm entry of "skin," code 172.8 results, but in this case we know that the chest wall is involved, so code 172.5 is assigned. If the neoplasm table were used exclusively, code 173.5 would result and reflect a malignant neoplasm of the skin of the chest wall, but not the fact that it was a malignant melanoma lesion. Turn to the tabular section of the ICD-9-CM book and note the differences between category 172 and 173 in the ICD-9-CM system.

1.44. 151.5

Rationale: The Alphabetic Index refers the coder to the neoplasm table and indicates that adenocarcinoma is considered malignant. When not further specified, the lesser curvature is reported with code 151.5.

1.45. 198.89

Rationale: Malignant neoplasms are the only diseases with "secondary" eligibility in the neoplasm table. In the table, go to salivary gland, subterm submandibular, and choose the code in the secondary column. Note that this code is the same as many others despite the difference in anatomic location. Turn to the Tabular List in ICD-9-CM and review the description of code 198.89, Other specified sites, other, which is very broad.

1.46. 211.3

Rationale: In the neoplasm table, reference the main term appendix, to select the code in the "benign" column

1.47. 233.0

Rationale: The term "in situ" indicates "in the original position." In other words, the cancer has not spread from the immediate area. ICD-9-CM has a specific location in the neoplasm table under malignancy. Because the exact location is not provided, the main term is breast, with no subterms. Note that regardless of anatomic site within the breast, the code for "in situ" disease is the same in ICD-9-CM—233.0.

1.48. b. Malignant

Rationale: The ICD-9-CM classification system often provides clues in the Alphabetic Index concerning the nature of a neoplasm. In this case, it is clear that this is a malignant neoplasm of the connective tissue.

1.49. Connective tissue

Rationale: The ICD-9-CM classification system often provides clues in the Alphabetic Index concerning the nature of a neoplasm. In this case, it is clear that this is a malignant neoplasm of the connective tissue.

1.50. Primary

Rationale: When the origin of the neoplasm is not known (that is, the physician has stated that there is an unknown [primary] location), there is a specific code for reporting—199.1. Metastatic spread of a primary malignancy is reported as a secondary neoplasm, with the appropriate code according to the location. Code 155.2 is an example of an ICD-9-CM code that is not specified as primary or secondary that allows reporting of malignancy in the liver.

1.51. 162.9

Rationale: The Alphabetic Index refers the coder to the neoplasm table. The main term is bronchus, resulting in code 162.9. It would be important to carefully review the documentation to determine if a more specific code could be reported because this code is unspecified and could refer to either the bronchus or the lung. The term "bronchogenic" suggests that the cancer originated at this location, so the choice of primary malignancy is appropriate.

1.52. 233.1

Rationale: The Alphabetic Index refers the coder to the neoplasm table. The main term is uterine cervix, and the "in situ" column is selected for code 233.1.

1.53. c. Lymph nodes of axilla and upper limb

Rationale: The ICD-9-CM codes for malignancies of the lymphatic systems use fifth digits to indicate the location of lymph node involvement. In this case, the digit 4 indicates the lymph nodes of the axilla and/or the upper limb. The lymph nodes of the inguinal region are reflected in fifth digit 5, the intrapelvic 6, and the head, face, and neck 1.

1.54. 203.01

Rationale: Following treatment, this disease may go into remission, where the patient is not considered cancer free, but is managing the disease or is symptom free. For coding, the Alphabetic Index main term Myeloma is reviewed. Note the nonessential modifier "multiple" and the code 203.0. A fifth digit is required to indicate whether or not the patient is in remission. In this case, 1 is assigned to reflect that status. If not mentioned in the documentation, 0 would be used. When in doubt, the physician should always be consulted to determine the correct code.

1.55. 205.02

Rationale: The Alphabetic Index main term is Leukemia, with subterms myelogenous, acute. Assign the fifth digit of 2 for the patient being in relapse.

Endocrine, Nutritional and Metabolic Diseases, and Immunity Disorders

1.56. 279.06

Rationale: The Alphabetic Index main term is dysgam-maglobulinemia.

1.57. 276.1

Rationale: The Alphabetic Index main term is the same.

1.58. 272.0

Rationale: The Alphabetic Index main term is the same, subterm primary, which results in the same code assignment.

1.59. b. Hyperaldosteronism

Rationale: The ICD-9-CM index also includes eponyms and provides clues to the nature of the disease. In this case, a description of the disease is also listed as secondary hyperaldosteronism. There are also listings under the main term Syndrome that are useful, in some cases, for locating a specific code. Code 255.13 is listed under Syndromes, Bartter's.

1.60. 250.43, 581.81

Rationale: Coding of diabetes will often involve recognition of diabetes-related complications. The fourth digit indicates the type of diabetes involved and the fifth whether or not the physician has indicated that the diabetes is out of control. Comments such as "under poor control" should not be considered synonymous with uncontrolled. Physician query would be indicated.

1.61. 250.00

Rationale: Without further qualification on the type of diabetes, the patient may have code 250.00. If the patient is treated with insulin, the physician should be asked if code 250.01 is appropriate. Insulin-requiring diabetics are not considered insulin dependent per ICD-9-CM coding guidelines.

1.62. 250.51, 362.02

Rationale: Alphabetic Index main term is Diabetes, subterm retinopathy. The fifth digit 1 is assigned because the patient is described as a type I (also referred to as juvenile onset). The ophthalmic manifestation is mentioned, which is reflected in the fourth digit, and the additional code, 362.02, is reported to specify what the complication is.

1.63. 250.11

Rationale: Type I diabetes is also known as insulin-dependent type. The Alphabetic Index term is Diabetes, subterms with and ketosis, ketoacidosis. The fifth digit of 1 is assigned because the patient is listed as type I.

1.64. 250.51

Rationale: Code 250.51 is assigned for this condition, although it would be very unusual not to also report the manifestation code that describes the complication. Coding professionals are expected to research the documentation for additional conditions that allow more granular data capture.

1.65. 251.3

Rationale: The Alphabetic Index term is Hypoinsulinemia, postsurgical, because the patient has had the pancreas removed.

1.66. d. All of the above

Rationale: Each condition mentioned is indexed and classified in ICD-9-CM to code 255.2, so the answer is all of the above.

1.67. 253.3

Rationale: The Alphabetic Index term is Dwarfism, subterm hypophyseal, or main term Hypophyseal and subterm dwarfism.

1.68. 276.8

Rationale: The Alphabetic Index main term is the same. Caution is required in assignment of codes based on abnormal findings without physician validation. If the condition is not listed in a diagnostic statement, the best practice is to ask the physician if the condition should be reported with a diagnosis code. Conditions that are integral to the disease process are not separately reported in ICD-9-CM, per coding guidelines.

1.69. 277.02

Rationale: The Alphabetic Index main term is Cystic, subterms fibrosis, with, manifestations, pulmonary.

1.70. Mucopolysaccharidosis

Rationale: The main term in ICD-9-CM is Syndrome, subterms Hurler's (-Hunter), or Sanfilippo's, or an alternative main term is Gargoylism. All are classified to code 277.5 along with other syndromes.

1.71. 278.01, V85.4

Rationale: The Alphabetic Index main term is Obesity, subterm morbid. ICD-9-CM defines morbid obesity as increased weight beyond the limits of skeletal and physical requirements (125 percent or more over ideal body weight), as a result of excess fat in subcutaneous connective tissues. Before this code is assigned, the diagnosis should be confirmed with the physician, rather than the coder making a judgment concerning whether the condition is morbid. Unspecified obesity is reported with code 278.00. An additional code should be assigned to identify the Body Mass Index, which is located under the main term Body, subterms mass index, 40 and over, to code V85.4.

1.72. 256.4

Rationale: The Alphabetic Index term is Polycystic, subterm ovary, ovaries, assigned to code 256.4.

1.73. 271.4

Rationale: The Alphabetic Index term is Glycosuria, subterm renal. If not designated as renal, this condition is classified as an abnormal finding with code 791.5.

1.74. 242.30

Rationale: The Alphabetic Index main term is Goiter, subterms nodular, with hyperthyroidism. Cross-reference ("*see also* Goiter, toxic"), produces the same code. There is no mention of thyrotoxic crisis or storm, so the correct fifth digit is 0.

1.75. 243

Rationale: The Alphabetic Index main term is Hypothyroidism, subterm congenital. This code would be assigned only to patients who were born with this condition.

Disorders of the Blood and Blood-Forming Organs

1.76. 280.0

Rationale: The Alphabetic Index main term is Anemia, subterms due to, blood loss (chronic). Note that this condition is classified with iron deficiency anemia. If the coder followed Anemia, deficiency, iron, as subterms, code 280.9 would result and not be as specific. The combination of the Alphabetic Index and the Tabular List is required for accurate code assignment.

1.77. b. Hereditary hemolytic anemias

Rationale: Both conditions are classified to category 282 (codes 282.60 and 282.4X) in the Alphabetic Index in ICD-9-CM. The main terms Sickle-cell and Thalassemia are indexed and are both hereditary hemolytic anemias.

1.78. 282.5

Rationale: Clinical disease is rarely present in patients who carry the sickle-cell trait. To locate this code in the Alphabetic Index, the main term is Sickle-cell, subterm trait, or main term Trait, subterm sickle-cell.

1.79.   285.1

Rationale: The Alphabetic Index main term is Anemia, subterms due to, blood loss, acute. Caution should be used in assignment of this code without confirmation from the physician that this is an appropriate diagnosis for reporting. Transfusions following surgery do not automatically mean the patient has suffered acute blood loss or has acute blood loss anemia. Also, diagnosis codes should not be assigned based on laboratory findings alone without physician confirmation of their significance. Best practice is to ask the physician if this condition is appropriate to add to the diagnostic statement and determine whether a code should be assigned.

1.80.   285.21, 585.6

Rationale: The Alphabetic Index main term is Anemia, subterms in, end-stage renal disease. When assigning code 285.21, coding guidelines indicate to also assign a code from category 585 to indicate the stage of chronic kidney disease. This diagnosis would not be reported based on laboratory findings alone. The physician should validate the diagnosis somewhere in the documentation used to select and justify the code assignment.

1.81.   a. Fanconi's anemia

Rationale: The Alphabetic Index directs assignment of code 284.09 for Fanconi's anemia. The main term is Anemia with subterm Fanconi's (congenital pancytopenia).

1.82.   286.4

Rationale: The Alphabetic Index main term is Disease, subterm von Willebrand's (angiohemophilia), or von Willebrand's (-Jurgens) (-Minot), subterm disease or syndrome.

1.83.   White

Rationale: The Alphabetic Index main term Agranulocytosis directs the coder to code 288.0. Note that category 288 is for diseases of the white blood cells. This condition is characterized by a reduced number of white cells in the blood.

1.84.   284.9

Rationale: To code aplastic anemia without further qualification, the main term is Anemia, subterm aplastic.

1.85.   281.2

Rationale: The Alphabetic Index main term is Anemia, subterms deficiency, folate. Note that the subterms under folate also are classified to the same code, 281.2, whether dietary or drug induced. An E code may be used to indicate that the condition is due to a poisoning or adverse reaction to medical treatment. Documentation must reflect the type of cause-and-effect relationship in order to assign the additional E code.

1.86. 281.3

Rationale: The Alphabetic Index main term is Anemia, subterm refractory (primary) megaloblastic, resulting in code 281.3.

1.87. 289.89

Rationale: The Alphabetic Index main term is Anemia, subterm osteosclerotic, or Osteosclerotic anemia, to assign code 289.89. Note that this code is not limited to this type of anemia but includes a variety of other specified diseases of blood and blood-forming organs that is quite broad.

1.88. 286.6

Rationale: The Alphabetic Index main term is Purpura, subterm fulminans (fulminous), resulting in code 286.6. The term "purpura" means hemorrhagic state characterized by patches of purplish discoloration in the skin and mucous membranes.

1.89. 287.30

Rationale: The Alphabetic Index main term is Purpura, subterm thrombocytopenic, or main term Thrombocytopenia, subterm purpura, to assign code 287.30. Note that this condition is classified as a primary thrombocytopenia and includes other conditions specified using different terms.

1.90. 287.4

Rationale: The Alphabetic Index main term is Thrombocytopenia, subterms due to, massive blood transfusion, or secondary, resulting in code 287.4. There are E codes that could also be assigned to reflect the fact that the condition is an adverse reaction to medical treatment. See code category E934.x. Documentation must reflect a cause-and-effect relationship to assign the secondary code and the E code for adverse reaction to substance properly administered.

1.91. 285.9

Rationale: This term is indexed as Anemia and is reported with 285.9. Care should be taken to determine if the condition is further specified within the health record for more specific coding than 285.9. Chronic simple anemia is classified to code 281.9 but should not be assigned without clear confirmation of the diagnosis. A fifth digit is required for codes that reflect anemia in chronic diseases but is not required for other specified anemia, 285.8, or the unspecified code in this exercise.

1.92. 284.01

Rationale: The main terms Anemia or Aplasia can be used in the Alphabetic Index to locate the correct code, 284.01, with the subterms congenital, aplastic, or congenital pure red cell. This condition is also called constitutional anemia.

1.93. 288.3

Rationale: The Alphabetic Index main term is Leukocytosis, with subterm eosinophilic to assign code 288.3.

1.94. 281.1

Rationale: The Alphabetic Index main term is Anemia, subterms vitamin, and B_{12} deficiency, to assign code 281.1 Using the subterm deficiency, you will note that pernicious anemia has a different fourth digit.

1.95. 286.0

Rationale: The Alphabetic Index includes this term for assignment of code 286.0. Note that many codes in this category are all congenital factor deficiencies in coagulation. If the coagulation deficiency is acquired and not congenital, code 286.7 applies. This may be due to liver disease or to a deficiency in vitamin K. An E code would be assigned if the cause were drug induced to reflect the drug involved.

Mental Disorders

1.96. b. Two codes

Rationale: Two ICD-9-CM codes are required. The Alphabetic Index main term Disease, subterm Jakob-Creutzfeldt (code 046.19), with dementia, offers code 294.11 as a manifestation code with behavioral disturbance, code 294.10 without.

1.97. 291.2

Rationale: The Alphabetic Index main term is Syndrome, brain, chronic alcoholic, resulting in code 291.2. When coding a health record, an additional ICD-9-CM code would be assigned for the alcoholism.

1.98. 295.34

Rationale: The Alphabetic Index main term is Schizophrenia, subterms paranoid (acute), with the fifth digit 4 added to reflect an acute exacerbation of a chronic condition with code 295.34.

1.99. 301.11

Rationale: The Alphabetic Index main term is Disorder, subterms personality and hypomanic (chronic), for assignment of code 301.11.

1.100. 300.01

Rationale: There are two ways to locate this code in the Alphabetic Index. One is under the main term Attack, subterm panic, and the second is found under the main term Panic, to locate code 300.01.

1.101. a. Dissociative identity disorder

Rationale: In the ICD-9-CM Alphabetic Index, look up Multiple, and note the code assignment under the subterm personality, 300.14. Note that ICD-9-CM includes the term "dissociative identity disorder." Looking up disorder, identity results in a different code. The index for Dissociative, subterm identity disorder, also results in code 300.14, so answer "a" is correct.

1.102. 301.51

Rationale: This mental illness is indexed under the main term Munchausen syndrome, for code 301.51. Note that other disorders described in different terms are also assigned to this code, such as hospital addiction syndrome and multiple operations syndrome.

1.103. d. All of the above

Rationale: The Alphabetic Index for any of these entries leads to category 302 for sexual deviations and disorders, along with other forms of psychosexual problems/disorders.

1.104. 303.00

Rationale: The Alphabetic Index main term is Intoxication, subterms acute, with alcoholism, to assign code 303.00. Fifth-digit assignments must be based on physician documentation rather than subjective assessment by the coder. Acute intoxication may occur in patients who do not have chronic alcoholism, and the code assignment is then 305.00.

1.105. 304.03

Rationale: Drug addiction is indexed under the main term Dependence in the ICD-9-CM Alphabetic Index. The subterm is morphine. The fifth digit 3 is used to denote that the patient is not currently using the drug and is considered by the physician to be in remission. Coders may not make assumptions about whether or not the patient is in remission from documentation found in the record. This is based on physician specification of the patient's status.

1.106. 304.70

Rationale: This combination of recreational drugs and prescription drugs is classified to code 304.70. Morphine or any other opioid type drug (such as heroin) in combination with any other type of drug is assigned to this category. Because the status of drug use is not known in this statement, the fifth digit 0 is assigned.

1.107. 306.0

Rationale: The Alphabetic Index main term is Torticollis, which may be a medical condition or psychogenic in origin. The subterm psychogenic results in code assignment of 306.0.

1.108. 307.23

Rationale: This mental illness is indexed in ICD-9-CM by the eponym for the disease rather than under Disorder and is assigned to code 307.23.

1.109. 300.4

Rationale: Nervous depression is indexed under the main term Depression, subterm nervous to code 300.4.

1.110. 309.21

Rationale: This condition is found in the Alphabetic Index under Disorder, subterms separation, anxiety, and assigned to code 309.21.

1.111. 318.0

Rationale: The Alphabetic Index main term is Retardation, with categories that describe the extent according to measured IQ ranges. Code 318.0 results, for moderate retardation, in a patient with this IQ measurement.

1.112. 314.01

Rationale: This condition is indexed under the main term Disorder, subterm attention deficit with hyperactivity, resulting in code 314.01.

1.113. 291.5

Rationale: The Alphabetic Index main term is Paranoia, subterm alcoholic, for code 291.5. An additional code would also be added to reflect alcoholism, according to the documentation provided in the actual health record.

1.114. 291.0

Rationale: Delirium tremens is a common side effect for a chronic alcoholic who is not drinking. The Alphabetic Index has an entry for the term, with the nonessential modifier (impending) listed, and code 291.0. The appropriate code for alcoholism would be assigned, based on the information available in the record that is not found in this short statement.

1.115. 290.43, 437.0

Rationale: This mental illness that follows cerebral infarctions is indexed under the main term Dementia, multi-infarct, with an instruction to "see also Dementia, arteriosclerotic." Going to this subterm shows additional choices including depressed features and depressed type, both assigned to code 290.43. If this is a late effect of cerebrovascular disease, an additional code should be added from the 438 category, based on the documentation in the health record. Note instructions to also assign 437.0 with this subcategory.

Nervous System and Sense Organs

1.116. 360.01

Rationale: Index the main term Endophthalmitis, subterm acute for code 360.01.

1.117. 359.1

Rationale: This condition is indexed under the main term Dystrophy, with subterms muscular or Duchenne's resulting in the same code, 359.1.

1.118. c. 250.50, 362.02

Rationale: When retinopathy is due to underlying diabetes, the diabetes code is sequenced first, followed by a manifestation code for the retinopathy, as in answer "c."

1.119. 362.31

Rationale: This condition is found in the Alphabetic Index under the main term Occlusion, subterms retina and artery, central to result in the selection of code 362.31.

1.120. 366.16

Rationale: The main term in the Alphabetic Index is Cataract, subterm nuclear, for code assignment 366.16.

1.121. 361.81

Rationale: To locate the correct code, use the main term Detachment, then retina, then traction, to assign code 361.81.

1.122. 366.14

Rationale: The Alphabetic Index main term is Cataract, subterms senile, posterior subcapsular. Assuming the cataract is "senile" on the basis of the patient's age is inappropriate. A specific diagnosis of senile cataract is required to assign a code from this category. A cataract without further specification as to type is reported with code 366.9.

1.123. 365.22

Rationale: The main term Glaucoma is indexed in the Alphabetic Volume II of ICD-9-CM, and subterms include angle closure, acute, for assignment of code 365.22. When specified as chronic, this code is not appropriate.

1.124. c. Blue and yellow

Rationale: To review this issue, go to the main term Color blindness in the index and locate code 368.59 in Volume I (Tabular List) of the classification system. There will be instances where the exact term in a diagnostic statement will not be included in the ICD-9-CM index, and you would scan the Tabular List to select an appropriate code after finding the general category. Note that code 368.53 is described as Tritan defect, with tritanomaly and tritanopia listed as alternative terms. You will find them listed as main terms that guide you to code 368.53, which involves blue/yellow determination.

1.125. 371.23

Rationale: The main alphabetic term is Keratopathy, subterm bullous, to indicate code 371.23. Note the "*see also* Keratitis" when this diagnosis is considered for coding.

1.126. 348.81

Rationale: The main alphabetic term is Sclerosis, subterm temporal for code 348.81.

1.127. c. Presbyopia

Rationale: Look up each term in the Alphabetic Index. The term "Presbyopia" (answer "c") does not result in a code from category 378, but rather code 367.4.

1.128. 381.10

Rationale: When otitis media is specified as chronic serous, code 381.10 results. If the documentation does not further specify this common ear infection in children, the code assignment defaults to 382.9. The main term is Otitis, subterms media, serous, chronic.

1.129. 382.01

Rationale: It is important to code this according to ICD-9-CM conventions. The main term is Otitis, subterms media, suppurative, acute with spontaneous rupture of eardrum. This may also be expressed as tympanic perforation. When this occurs postinflammation, the code is 384.20.

1.130. 385.33

Rationale: The Alphabetic Index main term is Cholesteatoma, with subterms middle ear, with involvement of mastoid cavity, for code 385.33.

1.131. 386.51

Rationale: The Alphabetic Index main term is Hyperactive, labyrinth (unilateral), so the code is 386.51. If present in both ears, code 386.52 is assigned. Take care not to confuse hyper with hypoactivity, which has a different code—386.53.

1.132. 379.41

Rationale: Anisocoria is the inequality in the size of the pupils of the eyes. The code assignment depends on whether the condition is congenital or not. Without further qualification, the code is 379.41.

1.133. 380.14

Rationale: The Alphabetic Index main term is Otitis, externa, malignant, resulting in code 380.14. This is a severe necrotic form due to bacteria.

1.134. 382.9

Rationale: Code 382.9 results when the physician does not further qualify whether this is an acute or chronic condition or specify the type of otitis media. In practice, the documentation should be reviewed for this information or the physician should be queried to determine the specifics so a more concise code may be reported.

1.135. 337.21

Rationale: The main term in the Alphabetic Index is Dystrophy, subterm sympathetic (reflex), upper limb, resulting in code 337.21. Even though the condition affects both arms, ICD-9-CM codes are not repeated. This is a convention of a classification system that is different from other coding systems, such as CPT, where a code may have a modifier appended or more than one code assigned when the procedure is performed in more than one location.

Circulatory System

1.136. 414.10

Rationale: The main term in the Alphabetic Index is Aneurysm, subterm ventricular, resulting in code 414.10. Follow the cross-reference instructions to "*see also* aneurysm, heart."

1.137. d. 402.01, 428.0

Rationale: Alphabetic Index main term is Hypertension, which takes you to the hypertension table. Note that hypertension with heart involvement has a note to "*see also* hypertension, heart." There is a specific code for malignant hypertension with heart failure in code 402.01. In the Tabular List there is an instruction to use an additional code to specify the type of heart failure, so code 428.0 is also assigned for that purpose. Answer "b" is incorrect because the code for the heart failure is not specific to congestive failure.

1.138. 396.1

Rationale: The ICD-9-CM classification system provides a specific category for valve disease that involves both structures and whether or not they are specified as rheumatic. In the Alphabetic Index, the main terms are Stenosis, subterms mitral, with aortic, insufficiency or incompetence, for code 396.1, or Insufficiency, aortic, with mitral valve disease, 396.1.

1.139. 410.21

Rationale: The Alphabetic Index main term is Infarct, subterm myocardium, inferolateral, with code 410.21 resulting. When a myocardial infarct is documented as acute, the initial episode of care fifth digit is assigned to a discharged patient. The use of the fifth digit 0 should not apply when a health record is available for coding.

1.140. 8

Rationale: This is an ICD-9-CM convention. The index guides the coder from the main term Infarct, myocardium, with symptoms after 8 weeks, to code 414.8. Turn to the Tabular List for category 410 (acute myocardial infarction). Note the definitions for the use of fifth digit 2 and also refer to the notes concerning "stated duration of 8 weeks or less."

1.141. 401.9

Rationale: Hypertension when not otherwise specified by the physician is reported with code 401.9. An assumption cannot be made by a coder that the hypertension is benign or malignant—this must be stated by the physician. The hypertension table in the Alphabetic Index may be referenced to locate this code.

1.142. Stenosis

Rationale: Selecting the main term in using ICD-9-CM is looking for the condition to be classified rather than the anatomic location or adjectives describing attributes of the disease or disorder. In this statement, the main term is Stenosis, with subterms subaortic, hypertrophic (idiopathic is a nonessential modifier) to locate code 425.1.

1.143. 427.32

Rationale: The main term is Flutter, subterm atrial or heart, atrial, resulting in code 427.32.

1.144. 427.41

Rationale: The Alphabetic Index main term is Fibrillation, subterm ventricular, to locate code 427.41.

1.145. 428.32

Rationale: The main term in the Alphabetic Index is Failure, subterms heart, diastolic, chronic, to locate code 428.32.

1.146. 411.1

Rationale: The Alphabetic Index main term is Angina, subterm preinfarctional. Angina that evolves into a myocardial infarction in the hospital setting would not be assigned a separate code. Rather, the code for the MI would be assigned because the angina in this circumstance would be considered integral to the disease process.

1.147. 415.19

Rationale: The Alphabetic Index main term is Infarct, subterm pulmonary. A fifth digit is assigned to reflect whether the event was iatrogenic (due to treatment) or not specified as iatrogenic in the "other" category, to result in code 415.19.

1.148. 414.06 (if native artery)

414.07 (if of bypass graft)

Rationale: Patients with a transplanted heart may also get arteriosclerotic heart disease in the new heart, either in the native artery or of a bypass graft. The Alphabetic Index main term is Arteriosclerosis, subterms, coronary, of transplanted heart, resulting in code 414.06 or 414.07 depending on the documentation.

1.149. 414.04

Rationale: The Alphabetic Index main term is Atherosclerosis, which refers you to arteriosclerosis, subterm bypass graft, coronary artery, autologous artery (internal mammary), to code 414.04. Autologous means that the artery was bypassed with tissue taken from another location in the patient's own body.

1.150. 438.13

Rationale: Late effects of a cerebral event that has occurred in the past are reported with a code from the 438 category in ICD-9-CM. Using Dysarthria as the main term results in code 784.5 in the Alphabetic Index, which is a symptom code. To locate the appropriate code, go to the index entry Late, subterms effect, cerebrovascular disease, with, dysarthria, resulting in code 438.13.

1.151. 433.21

Rationale: The Alphabetic Index entry is Stenosis, subterms precerebral, which refers you to narrowing, artery, precerebral, which suggests code 433.2, with the fifth digit of 1 added to show the presence of the infarction. If Infarct is used as the main term, subterm cerebral, code 434.91 is suggested, but the vertebral artery is not considered a cerebral artery, but rather a precerebral artery.

1.152. 416.2

Rationale: The Alphabetic Index main term is Embolism, subterms pulmonary, chronic, to assign the code 416.2.

1.153. 458.0

Rationale: The main term used in the Alphabetic Index is Hypotension.

1.154. 454.0

Rationale: The Alphabetic Index main term is Varicose, subterm vein, with, ulcer, resulting in code 454.0.

1.155. 441.3

Rationale: The Alphabetic Index main term is Aneurysm, subterms aorta, abdominal, ruptured, resulting in code 441.3.

Respiratory System

1.156. 466.0

Rationale: The Alphabetic Index main term is Bronchitis, subterm acute, resulting in code 466.0. Note that acute bronchitis with various forms of COPD results in a different code assignment. Bronchitis not specified as acute is classified to code 490.

1.157. 464.01

Rationale: The Alphabetic Index main term is Laryngitis, subterm with obstruction, resulting in code 464.01.

1.158. 474.10

Rationale: The main term in the Alphabetic Index is Hypertrophy, adenoids and tonsils, or tonsils and adenoids, resulting in code 474.10.

1.159. 471.8

Rationale: The Alphabetic Index main term is Polyp, subterm sinus or maxillary (sinus), resulting in code 471.8.

1.160. b. 480.1

Rationale: RSV is the abbreviation for respiratory syncytial virus. To code this condition, the main term is Pneumonia, subterm respiratory syncytial virus, resulting in code 480.1. Code 079.6 would not be needed to reflect the organism because it is specified in code 480.1. The 466.11 code is for bronchiolitis due to RSV, rather than pneumonia.

1.161. 482.81

Rationale: The Alphabetic Index main term is Pneumonia, subterm Gram-negative bacteria, anaerobic, resulting in code 482.81. In order to assign this code, physician documentation must be present, not just laboratory findings.

1.162. 491.21

Rationale: The Alphabetic Index main term is Disease, subterms pulmonary, obstructive (chronic), with acute exacerbation, resulting in code 491.21.

1.163. 492.8

Rationale: The Alphabetic Index main term is Emphysema. When not otherwise qualified, code 492.8 results. The health record should be evaluated for further specificity as to the type of emphysema when reporting for a healthcare episode or visit.

1.164. 486

Rationale: Although this diagnostic statement appears to be very specific, ICD-9-CM does not provide a specific code but rather classifies this condition to pneumonia, not elsewhere classified. The main term is Pneumonia, but it should be noted that bilateral, granulomatous, hemorrhagic, and septic are all nonessential modifiers.

1.165. 507.0

Rationale: The Alphabetic Index main term is Pneumonia, subterm aspiration, resulting in code 507.0.

1.166. 493.21

Rationale: The Alphabetic Index main term is Asthma, subterm with chronic obstructive pulmonary disease, resulting in code 493.21. The fifth digit 1 reflects the status asthmaticus.

1.167. 512.1

Rationale: The Alphabetic Index main term is Pneumothorax, subterm postoperative, resulting in code 512.1.

1.168. 518.83

Rationale: The Alphabetic Index main term is Failure, subterms respiration, chronic, resulting in code 518.83.

1.169. 519.02

Rationale: A tracheostomy is an artificial opening created in the trachea to facilitate breathing. The main term in the Alphabetic Index is Stenosis, subterm tracheostomy, resulting in code 519.02.

1.170. 494.0

Rationale: The Alphabetic Index main term is Bronchiectasis. Postinfectious is a nonessential modifier, so code 494.0 is appropriate. If documentation of an acute exacerbation was present, code 494.1 would be assigned.

1.171. c. 493.01

Rationale: The Alphabetic Index main term is Asthma, with subterm extrinsic adding the fourth digit 0. The fifth digit 1 reflects the status asthmaticus. The Official Coding Guidelines of ICD-9-CM states that it is inappropriate to assign an asthma code with a 5th digit of 2 (with acute exacerbation), together with an asthma code with a 5th digit of 1 (with status asthmaticus). Only the 5th digit of 1 should be assigned to indicate the status asthmaticus.

1.172. 512.8

Rationale: The main term in the Alphabetic Index is Pneumothorax, subterm spontaneous, resulting in code 512.8. If the patient were a newborn, code 770.2 would be assigned.

1.173. 493.00

Rationale: The main Alphabetic Index term is Asthma, subterm childhood, to assign 493.0x. The fifth digit describes with or without status asthmaticus or acute exacerbation. The appropriate fifth digit in this case is 0 because neither status asthmaticus nor acute exacerbation is mentioned.

1.174. 508.0

Rationale: The main term in the Alphabetic Index is Pneumonitis, subterm radiation, resulting in assignment of code 508.0. Depending on the reporting circumstances, an E code from the supplementary classification systems in the ICD-9-CM system might be added to reflect the external cause of this condition.

1.175. 460

Rationale: The Alphabetic Index main term is Cold, resulting in the three-digit category code 460. Acute upper respiratory illness is often used for patients who seek treatment in the emergency room or physician's office. This condition is classified to code 465.9 in ICD-9-CM, rather than code 460.

Digestive System

1.176. 521.00

Rationale: The Alphabetic Index main term is Caries, subterm tooth. Without further qualification, the ICD-9-CM code that results is 521.00.

1.177. 532.00

Rationale: The Alphabetic Index main term is Ulcer, subterm duodenum, acute, with hemorrhage. The fifth digit 0 reflects the fact that there was no mention of an obstruction in the documentation.

1.178. 531.90

Rationale: The Alphabetic Index main term is Ulcer, subterm stomach, resulting in code 531.90. The fifth digit 0 indicates there was no mention of obstruction in the source document used for coding.

1.179. 528.6

Rationale: The Alphabetic Index main term is Leukoplakia, subterm tongue, resulting in code 528.6.

1.180. b. 530.11

Rationale: The correct answer is "b" with code 530.11. The main term in the Alphabetic Index is Esophagitis, subterm reflux. Code 530.81 is assigned for esophageal reflux, and there is an "Excludes" note in the Tabular List for reflux esophagitis. The other choices are also not as specific as answer "b."

1.181. d. 531.10

Rationale: The main term in the Alphabetic Index is Ulcer, subterms stomach, with perforation (chronic), and no mention of obstruction, resulting in code 531.10. Category 533 in ICD-9-CM is reserved for a peptic ulcer with the site not specified enough to assign a more concise code. In this case, we know it is the stomach. The term "peptic" can refer to the esophagus, stomach, or duodenum.

1.182. 537.82

Rationale: The main term in the Alphabetic Index is Angiodysplasia, subterm stomach, resulting in code 537.82. When analyzing a health record, the documentation should be searched for evidence of hemorrhage because that would result in a different code assignment.

1.183. 535.31

Rationale: The main term in the Alphabetic Index is Gastritis, subterm alcoholic, with the fifth digit of 1 assigned to indicate hemorrhage, resulting in code 535.31. In reporting services for an encounter, it would also be appropriate to report an additional code for the alcoholism, if it could be verified in the documentation.

1.184. 540.9

Rationale: The main term in the Alphabetic Index is Appendicitis, subterm acute, resulting in code 540.9. Note that obstructive is a nonessential modifier.

1.185. 553.21

Rationale: The Alphabetic Index main term is Hernia, subterm incisional, resulting in code 553.21.

1.186. 550.93

Rationale: The main term in the Alphabetic Index is Hernia, subterm inguinal, for code assignment of 550.93. The fifth digit 3 indicates that both the right and the left sides are involved, and the hernia has recurred.

1.187. 552.00

Rationale: The main term in the Alphabetic Index is Hernia, subterms femoral, with obstruction. The term "incarcerated" describes an obstruction, so code 552.00 is assigned. The fifth digit 0 indicates that the source document did not indicate that the hernia involved both sides or was recurrent.

1.188. 555.0

Rationale: The main term from the Alphabetic Index is Disease, subterm Crohn's, or Crohn's disease. There is an instructional note to "see Enteritis, regional," so this term is referenced. When specified as located in the small bowel, this condition is reported with code 555.0.

1.189. 556.9

Rationale: The Alphabetic Index main term is Colitis, subterm ulcerative, resulting in code 556.9.

1.190. 560.31

Rationale: The main term in the Alphabetic Index is Ileus, subterm due to gallstone, resulting in code 560.31.

1.191. c. 562.10

Rationale: The answer "c" with code 562.10 is correct because the main term Diverticula, subterm colon, is classified there. The other choices involve diverticulitis or hemorrhage (not mentioned), or involve the small intestine.

1.192. 568.0

Rationale: The Alphabetic Index main term Adhesions, postoperative, results in code 568.0. There is an instructional note to "see also Adhesions, peritoneum," which provides additional choices. In a female, the postoperative peritoneal adhesions are reported with code 614.6. It is critical to consider all of the facts available in source documentation before assigning a diagnosis code.

1.193. 574.00, 574.10

Rationale: The main term in the Alphabetic Index is Cholelithiasis, with subterms cholecystitis, acute, resulting in code 574.00, and chronic, resulting in code 574.10. The fifth digit is 0, because there is no mention in the diagnostic statement of an obstruction. Careful analysis of the health record would be recommended to validate the code choice.

1.194. 577.0

Rationale: The main Alphabetic Index term is Pancreatitis, subterm acute.

1.195. 569.71

Rationale: Pouchitis is an inflammation of an internal pouch created in patients who have part of their colon removed to treat ulcerative colitis or familial adenomatous polyposis (FAP). This term is indexed in Volume II (Alphabetic Index), and code 569.71 is assigned.

Genitourinary System

1.196. 584.9

Rationale: This condition is indexed under the main term Failure, renal, acute, resulting in code 584.9.

1.197. 592.1

Rationale: The term, "ureterolithiasis," describes a stone or blockage in the ureter. It is indexed in the Alphabetic Index and results in code 592.1. Take care not to confuse with urethrolithiasis, which is assigned to code 594.2.

1.198. 590.10

Rationale: The Alphabetic Index main term is Pyelonephritis, subterm acute.

1.199. 594.2

Rationale: The term, "urethrolithiasis," describes a stone or blockage in the urethra. It is indexed in the Alphabetic Index and results in code 594.2. Take care not to confuse with ureterolithiasis, which is assigned to code 592.1.

1.200. 591

Rationale: Hydronephrosis occurs when, due to an occlusion or stricture, urine backs up into the kidney. It may result in pyelonephrosis.

1.201. 599.0

Rationale: Urinary tract infection is located in the Alphabetic Index under Infection as the main term, subterm urinary. Code 599.0 is an NEC code so when specified further, this code should not be assigned, but rather the more specific code. Also, this code must not be assigned based on laboratory results alone, but rather based on a diagnostic statement from the physician. When the organism responsible for the infection has been confirmed by the physician, an additional code may be assigned to reflect the source of the infection.

1.202. 596.51

Rationale: The main term in the Alphabetic Index is Overactive, subterm bladder, resulting in code 596.51.

1.203. 599.70

Rationale: This is a main term in the Alphabetic Index for ICD-9-CM. There are additional codes available when the etiology is known. This code is not assigned based on laboratory results alone but, instead, would require documentation of a diagnosis somewhere in the health record to justify reporting.

1.204. b. 598.9

Rationale: The main term in the Alphabetic Index is Stricture, with the subterm urethral, so answer "b" is correct. Code 598 is further specified. Code 598.00 indicates with infection, which is not stated, and the fourth digit of 8 would require a specified cause to be assigned.

1.205. b. The urinary tract infection

Rationale: The UTI is reported first because it is the root cause or etiology. Codes from category 041 are provided to be used as additional codes to identify the bacterial agent in diseases classified elsewhere or for bacterial infections of unspecified nature or sites. Answer "b" is correct.

1.206. c. 600.00

Rationale: The main Alphabetic Index term is Hypertrophy, subterms prostate, benign. Code 222.2 is not appropriate because prostatic hypertrophy is excluded from this category. The fourth digits of 2 or 9 are also not correct because the statement does not indicate localized hyperplasia and specifies the condition enough to assign 0. The fifth digit of "0" is assigned because there is no indication of obstruction.

1.207. 602.3

Rationale: The abbreviation PIN II refers to prostatic intraepithelial neoplasia, grade II. The Alphabetic Index main term is PIN II, resulting in code 602.3. Note that this is the appropriate code for grade I and II PIN, but grade III is reported with a code from the neoplasm section, 233.4, Carcinoma in situ of the prostate.

1.208. a. The tuberculosis

Rationale: In the ICD-9-CM classification system, when indicated in the Alphabetic Index, the etiology of a condition is reported first, followed by any manifestation codes. The correct answer is "a."

1.209. 611.82

Rationale: This term is found in the Alphabetic Index and assigned to code 611.82.

1.210. 614.3

Rationale: This abbreviation is for pelvic inflammatory disease. The main term in the Alphabetic Index is Disease, subterms pelvis, inflammatory (female), acute, code 614.3 results. Note that different codes result when the disease is further described as chronic or is due to another condition or complication.

1.211. 617.3

Rationale: The main Alphabetic Index term is Endometriosis, subterm broad ligament, resulting in code 617.3.

1.212. 620.1

Rationale: The main term in the Alphabetic Index is Cyst, subterms ovary, corpus, luteum, resulting in code 620.1.

1.213. 625.3

Rationale: This term is included in the Alphabetic Index and is assigned to 625.3. Use caution when reporting because this condition is often integral to other disease processes and may not always warrant separate reporting in ICD-9-CM.

1.214. 627.3

Rationale: The main term in the Alphabetic Index is Vaginitis, subterms postmenopausal, atrophic, resulting in code 627.3.

1.215. 622.12

Rationale: This is an abbreviation for cervical intraepithelial neoplasia II, which is indexed as such in Volume II of ICD-9-CM. Code 622.12 results.

Pregnancy, Childbirth, and the Puerperium

1.216. 653.11

Rationale: The Alphabetic Index process for a delivery is indexed under the main term Delivery, with the subterm complicated when there are factors that require treatment. In this case, the subterms contraction, contracted pelvis apply. The fifth digit assignment is 1, for delivered with or without mention of an antepartum condition.

1.217. 648.83

Rationale: This condition occurs during pregnancy and generally resolves following delivery. The Alphabetic Index main term is Diabetes, with subterm gestational, resulting in code 648.8, with the fifth digit 3 added to show that this was an antepartum condition in a patient not yet delivered. V58.67, Long-term (current) use of insulin, should also be assigned if the diabetes mellitus is being treated with insulin.

1.218. 669.22

Rationale: Codes from chapter 11 in ICD-9-CM are organized by antepartum and postpartum conditions. The main term in the Alphabetic Index is Syndrome, maternal hypotension, code 669.2, with the fifth digit 2 added to show that the condition occurred after the delivery (postpartum).

1.219. 6

Rationale: The chapter-specific guidelines general rules item C11, F.1, says, "The postpartum period begins immediately after delivery and continues for six weeks after delivery." The Official Guidelines are maintained by the National Center for Health Statistics and may be found at www.cdc.gov/nchs/data/icd9/icdguide.pdf.

1.220. 35

Rationale: To code this condition, the main term is Pregnancy, management affected by advanced maternal age, primigravida, resulting in code 659.5X. Note the definition of "elderly" in this code and the one for elderly multigravida. Supervision of a pregnancy of either is reported with V23.81 or V23.82.

1.221. 656.61

Rationale: The main term is Pregnancy, management, affected by large-for-dates fetus, resulting in code 656.6 with fifth digit 1 added because delivery occurred this admission.

1.222. 661.01

Rationale: The main term in the Alphabetic Index is Delivery (note that this complication is related to the delivery of the baby rather than to the pregnancy), with subterms inertia, uterine, primary, resulting in code 661.0 with the fifth digit 1 added to show the patient was delivered during this hospital stay.

1.223. 664.31

Rationale: The main term in the Alphabetic Index is Delivery, subterms complicated by, laceration, perineum, fourth degree, with fifth digit 1 assigned for an accomplished delivery during this admission. A corresponding procedure code from Volume III of ICD-9-CM would be expected for the laceration repair.

1.224. 670.24

Rationale: The main term in the Alphabetic Index is Sepsis, subterms puerperal, postpartum, resulting in code 670.2 with the fifth digit 4 assigned because the postpartum complication is for an episode of care following the admission for delivery.

1.225. 643.13

Rationale: The main term in the Alphabetic Index is Hyperemesis, subterms gravidarum, with dehydration, resulting in code 643.1 with fifth digit 3 added to show that the condition occurred before the delivery episode of care.

1.226. 644.13

Rationale: The main term in the Alphabetic Index is Pregnancy, subterms complicated by, false labor (pains), resulting in code 644.1 with the fifth digit 3 added for antepartum status. Note that category 644.1 is limited to a fifth digit of 0 or 3 only.

1.227. 654.03

Rationale: The main term in the Alphabetic Index is Bicornuate, subterms in pregnancy or childbirth, resulting in code 654.0, with the fifth digit added to show antepartum status.

1.228. 674.14

Rationale: The Alphabetic Index main term is Dehiscence, cesarean wound, reported with code 674.1, with fifth digit 4 added to indicate this is a postpartum condition subsequent to the delivery episode.

1.229. 673.12

Rationale: The Alphabetic Index main term is Embolism, subterms amniotic fluid (pulmonary), resulting in code 673.1, and fifth digit 2 added to reflect the postpartum condition during the delivery episode of care.

1.230. 2

Rationale: See the fifth-digit categories scattered throughout chapter 11 in Volume I of ICD-9-CM Tabular Lists. The correct answer is 2, delivered with mention of postpartum complication.

1.231. 3

Rationale: See the fifth-digit categories scattered throughout chapter 11 in Volume I of ICD-9-CM Tabular Lists. The correct answer is 3, antepartum condition or complication.

1.232. c. Deficient amount of amniotic fluid

Rationale: The correct answer is "c," deficient amount of amniotic fluid. The other conditions listed would result in different codes.

1.233. 632

Rationale: The Alphabetic Index entry is at the main term Missed, subterm abortion. If the patient has a history of this condition affecting the supervision/management of a current pregnancy, then code V23.1 is reported.

1.234. 5

Rationale: Look up the main term Abortion, subterms with complications, shock, (septic). Code 637.5 results, so the answer is 5.

1.235. d. a and b

Rationale: Any products of conception that are found outside the uterus are considered ectopic pregnancies, so answer "d" is correct because either a tubal (fallopian tube) or an abdominal pregnancy (outside the uterus) is ectopic.

Skin and Subcutaneous Tissue

1.236. 680.4

Rationale: The main term in the Alphabetic Index is Carbuncle, subterm hand, resulting in code 680.4.

1.237. 681.02

Rationale: The main term in the Alphabetic Index is Paronychia, subterm finger, resulting in code 681.02.

1.238. 692.71

Rationale: This term is listed in the Alphabetic Index. Code 692.71 results when the burn is first degree or not otherwise specified. For more serious burns (second or third degree), different codes are assigned.

1.239. 682.0

Rationale: The Alphabetic Index main term is Cellulitis, subterm face (there is no subterm chin, so the more general term of face is referenced), resulting in code 682.0.

1.240. 685.1

Rationale: The Alphabetic Index main term is Cyst, subterm pilonidal, resulting in code 685.1. When an abscess is involved, code 685.0 results.

1.241. 692.6

Rationale: The Alphabetic Index main term is indexed as Poison ivy, oak, sumac, or other plant dermatitis, and code 692.6 results for any of them.

1.242. 692.84

Rationale: The Alphabetic Index main term is Dermatitis, subterms due to, animal, dander (cat) (dog), resulting in code 692.84.

1.243. 695.4

Rationale: The main Alphabetic Index term is Lupus, subterm erythematosus, resulting in code 695.4.

1.244. 701.4

Rationale: The main Alphabetic Index term is Keloid (cheloid), subterm scar, resulting in code 701.4. The main term can also be scar, but the alternative cheloid is the term that results in the correct coding when you take this route.

1.245. 702.0

Rationale: The main Alphabetic Index term is Keratosis, subterm actinic, resulting in code 702.0. Note the various types of keratosis and the need for specificity in getting the correct code assigned. Without further qualification, code 701.1 results.

1.246. 704.01

Rationale: The main Alphabetic Index term is Alopecia, subterm areata, resulting in code 704.01.

1.247. 705.83

Rationale: The main Alphabetic Index term is Hidradenitis (suppurativa), resulting in code 705.83.

1.248. c. 707.07

Rationale: The Alphabetic Index main term is Pressure, subterm ulcer, resulting in code 707.07. This category is not specific to site. All of the codes except answer "c" are for nonpressure ulcers.

1.249. b. The diabetes mellitus

Rationale: Because the foot ulcer is a manifestation of the underlying diabetes, answer "b" is correct. A cause-and-effect relationship must be established for that rule to apply.

1.250. 697.0

Rationale: The Alphabetic Index main term is Lichen, subterm planus, resulting in code 697.0.

1.251. 692.0

Rationale: The Alphabetic Index main term is Dermatitis, subterms due to, detergent, resulting in code 692.0.

1.252. 682.3

Rationale: The Alphabetic Index main term is Abscess, subterm axilla, resulting in code 682.3.

1.253. 691.0

Rationale: The Alphabetic Index main term is Dermatitis, subterm diaper, resulting in code 691.0. Note that due to ammonia refers to household/liquid ammonia that is classified to code 692.4.

1.254. 695.10

Rationale: The Alphabetic Index main term is Erythema, subterm multiforme, resulting in code 695.10.

1.255. 692.76

Rationale: The Alphabetic Index main term is Sunburn, subterm second-degree, resulting in code 692.76.

Musculoskeletal System and Connective Tissue

1.256. 711.05

Rationale: The Alphabetic Index main term is Arthritis, subterm pyogenic or pyemic. The note at the beginning of the index entry for arthritis gives the fifth digits. The fifth digit designating hip (pelvic region and thigh) is 5. The resulting code is 711.05.

1.257. 714.0

Rationale: The Alphabetic Index main term is Arthritis, subterm rheumatoid, resulting in code 714.0. Subcategory 714.0 does not require a fifth digit to specify anatomic site involved.

1.258. 733.42

Rationale: The Alphabetic Index main term is Necrosis, subterm aseptic, bone, and femur, resulting in code 733.42, with the nonessential modifiers head and neck.

1.259. 715.36

Rationale: *Coding Clinic* (1995, 2Q:5), and *Coding Clinic* (2003, 4Q:118), state osteoarthrosis, localized, not specified whether primary or secondary, lower leg, is assigned for degenerative joint disease of the knee. The instructional note at the beginning of the index entry for osteoarthritis gives the fifth digit for knees ("lower leg") as 6, resulting in code 715.36.

1.260. 715.09

Rationale: The abbreviation DJD stands for degenerative joint disease. The Alphabetic Index main term is Degeneration, degenerative, subterm joint disease. A cross-reference note refers the coding professional to "*see also* osteoarthrosis." An entry for "multiple" results in the code 715.09. Review of this code in the Tabular List indicates that generalized DJD is synonymous with DJD of multiple joints.

1.261. 717.41

Rationale: The Alphabetic Index main term is Tear, subterm meniscus, lateral, bucket handle, old, resulting in code 717.41. Note the level of specificity available for injuries to the meniscal structures of the knee.

1.262. 717.7

Rationale: The Alphabetic Index main term is Chondromalacia, subterm knee or patella, resulting in code 717.7.

1.263. 719.11

Rationale: The Alphabetic Index main term is Hemarthrosis, subterm shoulder, resulting in code 719.11. Chronic is a nonessential modifier.

1.264. 720.0

Rationale: The Alphabetic Index main term is Spondylitis, subterm ankylosing, resulting in code 720.0. This subcategory does not require a fifth digit to identify anatomic site.

1.265. 721.1

Rationale: The Alphabetic Index main term is Spondylosis. The entry for Osteoarthritis, subterm spine, refers the coding professional to spondylosis, the term for arthritis of the spine. A search under spondylosis leads to subterm cervical, with myelopathy. The documented spinal cord compression constitutes myelopathy. This results in the code 721.1. This subterm does not require a fifth digit.

1.266. 722.10

Rationale: The abbreviation HNP stands for herniated nucleus pulposus. A search for Herniation, nucleus pulposus, in the Alphabetic Index results in a cross-reference note "*see Displacement, intervertebral disc.*" The main term is Displacement, subterms intervertebral disc, lumbar, lumbosacral. The presence of radicular symptoms does not constitute myelopathy, so the resulting code is 722.10.

1.267. 722.52

Rationale: The Alphabetic Index main term is Degeneration, subterm intervertebral disc. Review of the entry under main term Disease, subterm disc, degenerative, leads the coding professional to the above entry. The subterm lumbar, lumbosacral, results in code 722.52. There is no mention of cord compression in the diagnostic statement, so "with myelopathy" is not the appropriate code.

1.268. 724.2

Rationale: The Alphabetic Index main term is Pain, subterms back, low, resulting in code 724.2. The term "lumbago" is synonymous with low back pain.

1.269. 727.40

Rationale: The Alphabetic Index main term is Cyst, subterm synovial, resulting in code 727.40. Review of this code in the Tabular List shows that there is no specific code for the wrist.

1.270. 710.0

Rationale: The abbreviation SLE is for systemic lupus erythematosus. Although localized lupus is a disease of the skin, generalized or systemic lupus is included in the diseases of the musculoskeletal system as it primarily affects the joints. The Alphabetic Index main term is Lupus, subterm erythematosus, disseminated or systemic, resulting in code 710.0. This subcategory does not require a fifth digit.

1.271. 730.07

Rationale: The Alphabetic Index main term is Osteomyelitis, subterm acute or subacute. The instructional note at the beginning of the index entry for osteomyelitis indicates that a fifth digit of 7 is appropriate for the bones of the foot, resulting in code 730.07.

1.272. 733.01

Rationale: The Alphabetic Index main term is Osteoporosis (with nonessential modifier generalized), subterm postmenopausal, or senile, resulting in code 733.01.

1.273. 733.14

Rationale: The Alphabetic Index main term is Fracture, subterm pathologic, femur (neck), resulting in code 733.14. Traumatic fractures are coded to chapter 17, Injury and Poisoning, but pathological fractures, which are due to an underlying bone disease, are categorized to this chapter. Whenever a pathologic fracture code is assigned, the coding professional should also be alert for the presence of a concurrent bone disease, such as osteoporosis, malignancy, bone cyst, and so forth.

1.274. 735.0

Rationale: The Alphabetic Index main term is Hallux, subterm valgus, resulting in code 735.0. Acquired is a nonessential modifier, but congenital is an essential modifier and results in a different code. Because this diagnostic statement does not specify congenital, code 735.0 is appropriate. Note that hallux is not the name of a disease or condition, but merely the term for the big toe.

1.275. 737.10

Rationale: The Alphabetic Index main term is Kyphosis, resulting in code 737.10.

Newborn/Congenital Disorders

1.276. 741.93

Rationale: The Alphabetic Index main term is Spina bifida, subterm lumbar (fifth digit of 3). As there is no mention of hydrocephalus, the resulting code is 741.93.

1.277. 744.42

Rationale: The Alphabetic Index main term is Cyst, subterm branchial, with nonessential modifier cleft, resulting in code 744.42.

1.278. 745.4

Rationale: The abbreviation VSD stands for ventricular septal defect. The Alphabetic Index main term is Defect, subterm ventricular septal. With no further qualification, the appropriate code is 745.4.

1.279. 747.10

Rationale: The Alphabetic Index main term is Coarctation, subterm aorta, resulting in code 747.10. This code may also be located under main term Anomaly, subterm aorta, coarctation.

1.280. 749.03

Rationale: The Alphabetic Index main term is Cleft, subterms palate, bilateral, complete. All modifiers here are essential. As there is no mention of cleft lip, code 749.03 is assigned.

1.281. 752.61

Rationale: The Alphabetic Index main term is the same. As there is no sex designation in the diagnostic statement, code 752.61 is assigned because male is a nonessential modifier, but female is an essential modifier.

1.282. 753.12

Rationale: The Alphabetic Index main term is Disease, subterms kidney, polycystic, resulting in code 753.12. None of the essential modifiers that result in other codes are present in this diagnostic statement.

1.283. 754.35

Rationale: The Alphabetic Index main term is Dislocation, subterms hip, congenital (or congenital, hip), with subluxation of the other hip, resulting in code 754.35.

1.284. 755.11

Rationale: The Alphabetic Index main term is Syndactylism or syndactyly, subterms fingers, without fusion of bones, resulting in code 755.11.

1.285. 756.12

Rationale: The Alphabetic Index main term is Spondylolisthesis. In the absence of more information, code 756.12 is assigned.

1.286. 756.73

Rationale: The Alphabetic Index main term is Gastroschisis, resulting in code 756.73.

1.287. 758.7

Rationale: The Alphabetic Index main term is Syndrome, subterm Klinefelter's, resulting in code 758.7.

1.288. 756.51

Rationale: The Alphabetic Index main term is Osteogenesis imperfecta, resulting in code 756.51.

1.289. 771.1

Rationale: The abbreviation CMV stands for cytomegalovirus. The Alphabetic Index main term is Infection, subterms congenital, cytomegalovirus, resulting in code 771.1.

1.290. 770.12

Rationale: The Alphabetic Index main term is Syndrome, subterms meconium, aspiration, resulting in code 770.12. This code can also be accessed via main term Syndrome, subterms aspiration, of newborn, massive, or meconium.

1.291. 773.0

Rationale: The Alphabetic Index main term is Incompatibility, subterms Rh, fetus, or newborn, resulting in code 773.0. This code can also be accessed via main term Disease, subterms hemolytic, due to or with, incompatibility, Rh-negative mother.

1.292. 756.72

Rationale: The Alphabetic Index main term is Omphalocele, resulting in code 756.72.

1.293. 779.5

Rationale: The Alphabetic Index main term is Syndrome, subterm drug withdrawal, infant, of dependent mother, resulting in code 779.5. This code can also be accessed via main term Withdrawal symptoms or syndrome, subterm newborn, infant of dependent mother.

1.294. b. V30.00

Rationale: The Alphabetic Index main term is Newborn, subterm single, born in hospital. Per ICD-9-CM coding guidelines, the code for liveborn infant (V30–V39) is assigned as the principal diagnosis. See *Coding Clinic* 2002, 4Q. Additional codes would be assigned for all the complications of the newborn period.

1.295. 777.50

Rationale: The Alphabetic Index main term is Enterocolitis, subterms necrotizing, newborn, resulting in code 777.50.

Symptoms, Signs, and Ill-Defined Conditions

1.296. 783.0

Rationale: The Alphabetic Index main term is Anorexia. In the absence of either of the essential modifiers hysterical or nervosa, code 783.0 is assigned.

1.297. 783.7

Rationale: The Alphabetic Index main term is Failure, subterm to thrive, adult, resulting in code 783.7.

1.298. 780.91

Rationale: The Alphabetic Index main term is Fussy infant, resulting in code 780.91. This code can also be accessed via main term Infant, subterm fussy.

1.299. 780.60

Rationale: The Alphabetic Index main term is Fever. In the absence of any additional information, the code 780.60 is assigned.

1.300. 780.2

Rationale: The Alphabetic Index main term is Syncope. In the absence of any additional information, the code 780.2 is assigned.

1.301. 780.71

Rationale: The Alphabetic Index main term is Syndrome, subterm fatigue, chronic, resulting in code 780.71. This code can also be accessed via the main term Fatigue, subterms chronic or chronic syndrome, or main term Fatigue, subterm syndrome, chronic.

1.302. 786.50

Rationale: The Alphabetic Index main term is Pain, subterm chest. In the absence of any additional information, the code 786.50 is assigned.

1.303. 799.21

Rationale: The Alphabetic Index main term is Nervousness, resulting in code 799.21.

1.304. 783.5

Rationale: The Alphabetic Index main term is Polydipsia, resulting in code 783.5. This code can also be accessed via the main term Thirst, subterm excessive.

1.305. 790.29

Rationale: This code can be accessed via the main term Findings, abnormal, without diagnosis, subterms glucose, 790.29. If there was documentation that the findings were elevated, then code 790.22 (impaired glucose tolerance test) would be assigned.

1.306. 787.01

Rationale: The Alphabetic Index main term is Nausea, subterm with vomiting, resulting in code 787.01. This code can also be accessed via main term Vomiting, subterm with nausea.

1.307. 789.7

Rationale: The Alphabetic Index main term is Colitis, resulting in code 789.7.

1.308. 788.41

Rationale: The Alphabetic Index main term is Frequency (urinary) NEC, resulting in code 788.41. This same code can be accessed via the subterm micturition (synonym for urination).

1.309. 789.01

Rationale: The abbreviation RUQ stands for right upper quadrant of the abdomen. The Alphabetic Index main term is Pain, abdominal. The Alphabetic Index indicates the need for a fifth digit, and review of subcategory 789.0 reveals that the appropriate fifth digit for the right upper quadrant is 1.

1.310. 794.02

Rationale: The abbreviation EEG stands for electroencephalogram. The Alphabetic Index main term is Abnormal, subterm electroencephalogram (EEG), resulting in code 794.02.

1.311. 793.3

Rationale: The Alphabetic Index main term is Nonvisualization, subterm gallbladder, resulting in code 793.3. This code can also be accessed via the main term Abnormal, subterms radiologic examination, biliary tract.

1.312. 793.80

Rationale: The Alphabetic Index main term is Abnormal, subterm mammogram, resulting in code 793.80. This code can also be accessed via the main term Abnormal, subterms radiologic examination, breast, mammogram.

1.313. 798.0

Rationale: The abbreviation SIDS represents sudden infant death syndrome, considered a sign or symptom, rather than a specific diagnosis. The Alphabetic Index main term is Syndrome, subterm sudden infant death, resulting in code 798.0.

1.314. 799.4

Rationale: The Alphabetic Index main term is the same, resulting in code 799.4.

1.315. 786.01

Rationale: The Alphabetic Index main term is the same, resulting in code 786.01 in the absence of any additional diagnostic information.

Trauma/Poisoning

1.316. 803.75

Rationale: The Alphabetic Index main term is Fracture, subterms skull, open, with subarachnoid hemorrhage. An instructional note at the beginning of the index entry for fracture defines open vs. closed fractures, and another note at the entry for skull defines the appropriate fifth digits that describe loss of consciousness. The resulting code is 803.75.

1.317. 806.01

Rationale: The Alphabetic Index main term is Fracture, vertebra, with spinal cord injury, cervical. A note at the entry for fracture of vertebra defines the fifth-digit subclassifications that describe the extent of spinal cord injury. The appropriate code for a third cervical vertebra fracture, not specified as open, with a complete cord lesion, is 806.01.

1.318. 807.07

Rationale: The Alphabetic Index main term is Fracture, subterm ribs. The instructional table following the entry for Fracture, ribs, indicates that fifth digits are used to describe the number of ribs involved. Fracture, not specified as open, of seven ribs results in code 807.07.

1.319. 808.43

Rationale: The Alphabetic Index main term is Fracture, subterms pelvis, multiple, with disruption of pelvic circle, resulting in code 808.43.

1.320. 812.01

Rationale: The Alphabetic Index main term is Fracture, subterms humerus, surgical neck, resulting in code 812.01. The instructional note at the beginning of the index entry for fracture indicates that comminuted and impacted fractures are not open.

1.321. 813.47

Rationale: The Alphabetic Index main term is Fracture, subterms radius, with ulna, torus, resulting in code 813.47. A torus fracture is a type of incomplete break common in children, it is also known as a buckle fracture

1.322. 832.2

Rationale: The Alphabetic Index main term is Nursemaid's, subterm elbow, resulting in code 832.2.

1.323. 822.1

Rationale: A missile fracture is a type of open fracture. The Alphabetic Index main term is Fracture, subterms patella, open, resulting in code 822.1. An E code could also be reported to show that the injury was from a bullet.

1.324. 830.0

Rationale: The Alphabetic Index main term is Dislocation, subterm jaw. There is no indication that the dislocation is open or recurrent, so code 830.0 is appropriate.

1.325. 842.00

Rationale: The Alphabetic Index main term is Sprain, subterm wrist, resulting in code 842.00.

1.326. 860.1

Rationale: The Alphabetic Index main term is Pneumothorax, traumatic, with open wound into thorax, resulting in code 860.1. An E code could be added to report the stabbing with a knife.

1.327. 911.5

Rationale: The Alphabetic Index main term is Injury, superficial, buttocks. The instructional note at the entry for injury, superficial, indicates that the fifth digit to describe a bite by a nonvenomous insect, infected, is 5, resulting in code 911.5.

1.328. 944.35

Rationale: The Alphabetic Index main term is Burn, subterms hand, third-degree. Review of the Tabular List entry for category 944 indicates that the fifth digit to describe burn affecting the palm of the hand is 5, resulting in code 944.35.

1.329. 965.1

Rationale: The Alphabetic Index main term is Poisoning. There is no separate entry under poisoning for salicylate, and the coding professional is referred to the Table of Drugs and Chemicals. Review of the table shows that the appropriate code for salicylate poisoning is 965.1. If the circumstances of the poisoning were known, an E code could also be assigned.

1.330. 995.64

Rationale: The Alphabetic Index main term is Anaphylactic shock or reaction, subterms due to, food, nuts, resulting in code 995.64.

1.331. 991.0

Rationale: The Alphabetic Index main term is Frostbite, subterm face, resulting in code 991.0. An E code for adverse effect of exposure to cold might also be reported.

1.332. 996.02

Rationale: Search for the entry, Leakage of device or implant, leads to a cross-reference to "see Complications, mechanical." The main term is Complications, subterms mechanical, heart valve prosthesis, resulting in code 996.02.

1.333. 996.82

Rationale: The Alphabetic Index main term is Rejection, subterms transplant, organ, liver, resulting in code 996.82.

1.334. 998.2

Rationale: The Alphabetic Index main term is Laceration, accidental, complicating surgery, resulting in code 998.2.

1.335. 995.81

Rationale: The Alphabetic Index main term is Battered, subterm spouse.

E Codes

1.336. E886.0

Rationale: The Alphabetic Index main term is Tackle in sport, resulting in code E886.0.

1.337. E881.0

Rationale: The Alphabetic Index main term is Fall, subterms from, ladder, resulting in code E881.0.

1.338. E893.1

Rationale: The Alphabetic Index main term is Ignition, subterm clothes, (from controlled fire) in building. This leads to code E893.9. Review of category E893 shows that a more specific code, E893.1, exists for burns from ignition of clothing by controlled fire in a building other than a private dwelling. Thus, code E893.1 is the most appropriate code. It can also be found by accessing Ignition, subterm clothes (from controlled fire) in specified building or structure, except private dwelling E893.1.

1.339. E905.0

Rationale: The Alphabetic Index main term is Bite, subterm rattlesnake, resulting in code E905.0.

1.340. E909.2

Rationale: The Alphabetic Index main term is the same, Avalanche, resulting in code E909.2.

1.341. E917.3

Rationale: The Alphabetic Index main term is Bumping against, into, object, subterm furniture resulting in code E917.3.

1.342. E910.4

Rationale: Search for the entry, Drowning, leads the coding professional to a cross-reference to Submersion. Thus, the Alphabetic Index main term is Submersion, subterms in, bathtub, resulting in code E910.4.

1.343. E923.0

Rationale: The Alphabetic Index main term is the same, Fireworks, resulting in code E923.0.

1.344. E004.1

Rationale: The Alphabetic Index main term is Rappelling, resulting in code E004.1.

1.345. 882.0, E966

Rationale: The Alphabetic Index main term is Wound, open, hand. Without documentation of tendon involvement or complication of the wound, the resulting code is 882.0. The E code Alphabetic Index main term is Assault, subterms cut, knife, or stab, resulting in code E966.

1.346. 847.0, E816.0

Rationale: The Alphabetic Index main term is Sprain, subterms cervical or neck, resulting in code 847.0. The E code Alphabetic Index main term is accident, subterm motor vehicle, not involving collision with motor vehicle. A note refers the coding professional to categories E816–819. Review of these categories and the instructional note preceding category E810, which indicates that the appropriate fourth digit for driver of the motor vehicle is 0, results in code E816.0.

1.347. 813.82, E818.3

Rationale: The Alphabetic Index main term is Fracture, subterm ulna, resulting in code 813.82, without further information on the specific site of the fracture. The E code Alphabetic Index main term is accident, subterm motor vehicle, not involving collision. A note refers the coding professional to review categories E816–819. Review of these categories and the instructional note preceding category E810, which indicates that the appropriate fourth digit for passenger on a motorcycle is 3, results in code E818.3.

1.348. E017.0

Rationale: The Alphabetic Index main term is Roller coaster, resulting in code E017.0.

1.349. E906.0

Rationale: The Alphabetic Index main term is Bite, subterm dog, resulting in code E906.0.

1.350. E849.5

Rationale: The Alphabetic Index main term is Accident, subterms occurring at, street, resulting in code E849.5.

1.351. E871.0

Rationale: The Alphabetic Index main term is Misadventure to patients during surgical or medical care, subterms foreign object left in body during procedure, surgical operation, resulting in code E871.0. A search on the main term Foreign body leads to the cross-reference to Misadventure.

1.352. E909.0

Rationale: The Alphabetic Index main term is the same, Earthquake (any injury), resulting in code E909.0.

1.353. E919.3

Rationale: The Alphabetic Index main term is Accident, subterms machine, metal-working, resulting in code E919.3.

1.354. E924.0

Rationale: The Alphabetic Index main term is Burn, subterms, hot, liquid, resulting in code E924.0. This code may also be accessed from main term Burn, subterms substance, boiling, or molten.

1.355. 872.11, E928.3

Rationale: The Alphabetic Index main term is Wound, open, ear, external complicated. This leads to subcategory 872.1, where review shows that the appropriate code is 872.11, Auricle of ear. The E code main term is Bite, subterm human.

V Codes

1.356. V26.1

Rationale: The Alphabetic Index main term is Artificial, subterm insemination, resulting in code V26.1. This code can also be accessed via main term Insemination, artificial.

1.357. V02.61

Rationale: The Alphabetic Index main term is Carrier of, subterms, hepatitis, B, resulting in code V02.61. This code can also be accessed via the main term Hepatitis, subterms, viral, type B, carrier status.

1.358. V10.3

Rationale: The Alphabetic Index main term is History of, subterms malignant neoplasm of, breast, resulting in code V10.3.

1.359. V12.72

Rationale: The Alphabetic Index main term is History of, subterms polyps, colonic, resulting in code V12.72.

1.360. V16.41

Rationale: The Alphabetic Index main term is History of, subterms family, malignant neoplasm of, ovary, resulting in code V16.41.

1.361. V20.2

Rationale: The Alphabetic Index main term is Admission for, subterms well baby and child care, resulting in code V20.2.

1.362. V22.2

Rationale: The Alphabetic Index main term is Pregnancy, subterms incidental finding, resulting in code V22.2.

1.363. V33.01

Rationale: The Alphabetic Index main term is Newborn, subterms twin, born in hospital, with cesarean delivery or section, resulting in code V33.01.

1.364. V28.0

Rationale: The Alphabetic Index main term is Amniocentesis screening, subterm chromosomal anomalies, resulting in code V28.0.

1.365. V87.31

Rationale: The Alphabetic Index main term is Exposure, subterms to, mold, resulting in code V87.31.

1.366. V45.11

Rationale: The Alphabetic Index main term is Status, subterm renal dialysis, resulting in code V45.11.

1.367. V45.01

Rationale: The Alphabetic Index main term is Status (post), subterms cardiac, device, pacemaker, resulting in code V45.01. Code V53.31, Fitting or adjustment of cardiac pacemaker, is not appropriate here because there is no mention of such services, only that the pacemaker was present.

1.368. V53.32

Rationale: The abbreviation AICD represents an automatic, implantable cardioverter-defibrillator, a device that both detects and corrects cardiac rhythm abnormalities. The Alphabetic Index main term is Reprogramming, subterms cardiac pacemaker, resulting in code V53.31. When reviewing the code choices, code V53.32 is a better choice.

1.369. V54.27

Rationale: The Alphabetic Index main term is Aftercare, subterms fracture, healing, pathologic, vertebra, resulting in code V54.27. The aftercare codes are appropriate as principal diagnoses for home health agencies, skilled nursing facilities, rehabilitation facilities, and so forth.

1.370. V55.0

Rationale: The Alphabetic Index main term is Admission for, subterms attention to artificial opening, tracheostomy, resulting in code V55.0.

1.371. V55.3

Rationale: The Alphabetic Index main term is Admission for, subterms attention to artificial opening, colostomy, resulting in code V55.3. This code can also be accessed via the main term Colostomy, subterm attention to.

1.372. V58.11

Rationale: The Alphabetic Index main terms are either Admission for, subterm chemotherapy, or Chemotherapy, subterm encounter for, both resulting in code V58.11. If the purpose of an encounter is the administration of chemotherapy, this is the principal or primary diagnosis, rather than the malignancy, even if the malignancy is still present. An additional code for the malignancy is also used.

1.373. V59.4

Rationale: The Alphabetic Index main term is Donor, subterm kidney, resulting in code V59.4.

1.374. V71.4

Rationale: The Alphabetic Index main term is Admission for, subterms observation, following accident, resulting in code V71.4. This code may also be accessed via the main term Observation, subterm accident. The abbreviation MVA stands for motor vehicle accident.

1.375. V76.12

Rationale: The Alphabetic Index main term is Screening for, subterms malignant neoplasm, breast, mammogram NEC, resulting in code V76.12. This code is appropriate because there is no documentation that this was a patient at high risk for the development of breast cancer.

ICD-9-CM Procedure Coding

1.376. 63.73

Rationale: The Alphabetic Index main term is Vasectomy, resulting in code 63.73. The operative report should be thoroughly reviewed before assigning this code, as surgeons may use the term "vasectomy" synonymously with "ligation of the vas deferens" as a means of male sterilization. The appropriate code for ligation of the vas is 63.71.

1.377. 37.36

Rationale: The Alphabetic Index main term is Stapling, subterm left atrial appendage, resulting in code 37.36.

1.378. 06.2

Rationale: The Alphabetic Index main term is Lobectomy, subterms thyroid (unilateral), resulting in code 06.2.

1.379. 11.62

Rationale: The Alphabetic Index main term is Keratoplasty, subterm lamellar, resulting in code 11.62. Search on the main term Transplant, cornea, yields a code, 11.60, that is nonspecific and not appropriate for the degree of information that we have.

1.380. 20.01

Rationale: The Alphabetic Index main term is Myringotomy, subterms with insertion of tube or drainage device, resulting in code 20.01. This code can also be accessed via the main term Tympanotomy, subterm with intubation. The terms "myringotomy" and "tympanotomy" are synonymous and the physician's choice is usually based on the terminology used at the medical school he or she attended.

1.381. 27.62

Rationale: The Alphabetic Index main term is Repair, subterms cleft, palate, resulting in code 27.62.

1.382. 32.22

Rationale: The Alphabetic Index main term is Reduction, subterm lung volume, resulting in code 32.22.

1.383. 35.51

Rationale: The Alphabetic Index main term is Repair, subterms atrial septal defect, with, prosthesis (open-heart technique), resulting in code 35.51. Mesh is a type of bioinert, manufactured material that is used to patch a hole. Code 35.61, Repair with tissue graft, would not be appropriate as this would involve closure by patching with donor human tissue. Review the documentation in the record to see if 39.61, Cardiopulmonary bypass, is appropriate to use as an additional code.

1.384. 00.66

Rationale: The abbreviation PTCA stands for percutaneous transluminal coronary angioplasty. This is a technique for reducing plaque formation in an artery that is performed through the vessel (percutaneous) rather than via an incision. Search on the abbreviation PTCA leads to a cross-reference. The Alphabetic Index main term is Angioplasty, subterms balloon, coronary artery, resulting in code 00.66. This code can also be accessed via the same main term, subterms percutaneous transluminal, coronary. Only the right coronary artery was treated, so this is the appropriate code.

1.385. 36.16

Rationale: The Alphabetic Index main term is Bypass, subterms internal mammary-coronary artery, double vessel, resulting in code 36.16. The subterm aortocoronary bypass is inappropriate because the internal mammary arteries are sutured directly to the heart without harvesting. In aortocoronary bypass grafting, a segment of vein is sutured to the aorta at one end and to the affected coronary artery at the other end. With an internal mammary graft, the vessel is sutured to the coronary artery but remains attached to its native blood supply on the other end. Because both the left and right internal mammary arteries were used, this is a double-vessel graft, code 36.16. An additional code would be assigned for the use of cardiopulmonary bypass in actual practice. This code may also be accessed via the main term Revascularization, subterms cardiac, internal mammary-coronary artery, double vessel.

1.386. 40.42

Rationale: The Alphabetic Index main term is Dissection, subterms neck, radical, bilateral, resulting in code 40.42. This code may also be accessed via the main term Excision, subterms lymph, node, cervical, radical, bilateral. A search on the term lymphadenectomy, which may be used by the surgeon, leads to this second approach to the code.

1.387. 45.81

Rationale: The Alphabetic Index main term is Colectomy, subterms total, laparoscopic, resulting in code 45.81. This code may also be accessed via the main term Resection, subterms colon, total, laparoscopic.

1.388. 52.7

Rationale: The Alphabetic Index main term is Whipple operation, resulting in code 52.7.

1.389. 53.03

Rationale: The Alphabetic Index main term is Repair, subterms hernia, inguinal, direct unilateral, with prosthesis or graft, resulting in code 53.03.

1.390. 55.53

Rationale: The Alphabetic Index main term is Nephrectomy, subterm removal transplanted kidney, resulting in code 55.53.

1.391. 59.6

Rationale: The Alphabetic Index main term is Pereyra operation, resulting in code 59.6. This code may also be accessed via the main term Suspension, subterm paraurethral.

1.392. 68.8

Rationale: The Alphabetic Index main term is Exenteration, subterms pelvic, female, resulting in code 68.8.

1.393. 75.62

Rationale: Search on the main term Repair, laceration, leads to the cross-reference "see suture, by site." The Alphabetic Index main term is Suture, subterms rectum, obstetric laceration, resulting in code 75.62.

1.394. 81.51

Rationale: The Alphabetic Index main term is Replacement, subterms hip, total, resulting in code 81.51. Surgeons also use the term "total hip arthroplasty," and the code may also be accessed via the main term Arthroplasty, subterms hip, total replacement.

1.395. 84.24

Rationale: The Alphabetic Index main term is Reattachment, subterms arm, upper, resulting in code 84.24.

1.396. 72.21

Rationale: The Alphabetic Index main term is Delivery, subterms forceps, mid, with episiotomy, resulting in code 72.21.

1.397. 60.4

Rationale: The Alphabetic Index main term is Prostatectomy, subterm retropubic, resulting in code 60.4.

1.398. 45.62

Rationale: The Alphabetic Index main term is Jejunectomy, resulting in code 45.62. This code may also be accessed via the main term Resection, subterms intestine, small. An end-to-end anastomosis is not separately coded.

1.399. 36.32

Rationale: The Alphabetic Index main term is Revascularization, subterms cardiac, transmyocardial, percutaneous, resulting in code 36.32.

1.400. 36.07, 00.45

Rationale: The Alphabetic Index main term is Insertion, subterms stent, artery, coronary, drug eluting, resulting in code 36.07 and 00.45 to indicate the number of stents inserted.

Review Questions

1.401. b. 540.9

1.402. A code for the initiating underlying systemic infection followed by a code for SIRS (code 995.92) must be assigned before the code for septic shock. As noted in the sequencing instructions of the Tabular List, the code for septic shock cannot be assigned as a principal diagnosis.

1.403. In situ

1.404. Secondary

1.405. c. Dehydration

1.406. b. 491.22

1.407. a. Chronic kidney disease

1.408. Principal

1.409. c. Dependent on the circumstances of the admission

1.410. Manifestation

1.411. a. Codes from all other chapters

1.412. b. The mother's record

1.413. d. All of the above

1.414. d. All of the above

1.415. b. The primary hyperparathyroidism

1.416. c. Attending physician's documented clinical assessment of the maturity of the infant

1.417. Combination

1.418. c. There is no set time.

1.419. d. All of the above

1.420. b. The one most closely related to the principal diagnosis

1.421. b. 715.95, Osteoarthritis of the hip

1.422. b. Abdominal pain

1.423. a. Nausea with vomiting is reported as the principal diagnosis, and acute gastroenteritis and food poisoning are reported as secondary diagnoses.

1.424. d. Either a or b

1.425. a. It involves abnormal glucose tolerance test findings/results in pregnant women without previous history of diabetes.

1.426. c. Physician or any qualified healthcare practitioner who is legally accountable for establishing the patient's diagnosis

Chapter 2. Basic Principles of CPT Coding

CPT Organization, Structure, and Guidelines

2.1.   a. Patient management

Incorrect answer. This issue is addressed in the Category II codes.

b. New technology

Correct answer. New technology is addressed by the Category III codes.

c. Therapeutic, preventive, or other interventions

Incorrect answer. This issue is addressed in the Category II codes.

d. Patient safety

Incorrect answer. This issue is addressed in the Category II codes.

2.2.   a. Changes in verbiage within code descriptions

Incorrect answer. The symbol ▲ is used to indicate changes in verbiage in code descriptions.

b. A new code

Incorrect answer. The symbol ● is used to indicate a new code.

c. Changes in verbiage other than that in code descriptions, for example, changes in coding guidelines or parenthetical notes

Correct answer.

d. A code for which there is a corresponding HCPCS Level II code

Incorrect answer. There is no such indication in CPT.

2.3.   a. No. All diagnostic procedures are included in therapeutic interventional procedures.

Incorrect answer. This is one of the circumstances when the diagnostic procedure may be reported in addition to the therapeutic intervention.

b. Yes. Per revised coding guidelines, if there is a clinical change during an interventional procedure that requires further diagnostic study, the diagnostic angiogram may be reported in addition to the therapeutic procedure.

Correct answer.

2.4.   a. Kidneys, abdominal aorta, common iliac artery origins, inferior vena cava

Correct answer.

b. Kidneys, abdominal aorta, common iliac artery origins, inferior vena cava, and urinary bladder

Incorrect answer. The urinary bladder need be included only if there is a clinical history of urinary system pathology.

c. Liver, gallbladder, common bile duct, pancreas, spleen, kidneys, upper aorta, inferior vena cava

Incorrect answer. These organs are the components of a complete ultrasound of the abdomen.

d. Kidneys, abdominal aorta, common iliac artery origins

Incorrect answer. The inferior vena cava must also be evaluated to complete an examination.

2.5. a. Appendix E

Incorrect answer. Appendix E contains a list of CPT codes exempt from modifier -51. Appendix G is the correct answer.

b. Appendix F

Incorrect answer. Appendix F contains a list of CPT codes exempt from modifier -63. Appendix G is the correct answer.

c. Appendix G

Correct answer.

d. Appendix H

Incorrect answer. Appendix H contains an alphabetic listing of Category II codes. Appendix G is the correct answer.

2.6. a. True

Incorrect answer. Category II codes are never used alone. They are supplemental tracking codes and may never be reported first.

b. False

Correct answer.

2.7. a. Appendix J

Correct answer. Appendix J contains a listing of each of the nerve conduction studies and the nerve that is appropriately reported with that code.

b. Appendix K

Incorrect answer. Appendix K lists codes assigned in anticipation of FDA approval. Appendix J contains a listing of each of the nerve conduction studies and the nerve that is appropriately reported with that code.

c. Appendix I

Appendix I is a detailed listing of genetic testing code modifiers. Appendix J contains a listing of each of the nerve conduction studies and the nerve that is appropriately reported with that code.

d. Appendix L

Appendix L is a series of diagrams of vascular families. Appendix J contains a listing of each of the nerve conduction studies and the nerve that is appropriately reported with that code.

2.8. d. Both a and b

Rationale: Per CPT guidelines (see Introduction to CPT), in order to be included, a procedure must commonly be performed by many physicians across the country, and it must also be consistent with contemporary medical practice. Answer "c," it must be covered by Medicare, is not correct. Medicare coverage has no bearing upon the creation of CPT codes. Answer "d" is correct.

2.9. a. They are updated only once every two years.

Rationale: All the statements are true except this one. The Category III codes are updated every six months in order to reflect current advances in technology.

2.10. b. Is considered to be an integral part of another, larger service

Rationale: Because a separate procedure is considered a part of, and integral to, another, larger procedure, it is not coded when performed as part of the more extensive procedure. See Surgery Guidelines. It may, however, be coded when it is not performed as part of another, larger service, so answer "c" is not correct.

2.11. a. They are numeric.

Rationale: CPT Category I codes describe primarily physician services and are updated annually by the American Medical Association, so the other statements are all false.

2.12. d. The code has been revised in some way this year.

Rationale: The symbol ▲ is used to designate a code that has been revised this year. See Introduction to CPT for descriptions of the meanings of the various symbols used in the terminology.

2.13. a. The code is new for this year.

Rationale: The symbol ● appears before a code that is new with the current edition of CPT. See Introduction to CPT for descriptions of the meanings of the various symbols used in the terminology.

2.14. b. AMA

Rationale: The AMA developed and maintains CPT. CMS developed and maintains HCPCS level II codes. The Cooperating Parties and WHO have nothing to do with CPT.

2.15. a. Annually for the main body of codes and every 6 months for Category III codes

2.16. d. All of the above

Rationale: Unlike the Alphabetic Index to Procedures in ICD-9-CM, the Alphabetic Index in CPT includes listings by procedures and services, examinations, and anatomic sites, as well as abbreviations, eponyms, synonyms, and diagnoses.

2.17. b. The procedure can only be reported for that diagnosis.

Rationale: The use of the term "for" followed by a diagnosis means that the code can only be reported with that diagnosis. When a code descriptor contains the term "e.g." followed by one or more diagnoses, the manual is giving examples of the types of diagnoses for which the procedure may be performed.

2.18. b. An unlisted procedure code from the appropriate chapter of CPT

Rationale: There is no "generic" unlisted procedure code in CPT. The unlisted procedure code from the appropriate chapter should be reported. Physicians should never report ICD-9-CM procedure codes. These codes are used only for inpatient hospital coding purposes. The fact that a procedure does not have a code in CPT or HCPCS Level II does not mean that it should not be reported. All services rendered should be reported as specifically as possible. If an unlisted procedure code is reported, the payer will typically request further information, including the operative report.

2.19. Laboratory/Pathology

Rationale: See Introduction to CPT.

2.20. d. All of the above

Rationale: The + sign identifies an add-on code, which can never be reported alone or in the first position. All the statements are true.

2.21. a. Appendix A

2.22. c. Any physician

Rationale: Any physician may use the codes in any section of CPT.

Evaluation and Management (E/M) Services

2.23. a. 99304

Incorrect answer. Code 99304 is for a new patient, which this is not. Assuming that the documentation is supportive, code 99309 would be reported, as it reports subsequent services to a nursing facility patient who requires a detailed interval history, detailed examination and medical decision making of moderate complexity.

b. 99305

Incorrect answer. Code 99305 is for a new patient and one meeting more extensive criteria. Assuming that the documentation is supportive, code 99309 would be reported, as it reports subsequent services to a nursing facility patient who requires a detailed interval history, detailed examination and medical decision making of moderate complexity.

c. 99309

Correct answer.

d. 99310

Incorrect answer. Code 99310, which is for an established patient, requires more extensive criteria. Assuming that the documentation is supportive, code 99309 would be reported, as it reports subsequent services to a nursing facility patient who requires a detailed interval history, detailed examination and medical decision making of moderate complexity.

e. 99318

Incorrect answer. Code 99318 is used to report an annual assessment on an essentially stable patient for administrative reasons. Assuming that the documentation is supportive, code 99309 would be reported, as it reports subsequent services to a nursing facility patient who requires a detailed interval history, detailed examination and medical decision making of moderate complexity.

2.24. a. Documentation of history, examination, and medical decision making

Rationale: The documentation of history, physical examination, and medical decision making usually determines the level of E/M code because they are the three key components. The final diagnosis may support or justify the level but does not determine it. The amount of time spent with the patient is only a determining factor when more than half the visit is devoted to counseling. See E/M Services Guidelines.

2.25. 99205

Rationale: See E/M Services Guidelines, Instructions for Selecting a Level of E/M Service, in the CPT manual.

2.26. 99202

Rationale: See E/M Services Guidelines, Instructions for Selecting a Level of E/M Service, in the CPT manual.

2.27. 99213

Rationale: See E/M Services Guidelines, Instructions for Selecting a Level of E/M Service, in the CPT manual.

2.28. Time

Rationale: See E/M Services Guidelines, Instructions for Selecting a Level of E/M Service, in the CPT manual.

2.29. d. A patient is placed in designated observation status.

Rationale: See instructional notes preceding code 99217. In order to report these codes, the admission order must designate observation status. Whether or not the patient meets admission criteria or is admitted following surgery does not affect the observation code selection. If the patient is admitted/discharged on the same date, codes 99234–99236 are appropriate.

2.30. d. One code for the inpatient admission only

Rationale: All the E/M services "roll up into" the most intensive service, which is the hospital admission visit. See definitions preceding code 99201. Individual codes should not be assigned for the visits prior to the admission, although the medical decision making that occurred then would be a part of the medical decision making for the hospital admission.

2.31. Key

Rationale: See E/M Services Guidelines, Instructions for Selecting a Level of E/M Service, in the CPT manual.

2.32. d. a and b above

Rationale: Both the occupational history and the marital history are components of the social history. Allergic history is a component of past medical history. See E/M Services Guidelines, Instructions for Selecting a Level of E/M Service, in the CPT manual.

2.33. b. Social history

Rationale: Documentation of history of use of drugs, alcohol, and/or tobacco is considered part of the social history. The review of systems is a part of the history of present illness. See E/M Services Guidelines, Instructions for Selecting a Level of E/M Service, in the CPT manual.

2.34. d. Has a moderate risk of morbidity without treatment, a moderate risk of mortality without treatment, uncertain prognosis, or increased probability of functional impairment

Rationale: See E/M Services Guidelines, Instructions for Selecting a Level of E/M Service, in the CPT manual.

2.35. 99471

Rationale: Index Critical Care Services, pediatric, initial. Note that pediatric critical care is reported in units of days, unlike adult critical care, which is reported in increments of 30 minutes.

2.36. c. Subsequent hospital care codes

Rationale: The subsequent hospital care codes are used. Refer to the E/M Consultations instructional notes.

2.37. 99243

Rationale: See E/M Services Guidelines, Instructions for Selecting a Level of E/M Service, in the CPT manual.

2.38. b. Chief complaint

Rationale: See E/M Services Guidelines, Instructions for Selecting a Level of E/M Service, in the CPT manual.

2.39. d. All of the above.

Rationale: See E/M Guidelines, Instructions for Selecting a Level of E/M Service, in the CPT manual.

2.40. c. Domiciliary, rest home, or custodial care services

Rationale: See the instructional note preceding code 99324 for a definition of the care settings for which these codes are reported.

2.41. b. Age of the patient

Rationale: See definitions preceding code 99381.

2.42. b. Office or other outpatient services codes

Rationale: If the department is not open 24 hours, office or other outpatient services codes are used. See instructions preceding code 99281. The services are codable, but the outpatient services codes must be used.

2.43. 30 (thirty)

Rationale: See Guidelines for Critical Care Services in the CPT manual.

Anesthesia Services

2.44. b. When the anesthesiologist is no longer in personal attendance on the patient

Rationale: See Anesthesia Guidelines, Time Reporting.

2.45. b. Has severe systemic disease

Rationale: See Anesthesia Guidelines, Anesthesia Modifiers.

2.46. d. All of the above

Rationale: See Anesthesia Guidelines, Qualifying Circumstances.

2.47. 99140

Rationale: See Anesthesia Guidelines, Qualifying Circumstances.

2.48. 00172

Rationale: Index Anesthesia, cleft palate repair, resulting in code 00172.

2.49. 00326

Rationale: Index Anesthesia, trachea. The codes available are 00320, 00326, 00542. Index Anesthesia, trachea, reconstruction, results in code 00539, which appears to be the most appropriate code. Review of the available codes, however, shows that code 00326 is the correct code for a tracheal reconstruction on a patient under one year of age. A note instructs that code 99100 is not used with 00326.

2.50. 00530

Rationale: Index Anesthesia, pacemaker insertion, resulting in code 00530.

2.51. 00670

Rationale: Index Anesthesia, spine and spinal cord, lumbar, resulting in code range 00630–00670. Review of the available codes shows that code 00670 is appropriate for extensive procedures involving instrumentation.

2.52. 00832, 99100

Rationale: Index Anesthesia, hernia, abdomen, lower, resulting in code range 00830–00836. Review of the available codes indicates that code 00832 is the appropriate code for reporting ventral hernia repair. Because the patient is 76 years old, a qualifying circumstance code may also be assigned.

2.53. 00862

Rationale: Index Anesthesia, nephrectomy, resulting in code 00862. Anesthesia coding does not distinguish between donor nephrectomy and nephrectomy for disease.

2.54. 01400

Rationale: Index Anesthesia, arthroscopic procedures, knee, resulting in code 01382 or 01400. Review of the available codes indicates that code 01382 is used to report anesthesia for diagnostic knee arthroscopies, and 01400 is used for surgical arthroscopic procedures. Thus, code 01400 is the appropriate code.

2.55. 01214

Rationale: Index Anesthesia, hip, resulting in code range 01200–01215. Review of the available codes indicates that code 01214 is the appropriate code for anesthesia for a total hip replacement.

2.56. 00921

Rationale: Index Anesthesia, vasectomy, resulting in code 00921.

2.57. 01961, 01968

Rationale: Index Anesthesia, cesarean delivery, resulting in code 01961 or 01963. Review of the available codes indicates that code 01961 is appropriate for anesthesia for cesarean delivery. Further review of the section shows that code +01968 should also be reported for the failed attempt at vaginal delivery under spinal anesthesia.

2.58. 01232, 99140

Rationale: Index Anesthesia, leg upper, resulting in code range 01200–01274. Review of the available codes indicates that code 01232 is the appropriate code for anesthesia for a femoral amputation. Because the procedure is performed as an emergency, a qualifying circumstance code may also be reported.

2.59.   01480

Rationale: Index Anesthesia, tibia, resulting in code range 01390–01392 or code 01484. Review of the available codes indicates that none of the listed codes are appropriate. In fact, code 01480, Anesthesia for open procedures on bones of the lower leg, ankle, and foot; not otherwise specified, is the appropriate code. The abbreviation ORIF indicates open reduction, internal fixation, so this was an open procedure.

2.60.   00563

Rationale: Index Anesthesia, heart, resulting in code range 00560–00580. Review of the available codes indicates that code 00563 is the appropriate code for anesthesia for surgery on the heart involving the use of the heart-lung perfusion machinery and systemic hypothermia.

2.61.   00794

Rationale: Index Anesthesia, pancreas, resulting in code 00794. A Whipple procedure is a radical procedure for carcinoma of the pancreas, involving removal of the pancreas and the duodenum.

2.62.   00567

Rationale: Index Anesthesia, heart, coronary artery bypass grafting, resulting in code range 00566–00567. Review of the available codes indicates that code 00567 is the appropriate code for coronary artery bypass grafting with pump oxygenator.

2.63.   00944

Rationale: Index Anesthesia, hysterectomy, vaginal, resulting in code 00944.

Integumentary System

2.64.   a. Yes

Incorrect answer. The code for this procedure, 19298, is on the list of procedures that include conscious sedation if administered by the same physician who performed the procedure.

b. No

Correct answer.

2.65.   a. Autograft

Incorrect answer. An autograft is tissue transplanted from one part of an individual's body to another part. Tissue transplanted from one individual to another of the same species but different genotype is called an allograft or allogenic graft.

b. Xenograft

Incorrect answer. A xenograft, also called a heterograft, is a graft from another species.

Tissue transplanted from one individual to another of the same species but different genotype is called an allograft or allogeneic graft.

c. Allograft or allogeneic graft

Correct answer.

d. Heterograft

Incorrect answer. A heterograft, also called a xenograft, is a graft from another species.

Tissue transplanted from one individual to another of the same species but different genotype is called an allograft or allogeneic graft.

2.66. a. True

Correct answer.

b. False

Incorrect answer. Per the coding guidelines preceding code 15002, "These codes are not intended to be reported for simple graft application alone or application stabilized with dressings (e.g., by simple gauze wrap)." The skin substitute/graft is anchored using the surgeon's choice of fixation. When services are performed in the office, the supply of the skin substitute/graft should be reported separately. Routine dressing supplies are not reported separately.

2.67. a. A code for the Z-plasty only

Rationale: Per CPT guidelines, when a lesion is excised and the resultant defect is closed with adjacent tissue transfer, only the tissue transfer is coded. See definitions preceding code 14000. Examples of adjacent tissue transfers include Z-plasty, W-plasty, V–Y-plasty, rotation flap, advancement flap, and double-pedicle flap. It is inappropriate to assign an excision code along with an adjacent tissue transfer code.

2.68. b. Code each lesion separately.

Rationale: Each lesion is coded separately. Dimensions are only added together when coding repair of wounds. See definitions preceding code 11400. The dimensions that determine the code are now composed of the size of the lesion plus the circumferential margins.

2.69. a. 19120

Rationale: The fact that the lesion was completely excised makes 19120 the appropriate answer. Code 19125 is for excision of a lesion marked by a radiologic marker. Code 19301 is for a partial mastectomy.

2.70. b. Measurement of the lesion plus circumferential margins documented by the surgeon preexcision

Rationale: The code is determined by measurement of the lesion plus circumferential margins documented by the surgeon preexcision. See definitions preceding code 11400. This represents a change in the method of measuring excision sizes.

2.71. Shaving

Rationale: See guidelines preceding code 11300. Note that the surgical code includes the local anesthesia, as well as the cautery of the wound. By definition, shavings do not require suturing.

2.72. 11043

Rationale: Index Debridement, skin, subcutaneous tissue, resulting in code range 11042–11044. Review of the available codes indicates that code 11043 is the appropriate code for a debridement involving skin, subcutaneous, and muscle.

2.73. 11440

Rationale: Index Excision, skin, lesion, benign, resulting in code range 11400–11471. Review of the available codes indicates that code 11440 is the appropriate code for an excision involving the cheek (face), .5 cm or less. Note that the size of the lesion plus margins as well as the site of the lesion determine the code assignment. A solar keratosis is a type of benign skin lesion.

2.74. 11604

Rationale: Index Excision, skin, lesion, malignant, resulting in code range 11600–11646. Review of the available codes indicates that code 11604 is the appropriate code for a lesion of 3.2 cm (1.2 cm lesion plus 2 cm skin margins). Basal cell carcinoma is a type of malignant skin lesion.

2.75. 11462

Rationale: Index Hidradenitis, excision, resulting in code range 11450–11471. Review of the available codes indicates that code 11462 is the appropriate code for inguinal hidradenitis excision with an intermediate closure. Layered closure is a type of intermediate closure, and inguinal and groin are essentially synonymous.

2.76. 11960

Rationale: Index Tissue, expander, insertion, skin, resulting in code 11960. This code is appropriate for all tissue expander insertions other than the breast and includes the inflation of the tissue expander.

2.77. 12042

Rationale: Index Repair, skin, wound, intermediate, resulting in code range 12031–12057. This code may also be accessed via main term Repair, wound, intermediate, resulting in code in the same code range. Review of the available codes indicates that code 12042 is the appropriate code for a 5.2 cm laceration of the hand. Refer to the instructional notes preceding code 12001 for a definition of simple, intermediate, and complex repair.

2.78. 12002

Rationale: Index Repair, skin, wound, simple, resulting in code range 12020–12021. Indexing Repair, wound, simple, results in code range 12001–12021. Review of the available codes indicates that code 12002 is the appropriate code for this repair. These are both simple closures, and the lacerations are of the same body part (extremity), so they are added together, resulting in a total length of 5.4 cm.

2.79. 12004

Rationale: Index Repair, wound, simple, resulting in code range 12001–12021. In this case, because the repair is simple, and the scalp and extremities are the same body part, the sizes are summed. The total laceration length is thus 11.5 cm. Review of the available codes indicates that code 12004 is the appropriate code in this case (7.6 to 12.5 cm).

2.80. 12015, 13101, 13102, 13102

Rationale: Index Repair, skin, wound, simple, and Repair, skin, wound, complex. Review of the available codes indicates that code 12015 is the appropriate code for the 5.0 cm laceration of the cheek plus the 3.2 cm laceration of the forehead (total 8.2 cm from this body part). Codes 13101 and 13102 × 2 are required for the repair of the complex laceration of the chest wall. Code 13101 reports the first 7.5 cm. Code 13102 is reported for each additional 5 cm or less (13101 = 7.5 cm, 13102 = 5 cm, and 13102 = 3.5 cm, to report a total of 16 cm).

2.81. 12002

Rationale: Index Repair, wound, simple, resulting in code range 12001–12021. Review of the available codes indicates that code 12002 is the appropriate code assignment for a simple repair of the neck. Note that the dimensions documented in the record are in inches. One inch equals approximately 2.5 cm, so a 2 inch laceration would be approximately 5 cm.

2.82. Intermediate

Rationale: See definitions of simple, intermediate, and complex repair preceding code 12001.

2.83. 19125

Rationale: Index Breast, excision, lesion, by needle localization resulting in code range 19125–19126. Review of the available codes indicates that code 19125 is the appropriate code for reporting an excision of a single breast lesion.

2.84. b. Both surgeon and pathologist

Rationale: The physician must act as both surgeon and pathologist. See definitions preceding code 17311.

2.85. 19125

Rationale: Index Excision, breast, lesion, by needle localization, resulting in code range 19125–19126. Review of the available codes indicates that code 19125 is the appropriate code for the first lesion. If the needle was placed during the same session (and at the same site of service), a code for the needle placement (19290–19291) may also be reported. With needle localization excision, there is no discrete lesion identified but, rather, an area of somewhat abnormal appearance on mammography. The tissue at the tip of the needle is excised. If multiple areas are identified by needle placements, additional codes (19126) may be reported for each additional area.

2.86. 14000

Rationale: A V–Y plasty is a type of adjacent tissue transfer. Index Tissue, transfer, adjacent, skin, resulting in code range 14000–14350. Review of the available codes indicates that code 14000 is the appropriate code to report a less than 10 sq cm of the trunk. See the instructional note preceding code 14000 for guidelines on coding lesion excisions with repair by adjacent tissue transfer.

Musculoskeletal System

2.87. a. True

Correct answer.

b. False

Incorrect answer. The type of fracture treatment is based upon the physician's clinical judgment and not the type of fracture.

2.88. a. True

Incorrect answer. A bone biopsy performed in conjunction with a kyphoplasty procedure is not reported separately.

b. False

Correct answer.

2.89. a. CT angiography

Incorrect answer. 3D reconstruction is not to be reported with any of these modalities, nor with nuclear medicine studies or CT (virtual) colonoscopy.

b. MR angiography

Incorrect answer. 3D reconstruction is not to be reported with any of these modalities, nor with nuclear medicine studies or CT (virtual) colonoscopy.

c. PET scans

Incorrect answer. 3D reconstruction is not to be reported with any of these modalities, nor with nuclear medicine studies or CT (virtual) colonoscopy.

d. All of the above

Correct answer.

2.90.   b. Comminuted

Rationale: The other terms all describe open fractures.

2.91.   d. All of the above

Rationale: All of the scenarios describe open fracture treatment. See Musculoskeletal Guidelines, Definitions. The definitions of open vs. closed treatment of fractures have changed somewhat with CPT 2003, and the guidelines should be carefully reviewed.

2.92.   a. A "with manipulation" code

Rationale: The "with manipulation" code is used. The fracture was manipulated, even if the manipulation did not result in clinical anatomic alignment. See Musculoskeletal Guidelines, Definitions.

2.93.   28292

Rationale: Index Bunion Repair, Keller procedure, resulting in code 28292. In a Keller procedure, the base of the proximal phalanx is removed, and the alignment between the phalanx and the first metatarsal is maintained with Kirschner wires. This results in an essentially fused joint, with little motion, so this type of bunionectomy is not usually performed in more active patients.

2.94.   29881

Rationale: Index Arthroscopy, surgical, knee, resulting in code range 29871–29889. Review of the available codes indicates that code 29881 is the most appropriate code for a medial meniscectomy via the arthroscope. Consistent with guidelines throughout CPT, the diagnostic arthroscopy is not coded separately when performed as a part of a surgical procedure. See the instructional note preceding code 29800.

2.95.   27557

Rationale: Index Dislocation, knee, open treatment, resulting in code range 27556–27558, and individual code 27566 or 27730. Review of all the available codes indicates that code 27557, Open treatment, with or without internal fixation, with primary ligamentous repair, is the most appropriate code. There is no documentation of ligament augmentation (in which a portion of the lower leg musculature is brought up and sutured to the knee tendon structures) but rather use of a special suture (Anchor suture) to repair the ligament.

2.96.   22521

Rationale: Index Vertebra, osteoplasty, lumbar, resulting in code range 22521–22522. Because only one level was treated, code 22521 is appropriate. In this procedure, methylmethacrylate bone cement is injected into a fractured vertebral body percutaneously under imaging guidance.

2.97.   23031

Rationale: Index Incision and Drainage, shoulder, bursa, resulting in code 23031.

2.98. 23450

Rationale: Index Putti-Platt Procedure, resulting in code 23450. A Putti-Platt procedure is a type of open shoulder repair in which the joint capsule is sutured back to the glenoid labrum of the scapula.

2.99. 24515

Rationale: Index Fracture, humerus, shaft, open treatment, resulting in code 24515. The application of the initial cast is part of the code for the fracture treatment and should not be reported separately. Refer to the instructional note preceding code 29000.

2.100. 25810

Rationale: Index Arthrodesis, wrist, with graft, resulting in code 25810. The term "arthrodesis" is synonymous with fusion. The instructional note with code 25810 indicates that this code includes the harvesting of the graft, so no additional code should be reported for this procedure.

2.101. 25605

Rationale: Index Fracture, radius, with manipulation, resulting in codes 25565 or 25605. When a fracture is said to have been reduced, the "with manipulation" code is reported.

2.102. 27130

Rationale: Index Arthroplasty, hip, total replacement, resulting in code 27130. A total hip arthroplasty involves replacement of the femoral neck, femoral head, and acetabulum of the hip bone (ilium). This procedure is typically performed for bone diseases such as arthritis. When a fracture of the femoral neck is the reason for the surgery, a partial hip replacement (partial hip arthroplasty) involving replacement of only the femoral component, not including the acetabulum, is performed.

2.103. d. All of the above

Rationale: Casting is reported in all the listed circumstances. See instructional note for application of casts and strapping preceding code 29000.

2.104. 22864

Rationale: Index Removal, artificial intervertebral disc, cervical interspace, resulting in codes 0095T, 22864. Review of the available codes indicates that code 22864 is the correct code.

2.105. 20240

Rationale: Index Biopsy, bone, resulting in code range 20220–20245. Review of the available codes indicates that code 20240, Biopsy, bone, open, superficial, is the appropriate code because the ilium is listed as an example of a superficial bone structure.

2.106. 29425

Rationale: Index Cast, walking, resulting in code 29355 or 29425. Review of the available codes indicates that code 29425 is the appropriate code. Code 29355 is used to report a long-leg walking cast. Because this cast application was not part of initial fracture treatment, it is appropriate to code. Refer to the instructional note preceding code 29000.

2.107. 29827

Rationale: Index Arthroscopy, surgical, shoulder, resulting in code range 29806–29827. Review of the available codes indicates that code 29827 is the appropriate code for reporting an arthroscopic rotator cuff repair. Code 23412, Repair of ruptured musculotendinous cuff; chronic, is not appropriate because this code is used to report an open procedure.

2.108. 27590

Rationale: Index Amputation, leg, upper, resulting in code range 27590–27592. Review of the available codes indicates that code 27590 is the appropriate code for an amputation through the femur (the thigh bone).

2.109. 21480

Rationale: Index Dislocation, temporomandibular joint, closed treatment, resulting in code range 21480–21485. Review of the available codes indicates that code 21480 is the appropriate code because there is no documentation that this was a complicated reduction.

Respiratory System

2.110. a. Transbronchial lung biopsy

Rationale: If lung tissue is obtained via a puncture through the bronchus, a transbronchial biopsy is the appropriate procedure to report.

2.111. 30140

Rationale: Index Turbinate, submucous resection, nose excision, resulting in code 30140.

2.112. 30901

Rationale: Index Epistaxis, resulting in code range 30901–30906. Review of the available codes indicates that code 30901 is appropriate, even though both cautery and packing were used, because the code description states cautery and/or packing. There is no documentation that this was extensive.

2.113. 31255

Rationale: Index Sinuses, ethmoid, excision, endoscopy, resulting in code range 31254–31255. Review of the available codes indicates that code 31255 is appropriate because this is specified as a total ethmoidectomy, which is defined as anterior and posterior. Note that the FESS (functional endoscopic sinus surgery) codes are unilateral. If this procedure had been performed bilaterally, a modifier -50 would be appended.

2.114. 31365

Rationale: Index Laryngectomy, resulting in code range 31360–31382. Review of the available codes indicates that code 31365 is appropriate for a total laryngectomy with radical neck dissection (removal of regional lymph nodes).

2.115. 31541

Rationale: Index Laryngoscopy, operative, resulting in code range 31530–31561. Review of the available codes indicates that code 31541 is the appropriate code. The instructional note following this code indicates that it is not correct to also report code 69990 (use of operating microscope) with this code.

2.116. 31628

Rationale: Index Bronchoscopy, biopsy, resulting in code range 31625–31629 and code range 31632–31633. Review of the available codes indicates that code 31628 is the appropriate code to report when a transbronchial biopsy is performed. As always, any diagnostic endoscopy is included in the surgical endoscopy and not separately reported.

2.117. 32422

Rationale: Index Thoracentesis, resulting in code range 32421–32422. Review of the available codes indicates that code 32422 is appropriate when a tube is placed.

2.118. 32606

Rationale: Index Thoracoscopy, diagnosis, with biopsy, resulting in code 32602, 32604, or 32606. Review of the available codes indicates that code 32606 describes the procedure.

2.119. 31030

Rationale: Index Caldwell-Luc Procedure, sinusotomy, resulting in code range 31030–31032. Review of the available codes indicates that code 31030 is appropriate because there is no documentation of removal of polyps.

2.120. 31500

Rationale: Index Insertion, endotracheal tube, resulting in code 31500.

2.121. 31643

Rationale: Index Bronchoscopy, catheter placement, intracavity radioelement, resulting in code 31643.

2.122. 32480

Rationale: Index Lobectomy, lung, resulting in code range 32480–32482. Review of the available codes indicates that code 32480 is appropriate for reporting removal of a single lobe.

2.123. 32854

Rationale: Index Transplantation, lung, double, with cardiopulmonary bypass, resulting in code 32854.

2.124. 31276

Rationale: Index Sinuses, frontal, exploration, with nasal/sinus endoscopy, resulting in code 31276. In the case of the frontal sinus, CPT does not distinguish between procedures with removal of tissue and those without.

2.125. 31238

Rationale: Index Endoscopy, nose, surgical, resulting in code range 31237–31294. Review of the available codes indicates that code 31238 is appropriate when the endoscopy is performed for control of hemorrhage.

2.126. c. The fluoroscopy is included in the bronchoscopy and no code is assigned for it.

Rationale: See instructional note preceding code 31615.

2.127. 32560

Rationale: Index Pleurodesis, chemical, resulting in code 32560.

2.128. 31588

Rationale: Index Laryngoplasty, burns, resulting in code 31588.

2.129. 31380

Rationale: Index Larynx, excision, partial, resulting in code range 31367–31382. Review of the available codes indicates that code 31380 is the appropriate code for this particular approach.

Cardiovascular System

2.130. a. Intravascular ultrasound

Correct answer.

b. Angiography of the thoracic aorta

Incorrect answer. Per guidelines in CPT preceding code 33880, angiography of the thoracic aorta, fluoroscopic guidance in delivery of the endovascular components, and preprocedure diagnostic imaging are all included in the repair code. Intravascular ultrasound, if performed, may be separately coded.

c. Fluoroscopic guidance in delivery of the endovascular components

Incorrect answer. Per guidelines in CPT preceding code 33880, angiography of the thoracic aorta, fluoroscopic guidance in delivery of the endovascular components, and preprocedure diagnostic imaging are all included in the repair code. Intravascular ultrasound, if performed, may be separately coded.

d. Preprocedure diagnostic imaging

Incorrect answer. Per guidelines in CPT preceding code 33880, angiography of the thoracic aorta, fluoroscopic guidance in delivery of the endovascular components, and preprocedure diagnostic imaging are all included in the repair code. Intravascular ultrasound, if performed, may be separately coded.

2.131. a. True

Correct answer.

b. False

Incorrect answer. Code 37718 describes ligation, division and stripping of the short saphenous vein, and code 37722 describes treatment of the long saphenous vein.

2.132. a. Selective catheterization

Rationale: If the tip of the catheter is manipulated, it is a selective catheterization. In the case of a nonselective catheterization, the tip of the catheter remains in either the aorta or the artery that was originally entered.

2.133. 33030

Rationale: Index Pericardiectomy, subtotal, resulting in code range 33030–33031. Review of the available codes indicates that code 33030 is most appropriate because there is no documentation of cardiopulmonary bypass being used. Because this procedure is often performed under cardiopulmonary bypass, this might alert the coding professional to check the medical record for mention of bypass.

2.134. 33208

Rationale: Index Insertion, pacemaker, heart, resulting in code ranges 33202–33208 and 33212–33213. Review of all the available codes indicates that code 33208 is most appropriate for placement of this type of pacemaker, in which leads are inserted into both the atrium and the ventricle. Codes 33212 and 33213 are to report the placement of the pulse generator only, so are not appropriate in this case.

2.135. c. One code for the final vessel entered

Rationale: The only vessel coded is the final vessel entered. See instructional note preceding code 36000. Intermediate steps along the way are not reported.

2.136. 33430

Rationale: Index Replacement, mitral valve, resulting in code 33430.

2.137. 33510

Rationale: Index Coronary Artery Bypass Graft, venous, resulting in code range 33510–33516. Review of the available codes indicates that code 33510 is appropriate. The harvesting of the vein grafts is included (unless they are obtained from upper extremity veins). Only one artery, the left anterior descending, was grafted, so code 33510 is the correct code. Carefully review the instructional note preceding code 33510 for further discussion of coding of CABGs.

2.138. 33534

Rationale: The abbreviation LIMA stands for left internal mammary artery. Index Coronary Artery Bypass Graft, arterial, resulting in code range 33533–33536. Because two arteries were bypassed (the circumflex and the right), code 33534 is appropriate. Review the instructional note preceding code 33533 regarding coding of arterial conduits for coronary artery bypass grafting.

2.139. 33967

Rationale: Index Balloon Assisted Device, aorta, resulting in code range 33967–33974. Review of the available codes indicates that code 33967 is appropriate for the insertion of the device.

2.140. 36200

Rationale: Index Aorta, catheterization, catheter, resulting in code 36200. This procedure, in which a catheter is placed directly into the aorta and stays there, is an example of a nonselective catheterization.

2.141. 36425

Rationale: Index Venipuncture, child/adult, cutdown, resulting in code 36425.

2.142. 36561

Rationale: Index Insertion, Vascular Access Device, central, resulting in code range 36560–36566. The coding of a VAD is dependent on the type of insertion (central vs. peripheral), type of catheter (tunneled vs. nontunneled, port vs. pump), and patient age. A VAD is an implanted reservoir attached to a central venous catheter. To determine if the catheter is a VAD, look for an implant sticker in the medical record. Central venous catheters are not considered implants and do not carry implant stickers, while VADs do. Most VADs have the word "port" in their brand name. Some examples are Life-Port, PORT-A-CATH, and Infuse-A-Port. Devices such as pumps and ports always require a tunneled catheter.

2.143. 36821

Rationale: Index Brescia-Cimino Type Procedure, resulting in code 36821. This is a type of AV fistula for dialysis in which an artery and a vein are directly sutured together. The radial artery and cephalic vein are the first choice, followed by the brachial artery and vein.

2.144. 37718, 37722

Rationale: Index Varicose Vein, removal, resulting in code ranges 37718, 37722 and 37765–37785. Review of all the available codes indicates that codes 37718 and 37722 are the most appropriate because both the long and short saphenous veins were treated.

2.145. 38120

Rationale: Index Splenectomy, laparoscopic, resulting in code 38120. This code may also be accessed via the main term Spleen, excision, laparoscopic.

2.146. 38792

Rationale: Index Sentinel Node, injection procedure, resulting in code 38792.

2.147. 37609

Rationale: Index Biopsy, artery, temporal, resulting in code 37609.

2.148. 36558

Rationale: Index Central Venous Catheter Placement, insertion, central, resulting in code range 36555–36558. It is necessary to know if the catheter is tunneled or nontunneled. It is also necessary to know if the catheter is centrally or peripherally inserted and the age of the patient.

2.149. 36430

Rationale: Index Transfusion, blood, resulting in code 36430. For reporting blood transfusions in the hospital outpatient setting, in order to ensure appropriate reimbursement, this code must be assigned for the actual administration of the blood, along with one or more HCPCS level II codes from the "C" or "P" codes to describe the product.

2.150. 35646

Rationale: Index Bypass Graft, femoral artery, resulting in codes 35521, 35533, 35540, range 35551–35558, 35566, 35621, range 35646–35647, range 35651–35661, 35666, and 35700. Review of all the available codes indicates that code 35646 is appropriate for a graft from the aorta to both femoral arteries (a Y-type graft).

2.151. 35474

Rationale: Index Angioplasty, popliteal artery, percutaneous, resulting in code 35474.

Digestive System

2.152. 40701

Rationale: Index Repair, cleft lip, resulting in code ranges 40525–40527 and 40700–40761. Review of the available codes indicates that code 40701 is appropriate for a single-stage primary procedure.

2.153. 41108

Rationale: Index Biopsy, mouth, resulting in code 40808 or 41108. Because this biopsy is specified as involving the floor of the mouth, code 41108 is correct.

2.154. 42145

Rationale: Index Uvula, excision, resulting in code range 42140–42145. Review of the available codes indicates that code 42145 is the appropriate code.

2.155. 42820

Rationale: Index Tonsillectomy, resulting in code range 42820–42826. Indexing the main term Tonsils, excision, with adenoids, results in code range 42820–42821. Review of the available codes indicates that code 42820 is appropriate for a child less than 12 years of age.

2.156. 43239

Rationale: Index Endoscopy, gastrointestinal, upper, biopsy, resulting in code 43239. Note that the description states biopsy, single or multiple. This code is assigned once for taking of biopsies, no matter how many are performed. If the same lesion that is biopsied is subsequently excised, only an excision code is assigned. If one lesion is biopsied and another excised, two codes are assigned.

2.157. b. A code for the lesion excision only

Rationale: When a lesion is biopsied and the same lesion is excised, only the excision is coded. If one area is biopsied and a different area excised, codes for both the excision and the biopsy are reported.

2.158. 43215

Rationale: Index Esophagus, endoscopy, removal, foreign body, resulting in code 43215. This code may also be accessed by indexing the main term Endoscopy, esophagus, removal, foreign body.

2.159. 43248

Rationale: The abbreviation EGD stands for esophagogastroduodenoscopy, also called upper gastrointestinal endoscopy. Index Endoscopy, gastrointestinal, upper, dilation, resulting in code 43245, and code range 43248–43249. Review of the available codes indicates that code 43248 is appropriate for reporting dilation over a guidewire as part of an endoscopic procedure. Esophageal dilations can also be performed without an endoscope.

2.160. d. Query the physician as to the method used.

Rationale: It is not appropriate for the coder to assume that the removal was done by either snare or hot biopsy forceps. The ablation code is only assigned when a lesion is completely destroyed and no specimen is retrieved. The coding professional must query the physician to assign the appropriate code.

2.161. 43262

Rationale: The abbreviation ERCP stands for endoscopic retrograde cholangio-pancreatography (examination of the gallbladder, pancreas, and bile ducts). Index Bile Duct, endoscopy, sphincterotomy, resulting in code 43262.

2.162. 43280

Rationale: Index Fundoplasty, esophagogastric, laparoscopic, resulting in code 43280. Indexing the main term Nissen Operation results in this cross-reference. Indexing the main term Nissen procedure, laparoscopic, results in code 43280.

2.163. 43450

Rationale: Index Dilation, esophagus, resulting in code range 43450–43458. There is no mention of endoscopy in this procedure. Review of the available codes indicates that code 43450 is most appropriate. Bougies are small, weighted bags that are dropped down the esophagus in progressively larger sizes to dilate the lumen of the esophagus.

2.164. 43246

Rationale: Index Gastrostomy Tube, placement, percutaneous, endoscopic resulting in code 43246.

2.165. 44140

Rationale: Index Colectomy, partial, with anastomosis, resulting in code 44140. There is no mention of laparoscopy in this procedure or of the creation of any type of ostomy. The ends of the colon were simply sewed back together, which is possible if the segment removed is located in such a position that the ends can be mobilized and joined back together.

2.166. 44206

Rationale: Index Colectomy, partial, with colostomy, laparoscopic, resulting in code 44206 or 44208. Review of the available codes indicates that code 44206 is appropriate in this case because an end colostomy is specified.

2.167. 44346

Rationale: Index Colostomy, revision, paracolostomy hernia, resulting in code range 44345–44346. Review of the available codes indicates that code 44346 most accurately describes this procedure.

2.168. 44378

Rationale: Index Endoscopy, intestines, small, hemorrhage, resulting in code 44366 or 44378. Review of the available codes indicates that code 44378 is appropriate because the site of the bleeding is specified as being in the ileum. Code 44366 is for a small bowel endoscopy that does not include the ileum, so this cannot be the correct code.

2.169. 45384

Rationale: Index Endoscopy, colon, removal, polyp, resulting in code 44392 and range 45384–45385. Review of the available codes indicates that code 45384 describes polypectomy with hot biopsy forceps.

2.170. 45337

Rationale: Index Endoscopy, colon-sigmoid, volvulus, resulting in code 45337.

2.171. 47563

Rationale: Index Cholecystectomy, any method, with cholangiography, resulting in codes 47563, 47605, and 47620. Review of the available codes indicates that code 47605 and 47620 are for an open procedure, whereas code 47563 is for a laparoscopic procedure, which is the method described.

Urinary System

2.172. 50200

Rationale: Index Biopsy, kidney, resulting in code range 50200–50205. Review of the available codes indicates that code 50200 is appropriate for a percutaneous needle biopsy.

2.173. 50320

Rationale: Index Nephrectomy, donor, resulting in code range 50300–50320 or code 50547. Review of the available codes indicates that code 50320 is appropriate in this case involving a living donor and with no mention of laparoscopic assistance.

2.174. 50541

Rationale: Index Kidney, cyst, ablation, resulting in code 50541.

2.175. 50590

Rationale: Index Lithotripsy, kidney, resulting in code 50590 or 52353. Review of the available codes indicates that code 50590 is correct because there is no mention of cystourethroscopy.

2.176. 50688

Rationale: Index Ureterostomy Tube, change, resulting in code 50688.

2.177. 51596

Rationale: Index Cystectomy, complete, with continent diversion, resulting in code 51596. In this procedure, the ureters are implanted into a segment of the large or small intestine with an opening onto the skin.

2.178. 51702

Rationale: Index Bladder, catheterization, resulting in code 51045 and range 51701–51703. Review of the available codes indicates that code 51702 is most appropriate. Indexing the main term Catheterization, bladder, results in codes 51102 and 51045, neither of which is appropriate. Note that codes 51701–51703 should be reported only when performed independently. The insertion of a bladder catheter is an integral part of most genitourinary procedures.

2.179. 52234

Rationale: Index Fulguration, cystourethroscopy with, tumor, resulting in code range 52234–52240. Review of the available codes indicates that code 52234 is appropriate with bladder tumors less than 2 cm in size. Note that the code is assigned once, irrespective of the number of tumors treated. Each tumor should be measured individually to determine the appropriate category (e.g. small, medium, large). CPT code 52234 should be reported once for single or multiple tumors that individually measure 0.5–2.0 cm.

2.180. 52282

Rationale: Index Stent, urethra, insertion, resulting in code 52282. Be careful to distinguish between urethra and ureter.

2.181. 52332

Rationale: Index Cystourethroscopy, insertion, indwelling urethral stent, resulting in code 50947 or 52332. Review of the available codes indicates that code 52332 is appropriate. Code 50947 describes placement of a stent into a ureter via laparoscopy rather than cystoscopy. Indexing the main term Endoscopy, ureter, placement, stent, also results in code 50947, which is not correct for the procedure described.

2.182. 52342

Rationale: The abbreviation UPJ stands for ureteropelvic junction. Index Cystourethroscopy, dilation, ureter, resulting in code range 52341–52342, and range 52344–52345. Review of the available codes indicates that code 52342 is most appropriate. Once again, indexing the main term Endoscopy, ureter, will result in codes that describe laparoscopic procedures, rather than cystoscopic.

2.183. 52601

Rationale: Index Prostate, excision, transurethral, resulting in code 52402, 52601, or 52630. Review of the available codes indicates that code 52601 is correct because there is no mention of this being a staged procedure. The control of postoperative bleeding is included in code 52601, so it is not coded separately.

2.184. 53445

Rationale: Index Prosthesis, urethral sphincter, insertion, resulting in code range 53444–53445. Review of the available codes indicates that code 53445 is appropriate for insertion of a complete inflatable system.

2.185. 53621

Rationale: Index Dilation, urethral, stricture, resulting in code 52281 and range 53600–53621. Review of the available codes indicates that code 52281 is not correct because it describes a cystourethroscopic procedure. Review of codes 53600–53621 shows that code 53621 is correct for a subsequent dilation of a male patient.

2.186. 50945

Rationale: Index Laparoscopy, ureterolithotomy, resulting in code 50945. Note that in this case the procedure is performed laparoscopically, that is, by visualization through the abdomen. Ureterolithotomy can also be performed cystoscopically.

2.187. 51772

Rationale: Index Urethra, pressure profile, resulting in code 51772.

2.188. 51840

Rationale: Index Vesicourethropexy, resulting in code range 51840–51841. Review of the available codes indicates that code 51840 is appropriate because there is no documentation that this was a complicated or repeat procedure.

2.189. 52204

Rationale: Index Cystourethroscopy, biopsy, resulting in code choice of 52204 or 52354. Review of the available codes indicates that code 52354 is for a biopsy of the ureter and code 52204 is for biopsy of the bladder or urethra. Code 52204 is therefore the correct code.

2.190. 52352

Rationale: Index Endoscopy, ureter, removal, calculus, resulting in code 50961, 50980, or 52352. Review of the available codes indicates that code 50961 reports a ureteral endoscopy via an ureterostomy, which is not documented here. Code 50980 is for an endoscopy via an ureterotomy, an incision into the ureter, which is also not documented here. Code 52352 describes removal of a ureteral stone via a cystourethroscopy with ureteral catheterization and is the correct code.

2.191. 52630

Rationale: Index Excision, prostate regrowth, resulting in code 52630.

Male/Female Genital System and Laparoscopy

2.192. 54057

Rationale: Index Condyloma, destruction, resulting in code range 54050–54065. Review of the available codes indicates that code 54057 is the appropriate code to describe treatment with the laser.

2.193. 54401

Rationale: Index Prosthesis, penile, insertion, resulting in code range 54400–54405. Review of the available codes indicates that code 54401 describes insertion of an inflatable prosthesis. All the other codes describe more complex prostheses.

2.194. 54417

Rationale: Index Prosthesis, penile, removal, resulting in code 54406 or code range 54410–54417. Review of the available codes indicates that code 54417, which describes the infected field and need for debridement of infected tissues, is the most appropriate code.

2.195. 54692

Rationale: Index Laparoscopy, orchiopexy, resulting in code 54692.

2.196. 55250

Rationale: Index Vasectomy, resulting in code 55250.

2.197. 55700

Rationale: Index Biopsy, prostate, resulting in code range 55700–55705. Review of the available codes indicates that code 55700 is appropriate for reporting a needle biopsy. This code may also be accessed via the main term Needle biopsy, prostate, which leads directly to code 55700.

2.198. 55840

Rationale: Index Prostatectomy, retropubic, radical, resulting in code range 55840–55845 or code 55866. Review of the available codes indicates that code 55840 is correct because there is no mention of lymph node dissection and the procedure was not done laparoscopically (55866), according to the limited documentation provided here.

2.199. 56420

Rationale: Index Incision and Drainage, abscess, Bartholin's gland, resulting in code 56420.

2.200. 57456

Rationale: Index Colposcopy, cervix, resulting in code 57421 or code range 57452–57461. Review indicates that code 57456 is most appropriate for a colposcopy of the cervix with curettage. Code 57421 describes colposcopy of the vagina/cervix, and the other cervical colposcopy codes describe procedures other than biopsy with endocervical curettage.

2.201. 58152

Rationale: Index Hysterectomy, abdominal, total, with colpourethropexy, resulting in code 58152. This single code describes the entire procedure, and no separate code should be reported for the Marshall-Marchetti-Krantz procedure.

2.202. 58291

Rationale: Index Hysterectomy, vaginal, resulting in code ranges 58260–58270, 58290–58294, 58550, and 58554. Review of the available codes indicates that code 58291 describes the procedure on a uterus over 250 grams, with the only secondary procedure being the removal of the tubes and ovaries.

2.203. 58270

Rationale: Index Hysterectomy, vaginal, resulting in the same list of codes as above. In this case, code 58270 describes the procedure on the smaller uterus (under 250 grams), with concurrent enterocele repair.

2.204. 58546

Rationale: Index Myomectomy, uterus, resulting in code range 58140–58146 or 58545–58546. Review of the available codes indicates that codes 58140–58146 describe open myomectomy, and this procedure was performed laparoscopically. Because eight myomas were removed laparoscopically, code 58546 is correct.

2.205. 58600

Rationale: Index Ligation, fallopian tube, oviduct, resulting in code range 58600–58611 or code 58670. Review of the available codes indicates that code 58600 is the appropriate code because there is no documentation that this procedure was performed postpartum, nor was it performed laparoscopically (58670), based upon the available information.

2.206. 58671

Rationale: Index Laparoscopy, oviduct surgery, resulting in code range 58670–58671 or code 58679. Review of the available codes indicates that code 58671 describes occlusion of the fallopian tubes by a device, procedure performed laparoscopically.

2.207. 58943

Rationale: Index Ovary, excision, total, resulting in code range 58940–58943. Review of the available codes indicates that code 58943 describes the salpingo-oophorectomy and the biopsies.

2.208. 58340

Rationale: Index Hysterosalpingography, injection procedure, resulting in code 58340. In order to fully report this procedure, a radiological supervision and interpretation code would also be reported.

2.209. 54240

Rationale: Index Plethysmography, penis, resulting in code 54240. Note that all the other plethysmographic procedures are listed in the Medicine section of CPT.

2.210. 54318

Rationale: Index Hypospadias, repair, urethroplasty for third stage, resulting in code 54318.

2.211. 58662

Rationale: Index Laparoscopy, destruction, lesion, resulting in code 58662.

Endocrine System

2.212. 60000

Rationale: Index Incision and Drainage, cyst, thyroid gland, resulting in code 60000.

2.213. 60100

Rationale: Index Needle Biopsy, thyroid gland, resulting in code 60100.

2.214. 60200

Rationale: Index Thyroid Gland, tumor, excision, resulting in code 60200. An adenoma is a benign tumor, so searching on the main term Thyroid gland, excision, will not lead to the appropriate code.

2.215. 60210

Rationale: Index Thyroidectomy, partial, resulting in code range 60210–60225. Review of the available codes indicates that code 60210 is appropriate for this simple procedure.

2.216. 60212

Rationale: Index Thyroidectomy, partial, resulting in code range 60210–60225. Review of the available codes indicates that code 60212 is correct because there is documentation of isthmusectomy and subtotal resection on the opposite (contralateral) side.

2.217. 60220

Rationale: Index Thyroidectomy, partial, resulting in code range 60210–60225. Review of the available codes indicates that code 60220 is correct because it describes a unilateral complete lobectomy.

2.218. 60225

Rationale: Index Thyroidectomy, partial, resulting in code range 60210–60225. Review of the available codes indicates that code 60225 is correct because it describes a unilateral complete lobectomy and isthmusectomy with subtotal resection on the opposite (contralateral) side.

2.219. 60240

Rationale: Index Thyroidectomy, total, resulting in code 60240 or 60271. Review of the available codes indicates that code 60240 is correct, based upon the available information.

2.220. 60252

Rationale: Index Thyroidectomy, total, for malignancy, limited neck dissection, resulting in code 60252.

2.221. 60254

Rationale: Index Thyroidectomy, total, for malignancy, radical neck dissection, resulting in code 60254.

2.222. 60500

Rationale: Index Parathyroidectomy, resulting in code range 60500–60505. Review of the available codes indicates that code 60500 is appropriate, based upon the available documentation. The parathyroids are routinely removed along with the thyroid due to their proximity, and a separate code should not be reported for the parathyroidectomy in that circumstance.

2.223. 60271

Rationale: Index Thyroidectomy, total, cervical approach, resulting in code 60271.

2.224. 60281

Rationale: Index Thyroglossal Duct, cyst, excision, resulting in code range 60280–60281. Review of the available codes indicates that code 60281 is appropriate when the cyst is documented as recurrent.

2.225. 60505

Rationale: Index Parathyroid Gland, exploration, resulting in code range 60500–60505. Review of the available codes indicates that code 60505 is correct when a mediastinal exploration is documented.

2.226. 60521

Rationale: Index Thymus Gland, excision, resulting in code range 60520–60521. This code range can also be accessed via the main term Thymectomy. Review of the available codes indicates that code 60521 is appropriate when the approach is documented as transthoracic and there is no mention of mediastinal lymph node dissection.

2.227. 60540

Rationale: Index Biopsy, adrenal gland, resulting in code range 60540–60545. Review of the available codes indicates that code 60540 is appropriate when there is no documentation of excision of tumor. Note that adrenalectomy is a separate procedure. The adrenals are routinely removed with the kidneys and a separate code should not be reported for this.

2.228. 60650

Rationale: Index Laparoscopy, adrenal gland, excision, resulting in code 60650. Note that indexing Laparoscopy, adrenalectomy, results in code 50545. Review of the descriptor for this code, however, indicates that it describes a considerably more invasive procedure than a simple adrenalectomy. Code 50545 includes a radical nephrectomy (kidney and ureter), excision of fascia, lymph nodes, and adrenal glands. This illustrates how important it is to reference the Tabular List, even when the index directs the coder to one specific code.

2.229. 60605

Rationale: Index Carotid Body, lesion, carotid artery, resulting in code 60605.

2.230. 60522

Rationale: Index Thymectomy, resulting in code range 60520–60521. Review of the available codes indicates the code that actually best describes the procedure is 60522. This code may be accessed via the main term Thymectomy, sternal split/transthoracic approach, resulting in code range 60521–60522.

2.231. 60300

Rationale: Index Aspiration, cyst, thyroid, resulting in code 60300.

Nervous System

2.232. 61154

Rationale: Index Drainage, hematoma, brain, resulting in code range 61154–61156. Review of the available codes indicates that code 61154 describes the procedure for drainage of hematoma.

2.233. 61322

Rationale: Index Craniectomy, decompression, resulting in code range 61322–61323, or code range 61340–61343. Review of all the available codes indicates that code 61322 is appropriate when the procedure is performed for intracranial hypertension and there is no documentation of lobectomy. Note the use of the term "for treatment of intracranial hypertension" in the descriptors for 61322 and 61323. This means that these codes can only be used with that diagnosis.

2.234. 61519

Rationale: Index Brain, meningioma, excision, resulting in codes 61512 and 61519. Review of the available codes indicates that code 61519 is the appropriate code to report excision of a posterior fossa meningioma.

2.235. 61626

Rationale: Index Transcatheter, embolization, percutaneous, cranial, resulting in code range 61624–61626. Code 61626 lists the brachiocephalic artery among the treatment areas and is the appropriate code.

2.236. 61798

Rationale: Index Brain, stereotactic, radiosurgery, resulting in code range 61796–61800 in the surgery section. Review of the available codes indicates that code 61798 is correct because the notes prior to code 61795 states that a pituitary tumor is always considered complex, regardless of the size of the tumor.

2.237. 62223

Rationale: Index Shunt, brain, creation, resulting in code range 62180–62223. Review of the available codes indicates that code 62223 describes creation of a shunt from the ventricle of the brain to the peritoneal cavity.

2.238. 62270

Rationale: Index Puncture, spinal cord, diagnostic, resulting in code 62270.

2.239. 61885

Rationale: Index Implantation, neurostimulator, pulse generator, resulting in code 61885.

2.240. 64475

Rationale: Index Epidural, injection, resulting in code ranges 62281–62282, 62310–62319, and 64479–64484. Review of all the available codes indicates that code 64475 appropriately describes injection of a steroid (Depo-Medrol) and anesthetic (bupivacaine) into a facet joint.

2.241. 64479

Rationale: Index Epidural, injection, resulting in code ranges 62281–62282, 62310–62319, and 64479–64484. Review of all the available codes indicates that codes 64479–64484 report transforaminal injections. Code 64479 is correct for a cervical injection by this approach.

2.242. 64776-F8

Rationale: Index Excision, lesion, nerve, resulting in code range 64774–64792. Review of the available codes indicates that code 64776 describes excision of a neuroma of a digital nerve. The modifiers for the fingers begin with FA for the left thumb and progress to F9 for the right little finger. The appropriate modifier for the right fourth (ring) finger is F8.

2.243. 61340

Rationale: Index Decompression, skull, resulting in code range 61322–61323 or 61340–61345. Review of the available codes indicates that codes 61322–61323 can only be used for a diagnosis of intracranial hypertension, which is not documented here. Code 61340 is the appropriate code. Code 61345 includes a laminectomy of the upper cervical vertebra, which is not documented in the available information.

2.244. 61698

Rationale: Index Aneurysm Repair, vertebral artery, resulting in code 61698 or 61702. Review of both codes shows that code 61698 is the more appropriate code. The instructional note following code 61698 indicates that resection of an aneurysm larger than 15 mm would constitute a complex surgery. The aneurysm in this case is documented at 20 mm.

2.245. 61751

Rationale: Index Biopsy, brain, stereotactic, resulting in code range 61750–61751. Review of the available codes indicates that code 61751 is correct because there is documentation of magnetic resonance imaging guidance.

2.246. 62165

Rationale: Index Neuroendoscopy, intracranial, resulting in code range 62160–62165. Review of the available codes indicates that code 62165 is the correct code for excision of a pituitary tumor via intracranial neuroendoscopy.

2.247. 62252

Rationale: Index Reprogramming, shunt, brain, resulting in code 62252.

2.248. 63077

Rationale: Index Diskectomy, resulting in code range 63075–63078. Review of the available codes indicates that code 63077 is the appropriate code for an anterior diskectomy. Note that indexing Diskectomy, thoracic, leads to code 22222. Review of this code indicates that it includes an osteotomy, which is not documented in this case.

2.249. 64415

Rationale: Index Injection, nerve, anesthetic, resulting in code range 01991–01992 or 64400–64530. Review of the codes indicate that code 64415 is appropriate for the brachial plexus.

2.250. 64831-F2, 64832-F3

Rationale: Index Suture, nerve, resulting in code range 64831–64876. Review of the available codes indicates that code 64831 is appropriate for reporting the suture of the first digital nerve, and add-on code 64832, reported once, for the second digital nerve repair. The modifiers for the fingers begin with FA for the left thumb and progress to F9 for the right little finger. The appropriate modifier for the left third (long) finger is F2, and for the left fourth (ring) finger, F3.

2.251. 64600

Rationale: Index Destruction, nerve, resulting in code range 64600–64681. Review of the available codes indicates that code 64600 is appropriate to report the destruction of this branch of the trigeminal nerve.

Eye/Ocular Adnexa

2.252. 65222

Rationale: Index Removal, foreign bodies, cornea, with slit lamp, resulting in code 65222.

2.253. 65750

Rationale: Index Keratoplasty, penetrating, in aphakia, resulting in code 65750.

2.254. 65771

Rationale: Index Keratotomy, radial, resulting in code 65771.

2.255. 66984

Rationale: Index Cataract, removal/extraction, extracapsular, resulting in code 66982 or 66984. Review of both codes shows that code 66984 is appropriate because there is no documentation of special equipment being used or that this was a more than usually complex procedure.

2.256. 67107

Rationale: Index Retina, repair, detachment, by scleral buckling, resulting in code 67112. Review of this code, however, indicates that it is to be used for a repeat procedure, which is not documented to be the case here. Review of the other codes in the Repair of Retinal Detachment section reveals that actually code 67107 is most appropriate in this case.

2.257. 67228

Rationale: Index Retina, retinopathy, treatment, photocoagulation, resulting in code 67228.

2.258. 67312

Rationale: Index Strabismus, repair, two horizontal muscles, resulting in code 67312. The horizontal muscles of the eyeball are the lateral and medial recti. The vertical muscles are the superior and inferior recti. The superior and inferior oblique muscles are located on the back portion of the eyeball.

2.259. 67318

Rationale: Index Strabismus, repair, superior oblique muscle, resulting in code 67318.

2.260. 67316, 67335

Rationale: Index Strabismus, repair, two vertical muscles, and Strabismus, repair, adjustable sutures, resulting in code 67316 for the primary procedure and add-on code 67335 to report that adjustable sutures were used. This allows for "fine-tuning" the alignment when the patient has awakened from anesthesia and is moving the eyeball. Because code 67335 is an add-on code, no modifier such as -51 or -59 is needed.

2.261. 67902

Rationale: Index Blepharoptosis, repair, frontalis muscle technique with fascial sling, resulting in code 67902. Although this is the appropriate code to describe this type of procedure to correct blepharoptosis (droopy eyelids), note that Medicare or other insurance companies may not cover it if performed for purely cosmetic purposes. Documentation of loss of visual fields is usually required to obtain insurance coverage. This does not affect the code assignment, however.

2.262. 67922

Rationale: Index Entropion, repair, thermocauterization, resulting in code 67922.

2.263. 68720

Rationale: Index Dacryocystorhinostomy, resulting in code 68720. Note that some physicians use the term "dacryorhinocystostomy," which means the same thing.

2.264. 68815

Rationale: Index Nasolacrimal Duct, insertion, stent, resulting in code 68815.

2.265. 67805

Rationale: Index Chalazion, excision, multiple, different lids, resulting in code 67805.

2.266. 67145

Rationale: Index Retina, repair, prophylaxis, detachment, resulting in code range 67141–67145. Review of the available codes indicates that code 67145 is the appropriate code when the laser is used for the procedure.

2.267. 66170

Rationale: Index Trabeculectomy ab Externo, in absence of previous surgery, resulting in code 66170. If you arrived at code 65850, you have indexed the term "trabeculotomy ab externo," rather than trabeculectomy.

2.268. 65105

Rationale: Index Enucleation, eye, with implant, muscles attached, resulting in code 65105. There are three terms used for removal of the eyeball: evisceration, enucleation, and exenteration. Evisceration is removal of the contents of the eyeball, leaving the sclera and sometimes the cornea. Enucleation is removal of an entire eyeball, without rupture, leaving the muscles intact to attach to an implant. Exenteration is removal of the entire contents of the orbit, usually including the muscles.

2.269. 65260

Rationale: Index Removal, foreign bodies, posterior segment, magnet extraction, resulting in code 65260.

2.270. 65426

Rationale: Index Pterygium, excision, with graft, resulting in code 65426. The graft is typically obtained from the conjunctiva, and no additional code is assigned for its harvesting.

2.271. 67040

Rationale: Index Vitrectomy, subtotal, with endolaser panretinal photocoagulation, resulting in code 67040.

Auditory System

2.272. 69140

Rationale: Index Exostosis, excision, resulting in code 69140. Although exostosis can occur in any part of the body, this code is, in fact, correct for the external auditory canal.

2.273. 69421

Rationale: Index Myringotomy, resulting in code range 69420–69421. Review of the available codes indicates that code 69421 is appropriate when general anesthesia is used. Note that some physicians use the term "tympanotomy," which is synonymous with myringotomy. ("Myrinx" is the Greek root for eardrum; "tympanum" is the Latin root for eardrum.)

2.274. 69433

Rationale: Index Tympanic Membrane, create stoma, resulting in code range 69433–69436. Review of the available codes indicates that code 69433 is appropriate because the use of general anesthesia is not documented.

2.275. 69642

Rationale: Index Tympanoplasty, with mastoidectomy, with ossicular chain reconstruction, resulting in code 69642.

2.276. 69960

Rationale: Index Decompression, auditory canal, internal, resulting in code 69960.

2.277. 69020

Rationale: Index Auditory Canal, external, abscess, incision and drainage, resulting in code 69020.

2.278. 69200

Rationale: Removal, foreign bodies, auditory canal, external, resulting in code 69200, which is appropriate because there is no documentation of use of general anesthesia (code 69205).

2.279. 69300

Rationale: Index Ear, external, reconstruction, resulting in code 69300. This code can also be accessed via the main term Otoplasty.

2.280. 69210

Rationale: Index Cerumen, removal, resulting in code 69210. Review of the descriptor for this code shows that it is bilateral or unilateral in nature, and no modifier is added if the procedure is done bilaterally.

2.281. 69633

Rationale: The abbreviation PORP stands for partial ossicular replacement prosthesis. PORPs are ossicular chain replacements that do not include the stapes. If the prosthesis includes a stapes reconstruction, it is referred to as a total ossicular replacement prosthesis, or TORP. Index Tympanoplasty, without mastoidectomy, with synthetic prosthesis, resulting in code 69633.

2.282. 69436

Rationale: Index Tympanostomy, resulting in code range 69433–69436. Note that the terms "tympanostomy" and "myringotomy" are synonymous. Review of the available codes indicates that code 69436 is appropriate when general anesthesia is used.

2.283. 69552

Rationale: Index Excision, tumor, ear, middle, transmastoid, resulting in code 69552.

2.284. 69610

Rationale: Index Tympanic Membrane, repair, resulting in code 69450 or 69610. Review of both codes reveals that 69450 actually refers to a tympanolysis (freeing of the membrane), and code 69610 is the correct code.

2.285. 69661

Rationale: Index Stapedotomy, with footplate drillout, resulting in code 69661. This procedure is frequently performed with the use of the operating microscope, which may be coded in addition if it is used.

2.286. 69930

Rationale: Index Cochlear Device, insertion, resulting in code 69930.

2.287. 69666

Rationale: Index Oval window, repair fistula, resulting in code 69666.

2.288. 69910

Rationale: Index Labyrinthectomy, with mastoidectomy, resulting in code 69910.

2.289. 69710

Rationale: Index Temporal Bone, electromagnetic bone conducting hearing device, implantation/replacement, resulting in code 69710.

2.290. 69222

Rationale: Index Debridement, mastoid cavity, complex, resulting in code 69222. Review of the descriptor for the code verifies that the need for general anesthesia constitutes a "complex" debridement.

2.291. 69424

Rationale: Index Removal, ventilating tube, ear, middle, resulting in code 69424.

Radiology Services

2.292. a. True

Correct answer.

b. False.

Incorrect answer. When applied to the male pelvis, this examination includes the urinary bladder, prostate, seminal vesicles, and any identified pelvic pathology.

2.293. 70110

Rationale: Index Mandible, x-ray, resulting in code range 70100–70110. Review of the available codes indicates that code 70110 is the appropriate code when four or more views are obtained.

2.294. 70370

Rationale: Index Pharynx, x-ray, resulting in codes 70370 and 74210. Review of the available codes indicates that code 70370 is the appropriate code since fluoroscopy was utilized.

2.295. 70470

Rationale: Index CT Scan, without and with contrast, brain, resulting in code 70470 or 70496. Review of both codes shows that code 70496 is actually the code for CT angiography. Code 70470 is the correct code.

2.296. 71020

Rationale: Index Chest, x-ray, resulting in code range 71010–71035. Review of the available codes indicates that code 71020 is appropriate for reporting a front-to-back (AP, anteroposterior) and side-to-side (lateral) two-view x-ray.

2.297. 70552

Rationale: Index Magnetic Resonance Imaging, brain, resulting in code range 70551–70555. Review of the available codes indicates that code 70552 is the appropriate code for brain MRI with contrast.

2.298. 72052

Rationale: Index Spine, x-ray, cervical, resulting in code range 72040–72052. Review of the available codes indicates that code 72052 is appropriate when a complete study, including oblique and flexion views, is done.

2.299. 72240

Rationale: Index Myelography, spine, cervical, resulting in code 72240. Note that to fully report the procedure, a code for the injection of the contrast material must also be reported per the instructional note following code 72240.

2.300. 73040

Rationale: Index Arthrography, shoulder, resulting in code 73040.

2.301. 73530

Rationale: Index Hip, x-ray, intraoperative, resulting in code 73530.

2.302. 74270

Rationale: Index Barium Enema, resulting in code range 74270–74280. Review of the available codes indicates that code 74270 is appropriate. Note that abbreviation KUB stands for kidneys, ureters, and bladder, which may or may not be visualized as a part of a barium enema.

2.303. 74320

Rationale: Index Cholangiography, percutaneous, resulting in code 74320. Note that to fully describe the procedure, an injection code must be reported as well.

2.304. 74400

Rationale: Index Urography, intravenous, resulting in code range 74400–74415. Review of the available codes indicates that code 74400 is appropriate for an IVP (intravenous pyelogram) whether or not tomograms are performed.

2.305. 75660

Rationale: Index Angiography, carotid artery, resulting in code range 75660–75671. Review of the available codes indicates that code 75660 is the most appropriate code to describe this procedure.

2.306. 76801

Rationale: Index Ultrasound, pregnant uterus, resulting in code range 76801–76817. Review of the available codes indicates that code 76801 is the appropriate code.

2.307. 75746

Rationale: Index Angiography, pulmonary, resulting in code range 75741–75746. Review of the available codes indicates that code 75746 is the appropriate code when the catheterization is documented to be nonselective. Per the instructional note following code 75746, an injection code is needed to completely report the procedure.

2.308. 78320

Rationale: Index Bone, nuclear medicine, SPECT, resulting in code 78320. The acronym SPECT stands for single photon emission computed tomography and is a more sophisticated form of CT scanning. Unlike basic x-ray CT scanning, SPECT involves injected radionuclides, and is considered a form of nuclear medicine. It is being supplanted to some extent now by PET (positron emission tomography) scanning, which is capable of better resolution and sensitivity.

2.309. 75960

Rationale: Index Transcatheter, placement, intravascular stents, resulting in code range 37205–37208, 37215–37216, 0075T–0076T, or 0005T–0007T. These latter codes are Category III CPT codes which will be addressed below. Review of the available codes indicates that code 75960 is the appropriate code for the radiological supervision and interpretation. See note with code 37205. A code from the Cardiovascular section will be assigned to report the actual procedure.

2.310. 77032

Rationale: Index Mammogram, breast, localization nodule, resulting in code 77032.

2.311. 76770

Rationale: Index Ultrasound, retroperitoneal, resulting in code range 76770–76775. Review of the available codes indicates that code 76770 is correct. Code 76775 reports a limited retroperitoneal ultrasound, such as of one organ, but that is not documented here.

2.312. 78278

Rationale: Index Nuclear Medicine, gastrointestinal, blood loss study, resulting in code 78278.

Pathology/Laboratory Services

2.313. a. This is an add-on laboratory code.

Incorrect answer. The symbol ⊬ designates a laboratory test that has been assigned a Category I code in anticipation of receipt of FDA approval. Ordinarily, AMA does not assign Category I codes to procedures that have not actually received FDA approval.

b. The code is sex specific.

Incorrect answer. The symbol ⊬ designates a laboratory test which has been assigned a Category I code in anticipation of receipt of FDA approval. Ordinarily, AMA does not assign Category I codes to procedures that have not actually received FDA approval.

c. This code should only be reported for Medicare patients.

Incorrect answer. The symbol ⊬ designates a laboratory test which has been assigned a Category I code in anticipation of receipt of FDA approval. Ordinarily, AMA does not assign Category I codes to procedures that have not actually received FDA approval.

d. FDA approval of the vaccine is pending.
Correct answer.

2.314. a. 82270
Correct answer.

b. 82271

Incorrect answer. Code 82271 is occult blood sampling from a site other than fecal. Occult blood assay using multiple samples to screen for colorectal cancer is reported with code 82270.

c. 82272

Incorrect answer. Code 82272 reports fecal occult blood sampling by 1–3 simultaneous determinations for screening of a condition other than colorectal cancer. Occult blood assay using multiple samples to screen for colorectal cancer is reported with code 82270.

d. 82274

Incorrect answer. Code 82274 is for 1–3 simultaneous determinations by immunoassay, not three consecutive collected specimens. Occult blood assay using multiple samples to screen for colorectal cancer is reported with code 82270.

2.315. a. True

Incorrect answer. Organ and disease-oriented panel codes, 80047–80076, can only be assigned if all of the tests included in the panel are performed. If one or more of the tests were not performed, each individual test must be coded separately.

b. False

Correct answer.

2.316. a. Cancer patients on toxic chemotherapy agents

Incorrect answer. 87900 Infectious agent drug susceptibility phenotype prediction using regularly updated genotypic bioinformatics is used in the management of HIV patients on antiretroviral therapy.

b. HIV patients on antiretroviral therapy

Correct answer.

c. Tuberculosis patients on rifampin therapy

Incorrect answer. 87900 Infectious agent drug susceptibility phenotype prediction using regularly updated genotypic bioinformatics is used in the management of HIV patients on antiretroviral therapy.

d. Organ transplant patients on immunosuppressive therapy

Incorrect answer. 87900 Infectious agent drug susceptibility phenotype prediction using regularly updated genotypic bioinformatics is used in the management of HIV patients on antiretroviral therapy.

2.317. 82552

Rationale: Index CPK, blood, resulting in code range 82550–82552. Review of the available codes indicates that code 82552 is the appropriate code for reporting complete fractionation into isoenzymes.

2.318. 83550

Rationale: Index Iron Binding Capacity, resulting in code 83550.

2.319. 83015

Rationale: Index Mercury, resulting in code choice of 83015 or 83825. Review of both codes shows that code 83825 is for quantitative mercury. The terms "screen for" and "qualitative" are essentially synonymous, meaning that a specimen is evaluated for the presence of a substance. "Quantitative" means that the amount of the identified substance in the specimen is directly or indirectly measured. A quantitative measurement may also be called a "titer." Thus code 83825 is inappropriate and code 83015, Heavy metal screen, is the correct choice.

2.320. 83986

Rationale: Index pH, other fluid, resulting in code 83986.

2.321. 84160

Rationale: Index Protein, total, resulting in codes 84155–84160. Review of the codes indicates that code 84160 is the correct code for refractometric protein measurement.

2.322. 84300

Rationale: Index Sodium, urine, resulting in code 84300.

2.323. 85025

Rationale: Index Blood Cell Count, hemogram, added indices, resulting in code range 85025–85027. The codes for reporting CBCs (complete blood counts) are very specific and should be carefully reviewed. The appropriate code for a CBC with automated white blood cell differential is 85025.

2.324. 85002

Rationale: Index Bleeding, time, resulting in code 85002.

2.325. 85610

Rationale: Index Prothrombin Time, resulting in code range 85610–85611. Review of the available codes indicates that code 85610 is the appropriate code. There is no documentation of plasma fractionation here.

2.326. 86039

Rationale: Index Antinuclear Antibodies, resulting in code range 86038–86039. Review of the available codes indicates that code 86039 is specified as the titer.

2.327. 86592

Rationale: Index VDRL, resulting in code range 86592–86593. The abbreviation VDRL stands for Venereal Disease Research Laboratory slide test, which is specified as one of the qualitative syphilis tests. Thus, code 86592 is correct.

2.328. 86706

Rationale: In this abbreviation, H stands for hepatitis, b for type B, s for surface, and Ab for antibody. Index Hepatitis Antibody, B surface, resulting in code 86706.

2.329. 86632

Rationale: Index Chlamydia, antibody, resulting in code range 86631–86632. Review of the available codes indicates that code 86632 is appropriate when the IgM antibody is studied. The abbreviation IgM means the "M" immunoglobulin (Ig). Immunoglobulins are protein groups that react in different ways with infectious agents.

2.330. 85652

Rationale: Index Sedimentation Rate, automated, resulting in code 85652.

2.331. 88305

Rationale: Index Pathology, surgical, gross and micro exam, level IV resulting in code 88305. In practice, each entry in the Surgical Pathology section should be reviewed to determine the appropriate level. An arterial biopsy is categorized to a level IV. Review the instructional note preceding code 88300. Note that the unit of service is the specimen, not the number of slides or cell blocks.

2.332. 88309

Rationale: Index Pathology, surgical, gross and micro exam, level VI resulting in code 88309. In practice, each entry in the Surgical Pathology section should be reviewed to determine the appropriate level. A specimen consisting of breast and regional lymph nodes is categorized to a level VI. Review the instructional note preceding code 88300. Note that the unit of service is the specimen, not the number of slides or cell blocks.

2.333. 86618

Rationale: Index Antibody, Lyme disease, resulting in code 86617. Review of this code, however, shows that this is a confirmatory test, which is not specified here. The next listed code, 86618, is, in fact, the appropriate code.

2.334. 84203

Rationale: Index Protoporphyrin, resulting in code range 84202–84203. Review of the available codes indicates that code 84202 is for a quantitative test, so code 84203, Screen, is correct.

2.335. 82365

Rationale: Index Calculus, analysis, resulting in code range 82355–82370. Review of the available codes indicates that when infrared spectroscopy is used to perform chemical analysis of a kidney stone, the appropriate code is 82365.

2.336. 87040

Rationale: Index Culture, bacteria blood, resulting in code 87040.

Medicine

2.337. a. Intravenous infusion

Incorrect answer. An infusion that lasts for less than 15 minutes should be reported with an IV push code per CPT coding guidelines.

b. Intravenous piggyback

Incorrect answer. An infusion that lasts for less than 15 minutes should be reported with an IV push code per CPT coding guidelines.

c. Intravenous or intra-arterial push

Correct answer.

d. Intravenous hydration

Incorrect answer. An infusion that lasts for less than 15 minutes should be reported with an IV push code per CPT coding guidelines.

2.338. a. Chemotherapeutic agents

Incorrect answer. Codes 96360 and 96361 are used to report intravenous infusions for hydration, consisting of prepackaged fluids and/or electrolytes. These codes are not used for infusion of any other types of medications.

b. Sequential drugs of the same drug family

Incorrect answer. Codes 96360 and 96361 are used to report intravenous infusions for hydration, consisting of prepackaged fluids and/or electrolytes. These codes are not used for infusion of any other types of medications.

c. Hormonal antineoplastics

Incorrect answer. Codes 96360 and 96361 are used to report intravenous infusions for hydration, consisting of prepackaged fluids and/or electrolytes. These codes are not used for infusion of any other types of medications.

d. Prepackaged fluids and/or electrolytes

Correct answer.

2.339. a. Who administers the sedation

Incorrect answer. All three criteria are used to determine which moderate conscious sedation code to assign.

b. The age of the patient

Incorrect answer. All three criteria are used to determine which moderate conscious sedation code to assign.

c. The duration of the sedation

Incorrect answer. All three criteria are used to determine which moderate conscious sedation code to assign.

d. All of the above

Correct answer.

2.340. a. 96401

Incorrect answer. 96401 reports nonhormonal antineoplastic. This is a hormonal antineoplastic, as its name suggests, so code 96402 is appropriate.

b. 96402

Correct answer.

c. 96413

Incorrect answer. Code 96402 is specific for hormonal antineoplastic, given subcutaneous tissue. This code reports an intravenous infusion.

d. 96405

Incorrect answer. This code reports intralesional injections of antineoplastics. Code 96402 is specific for hormonal antineoplastic, given subcutaneous tissue.

2.341. a. True

Incorrect answer. It is based upon the primary reason for the encounter.

b. False

Correct answer.

2.342. c. 90375, 96372

Rationale: In order to appropriately report administration of vaccines, both the product administered and the method of administration must be reported. See the instructional note preceding code 90281.

2.343. Interactive

Rationale: See instructions, Psychiatric Diagnostic or Evaluative Interview Procedures, in CPT.

2.344. 90818

Rationale: Index Psychiatric Treatment, individual, insight-oriented, hospital or residential care, resulting in code range 90816–90822. Review of the available codes indicates that code 90818 is appropriate for a 45 to 50 minute session.

2.345. 91012

Rationale: Index Esophagus, motility study, resulting in code 78258 and code range 91010–91012. Code 78258 is a nuclear medicine study, which is not documented here. Review of the other available codes indicates that code 91012 is appropriate when an esophageal motility study is performed with acid perfusion testing.

2.346. 92235

Rationale: Index Angiography, Fluorescein, resulting in code 92235.

2.347. 92602

Rationale: Index Cochlear Device, programming, resulting in code range 92601–92604. Review of the available codes indicates that code 92602 is reported for a subsequent reprogramming of such a device in a child less than seven years of age.

2.348. 92980

Rationale: Index Coronary Artery, insertion, stent, resulting in code range 92980–92981. Review of the available codes indicates that code 92980 is appropriate for the first artery treated. It would be appropriate to add modifier -RC to this code to show that the right coronary artery was the one treated in this manner. In addition, radiological supervision and interpretation codes would be reported, as well as catheter placement codes from the cardiovascular chapter.

2.349. 93010

Rationale: Index Electrocardiography, evaluation, resulting in code 93000, 93010, or 93014. Review of the available codes indicates that code 93010 is appropriate. Note that EKG has separate codes for reporting by the physician and the hospital, when a physician reads EKGs performed on hospital equipment.

2.350. 93526

Rationale: Index Catheterization, cardiac, combined left and right heart, resulting in code range 93526–93529. Review of the available codes indicates that code 93526 is appropriate because there is no documentation of septal perforation or left ventricular puncture. In addition to the catheterization code, codes for opacification of the coronary structures (93539–93545), as well as radiological supervision and interpretation (93555 and/or 93556) are reported.

2.351. 93283

Rationale: Index Analysis, electronic, pacing cardioverter-defibrillator, evaluation of programming resulting in codes 93282–93284, 93287, 93641–93642. Review of the available codes indicates that based upon the fact that this is a dual-chamber device and reprogramming was required, code 93283 is correct.

2.352. 93925

Rationale: Index Duplex Scan, arterial studies, lower extremity, resulting in code range 93925–93926. Review of the available codes indicates that code 93925 is correct for reporting a bilateral study.

2.353. 94621

Rationale: Index Pulmonology, diagnostic, stress test, resulting in code 94621. Review of this code and surrounding codes shows another code, 94620, for reporting simple pulmonary stress testing, but this is considered a complex test since the measurements of CO_2 production, O_2 uptake, and electrocardiographic recordings.

2.354. 95819

Rationale: Index Electroencephalography, standard, resulting in code 95819. Review of this code descriptor confirms that standard EEG is awake and asleep.

2.355. 97110x2 or 97110+97110

Rationale: Index Physical Medicine/Therapy/Occupational Therapy, procedures, therapeutic exercises, resulting in code 97110. Review of the code indicates that it is reported in 15-minute increments. Thus, a 23-minute session would be reported with code 97110 twice.

2.356. 98941

Rationale: Index Manipulation, chiropractic, resulting in code range 98940–98943. Review of the available codes indicates that code 98941 is appropriate in this case, where four areas of the spine were manipulated.

2.357. 95861

Rationale: Index Electromyography, needle, extremities, resulting in code range 95861–95864. Review of the available codes indicates that code 95861 is appropriate to report an EMG of two extremities with the related paraspinous muscles.

2.358. 94070

Rationale: Index Pulmonology, diagnostic, spirometry, resulting in code range 94010–94070. Review of the available codes indicates that code 94070 is the appropriate code for a bronchospasm provocation evaluation. There is a note to report the bronchodilator antigen administration separately with 99070 or appropriate supply code.

2.359. 97140

Rationale: Index Physical Medicine/Therapy/Occupational Therapy, procedures, traction therapy, resulting in code 97140.

2.360. 96409

Rationale: Index Chemotherapy, intravenous, resulting in code range 96409–96417. Review of the available codes indicates that code 96409 is appropriate when intravenous push technique is used.

2.361. 93620

Rationale: Index Electrophysiology Procedure, resulting in code range 93600–93660. The electrophysiology (EP) studies are complex. The induction of arrhythmia determines the code in this case, which is 93620.

Modifiers

2.362. 51 or -51

Rationale: See instructions for use of modifiers in appendix A.

2.363. RC or -RC

Rationale: See instructions for use of modifiers in appendix A.

2.364. d. All of the above.

Rationale: All of the answers reflect circumstances that can be described with the use of a modifier. See instructions for use of modifiers in appendix A.

2.365. 26 or -26

Rationale: See instructions for use of modifiers in appendix A.

2.366. 67916E1 or 67916-E1

Rationale: Index Ectropion, repair, and see instructions for use of modifiers in appendix A.

2.367. 54 or -54

See instructions for use of modifiers in appendix A.

2.368. 26045RT or 26045-RT

Rationale: Index Fasciotomy, palm, and see instructions of use of modifiers in appendix A.

2.369. a. Assign the code for a colonoscopy with modifier -74.

Rationale: Per CPT coding guidelines, when a planned procedure is terminated prior to completion for cause, the intended procedure is coded with a modifier. Rationale: See instructions for use of modifiers in appendix A. Because general anesthesia was used, modifier -74 would be appropriate in this case. See Medicare billing guidelines, which have specific requirements for canceled endoscopic procedures.

2.370. 91, -91

Rationale: See instructions for use of modifiers in appendix A.

2.371. c. Assign a code for the procedure and one for the E/M service, with modifier -25 appended to the E/M code.

Rationale: Per coding guidelines, both the procedure and the E/M service should be coded, with modifier -25 appended to the E/M code.

2.372. 50 or -50

Rationale: See instructions for use of modifiers in appendix A.

2.373. 45307-53

Rationale: Index Proctosigmoidoscopy, removal, foreign body, and see instructions for use of modifiers in appendix A.

2.374. 25 or -25

Rationale: See instructions for use of modifiers in appendix A.

2.375. 32 or -32

Rationale: See instructions for use of modifiers in appendix A.

2.376. 27 or -27

Rationale: See instructions for use of modifiers in appendix A.

2.377. QM, -QM

Rationale: See instructions for use of modifiers in appendix A.

2.378. 21 or -21

Rationale: See instructions for use of modifiers in appendix A.

2.379. 80 or -80

Rationale: See instructions for use of modifiers in appendix A.

2.380. 62 or -62

Rationale: See instructions for use of modifiers in appendix A.

2.381. 58 or -58

Rationale: See instructions for use of modifiers in appendix A.

Category III Codes

2.382. d. All of the above.

Rationale: All the statements are true. See Introduction to Category III codes.

2.383. b. Report the Category III code.

Rationale: See Introduction to Category III codes. The Category III code should be assigned without modifier.

2.384. a. Will be archived unless there is evidence that a temporary code is still needed

Rationale: They will be archived unless there is evidence that a temporary code is still needed. See Introduction to Category III codes.

2.385. 00171T, 0172T

Rationale: Index Vertebra, lumbar, distraction device, resulting in codes 0171T–0172T.

2.386. 0103T

Rationale: Index Holotranscobalamin, resulting in code 0103T.

2.387. 0184T

Rationale: Index: Index Rectum, tumor, excision, transanal endoscopic, resulting in code 0184T. TEMS stands for transanal endoscopic microsurgical approach.

2.388. 0195T

Rationale: Index Arthrodesis, vertebra, lumbar, pre-sacral interbody, resulting in codes 0195T, 0196T. Review of the codes indicates that code 0195T is correct for one arthrodesis of a single interspace.

2.389. b. Semiannually

Rationale: See Introduction to Category III codes. They are updated more frequently than the main body of CPT in order to better reflect advances in technology.

2.390. 0030T

Rationale: Index Antiprothrombin Antibody resulting in code 0030T.

2.391. 0188T

Rationale: Index Critical care services, remote, video-conferenced evaluation and management, resulting in codes 0188T, 0189T. Review of the codes indicates that code 0188T is the correct code for 60 minutes.

2.392. 0170T

Rationale: Index Fistula, anal, repair, resulting in codes 0170T, 46288.

2.393. 0186T

Rationale: Index Eye, injection, medication, suprachoroidal delivery, resulting in code 0186T.

2.394. 22856, 0092T

Rationale: Index Arthroplasty, intervertebral disk, total replacement, resulting in codes 0163T, 22856–22857. Review of these codes reveals that the correct codes are 22856, 0092T.

2.395. c. Hospitals, physicians, insurers, health services researchers

Rationale: Hospitals, physicians, insurers, and health services researchers may use the codes. See Introduction to Category III Codes.

2.396. 0179T

Rationale: Index Cardiology, electrocardiogram, evaluation, resulting in codes 93000, 93010, 93014, 93660, 0178T–0180T. Review of the codes indicates that code 0179T is the most appropriate code for this scenario.

2.397. 0017T

Rationale: Index Photocoagulation, lesion, retina, resulting in code 0017T, 67210, 67227–67228.

2.398. 0158T

Rationale: Index Laparotomy, electrode removal gastric, resulting in codes 43882, 0158T. Review of the codes indicates that code 0158T is the correct code for removal of electrodes from the lesser curvature of the stomach.

2.399. 0067T

Rationale: Index Colonoscopy, virtual, resulting in codes 0066T, 0067T.

2.400. 0140T

Rationale: Index pH, exhaled breath condensate, resulting in code 0140T.

2.401. 0042T

Rationale: Index Cerebral Perfusion Analysis, resulting in code 0042T.

Review Questions

2.402. 29881, 29873

2.403. 31254-50, 31267-50

2.404. 14020

2.405. 12032, 12042, 12006

Note that the simple repairs are sequenced after more complex repairs.

2.406. 22630, 22632, 20936

2.407. 25025

2.408. 33690

2.409. 33533, 33517, 35500

2.410. 37205, 36200, 37250, 75960, 75945

2.411. 43243, 43239

2.412. 45308, 45305

2.413. 31631, 31625

2.414. 38505

2.415. 43264

2.416. 52235, 52330

2.417. 55815

2.418. 57456

2.419. 59610

2.420. 61548

2.421. 65285

2.422. 23350-RT, 73040

2.423. 78216

2.424. 86141

2.425. 93316

2.426. 90748, 90471

Chapter 3. HCPCS Level II Coding

Drugs

3.1. d. All of the above

Rationale: HCPCS contains codes for drugs that can be administered by all of these routes. See introduction to J codes.

3.2. J0295

Rationale: Index Unasyn.

3.3. J0476

Rationale: Index Baclofen.

3.4. J0585, J0585, J0585, or J0585x3

Rationale: Index Botulinum Toxin. Code J0585 reports Botox per unit. To report three units, the code should be reported three times, or once with a unit of "3" in FL 46 (Serv Units) of the UB-92 claim form.

3.5. J1260

Rationale: Index Anzemet.

3.6. J2790

Rationale: Index RhoGAM.

3.7. J9100

Rationale: Index Cytosar-U.

3.8. J9291

Rationale: Index Mitomycin, resulting in code range J9280–J9291. Review of the available codes indicates that code J9291 reports a 40 mg dose of Mitomycin and is the appropriate code.

3.9. J1160

Rationale: Index digoxin.

3.10. J7322

Rationale: Index Synvisc.

Supplies

3.11. E0601

Rationale: Index Continuous positive airway pressure (CPAP) device, resulting in code E0601.

3.12. A4750

Rationale: Index Blood, tubing, resulting in code A4750 or A4755. Review of the available codes indicates that code A4755 is used to report blood tubing for both the arterial and venous limbs of a hemodialysis access. The order specifies venous tubing only, so code A4750, Blood tubing, arterial or venous, is appropriate.

3.13. A5071

Rationale: Index Pouch, urinary, resulting in code range A4379–A4383, A4391, A5071, or A5073. Review of the available codes indicates that codes A4379–A4383 refer to ostomy pouches with face plates attached, and A4391 is for a pouch with extended-wear barrier, which is not specified here. Code A5071 is appropriate for a urinary ostomy pouch with unspecified barrier attached.

3.14. A6197

Rationale: Index Alginate dressing, resulting in code range A6196–A6199. Review of the available codes indicates that code A6197 is the appropriate code for a dressing of 16–48 sq in. Examples of alginate dressings include AlgiSite, Kalginate, and Tegagen. Alginate dressings are more absorbent than standard dressings and are used for wounds with heavy exudates to decrease the need for frequent dressing changes and to speed healing.

3.15. A9503

Rationale: Index Technetium-99 medronate (Tc-99m). There are multiple analogs of technetium-99m, many of which have their own codes. Care must be taken in assigning these codes. More information may be needed to assign the appropriate code, and input of the nuclear medicine technician and/or the manufacturer may be needed.

3.16. A9600

Rationale: Index Strontium 89 chloride.

3.17. A4605

Rationale: Index Tracheal suction catheter, resulting in code A4624. Code A4624 refers to a tracheal suction catheter, any type other than closed system; therefore, another code (A4605) was referenced for the closed system.

3.18. A4253

Rationale: Index Blood, glucose test strips.

3.19. A7018

Rationale: Index Nebulizer, water

3.20. A4550

Rationale: Index Surgical, tray

Ambulance

3.21. A0384

Rationale: Index Ambulance, resulting in code range A0021–A0999. Review of the descriptions of the available codes indicates that code A0384 is the appropriate code for BLS defibrillation supplies.

3.22. -HN

Rationale: See instructional notes regarding ambulance coding preceding code A0021.

3.23. A0380

Rationale: Index Ambulance, resulting in code range A0021–A0999. Review of the descriptions of the available codes indicates that code A0380 is the appropriate code for BLS (basic life support) transport.

3.24. b. Per mile

Rationale: Ambulance services are reported per mile. See instructional notes regarding ambulance coding preceding code A0021.

3.25. A0436

Rationale: Index Ambulance, air.

3.26. A0424

Rationale: Index Ambulance, resulting in code range A0021–A0999. Review of the descriptions of the available codes indicates that code A0424 is the appropriate code for reporting the circumstance where an extra attendant is required based upon the patient's medical condition.

3.27. c. Half hours

Rationale: Waiting time is measured in half-hour increments. See instructional note preceding code A0420.

3.28. A0382

Rationale: Index Ambulance, disposable supplies, resulting in code range A0382–A0398. Review of the available codes indicates that code A0382 is the appropriate code to report routine disposable supplies, lacking further information.

3.29. A0225

Rationale: Index Ambulance, resulting in code range A0021–A0999. Review of the descriptions of the available codes indicates that code A0225 is the appropriate code for reporting neonatal transport.

3.30. A0422

Rationale: Index Ambulance, oxygen.

Durable Medical Equipment

3.31. E0434

Rationale: Index Oxygen, supplies and equipment, resulting in a number of code ranges. Review of the available codes indicates that code E0434 describes rental of a complete liquid oxygen system.

3.32. E0297, E0277

Rationale: Index Bed, hospital, full electric, home care, without mattress, and Mattress, alternating pressure.

3.33. E1594

Rationale: Index Dialysis, peritoneal, resulting in several individual codes and code ranges. Review of all the available codes indicates that code E1594 is the only code that correctly describes the equipment specified here.

3.34. E1300

Rationale: Index Whirlpool equipment, resulting in code range E1300–E1310. Review of the available codes indicates that code E1300 is appropriate to describe a portable unit.

3.35. E1180

Rationale: Index Wheelchair, amputee, resulting in code range E1170–E1200. Review of the available codes indicates that code E1180 describes a chair with the particular combination of accessories detailed above.

3.36. E1038

Rationale: Index Transport chair, resulting in code E1037 or E1038. Review of both the available codes indicates that code E1037 reports a pediatric chair, and code E1038 is appropriate for an adult chair.

3.37. E0950

Rationale: Index Wheelchair, accessories, tray.

3.38. E0184

Rationale: Index Eggcrate dry pressure pad/mattress, resulting in code E0184 or E0199. Review of both the available codes indicates that the appropriate code is E0184.

3.39. E0730

Rationale: Index TENS, resulting in code A4595 or code range E0720–E0749. Review of the available codes indicates that code A4595 is used to report the leads, not the unit. Review of the E codes indicates that code E0730 is appropriate to report a four-lead TENS unit.

3.40. E0619

Rationale: Index Monitor, apnea, resulting in code E0618. Review of the description of this code, however, shows that E0618 reports a nonrecording apnea monitor. Review of other codes in this section leads to code E0619 for a recording apnea monitor, which is the correct code. This code may also be accessed by indexing Apnea monitor, which results in code E0618 or E0619.

Procedures/Services

3.41. G0117

Rationale: Index Screening, glaucoma, resulting in codes G0117 or G0118.

3.42. G0122

Rationale: Index Screening examination, colorectal cancer, resulting in a series of code listings. Review of the available codes indicates that code G0122 is the appropriate code for reporting barium enema as a means for screening for colorectal cancer.

3.43. G0206

Rationale: Index Mammography, resulting in code range G0202–G0206. Review of the available codes indicates that code G0206 is appropriate to describe a unilateral diagnostic mammography.

3.44. G0219

Rationale: Index PET imaging, whole body, resulting in code G0219.

3.45. G0379

Rationale: Index Hospital, observation, direct admit.

3.46. G0290

Rationale: Index Stent placement, transcatheter, intracoronary, resulting in code G0290 or G0291. Review of the available codes indicates that code G0290 is the appropriate code for the first stent placement, and G0291 for each additional stent.

3.47. G0155

Rationale: Index Social worker, home health setting.

3.48. G0109

Rationale: Index Training, diabetes, resulting in code G0108 or G0109. Review of the available codes indicates that the code for group training is G0109.

3.49. G0127

Rationale: Index Trim nails.

3.50. G0008

Rationale: Index Vaccination, administration, influenza virus, resulting in code G0008.

Part II

Intermediate Coding Exercises

Chapter 4. Case Studies from Inpatient Health Records

Disorders of the Blood and Blood-Forming Organs

4.1.   a. 285.1

Incorrect answer. The anemia may be acute blood loss or a complication due to the surgery, but it is not stated by the physician. Due to incomplete physician documentation, query the physician. *Coding Clinic* (2004, 3Q:4; 2000, 3Q:6; and 1992, 2Q:15–16).

   b. 998.11

Incorrect answer. The anemia may be acute blood loss or a complication due to the surgery, but it is not stated by the physician. Due to incomplete physician documentation, query the physician. *Coding Clinic* (2004, 3Q:4; 2000, 3Q:6, and 1992, 2Q:16).

   c. 998.11, 285.1

Incorrect answer. The anemia is not documented as a complication of the surgery nor is the anemia documented as acute blood loss. Due to incomplete physician documentation, query the physician. *Coding Clinic* (2004, 3Q:4; 2000, 3Q:6; and 1992, 2Q:16).

   d. Unable to code, the physician must be queried.
   Correct answer.

4.2.   a. 491.21, 284.1, 99.03
   Correct answer.

   b. 491.21, 284.1, 285.9, 288.0, 287.5, 99.03

Incorrect answer. Pancytopenia is a deficiency of all three blood components: white blood cells (neutropenia), red blood cells (anemia), and platelets (thrombocytopenia). Therefore, only the code for pancytopenia (284.1) is assigned.

   c. 496, 284.1, 99.03

Incorrect answer. The correct code for an acute exacerbation of COPD is 491.21.

d. 491.21, 285.9, 288.00, 287.5, 99.02

Incorrect answer. Pancytopenia is a deficiency of all three blood components: white blood cells (neutropenia), red blood cells (anemia), and platelets (thrombocytopenia). Therefore, only the code for pancytopenia (284.1) is assigned. The transfusion was not with previously collected autologous blood.

4.3. 174.4-Y, 85.21, 40.23

Note: When a sentinel lymph node biopsy is performed, an excision of the sentinel node is examined to determine the presence of malignancy. *Coding Clinic* (2002, 2Q:7).

4.4. a. 286.0, 99.06, 99.03

Incorrect answer. The anemia code of 285.1 would be coded as the principal diagnosis.

b. 285.1, 286.0, 99.06, 99.03

Correct answer.

c. 286.0, 285.1, 99.06, 99.03

Incorrect answer. In accordance with UHDDS definition for principal diagnosis, the anemia (not the hemophilia), is the reason for admission and sequenced as the principal diagnosis (*ICD-9-CM Official Guidelines for Coding and Reporting*).

d. 285.1, 99.06, 99.03

Incorrect answer. There is a hemophilia code of 286.0 that is needed as a secondary diagnosis code.

4.5. 284.89-Y, E933.1-Y MS-DRG: 810

Note. The "Excludes" note under V58.1 states that when chemotherapy is given for a nonneoplastic condition, the condition is coded. In this case, you would not code the chemotherapy diagnosis code. The procedure code would indicate that the chemo had been given.

Disorders of the Cardiovascular System

4.6. a. The conditions are reported with two separate codes unless the physician specifically states that there is a cause-and-effect relationship.

Incorrect answer. A cause-and-effect relationship is assumed unless the physician states otherwise.

b. Code 403.9X is assigned, with an additional code for chronic kidney disease.

Correct answer.

c. A cause-and-effect relationship is never assumed.

Incorrect answer. A cause-and-effect relationship is assumed unless the physician states otherwise.

d. Code 403.9X is assigned, with an additional code to specify the type of hypertension.

Incorrect answer. Code 403.9X is assigned with an additional code to specify the stage of the chronic kidney disease.

4.7. 410.41-Y, 427.31-N, 37.23, 88.54, 88.56

Note: The fifth digit of 1 is assigned for the MI because the patient was transferred, so this is considered the initial episode of care. The atrial fibrillation was new onset diagnosed during the hospital stay; therefore, POA indicator is N.

4.8.   a. 428.21, 428.31, 410.12, 599.0, 041.4, 89.54

Incorrect answer. It is incorrect to use systolic and diastolic heart failure codes together. The combined code is used in this case.

b. 428.41, 410.12, 599.0, 041.4, 89.54

Correct answer.

c. 428.0, 412, 599.0, 041.4, 89.54

Incorrect answer. The heart failure is not stated as congestive but, rather, the specific types of failure are documented. The MI would be coded as acute-subsequent admission because it is within the eight-week time frame.

d. 428.41, 410.11, 599.0, 041.4, 89.54

Incorrect answer. It is not correct to use the initial episode fifth digit for the MI because the initial episode of care was completed. The subsequent episode of care fifth digit of 2 should be used instead.

4.9. 414.01-Y, 415.19-N, 496-Y, 36.14, 39.61, MS-DRG: 235

Note. In accordance with the UHDDS guidelines for principal diagnosis assignment, the ASHD is the reason for admission, and is sequenced as the principal diagnosis (*ICD-9-CM Official Guidelines for Coding and Reporting*).

4.10.   a. Acute myocardial infarction, congestive heart failure, Parkinson's disease, emphysema

Correct answer.

b. Acute myocardial infarction, congestive heart failure

Incorrect answer. The Parkinson's disease, congestive heart failure, and emphysema are reported as secondary diagnoses based on the UHDDS additional diagnosis guidelines (*ICD-9-CM Official Guidelines for Coding and Reporting* and *Coding Clinic* 2006, 4Q:234).

c. Acute myocardial infarction, congestive heart failure, Parkinson's disease, emphysema, pneumonia, bleeding ulcer

Incorrect answer. The pneumonia and bleeding ulcer are not current conditions nor evaluated or treated during the hospitalization and should not be coded as secondary diagnoses.

d. Acute myocardial infarction, pneumonia, congestive heart failure, emphysema

Incorrect answer. The pneumonia is not a current condition nor evaluated or treated during this hospitalization and should not be coded as a secondary diagnosis. The Parkinson's disease should be added as a secondary diagnosis as a chronic condition requiring monitoring and nursing resources.

4.11. 414.01-Y, 427.81-Y, 37.83, 37.72, 00.66, 36.07, 00.40, 00.45, MS-DRG: 244

Note: In accordance with UHDDS definition for principal diagnosis, the reason (after study) the patient is admitted to the hospital is to undergo the PTCA for the CAD; therefore, the 414.01 is the principal diagnosis

4.12. a. 411.0, 412

Incorrect answer. The angina was documented as "crescendo" and should be assigned to code 411.1, coding to the highest degree of code specificity.

b. 413.9, 412

Incorrect answer. The angina was documented as "crescendo" and should be assigned to code 411.1, coding to the highest degree of code specificity.

c. 411.1, 412

Correct answer.

d. 413.0, 412

Incorrect answer. The angina was documented as "crescendo" and should be assigned to code 411.1, coding to the highest degree of code specificity.

4.13. 434.91-Y, 438.21, MS-DRG: 065

Note: Code 436 would not be assigned if there is documentation of infarction. Code V12.59 would not be assigned because it is only for those instances where there are no residual neurologic deficits from a previous stroke. Residual conditions from a previous stroke may be reported with another acute infarct. Category 438 is exempt from the POA requirement.

4.14. a. V58.64

Incorrect answer. Code V58.64 is used to report long-term (current) use of nonsteroidal anti-inflammatories (NSAID). There is no documentation that support the patient is taking aspirin as an anti-inflammatory for osteoarthritis.

b. V58.61

Incorrect answer. Code V58.61 is used to report long-term (current) use of anticoagulants. There is no documentation that supports the patient is taking aspirin as an anticoagulant.

c. V58.69

Incorrect answer. Long-term (current) use of other medication is incorrect code assignment based on a more accurate code match of V58.66 long term (current) use of aspirin in accordance with the documentation.

d. V58.66

Correct answer.

4.15. a. 00.66

Incorrect answer. Coder should reference the "Code Also" instructional note to code: number of stents, insertion of stents, infusion of thrombolytic, and number of arteries.

b. 00.66, 00.47, 00.41, 99.10

Incorrect answer. See "Code Also" note: The insertion of the stent should also be coded in addition to the numbers of stents.

c. 00.66, 36.06, 00.47, 00.41, 99.10

Correct answer.

d. 36.06

Incorrect answer. Incomplete coding. Coder should reference the "Code Also" instructional note to code: PTCA, number of stents, infusion of thrombolytic, and number of arteries.

Disorders of the Digestive System

4.16. 569.85-Y, 562.11-Y, 45.23

Note: The source of the bleeding is angiodysplasia. Therefore, the code with hemorrhage is assigned based on *Coding Clinic* (2005, 3Q:17–18), GI bleeding with multiple possible causes. The diverticulitis was not the source of bleeding; therefore code is assigned without bleeding. The 578.1 code is not reported in addition because it is included in the 569.85 code.

4.17. 531.20-Y, 44.41

Note: The ulcer was an acute gastric ulcer with perforation and hemorrhage. The procedure was suture of gastric ulcer. There was no documentation that it was done laparoscopically, therefore, the open technique is coded.

4.18. 578.1-Y, 428.22-Y, 428.0-Y, 45.16, MS-DRG: 378

Note: The melena is listed as the principal diagnosis. No documented cause is identified for the bleeding. Therefore, melena is the most specific code available. It is correct to add 428.0 with another specified type of heart failure (chronic systolic) based on *Coding Clinic* (2004, 4Q:140) that states CHF is not an inherent component of diastolic or systolic heart failure; therefore, two codes are required.

4.19. a. 003.0, 276.51

Incorrect answer. The patient was admitted for treatment of dehydration. The circumstances of inpatient admission always govern the selection of principal diagnosis (*Coding Clinic* 2008, 1Q:10–11).

b. 558.9, 003.0, 276.51

Incorrect answer. The patient was admitted for treatment of dehydration. The circumstances of inpatient admission always govern the selection of principal diagnosis. *Coding Clinic* 2008 (1Q:10–11). Code 558.9 would not be assigned as the cause of the gastroenteritis is Salmonella.

c. 003.0, 578.9, 276.51, 787.91

Incorrect answer. Acute symptoms of Salmonella gastroenteritis include the sudden onset of nausea, abdominal cramping, and bloody diarrhea. Signs and symptoms that are integral to the disease process should not be assigned as additional codes (*ICD-9-CM Official Guidelines for Coding and Reporting*). Use of category 578, Gastrointestinal hemorrhage, is limited to cases where a G.I. bleed is documented but no bleeding site or cause is identified (*Coding Clinic* 1992, 2Q:9–10).

d. 276.51, 003.0

Correct answer.

4.20. 550.93-Y, 496-Y, 403.91-Y, 585.6-Y, 53.16, MS-DRG: 350

Note: According to ICD-9-CM, hypertension and end-stage renal disease is a presumed cause and effect relationship. Therefore, a combination code is assigned, along with a code specifying the stage of the kidney failure. COPD meets additional diagnosis reporting. There is a combination code available for the hernia to show that it is bilateral and at least one side is recurrent. The combination procedure code shows that the hernia is bilateral, with one direct and one indirect, and that a graft was used.

4.21. 574.80-Y, 401.9-Y, 51.22, 51.41

Note: It is important to review all of the choices at category 574. One code can be selected to show the cholelithiasis, the choledocholithiasis, and the acute and chronic cholecystitis. Hypertension meets UHDDS definition for reporting additional diagnosis.

4.22. 153.3-Y, 197.7-Y, 45.76, MS-DRG: 330

Note: Subcategory code 45.9 excludes note states "end-to-end anastomosis —omit code." Therefore the anastomosis code is not assigned as a separate code.

4.23 a. 410.42, 414.01, 729.5, 782.5, 305.1, V17.3, 00.66, 00.40, 37.22, 88.56, 88.53

Incorrect answer. The patient was transferred to the facility while in the acute phase of a myocardial infarction. The fifth digit 2 is assigned to a myocardial infarction code for a subsequent episode of care within 8 weeks of the initial episode.

b. 410.41, 414.01, 729.5, 782.5, 305.1, V17.3, 00.66, 00.40, 37.22, 88.56, 88.53

Correct answer. It is appropriate to code an acute myocardial infarction, initial episode of care, when a patient is transferred for further treatment of the myocardial infarction. ICD-9-CM coding conventions require coding of procedures to the fullest extent they were performed. Therefore, it is appropriate to code the PTCA of the single artery.

c. 410.41, 414.01, 305.1, V17.3, 37.22, 88.56, 88.53

Incorrect answer. In ICD-9-CM coding, procedures are coded to the extent they are performed regardless whether they were successful for treatment of the condition. The source document indicates a rocket balloon was inflated 4 times in the right posterior lateral branch. Therefore, it is appropriate to assign the codes for PTCA of one coronary artery. The patient had a work up for the pain and cyanosis of toes. No definitive diagnosis was documented; however, the symptoms are reported.

d. 410.42, 414.01, 305.1, V17.3, 37.22, 88.56, 88.53

Incorrect answer. See incorrect answers a and c.

Endocrine, Nutritional and Metabolic Diseases, and Immunity Disorders

4.24. 276.51-Y, 787.91-Y, 280.9-Y, 486-Y, 344.40-Y, 353.8-Y, 139.8, 45.25, MS-DRG 640

Note: In accordance with *ICD-9-CM Official Guidelines for Coding and Reporting* and *Coding Clinic* (2008, 4Q:206–211), a late effect is the residual effect after the acute phase has ended. Coding requires two codes: one for the condition(s) produced and the late effect code. The pneumonia was being treated prior to admission and is still present. Code 139.8 is POA exempt. All other diagnoses were present on admission.

4.25. a. 250.30, 250.40, 581.81, 250.70, 785.4

Correct answer.

b. 250.30, 581.81, 785.4

Incorrect answer. The DM etiology codes for renal complications and peripheral circulatory disorders (gangrene) should be coded as well. Per *Coding Clinic* (1986, March/April:12), if no other "cause-and-effect" relationship has been established for gangrene, assume that the gangrene is the consequence of diabetic peripheral vascular circulatory disorder. This is especially true when the gangrene is in the lower extremity.

c. 250.30, 250.41, 581.81, 785.4

Per *Coding Clinic* (1986, March/April:12), if no other "cause-and-effect" relationship has been established for gangrene, assume that the gangrene is the consequence of diabetic peripheral vascular circulatory disorder. This is especially true when the gangrene is in the lower extremity. The DM is specified as type II, so the fifth digit of 1 (type I) is incorrect. The DM etiology code should be assigned for the peripheral vascular circulatory disorder.

d. 250.31, 250.41, 250.71

Incorrect answer. The DM is specified as type II, so the fifth digit of 1 (type I) is incorrect. The instruction note states "Code Also" the specific renal manifestations of the diabetes (nephrotic syndrome) and circulatory manifestations of diabetes (gangrene). Both should also be coded.

4.26. 250.13-Y, 276.51-Y

Note: The diabetes is coded as the principal diagnosis as it meets definition of UHDDS condition, after study, to be the reason the patient was admitted. The fifth digit is 3 because the DM is type I and it is documented as uncontrolled. The symptoms such as polydipsia would not be coded as this symptom is integral to the diabetes. Dehydration meets reporting guidelines as a secondary diagnosis as patient's dehydration was evaluated and treated during the hospitalization. Both conditions were present at the time of admission.

4.27. 193-Y, 196.0-Y, 06.4 MS-DRG: 626

Note: There was documented metastasis to the cervical lymph node, therefore, this meets reporting as a secondary diagnosis. Initially the left lobe was removed, but because of the carcinoma, a total thyroidectomy was done.

4.28. a. 250.71, 440.23, 250.61, 357.2, 86.28

Incorrect answer. Code 440.24 includes any condition classifiable to 440.23 with ischemic gangrene. Assign an additional code for the foot ulceration.

b. 250.71, 440.24, 250.61, 357.2, 707.15, 86.28

Correct answer.

c. 250.01, 440.20, 785.4, 357.2, 707.15, 86.22

Incorrect answer. The gangrene is included in the fifth digit for subcategory 440.2. The debridement was nonexcisional.

d. 250.71, 440.24, 250.61, 707.15, 86.22

Incorrect answer. Assign code 250.6X, Diabetes with neurological manifestations, and code 357.2, Polyneuropathy in diabetes, for diabetic neuropathy. *Coding Clinic* (1991, 3Q:9–11). The debridement was nonexcisional.

Disorders of the Genitourinary System

4.29. a. 614.9, 079.98, 59.02

Incorrect answer. Code 614.9 is not specific, while code 614.6 specifies pelvic adhesions and more closely describes the findings at time of surgery. INTERCEED is an adhesion barrier that should be coded.

b. 614.6, 079.98, 59.02, 99.77

Correct answer.

c. 614.6, 079.88, 54.59, 99.77

Incorrect answer. The chlamydia is unspecified, code 079.98. Code 54.59 is incorrect choice as "Excludes" note directs code assignment to "lysis of adhesions kidney 59.02 and ureter 59.02–59.03" as the lysis was performed around the kidney and uteter.

d. 614.3, 079.98, 59.02, 99.77

Incorrect answer. Documentation does not state acute inflammatory process.

4.30.   a. 183.0, 68.41, 65.61, 40.3

Incorrect answer. Documentation states a radical abdominal hysterectomy was done, coded 68.69, not a laparoscopic total abdominal hysterectomy.

b. 183.0, 68.69, 65.61, 40.3

Correct answer.

c. 198.6, 68.61, 65.61, 40.3

Incorrect answer. Ovarian cancer is a primary cancer, not a secondary one, so the correct code is 183.0. Documentation states a radical abdominal hysterectomy was done, coded 68.69, not a laparoscopic radical abdominal hysterectomy.

d. 183.0, 68.69, 65.61, 40.59

Incorrect answer. Documentation states regional lymph node dissection was done, which would be coded 40.3.

4.31.   599.0-Y, 041.4-Y, 491.21-N, 414.01-Y, 401.9-Y, MS-DRG: 690

Note: The symptoms of the UTI are not coded as they are integral to the UTI. The additional conditions meet reporting guidelines as secondary diagnoses because they are current conditions evaluated and/or treated during the hospitalization. Assign 414.01 if the patient has coronary artery disease and past history does not show coronary artery bypass grafting (*Coding Clinic* 1997, 3Q:15). All conditions EXCEPT the exacerbation of COPD were present at the time of admission. POA reporting guidelines for combination codes instructs coder to report N (no) if any part of the combination code was not present on admission and assign Y (yes) if all parts of the combination code were present on admission.

4.32.   600.11-Y, 185-Y, 60.29

Note: Code 600.11 is assigned because of the documentation of nodular hyperplasia and meets reporting guidelines and UHDDS definition of principal diagnosis as the condition, after study, as the reason for admission. The microscopic foci adenocarcinoma meets reporting guidelines as a secondary diagnosis for a condition identified during treatment and may impact future care. See *Coding Clinic* (1992, 3Q:7).

4.33.   610.1-Y, V16.3, 85.42

Note: This is one procedure code that has a differentiation in ICD-9-CM for bilateral procedures. There is also distinction between simple and other types of mastectomy. Report secondary diagnosis code V16.3 for family history of breast cancer. V16.3 is exempt from POA reporting per the national guidelines.

4.34.   584.9-Y, 276.1-Y, 401.9-Y, MS-DRG: 683

Note: The acute renal failure and hypertension are coded individually and not combined. The category for hypertensive renal disease does not include "acute" renal failure. Dehydration "with" hyponatremia coded to the highest degree of code specificity is reported as 276.1 (not 276.51). All conditions were present at the time of admission.

4.35. 584.9-Y, 403.90-Y, 585.4-Y, 250.41-Y, MS-DRG: 684

Note: Code 403.90 is assigned to report hypertensive chronic kidney disease stage IV, and the stage (585.4) is assigned as an additional code. Code 583.81 is not reported because the nephritis/nephropathy is specified as acute and chronic.

4.36. a. V50.41, V84.01, V16.3

Correct answer.

b. V16.3, V84.01

Incorrect answer. Incomplete coding. For complete coding, report the genetic susceptibility code V84.01 as a secondary diagnosis. Report admission for prophylactic organ removal of breast as principal diagnosis, code V50.41.

c. 174.9, V16.3

Incorrect answer. Code 174.9 is for breast cancer and the patient does not have breast cancer. She is having her breasts prophylactically removed to prevent breast cancer since she is genetically susceptible to the disease. For complete coding, report the genetic susceptibility code V84.01 as a secondary diagnosis. Report admission for prophylactic organ removal of breast as principal diagnosis, code V50.41.

d. V50.41, V84.01, V10.3

Incorrect answer. Secondary diagnosis code is reported incorrectly as a personal history of breast cancer (and not family history of breast cancer).

Infectious Diseases

4.37. 042-Y, 012.13-Y, 014.83-Y, 017.23-Y, 729.81-N, 40.11, 88.77, 87.41, 88.01, 88.38, 87.03, MS-DRG 976

Note: In accordance with *ICD-9-CM Official Guidelines for Coding and Reporting* and *Coding Clinic* (2006, 4Q:152), report code 042 as the principal diagnosis when a patient is admitted for an HIV-related condition. The HIV-related conditions are reported as secondary diagnoses. All locations of the lymph node tuberculosis should be coded. Except the swelling of the extremities, all conditions are present on admission.

4.38. 038.0-Y, 995.91-Y, 599.0-Y, 041.02-Y, MS-DRG: 872

Note: The term "urosepsis" should be queried to determine if the patient has sepsis. Physician response documented sepsis with streptococcal septicemia and urinary tract infection with streptococcus B. In accordance with *ICD-9-CM Official Guidelines for Coding and Reporting* and *Coding Clinic* (2006, 4Q:154–160), report the streptococcal septicemia as the underlying infection and the 995.91 sepsis as the systemic inflammatory response syndrome due to the infectious process without acute organ dysfunction. Urinary tract infection and the causative organism meet secondary diagnosis reporting. All conditions were present at the time of admission.

4.39. 647.63-Y, 042-Y, 647.83-Y, 136.3-Y, MS-DRG: 781

Note: In accordance *ICD-9-CM Official Guidelines for Coding and Reporting* and *Coding Clinic* 2006 (4Q:153–154), during pregnancy, a patient admitted because of an HIV-related illness is reported with the principal diagnosis of 647.6x followed by 042. The pregnancy is also complicated by the Pneumocystis carinii pneumonia which meets reporting guidelines for a secondary diagnosis.

4.40. 042-Y, 078.5-Y, 011.03-Y, 492.8-Y, V42.6, 33.24, MS-DRG: 975

Note: In accordance with *ICD-9-CM Official Guidelines for Coding and Reporting* and *Coding Clinic* (2006, 4Q:152), report code 042 as the principal diagnosis when a patient is admitted for an HIV-related condition. The HIV-related conditions are reported as secondary diagnoses. Code 33.24 is correct for bronchoscopy with bronchoalveolar lavage (*Coding Clinic* 2006, 2Q:20). Code V42.6 is POA exempt. All other diagnoses were present on admission.

4.41. 482.31-Y, 054.11-Y

Note: There is documentation of the cause of the pneumonia. Therefore, the pneumonia due to group A streptococcus is coded. The underlying cause of the vulvovaginitis is determined to be herpes. Therefore, this is reported as a secondary diagnosis. All conditions are present on admission.

Disorders of the Skin and Subcutaneous Tissue

4.42. 507.0-Y, 438.82, 707.04-Y, 707.21-Y, MS-DRG: 179

Note: The documentation links the aspiration to the pneumonia and meets principal diagnosis reporting guidelines. Secondary diagnosis reporting of the dysphagia due to old stroke and stage one decubitus ulcer were evaluated and utilized nursing resources. Code 438.82 is POA exempt. If the documentation had provided further detail about the dysphagia, an additional code from subcategory 787.2 would be assigned.

4.43. 998.59-Y, 682.2-Y, 041.11-Y, 250.00-Y

Note: In accordance with UHDDS definition for principal diagnosis, the postoperative wound infection meets reporting as principal diagnosis because the condition, after study, caused the admission. Secondary diagnosis reporting of the cellulitis, infectious organism, and diabetes meet secondary reporting guidelines as conditions that were evaluated, treated, or increased nursing care during the hospital stay.

4.44. 682.6-Y, 707.05-Y, 707.20-Y. 438.20, 041.02-Y, MS-DRG: 603

Note: The cellulitis is listed in the first position. The infectious organism should be coded as well as the hemiplegia and the decubitus ulcer. Code 438.20 is POA exempt.

4.45.   707.05-Y, 707.22-Y, 707.14-Y, 331.0-Y, 83.45, 86.22, MS-DRG: 574

Note: The most extensive procedure went into the muscle, so both procedures should be coded. The decubitus as well as the chronic heel ulcer should be coded.

4.46.   172.5-Y, 493.92-N, 86.4, 86.63, 93.94

Note: The melanoma is listed first. The procedure codes reflect the wide excision and the full-thickness skin graft.

Behavioral Health Conditions

4.47.   a.   291.81, 303.01, 94.63

Incorrect answer. When a patient experiences alcohol withdrawal symptoms, one of three codes will apply (291.0, 291.3 or 291.81). Code 291.0 takes precedence over the other two, and 291.3 takes precedence over 291.81. In this case, the patient experienced delirium tremens (DTs); code 291.0 is assigned. See "Excludes" note for 291.3 and 291.81 (*Coding Clinic* 1991, 2Q:9–13).

b.   291.81, 303.90, 94.62

Incorrect answer. When a patient experiences alcohol withdrawal symptoms, one of three codes will apply (291.0, 291.3 or 291.81). Code 291.0 takes precedence over the other two, and 291.3 takes precedence over 291.81. In this case, the patient experienced delirium tremens (DTs) and code 291.0 is assigned. See "Excludes" note for 291.3 and 291.81 (*Coding Clinic* 1991, 2Q:9–13). Code 303.9x is assigned with the fifth digit of 3, remission, which refers to either a complete cessation of alcohol intake or the period during which a decrease toward cessation is taking place. The documentation supports assignment of code 303.01 which indicates acute alcoholic intoxication, continuous. Code 94.63 is correct as patient was admitted for both rehab and detox.

c.   291.0, 303.93, 94.63

Correct answer.

d.   291.0, 303.90, 94.62

Incorrect answer. Code 303.9x is assigned with the fifth digit of 3, remission, which refers to either a complete cessation of alcohol intake or the period during which a decrease toward cessation is taking place. The documentation supports assignment of code 303.01, which indicates acute alcoholic intoxication, continuous. Code 94.63 is correct as patient was admitted for both rehab and detox.

4.48.   296.24-Y, 94.27, 94.22, 94.08, MS-DRG: 885

Note: The procedures assigned would be according to the hospital policy for assigning ICD-9-CM codes for nonsurgical procedures.

4.49. 331.0-Y, 294.11-Y, 891.0-Y, E888.9-Y, E849.4, E000.9, 86.59, MS-DRG: 057

Note: The dementia with behavioral disturbance is assigned because wandering off is included in this code.

4.50. 303.01-Y

Note: Only one code is assigned for acute and chronic alcoholism, and it was present at the time of admission. The acute inebriation is included in code 303.01. It would be incorrect to assign a code from the 305 category (*Coding Clinic* 1991, 2Q:9–13).

4.51. 491.21-Y, 293.84-Y, 244.9-Y, 305.1-Y, MS-DRG: 192

Note: Code 293.84 is assigned when the anxiety is due to an organic condition (hypothyroidism) (*Coding Clinic* 1996, 4Q:29). POA indicator is assigned a Y (yes) according to POA guidelines for combination codes that identify both the chronic condition and the acute exacerbation if all parts of the combination code were present on admission.

Disorders of the Musculoskeletal System and Connective Tissue

4.52. 825.25-Y, E000.9, 79.37, 78.18

Note: Fracture does not include tarsals. Open reduction, internal fixation should be coded.

4.53. 996.66-Y, V43.64, 81.53, MS-DRG: 468

Note: "Any time the joint is replaced or revised after the initial replacement would be considered a revision." (*Coding Clinic* 1996, 2Q:13, 1997 3Q:13).

4.54. a. 718.31, 81.82

Correct answer.

b. 718.31, 81.82, 83.5

Incorrect answer. Bursectomy is included in acromioplasty.

c. 831.00, 81.82, 83.5

Incorrect answer. Dislocation is not acute, it is stated as recurrent. Bursectomy is included in acromioplasty.

d. 831.00, 81.82, 83.5, 80.41

Incorrect answer. Dislocation is not acute, it is stated as recurrent. Bursectomy and division of ligament are included in acromioplasty.

4.55. a. 722.52, 721.3, 414.00, 401.9, 03.92, 99.23, 88.93

Correct answer.

b. 722.52, 721.3, 724.02, 724.4, 414.00, 401.9, 03.92, 99.23, 88.93

Incorrect answer. Codes 724.02 and 724.4 should not be assigned. Symptoms and signs associated with (due to) spondylosis and allied disorders or intervertebral disc disorders are included in the 721–722 code series (*Coding Clinic* 1989, 2Q:14). If the physician had stated the lumbar stenosis was not attributable to the displaced disc it would have been assigned (*Coding Clinic* 1994, 3Q:14).

c. 724.4, 414.00, 401.9, 03.92, 99.23, 88.93

Incorrect answer. The patient has lumbar degenerative disc disease. Code 722.52 should be assigned as the principal diagnosis. Codes 724.4 should not be assigned. Symptoms and signs associated with (due to) intervertebral disc disorders are included in the 721–722 code series (*Coding Clinic* 1989, 2Q:14). The arthritis requires a code assignment also.

d. 722.52, 721.3, 414.00, 401.9, 03.91, 88.93

Incorrect answer. The procedure performed was steroid injections, code 03.92. Code 03.92 does not identify the specific agent injected. Therefore, it would be appropriate to assign both codes 03.92 and 99.23, Injection of steroid, for a single injection of steroid into the spinal canal. This code assignment may be repeated for each injection (*Coding Clinic* 2000, 3Q:15).

4.56. 733.13-Y, 733.01-Y, 03.91

Note: This is coded as a pathologic fracture because it is due to disease process rather than trauma. Both conditions present on admission.

4.57. a. 80.51

Incorrect answer. The discectomy only includes the removal of the disc, but not the insertion of the prosthetic device.

b. 80.51, 84.65

Incorrect answer. The discectomy is included in the spinal disc replacement device codes and is not separately assigned.

c. 84.65, 80.51

Incorrect answer. The discectomy is included in the spinal disc replacement device codes and is not separately assigned.

d. 84.65

Correct answer.

4.58. a. 84.53, 78.37

Correct answer.

b. 84.53

Incorrect answer. There is a code also note with code 84.53 indicating the need to assign a code from 78.3x for limb lengthening procedure.

c. 78.37

Incorrect answer. Missing the code for the principal procedure, implantation of the limb lengthening device.

d. 84.54, 78.37

Incorrect answer. There is documentation this was kinetic distraction. Therefore, code 84.54 is an incorrect representation of procedure performed.

4.59. Principal diagnosis: 820.8-Y

Additional diagnoses: 428.0-Y, 492.8-Y, 714.0-Y, 733.00-Y, V15.82, V58.65, E884.5-Y, E849.0, E000.8, E013.4

Procedure: 81.52

MS-DRG: 470

Note: It is appropriate to code an acute fracture in this case because the physician did not identify the fracture as pathological or correlate the osteoporosis to the fracture in any way. All conditions were present on admission. Code V15.82 is exempt from POA reporting. Category V58 is exempt from POA reporting. Code E849.0 is exempt from POA reporting.

Neoplasms

4.60. a. 338.3, 199.0, V10.3, 276.51, 250.02, 428.0

Correct answer.

b. 174.9, 276.51, 250.02, 428.0

Incorrect answer. The breast carcinoma was excised three years ago. Therefore, report history of breast cancer V10.3. The widespread metastatic carcinoma, 199.0 is causing the pain and is sequenced as a secondary diagnosis. The reason for the admission is the neoplasm-related pain. Sequence the 338.3 as the principal diagnosis. See *Coding Clinic* (2008, 4Q:231–235). Secondary diagnoses of dehydration, diabetes, and CHF were all treated during the stay and meet secondary reporting guidelines. See *ICD-9-CM Official Guidelines for Coding and Reporting*.

c. 199.0, V10.3, 276.51, 250.02, 428.0

Incorrect answer. The breast carcinoma was excised three years ago. Therefore, report history of breast cancer V10.3. The widespread metastatic carcinoma, 199.0 is causing the pain and is sequenced as a secondary diagnosis. The reason for the admission is the neoplasm-related pain, sequence the 338.3 as the principal diagnosis. See *Coding Clinic* (2008, 4Q:231–235). Secondary diagnoses of dehydration, diabetes, and CHF were all treated during the stay and meet secondary reporting guidelines. See *ICD-9-CM Official Guidelines for Coding and Reporting*.

d. 786.59, 199.0, 276.51, 250.02, 428.0

Incorrect answer. Per *ICD-9-CM Official Guidelines for Coding and Reporting*, "General Coding Guidelines" state that signs and symptoms are acceptable for reporting when a related definitive condition has not been established (confirmed) by the provider. The neoplasm-related pain is documented by the physician, therefore, delete the 786.59 symptom code and assign 338.3 as the principal diagnosis. The breast carcinoma was excised three years ago. Therefore, report history of breast cancer V10.3.

4.61. V58.11, 162.3-Y, 198.5-Y, 99.25

Note: Because the reason for admission is to receive chemotherapy, V58.11 is sequenced in the first position. Category V58 is on the POA exempt list and no indicator is assigned to V58.11.

4.62. 276.51-Y, 174.9-Y, 197.7-Y, 198.3-Y, MS-DRG: 641

Note: See *ICD-9-CM Official Guidelines for Coding and Reporting* "Neoplasm" guidelines. Because the focus of the admission and treatment was for the dehydration, it meets principal diagnosis reporting. There is no mention that the breast cancer has been resected, therefore, it is coded as current. All conditions were present on admission with a Y indicator assigned.

4.63. 198.3-Y, 196.3-Y, V10.3

Note: The reason for admission is the metastatic brain cancer. The breast cancer was excised, so it is coded as history. The mets to the axillary lymph nodes should be coded. Both metastatic conditions were present at the time of admission and POA indicator of Y is assigned. Category V10 is on the POA exempt list. Therefore, no indicator is assigned to V10.3

4.64. V58.11, 152.8-Y, 276.51-N, 787.01-N, 99.25, MS-DRG: 847

Note: Even though the dehydration extended the stay, the reason for admission (chemotherapy) is listed as the principal diagnosis. Even though the N/V led up to the dehydration, it is not always an integral component of the dehydration. Therefore, it may be added. The neoplasm is coded as current (even though it was excised) because she is still receiving chemotherapy. The contiguous site code is used because the cancer is part in the duodenum and part in the jejunum. Category V58 is on the POA exempt list and no indicator is assigned to V58.11.

4.65. 183.0-Y, 197.6-Y, 68.69, 65.61, 54.4, MS-DRG: 734

Note: The hysterectomy was a radical one, the "Code Also" note instructs the coder to assign BSO in addition and the omentectomy meets procedure coding guidelines.

4.66. 338.3-Y, 197.7-Y, 185-Y, 198.5-Y, 86.07

Note: The documentation indicates that the main reason for the extreme pain is the liver mets. Therefore, neoplasm-related pain is reported as the principal diagnosis (*Coding Clinic* 2008, 4Q:231–235). Both metastases meet secondary reporting guidelines. The prostate cancer would be coded as current because there is no documentation to indicate that it was eradicated or excised. VAD is coded to 86.07.

Disorders of the Nervous System and Sense Organs

4.67. a. 996.2, 331.4, 326, 02.42, 87.02, 87.03

Correct answer.

b. 331.4, 326, 02.42, 87.02, 87.03

Incorrect answer. The reason for admission was for the shunt malfunction (code 996.2).

c. 996.63, 331.4, 02.42

Incorrect answer. The shunt was not infected. Additional codes should be assigned for the late effect of meningoencephalitis, CT scan, and pneumocisternogram.

d. 996.2, 02.42, 87.03

Incorrect answer. Additional codes should be assigned for the hydrocephalus, late effect of meningoencephalitis, and pneumocisternogram.

4.68. 345.51-Y, 01.59, 01.18

Note: The epilepsy is documented as intractable, partial. Subcategory 345.4 would not be correct because there was not documentation of impairment of consciousness. The procedure code is 01.59. Code 01.39 is not correct because it is for amygdalohippocampotomy. POA indicator of Y as epilepsy was present on admission.

4.69. 320.1-Y, 481-Y, 03.31, MS-DRG: 094

Note: The patient had both meningitis and pneumonia, so both should be coded. The spinal tap should also be coded. Both conditions were present at the time of admission. Therefore, POA indicator is Y.

4.70. 437.3-Y, 38.41, 88.41

Note: If the aneurysm was ruptured, then code 430 would be assigned, but in this case documentation states that it is nonruptured. POA indicator Y as condition is present on admission.

4.71. a. 434.91, 438.21, 438.12, 250.00, 305.1, 88.91, 93.39, 93.72

Incorrect answer. This is an acute event. Therefore, code 342.91 and code 784.5 are assigned as additional diagnoses to identify the current neurologic deficits that resulted from the cerebral infarction. When codes from the 430–437 series are used, additional codes are needed to identify any sequelae present, such as category 342 for any associated hemiplegia. (*Coding Clinic* 1998, 4Q:87).

b. 434.91, 342.91, 784.5, 250.00, 305.1, 88.91, 93.39, 93.74

Incorrect answer. The patient was receiving speech therapy for dysphasia.

c. 436, 250.00, 305.1, 88.91, 93.39, 93.74

Incorrect answer. The terms stroke and CVA are often used interchangeably to refer to a cerebral infarction. The terms stroke, CVA, and cerebral infarction NOS are all indexed to the default code 434.91, Cerebral artery occlusion, unspecified, with infarction. Code 436, Acute, but ill-defined, cerebrovascular disease, should not be used when the documentation states stroke or CVA (*ICD-9-CM Official Coding Guidelines*). Code 342.91 and code 784.5 are assigned as additional diagnoses to identify the current neurologic deficits that resulted from the cerebral infarction. When codes from the 430–437 series are used, additional codes are needed to identify any sequelae present, such as category 342 for any associated hemiplegia (*Coding Clinic* 1998, 4Q:87).

d. 434.91, 342.91, 784.5, 250.00, 305.1, 88.91, 93.39, 93.72
Correct answer.

Newborn/Congenital Disorders

4.72.   a. 749.02, 749.12, 27.62, 27.54

Incorrect answer. There is one diagnosis code that includes both the cleft lip and palate, 749.22.

b. 749.22, 27.54, 27.63

Incorrect answer. The 27.63 code is for revision of a previous cleft palate repair.

c. 749.02, 749.12, 27.69

Incorrect answer. There is one diagnosis code that includes both the cleft lip and palate, 749.22. The procedure code 27.69 is an unspecified code. The more specific procedure codes of 27.62 and 27.54 should be used.

d. 749.22, 27.62, 27.54
Correct answer.

4.73.   771.4-Y, 041.11-Y, 041.09-Y

Note: Category 041 codes are used as an additional code to identify the bacterial agent in diseases classified elsewhere. ICD-9-CM does not have a specific code for Group H Streptococcus. Therefore, code 041.09, other Streptococcus, is correct. All conditions are present on admission.

4.74.   a. V30.01, 765.03, 765.24

Incorrect answer. A diagnosis code is needed for the respiratory distress syndrome, 769.

b. 765.03, 769

Incorrect answer. A birth code of V30.01 is reported as principal diagnosis (*ICD-9-CM Official Guidelines for Coding and Reporting*; *Coding Clinic* 2006, 4Q:190). See instructional note under 765.0x to Use Additional Code for weeks of gestation.

c. V30.01, 765.03, 765.24, 769

Correct answer.

d. V30.01, 769

Incorrect answer. Code for prematurity, 765.03, and code 765.24 for weeks of gestation meet reporting guidelines as additional diagnoses.

4.75.   a. 389.9, 20.96

Incorrect answer. The 389.9 is for unspecified deafness. The 759.89 code is needed to indicate the Usher syndrome. Bilateral implants were performed, in which case they are coded twice.

b. 389.22, 759.89, 20.96, 20.96

Correct answer.

c. 389.20, 759.89, 20.95

Incorrect answer. The fifth digit for the principal diagnosis is incorrectly reported as unspecified mixed hearing loss. Documentation supports code for bilateral mixed hearing loss with a fifth digit of 2. This procedure code does not indicate a cochlear implant.

d. 389.22, 20.96, 20.96

Incorrect answer. Usher syndrome 759.89 meets reporting as an additional diagnosis. Alphabetical look-up: Syndrome, congenital, specified type NEC— Codes to 759.89.

4.76.   V30.00, 760.71-Y

Note: Because there is no documentation of drug withdrawal, code 760.71 is the best choice. The physician could be queried when reviewing the actual medical record. No POA indicator assigned to V30.00 as V30–V39 are listed on the POA exempt list.

Pediatric Conditions

4.77.   945.34-Y, 942.34-Y, 948.10-Y, MS-DRG: 934

Note:. The highest degree burn on the lower leg is reported with code 945.34, and the highest degree burn on the back should also be coded.

4.78.   a. 201.21, 40.40, 92.29

Incorrect answer. Lymph node biopsy is coded to 40.11. Megavoltage radiotherapy is assigned to a more specific code of 92.24.

b. 201.91, 40.40, 92.29

Incorrect answer. Hodgkin's sarcoma is assigned to code 201.21. Lymph node biopsy is coded to 40.11. Megavoltage radiotherapy is assigned to a more specific code of 92.24.

c. 201.21, 40.11, 92.24

Correct answer.

d. 201.91, 40.11, 92.24

Incorrect answer. Hodgkin's sarcoma is assigned to code 201.21.

4.79. 493.91-Y

Note: *Coding Clinic* (1988, 3Q:9–10) states that refractory is another term for intractable and should be assigned the fifth digit of 1. It is not correct to assign bronchospasm with asthma because bronchospasm is a component of an acute asthmatic attack and is included in the code assignments under category 493 (*Coding Clinic* 1993, 4Q:6–7). POA indicator assigned Y (yes) as this condition and the acute phase were present at the time of admission.

4.80. a. 008.61, 276.51

Incorrect answer. The patient was admitted for treatment of dehydration. The circumstances of inpatient admission always govern the selection of principal diagnosis (*Coding Clinic* 2008, 1Q:10–11).

b. 276.51, 558.9

Incorrect answer. The cause of the gastroenteritis was determined to be Rotavirus.

c. 276.51, 008.61

Correct answer.

d. 008.8

Incorrect answer. The cause of the gastroenteritis was determined to be Rotavirus. The dehydration should also be coded as principal diagnosis.

4.81. 995.55-Y, 852.23-Y, 361.05-Y, E968.8-Y, E967.8-Y, MS-DRG: 922

Note: The shaken infant syndrome code is reported as the principal diagnosis. Instructional note states Use additional Code(s) to identify associated injuries and Use Additional E-code to identify both the nature of the abuse and the perpetrator per *Coding Clinic* (1996, 4Q:38–43). *ICD-9-CM Official Coding Guidelines for Coding and Reporting* and *Coding Clinic* (2006, 4Q:228) state that category E967, Perpetrator, goes after the type of assault. The unconsciousness is not separately coded because it is included as part of the fifth digit reporting in code 852.23. POA indicators are Y (yes) as all were present on admission and none of the codes are on the POA exempt list.

Conditions of Pregnancy, Childbirth, and the Puerperium

4.82. a. 633.80, 66.62

Incorrect answer. The ectopic pregnancy was documented as tubal.

b. 633.10, 66.62

Correct answer.

c. 633.10, 66.4

Incorrect answer. The salpingectomy was "with removal of tubal pregnancy."

d. 633.10, 66.02

Incorrect answer. The procedure performed was a salpingectomy, not a salpingostomy.

4.83. a. 635.91, 69.09

Incorrect answer. This was a spontaneous abortion. The D&C should be assigned to code 69.02.

b. 634.91, 69.09

Incorrect answer. The D&C should be assigned to code 69.02.

c. 634.91, 69.02

Correct answer.

d. 635.91, 69.02

Incorrect answer. This was a spontaneous abortion.

4.84. 664.01-N, V27.0, 75.69

Note: It would be incorrect in this case to use the 650 code. Even though everything seemed to be normal, the perineal laceration is coded to a complication of delivery and would not be included in the criteria for assigning 650. The procedure performed was repair of perineum. No POA indicator assigned to V27.0 as category V27 is on the POA exempt list.

4.85. 654.21-Y, 646.81-N, V27.0, 72.1, MS-DRG: 775

Note: The previous cesarean delivery code, which is present on admission, is assigned POA indicator of Y. The fatigue was not present on admission so POA indicator of N is assigned. No POA indicator assigned to V27.0 as category V27 is on the POA exempt list.

4.86. 660.11-Y, 653.51-Y, 648.81-Y, V27.0, 74.1, MS-DRG: 766

Note: The note with code 660.11 indicates that the code from category 653 is used as an additional code, so the sequencing in this case must be in this order. If the patient was on insulin during her pregnancy, an additional code for long-term (current) insulin use would also be assigned, V58.67. No POA indicator assigned to V27.0 as category V27 is on the POA exempt list. All remaining diagnoses are present on admission. Therefore assign POA indicator of Y.

Disorders of the Respiratory System

4.87. a. 491.21

Correct answer.

b. 491.21, 518.82

Incorrect answer. Acute respiratory insufficiency is an integral part of COPD and is, therefore, not coded.

c. 518.81, 491.21

Incorrect answer. The patient had acute respiratory insufficiency, not acute respiratory failure. Acute respiratory insufficiency is an integral part of COPD and is, therefore, not coded.

d. 518.82, 491.21

Incorrect answer. Acute respiratory insufficiency is an integral part of COPD and is, therefore, not coded.

4.88.   a. 492.8, 276.51, 96.72

Incorrect answer. The dehydration is the reason for admission and should be listed as the principal diagnosis. The code for ventilator-dependent (V46.11) should be listed.

b. 276.51, 492.8, V46.11, 96.72

Correct answer.

c. 276.51, 496, V46.11, 96.71

Incorrect answer. The COPD emphysema should be coded to 492.8. The mechanical ventilation was for 96 continuous hours or more, code 96.72

d. 492.8, 276.51, V46.11, 96.72

Incorrect answer. The dehydration is the reason for admission and should be listed as the principal diagnosis.

4.89.   486-Y, 276.51-Y, 344.03-Y or 344.04-Y depending on results of physician query, 907.2, V14.0, E929.0, MS-DRG 193

Note: Query the physician to find out if the spinal cord injury was complete or incomplete in order to select the correct code for the quadriplegia. In accordance with *ICD-9-CM Official Guidelines for Coding and Reporting* and *Coding Clinic* (2008, 4Q:206–211), a late effect is the residual effect after the acute phase has ended. Coding requires two codes: one for the condition(s) produced and the late effect code. A late effect E code should be used with any report of a late effect or sequela resulting from a previous injury (*Coding Clinic* 2005, 1Q:90–91). Do not assign a code for hypokalemia unless the physician has included the condition in the discharge statement. There are many factors which may influence a physician's decision to prescribe a medication. It is inappropriate for the coder to assign a code based on the administration of any medication. Query the physician to determine if the patient has hypokalemia and if so have it added as a final diagnosis (*Coding Clinic* 1994, 5Q:11). Codes 907.2, V14.0, and E929.0 are POA exempt. All other diagnoses were present on admission.

4.90.   507.0-Y, 482.40-Y, 438.82, MS-DRG: 179

Note: It is correct to code aspiration pneumonia along with a bacterial pneumonia when documented according to *Coding Clinic* (1991, 3Q:16–17). All codes except 438.82 are present on admission and assigned POA indicator of Y (yes). Category 438 is on the POA exempt list and no indicator is assigned to 438.82. If the documentation had provided further detail about the dysphagia, an additional code from subcategory 787.2 would be assigned.

4.91. 518.81-Y, 482.31-Y, 492.8-Y, 305.1-Y, 96.71, 96.04, MS-DRG: 208

Note: *ICD-9-CM Official Guidelines for Coding and Reporting* and *Coding Clinic* (2006, 4Q:178) state acute respiratory failure may be assigned as the principal diagnosis when it is the condition established, after study, to be chiefly responsible for occasioning the admission to the hospital and the selection is supported by the alphabetic index and tabular list. All conditions are present on admission and assigned POA indicator of Y (yes).

Trauma and Poisoning

4.92. a. 852.23, E886.0, E849.4, E007.0, E000.8, 01.31, 88.91, 88.91

Incorrect answer. The patient was unconscious, but the duration is unspecified, so code 852.26 is correct.

b. 852.26, E886.0, E849.4, E007.0, E000.8, 01.31, 88.91, 88.91

Correct answer.

c. 852.33, E886.0, E849.4, E007.0, E000.8, 01.39, 88.91, 88.91

Incorrect answer. This is specified as a subdural hematoma without mention of an open intracranial wound, so code 852.26 is correct. Evacuation of a subdural hematoma is indexed as incision, subdural space, cerebral. Code 01.31 is correct.

d. 852.26, E886.0, E849.4, E007.0, E000.8, 01.39, 88.91, 88.91

Incorrect answer. Evacuation of a subdural hematoma is indexed as incision, subdural space, cerebral. Code 01.31 is correct.

4.93. a. 997.61, E929.0; 84.3

Correct answer.

b. 905.9, E929.0; 84.3

Incorrect answer. The residual condition is the neuroma of the stump (997.61). A separate late effect code is not reported because code 997.61 is considered a late effect code.

c. 997.61, 905.9, E929.0; 84.3

Incorrect answer. A separate late effect code (905.9) is not reported because code 997.61 is considered a late effect code.

d. 997.61, V49.76; 84.10

Incorrect answer. The V code merely indicates the status of an amputation, which is unnecessary as this is clear from code 997.61. Code E929.0 is also reported. The procedure code 84.10 is used for a revision of the stump during the acute phase of the injury. Revision after the acute phase is coded 84.3 (see "Excludes" notes).

4.94. 813.33-Y, 847.0-Y, E812.0, 79.32

Note: A compound fracture is an open fracture. The site of the fractures was specified. The procedure is ORIF. POA status indicator Y for diagnoses codes as both were present on admission. No POA indicator is assigned to E812.0 as E810–E819 are included on the POA exempt list.

4.95.   942.34-Y, 948.22-Y, E923.2-Y, E849.0, E030, MS-DRG: 933

Note: The 948 category is used whenever the percent of body surface is documented. The E code selected is based on the documentation in this scenario that states only that there was an explosion. Be advised that if the documentation, such as the actual medical record, states that there was a resultant fire, then a code from category E890 would be correct. All diagnoses are present at the time of admission and assigned indicator Y (yes). Code E849.0 is not assigned an indicator as E849.0 is on the POA exempt list.

4.96.   536.41-Y, 682.2-Y, 041.11-Y, 150.4-Y, MS-DRG: 394

Note: The infection of the gastrostomy is sequenced first. See the note under the code: Use additional code to specify type of infection, such as: abscess or cellulitis of abdomen (682.2). The organism is also coded. The cancer of the esophagus is coded as current because there is no documentation that it has been excised. All diagnoses are reported with status indicator Y (yes) as they were present at the time of admission.

4.97.   897.7-Y, E805.2, E001.0, 84.10, 84.10, MS-DRG: 909

Note: The complicated code is used because there was documentation of delayed healing. Code 84.3 is not correct for the procedure because it is used for amputation stumps that are not current. Index: Revision, current traumatic, *see* amputation. The notes under code 84.10 show that it includes revision of current traumatic amputation. The procedure code may be repeated because it was bilateral (*Coding Clinic*: 1985, Nov/Dec:11). E805.2 is not assigned a status indicator because categories E800–E807 are on the POA exempt list.

4.98.   996.43-Y, V43.64, 81.53, 93.22

Note: Because this is a mechanical complication, the index entries are as follows: Complications, mechanical, prosthetic, joint, failure, 996.43.

4.99.   824.6-Y, 850.0-Y, E880.9-Y, E001.0, E849.0, 79.36, MS-DRG: 494

Note: The trimalleolar fracture is closed and there is no documentation to the contrary. There was no loss of consciousness, so code 850.0 is assigned for the concussion. E885.9 was not selected because that indicates a fall on the same level. Even though she slipped on ice, she fell down the steps. E880.9 is more correct. To show that it happened at home, E849.0 should be used, but it needs to go in the second E code position, according to coding guidelines. All diagnoses are present at the time of admission and assigned indicator Y (yes). Code E849.0 is not assigned an indicator as it is on the POA exempt list.

Chapter 5. Case Studies from Ambulatory Health Records

Disorders of the Blood and Blood-Forming Organs

5.1.   a. 569.85, 45382, 36430

Correct answer.

b. 578.9, 569.84, 45382, 36430, 36430, 36430

Incorrect answer. The 36430 is only reported one time. The angiodysplasia of the colon is listed first, and the only code required is the combined code for the angiodysplasia with hemorrhage.

c. 578.9, 45382, 36430

Incorrect answer. The GI bleed would be reported with the angiodysplasia code with hemorrhage.

d. 569.84, 578.9, 45382

Incorrect answer. Code 578.9 is not required with 569.84. Code 36430 also should be reported for the administration of the transfusion.

5.2.   a. 285.9, 38220

Incorrect answer. The admitting diagnosis was anemia, but the pathologist gave more clarification by providing the diagnosis of iron deficiency anemia.

b. 280.9, 38220

Correct answer.

c. 285.9, 38220, 38221-59

Incorrect answer. The admitting diagnosis was anemia, but the pathology report states bone marrow aspiration and biopsy; however, the technique reported by the surgeon shows that the procedure performed was a bone marrow aspiration, bone trabecula not seen. Code 38221 would not be reported.

d. 280.8, 38230

Incorrect answer. The iron deficiency anemia has not been specified as to the type, so code 280.8 is not correct. The procedure codes listed here would only be used for bone marrow harvesting for transplantation purposes.

5.3.   204.00, 38220

Note: Acute lymphocytic leukemia is coded to 204.00. There is no remission because this is a new diagnosis. The procedure described is bone marrow aspiration. The code is only assigned once, even though the needle was repositioned to obtain more than one specimen. This is common in this procedure.

5.4.   172.6, 196.3, 38525-LT, 38792, 78195

Note: CPT codes are assigned for the excision and injection procedure. The radiology procedure is also added in the example, but the HIM coder would probably not assign that—it would probably be assigned by the chargemaster. Assign modifier -LT to show that the left axillary lymph node was biopsied.

5.5.   Reason for visit code(s): 786.50, 518.3.

Code(s): 282.62, 517.3

Note: Acute chest syndrome (517.3) is to be assigned as an additional code for sickle-cell codes with crisis per instructional note.

Disorders of the Cardiovascular System

5.6.   a. 454.9, 37718-50

Incorrect answer. Although both legs were operated on at the same session, only the long veins were involved in the right leg, while the long and short veins were involved on the left. The best way to report this is using HCPCS modifiers for left and right. If these are not acceptable, modifier -59 may be reported to show that the services are separate from each other, rather than one being a component of the other. The ICD-9-CM code is not as specific as possible because there is documentation of edema and pain.

b. 454.8, 37722-50

Incorrect answer. Although both legs were operated on at the same session, only the long veins were involved in the right leg, while the long and short veins were involved on the left. The best way to report this is using HCPCS modifiers for left and right. If these are not acceptable, modifier -59 may be reported to show that the services are separate from each other rather than one being a component of the other.

c. 454.8, 37722-50, 37718-LT

Correct answer.

Note: Use modifier -59 to denote a distinct procedural service and -LT to indicate left side for code 37718 if NCCI edit appears for this code.

d. 454.2, 37722-50, 37718-50

Incorrect answer. Severe does not necessarily mean inflamed or ulcerated, so code 454.8 is as specific as possible for this documentation. Stripping of the short veins was only done on the left leg.

5.7.   a. 745.4, 93315

Incorrect answer. The diagnosis code is not specific to an AV canal defect.

b. 745.69, 93315

Correct answer. The CPT code may be assigned by the chargemaster.

c. 745.69, 93312

Incorrect answer. Conditions present at birth are considered congenital, so the CPT code would be 93315.

d. 429.71, 93312

Incorrect answer. Conditions present at birth are considered congenital, so the CPT code would be 93315. The ICD-9-CM code is for an acquired cardiac septal defect, which means it is not present at birth.

5.8.   155.0, 36563

Note: Code 155.0 is assigned because there is documentation that it is primary. Reporting of the chemotherapy agent 5-FU is reported with a HCPCS "J" code and usually assigned by the chargemaster.

5.9.   Reason for visit code(s): 786.50

Code(s): 410.11, 428.22, 401.9, 93510, 93543, 93545, 93555, 93556

Note: The angina is not coded during the same episode of care as an acute myocardial infarct because the patient was admitted with symptomatic angina that evolved into or, after study, is found to have an AMI. In this case, the AMI is sequenced as the principal diagnosis and no additional code would be assigned as the angina is an inherent part of this condition (*Coding Clinic* 1993, 5Q:17–24).

The chronic systolic heart failure and hypertension meeting additional diagnosis reporting to describe co-existing conditions that require and/or affect patient care treatment or management. The hypertension is coded separately because there is no cause-effect documentation provided. The correct codes for the cardiac cath are 93510, 93543, 93545, 93555, 93556 (*CPT Assistant* [1994, April]).

5.10.   Reason for visit code(s): 427.5

Note: The probable MI may not be coded on an outpatient record per *ICD-9-CM Official Guidelines for Coding and Reporting* of Outpatient Services that states "coding for inconclusive diagnoses (probable, suspected, rule out, etc.) were developed for inpatient reporting and do not apply to outpatients."

5.11.   a. 36475-RT

Correct answer.

b. 36475-RT, 36000

Incorrect answer. The introduction of the catheter into the vein is included in the procedure code, per the instructional note following code 36476.

c. 36478-RT

Incorrect answer. Code 36478 describes laser ablation of incompetent veins. The scenario for coding specifies radiofrequency ablation, 36475.

d. 36475-RT, 76942

Incorrect answer. Per the description of code 36475, the procedure code is inclusive of all imaging guidance and monitoring.

Disorders of the Digestive System

5.12.   a. 553.3, 39502

Incorrect answer. The diagnosis code is correct, but the procedure code is an open abdominal procedure. Because a laparoscopic approach is described for this Nissen procedure, code 43280 is reported.

b. 553.3, 43280

Correct answer. The procedure describes a Nissen fundoplication performed via a laparoscope.

c. 551.3, 43280

Incorrect answer. Code 551.3 would be assigned only when gangrene was documented. The procedure code is correct.

d. 553.3, 43324

Incorrect answer. The CPT code is for an esophagogastric fundoplasty. When the procedure is performed via a laparoscope, designated in this operative report by the use of insufflation, trocars, ports, and direct visualization, code 43280 is reported.

5.13.   Reason for visit code(s): 578.1

Code(s): 578.1, 43235

Note: The duodenal ulcer is not coded because it has not been confirmed. Coding guidelines for outpatients state that rule-outs or possible diagnoses are not coded. Code to the highest degree of certainty. The patient had an esophagoscopy, but the scope also went into the stomach and duodenum. Code 43235 is correct. Code 43200 is a separate procedure code, and the esophagoscopy is included in code 43235. It would be incorrect to assign the separate procedure code in this case. Documentation only states that the endoscopy was done. It does not specify that any techniques were used to control the bleeding.

5.14.   263.0, 438.21, 43246, 49440

Note: The percutaneous endoscopic gastrostomy (PEG) tube placement is coded 43246. V12.59 is for old stroke without residuals, so it is not appropriate. This patient has hemiparesis.

5.15.   574.20, 47562

Note: The adhesions did not prevent the surgeon access to the organ and were not documented to be significant. Per ICD-9-CM guidelines, they would not be coded in this instance. Code 44180 is a separate procedure code and per CPT guidelines would not be added on when part of a more extensive, related procedure.

5.16. 569.1, 569.0, 562.10, 558.9, 45380

Note: The polyps are stated to be nonadenomatous. *CPT Assistant* (1996, Jan) states that the correct code for a cold biopsy is 45380 or 45385, depending on the technique used, and in this case it was 45380. The biopsy code is used only once. The entire polyps were not removed. Code the postoperative diagnosis rather than the preoperative diagnosis.

5.17. 550.90, 49505-RT

Note: In CPT, it is not correct to code the implantation of the mesh except for incisional or ventral hernia repairs. Assign HCPCS level II modifier of RT to indicate the right inguinal hernia.

5.18. 574.00, 574.10, 47563

Note: Subacute is a nonessential modifier to acute and listed in parenthesis; therefore, subacute is coded to acute. It is correct to code the acute and chronic cholecystitis because there is documentation of both. The cholecystectomy includes cholangiography.

5.19. a. 45384, 45342

Incorrect answer. Code 45384 describes biopsy using a hot biopsy forceps, not the cold forceps mentioned here. In addition, code 45342 is used to report a sigmoidoscopic ultrasound, not ultrasound with colonoscopy.

b. 45380, 45391

Incorrect answer. Code 45391 does not include the transmural biopsy that was performed via the ultrasonic endoscope. Code 45392 is the correct code.

c. 45384, 45392

Incorrect answer. Code 45384 describes biopsy using a hot biopsy forceps, not the cold forceps mentioned here.

d. 45380, 45392
Correct answer.

5.20. a. 558.9, 211.3, 569.0, 562.10, 45384, 45380-59
Correct answer.

b. 558.9, 211.3, 569.0, 562.10, 45380

Incorrect answer. An additional procedure code for the forceps removal of the colon polyp should be assigned as a separate procedure.

c. 787.3, 211.3, 569.0, 562.10, 45384, 45380-59

Incorrect answer. There is an addendum added to indicate that the patient has "eosinophilic colitis," so this may be coded rather than the abdominal bloating and gas symptom code.

d. 558.9, 211.3, 562.10, 45384, 45380

Incorrect answer. An additional diagnosis code should be added for the rectal polyp that was indicated on the addendum. Modifier -59 is added to reflect that the colonoscopy with biopsy is a separate procedure from the colonoscopy with removal of polyp.

Endocrine, Nutritional and Metabolic Diseases, and Immunity Disorders

5.21.   271.3, 625.3

Note: In this case, lactose intolerance is confirmed. It would be inappropriate to code right lower quadrant abdominal pain or cramping because two sources of pain are documented.

5.22.   250.01

Note: In this case, the diabetes is confirmed. It would be inappropriate to add the V72.6 as an additional code or to use it in the first position. The code for screening would also be incorrect.

5.23.   202.00, 60100

Note: The lymphoma is in the thyroid gland, which is an organ, so diagnosis code 202.00 is correct. This is not a fine needle aspiration. A large hollow core needle is inserted percutaneously. Code 60100 is correct. If needle placement were guided by ultrasound or by computerized tomography, code 76942 or 76360 would also be reported.

Disorders of the Genitourinary System

5.24.   a. 625.6, 618.01, 618.2, 57284, 51840

Incorrect answer. Because the cause of the incontinence is likely the vaginal prolapse/cystocele, the reason for visit should be 618.01 followed by the stress incontinence code. Diagnosis code 618.2 is not needed because code 618.01 represents both the cystocele and vaginal prolapse. See *CPT Assistant* (1997, Jan) regarding the procedure. Additional codes such as 51840 and 51841 should not be reported separately when performed with a paravaginal defect repair

b. 625.6, 57284-50

Incorrect answer. The diagnosis code (618.01) should be reported first to reflect the incomplete vaginal prolapse and the resulting cystocele, contributing to the stress incontinence. According to *CPT Assistant*, this procedure is inherently bilateral, so a modifier is inappropriate. Also, codes 51845, 57289, and 57240 may be reported in addition to code 57284 if the paravaginal defect repair is performed in conjunction with an abdomino-vaginal vesical neck suspension, such as Stamy, Raz, or a modified Pereyra (*CPT Assistant*, 1997, Jan). These more complicated procedures are more likely to be performed on an inpatient basis. Careful review of the operative note is required to see if there is enough justification to assign a code for anterior colporrhaphy.

c. 618.02, 57240

Incorrect answer. Urinary incontinence should be added as an additional code per ICD-9-CM coding conventions, by reporting code 625.6. Paravaginal defect repair is reported with CPT code 57284. More documentation would be required to support reporting of anterior colporrhaphy with code 57240.

d. 618.01, 625.6, 57284

Correct answer.

5.25.   a. 788.37, 53445, 51715

Correct answer.

b. 788.39, 51715

Incorrect answer. The diagnosis code can be more specific by reporting code 788.37. Additional procedure code 53445 is required to show the incision of the perineum, with the placement of the artificial sphincter.

c. 788.37, 53440

Incorrect answer. Code 53440 describes a sling operation.

d. 788.37, 53445

Incorrect answer. Code 51715 is reported.

5.26.   a. 592.1, 52353, 52332

Incorrect answer. The documentation provided does not support the fact that the calculus was ureteral. Code 592.0 is assigned

b. 592.0, 52353-RT

Incorrect answer. The RT modifier may apply, but the documentation does not indicate whether this was the right or left side (these CPT codes are considered unilateral). The insertion of the ureteral stent should also be reported with code 52332.

c. 592.0, 52353, 52332

Correct answer.

d. 592.0, 52352, 52332-51

Incorrect answer. The correct CPT code in this scenario is the one including the lithotripsy, which is code 52353. A facility would not report modifier -51, which is reserved for physician reporting according to CMS guidelines. If a distinct procedural service was provided in the hospital outpatient setting, then modifier -59 is assigned.

5.27.   a. 600.20, 53852

Correct answer.

b. 600.20, 52601

Incorrect answer. When thermotherapy is used, code 53852 is reported. Code 52601 is reported only for electrosurgical resection.

c. 600.00, 53852

Incorrect answer. Adenoma of the prostate is reported with 600.20.

d. 222.2, 53850

Incorrect answer. Adenoma of the prostate is reported with 600.20. Code 53852 is for microwave thermotherapy. In this procedure radiofrequency was used.

5.28. Reason for visit code(s): 608.9

Code(s): 608.20, 54699

Note: There is no specific CPT code describing the process of manual detorsion of a testicle, therefore code 54699 is assigned.

5.29. Reason for visit code(s): 780.6, 789.07

Code(s): 780.6, V13.02, 290.3, 81000

Note: A urinary tract infection was not established, so it is not coded. It may be useful to also report the history of UTI with code V13.02 to establish medical necessity for the urinalysis. It is appropriate to add all diagnoses that affect current patient management. In this case, the fact that the patient has dementia does impact the care and should be reported with code 290.3 (with delirium).

5.30. 250.41, 585.6, 583.81, 36821

Note: It is correct to report all codes for diagnoses that impact the care or treatment of this patient: nephropathy manifestation code and end-stage renal disease.

5.31. 614.6, 58660

Note: The adhesions would be considered pelvic, not abdominal.

5.32. 600.01, 596.0, 52500.

5.33. 50592

Note: Code 50592 describes percutaneous radiofrequency ablation of four tumors. The code description states "Ablation, one or more renal tumor(s). . . ." so it is not appropriate to report it more than once for multiple tumor ablations. Code 50250 reports an open procedure, and code 50542 a laparoscopy with tumor ablation, so neither is correct to report a percutaneous procedure. The CPT description for 50592 describes this procedure as "unilateral;" therefore no RT modifier is required. CPT code 50592 includes moderate sedation, and it is not appropriate for separate reporting of sedation codes 99143–99145.

Infectious Diseases

5.34. Reason for visit code(s): 789.01, 780.6, 780.79

Note: Coder may select any three admitting symptoms as the reason for visit codes: right upper quadrant pain, fever, profound malaise, and bloody diarrhea 006.0.

Note: The correct code would be 006.0. Symptoms are not reported separately as they are integral to the Entamoeba histolytica dysentery.

5.35. Reason for visit code(s): 698.1, 709.8

Code(s): 133.0.

Note: Code 133.0 is reported for scabies of any site.

5.36. Reason for visit code(s): 787.91

Code(s): 008.02.

Note: Enteritis due to enterotoxigenic E. coli is assigned to 008.02.

5.37. Reason for visit code(s): 795.5

Code(s): 795.5. 296.52

Note: Latent TB means that the patient has had a positive TB test but has no active disease. INH is given prophylactically to keep the patient from converting to active disease later in life. The only code available is 795.5 for a positive PPD. The bipolar disease is coded because this disease process affects the patient's ability to continue taking medication as prescribed.

Disorders of the Skin and Subcutaneous Tissue

5.38. a. 172.5, 11603

Incorrect answer. An additional code is required for reporting the layer closure: 12032 for a 3 cm repair.

b. 709.9, 11603

Incorrect answer. When a malignant lesion has been excised and the patient presents for wide excision, the malignant lesion is coded for each case. An additional code is required for reporting the layer closure: 12032 for a 3-cm repair.

c. 172.5, 11603, 12032

Correct answer.

d. V76.43, 11603, 13121

Incorrect answer. When a malignant lesion has been excised and the patient presents for wide excision, the malignant lesion is coded for each case. The code for the layer closure should be reported with 12032. Intermediate repair is generally what is reported for layer closure, unless the report indicates a complicated wound closure involving the procedures described in the CPT manual as complex.

5.39. a. 173.3, 15240, 11646

Incorrect answer. Code 11646 is incorrect because the size of the lesion was only 3.2. The size of graft was 10 sq cm.

b. 173.3, 15240, 15004

Incorrect answer. CPT code 15004 is reported for the surgical preparation or creation of a recipient site by excision of open wounds, burn eschar, or scar; therefore it is not accurate to report this code for the malignant lesion excision. Report code 11644 for the 3.2 cm malignant lesion.

c. 173.3, 15350, 15004, 11644

Incorrect answer. The CPT code for the graft is for an allograft. This uses a homograft from healthy/cadaver skin from another person. When the patient's own tissue is grafted, code 15240 is reported for this size of graft. CPT code 15004 is reported for the surgical preparation or creation of a recipient site by excision of open wounds, burn eschar, or scar; therefore it is not accurate to report this code for the malignant lesion excision.

d. 173.3, 15240, 11644

Correct answer.

5.40.   Reason for visit code(s): 703.0

Code(s): 703.0, 281.0, 334.0, 429.9, 11750

Note: The digital block is included in the procedure and therefore not coded separately. Code 11750 is reported because the nail matrix is destroyed to achieve permanent removal, even though the physician describes the procedure as a wedge resection. Code 11765 is not used because the nail and the matrix are both removed, not just the skin of the nail fold.

5.41.   078.10, 17110

Note: The code 17110 includes cryosurgery and curettement of up to 14 lesions, so no other code is assigned.

5.42.   Reason for visit code(s): 884.0, 882.0, 891.0

Code(s): 891.0, 884.0, 882.0, E920.8, E849.0, 12031, 12002.

Note: The intermediate repair is reported in the first position as the most resource-intensive code. The lacerations repaired with simple repair are added together to total 5 cm as all anatomic sites are listed in code 12002.

5.43.   701.4, 709.2, 15004, 15005, 15175, 15176

Note: Contracture of the burn scar is coded as a cicatrix, 709.2. The hypertrophy of the scar/keloid is coded as 701.4. Integra is an acellular dermal replacement that does not require a concurrent epidermal cover.

5.44.   a. 19297-LT

Incorrect answer. Also assign a code for the lumpectomy (partial mastectomy), 19301. Code 19297 is an add-on code and must be reported with the primary procedure code.

b. 19301-LT, 19297-LT

Correct answer.

c. 19301-RT

Incorrect answer. Modifier is reported as -RT (right) and documentation supports procedure on the -LT (left) breast. Report primary procedure and add-on code for the placement of the radiotherapy afterloading balloon catheter.

d. 19120-LT

Incorrect answer. Code 19120 is used to report an excisional biopsy of the breast. A lumpectomy is considered a form of partial mastectomy and is reported with code 19301.

5.45.   a. 707.0, 97602

Incorrect answer. Fifth digits are required for coding to the highest level of specificity. Both sites are reported even though only one had a debridement: sacrum 707.03 and buttock 707.05. CPT procedure code assigned is non-selective wound debridement (nonsurgical) and surgeon performed a full thickness excisional debridement (surgical) (*Coding Clinic* 2000, 2Q:9).

b. 707.03, 707.05, 11040

Incorrect answer. Fifth digits are required for coding to the highest level of specificity. Excisional debridement code is coded incorrectly as partial thickness (11040) rather than full thickness (11041) (*Coding Clinic* 2000, 2Q:9).

c. 707.03, 97597

Incorrect answer. Both decubitus sites are reported even though only one had a debridement: sacrum 707.03 and buttock 707.05. CPT procedure code assigned is for a selective debridement (nonsurgical). Surgeon performed a full thickness excisional debridement (surgical) (*Coding Clinic* 2000, 2Q:9).

d. 707.03, 707.05, 11041

Correct answer.

Behavioral Health Conditions

5.46.   a. 301.4, 90853

Incorrect answer. The diagnosis reported is a personality disorder (301.4, obsessive compulsive) and is more accurately reported as a phobic disorder (300.3, obsessive-compulsive disorder).

b. 300.3, 90857

Incorrect answer. The diagnosis code is correct, however, documentation does not support interactive group psychotherapy.

c. 300.3, 90853

Correct answer.

d. 300.3, 90847

Incorrect answer. The service was for a group, not an individual, and there is no documentation of the patient's family being present.

5.47.   309.81, 90804

Note: Code 90804 describes individual psychotherapy for 20–30 minutes.

5.48.   Reason for visit code(s): 881.02

Code(s): 881.02, 296.23, E956, E849.0, 12002.

Note: The E956 code identifies that it is a suicide attempt.

5.49. Reason for visit code(s): 969.0, 969.4

Code(s): 969.05, 969.4, 980.0, 311, E950.3, E950.9, E849.0, 91105, 92950. Note: Both drugs and the alcohol are coded to the poisoning codes with the respective E codes denoting a suicide attempt. The depression is also reported. Report procedure codes for gastric lavage and CPR.

Disorders of the Musculoskeletal System and Connective Tissue

5.50. a. 805.5, E881.0, 22325

Incorrect answer. Code 805.5 is for open fractures of the lumbar spine. There would have to be a mention of an open wound communicating with the fracture site for this to be correct. Code 22325 is for open treatment of a fracture, which also is not documented here. The E code to show that the accident happened at home could be assigned.

b. 805.4, E881.0, E849.0, 22310

Correct answer. The fracture care code 22310 includes the initial application of casts and strapping. Code 22310 includes those requiring a brace.

c. 806.4, E881.0, E849.0, 22315

Incorrect answer. The 806 category includes those fractures with spinal cord injury, which is not mentioned here. Code 22315 includes manipulation, which is also not mentioned.

d. 805.01, 805.02, E881.0, E849.0, 22326

Incorrect answer. Code 805.01 is for cervical vertebrae, and this patient's injury was to the lumbar vertebral bodies. Code 22326 is for open treatment of a cervical fracture, which is not the case here.

5.51. a. 812.52, 24577, 29065

Incorrect answer. The diagnosis code is for an open fracture, which is not described here. The CPT code 24577 describes closed reduction of a humeral fracture, rather than the open reduction and internal fixation procedure documented. CPT 29065 should not be assigned with a fracture care code because casting is included in the initial fracture service per CPT guidelines. The HCPCS level II modifier of RT (right) is added to show laterality.

b. 812.42, 24579, 29065

Incorrect answer. The diagnosis code and CPT code 24579 are correct. CPT 29065 should not be assigned with a fracture care code because casting is included in the initial fracture service per CPT guidelines. The HCPCS level II modifier or RT (right) is added to show laterality.

c. 812.42, 24579-RT

Correct answer. The HCPCS level II modifier of RT (right) is added to show laterality.

d. 812.52, 24579-RT

Incorrect answer. The diagnosis code is for an open fracture, which is not described here.

5.52. Reason for visit code(s): 873.41

Code(s): 873.41, 802.0, E917.0, E007.5, E849.4, 21320, 12011

Note: The fracture is presumed closed. The ER provided fracture care of stabilization, splinting and taping. This is frequently the only care needed for a nondisplaced nasal fracture. The physician did repair the superficial laceration of the cheek.

5.53. 816.12, E919.8, E849.3, 26765-F6

Note: The fracture is open, and it is documented as distal phalanx; therefore fifth digit of 2 is assigned. The CPT code would be assigned for each finger, and in this case there is no documentation that multiple fingers are involved; therefore one code is assigned with the HCPCS level II modifier to show which finger was treated.

5.54. V54.01, 20680-LT

Note: The fracture is not current, so the V54.01 is assigned as the primary diagnosis for removal of internal fixation device. The removal of the hardware is documented as deep (plate and pins) so CPT code 20680 is correct. Add HCPCS level II modifier of LT (left) to report laterality.

5.55. a. Osteochondral autograft

Incorrect answer. An osteochondral autograft involves harvesting of tissue from the patient himself or herself. When the graft comes from a cadaver, it is an osteochondral allograft.

b. Osteochondral allograft

Correct answer.

c. Autologous chondrocyte implantation

Incorrect answer. This procedure involves harvesting of cells from the patient, growing them to maturity in a laboratory setting, and reinjecting them. When a full osteochondral graft is obtained from a cadaver, it is an osteochondral allograft.

d. Anterior cruciate ligament repair

Incorrect answer. When an osteochondral graft is obtained from a cadaver, it is an osteochondral allograft. A ligament repair may involve cadaveric ligament, but not osteochondral tissue.

5.56. a. 719.46, 717.7, 29873-RT, 29877-RT-59,

Correct answer. In a Medicare OPPS case, HCPCS Code Level II code G0289 would be used in lieu of CPT code 29877-RT-59, since chondroplasty was performed in separate compartments as per the source document.

b. 719.46, 717.7, 27425-RT

Incorrect answer. Diagnosis codes 717.7 and 719.46 are correct. CPT code 27425 is used to report an open retinacular release, rather than the retinacular release via arthroscopy described in the source document.

c. 717.7, 29877-RT

Incorrect answer. Diagnosis and procedure codes are missing. The source document indicates a lateral retinacular release of the right knee was performed to correct lateral patellar compression syndrome in addition to the chondroplasty performed.

d. 719.46, 717.7, 29999-RT, 29877-RT

Incorrect answer. CPT code 29999 is used only when an unlisted arthroscopic procedure is performed. In this case, CPT code 29873 identifies arthroscopic retinacular release described in the source document.

Neoplasms

5.57. a. V58.0, 77413

Incorrect answer. The malignancy must be reported (149.0 and 196.0) as well as the V code for the encounter.

b. 149.0, 77408

Incorrect answer. The encounter for radiation therapy, V58.0, should be the first-listed code. In addition to the primary malignancy code, the lymph node metastasis should also be reported because this is also treated by radiation (196.0). The radiation treatment CPT code must be 77413 because three treatment areas are involved and custom blocking was employed.

c. V58.0, 149.0, 196.0, 77413

Correct answer.

d. 149.0, 196.0, 77412

Incorrect answer. Encounters for radiotherapy are always coded V58.0, followed by the neoplastic disease. The CPT code is not appropriate for the 6-MV linear accelerator; code 77413 is assigned.

5.58. a. 162.9, 31629

Correct answer.

b. 162.9, 31629, 77002

Incorrect answer. Fluoroscopic guidance is included in all endoscopic biopsy codes in the range of 31622–31646 and is not assigned as an additional code.

c. 162.9, 31625

Incorrect answer. The procedure code is incorrect for a transbronchial aspiration biopsy of lung tissue. Code 31629 is assigned.

d. 235.7, 31629, 77002

Incorrect answer. The carcinoma was not specified as a neoplasm of uncertain behavior, and Volume II of ICD-9-CM directs the coder to malignant neoplasm of the site or, when the site is unspecified, to 162.9. Fluoroscopic guidance is not reported separately in the endoscopic biopsy code range of 31622–31646. This code is also not specific to an intrathoracic needle biopsy.

5.59.   a.   174.9, 610.1, 19120-RT, 19125-LT, 19290-LT

Correct answer. HCPCS Level II modifiers are used to show that the lesions were not in the same breast and different techniques with separate incisions were employed.

b.   611.72, 610.1, 19120-50

Incorrect answer. When a definitive diagnosis is known, it is reported, so 174.9 for the primary malignancy would be the first-listed code and the breast lump would not be reported. A bilateral modifier -50 applies only to identical procedures on paired organs. The breasts are paired organs, but the procedures involved here are not the same. HCPCS Level II modifier -RT identifies the 19120 procedure on the right breast, while the LT modifier is appended to CPT codes 19125 and 19290 to show that procedure occurred on the left breast.

c.   174.9, 610.1, 19120-50, 19125-50, 19290-50

Incorrect answer. Appropriate use of the bilateral modifier has it appended to only one CPT code with identical procedures performed on paired organs. Although the breasts may have bilateral procedures using modifier -50, it is only assigned to one code, which communicates to Medicare that 150 percent of the allowed amount should be provided in reimbursement for the case. The correct way to code the procedures is by use of the RT and LT Level II HCPCS codes to show that different breasts were involved. Codes 19120 and 19125 would be mutually exclusive otherwise.

d.   174.9, 610.2, 19120, 19125-59, 19290

Incorrect answer. The fibrocystic disease was not stated to be fibroadenosis, so code 610.1 is as specific as the documentation allows. The use of modifier -59 is not appropriate for this case because HCPCS Level II modifiers RT and LT would describe the services more concisely.

5.60.   153.3, 235.2, 45384, 45380-59

Note: Villous adenoma (polyps) is a neoplasm of uncertain behavior. These codes are only appropriately reported when specified as such by a pathologist. Code 235.2 is assigned. Two separate procedures were performed in two distinct locations, so two codes are required—the excision of the polyps by hot biopsy forceps are coded (with one code), and the biopsy of the sigmoid colon is assigned a code because it is a separate lesion. Modifier -59 designates that the two procedures are not components of one another, but distinct.

5.61.   V58.11, 204.00, 96409, J9094

Note: The leukemia is documented as acute lymphocytic (without remission documented), so code 204.00 is correct. The V58.11 code is listed in the first position. Typically the J code is assigned by the chargemaster.

Disorders of the Nervous System and Sense Organs

5.62. 996.2, E878.1, 331.5, 62252

Note: Malfunction of the CSF shunt is coded as a complication, mechanical, shunt, ventricular, code as 996,2 and E878,1. Headache is not coded as this is a symptom of the hydrocephalus. Reprogramming of a programmable shunt is coded as 62252.

5.63.   a. 335.20, 92265-50, 95861

Incorrect answer. A bilateral modifier is not appropriate for the eye muscle EMG because the code description states "one or both eyes."

b. 335.24, 95868-59, 95861

Incorrect answer. The diagnosis code is incorrect because this is the code for primary lateral sclerosis. ALS is coded 335.20. The CPT code for the EMG of the eye muscles is 92265 and for the legs (two extremities) is 95861. No modifier is needed for reporting these procedures together because they are for separate sites.

c. 335.20, 95861, 92265

Correct answer.

d. 335.29, 95861

The diagnosis code requires a fifth digit of 0 for ALS. The correct CPT codes are 95861 for the extremity testing and 92265 for the eye muscle testing.

5.64.   a. 250.51, 362.01, 67040-50

Correct answer.

b. 362.01, 362.81, 67040-50

Incorrect answer. When diabetic complications are involved, the code for the diabetes is always listed first, followed by the manifestation codes. Code 250.51 is the reason for service in this case. Although a separate code is available for retinal hemorrhage, this condition is included in the code for diabetic retinopathy, and no additional code is required.

c. 250.50, 362.02, 67039-LT-RT

Incorrect answer. The diabetic code requires a fifth digit of 1 to reflect type I diabetes. The retinopathy should be assigned to code 362.01. The CPT code is for a procedure limited to a small area, such as one or two areas (focal), rather than the increased amount of laser energy required to treat all four quadrants. Correct modifier assignment when both sides are treated is 50.

d. 250.51, 362.02, 67105, 67145

Incorrect answer. The retinopathy should be assigned to code 362.01. The CPT coding is incorrect in this code set. Code 67040 includes the vitrectomy with panretinal laser treatment. The CPT codes listed in this set are for reporting of retinal detachment repairs and prophylaxis of retinal detachment, which would not occur together.

5.65. 366.9, 66984-LT

Note: There is no further documentation about the type of cataract, so code 366.9 is correct. The CPT code 66984 describes an extracapsular cataract removal. The insertion of the intraocular lens is included in the code. There is no documentation that this was a complex procedure.

5.66. Reason for visit: 345.10

Code(s): 345.11.

Note: There is physician documentation of intractable epilepsy to support the fifth digit of 1.

5.67. a. 66710-LT

Incorrect answer. This code describes a procedure not involving the use of the ophthalmic endoscope. Code 66711 is the correct code.

b. 66711-LT

Correct answer.

c. 66720-LT

Incorrect answer. This code describes destruction of the ciliary body by cryotherapy. Code 66711 is the correct code.

d. 66700-LT

Incorrect answer. This code describes destruction of the ciliary body by diathermy. Code 66711 is the correct code.

5.68. a. 360.00, 67036-LT, 66030-LT

Correct answer. The patient underwent a pars plana vitrectomy with injection of medications for endophthalmitis.

b. 360.03, 67036-LT, 66030-LT

Incorrect answer. The source documentation does not provide specificity of the type of endophthalmitis the patient had.

c. 360.00, 67036-RT

Incorrect answer. The additional code for the injection is needed to completely identify the procedure performed. Procedure performed on the Left eye; therefore correct modifier is LT.

d. 998.59, 360.00, 67036-LT, 66030-LT

Incorrect answer. Diagnosis code 998.59 is coded when a postoperative infection is documented by the physician. The source document indicates the patient is status post a procedure; however does not link the current infection as a complication of that procedure.

Newborn/Congenital Disorders

5.69.   a. 743.30, 760.2, 66984-50

Incorrect answer. The information provided allows greater specificity in the diagnosis code selection. Code 743.32 is the correct code. Category 760 is used to report maternal conditions that affect the fetus or newborn. This was likely reported during the birth episode but is not a reason for health services at this time (evaluation and management are directed at the congenital cataract). Documentation supports the left eye and not bilateral; therefore correct HCPCS Level II modifier is -LT.

b. 366.03, 66984-LT

Incorrect answer. There is a specific ICD-9-CM code for congenital cataracts. Code 743.32 is the correct code.

c. V30.00, 771.0, 743.32

Incorrect answer. This is a subsequent episode of care for a seven-month-old, so the V30 code is inappropriate. Code 771.0 is no longer under evaluation or management. CPT code 66984 should be reported.

d. 743.32, 66984-LT

Correct answer.

5.70.   a. 755.02, 11200

Correct answer.

b. 755.02, 11200-RT, 11200-59

Incorrect answer. The CPT code includes up to 15 lesions, so it is not repeated. This makes the use of modifier -59 inappropriate to represent a separate site. The skin does not have a "right" or "left" to it, so addition of modifier LT is inappropriate. CMS guidelines state that -RT and -LT modifiers are not to be used for CPT codes with more than one anatomic location included. Code 11200 is such a code.

c. 755.00, 28899

Incorrect answer. The diagnosis code may be specific to the toes in code 755.02. The unlisted code is required only if the procedure involved more than soft tissue removal. In a two-week-old child, this likely is a very small lesion to remove. Code 11200 is used to report this service.

d. 755.02, 26587

Incorrect answer. The procedure code listed is for procedures involving reconstruction of tissue and bone for extra digits found on the hand. Because there is no bone in this case, code 11200 is adequate to report the service.

5.71.   752.61, 54304

Note: Hypospadias is a congenital condition reported with code 752.61. The CPT code 54304 is the correct procedure to report because it is a first-stage procedure requiring transposition of the prepuce.

5.72. 778.6, 550.92, 49500-50

Note: There is a specific code for congenital hydrocele. The 550.92 code includes hernias that are congenital. Because a combination code exists and the procedure is performed on both sides, CPT code 49500 is correct.

Pediatric Conditions

5.73. a. 487.0, 482.2

Correct answer.

b. 487.0

Incorrect answer. An additional code to identify the type of pneumonia is also reported with code 482.2

c. 482.2, 487.0

Incorrect answer. The first listed code is 487.0 and code 482.2 to identify the type of pneumonia is listed as a secondary code.

d. 485, 482.2

Incorrect answer. Pneumonia caused by H. influenzae is coded to 487.0 and 482.2.

5.74. 493.02, 94640 x2, J7611

Note: Cough is integral to asthma and therefore not coded. Allergic asthma is coded as 493.0X with a 5th digit of 2 for acute exacerbation. The nebulizer treatments are coded as 94640 (nonpressurized inhalation treatment for acute airway obstruction) with units of 2. Some insurers may require that the nebulizers be reported as 94640 and 94640-76 for repeat procedure by the same physician. J7611 is reported for the 1 mg of Albuterol. Note that the medication may be reported as a pharmacy service.

5.75. a. 550.91, 49520-RT

Incorrect answer. The hernia is not specified as recurrent, the fifth digit of 0 should be used for the diagnosis, and the correct procedure code is 49505.

b. 550.90, 49525-RT

Incorrect answer. This is a reducible inguinal hernia, not a sliding hernia. Code 49505 is the correct code.

c. 550.92, 49505-50

Incorrect answer. The hernia is unilateral, not bilateral. Code 550.90 is correct. Modifier -50 is not correct.

d. 550.90, 49505-RT

Correct answer.

5.76. Reason for visit code(s): 780.6, 786.2

Code(s): 465.9, 372.00.

Note: The conjunctivitis is unspecified as to the cause.

Conditions of Pregnancy, Childbirth, and the Puerperium

5.77.   a. 790.22, V22.2, 82951

Incorrect answer. Code 790.22 excludes that complicating pregnancy and refers the coder to subcategory 648.8. The V code is not appropriate for this encounter because the pregnancy is not incidental. The correct codes are 648.83 and 82951 but laboratory codes are typically coded by the chargemaster.

b. 648.83, 82951

Correct answer. Laboratory codes are typically coded by the chargemaster.

c. 648.83, 82950

Incorrect answer. CPT code 82951 is the appropriate code for this test, which involves obtaining three separate specimens for testing the glucose levels at 1 hour, 2 hours, and 3 hours after the patient drinks the glucose mixture. Laboratory codes are typically coded by the chargemaster.

d. 648.80, 82951, 82952, 82952

Incorrect answer. The fifth digit of 0 is unspecified. This is an antepartum condition. Code 648.83 is the correct code. Three specimens are included in code 82951. CPT code 82952 would only be reported if additional tests, beyond three, are performed. Laboratory codes are typically coded by the chargemaster.

5.78.   a. 637.91, 58120

Incorrect answer. The abortion was specified as spontaneous; therefore, the diagnosis code 634.91 is reported. Code 58120 is incorrect because this is surgical completion of an incomplete abortion. The correct CPT code is 59812.

b. 634.91, 59812

Correct answer.

c. 634.91, 58120

Incorrect answer. The CPT code 58120 is used for a nonobstetric procedure. Because this procedure is done for treatment of an incomplete spontaneous abortion, code 59812 is reported.

d. 634.92, 59812

Incorrect answer. The fifth digit is incorrect for the diagnosis of an incomplete abortion.

5.79.   V28.4, 76805

Note: Because the purpose of the test is antenatal screening, code V28.4 is reported as the reason for the test. It is incorrect to assign V22.0 in this case.

5.80.   628.2, 58340, 74740, 77002

Note: Code 58340 is reported for the injection. Code 74740 is reported for a hysterosalpingogram. The use of the fluoroscope would be reported with code 77002.

Disorders of the Respiratory System

5.81. a. 493.22

Correct answer.

b. 493.21, 491.21

Incorrect answer. When the two conditions occur together, code 493.22 is the only code to report.

c. 493.20

Incorrect answer. The fifth digit should be 2 to show acute exacerbation.

d. 491.21

Incorrect answer. A note under 493.2 includes chronic asthmatic bronchitis, and asthma with chronic obstructive pulmonary disease.

5.82. 162.3, 305.1, 31625

Note: The site is specified as upper lobe of bronchus. The hemoptysis and cough would be integral to the carcinoma.

5.83. Reason for visit code(s): 784.7

Code(s): 784.7, 30903-50.

Note: Because the procedure was a bilateral procedure and the code is considered unilateral, modifier -50 is required. The procedure is documented to be extensive, and it is an anterior pack, so code 30903 is assigned.

Trauma and Poisoning

5.84. a. 934.0, E912, E849.4, 31577

Correct answer.

b. 934.0, E912, E849.4, 31511

Incorrect answer. Code 31511 is for an indirect laryngoscopy rather than the fiberoptic type of scope indicated. Code 31577 is correct.

c. 784.99, E912, E849.4, 31530

Incorrect answer. An operative laryngoscopy requires anesthetic support not available in the ED. CPT code 31577 is the correct code for a fiberoptic scope with local anesthesia used. Also, when choking occurs from a foreign body lodged in the airway, the foreign body should be coded rather than the symptom code for choking sensation.

d. 933.1, 31577

Incorrect answer. Code 934.0 is specific to the trachea, while code 933.1 is for a foreign body in the larynx. An E code should be assigned (E912) to show the cause of the problem and E849.4 to report the place of occurrence.

5.85.   972.9, E950.4, 91105, 96374, 96367, 96366, J1610 x 20, J7060

Note: Verapamil is not listed specifically in the Table of Drugs and Chemicals but is a cardiovascular medication and can be accessed in the Table under that term. For a suicide attempt, the code is 972.9 with an E-code of E950.4. The initial IV is a push of Glucagon (96374) with 2 additional hours of sequential IV (96367 and 96366). The Glucagon HCl is J1610 for 20 units (10 mg push and 5 mg per hour over 2 hours) and D5W is J7060.

5.86.   V58.30 16030

Note: The specific site of the burns is not documented, so code 943.20 is the most specific code. However, the patient is being seen in aftercare (after acute phase of injury was treated) for dressing changes. The correct code to report is V58.3X (attention to dressing and sutures) with fifth digit of 0 to denote encounter for change or removal of nonsurgical wound dressing; therefore code 943.20 (second degree burn of upper extremity) would not be reported. E codes are not assigned for subsequent visits of an accident, only the initial visit, or when a late effect applies. Code 16030 was selected because dressings were applied to more than one extremity.

5.87.   162.9, 511.81, 32421, 32421-76

Note: The thoracentesis was repeated in the same day by the same physician. The procedure code is reported twice with modifier -76 reported on the second procedure. The malignant pleural effusion is coded as 511.81.

5.88.   Reason for visit code(s): 882.0, 881.0, 890.0
Code(s): 882.0, 881.00, 890.0, E888.0, E920.9, E849.1, 12042, 12004.

Note: When the sites of the open wounds are known, do not assign a code for multiple. Code the sites individually. The External cause of injury code E888.0 instructs the coder to use an additional E code to identify the sharp object (E920.9). Place of occurrence is a farm (E849.1).The lengths of all three wounds are not added together. Only the lengths of wounds that are in the same repair category and anatomic site are added together. In this case, the forearm and thigh are both simple repairs, while the hand is an intermediate repair, which is separately reported. The intermediate repair is listed as the first procedure since it is the more resource-intensive procedure.

5.89.   a. 961.0 786.09, 995.1, 693.0, E857, E849.0

Incorrect answer. There is no evidence in the source document of an overdose of the medication, therefore an ICD-9-CM code for poisoning is inappropriate.

b. 995.20, E931.0, E849.0

Incorrect answer. Code 995.20 is less specific and 995.1 accurately reflects documentation.

c. 995.1, 786.09, E931.0, E849.0

Correct answer.

d. 995.1, 786.09, 693.0, E930.9, E849.0

Incorrect answer. The diagnosis codes are correct except the E-code. According to the source document, the antibiotic Bactrim (sulfonamide) was the cause of the adverse reaction, requiring assignment of an E-code with a higher level of specificity

5.90. Reason for visit code(s): 959.5

Code(s): 816.11, E919.4, E849.0, 26418-F1, 26540-F1, 11012-F1

Note: The source document reveals the patient had a compound fracture that was debrided down to the bone with extensor tendon and collateral ligament repair. The left hand modifiers are as follows: 1st digit (thumb) is -FA, 2nd digit (index) is -F1, 3rd digit (middle finger) is -F2, 4th digit (ring finger) is -F3, and 5th digit (pinky) is -F4.

Chapter 6. Case Studies from Physician-Based Health Records

Anesthesia Services

6.1.   a. 00404

Incorrect answer. Code 00402 specifies reconstructive procedures on the breast.

b. 00406

Incorrect answer. Code 00402 specifies reconstructive procedures on the breast.

c. 00402

Correct answer.

d. 00400

Incorrect answer. Code 00402 specifies reconstructive procedures on the breast.

6.2.   a. 660.11, 653.41, 64475

Incorrect answer. This is for a nerve block of the facet joint or facet nerve. The correct answer is 01967 and 01968.

b. 660.11, 653.01, 01961

Incorrect answer. This is for a C-section delivery that does not involve an epidural; (that is, general anesthesia). The correct answer is 01967 and 01968. The disproportion was specified as cephalopelvic, thus the correct ICD-9-CM code is 653.41.

c. 660.11, 653.41, 01967, 01968

Correct answer.

d. 660.11, 653.91, 01996

Incorrect answer. The code 01996 should be used only for each subsequent day if a long-term epidural is used for pain control. The correct answer is 019167 and 01968. The disproportion was specified as cephalopelvic; thus the correct ICD-9-CM code is 653.41.

6.3.   a. 521.00, 00170-AA-23

Correct answer.

b. 521.00, 00170-AA, 99100-23

Incorrect answer. The patient was not under one year of age. Modifiers should be attached to the anesthesia code.

c. 520.7, 00170-P1-23-AA

Incorrect answer. The diagnosis code should be 521.00, and the P1 modifier may not be required if it does not add additional unit value.

d. 521.30, 00170, 99100-23-AA

Incorrect answer. The diagnosis code should be 521.00. The patient was not under one year of age. Modifiers should be attached to the anesthesia code.

6.4.   a. 12031, 99143

Incorrect answer. The patient age of 5 years is reported with code 99144.

b. 12031, 99144

Correct answer.

c. 12031-47

Incorrect answer. Neither regional nor general anesthesia was given to the patient, so modifier -47 is not appropriate. The code for conscious sedation with Versed, 99144, must be reported.

d. 12031-QS

Incorrect answer. The QS modifier for monitored anesthesia care applies to anesthesia providers who are monitoring the patient. In this case, the staff nurse monitored the patient. The code for conscious sedation with Versed, 99144, must be reported.

6.5.   747.10, 00561-AA-P5

Note: The physical status modifier would be P5 because the patient is not expected to survive without the surgery. Code 99100 is not assigned due to an instructional note under 00561 that states "do not report 00561 in conjunction with 99100).

Disorders of the Blood and Blood-Forming Organs

6.6.   a. 204.90, 38221

Incorrect answer. The leukemia is specified as acute, so the fourth digit of 9 is not the best choice. The procedure was bone marrow aspiration. Code 38221 is used for bone marrow biopsy.

b. 208.00, 20220

Incorrect answer. The leukemia is specified as acute lymphocytic. The unspecified code of 208.00 would not be correct. Code 20220 is used when a biopsy of the bone is performed.

c. 204.90, 38220

Incorrect answer. The leukemia is specified as acute, so the fourth digit of 9 is not the best choice.

d. 204.00, 38220

Correct answer.

6.7.   a. 201.21, 38505

Correct answer.

b. 201.91, 38505

Incorrect answer. Hodgkin's sarcoma is assigned to code 201.21.

c. 201.21, 38500

Incorrect answer. The biopsy was performed with a needle, so code 38500 is not correct.

d. 785.6, 38510

Incorrect answer. Because the Hodgkin's sarcoma was confirmed by a pathologist, the definitive diagnosis should be coded. There is no documentation that the lymph node is deep, and it was biopsied with a needle, so code 38510 is not correct.

6.8.   a. 282.61, 789.09, 427.31, 250.00

Incorrect answer. The sickle-cell anemia is in crisis, so 282.61 is not correct. It would not be necessary to code the inguinal pain because pain, fever, and so forth are part of a sickle-cell crisis.

b. 282.62, 733.42, 427.31, 250.00

Incorrect answer. The avascular necrosis was not confirmed, but only documented as "rule-out." This would not be coded in the physician setting.

c. 282.62

Incorrect answer. The atrial fib and diabetes should be coded.

d. 282.62, 427.31, 250.00
Correct answer.

6.9.   36415, 82951

Note: The correct code assignment would be code 36415 for the venipuncture, all three specimens, and code 82951 for the glucose tolerance test, three specimens.

6.10.   a. 38206, 38210, 38241

Incorrect answer. The physician did not harvest the stem cells during this encounter. The stem cells were previously harvested and were being thawed for transplantation, therefore code 38208 is correct.

b. 38208, 38210, 38241
Correct answer.

c. 38209, 38211, 38240

Incorrect answer. The physician did not wash the cells after they were thawed, therefore code 38208 is correct. The T cells were depleted from the sample, not the tumor cells. This sample was obtained from the patient and frozen, making this an autologous sample, not an allogenic sample. 38241 is the correct code.

d. 38209, 38241

Incorrect answer. The physician did not wash the cells after they were thawed, therefore code 38208 is correct. The T cells were depleted from the sample, therefore code 38210 should be reported.

Disorders of the Cardiovascular System

6.11. 458.9, 427.89, 787.91, 715.36

Symptoms of hypotension and sinus bradycardia are coded because the cause is not established. Diarrhea is coded. GI bleed is stated a "potential" and is not an established diagnosis. Osteoarthrosis is localized to the knee and therefore coded as 715.36.

6.12. a. 427.0, 414.01, 92982, 33206

Incorrect answer. Patient had sick sinus syndrome (not paroxysmal supraventricular tachycardia), which should be listed as a secondary diagnosis code. The pacemaker is documented as AV, which means atrial-ventricular or dual chamber. Code 33208 is correct.

b. 414.01, 427.81, 92995, 33208

Incorrect answer. The angioplasty is not documented as with atherectomy. The correct code is 92982.

c. 414.01, 427.81, 92982, 33208

Correct answer.

d. 427.81, 414.01, 92982, 33200

Incorrect answer. The documentation states that the patient was transferred to the hospital specifically to undergo the PTCA for the CAD, so the 414.01 should be sequenced first. The documentation shows that the pacemaker was inserted percutaneously. The correct code is 33208.

6.13. 404.93, 428.0, 585.5, 250.01

Note: The combination code for hypertensive heart and renal disease is used because the hypertension was documented as the cause of the heart disease. The fifth digit of 3 is assigned and code 585.5 is assigned to identify the stage of chronic kidney disease. A separate code is not assigned for the hypertension. The type of heart failure (428.0) should be a second code. The DM should also be coded.

6.14. 411.1

Note: The patient did not have a myocardial infarction. See Syndrome, preinfarction.

6.15. V58.81, 153.3, 36589

Note: The V code is used because the episode was not directed at the cancer. The cancer is coded as current because it has not been resected. It is appropriate to assign a procedure code for removal of an implantable venous access device. The coding of the removal of a VAD is dependent on a tunneled central venous catheter and whether or not a port or pump was present.

Disorders of the Digestive System

6.16.   a. 278.00, 43842, 43846-51

Incorrect answer. Documentation states that the patient has morbid obesity, so code 278.01 is correct. The contributing risk factors should be coded because they were treated and affect the care of the patient. The CPT code 43846 should not be added because there was no documentation that a bypass was also performed.

b. 278.01, 401.9, 272.0, 43842

Correct answer.

c. 278.01, 401.1, 272.0, 43842, 43843-59

Incorrect answer. The hypertension was not documented as benign; therefore, it should be coded 401.9 without further query to the physician. 43842 is the only procedure that is needed.

d. 278.01, 43848

Incorrect answer. The contributing risk factors should be coded because they were treated and affect the care of the patient. CPT code 43848 is incorrect because this is the original procedure, not a revision.

6.17.   a. 560.89, 555.0, 44120, 44121-51

Incorrect answer. *Coding Clinic* (1997, 2Q) states that the regional enteritis is sequenced first followed by the bowel obstruction. Code 44121 is an add-on code and therefore the modifier -51 is not appropriate.

b. 555.0, 560.89, 44120, 44121-51

Incorrect answer. Code 44121 is an add-on code and therefore the modifier -51 is not appropriate.

c. 555.0, 560.89, 44120, 44121

Correct answer.

d. 555.2, 560.89, 44020

Incorrect answer. The correct code for Crohn's disease of the small intestine is 555.0. There is no documentation of exploration, biopsy or removal of foreign body. The correct code for the enterectomy, which is excision, is 44120.

6.18.   45384, 45380-51

Note: Because the biopsy and the polypectomy were done of different sites, they should both be coded. The polypectomy was done by hot biopsy forceps. Some payers may require a -59 modifier appended to code 45380.

6.19.   789.00, 578.1, 91110

Note: The procedure is located in the index under Gastrointestinal tract, Imaging and the Intraluminal. The physician documents a site "suggestive of possible...." and therefore the erosion is not coded.

6.20. 47610, 44950-52

Note: For reporting purposes, some payers require that the appendectomy be identified. In those cases, CPT code 44950-52 would be reported, in addition to the major abdominal procedure performed, to identify that the appendectomy was lesser than that usually performed. The correct code for cholecystectomy with common duct exploration is 47610. The appendectomy code 44955 is not correct because there is no documentation that the patient had a condition of the appendix. Documentation states incidental.

6.21. 455.4, 46083, 46083-51

Note: If multiple hemorrhoids are incised, you may report the code 46083 more than once with the use of modifier -51. Review *CPT Assistant* (1997, June). Because the words "incision" and hemorrhoid" are singular in the CPT description, it implies one hemorrhoid is being treated.

6.22. 574.00, 574.10, 47563

Note: Coding guidelines state that when an acute and a chronic condition are both present, and there is no combination code, you code both with the acute condition sequenced first. The procedure was done via laparoscope.

6.23. a. 43773

Correct answer. Code 43773 describes removal and replacement of an adjustable gastric band.

b. 43771, 43770.

Incorrect answer. Reporting both codes 43771 and 43770 for removal of a band and placement of a band could be construed as unbundling, since there is a single code that reports the procedure.

c. 43774, 43770

Incorrect answer. Code 43774 is inappropriate as it describes removal of both the band and subcutaneous port, which was not done here.

d. 43888

Incorrect answer. Code 43888 describes removal and replacement of a gastric band, but this is the code for an open procedure, not the laparoscopic procedure noted here.

Evaluation and Management (E/M) Services

6.24. a. 99284

Incorrect answer. Note the description for code 99285, "with the constraints imposed by the urgency of the patient's clinical condition and/or mental status."

b. 99285

Correct answer.

c. 99285-52

Incorrect answer. Description for code 99285 allows for constraints. Modifier -52 for reduced services is not necessary.

d. 99291

Incorrect answer. No mention was made of critical care services being provided and time spent performing critical care is not documented.

6.25. a. 784.99, 783.3, 99335

Incorrect answer. The choking was caused by foreign body, code 933.1.

b. 933.1, 99334

Incorrect answer. The correct CPT code for the key components listed is 99335 as this is an established patient with two out of the three components being met (expanded problem focus exam and low complexity MDM).

c. 933.1, 99335

Correct answer.

d. 783.3, 99334

Incorrect answer. Choking was caused by foreign body, code 933.1. The correct CPT code for the key components listed is 99335 as this is an established patient with two out of the three components being met (expanded problem focus exam and low complexity MDM).

6.26. 99396, 99214-25

Note: The physician codes 99396 for the preventive medicine visit, and 99214-25 for the additional diagnosis and workup related to the mass.

6.27. 427.5, 99291, 99292 × 2

Note: Reference the Critical Care Services section preceding the critical care codes. Codes 99291 and 99292 are used to report the total duration of time spent by the physician providing critical care to the patient even if the time spent is not continuous for that date. This requires that the physician devote his or her full attention to the patient and therefore cannot provide services to any other patient during the same period of time. Critical care time may or may not be direct bedside care, but also includes nursing unit time for care assessment and planning that contributes directly to the treatment of the patient.

6.28. 381.00, 786.07, 787.03, 758.0, 99214-25, 94664, 96372, J0696 × 2 units

Note: The otitis is documented as acute and with effusion, so code 381.00 is correct. The documented components support 99214 as the E/M code assignment. The patient received an IM injection, 96372 with 2 units of Ceftriaxone sodium, J0696, because each unit is worth 250 mg. The patient and mother are taught how to use the inhaler, which is coded as 94664.

6.29.   a. 99304

Incorrect answer. This reports initial evaluation and management services to a nursing facility patient. 99318 is the appropriate code for an annual physical examination.

b. 99308

Incorrect answer. This reports subsequent evaluation and management services that are performed to assess a change in the patient. Annual examinations performed for administrative reasons are reported with code 99318.

c. 99318

Correct answer.

d. 99306

Incorrect answer. 99306 reports an initial new or established nursing facility evaluation meeting comprehensive history, comprehensive exam, and high complexity MDM.

Endocrine, Nutritional and Metabolic Diseases, and Immunity Disorders

6.30.   a. 60220-50

Incorrect answer. 60220 describes the removal of one lobe of the thyroid. This is correct on the left side but the right side is more appropriately coded with 60260 because part of the right thyroid was previosuly removed. In addition, a code is needed for sparing the parathyroid glands and the replantation into the local tissue.

b. 60240

Incorrect answer. Code 60240 describes a total thyroidectomy. However, in this case, a portion of the right thyroid gland has already been removed. Codes 60260 and 60220 more appropriately describe this procedure. In addition, a code is needed for sparing the parathyroid glands and the replantation into the local tissue.

c. 60260-50, 60512

Incorrect answer. Code 60260 describes removal of the remaining portion of the thyroid when a portion has been previously removed. This describes the procedure on the right but not on the left. Codes 60260 and 60220 more appropriately describe this procedure. The parathryoid procedure is correct.

d. 60260-RT, 60220-LT, 60512

Correct answer.

6.31.   a. 90467, 90700

Incorrect answer. Code 90467 is used to report intranasal or oral vaccine administration; however, this was intramuscular. The code for the vaccine is appropriate.

b. 99213, 90465, 90700

Incorrect answer. An evaluation and management code should not be reported in addition to the code from the range 90465–90468.

c. 90465, 90700

Correct answer.

d. 90465

Incorrect answer. This code is appropriate for reporting the administration, but an additional code should be reported for the vaccine itself, 90700.

6.32.   a. 253.0, 225.0

Incorrect answer. A pituitary tumor is not confirmed and would not be coded until it is confirmed. If it is confirmed, a pituitary adenoma would be coded to 227.3, rather than 225.0.

b. 253.0

Correct answer.

c. 227.3

Incorrect answer. A pituitary tumor is not confirmed and would not be coded until it is confirmed. Code only the known diagnosis at the time of the visit; in this case, the acromegaly.

d. 253.0, 227.3

Incorrect answer. A pituitary tumor is not confirmed and would not be coded until it is confirmed.

6.33.   a. V07.4, V49.81, 99212

Correct answer. Based on the limited information in this scenario, these are the correct codes. It is unclear whether the menopause occurred naturally, and there is no documentation of any symptomatology to support a code in category 627. It is advisable to query the physician to clarify this case.

b. 627.2, 99212

Incorrect answer. There is no documentation of any disorder or symptoms related to the menopause. From this limited information, the estrogen patch appears be prophylactic (V07.4).

c. 256.31, 99212

Incorrect answer. There is no indication that the patient suffered premature menopause.

d. V58.69, V49.81, 99212

Incorrect answer. Based on the limited information in this scenario, the correct diagnosis code is V07.4 rather than V58.69 as V58.69 is valid as an additional diagnosis only. It is unclear whether the menopause occurred naturally, and there is no documentation of any symptomatology to support a code in category 627. It is advisable to query the physician to clarify this case.

6.34. 250.41, 583.81, 250.51, 362.01

Note: Both diabetic complication codes are assigned with the fifth digit of 1.

6.35. 250.11, 276.51

Note: The ketoacidosis should be sequenced first and the DM is not specified as uncontrolled, so fifth digit of 1 is used. The symptoms of increased urination and polydipsia are related to the diabetic condition. The dehydration, however, is treated separately.

6.36. a. 250.60, 536.3, V58.67

Correct answer.

b. 250.60, 586.3, 337.1, V58.67

Incorrect answer. *Coding Clinic* (2nd Q 2004), published as superseding advice, states that only 2 codes are needed for this condition. Code 337.1 is no longer assigned.

c. 250.61, 536.3

Incorrect answer. The patient is a type II diabetic who is on insulin. This is not the same as a type I diabetic. The fifth digit of 0 is assigned. The V58.67 is reported to show the current insulin usage.

d. 250.62, 536.3, V58.67

Incorrect answer. Just because the patient is on insulin, it cannot be presumed that the diabetes is uncontrolled.

6.37. a. 250.50, 362.07

Incorrect answer. The diabetes needs to be listed first, followed by the code for the proliferative retinopathy (362.02). Per the coding notes, the code for macular edema would be added (362.07), along with a code from 362.01–362.06.

b. 250.50, 362.06, 362.07

Incorrect answer. The diabetes needs to be listed first, followed by the code for the proliferative retinopathy (362.02). Per the coding notes, the code for macular edema would be added (362.07), along with a code from 362.01–362.06.

c. 250.50, 362.02, 362.07

Correct answer.

d. 362.02, 363.07

Incorrect answer. The diabetes needs to be listed first, followed by the code for the proliferative retinopathy (362.02). Per the coding notes, the code for macular edema would be added (362.07), along with a code from 362.01–362.06.

Disorders of the Genitourinary System

6.38.   a. 585.6, 90970

Incorrect answer. The services are for a month, so 90970 is incorrect.

b. V56.0, 90960

Incorrect answer. The patient is receiving dialysis, but for physician services, the ESRD code would be used, not V56.0. When the facility performs dialysis, they would use the V56.0 code.

c. 585.6, V56.8, 90999

Incorrect answer. The V56.8 code is not needed. The procedure code is incorrect and is more appropriately coded as 90960.

d. 585.6, 90960

Correct answer. Any E/M services that are unrelated to the dialysis care may be reported in addition.

6.39.   a. V67.6, V10.51, 600.00, 52000

Correct answer.

b. 188.9, 600.00, 52000

Incorrect answer. The cancer has been resected and has not recurred in seven years. This encounter is for follow-up after combined therapy (surgery and chemotherapy). The cancer is expressed as a history code using V10.51. The procedure code is correct.

c. 600.00, V10.51, 52010

Incorrect answer. Code V67.6 is the appropriate code to report because this procedure is for surveillance only following completed treatment. The procedure code is incorrect. Code 52000 is appropriate for this follow-up diagnostic procedure.

d. V67.00, 188.9, 52000

Incorrect answer. It is mentioned that the patient was treated with both surgery and chemotherapy, so the follow-up code V67.6 is a better choice. If the patient still had cancer, the 188.9 would be assigned instead of follow-up. Code V10.51 is assigned because the cancer was resected and there has been no recurrence. The additional code of prostatic hypertrophy should also be reported because it may require future follow-up. The other codes are correct.

6.40.   592.1, 52325, 52320-51

Note: Some payers might want the -59 modifier reported to show that these were distinct procedures and independent from each other. To show that an ultrasonic fragmentation was also performed, it is correct to report code 52325. To show that one calculus was removed, code 52320 should be reported.

6.41. V25.2, V61.5, 58671

Note: The tubal ligation was performed with Falope Rings and was performed laparoscopically. Code V61.5 identifies the multiparity as the reason for desiring the tubal ligation.

6.42. 078.0, 54057, 54056-51

Note: It is appropriate to assign both techniques when performed. Some payers may require the use of the -59 modifier to show that the procedures were done independently. Because there is documentation that cryosurgery and laser was used, they both should be coded.

Infectious Diseases

6.43. 034.0, 034.1, 99214, 87880, 96372, J0550

Note: Penicillin G/Penicillin G Procaine has a specific HCPCS code, J0550 for the dosage of 2,400,000 units.

6.44. V05.3, 90471, 90746

Code V05.3 is used for this purpose. CPT codes for the injection and for the hepatitis B are assigned.

6.45. V20.2, 90707, 90471, 99393

Note: It is correct to assign the immunizations with the preventive medicine visit and V20.2 is the only diagnosis required.

Disorders of the Skin and Subcutaneous Tissue

6.46. a. 996.61, 682.2, 33222
Correct answer.

b. 682.2, 33222

Incorrect answer. Devices that cause inflammation or infection are coded to the 996 category in ICD-9-CM. The correct code is 996.61. The procedure code is correct.

c. 996.61, 33233

Incorrect answer. This CPT code is for a revision of the skin pocket for a cardioverter-defibrillator. Code 33222 is the correct code. Code 682.2 is coded per the instructions under code 996.6.

d. 996.72. 682.2, 33999

Incorrect answer. An abscess is an infection, so subcategory 996.6 is more applicable than 996.7. The unlisted code is not appropriate, because there is a specific CPT code available for relocation of a pacemaker pocket. Code 33222 is correct.

6.47. 706.1, 10040

Note: Pustular acne is classified to ICD-9-CM code 706.1. Acne surgery is reported with code 10040. An evaluation and management service (even the lowest level) is not reported when no separate E/M services are rendered.

6.48. 701.1, 15786, 15787, 15787

Note: Keratosis, NOS, is assigned to 701.1. To correctly report the abrasion of the keratoses, code 15786 is reported for the first lesion. Add-on code 15787 is used for each additional four lesions. The 15787 code needs to be repeated one additional time for the sixth lesion. The add-on code is exempt from modifier -51 use.

6.49. 15002, 15003, 15400, 15401, 15401, 15401

Note: The documentation supports assignment of codes 15002 and 15003, since it states that necrotic eschar was debrided to bleeding subcutaneous tissue. Code 15400 describes application of the first 100 sq cm of Mediskin, which is a type of xenogeneic (porcine) dermis. Code 15401 is reported three times to report sq cm 100–200, 200–300, and >300.

6.50. 15365

Note: TranCyte is an example of tissue-cultured allogeneic dermal substitute, most often used to treat diabetic foot ulcers. It is reported with codes in the range 15360–15366. Because this graft involved the foot, code 15365 is correct. There is no documentation of preparation of the recipient site by excision of tissue, so the reporting of code 15004 is not correct.

Behavioral Health Conditions

6.51. a. 90805

Correct answer.

b. 90804, 99212

Incorrect answer. The combination code for psychotherapy and E/M service is reported, 90805.

c. 90811

Incorrect answer. The psychotherapy is described as insight-oriented, not interactive type. Code 90805 is correct.

d. 90810, 99212

Incorrect answer. The combination code for insight-oriented type of psychotherapy with E/M service is reported, 90805.

6.52. a. 314.00, 99214

Incorrect answer. A new patient visit code should be reported, 99204.

b. 314.00, 99204

Correct answer.

c. 314.01, 99204

Incorrect answer. The diagnosis does not include hyperactivity. The correct code is 314.00.

d. 314.9, 99214

Incorrect answer. The DSM-IV code for ADD is 314.9; however, the correct code in ICD-9-CM is 314.00. Also, a new patient visit code should be reported, 99204.

6.53. 303.01

Note: The alcoholism is documented as continuous so the fifth digit of 1 is correct. When there is acute intoxication in alcoholism, a code from subcategory 303.0 is assigned.

6.54. 331.0, 294.11

Note: The dementia is coded as that with behavioral disturbance because of the wandering off. Assign code 294.11. It is very clear in the tabular notes under subcategory 294.1 that the Alzheimer's disease is listed first.

Disorders of the Musculoskeletal System and Connective Tissue

6.55. a. 739.7, 99213-25, 98925

Correct answer. Somatic dysfunction is found in ICD-9-CM under the main term "dysfunction" and subterm "somatic." E/M services on the same day must have documentation that show they are separate from the procedure and include the key elements of an evaluation and management code (history, exam, and medical decision making).

b. 739.2, 98925

Incorrect answer. The wrong region is described by this ICD-9-CM code. Also not reporting the E/M service with the procedure is underreporting the physician work for the visit.

c. 786.59, 99212-25, 98925

Incorrect answer. The ICD-9-CM code is too vague and the E/M service level is not as high as the documentation supports.

d. 739.8, 99213

Incorrect answer. The ICD-9-CM code is not as specific as the documentation allows. Failure to report the osteopathic manipulation in addition to the E/M service is underreporting the physician service.

6.56.   a. 824.8, E917.0, 27788, Q4046

Correct answer.

b. 824.2, E917.0, 27788, 29515-51

Incorrect answer. The diagnosis code is specific to the lateral malleolus, which is not documented. Code 29515 should not be reported with a fracture care code because casts and strapping are included with initial fracture care.

c. 823.81, E917.0, 27786, L4350

Incorrect answer. Code 823.81 is not the correct classification for distal fibula. The CPT code for fracture care is for closed treatment without manipulation. The HCPCS code is for an air splint but this splint is molded from fiberglass.

d. 824.4. E917.0, 27810, 29515-51, L4396

Incorrect answer. The diagnosis code is specific to a bimalleolar fracture, which is not documented. CPT code 27810 is for fracture care of a bimalleolar fracture with manipulation, so it is also inappropriate. Code 29515 for the splint should not be reported with a fracture care code, and the supply code L4396 is not appropriate because it is a splint for ankle contracture, not a fracture.

6.57.   V54.16, 29440, 73590

Note: It is correct to use the orthopedic aftercare code. The CPT codes would be for conversion to a walking cast and the x-ray. It is incorrect to code fracture care codes in this scenario. Do not report an E code because this is not the first encounter for the injury.

6.58.   a. 23140

Incorrect answer. Code 23140 describes the excision of a bone cyst or tumor. In this case, the physician excises a piece of dead bone, not a cyst or tumor.

b. 23172

Correct answer. A sequestrum is a piece of dead bone that has become separated during the process of necrosis from normal/sound bone. It is a complication (sequela) of osteomyelitis. A sequestrectomy is the removal of this dead bone.

c. 23182

Incorrect answer. Code 23182 describes the process of creating a crater or saucer on the body of the scapula. Code 23172 describes the exact procedure performed on the scapula and is therefore, a better choice.

d. 23190

Incorrect answer. Code 23190 describes the removal of a portion of the scapula but does not address the specific reason why the bone was removed. Code 23172 describes the exact procedure performed on the scapula and is therefore, a better choice.

6.59. 729.6, 26075

Note: This foreign body is a retained foreign body because the wound healed around the foreign body.

6.60. a. 724.5

Incorrect answer. The site of the pain is coded first followed by the 307.89 code. Because of the note, the site of the pain is sequenced first.

b. 724.5, 307.89

Correct answer. Instructional note under code 307.89 states to code first the type or site of pain.

c. 307.89

Incorrect answer. The site of the pain is coded first followed by the 307.89 code. Because of the note, the site of the pain is sequenced first.

d. 307.89, 724.5

Incorrect answer. The site of the pain is coded first followed by the 307.89 code. Because of the note, the site of the pain is sequenced first.

Neoplasms

6.61. a. V58.11, 149.8, 96401, J9213

Incorrect answer. Interferon is considered an immunotherapy agent, not chemotherapy. *See Coding Clinic* (1994, 4Q). When a patient is treated with immunotherapy, the code for the neoplasm should be assigned as the first diagnosis. Interferon is an immunotherapy antineoplastic agent, so the correct procedure code is 96372. Medicare rules may be different, so consult your Medicare manual for the correct coding of this service for Medicare beneficiaries.

b. 149.8, 96372, J9213

Correct answer.

c. 145.9, 140.9, 96372

Incorrect answer. The cancer is reported with one code because the lip and oral cavity are contiguous sites. Code 149.8 is correct. Also, the J9213 code is required to report the agent administered.

d. V58.11, 96549

Incorrect answer. Interferon is considered an immunotherapy agent, not chemotherapy. *See Coding Clinic* (1994, 4Q). When a patient is treated with immunotherapy, the code for the neoplasm (149.8) should be assigned as the first diagnosis. Interferon is an immunotherapy antineoplastic agent, so the correct procedure code is 96372. Medicare rules may be different, so consult your Medicare manual for the correct coding of this service for Medicare beneficiaries. A HCPCS code (J9213) to describe the agent administered should be reported as well.

6.62. 233.1, 493.90, 57454

Note: Cervical dysplasia is a precursor condition of carcinoma in situ of the cervix and should not be coded. Carcinoma in situ (233.1) should be assigned. The endocervical biopsy was performed endoscopically. Code 57454 is correct, and it includes endocervical curettage. Other pre- and postoperative services are not included and are reported separately.

6.63. 214.3, V10.05, 50543

Note: Lipoma of the kidney is assigned to code 214.3; history of colon cancer is assigned to code V10.05; laparoscopic partial nephrectomy is assigned to code 50543.

6.64. 155.0, 47120

Note: Hepatocellular carcinoma is a primary site coded to 155.0; wedge resection of the liver is coded to 47120.

6.65. 183.0, 250.03, 58943

Note: Ovarian carcinoma is assigned to code 183.0. The diabetes is insulin dependent and was out of control. The staging of the ovarian malignancy and excision for malignancy CPT code is 58943.

Disorders of the Nervous System and Sense Organs

6.66. a. 61796, 20660

Incorrect answer. CPT code 20660 is a separate procedure that is a component part of 61796, so no separate code is reported.

b. 61796, 61800

Correct answer.

c. 64600, 61795

Incorrect answer. The correct CPT code for this procedure is 61796; code 64600 is for destruction by a neurolytic agent, not a gamma knife. Computer assistance was not documented.

d. 61795

Incorrect answer. The correct code for the stereotactic radiosurgery is 61796. Code 61795 is for the stereotactic computer-assisted volumetric measurement. If documented, it may be listed separately in addition to the code for the primary procedure.

6.67. a. 63655

Incorrect answer. This CPT code is for reporting laminectomy for implantation of neurostimulator electrodes, plate/paddle, epidural.

b. 63685

Correct answer.

c. 63650

Incorrect answer. This CPT code is for reporting percutaneous insertion of a catheter with electrodes generally performed under fluoroscopic guidance.

d. 63688

Incorrect answer. This CPT code is for a revision or removal of implanted spinal neurostimulator pulse generatory or receiver.

6.68. a. 365.9, 250.00, 66172-RT

Incorrect answer. The glaucoma is specified as being open angle, so code 365.10 is correct. The diabetes mellitus is documented as type I, so the correct fifth digit is 1. This is the initial procedure according to the documentation, so code 66170 is correct.

b. 365.11, 250.01, 65850

Incorrect answer. Documentation only specifies the glaucoma as open angle, not primary open angle, so code 365.10 is correct. The section of codes 66150–66172 is for treatment of glaucoma, and code 66170 describes the procedure.

c. 250.51, 365.44, 66170-52

Incorrect answer. The patient has diabetes mellitus, but there is no cause-effect stated as to the cause of the glaucoma. In order to use this diagnosis coding, the physician would need to state "diabetic glaucoma" or "glaucoma due to diabetes." Each disorder needs to be separately coded. The procedure does not need the modifier -52 because these are inherently unilateral procedures.

d. 365.10, 250.01, 66170-RT

Correct answer. If the payer accepts HCPCS Level II modifiers, the -RT gives information about the side operated on.

6.69. a. 374.00, 67921-RT

Correct answer. Entropion is the turning inward of the eyelid edge toward the eyeball. If the payer accepts HCPCS Level II modifiers, modifier -RT gives information about the correct site of the procedure.

b. 374.00, 67921-50

Incorrect answer. It is incorrect to use the modifier -50 with this procedure. It is inherently a unilateral procedure. This patient has bilateral entropion, but only the right side was repaired at this session. If the payer accepts HCPCS Level II modifiers, the RT gives information about the correct site of the procedure.

c. 374.10, 67921-RT

Incorrect answer. Code 374.10 is the code for ectropion, the turning outward (eversion) of the eyelid edge causing the palpebral conjunctiva to be exposed. Code 374.00 is correct. The CPT code is correct.

d. 374.00, 67923

Incorrect answer. Code 374.00 is correct. The CPT code is incorrect because this would describe an entropion repair with tarsal wedge excision, which is not documented. The correct code is 67921-RT.

6.70. 438.20, 438.11, 401.9, 250.00

Note: The dominant side is not specified, so code 438.20 is the most specific code for this scenario. The aphasia is coded because it is still current, and the hypertension and DM should be coded.

Newborn/Congenital Disorders

6.71. a. 773.0, 770.84, 99469

Incorrect answer. For a birth episode, code V30.00 is reported in the first position for a spontaneous vaginal delivery. The management of the ventilator is included with the intensive care code, but the exchange transfusion is not included per the CPT manual. Code 36450 is assigned in addition.

b. V30.00, 99468 , 36450, 94657

Incorrect answer. Code 99469 is the appropriate choice for the second day of care. Code 99468 is used to report initial services, which in this case would be the date of birth. Code 94657 is not reported with neonatal intensive care because the listed services are considered bundled. The exchange transfusion is not a bundled service, so it is correctly reported as a separate code.

c. V30.00, 773.0, 770.84, 99469, 36450

Correct answer.

d. 773.0, 770.84 and 99499.

Incorrect answer. The exchange transfusion procedure, code 36450, should also be reported in CPT because it is not bundled with the intensive care services like the CPAP management. ICD-9-CM code V30.00 must be reported in first position when reporting an episode of care where a birth occurred.

6.72. a. 33813

Incorrect answer. CPT code 33813 is the repair of the aortopulmonary septal defect, or window, that is a communication between the ascending aorta and the main pulmonary artery above the two distinct semilunar valves. A patent ductus arteriosus is a connect between the aorta and the pulmonary artery within the aortic arch, well above the heart. PDA closure is described by 33820–33824, based on the method used for closure. In this case, the physician divides the connection and suturing each of the defects closed. CPT code 33824 describes this service for this 22-year-old patient.

b. 33820

Incorrect answer. This code describes a closure method by ligation, or tying off the connect with several heavy sutures. In this case, the physician divides the connection and suturing each of the defects closed. CPT code 33824 describes this service for this 22-year-old patient.

c. 33822

Incorrect answer. This codes describes the correct method of closure but the patient in this case is 22 years old. CPT code 33824 describes this service for this 22-year-old patient.

d. 33824

Correct answer.

6.73.   a. 49495-50, 55041-51

Incorrect answer. Codes from the 55040–55041 series are not reported when a hernia repair is also performed. Code 49495 is incorrect due to the patient's age of 2 years.

b. 49500-50

Correct answer. Because a combination code exists and the procedure is performed on both sides, this is the only correct code.

c. 49500-RT, 49500-LT

Incorrect answer. When surgery is performed on a paired organ, modifier -50 is used when both sides are operated on, unless the CPT codes contain "unilateral or bilateral" within the code description.

d. 55041, 49500

Incorrect answer. Code 55041 is not reported when hernia repair is involved. Because in this case the operation was bilateral, modifier -50 is appended to the 49500 code, which represents that the procedure involved both sides of the body.

6.74.   a. 754.69, 29450

Incorrect answer. The diagnosis code reported is for equinovarus, which is not what the documentation states and represents a different type of clubfoot. The evaluation and management service should also be reported with a -25 modifier to show that it is distinct from the cast replacement.

b. 736.71, 29405

Incorrect answer. The condition is congenital, not acquired, if the patient is a newborn. Clubfoot manipulation and casting has a specific CPT code to report, which is 29450. In addition, if the evaluation and management service is distinct from the procedure, it may be reported separately with modifier -25.

c. 754.51. 29405

Incorrect answer. Clubfoot manipulation and casting has a specific CPT code to report, which is 29450. In addition, if the evaluation and management service is distinct from the procedure, it may be reported separately with modifier -25.

d. 754.51, 99212-25, 29450

Correct answer. Selected payers may question or refuse to reimburse for an E/M service on the same date as a procedure, but it is correct from a CPT coding standpoint if the E/M service is above and beyond what is provided as part of the routine pre- and postop services connected with the procedure.

6.75.   a. V30.2, 99460 , 99238

Incorrect answer. When admission and discharge occur on the same date, code 99463 is reported. Code 99238 is not used when admission and discharge occur on the same day.

b. V30.00, 99463

Incorrect answer. A birthing center is not a hospital birth. The correct code is V30.2.

c. V30.2, 99460

Incorrect answer. Code 99460 is used in birthing room deliveries but not when the admission and discharge services occur on the same date. Code 99463 is the correct CPT code for this service.

d. V30.2, 99463

Correct answer. A birthing center is not considered a hospital birth, so the fourth digit is 2 for the liveborn infant type of birth.

Pediatric Conditions

6.76.   a. 99212, 90378, 96372

Incorrect answer. There is nothing in the brief description of this service to substantiate a Level II office visit (99212).

b. 90378, 90471

Incorrect answer. This is not a vaccine. Administration via IM injection of an immune globulin is reported with code 96372.

c. 99212, J1565

Incorrect answer. This J code is for intravenous administration of RSV immune globulin, not an intramuscular injection. There is nothing in the brief description of this service to substantiate a Level II office visit (99212). Administration of the IM injection is reported with code 96372.

d. 90378, 96372

Correct answer.

6.77.   382.01, 99213

Note: The otitis media is documented as acute with perforation of eardrum. The highest level of E/M code that could be assigned is 99213.

6.78.   382.3, 69436-50

Note: The procedure was performed bilaterally, so modifier -50 would apply.

6.79.   493.01, 99283, 94060.

The intractable wheezing would be assigned to the fifth digit of 1.

Conditions of Pregnancy, Childbirth, and the Puerperium

6.80.   a. 654.53, 59871

Correct answer.

b. 654.53 (The cerclage removal is part of the global package.)

Incorrect answer. CPT guidelines state that the cerclage removal may be coded if done under anesthesia other than local.

c. 622.5, with appropriate E/M procedure

Incorrect answer. Code 622.5 is used for incompetent cervix when the patient is not pregnant. CPT guidelines state that the cerclage removal may be coded if done under anesthesia other than local.

d. 622.5, 59871

Incorrect answer. Code 622.5 is used for incompetent cervix when the patient is not pregnant.

6.81.   a. 632, 59820

Incorrect answer. The CPT code is coded as a missed abortion, but the ICD-9-CM code can be more specific for a blighted ovum. It would be appropriate to also code the antepartum care provided.

b. 632, 59851, 59425

Incorrect answer. The CPT code is coded as a missed abortion, but the ICD-9-CM code can be more specific for a blighted ovum. CPT guidelines state to code a blighted ovum as a missed abortion treatment. Code 59851 is for other induced abortions and is not appropriate. It would be appropriate to also code the antepartum care provided.

c. 631, 59820

Incorrect answer. An E/M code is required to report the antepartum visits.

d. 631, 59820, plus appropriate E/M codes

Correct answer.

6.82.   a. 637.91, 59812

Incorrect answer. The abortion was specified as spontaneous. It is appropriate to also report the antepartum visits.

b. 634.91, 59812, 59425

Correct answer.

c. 634.91, 58120

Incorrect answer. 58120 is incorrect because this is an abortion. The correct code is found under the abortion subheading. It is correct to also report the antepartum visits.

d. 634.92, 58120, 59425

Incorrect answer. The abortion was incomplete, so the fifth digit is incorrect. 58120 is incorrect because this is an abortion. The correct code is found under the abortion subheading.

6.83. 643.23

Note: Because this started after the 22 completed week of gestation, it is considered to be excessive vomiting of late pregnancy.

6.84. 647.63, 042, 136.3

Note: According to the coding guidelines, when a pregnant female with AIDS is admitted with a related condition to the AIDS, code 647.6X is assigned, followed by 042 and the condition being treated.

Disorders of the Respiratory System

6.85. a. 519.00, V46.11, 31614

Incorrect answer. This was not a complication of the tracheostomy, such as an infection or a mechanical breakdown of the tube or tracheal stenosis. Code V55.0 is more appropriate for scar tissue redundancy.

b. V55.0, V46.11, 31614

Correct answer. Because the scar tissue is not a true complication of the stoma, the V code is the correct code to communicate the reason for the service.

c. V55.0, 31610

Incorrect answer. An additional code could be assigned for the respirator dependence because it would affect the evaluation and management of the case. Code 31610 is incorrect because this is a revision of a tracheostomy already established, not a fenestration procedure.

d. 519.00, 31613

Incorrect answer. This was not a complication of the tracheostomy, such as an infection or a mechanical breakdown of the tube or tracheal stenosis. Code V55.0 is more appropriate for scar tissue redundancy. The CPT code is also incorrect. Because flap rotation was documented, code 31614 is warranted. Also code V46.11 could be added because the respirator dependence is likely to affect evaluation and management of the case.

6.86. a. 518.89, 32657

Incorrect answer. The emphysematous nodules are assigned to code 492.8.

b. 492.8, 32657, 32657-51

Incorrect answer. The procedure code is correct, but it should only be reported one time because the description states "single or multiple."

c. 518.89, 32500

Incorrect answer. The emphysematous nodules are assigned to code 492.8. The procedure was done endoscopically with a thoracoscope. The open procedure code is not used. The correct CPT code is 32657.

d. 492.8, 32657

Correct answer.

6.87.   a. 231.2, 31641

Correct answer. Per individual payer guidelines, review should be done of the postop period because the diagnostic procedure was done. If the criteria are met, then modifier -58 might be appropriate.

b. 162.2, 31641, 31623-59

Incorrect answer. The lesions were not described as a primary neoplasm, so code 162.2 is not accurate. Code 231.2 is assigned. The CPT code for the bronchial washings is incorrect because the lesions were identified by this means in a previous bronchoscopy, and this episode was for the laser treatment through a rigid scope.

c. 231.2, 31641, 31623-59

Incorrect answer. The only CPT code to report for this session is 31641. The CPT code for the bronchial washings is incorrect because the lesions were identified by this means in a previous bronchoscopy, and this episode was for the laser treatment through a rigid scope.

d. 162.2, 31641

Incorrect answer. The lesions were not described as a primary neoplasm, so code 162.2 is not accurate. Code 231.2 is assigned.

6.88.   428.0

Note: Acute pulmonary edema with CHF is coded to 428.0. Respiratory distress is not separately coded (*Coding Clinic* 1991, 3Q:19–21).

6.89.   507.0, 482.40

Note: It is correct to code the aspiration pneumonia along with the superimposed staphylococcal bacterial pneumonia (*Coding Clinic* 1991, 3Q:16–17).

6.90.   a. 31622, 31625, 31636, 99144

Incorrect answer. The code for the diagnostic bronchoscopy (31622, designated as a separate procedure) should not be assigned when more extensive procedures are performed at the same session. In addition, the code for conscious sedation is included in the procedure when performed by the same physician as performs the procedure. This is indicated by the symbol ⊙ preceding the code.

b. 31628, 31632, 31636

Incorrect answer. Biopsies were taken of the walls of the bronchi, not through the walls. Code 31628 is the appropriate biopsy code. Code 31632 is also not appropriate.

c. 31625, 31636

Correct answer.

d. 31625, 31636, 99144

Incorrect answer. The endoscopic codes are appropriate, but the code for conscious sedation is included in the procedure when performed by the same physician as performs the procedure. This is indicated by the symbol ⊙ preceding the code.

Trauma and Poisoning

6.91. 942.42, 945.40, 948.22, E890.3, E849.0

Note: The burns are third degree but are specified as deep. The burn on the leg is of an unspecified site. The percent of body surface burned is 25 percent so the fourth digit of 2 is assigned with code 948; and the percent of third-degree burn is 25 percent, so the fifth digit is 2. Because the fire was in a house, category E890 would be used.

6.92. 709.2, 906.7, 906.8, E929.4

Note: It is incorrect to assign a current burn code for a late effect. Index the term "late." The residual of a late effect is listed in the first position, followed by the late effect code. The late effect E code could also be added in this case.

6.93. 536.41, 682.2, 041.11, 438.82

Note: The infection of the gastrostomy code is listed first. The note in the tabular of the book instructs that an additional code is used to specify cellulitis, and the organism, if known. Both are present here and should be coded. The dysphagia due to the old stroke is also coded.

6.94. 12041, 12001-51

Note: The intermediate repair is listed first. It is of the hand and is 1 cm, so code 12041 is correct. These repairs are not added together because they are different types of repair. The simple laceration of the arm is reported with 12001. Modifier -51 can be appended.

6.95. 928.21, E919.3, E849.3

Note: This is confusing to look up in the index. If you look in the index under ankle with other parts of foot, it gives you 928.20. If you look in the index under foot, excluding toe(s) alone (with ankle) the code is 928.20. However, if you look in the index under toe(s) with foot and ankle, the code assigned is 928.21. This seems like the most specific code. In the Index undercrushed, by machinery, it says *see* accident, machine.

Part III

Advanced Coding Exercises

Chapter 7. Case Studies from Inpatient Health Records

Disorders of the Blood and Blood-Forming Organs

7.1.   a. 428.0, 276.51, 287.30, 599.0, 250.00

Correct answer. The physician could be queried as to the use of V58.66, Long term use of aspirin.

b. 428.0, 276.51, 287.5, 599.0, 250.00

Incorrect answer. The documentation states primary thrombocytopenia, so code 287.5 is not the best choice.

c. 428.0, 511.9, 276.51, 287.30, 599.0, 250.00

Incorrect answer. Pleural effusion is not separately coded when present with CHF (*Coding Clinic* 1991, 3Q:19–20).

d. 276.51, 511.9, 428.0, 287.30, 782.7, 599.0, 250.00

Incorrect answer. The principal diagnosis should be the CHF because it was present on admission and the main focus of treatment during the inpatient stay. Pleural effusion is not separately coded when present with CHF. The petechia is not coded because it is part of the thrombocytopenia and is excluded as an additional code.

Optional MS-DRG Exercise (for users with access to MS-DRG software or tables)

The correct MS-DRG assignment is 292, Heart Failure and Shock with CC,

a. MS-DRG assignment in this case is based on the principal diagnosis; the secondary codes do not impact the MS-DRG.

Correct answer. Urinary tract infection (599.0) impacts this MS-DRG.

b. A principal diagnosis of CHF results in a higher-paying MS-DRG than a principal diagnosis of dehydration.

Incorrect answer. This is true.

c. This patient's LOS exceeded the average length of stay for the assigned MS-DRG.

Incorrect answer. This is true.

d. All of the above are true statements.

Incorrect answer. A is a false statement as secondary codes do impact this MS-DRG assignment.

7.2. Principal diagnosis: Sickle cell pain crisis, 282.62

Additional diagnoses:

Staphylococcus aureus bacteremia, 790.7, 041.11

Priapism, 607.3

Asthma, 493.90

Gastroesophageal reflux disease, 530.81

Hemorrhoids, 455.6

Procedures:

PICC line placement, 38.93

Bone scan, 92.14

Transesophageal echocardiogram, 88.72

Injection or infusion of other therapeutic or prophylactic substance, 99.29

Note: Pain is included in the code for sickle cell disease with crisis. According to *Coding Clinic* (2003, 4Q:79–81), Bacteremia is defined as the presence of bacteria in the blood.

Issues to clarify: The physician should be queried about the type of crisis if the full record does not provide this detail.

7.3. Principal diagnosis: Anemia of chronic disease 285.29-Y

Additional diagnoses:

Hypertension and Chronic renal insufficiency 403.90-Y and 585.9-Y

Diabetes 250.00-Y

Long term (current use) of insulin V58.67 (exempt)

Coronary artery disease 414.01-Y

Congestive heart failure 428.0-Y

Hypokalemia 276.8-N

Principal procedure: Transfusion of packed cells 99.04

Additional procedures: Not applicable

Note: The chronic renal insufficiency is not documented as the cause of the anemia, as chronic renal insufficiency is just one of the patient's chronic conditions. A history of coronary artery bypass graft is not documented so the disease is of the native arteries. *Coding Clinic* (2004, 1Q:24). An additional code specifying the stage of renal insufficiency needs to be added per "use additional code" instructional note under 403.90.

Procedure 99.04 s reported once in ICD-9-CM.

Disorders of the Cardiovascular System

7.4.   a. 414.01, 414.05, 410.12, 411.1, V45.82, 36.11, 36.15, 39.61, 37.22, 88.53, 88.57

Correct answer.

b. 414.01, 414.05, 410.12, 411.1, V45.81, 36.12, 39.61, 37.22, 88.53, 88.57

Incorrect answer. The bypass consisted of one coronary (36.11) and one mammary (36.15). V codes indicating CABG status are redundant when the diagnosis code itself indicates that the status exists. Therefore, only code 414.05 needs to be reported. Report V45.82 for the angioplasty status.

c. 414.00, 414.05, 410.11, 411.1, 36.11, 36.15, 39.61, 37.22, 88.53, 88.57

Incorrect answer. The coronary atherosclerosis should be coded to 414.01 since there was documentation in the native marginal circumflex of 80% stenosis. The MI of the anterior wall occurred prior to transfer; therefore, code to the fifth digit of 2 (410.12).

d. 414.01, 414.05, 410.12, 411.1, 412, V45.81, 36.11, 36.15, 39.61, 37.22, 88.53, 88.57

Incorrect answer. The MI was recent, not old, so code 412 should not be coded. V codes indicating CABG status are redundant when the diagnosis code itself indicates that the status exists. Therefore, only code 414.05 needs to be reported.

Optional MS-DRG Exercise (for users with access to MS-DRG software or tables)

The principal diagnosis is 414.01, Coronary atherosclerosis of native coronary artery.

In addition to the principal diagnosis, the procedure codes 36.11 and 37.22. This case groups to MS-DRG 234 Coronary Bypass with Cardiac Catheterization without MCC .

False: The presence or absence of the CC codes does not change the MS-DRG assignment; a major complication/comorbid condition does change the assignment.

7.5.   a. 37.26 Catheter-based invasive electrophysiologic testing

Incorrect answer. This is the ICD-9-CM code for a full catheter-based electrophysiological testing. Code 89.49 Automatic implantable cardioverter-defibrillator (AICD) check is the appropriate code for the post insertion lead check.

b. There is no ICD-9-CM code to report a lead check; it is included in the lead insertion.

Incorrect answer. 89.49 Automatic implantable cardioverter-defibrillator (AICD) check is the appropriate code for the post insertion lead check.

c. 89.49 Automatic implantable cardioverter-defibrillator (AICD) check

Correct answer.

d. Either code 89.49 or 37.26 may be assigned to report the lead check; they are essentially synonymous.

Incorrect answer. Code 37.26 is for a full catheter-based electrophysiological testing. Code 89.49 Automatic implantable cardioverter-defibrillator (AICD) check is the appropriate code for the post insertion lead check.

7.6. a. 00.61, 99.10, 00.63

Correct answer.

b. 00.61, 99.10, 00.64

Incorrect answer. Code 00.64 reports insertion of stents into other precerebral extracranial arteries than the carotid. Code 00.63 is specific for stenting of the carotid artery.

c. 00.61, 00.63

Incorrect answer. These codes are appropriate, but code 99.10 should also be reported as indicated in the Code Also note. Since streptokinase is considered a thrombolytic agent, as are urokinase, alteplase, anistreplase, and reteplase. Note that routine injection of heparin during a procedure is not considered injection of a thrombolytic agent.

d. 00.61

Incorrect answer. Code Also note instructs the following to be coded: injection of the thrombolytic agent (99.10) and placement of the carotid artery stent (00.63).

7.7. a. 00.66, 00.40, 36.07, 36.07, 99.10

Incorrect answer. Code 36.07 is appropriate for the atherectomy, and 99.10 for the urokinase infusion, but code 36.07 should be reported only once since the descriptor for this code is "Insertion of drug-eluting coronary artery stent(s)." The code is assigned once irrespective of the number of stents placed. The code 00.46 identifies the number of stents inserted.

b. 00.66, 36.07

Incorrect answer. These codes are appropriate, but code 99.10 should also be reported for the infusion of urokinase, which is considered a thrombolytic agent. The code for the number of vessels treated and number of stents inserted should also be assigned, 00.40 and 00.46.

c. 00.66, 00.40, 00.46, 36.07, 99.10

Correct answer.

d. 36.09, 00.40, 00.46, 36.06, 99.10

Incorrect answer. Code 00.40 and 00.46 are appropriate for the number of vessels treated and number of stents inserted and 99.10 for the urokinase infusion, but code 36.06 is used to report insertion of non-drug-eluting stents. Stents that are impregnated with sirolimus are by definition drug-eluting stents and should be reported with code 36.07. Sirolimus is an immunosuppressive drug that has been found to prevent or dramatically slow restenosis within atherectomized or angioplastied arteries. The principal procedure, atherectomy, should be coded 00.66, not 36.09.

7.8.   a. 38.44

Incorrect answer. Code 38.44 reports resection of the aneurysm of the aorta and replacement with a graft. This is an open, not a percutaneous endovascular procedure. Code 39.71 Endovascular implantation of graft in abdominal aorta, is the appropriate code.

b. 39.79

Incorrect answer. Code 39.79 reports an endovascular repair of vessels other than the aorta and vessels of the head and neck. Code 39.71 Endovascular implantation of graft in abdominal aorta, is the appropriate code.

c. 39.71

Correct answer.

d. 39.7

Incorrect answer. Code 39.7 is a truncated code; a fourth digit is required. Code 39.71 Endovascular implantation of graft in abdominal aorta, is the appropriate code.

7.9.   a. 411.1, 414.01, 250.00, 272.0, 36.12, 36.15, 39.61

Incorrect answer as the reason the patient was admitted is due to his coronary artery disease, therefore, 414.01 is sequenced as the principal diagnosis.

b. 414.01, 411.1, 250.00, 272.0, 36.12, 36.15, 39.61

Correct answer.

c. 414.00, 413.9, 995.89, 250.00, 36.12, 36.15, 39.61

Incorrect answer as the patient's coronary artery disease is identified as his native arteries. The angina is documented as being unstable. Hypothermia should not be coded as it is considered integral to the bypass surgery (*Coding Clinic* 1995, 1Q:5–6). Hypercholesterolemia meets reporting guidelines as a secondary procedure.

d. 414.01, 411.1, 272.0, 250.00, 36.13, 39.61

The patient actually had two vein graft bypass and one internal mammary artery. Therefore, the procedure code 36.13 is incorrect. The correct codes are 36.12 and 36.15.

7.10.   a. 411.1, 424.0, 429.81, 36.12, 36.15, 39.61, 35.12, 35.31

Correct answer.

b. 411.1, 424.0, 36.12, 36.15, 39.61, 35.12, 35.31

Incorrect answer. An additional code should be assigned for the papillary muscle tethering since it had to be repaired.

c. 411.1, 424.0, 429.81, 36.13, 39.61, 35.12, 35.31

Incorrect answer. The patient had two aortocoronary vein bypass grafts and one internal mammary artery bypass graft. The correct codes are 36.12 and 36.15 and not 36.13.

d. 411.0, 424.0, 429.81, 36.12, 36.15, 39.61, 35.12, 35.31

Incorrect answer. The documentation states "unstable postinfarct angina" which indexes to Angina—unstable—411.1.

Disorders of the Digestive System

7.11.　Principal diagnosis: Acute cholecystitis, 575.0-Y

Additional diagnoses:

　　Acute pancreatitis, 577.0-Y

　　Bile duct obstruction, 576.2-Y

Note: Cholecystitis is documented as acute. Review of the operative report confirms that no stones were found in the gallbladder. Though the physician suspected a stone in the bile duct, none was found and the diagnosis after study is "evidence of bile duct obstruction." POA indicator Y (yes) assigned to diagnoses codes as all conditions were present on admission.

Principal procedure: Cholecystectomy, 51.22

Additional procedures:

　　Common duct exploration for relief of obstruction, 51.42

　　Choledochoscopy, 51.11

　　Feeding jejunostomy, 46.39

　　Intraoperative cholangiogram, 87.53

Note: The cholecystectomy was performed open, not laparoscopically.

7.12.　a. 574.70, 577.0, 250.00, 401.9, 278.00, 52.93, 51.85, 51.10

Incorrect answer. The common bile duct stones are stated to have caused obstruction in the body of the operative report; the fifth digit should be 1. The ERCP (51.10) is not separately reported. An ERCP with cannulation of the pancreatic duct is coded to 52.93. The intraoperative cholangiogram (87.53) should also be reported. The balloon extraction of common bile duct stones (51.88) should also be coded.

b. 574.71, 577.0, 250.00, 401.9, 278.00, 52.93, 51.85, 51.88, 87.53

Correct answer.

c. 574.81, 577.0, 52.93, 51.85, 87.53

Incorrect answer. There is no documentation to support both acute and chronic cholecystitis. Code 574.71 is appropriate. The diabetes, hypertension, and obesity were documented and are current chronic conditions that would affect the treatment of a surgical patient and should be coded. The balloon extraction of common bile duct stones (51.88) should be coded.

d. 574.80, 577.2, 250.00, 401.9, 278.00, 52.93, 51.85, 51.88

Incorrect answer. There is no documentation to support both acute and chronic cholecystitis, and the common bile duct stones are stated to have caused obstruction in the body of the operative report. Code 574.71 is appropriate. The pancreatitis is documented as biliary, but not cystic. Because there is no entry for biliary, the 577.0 is correct. The intraoperative cholangiogram should be reported with code 87.53.

Optional MS-DRG Exercise (for users with access to MS-DRG software or tables)

MS-DRG assignment with the intraoperative cholangiogram code: 420 Hepatobiliary diagnostic procedure with MCC

MS-DRG assignment without the intraoperative cholangiogram code: 444, Disorders of the biliary tract W MCC

MS-DRG 420 is the correct MS-DRG assignment.

The code 577.0 is a MCC which affects the MS-DRG assignment.

7.13. Principal diagnosis: Morbid obesity 278.01-Y

Additional diagnoses:

Gastroesphogeal Reflux 530.81-Y

Obstructive Sleep Apnea 327.23-Y

Principal procedure: Revision gastroplasty converted to Roux-en-Y 44.39

Additional procedures:

Removal of ring 44.99

Liver biopsy 50.11

Gastroscopy 44.13

The eroded ring is not a complication because the reason the ring eroded was due to her increased weight. See *Coding Clinic* (2003, 3Q:3–8) for reference. Code 278.01 is reported for the morbid obesity. Code 327.23 is reported for Obstructive sleep apnea. Code 44.39, Other gastroenterostomy is reported when a gastroplasty is converted to Roux-en-Y procedure per *Coding Clinic* (2003, 3Q:3–8). The endoscopy procedure and the procedure to remove the ring should also be coded, 44.99. A liver biopsy was also performed in addition to removal of the ring and endoscopy.

Optional MS-DRG Exercise (for users with access to MS-DRG software or tables)

MS-DRG 621 O.R. Procedures for Obesity without CC/MCC

a. Secondary diagnosis of a complication/comorbid condition or a major complication/comorbid condition.

Correct answer. Addition of a CC/MCC would change the current MS-DRG.

b. Additional procedure codes

Incorrect answer. The principal procedure in addition to principal diagnosis is generating the MS-DRG.

c. If one of the current diagnoses was not present on admission

Incorrect answer The secondary diagnoses are not designated as a CC/MCC, so if they were identified as hospital-acquired conditions in addition to being NOT present on admission, the MS-DRG would remain the same.

d. All of the above

Incorrect answer, only "a" would change the MS-DRG assignment of this admission.

Endocrine, Nutritional and Metabolic Diseases, and Immunity Disorders

7.14.   a. 239.7, 255.0, 401.9, 785.1, 07.21

Incorrect answer. The alphabetic index directs the coder accordingly: Tumor, cortical (benign) 227.0, malignant cortical 194.0, and rest—see Neoplasm by site benign. Code 239.7 is coded to an adrenal neoplasm of uncertain behavior. There is no documentation to support this code selection.

b. 194.0, 401.9, 785.1, 07.22

Incorrect answer. The alphabetic index directs the coder accordingly: Tumor, cortical (benign) 227.0, malignant cortical 194.0, and rest—see Neoplasm by site benign. The type of tumor has not been identified and thus 194.0 malignant tumor of the adrenal is incorrectly reported. Cushing Syndrome meets secondary reporting as it is not inherent to the tumor. The tumor is unilateral, but there is no indication that a unilateral adrenalectomy was performed. Code 07.21 is correct.

c. 227.0, 255.0, 401.9, 785.1, 07.21

Correct answer.

d. 227.0, 255.0, 07.29

Incorrect answer. Hypertension 401.9 and palpitations 785.1 meet reporting guidelines as secondary diagnoses as patient discharged on Toprol used to treat both hypertension and palpitations. Code 07.21 is correct for excision of lesion of adrenal gland and thus other partial adrenalectomy 07.29 is incorrect reporting.

Optional MS-DRG Exercise (for users with access to MS-DRG software or tables)

a. 644, Endocrine Disorders with CC

Incorrect answer as the procedure code 07.21 was performed.

b. 615, Adrenal and Pituitary Procedures without CC/MCC

Incorrect answer as this admission has a CC (255.0).

c. 614, Adrenal and Pituitary Procedures with CC/MCC

Correct answer.

d. 628, Other Endocrine, Nutritional and Metabolic OR Procedures with MCC

Incorrect answer. The procedure code is 07.21 which groups in this instance to 614.

7.15. Principal diagnosis: Diabetic hypoglycemia, 250.82-Y

Additional diagnoses:

Diabetic neuropathy, 250.62-Y, 357.2-Y

Diabetic nephropathy, 250.42-Y, 583.81-Y

Long term (current use) of insulin, V58.67

Lung cancer, 162.9-Y

Hepatomegaly, 789.1-Y

Note: According to the *ICD-9-CM Official Guidelines for Coding and Reporting*, when a patient is admitted for the purpose of chemotherapy and develops complications, the principal diagnosis is V58.11, Encounter for chemotherapy. In this case, the patient initially presented to the facility as an outpatient for chemotherapy, but then was admitted as an inpatient to control his diabetes. The same fifth digit for diabetes mellitus should be used for all of the applicable diabetic manifestations coded in the hospital admission. According to *Coding Clinic* (2002, 2Q:13), a physician statement of "poorly controlled" diabetes should be clarified to determine if the diabetes is, in fact, uncontrolled. Query the physician to determine if "not controlled," "Admitted for control of his diabetes," and "due to poor diabetes control" means uncontrolled before fifth digit assignment is made. If physician responds to query as "uncontrolled," then fifth digit of 2 (type II or unspecified, uncontrolled) is assigned to all three diabetes codes. Otherwise, all three diabetes codes are assigned a fifth digit of 1 (type II diabetes not stated as uncontrolled). Manifestation codes for the diabetic neuropathy and diabetic nephropathy are assigned as secondary diagnoses. According to *Coding Clinic* (2005, 1Q:43–45), V58.67 is reported for type II patients who routinely use insulin.

Documentation states "He has been on 70/30 insulin, 25 units in the morning and 15 units in the evening." A physician query may be appropriate to determine if the hypoglycemia is due to chemotherapy treatment based on the documentation "One difficulty here is the cyclic nature of his chemo treatment regimen, likely to produce major shifts in his glucose, which is already difficult to control. Patient will need to monitor his glucose levels closely." See instructional note under 250.8x "Use Additional E code to identify cause if drug induced." If physician response to the query is that the chemotherapy is the cause of the hypoglycemia, then add E933.1. If not, then do not assign the E code. The patient has previously had surgery for the lung cancer; however, the cancer is still under treatment so the V code for "history of" is not appropriate and the cancer code of 162.9 is reported. Hyperlipidemia is not reported as it was not evaluated or treated in the hospital and did not meet reporting guidelines for additional diagnoses. See *ICD-9-CM Official Guidelines for Coding and Reporting* and *Coding Clinic* (2006, 4Q:234–235). All diagnoses codes are present on admission and require POA indicator of Y (yes); except V58.67. No POA indicator is assigned as category V58 if listed on the POA Exempt list.

Procedures: No reportable procedure; medical treatment only.

Note: There is no documentation to indicate that chemotherapy (99.25) was administered during this inpatient hospitalization.

Issues to clarify: The coding professional is advised to review the health record on this case to verify that physician documentation is consistent and supports the assignment of the fifth digit for uncontrolled diabetes. If there is any uncertainty, the physician should be queried for clarification.

7.16.   Principal diagnosis: Diabetes with ketoacidosis, type I, 250.13-Y
Additional diagnoses:

   Dehydration, 276.51-Y

   Congestive heart failure, 428.0-Y

   Aortic valve disorder, 424.1-Y

   Urinary tract infection, 599.0-Y

   E. coli infection, 041.4-Y

   Hyperkalemia, 276.7-Y

   Peripheral vascular disease, 443.9-Y

   Hypertension, 401.9-Y

   Hyperlipidemia, 272.4-Y

   Renal ureteral disease, 593.9-Y

   Old myocardial infarction, 412-Y

   Tobacco use, 305.1-Y

   Coronary artery disease, 414.01-Y

Issues to clarify: According to *Coding Clinic* (2Q, 2006), "Diabetic ketoacidosis is by definition uncontrolled and code 250.13 is the default."

Disorders of the Genitourinary System

7.17.   Principal diagnosis: Bleeding, postmenopausal, 627.1-Y
Additional diagnoses:

   Anemia due to blood loss, 280.0-Y

   Long-term current use of anticoagulants, V58.61 (exempt)

   Status heart valve, V43.3 (exempt)

Procedures:

   Endometrial ablation; Dilation and curettage, 68.23

   Transfusion packed cells, 99.04

Issues to clarify: Query the physician with regards to the anemia in order to select the best code for the patient's condition. Per *Coding Clinic* (1993, 4Q:3), if the physician clearly documents the anemia is due to acute blood loss, code 285.1 should be assigned. Anemia due to chronic blood loss is coded to 280.0 Secondary to blood loss (chronic). The physician should always be queried if there is a lack of sufficient documentation.

Note: History of present illness states "bleeding after being menopausal for approximately one year." The endometrial biopsy was performed prior to admission. The code for the endometrial ablation includes D&C.

Optional MS-DRG Exercise (for users with access to MS-DRG software or tables)

> MS-DRG assignment with the acute blood loss anemia code: MS-DRG 742 - UTERINE & ADNEXA PROC FOR NON-MALIGNANCY W CC/MCC
>
> MS-DRG assignment with anemia due to blood loss code: MS-DRG 743 - UTERINE & ADNEXA PROC FOR NON-MALIGNANCY W/O CC/MCC
>
> MS-DRG appropriate for this case: MS-DRG 743

7.18. Note: *Official Coding Guidelines* state: "If the diagnosis documented at the time of discharge is qualified as "probable", "suspected", "likely", "questionable", "possible", or "still to be ruled out", or other similar terms indicating uncertainty, code the condition as if it existed or was established."

Principal diagnosis: Probable urosepsis with streptococcal bacteremia, 599.0-Y, 041.03-Y

Note: According to *Coding Clinic* 2003, 4Q:79–81 Bacteremia is defined as the presence of bacteria in the blood.

Additional diagnoses:

> Left lower extremity cellulitis, 682.6-Y
>
> Status post acute renal failure likely secondary to acute tubular necrosis, 584.5-Y
>
> Insulin requiring diabetes mellitus, 250.00-Y, V58.67 (exempt)
>
> Probable chronic obstructive pulmonary disease, 496-Y
>
> Hypothyroidism, 244.Y
>
> Hypertension, 401.9-Y
>
> Probable iron deficiency anemia, 280.9-Y

Procedures: Doppler ultrasound of the left lower extremity which showed no evidence of DVT, 88.77

Issues to clarify: The physician should be queried to determine if a code should be assigned for the pulmonary edema and, if so, whether it is acute (of cardiac origin or not) or chronic (*Coding Clinic* 1988, 4Q:3–5).

7.19. a. 996.81, 586, 55.53, 55.69, 39.95 × 2

Correct answer.

b. 586, 996.81, 55.69, 39.95 × 2

Incorrect answer. The complication of the transplanted organ is reported as the principal diagnosis in accordance with the *ICD-9-CM Official Guidelines for Coding and Reporting* and *Coding Clinic* (2006, 4Q:231–232) that states "When the admission is for treatment of a complication resulting from surgery or other medical care, the complication code is sequenced as the principal diagnosis." Removal of the previously transplanted or rejected kidney is reported.

c. 586, V42.0, 55.53, 55.69, 39.95

Incorrect answer. Code V42.0 is used only to report transplant organ status when there are no complications. In this, case the principal diagnosis is the complication of the transplanted organ (996.81). Dialysis was done before and after surgery, therefore, it would be reported twice.

d. 584.9, V42.0, 55.69, 39.95

Incorrect answer. Coding is based on physician documentation and there is no documentation of "acute" renal failure (584.9); therefore, renal failure unspecified (586) is coded to report the renal failure. Code V42.0 is used to report transplant organ status when there are no complications. In this case, the first-listed code should be complication of the transplanted organ (996.81). Removal of the previously transplanted or rejected kidney is reported. Dialysis was done before and after surgery, therefore, it would be reported twice.

7.20   a. 584.9, 428.0, 496, 345.90, 459.81, 721.90, 715.89, 278.01, 275.49, 712.37, 401.9

Correct answer.

b. 403.90, 584.9, 428.0, 496, 345.90, 459.81, 721.90, 715.89, 278.01, 275.49, 712.37

Incorrect answer. The category 403 may only be used in instances of chronic kidney disease. This patient has acute renal failure and hypertension, which are not classified to category 403. Hypertension must be coded separately.

c. 586, 428.0, 496, 345.90, 459.81, 721.90, 715.89, 278.01, 275.49, 712.37

Incorrect answer. The renal failure is specified as acute. The patient has a history of hypertension and is currently on medication for hypertension, so this should be coded.

d. 404.90, 584.9, 428.0, 496, 345.90, 459.81, 721.90, 715.89, 278.01, 275.49, 712.37

Incorrect answer. There is not an assumed causal relationship between hypertension and congestive heart failure nor is there a relationship between acute renal failure and hypertension.

Issue to clarify: Is the renal failure also chronic as noted in chief complaint since it's not documented anywhere else?

Optional MS-DRG Exercise (for users with access to MS-DRG software or tables)

False: The MS-DRG for this admission is 684, Renal Failure without CC/MCC.

Infectious Diseases

7.21. Principal diagnosis: Septicemia due to E. coli, 038.42-Y

Additional diagnoses:

> UTI, 599.0-Y
>
> Group D strep, 041.04-Y
>
> Renal insufficiency, 593.9-Y
>
> Chronic obstructive lung disease, 496-Y
>
> Previous CVA with residual of hemiplegia, 438.20
>
> Previous CVA with aphasia, 438.11

Issues to clarify: According to *Coding Clinic* (2003, 4Q:79–81) and *Coding Clinic* (2006, 4Q:154–160), septicemia is often used interchangeably by physicians. However, the term septicemia and sepsis are no longer synonymous. A query is appropriate for this record. The physician should also be queried to confirm if the E. coli as well as Group D strep were causative agents for the UTI. During the course of stay in the hospital, the patient underwent "fluid rehydration." The coding professional may want to initiate a separate query to the physician to determine if dehydration meets secondary diagnosis reporting. The EKG showed sinus tachycardia; unless the physician indicates this is a significant finding, it would not be coded. The patient is on tube feedings; therefore, review the remainder of the health record to determine if the patient has a gastrostomy (V44.1).

Optional MS-DRG Exercise (for users with access to MS-DRG software or tables)

> The MS-DRG assignment is 872 Septicemia without Mechanical Ventilation 96+Hours without MCC.

7.22.   a. 042, 136.3, 276.2, 581.89, 585.9, 280.0, 305.61, 305.51, 455.5, 305.1, 33.24, 99.04

Correct answer.

b. 042, 136.3, 276.2, 581.89, 585.9, 280.0, 455.5, 33.24, 99.04

Incorrect answer. The heroin, cocaine, and tobacco abuse should be assigned codes to describe these additional conditions.

c. 042, 136.3, 581.89, 585.9, 280.0, 305.61, 305.51, 305.1, 33.24, 99.04

Incorrect answer. The metabolic acidosis and bleeding external hemorrhoids should be assigned codes to describe these additional conditions.

d. 136.3, 042, 581.89, 585.9, 280.0, 305.61, 305.51, 305.1, 33.24, 99.04

The principal diagnosis is AIDS, 042. In accordance with *ICD-9-CM Official Guidelines for Coding and Reporting* and *Coding Clinic* (2006, 4Q:152), report code 042 as the principal diagnosis when a patient is admitted for an HIV-related condition. The HIV-related conditions are reported as secondary diagnoses. The metabolic acidosis and bleeding external hemorrhoids should be assigned codes to describe these additional conditions.

7.23. a. 523.10, 054.9, 745.4, 446.1, 034.0

Incorrect answer. There is a combination code for the herpetic gingivostomatitis.

b. 054.2, 745.4, 034.0, 446.1, 785.6, 372.30, 782.1

Incorrect answer. Kawasaki's disease includes the lymphadenopathy, conjunctivitis, and rash, so these would not be coded separately.

c. 054.2, 745.4, 446.1, 034.0

Correct answer.

d. 054.2, 446.1, 034.0

Incorrect answer. The ventriculoseptal defect (VSD) should also be coded.

7.24. a. 038.9, 995.91, 599.0, 434.11, 394.1, 397.0, 398.91, 427.31, 287.5, 285.9

Incorrect answer. Because organ dysfunction (renal failure) is present with the sepsis, 995.92 is reported as Severe Sepsis.

b. 995.91, 599.0, 586, 434.11, 424.0, 397.0, 428.0, 427.31, 287.5, 285.9

Incorrect answer. 038.9 is reported as the principal diagnosis per Excludes note under 995.91 that instructs coder to Code First underlying infection (038.9). Because organ dysfunction (renal failure) is present with the sepsis, 995.92 is reported as Severe Sepsis. The congestive heart failure is presumed to be rheumatic in nature per *Coding Clinic* (1995, 1Q:6) when mitral valve and aortic valve insufficiency is present with congestive heart failure. ICD-9-CM classifies the congestive heart failure as rheumatic 398.91.

c. 038.9, 995.92, 599.0, 586, 434.11, 396.3, 397.0, 398.91, 427.31, 287.5, 285.9

Correct answer.

d. 434.11, 038.9, 995.92, 586, 428.0, 424.0, 397.0, 427.31, 287.5, 285.9

Incorrect answer. Sepsis is the reason the patient was admitted to the facility. The code 599.0 for urinary tract infection meets additional diagnosis reporting. Per *Coding Clinic* (1995, 1Q:6), the congestive heart failure is presumed to be rheumatic in nature when mitral valve and aortic value insufficiency is present with congestive heart failure. ICD-9-CM classifies the congestive heart failure as rheumatic 398.91.

Optional MS-DRG Exercise (for users with access to MS-DRG software or tables)

a. 064, Intracranial Hemorrhage or Cerebral Infarction with MCC

Incorrect answer as the patient's cerebral infarct developed after admission.

b. 871, Septicemia without mechanical ventilation 96+hours with MCC

Correct answer.

c. 872, Septicemia without mechanical ventilation 96+hours without MCC
Incorrect answer as a MCC is present (434.11).

d. 868, Other Infectious and Parasitic Disease Diagnoses with CC
Incorrect answer as the correct diagnoses codes group to MS-DRG 871.

7.25. Principal diagnoses:

038.42-Y Escherichia coli sepsis (either this or 038.11 may be principal diagnosis)

038.11-Y Staphylococcus aureus sepsis (either this or 038.42 may be principal diagnosis)

Secondary Diagnoses:

995.91 Sepsis

599.0-Y Urinary tract infection

294.8-Y Dementia

244.9-Y Hypothyroidism

401.9-Y Hypertension

263.9-Y Protein calorie malnutrition

787.20-Y Dysphagia

Behavioral Health Conditions

7.26. a. 296.24, V62.84, 94.27, 94.22, 94.08
Correct answer.

b. 296.23, V62.84, 94.27, 94.22, 94.08
Incorrect answer. The admitting diagnosis specified the major depressive disorder as with psychotic features, therefore, 5th digit of 3 (without psychotic features) is incorrect.

c. 296.24, V62.84, 427.9, 94.26, 94.22, 94.08
Incorrect answer. The cardiac arrhythmia may be an incidental symptom or a complication that should be reported. The physician may be queried for clinical significance and impact to the patient's care. ECT is coded 94.27.

d. 296.23, V62.84, 997.1, 427.9, 94.27, 94.22, 94.08
Incorrect answer. The admitting diagnosis specified the major depressive disorder as with psychotic features, therefore, 5th digit of 3 (without psychotic features) is incorrect. The cardiac arrhythmia may be an incidental symptom or a complication that should be reported. The physician may be queried for clinical significance and impact to the patient's care.

7.27. a. 295.34, 425.4, 401.9, 496, 250.01, 94.25

Incorrect answer. Alphabetical index: Cardiomyopathy, due to, hypertension—see Hypertension with heart involvement. A combination code exists for cardiomyopathy due to hypertension; code 402.90 is reported rather than 425.4 and 401.9. The diabetes is specified as type 2, therefore, the 5th digit of 1 (type I) is incorrect.

b. 295.32, 402.90, 496, 250.01, 94.25

Incorrect answer. The correct fifth digit for schizophrenia is 4 as the physician documented chronic with acute exacerbation. The diabetes is specified as type 2, therefore, the 5th digit of 1 (type I) is incorrect.

c. 295.34, 402.90, 496, 250.00, 94.25

Correct answer.

d. 295.84, 402.90, 496, 250.00, 94.25

Incorrect answer. The schizophrenia was specified as paranoid type, which is coded to subcategory 295.3.

7.28. a. 969.72, 785.0, 304.40, E950.3, 980.0, 303.00, E950.9, 314.01, 312.00

Correct answer. In real practice, the coding professional would review the consultation report and other relevant documentation in the health record for confirmation of the ADHD, aggressive behavior, or other applicable psychiatric diagnoses. The coding professional may also want to query the physician to determine if the diagnosis of dehydration is applicable.

b. 785.0, E939.7, 305.90, 314.01, 312.00

Incorrect answer. The coding guidelines for a poisoning, rather than adverse effect, should be followed. The amphetamine poisoning and drug dependence should be coded. Any time alcohol is involved with another drug, it is coded as a poisoning. The alcohol code is incorrect; when there is documentation of drug dependence, drug abuse codes are not used.

c. 969.72, 785.0, 304.00, E980.3, 303.00, 314.01, 312.00

Incorrect answer. The E code for suicide attempt should be assigned. Any time alcohol is involved with another drug, it is coded as a poisoning. The drug the patient was dependent on was amphetamines.

d. 785.0, 303.00, 304.40, 969.72, E950.3, 980.0, E950.9, 314.01, 312.00

Incorrect answer. The poisoning codes are incorrectly sequenced as a secondary diagnoses.

Disorders of the Musculoskeletal System and Connective Tissue

7.29. a. 816.01, 813.18, 79.24, 79.22

Incorrect answer. Per *Coding Clinic* (2003, 4Q:76–78), crush injury should be sequenced first. Fractures were open, not closed. Reductions were open, not closed. Code the suture of the tendon, also.

b. 816.01, 813.08, 79.34, 79.32, 82.45

Incorrect answer. Per *Coding Clinic* (2003, 4Q:76–78), crush injury should be sequenced first. Fractures were open, not closed.

c. 927.3, 816.11, 813.18, 79.24, 79.22, 82.45

Incorrect answer. Reductions were open, not closed.

d. 927.3, 816.11, 813.18, 79.34, 79.32, 82.45

Correct answer.

Optional MS-DRG Exercise (for users with access to MS-DRG software or tables)

906, Hand Procedures for Injuries
MS-DRG belongs to MDC 21

7.30. a. 806.00, E819.9, 344.61, 599.0, 787.20, 604.90, 041.7, 81.01, 93.41, 02.94

Incorrect answer. The C7 fracture specifies the spinal cord involvement as both central and ventral (anterior). There is also a C1 fracture that should be reported. The halo device was placed at another facility, there is no documentation to support that the device was placed or reinserted at this facility. In practice, the coding professional would analyze the remainder of the health record and/or query the physician to verify this.

b. 806.09, 805.01, E819.9, 344.61, 599.0, 604.90, 81.01, 93.41, 02.94

Incorrect answer. Ventral is the same as anterior, so the C7 fracture with central and ventral spinal cord defects is coded 806.08 and 806.07. The patient received therapy for difficulty swallowing; this should be coded (787.20). The pseudomonas should also be coded (041.7). The halo device was placed at another facility, there is no documentation to support that the device was placed or reinserted at this facility. In practice, the coding professional would analyze the remainder of the health record and/or query the physician to verify this.

c. 806.08, 805.01, E819.9, 344.61, 599.0, 787.20, 604.90, 041.7, 81.00, 93.42

Incorrect answer. The fracture at C7 involves injury of the spinal cord both central (806.08) and ventral (that is, anterior 806.07). The spinal fusion is specified as posterior C1–C2 (81.01). Spinal traction was via a halo device (93.41).

d. 806.08, 806.07, 805.01, E819.9, 344.61, 599.0, 787.20, 604.90, 041.7, 81.01, 93.41

Correct answer. The patient had two cervical fractures: one at C7 involving both central and ventral (that is, anterior) spinal cord injury; the other was an odontoid fracture at C1 with no mention of spinal cord injury at this level.

7.31.   a. 812.52, 401.9, 250.01, 79.32

Incorrect answer. The diagnosis code is for an open fracture, which is not described here. The hypertension should be specified as malignant. The procedure code is not specific to the humeral condyle.

b. 812.42, 401.0, 250.01, 79.31

Correct answer.

c. 812.42, 401.0, 250.01, 78.52

Incorrect answer. The procedure code is for internal fixation without fracture reduction. In this case, a fracture was manually reduced.

d. 812.52, 401.9, 250.00, 79.32

Incorrect answer. The diagnosis code is for an open fracture, which is not described here. The hypertension should be specified as malignant. The diabetes should be specified as type 1. The procedure code is not specific to the humeral condyle.

7.32.   Principal diagnosis: 722.10-Y

Additional diagnoses: 338.18-N, 998.2-N, 722.52-Y, E870.0-N

Procedures: 80.51, 78.59

Note: Displacement of L5-S1 intervertebral disc meeting reporting guidelines for principal diagnosis. The acute pain documented as occurring after surgery and the laceration during surgery meeting reporting guidelines for secondary diagnoses along with the degenerative lumbar disc disease. For diagnoses 338.18, 998.2 and E870.0, a POA indicator of N (no) is assigned as the pain occurred postoperatively and accidental laceration occurred during the procedure and was not present at the time of admission. Diagnoses 722.10 and 722.52 were present at the time of admission and assigned POA indicator of Y (yes).

Neoplasms

7.33.   a. 198.5, 733.13, 198.3, 198.82, 196.5, 185

Incorrect answer. The principal diagnosis is the pathological fracture. The primary prostate cancer is no longer under treatment; V10.46 is the appropriate code.

b. 198.3, 805.4, 198.5, 198.82, 196.5, V10.46

Incorrect answer. The principal diagnosis is the vertebral fracture, which is coded as a pathologic, nontraumatic fracture (733.13).

c. 805.4, 198.5, 198.3, 198.82, 196.5, 185

Incorrect answer. The vertebral fracture is coded as a pathologic, nontraumatic fracture (733.13). The primary prostate cancer is no longer under treatment; V10.46 is the appropriate code.

d. 733.13, 198.5, 198.3, 198.82, 196.5, V10.46

Correct answer.

Optional MS-DRG Exercise (for users with access to MS-DRG software or tables)

1. The principal diagnosis is defined in the Uniform Hospital Discharge Data Set as "that condition established after study to be chiefly responsible for occasioning the admission of the patient to the hospital for care." The principal diagnosis on this case is the pathological fracture of the L4 vertebrae (733.13).

2. The correct MS-DRG assignment is 543, Pathological Fractures & Musculoskeletal & Connective Tissue Malignancy with CC.

3. The MS-DRG assignment would change if a major complication or comorbid condition was present but would not change if additional complications/comorbidities were present.

7.34.   Principal diagnosis: Adenocarcinoma of the lung, 162.9-Y

Additional diagnoses:

Acute (malignant) pericardial effusion, 420.90-Y *Coding Clinic* (1989, 2Q:12)

Chronic obstructive pulmonary disease, 496-Y

Former 50-pack/year smoker, V15.82

Procedures:

Pericardial window, 37.12

Transbronchial biopsy, 33.27

Percutaneous drainage of pericardial fluid, 37.0

Administration of chemotherapy, 99.25

Note: All diagnosis codes assigned POA indicator of Y (yes) except for V15.82 as category V15 is on the POA Exempt List.

Issues to clarify: The coding professional should check the rest of the health record, and perhaps query the physician, to determine if the carcinoma is identified in a specific site of the lung.

Optional MS-DRG Exercise (for users with access to MS-DRG software or tables)

a. 164, Major chest procedures with CC

Correct answer.

b. 167, Other respiratory system OR procedures with CC

Incorrect answer. Without the pericardial window procedure (code 37.12), the case would be assigned to MS-DRG 167. However, this procedure was done, which changes the MS-DRG assignment to 164.

c. 163, Major chest procedures with MCC

Incorrect answer. The diagnosis codes on this case would group to MS-DRG 164 as a major complication or comorbid condition is not present.

d. 181, Respiratory neoplasms with CC

Incorrect answer. The diagnosis codes group to this MS-DRG; however procedures were performed.

7.35. a. 233.0, 491.9, 401.9, 85.41, 40.23, 85.12

Incorrect answer. The bronchitis is described as chronic obstructive bronchitis and the patient has a history of COPD, so code 491.20 is more accurate than 491.9. Smoker and chronic alcohol dependence meet reporting guidelines as secondary diagnoses. There is a combination code for a simple mastectomy with lymph node dissection (85.43). From the documentation in this report, it appears that a local excision of the lesion of the right breast was done (85.21) rather than an open biopsy (85.12). The coding professional should check the procedure report to verify which code is correct.

b. 174.9, 491.20, 401.9, 305.1, 303.90, 85.43, 85.21

Incorrect answer. The carcinoma is specified as in situ (coded 233.1).

c. 233.0, 491.20, 401.9, 305.1, 303.90, 85.43, 85.21

Correct answer.

d. 174.9, 491.9, 401.9, 85.41, 40.23, 85.21

Incorrect answer. The carcinoma is specified as in situ (coded 233.1). The bronchitis is described as chronic obstructive bronchitis and the patient has a history of COPD, so code 491.20 is more accurate than 491.9. Smoker and chronic alcohol dependence meet reporting guidelines as secondary diagnoses. There is a combination code for a simple mastectomy with lymph node dissection (85.43).

7.36. Principal diagnosis: Pathological fracture L2, 733.13-Y

Additional diagnoses:

Metastasis to the bone, 198.5-Y

Metastasis to the lung, 197.0-Y

Metastasis left celiac ganglion node plexus, 198.89-Y

History of primary colon cancer, V10.05

Cord compression from underlying neoplastic disease, 336.3-Y

UTI, 599.0-Y

Pseudomonas aeruginosa, 041.7-Y

Hypertension, 401.9-Y

Colostomy from previous colon cancer surgery, V44.3

Procedures:

Anterior allograft bone fusion at L2, 81.06

L2 laminectomy with decompression, 03.09

Physical therapy, 93.39

Note: All diagnoses assigned POA indicator Y (yes) except V10.05 and V44.3 as these codes are on the POA Exempt List; therefore, no indicator is attached.

7.37. a. 198.3, 189.0, 780.39, 414.01

Correct answer.

b. 780.39, 198.3, 189.0, 414.01

Incorrect answer. The seizures are a result of the metastatic brain cancer, therefore, the metastatic brain cancer should be the principal diagnosis.

c. 189.0, 198.3, 780.39, 414.01

Incorrect answer. This admission is directed at the metastatic brain cancer rather than the kidney carcinoma, therefore, the metastatic brain cancer should be the principal diagnosis.

d. 198.3, 189.0, 414.01

Incorrect answer. The patient is experiencing seizures due to the metastatic brain cancer, therefore, the seizure disorder should be coded as a secondary diagnosis.

Optional MS-DRG Exercise (for users with access to MS-DRG software or tables)

> 055, Nervous System Neoplasms without MCC
> MDC 1: Diseases and Disorders of the Nervous System (medical)

Disorders of the Nervous System and Sense Organs

7.38. Principal diagnosis: Transient vertigo versus posterior circulation transient ischemic attack. 780.4, 435.9

Note: Official Coding Guidelines for two or more comparative or contrasting conditions state "In those rare instances when two or more contrasting or comparative diagnoses are documented as "either/or" (or similar terminology), they are coded as if the diagnoses were confirmed and the diagnoses are sequenced according to the circumstances of the admission. If no further determination can be made as to which diagnosis should be principal, either diagnosis may be sequenced first."

Additional diagnoses:

> Noninsulin dependent diabetes, 250.00
> Coronary artery disease status post coronary bypass grafting, 414.00
> Hyperlipidemia, 272.4
> Smoker, 305.1
> Past MI, 412
> Hypertension, 401.9
> Old lacunar infarct—V12.54

Note: According to *Coding Clinic* (1997, 3Q:15), assign 414.00 when a patient has coronary artery disease and has had a previous CABG. Code 414.05 would be used if the physician confirmed that CAD had developed over the previous bypass graft. As stated in Coding Clinic (1994, 4Q:49), CAD of bypass graft should not be assigned based solely on the fact that the patient has atherosclerosis and has a history of bypass surgery.

Issues to clarify: ER note lists mild neuropathy secondary to his diabetes mellitus. The physician should be queried if the full record does not provide further substantiation of this diagnosis.

7.39.   a. 722.52, 721.3, 724.02, 724.4, 414.00, 401.9, V45.81, V45.82, 03.92, 99.23, 88.91

Incorrect answer. The codes from category 724 should not be reported. Per *Coding Clinic* (1989, 2Q:14), pain or neuritis due to spondylosis or intervertebral disc disorder is included in the 721–722 categories. Spinal stenosis due to degeneration (arthritic) of the intervertebral disc is classified to the 722 category. Review excludes notes.

b. 724.4, 414.00, 401.9, V45.81, V45.82, 03.92, 99.23, 88.91

Incorrect answer. Degenerative disc disease is the principal diagnosis and is coded 722.52. The lumbar arthropathy should also be reported, 721.3. Lumbar radiculopathy (724.4) is included in the codes in category 722–721. See *Coding Clinic* reference and rationale above.

c. 722.52, 721.3, 414.00, 401.9, V45.81, V45.82, 03.92, 99.23, 88.91

Correct answer.

d. 722.52, 721.3, 414.00, 401.9, V45.81, V45.82, 03.91, 88.91

Incorrect answer. The procedure code for lumbar epidural steroid injection is 03.92 and 99.23.

Optional MS-DRG Exercise (for users with access to MS-DRG software or tables)

a. True

b. False. The correct MS-DRG assignment is 552, medical back problems without MCC.

c. False. MS-DRG assignment is the same with or without this procedure code.

d. False. MS-DRG 552, medical back problems without MCC, is in MDC 8, diseases and disorders of the musculoskeletal system and connective tissue.

Newborn/Congenital Disorders

7.40.   a. 771.2, 041.09

Incorrect answer. This is not a specific umbilical cord infection code. Staphylococcus aureus should also be coded.

b. 686.9, 041.11, 041.09

Incorrect answer. This code, 686.9, is for omphalitis, but not of a newborn.

c. 771.4

Incorrect answer. The organisms identified in the culture would be separately coded.

d. 771.4, 041.11, 041.09

Correct answer.

7.41. a. 770.6, V30.10, V50.2, 96.04

Incorrect answer. The birth code should be the principal diagnosis code, and the fifth digit of 0 only applies to V30.0. The correct code is V30.1. There is no documentation to indicate the baby was intubated. Manual resuscitation (93.93) and oxygen therapy (93.96) should be coded. The circumcision should also be coded.

b. V30.1, 770.6, V50.2, 64.0, 93.93, 93.96
Correct answer.

c. V30.1, 769, V50.2, 64.0, 96.04

Incorrect answer. Because the chest x-ray stated wet lungs and the patient was only in NICU for about one day, the code 770.6 for wet lung syndrome is more appropriate than the 769 code for respiratory distress syndrome. There is no documentation to indicate the baby was intubated. Manual resuscitation (93.93) and oxygen therapy (93.96) should be coded.

d. V30.10, 768.6, V50.2, 64.0, 96.05, 93.96

Incorrect answer. The correct birth code is V30.1 as the fifth digit only applies to V30.0. Code 768.6 is incorrect as there is no mention of asphyxia at the time of birth. Documentation does not support intubation, only resuscitation (93.93).

Optional MS-DRG Exercise (for users with access to MS-DRG software or tables)

a. Complication or Comorbid condition
Incorrect answer as this MS-DRG is not subdivided based upon a CC.

b. Major complication or comorbid condition
Incorrect answer as this MS-DRG is not subdivided based upon a MCC.

c. Procedure code
Incorrect answer as this MS-DRG is not subdivided based upon a procedure.

d. Other significant problems
Correct answer, other significant problems also drive this MS-DRG assignment.

7.42. a. 747.0, 765.10, 765.27, 38.85

Incorrect answer. Codes in category 765 are assigned for conditions arising in the perinatal period. The includes note at category 765 also indicates that the listed conditions are reported in a fetus or newborn. The codes are not applicable on this three-year-old's admission.

b. 745.9, 35.39

Incorrect answer. Patent ductus arteriosus is a specific congenital anomaly that is reported with code 747.0. Procedure code 38.85 is a more specific code to reflect the procedure described.

c. 747.0, 38.85

Correct answer.

d. 745.0, 38.85

Incorrect answer. The patient's condition is specified as patent ductus arteriosus (747.0).

7.43.   a. 996.75, 741.03, 02.42

Correct answer.

b. 996.2, 741.03, 02.41, 02.42

Incorrect answer. This is not a mechanical complication; the shunt is occluded. Code 996.75 is more appropriate. The irrigation was unsuccessful; therefore, it is not coded.

c. 741.03, V45.2, 02.42, 02.43

Incorrect answer. The plugged shunt is the reason for admission and should be coded and sequenced first (996.75). V45.2 reflects status only and is not used, as there is a complication present. Removal of the old shunt is assumed in the replacement code and does not need to be coded separately, so the 02.43 code is not needed.

d. 996.75, 742.3, 741.00, 02.42

Incorrect answer. The spina bifida can be classified at the lumbar region because the physician states that the defect is at the bottom of her spine. The hydrocephalus is included in code 741.0x and would not be separately reported.

Pediatric Conditions

7.44.   a. 752.61, 550.91, 752.69, 58.49, 53.02, 64.0, 57.94

Incorrect answer. The hernia is not specified as recurrent, so a fifth digit of 0 should be used (550.90). Redundant preputial tissue is coded 605. Hypospadias repair is coded 58.45. Excision of the nevus is also reported (222.1, 64.2).

b. 752.61, 605, 550.90, 239.5, 58.47, 53.01, 64.2, 57.94

Incorrect answer. A nevus is coded as a benign neoplasm of the skin (222.1). In real practice, the coding professional would, of course, confirm this by checking the pathology report. Hypospadias repair is coded 58.45. This is an indirect hernia (determined because descriptions of the hernia sac, external oblique, and inguinal ring are mentioned. A direct hernia would be between the inferior epigastric artery and the edge of the rectus muscle.) Code 53.02 is reported. The circumcision is also reported, 64.0.

c. 752.61, 550.91, 752.69, 58.49, 53.00, 57.94

Incorrect answer. The hernia is not specified as recurrent, so a fifth digit of 0 should be used (550.90). Redundant preputial tissue is coded 605.

Excision of the nevus is also reported (222.1, 64.2). Hypospadias repair is coded 58.45. This is an indirect hernia (determined because descriptions of the hernia sac, external oblique, and inguinal ring are mentioned. A direct hernia would be between the inferior epigastric artery and the edge of the rectus muscle.) Code 53.02 is reported. The circumcision is also reported, 64.0.

d. 752.61, 605, 550.90, 222.1, 58.45, 53.02, 64.0, 64.2, 57.94
Correct answer.

7.45. a. 170.4, 758.0, 77.41

Incorrect answer. A vascular access device is implanted, 86.07.

b. 170.4, 170.3, 170.2, 77.81

Incorrect answer. The bone scan showed some questionable areas, but the physician does not document a diagnosis of sarcoma of the ribs and vertebra. The physician would have to be queried before these additional diagnosis codes could be added. The biopsy is not specified as excisional; code 77.41 is correct. Down syndrome is also reported, 758.0. A vascular access device is implanted, 86.07.

c. 170.4, 758.0, 77.61, 86.07

Incorrect answer. The biopsy is not specified as excisional, so code 77.41 is correct.

d. 170.4, 758.0, 77.41, 86.07
Correct answer.

Optional MS-DRG Exercise (for users with access to MS-DRG software or tables)

a. 517, Other musculoskeletal system and connective tissue OR procedure without CC/MCC

Incorrect answer as the procedure code is 77.41.

b. 497, Local excision and removal internal fixation devices except hip and femur without CC/MCC

Incorrect answer as the procedure code is 77.41

c. 479, Biopsies of musculoskeletal system and connective tissue without CC/MCC
Correct answer.

d. 477, Biopsies of musculoskeletal system and connective tissue with MCC

Incorrect answer as neither a CC nor MCC are present on this admission.

Conditions of Pregnancy, Childbirth, and the Puerperium

7.46. Principal diagnosis: Occiput posterior position, 660.31, 652.81

Additional diagnoses:

Arrest of descent, 661.11

Premature rupture of membranes, 658.11

Failed attempt at vaginal birth after C-section, 659.11

Previous cesarean section, 654.21

Positive group B strep, 648.91, V02.51

Delivery of a live infant, V27.0

Note: According to *Coding Clinic* (2006, 3Q:14), Assign code 648.9X, Other current conditions in the mother, classifiable elsewhere, but complicating pregnancy, childbirth, or the puerperium, and code V02.51, Carrier or suspected carrier of infectious diseases, Group B streptococcus, to identify group B strep carriers in pregnancy.

Procedures:

Low transverse cesarean delivery, 74.1

Pitocin for induction of labor, 73.4

7.47. a. 648.83, V58.67, 73.4

Incorrect answer. The patient was not induced this episode.

b. 648.81, V58.67, 73.01

Incorrect answer. The patient was not induced and did not deliver in this episode.

c. 648.83, V58.67

Correct answer.

d. 659.13, 648.83

Incorrect answer. The patient was not induced in this episode.

Optional MS-DRG Exercise (for users with access to MS-DRG software or tables)

781, Other Antepartum Diagnoses with Medical Complications

7.48. Diagnoses:

Prolonged first stage, 662.01-Y

Fourth-degree laceration, 664.31-N

Postpartum anemia, 648.22-N, 285.9-N

Maternal exhaustion, 669.81-Y

Single liveborn infant, V27.0 (exempt list)

Procedures:

Vacuum extraction with episiotomy, 72.71

Repair of fourth-degree laceration, 75.62

7.49. Principal diagnosis: Long labor, prolonged 2nd stage, delivered, 662.21-N

Additional diagnoses:

Problem amniotic membrane delayed delivery after AROM, 658.31-N

Septic thrombophlebitis, PP, delivered w/ PP comp, 670.32-N

Endomyometritis , delivered w/ PP comp, 670.12-N

Anemia, delivered w/ postpartum complication, 648.22-N, 285.9-N

Obstetrical surgery, delivered w/ PP complication, 669.42-N

Ileus, 560.1-N

Comp of L&D, delivered w/ postpartum complication, 669.82-N

Hypokalemia, 276.8-N

Comp obstetrical surgical wounds, del w/ PP comp, 674.32-N

Outcome of delivery, single liveborn, V27.0 (exempt list)

Procedures: 74.0, 73.09

Disorders of the Respiratory System

7.50. Principal diagnosis: Acute respiratory failure, 518.81-Y

Additional diagnoses:

Asthma with COPD and acute exacerbation, 493.22-Y

Metabolic alkalosis, 276.3-N

Gram-negative herpetic tracheobronchitis, 054.79-N

Acute cholecystitis and cholelithiasis, 574.00-N

Anemia due to GI bleed from undetermined cause, 280.0-N, 578.9-N

Maxillary and ethmoidal sinusitis, 473.0-N, 473.2-N

Pneumothorax, 512.0-N

Premature atrial contractions, 427.61-N

Cystadenofibroma right ovary, 236.2-N

Hypokalemia, 276.8-N

Note: Tracheobronchitis is categorized in code category 466, which would not be reported with asthma; instead, the fifth digit of 2 is assigned on the asthma code. The pneumothorax is further specified as a tension pneumothorax. Cystadenofibroma is specified as borderline malignancy. This is indexed under Cystadenofibroma, endometrioid, borderline malignancy.

Procedures:

Mechanical ventilation, 96.72

Intubation, 96.04

Tracheostomy, 31.1

Fiberoptic bronchoscopy × , 33.22

Cholecystectomy, 51.22

Cholangiogram, 87.53

Bilateral salpingo-oophorectomy, 65.61

Omental biopsy, 54.23

Thoracentesis, 34.91

Chest tube, 34.04

Tube feedings, 96.6

Transfusion of packed red blood cells, 99.04

Note: Documentation indicates that the patient was ventilator dependent for a week or more, so the mechanical ventilation can be coded as continuous for 96 hours or more. An exploratory laparotomy was performed, so the cholecystectomy was an open procedure. The cholangiogram is intraoperative.

Optional MS-DRG Exercise (for users with access to MS-DRG software or tables)

003, ECMO or tracheostomy with mechanical ventilation 96+ hours or principal diagnosis except face, mouth, and neck with major OR

a. The principal diagnosis of acute respiratory failure

Incorrect answer. Assignment of MS-DRG 003 depends upon the patient having a tracheostomy and/or mechanical ventilation for 96+ hours and any diagnosis except mouth, larynx and pharynx disorders.

b. There was an extensive OR procedure unrelated to the principal diagnosis.

Incorrect answer. There are extensive OR procedures unrelated to the principal diagnosis, but MS-DRG assignment is related to the tracheostomy.

c. The fact that the patient had a tracheostomy has the greatest impact on MS-DRG assignment for this case.

Correct answer.

d. All of the above

Incorrect answer. Assignment of MS-DRG 003 depends upon the patient having a tracheostomy and/or mechanical ventilation for 96+ hours.

7.51. Principal diagnosis:

Pneumonia, due to Gram-negative bacteria, 482.83-Y

Additional diagnoses:

Acute respiratory failure, 518.81-N

Cardiac arrest, 427.5-N

Cryptococcal meningitis, 117.5-N [321.0-N]

Severely malnourished, 261-Y

Note: It is important that the coding professional confirm that the cryptococcal organism is causing the meningitis only and not systemic or a causative agent of the pneumonia. The pneumonia is coded differently if caused by the cryptococcus. Streptococcus A organism as well as Proteus mirabilis is mentioned on the culture from the bronchoalveolar lavage. The coding professional may want to query the physician to determine if this was also a causative agent of the pneumonia before assigning code 482.31. Results of the open lung biopsy showed advanced fibrosis. The coder should query the physician to determine if pulmonary fibrosis (515) should also be coded. The patient was rehydrated and treated for a low albumin, so the coder would also need physician input to assign codes for dehydration (276.51) and low albumin (273.8).

Procedures:

Open lung biopsy, 33.28

Continuous mechanical ventilation, 96.70

Intubation, 96.04

Bronchoalveolar lavage, 33.24

Spinal tap, 03.31

Note: The discharge summary does not indicate how long the patient was on continuous mechanical ventilation. The coding professional would check the ventilation flow sheet, or other source document within the health record, to determine how long the patient was on continuous ventilatory support in order to assign a more specific code.

Optional MS-DRG Exercise (for users with access to MS-DRG software or tables)

a. 163, Major Chest Procedure with MCC

Correct answer.

b. 853, Infectious and parasitic diseases with OR Procedure with MCC

Incorrect answer. Without further information from the physician, this case is assigned to MS-DRG 163. If the physician indicated that the pneumonia was due to a cryptococcal organism, then the principal diagnosis code would change, perhaps to 117.5 and the MS-DRG would likely be 853. From the information provided here, the cryptococcal organism appears to be causing the meningitis only.

c. 178, Respiratory infections and inflammations with CC

Incorrect answer. The MS-DRG is 163, based on the open lung biopsy.

d. MS-DRG 003, ECMO or Tracheostomy with Mechanical Ventilation 96+ Hours or Principal Diagnosis Except Face, Mouth and Neck with Major O.R.

Incorrect answer, MS-DRG assignment is based on the open lung biopsy and is unaffected by the length of time the patient was on continuous mechanical ventilation.

7.52. a. 482.89

Incorrect answer. The documentation states lobar pneumonia (481). The patient experienced episodes of tachycardia of unknown etiology (785.0).

b. 483.8, 427.2

Incorrect answer. The final impression is lobar pneumonia. The patient experienced episodes of tachycardia of unknown etiology (785.0).

c. 481, 785.0

Correct answer.

d. 482.9, 785.0

Incorrect answer. The documentation states lobar pneumonia (481).

7.53. Principal diagnosis: Acute respiratory failure, 518.81-Y

Additional diagnoses:

MRSA Pneumonia, 482.42-Y

Congestive heart failure, 428.0-Y

Cerebral vascular accident with infarction, 433.11-N

Acute renal failure, 584.9-N

Hemiplegia secondary to stroke, 342.90-N

Procedures:

Mechanical ventilation, 96.72

TPN, 99.15

Packed red blood cell transfusion, 99.04

Note: Per *ICD-9-CM Official Guidelines for Coding and Reporting* and *Coding Clinic* (4Q:178–179), the acute respiratory failure may be assigned as the principal diagnosis if it is responsible for occasioning the admission to the hospital, which it was in this particular case. The chart should be reviewed to determine the cause of the lung mass for a more specific code or if it is incidental to the patient's CHF or pneumonia. More information is needed to code the placement of the central venous line. The coding of transfusions is facility-specific and may not be coded at all hospitals. Do not assign a code from category V09 since code 482.42 includes information about the organism being resistant to Methicillin (ICD-9-CM Official Coding Guidelines). Per *Coding Clinic* (1998 4Q:87), code 342.90, Hemiplegia, unspecified may be assigned as additional diagnosis to identify the current neurologic deficits that resulted from the cerebral infarction. When codes from the 430-437 series are used, additional codes are needed to identify any sequelae present, such as category 342 for any associated hemiplegia.

Optional MS-DRG Exercise (for users with access to MS-DRG software or tables)

a. 189, Pulmonary Edema and Respiratory Failure

Incorrect answer. The principal diagnosis is Respiratory Failure and with the ventilator, the correct MS-DRG is 207, Respiratory System Diagnosis with Ventilator Support 96+ Hours.

b. 291, Heart Failure and Shock with MCC

Incorrect answer. The principal diagnosis is Respiratory Failure and with the ventilator, the correct MS-DRG is 207, Respiratory System Diagnosis with Ventilator Support 96+ Hours.

c. 207, Respiratory System Diagnosis with Ventilator Support 96+ Hours

Correct answer.

d. 064, Intracranial Hemorrhage or Cerebral Infarction with MCC

Incorrect answer. The principal diagnosis is Respiratory Failure and with the ventilator, the correct MS-DRG is 207, Respiratory System Diagnosis with Ventilator Support 96+ Hours.

7.54.   a. 466.0, 515, 428.0

Correct answer.

b. 491.22, 428.0

Incorrect answer. Pulmonary fibrosis is not considered to be COPD, therefore, the codes are reported separately.

c. 491.22, 466.0, 515, 428.0

Incorrect answer. Pulmonary fibrosis is not considered to be COPD, therefore, the codes are reported separately.

d. 428.0, 466.0, 515

Incorrect answer. Bronchitis is the reason for admission after study. The pneumonia was ruled out.

7.55.   Principal diagnosis: 486-Y, pneumonia

Note: Query physician for presence of respiratory failure at the time of admission based on the following documentation: Discharge diagnosis: respiratory failure. Admitted to the hospital for treatment of pneumonia and hypoxemia. Her pO_2 in the ER was 50 on room air. Quadriplegic affects her ability to breath and contributes to respiratory infections. ABG pH 7.482, pCO2 33, pO2 low at 50, HCO3 324 and total CO2 was 55. Her O2 sat was only 88% on room air. Do not code the respiratory failure without further clarification from the physician, as it clinically does not appear that the patient was in failure.

Secondary diagnoses:

276.51-Y dehydration

344.00-Y quadriplegia (Fifth digit of 0 unspecified as documentation does not state complete or incomplete)

596.4-Y atonic bladder

305.1-Y tobacco use

276.8-Y hypokalemia

799.02-Y hypoxemia

Note: According to *Coding Clinic* (2006, 2Q:24–25), it is appropriate to code hypoxemia along with pneumonia as it is not inherent to pneumonia and it indicates a deficient oxygenation of the blood. However, if the physician is queried for the presence of acute respiratory failure and the physician confirms this diagnosis, hypoxemia is not coded since it is inherent to respiratory failure.

7.56. What is the correct code assignment for this admission?

a. 493.91, 305.1, V07.4

Incorrect as the asthma and COPD is a combination code 493.22.

b. 466.0, 493.22, 305.1, V07.4

Incorrect as the acute bronchitis is included in the asthma and COPD combination code.

c. 493.22, 491.22. 305.1, V07.4

Correct answer.

d. 493.21

Incorrect because the patient was not admitted as an inpatient with status asthmaticus. Status asthmaticus (fifth digit of 1) is documented in the ER and patient initially admitted to observation. When the patient's condition did not resolve as an observation, the H&P documents acute exacerbation of asthma/chronic obstructive pulmonary disease/acute bronchitis (fifth digit of 2). See *Coding Clinic* (2006, 3Q:20). Codes for tobacco use and hormone replacement therapy meet additional diagnoses reporting guidelines.

7.57. 486-Y, 491.21-Y, V15.82-Y, 33.24

This patient was admitted primarily for post obstructive pneumonia according to the source document. The patient was admitted with an additional diagnosis of a lung mass, however, this is ruled out by bronchoscopy. The COPD is exacerbated as documented in discharge summary. The two conditions are reported separately even though the physician documents post obstructive pneumonia as a diagnosis. See *Coding Clinic* (1998, 1Q:8 and 1997, 3Q:9). All diagnoses were present on admission and therefore, a Y (yes) indicator is attached to each code.

Optional MS-DRG Exercise (for users with access to MS-DRG software or tables)

194, Simple Pneumonia and Pleurisy with CC _____

Trauma and Poisoning

7.58. a. 709.2, 909.1, E929.2

Incorrect answer. This is a late effect of a poisoning; however, there is a more specific code for scar of the trachea (478.9) and the late effect of a burn should also be assigned (906.8).

b. 478.9, 909.1, 906.8, E929.2

Correct answer.

c. 709.2, 909.5, 906.8, E864.2

Incorrect answer. This code sequence reflects an adverse effect, and this scenario represents a late effect of a poisoning. Also, there is a more specific code for scar of the trachea. (See scar, trachea, in the Alphabetic Index.)

d. 478.9, 909.5, E864.2

Incorrect answer. This code sequence reflects an adverse effect, and this scenario represents a late effect of a poisoning. You'll notice in trying to assign the E code for an adverse effect of drain cleaner there is no code in the therapeutic use column of the table of drugs and chemicals. If there is no therapeutic use of a drug/chemical, there cannot be an adverse effect.

Optional MS-DRG Exercise (for users with access to MS-DRG software or tables)

153, Otitis Media and Upper Respiratory Infection without MCC

7.59. a. 804.45, E815.2, E849.5 96.72

Incorrect answer. The skull is the only bone fractured, so code category 804 is not applicable. The skull fractures are reported by site (temporal bone, orbital roof, and zygomatic arch). The friction burns are also reported. Also, additional procedures are coded, endotracheal intubation and monitoring of intracranial pressure.

b. 803.45, 919.0, E815.2, E849.5 96.72, 96.04

Incorrect answer. More specific skull fractures are reported for the temporal bone and orbital roof (category 801) and the zygomatic arch (category 802). Monitoring of intracranial pressure is also reported (01.18).

c. 801.05, 802.85, 802.45, E815.2, E849.5, 96.72, 96.04, 01.18

Incorrect answer. The temporal bone fracture should be coded with intracranial injury (801.45). Codes 802.8 and 802.4 do not have a fifth digit. The orbital roof is excluded from code category 802 and included in code category 801, so no separate code is reported. The friction burns are also reported (919.0).

d. 801.45, 802.4, 919.0, E815.2; E849.5, 96.72, 96.04, 01.18
Correct answer.

7.60. Principal diagnosis: Laceration of liver, 2 cm deep, 864.03-Y

Additional diagnoses:

Dehiscence of operative wound, 998.32-N

Infection of operative wound, 998.59-N

Passenger in MVA, E819.1 (exempt list)

Place of occurrence highway or street, E849.5 (exempt list)

Procedures:

Liver lobectomy, 50.3

Reopening and drainage of operative wound, 54.12

Issues to clarify: It is unknown from this brief case summary whether the dehiscence was internal or external. In real practice, the coding professional would review the operative report and other documentation to discern this and assign the most specific code. The coder would also look for documentation that might indicate the causative organism of the infection in the operative wound.

Note: The coder would not assign a code for an organism based on culture results alone; the physician must document the causative agent.

7.61.   a. 865.11

Incorrect answer. In this case, there is no documentation of open wound into cavity. Also, because there is a laceration, 865.02 would be assigned. It would also be appropriate to code the concussion and the E code for the cause of the accident and the E code for the place of occurrence.

b. 865.02, 850.9, E816.1, E849.5

Incorrect answer. The concussion was documented with a loss of consciousness of 10 minutes.

c. 865.02, 850.11, E816.1, E849.5

Correct answer.

d. 865.01, 865.02, 850.11, E816.1, E849.5

Incorrect answer. In this case, when the spleen has a hematoma and a laceration, only one code is used because code 865.01 states hematoma without rupture of capsule.

Chapter 8. Case Studies from Ambulatory Health Records

Disorders of the Blood and Blood-Forming Organs

8.1.   a. 282.61, 789.09, 427.31, 250.00, 99285

Incorrect answer. The sickle-cell anemia is in crisis, so 282.61 is not correct. It would not be necessary to code the inguinal pain because pain, fever, and so on, are part of a sickle-cell crisis. The level is four for the E/M code per the documentation, so code 99285 is not correct. It is also correct to add the x-ray codes.

b. 282.62, 733.42, 99284, 73550, 73510

Incorrect answer. The avascular necrosis was not confirmed, but only documented as "rule out." This would not be coded in the outpatient setting. The atrial fib and diabetes should be coded. A modifier -25 should be appended to the 99284 code.

c. 282.62, 427.31, 250.00, 73550, 73510

Incorrect answer. The emergency department service should be reported with 99284-25.

d. 282.62, 427.31, 250.00, 99284-25, 73550, 73510

Correct answer.

Note: The CMS Web site (www.cms.hhs.gov/manuals/pm_trans/A0040.pdf) states that modifier -25 should be appended to an evaluation and management code when reported with significant procedure (status indicator S or T) on the same day of service. Different fiscal intermediaries may have varying requirements for use of modifier -25.

8.2.   a. 280.0, 792.1, 414.01, 250.00, V45.81, V17.40, 36430, P9051 (x 3 units)

Correct answer.

Note: The physician may be queried for the underlying cause of the chronic blood loss.

b. 285.9, 780.79, 36430, P9051 (3 units)

Incorrect answer. The anemia is specified as severe chronic blood loss anemia, so code 285.9 is not the correct answer. Indexing Anemia, blood loss, chronic, results in code 280.0. It is not correct to code the weakness because it is a symptom of the more definitive diagnosis of anemia. The additional diagnoses of diabetes, ASHD, status bypass, and family history of cardiovascular disease may be coded because they were treated and/or are applicable to the case.

c. 280.0, 578.1, 414.01, 250.00, V45.81, V17.40, 36430

Incorrect answer. It is not correct to assume that the patient has GI bleeding, and the physician should be asked to add occult blood as a final diagnosis, if appropriate, which is coded to 792.1. The HCPCS Level II code with the number of units should also be added to account for the purchase of the packed cells from the blood bank. This code may generate an additional reimbursement under the APC system.

d. 285.9, 792.1, 414.01, 250.00, V45.81, V17.49, P9051 (3 units)

Incorrect answer. The anemia is specified as severe chronic blood loss anemia, so code 285.9 is not the correct answer. Family history of other specified cardiovascular disease V17.49 is not reflective of documentation that is unspecified as to the type of cardiovascular disease V17.40. The transfusion administration code must be assigned with a CPT code in order for the APC to be generated. The physician should be asked to add occult blood as a final diagnosis, if appropriate.

8.3.　　a. 599.0, 276.51, 428.0, 287.5, 250.00

Incorrect answer. The thrombocytopenia was specified as primary, so code 287.5 is not the best choice.

b. 599.0, 276.51, 428.0, 511.9, 287.5, 250.00

Incorrect answer. Pleural effusion is not separately coded when present with CHF. *Coding Clinic* (1991, 3Q:19–20). The thrombocytopenia was specified as primary, so code 287.5 is not the best choice.

c. 599.0, 276.51, 428.0, 287.30, 250.00

Correct answer.

d. 599.0, 276.51, 428.0, 511.9, 287.30, 782.7, 250.00

Incorrect answer. Pleural effusion is not separately coded when present with CHF. The petechia is not coded. It is part of the thrombocytopenia and is excluded as an additional code.

8.4.　　a. 285.22, 197.7, V10.3, E933.1

Correct answer.

b. 285.9, 197.7, V10.3, E933.1

Incorrect answer. The anemia is documented as due to the neoplasm, so code 285.9 is not the most specific choice. The anemia in chronic illness codes would be a better choice.

c. 197.7, 285.22, V10.3, E933.1

Incorrect answer. The patient is admitted for blood transfusion, so the anemia would be listed as the first diagnosis.

d. 285.9, 197.7, V10.3

Incorrect answer. The anemia is documented as due to the neoplasm, so code 285.9 is not the most specific choice. The anemia in chronic illness codes would be a better choice. It would also be appropriate to add the E code to show that the chemotherapy also helped cause the anemia.

Disorders of the Cardiovascular System

8.5. a. 786.50, 796.3, 93015, 96360

Incorrect answer. The patient's presenting symptom was arm pain, not chest pain, so code 729.5 is the primary diagnosis. The correct code is 458.9, not 796.3, according to the index. Low, blood pressure takes you to code 458.9. The hospital is providing only the technical component of the test, so code 93015 is inappropriate. Code 93017 is correct.

b. 729.5, 796.3, 93015, 96360

Incorrect answer. The correct code is 458.9 not 796.3 according to the index. Low blood pressure takes you to code 458.9. The hospital is providing only the technical component of the test, so code 93015 is inappropriate. Code 93017 is correct.

c. 414.8, 458.29, 93017, 96365

Incorrect answer. The procedure code is correct, but the diagnosis codes are not. The patient's presenting symptom was arm pain, not chest pain, indicating ischemic heart disease, so code 729.5 is the primary diagnosis. Although it appears that the hypotension may have been iatrogenic (induced by the stress test), physician query would be required. Code 458.9 is more appropriate for this documentation. No medication was included with the IV solution; therefore correct code is 96360.

d. 729.5, 458.9, 93017, 96360

Correct answer.

8.6. a. 404.92, 36830

Incorrect answer. The documentation supports heart failure so the correct combination fifth digit code is "3" (404.93). Additional codes are reported to specify the type of heart failure, in this case, congestive (428.0) and stage of chronic kidney disease (585.6).

b. 404.93, 585.6, 428.0, 36830

Correct answer.

c. 585.6, 428.0, 401.9, 36821

Incorrect answer. There is a combination code for the hypertensive heart and chronic kidney disease with heart failure. Code 36821 is incorrect because a Gore-Tex graft was required. Because direct connection was not possible, code 36830 is the correct CPT code.

d. 404.93, 36821

Incorrect answer. Additional codes are reported to specify the type of heart failure, in this case, congestive (428.0) and stage of chronic kidney disease (585.6). A Gore-Tex graft was required and direct connection was not possible; code 36830 is the correct CPT code.

8.7.   a. 414.00, 413.9, V45.81, 93526, 93543, 93540, 93544, 93555, 93556
Correct answer.

b. 414.01, 414.02, 93526, 93543, 93540, 93544, 93555, 93556

Incorrect answer. It is not known if arteriosclerosis was found in the native arteries or the grafts. Because grafts are examined, it can be assumed that patient is post CABG, so that should be coded also, but 414.00 is as specific as we can get without further physician clarification. The angina should be coded. The procedure codes are correct.

c. 414.00, 413.9, V45.81, 93526, 93543, 93540, 93544

Incorrect answer. The diagnosis codes are correct, but the imaging CPT codes have been omitted. CPT codes 93555 and 93556 are added for the imaging procedures performed for ventricular angiography and coronary angiography, including grafts and aortography.

d. 414.01, 414.02, 413.9, V45.81, 93510, 93543, 93544

Incorrect answer. It is not known if arteriosclerosis was found in the native arteries or the grafts. Because grafts are examined, it can be assumed that patient is post CABG, so that should be coded also, but 414.00 is as specific as we can get without further physician clarification. The imaging codes 93555 and 93556 have been omitted. The catheterization codes in this answer are for left heart cath rather than the combined procedure documented.

8.8.   a. 279.3, 558.9, 748.3, V13.69, V15.1, V44.1
Correct answer.

b. 558.9, 790.7, V15.1, V44.1

Incorrect answer. Differential diagnoses of bacteremia or septicemia are not coded until confirmed. Personal history of congenital malformation, V13.69, should be coded once the congenital malformation is repaired. In addition, V15.1 should be coded to specify that the surgery was of the heart and great vessels. Both larygnomalacia, 748.3 and unspecified immunodeficiency, 279.3 should be reported.

c. 787.01, 558.9, V44.1

Incorrect answer. Nausea and vomiting are integral to acute gastroenteritis and are therefore not coded. Personal history of congenital malformation, V13.69, should be coded once the congenital malformation is repaired. In addition, V15.1 should be coded to specify that the surgery was of the heart and great vessels. Both larygnomalacia, 748.3 and unspecified immunodeficiency, 279.3 should be reported.

d. 787.03, 780.60, 558.9, 745.2, V15.1, V44.1

Incorrect answer. Vomting and fever are integral to acute gastroenteritis and are therefore not coded. Personal history of congenital malformation, V13.69, should be coded once the congenital malformation is repaired. Tetralogy of Fallot is no longer coded once the malformation is repaired. Both larygnomalacia, 748.3 and unspecified immunodeficiency, 279.3 should be reported.

Note: Some Children's Hospitals do continue to report the congenital malformations once they are repaired, for research purposes.

8.9. a. 93650, 93620

Incorrect answer. Because the electrophysiological study was not complete, but was only done for identification of the appropriate area for ablation, it should not be reported. Only the code for the ablation itself, 93650, should be reported.

b. 93650, 93620-59

Incorrect answer. Because the electrophysiological study was not complete, but was only done for identification of the appropriate area for ablation, it should not be reported, even with a modifier. Only the code for the ablation itself, 93650, should be reported.

c. 93650

Correct answer.

d. 93650, 93620, 93622

Incorrect answer. Because the electrophysiological study was not complete, but was only done for identification of the appropriate area for ablation, it should not be reported. The left ventricular pacing (93622) was also done to enable the therapeutic part of the procedure to be completed, and should not be reported. Only the code for the ablation itself, 93650, should be reported.

8.10. 427.41, 427.5, 412, 414.01, 99291, 92960, 92950

Symptoms of palpitations, lightheadedness, syncope, and hypotension are all symptoms of ventricular arrythmia and ventricular fibrillation and are therefore, not coded. Cardiac arrest is coded based on *Coding Clinic* guidance from 2nd Quarter, 1988, page 8. CPR, 92950, is coded separately from the provision of critical care services.

8.11. a. 437.3, 36100, 37204, 75894

Incorrect answer. The diagnosis code is for the intracranial internal carotid. The correct code is 442.81. Code 37204 is for a nonhead and neck vessel, so code 61626 is required.

b. 442.81, 36620

Incorrect answer. The correct CPT codes are 61626 and 36100 for the injection of the contrast media with code 75894 added from the chargemaster for the x-ray component.

c. 442.81, 36100, 37204, 75894

Incorrect answer. Code 37204 is for nonhead and neck vessels. Code 61626 is used in this case.

d. 442.81, 61626, 36100, 75894

Correct answer.

8.12. Principal diagnosis: 414.01

Additional diagnosis: 997.1, 414.12, V45.82, E870.6, E849.7

Procedures: 92980-RC, 93510, 93545, 93556-59

Note: Since a diagnostic cardiac catheterization with injections and imaging were performed prior to the stent placement, it is necessary to code the diagnostic procedures in addition to the stent. Modifier 59 is required on 93556 to show that the imaging and angiography were performed separately as a diagnostic procedure since these codes are typically inherent to the angioplasty with placement of a stent. Diagnosis code 414.12, dissection, is not a normal result of a PTCA procedure and the physician inserted a stent to cover/protect the dissection; therefore this condition is reported as a secondary diagnosis that impacted care. There is no documentation to support a ventriculogram; therefore, 93543 and 93555 are not coded. Infusion codes integral to surgery/anesthesia would not be reported separately; however, if an infusion provided to a patient is not routinely part of the procedure, then an appropriate infusion code with modifier -59 may be added to show that it was a separate procedure. The HCPCS level II C-code for the stent device is also reported and not included in this example.

Disorders of the Digestive System

8.13. a. V55.1, 191.9, 345.90, 43246, 43246

Incorrect answer. Code V55.1 would be assigned if the tube had fallen out and no other complications existed. There is a specific diagnosis code for infection of a gastrostomy. The organism and the dysphagia would also be coded. The modifier -52 is attached to the 11/30 service because it had to be discontinued before completion. The tube was not removed and replaced until the next day by endoscope. CPT code 43246 is for a percutaneous placement of a tube that was not previously present. CPT code 43760 is correct for a change of tube.

b. 191.9, 345.90, V55.1, 43246, 43760-74

Incorrect answer. Although the neoplasm could be related, it is not the reason for the encounter. *Coding Clinic* advises assignment of the malignancy if it is the direct cause of the feeding problems (that is, carcinoma of the soft palate). In this case, there is a complication of the gastrostomy that should be coded as 536.41 with additional codes for the organism cultured (041.11) and the dysphagia (787.20). The code for attention to artificial openings is used only when no complications are present. The procedure codes are correct, but modifier -74 is not applicable. Medicare does not consider conscious sedation to be anesthesia, so modifiers -73 and -74 are not applicable. Modifier -52 should be reported.

c. 536.41, 041.11, 787.20, 191.9, 345.90, 43246, 43760-52

Correct answer. The applicable E/M codes for observation would also be reported according to the facility's acuity model. In addition, the codes for the IV infusion may also be reported if not reported from the chargemaster.

d. 996.69, 041.11, 787.20, 191.9, 345.90, 43246, 43246-53

Incorrect answer. There is a specific code for infection of a gastrostomy (536.41). Code 43246 is for initial placement of a G-tube percutaneously and what was planned was a change of tube. The modifier -53 is not available for hospital reporting (physician services only) and instead should be modifier -52, which explains an attempted 43760 (a procedure that does not require anesthesia, only conscious sedation).

8.14. a. 550.90, 562.10, V10.05, 49505-RT, G0105

Incorrect answer. Although the header did not include screening colonoscopy, this information was available in the body of the report. Diverticulosis was not confirmed, so it is not appropriate to report. Because the resection at the rectosigmoid junction was mentioned, code V10.06 was used for the history of CA. Although the HCPCS Level II code is correct for Medicare reporting, there is no information indicating that this is a Medicare patient, so CPT code 45378 is the correct choice.

b. 550.90, V76.51, V10.06, 49505-RT, 45378

Correct answer. If the patient were specified as Medicare, a HCPCS Level II procedure code (G0105) would be used, rather than the CPT code, for the colonoscopy. Because the resection at the rectosigmoid junction was mentioned, code V10.06 was used for the history of CA.

c. 550.91, V76.51, V10.05, 49505-RT, 49568-RT

Incorrect answer. The fifth digit used for the hernia code should be 0 because there is no documentation in this report of previous surgical repair. The V10.05 is for a history of colon cancer. Because the anastomosis examined is at the rectosigmoid junction, code V10.06 is more accurate. Code 49568 is never reported with inguinal hernia repair, so it should not appear. Lastly, the colonoscopy procedure code does not appear in the list, and it should be reported even though the physician did not list it in the procedure heading.

d. 550.90, V10.06, 49520-RT, 45330

Incorrect answer. Because the colonoscopy was performed for screening to rule out recurrent malignancy, code V76.51 should be added. The CPT code for the hernia repair is for a recurrent hernia that was not documented in this record, so code 49505 is used. The CPT code 45330 is for a sigmoidoscopy, and the documentation clearly described an exam to the ileocecal valve, which is a colonoscopy (45378).

8.15. a. 789.00, 787.99, 280.0, 796.2, 785.0, V64.3, 45378-74

Correct answer. CMS Transmittal 442 requires that the intended colonoscopy is reported with modifiers -73 or -74 appended as appropriate. For hospital outpatient Medicare billing purposes, anesthesia is defined to include local, regional block(s), moderate sedation/analgesia (conscious sedation), deep sedation/analgesia, and general anesthesia. The CMS Transmittal 442 is available online from: www.cms.hhs.gov/transmittals/downloads/R442CP.pdf

b. V71.1, V64.3, 45378-52

Incorrect answer. The patient had symptoms that were the reason for service, even though a definitive diagnosis could not be made. V codes from this category are assigned only when no other symptoms are documented and the patient is observed for suspected malignancy. Codes 789.00, 787.99, and 280.0, as well as 796.2 and 785.0, are assigned for all of the conditions documented that affected the care and treatment. The correct modifier is -74. CMS Transmittal 442 requires that the intended colonoscopy is reported with modifiers -73 or -74 appended as appropriate. For hospital outpatient Medicare billing purposes, anesthesia is defined to include local, regional block(s), moderate sedation/analgesia (conscious sedation), deep sedation/analgesia, and general anesthesia. Under the CMS policy modifier -52 is used to indicate partial reduction or discontinuation of radiology procedures and other services that do not require anesthesia. The CMS Transmittal 442 is available online from: www.cms.hhs.gov/transmittals/downloads/R442CP.pdf

c. 789.00, 787.99, 280.0, 796.2, 785.0, V64.3, 45378

Incorrect answer. CMS Transmittal 442 requires that the intended colonoscopy is reported with modifiers -73 or -74 appended as appropriate. For hospital outpatient Medicare billing purposes, anesthesia is defined to include local, regional block(s), moderate sedation/analgesia (conscious sedation), deep sedation/analgesia, and general anesthesia. The CMS Transmittal 442 is available online from: www.cms.hhs.gov/transmittals/downloads/R442CP.pdf

d. 789.00, 787.99, 280.0, 997.1, V64.3, 45330

Incorrect answer. The 997.1 code is for cardiac complications specifically stated to be due to a procedure. This is an assumption in this case because no cause and effect is documented. The conditions of elevated blood pressure and tachycardia would be coded, using 785.0 and 796.2, because they did affect the decision to terminate the procedure. The correct procedure code is 45378-74. CMS Transmittal 442 requires that the intended colonoscopy is reported with modifiers -73 or -74 appended as appropriate. For hospital outpatient Medicare billing purposes, anesthesia is defined to include local, regional block(s), moderate sedation/analgesia (conscious sedation), deep sedation/analgesia, and general anesthesia. The CMS Transmittal 442 is available online from: www.cms.hhs.gov/transmittals/downloads/R442CP.pdf

8.16. a. 211.3, 211.4, 562.10, 45385, 45384-59, 45380-59
Correct answer.

b. 211.3, 569.0, 45384

Incorrect answer. The code for adenomatous rectal polyp (211.4) is added because the polyp at 20 cm is from the rectum. Each procedure performed by a separate technique is reported in CPT. Code 45384 is reported for the polyp removal via cautery at 60 cm. Code 45385 is reported for the polyp removal via snare at 20 cm. Code 45380 is reported for the biopsy at 80 cm. Modifier -59 is applied to the subsequent CPT codes to show distinct and separate sites were involved.

c. 211.3, 569.0, 45385, 45384-59, 45380-59

Incorrect answer. Adenomatous rectal polyp should be coded. The diverticulosis code 562.10 was omitted from this list.

d. 792.1, 211.3, 569.0, 562.10, 45385, 45384

Incorrect answer. Code 792.1 would not be reported when the etiology (polyps) is known. Code 211.4 should be assigned for the adenomatous polyp from the 20-cm location. Also, modifier -59 should be added to all subsequent CPT codes to show that they are distinct from each other due to separate sites and techniques involved. CPT code 45380-59 is needed to report the biopsy of the lesion mentioned. When a biopsy and a polypectomy are not of the same location, they may be separately reported.

8.17.　a. 237.4, 573.8, 275.42, 276.51, 787.91, 276.8, 275.2, 626.0

Correct answer.

b. 211.6, 227.3, 197.7, 275.42, 276.51, 787.91, 276.8, 275.2, 626.0

Incorrect answer. Codes 211.6 and 227.3 are incorrect because the Alphabetic Index instructs the coding professional to code adenoma, multiple, endocrine two or more specified sites, to 237.4. In addition, the lesions in the liver are not yet confirmed as metastatic neoplasms, so code 573.3 is used rather than 197.7 in the outpatient setting.

c. 235.5, 237.0, 197.7, 275.42, 276.51, 787.91, 276.8, 275.2, 626.0

Incorrect answer. Codes 235.5 and 237.0 are incorrect because the Alphabetic Index instructs the coding professional to code adenoma, multiple, endocrine two or more specified sites, to 237.4. In addition, the lesions in the liver are not yet confirmed as metastatic neoplasms, so code 573.3 is used rather than 197.7 in the outpatient setting.

d. 237.4, 573.8, 259.2, 275.42, 276.51, 787.91, 276.8, 275.2, 626.0

Incorrect answer. The carcinoid syndrome is documented as "probable" at this point and has not been confirmed. Outpatient coding guidelines direct not to code probable diagnoses as if confirmed. Code 259.2 would not be reported until the MEN-1 has been confirmed.

8.18.　a. 162.9, 250.62, 357.2, 250.42, 583.81, V58.67, 272.4, 789.1

Incorrect answer. The patient was admitted for chemotherapy. Code V58.11 should be reported as the principal diagnosis. See *Coding Clinic* (2003, 4Q).

b. V58.11, 250.62, 250.42, V58.67, 272.4, 789.1

Incorrect answer. The reason for the chemotherapy, lung cancer, should also be coded. Diabetic neuropathy and nephropathy both require two codes to report both the diabetes with the specific complications and the manifestations of the diabetic complications.

c. V58.11, 162.9, 250.62, 357.2, 250.42, 583.81, V58.67, 272.4, 789.1

Correct answer.

d. 162.9, 250.02, V58.67, 272.4, 789.1

Incorrect answer. The patient was admitted for chemotherapy. Code V58.11 should be reported as the principal diagnosis. See *Coding Clinic* (2003, 4Q).

Diabetic neuropathy and nephropathy are documented, were addressed during the stay, and should be coded as 250.62 with 357.2 and 250.42 with 583.81, respectively.

Disorders of the Genitourinary System

8.19.　　a. 585.6, 401.1, 36830, 90935

Incorrect answer. There is a combination diagnosis code for chronic kidney disease associated with hypertension in code 403.11. ICD-9-CM presumes a cause-and-effect relationship. See *Coding Clinic* (2002, 4Q). An additional procedure code is required for the replacement of the centrally-inserted central venous access device (CPT code 36581). Modifier -59 may be needed on code 36581 to show that the procedure was distinct and not a component of the other procedure.

b. 403.90, 36825, 90935

Incorrect answer. Because we know that the hypertension is benign, we can use code 403.11 for this condition. A fifth digit of 1 is required to report the type of chronic kidney disease. An additional diagnosis code is reported to identify the stage of chronic kidney disease requiring dialysis (585.6). An additional procedure code is required for the replacement of the centrally-inserted central venous access device (CPT code 36581).

c. 403.11, 585.5, 36830, 36581-59

Incorrect answer. When dialysis is provided during the same encounter, it is reported separately (90935). Stage V chronic kidney disease requiring chronic dialysis is reported with code 585.6.

d. 403.11, 585.6, 36830, 36581-59, 90935

Correct answer. The replacement of the Quinton catheter is reported with code 36581 because it is a venous catheter. The new replacement code includes the removal and the insertion of the new catheter.

8.20.　　a. V55.6, V45.74, V10.51, 50684, 74425

Correct answer.

b. V55.2, V10.51, 74425

Incorrect answer. An ileal conduit is an artificial opening for the urinary tract, not the digestive tract; although the urine is diverted into an isolated segment of the ileum following cystectomy (bladder removal). Code 50684 is required for injection of the contrast material. Diagnosis code V45.74 can be added to reflect the acquired absence of the bladder.

c. 596.8, 188.9, 74425

Incorrect answer. The reason for the test was to check on the patency of the ileal conduit. ICD-9-CM provides V codes for attention to artificial openings. Because an ileal conduit is an artificial opening for the urinary tract, code V55.6 is reported along with code V45.74 to reflect the acquired absence of the bladder. Code 188.9 presumes that the patient still has the disease. When the malignancy has been eradicated, a V code for "personal history of malignancy" should be assigned, in this case, V10.51. Code 50684 is required for injection of the contrast material, in addition to the radiology code, which can be assigned from the hospital chargemaster.

d. Contact the ordering physician to obtain a diagnosis before coding this encounter.

Incorrect answer. If the indication for the test was to check for patency of the conduit, then the code for attention to artificial opening can be assigned. If there were any other results documented following the test, then they could be coded as well. See *Coding Clinic* (2000, 1Q) for more information about reporting reason for visit vs. results available from the radiologist. Diagnosis codes V55.6, V45.74, and V10.51 would be appropriate in this case, based upon the information available.

8.21. a. 626.2, 618.4, 618.6, 616.0, 58558

Correct answer.

b. 626.2, 58558

Incorrect answer. Additional conditions were identified in the body of the operative report that merit coding. Codes 618.4 and 618.6 should be added for the cystocele/rectocele and cervical erosion because the surgeon documented these conditions and they were not simply incidental findings noted on pathological examination. The documentation indicates "uterine prolapse."

c. 626.2, 618.4, 618.6, 616.0, 58100, 58120

Incorrect answer. A combination code is available in CPT for an endometrial biopsy, D&C, and hysteroscopy examination in code 58558. To report separate codes for the components of the procedure would constitute unbundling.

d. 618.4, 618.6, 616.0, 58558

Incorrect answer. The focus of the procedure was to investigate and/or treat the menorrhagia. The other conditions were not the cause of the bleeding but are documented findings that merit coding as secondary diagnoses.

Infectious Diseases/Disorders of the Skin and Subcutaneous Tissue

8.22.   a. 173.3, V10.42, 30118, 30400

Incorrect answer. The cancer is on the inside of the nose at the very tip and requires an extensive resection to treat, with a composite skin graft for reconstruction. Code 173.3 is the code to report malignancy of the skin of the nose. Code 160.0, Malignant neoplasm of nasal cavities, is the more appropriate code. Code 30118 describes excision of a lesion but is generally limited to laser or cryosurgery, without any wound repair required. Code 30150 is more descriptive of the procedure required in this case because a full-thickness resection was done and grafting was required. The reconstruction code 30400 is for plastic repair of this area not involving a skin graft.

b. 160.0, V10.42, 305.1, 30150, 15760

Correct answer.

c. 160.0, 15760, 30150

Incorrect answer. Although the history of carcinoma and the tobacco abuse do not directly affect this episode of care, they may be important data elements for research or patient care tracking. Code V10.42 is assigned for the history of uterine cancer, and tobacco abuse is reported with code 305.1. The CPT code for the resection is correct, but an additional code is required to reflect the skin graft needed for closure of the defect (15760).

d. 173.3, V10.42, 305.1, 14060

Incorrect answer. The cancer is on the inside of the nose at the very tip and requires an extensive resection to treat, with a composite skin graft for reconstruction. Code 173.3 is the code to report malignancy of the skin of the nose. Code 160.0, Malignant neoplasm of nasal cavities, is the more appropriate code. The procedure codes listed here are for adjacent tissue transfer rather than full-thickness composite grafting. Skin grafting to the nose is coded in the respiratory system rather than in the integumentary system in CPT.

8.23.   a. 998.59, E878.8, 15100

Incorrect answer. No mention is made of a wound infection, but rather, that the wound was failing to heal (998.83). The CPT code for the preparation of the recipient site is reported as code 15002, and is reported in addition to the grafting code.

b. 998.59, 15002, 15100

Incorrect answer. No mention is made of wound infection, but rather, failure to heal (998.83). The primary procedure 15100 should be listed before the preparation in sequence to reflect the most resource-intensive procedure. An E code to report the surgical procedure as a cause of abnormal reaction in a patient may be added when consistent with regulatory or hospital policy.

c. 998.83, E878.8, 15100, 15002

Correct answer.

d. 998.83, 278.01, 15200

Incorrect answer. A code for morbid obesity (278.01) is not warranted because the patient may no longer be overweight. The codes reported for the procedure are for full-thickness grafts, and this is a split-thickness graft procedure. Use of full-thickness grafts is generally reserved for the face and other cosmetically sensitive areas. Codes 15100 and 15002 are appropriate. An E code to report the surgical procedure as a cause of abnormal reaction in a patient may be added when consistent with regulatory or hospital policy.

8.24. a. 172.6, 216.7, 14001, 15002

Incorrect answer. A pigmented nevus is reported as a neoplasm of uncertain behavior with code 238.2. Code 15002 is used for site preparation for free skin grafts, not advancement flaps. CPT code 11423 is reported for the removal of the heel lesion with an additional code for the layer closure (12041).

b. 216.7, 216.6, 14000

Incorrect answer. The melanoma is the reason for excision of further tissue, so it should be reported (172.6) even though the pathology report does not mention the malignancy. A pigmented nevus is reported as a neoplasm of uncertain behavior with code 238.2. Because the surgeon documented that the graft was over 10.2 sq cm, the code to report is 14001. Code 11423 must be reported for the heel lesion excision performed separately from the shoulder graft, and code 12041 should be reported for the layer closure of this excision site.

c. 216.6, 238.2, 14001, 11606, 11423

Incorrect answer. The melanoma is the reason for excision of further tissue, so it should be reported (172.6) even though the pathology report does not mention the malignancy. It is documented that this diagnosis had been confirmed by biopsy. It is incorrect to report lesion removal when the resultant defect is repaired with an advancement flap closure because any excision is included in the codes in this section. See instructional note preceding code 14000. An additional code is required for the layered closure of the excision site of the heel lesion. Although the surgeon did not document the length of this repair, the pathology report shows us that it was less than 2.5 cm, so code 12041 is reported.

d. 172.6, 238.2, 14001, 11423-59, 12041

Correct answer.

Note: A modifier is necessary for code 11423 as the excision of lesions are usually included in 14001. Modifier -59 is reported to indicate a different site or lesion. The documentation in the description of the procedure does not support the advancement flap of the heel lesion although the name of the operation stated advancement flap reconstruction. Coding is based on the detailed description of the operation as documented in the body of the operative report.

8.25. a. 216.8, 15240, 15004, 12051

Incorrect answer. The lesion is located on the auricle of the ear, not the skin of the neck/scalp behind it. The skin graft was taken from this area. Although a layer closure was used to repair the defect from the donor site, no skin graft or local flap was used, so no additional code is warranted for this repair. Note that the size of the lesion and the graft are documented in millimeters, which are 1/10 the size of the centimeters used in the CPT system.

b. 216.2, 15260, 11442

Correct answer.

c. 173.2, 15260, 11442

Incorrect answer. The pathology report confirms that the lesion was benign, even though margins were taken and the resultant defect required a skin graft. The lesion code is 216.2.

d. 216.2, 14060

Incorrect answer. This was a full-thickness graft rather than an advancement graft. The appropriate codes are 15260 and 11442.

8.26. a. 054.10, 782.4, 794.8, 042, 99284

Incorrect answer. Documentation of lesions of both the penis and the scrotum is present, so codes 054.13 and 054.19 should be reported. Febrile jaundice is assigned code 070.1, so this is appropriate to report because the physician has used "suspected" with the hepatitis. Testing positive for HIV is not assigned to category 042 without confirmation of symptoms and infection. 795.71 is the appropriate code at this stage. Additional codes should be assigned for the drug addiction (opiates, continuous) and the lifestyle risks because they are clearly delineated by the attending physician and affect the management of the patient.

b. 054.19, 573.3, 795.71, 305.51, V69.8, 99214

Incorrect answer. Two codes from the 054 category should be used to show that both the penis and the scrotum were involved with the herpes outbreak. Code 573.3 is for noninfective hepatitis, but the documentation states that the patient had experienced febrile jaundice with "suspected" hepatitis. Code 070.1 should be used to report the febrile jaundice. Code 794.8 should also be added because the type of hepatitis is not confirmed. Code V69.2 is more specific than code V69.8. Because the drug dependence is already coded, the V code indicates the high-risk sexual behavior. Type A provider-based emergency room visits are reported with codes from the range 99281–99285, so code 99214 is not appropriate. This code would be used for a facility clinic visit.

c. 054.13, 054.19, 070.1, 794.8, 795.71, 305.51, V69.2, 99284

Correct answer. The use of two codes from the 054 category shows that both the penis and the scrotum were involved with the herpes outbreak. Hepatitis is not coded because it is not confirmed; instead, the symptoms are coded (febrile jaundice and abnormal liver function tests).

d. 042, 305.51, 070.1, 99291

Incorrect answer. No diagnosis of HIV has been made, based upon the documentation present. If additional information were available, or symptoms of HIV could be confirmed, then the 042 code could be used. When a patient is HIV seropositive, the correct code to report is 795.71.

The patient does have HSV-2, or genital herpes, which is reported with 054.13 and 054.19. These would be reported in the first position because they were the reason that the patient sought care. The code for febrile jaundice is correct, but the additional code 794.8 should also be reported because the type of hepatitis is not confirmed. A V69.2 code may be added for the high-risk sexual behavior, and code 305.51 is justified because the heroin addiction affected the management and treatment plans of the patient. Code 99291 should not be reported without additional documentation because critical care requirements were apparently not met. An emergency department visit code, 99284, is the appropriate code to report.

Behavioral Health Conditions

8.27.   a. 296.24, 90870

Correct answer.

b. 296.24, 90870, 95812, 93040

Incorrect answer. The EEG and EKG are integral to the electroconvulsive therapy and should not be reported separately. Note that the description for code 90870 reads "includes necessary monitoring."

c. 296.24, 90870, 99211-25

Incorrect answer. Without further documentation of a distinct evaluation and management service, separately identifiable from the procedure, code 99211 should not be reported, even with a modifier.

d. 296.24, 90870, 95812, 93040, 99234-25

Incorrect answer. Code 90870 is correct. The EEG and EKG are integral to the electroconvulsive therapy and should not be reported separately. Without further documentation of a distinct evaluation and management service, separately identifiable from the procedure, code 99211 should not be reported, even with a modifier.

8.28.   a. 295.34, 428.0, 99201

Incorrect answer. The evaluation and management service selected should be 99284 because this was an ED visit. In addition, a code might be required for the observation services. Individual payers have different requirements for reporting of observation services, and payer guidelines should be followed. Medicare has issued several program memoranda describing reporting of observation services for Medicare patients. These can be accessed on the CMS website at www.cms.hhs.gov.

b. 295.32, 99283

Incorrect answer. The appropriate fifth digit for the schizophrenia is 4 because the attending physician documented chronic with acute exacerbation. The emergency department evaluation and management service code is one level too low; 99284 would be reported with an acuity level of 4 documented. In addition, a code might be required for the observation services. Individual payers have different requirements for reporting of observation services and payer guidelines should be followed.

c. 295.34, 428.0, 99284

Correct answer. A code for the observation services might also be appropriate, depending upon the payer. More information regarding observation is located in the *2005 OPPS Final Rule,* which can be accessed at www.cms.hhs.gov.

d. 295.84, 99234

Incorrect answer. The schizophrenia is documented as paranoid type, which is coded to subcategory 295.3. The diagnosis of CHF should be added because a digoxin level was mentioned to evaluate the patient's management. The appropriate emergency department evaluation and management code to assign is 99284. In addition, a code might be required for the observation services. Individual payers have different requirements for reporting of observation services, and payer guidelines should be followed. Medicare has issued several program memoranda describing reporting of observation services for Medicare patients. These can be accessed at www.cms.hhs.gov.

8.29.   a. 296.20, 309.81, 303.92, 301.83, 300.9, 90819

Incorrect answer. The code for psychotherapy with medical evaluation and management services is not appropriate because there is no documentation of E/M services in addition to the psychotherapy in this note. Code 296.30 is appropriate because the diagnostic statement specifies the major depressive disorder as recurrent. Also, code 303.90 is reported rather than 303.92 because the alcohol dependence is not specified as episodic.

b. 296.30, 309.81, 303.90, 301.83, 300.9, 90845

Incorrect answer. The service provided was specified to be individual dialectical behavior therapy, which is a type of psychotherapy, not psychoanalysis.

c. 296.30, 309.81, 303.90, 301.83, 90818

Incorrect answer. The attending physician noted 45 minutes spent with the patient one-on-one (1:1). Also, the suicidal risk, which affected the patient's management, is reported with code 300.9.

d. 296.30, 309.81, 303.90, 301.83, 300.9, 90818
Correct answer.

8.30.   a. 295.33, 272.0, 90862
Correct answer.

b. 295.30, 272.0, 90862

Incorrect answer. The physician specified subchronic schizophrenia in the body of the note, and the diagnostic statement specified acute exacerbation. The fifth digit of 3 is appropriate. Code 295.33 is correct.

c. 295.30, 272.0, 90862, 99231

Incorrect answer. Neither 90862 nor M0064 is reported along with the evaluation and management service codes. In this case, code 90862 is the most appropriate code, particularly because the physician specifies that the purpose of the visit was a 20-minute medication review. Also, the physician specified subchronic schizophrenia in the body of the note, and the diagnostic statement specified acute exacerbation. The fifth digit of 3 is appropriate. Code 295.33 is correct.

d. 295.33, 272.0, M0064, 99231

Incorrect answer. Neither 90862 nor M0064 is reported along with the evaluation and management service codes. In this case, code 90862 is the most appropriate code, particularly because the physician specifies that the purpose of the visit was a 20-minute medication review.

8.31. a. 301.83, 296.30, 304.31, 99214

Incorrect answer. Time is not a determining factor in assigning an evaluation and management level unless counseling and coordination of care constitute more than 50 percent of the encounter. Code 99212 is assigned according to the documented extent of the three key elements (history, physical examination, and medical decision making). Also, the cannabis dependence is not specified as continuous. Even though the physician notes recent use of marijuana, the coding professional cannot assume continuous vs. episodic. The fifth digit for unspecified is used; code 304.30 is appropriate.

b. 301.83, 296.30, 304.30, 99212

Correct answer.

c. 301.83, 296.30, 304.30, 90805

Incorrect answer. Psychotherapy services were not provided. The focus of this visit was not to attempt to change maladaptive behavior patterns, and there is no mention of specific treatment goals or progress toward goals. This is a hospital outpatient visit summarizing the patient's progress to date. Based upon the documented extent of history, physical examination, and medical decision making, the evaluation and management code 99212 is reported with the diagnoses listed.

d. 301.83, 296.30, 304.31, 90805

Incorrect answer. The patient is an outpatient (CMHC), but the psychotherapy code is not appropriate because psychotherapy services were not provided. The focus of this visit was not to attempt to change maladaptive behavior patterns, and there is no mention of specific treatment goals or progress toward goals. This is a hospital outpatient visit summarizing the patient's progress to date. The evaluation and management code 99212 is reported. Also, the cannabis dependence is not specified as continuous. Even though the physician notes recent use of marijuana, the coding professional cannot assume continuous vs. episodic. The fifth digit for unspecified is used; code 304.30 is appropriate.

Disorders of the Musculoskeletal System and Connective Tissue

8.32.   a. 840.4, 29822

Incorrect answer. The code for chronic bursitis has been omitted and the code for hypertension may also be added. The CPT code 29822 reflects only debridement of the joint through the arthroscope; although the physician documents additional work, including an arthroscopic coracoacromial ligament release in the operative report. Code 29826 is appropriate to report this procedure.

b. 726.10, 401.9, 23415-RT, 23120-RT

Incorrect answer. A current tear of the rotator cuff is reported with code 840.4. Rotator cuff syndrome, including chronic bursitis, is classified in code 726.10. The CPT code 23415 is for a coracoacromial ligament release, which is an open procedure, rather than an endoscopic one. Code 29826 is used when repairs are accomplished through the endoscope. 23120 is an open approach to the claviculectomy; 29824 is the endoscopic approach.

c. 840.4, 726.10, 29820, 29805-59

Incorrect answer. The diagnosis codes are correct, but the CPT codes are components of the procedure described. Modifier -59 is inappropriate to use when one procedure is integral to another and separate approaches or separate sites are not documented.

d. 840.4, 726.10, 401.9, 29826-RT, 29824-RT

Correct answer. The injury is documented as current (one week), so a code from this category is correct. Code 726.10 is added as an additional code for the chronic bursitis mentioned. The HCPCS modifier is added for accurate reporting of laterality.

8.33.   a. 717.2, 717.6, 715.96, 29881-RT

Correct answer. The presence of degenerative disease implies that this is not a current injury; however, the coding professional would review the history and other portions of the health record to verify that the torn meniscus is not the result of a current injury. If the tear is due to a current injury, code 836.0 is reported rather than code 717.2. If there is any inconsistency or uncertainty, the physician should be queried for clarification. The physician may also be queried to clarify if the arthritis is localized to the knee joint. If documentation supports this, code 715.36 is more specific than code 715.96. See *Coding Clinic* (1995, 2Q) for an article on the coding of arthritis.

b. 717.43, 718.16, 29881-RT, 29874-RT

Incorrect answer. Code 717.43 describes derangement of the posterior horn of the lateral meniscus, and the medial meniscus was the structure involved. Codes in subcategory 718.1X are used to report a loose body of joints other than the knee. A fifth digit of 6 is not applicable to this subcategory. See the excludes note, which refers the coder to code 717.6 for knee. CPT code 29874 is included in 29881 except when different compartments of the knee are involved per National Correct Coding Initiative edits.

c. 844.8, 717.6, 29881-RT, 29877-RT

Incorrect answer. The diagnosis code reported here indicates a current injury rather than degenerative disease. CPT code 29877 is included in the meniscectomy code (29881) and should not be reported separately unless different compartments of the knee are involved per National Correct Coding Initiative edits reported for Medicare patients with HCPCS Level II code G0289.

d. 717.2, 715.96, 29881-RT, 29874-RT

Incorrect answer. The diagnosis code for loose body of the knee was omitted. CPT code 29874 is included in 29881 except when different compartments of the knee are involved per National Correct Coding Initiative edits.

8.34. a. 727.1, 735.4, 99242-25, 28202, 28285

Incorrect answer. Diagnosis codes 715.97, 754.52, and 754.59 were omitted. The CPT code 28202 is inappropriate because the tendon repair is included in the other procedure codes, 28299-TA, 28285-T1.

b. 727.1, 715.97, 754.52, 735.4, 754.59, 28299-TA, 28285-T1

Correct answer.

c. 735.4, 754.52, 28296

Incorrect answer. Diagnosis codes 715.97, 727.1, 735.4, and 754.59 were omitted. CPT code 28299-TA represents the combined procedure (Keller + Austin) and CPT code 28285-T1 was omitted for the hammertoe repair. Note that code 28299 is not an unlisted procedure code but represents a double osteotomy.

d. 727.2, 715.97, 754.52, 735.4, 754.59, 28296-TA and 28292-TA-59, 28285-T1

Incorrect answer. Code 727.2 is the code for specific bursitis, often with occupational origin, rather than the code for a bunion. CPT code 28299 exists for severe cases where combined techniques are needed for correction, so it is not appropriate to assign two bunionectomy codes for the same foot.

8.35. a. 882.1, 817.1, 26418, 26735, 26746, 11012

Incorrect answer. Code 882.1 does not include the tendon involvement that required repair. Code 817.1 is for an open fracture of hand bones, which is not documented in this case. The correct CPT codes are 26418-F1, 26418-F2, 26418-F3, 26418-F5, 11010-F1, 11012-F4. Failure to report the debridements and duplication of the same procedure on different fingers constitutes underreporting and may result in inappropriately low reimbursement for the surgery. As no fracture reduction is described, only debridement is reported.

b. 842.12, 817.0, 26746-F4, 11010-F1, 11012-F4

Incorrect answer. Code 842.12 is for a sprain, rather than a fracture of the metacarpophalangeal joint. No fracture treatment was rendered except for debridement. The correct codes for the procedure are 26418-F1, 26418-F2, 26418-F3, 26418-F5, 11010-F1, 11012-F4. Failure to report the duplication of the same procedure on different fingers constitutes under-reporting and may result in inappropriately low reimbursement for the surgery.

c. 842.12, 817.1, 26418-F1, 26418-F2, 26418-F3, 26418-F4

Incorrect answer. Code 842.12 is for a sprain, rather than a fracture of the metacarpophalangeal joint. Code 817.1 is for an open fracture of hand bones, which is not documented in this case. The debridement codes (11010-F1, 11012-F4) were omitted.

d. 882.2, 816.11, 26418-F1, 26418-F2, 26418-F3, 26418-F5, 11010-F1, 11012-F4

Correct answer.

Neoplasms

8.36.   a. 185, 55700

Incorrect answer. Carcinoma in situ is coded as 233.4 because the malignancy has not spread to any surrounding tissue and has been detected early. CPT codes are required for the placement of the ultrasound probe (76872) and the actual provision of the ultrasonic guidance for the biopsy (76942). Stones of the prostate have a code assigned because they may affect current or future management of the patient (602.0).

b. 233.4, 790.93, 55705, 76872

Incorrect answer. The biopsy code in CPT is 55700 because no incision is documented. The placement of the ultrasound probe is only one component of the procedure performed. An additional code (76942) is required for the guidance of the needle to the prostate for the biopsy. Stones of the prostate have a code assigned because they may affect current or future management of the patient (602.0). Abnormal laboratory findings are not assigned an additional code when the etiology has been confirmed and a definitive diagnosis assigned by the close of the encounter.

c. 233.4, 602.0, 55700, 76872, 76942

Correct answer.

d. 185, 790.93, 602.0, 55700, 76872, 76942

Incorrect answer. The neoplasm is specified as carcinoma in situ of the prostate, so code 233.4 is assigned because the malignancy has not spread to any surrounding tissue and has been detected early. Abnormal laboratory findings are not assigned an additional code when the etiology has been confirmed and a definitive diagnosis assigned by the close of the encounter.

8.37.   a. 203.01, 199.1, 38221

Incorrect answer. ICD-9-CM coding guidelines require reporting to the highest degree of specificity at the close of the encounter, and the melanoma has not yet been confirmed. Metastatic disease in the bone has been documented, but there is no confirmation of the primary neoplasm (198.5 for the bone metastases and 199.1 for the unknown primary). The history of breast cancer (V10.3) is known, and the pathologic fractures (733.19), osteoporosis (733.00), and urinary tract infection (599.0 and 041.4) also affect the patient's management and should be coded.

b. 198.5, 199.1, 733.19, 733.00, V10.3, 599.0, 041.4, 38221

Correct answer.

c. 199.0, 27299

Incorrect answer. There is no documentation to support the code for carcinomatosis. ICD-9-CM coding guidelines require reporting to the highest degree of specificity at the close of the encounter. We know that there is metastatic disease in the bone but do not have confirmation of the primary neoplasm (198.5 and 199.1). The history of breast cancer (V10.3) is known, and the pathologic fractures (733.19), osteoporosis (733.00), and urinary tract infection (599.0 and 041.1) also affect the patient's management and should be coded. A bone marrow biopsy was performed and should be coded (38221).

d. 198.5, 203.01, 174.9, 38221

Incorrect answer. If this were an inpatient visit, the diagnosis reported as "suspected" or "rule out" could be coded as if present, but because this is an ambulatory service, this code assignment is inappropriate. Correct reporting is the established bone metastatic disease (198.5) and an additional code for the unknown primary site (199.1). The history of breast cancer (V10.3) is known, and the pathologic fractures (733.19), osteoporosis (733.00), and urinary tract infection (599.0 and 041.4) also affect the patient's management and should be coded.

8.38. a. 153.3, 197.4, 49329

Incorrect answer. Code 197.4 is incorrect. The metastasis is to the abdominal pericolic adipose tissue (198.89). The evaluation of the pericolic lesions is considered a peritoneal biopsy. The appropriate code is 49321. With confirmation from the physician, a case may be made for assigning 49329 because more than just a biopsy was performed (some dissection). The colonoscopy with biopsy must also be reported in this case with 45380.

b. 153.9, 49321-74, 45380-59

Incorrect answer. The first-listed diagnosis is not as specific as possible (report 153.3 for sigmoid colon). The modifiers appended to the CPT codes are not necessary. The procedure was not discontinued before completion, only changed due to the nature of the pathology discovered, so modifier -74 is not correct. Modifier -59 is not necessary because the colonoscopy would not be considered a component of the laparoscopic surgery. The metastases to the abdominal pericolic adipose tissue should also be coded.

c. 197.4, 153.3, 197.7, 49321, 45380

Incorrect answer. An initial diagnosis of cancer generally shows the primary carcinoma code in the first position, unless the diagnosis or treatment was focused on the metastases. The liver metastasis is not yet confirmed and cannot be reported for an outpatient encounter. Code 197.4 is incorrect. The metastasis is to the abdominal pericolic adipose tissue (198.89). The procedure codes are correct.

d. 153.3, 198.89, 49321, 45380

Correct answer.

8.39. a. 239.5, 250.00, 332.0, 278.00, 57410, 56620

Incorrect answer. Based on the tissue report, the lesion is VIN III or Carcinoma in situ of the vulva, coded as 233.32. The remainder of the diagnoses are correct. Code 57410 for pelvic exam under anesthesia is included in the main procedure of 56620.

b. 624.02, 250.00, 332.0, 278.00, 56630

Incorrect answer. Based on the tissue report, the lesion is VIN III or Carcinoma in situ of the vulva, coded as 233.32. Code 624.02 is for VIN II of the vulva. The procedure performed was a simple, partial vulvectomy based on the definitions in the CPT book. The correct code is 56620.

c. 233.32, 250.00, 57410, 11626, 12042

Incorrect answer. Parkinsonism 332.0 and obesity 278.00 should both be reported. The pelvic exam under anesthesia should be coded as part of the major procedure, a simple partial vulvectomy. This lesion was not described as a skin lesion and therefore integumentary codes are not correct. The correct code is 56620.

d. 233.32, 250.00, 332.0, 278.00, 56620

Correct answer.

Disorders of the Nervous System and Sense Organs

8.40. a. 956.5, E920.4, E849.0, 64831, 28200

Incorrect answer. The complicated open wound would be reported as the reason for the visit. Although a digital nerve repair was performed, this also involved a nerve graft, so code 64890 is assigned. The -LT modifier may be assigned to the CPT codes to show that the repair was to the left foot. An additional code should also be assigned for the use of the operating microscope (69990).

b. 892.2, 956.5, E920.4, E849.0, 64891, 28202, 69990

Incorrect answer. The nerve was grafted, but the graft did not measure more than 4 mm, so code 64890 is reported. There was no tendon graft, so code 28202 is inappropriate; code 28200 should be assigned. The -LT modifier may be assigned to the CPT codes to show that the repair was to the left foot.

c. 892.2, 956.5, E920.4, E849.0, 64890-LT, 28200-LT, 69990

Correct answer.

d. 956.5, 64890-LT, 28200-LT

Incorrect answer. The complicated open wound would be reported as the reason for the visit, so code 892.2 should be reported as the primary diagnosis, with 956.5 as a secondary diagnosis. Codes E920.4 and E849.0 are added to show the cause of the injury. The procedure codes are correct, except that an additional code should also be assigned for the use of the operating microscope (69990).

8.41. Diagnosis code: 337.20

Note: This condition is located in the Alphabetic Index under Dystrophy, sympathetic. Code 337.20 is all that can be reported without further documentation because no specific site is specified.

Procedure code: 64510

Note: The stellate ganglion is a sympathetic nerve, not a peripheral nerve. Code 64510 is the correct code for the stellate ganglion, which is also called the cardiothoracic plexus.

8.42. a. 436, 99284-25, 70450

Incorrect answer. There are documented residuals of the CVA with infarct (434.91), which need to be reported with codes 342.90 and 784.5. Coexisting conditions may impact patient management, so 305.1 should be reported for tobacco use and 250.00 for diabetes.

Note: The CMS Web site (www.cms.hhs.gov/manuals/pm_trans/A0040.pdf) states that modifier -25 should be appended to an evaluation and management code when reported with another procedure on the same day of service. Different fiscal intermediaries may have varying requirements for use of modifier -25.

b. 434.91, 99283, 70470

Incorrect answer. The residual conditions should be coded by assignment of 342.90 and 784.5. Comorbid conditions are reported also with 305.1 for tobacco use and 250.00 for type II diabetes. The wrong code is used for the CT scan because no contrast was employed. In this case, code 70450 is appropriate. For facility reporting, the acuity level established by the facility is reported, rather than any use of the key elements of CPT code reporting. Level IV acuity is 99284.

c. 434.91, 342.90, 784.5, 305.1, 250.00, 99284-25, 70450

Correct answer.

Note: The CMS Web site (www.cms.hhs.gov/manuals/pm_trans/A0040. pdf) states that modifier 25 should be appended to an evaluation and management code when reported with another procedure on the same day of service. Different fiscal intermediaries may have varying requirements for use of modifier -25.

d. 436, 342.90, 784.5, 305.1, 250.00, 99284, 70470

Incorrect answer. The diagnosis listed is not as specific as it should be. When an infarction is established, code 436 is not used, but a code from category 434 is reported. In this case, we know it is an arterial occlusion with an infarct, so code 434.91 is assigned. The wrong code is used for the CT scan because no contrast was employed. In this case, code 70450 is appropriate.

8.43.   a. 350.1, 64600, 77003

Incorrect answer. The foramen ovale was involved and the use of radiologic monitoring results in code 64610. The other codes are appropriate.

b. 350.1, 64610, 77003
Correct answer.

c. 350.1, 64610

Incorrect answer. For ambulatory reporting, it is important to include radiologic guidance. Per CPT guidelines, code 77003 is appropriate for reporting fluoroscopic guidance in this procedure.

d. 350.1, 64605

Incorrect answer. Code 64610 is required for the procedure described. Per CPT guidelines, code 77003 is appropriate for reporting fluoroscopic guidance in this procedure.

8.44.   CPT code assignment:

61750, Stereotactic biopsy, aspiration, or excision, including burr hole(s), for intracranial lesion

Note: See *CPT Assistant* (1996, June). When the attachment of the stereotactic frame is a component of a more comprehensive procedure, it is not reported separately. Code 20660 should not be reported because it is considered to be a part of the biopsy procedure.

70450, Computed tomography, head or brain; without contrast material

Note: CT mapping was performed, rather than MRI, so code 70450 would be appropriate. The CT mapping was performed prior to the procedure; therefore, reporting Intraoperative use of CT or MRI guidance (code 61751) is not accurate.

8.45.   a. 361.02, 379.23, 364.3, 67108
Correct answer.

b. 361.9, 379.23, 364.3, 67108

Incorrect answer. The body of the operative report states multiple tears of the retina, so this can be classified as 361.02 rather than 361.9 unspecified.

c. 361.02, 364.3, 67108

Incorrect answer. An additional diagnosis code for the vitreous hemorrhage should be assigned.

d. 361.02, 379.23, 364.10, 67107, 67036

Incorrect answer. This is a traumatic iritis, not chronic. Code 67108 includes all the procedures the repair of the retinal detachment (scleral buckle) and the vitrectomy.

8.46.   a. 470, 478.0, 519.8, 473.0, 473.2, 473.1, 471.8, 31276-50, 31255-50, 30140-50-59, 30520, 31256-50
Correct answer.

b. 470, 478.0, 519.8, 473.0, 473.2, 473.1, 471.8, 31276, 31255, 30140, 30520, 31256

Incorrect answer.

Note: CPT codes for sinus endoscopy require modifiers to identify whether the procedure was performed on the left side (LT), right side (RT), or bilaterally (50). See *CPT Assistant* (2003, April:25).

c. 470, 478.0, 519.8, 461.0, 461.1, 461.2, 471.8, 31276-50, 31255-50, 30520, 31256-50

Incorrect answer.

Note: According to CPT coding guidelines, it is inappropriate to report CPT code 30140 in addition to CPT code 31255 since the middle turbinate is part of the ethmoid bone and the approach to access procedures performed in the sphenoid, maxillary, or frontal sinus procedures. Therefore, in this case, the inferior turbinate resection is coded with modifier -59 to show that it is a distinct procedure. In addition, the source document identified the patient's sinusitis as chronic, not acute. See *CPT Assistant* (2003, May:5–6).

d. 470, 478.0, 519.8, 461.0, 461.1, 461.2, 471.8, 31276-50, 31255-50, 30140-50-59, 30520, 31256-50

Incorrect answer.

Note: The source document indicates the patient's sinusitis is chronic, not acute.

Newborn/Congenital Disorders

8.47.   a. V53.01, 62230

Incorrect answer. In this situation the physician indicates there is a malfunction of the shunt. Therefore, 996.2 should be reported as the first-listed code for the shunt valve malfunction, followed by the congenital hydrocephalus (742.3), which is not resolved (or he would not require the shunt).

b. 996.2, 742.3, 62230

Correct answer.

c. 742.3, V53.01, 62225

Incorrect answer. Aftercare codes are assigned in secondary position only when aftercare is provided during an episode of care for an unrelated diagnosis. If the patient had presented to a facility for the purpose of aftercare (shunt maintenance) without any additional management or treatment, code V53.01 would be the appropriate code for the reason for the visit. In this case, the patient was evaluated by a consulting physician who concurred with the pediatrician's analysis that the shunt catheter should be replaced with a longer one because the child had grown. Code 62225 is the code for reporting the ventricular catheter, rather than the peritoneal catheter, and would not include the valve replacement. Code 62230 is the appropriate code.

d. 742.3, 62230

Incorrect answer. The consulting physician found that the shunt valve was malfunctioning. Code 996.2 should be reported as the first-listed code.

8.48. a. Diagnoses: 770.84, 765.19; 99285

Incorrect answer. The code for prematurity is based on birth weight, not current weight, so code 765.18 is the correct code. An additional code should be assigned for cardiac arrest, which in a newborn is 779.84, with a code from the circulatory system to further describe the specific condition, 427.5. The CPT codes for hospital and physician reporting are incorrect. Both would report code 99291 for services where critical care is provided in the emergency department, regardless of the age of the patient. The hospital would also report the CPR procedure with code 92950.

b. Diagnoses: 770.84, 779.89, 427.5, 765.18; 99291, 92950, 31500.

Correct answer. Hospitals report only one critical care code, 99291, irrespective of the length of time critical care is rendered. Critical care for outpatient services is reported with 99291 regardless of age of the patient.

c. Diagnoses: 770.84, 779.89, 765.18; 99468, 92950

Incorrect answer. The diagnosis of cardiac arrest (427.5) from the circulatory system chapter may be added to the codes for greater specificity behind the perinatal condition codes. CPR is reported with code 92950 (CPR) and 31500 (intubation) because they are not included as bundled services in critical care.

d. Diagnoses: 770.84, 779.89, 427.5, 765.18, 99291

Incorrect answer. The CPR procedure (CPT code 92950) and the intubation (31500) are not bundled codes with critical care, so they would be reported separately for both the physician and the hospital. The patient is still considered neonatal, as the age of the infant is 28 days.

Pediatric Conditions

8.49. a. 813.41, E886.0, E849.4, 29075-LT, 99283.

Incorrect answer. The x-ray further specifies that the fracture involves both the distal radius and ulna. Code 813.44 is more specific. Modifier -25 is needed on the E/M code.

b. 813.44, E886.0, E849.4, 29075-LT, 99283-25

Correct answer.

c. 813.44, E886.0, E849.4, 25600-LT, 99283-25

Incorrect answer. The fracture is not treated. The cast is applied for comfort only. The orthopedic surgeon will determine what treatment is appropriate. Code 29075 is correct.

d. 813.41, E886.0, E849.4, 25600-LT, 99283-25

Incorrect answer. The x-ray further specifies that the fracture involves both the distal radius and ulna. Code 813.44 is more specific. The fracture is not treated. The cast is applied for comfort only. The orthopedic surgeon will determine what treatment is appropriate. Code 29075 is correct.

Conditions of Pregnancy, Childbirth, and the Puerperium

8.50. a. 648.81, 250.01, V58.67, 99235

Incorrect answer. The fifth digit of 1 is incorrect because the patient did not deliver during this episode of care. 250.01 is not used for gestational diabetes. Refer to the excludes note at category 250 in the tabular volume of ICD-9-CM. Code 99235 is the correct code if the payer requires evaluation and management codes for observation patients. The coding professional should always verify payer reporting guidelines.

b. 648.83, 250.81, 99235

Incorrect answer. Codes in category 250 are not used for gestational diabetes. Refer to the excludes note at category 250 in the tabular volume of ICD-9-CM. Code V58.67 should be assigned to indicate the use of insulin. Code 99235 is the correct code if the payer requires evaluation and management codes for observation patients. The coding professional should always verify payer reporting guidelines.

c. 648.83, V58.67, 99235

Correct answer. Code 99235 is the correct code if the payer requires evaluation and management codes. The coding professional should always verify payer reporting guidelines.

d. 648.83, 790.29, V58.67, 99235

Incorrect answer. 790.29 is not used for gestational diabetes. The excludes note refers the coding professional to use code 648.8x. Code 99235 is the correct code if the payer requires evaluation and management codes. The coding professional should always verify payer reporting guidelines.

8.51. 640.03, V23.41, 923.11, E819.1

Note: The patient has a history of pre-term labor and is currently pregnant. Therefore, code V23.41 is assigned. 389.05, unilateral conductive hearing loss is not coded as it was not treated and has no impact on the care of the patient.

8.52. a. 633.20, 620.2, 59121, 49320

Incorrect answer. The ectopic pregnancy is located at the fimbriated end of the left tube. Code 633.10 is therefore the correct choice. The diagnosis code for peritubular cyst would also be reported (620.8). The CPT code for laparoscopic treatment of an ectopic pregnancy (59150) would be reported rather than 59121, which is the code for reporting an open procedure. Drainage of the ovarian cyst would be reported with CPT code 58662. The diagnostic laparoscopy is included in the surgical laparoscopy (code 59150), so CPT code 49320 would not be reported.

b. 633.10, 620.2, 620.8, 59150, 58662

Correct answer.

c. 633.10, 620.2, 58673, 49320

Incorrect answer. The diagnosis code for peritubular cyst would also be reported (620.8). This is a laparoscopic salpingostomy, but it is for the treatment of an ectopic pregnancy. CPT code 59150 is the correct choice rather than 58673. The diagnostic laparoscopy is included in the surgical laparoscopy (code 59150), so CPT code 49320 would not be reported.

d. 633.20, 654.43, 58673, 58662

Incorrect answer. The ectopic pregnancy is located at the fimbriated end of the left tube. Code 633.10 is therefore the correct choice. The ovarian cyst is not complicating a pregnancy. Code 620.2 is reported rather than 654.43. This is a laparoscopic salpingostomy, but it is for the treatment of an ectopic pregnancy. CPT code 59150 is the correct choice rather than 58673.

Disorders of the Respiratory System

8.53. Diagnosis codes:

V55.0 Attention to artificial openings, tracheostomy

V46.11 Other dependence on machines, respirator

Note: This is not a complication of the tracheostomy, such as an infection or a mechanical breakdown of the tube or tracheal stenosis. Code V55.0 is the most appropriate code for scar tissue redundancy. An additional code could be assigned for the respirator dependence because it would affect the evaluation and management of the case.

Procedure code:

31614 Tracheostomy revision, complex, with flap rotation

Note: This is a revision of a tracheostomy already established. Flap rotation is supported by documentation. This is not a fenestration procedure.

8.54. a. 784.7, 30901-RT, 30903-RT, 30905-RT, 36430-RT

Incorrect answer. The diagnosis code is correct, but the additional conditions should also be coded (280.0 for the blood loss anemia and 496 for the COPD). Modifier -59 should be appended to the second anterior packing with cauterization and the posterior packing to show that separate and distinct sessions were involved. Normally, these CPT codes would not appear on the same claim. HCPCS Level II codes with the number of units should be added to account for the blood products that were transfused. These codes would generate additional reimbursement under the APC system.

b. 784.7, 280.0, 496, 30901-RT, 30901-RT-76, 30905-RT-77, P9021

Incorrect answer. The procedure codes are incorrect because the second procedure involved the cauterization, and the first was limited to simple packing. Only if both procedures were the same should modifier -76 appear. Also, the -77 would not be needed for code 30905 because there was no other code reported for that number. The number of units would be reported for P9021 to account for the blood product. The transfusion administration code (36430) must be assigned in order for the additional APC to be generated.

c. 784.7, 285.9, 30901-RT, 30903-RT-59, 30905-RT-77, 36430-RT, P9021 (2 units)

Incorrect answer. Blood loss anemia has a specific code, 280.0. COPD may be coded, even if it is mentioned in the history portion of the procedure, according to *Coding Clinic* (1992, 2Q). Modifier -59, rather than -77, should be appended to code 30905, because it is a distinct session from the other procedures and normally the codes would not appear on the same claim.

d. 784.7, 280.0, 496, 30901-RT, 30903-RT-59, 30905-RT-59, 36430-RT, P9021 (2 units)

Correct answer. The appropriate E/M code(s) for the observation service should also be reported if the payer requires evaluation and management codes.

Note: Coder may query physician for acute blood loss anemia (285.1) due to clinical indicators and documentation of drop in hematocrit, extensive bleeding, and transfusion.

8.55. a. 486, 692.3, V10.11, E879.2, 71010

Incorrect answer. The pneumonitis is stated as being caused by radiation therapy and is therefore, 508.0. The dermatitis is also caused by the radiation therapy and is coded as 692.82. In addition, the atrial fibrillation and long term use of anti-coagulant should be reported as 427.31 and V58.61. The two-view chest x-ray is coded as 71020.

b. 508.0, 692.82, 427.31, V58.61, V10.11, E879.2, 71020

Correct answer.

c. 508.0, 990, E926.5, 162.4, 427.31, V58.69, 71030

Incorrect answer. This patient has specific complications of radiation therapy. Code 990 is only coded when the documentation does not indicate a specific side effect. Rather, 692.82 should be coded for the radiation dermatitis. The exclusion note under E926.5 refers the coder to E879.2 for abnormal reactions to radiation therapy without mention of a misadventure. The patient has completed the treatment for the lung cancer, and the tumor was eradicated. A history of lung cancer is coded as V10.11. The two-view chest x-ray is coded as 71020.

d. 508.1, 692.82, 162.4, 427.31, V58.69, E926.5, 71020

Incorrect answer. The radiation pneumonitis is coded as 508.0. Code 508.1 describes the condition of radiation fibrosis, which is a long term complication of radiation therapy with permanent damage to the lungs. The patient has completed the treatment for the lung cancer, and the tumor was eradicated. A history of lung cancer is coded as V10.11. The exclusion note under E926.5 refers the coder to E879.2 for abnormal reactions to radiation therapy without mention of a misadventure.

8.56. a. 473.9, 31256-50, 31287

Incorrect answer. The code reported is for unspecified sinusitis. Separate codes should be assigned for the sinusitis to fully describe what areas are involved (473.0, 473.2, and 473.3). The code for polyps (471.8) should also be reported because a polypectomy was described, even though it is included in the more extensive CPT codes. The CPT codes that should be reported are 31255-50, 31267-50, and 31288-50 because tissue removal was described for the maxillary and sphenoid areas, and the physician described the procedure as ethmoidectomy (on both sides), not ethmoidotomy.

b. 473.0, 473.2, 473.3, 471.8, 31256-50, 31287-50

Incorrect answer. The CPT codes reported should be 31255-50, 31267-50, and 31288-50 because tissue removal was described for the maxillary and sphenoid areas, and the physician described the procedure as ethmoidectomy, anterior and posterior (on both sides), not ethmoidotomy. Tissue removal was part of each procedure, so codes 31267 and 31288 are required instead of the codes reported, which are without mention of tissue removal.

c. 473.0, 473.2, 473.3, 471.8, 31255-50, 31267-50, 31288-50

Correct answer.

d. 473.0, 473.2, 473.3, 471.8, 31255, 31267

Incorrect answer. The diagnosis codes are correct and the procedure codes are correct, but modifier -50 must be appended to each procedure to reflect that these were carried out bilaterally. Per the instructional note preceding code 31231, the endoscopic sinus procedures are unilateral in nature. CPT code 31288-50 is also assigned for the sphenoidotomy, with tissue removal.

Trauma and Poisoning

8.57. a. 805.04, 344.01, E828.2, 99291, 31500

Incorrect answer. For facility reporting, the first hour of critical care is reported. There is a combination code for fracture with spinal cord injury. (See the includes note at code 806.)

b. 805.04, 344.01, E828.2, 99291, 31500

Incorrect answer. There is a combination code for fracture with spinal cord injury. (See the includes note at code 806.)

c. 806.01, E828.2, 99291, 31500

Correct answer.

d. 806.01, E828.2, 99291, 31500, 22305

Incorrect answer. Code 22305 is not reported because fracture care was not performed at this initial visit. The patient was transferred to another hospital for definitive fracture care.

8.58.   a. 816.00, 26756-F4, 13131-F4

Incorrect answer. This fracture is documented as an open fracture of the middle phalanx. Therefore, the correct code is 816.11. E codes should be reported for the cause of injury on this case. The appropriate codes are E920.1 for injury with a power hedge cutter and E849.0 for place of occurrence in the home. While the fracture was aligned with a pin, it states that this was done in an open fashion, or by visualizing the fracture site. Code 26756 describes a percutaneous pinning of the fracture, or through the skin at the end of the finger. This is an open repair and the closure code is included in the procedure. The correct CPT code is 26735.

b. 816.01, E920.1, 11012, 26735-F4

Incorrect answer. This fracture is documented as an open fracture of the middle phalanx, not a closed fracture. The correct code is 816.11. The E code for the place of occurrence should be reported as E849.0 for home. The CPT code is correct.

c. 816.11, E920.1, E849.0, 26735-F4

Correct answer.

d. 816.11, E920.1, E849.0, 26756-F4, 26418-F4, 26540-F4, 11012, 13131

Incorrect answer. While the fracture was aligned with a pin, it states that this was done in an open fashion, or by visualizing the fracture site. Code 26756 describes a percutaneous pinning of the fracture, or through the skin at the end of the finger. When the correct CPT code for open repair of the fracture is coded as 26735-F4, all of the other procedures are included in the fracture repair. All of the other codes are included per the NCCI edits.

Chapter 9. Case Studies from Physician-Based Health Records

Anesthesia Services

9.1.   a. 745.10, 00562-AA-23, 99100

Incorrect answer. The correct anesthesia code is 00561 for procedures on the heart using the pump oxygenator on patients under 1 year of age. No mention is made of unusual anesthesia circumstances. The infant's physical status was P5. Code 99100 is not to be reported with 00561 per instructional note under 99100: Do not report 00561 in conjunction with 99100.

b. 745.11, 00561-AD-P5, 99140

Incorrect answer. The correct ICD-9-CM code for transposition of the great vessels is 745.10. The appropriate modifier for the anesthesiologist is -AA. There is no mention of emergency circumstances. The qualifying circumstance is 99100 for a patient under one year of age and should not be reported with 00561 per instructional note: Do not report 00561 in conjunction with 99100.

c. 745.10, 00561-AA-P5

Correct answer.

d. 745.19, 00563-AA-P5, 99100, 99140

Incorrect answer. The correct ICD-9-CM code for transposition of the great vessels is 745.10. The correct anesthesia code is 00561 for procedures on the heart using the pump oxygenator, but without mention of systemic hypothermia. There is no mention of emergency circumstances, so qualifying circumstance code 99140 is not appropriate here, and it is inappropriate to report 99100 with 00561.

9.2.   a. 723.3, 907.3, E929.0, 99241, 64413

Correct answer.

Note: The supply code for the medication (J code) for the Marcaine and steroid injection also is reported per payer guidelines.

b. 907.3, 723.3, E929.0, 99242, 64413

Incorrect answer. The residual cervicobrachial syndrome should be sequenced before the late effect code per ICD-9-CM coding guidelines. All three key components of history, physical examination, and medical decision making must be met or exceeded to assign an evaluation and management code. The brief history makes 99241 the appropriate consultation code. The procedure code is correct.

c. 723.3, 907.3, E929.0, 99212, 64415

Incorrect answer. This was not an established patient office visit, but an outpatient consultation. Based upon the documentation of history, physical examination, and medical decision making, 99241 is the appropriate evaluation and management code. The injection was of the cervical rather than the brachial plexus, so code 64413 is the correct CPT procedure code.

d. 907.3, E929.0, 99245, 64470

Incorrect answer. The residual cervicobrachial syndrome should be sequenced before the late effect code, per ICD-9-CM coding guidelines. Based upon the documentation of history, physical examination, and medical decision making, 99241 is the appropriate evaluation and management code. The injection was of the cervical rather than the brachial plexus, so code 64413 is the correct CPT procedure code.

9.3.   a. 354.0, 64719

Incorrect answer. The report specifies the median nerve. The surgeon provided the regional anesthesia, so modifier -47 is reported with code 64721.

b. 354.0, 64722-47

Incorrect answer. The median nerve was specified, so code 64721 is correct. The surgeon provided the regional anesthesia, so modifier -47 is reported with code 64721.

c. 354.0, 64721-47

Correct answer.

d. 354.1, 64721, 01810

Incorrect answer. Carpal tunnel syndrome is reported with ICD-9-CM code 354.0. The regional anesthesia was provided by the surgeon, so modifier -47 is reported with code 64721, rather than reporting a separate anesthesia code.

Disorders of the Blood and Blood-Forming Organs

9.4.   a. 173.6, 38525

Incorrect answer. The codes for malignant neoplasm of the skin (category 173.X) exclude malignant melanoma, which is reported with a code from category 172.X, in this case, 172.6. A code should also be reported for the injection of the dye (38792).

b. 172.6, 38525, 38792

Correct answer.

c. 172.6, 38525, 38792-51, 78195

Incorrect answer. The lymphoscintigraphy (78195) was performed by the radiologist, and the surgeon should not report the code. Code 38792 is identified in the CPT manual as being exempt from modifier -51 reporting requirements.

d. 172.9, 38525, 38790-51

Incorrect answer. The site of the melanoma is specified (arm), so code 172.9 is incorrect. The dye was injected for identification of sentinel node, so code 38790 is not correct. Refer to the instructional note preceding code 38500, which specifies code 38792 as the appropriate code for injection of dye for identification of sentinel node. Code 38792 is identified in the CPT manual as being exempt from modifier -51 reporting requirements.

9.5.   a. 280.0, 792.1, 414.01, 250.00, V45.81
Correct answer.

b. 285.9, 780.79

Incorrect answer. The anemia is specified as due to chronic blood loss, so code 285.9 is not correct. It is also not correct to code the weakness because it is a symptom of the more definitive diagnosis of anemia. The positive hemoccult would be reported because the etiology is still uncertain (792.1). The additional diagnoses of diabetes, ASHD, and status post coronary artery bypass may be coded because they were treated and/or are applicable to the case.

c. 280.0, 578.1, 414.01, 250.00, V45.81

Incorrect answer. It is not correct to assume that the patient had GI bleeding. Occult blood in the stool is reported with code 792.1.

d. 998.11, 285.1, 792.1, 414.01, 250.00, V45.81

Incorrect answer. There is no documentation that the bleeding was a complication of the surgical procedure to substantiate the use of code 998.11. The anemia is specified as severe, but not acute, so code 285.1 would not be used even though the hemoglobin was 5.7. Code 280.0 is appropriate for reporting chronic blood loss anemia.

Disorders of the Cardiovascular System

9.6.   a. 972.1. E858.3, 787.01

Incorrect answer. Toxicity from digitalis use is coded as an adverse effect by assigning the codes for the manifestations of the adverse effect (787.01 and 780.79) as the primary diagnoses, followed by the E code that represents the agent in therapeutic use (E942.1). There is no suggestion that the drug was taken inappropriately. Additional codes are assigned for the MI (subsequent episode of care, 410.12) and the CHF (428.0).

b. 410.12, 428.0

Incorrect answer. The treatment in this case was focused on medication management, not the MI or the CHF. Toxicity from digitalis use is coded as an adverse effect by assigning the codes for the manifestations of the adverse effect (787.01 and 780.79) as the primary diagnoses, followed by the E code that represents the agent in therapeutic use (E942.1). There is no suggestion that the drug was taken inappropriately.

c. 787.01, 780.79, E858.3

Incorrect answer. The manifestation codes for the adverse effects of digitalis are correct and are appropriately sequenced as the primary diagnoses, but the E code is that used for a poisoning. The E code that represents the agent in therapeutic use (E942.1) is the appropriate E code. Additional codes are assigned for the MI (subsequent episode of care, 410.12) and the CHF (428.0).

d. 787.01, 780.79, E942.1, 410.12, 428.0
Correct answer.

9.7. a. 429.9, 424.0, 92961

Incorrect answer. The atrial flutter (427.32) should be assigned as the principal diagnosis. The excludes note at code 424.0 directs the coding professional to category 396 when both mitral and aortic valve disorders are present, whether or not the cause is specified as rheumatic. The cardioversion was external, so CPT code 92960 should be reported.

b. 429.9, 394.1, 33240

Incorrect answer. The atrial flutter (427.32) should be assigned as the principal diagnosis. There is a combination code (396.3) for reporting both mitral and aortic regurgitation. Code 429.9 is reported for the ventricular dysfunction. The procedure was an external cardioversion, not insertion of a pacing cardioverter-defibrillator pulse generator, so code 33240 is not correct. CPT code 92960 is the appropriate code for reporting an external cardioversion.

c. 427.32, 394.1, 429.9, 33211

Incorrect answer. The regurgitation is not specified as rheumatic, and both the mitral and aortic valves are involved, so code 396.3 is correct. The procedure performed was an external cardioversion, not placement of temporary pacemaker, so CPT code 92960 is reported.

d. 427.32, 396.3, 429.9, 92960
Correct answer.

9.8. a. 414.01, 414.05, 410.12, 411.1, V45.81, 33517, 33533, 33530
Correct answer.

b. 414.01, 414.05, 410.12, 411.1, V45.81, 33510, 33533

Incorrect answer. The bypass consisted of one venous graft and one mammary (arterial) graft, so codes from 33517–33523 must be used for the venous portion of the bypass per CPT coding guidelines. See instructional note preceding code 33510. The fact that this was a redo procedure should also be coded (33530).

c. 414.00, 414.05, 410.11, 411.1, V45.81, 33530

Incorrect answer. The coronary atherosclerosis involving the native artery should be coded to 414.01. Code 414.05 for the graft stenosis is correct. The MI was specified as involving the anterior wall (410.12). Code 33530 reports the reoperation only and is an add-on code that should not be reported alone. Codes 33517 and 33533 should be reported in the first two positions for the actual bypass procedure.

d. 414.01, 414.05, 410.12, 412, V45.81, 33518, 33530

Incorrect answer. The MI was recent (10 days), not old, so code 412 should not be used. The preinfarction angina should also be reported with code 411.1. The bypass was done with one artery and one vein, so the correct codes are 33517 and 33533.

9.9.   a. 428.0, 486, 496, 290.0

Correct answer.

b. 428.0, 518.4, 486, 496, 290.0

Incorrect answer. According to *Coding Clinic* (1988, 3Q), acute pulmonary edema of cardiac origin is a manifestation of CHF, category 428, and as such is included in the code.

c. 428.0, 410.91, 486, 496, 290.0

Incorrect answer. The MI was ruled out and should not be coded as if present.

d. 518.4, 428.0, 486, 496, 290.0

Incorrect answer. According to *Coding Clinic* (1988, 3Q), acute pulmonary edema of cardiac origin is a manifestation of CHF, category 428, and as such is included in the code. The CHF would be assigned alone, and in the principal diagnosis position.

9.10.   a. 33880

Incorrect answer. This code is appropriate for coverage of the left subclavian artery origin. The correct code assignment is 33881.

b. 33779

Incorrect answer. The correct code assignment is 33881.

c. 33881

Correct answer.

d. 33881, 33883, 33884

Incorrect answer. The extensions are included in code 33881 and are not reported separately with 33883 and 33884.

9.11.   a. 35454, 34900, 37205, 37250

Incorrect answer. Code 34900 is appropriate for the endovascular repair of the pseudoaneurysm, 37205 is appropriate for the stent placement because the pseudoaneurysm is proximal to the occlusion and therefore a separate target treatment area. Code 37250 is appropriate for the endovascular ultrasound, but code 35454 reports an open balloon angioplasty of the iliac artery. Code 35473 is the appropriate code to report a percutaneous balloon angioplasty of the iliac artery.

b. 35473, 34900, 37205, 37250

Correct answer.

c. 35454

Incorrect answer. This code is appropriate for the percutaneous balloon angioplasty, but codes for the stent placement (37205), the endovascular ultrasound (37250), and the endovascular repair of the pseudoaneurysm (34900) should also be reported.

d. 35492, 34900, 37205

Incorrect answer. Code 35492 reports a percutaneous transluminal atherectomy of the iliac artery, not a balloon angioplasty, which is reported with code 35473. Code 37250 should also be reported for the endovascular ultrasound. The other codes are correct.

9.12.   a. 93508, 92980-RC, 92981-LC

Correct answer.

b. 93508, 92982-RC, 92984-LC, 92980-RC, 92981-LC × 2

Incorrect answer. Codes 92982 and 92984 (angioplasty) are not reported in addition to 92980 and 92981 (stenting) per instructional note listed under codes 92980 and 92981: Coronary angioplasty (92982, 92984) in the same artery is considered part of the stenting procedure and is not reported separately. Stenting in the left circumflex coronary artery reported as 92981-LC × 2 is incorrect as the code is not reported based on the number of stents, it is reported based on the number of vessels stented (add on-code states: each additional vessel).

c. 93510, 92980-RC, 92981-LC

Incorrect answer. The codes for the interventional portions of the procedure are appropriate, but the code for the cardiac catheterization is not. Code 93510 is reported only when a full left heart catheterization is done and documentation states full cath was performed yesterday. Code 93508 is the appropriate code when catheters are placed into the coronary arteries for interventional procedures without a concomitant left heart catheterization.

d. 93510, 92982-RC, 92984-LC, 92980-RC, 92981-LC × 2

Incorrect answer. Code 93510 is reported only when a full left heart catheterization is done. Code 93508 is the appropriate code when catheters are placed into the coronary arteries for interventional procedures without a concomitant left heart catheterization. Codes 92982 and 92984 (angioplasty) are not reported in addition to 92980 and 92981 (stenting) per instructional note listed under codes 92980 and 92981: Coronary angioplasty (92982, 92984) in the same artery is considered part of the stenting procedure and is not reported separately. Stenting in the left circumflex coronary artery reported as 92981-LC × 2 is incorrect as the code is not reported based on the number of stents, it is reported based on the number of vessels stented (add on-code states: each additional vessel).

Disorders of the Digestive System

9.13.   a. 578.0, 285.1, 789.59, 99285, 43752

Incorrect answer. The only key component of history, physical examination, and medical decision making that meets criteria for 99285 is the high-complexity medical decision making. In assigning ED codes, all three elements must be met or exceeded unless there is clear documentation of patient inability to cooperate with history and physical examination, which is not present here. Code 99284 is the correct code. The evaluation and management code should have modifier -25 assigned.

b. 578.0, 789.00, 780.4, 99284-25, 91105

Incorrect answer. The abdominal pain is an integral part of the hematemesis, so code 789.00 should not be assigned. The dizziness and light-headedness are both due to the documented blood loss anemia and also should not be coded. The codes for anemia (285.1) and ascites (789.59) should be reported. The gastric tube was inserted by the emergency department physician and left in place to continue draining stomach contents, so code 43752 should also reported, rather than 91105.

c. 789.51, 578.0, 280.0, 99284, 43752

Incorrect answer. There is no documentation of malignant ascites, 789.51. The hematemesis is the reason for the patient seeking medical care, so this should be reported as the primary diagnosis. The anemia is due to the current episode of acute blood loss and should be assigned code 285.1. The evaluation and management code should have modifier -25 assigned.

d. 578.0, 285.1, 789.59, 99284-25, 43752

Correct answer.

9.14.   a. 562.12, 211.3, 45385, 45384-51 or 45384-59

Correct answer. Either modifier -59 or -51 may be used, depending upon specific payer requirements.

b. 211.3, 562.10, 578.1, 45384

Incorrect answer. Per *CPT Assistant* (1998, July), both 45384 and 45385 should be coded because two lesions were addressed with two different techniques. The diverticulosis is the cause of the bleeding and should be coded as "with hemorrhage" (562.12). This code should be listed first because it was the cause of the patient's seeking attention and undergoing the procedure. The GI bleeding code is not needed with code 562.12 because it is included in the fifth digit.

c. 562.12, 211.3, 578.9, 45385

Incorrect answer. Per *CPT Assistant* (1998, July), both 45384 and 45385 should be coded because two lesions were addressed with two different techniques. The GI bleeding code is not needed with code 562.12 because it is included in the fifth digit.

d. 562.12, 211.3, 45384

Incorrect answer. Per *CPT Assistant* (1998, July), both 45384 and 45385 should be coded because two lesions were addressed with two different techniques.

9.15.   a. 530.81, 530.85, 47562, 43289-51

Incorrect answer. The documentation states "with esophagitis," so code 530.11 is correct. The chronic cholecystitis should also be coded. CPT code 43280 includes laparoscopic Nissen procedures, so the unlisted procedure code is not appropriate.

b. 530.11, 530.85, 574.10, 43324, 47600-52

Incorrect answer. The cholecystitis is not specified as being calculous, so code 574.10 is not correct. Codes 43324 and 47600 are open procedures. It is never appropriate to assign an open procedure code when a laparoscopic approach is specified.

c. 530.11, 530.89, 575.11, 43326

Incorrect answer. Barrett's esophagus codes to 530.85. The correct procedure code is 43280 because there is no documentation of a gastroplasty being performed. The laparoscopic cholecystectomy should also be reported (47562-51).

d. 530.11, 530.85, 575.11, 43280, 47562-51
Correct answer.

9.16.   a. 574.11, 47564

Incorrect answer. Code 574.71 describes chronic cholecystitis with cholelithiasis and bile duct calculus with obstruction. The common bile duct was not explored with the cholecystectomy, but rather was done via ERCP. Codes 43265, 43262, and 43264 are also reported per *CPT Assistant* (1994, April).

b. 574.70, 47562, 43265-51

Incorrect answer. Code 574.71 describes chronic cholecystitis with cholelithiasis and bile duct calculus with obstruction. Codes 43262 and 43264 are also reported per *CPT Assistant* (1994, April).

c. 574.71, 47562, 43265-51, 43264-51

Incorrect answer. It is appropriate to code each procedure separately. The CPT manual also instructs the coding professional to add code 43262 to code 43265 or 43264 when performed.

d. 574.71, 47562, 43265-51, 43262-51, 43264-51
Correct answer.

9.17.   a. 455.2, 46221, 45300-51, 46600-51
Correct answer.

b. 455.2, 46221, 46221-59, 45300

Incorrect answer. Per *CPT Assistant* (1997, Oct.), even though there are multiple ligations done, only one is coded. The anoscopy should also be coded per the same reference, even though some payers may not reimburse for this.

c. 455.0, 46945, 45300

Incorrect answer. The hemorrhoids are documented as prolapsed and bleeding, which constitutes a complication. Code 455.2 is the correct diagnosis code. Per *CPT Assistant* (1997, Oct.), the appropriate CPT code for rubber band ligation of hemorrhoids is 46221. The anoscopy should also be coded per the same reference, even though some payers may not reimburse for this.

d. 455.8, 46083, 45300-51, 46600-51

Incorrect answer. There is documentation that the hemorrhoids were internal; therefore 445.2 is the correct ICD-9-CM diagnosis code. Per *CPT Assistant* (1997, Oct.), the appropriate CPT code for rubber band ligation of hemorrhoids is 46221.

Evaluation and Management (E/M) Services

9.18.   a. 99219, 99231, 99217

Incorrect answer. An inpatient code (99231) is not appropriate for the place of service for a hospital outpatient.

b. 99219, 99499, 99217

Correct answer. *CPT Assistant* (1996, April) advises the use of code 99499 to report this unusual circumstance. Note that specific payers may publish other requirements.

c. 99283, 99219, 99217

Incorrect answer. The emergency department visit should be bundled into the initial observation day code, and a separate outpatient care code is needed for day two.

d. 99283, 99231, 99217

Incorrect answer. An inpatient code (99231) is not appropriate for the place of service for a hospital outpatient. The emergency department visit should be bundled into the initial observation day code, and a separate outpatient care code is needed for day two.

9.19.   a. Dr. Smith: 99315, 99219; Dr. Johnson: 99236

Incorrect answer. No mention is made of discharge from the nursing facility.

b. Dr. Smith: 99219; Dr. Johnson: 99217, 99236

Incorrect answer. Observation discharge is not coded when the patient is admitted and discharged on the same day.

c. Dr. Smith: 99219; Dr. Johnson: 99236

Correct answer.

d. Dr. Smith 99315, 99222; Dr. Johnson: 99238

Incorrect answer. None of these codes is correct. No mention is made of discharge from the nursing facility, nor was the patient admitted to inpatient status on the first day. Instead of hospital discharge 99238, Dr. Johnson's services require code 99236, Observation or inpatient hospital care, for admission and discharge on the same day.

9.20. a. 99214, 99222, 99239, 99305

Incorrect answer. The office visit should be bundled into the initial hospital care code.

b. 99222, 99239, 99305

Correct answer.

c. 99214, 99235, 99305

Incorrect answer. The patient was not admitted and discharged on the same day. Separate codes are needed for the admission and discharge. The office visit should be bundled into the initial hospital care code.

d. 99222, 99305

Incorrect answer. A code for the hospital discharge day is also needed.

9.21. a. 99204, 99354

Incorrect answer. Because there is documentation that counseling comprised more than 50 percent of the total time of the visit, time may be used as the determining factor, resulting in code 99205. The total time of the visit should be used in calculating the evaluation and management code, not the amount of time spent in counseling.

b. 99205, 99354, 99355

Incorrect answer. Documentation states that 50 minutes was spent counseling and coordinating care with a total of 95 minutes. This does not support the use of an additional 30 minutes of prolonged care.

c. 99205, 99354

Correct answer.

d. 99204

Incorrect answer. Because there is documentation that counseling comprised more than 50 percent of the total time of the visit, time may be used as the determining factor, resulting in code 99205. Because code 99205 suggests a time of approximately 60 minutes, there are an additional 35 minutes to be reported, which should be reflected with the prolonged service code 99354.

9.22. a. V72.31, V76.47, V45.77, 99396; 784.0, 99213-25

Correct answer.

b. V70.9, 99396, 784.0, 99213

Incorrect answer. A vaginal pap smear and pelvic examination were performed, so code V72.31 followed by V76.47 is the best choice for the primary diagnosis. A modifier -25 is needed on the evaluation and management code for the office visit for evaluation of the headache complaint. Acquired absence of the uterus may also be reported (V45.77).

c. V76.2, V76.47, V45.77, G0101, Q0091; 784.0, 99213-25

Incorrect answer. The patient is 56 years old and is not a Medicare beneficiary. Acquired absence of the uterus may also be reported (V45.77).

d. 784.0, V72.31, V76.47, V45.77, 99214

Incorrect answer. A complete preventative medicine examination was performed as scheduled. The patient had an incidental complaint of headache after she arrived, which was evaluated, and this should be coded as a separately identifiable evaluation and management service with modifier -25.

9.23. a. 99233

Incorrect answer. Critical care services were rendered, with one hour documented. The correct code is 99291.

b. 99291, 99292

Incorrect answer. Only one hour of critical care is documented. The appropriate code is 99291.

c. 99233, 99354

Incorrect answer. Critical care services were rendered, with one hour documented. The correct code is 99291.

d. 99291

Correct answer.

9.24. a. 99205

Incorrect answer. This E/M service is reported for an office visit, new patient, and not appropriate reporting for the consultant seeing a patient for the first time. Use office or other outpatient consult codes 99241–99245. The follow-up visit(s) by that same consultant would report other office or outpatient visit codes 99211–99215.

b. 99244

Correct answer.

c. 99243

Incorrect answer. Although documentation of history, physical examination, and medical decision making meets the criteria for code 99242, because more than 50 percent of the total time was spent in counseling the patient, time is the determining factor and meets the criteria for code 99244.

d. 99354

Incorrect answer. Code 99354 is an add-on code and is not reported separately without being used in conjunction with 99201–99215 or 99241–99245 or 99304–99350.

Endocrine, Nutritional and Metabolic Diseases, and Immunity Disorders

9.25.   a. First visit: 259.4, 259.0; second visit: 253.3

Incorrect answer. There is no mention made of any type of dwarfism. Short stature should be coded.

   b. First visit: 783.43, 259.0; second visit: 253.3

Correct answer.

   c. First visit: 259.0. second visit: 253.4

Incorrect answer. Short stature should also be coded for the first visit. Code 253.4 describes "deficiency . . . other than growth hormone." Code 253.3 is the appropriate code.

   d. First visit: 259.4; second visit: 253.4

Incorrect answer. There is no mention made of any type of dwarfism. Short stature and delay in sexual development should be coded. Code 253.4 describes "deficiency . . . other than growth hormone." Code 253.3 is the appropriate code.

9.26.   a. 611.1, 257.2

Correct answer.

   b. 257.1, 611.1, 259.0

Incorrect answer. No mention is made of postablative status, so code 257.1 is not appropriate. The failure to develop secondary sexual characteristics is inherent to hypogonadism and should not be coded separately.

   c. 257.8, 909.1

Incorrect answer. Code 257.2 more specifically describes the hypogonadism, and code 611.1 accurately reports the gynecomastia. Possible pesticide exposure is not a confirmed diagnosis and would not be reported per ICD-9-CM outpatient (physician) coding guidelines. *ICD-9-CM Official Guidelines for Coding and Reporting*: Section IV. Diagnostic Coding and Reporting Guidelines for Outpatient Services. These guidelines apply to hospital-based outpatient and provider-based office visits. Inconclusive diagnoses (probable, suspected, rule out, and so on) were developed for inpatient reporting and do not apply to outpatient. *Coding Clinic* (2006, 4Q:236).

   d. 257.2, 259.0

Incorrect answer. The failure to develop secondary sexual characteristics is inherent to hypogonadism and should not be coded separately. A code for the gynecomastia (611.1) should be reported.

9.27.   a. 227.3, 162.9, V77.1

Incorrect answer. It is unclear whether this tumor was benign or malignant. Code 239.7 is the appropriate neoplasm code when the nature of the tumor has not been determined. The patient will be followed for possible development of diabetes insipidus. No screening was done for diabetes.

b. 194.3, 162.9

Incorrect answer. There is no mention of whether the pituitary tumor was benign or malignant. Code 239.7 is the appropriate neoplasm code when the nature of the tumor has not been determined.

c. 239.7, 162.9, 253.5

Incorrect answer. The patient will be followed for possible development of diabetes insipidus, but it has not yet been diagnosed.

d. 239.7, 162.9

Correct answer. If this is a case where an oncologist is providing care for the lung cancer and an endocrinologist is addressing the pituitary tumor concurrently, it would be important for each specialist to report only the specific condition(s) that he or she is following in order to avoid the appearance of duplicate coding and billing.

Disorders of the Genitourinary System

9.28.   a. 233.4, 55875, 52000, 77763, 76000

Incorrect answer. Although the physician states that the cancer is localized, carcinoma in situ would not be assumed without being directly stated as such. The primary malignancy should be reported as the reason for the radiation therapy. Code 77778 would be appropriate, rather than 77763, because the treatment of the prostate would be interstitial rather than intracavitary because the prostate is a solid organ. See the note in the CPT manual with code 55875 instructing the coding professional to use codes 77776–77787 for interstitial radioelement application. According to the NCCI, code 52000 is bundled into the procedure code 55875 and is not listed separately. Review of code 55875 in the CPT manual states "with or without cystoscopy," which indicates that whether the cystoscopy was performed or not, the code and reimbursement for 55875 are the same.

b. 185, 55875, 77778, 76965, 76000

Correct answer. Modifier -51 may be used if accepted by the payer. Depending upon the physician's arrangements with the cancer center, modifier -26 may be needed.

c. 185, 55875, 77787, 76872, 77790

Incorrect answer. There is a specific code for interstitial radioelement application. Code 77787 is used to report remote application using catheters. Code 77778 is the correct code. The ultrasound code should be 76965, which is the specific code for guidance for interstitial application. The fluoroscopy (76000) should also be reported. The port films would not be coded in this case. This is brachytherapy, not radiation therapy, and there is no documentation of films being performed. Also, the code reported is for each five days, and this procedure has a different treatment plan.

d. 185, 52000, 77762

Incorrect answer. We need to report the surgical implantation code (55875) with ultrasonic guidance (76965) and the fluoroscopy (76000) codes. This procedure on the prostate, a solid organ, is an interstitial application, rather than an injection (intravenous) or intracavitary insertion, which is used only for hollow organs such as the bladder.

9.29.   a. 611.72, 610.1, 19120-50

Incorrect answer. When a definitive diagnosis is known, it is reported, so code 174.9 for the primary malignancy would be the first code reported, followed by the code for the fibrocystic disease, and the breast lump would not be coded. A bilateral modifier -50 applies only to identical procedures on paired organs. The breasts are paired organs, but the procedures involved here were not the same. HCPCS Level II modifier -RT identifies the 19120 procedure on the right side, while the -LT procedure is appended to CPT codes 19125 and 19290 to report the procedure on the left breast.

b. 174.9, 610.1, 19125-50, 19290-50, 19120-50

Incorrect answer. Appropriate use of the bilateral modifier has it appended to only one CPT code when identical procedures are performed on paired organs. Although identical procedures may be performed on the breasts, the code is reported only once with modifier -50. In the case described in this source document, identical procedures were not performed, so the appropriate modifier assignment in this case is -RT and -LT for the two different procedures. Codes 19120 and 19125 would be mutually exclusive under the NCCI otherwise; therefore, they require an additional modifier -51 to differentiate that a separate procedure was performed on the right breast from the procedure performed on the left breast.

c. 174.9, 610.1, 19120-RT, 19125-LT-51, 19290-LT-51

Correct answer.

d. 174.9, 610.2, 19120, 19125-59, 19290-59

Incorrect answer. The fibrocystic disease was not stated to be fibroadenosis, so code 610.1 is as specific as the documentation here allows. The use of modifier -59 is not appropriate for this case because HCPCS Level II modifiers -RT and -LT would describe the services more accurately.

9.30. a. 626.8, 218.1, 58558
Correct answer.

b. 626.8, 218.9, 57800, 58558

Incorrect answer. This patient has intramural fibroids. While intramural is not a subterm listed under Fibroids in the index, it is listed as a specific type of uterine fibroid when you view the index. Therefore, 218.1 for intramural fibroids should be chosen as the code. CPT code 57800 is for dilation of the cervical canal and is a separate procedure. Therefore, this cannot be used with another procedure code and is not correct.

c. 627.0, 218.9, 58558, 58120

Incorrect answer. The physician states that this patient has dysfunctional bleeding but does not link it to a premenopausal state. The physician states that the lab work suggests a perimenopausal state but this does not support the use of this code. CPT code 58120 is not coded separately as code 58558 states "with or without D&C" in the description.

d. 627.0, 218.1, 58558

Incorrect answer. The physician states that this patient has dysfunctional bleeding but does not link it to a premenopausal state. The physician states that the lab work suggests a perimenopausal state but this does not support the use of this code. The CPT code is correct.

9.31. a. 188.6, 52354-RT

Incorrect answer. The report states that one of the tumors was in the ureteropelvic junction, not the ureterobladder junction coded with 188.6. Code 189.2 is the appropriate ICD-9-CM diagnosis code. Procedure performed on right ureter; therefore modifier RT (right) is added to show procedure was performed on the right ureter.

b. 188.6, 52224-RT

Incorrect answer. This operation involved the ureters, not the bladder. Code 189.2 is the correct diagnosis code for a primary malignancy of the ureter, and code 52354 describes the fulguration of such lesions. Procedure performed on right ureter; therefore modifier RT (right) is added to show procedure was performed on the right ureter.

c. 189.2, 52354-RT
Correct answer.

d. 189.2, 52354-RT, 52330-RT

Incorrect answer. CPT code 52330 is not separately reported because it represents the approach and is a component of the more extensive procedure. Procedure performed on right ureter; therefore modifier RT (right) is added to show procedure was performed on the right ureter.

9.32.   a. 185, 55700

Incorrect answer. Carcinoma in situ of the prostate is coded 233.4 because the malignancy has not extended into any surrounding tissue and is detected early. CPT codes are required for the placement of the ultrasound probe (76872) and the actual provision of ultrasonic guidance for the biopsy (76942). Stones of the prostate (602.0) should also have a code assigned because they may affect current or future care of the patient.

b. 233.4, 790.93, 55705, 76872

Incorrect answer. The biopsy code in CPT is 55700 because no incision is documented. The placement of the transrectal probe is only one component of the procedure. An additional code (76942) is required for the needle guidance for the prostatic biopsy. Stones of the prostate (602.0) should also have a code assigned because they may affect current or future care of the patient. Abnormal laboratory tests are not assigned an additional code when the etiology has been confirmed by the close of the encounter.

c. 185, 790.93, 602.0, 55700, 76872, 76942

Incorrect answer. The neoplasm is specified as carcinoma in situ of the prostate, so code 233.4 is assigned, rather than the code for a primary malignant neoplasm of the prostate. Abnormal laboratory tests are not assigned an additional code when the etiology has been confirmed by the close of the encounter. The other codes are correct.

d. 233.4, 602.0, 55700, 76872, 76942

Correct answer.

Infectious Diseases/Disorders of the Skin and Subcutaneous Tissue

9.33.   a. 686.9, V12.04. 250.00, 443.81, 99214, 96372

Incorrect answer. 686.9 is found in the index under Infection, leg. However, the specific disease process is cellulitis. When this is found in the index, the subterm entry of leg provides the code of 682.6. This patient has diabetic peripheral vascular disease and therefore the correct codes are 250.70 for the complicated diabetes and 443.81 as the secondary code to describe the type of complication. The E/M code for this visit is 99215 because only two key components are required and this documentation includes a comprehensive examination and high-level medical decision making (a new problem with risk to life or bodily function). The antibiotic is administered through the IV route and not the intramuscular route. A HCPCS code is required to report the medication and the dosage administered.

b. 682.6, V02.54, 250.70, 443.81, 99214, 96374, S0077

Incorrect answer. The cellulitis code is correct but the patient has a personal history of MRSA and is not a suspected carrier of MRSA, therefore V12.04 is the correct code. The E/M code for this visit is 99215 because only two key components are required and this documentation includes a comprehensive examination and high level medical decision making (a new problem with risk to life or bodily function). The antibiotic and the administration is coded correctly.

c. 682.6, V12.04, 250.70, 443.81, 99215, 96374, S0077
Correct answer.

d. 891.1, V02.54, 250.70, 443.81, 99215, 96372, J3490

Incorrect answer. Code 891.1 represents a complicated open wound of the leg. While the leg has an open wound, it did not start as an open wound, it started as mild redness and not an open wound. The cellulitis code of 682.6 is the most appropriate code. The patient has a personal history of MRSA and is not a suspected carrier of MRSA, therefore V12.04 is the correct code. The remainder of the coding is correct.

9.34. a. 891.0, 882.0, E920.8, E849.0, 12004

Incorrect answer. The left ankle laceration was repaired with a layered closure, which constitutes an intermediate repair. It would not be added to the code for the simple closure.

b. 891.1, 882.0, 12002, 12032-51

Incorrect answer. The repair of the wound of the left ankle, even though it required a layered closure, did not meet the criteria for a complex repair. External cause of injury codes (E-codes) may be reported to show how the accident occurred and the place of occurrence for full reporting purposes. Because of the age of the patient, he is assumed to be a Medicare beneficiary and a HCPCS Level II code, G0168, is used to report repairs using only tissue adhesive.

c. 894.0, 12032, 12002, supply code for the DERMABOND tissue adhesive

Incorrect answer. The use of the multiple open wound ICD-9-CM diagnosis code is incorrect when specified sites are documented. E codes may be reported to show how the accident occurred for full reporting purposes. Because of the age of the patient, he is assumed to be a Medicare beneficiary and a HCPCS Level II code, G0168, is used to report repairs using only tissue adhesive. The supply is included in this code.

d. 891.0, 882.0, E920.8, E849.0, 12032, 12002-51, G0168
Correct answer.

9.35.   a. 173.3, 214.1, 11641, 11403-51, 12031-51

Correct answer. Some payers may require the use of modifiers. Depending on payer requirements, code 11641 may have modifier -59 appended to show that it is a distinct procedure. Code 12031 may require the use of modifier -51 to show multiple procedures.

b. 173.3, 214.9, 11403, 11441-51

Incorrect answer. The lipoma is specified as of the skin, so code 214.1 is correct and more specific. The lesion of the cheek is a squamous cell carcinoma, a type of malignant neoplasm. The layered closure should also be reported, per the instructional note preceding code 11600.

c. 214.1, 195.0, 11603, 11641-51, 12031-51

Incorrect answer. The squamous cell carcinoma is specified as left cheek, so it would be coded as 173.3, Skin of the face, rather than unspecified site. The lesion on the right shoulder is a lipoma, which is benign. Code 11403 is used rather than 11603.

d. 173.3, 11643, 12031-51

Incorrect answer. Each lesion should have a diagnosis code assigned when available. One lesion is a lipoma, a type of benign lesion, and the other is a squamous cell carcinoma, a type of malignant lesion. Lesion excision codes are never added together in CPT like repair codes are. Each lesion excision should be assigned a separate code. One code should be assigned for the benign lesion and one for the malignant lesion.

9.36.   a. 15220, 15221-51, 15002-51

Incorrect answer. Codes 15220 and 15221 are incorrect. These are the codes for a full-thickness graft, but the graft documented in this source document was a split-thickness graft. Also, code 15221 is an add-on code and is exempt from modifier -51 use.

b. 15100

Incorrect answer. The preparation of the burn site should also be coded with code 15002 with modifier -51 multiple procedure.

c. 14021, 15002-51

Incorrect answer. Code 14021 would be used when a flap of tissue is advanced into the site of the defect but remains attached. This report documents a free graft.

d. 15100, 15002-51

Correct answer.

9.37.   a. 195.0, 15120

Incorrect answer. The neoplasm code is indexed under forehead, and 195.0 is not the most specific code possible. The excision of the lesion should also be coded per CPT guidelines. The split thickness autograft was performed on the thigh (15100—trunk, arms, legs) not face, scalp, eyelids, mouth, neck, ears, orbits, genitalia, hands, feet or multiple digits (15120).

b. 173.3, 15120

Incorrect answer. The excision of the lesion should also be coded per CPT guidelines. The split thickness autograft was performed on the thigh (15100—trunk, arms, legs) not face, scalp, eyelids, mouth, neck, ears, orbits, genitalia, hands, feet or multiple digits (15120).

c. 173.3, 15100, 11646

Correct answer.

d. 195.0, 15004, 15120

Incorrect answer. The neoplasm code is indexed under forehead, and 195.0 is not the most specific code possible. It is not appropriate to assign code 15004 when an excision of a lesion is performed. The excision of the malignant lesion should be coded instead (11646). The split thickness autograft was performed on the thigh (15100—trunk, arms, legs) not face, scalp, eyelids, mouth, neck, ears, orbits, genitalia, hands, feet or multiple digits (15120).

9.38.   a. 599.0, 682.5, 780.60, 493.90, 99214-25, 99143, 10061, 99000

Incorrect answer. The symptom of fever is not coded with an established diagnosis of an infective process. The asthma is not coded because the condition was not treated during the encounter. The incision and drainage of the abscess should be coded as 10060 because the abscess is not described as complicated and a drain is not left in the wound.

b. 599.0, 682.5, 780.61, 99215, 99143, 10061, 36415, 85025, 85009, 81001

Incorrect answer. The symptom of fever is not coded with an established diagnosis of an infective process. Code 780.61 is used to describe fever when present in conditions where fever establishes the severity of the condition. In this case, fever is integral to an infection and therefore, not coded separately. The E/M code of 99215 is not supported by documentation. An encounter with a detailed history, comprehensive exam, and moderate decision making is coded as 99214. In this case, a procedure is performed in addition to a significant, separately identifiable E/M service and therefore, a 25 modifier is necessary. The code for a manual differential, 85009, should not be coded as an automated differential is included in the CBC code, 85025.

c. 599.0, 682.2, 99214, 99144, 10060, 99000, 36415, 85025, 81003

Incorrect answer. The abscess is of the buttock and not of the trunk and therefore, code 682.5 is correct. The E/M code is correct but requires the addition of a 25 modifier to show that a significant, separately identifiable E/M service was performed. The conscious sedation code should be 99143 because the physician performing the procedure did the conscious sedation with the assistance of a trained staff observer. The urinalysis code should be 81001 because the performance of a microscopy is documented.

d. 599.0, 682.5, 99214-25, 99143, 10060, 99000, 36415, 85025, 81001

Correct answer.

Behavioral Health Conditions

9.39. a. 965.1, 780.4, 388.30, E950.0, 99284-25, 91105

Correct answer.

b. 965.1, 780.4, E980.0, 99284

Incorrect answer. Tinnitus is coded as 388.30. A suicide attempt is clearly documented in the source document, and code E950.0 is more appropriate than the undetermined code. The gastric tube insertion should also be coded.

c. 780.4, 388.30, E935.3, 99284-25, 43752

Incorrect answer. This would be the appropriate code assignment for an adverse effect of aspirin therapy. The poisoning code, 965.1, should be primary in this case and the manifestations secondary. The gastric tube insertion was done therapeutically and should be coded with code 91105. Modifier -25 significant, separately identifiable E/M service by same physician on same date of procedure or other service is added to the E/M code.

d. 780.4, 388.30, 965.1, E935.3, 99284, 43752

Incorrect answer. The poisoning code, 965.1, should be the primary diagnosis and the manifestations secondary. The E code reported here reflects an adverse effect, and code E950.0 is more appropriate with the documented suicide attempt. The gastric tube insertion was done therapeutically and should be coded with code 91105. Modifier -25 significant, separately identifiable E/M service by same physician on same date of procedure or other service is missing from the the E/M code.

9.40. a. 303.00, 980.9, 99291, 99292

Incorrect answer. The poisoning code should be the primary diagnosis. Alcoholic beverages were specified, so the correct code is 980.0. There is no documentation of alcoholism in the patient, only acute alcohol intoxication. There is no mention of critical care being performed in the emergency department. An E code is needed for the external cause of injury (E860.0).

b. 980.9, 305.00, 99285-25, 12011

Incorrect answer. The laceration was closed with Steri-Strips, which is not coded as a laceration repair per the instructional note preceding code 12001. CPT guidelines state that a wound closure utilizing adhesive strips as the sole means of repair should be reported with an appropriate evaluation and management code. An E code is needed for the external cause of injury (E860.0).

c. 980.0, 305.00, 873.42, E860.0, 99285

Correct answer.

d. 980.0, 303.00, 99291, 12011

Incorrect answer. There is no documentation of alcoholism in the patient, only acute alcohol intoxication. There is no mention of critical care being performed in the emergency department. An E code is needed for the external cause of injury (E860.0). CPT guidelines state that a wound closure utilizing adhesive strips as the sole means of repair should be reported with an appropriate evaluation and management code.

9.41. a. 307.1, 314.01, 301.83, 493.90, V17.0, 90801

Correct answer.

b. 301.1, 314.01, 301.83, 276.8, 493.90, 359.3, 90801

Incorrect answer. The hypokalemia is stated as "history of." There is no documented evidence that the patient is currently hypokalemic, so code 276.8 is not reported for this admission. The statement of hypokalemic periodic paralysis "per patient report" would not be reported unless confirmed by the attending physician. The family history of psychiatric conditions may also be reported (V17.0).

c. 307.1, 314.01, 301.83, 493.90, V17.0, 99223

Incorrect answer. This is a psychiatric diagnostic/evaluative interview, also known as an Initial Psychiatric Evaluation (IPE), rather than a hospital admission service. The appropriate code is 90801.

d. 301.1, 314.01, 301.83, 276.8, 493.90, 359.3, 99223

Incorrect answer. This is a psychiatric diagnostic/evaluative interview, also known as an Initial Psychiatric Evaluation (IPE), rather than a hospital admission service. The appropriate code is 90801. The hypokalemia is stated as "history of." There is no documented evidence that the patient is currently hypokalemic, so code 276.8 is not reported for this admission. The statement of hypokalemic periodic paralysis "per patient report" would not be reported unless confirmed by the attending physician. The family history of psychiatric conditions may also be reported (V17.0).

Disorders of the Musculoskeletal System and Connective Tissue

9.42. a. 813.32, 24650, 11010-51, 20692-51

Incorrect answer. The diagnosis code is inappropriate because it identifies the ulnar shaft rather than the location near the head, with dislocation of the radial head. The CPT code is also incorrect for the fracture repair as this code describes repair of a fracture of the radial head or neck. Code 20692 is incorrect; there is no combination code available for this fracture repair. Note that code 20692 is exempt from modifier -51 use.

b. 813.18, 24685, 11010-51, 29105-51

Incorrect answer. The diagnosis code is not as specific as possible on the basis of the documentation provided. The CPT code is for repair of the olecranon process and the splint application code is inappropriately assigned. Codes for splinting, casting, and strapping are included in the initial fracture care codes and are not to be reported separately.

c. 813.02, 24635, 20692, 29105-51

Incorrect answer. The diagnosis code is not as specific as possible on the basis of the documentation provided. The CPT code for the fracture care is correct, but the additional codes 20692 and 29105 should not be reported separately. In addition, the fracture debridement should be coded.

d. 813.13, 24635, 11010-51

Correct answer.

9.43. a. 170.7, 27360, 27447, 35721, 27448, 76000

Incorrect answer. The resection of the femur tumor was considered radical resection because the entire proximal femur was removed. Code 27360 describes removal of small pieces of bone, not the entire proximal femur. Code 27445 describes the hinge prosthesis used in this case, rather than a total knee arthroplasty described in 27447. The surgeon performed a lateral retinacular release, which should be reported to correctly describe the case. Fluoroscopy was used but the surgeon should correctly report the professional component only by appending modifier 26 to 76000.

b. 170.7, 27365, 27445, 35721, 27448, 27425, 76000-26

Correct answer.

c. 238.0, 27329, 27445, 27448, 76000-26

Incorrect answer. An osteosarcoma is a malignant bone tumor. The ICD-9-CM index directs the coder to the malignant column in the neoplasm table for code 170.7. CPT code 27329 describes the excision of a tumor of the soft tissue of the thigh or knee, not a bone tumor. Therefore, 27365 is the correct code. The surgeon performed a lateral retinacular release, which should be reported to correctly describe the case. The femoral artery was explored during the procedure, and code 35721 must be reported to correctly describe the case.

d. 239.2, 27360, 27447, 27448, 27425, 76000

Incorrect answer. An osteosarcoma is a malignant bone tumor. The ICD-9-CM index directs the coder to the malignant column in the neoplasm table for code 170.7. The resection of the femur tumor was considered radical resection because the entire proximal femur was removed. Code 27360 describes removal of small pieces of bone, not the entire proximal femur. Code 27445 describes the hinge prosthesis used in this case, rather than a total knee arthroplasty described in 27447. Fluoroscopy was used but the surgeon should correctly report the professional component only by appending modifier 26 to 76000.

9.44. a. 722.52, 401.9, 63047

Incorrect answer. The diagnosis code 722.52 reports degenerative disc disease rather than disc displacement. CPT code 63047 is used to report laminectomy, facetectomy, and foraminotomy, rather than the partial facetectomy documented in this source document.

b. 722.73, 401.9, 63030

Incorrect answer. Diagnosis code 722.72 is used to report disc disorder with myelopathy. Although there is disc encroachment upon the nerve root, there is no documentation of compression of the spinal cord, which is required to assign a "with myelopathy" code. The CPT code is correct.

c. 722.10. 63047

Incorrect answer. The ICD-9-CM diagnosis code is correct. CPT code 63047 is used to report laminectomy, facetectomy, and foraminotomy, rather than the partial facetectomy documented in this source document.

d. 722.10. 401.9, 63030

Correct answer.

9.45. First listed diagnosis: 844.2

Additional diagnoses: 836.1, 836.0

Procedures: 29888-RT, 29880-RT-51

Note: It is appropriate to report code 29880 in addition to code 29888 since the meniscectomy is not considered an integral component of the anterior cruciate ligament repair/reconstruction. Modifier -51 should be appended to the secondary code to report multiple procedures were performed at the same session.

9.46. 733.42, 733.49, 27130-RT

Note: The patient was noted to have avascular necrosis of the hip. Because there is no one ICD-9-CM diagnosis code to identify both components of the hip, two diagnosis codes are needed to identify the bones which comprise the hip. (femur and acetabulum)

Neoplasms

9.47. a. 204.00, 996.62, 780.60, 99284-25, 96374

Incorrect answer. This patient has a central venous catheter. Infections of central venous catheters are coded as 999.31. Code 780.60 is not reported in this case because fever is integral to the infective process. The CPT code for the IV push is not reported as this service was provided by facility nursing staff. In addition, the CPT book states in the notes within this section that these codes are not to be reported by physicians in the facility setting. The 25 modifier is not appropriate because no physician-performed procedure was provided.

b. 204.00, 999.31, E878.2, 99284

Correct answer.

c. 208.00, 996.69, 780.61, 99285

Incorrect answer. Acute lymphocytic leukemia is coded as 204.00 by accessing the index under Leukemia, lymphocytic, and then the subterm of acute. This patient has a central venous catheter. Infections of central venous catheters are coded as 999.31. Code 996.69 is used to report an infection of an unspecific catheter. CPT code 99285 is incorrect because documentation states that the medical decision making was moderate. This limits the emergency department code to 99284.

d. 208.00, 999.31, 99285-25, 96374

Incorrect answer. Acute lymphocytic leukemia is coded as 204.00 by accessing the index under Leukemia, lymphocytic, and then the subterm of acute. CPT code 99285 is incorrect because documentation states that the medical decision making was moderate. This limits the emergency department code to 99284. The CPT code for the IV push is not reported as this service was provided by facility nursing staff. In addition, the CPT book states in the notes within this section that these codes are not to be reported by physicians in the facility setting. The 25 modifier is not appropriate because no physician-performed procedure was provided.

9.48. a. 162.9, 32400, 77002

Incorrect answer. The diagnosis code may be further specified in location to the lower lobe with code 162.5. Also, the CPT code reported here reflects a pleural biopsy (surface area) rather than deeper into lung tissue as described. Code 32405 is the appropriate code to describe the procedure performed.

b. 786.09, 786.2, 32405

Incorrect answer. Symptoms are not reported when the etiology is established by the close of the visit. The CPT code is correct, but the coding professional should also add the code for fluoroscopic guidance for the procedure. This is reported with code 76003, which is not included in the code for the needle biopsy.

c. 162.5, 32405, 77002-26

Correct answer. The use of modifier -26 on the fluoroscopic guidance code is appropriate. This code is for the radiological supervision and interpretation only; however, it must be billed with a -26 to show the professional component and the facility bills the same code 77002 with modifier -TC for technical component (owns the equipment).

d. 162.5, 786.09, 786.2, 32405, 77002-26

Incorrect answer. Symptoms are not reported when the etiology is established by the close of the visit. The remainder of the codes are correct.

9.49. a. 197.3, 199.1, 796.2, 31576, 99144

Correct answer. Because the primary site has not been established, diagnosis code 199.1 may be reported following the code for the confirmed metastatic disease. Though the procedure was discontinued, the planned procedure was carried out, so no modifier is necessary.

b. 161.8, 198.89, 401.9, 31510

Incorrect answer. The pathology report indicates that the laryngeal malignancy is metastatic. If the malignancy were primary to the larynx, this would be the correct diagnosis code. Hypertension cannot be coded on the basis of an elevation of blood pressure, so code 796.2 is assigned to reflect that complication. Code 197.3 is the only code that can be assigned because the esophageal primary has yet to be confirmed. Because the primary site has not been established, diagnosis code 199.1 may be reported following the code for the confirmed metastatic disease. Code 198.89 is not the correct code for thyroid cartilage, which is an anatomic portion of the larynx. Code 197.3 is assigned for metastatic disease in this location. The CPT code is for an indirect laryngoscopy with biopsy rather than the flexible fiberoptic procedure described. Code 31576 is the correct code. IV sedation was administered by the physician and code 31576 does not include moderate (conscious) sedation; therefore code 99144 is reported for IV sedation.

c. 150.9, 197.3, 197.3, 197.3, 197.3, 997.1, 31576-53

Incorrect answer. Because the primary site has not been confirmed, it is not appropriate to assign the code for primary carcinoma of the esophagus. The metastatic disease would not be coded multiple times for the various sites because ICD-9-CM is a classification system. The correct reporting is 197.3, 199.1, and 796.2 to report the increased blood pressure episode. Code 997.1 is inappropriate in this circumstance because neither the diagnosis of hypertension nor a cause-and-effect relationship between the procedure and the elevated blood pressure reading has been documented. Modifier -53 is not needed for the procedure code because the laryngoscopy and biopsies had been accomplished before the procedure was discontinued. IV sedation was administered by the physician and code 31576 does not include moderate (conscious) sedation; therefore code 99144 is reported for IV sedation.

d. 150.9, 161.8, 796.2, 31576, 99144, 99145

Incorrect answer. It is rarely appropriate to assign two codes for primary neoplasm in the same case and would never be appropriate without physician documentation that two primary sites with different morphology were present. In this case, the laryngeal malignancy is stated to be metastatic, with a suspected primary in the esophagus. Because this is an outpatient case, we cannot code any diagnosis that is not confirmed. And in any event, physician-reporting guidelines preclude reporting unconfirmed diagnoses in any setting. The correct diagnosis codes, in addition to the elevated blood pressure reading, are 197.3 and 199.1 for the unknown primary. IV sedation was administered by the physician for 16 minutes and code 99144 includes the first 30 minutes; therefore code 99145 (each add'l 15 minutes) is not reportable based on the documentation.

9.50. a. 153.2, 45384

Incorrect answer. The procedures involve different sites and have different diagnosis codes. The modified code 45380-59 is assigned to show that separate sites were involved in this case. Code 211.3 should also be reported.

b. 153.2, 211.3, 45384, 45380-59

Correct answer. Modifier -59 is required to show that the biopsy and the polypectomy were performed at different sites.

c. V67.09, V10.05, 153.2, G0105, 45384-59

Incorrect answer. Medicare requires that specific HCPCS Level II codes be used to report screening colonoscopy in a high-risk patient, but the codes are used only when no recurrence of disease is found or no procedure is carried out beyond the description of code 45378. The V code for the reason for visit is also incorrect because a recurrence of the primary neoplasm at the same site is documented, which is assigned the code for the malignancy, rather than the V code.

d. 153.9, V10.05, V45.89, 45384, 45380

Incorrect answer. There is more definitive location information available, so code 153.2 may be assigned instead of the unspecified code. The "history of" V code is not assigned as an additional code, but it is assigned in a case where the malignancy has been surgically removed and has not recurred. Addition of the V45.89 code does not add any information, so it is not recommended. The CPT codes are not completely correct because it is appropriate to code both a biopsy and a polypectomy when different sites are involved. To show the payer that these are different sites, modifier -59 should be appended to the lesser procedure (the biopsy).

9.51. a. 182.0, 627.1, V10.3, 58558, 99214-59

Incorrect answer. An additional diagnosis code should be reported for the mass, which contributes to the separately identifiable services required above and beyond the services normally associated with a diagnostic hysteroscopy. The modifier assigned would be -25 rather than -59 because modifier -59 is not used when another, more specific modifier is appropriate. The postmenopausal bleeding in this case would not be separately reported because the etiology is known by the end of the session.

b. 182.0, 785.6, V10.3, 58558, 99214-25

Correct answer. Modifier -25 shows that a significant and separately identifiable evaluation and management service occurred on the same date as the procedure.

c. 182.0, 785.6, V10.3, 58558-25

Incorrect answer. Modifier -25 is only appended to an evaluation and management code. Code 99214 is assigned for an established patient who has the level of examination described in this scenario, based upon documentation of history, physical examination, and medical decision making.

d. 182.0, 785.6, V10.3, 58555, 58100, 99214-25

Incorrect answer. When a biopsy is performed via a hysteroscope, the combination code 58558 is reported. The other codes are correct.

9.52. a. 199.0, 153.9, 36561, 36556-59

Incorrect answer. Two procedures were actually performed, although the left subclavian VAD placement was aborted before completion. Due to the limited aborted procedure documentation, a physician query is required to determine if the left subclavian vein catheter insertion was nontunneled in order to meet the criteria for code 36556. The venipuncture should be reported with modifier 59 to show that code 36410 is a separate procedure at a different site.

b. 153.9, 36563, 36410-53

Incorrect answer. The disseminated disease should be coded as 199.0, although the sequencing is probably not significant because the reason for the visit is the insertion of the port. The CPT codes must reflect the insertion of the port in the right subclavian, as well as the cannulation of the left subclavian. The code 36563 is for an infusion pump, not a VAD with a port. Modifier -59 is assigned rather than -53 to report that code 36410 is a separate procedure at a different site rather than a discontinued procedure.

c. 199.0, 153.9, 36561, 36410-59

Correct answer. The physician would only report fluoroscopy if he had utilized his own equipment. This procedure is performed at the hospital, so the hospital will report the imaging guidance (likely 77002). Due to the limited aborted procedure documentation, a physician query is required to determine if the left subclavian vein catheter insertion was nontunneled in order to meet the criteria for code 36556.

d. V58.81, 199.0, 153.9, 36561, 12031

Incorrect answer. The Code V58.81 is used for removal or replacement of a catheter. The neoplasm is sequenced first when the reason for the visit is initial insertion. The catheterization of the left subclavian may also be reported as 36556-59, with the modifier showing that it was not a component of the VAD procedure, but involved a different site. Layered closure (12031) is included in code 36561 and would not be reported separately. The venipuncture should be reported with modifier -59 to show that code 36410 is a separate procedure at a different site.

9.53. a. 172.7

Correct answer.

b. 232.7

Incorrect answer. This is a melanoma, which is classified to category 172.

c. 232.7, 172.7

Incorrect answer. Only one code for the melanoma is necessary. Code category 172 is for melanoma of the skin, which is the most specific code for this patient.

d. 172.7, 709.9

Incorrect answer. The skin lesion was identified as melanoma. Only a code from category 172 is necessary.

Disorders of the Nervous System and Sense Organs

9.54. a. 438.11, 438.81, 99203, 96105

Incorrect answer. The evaluation and management service described is a consultation and should be reported with code 99243-25.

b. 784.3, 784.69, 99244

Incorrect answer. When neurological problems remain following a CVA, a code from the late effects section of ICD-9-CM is used. In this case, codes 438.11 and 438.81 are used to reflect the aphasia and apraxia. The consultation code is one level too high, based upon documentation of history, physical examination, and medical decision making, and should be 99243, based upon the low-complexity medical decision making. Modifier -25 is added to show that an assessment reported with code 96105 was also provided on the same date in addition to the evaluation and management service.

c. 438.81, 99243

Incorrect answer. There are actually two residual conditions present that warrant coding, the aphasia and the apraxia. Code 438.11 should be assigned in addition to 438.81. The clinic service described is a consultation service, with an additional neurocognitive test performed, reported with code 96105. Modifier -25 may be helpful with code 99243 for the evaluation and management service to show that both services were provided and are separately identifiable.

d. 438.11, 438.81, 99243-25, 96105

Correct answer.

9.55. a. 437.3, 61700

Incorrect answer. Because of the term "microdissection," the code for use of the operating microscope should be assigned. Additional codes should be reported to reflect the postoperative pneumonia, which would be codes 997.3 and 482.1.

b. 430, 482.1, 61700, 69990-51

Incorrect answer. Code 69990 is exempt from modifier -51 use because the + symbol in the CPT manual signifies an add-on code. Such procedures are never reported alone, so modifier -51 is not used. The aneurysm is not described as ruptured, so code 437.3 is the appropriate code. To show that the pneumonia was documented as due to the surgery, code 997.3 should also be reported.

c. 437.3, 997.3, 482.1, 61700, 69990

Correct answer.

d. 747.81, 997.3, 61703, 69990

Incorrect answer. The procedure code is incorrect. Code 61700 correctly describes the procedure performed. Even though the patient is 35 years old, we cannot presume that the aneurysm is congenital. Code 437.3 is correct with this documentation. Code 997.3 identifies that the pneumonia was due to the procedure, but an additional code of 482.1 should be reported to show the organism (Pseudomonas) responsible.

9.56.   a. 333.1, 728.9, 99244-25, 95925, 95927-51

Correct answer. The modifier -25 may or may not be required to show that both an evaluation and management service and a diagnostic procedure were performed at the same time, depending upon payer reporting requirements. For codes 95925 and 95927, care should be taken to report exactly what the physician does. The use of the -26 or -TC modifiers may be indicated if only the supervision or only the equipment were provided. For a unilateral procedure, use the -52 modifier. Code 95920 may also be reported, if documented.

b. 340, 99245-25, 95927

Incorrect answer. For physician reporting, a diagnosis qualified as "rule out" cannot be assigned a definitive code. The symptoms prompting the service are reported instead: 333.1 for intention tremor, and 728.9 for muscle weakness. An additional CPT code should be reported for the testing on the upper limbs (95925). The evaluation and management consultation code may not be higher than level 4 when moderate medical decision making is documented. Code 99245 requires complex medical decision making.

c. 333.1, 728.9, 99204, 95925, 95927-51

Incorrect answer. Consultation services are assigned to a different category of the evaluation and management section of CPT. Modifier -25 may or may not be required to show that both an evaluation and management service and a diagnostic procedure were performed at the same time, depending upon payer reporting requirements.

d. 728.9, 781.0, 99244-25, 95927

Incorrect answer. The ICD-9-CM code for intention tremor has a code from the nervous system chapter (333.1). Tremor NOS would be assigned the symptom code 781.0. Procedure codes are required for both the EMG tests (95925 and 95927).

9.57.   a. 64449

Incorrect answer. Code 64449 is for continuous administration of a local anesthetic agent through a catheter, not a single injection by a needle approach.

b. 62319

Incorrect answer. Code 62319 is for continuous infusion through a catheter, not a single injection by a needle approach.

c. 62311

Correct answer. A caudal injection is in the lumbosacral region.

d. 62311, 77003

Incorrect answer. Fluoroscopy was not mentioned in this case, so it is not appropriate to report this code. Because many such procedures are performed under fluoroscopy, it may be appropriate to query the physician about this. Also the physician would only report fluoroscopy if he had utilized his own equipment. This procedure is performed at the hospital, so the hospital would report the fluoroscopy.

9.58.   a. 387.9, 997.1, 427.31, 69661-LT

Correct answer. Medicare probably does not cover this patient, but it is possible. If the payer allows the reporting of HCPCS Level II modifiers, the -LT will indicate which side had surgery. If the payer does not allow the use of modifier -LT, it should be deleted.

b. 387.9, 69661-LT

Incorrect answer. The patient was admitted to the hospital after the procedure, and the postoperative atrial fibrillation should be reported. Even though the cardiologist will follow the patient, these codes should also be reported to show why the patient was admitted to the hospital and why any additional evaluation and management codes will be submitted for the stay.

c. 387.9, 427.31, 69661-LT

Incorrect answer. Because the physician documented that the atrial fibrillation was due to the surgery, code 997.1 should also be assigned, followed by the 427.31.

d. 387.9, 69660-LT

Incorrect answer. According to documentation, the footplate was drilled out. Code 69661 is correct for reporting this procedure. The complications requiring admission to the hospital should also be reported.

Newborn/Congenital Disorders

9.59.   a. 99460, 99462, 99238

Incorrect answer. The physician's attendance at delivery on 11/20 with initial care to the newborn should also be reported with code 99464.

b. 99460, 99464, 99462, 99238

Correct answer.

c. 99460, 99360, 99233, 99238

Incorrect answer. Physician standby (99360) is reported for prolonged attendance without direct patient contact. In this case, the physician did provide the initial care to the newborn. Code 99464 is reported. Also, subsequent hospital care is reported for the normal newborn (99462) rather than the usual hospital inpatient care (99233).

d. 99464, 99232, 99238

Incorrect answer. Code 99464 is correct; however, 99460 should also be reported on 11/20 because the physician initiated the newborn's diagnostic and treatment plan on that date. Also, subsequent hospital care is reported for the normal newborn (99462) rather than the usual inpatient hospital care (99232).

9.60.   a. 381.01, 462, 758.0, V45.89, 99214, 96372, J0530
Correct answer.

b. V20.2, 381.01, 462, 758.0, V45.89, 99392, 99214-25

Incorrect answer. Although the chief complaint in this note indicates routine or "preventative" service, there are symptoms and problems indicated in the history of present illness that actually precipitated the visit. Also, CPT instructions state that when less than the code description for preventative care is provided, the usual evaluation and management codes are reported. With a detailed history and physical examination and moderate level medical decision making (for example, medication management and review of records), code 99214 may be supported. Without the 99392 code, no modifier is needed. The administration of the injection should be reported with the appropriate materials code. This may be J0530 if the payer accepts HCPCS Level II codes, or 99070 in CPT. Code 96372 may be bundled with the evaluation and management code but is appropriately assigned when performed. Because this is not a "well-child" visit, code V20.2 is not appropriate to report. Reporting both services together would be reserved for an instance in which a preventative examination is scheduled for an asymptomatic patient, and, in the course of the evaluation, a condition is identified that requires significant and separately identifiable physician work that is performed for the identified condition, in addition to completion of the components of the preventative service. In that case, the V code is listed first, followed by the identified condition, and both evaluation and management services are reported, with the preventative service reported first and modifier -25 on the office visit code.

c. 381.01, 462, 99214, 96372

Incorrect answer. The Down syndrome code is important to report because the physician did evaluate development and spent part of the visit counseling the mother about the condition. The code for the ventricular septal defect may not be coded for this visit because it was not evaluated and did not affect management. Code V45.89 could be reported to show that the child was status post surgery. It is important for physician office reporting to capture all services including drugs. Third-party payers differ in their policies of accepting HCPCS Level II codes (J0530 in this case), and some might expect CPT code 99070 to be reported, with a description of the drug injected.

d. 758.0, V45.89, 99213, J0530

Incorrect answer. The child presented with symptoms of otitis media and was also followed for developmental and other health concerns surrounding Down syndrome and the cardiac surgery required for repair of the ventricular septal defect. The otitis media (381.01) and sore throat (462) codes are reported as the reason for visit and to explain the need for antibiotic administration. This should also be reported with a CPT code 96372, even though some payers will bundle this service into the evaluation and management code and not allow separate reimbursement. The code for Down syndrome (758.0) and status post surgery (V45.89) should also be reported. The evaluation and management value is one level too low because a detailed history and physical examination and moderate-level medical decision making are documented, which would allow reporting of 99214.

9.61. a. 749.04, 42225, 42825

Incorrect answer. It would be important to assign code 474.00 as the reason for the tonsillectomy. The physician would add modifier -51 to the tonsillectomy code to reflect multiple procedures at the same operative session.

b. 749.04, 474.00, 42225

Incorrect answer. The tonsillectomy, although "incidental," is reported with CPT code 42825. See *CPT Assistant* (1997, August). The physician would add modifier -51 to the tonsillectomy code to reflect multiple procedures at the same operative session.

c. 749.04, 474.00, 42225, 42825-51

Correct answer.

d. V50.8, 749.04, 474.00, 42200, 42826-51

Incorrect answer. A diagnosis code from the V50 category is used only to report services where there is no medical necessity for a procedure, but a cosmetic or other elective benefit, such as an encounter for circumcision. Revision palatoplasty procedures have specific codes, and in this case code 42225 is the correct code because a pharyngeal flap was employed. A tonsillectomy would not be an integral part of a palatoplasty and is always reported separately; however, the appropriate code is 42825 because the patient is 10 years old. See *CPT Assistant* (1997, August).

9.62. a. 536.49, 079.99, 530.81, 49440

Incorrect answer. No complication of the gastrostomy is documented. The child pulled the tube out, which is not a complication. Attention to the G tube should have been reported as V55.1. Congenital cytomegalovirus infection is coded as 771.1 and not a nonspecific viral infection code. The code is located in the index under Infection, then Congenital and then cytomegalovirus. This condition will affect the child for his entire life and can be coded even though he is no longer a newborn. Erosion of the esophagus should be coded as 530.89 because this is a complication of gastroesophageal reflux disease, not a symptom. The CPT code should be 49450 to report a replacement of a G tube. Even though the physician did not remove the G tube, the tube is replaced using the same gastrostomy site. See *CPT 2008 Changes: An Insider's View* for the description of this procedure.

b. 536.41, 771.1, 530.81, 530.89, 43760, 76000-26

Incorrect answer. No infection of the gastrostomy is documented. The congenital cytomegalovirus infection is not a localized infection of the G tube site. Attention to the G tube should have been reported as V55.1. The CPT code should be 49450 to report a replacement of a G tube. Even though the physician did not remove the G tube, the tube is replaced using the same gastrostomy site. See *CPT 2008 Changes: An Insider's View* for the description of this procedure. Fluoroscopic guidance is included in code 49450.

c. V55.1, 530.81, 530.89, 771.1, 49450

Correct answer.

d. V55.1, 530.81, 079.99, 49450, 76000-26

Incorrect answer. Congenital cytomegalovirus infection is coded as 771.1 and not a nonspecific viral infection code. The code is located in the index under Infection, then Congenital and then cytomegalovirus. This condition will affect the child for his entire life and can be coded even though he is no longer a newborn. Erosion of the esophagus should be coded as 530.89 because this is a complication of gastroesophageal reflux disease, not a symptom. The CPT code is correct, however, fluoroscopic guidance is included in code 49450.

Pediatric Conditions

9.63.   a. 99281-25, 31505

Correct answer.

b. 99281-25, 31511

Incorrect answer. The removal of the foreign body could not be completed by the ED physician. The diagnostic scope was completed, so this code would be reported instead.

c. 99282, 31505

Incorrect answer. All three elements of history, physical examination, and medical decision making must be met or exceeded to assign an emergency department code. The documentation met a level 1 (99281) on the basis of a problem-focused physical examination. A -25 modifier should be added to the evaluation and management code.

d. 99281, 31511

Incorrect answer. The removal of the foreign body could not be completed. The diagnostic scope was completed, so this code would be reported instead. A -25 modifier should be added to the evaluation and management code.

9.64.   a. 770.83, 079.6, 933.1, E911, 99284

Incorrect answer. This infant is not a newborn. The newborn period extends through the 28th day of life. RSV infection (079.6), and Asphyxia by aspiration (933.1) cannot be coded as they are documented as "rule out" conditions. Documentation for this case supports a level 99285 because the history is comprehensive, the exam is comprehensive, and the medical decision making is high (new problem with risk to life or bodily function).

b. 782.5, 786.03, 799.82, 99285

Correct answer. The tabular instructs the coder to use additional code(s) for associated signs and symptoms.

c. 799.82, 99285

Incorrect answer. The CPT code is correct. The ALTE code is correct, however the tabular instructs the coder to use additional code(s) for associated signs and symptoms. This means that cyanosis and apnea must also be coded.

d. 782.5, 799.82, 99291

Incorrect answer. Cyanosis and ALTE are correct but the symptom of apnea must also be coded. Critical care is not provided or documented in this case, and the documentation supports a 99285 service.

9.65.   a. 3/31: 813.43, 25600, A4580

4/1: 813.43, 840.9, 99024

4/2: 813.44, 99024, A4580.

Incorrect answer. The cast application on 3/31 was for the purpose of pain management. Restorative treatment had not been determined at that point. Code 29075 is reported for the 3/31 services. The global period had not yet begun, so 99024 is not applied on 4/1. The visit on 4/1 was for treatment of a complication, and the office visit can be reported (99213). The global fracture treatment (25600) begins on 4/2. At this point, restorative treatment is done and a treatment plan is established.

b. 3/31: 813.43, 29075, A4580

4/1: 840.9, 813.43, 99213

4/2: 813.44, 25600, A4580

Correct answer.

c. 3/31: 813.43, 25605, A4580

4/1: 840.9, 813.43, 99213

4/2: 813.44, 29075, A4580

Incorrect answer. The cast application on 3/31 was for the purpose of pain management. Restorative treatment had not been determined at that point. Code 29075 is reported for the 3/31 service. Coding for 4/1 is correct. The global fracture treatment (25600) begins on 4/2. At this point, restorative treatment is done and a treatment plan is established. Code 25600 is the appropriate code because no manipulation (reduction) was done.

d. 3/31: 813.43, 29075, A4580

4/1: 840.9, 813.43, 99213

4/2: 813.44, 25605, A4580

Incorrect answer. The fracture treatment on 4/2 did not include manipulation. Code 25600 is the appropriate code.

9.66.   a. 475, 474.00, 075, 250.01, 99239
Correct answer.

b. 475, 474.00, 075, 250.81, 99238

Incorrect answer. Hypoglycemia is mentioned in evaluating the laboratory values; however, no definitive diagnosis is documented. The correct code for diabetes is 250.01. The discharge code 99239 would be reported because the physician has documented more than 30 minutes spent in discharging the patient.

c. 475, 075, 250.01, 99238

Incorrect answer. The chronic tonsillitis is specifically excluded from code 475 and is reported separately with code 474.00. The discharge code 99239 would be reported because the physician has documented more than 30 minutes spent in discharging the patient.

d. 475, 474.0, 075, 250.81, 99239

Incorrect answer. The correct diagnosis code is 474.00. Hypoglycemia is mentioned in evaluating the laboratory values; however, no definitive diagnosis is documented. The correct code for diabetes is 250.01.

Conditions of Pregnancy, Childbirth, and the Puerperium

9.67.   a. 667.02646.62, 670.02, 664.31, 663.31, V27.0; 59400, 59160-78
Correct answer.

b. 667.04, 646.62, 670.02, 664.31, 663.31, V27.0; 59400, 59300-51, 58120-78

Incorrect answer. The patient delivered during this admission, so the fifth digit of 1 or 2 must be used on the pregnancy codes. Code 667.02 is correct because this is a postpartum complication. The episiotomy and repair are not separately reported. A postpartum curettage is coded 59160.

c. 667.02, 664.31, 663.31, V27.0; 59400, 59300, 59160

Incorrect answer. The endometriosis should be coded. The episiotomy and repair are not separately reported. Modifier -78 should be appended to 59160.

d. 667.04, 646.62, 670.02, 664.31, V27.0; 59400, 58120

Incorrect answer. The patient delivered during this admission, so the fifth digit of 1 or 2 must be used. Code 667.02 is correct. Documentation also states that there was a nuchal cord. A postpartum curettage is coded 59160, and modifier -78 should be appended.

9.68.   a. 632, 493.90, 59820, 59200-51

Incorrect answer. The excludes note at code 632 directs the coding professional to use either 630 or 631 when there is an abnormal product of conception. This anembryonic gestation would be coded as 631. Procedure codes for the insertion of laminaria would not be reported because that procedure was done prior to this episode of care.

b. 630, 493.90, 59870

Incorrect answer. Although the pathology report shows chorionic villi, which would be consistent with a molar pregnancy, the code 630 should not be assigned without the physician's diagnosis. With the diagnosis of anembryonic gestation, code 631 is the correct code. CPT coding guidelines state that if the molar pregnancy is unspecified, code 59820 for treatment of missed abortion is reported. See *CPT Assistant* (1999, February).

c. 631, 59856, 59200

Incorrect answer. Diagnosis code 631 is correct. The asthma should also be reported (493.90). This is not an induced abortion but, rather, treatment for a missed abortion (59820). Procedure codes for the insertion of laminaria would not be reported because that procedure was done prior to this episode of care.

d. 631, 493.90, 59820

Correct answer.

Disorders of the Respiratory System

9.69. a. 491.21, 518.82, 99214

Incorrect answer. Acute respiratory insufficiency is an integral part of COPD and is not coded separately.

b. 518.81, 491.21, 99213

Incorrect answer. The patient had acute respiratory insufficiency, not acute respiratory failure. Acute respiratory insufficiency is an integral part of COPD and is not coded separately. Because this is an established patient, only two out three of the components of history, physical examination, and medical decision making must be met to assign an evaluation and management level code. Code 99214 is correct.

c. 518.82, 491.21, 99203

Incorrect answer. Acute respiratory insufficiency is an integral part of COPD and is not coded separately. The CPT code for a new patient visit is incorrect because the patient has been seen many times by this practitioner for this condition.

d. 491.21, 99214

Correct answer.

9.70. a. 473.8, 471.8, 349.81, 31201-50, 31051-50, 31020-50, 69990

Correct answer. The excision of the uncinate process is a component of the sinus surgeries and would not be separately reported.

b. 473.8, 471.8, 998.2, E870.0, E849.7, 31201-50, 31051-50, 31020-50

Incorrect answer. The complication code is not appropriate in this case because the surgeon indicated that no instruments were used in this area. The coding professional should not assume that a condition is a "complication" of a procedure. Refer to *Coding Clinic* (1990, 3Q and 1992, 2Q) for more information on coding complications. The cerebrospinal fluid leak is then coded to 349.81. Code 69990 should be reported as well because there is documentation of the use of the operating microscope.

c. 478.19, 473.8, 31267-50, 31288-50, 31254-50, 69990

Incorrect answer. The approach for the procedures is intranasal and not endoscopic, so the CPT codes are incorrect. An additional diagnosis code is assigned for the CSF leak (349.81). Code 471.8 is the appropriate code for polyposis of the sinuses rather than 478.19.

d. 473.8, 471.8, 998.11, 998.2, E870.0, E849.7, 31090-50, 69990

Incorrect answer. Neither the CSF leak nor the blood loss should be coded as surgical complications. The surgeon indicated that no instrumentation was used in this area of the CSF leak, and there was no documentation to indicate that the moderate bleeding complicated the surgical procedure. The CPT code used is for a unilateral sinusotomy involving three or more sinuses. Codes 31201, 31051, and 31020 are more descriptive of this complex procedure and may be modified to show that the procedure was bilateral.

9.71. a. 478.33, 31561, 31600

Incorrect answer. Code 31600 is not reported in addition to 31561 because it is designated as a "separate procedure" in CPT.

b. 478.30, 31560

Incorrect answer. The diagnosis code is not as specific as it could be. Because bilateral partial paralysis is documented, code 478.33 may be reported. The correct procedure code is 31561 because the microscopy was used.

c. 478.33, 31561

Correct answer.

d. 478.33, 31560, 69990

Incorrect answer. There is a combination code for laryngoscopy with use of the operating microscope, 31561, which is reported instead of 31560 and 69990.

9.72. a. 162.5, 31641, 99144

Correct answer. The drug should also be coded. The entire record should be reviewed to identify the drug given and the dosage. If this were a Medicare patient, a HCPCS Level II code could be assigned. If Versed were given, for example, code J2250 would be used and repeated for each mg given.

b. 162.5, 31641, 76001

Incorrect answer. Code 99144 should be reported for the conscious sedation (if criteria for its reporting are met). Code 76001 is not separately reported, per CPT guidelines. CPT codes 31622–31646 include fluoroscopy when performed.

c. 239.1, 31640, 99144-51

Incorrect answer. Carcinoma is a malignant neoplasm of the bronchus and should be reported using code 162.5 for the lower lobe. The CPT code is for excision by forceps, and in this situation a laser probe was used, so code 31641 would be assigned.

d. 239.1, 31641, 99144, 76001

Incorrect answer. Carcinoma is a malignant neoplasm of the bronchus and should be reported using code 162.5 for the lower lobe. Code 76001 is not separately reported, per CPT guidelines. CPT codes 31622–31646 include fluoroscopy when performed.

9.73. a. 239.1, V64.1, 31629, 76000

Incorrect answer. The diagnosis code is too presumptive. All masses are not neoplasms and should not be coded from the neoplasm table unless so stated by the physician. The atrial fibrillation code 427.31 should be added to show a condition that affected patient management. The CPT code is correct but requires a modifier to show that the procedure was terminated before completion. Code 76000 is not assigned because fluoroscopy is always included in this code range when performed.

b. 786.6, 427.31, 31629-52

Incorrect answer. Modifier -53 is correct because the procedure was terminated due to circumstances that threatened the well-being of the patient. Code V64.1 is added to show that the procedure was not carried out because of the contraindication of atrial fibrillation.

c. 786.6, 427.31, V64.1, 31628-53

Incorrect answer. The CPT code reported is for transbronchial lung biopsy, which would be performed with biopsy forceps rather than a needle aspiration process. Code 31629 is the appropriate CPT code.

d. 786.6, 427.31, V64.1, 31629-53

Correct answer. If modifiers are accepted, the -53 will show that the physician terminated the procedure due to extenuating circumstances.

9.74. a. 32480, 32663-53

Correct answer.

b. 32663, 32480

Incorrect answer. The open procedure is listed first, and the converted endoscopic procedure is listed second per *CPT Assistant* (1994, Fall).

c. 32480

Incorrect answer. The open procedure is listed first, and the converted endoscopic procedure is listed second per *CPT Assistant* (1994, Fall).

d. 32484, 32663-52

Incorrect answer. The open procedure is listed as a lobectomy, not a segmentectomy. Code 32480 is correct. The appropriate modifier is -53. Modifier -52 is close, but the procedure was terminated because of extenuating circumstances, not reduced.

9.75.   a. 466.0

Correct answer.

b. 466.0, 519.11

Incorrect answer. The bronchospasm is included in the acute bronchitis and is not coded separately. Refer to the alphabetic index: Bronchitis, acute or subacute, with, bronchospasm—466.0

c. 519.11

Incorrect answer. A code for acute bronchitis should be assigned, which includes bronchospasm.

d. 466.19

Incorrect answer. This is the code for bronchiolitis, this patient has acute bronchitis.

Trauma and Poisoning

9.76.   a. 942.32, 943.29, 948.10, E924.0, E015.2, 99283-25, 16030

Correct answer.

b. 942.32, 948.00, E924.0, 16025

Incorrect answer. The total burned area (both second and third degree) was greater than 10 percent, therefore 948.10 is correct. An E/M code (99283-25) would be reported for the care provided before the burns are treated. These burns are considered large, and code 16030 is most appropriate. An E-code to describe that the patient was involved in the activity of cooking should be reported.

c. 942.23, 942.33, E924.0, E015.2, 99284, 16025

Incorrect answer. The burn of the chest was described as full thickness or third degree and should be coded as 942.32. The other burn was a partial thickness burn of the arm and is coded as 943.29 because of the multiple locations on the same arm. Only code 99283 can be justified by the documentation and requires a -25 modifier.

d. 942.22, 943.20, 948.10, E924.0, 11000, 11001

Incorrect answer. The burn of the chest was described as full thickness or third degree and should be coded as 942.32. The second degree burn is of both the upper and lower arm and is therefore coded to the multiple location code of 943.29. An E-code to describe that the patient was involved in the activity of cooking should be reported. An E/M code (99283-25) would be reported for the care provided before the burns are treated. Codes 11000 and 11001 describe debridement of infected skin and are not appropriate here. The codes for debridement of burn wound should be used, and these burns are considered large, or 16030.

9.77.   a. 823.10, E819.2, 27535, 11011-51

Incorrect answer. The orthopedic surgeon performed the fracture reduction. The emergency department physician would report the CPT code 11011 in addition to the appropriate level of evaluation and management service for the medical evaluation of the patient prior to the surgical procedure. Modifier -51 is used only when one physician performs more than one procedure at the same operative session. Two different physicians were involved here, so no modifier is required. Diagnosis codes are correct.

b. 823.12, E819.2, 11043

Incorrect answer. Codes from the range 11010–11012 are assigned for debridement associated with open fractures. The emergency department physician would report the appropriate evaluation and management service code and 11011 for the debridement procedure. The diagnosis is an open fracture of the tibia. There is no mention of fibular fracture, so 823.10 is the correct diagnosis code.

c. 823.10, E819.2, 11011

Correct answer.

d. 823.90, E819.2, 27535, 11043-51

Incorrect answer. The orthopedic surgeon performed the fracture reduction. The emergency department physician performed the debridement, but this code is incorrect. Code 11011 is the appropriate code. Modifier -51 is used only when one physician performs more than one procedure at the same operative session. Two different physicians were involved here, so no modifier is required. A more specific diagnosis code for the fracture of the proximal end of the tibia should be used.

9.78.   a. 512.0, 821.01, 807.03, E819.3; 99284-25, 32551

Incorrect answer. This is a traumatic pneumothorax; code 860.0 is correct. All three key components for evaluation and management code 99285 were met, so that would be the appropriate code.

b. 860.0, 821.01, 807.03, E819.3; 99285-25, 32551

Correct answer.

c. 860.0, 821.00, 807.09, E819.3; 99285, 32422

Incorrect answer. The femur fracture is specified as midshaft. The final diagnosis indicates multiple rib fractures, but review of the rest of the note reveals that three ribs were fractured. Modifier -25 is needed to report a significant, separately identifiable evaluation and management service. No mention of a thoracentesis is made. The chest tube is coded 32551.

d. 512.0, 821.00, 807.09, E819.3; 99284, 32422

Incorrect answer. This is a traumatic pneumothorax; code 860.0 is correct. All three key components for evaluation and management code 99285 were met, so that would be the appropriate code. The final diagnosis indicates multiple rib fractures, but review of the rest of the note reveals that three ribs were fractured. Modifier -25 is needed to report a significant, separately identifiable evaluation and management service. No mention of a thoracentesis is made. The chest tube is coded 32551.

9.79.   a. 803.06, E819.2, 99291, 36556

Incorrect answer. Critical care was less than 30 minutes, so evaluation and management codes should be used. Head injury was diagnosed with a skull fracture, so 803.46 would be the correct code. The intubation should also be coded.

b. 803.46, E819.3, 99291, 31500

Incorrect answer. Critical care was less than 30 minutes, so evaluation and management codes should be used. The central line is also coded unless it was done in connection with critical care codes. The patient was the vehicle driver; the fourth digit on the E code should be 2.

c. 803.33, E819.2, 99285, 31500, 36556-51

Incorrect answer. There is no mention of intracranial hemorrhage in the documentation.

d. 803.46, E819.2, 99285, 31500, 36556-51

Correct answer.

9.80.   a. 99291, 99292, 32160, 31500

Correct answer.

b. 99291, 99292, 32160

Incorrect answer. The intubation is not bundled into critical care and should be separately coded.

c. 99291, 99292, 31500-51

Incorrect answer. The cardiac massage should be coded. In addition, code 31500 is exempt from modifier -51 use.

d. 99291, 32160, 31500

Incorrect answer. According to the table provided in the CPT book: critical care time of 30 to 74 minutes (total time of 1 hr 14 minutes is reported with code 99291; and each additional 30 minutes beyond the first 74 minutes (1 hr and 14 minutes), report 99292 for each additional 30 minute block of time. Therefore, 85 minutes of critical care time in the ER requires add-on code 99292 to be reported with 99291.

9.81.   a. 852.40, 61154
Correct answer.

b. 853.00, 61108

Incorrect answer. This CPT code would be used to report a subdural hematoma evacuated via twist drill hole. This case is an epidural hematoma evacuated via burr hole (61154). The diagnosis code 852.40 is more specific.

c. 852.40, 61156

Incorrect answer. This CPT code would be used for treatment of an intracerebral hematoma. This case is an epidural hematoma.

d. 853.00, 61156

Incorrect answer. This CPT code would be used for treatment of an intracerebral hematoma. This case is an epidural hematoma. The diagnosis code 852.40 is more specific.

9.82.   a. 945.50, 942.44, 942.43, 11100-59, 15150, 15151, 15152 × 7, 15100, 15101 × 3
Correct answer.

b. 945.50, 942.49, 11100-59, 15150, 15151, 15152 × 7, 15100, 15101 × 3

Incorrect answer. The sites of the burns to the trunk are specified as the buttocks and left flank, so they may be coded separately with specific codes.

c. 945.50, 942.44, 942.43, 11100, 15150, 15151, 15152 × 7, 15100, 15101 × 3

Incorrect answer. A modifier should be added to code 11100 to indicate that this was a distinct procedure that was separate from the others.

d. 945.50, 942.44, 942.43, 11100-59, 15150, 15151, 15152, 15100, 15101 × 3

Incorrect answer. There was 720 sq cm of tissue cultured skin graft. 15151 covers the first 25 sq cm and 15151 indicates there was an additional 75 sq cm, which equals 100 sq cm. Code 15152 needs to be assigned 7 times to get to 720 sq cm.

Part IV

Coding Challenge

Chapter 10. Coding Challenge: Nonacute Settings; ICD-10-CM and ICD-10-PCS Code Sets; CPT Modifiers, HCPCS Level II Modifiers

Home Health

10.1.   a. V-code for aftercare of surgery

Rationale: Bleeding gastric ulcer is not current and would not be coded. Traumatic wounds are not coded for surgical wounds.

10.2.   c. Diabetes mellitus

Rationale: The diabetes mellitus would be reported in M0240 as a secondary diagnosis. The diverticulitis is not a current condition and would not be reported. The pneumonia is still present and the focus of care, and is reported in M0230 as the primary diagnosis.

10.3.   a. 438.20 (hemiplegia)

Incorrect answer. This code would be reported in M0240, but it is not the focus of the care.

b. 153.1 (Ca of transverse colon)

Incorrect answer. Because the focus of care is the result of the patient's recent surgery for cancer, the patient's primary diagnosis is V58.42, Aftercare following surgery for neoplasm. ICD-9-CM coding guidelines stipulate that code V58.42 is sequenced before the malignancy code, if the focus of care is aftercare.

c. V58.42 (Aftercare following surgery for neoplasm)

Correct answer. Because the focus of care is the result of the patient's recent surgery for cancer, the patient's primary diagnosis is V58.42, Aftercare following surgery for neoplasm. ICD-9-CM coding guidelines stipulate that code V58.42 is sequenced before the malignancy code, if the focus of care is aftercare.

d. V58.31 (Attention to surgical wound dressings)

Incorrect answer. This code was also a focus of the care, but code V58.42 was selected in the first position because it provides more detailed information.

10.4. a. M0230: V58.42; M0240: 154.1, V55.3

Incorrect answer. It appears that most of the care is directed at the colostomy care, so it would be the most specific code to use for the primary.

b. M0230: V55.3; M0240: 154.1, V58.42

Correct answer.

c. M0230: 154.1; M0240: V55.3, V58.42

Incorrect answer. The treatment is directed at the colostomy care.

d. M0230: V55.3; M0240: V10.06, V58.42

Incorrect answer. The cancer has been resected, but according to coding guidelines, if there is treatment directed to it, then it is coded as a current cancer.

10.5. a. 185

Incorrect answer. It would not be correct to report the cancer code since it has been excised and is not currently being treated.

b. V10.46

Correct answer.

c. V16.42

Incorrect answer. The patient has a personal history not family history.

d. The status of the cancer would not be reported.

Incorrect answer. It would be correct to report the status code.

10.6. a. 998.59

Correct answer.

b. V58.31

Incorrect answer. The patient is having surgical wound dressing changes, but it is not the only focus of care. Treatment appears to be centered around the postoperative wound infection. Use V58.31 in M0240.

c. 879.2

Incorrect answer. It is incorrect to code open wound for surgical wounds.

d. 574.10

Incorrect answer. The gallbladder has been removed, so this is not the appropriate diagnosis.

10.7. M0230: V54.81; M0240: V43.64, 781.2; M0246: 781.2

Rationale: Assign code V54.81, Aftercare following joint replacement, as the first-listed code for the home health care visit. Codes V43.64, Organ or tissue replaced by other means, Joint hip; and 781.2, Abnormality of gait, should be assigned as additional diagnoses.

Discussion: Code 781.2 is appropriate as an additional diagnosis because it describes the current symptom being addressed. Code 719.7, Difficulty in walking, would not be appropriate because codes in this category describe disorders of the joints. This problem does not represent a disorder of the joint.

Code 717.35 should not be assigned for osteoarthritis in the hip joint that was replaced, since the patient no longer has osteoarthritis in this joint after the hip replacement. If the patient still has osteoarthritis in other joints, such as the other hip, then the appropriate code from category 715 should be assigned. See *Coding Clinic* (2004, 2Q).

10.8. M0230: 454.0; M0240: 250.80, 707.15, 428.0, 401.9

Rationale: M0230: 454.0, Stasis ulcer of the leg

M0240: 250.80, Diabetes with other specified manifestations

M0240: 707.15, Diabetic ulcer of toe

M0240: 428.0, Congestive heart failure

M0240: 401.9, Hypertension

There is no need to complete M0246 because the patient's primary diagnosis, 454.0, Stasis ulcer of the leg, is not a V-code and is not a case mix diagnosis.

Discussion: The most intensive skilled service is provided to the leg dressing related to the stasis ulcer. The stasis ulcer is the appropriate principal/primary diagnosis rather than diabetic ulcer, since the documentation indicates he has a stasis ulcer. The diabetic toe ulcers are reported using the coding sequence 250.80, 707.15. Edema would not be coded and reported because it is integral to CHF. ICD-9-CM coding guidelines indicate that conditions integral to a diagnosis are not coded separately. The CHF and HTN are mentioned as secondary diagnoses because they contribute to the need for medication and physical therapy.

10.9. M0230: V58.42; M0240: 174.9, 438.31, V58.31

Rationale: M0230: V58.42, Aftercare following surgery for neoplasm

M0240: 174.9, Malignant neoplasm of female breast, unspecified

M0240: 438.31, Late effects of cerebrovascular disease, monoplegia of upper limb

M0240: V58.31, Attention to surgical wound dressings

There is no need to complete M0246 because the patient's primary diagnosis, V58.42, Aftercare following surgery for neoplasm, is a V code that is not replacing a case mix diagnosis.

Discussion: The most intensive skilled service that is being provided to this patient is the skilled home health treatment activity for the care of her surgical wound. Since the specific focus of care for this patient is the result of the patient's recent surgery for breast cancer, the patient's primary diagnosis is V58.42, Aftercare following surgery for neoplasm. ICD-9-CM coding guidelines stipulate that code V58.42 is sequenced before the malignancy code if the focus of care is aftercare, which it is in this case. Therefore, 174.9, Malignant neoplasm of the female breast, unspecified, is the patient's secondary diagnosis. Since code 174.9 is not a case mix diagnosis, M0246 does not need to be completed, as a V code is not replacing a case mix diagnosis. In addition, the breast cancer is not resolved, as evidenced by the tamoxifen treatment.

The diagnosis of neoplasm will vary depending on the patient's type of neoplasm; ICD-9-CM code 217 would be indicated if the neoplasm was determined to be benign.

The diagnoses that follow will vary depending on the conditions that coexist at the time the Patient's Plan of Care is established, or which have developed subsequently, or that affect the treatment of care. These diagnoses are listed on the Plan of Care in order to best reflect the seriousness of the patient's condition and to justify the disciplines and services provided. The diagnosis responsible for the patient's inability to perform the wound care, late effect of stroke, is reflected as a secondary diagnosis. The patient may not necessarily have a physical inability to perform the wound care. (If she is incapable of performing the procedure due to a learning deficit or a refusal, this requires documentation of the skilled nurse's attempts to teach and the result of the teaching.) The fifth digit for late effects signifies dominant/nondominant/nonspecified side.

10.10. d. All of the above

Rationale: As explained on the first page of the Official Coding Guidelines, all facilities must follow Section I.

10.11. M0230: V58.78; M0240: 250.80, 731.8, 781.2, V58.31; M0246: 250.80, 731.8

Rationale: M0230: V58.78, Aftercare following surgery of the musculoskeletal system, NEC

M0240: 250.80, Diabetes with other specified manifestations

M0240: 731.8, Other bone involvement in diseases classified elsewhere

M0240: 781.2, Abnormality of gait

M0240: V58.31, Attention to surgical dressings and sutures

M0246: 250.80, Diabetes with other specified manifestations

M0246: 731.8, Other bone involvement in diseases classified elsewhere

There is a need to complete M0246 because V58.78 is a V code that is replacing a case mix diagnosis (250.80). In this case, the case mix diagnosis, diabetic osteomyelitis, requires multiple coding (250.80 and 731.8).

Discussion: As you can see from this example, diabetic osteomyelitis is at the root of the patient's current problem, which is the loss of the patient's right foot by amputation. Diabetic osteomyelitis is not a direct cause of the treatment need so it is not the primary diagnosis. The primary diagnosis that is associated with the most intensive skilled service provided to this patient is V58.78, Aftercare following surgery of the musculoskeletal system.

Because an aftercare V-code is replacing a case mix diagnosis, the agency would be expected to complete M0246 with the case mix diagnosis, which in this case requires multiple coding (250.80, Diabetes with other specified manifestations, and 731.8, Other bone involvement in diseases classified elsewhere). Therefore, because the case mix diagnosis requires a manifestation code, the home health agency is expected to complete both M0246 codes as stated above.

10.12. M0230: V57.1; M0240: 781.2, V54.13; M0246: 781.2

Rationale: M0230: V57.1, Physical therapy

M0240: 781.2, Abnormality of gait

M0240: V54.13, Aftercare for healing traumatic fracture of hip

M0246: 781.2, Abnormality of gait

There is a need to complete M0246 because the patient's primary diagnosis is a V-code, (V57.1), which replaces a case mix diagnosis.

Discussion: The most intensive skilled service that is being provided to this patient is the skilled physical therapy services for gait training. V57.1, physical therapy is selected as this patient's primary diagnosis because his treatment is directed at rehabilitation following his hip fracture and surgery. Coding guidelines stipulate that the acute fracture code may only be used for the initial, acute episode of care. The acute fracture code is no longer appropriate once the patient has been discharged from the hospital to home health care. Abnormality of gait (781.2) was selected as the first secondary diagnosis because it accurately describes this patient's current condition and his need for therapy (technically, he no longer has a hip fracture, which was resolved by the hospital surgical treatment) and because the physician specified gait training.

10.13. a. V58.44

Incorrect answer. Code V58.44 is correct, but the instructional note states to "Use additional code to identify the organ transplanted (V42.0–V42.9). Code V42.0 should also be assigned.

b. V58.44, V42.0

Correct answer. This is correct coding from the provided documentation. If there is any other medical condition still present, for example in the other kidney, then it should be added as secondary codes. Any dressing change codes or any other applicable codes should also be added. Limited documentation was used here to illustrate the new aftercare code.

c. 585.6

Incorrect answer. There is documentation that there is renal failure. The aftercare code should be listed.

d. V42.0

Incorrect answer. This would be a secondary code according to the note. The aftercare code is listed first.

10.14. a. 3

Incorrect answer. There are four categories of neurology disorders in the HH-PPS.

b. 4

Correct answer. The four categories are: Neuro 1—Brain disorders and paralysis; Neuro 2—Peripheral neurological disorders; Neuro 3—Stroke; Neuro 4—Multiple Sclerosis

c. 5

Incorrect answer. There are four categories of neurology disorders in the HH-PPS.

d. 6

Incorrect answer. There are four categories of neurology disorders in the HH-PPS.

ICD-10-CM

10.15. b. 4

Rationale: According to the ICD-10-CM Official Guidelines for Coding and Reporting, a myocardial infarction is acute for 4 weeks. In ICD-9-CM, a myocardial infarction is acute for 8 weeks.

10.16. d. Emphysema

Rationale: Emphysema is found in category J43.

10.17. a. True

Rationale: ICD-10-CM codes will be utilized by all healthcare settings to assign diagnosis codes. ICD-10-PCS codes will be utilized by inpatient hospital settings to assign procedure codes.

10.18. a. K81.0

Rationale: Index the main term Cholecystitis, subterm, acute to assign code K81.0. Note that "gangrenous" is a nonessential modifier, so it does not change the code assigned.

10.19. c. E20.9, H28

Rationale: Index the main term Cataract, subterms, in (due to), hypoparathyroidism to assign codes E20.9, H28. The underlying condition of hypoparathyroidism (E20.9) should be assigned first, followed by the cataract code (H28).

10.20. b. J69.0

Rationale: Index the main term Pneumonia, subterms, aspiration, due to, food to assign code J69.0.

ICD-10-PCS

10.21. a. True

Rationale: All ICD-10-PCS codes contain 7 alphanumeric characters. The meaning of each character may differ by section. For example, the third character in the Medical and Surgical section means "root operation," whereas the third character in the Mental Health section means "root type."

10.22. a. 0 (Medical and surgical)

       b. 0 (Medical and surgical)

       c. F (Physical rehabilitation and diagnostic audiology)

       d. B (Imaging)

       e. 2 (Placement)

       f. 8 (Other procedures)

10.23. a. Y (Transplantation)

       b. T (Resection) or B (Excision)

       c. J (Inspection)

       d. F (Fragmentation)

       e. D (Extraction)

       f. L (Occlusion)

10.24. a. 3 (Percutaneous)

       b. 7 (Via Natural or Artificial Opening)

       c. 0 (Open)

       d. 2 (Open Endoscopic)

       e. 4 (Percutaneous Endoscopic)

       f. 8 (Via Natural or Artificial Opening Endoscopic)

       g. X (External)

10.25. a. 2 (Open)

       b. 4 (Percutaneous)

       c. 1 (Via Natural or Artificial Opening)

       d. 3 (Percutaneous Endoscopic)

10.26. Code 0DTJ4ZZ

Rationale:

    0   Medical and surgical section

    D   Gastrointestinal body system

    T   Resection root operation

    J   Appendix body part

    4   Percutaneous endoscopic approach

    Z   No device

    Z   No qualifier

ICD-10-CM/PCS Application Exercise

10.27. a. Search the registry by date, looking for the presence of code 410.11 when ICD-9-CM was used and code I21.0 when ICD-10-CM was used.

b. Search the registry by date, looking for the presence of code 51.51 when ICD-9-CM was used and code 0FJ90ZZ when ICD-10-PCS was used.

CPT Modifiers

10.28. a. No modifier is necessary because Dr. R interpreted the x-ray under contract with the hospital. The hospital will bill the global and pay Dr. R from the reimbursement.

Incorrect answer. Dr. R should report the chest x-ray code with modifier -26, professional component. If he had performed the service with equipment he owned and staff that he employed, he could have reported the global; but because the hospital assumed the technical overhead, he can only report the professional component.

b. Modifier -26, Professional component.

Correct answer.

c. Modifier -TC, Technical component.

Incorrect answer. Dr. R performed the professional component of the split service, not the technical component. He should report modifier -26.

d. Modifier -59.

Incorrect answer. Modifier -26 is the appropriate modifier to report the professional component of a split service. Modifier -59 is reported only when a specific modifier does not exist.

10.29. a. No modifier is needed for the surgery; although the anesthesiologist might need a modifier.

Incorrect answer. Modifier -63, Procedure performed on infants less than 4 kg, should be reported.

b. Modifier -63 is reported because the baby weighs less than 4 kg and thus is a higher surgical risk than a larger neonate.

Correct answer.

c. No modifier is needed because code 44120 already applies to neonates who are very low weight.

Incorrect answer. Code 44120 is not exempt from the assignment of modifier -63, and this modifier should be assigned.

d. A modifier is optional and may or may not be assigned depending upon the departmental coding guidelines.

Incorrect answer. Modifier -63, Procedure performed on infants less than 4 kg, should be reported in this case.

10.30. a. Modifier -59, to show that these were not duplicate charges, but indeed separate incidents.

Incorrect answer. Modifier -91 is specific for repeat laboratory tests.

b. No modifier is necessary for repeat laboratory tests, only for repeat surgical procedures.

Incorrect answer. Modifier -91 is specific for repeat laboratory tests.

c. Modifier -91.

Correct answer.

d. Modifier -91 and -59 should be reported for the second and third determinations.

Incorrect answer. Only modifier -91 is necessary, as it is specific for repeat laboratory tests.

10.31. a. Modifier -76, Repeat procedure by the same physician, should be reported for each chest tube insertion.

Incorrect answer. Modifier -76 is the appropriate modifier, but it should be appended only to the second procedure. No modifier is needed on the first procedure.

b. Modifier -76 should be reported with the second procedure, no modifier on the first procedure.

Correct answer.

c. Modifier -59 should be reported with the second procedure, no modifier with the first procedure.

Incorrect answer. Modifier -76 is specific for repeat of an identical procedure by the same physician and should be reported with the second procedure.

d. Either modifier -59 or -76 may be reported on the first and second procedure.

Incorrect answer. Modifier -76 is specific for repeat of an identical procedure by the same physician, and should be reported with the second procedure. Modifier -59 should be used only when a more specific modifier is not available. No modifier should be reported with the first procedure.

10.32. a. No modifier is needed because the ICD-9-CM diagnosis code and the CPT procedure code clearly identify that this was a procedure not related to the cholecystectomy.

Incorrect answer. Even though the procedure is clearly not related, modifier -79, Unrelated procedure or service by the same physician during the postoperative period, should be reported to make the circumstances completely clear to the payer.

b. Modifier -79, Unrelated procedure or service by the same physician during the postoperative period, should be reported with the appendectomy code.

Correct answer.

c. Modifier -78, Return to the operating room for a related procedure during the postoperative period, should be reported with the appendectomy code.

Incorrect answer. There is nothing to suggest that the acute appendicitis was related to the cholecystectomy. Modifier -79, Unrelated procedure or service by the same physician during the postoperative period, should be reported with the appendectomy code.

d. Modifier -58, Staged or related procedure or service by the same physician during the postoperative period.

Incorrect answer. This was not a related or stated procedure, but an unrelated procedure for an unrelated diagnosis. Modifier -79, Unrelated procedure or service by the same physician during the postoperative period, should be reported with the appendectomy code.

HCPCS Level II Modifiers

10.33. a. No, if an "inpatient only" procedure is performed on an outpatient basis, the hospital cannot obtain reimbursement under any circumstances.

Incorrect answer. Modifier -CA may be assigned when a patient expires prior to admission when an "inpatient only" procedure is performed on an emergency basis.

b. Modifier -CA, Procedure payable only in the inpatient setting when performed emergently on an outpatient who expires prior to admission, may be appended to the CPT procedure code.

Correct answer.

c. Modifier -ST, Related to trauma or injury, may be appended and a 50 percent reimbursement will be available to the hospital.

Incorrect answer. Modifier -CA may be assigned when a patient expires prior to admission when an "inpatient only" procedure is performed on an emergency basis.

d. Modifier -SC, Medically necessary service or supply, may be appended and a 25 percent reimbursement will be available to the hospital.

Incorrect answer. Modifier -CA may be assigned when a patient expires prior to admission when an "inpatient only" procedure is performed on an emergency basis.

10.34. a. No modifier. By definition, bunionectomy is performed on the big toe.

Incorrect answer. Modifier -T5, Right foot, great toe, is the appropriate modifier.

b. Modifier -T5

Correct answer.

c. Modifier -RT

Incorrect answer. Modifier -T5, right foot, great toe, is the appropriate modifier, as it is more specific.

d. Modifier -TA

Incorrect answer. Modifier -TA reports the left foot, great toe.

10.35. a. Modifier -GW

Correct answer.

b. Modifier -AT

Incorrect answer. Modifier -GW is specific for identifying services not related to a hospice patient's terminal condition.

c. Modifier -GZ

Incorrect answer. Modifier -GW is appropriate for reporting services that are not part of a patient's terminal condition.

d. Modifier -SC

Incorrect answer. Modifier -GW is specific for identifying services not related to a hospice patient's terminal condition.

10.36. a. CPT codes

Incorrect answer. They can be used with both CPT and HCPCS Level II codes.

b. HCPCS Level II codes

Incorrect answer. They can be used with both CPT and HCPCS Level II codes.

c. ICD-9-CM Volume III codes

Incorrect answer. They can be used with both CPT and HCPCS Level II codes, but not with ICD-9-CM procedure codes.

d. Both a and b

Correct answer.

10.37. a. Laboratory tests

Incorrect answer. They are reported with dialysis codes.

b. Dialysis codes

Correct answer.

c. Coronary artery interventional procedures

Incorrect answer. They are reported with dialysis codes.

d. Oxygen therapy

Incorrect answer. They are reported with dialysis codes.

10.38.
1. f
2. g
3. i
4. b
5. j
6. h
7. c
8. a
9. e
10. d

10.39. V2523-VP-H9

Rationale: V2523-VP-H9 Contact lens, hydrophilic, extended wear, per lens; aphakic patient; court ordered. The modifier -VP, Aphakic patient, is the most specific and the most important so it is placed closest to the procedure code. For a Medicare benficiary, this information is critical to reimbursement because Medicare will only pay for this service (the hydrophilic contact lens) for aphakic patients.

Long-Term Acute Care (LTAC) Coding

10.40. a. 433.00, 438.21, 438.11, 438.82

Incorrect answer. The acute bleed (433.00) is completed, and the patient is admitted for therapy for management of the various late effects—the hemiplegia (438.21), the aphasia (438.11), and the dysphagia (438.82)—which should be sequenced as the principal and secondary diagnoses.

b. V57.89, 438.21, 438.11, 438.82

Correct answer.

c. V58.9, 438.21, 438.11, 438.82

Incorrect answer. The admission conditions are the late effects of the bleed and rehabilitation for the same. No specific after-care is documented.

d. V57.2, V57.3, V57.89

Incorrect answer. The individual types of rehabilitation need not be reported. Code V57.89, followed by the specific sequelae of the bleed, are the appropriate principal and secondary diagnoses.

10.41. a. 707.05, 707.07, 707.22, 250.00, 496, 86.28

Correct answer.

b. V57.89, 707.05, 707.07, 707.22, 250.00, 496, 86.28

Incorrect answer. No specific therapy is documented. The patient is admitted for management of the continued acute condition of the decubitus ulcers, which should be assigned as the principal diagnosis.

c. 707.05, 707.07, 707.22, 86.28

Incorrect answer. Although these codes are appropriate, the codes for the concomitant chronic conditions of diabetes and COPD should also be coded as they impact the patient's response to treatment.

d. 707.05, 707.07, 707.22, 86.22

Incorrect answer. The diagnosis codes are appropriate, but the procedure code, 86.22, reports excisional debridement, not nonexcisional debridement. Code 86.28 is the appropriate code. As this code assignment impacts MS-DRG grouping, this coding error would constitute a significant compliance issue for the hospital.

10.42. a. 496, 414.00, 250.60, 337.1

Incorrect answer. The patient is specifically admitted for pulmonary rehabilitation. V57.89 is the appropriate principal diagnosis in this case. The COPD should be reported as a concomitant secondary diagnosis.

b. V57.0, 496

Incorrect answer. V57.0 reports only breathing exercises. Pulmonary rehabilitation is a multidisciplinary rehabilitation involving pulmonary, physician and occupational therapy and sometimes speech-language therapy. V57.89 is the appropriate principal diagnosis. The COPD is appropriately reported as a secondary diagnosis. The ASHD and diabetes with neurological manifestations in the form of peripheral neuropathy should also be reported, as they currently affect the patient's condition. Add codes 414.00, 250.60, 337.1.

c. V57.89, 496, 414.00, 250.60, 337.1

Correct answer.

d. V57.89

Incorrect answer. The rehabilitation is the appropriate principal diagnosis code, but the underlying pulmonary condition for which the rehabilitation is given (496), as well as the concomitant chronic conditions (414.00, 250.60, 337.1), should also be coded.

10.43. a. V57.89

Incorrect answer. Although the patient may eventually receive therapy, management of the stump infection is the primary focus of her admission. Assign code 997.62 as the principal diagnosis.

b. V52.1

Incorrect answer. Although the patient may eventually be fitted with a prosthesis, the main reason for her admission is to resolve the stump infection. Assign code 997.62 as the principal diagnosis.

c. 904.53

Incorrect answer. Although the injury to the posterior tibial artery precipitated the amputation, this episode of care is over. The patient is admitted to the LTAC for management of the stump infection. Assign code 997.62 as the principal diagnosis.

d. 997.62

Correct answer.

Outpatient Rehabilitation Cases

10.44. V57.1, 343.9, 737.30, 754.31

10.45. V57.1; 723.1

Inpatient Rehabilitation Cases

10.46. a. Admit: 821.00

     Principal: V57.89

     Secondary: V54.13
                         V58.43
                         E929.3
                         427.31
                         317
                         V58.61
                         530.81
                         457.1

     b. Etiology: 820.21

       Comorbidities: E929.3
                              427.31
                              317
                              V58.61
                              530.81
                              457.1

10.47. a. Admit: 952.9

     Principal: V57.89

     Secondary: 907.2
                         E929.0
                         596.54
                         564.81
                         344.02

     b. Etiology: 952.03

       Comorbidities: E929.0
                              596.54
                              564.81
                              344.02

10.48. a. Admit: 438.9
     Principal: V57.89

Secondary: 438.20
438.6/781.8
438.19
438.82
438.83
250.00
272.4
427.31
276.1
278.01
414.00
715.35
V58.61
726.10

b. Etiology: 434.91
    Comorbidities: 781.8
787.2
784.59
427.31
250.00
272.4
278.01

Skilled Nursing Facility (SNF) Cases

10.49. a. V54.25, 198.5, V10.3

Correct answer.

b. 733.14, 198.5, V10.3

Incorrect answer. The pathological fracture treatment was carried out in the acute hospital, and the patient is admitted to the skilled nursing facility for aftercare. Assign a code from the "Aftercare for pathological fracture" series as the principal diagnosis, in this case, V54.25.

c. V57.89, 733.14, 198.5, V10.3

Incorrect answer. The patient is not admitted specifically for rehabilitation; she is nonambulatory and is admitted for continued healing of the fracture. Assign a code from the "Aftercare for pathological fracture" series as the principal diagnosis, in this case, V54.25.

d. V54.15, 821.00

Incorrect answer. Code V54.15 reports aftercare for a healing traumatic fracture, but this is documented as a pathological fracture. In addition, code 821.00 reports a traumatic fracture. Codes V54.25, 198.5, V10.3 are the correct codes to report for this admission.

10.50. a. 486, 496, 401.9, 414.00

Incorrect answer. The pneumonia had resolved in the acute hospital, and no treatment was needed in the skilled nursing facility. The patient was admitted because of Alzheimer's dementia, which should be sequenced as the principal diagnosis, along with the behavior disturbance manifested as wandering off (331.0, 294.11). The other diagnosis codes (496, 401.9, 414.00) are appropriate, if nonspecific.

b. 331.0, 294.11

Incorrect answer. These are appropriate codes for the principal diagnosis, but the underlying chronic diseases of COPD, hypertension and ASHD should also be coded, as they affect the patient's management. Add codes 496, 401.9, 414.00.

c. 331.0, 294.11, 496, 401.9, 414.00
Correct answer.

d. V57.89, 331.0, 294.11, 496, 401.9, 414.00

Incorrect answer. There is no documentation of any therapy being ordered. The patient is essentially custodial. Assign the Alzheimer's dementia with behavioral disturbance as the principal diagnosis and the underlying chronic conditions as secondary diagnoses.

10.51. a. V58.75, 780.79, V10.05
Correct answer.

b. V58.75, 997.99, 780.79, V10.05

Incorrect answer. Although the principal diagnosis code is appropriate, there is no documentation that the weakness was a postoperative complication. Delete code 997.99. The remainder of the codes are correct.

c. V10.05, 780.79

Incorrect answer. The patient was admitted for aftercare following the surgery for the carcinoma, not because she had a history of colon cancer. Assign V58.75 as the principal diagnosis.

d. V58.75, 780.79, 153.1

Incorrect answer. Code 153.1 is not appropriate, as the malignancy has been eradicated by the surgery, and the patient is not receiving any treatment at this time. Change to code V10.05. The rest of the codes are correct.

Secondary:	438.20
	438.6/781.8
	438.19
	438.82
	438.83
	250.00
	272.4
	427.31
	276.1
	278.01
	414.00
	715.35
	V58.61
	726.10

b. Etiology:	434.91
Comorbidities:	781.8
	787.2
	784.59
	427.31
	250.00
	272.4
	278.01

Skilled Nursing Facility (SNF) Cases

10.49. a. V54.25, 198.5, V10.3

Correct answer.

b. 733.14, 198.5, V10.3

Incorrect answer. The pathological fracture treatment was carried out in the acute hospital, and the patient is admitted to the skilled nursing facility for aftercare. Assign a code from the "Aftercare for pathological fracture" series as the principal diagnosis, in this case, V54.25.

c. V57.89, 733.14, 198.5, V10.3

Incorrect answer. The patient is not admitted specifically for rehabilitation; she is nonambulatory and is admitted for continued healing of the fracture. Assign a code from the "Aftercare for pathological fracture" series as the principal diagnosis, in this case, V54.25.

d. V54.15, 821.00

Incorrect answer. Code V54.15 reports aftercare for a healing traumatic fracture, but this is documented as a pathological fracture. In addition, code 821.00 reports a traumatic fracture. Codes V54.25, 198.5, V10.3 are the correct codes to report for this admission.

10.50. a. 486, 496, 401.9, 414.00

Incorrect answer. The pneumonia had resolved in the acute hospital, and no treatment was needed in the skilled nursing facility. The patient was admitted because of Alzheimer's dementia, which should be sequenced as the principal diagnosis, along with the behavior disturbance manifested as wandering off (331.0, 294.11). The other diagnosis codes (496, 401.9, 414.00) are appropriate, if nonspecific.

b. 331.0, 294.11

Incorrect answer. These are appropriate codes for the principal diagnosis, but the underlying chronic diseases of COPD, hypertension and ASHD should also be coded, as they affect the patient's management. Add codes 496, 401.9, 414.00.

c. 331.0, 294.11, 496, 401.9, 414.00

Correct answer.

d. V57.89, 331.0, 294.11, 496, 401.9, 414.00

Incorrect answer. There is no documentation of any therapy being ordered. The patient is essentially custodial. Assign the Alzheimer's dementia with behavioral disturbance as the principal diagnosis and the underlying chronic conditions as secondary diagnoses.

10.51. a. V58.75, 780.79, V10.05

Correct answer.

b. V58.75, 997.99, 780.79, V10.05

Incorrect answer. Although the principal diagnosis code is appropriate, there is no documentation that the weakness was a postoperative complication. Delete code 997.99. The remainder of the codes are correct.

c. V10.05, 780.79

Incorrect answer. The patient was admitted for aftercare following the surgery for the carcinoma, not because she had a history of colon cancer. Assign V58.75 as the principal diagnosis.

d. V58.75, 780.79, 153.1

Incorrect answer. Code 153.1 is not appropriate, as the malignancy has been eradicated by the surgery, and the patient is not receiving any treatment at this time. Change to code V10.05. The rest of the codes are correct.